www.wadsworth.com

www.wadsworth.com is the World Wide Web site for
Wadsworth and is your direct source to dozens of online
resources.

At *www.wadsworth.com* you can find out about supplements, demonstration software, and student resources.
You can also send e-mail to many of our authors and
preview new publications and exciting new technologies.

www.wadsworth.com
Changing the way the world learns®

SIXTH EDITION

Concepts of Chemical Dependency

Harold E. Doweiko

THOMSON

BROOKS/COLE

Australia • Brazil • Canada • Mexico • Singapore • Spain • United Kingdom • United States

THOMSON

BROOKS/COLE

Conepts of Chemical Dependency, Sixth Edition

Harold E. Doweiko

Publisher/Executive Editor: *Lisa Gebo*
Senior Acquisitions Editor: *Marquita Flemming*
Assistant Editor: *Monica Arvin*
Editorial Assistant: *Christine Northup*
Technology Project Manager: *Barry Connolly*
Marketing Manager: *Caroline Concilla*
Marketing Assistant: *Rebecca Weisman*
Marketing Communications Manager: *Tami Strang*
Project Manager, Editorial Production: *Megan E. Hansen*
Art Director: *Vernon Boes*
Print Buyer: *Doreen Suruki*

Permissions Editor: *Joohee Lee*
Production Service: *Anne Draus, Scratchgravel Publishing Services*
Copy Editors: *Patterson Lamb and Linda Ruth Dane*
Illustrator: *Greg Draus, Scratchgravel Publishing Services*
Cover Designer: *Larry Didona*
Cover Images: *Marijuana and Paraphernalia,* © *Comstock Images/Getty Images; Cigarette Butts,* © *Enrique Algarra/Pixtal/ Agefotostock; Drug Works and Needle,* © *AbleStock/Index Stock; Woman under a pill-covered glass table,* © *Amy Illardo/Photonica*
Compositor: *Integra*
Printer: *Malloy Incorporated*

For more information about our products, contact us at:
Thomson Learning Academic Resource Center
1-800-423-0563

For permission to use material from this text or product, submit a request online at
http://www.thomsonrights.com.
Any additional questions about permissions can be submitted by email to
thomsonrights@thomson.com.

Library of Congress Control Number: 2005923112

ISBN 0-534-63284-X

Thomson Higher Education
10 Davis Drive
Belmont, CA 94002-3098
USA

Asia (including India)
Thomson Learning
5 Shenton Way
#01-01 UIC Building
Singapore 068808

Australia/New Zealand
Thomson Learning Australia
102 Dodds Street
Southbank, Victoria 3006
Australia

Canada
Thomson Nelson
1120 Birchmount Road
Toronto, Ontario M1K 5G4
Canada

UK/Europe/Middle East/Africa
Thomson Learning
High Holborn House
50/51 Bedford Row
London WC1R 4LR
United Kingdom

Latin America
Thomson Learning
Seneca, 53
Colonia Polanco
11560 Mexico
D.F. Mexico

In loving memory of my wife, Jan

CONTENTS

5 Addiction as a Disease of the Human Spirit   44

6 An Introduction to Pharmacology   55

7 Alcohol: Humans' Oldest Recreational Chemical   70

15 Hallucinogen Abuse and Addiction   197

16 Abuse of and Addiction to the Inhalants and Aerosols   213

17 The Unrecognized Problem of Steroid Abuse and Addiction   221

18 The Over-the-Counter Analgesics: Unexpected Agents of Abuse   229

19 Tobacco Products and Nicotine Addiction   245

20 Chemicals and the Neonate: The Consequences of Drug Abuse During Pregnancy   260

21 Hidden Faces of Chemical Dependency 275

22 The Dual-Diagnosis Client: Chemical Addiction and Mental Illness 290

23 Chemical Abuse by Children and Adolescents 304

24 Codependency and Enabling   320

25 Addiction and the Family   330

26 The Evaluation of Substance-Use Problems   341

27 The Process of Intervention   356

In the years since the terrorist attacks on the World Trade Center on September 11, 2001, national priorities have shifted away from the drug-abuse problem to the war against terrorism. This shift in focus does not mean that the abuse of chemicals has disappeared. Indeed, although the number of adolescents who admit to abusing cannabis has leveled off, it is at a level *more than three times as high* as that seen in the 1980s. Heroin remains plentiful and cheap. Evidence suggests that the amount of cocaine under cultivation has remained stable and might even be on the increase, in spite of efforts to persuade local farms to switch to other crops. These signs indicate that the drug-abuse problem has not disappeared.

The field of addiction treatment is constantly changing. New discoveries in the fields of neurology, neuropsychology, and neuropsychopharmacology have provided new insights into the effects of recreational chemicals on the user's brain and how the drugs of abuse disrupt the normal function of the user's neurons. Compounds that were viewed as emerging drugs of abuse just five or six years ago have faded into obscurity, whereas emerging chemicals hold the potential to become the latest trend. Pharmaceuticals that once held great promise in the fight against drug abuse, such as LAAM (see Chapter 32), have been found to pose significant health risks for the user and have been removed from the arsenal of medications used to treat alcohol and drug addiction. Access to inpatient rehabilitation centers has been further curtailed since the fifth edition of this text appeared, and methamphetamine use continues to spread from the west to the east coast. These conditions made a new edition of this text imperative.

In order to keep pace with the world of addictions, more than 450 changes have been made to this text. New data have been added in all chapters, many of which have been extensively rewritten, and older, obsolete material has been deleted. A new section on the emerging "Drug Court" movement, a new form of legal intervention, has been added to Chapter 27, for example. Chapter 36 includes new information on tryptamines and phenethylamines, families of chemicals that include many potential or emerging drugs of abuse. The section on gamma hydroxybutyrate (GHB) has also been revised as more information about this and other "date rape" drugs has been uncovered. The material on "ecstasy" has been updated as scientists explore the possibility that this popular drug of abuse might actually be a selective neurotoxin in primates and possibly humans. Two new chapters have been added. Chapter 35 addresses the growing debate on the question of legalization, and Chapter 36 explores the debate on the relationship between substance abuse and criminal behavior. Issues such as the difference between *medicalization* and full *legalization* are investigated, and questions are raised about how the Constitution has been reinterpreted in light of the "war on drugs."

The fast pace of research and the evolving social response to the problem of substance abuse and addiction are two reasons why the field of addictive medicine is so exciting: It is constantly changing. There are few generally accepted answers, a multitude of unanswered questions, and, compared to the other branches of science, few interdisciplinary boundaries to limit exploration of the field. This text has tried to capture the excitement of this process while providing an overview of the field of substance abuse and rehabilitation.

Disclaimer

This text was written in an attempt to share the knowledge and experience of the author with others interested in the field of substance abuse. Every effort has been made to ensure that the information reviewed in this text is accurate, but this book is *not* designed for, nor should it be used as, a guide to patient care. Furthermore, this text provides a great deal of information about the current drugs of abuse, their dosage levels, and their effects. This information is provided not to advocate or encourage the use or abuse of chemicals. Rather, this information is reviewed to inform the reader of current trends in the field of drug abuse/addiction. The text is not intended as a guide to self-medication, and neither the author nor the publisher assumes any responsibility for individuals who attempt to use this text as a guide for the administration of drugs to themselves or others or as a guide to treatment.

Acknowledgments

It would not be possible to mention every person who has helped to make this book a reality. However, I must mention the library staff at Lutheran Hospital, La Crosse, for their continued assistance in tracking down obscure references, many of which have been used in this edition of *Concepts of Chemical Dependency*. I also thank the following reviewers who offered comments: Riley Venable, Texas Southern University; Maria Saxionis, Bridgewater State College; Fred T. Ponder, Texas A&M University; John B. McIntosh, Penn State University, Altoona; John Jung, California State University, Long Beach; Suzanne Lenhart, Tri-State University; James F. Scorzelli, Northeastern University, Boston; and Yolanda V. Edwards, University of South Carolina School of Medicine.

Finally, I would like to point out that without the support of my late wife, Jan, the earliest editions of this text would never have been published. Until her untimely death, she happily read each chapter of each edition. She corrected my spelling (many, many times over) and encouraged me when I was up against the brick wall of writer's block. Her feedback was received with the same openness that any author receives "constructive criticism" when she offered it the first time around. But in spite of that she persisted with her feedback about each edition, and more often than not she was right. She was indeed my best friend and my "editor in chief." Although I have attempted to complete the revisions to this sixth edition in such a manner as to remain true to what I think she would have liked, I do wonder what she would have had to say about this edition of *Concepts of Chemical Dependency*, and I miss her input.

Concepts of Chemical Dependency

Why Worry About Recreational Chemical Abuse?

Introduction

Collectively, the substance-use disorders are *the* most prevalent mental health problem in the United States today (Vuchinich, 2002). But in spite of a "war" on drug abuse that has spanned the last three decades, people still insist on abusing chemicals that change their conscious perception of the world (Schuckit, 2001). In spite of an expenditure of hundreds of billions of dollars in an effort to eliminate recreational chemical abuse, the substance-use disorders continue to be a major problem in this country. Although the frequency of abuse of such substances as cannabis has leveled off, substance use is at levels far above those seen in the 1980s and 1990s. Further, while the abuse of some compounds such as PCP have become rare, the misuse of other chemicals, such as MDMA and heroin, is on the increase.

Proponents of the "war on drugs" point to these trends as evidence that the current approach, a legal approach that seeks to incarcerate those who abuse illicit chemicals, is working. Detractors of this policy point to these same trends as evidence that the war on drugs is a dismal failure and that other approaches to the problem of alcohol/drug abuse must be tried. They defend this position by observing that after more than a century's effort, virtually every drug that was ever discovered is both easily available and commonly abused by illicit drug abusers in the United States (Hopkins, 1998).

In reality, recreational substance abuse is deeply ingrained in the social life of the United States. For example, the challenge of providing affordable, effective health care to the citizens of the United States has been compounded by the alcohol/drugs in a number of ways:

- Approximately 25% of patients seen by primary care physicians have an alcohol or drug problem (Jones, Knutson, & Haines, 2003)
- Between 20% and 50% of *all* hospital admissions are related to the effects of alcohol abuse/addiction (Greenfield & Hennessy, 2004; McKay, Koranda, & Axen, 2004).
- The abuse of illicit drugs is a major cause of ischaemic stroke in adults, increasing the individual's risk of such an event 1,100% (Martin, Enevoldson, & Humphrey, 1997).

Recreational drug use is not simply a drain on the general medical resources of the United States but is also a significant contributing factor to psychiatric problems that people experience. For example:

- The most common cause of psychosis in young adults is alcohol/drug abuse (Cohen, 1995).
- Suicide is 30 times as common among alcohol-dependent people as it is in the general population (Mosier, 1999). Between 20% and 35% of completed suicides are carried out by alcohol-dependent individuals (Lester, 2000; Preuss et al., 2003).
- Suicide is the cause of death in 35% of all intravenous drug abusers (Neeleman & Farrell, 1997) and 5% of all alcohol-dependent people (Preuss et al., 2003).

The problem of interpersonal violence has contributed to untold suffering in the United States for generations. Fully 56% of all assaults are alcohol-related (Dyehouse & Sommers, 1998). Further, research has found that adults with an alcohol or drug-use disorder were 2.7 times as likely to report having engaged in the physical abuse of a child and 4.2 times as likely to report child neglect as nonusing control subjects (Ireland, 2001). There is a known relationship between substance abuse and homicide (Rivara et al., 1997). The authors found that illicit drug use in the home increased a woman's chances of being murdered by a significant other by a factor of 28, even if she herself was not using drugs. Alcohol alone is implicated in half of all homicides committed in the United States (National Foundation for Brain Research, 1992). The role of alcohol/drugs in the process of victimization has been underscored by study after study:

- The team of Liebschutz, Mulvey, and Samet (1997) found that 42% of a sample of 2,322 women who were seeking treatment for substance-use problems had a history of having been physically or sexually abused at some point in their lives. A quarter of these women said that they were in danger of being revictimized again in the near future.
- Of a sample of 802 inpatients being treated for alcoholism, 49% of the women and 12% of the men reported that they had been the victim of some form of sexual abuse (Windle, Windle, Scheidt, & Miller, 1995).

The impact of alcohol/drug abuse on the health care crisis facing the United States in the early years of the 21st century is not limited to the problem of interpersonal violence. For example, between 40% (Liu et al., 1997) and 60% (Hingson, 1996) of the population of the United States will be involved in an alcohol-related motor vehicle accident at some point in their lives. The list goes on and on. Indeed, as one examines the full scope of recreational chemical use/abuse in this country, it becomes increasingly clear that recreational substance abuse extracts a terrible toll from each individual living here. It is a problem that, directly or indirectly, touches every individual in the nation.

Who Treats Those Who Abuse or Are Addicted to Chemicals?

In spite of the damage done by alcohol/drug abuse or addiction, only 4 cents of every dollar spent by the 50 states was devoted to prevention and treatment of substance-use problems (Grinfeld, 2001). Nor are the various state governments alone in not addressing the issue of substance abuse. Nationally, less than one-fifth of the physicians surveyed considered themselves prepared to deal with alcohol-dependent patients, whereas less than 17% thought they had the skills necessary to deal with prescription drug abusers (National Center on Addiction and Substance Abuse at Columbia University, 2000). These findings are understandable considering that few "medical schools or residency programs have an adequate required course in addiction." Further, "most physicians fail to screen for alcohol or drug dependence during routine examinations. Many health professionals view such screening efforts as a waste of time" (McLellan, Lewis, O'Brien, & Kleber, 2000, p. 1689).

As a result of this professional pessimism, physicians tend to "resist being involved in negotiating a referral and brokering a consultative recommendation when alcoholism is the diagnosis" (Westermeyer, 2001, p. 458). Bernstein, Tracey, Bernstein, and Williams (1996) investigated the outcome of this neglect. The authors examined the ability of emergency department physicians to detect alcohol-related problems in over 210 patients. The patients completed an evaluation process that included three different tests: the Ever A Problem (EAP) quiz, the CAGE (discussed in Chapter 26), and the QED Saliva Alcohol Test (SAT). Forty percent of the patients were found to have an alcohol-use problem on at least one of the three measures utilized, yet less than a quarter of these patients were referred for further evaluation or treatment. The authors concluded that professional beliefs about the hopelessness of attempting to intervene when the patient had an alcohol-use problem was still a major reason that physicians did not refer that patient to treatment.

In spite of the known relationship between substance abuse and traumatic injury, alcoholism remains undetected or undiagnosed by physicians (Greenfield & Hennessy, 2004). This suggests that although the benefits of professional treatment for alcohol abuse/addiction have been demonstrated time and again, many physicians continue to consider alcohol and illicit drug-use problems to be virtually untreatable (National Center on Addiction and Substance Abuse at Columbia University, 2000).

However, this diagnostic blindness is not limited to physicians. The typical training program for registered nurses includes fewer than 2 to 4 hours of classwork on addictive diseases, and many programs have no formal training at all on this disorder (Coombs, 1997). Further, even though alcohol use/abuse is a known risk factor for violence within the family, marital/family therapists only rarely ask the proper questions to identify alcohol/drug abuse/dependence. When a substance-use problem within a marriage or family is not uncovered, therapy proceeds in a haphazard fashion. Vital clues to a very real illness within the family are missed, and the attempt at family or marital therapy is ineffective unless the addictive disorder is identified and addressed.

In spite of the obvious relationship between substance abuse and the various forms of psychopathology, 74% of the psychologists surveyed admitted that they had had no formal education in the area of the addictions (Aanavi, Taube, Ja, & Duran, 2000). Most psychologists in practice rate their graduate school training in the area of drug addiction as inadequate (Cellucci & Vik, 2001). In a very real sense, no matter whether substance abuse/addiction is a true "disease" or not, the health care and mental health professions have responded to this disorder by not training practitioners to recognize its signs or how to treat it.

These findings are important because they show the marked lack of attention or professional training the mental health and health care professions have given to the problem. But perhaps this is because drug use/abuse in the United States is such a minor problem that dealing with it does not require the training of large numbers of professionals. In the next section, the scope of substance abuse/addiction will be examined, and you decide if it *really* is as serious as it appears.

The Scope of the Problem of Chemical Abuse/Addiction

Globally, 3% of the population, or 185 million people, are estimated to use an illicit substance at least once each year (United Nations, 2004). In the United States, 35% of men and 18% of women are predicted to develop a substance-use disorder at some point during their lives (Rhee et al., 2003). At first glance, these estimates seem to suggest that substance-use problems are more common in the United States than elsewhere in the world, but keep in mind that these two research studies utilize two different measures: annual drug use versus estimated lifetime prevalence of substance-use problems. The underlying assumptions on which the two studies are based are often vastly different.

One dramatic and frightening estimate of the scope of substance-use problems in the United States was offered by Wilens (2004a, b), who suggested that between 10% and 30% of adults have a substance-use disorder. These figures are indeed quite alarming and were consistent with the findings of other research studies (Kessler et al., 1994; Kessler et al., 1997). The data from each of these studies was based on the responses of a sample of 8,098 individuals, who took part in the National Comorbidity Survey. The sample was selected to approximate the characteristics of the population of the United States as a whole (in terms of age, sex, and so on), providing an overview of the population that would meet criteria for a diagnosis of one of 14 separate psychiatric conditions both in the preceding 12 months and during the respondent's lifetime.

People in the United States are curious about illicit drugs: An estimated 70 million people in this country have used an illicit substance at least once (Leshner, 1997b). In contrast to this number, only about 19.5 million people in the United States above the age of 12 were thought to have abused an illicit chemical at some point, and only 5.3 million of this number were addicted to a drug(s) (Office of National Drug Control Policy, 2004). These figures were similar to those suggested a decade earlier in the *Harvard Mental Health Letter* ("Strong medicine," 1995) that 5% to 10% of the adults in the United States had a "serious alcohol problem" (p. 1) and that another 1% to 2% had "a serious illicit drug problem" (p. 1).

The intravenous drug addict is often seen as a stereotype of the addicted person. Yet only 1.5 million people in the entire United States are estimated to be intravenous drug users (Work Group on HIV/AIDS, 2000). This estimate includes both drug abusers and addicts, yet this total is less than 1% of the estimated population of the country. However, the wide differences between the various estimates of those who are substance abusers or are addicted to drugs in this country underscore one serious shortcoming in the field of substance-abuse rehabilitation: the lack of clear data. Depending on the research study cited, substance abuse is or is not a serious problem, is or is not getting worse (or better), will or will not be resolved in the next decade, and is something that parents should or should not worry about. The truth is that large numbers of people use one or more recreational chemicals, but only a small percentage of these people will ultimately become addicted to the chemical(s) being abused (Peele, Brodsky, & Arnold, 1991). In the next section, we look at an overview of substance abuse in this country.

Estimates of the problem of alcohol use, abuse, and addiction. Surprisingly, the use of alcohol in the United States has been declining since around 1980 and has actually dropped about 15% since then (Musto, 1996). But alcohol remains a popular recreational chemical in the United States, used by an estimated 119 million people (Office of National Drug Control Policy, 2004). Of this number, 16.27 million are thought to be physically dependent on it (Office of National Drug Control Policy, 2004).

There is a discrepancy in the amount of alcohol consumed by casual drinkers compared to problem drinkers: Only 34% of the population in this country consumes 62% of all of the alcohol produced (Kotz & Covington, 1995). Approximately 10% of those who drink alcohol on a regular basis will become alcohol dependent (Kotz & Covington, 1995). However, researchers disagree on the exact scope of alcohol addiction in the United States. Estimates range from 9 million (Ordorica & Nace, 1998) to 12 million (Siegel, 1989) to perhaps as many as 16.27 million people (Office of National Drug Control Policy, 2004).

The majority of those who abuse or are addicted to alcohol in the United States are male. But this does not mean that alcohol abuse/addiction is *exclusively* a male problem. The ratio of male to female alcohol abusers/addicts is thought to fall between 2:1 and 3:1 (Blume, 1994; Cyr & Moulton, 1993; Hill, 1995). These figures suggest that significant numbers of women are also abusing or addicted to alcohol. Because it can be purchased legally by adults over the age of 21, many people tend to forget that it is also a drug. However, the grim reality is that this "legal" chemical makes

up the greatest part of the drug abuse/addiction problem in this country. Franklin (1987) stated, for example, that alcoholism alone accounts for 85% of drug addiction in the United States. This is not surprising, as alcohol is the most commonly abused chemical in the world (Lieber, 1995).

Estimates of the problem of narcotics abuse and addiction. When many people hear the term *drugs of abuse*, narcotics are the drugs people think of, especially heroin. Although narcotic analgesics have the reputation of being quite addictive, only about half of those who abuse these drugs become addicted to them (Jenike, 1991). Globally, around 10 million people are estimated to abuse or be addicted to heroin (Milne, 2003). In the United States, 810,000 people are estimated to be dependent on opiates, and the problem of opiate addiction probably costs society about $21 billion annually (Fiellin, Rosenheck, & Kosten, 2001). This is a far different estimate from the one offered by Herbert Kleber (quoted in Grinfeld, 2001)—that there are approximately 1 million heroin-dependent people in the United States.

About half of the heroin-addicted individuals in the United States are thought to live in New York City (Kaplan, Sadock, & Grebb, 1994; Witkin & Griffin, 1994). Approximately 20% of those addicted to opiates are women (Krambeer, von McKnelly, Gabrielli, & Penick, 2001). Given a median estimate of 800,000 heroin-dependent people in the United States, this would mean that approximately 160,000 women in this country are addicted to opiates. There is a hidden population of opiate abusers in the United States, however: individuals who have regular jobs, and thus have private health care insurance, but who abuse or are addicted to opiates. Fully 76% of illicit drug abusers in the United States are employed, as are 81% of the binge drinkers and 81% of the heavy drinkers (Lowe, 2004). It is unlikely that these individuals will appear in estimates of drug addiction, and very little is known about this particular population. There are other aspects of opiate abuse/addiction that also have never been studied. For example, some pharmaceutical narcotic analgesics are known to be diverted to the illicit drug market. However, virtually no information is available on this problem, and we don't know whether the person who abuses pharmaceuticals is similar to, or markedly different from, the person who abuses illicit narcotics. Thus, the estimate of 500,000–1,000,000 intravenous heroin addicts must be accepted as only a minimal estimate of the narcotics-abuse/addiction problem in the United States.

Estimates of the problem of cocaine abuse and addiction. Cocaine abuse in the United States peaked in the mid-1980s, but cocaine remains a popular drug of abuse. Globally, an estimated 15 million people abuse or are addicted to cocaine, the vast majority of whom are thought to live in North America (Milne, 2003). In contrast, Grinfeld (2001) estimated that there were 2.5 million cocaine addicts in the United States.

Surprisingly, in spite of cocaine's reputation as an addictive substance, only a fraction of those who use it ever actually become addicted to it. Researchers now believe that only 3% to 20% of users go on to become addicted to this substance (Musto, 1991). Other researchers have suggested that only one cocaine user in six (Peele, Brodsky & Arnold, 1991) to one in twelve (Peluso & Peluso, 1988) was actually addicted to the drug.

Estimates of the problem of marijuana abuse/addiction. Marijuana is the most commonly abused *illegal* drug in the United States (Kaufman & McNaul, 1992) as well as Canada (Russell, Newman, & Bland, 1994). Some estimate that approximately 25% of the entire population of the United States, or more than 70 million people, have used marijuana at least once, and that there are 9 million "regular" users of marijuana in this country (Angell & Kassirer, 1994, p. 537). Of this number, approximately 3 million are thought to be addicted to the drug (Grinfeld, 2001).

Estimates of the problem of hallucinogenic abuse. As with marijuana, there are questions about whether hallucinogenics may be addictive. For this reason, this text speaks of the "problem of hallucinogenic abuse." Perhaps 10% of the entire population of the United States have used a hallucinogen at least once (Sadock & Sadock, 2003). However, hallucinogenic use is actually quite rare, and of those young adults who have used hallucinogenic drugs, only 1% or 2% will have done so in the past 30 days, according to the authors. These data suggest that the problem of *addiction* to hallucinogenics is exceedingly rare.

Estimates of the problem of tobacco addiction. Tobacco is a special product. Like alcohol, it is legally sold to adults. Unfortunately, tobacco products are also readily obtained by adolescents, who make up a significant proportion of those who use tobacco. Researchers estimate that approximately 46 million Americans smoke cigarettes (Brownlee et al., 1994). Of this number, an estimated 24 million smokers are male, and 22.3 million are female.

The Cost of Chemical Abuse/Addiction in the United States

Although the total number of people in this country who abuse or are addicted to recreational chemicals is limited, recreational substance use still extracts a terrible toll from society. Alcohol and drug abuse by some estimates cost $81 billion in lost productivity each year in the United States: $37 billion because of premature death and $44 billion because of illness (Lowe, 2004). Each year in the this country an estimated 420,000 smokers die from tobacco-related illness, and an additional 35,000 to 56,000 nonsmokers die each year as a result of their exposure to second-hand cigarette smoke (Mokdad, Marks, Stroup, & Gerberding, 2004; Benson & Sacco, 2000). Each year, an estimated 100,000 (Fleming, Mihic, & Harris, 2001; Naimi et al., 2003; Small, 2002;) to 200,000 (Hyman & Cassem, 1995; Kaplan, Sadock, & Grebb, 1994) die from alcohol-related illness or accidents. The annual drug-related death toll as a result of drug-related infant deaths, overdose-related deaths, suicides, homicides, motor vehicle accident deaths, and the various diseases associated with drug abuse in the United States is estimated at 16,000 (Craig, 2004) to 17,000 (Mokdad et al., 2004) people a year. However, even this number is still one-sixteenth as many people as are thought to die as a result of just tobacco use each year in this country, yet tobacco remains legal for individuals over the age of 21.

Collectively, all forms of recreational chemical abuse account for one-fourth to one-third of all deaths in the United States each year (Hurt et al., 1996). The majority of these substance-related deaths are caused by alcohol/tobacco abuse. As these figures suggest, chemical use, or abuse, is a significant factor in premature death, illness, loss of productivity, and medical expenses. However, because chemical abuse/addiction has so many hidden faces, behavioral scientists believe that these are only rough estimates of the annual impact of alcohol/drug use problems in the United States. Consider, for example, the hidden facet of substance abuse as a background cause of traumatic injuries. For example, 71% of patients admitted to a major trauma center had evidence of alcohol/illicit drugs in their bodies at the time (Cornwell et al., 1998).

The cost of alcohol abuse in the United States. A number of factors must be considered in attempting to calculate the annual financial cost of alcohol abuse and addiction in this country. Included in this list are direct and indirect costs, such as the cost of alcohol-related criminal activity, motor vehicle accidents, destruction of property, the cost of social welfare programs, private and public hospitalization costs for alcohol-related illness, and the cost of public and private treatment programs. Alcohol abuse/addiction is thought to cost society $185 billion/year in the United States alone, of which $26 billion is for direct health care costs (Petrakis, Gonzalez, Rosenheck, & Krystal, 2002; Smothers, Yahr, & Ruhl, 2004). The cost of alcohol-related lost productivity in this country alone is estimated at $67.7 billion (Craig, 2004) to $138 billion per year (Brink, 2004).

In recent years, politicians have spoken at length about the need to control the rising cost of health care in the United States. Alcohol-use disorders are significant factors in the growing health care financial crisis. Although only 5% to 10% of the general population has an alcohol-use problem, 10% to 20% of the ambulatory patients and 25% to 40% of the patients in hospitals suffer from some complication of alcohol use/abuse (Mersey, 2003; Weaver, Jarvis, & Schnoll, 1999). Further, 15% to 30% of the nursing home beds in this country are occupied by individuals whose alcohol use has contributed in part to their need for placement in a nursing home (Schuckit, 2000). Many of these nursing home beds are supported partly by public funds, making chronic alcohol abuse a major factor in the growing cost of nursing home care for the elderly.

Alcohol-related costs of vehicle and property destruction amount to $24.7 billion a year in the United States,

according to Craig (2004), with alcohol being a factor in approximately 40% of all fatal motor vehicle accidents. Alcohol abuse is thought to be a factor in 25% to 60% of all accidents resulting in traumatic injuries (Dyehouse & Sommers, 1998). Each year, an estimated 85,000 to 140,000 people in this country lose their lives because of alcohol use/abuse (Mokdad et al., 2004).

Individuals who have been injured as a result of alcohol use/abuse require medical treatment. Ultimately, this medical treatment is paid for by the public in the form of higher insurance costs and higher taxes. Indeed, alcohol-use disorders are thought to account for 15% of the money spent for health care in the United States each year (Schuckit, 2000). Yet in spite of the pain and suffering that alcohol causes, only 5% (Prater, Miller, & Zylstra, 1999) to 10% of alcohol-dependent individuals are *ever* identified and referred to a treatment program (Wing, 1995).

The cost of tobacco use. Although it is legally produced and might be consumed by adults without legal problems, tobacco extracts a terrible cost. Estimates of the economic cost of cigarette smoking range from $53 to $73 billion in just direct medical costs in the United States, plus an additional $47 to $82 billion a year in lost productivity (Anczak & Nogler, 2003; Patkar, Vergare, Batka, Weinstein, & Leone, 2003; "Cigarette Smoking Attributable Morbidity . . . ," 2004). Globally, more than 3 million people, die each year as a result of smoking-related illness; 435,000 of these live in the United States (Mokdad et al., 2004; Patkar et al., 2003). It is believed that one in every five deaths in the United States can be traced to smoking-related disease (Miller, 1999).

The cost of illicit substance abuse. A number of factors must be included in any estimate of recreational drug use in the United States, including the estimated financial impact of premature death or illness caused by substance abuse, lost wages from those who lose their jobs as a result of substance abuse, the financial losses incurred by victims of drug-related crimes, and the expected costs of drug-related law-enforcement activities. With this in mind, researchers have suggested that the annual economic cost of recreational chemical use in the United States is approximately $383 per person (Swan, 1998). The total annual economic impact of illicit chemical use/abuse is estimated at between $110 billion (Connors, Donovan, & DiClemente, 2001) and $276 billion per year (Stein, Orlando, & Sturm, 2000). No matter which of these estimates you accept as most accurate, drug abuse is clearly an expensive luxury.

Drug use as an American way of life. Notice that in the last paragraph drug abuse was identified as a "luxury." To see how we as a nation have come to value recreational chemical use, consider that money spent on illicit recreational chemicals is not used to buy medical care, food, shelter, or clothing, but spent simply for personal pleasure. In the last years of the 20th century, the annual expenditure for illicit recreational chemicals in the United States was a sum greater than *the total combined income* of the 80 poorest Third World countries (Corwin, 1994).

In conclusion, there is no possible way to estimate fully the personal, economic, or social impact that these various forms of chemical addiction have had on society When one considers the possible economic impact of medical costs incurred, lost productivity, or other indirect costs from such "hidden" drug abuse and addiction, one can begin to appreciate the impact that chemical abuse and addiction has inflicted.

Why Is It So Difficult to Understand the Drug Abuse Problem in the United States?

For the past two generations, politicians have spoken about society's war on drug use/abuse. One of the basic strategies of this ongoing war has been the exaggeration of the dangers associated with chemical use (Musto, 1991; Peele, 1994). This technique is known as *disinformation*, and it seems to have been almost an unofficial policy of the government's antidrug efforts to distort and exaggerate the scope of the problem and the dangers associated with recreational drug use.

An excellent example of this "disinformation policy" is the statement made by U.S. Representative Vic Fazio, who, in calling for legislation to control access to certain chemicals that might be used to manufacture illicit methamphetamine, spoke of "a generation of meth-addicted crank babies . . .

rapidly filling our nation's hospitals" ("Politicians discover," 1996, p. 70). This statement came as a surprise to health care professionals: There was no epidemic of methamphetamine addicted babies. But this did not prevent the false statement from being offered as a "fact" in the United State House of Representatives.

For more than two generations, the media have presented drugs in such a negative light that "anyone reading or hearing of them would not be tempted to experiment with the substances" (Musto, 1991, p. 46). Unfortunately, such scare tactics have not worked. For example, in the mid-1980s the media presented report after report of the dangers of chemical addiction yet consistently failed to point out that only 5.5 million Americans (or about 2% of the then-current population of approximately 260 million) was addicted to illegal drugs (Holloway, 1991).

It is not the goal of this text to advocate substance use, but there are wide discrepancies between the scope of recreational drug use as reported in the mass media and that reported in the scientific research. For example, Wilens (2004a, b) suggested that between 10% and 30% of the adults in the United States have a substance-use disorder of some kind. In contrast, other researchers have suggested that only a small percentage of the U.S. population was using illicit chemicals. Given these wide discrepancies, the most plausible conclusion is that much of what has been said about the drug-abuse "crisis" in the United States has been tainted by misinformation, or disinformation. To understand the problem of recreational chemical use/abuse, it is necessary to look beyond the "sound bytes" or the "factoids" of the mass media and the politicians.

Summary

Researchers estimate that at any point in time, 2% to 10% of American adults either abuse or are addicted to illegal drugs. Although this percentage would suggest that large numbers of people are using illicit chemicals in this society, it also suggests that the drugs of abuse are not universally addictive. The various forms of chemical abuse/addiction discussed here reflect different manifestations of a unitary disorder: chemical abuse/addiction. Finally, although drug addiction is classified as a disease, most physicians are ill-prepared to treat substance-abusing patients. In this chapter, we have examined the problem of recreational drug use and its impact on society. In later sections of this book, we will explore in detail the various drugs of abuse, their effects on the user, the consequences of their use, and the rehabilitation process available for those who are abusing or addicted to chemicals. This information should help you to better understand the problem of recreational substance use in this country.

CHAPTER TWO

What Do We Mean When We Say Substance Abuse and Addiction?

Introduction

The last chapter examined substance abuse/addiction as an under-recognized social problem. Like many problem areas, the world of substance abuse and drug rehabilitation has its own language. This chapter presents some of the more common concepts and terms used in this field.

The Continuum of Chemical Use

People frequently confuse chemical *use* with *abuse* and *addiction*. Indeed, these terms are often mistakenly used as if they were synonymous, even in clinical research studies (Minkoff, 1997). In reality, recreational alcohol/drug use, like most forms of human behavior, falls on a continuum (Kaminer, 1999). Complete abstinence is at one end of the continuum; physical addiction to a chemical is the opposite end (McCrady & Epstein, 1995). Between these two extremes are various patterns of chemical use that differ in the intensity with which people engage in substance use and the consequences of this behavior. In their discussion of illegal substance use, Cattarello, Clayton, and Leukefeld (1995) suggested that "people differ in their illicit drug use. Some people never experiment; some experiment and never use again. Others use drugs irregularly or become regular users, whereas others develop pathological and addictive patterns of use" (p. 152). In this statement, the authors identified five different patterns of recreational chemical use: (a) total abstinence, (b) a brief period of experimentation, followed by a return to abstinence, (c) irregular, or occasional, use of illicit chemicals, (d) regular use of chemicals, and (e) the pathological or addictive pattern of use that is the hallmark of physical dependence on chemicals.

Even the stage of addiction to alcohol/drugs is not uniform. Rather, "drug use is considered a normal learned behavior that falls along a continuum ranging from patterns of little use and few problems to excessive use and dependence" (Budney, Sigmon, & Higgins, 2003, p. 249). Unfortunately, there are no firm boundaries between the points on a substance-use continuum (Sellers et al., 1993). Only the end points—total abstinence, and active physical addiction to chemicals—remain relatively fixed. The main advantage of a drug-use continuum is that it allows us to classify chemical use of various intensities and patterns. Drug use/abuse/addiction thus becomes a behavior with a number of possible intermediate steps between the two extreme points, not a "condition" that either is or is not present. For the purpose of this text, we will view the phenomenon of recreational alcohol/drug use along the continuum shown in Figure 2.1.

The first point in the continuum presented in Figure 2.1 is *Level 0: Total abstinence*. Individuals whose substance use falls in this category abstain from all alcohol/drug abuse, and they present no immediate risk for substance-use problems (Isaacson & Schorling, 1999).

The second category is *Level 1: Rare/social use*. This level includes experimental use and presents a low risk for a substance-use disorder on the continuum suggested by Isaacson and Schorling (1999). Individuals in this category would only rarely use alcohol or chemicals for recreational purposes. They would not experience any of the social, financial, interpersonal, medical, or legal problems that are the hallmark of the pathological use of chemicals. Further, people whose substance use is at this level would not demonstrate the loss of control over their chemical use that is found at higher levels of the continuum. Their chemical use would not pose any threat to their lives.

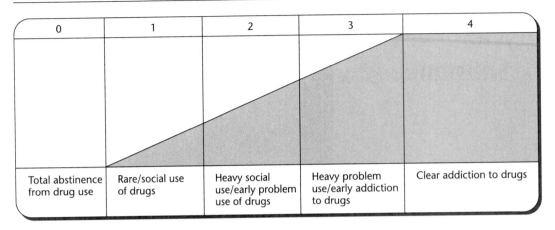

0	1	2	3	4
Total abstinence from drug use	Rare/social use of drugs	Heavy social use/early problem use of drugs	Heavy problem use/early addiction to drugs	Clear addiction to drugs

FIGURE 2.1   The continuum of chemical use.

Level 2: Heavy social use/early problem drug use. A person whose chemical use falls at this point in the continuum would (a) use alcohol/drugs in a manner that is clearly above the norm for society, and/or (b) begin to experience various combinations of legal, social, financial, occupational, and personal problems associated with chemical use. Individuals whose substance use falls in this range could be classified as being at risk for a substance-use disorder (Isaacson & Schorling, 1999), for being substance abusers, or for being problem drinkers.

Individuals in this category are more numerous than those who are clearly addicted to chemicals. Sobell and Sobell (1993) found, for example, that problem drinkers were four times as numerous as alcohol-dependent individuals. At this level of chemical use, individuals begin to manifest symptoms of a behavioral disorder in which they make poor choices about their use of a recreational chemical, but are potentially still able to control their use (Minkoff, 1997). They might try to hide or deny the problems that arise from their chemical use. Fortunately, many of those who reach this point in the drug-use continuum will learn from their experience and alter their behavior to avoid future problems. Thus, at this level of use, the individual is not addicted to chemicals.

Level 3: Heavy problem use/early addiction. At level 3, the alcohol or chemical use has clearly become a problem. Indeed, this person may have become addicted to chemicals, although he or she may argue the point.

Someone whose chemical abuse is at this level has started to experience medical complications as well as classic withdrawal symptoms when he or she is unable to continue the use of drugs/alcohol. Isaacson and Schorling (1999) classified individuals at this level as engaging in "problem use." They are often preoccupied with substance use and have *lost control* over their chemical use (Brown, 1995; Gordis, 1995). Shute and Tangley (1997) estimated that 40 million people in the United States abuse alcohol but are not dependent on it. These individuals would fall into categories 3 and 4 on the continuum.

Level 4: Clearly addicted to drugs. At this point the person demonstrates all of the symptoms of the classic addiction syndrome, in combination with multiple social, medical, legal, financial, occupational, and personal problems that are the hallmark of an alcohol/drug dependency. A person whose chemical use falls at this point in the continuum would clearly have the physical disorder of alcohol/drug *dependency* (Minkoff, 1997). This individual is clearly addicted in the assessor's mind. Even at this level of substance use, the addicted individual might try to rationalize away or deny problems associated with his or her alcohol or drug use. More than one elderly alcoholic, for example, has tried to explain away an abnormal liver function as being the aftermath of a childhood illness. However, to an impartial observer, the person at this level is clearly addicted to alcohol or drugs.

Admittedly, this classification system, like all others, is imperfect. The criteria used to determine an individual's level of use are arbitrary and subject to discussion. It is often "the variety of alcohol related problems, not any unique criterion, that captures what clinicians really mean when they label a person alcoholic" (Vaillant, 1983, p. 42). However, even in the case of the opiates, some individuals will use these drugs, perhaps even on a regular basis, and not become *addicted*. Physical addiction is just one point on the continuum of drug-use styles.

Definitions of Terms Used in This Book

To understand each other when they communicate about the phenomenon of substance abuse, the people who study this problem need a common language. This section presents definitions of some of the most common terms in this field.

Social use. "Social use" of a substance is defined by traditional social standards. Currently, alcohol is the chemical most frequently found within a social context, often being used in religious or family functions. In some circles, marijuana is also used in a social context, although it is a controlled substance[1], and thus it is less acceptable than alcohol.

Substance abuse. Substance abuse occurs when an individual uses a drug without a legitimate medical need to do so. In the case of alcohol, the person is drinking in excess of accepted social standards (Schuckit, 1995b). Thus the definition of substance *abuse* is based on current social standards. The individual who abuses a chemical might be said to have made *poor choices* regarding use of that substance, but he or she is not addicted to it (Minkoff, 1997).

Drug-of-choice. Clinicians once spoke about the individual's *drug of choice* as an important component of the addictive process. They assumed that the drug a person would use given the choice was an important clue to the nature of his or her addiction. However, little emphasis is currently put on the individual's drug of choice (Walters, 1994). One reason for this change is that the nature of addiction itself is changing. In this era of polyphar-

macology,[2] it is rare for a person to be addicted to just one chemical. For example, many stimulant users will drink alcohol or use benzodiazepines to control the side effects of cocaine or amphetamines.

Addiction/dependence. Technically, *addiction* is a term that is poorly defined, and most scientists prefer the more precise term *dependence* (Shaffer, 2001). In this text, these terms will be used interchangeably. Physical dependence on alcohol or drugs might be classified as

a primary, chronic, disease with genetic, psychosocial and environmental factors influencing its development and manifestations. The disease is often progressive and fatal. It is characterized by impaired control over drinking, preoccupation with the drug alcohol, use of alcohol despite adverse consequences, and distortions in thinking. (Morse & Flavin, 1992, p. 1013)

This definition contains all of the core concepts used to define drug addiction. Each form of drug addiction is viewed as a (a) primary disease (b) with multiple manifestations in the person's social, psychological, spiritual, and economic life; the disease (c) is often progressive, (d) potentially fatal, and (e) marked by the individual's inability to control the use of the drug; the person has (f) a preoccupation with chemical use, and in spite of its many consequences, (g) develops a distorted way of looking at the world that supports continued use of that chemical. In addition, dependence on a chemical is marked by (a) the development of *tolerance* to its effects and (b) a *characteristic withdrawal syndrome* when the drug is discontinued (Schuckit, 2000). Each of these symptoms of addiction will be discussed later in more detail.

Tolerance develops over time, as the individual's body struggles to maintain normal function in the presence of one or more foreign chemicals. Technically, there are several different types of tolerance. In this text, we will limit our discussion to just two: (a) metabolic tolerance and (b) pharmacodynamic tolerance. *Metabolic tolerance* develops when the body becomes effective in biotransforming a chemical into a form that can be

---

[1] See Appendix 3.

[2] See Glossary.

easily eliminated from the body. (The process of biotransformation will be discussed in more detail in Chapter 6). The liver is the main organ involved in biotransformation. In some cases, constant exposure to a chemical causes the liver to become more efficient at breaking it down, making a given dose less effective over time.

Pharmacodynamic tolerance describes the increasing insensitivity of the central nervous system to the drug's effects. When the cells of the central nervous system are continuously exposed to a chemical, they will often try to maintain normal function by making minute changes in their structure to compensate for the drug's effects. These cells then become less sensitive to the effects of that chemical, and the person must use more of the drug to achieve the initial effect.

If used for a long enough period of time, the major recreational chemicals will bring about a characteristic *withdrawal syndrome*. The exact nature of withdrawal will vary depending on the class of drugs being used, the length of time the drug is used, and other factors such as the individual's state of health. But each group of drugs will produce certain physical symptoms when the person stops taking them. A rule of thumb is that the withdrawal syndrome will include symptoms that are opposite to those induced by the drug. In clinical practice, the existence of a withdrawal syndrome is evidence that pharmacodynamic tolerance has developed. The withdrawal syndrome is caused by the absence of the chemical to which the central nervous system had previously adapted. When the drug is discontinued, the central nervous system will go through a period of readaptation, as it learns to function normally without the drug being present. During this period of time, the individual will experience the physical signs of withdrawal.

This process is clearly seen during alcohol withdrawal. Alcohol functions on the cells of the central nervous system much like the brakes on your car. If you attempt to drive while the brakes are engaged, you might eventually force the car to go fast enough to meet the posted speed limits; but if you were to release the pressure on the brakes suddenly, the car would leap ahead because the brakes would no longer be impeding its forward motion. You would have to ease up on the gas pedal so the engine would slow enough to keep you within the posted speed limit.

During that period of readjustment, the car would, in a sense, be going through withdrawal. Much the same thing happens in the body when the individual stops using drugs. The body must adjust to the absence of a chemical that, previously, it had learned would always be there. This withdrawal syndrome, like tolerance of the drug's effects, provides strong evidence that the individual is addicted to one or more chemicals.

The Growth of New "Addictions"

Not only does the popular press exaggerate the dangers of chemical abuse, but society also tends to speak of "addictions" to a wide range of behaviors/substances, including food, sex, gambling, men, women, play, television, shopping, credit cards, making money, carbohydrates, shoplifting, unhappy relationships, french fries, lip balm, and a multitude of other "non-drug" behaviors or substances (Shaffer, 2001). This expanded use of the term *addiction* does not appear to have an end in sight, although it may have reached its zenith with the formation of "Lip Balm Anonymous" (Shaffer, 2001).

Fortunately, there is little evidence that non-drug centered behaviors can result in physical addiction. In this text, the term *addiction* will be limited to physical dependence on alcohol and chemical agents commonly known as "drugs of abuse."

What Do We *Really* Know About the Addictive Disorders?

If you were to watch television talk shows or read a small sample of the self-help books on the market, you would think that researchers fully understand the causes and treatment of drug abuse. *Nothing could be further from the truth!* Much of what is "known" about addiction is based on mistaken assumptions, clinical theory, or, at best, incomplete data.

An excellent example of how incomplete data might influence treatment theory is that much of the research on substance abuse is based on a distorted sample of people: those who are in treatment for substance-abuse problems (Gazzaniga, 1988). Virtually nothing is known about people who use chemicals on a social basis but never become addicted, or those who are addicted to chemicals but recover from their chemical-use problems without formal intervention or treatment. A serious question that must be asked is whether individuals in treatment are representative of *all* drug/alcohol addicted persons.

For example, individuals who seek treatment for a substance-use disorder are quite different from those who do not (Carroll & Rounsaville, 1992). As a group, alcohol/drug addicted people who do not seek treatment seem better able to control their substance use and to have shorter drug-use histories than people who seek treatment. This may be why the majority of those who abuse chemicals either stop or significantly reduce their chemical use without professional intervention (Carroll & Rounsaville, 1992; Humphreys, Moos, & Finney, 1995; Mayo Foundation for Medical Education and Research, 1989; Peele, 1985, 1989; Tucker & Sobell, 1992). It appears that only a minority of those who begin to use recreational chemicals lose control over their substance use and require professional intervention. Yet it is on this minority that much of the research on recognition and treatment of substance-abuse problems is based.

Consider, for a moment, the people known as "chippers." They make up a subpopulation of drug users about whom virtually nothing is known. They seem to be able to use a chemical, even one supposedly quite addictive, only when they want to, and then to discontinue its use when they wish to do so. Researchers are not able to make even an educated guess as to their number. Chippers are thought to use chemicals in response to social pressure, and then to stop using when the social need has passed. But this is only a theory, and it might not be supported by research.

Another reason that much of the research in substance abuse rehabilitation is flawed is that a significant proportion is carried out either in Veterans Administration (VA) hospitals or in public facilities such as state hospitals. However, individuals in these facilities are not automatically representative of the "typical" alcohol/drug dependent person. For example, to be admitted to a VA hospital, the individual must have successfully completed a tour of duty in the military. This means that the person is quite different from those who either never enlisted in the military or who enlisted but were unable to complete a tour of duty. The alcohol/drug addict who is employed and able to afford treatment in a private treatment center might be far different from the indigent alcohol/drug dependent person who must be treated in a publicly funded treatment program. Further, only a small proportion of the available literature on the subject of drug addiction addresses forms of addiction other than alcoholism. An even smaller proportion addresses the impact of recreational chemical use on women (Cohen, 2000). Much of the research conducted to date has assumed that alcohol/drug use is the same for men and women, overlooking possible differences in how men and women come to use chemicals and the differing ways addiction affects them.

Further, although children and adolescents have long been known to abuse chemicals, there is still virtually no research on drug abuse/addiction in this group. Yet, as will be discussed in Chapter 21, drug abuse in this population is a serious problem. Children and adolescents who abuse chemicals are not simply small adults, and research done on adults cannot be accurately generalized to them.

Thus, much of what we think we know about addiction is based on research that is quite limited, and many important questions remain to be answered. Yet this is the foundation on which an entire industry of treatment has evolved. It is not our purpose to deny that large numbers of people abuse drugs or that such drug abuse carries with it a terrible cost in personal suffering. It is also not our purpose to deny that many people are harmed by drug abuse. We know that people become addicted to chemicals. The purpose of this section is to make the reader aware of the shortcomings of the current body of research on substance abuse.

The State of the Art: Unanswered Questions, Uncertain Answers

As you have discovered by now, there is much confusion in the professional community over the problems of substance abuse/addiction. Even in the case of alcoholism, the most common of the drug addictions, there is an element of confusion or uncertainty over what the essential features of alcoholism might be. For example, 30% to 45% of all adults will have at least one transient alcohol-related problem (blackout, legal problem, etc.)

at some point in their lives (Sadock & Sadock, 2003). Yet this does not mean that 30% to 45% of the adult population is alcohol dependent! Rather, this fact underscores the need for researchers to more clearly delineate the features that might identify the potential alcoholic.

What constitutes a valid diagnosis of chemical dependency? Ultimately, the definitions of substance *abuse* or *addiction* are quite arbitrary (O'Brien, 2001). A generation ago, George Vaillant (1983) suggested that "it is not who is drinking but *who is watching*" (p. 22, italics added for emphasis) that defines whether a given person is alcohol dependent. The same is true for other drugs of abuse. In the end, a diagnosis of drug addiction is a value judgment. This professional opinion might be made easier by suggested criteria such as those for mental illnesses in the American Psychiatric Association's *Diagnostic and Statistical Manual of Mental Disorders* (4th edition, 2000; *DSM-IV*); but even in rather advanced cases of drug dependency, the issue of whether the individual is addicted is not always clear-cut.

Let us, for the moment, focus on the problem of alcoholism, or drug addiction, and its diagnosis. There are three elements necessary to the diagnosis of alcoholism or drug addiction (Shaffer, 2001):

1. *Craving/compulsion:* the individual's thoughts become fixated on obtaining and using the chemical(s) he or she has become dependent on.
2. *Loss of control:* the person will use more of the chemical than he or she intended, is unable to cut back on the amount used, or is unable to stop using it.
3. *Consequences:* the individual will use the drug regardless of the results of this use. Such consequences might include impairment of social, vocational, or physical well-being as well as possible legal or financial problems.

Although these criteria provide some degree of consistency between diagnoses, ultimately, the diagnosis of chemical dependency is one person's opinion about another person's chemical use. The issue of assessing another individual's substance-use pattern will be discussed in a later chapter. The point here is that we still have much to learn and many questions to answer about how to best assess a person's chemical-use pattern and provide an accurate diagnosis.

What is the true relationship between alcohol/drug use and violence within the family? In the last chapter, we noted a relationship between alcohol/drug use and violence in the family. It is wrong to assume automatically, however, that the drug use *caused* the violence. Indeed, there is evidence to suggest that at least in some families the violence might have taken place regardless of whether drugs or alcohol were involved (Steinglass, Bennett, Wolin, & Reiss, 1987). In such families, alcohol use and violence reflect the presence of another form of familial dysfunction that has yet to be identified. The point to keep in mind is that we cannot see a relationship between alcohol/drug use and violence within the family and assume that the drug use caused the violence. Behavioral science has a great deal more to learn about the true relationship between violence and alcohol/drug abuse.

What is the role of news media in the development of new chemical use trends? One of the most serious of the unanswered questions facing mental health or substance abuse professionals is whether the media have been a positive or a negative influence on people who have not started to experiment with alcohol or drugs. There is a prohibition against chemical use, coupled with legal sanctions against the importation or use of many drugs. Because of this prohibition, the sale, or use of drugs or alcohol (for those who are under the legal drinking age), is "newsworthy."

Some have charged that media reports, rather than making drug use unattractive, have actually enhanced its appeal to many who might otherwise not have been motivated to experiment. Media coverage of drug arrests, the "dangers" associated with the use of various chemicals, not to mention the profits associated with the sale of controlled substances, all contribute to a certain "aura" that surrounds drug abuse. The experience of the Netherlands in dealing with the drug problem (discussed in Chapter 35) suggests that when the legal sanctions against drug use are removed, drugs actually become *less* attractive to the average individual, and casual drug use declines.

In the Netherlands, substance abuse was originally seen as a public health issue rather than a legal problem.

Only after large numbers of chemical-using foreigners moved to the Netherlands to take advantage of this permissiveness which had been widely reported in the media, did Dutch authorities begin to utilize law enforcement as a means of controlling substance use. The point is that much evidence suggests the media reports have actually contributed to the problem of substance by adding to the aura of mystery and "charm" that surrounds the street drug world. Thus, the question must be asked: Whose side are the media on?

Summary

In this chapter, a continuum of drug use was introduced and terms common to the study of substance abuse were presented. There is a problem of inadequate research in chemical dependency, and this was explored, as well as the role of drug use in family violence and the part played by the media in inadvertently encouraging drug experimentation through wide-scale reporting about the drug scene.

CHAPTER THREE

The Medical Model of Chemical Addiction

Introduction

Later in this text, the various major drugs of abuse will be discussed. However, knowledge of what each drug might do to the user does not answer a simple yet very difficult set of questions: (a) Why do people *begin* to use these chemicals, (b) why do they *continue* to use recreational chemicals, and (c) why do some *become addicted* to them? In this chapter, the answers to these questions will be examined from the perspective of the "medical," "biomedical," or "disease" model of addiction.

Why Do People Abuse Chemicals?[1]

At first, to ask why people abuse chemicals might seem rather simplistic. People use drugs because the drugs make them feel good. Because they feel good after using the drug, some people wish to repeat the experience. As a result of this continual search for drug-induced pleasure, the drugs of abuse have become part of our environment. The prevailing atmosphere of chemical use/abuse then forces each one of us to make a decision to use or not use recreational chemicals every day. For most of us, the choice is relatively simple. Usually the decision not to use chemicals does not even require conscious thought. But regardless of whether we acknowledge the need to make a decision, each of us is faced with the opportunity to use recreational chemicals each day and we must decide whether or not to do so.

Some people might challenge the issue of personal choice, but stop for an instant, and think: Where is the nearest liquor store? If you wanted it, where could you buy some marijuana? If you are above the age of about 15, the odds are very good that you could answer either of these questions. But why didn't you buy any of these chemicals on your way to work or to school this morning? Why did you, or didn't you, buy a recreational drug or two on your way home last night? The answer is that you made a choice. So, in one sense, people use the drugs of abuse because they choose to do so. But a number of factors influence the individual's decision to use or not use recreational chemicals, and these will be discussed in the next section of this chapter.

Factors That Influence Recreational Drug Use

The physical reward potential. The reasons a person might use alcohol or another drug of abuse are complex. The novice chemical user may make the decision to try one or more drugs in response to peer pressure or because that individual expects the drug will have pleasurable effects. Researchers call this the "pharmacological potential," or the "reward potential" of the chemical (Budney, Sigmon, & Higgins, 2003; Kalivas, 2003; Monti, Kadden, Rohsenow, Cooney, & Abrams, 2002; Meyer, 1989). As virtually all the drugs of abuse have a high reinforcement potential (Crowley, 1988), it is easy to understand how the principles of operant conditioning might apply to the phenomenon of drug abuse/addiction (Budney et al., 2003).

According to the basic laws of behavioral psychology, if something (a) increases the individual's sense of pleasure or (b) decreases his or her discomfort, then he or she is likely to repeat that behavior. This is called the *reward process.* In contrast, if a certain behavior (c) increases the individual's sense of discomfort or (d) reduces the person's sense of pleasure, he or she would be unlikely to repeat that behavior. This is called the *punishment*

---

[1]This question is a reference not to those people who are addicted to chemicals, but to those who use chemicals for recreational purposes.

potential of the behavior in question. Finally, the immediate consequence (either reward or punishment) has a stronger impact on behavior than delayed consequence. When these rules of behavior are applied to the problem of substance abuse such as cigarette smoking, one discovers that the immediate consequences of chemical use (that is, the immediate pleasure) has a stronger impact on behavior than the delayed consequences (i.e., possible development of disease at a later date). Therefore, it should not be surprising that because many people find the effects of the drugs of abuse[2] to be pleasurable, they will be tempted to use the drugs again and again. But the reward potential of a chemical substance, while a powerful incentive for its repeated use, is not sufficient in itself to cause addiction (Kalivas, 2003).

The social learning component of drug use. Individuals do not start life expecting to abuse chemicals. Alcohol/drug abusers must be taught (a) that substance use is acceptable, (b) to recognize the effects of the chemical, and (c) to interpret them as pleasurable. All of these tasks are accomplished through social learning. For example, in addition to the influence of peer groups on the individual's chemical-use history (discussed later in this chapter), how substance use is portrayed in the movies or other forms of mass media impacts how the individual perceives the abuse of that chemical (Cape, 2003).

Marijuana abuse provides a good illustration of points "b" and "c" (above). First time marijuana users must be taught by their drug-using peers (1) how to smoke it, (2) how to recognize the effects of the drug, and (3) why marijuana intoxication is so pleasurable (Kandel & Raveis, 1989). The same learning process takes place with the other drugs of abuse, including alcohol (Monti et al., 2002). It is not uncommon for a novice drinker to become so ill after a night's drinking that he or she will swear never to drink again. However, more experienced drinkers will help the novice learn such things as how to drink, what effects to look for, and why these alcohol-induced physical sensations are so pleasurable. This feedback is often informal and comes

through a variety of sources such as a "drinking buddy," newspaper articles, advertisements, television programs, conversations with friends and coworkers, and casual observations of others who are drinking. The outcome of this social learning process is that the novice drinker is taught how to drink, and how to enjoy the alcohol he or she consumes.

Individual expectations as a component of drug use. The individual's expectations for a drug are a strong influence on how that person interprets the effects of the chemical. These expectations evolve in childhood or early adolescence as a result of multiple factors, such as peer group influences, the child's exposure to advertising, parental substance use behaviors, and mass media (Cape, 2003; Monti et al., 2002). To understand this process, consider the individual's expectations for alcohol. Research has shown that these are most strongly influenced by the context in which the individual uses alcohol and by his or her cultural traditions rather than the pharmacological effects of the alcohol consumed (Lindman, Sjoholm, & Lang, 2000).

These drug use expectations play a powerful role in shaping the individual's drug- or alcohol-use behavior. For example, for people who became "high-risk drinkers" (Werner, Walker, & Greene, 1995, p. 737), by the end of their junior year of college their expectations that alcohol use would be a positive experience for them were significantly stronger than those of nondrinkers or those the authors classified as "low risk" drinkers (p. 737). In the case of LSD abuse, the individual's negative expectations are a significant factor in the development of a "bad trip." Novice LSD users are more likely to anticipate negative consequences from the drug than are more experienced users. This anxiety seems to help set the stage for the negative drug experience known as the "bad trip."

Although people's expectations about the effects of alcohol or drugs play a powerful role in shaping their subsequent alcohol/drug use behavior, they are not fixed. In some cases, the expectations about the use of a specific drug are so extremely negative that people will not even contemplate the use of that compound. This is frequently the case for children who grow up with a violent, abusive alcoholic parent; often these children vow *never* to use alcohol themselves. This is an extreme adaptation to the problem of personal alcohol use, but it is not uncommon.

---

[2]Obviously, the over-the-counter analgesics are exceptions to this rule, since they do not cause the user to experience "pleasure." However, they are included in this text because of their significant potential to cause harm.

More often, the individual's expectations about alcohol/drugs can be modified by both personal experience and social feedback. For example, if an adolescent with initial misgivings about drinking finds alcohol's effects to be pleasurable, he would be more likely to continue to use alcohol during adolescence (Smith, 1994). After his first use of a recreational chemical, his preconceptions, combined with feedback from others, will help shape his interpretation of the chemical's effects. Based on his subjective interpretation of the alcohol's effects, he becomes more willing to use that compound in the future.

Cultural/social influences on chemical use patterns. People's decision to use or not use a recreational chemical is made within the context of their community and the social groups to which they belong (Monti et al., 2002; Rosenbloom, 2000). A person's cultural heritage can impact his or her chemical use at five levels (Pihl, 1999): (a) the general cultural environment, (b) the specific community in which the individual lives, (c) subcultures within the specific community, (d) family/peer influences, and (e) the context within which alcohol/drugs are used. At each of these levels, factors such as the availability of recreational substances and prevailing attitudes and feelings combine to govern the individual's use of mood-altering chemicals (Kadushin, Reber, Saxe, & Livert, 1998; Westermeyer, 1995). Thus, in "cultures where use of a substance is comfortable, familiar, and socially regulated both as to style of use and appropriate time and place for such use, addiction is less likely and may be practically unknown" (Peele, 1985, p. 106). Unfortunately, in contrast to the rapid rate at which new drug use trends develop, cultural guidelines might require generations or centuries to develop (Westermeyer, 1995).

An interesting transition is emerging from the Jewish subculture, especially in the ultraorthodox sects. Only certain forms of alcohol are blessed by the local rabbi as having been prepared in accordance with Jewish tradition and thus are considered "kosher." Recreational drugs, on the other hand, are not considered kosher, and are forbidden (Roane, 2000). Yet as the younger generation explores new behaviors, many are turning toward experimental use of the "unclean" chemicals that they hear about through non-Jewish friends and the mass media. Significant numbers of these individuals are becoming addicted to recreational chemicals in spite of the religious sanction against their use, in large part because their education failed to warn them of the addictive powers of these compounds (Roane, 2000).

In the Italian American subculture, drinking is limited mainly to religious or family celebrations, and excessive drinking is strongly discouraged. The "proper" (i.e., socially acceptable) drinking behavior is modeled by adults during religious or family activities, and there are strong familial and social sanctions against those who do not follow these rules. As a result of this process of social instruction, the Italian American subculture has a relatively low rate of alcoholism.

More than a generation ago, Kunitz and Levy (1974) explored the different drinking patterns of the Navaho and Hopi Indian tribes. This study is significant as the cultures co-exist in the same part of the country and share similar genetic histories. However, Navaho tribal customs see public group drinking as acceptable and solitary drinking as a mark of deviance. For the Hopi, however, drinking is more likely to be a solitary experience, for alcohol use is not tolerated within the tribe, and those who drink are shunned. These two groups, who live in close geographic proximity to each other, clearly demonstrate how different social groups develop different guidelines for alcohol use for their members.

For the most part, the discussion in this section has been limited to the use of alcohol. This is because alcohol is the most common recreational drug used in the United States. However, this is not true for all cultural groups. The American Indians of the Southwest will frequently ingest mushrooms with hallucinogenic potential as part of their religious ceremonies. In many cultures in the Middle East, alcohol is prohibited but the use of hashish is quite acceptable. In both cultures, strict social rules dictate the occasions when these substances might be used, the conditions under which they might be used, and the penalties for unacceptable use.

The point to remember is that cultural rules provide the individual with a degree of guidance about acceptable and unacceptable substance use. But within each culture, there are various social groups which may, only to a limited degree, adopt the standards of the parent culture. The relationship between different social groups and the parent culture is illustrated in Figure 3.1.

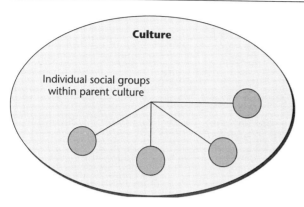

FIGURE 3.1 Relationship between different social groups and the parent culture.

Social feedback mechanisms and drug use. There is a subtle, often overlooked feedback mechanism that exists between the individual and the social group to which she belongs. Whereas the individual's behavior is shaped, at least in part, by her social group, she will also help to shape the behavioral expectations of the group by choosing which groups to associate with. In other words, individuals who abuse certain chemicals tend to associate with others who abuse those same compounds and to avoid those whose substance abuse pattern is different. An example of this is the pattern of cocaine abuse that has evolved in the United States: "Crack" cocaine is found mainly in the inner cities, whereas powdered cocaine is found more often in the suburbs.

Although most people do not think in terms of cultural expectations, their behavior *does* parallel these themes. Consider the "closet" alcohol abuser, who might go a different liquor store each day to hide the extent of his drinking from sales staff (Knapp, 1996), or who might sneak around the neighborhood at night hiding empty alcohol bottles in the neighbors' trash cans. In each case, the individual is attempting to project an image of his alcohol use that is closer to social expectations than to reality.

A fact often overlooked in substance abuse research is that chemical use patterns are not fixed. People often change their alcohol/drug use pattern over time. For example, if you were to question large numbers

of people who used marijuana and hallucinogenics during the "hippie" era (late 1960s to the mid 1970s), most would say the drug use was simply a "phase I was going through." Unfortunately, some people find the chemical's effects desirable enough to encourage further abuse in spite of social sanctions against it. In such cases it is not uncommon for the individual to drift toward a social group that encourages and supports use of that drug in what amounts to either a conscious or unconscious attempt to restructure his or her social environment so that it supports the chemical use.

Individual life goals as helping to shape chemical use. Another factor that also influences the individual's decision to either begin or continue the use of chemicals is whether use of a specific drug is consistent with the person's long-term goals or values. This is rarely a problem with socially approved drugs, such as alcohol—and to a smaller degree tobacco. But consider the junior executive who has just won a much hoped for promotion, only to find that the new position is with a division of the company with a strong "no smoking" policy.

In this hypothetical example, the executive might find that giving up smoking is not as serious a problem as he had once thought, if this is part of the price he must pay to take the promotion. In such a case, the individual has weighed whether further use of that drug (tobacco) is consistent with his life goal of a major administrative position with a large company. However, there are also cases in which the individual will search for a new position rather than accept the restriction on his cigarette use. A flow chart of the decision-making process to use or not use alcohol or drugs is shown in Figure 3.2.

Note, however, that we are discussing the individual's decision to use alcohol or drugs on a recreational basis. People do not plan to become addicted to alcohol or drugs. Thus, the factors that *initiate* chemical use are not the same as factors that *maintain* chemical use (Zucker & Gomberg, 1986). A person might begin to abuse narcotic analgesics because these chemicals help her deal with painful memories. However, after she has become physically addicted to the narcotics, her fear of withdrawal may be one reason that she continues to use the drugs.

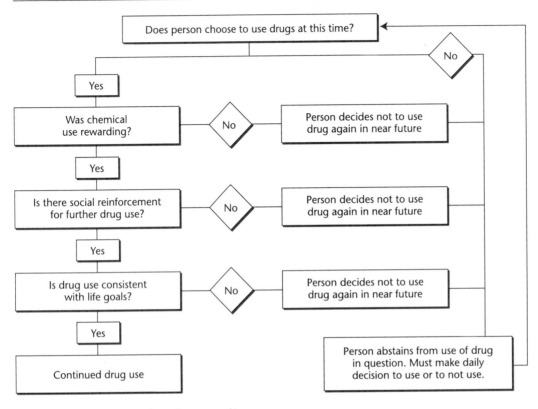

FIGURE 3.2 The chemical use decision-making process.

What Do We Mean When We Say That Someone Is "Addicted" to Chemicals?

Surprisingly,. in light of the ease with which people speak of the "medical model" of alcohol/drug addiction, there is no single definition of addiction to alcohol/drugs. Rather, there are a number of competing definitions. Although many of these appear to have some validity in certain situations, a universally accepted comprehensive theory of addiction has yet to be developed. In this text, addiction will be defined by the criteria outlined in the American Psychiatric Association's (2000) *Diagnostic and Statistical Manual of Mental Disorders* (4th edition - Text Revision; 2000) (or *DSM-IV-TR*). According to the *DSM-IV-TR*, the following are some of the signs of alcohol/drug addiction:

1. *Preoccupation* with use of the chemical between periods of use.

2. *Using more of the chemical* than had been anticipated.
3. *The development of tolerance* to the chemical in question.
4. A *characteristic withdrawal syndrome* from the chemical.
5. *Use of the chemical to avoid or control withdrawal symptoms.*
6. *Repeated efforts to cut back or stop* the drug use.
7. *Intoxication at inappropriate times* (such as at work), or when *withdrawal interferes with daily functioning* (hangover makes person too sick to go to work, for example).
8. A *reduction in social, occupational, or recreational activities* in favor of further substance use.
9. *Continued chemical use* in spite of having suffered social, emotional, or physical problems related to drug use.

Any combination of four or more of these signs is used to identify the individual who is said to suffer from the "disease" of addiction. In the *disease model* of substance abuse, or the *medical model* as it is also known, (a) addiction is a medical disorder, as much as cardiovascular disease or a hernia might be; (b) there is a biological predisposition toward addiction; (c) the disease of addiction is progressive. An unspoken assumption on which the disease model of drug addiction rests is that some people have a biological vulnerability to the effects of chemicals that is expressed in the form of a loss of control over the use of that substance (Foulks & Pena, 1995).

The Medical Model of Drug Addiction

The medical model accepts as one of its basic tenets the belief that much of behavior is based on the individual's biological predisposition. Thus, if the individual behaves in a way that society views as inappropriate, the medical model assumes that there is a biological dysfunction that causes this "pathology." But the reader must remember that there is no single, universally accepted disease model that explains alcohol/drug use problems. Rather, there is a group of loosely related theories stating that alcohol/drug abuse/addiction is the outcome of an unproven biomedical or psychobiological process, and thus can be called a "disease" state.

The disease model of chemical dependency has not met with universal acceptance. Indeed, for decades the treatment of those who suffered from a chemical dependency rested not with physicians but with substance abuse counselors and mental health professionals (Stein & Friedmann, 2001). Only now are physicians starting to claim that patients with addictive disorders suffer from a chronic, relapsing disorder that falls in their purview (Stein & Friedmann, 2001). In this section, the disease model of addiction is discussed, along with some of the research that, according to proponents of this model, supports their belief that the compulsive use of chemicals is a true disease.

Jellinek's work. The work of E. M. Jellinek (1952, 1960) has had a profound impact on how alcoholism[3] is viewed by physicians in the United States. Prior to the American Medical Association's decision to classify alcoholism as a formal disease in 1956, the condition was viewed as a moral disorder. Alcoholics were considered immoral individuals both by society in general and by the majority of physicians. In contrast to this, Jellinek (1952, 1960) and a small number of other physicians argued that alcoholism was a disease, like cancer or pneumonia. Certain characteristics of the disease, according to Jellinek, included (a) the individual's loss of control over his or her drinking, (b) a specific progression of symptoms, and (c) death if the alcoholism was left untreated.

In an early work on alcoholism, Jellinek (1952) suggested that the addiction to alcohol progressed through four different stages. The first, which he called the *Prealcoholic* phase, was marked by the individual's use of alcohol for the relief from social tensions encountered during the day. In the prealcoholic stage, one sees the roots of the individual's loss of control over her drinking, as she is no longer drinking on a social basis but has started to drink for relief from stress and anxiety. As she continues to engage in "relief drinking" for an extended period of time, she enters the second phase of alcoholism: the *Prodromal* stage (Jellinek, 1952). This is marked by memory blackouts, secret drinking (also known as hidden drinking), a preoccupation with alcohol use, and feelings of guilt over her behavior while intoxicated.

With continued use, the individual would eventually become physically dependent on alcohol, a hallmark of what Jellinek (1952) called the *Crucial* phase. Other symptoms of this third stage are a loss of self-esteem, a loss of control over one's drinking, social withdrawal in favor of alcohol use, self-pity, and a neglect of proper nutrition while drinking. During this phase, the individual would attempt to reassert her control over the alcohol by entering into periods of abstinence, only to return to its use after short periods of time. Finally, with continued alcohol use, Jellinek (1952) thought that the alcoholic would enter the *Chronic* phase. The symptoms of this phase include a deterioration of the person's morals, drinking with social inferiors, the development of motor tremors, an obsession with drinking, and for some, the use of "substitutes" when alcohol is not available (e.g., drinking rubbing alcohol). A graphic representation of these four stages of alcoholism is shown in Figure 3.3.

[3]See Appendix 3.

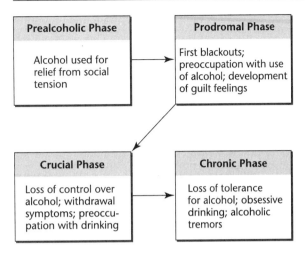

Prealcoholic Phase	Prodromal Phase
Alcohol used for relief from social tension	First blackouts; preoccupation with use of alcohol; development of guilt feelings

Crucial Phase	Chronic Phase
Loss of control over alcohol; withdrawal symptoms; preoccupation with drinking	Loss of tolerance for alcohol; obsessive drinking; alcoholic tremors

FIGURE 3.3 Jellinek's four stages of alcoholism.

In 1960, Jellinek presented a theoretical model of alcoholism that was both an extension and a revision of his earlier work. According to Jellinek (1960), the alcoholic was unable to consistently predict in advance how much he or she would drink at any given time. Alcoholism, like other diseases, was viewed by Jellinek as having specific symptoms, which included the physical, social, vocational, and emotional complications often experienced by the compulsive drinker. Further, Jellinek continued to view alcoholism as having a progressive course that if not arrested would ultimately result in the individual's death.

In his 1960 book, Jellinek went further by attempting to classify different patterns of addictive drinking. Like Dr. William Carpenter in 1850, Jellinek came to view alcoholism as a disease that might be expressed in a number of different forms, or styles, of drinking (Lender, 1981). Unlike Dr. Carpenter, who thought there were three types of alcoholics, Jellinek identified five subforms of alcoholism. Jellinek used the first five letters of the Greek alphabet to identify the most common forms of alcoholism found in the United States. Table 3.1 provides a brief overview of his theoretical system.

Advanced in an era when most physicians viewed alcohol dependence as being caused by a moral weakness, Jellinek's (1960) model of alcoholism offered a new paradigm. First, it provided a diagnostic framework within which physicians could classify different

patterns of drinking, as opposed to the restrictive dichotomous view—in which the patient was either alcoholic or not—that had previously prevailed. Second, Jellinek's (1960) model of alcoholism as a physical disease made it worthy of study, and the person with this disorder was worthy of "unprejudiced access" (Vaillant, 1990, p. 5) to medical treatment. Finally, the Jellinek model attributed the individual's use of alcohol *not* to a failure of personal willpower, but to the drinker's suffering from a medical disorder (Brown, 1995).

Since the time that the Jellinek (1960) model was introduced, researchers have struggled to determine whether it is valid. Sobell and Sobell (1993) found that there was a clear-cut progression in the severity of the individual's drinking in only 30% of the cases. In the same year, Schuckit, Smith, Anthenelli, and Irwin (1993) found clear evidence of a progression in the severity of problems experienced by the alcohol-dependent men in their research sample; but the authors concluded that there was remarkable variation in the specific problems encountered by their subjects, suggesting that alcohol-dependent individuals do not follow a single progressive pattern. Thus, the research data supporting the Jellinek model continue to be mixed.

The genetic inheritance theories. In the last 20 years of the 20th century, researchers began to identify genetic patterns that seemed to predispose some individuals to develop alcohol-use patterns. Early evidence suggested that a gene called *slo-1*, which controls the activity of a certain protein known as the BK channel, seemed to mediate the individual's sensitivity to alcohol's effects (Lehrman, 2004). The BK channel protein normally controls the flow of ions out of the neuron during the normal cycle of neural "firing." When alcohol binds at this protein complex, it holds the ion channel open for far longer than is normal, slowing the rate at which that neuron can prepare for the next firing cycle and thus slowing the level of activity for that neuron (Lehrman, 2004).

The team of Tsuang et al. (1998) examined the issue of genetic predisposition toward substance abuse and concluded that both genetic *and* environmental factors predisposed their subjects toward the abuse of *classes* of chemicals. The authors also found variations in how either the environment or genetic inheritance influenced the use of a specific compound. Each class of drug had a unique genetic predisposition according to

TABLE 3.1   Comparison of Jellinek's Drinking Styles

Type of alcoholism	Alpha	Beta	Delta	Gamma	Epsilon
Psychological dependence on alcohol?	Yes	Yes	Yes	Yes	Possibly but not automatically
Do physical complications develop?	No	Yes	Minimal to no physical complications	Multiple and serious physical problems from drinking	Possibly, but rare because of binge pattern of alcohol use
Tolerance to the effects of alcohol?	No	No	Yes. Person will "crave" alcohol if forced to abstain from use.	Yes. Person will "crave" alcohol if forced to abstain from use.	Possibly, but rare because of binge pattern of alcohol use
Can the individual abstain from alcohol use?	For short periods of time, if necessary	For short periods of time, if necessary	No. Person has lost control over his or her alchohol use	No. Person has lost control over his or her alcohol use	Yes. Person is able to abstain during periods between binges
Is this pattern of drinking stable?	Yes	Yes	Yes	Yes	Unknown*
Is this pattern of drinking progressive?	In rare cases, but not automatically	Possibly, but not automatically	Strong chance of progression to gamma, but not automatic	No. This is an end-point style of drinking	Unknown*
If so, to what pattern will this style of drinking progress?	Gamma	Gamma	Gamma	Not applicable	Unknown*

*According to Jellinek (1960), the epsilon style of drinking was the least common in the United States and only limited information about this style of drinking was available to him.

the authors, possibly explaining why different individuals seem "drawn" to very specific drugs of abuse.

Researchers have found cultural factors to be one factor that helps to determine whether the genetic predisposition for cigarette smoking is activated (Kendler, Thornton, & Pedersen, 2000). In Sweden, as the social restrictions against the use of tobcacco products by women slowly relax, more and more women, including those with the suspected genetic predisposition and who may become dependent, are able to indulge in the use of tobacco products. Nor are environmental influences limited to the use of tobacco products. The team of Gruber and Pope (2002) suggested that unspecified "genetic factors" (p. 392) accounted for 44% of the risk

for marijuana abuse, whereas "family environmental factors" (p. 392) accounted for 21% of the risk.

A quarter of a century ago, Cloninger, Bohman, and Sigvardsson (1981) uncovered inheritance patterns in families that continued to express themselves even in cases where the child was adopted shortly after birth and was not brought up with the biological family. Drawing on the records of 3,000 individuals who were adopted, the authors discovered that the children of alcoholic parents were likely to grow up to become dependent on alcohol themselves, even when the children were reared by nonalcoholic adoptive parents almost from birth. The authors also found that the children who grew up to be alcoholic essentially fell into two groups. In the first subgroup, three-quarters of the children had biological parents who were alcoholic, and these children went on to develop alcohol-use disorders. During young adulthood, these individuals would drink only in moderation. Only later in life did their drinking progress to the point that they could be classified as alcohol dependent. Even so, Cloninger et al. (1981) found that these individuals tended to function within society and were only rarely involved in antisocial behaviors. The authors classified these individuals as "Type I" (or "Type A" or "late onset") alcoholics (Gastfriend & McLellan, 1997; Goodwin & Warnock, 1991).

Cloninger et al. (1981) found that there was a strong environmental impact on the possibility that the adopted child whose biological parents were alcoholic would also be alcoholic. For example, the authors found that children of alcoholic parents, if adopted by a middle-class family in infancy, actually had only a 50–50 chance of being alcoholic in adulthood. Although this is still markedly higher than what one would expect based on the knowledge that only 3% of the general population is alcohol dependent, it is still lower than the outcome found for children of alcoholic parents who were adopted and raised by parents of lower socioeconomic status. In this case, the chances were greater that the child would grow up to be an alcoholic. The authors interpreted these findings as evidence of a strong environmental influence on the evolution of alcohol use, in spite of the individual's genetic inheritance.

The second, smaller group of alcoholics found by the research team of Cloninger et al. (1981) were male, more violent alcoholics who tended to be involved in criminal activity. These individuals were classified as having "Type II" (or "male limited," "Type B," or "early onset") alcoholism (Gastfriend & McLellan, 1997; Goodwin & Warnock, 1991). A male child born to a "violent" alcoholic ran almost a 20% chance of himself becoming alcoholic, no matter what social status the child's adoptive parents had. Because a male child whose father was a violent alcoholic stood a significantly greater chance of himself becoming dependent on alcohol than what one would expect on the basis of chance alone, the authors concluded that there was a strong genetic influence for this subgroup of alcoholics.

The team of Sigvardsson, Bohman, and Cloninger (1996) successfully replicated this earlier study on the heritability of alcoholism. The authors examined the adoption records of 557 men and 600 women who were born in Gothenburg, Sweden, and who were adopted at an early age by nonrelatives. A significant percentage of the adopted children had alcoholic biological fathers, allowing for a good-sized research sample. The authors confirmed their earlier identification of two distinct subtypes of alcoholism for men. Further, the authors found that the "Type I" and "Type II" subtypes appear to be independent, but possibly related, forms of alcoholism. Where one would expect 2% to 3% of their sample to have alcohol-use problems on the basis of population statistics, the authors found that 11.4% of their male sample fit the criteria for Type I alcoholism, and 10.3% of the men in their study fit the criteria for Type II alcoholism. But in contrast to the original studies, which suggested that Type II alcoholism was limited to males, there is now evidence that a small percentage of alcohol-dependent women might also be classified as Type II alcoholics (Cloninger et al., 1996; Del Boca & Hesselbrock, 1996).

The distinction between Type I and Type II alcoholics has lent itself to a series of research studies designed to identify possible personality traits unique to each group of alcohol dependents. Researchers have found that, as a group, Type I alcoholics tend to engage in harm-avoidance activities, whereas Type II alcoholics tend to be high in the novelty seeking trait (Cloninger et al., 1996). Other researchers have found differences in brainwave activity, using the electroencephalograph (EEG), between the Type I and Type II alcoholics. Further, as a group, Type I alcoholics tend to have higher levels of the enzyme monoamine oxidase (MAO) than Type II alcoholics do. The researchers hypothesized that this lower MAO level in Type II alcoholics might account for their tendency to be more violent than Type I alcoholics (Cloninger et al., 1996). Thus, the Type I–Type II typology seems to have some validity as a way of classifying different patterns of alcohol use/abuse.

Using a different methodology and a research sample of 231 substance abusers, 61 control subjects, and 1,267 adult first-degree relatives of these individuals, the team of Merikangas et al. (1998) found evidence of "an 8-fold increased risk of drug [use] disorders among relatives of probands[4] with drug disorders" (p. 977). According to the authors, there was evidence of familial predisposition toward the abuse of specific substances, although they did admit that the observed familial "clustering of drug abuse could be attributable to either common genetic or environmental factors" (p. 977). Such environmental factors might include impaired parenting skills, marital discord, stress within the family unit, and/or physical/emotional/sexual abuse as well as exposure to parental chemical abuse at an early age, according to the authors. These findings were supported by an independent study conducted by Bierut et al. (1998), who suggested that there was "a general addictive tendency" (p. 987) that was transmitted within the family unit. However, they could not be more specific about the nature of this genetic predisposition toward alcohol/substance abuse. Other researchers have concluded that 48% to 58% of the risk for alcoholism is based on the individual's genetic inheritance, at least for males (Prescott & Kendler, 1999). Further, researchers have found evidence that within each family forces are at work that seem to help shape the individual's choice of recreational chemical(s) to abuse (Bierut et al., 1998; Merikangas et al., 1998).

The biological differences theories. Over the past 50 years, a number of researchers have suggested that people who are alcohol dependent are somehow different biologically from those who are not. The range of this research is far too extensive to discuss in this chapter, but the general theme is that alcohol-dependent individuals seem to metabolize alcohol differently from nondependent drinkers, that the site/mechanism of alcohol biotransformation is different for the alcohol-dependent person compared to the nonalcoholic, or that the alcohol-dependent person seems to have a reaction to the effects of that chemical that are different from the reaction of those who are not dependent on it.

The general thrust of these research articles is that there is a biological difference between the alcoholic and the nonalcoholic. This assumption has resulted in studies by various researchers who have attempted to identify the exact difference that might exist between alcoholic and nonalcoholic individuals. One example

[4]See Glossary.

is the study conducted by the team of Ciraulo et al. (1996). They selected a sample of 12 women who were adult daughters of alcoholic parents, and 11 women whose parents were not alcohol dependent, and then administered either a 1mg dose of the benzodiazepine alprazolam or a placebo to their subjects. The authors found that the women of alcoholic parents who received the alprazolam found it to be more enjoyable than did those women whose parents were not alcohol dependent. This finding, along with an earlier study using male subjects conducted by the same team, was consistent with the findings of Tsaung et al. (1998), who suggested on the basis of their research that people developed vulnerabilities to classes of drugs rather than to a specific substance.

An interesting approach is that of Goldstein and Volkow (2002), who used neuro-imaging technology to explore which areas of the brain become active during the experience of "craving" and intoxication. The authors noted that some of the same regions of the brain activated during these drug-use experiences, such as the orbitofrontal cortex and the anterior cingulate gyrus, are both connected with the limbic system and cognitive-behavioral integration activities such as motivation and goal-directed behavior. The authors suggest that through repeated exposure to the chemical, the individual comes to expect certain effects from that chemical. Finally, as a result of repeated drug-induced episodes of pleasure, the individual becomes less sensitive to normal reward experiences, and through both a cognitive and neurobehavioral process comes to overvalue the reinforcing effects of alcohol/drugs. This theory, although still in its formative stages, would seem to account for many of the facets of alcohol/drug use disorders.

Starting in the early 1990s, several different teams of researchers began to explore the possibility that one of the five dopamine receptor subtypes might play a critical role in the development of alcohol/drug use problems. Much of this research centered around the *dopamine D2 receptor gene* and its role in alcohol dependence. Research has found that those individuals who have lower levels of dopamine D2 receptor sites are more likely to respond with pleasure to an intravenous injection of a stimulant such as methylphenidate than are those individuals with high levels of dopamine D2 receptor sites (Volkow, 2004).

The team of Cheng, Gau, Chen, Chang, and Chang (2004) followed a sample of 499 individuals in Taiwan for a period of 4 years, and found strong evidence supporting the genetic inheritance theory for alcoholism for the men in their study.

In the early 1990s, the team of Blum et al. (1990) published the results of their research into the prevalence of the dopamine D2 receptor gene in samples of brain tissue from 70 cadavers, half of which were known to be alcohol dependent in life. The authors found that 77% of the brains from alcohol-dependent people, but only 28% of the nonalcoholic brains, possessed the dopamine D2 receptor gene. In an extension of the original research, Noble, Blum, Ritchie, Montgomery, and Sheridan (1991) utilized tissue samples from the brains of 33 known alcohol-dependent people and a matched group of 33 nonalcoholic controls. The authors concluded, on the basis of their "blind" study of the genetic makeup of the tissue samples, that there was strong evidence of a genetic foundation for severe alcoholism involving the D2 dopamine receptor. As will be discussed in the next chapter, however, these studies have been challenged by other researchers.

On the basis of such research, Blum, Cull, Braverman, and Comings (1996) argued that such behavioral disorders as alcoholism, drug abuse/addiction, cigarette smoking, pathological gambling, Tourette's Syndrome, and obesity were all reflections of a "reward deficiency syndrome" in which the brain's reward system failed to function appropriately. The authors hypothesized that a defect in the A1 subtype of the dopamine D2 receptor gene was pivotal for the development of the so-called reward deficiency syndrome, which expressed itself behaviorally as an inability of the individual to derive pleasure from everyday activities.

Marc Schuckit (1994) utilized a different approach to try to identify biological predictors of alcoholism. In the early 1980s, the author tested 227 men who were the sons of alcoholics along with a control group. He found that 40% of the sons of alcholics, but only 10% of the men who did not have an alcoholic parent (from the control group), were "low responders" to a standard dose of alcohol. The author found that the "low responders" did not seem to have been as strongly affected by the alcohol that they had received as were the individuals in the control group. Ten years later, the author again was able to contact 223 of the original sample of men who

were raised by alcoholic parents. He found that of the men who had an abnormally low response to the alcohol challenge test, 56% had become alcoholic. Of the men raised by alcoholic parents who did not demonstrate an abnormally low physiological response to a standard dose of alcohol when originally tested, only 14% had become alcoholic in the decade between the original examination and the follow-up studies (Schuckit & Smith, 1996; Schuckit, 1994).

These data were interpreted to suggest that low responders were insensitive to the effects of alcohol. In turn, this insensitivity was hypothesized to contribute to a tendency for the individual to drink more often and to consume more alcohol per session than individuals who were not low responders (Schuckit, 1994). Thus, there is strong evidence for a genetic predisposition toward addictive disorders. But researchers also believe that environmental factors must interact with the individual's genetic heritage to allow that disorder to develop (Monti et al., 2002). To date, no *unequivocal* biochemical or biophysical difference between those who are or are not addicted to one or more chemicals has been identified by researchers.

The Personality Predisposition Theories of Substance Abuse

Many researchers believe that substance abuse might be traced back to the individual's personality structure. This perspective is known as the *characterological model* of addiction (Miller & Hester, 1995). An example of this perspective on substance-use disorders is the theory that individuals might turn to alcohol/drugs as a result of a self-regulation disorder (Khantzian, 2004). According to this theory, individuals engage in harmful or self-destructive behaviors because they lack the ability to meet their emotional needs in appropriate ways. Their drug of choice is viewed as having specific properties that allow them to more effectively cope with unpleasant emotional states that threaten to overwhelm them (Khantzian, 2003a, 2004; Murphy & Khantzian, 1995; Shaffer & Robbins, 1995).

An early proponent of this model was Karen Horney (1964), who spoke of alcohol as being a way to "narcotize" (p. 45) anxiety. The specific compounds being abused are viewed as providing at least short-term relief over these painful internal affect states either through the pharmacological effects of the chemicals or the attendant rituals, practices, and drug-centered pseudo-culture (Khantzian, Mack, & Schatzberg, 1999). The addiction to the chemical is viewed as an unintended side effect of the individual's use of that compound in the struggle to deal with these painful emotional states (Khantzian, Mack, & Schatzberg, 1999; Murphy & Khantzian, 1995). Table 3.2 provides a summary of the psychoanalytic perspective of addiction.

In support of the psychoanalytic model of addictions, an impressive body of evidence suggests that certain personality traits do seem to predispose the individual to specific forms of drug abuse. When forces conspired to limit the amount and quality of heroin available in Australia's capital territory, heroin addicts did not appear to switch their drug of choice in large numbers, suggesting that the particular drug played a specific role in their lives that could not be fulfilled by other chemicals (Smithson, McFadden, Mwesigye, & Casey, 2004). The team of LeBon et al. (2004) found that heroin-dependent people demonstrated higher scores for the traits of Novelty-seeking and Self-directedness on the Cloninger TCI personality test than did alcohol-dependent people, suggesting that those who abuse or become addicted to heroin might differ from alcohol-dependent people in fundamental ways. Further, there is evidence suggesting a relationship between psychological trauma and later substance-use problems. Individuals who experienced physical and/or sexual abuse in childhood or adolescence, for example, seem prone to substance-use problems in later life (Khantzian, 2004; Miller & Downs, 1995).

TABLE 3.2 Ego State and Drug of Choice

Class of chemical being abused	Affective state that chemical of abuse is thought to control
Alcohol and CNS depressants (barbiturates, benzodiazepines, etc.)	Loneliness, emptiness, isolation
Opiates (heroin, morphine, etc.)	Rage and aggression
CNS stimulants (cocaine, amphetamines, etc.)	Depression, a sense of depletion, anergia (sense of no energy), low self-esteem

Source: Based on Murphy & Khantzian (1995).

A small number of theorists have come to view the painful affective state known as *shame* as being a central factor for at least a subgroup of substance abusers (Bradshaw, 1988a; Sanford, 2004). Although the chemical offers the illusion of helping people escape from this painful affective state at least for a brief time, their compulsion to use the same method to cope with the shame plants the seed of addiction—for it is when people compulsively use one and only one method of escaping from emotional distress that they are in danger of becoming addicted to that system of control.

A number of studies have found that abnormal risk taking seems to identify children who have the potential for later substance-use problems. The team of Dobkin, Tremblay, and Sacchitelle (1997) found that their data, drawn from a pool of 13-year-old boys, some of whom had alcoholic fathers and some of whom did not, failed to suggest which of these boys were at risk for later alcohol-use disorders. But on the basis of their research the authors concluded that the *mother's* parenting style and whether the boy engaged in disruptive behaviors were more indicative of increased risk for alcohol-use disorders than was the father's drinking status. Partial support for this study was provided by Masse and Tremblay (1997), who examined the personality characteristics of students at ages 6, 10, and adolescence to learn whether certain personality features predicted which individuals would engage in recreational drug use later in life. The authors found that students highest in the characteristic of novelty seeking and lowest on harm avoidance were most likely as adolescents to engage in cigarette and recreational drug use. Low harm avoidance is a trait that might express itself through disruptive behaviors, providing partial support for the study completed by Dobkin et al. (1997).

Section summary. A number of researchers have suggested that certain personality characteristics predispose the individual toward alcoholism or other forms of chemical abuse. There do appear to be certain personality traits that are associated with substance use disorders, but it is difficult to determine whether these personality traits precede the development of the drug dependency or if they are a result of the frequent use of illicit chemicals. To date, no clearly identified causal factor has been found, and research into possible personality factors that might predispose one toward alcohol or substance abuse continues.

Summary

This chapter has explored some of the leading theories that attempt to explain why people use recreational chemicals and why they might become addicted to these drugs. Several factors that help to modify the individual's substance-use pattern were explored, including the physical reinforcement value of the drugs being abused, the social reinforcement value, cultural rules that govern recreational chemical use, and the individual's life goals.

The medical or disease model of addiction has come to play an important role in the treatment of substance abuse in this country. Based on the work of E. M. Jellinek, the disease model of alcoholism has come to be applied to virtually every other form of substance abuse in addition to alcohol. Jellinek viewed alcoholism as being a progressive disorder, which moved through specific stages. In a time when the alcoholic was considered a social failure who resorted to the bottle, Jellinek suggested that the individual suffered from a disease that would, if not treated, result in death. In time, the field of medicine came to accept this new viewpoint, and alcoholism was seen as a medical disorder.

Since the early work of Jellinek, other researchers have attempted to identify the specific biophysical dysfunction that forms the basis for the addictive disorders. Most recently, drawing on medicine's growing understanding of human genetics, scientists have attempted to identify the genetic basis for alcoholism and the other forms of drug addiction. To date, however, the exact biochemical or genetic factors that predispose one to become addicted have not been identified.

Are People Predestined to Become Addicted to Chemicals?

Introduction

The disease model of substance addiction, which was discussed in the last chapter, has not met with universal acceptance. Indeed, many health care professionals and scientists maintain that there are no biological or personality traits that *automatically* predispose the individual to abuse chemicals. Some researchers question the possibility that alcohol/drug addiction is a true "disease"; others concede that there is evidence of biological or psychosocial predispositions toward substance abuse but that certain environmental forces are needed to activate this predisposition toward addiction. In this chapter, some of these reactions against the "disease" model of substance abuse will be examined.

Multiple Models

Although the medical model predominates the field of substance-abuse rehabilitation in the United States, several theoretical systems address the problem of alcohol/drug abuse. Some of the more important theoretical models are reviewed in Table 4.1. Although each of these theoretical models has achieved some degree of acceptance in the field of substance-abuse rehabilitation, no single model has come to dominate the field as has the disease model.

Reaction Against the Disease Model of Addiction

It is tempting to speak of the "disease model" of alcohol/drug abuse as if there were a single, universally accepted definition of substance-use problems. But in reality, there are often subtle and sometimes not so subtle philosophical differences between the ways physicians view the same disease. For example, treatment protocols for a condition such as a myocardial infarction might vary from one hospital to another because of the differing treatment philosophies for that disorder at the different health care facilities (or between physicians who follow different treatment philosophies).

Advocates for the disease model of alcoholism point out that alcohol dependence (and, by extension, the other forms of drug dependence) have strong similarities to other chronic, relapsing disorders such as asthma, hypertension, or diabetes, and that the addictions are *medical* disorders (Marlowe & DeMatteo, 2003). In contrast, others argue that the substance-use disorders are forms of reckless misconduct such as speeding, and that individuals who engage in these behaviors should be treated as criminals by the court system (Marlowe & DeMatteo, 2003).

Critics of the disease model often center their attack on how *disease* is defined. In the United States, disease is seen as reflecting a biophysical dysfunction of some kind that interferes with the normal function of the body. In an infectious process, a bacterium, virus, or fungus invading the host organism would be classified as a disease by this criterion. Another class of disease is those caused by a genetic disorder that leads to abnormal growth or functioning of the individual's body. A third class is those in which the optimum function of the body is disrupted by acquired trauma.

As noted in previous chapters, behavioral scientists agree that there is a genetic "loading" for alcoholism that increases the individual's risk for developing this disorder (O'Brien, 2001). They argue that if such

TABLE 4.1   Theoretical Models of Alcohol/Drug Abuse

	Moral model	*Temperance model*	*Spiritual model*	*Dispositional disease model*
Core Element	The individual is viewed as choosing to use alcohol in problematic manner.	This model advocates the use of alcohol in moderate manner.	Drunkenness is a sign that the individual has slipped from his or her intended path in life.	The person who becomes addicted to alcohol is somehow different from the nonalcoholic. The alcoholic might be said to be allergic to alcohol.
	Educational model	*Characterological model*	*General systems model*	*Medical model*
Core Element	Alcohol problems are caused by a lack of adequate knowledge about harmful effects of this chemical.	Problems with alcohol use are based on abnormalities in the personality structure of the individual.	People's behavior must be viewed within context of social system in which they live.	The individual's use of alcohol is based on biological predispositions, such as his or her genetic heritage, brain physiology, and so on.

Source: Chart based on material presented by Miller & Hester (1995).

a genetic predisposition exists for alcoholism, then one must exist for all forms of substance addiction, as alcohol is just one of a variety of recreational chemicals. If there is a genetic predisposition for addictive behaviors, then chemical dependency is very much like the other physical disorders for which there is a genetic predisposition. In this sense, substance abuse might be said to be a disease, and this is what E. M. Jellinek proposed in 1960.

Reaction to the Jellinek model.[1] Recall that Jellinek (1960) proposed a theoretical model for *alcohol dependence* only. In spite of this, his model has been applied to virtually every other pattern of drug abuse/addiction, even though doing so has exposed some serious flaws.

First, there were problems in the way Jellinek (1960) carried out his research. He based his work on surveys that were mailed out to 1,600 members of Alcoholics Anonymous (AA) and of the 1,600 surveys sent, only 98 were returned (a return rate of just 6%). Such a low return rate is rarely accepted as the foundation for a research study. Further, researchers must assume that those individuals who chose to participate in the study were different from those who decided not to do so, if only because they participated

in the study. Also, members of a self-help group such as AA should be viewed as being different from nonmembers, because they made the decision to join the self-help group whereas nonmembers did not.

Jellinek (1960) violated a number of basic rules of statistical research when he designed his model of alcoholism. He assumed that (a) AA members were the same as nonmembers, and (b) those people who returned the survey were the same as those who did not return the survey. Further, Jellinek utilized a cross-sectional research design. While this does not violate any rule of statistical research, cross-sectional research may not yield the same results as a life-span (longitudinal) research design. The Jellinek (1960) model tends to break down when it is used to examine the alcohol-use patterns of alcohol-dependent persons over the course of their lifetime (Vaillant, 1995).

In challenging the Jellinek (1960) model, Skog and Duckert (1993) pointed out that alcoholism is not automatically progressive. A number of researchers have observed that the progression in the severity of alcoholism suggested by Jellinek develops in only a minority (25%–30%) of the cases (Sobell & Sobell, 1993; Toneatto, Sobell, Sobell, & Leo, 1991). In reality, positions "taken on the progressive nature of

[1]See Appendix 3.

alcoholism often depend more on the treatment orientation of the observers than upon the adequacy of their data" (Vaillant, 1995, p. 5). There is little research data supporting the theory that alcoholism is a progressive disorder, and many studies have shown that alcohol-dependent individuals alternate between periods of abusive and nonabusive drinking or even total abstinence. Illicit drug use also tends to follow a variable course (Toneatto, Sobell, Sobell, & Rubel, 1999). These findings challenge Jellinek's conclusion that alcohol dependence was automatically a progressive disorder.

Further, the concept of *loss of control* over alcohol use, a central feature of Jellinek's theory, has been challenged (Schaler, 2000). Research suggests that chronic alcohol abusers drink to achieve and maintain a desired level of intoxication (Schaler, 2000), suggesting that the alcohol abuser has significant control over his alcohol intake. At this time, most professionals in the field accept that alcohol-dependent individuals have *inconsistent* control over their alcohol intake rather than a total loss of control (Toneatto et al., 1991; Vaillant, 1990, 1995).

The genetic inheritance theories. In the last half of the 20th century and the first years of the 21st century, a significant body of evidence has suggested that the addictive disorders have a genetic basis. However, research has failed to identify a single "alcohol gene," and it has become necessary to hypothesize that alcoholism, and by extension the other addictive disorders, were "polygenetic" rather than monogenetic in nature (Krishnan-Sarin, 2000).

For more than a generation proponents of genetic inheritance theories have pointed to the work of Cloninger, Bohman, and Sigvardsson (1981) to support their contention that there is a biological predisposition for alcoholism. Yet it has been suggested that the methodology utilized by Cloninger et al. was flawed (Hall & Sannibale, 1996). Whereas Cloninger and colleagues claimed that the alcohol-dependent males in their study fell into two different subgroups, the Type I/Type II typology discussed in the last chapter, Hall and Sannibale (1996) found that *fully* 90% of the alcohol-dependent individuals who are admitted to treatment actually have characteristics of *both* Type I *and* Type II alcoholics, a finding that raises questions as to the validity of this distinction.

Further, Cloninger et al. (1981) uncovered strong evidence suggesting that environmental forces also help to shape alcohol-use disorders. Subsequent research has found that while genetic inheritance seems to account for 40%–60% of the variance for alcohol dependence, environmental forces can do much to mitigate the impact of the individual's biological heritage (Jacob et al., 2003). Indeed, after examining the histories of over 1,200 pairs of monozygotic and dizygotic twins born in the United States between 1939 and 1957 and conducting structured psychiatric interviews with these individuals, the authors concluded that the individual's "genetic risk [for alcoholism] in many cases becomes actualized *only* if there is some significant environmental sequela to the genetic vulnerability" (Jacob et al., 2003, p. 1270, italics added for emphasis).

Currently, the evidence suggests a strong environmental influence on the evolution of alcoholism, in spite of the individual's genetic inheritance, for those individuals whom Cloninger et al. (1981) classified as having "Type I" alcoholism. Because of this environmental influence, Type I alcoholism is also called *milieu-limited alcoholism* by some researchers. In contrast to the Type I alcoholics identified by Cloninger and colleagues were the Type II , or *male-limited* alcoholics. These individuals tend to be both alcoholic and involved in criminal behaviors. The male offspring of a "violent" alcoholic adopted in infancy ran almost a 20% chance of himself becoming alcohol dependent regardless of the social status of the child's adoptive parents. However, here again the statistics are misleading. Although almost 20% of the male children born to a "violent alcoholic" themselves eventually became alcoholic, more than 80% of the male children born to these fathers do *not* follow this pattern. This would suggest that additional factors, such as environmental forces may play a role in the evolution of alcoholism for Type II alcoholics.

Perhaps the strongest evidence of an environmental impact on the development of alcoholism is the significant variation in the male:female ratio of those who are alcohol dependent in different cultures around the world. In the United States, the male:female ratio for alcohol use disorders is about 5.4:1. In Israel, this same ratio is approximately 14:1, whereas in

Puerto Rico it is 9.8:1, and 29:1 in Taiwan. In South Korea the male:female ratio for alcohol-use disorders is 20:1, and it is 115:1 in the Yanbian region of China (Hill, 1995). If alcoholism were simply a matter of genetic inheritance, one would not expect a significant variation in the male: female ratio. As a comparison, approximately 1% of the population has schizophrenia in every culture studied, and the male:female ratio for schizophrenia is approximately the same around the globe.

Thus, on the basis of research to date, it is clear that *both* a biological predisposition toward alcohol addiction and strong environmental influences help to shape the individual's alcohol-use pattern. But there is still a great deal to be discovered about the evolution of substance-use disorders; as evidence of this, for reasons that are not understood up to 60% of known alcoholics come from families in which there is no prior evidence of alcohol dependence (Cattarello, Clayton, & Leukefeld, 1995).

Do genetics rule? A great deal of research has been conducted with the goal of isolating the "alcohol gene." Such a simplistic view of alcoholism as being caused by a genetic disorder serves only to confuse the average person. In reality, nonfamilial alcoholism accounts for 51% of all alcohol-dependent persons, a finding that is unlikely if the genetic predisposition for alcoholism is transmitted in families (Renner, 2004). This finding reinforces the truism that "genes confer vulnerability to but not the certainty of developing a mental disorder" (Hyman & Nestler, 2000, p. 96).

Another popular misconception is that genetic predisposition is unalterable. This is clearly seen in the field of substance-abuse rehabilitation, where counselors speak knowingly of a patient's "genetic loading" for an addictive disorder because relatives are themselves addicted to alcohol/drugs. In reality, the popular belief that "one gene = one unchangable behavior" is in error (Alper & Natowicz, 1992; Sapolsky, 1997). Admittedly, there does appear to be a genetic predisposition, or a "loading," for alcohol/drug dependence. But the genetic "loading" for a certain condition does not guarantee that it will develop (Holden, 1998; Sapolsky, 1997, 1998), and to predict who will or will not develop a substance-use disorder on the basis of genetic predisposition is not possible

at this time (Madras, 2002). The individual's genetic predisposition should be viewed only as a rough measure of his/her degree of risk, not the individual's predestination (Cattarello et al., 1995; Gordis, 1996). Social, environmental, historical, and cultural forces all play a role in determining whether the genetic potential toward alcohol/drug addiction will or will not be activated.

Arguing against the biological determinist theories of alcoholism, Greene and Gordon (1998) stated: "No 'alcoholism gene' has been discovered, just a bundle of biological risk factors that make alcoholism more or less likely" (p. 35). Popular opinion to the contrary, "to say that some behavior is 'genetic' rarely means it is inevitable" (Tavris, 1988, p. 42). This was seen in the results of an experiment in which genetically identical rats were sent to a number of different laboratories and then administered standard doses of alcohol under rigidly controlled conditions. Rather than respond to the alcohol in a uniform manner, the rats in the various laboratories had different responses to their exposure to alcohol (Tabakoff & Hoffman, 2004). This outcome would hardly have been seen if the rats' reaction to alcohol was determined by their genetic heritage alone, since they were genetically identical.

Thus, while there is evidence to suggest a genetic component to alcoholism, there is also strong evidence suggesting that cultural, social, and environmental forces play an equally strong role in the evolution of substance-use disorders. The identification of a genetic pattern that predisposes the individual toward addictive disorders would simply indicate the presence of a *risk factor* for the development of a substance-use disorder, not predestination.

The dopamine D_2 receptor site connection. A number of research studies have found that individuals who are alcohol or cocaine dependent seem to have fewer dopamine D_2 receptor sites than do individuals who are not dependent on these chemicals. The clinical importance of these studies remains unclear, as it is possible that the observed findings reflect not preexisting condition but the brain's protective down regulation of receptor sites in response to the substance-induced release of dopamine (O'Brien, 2004). Evidence supporting the dopamine

D_2 hypothesis—that the observed deficit of dopamine D_2 receptor sites predates the development of alcohol or cocaine addiction—has received only limited support (Krishnan-Sarin, 2000). Even if the dopamine D_2 connection does play a major role in the biochemistry of addiction, "finding genetic differences in susceptibility to drug abuse or addiction does not imply that there is an 'addiction gene' which dooms unfortunate individuals to become hopeless drug addicts" (George, 1999, p. 99).

In the last chapter, a recent study by Marc Schuckit (1994) was presented as evidence of a biological predisposition toward alcohol abuse/dependence in certain men. The author based the study on 223 men who, when tested a decade earlier, had demonstrated an abnormally low physical response to a standard dose of an alcoholic beverage. At the time of his earlier study, Schuckit had found that fully 40% of the men who had been raised by alcoholic parents, but only 10% of the control group, demonstrated this unusual response. A decade later, in 1993, the author found that 56% of the men who had the abnormally low physiological response to alcohol had progressed to alcohol dependence. The author interpreted this finding as evidence that the abnormally low physical response to a standard dose of an alcoholic beverage that he had found might identify a biological "marker" for alcoholism. But only a minority of the men who had been raised by an alcoholic parent demonstrated this abnormally low physiological response to the alcohol challenge test—91 of 227. Further, a full decade later, only 56% of these 91 men (just 62 men of the original sample) appeared to have become dependent on alcohol. Although this study is suggestive of possible biochemical mechanisms that might predispose the individual toward alcoholism, it also illustrates quite clearly that biological predisposition does not predestine the individual to develop an alcohol-use disorder.

Other challenges to the disease model of addiction. No matter how you look at it, addiction remains a most curious "disease." Even Vaillant (1983), who has long been a champion of the disease model of alcoholism, had to concede that to make alcoholism fit into the disease model, it had to be "shoehorned" (p. 4). Further, even if alcoholism is a disease, "both

its etiology and its treatment are largely social" (Vaillant, 1983, p. 4). This trait would suggest that alcohol dependence is an unusual disorder. For example, after following a group of alcoholic males for 50 years, Vaillant (1995) concluded that in at least some cases genetics determine whether an individual is going to become dependent on alcohol, while the social environment determines when this transition might occur.

The possibility has been suggested that what we call "addictions" are actually a misapplication of existing neurobiological reward systems (Rodgers, 1994). The "reward system" provides reinforcement when the individual engages in a life-sustaining behavior. Unfortunately, the drugs of abuse overwhelm the brain's normal reward mechanism to trick it into believing that chemical use is the most important priority for the organism (Leshner, 2001b). From this perspective, we might all be said to have the potential to become addicted because we are all biologically "wired" with a "reward system." However, at this time, it is not known why some people are more easily trapped than are others by the ability of chemicals to activate the reward system.

In the United States, an estimated $1 billion per year is spent by the manufacturers of alcohol-containing beverages to promote their product. If alcohol abuse/dependence is indeed a disease, why is the use of the offending agent, alcohol, promoted through commercial means? The answer to this question raises some interesting points about the role of alcohol within this society and the classification of excessive alcohol use as a disease.

The medical model and individual responsibility. For some unknown reason, "we exempt addiction from our beliefs about change. In both popular and scientific models, addiction is seen as locking you into an inescapable pattern of behavior" (Peele, 2004a, p. 36). One of the reasons for this misperception is that modern medicine "always gives the credit to the disease rather than the person" (B. Siegel, 1989, p. 12). Given this initial assumption, it is only natural for clinicians to believe that

in the gradation between determinism and free will, the initiation of substance use may occur toward the free-will end of the spectrum, whereas continued abuse may fall more toward the deterministic end, after certain neurochemical changes have taken place in the brain. Once the addictive process begins, neurobiological mechanisms make it increasingly difficult for the individual to abstain from the drug. (Committee on Addictions of the Group for the Advancement of Psychiatry, 2002, p. 706)

The medical model thus proposes that people *freely* choose to initiate the substance use, but once entangled they increasingly become helpless victims of their biology. From this perspective, the individual essentially ceases to exist except as a genetically preprogrammed disease process!

Consider the following case summary of an adolescent who developed a chemical use problem: One parent is identified as being a pharmacist; the other is a physician. The parents, identified as the "Lowells" were "well-versed in the clinical aspects of substance abuse, [but were] . . . outmaneuvered by the cunning that so often accompanies addiction" (Comerci, Fuller, & Morrison, 1997, p. 64). In this clinical summary, the child is totally absolved of any responsibility for attempting to manipulate his parents! It is the *addiction* that caused the adolescent to outmaneuver/manipulate the parents, not the adolescent! In a very real sense, the same process might be seen in the concept behind methadone maintenance. Proponents of the methadone maintenance concept suggest that even a single dose of narcotics would forever change the brain structure of the opiate-dependent individual, making that person crave more opiates (Dole, 1988; Dole & Nyswander, 1965).

Now, if narcotics are so incredibly powerful, how does one account for the thousands of patients who receive narcotics for the control of pain, for extended periods of time, without developing a "craving" for opioid after their treatment is ended? Even patients who receive massive doses of narcotic analgesics for the control of pain only rarely report a sense of euphoria, or feel the urge to continue their use of opioids (Rodgers, 1994). In addition to this, Dole and Nyswander's (1965) theory has no explanation for the many individuals who "chip" (occasionally use) narcotics for years without becoming addicted to these drugs. The whole concept on which methadone maintenance is based is the belief that narcotics are so powerful that just a single dose takes away all of the individual's power of self-determination. Finally, one must explain how the majority of people with a chemical dependency problem come to terms with it on their own, without any form of professional or para-professional assistance (Peele, 2004a).

Many view the addictive disorders as being "a brain disease. The behavioral state of compulsive, uncontrollable drug craving, seeking, and use comes about as a result of fundamental and long-lasting changes in brain structure and function" (Leshner, 1997a, p. 691). Yet, when one speaks with alcohol-dependent people, they readily agree that they can resist the craving for alcohol, *if the reward for doing so is high enough*. Many alcohol-dependent people successfully resist the desire to drink for weeks, months, years, or decades, casting doubt on the concept of an "irresistible" craving for alcohol or the other drugs of abuse. If one can resist the impulse to use, *if the reward is high enough*, does the substance rob the individual of all willpower?

One central feature of the medical model of illness is that once a person has been diagnosed as having a certain "disease," he or she is expected to take certain steps toward recovery. According to the medical model, the "proper way to do this is through following the advice of experts (e.g., doctors) in solving the problem" (Maisto & Connors, 1988, p. 425). Unfortunately, as was discussed in Chapter 1, physicians are not required to be trained in either the identification or the treatment of the addictions. The medical model of addiction thus lacks internal consistency in that while medicine claims that addiction is a disease, it does not routinely train its practitioners in how to treat this ailment.

What Exactly *Are* the Addictive Disorders?

Proponents of the disease model often note that Dr. Benjamin Rush was the first to suggest that alcoholism was a disease more than 200 years ago. What is overlooked is that the very definition of "disease" has changed since the time of Dr. Rush. In his day, a disease was anything classified as being able to cause an imbalance in the nervous system (Meyer,

1996). Most certainly, alcohol appears capable of causing such an imbalance or disruption in the normal function of the central nervous system (CNS). Thus, by the standards of Benjamin Rush in the 1700s, alcoholism was indeed a disease.

However, in the first decade of the 21st century, the issue is hardly as clear. The branch of medicine charged with the treatment of the addictions, psychiatry, is still in the process of defining what is, and is not, a manifestation of mental illness (Bloch & Pargiter, 2002). This ongoing process is clearly seen in the debate of whether substance abuse/addiction is or is not an actual form of mental illness (Kaiser, 1996; Schaler, 2000; Szasz, 1972, 1988). At what point does a "bad habit" become a disease? If a bad habit such as alcoholism were to be classified as a disease, then where do we draw the line between other unacceptable behaviors and disease? This issue has become so muddled that

> today *any* socially-unacceptable behavior is likely to be diagnosed as an "addiction." So we have shopping addiction, videogame addiction, sex addiction, Dungeons and Dragons addiction, running addiction, chocolate addiction, Internet addiction, addiction to abusive relationships, and so forth. . . . All of these new "addictions" are now claimed to be medical illnesses, characterized by self-destructiveness, compulsion, loss of control, and some mysterious, as-yet-unidentified physiological component. (Schaler, 2000, p. 18, italics added for emphasis)

Through this process of blurring the distinction between unacceptable behavior and actual disease states a number of "pseudo ailments" (Leo, 1990, p. 16) have evolved. These new "diseases" show that we have "become a nation of blamers, whiners, and victims, all too happy, when we get the chance, to pass the buck to someone else for our troubles" (Gilliam, 1998, p. 154). Consider that the 12-Step model pioneered by AA has now been applied to more than 100 different conditions that at least some people believe are a form of addiction (Addiction—Part II, 1992b).

One point often misunderstood by those both outside and within the medical field is that the concept of a "disease" and its treatment are fluid and that they change in response to new information. Stomach ulcers, once thought to be the consequence of stress-induced overproduction of gastric acids, are now viewed as the site of a bacterial infection in the stomach wall and are treated with antibiotics, not tranquilizers. The very nature of the concept of disease makes it vulnerable to misinterpretation, and a small but vocal minority within and outside the field of psychiatry question whether the medical model should be applied to behavioral disorders.

Another overlapping point that is often overlooked in the debate over whether the addictions are actual diseases is the financial incentive to "discovering" a new disease, especially for those who have developed a treatment for it. This was clearly seen in the first decade of the 21st century. Following the aggressive marketing of compounds such as methylphenidate for the treatment of childhood attention deficit hyperactivity disorder (ADHD) in the last decade of the 20th century, some pharmaceutical companies began a media campaign suggesting that adults who had difficulty concentrating and who were easily distracted should discuss with their physician whether they needed methylphenidate. This media campaign did not mention (a) that the diagnosis of ADHD is quite difficult, (b) that questions have been raised about whether ADHD is even a real disorder, (c) and that some have challenged the appropriateness of using compounds such as methylphenidate in treating ADHD—if it exists.

Another complicating issue is that *neither alcohol nor drugs are the enemy*. By itself, a chemical compound has no inherent value (Shenk, 1999; Szasz, 1997, 1996, 1988). Drug molecules are neither "good" nor "evil." *It is the manner in which they are used by the individual* that determines whether they are helpful or harmful. To further complicate matters, society has made an arbitrary decision to classify some drugs as dangerous and others as being acceptable for social use. The antidepressant medication Prozac (fluoxetine) and the hallucinogen MDMA both cause select neurons in the brain to release the neurotransmitter serotonin and then block its reabsorption. Surprisingly, although fluoxetine is an antidepressant, a small but significant percentage of those patients taking this drug do so because they desire its mood-enhancing effects rather than its antidepressant properties ("Better than well," 1996). This raises a dilemma: If a pharmaceutical is being used by people only because they enjoy its effects, where is the line between the legitimate need for that medication and its abuse?

The basis for making this distinction is often not based on scientific studies but on "religious or political (ritual, social) considerations" (Szasz, 1988, p. 316). As it is more than apparent that people *desire* the recreational drugs for their effects, it would seem that the current "war" on drugs was really a "war on human desire" (Szasz, 1988, p. 322). The dilemma is not so much that people use chemicals, according to Szasz, but that people desire to use them for personal pleasure. Indeed, it "is hard, in fact, to think of a single social ritual that does not revolve around some consciousness-altering substance" (Shenk, 1999, p. 43).

As further evidence supporting Szasz's position, 1 out of every 131 outpatient deaths in the United States is caused by "drug mistakes" (Friend, 1998). An estimated 300 deaths per day or 125,000 deaths per year occur in this country alone as a result of adverse reactions to prescribed medications (Graedon & Graedon, 1996; Lazarou, Pomeranz, & Corey, 1998; Pagliaro & Pagliaro, 1998). Another 2.21 million people are injured each year in the United States as a result of mistakes made in the prescription of legitimate pharmaceuticals by health care professionals (Lazarou et al., 1998). The annual death toll caused by such drug mistakes in this country is five times the number of deaths caused each year by recreational drug use. Yet there is hardly a whisper from Washington about the impact of drug mistakes, whereas thousands of speeches have been made about the problem of drug misuse. If the priority is to save lives, why is there so little attention to drug-prescribing mistakes as a source of premature death?

The unique nature of addictive disorders. In spite of all that has been written about the problem of alcohol/drug use/abuse over the years, researchers continue to overlook a very important fact. Unlike the other diseases, the substance use disorders require the *active participation* of the "victim" in order to exist. The capacity for addiction rests with the individual, not (as so many would have us believe) with the drug itself (Savage, 1993). The addictive disorders do not force themselves on the individual in the same sense that an infection might. Alcohol or drugs do not magically appear in the individual's body. Rather, the "victim" of this disorder must go through several steps to introduce the chemical into his or her body.

Consider heroin addiction: The addict must obtain the money to buy the drug. Then, he or she must find somebody who is selling heroin and actually buy some for use. Next, the "victim" must prepare the heroin for injection, mixing the powder with water, heating the mixture, pouring it into a syringe; find a vein to inject the drug into; and then insert the needle into the vein. Finally, after all of these steps, the individual must actively inject the heroin into his or her own body. This is a rather complicated chain of events, each of which involves the active participation of the individual, who is then said to be a "victim" of a disease process. If it took as much time and energy to catch a cold, pneumonia, or cancer, it is doubtful that any of us would ever be sick a day in our lives!

The team of O'Brien and McLellan (1996) offered a modified challenge to the disease model of the addictions as it now stands. The authors accepted that drug/alcohol addiction is a form of chronic disease; but whereas the addictive disorders were chronic diseases like adult-onset diabetes or hypertension, there also were behavioral factors that helped to shape the evolution of these disorders. Thus, according to the authors, "although a diabetic, hypertensive or asthmatic patient may have been genetically predisposed and may have been raised in a high-risk environment, it is also true that behavioral choices . . . also play a part in the onset and severity of their disorder" (p. 237). It is people's behavior, the decisions they make, that will help to shape the evolution of the addictive disorders. Ultimately, the people retain responsibility for their behavior, even if they have a "disease" such as addiction (Vaillant, 1983, 1990).

In the past 60 years, proponents of the medical model of alcoholism have attempted to identify the biological foundation for abusive drinking. Over the years, a large number of research studies have been published, many of which have suggested that alcoholics (a) seem to metabolize alcohol differently than nonalcoholics, or (b) seem to be relatively insensitive (or, depending on the research study, more sensitive) to the effects of alcohol, compared to nonalcoholics. Proponents of the medical model of addiction often point to these studies as evidence of a biological predisposition toward alcoholism.

However, in spite of a significant amount of research, no *consistent* difference has been found in the rate of metabolism, the route by which addicted and nonaddicted individuals biotransform chemicals, or the susceptibility of addicted/nonaddicted individuals to the effects of recreational chemicals. Although substance abuse-rehabilitation professionals talk about the "genetic predisposition" toward alcohol/drug use disorders as if this were a proven fact, the truth is that scientists still have virtually no idea how individual genes, or groups of genes, affect the individual's behavior (Siebert, 1996). As David Kaiser (1996) observed,

> Modern psychiatry has yet to convincingly prove the genetic/biologic cause of any single mental illness. However, this does not stop psychiatry from making essentially unproven claims that . . . alcoholism . . . [is] in fact primarily biologic and probably genetic in origin, and that it is only a matter of time until . . . this is proven. (p. 41)

Thus, at this time, it does not appear that the disease model of addiction as it now stands provides the ultimate answer to the question of why people become addicted to chemicals.

The disease model as theory. Since it was first introduced, the disease model of chemical dependency has experienced a remarkable metamorphosis: Although it was first introduced as a *theoretical* model of alcoholism, it has evolved into the standard model for the treatment of virtually all forms of drug addiction. Further, although the medical model of addiction is but one of several competing theoretical models, proponents do not speak of it as a *theoretical* model, but as an established fact. In part, this reflects the impact of the medical diagnosis process on the evolution of the disease model, for within this context a disease is

viewed as a clinical entity with a predictable course (Rosenberg, 2002). The diagnostic process provides an avenue of communication between the clinician and the bureaucrat, and it legitimatizes specific illnesses as being worthy of social approval or acceptance (Rosenberg, 2002). When viewed in this light, the disease model of the addictions might be seen as having value, providing "a useful metaphor or reframe for many clients" (Treadway, 1990, p. 42). But it is only an analogy, which has contributed little in the way of new, effective, treatment methods for those who are addicted (Marlowe & DeMatteo, 2003).

In reality, the disease model of alcohol/drug addiction reflects the unproven tenet of modern medicine: *All forms of suffering are caused by a physical disorder of some kind* (Breggin, 1998). In spite of rather vocal claims as to the scientific nature of the medical model,

> psychiatrists as medical doctors have always claimed that everything they happen to be treating is biological and genetic. [These] claims, in other words, are nothing new. . . . They are inherent in the medical viewpoint. In reality, not a single psychiatric diagnosis, including schizophrenia and manic-depressive disorder have been *proven* to have a genetic or biochemical origin. (Briggin, 1998, p. 173, italics added for emphasis)

Thus, the theory of the biogenetic foundation of alcoholism, and by extension the other forms of drug addiction, has become dogma. Unfortunately, dogmatists tend to rarely, if ever, question their basic assumptions (Kaiser, 1996). For example, proponents of the disease model seem determined to defend it from *all* criticism. This process is not uncommon. History has demonstrated time and time again that once a certain theoretical viewpoint has become established, proponents of that position work to protect it from both internal and external criticism (Astrachan & Tischler, 1984). This process may clearly be seen in the disease model of addiction. The current atmosphere is one in which legitimate debate over strengths and weaknesses of the different models of addiction is discouraged. There is only one "true" path to enlightenment, according to proponents of the disease model, and you should not question its wisdom.

In this country the disease model has become "big politics and big business," a situation that encourages its proponents to turn a deaf ear to other viewpoints (Fingarette, 1988, p. 64). The disease model has formed the basis of a massive "treatment" industry, into which many billions of dollars and thousands of man-years have been invested. In a very real sense, the biogenetic model has taken on a life of its own (Vaillant, 1983).

In reality, what is surprising is not that the disease model exists, but that it has become so politically successful in this country. Consider that the treatment methods currently in use are those advocated by the proponents of the disease model and they have not changed significantly in 40 years (Rodgers, 1994). Further, practitioners commonly have had little training in the application of scientific theories to treatment settings and frequently have only their own history of alcohol/drug addiction as a guide to how to proceed with the treatment process (Marinelli-Casey, Domier, & Rawson, 2002).

Many current treatment methods are based not on clinical research but on somebody's belief that those methods should work (Gordis, 1996). Not surprisingly, strong evidence shows that current treatment methods for the addictions are possibly less effective than doing *nothing* for the individual (Larimer & Kilmer, 2000).

Proponents of the medical model are hardly likely to go to insurance companies or the public after 60-odd years of claiming that the addictions are diseases and admit that treatment does not work. Rather, as Peele (1989) pointed out, when the "treatment" of an addictive disorder is unsuccessful, the blame is usually put on the patient through such claims as "She did not want to quit," or on the existence of unproven "overwhelming and uncontrollable impulses" (Shaffer, 2001, p. 2). But the blame is never placed on the disease model, in spite of an extensive body of evidence that suggests it has not been successful in the treatment of the addictive disorders.

Summary of reaction to the disease model of addiction. A welcome breath of fresh air was offered by Miller (1998) who observed,

In the end, even in more biologically oriented treatment programs, clients in effect are left to use their rational capacities of deciding, accepting, choosing, and controlling themselves. And so they do, by the millions, with or more often without treatment. . . . Motivation [to quit using chemicals] does not seem to be a matter of insurmountable biology. (p. 122)

People in the United States seem to be fascinated with biological explanations for addictive disorders. Although the available data do seem to point to a biological factor in substance abuse, researchers have not been able to identify the specific biological mechanism or genetic pattern that seems to predispose the individual to the addictive use of chemicals. Indeed, researchers in the field of behavioral genetics are viewing alcohol dependence as being "polygenic," a behavior that reflects the input of a number of different genes (Gordis, 1996). Each of these genes then adds or subtracts a degree of risk to the individual's total potential for developing an addiction to alcohol.

But genetic *predisposition* does *not* mean *predestination* (Schuckit, 2001). Rather, it is wise to remember that "in no mental illness is there expected to be a one-to-one relationship between the genes and disease. Instead, genes are thought of as 'risk factors' that increase the probability that mental illness will occur but that do not determine it" (McMahon, 2003, pp. 63–64). For example, although Schuckit's (1994) study was suggestive of possible genetic factors that might predispose the individual to alcohol dependence, the combination of low response to the test dose of alcohol *and* having a family history of alcoholism still only accounted for approximately 22% of the individual's later risk for an alcohol-use disorder (Lehrman, 2004). Environmental forces such as an adverse childhood environment must also be present for the individual to develop an alcohol-use disorder (Schuckit, 2001; Small, 2002). Currently, the evidence suggests that the individual's genetic heritage accounts for about 60% of the ultimate risk for alcoholism, whereas the environment contributes the remainder (Schuckit, 2001).

The Personality Predisposition Theories of Substance Abuse

Personality factors have long been suspected of playing a role in the development of the substance-use disorders, but research has failed to isolate a prealcoholic personality (Renner, 2004). In spite of this, certain constellations of personality patterns seem to be associated with some subtypes of alcoholism. Type II alcoholic males, for example, were found by Cloninger, Sigvardsson, and Bohman (1996) to be three times more likely to be depressed and four times more likely to have attempted suicide as Type I alcoholic males.

There are a number of variations on this "predisposing personality" theme, but as a group they all are strongly deterministic in the sense that people are viewed as being powerless to avoid the development of an addictive disorder because of their personality predisposition if they are exposed to certain conditions. This is clearly seen in the "very word *addict* [which] confers an identity that admits no other possibilities" (Peele, 2004a, p. 43, italics in original). For example, a number of researchers have suggested that the personality traits of impulsiveness, thrill seeking, rebelliousness, aggression and nonconformity were "robust predictors of alcoholism" (Slutske et al., 2002, p. 124). Other researchers, however, found little evidence to suggest personality factors represent familial or heritable risk factors (Swendsen, Conway, Rounsaville, & Merikangas, 2002). Thus, the role of personality as a possible predisposing factor for substance use disorders remains elusive at best.

Some researchers investigated whether the personality traits of nonconformity, risk taking, and rebelliousness might reflect disturbances in the dopamine utilization system in the brains of individuals who were alcohol abusers/addicts. To test this hypothesis, the team of Heinz and colleagues (1996) examined the clinical progress of 64 alcohol-dependent individuals and attempted to assess their sensitivity to dopamine through various biochemical tests. Although the researchers expected to find an association between depression, anxiety, disturbances in dopamine utilization, and alcohol-use problems, there was little evidence to support the popular beliefs that alcoholism is associated with depression, high novelty seeking, or anxiety.

The work of Cloninger et al. (1996) seemed to point to the personality characteristics of Harm Avoidance (HA) and Reward Dependency (RD) as predisposing the individual to substance use disorders. But when the team of Howard, Kivhahan, and Walker (1997) examined a series of research studies that attempted to relate Cloninger's theory of personality to the development of alcohol abuse/addiction, the authors found that even when a test specifically designed to test Cloninger's theory of personality was used, the results did not clearly support the theory that individuals high in the traits of Harm Avoidance and Reward Dependency were significantly more likely to have an alcohol-use disorder. Thus, to date the personality predisposition theoretical models do not allow for more than a general statement that some personality characteristics might increase the long-term risk that a person will become addicted to chemicals. However, which personality characteristics might predispose the individual to become addicted to alcohol and/or drugs is still not clear.

At this time, the "alcoholic personality" is viewed as nothing more than a clinical myth that has developed within the field of substance-abuse rehabilitation (Stetter, 2000). Even though there is limited evidence to support these beliefs, clinicians continue to operate on the assumption (a) that alcoholics are developmentally immature, (b) that the experience of growing up in a disturbed family helps to shape the personality growth of the future alcoholic, and (c) that alcohol-dependent individuals tend to overuse ego defense mechanisms such as denial. Unfortunately, much of what is called "treatment" in the United States rests on such assumptions about the nature of the personality of addicted people, which have not been supported in the clinical research. Traits identified in one research study as being central to the personality of addicted people are found to be of peripheral importance in subsequent studies.

In the face of this evidence, then, one must ask how the myth of the "alcoholic personality" evolved. One possibility is that researchers became confused by the high comorbidity levels between alcohol/drug-use disorders and antisocial personality disorder (ASPD), especially as 84% (Ziedonis & Brady, 1997) to 90% of individuals with ASPD will have an alcohol/drug use problem at some point in their lives (Preuss & Wong, 2000). This is not to suggest that the antisocial personality disorder *caused* the substance use. Rather, ASPD and the addiction to chemicals are postulated to be two separate disorders, which may co-exist in the same individual (Schuckit, Klein, Twitchell, & Smith, 1994; Stetter, 2000).

An alternate theory about how people began to believe that there was an "addictive personality" might be traced to the impact of psychoanalytic thought in the first half of the 20th century. There is no standard definition or form of psychoanalysis, but as a group the psychoanalytic schools postulated that substance abuse is a symptom of an underlying disorder that motivates the individual to abuse chemicals in an attempt to calm these inner fires (Leeds & Morgenstern, 2003). Various psychoanalytic theorists offered competing theories as to the role of substance misuse in the personality of the addicted person, but essentially all major psychoanalytic theories suggest that there is an "addictive personality" that suffers from an internal conflict that paves the ground for addictive behavior. While this is theoretically appealing, psychoanalytic inquiry has failed to agree on the nature of this conflict or how it might be addressed (Leeds & Morgenstern, 2003). In spite of these failings, psychoanalytic theories have continued to influence the way addictive behaviors are viewed.

Another theory suggesting that the "addictive personality" might be a research artifact was advanced by Pihl (1999). The author, drawing on earlier research, pointed out that 93% of the early research studies that attempted to isolate the so-called addictive personality were based on samples drawn from treatment centers. Unfortunately, there are major differences between those people who are and are not in treatment for a substance-use problem. One major difference is that some people *are* in a treatment program for a substance-use problem whereas others are not. The early studies cited by Pihl (1999) might have isolated a "treatment personality" more than an "addictive" personality, with those people who enter formal rehabilitation programs having

common personality traits as compared with those who did not enter treatment. Ultimately, however, the study of the whole area of personality growth and development, not to mention the study of those forces that initially shape and later maintain addiction, are still so poorly defined that it is quite premature to answer the question of whether there are personality patterns that may precede the development of substance-use disorders.

The abuses of the medical model. Unfortunately, since the time of its introduction, the disease model of alcoholism has been misused—or perhaps "misapplied" might be a better term—to the point that "judges, legislators, and bureaucrats . . . can now with clear consciences get the intractable social problems caused by heavy drinkers off their agenda by compelling or persuading these unmanageable people to go elsewhere—that is, to get 'treatment'" (Fingarette, 1988, p. 66). This is because the substance-use disorders exist in the boundary between biological facts and social values (Rosenberg, 2002; Wakefield, 1992). Indeed, it has been argued that the term

> "mental disorder" is merely an evaluation label that justifies the use of medical power (in the broad sense, in which all the professions concerned with pathology, including psychiatry, clinical psychology, and clinical social work, are considered to be medical) to intervene in socially disapproved behavior. (Wakefield, 1992, p. 374)

This statement remains no less true in today's world and is supported by writers such as Bracken (2002), who observed that "psychiatric classification systems do not hold some universal truth about madness and distress" (p. 4). Rather, such systems are arbitary classification systems designed to provide a way to understand the individual's experiences and problems. Such classification systems are useful but hold significant dangers as well. There is the ever-present danger that they might be used as weapons to silence those who disagree with the authorities (Bracken, 2002). For example, the "patient" suffers from a profound schizophrenia, which by definition means that she is unable to correctly interpret reality, and so her observations about her treatment are inherently incorrect. Also, the emphasis of a psychiatric classification system on psychopathology "can be profoundly disempowering and stigmatizing" (Bracken, 2002, p. 4).

Thus, although this was not the original intent, the medical (psychiatric) diagnostic system has become a way to control social deviance (Bracken, 2002; Rosenberg, 2002). Armed with a diagnosis of abnormality, the guardians of social order, the courts and the lawyers, have assumed the power to define how this deviant behavior is to be treated. Within this context, one could argue that the "war on drugs" is nothing more than a politically inspired program to control individuals who were defined by conservative Republicans as social deviants (Humphreys & Rappaport, 1993). According to the authors, the war on drugs essentially served the Reagan administration as a "way to redefine American social control policies in order to further political aims" (p. 896). By shifting the emphasis of social control away from the community mental health center movement to the war on drugs, the authors suggested, justification was also found for a rapid and possibly radical expansion of the government's police powers, and the "de facto repeal of the Bill of Rights" (Duke, 1996, p. 47).

Indeed, the charge has been made that the community mental health movement itself has been subverted by government rules and regulations until it has become little more than "an arm of government enforcement" (Cornell, 1996, p. 12). As part of this process, many forms of nonconformist behaviors, including substance misuse, are now mistakenly classified not as political inconvenience but as psychiatric problems (Wilson & Trott, 2004). But the medical model of the addictive disorders might be viewed as having evolved into an excuse to extend the government's police powers by making nonconformist behavior a medical disorder. Most certainly, the problem of drivers who operate motor vehicles while intoxicated present a very real problem of social deviance. However, one must question the wisdom of sending the chronic offender to "treatment" time and time again, when his or her acts warrant incarceration, and it has been argued that incarceration may help bring about a greater behavior change in these people than

would repeated exposure to short-term treatment programs (Peele, 1989).

In an ideal world, one question that would be considered is this: At what point should treatment be offered as an alternative to incarceration, and when should incarceration be imposed on the chronic offender? Unfortunately, all too often, the courts fail to consider this issue before sending the offender to "treatment" once more.

The Final Common Pathway Theory of Addiction

As should be evident by now, most practitioners in the field view the addictions to be a multimodal process, resting on a foundation of genetic predisposition and a process of social learning (Monti et al., 2002). But to date both the biological and the psychosocial theories of addiction have failed to explain all of the phenomena found in substance abuse/addiction, and a grand unifying theory of addiction has yet to evolve.

But there is another viewpoint to consider, one called the *final common pathway* (FCP) theory of chemical dependency. In a very real sense, FCP is a non-theory: It is not supported by any single group or profession. However, the final common pathway perspective holds that substance use/abuse is not the starting point but a common *endpoint* of a unique pattern of growth. According to the FCP theory, there is no single "cause" of drug dependency but a multitude of different factors that may contribute to or detract from an individual's chance of becoming addicted to chemicals. These might include social forces, psychological conditioning, how the person copes with internal pain, a spiritual shortcoming, or some combination of other factors. The proponents of this position acknowledge a possible genetic predisposition toward substance abuse. But the FCP theory also suggests that it is possible for a person who lacks this genetic predisposition for drug dependency to also become addicted to chemicals, if he or she has the proper life experiences.

Strong support for the final common pathway model of addiction might be found in the latest neurobiological research findings. Over time, evolution has equipped humans (and many other species) with a "reward system" that is activated when the individual engages in some activity that enhances survival (Nesse & Berridge, 1997; Nestler, Hyman, & Malenka, 2001; Selim, 2001; Stahl, 2000). The drugs of abuse seem to activate this so-called pleasure center or the reward system of the brain (Gardner, 1997; Reynolds & Bada, 2003). This is often called the pharmacological reward potential of the drugs being used. In effect, the final common pathway theory of addiction holds that the various drugs of abuse "create a signal in the brain that indicates, falsely, the arrival of a huge fitness benefit" (Nesse & Berridge, 1998, p. 64; Reynolds & Bada, 2003). This signal involves, at least in part, a spike in the dopamine levels of the ventral tegmentum (Saal, Dong, Bonci, & Malenka, 2003) and nucleus accumbens (Leshner, 2001b) regions of the brain. These regions of the brain are interconnected and form part of the brain's reward system (Salloway, 1998; O'Brien, 1997; Fleming, Potter, & Kettyle, 1996; Hyman, 1996; Blum, Cull, Braverman, & Comings, 1996; Restak, 1994), which is part of what is known as the mesolimbic dopamine system of the brain (Leshner, 1998; Stahl, 2000).

The "mesolimbic reward system . . . extends from the ventral tegmentum to the nucleus accumbens, with projections to areas such as the limbic system and the orbitofrontal cortex"(Leshner, 1998, p. 46). The meso-limbic dopamine system seems to function as a focal point for the brain's reward system, projecting electrochemical messages to the limbic system (where emotions are thought to be generated), and the frontal cortex (a region of the brain involved with consciousness and planning). Research has demonstrated that the drugs of abuse cause a five- to tenfold increase in the dopamine levels in these regions of the brain at least at first, and it is theorized that when the dopamine levels fall after the individual stops using drugs for a period of time that the subjective experience is that of a sense of "craving" (Anthony, Arria, & Johnson, 1995; Nutt, 1996; O'Brien, 1997).

There still is much to learn about how the drugs of abuse alter brain function. For example, we know that the current drugs of abuse alter the function of the *locus ceruleus*. This appears to be the region of the brain that coordinates the body's response to both novel external stimuli and to internal stimuli that might signal a danger to the individual (Gourlay & Benowitz, 1995). Thus, the locus ceruleus will respond to such internal stimuli as blood loss, hypoxia, and pain. The locus ceruleus is also involved in the "fight-or-flight" response of fear and anxiety. This makes clinical sense, as in ages past novel stimuli might prove dangerous to the individual (such as the first time the observer sees a mountain lion running at him). It also is not surprising that this region of the brain is involved in the body's response to the various drugs of abuse.

Last, the final common pathway model of addiction views substance dependence as a common endpoint. Earlier editions of this text had suggested that the different drugs of abuse might activate different nerve pathways but that the final step was the activation of the brain's "reward" or "pleasure" center, and that this was where the phemonenon of addiction was centered. The team of Saal et al. (2003) arrived at this same conclusion on the basis of their clinical research on brain function. The various drugs of abuse might follow different nerve pathways, but they all eventually activate the same regions of the brain's pleasure center.

This, then, is the core element of addiction according to the final common pathway theory of addiction: Addiction is the common endpoint for each individual who suffers from the compulsion to use chemicals. To treat the addiction, the chemical dependency counselor must identify the forces that brought about and support this individual's addiction to chemicals. With this understanding, the counselor might establish a treatment program that will help the individual abstain from further chemical abuse.

Summary

Although the medical model of drug dependency has dominated the treatment industry in the United States, this model is not without its critics. For each study that purports to identify a biophysical basis for alcoholism or other forms of addiction, other studies fail to document such a difference. For each study that claims to have isolated personality characteristics that seem to predispose one toward addiction, other studies fail to find that predictive value in these characteristics, or find that the personality characteristic in question is brought about by the addiction, not one that predates it.

Some researchers see the medical model of addiction as a metaphor through which people might better understand their problem behavior. However, the medical model of addiction is a theoretical model, one that has not been proven and one that does not easily fit into the concept of *disease* as medicine in this country understands the term. Indeed, it was suggested that drugs were themselves valueless, and that it was the use to which people put the chemicals that was the problem, not the drugs themselves.

CHAPTER FIVE

Addiction as a Disease of the Human Spirit

Introduction

To some, addiction is best understood as a disease of the "spirit," a disconnection syndrome in which the person's relationship with "self" and a higher power is replaced with the false promises of the chemical (Alter, 2001). The concept of alcoholism as a spiritual disorder forms the basis of the Alcoholics Anonymous program (Miller & Hester, 1995; Miller & Kurtz, 1994). From this perspective, to understand the reality of addiction is, ultimately, to understand something of human nature. In this chapter, the spiritual foundation for the addictive disorders will be explored.

The Rise of Western Civilization, or How the Spirit Was Lost

Throughout the 20th century and the first decade of the 21st century, science and spirituality have been moving farther and farther apart. Although spirituality is recognized as one of the factors that helps to define, give structure to, and provide a framework within which to interpret human existence (Mueller, Plevak, & Rummans, 2001), in today's world of medicine many "physicians question the appropriateness of addressing religious or spiritual issues within a medical setting" (Koenig, 2001, p. 1189). The physician's discomfort reflects the attitude of "enlightened" society, which turns away, as if embarrassed by the need to discuss "spiritual" matters. To such a person, the "spirit" is viewed as a remnant of man's primitive past, just like spears or clothing made of animal skins. In this way, the "enlightened" person turns away from his or her roots.

The word *spirit* is derived from the Latin word *spiritus*, which on one level simply means "breath" (Mueller et al., 2001). On a deeper level, however, spiritus refers to the divine, living force within each of us. Yet human beings hold a unique position in the circle of life on Earth. In humankind, life, spiritus, has become aware of itself as being apart from nature, and we are all aware of our isolation from one other (Fromm, 1956). This awareness is known as "self-awareness." But with the awareness of "self" comes the painful understanding that each of us is forever isolated from his fellows. Fromm termed this awareness of one's basic isolation as being an "unbearable prison" (p. 7), in which are found the roots of anxiety and shame. "The awareness of human separation," wrote Fromm, "without reunion by love is the source of shame. It is at the same time the source of guilt and anxiety" (p. 8).

A flower, bird, or tree cannot help being what its nature ordains: a flower, bird, or tree. A bird does not think about being a bird or what kind of a bird it might become. The tree does not think about "being" a tree. Each behaves according to its gifts to become a specific kind of bird or tree. Arguably, each must live the life that it was predestined to live. But man possesses the twin gifts of self-awareness and self-determination. These gifts, however, carry a price. Fromm (1956, 1968) viewed humans' awareness of their fundamental aloneness as being the price they had to pay for the power of self-determination. Humans, by self-awareness, have come to know that they are different from the animal world. With the awareness of "self" comes the power of self-determination. But self-awareness also brought a sense of isolation from the rest of the universe. People became aware of "self," and in so doing came to know loneliness. It is only through the giving of "self" to another through love that Fromm (1956, 1968) envisioned man as transcending his isolation to become part of a greater whole.

Merton (1978) took a similar view on the nature of human existence. Yet Merton clearly understood that one could not seek happiness through the compulsive use of chemicals. He discovered that "there can never be happiness in compulsion" (p. 3). Rather, happiness may be achieved through the love that is shared openly and honestly with others. Martin Buber (1970) took an even more extreme view, holding that only through our relationships does our life have definition. Everyone stands "in relation" to another. The degree of relation, the relationship, is defined by how much of the "self" one offers to another, and what flows back in return.

The reader might question what relevance this material has to a text on chemical dependency. The answer is found in the observation that the early members of Alcoholics Anonymous came to view alcoholism (and by extension, the other forms of addiction) as a "disease." The disease of addiction to alcohol (and the other drugs of abuse) was viewed as being unique. In their wisdom, these early members saw alcoholism as a disease not only of the body but also of the spirit. In so doing, they transformed themselves from helpless victims of alcoholism into active participants in the healing process of recovery.

Out of this struggle, the early members of Alcoholics Anonymous came to share an intimate knowledge of the nature of addiction. They viewed addiction not as a phenomenon to be dispassionately studied but as an elusive enemy that had a firm hold on each member's life. Rather than focusing on the smallest common element that might "cause" addiction they sought to understand and share in the healing process of sobriety. In so doing, these early pioneers of AA learned that recovery was a spiritual process through which the individual recaptured the spiritual unity that he or she could not find through chemicals.

Self-help groups such as Alcoholics Anonymous and Narcotics Anonymous[1] do not postulate any specific theory of how chemical addiction comes about (Herman, 1988). They assume that any person whose chemical use interferes with his or her life has an addiction problem. The need to attend AA was, to its founders, self-evident to the individual in that either you were addicted to alcohol or you were not.

Addiction itself was viewed as resting on a spiritual flaw within the individual. Those who were addicted were viewed as being

> on a spiritual search. They really are looking for something akin to the great hereafter, and they flirt with death to find it. Misguided, romantic, foolish, needful, they think they can escape from the world by artificial means. And they shoot, snort, drink, pop or smoke those means as they have to leave their pain and find their refuge. At first, it works. But, then it doesn't. (Baber, 1998, p. 29)

In a very real sense, the drugs do not bring about addiction; rather, the individual comes to abuse or be addicted to drugs because of what he or she believes to be important (Peele, 1989). Such spiritual flaws are not uncommon, and they usually pass unnoticed in the average person. But for the alcohol/drug-addicted person, his or her spiritual foundation is such that chemical use is deemed acceptable, appropriate, and desirable as a means to reach a goal that is ill-defined at best.

One expression of this spiritual flaw is the individual's hesitation to take responsibility for the "self" (Peele, 1989). Personal suffering is, in a sense, a way of owning responsibility for one's life. Most certainly, suffering is an inescapable fact of life. We are thus granted endless opportunities to take personal responsibility for our lives. Unfortunately, modern society looks down on the process of individual growth and the pain inherent in growth. With its emphasis on individual happiness, society views any pain as unnecessary, if not dysfunctional. Further, modern society advocates that pain *automatically* be eradicated through the use of medications, as long as the pills are prescribed by a physician (Wiseman, 1997).

A reflection of this modern neurosis is that many people are willing to

> go to quite extraordinary lengths to avoid our problems and the suffering they cause, proceeding far afield from all that is clearly good and sensible in order to find an easy way out, building the most

---

[1] Although there are many similarities between AA and NA, these are separate programs. On occasion, they might cooperate on certain matters, but each is independent of the other.

elaborate fantasies in which to live, sometimes to the total exclusion of reality. (Peck, 1978, p. 17)

In this, the addicted person is not unique. Many people find it difficult to accept the suffering that life offers to us. We all must come to terms with personal responsibility and with the pain of our existence. But the addicted person chooses a different path from that of the average person. Addiction might be viewed as an outcome of a process through which the individual utilizes chemicals to avoid acknowledging and accepting life's problems. The chemicals lead the individual away from what he or she believes is good and acceptable in return for the promise of comfort and relief.

Diseases of the Mind—Diseases of the Spirit: The Mind-Body Question

As B. S. Siegel (1986) and many others have observed, modern medicine enforces an artificial dichotomy between the individual's "mind" and "body." As a result, modern medicine has become rather mechanical, with the physician treating "symptoms," or "diseases," rather than the "patient" as a whole (Cousins, 1989; B. S. Siegel, 1989).

In a sense, the modern physician has become a very highly skilled technician who often fails to appreciate the unique person now in the role of a patient. Diseases of the body are viewed as falling in the realm of physical medicine, whereas diseases of the mind fall into the orbit of the psychological sciences. Diseases of the human spirit, according to this view, are the specialty of clergy (Reiser, 1984). The problem with this perspective is that the patient in reality is not a "spiritual being" or a "psychosocial being" or a "physical being" but a unified whole. Thus, when a person abuses chemicals, the drug use will affect that person "physically, emotionally, socially, and spiritually" (Adams, 1988, p. 20). Unfortunately, society has difficulty accepting that a disease of the spirit—such as addiction—is just as real as a disease of the physical body.

But we are indeed spiritual beings, and self-help programs such as Alcoholics Anonymous and Narcotics Anonymous view addiction to chemicals as spiritual illnesses. Their success in helping people to achieve and maintain abstinence suggests that there is some validity to this claim. However, society struggles to adhere to the artificial mind-body dichotomy and in the process, to come to terms with the disease of addiction, which is neither totally a physical illness nor exclusively one of the mind.

The Growth of Addiction: The Circle Narrows

As the disease of alcoholism progresses, the individual comes to center his or her life around the use of the alcohol. Indeed, one might view alcohol as being the "axis" (Brown, 1985, p. 79) around which the alcoholic's life revolves. Alcohol comes to assume a role of "central importance" (p. 78) both for the alcoholic and the family. It is difficult for those who have never been addicted to chemicals to understand the importance that the addict attaches to the drug of choice. Those who are addicted will demonstrate a preoccupation with their chemical use and will protect their source of chemicals. To illustrate, it is not uncommon for cocaine addicts to admit that if it they had to make a choice, they would choose cocaine over friends, lovers, or even family. In many cases, the drug-dependent person has already made this choice—in favor of the chemicals.

The grim truth is that the active addict is, in a sense, insane. One reflection of this moral insanity is that the drug has taken on a role of central importance in the addict's life. Other people, other commitments, become secondary. Addicted people might be said "never . . . to outgrow the self-centeredness of the child" (Narcotics Anonymous World Service Office, Inc., 1983, p. 1). In exploring this point, the book *Narcotics Anonymous* (Narcotics Anonymous World Service Office, Inc., 1982) noted:

> Before coming to the fellowship of NA, we could not manage our own lives. We could not live and enjoy life as other people do. We had to have something different and we thought we found it in drugs. We placed their use ahead of the welfare of our families, our wives, husbands, and our children. We had to have drugs at all costs. (p. 11, italics in original deleted)

As experienced mental health professionals can affirm, there are many people whose all-consuming interest is themselves. They care for nothing outside that little portion of the universe known as "self." In this sense, chemical addiction is a form of self-love, or perhaps more accurately, a perversion of self-love. It is through the use of chemicals that such people seek to cheat themselves of the experience of reality, replacing it with the distorted desires of the "self."

To say that those who are addicted demonstrate an ongoing preoccupation with chemical use is something of an understatement. They generally demonstrate an exaggerated concern about maintaining their supply of the drug, and they may avoid those who might prevent further drug use. For example, consider an alcoholic who, with six or seven cases of beer in storage in the basement, goes out to buy six more "just in case." This behavior demonstrates the individual's preoccupation with maintaining an "adequate" supply. Other people, when their existence is recognized at all, are viewed by the addict either as being assets in the continued use of chemicals or impediments to drug use. But nothing is allowed to come between the individual and his or her drug, if at all possible. It is for this reason that recovering addicts speak of their still-addicted counterparts as being morally insane.

The Circle of Addiction: Addicted Priorities

The authors of *Narcotics Anonymous* concluded that addiction was a disease composed of three elements: (a) a compulsive use of chemicals, (b) an obsession with further chemical use, and (c) a spiritual disease that is expressed through a total self-centeredness. It is this complete self-absorption, the spiritual illness, that causes the person to demand "what *I* want when *I want* it!" and makes the individual vulnerable to addiction. But for the person who holds this philosophy to admit to it would mean that he or she would have to face the need for change. So those who are addicted to chemicals will use the defense mechanisms of denial, rationalization, projection, and/or minimization to justify their increasingly narrow range of interests both to themselves and to significant others.

To support their addiction, people must renounce more and more of the "self" in favor of new beliefs and behaviors that make it possible to continue to use chemicals. This is the spiritual illness of addiction, for the individual comes to believe that "nothing should come between me and my drug use!" No price is too high nor is any behavior unthinkable if it allows for further drug use. People will be forced to lie, cheat, and steal to support their addiction, and yet they will seldom count the cost—as long as they can obtain the alcohol/drugs that they crave.

Although many addicts have examined the cost demanded of their drug use and have turned away from chemicals with or without formal treatment, there are others who accept this cost willingly. These individuals will go through great pains to hide the evidence of their drug addiction so that they are not forced to look at the grim reality that they *are* addicted.

Those who are alcohol/drug addicts are active participants in this process, but they are also blinded to its existence. If you were to ask them why they use alcohol, you would be unlikely to learn the real reason. As one individual said at the age of 73, "You have to understand that the reason I drink now is because I had pneumonia when I was 3 years old." For her to say otherwise would be to admit that she had a problem with alcohol, an admission that she had struggled very hard to avoid for most of her adult life.

As the addiction comes to control more and more of their lives, those who are addicted must expend greater and greater effort to maintain the illusion that they are living normally. Gallagher (1986) told of one physician, addicted to a synthetic narcotic known as fentanyl, who ultimately would buy drugs from the street because he could no longer divert enough drugs from hospital sources to maintain his drug habit. When the tell-tale scars from repeated injections of street drugs began to form, this same physician intentionally burned himself on the arm with a spoon to hide the scars.

Addicted people also find that as the drug comes to control more and more of their existence, they must invest significant effort in maintaining the addiction itself. More than one cocaine or heroin addict has had to engage in prostitution (homosexual or heterosexual) to earn enough money to buy more chemicals.

Everything is sacrificed to obtain and maintain what the addict perceives as an "adequate" supply of the chemicals.

Some Games of Addiction

One major problem in working with those who are addicted to chemicals is that these individuals will often seek out sources of legitimate pharmaceuticals either to supplement their drug supply or to serve as their primary source. There are many reasons for this. First, as Goldman (1991) observed, they may purchase pharmaceuticals legally if there is a legitimate medical need for the medication. The drug user does not need to fear arrest with a legitimate prescription for a medication signed by a physician.

Second, for the drug-addicted person who is able to obtain pharmaceuticals, the medication is of a known product, at a known potency level. The drug user does not have to worry about low potency "street" drugs, impurities that may be part of the drugs purchased on the street (as when PCP is mixed with low-potency marijuana), or misrepresentation (as when PCP is sold as "LSD"). Also, the pharmaceuticals are usually much less expensive than street drugs. For example, the pharmaceutical analgesic hydromophone costs about $1 per tablet at a pharmacy. On the street, each tablet might sell for as much as $45 to $100 (Goldman, 1991).

To manipulate physicians into prescribing desired medications, addicts are likely to "use ploys such as outrage, tears, accusations of abandonment, abject pleading, promises of cooperation, and seduction" (Jenike, 1991, p. 7). The physician who works with addicted individuals must remember that they care little for the physician's feelings. For them, the goal is to obtain more drugs at virtually any cost. One favorite manipulative ploy is for the addict (or an accomplice) to visit the hospital emergency rooms (Klass, 1989) or the physician's office in an attempt to seek medication. The addict will then either simulate an illness or use a real physical illness, if one is present, as an excuse to obtain desired medications. Sometimes the presenting complaint is "kidney stones," or a story about how other doctors or emergency room personnel have not been able to help the patient, or a story about how the individual "lost" the medication, or how the "dog ate it," and so on.

Patients who have been asked to submit a urine sample for testing have sometimes secretly pricked their fingers with needles to squeeze some blood into the urine to support their claim that they were passing a kidney stone. Others have inserted foreign objects into the urethra to irritate the tissues lining it so they could provide a "bloody" urine sample. The object of these games is to obtain a prescription for narcotics from a sympathetic doctor who wants to treat the patient's obvious "kidney stone." Addicted individuals have been known to go to an emergency room with a broken bone, have the bone set, and go home with a prescription for a narcotic analgesic (provided to help the patient deal with the pain of a broken bone). Once at home, the patient (or an accomplice) removes the cast and the patient goes to another hospital emergency room to have yet another cast applied to the injured limb, in the process receiving another prescription for a narcotic analgesic. In a large city, this process might be repeated 10 times or more (Goldman, 1991).

It is also not unusual for addicted persons to study medical textbooks to learn what symptoms to fake and how to provide a convincing presentation of these symptoms to health care professionals. In many cases, the addicted person knows more about the simulated disorder than does the physician who is treating it!

A Thought on Playing the Games of Addiction

A friend who worked in a maximum security penitentiary for men was warned by older, more experienced corrections workers not to try to "out con a con"—that is, don't try to out-manipulate the individual whose entire life centers on manipulating others. "Remember that while you are home watching the evening news, or going out to see a movie, these people have been working on perfecting their 'game.' It is their game, their rules, and in a sense their whole life." This lesson applies when working with addicted individuals, for addiction is a lifestyle, one that involves to a large degree the manipulation of others into supporting the addiction. Of course, the addict can, if necessary, "change his spots," at least for a short time. This is especially true early in the addiction process or during the early stages of treatment.

Often, addicts will go "on the wagon" for a few days, or perhaps even a few weeks, to prove both to themselves and to others that they can "still control it." Unfortunately, they fail to realize that by attempting to "prove" their control, they are actually demonstrating their lack of control over the chemicals. However, as the addiction progresses, more and more effort is required to motivate these people to give up their drug, even for a short time. Eventually, even "a short time" becomes too long.

There is no limit to the manipulations that addicted individuals will use to support their addiction. Vernon Johnson (1980) spoke at length of how they will even use compliance as a defense against treatment. Overt compliance is often utilized as a defense against acceptance of their own spiritual, emotional, and physical deficits (Johnson, 1980).

Honesty as a Part of the Recovery Process

One of the core features of the physical addiction to a chemical is "a fundamental inability to be honest . . . with the *self*" (Knapp, 1996, p. 83, italics in original). Honesty is the way to break through this deception, to bring the person face to face with the reality of the addiction. The authors of *Narcotics Anonymous* (1982) warned that progression toward the understanding that one was addicted was not easy. Indeed, self-deception was part of the price the addict paid for addiction; "only in desperation did we ask ourselves, 'Could it be the drugs?' " (pp. 1–2).

Addicted people will often say with pride that they have been more or less "drug free" for various periods of time. The list of reasons the individual is drug free is virtually endless. This person is drug free because her husband threatened divorce if she continued her use of chemicals. (But she secretly longs to return to chemical use and will do so if she can find a way.) Another person is drug free because his probation officer has a reputation for sending people to prison if their urine sample (drawn under strict supervision) is positive for chemicals. (But he is counting the days until he is no longer on probation and possibly will even sneak an occasional drink or episode of drug use if he thinks he can get away with it.)

In each instance, the person is drug free only because of an external threat. In virtually every case, as soon as the external threat is removed, the individual will usually drift back to chemicals. It is simply impossible for one person to provide the motivation for another person to remain drug free forever. Many addicted people have admitted, often only after repeated and strong confrontation, that they had simply switched addictions to give the appearance of being drug free. It is not uncommon for an opiate addict in a methadone maintenance program to use alcohol, marijuana, or cocaine. The methadone does not block the euphoric effects of these drugs as it does the euphoria of narcotics. Thus, the addicted person can maintain the appearance of complete cooperation, appearing each day to take the methadone without protest, while still using cocaine, marijuana, or alcohol at will.

In a very real sense, the addicted person has lost touch with reality. Over time, those who are addicted to chemicals come to share many common personality traits. There is some question whether this personality type, the so-called addicted personality, predates addiction or evolves as a result of the addiction (Bean-Bayog, 1988; Nathan, 1988). However, this chicken-or-egg question does not alter the reality that for the addict, the addiction always comes first.

Many addicted people have admitted going without food for days, but very few would willingly go without using chemicals for even a short period of time. A cocaine addict will admit to avoiding sexual relations with a spouse or significant other in order to continue using cocaine. Just as the alcoholic will often sleep with an "eye opener" (an alcoholic drink) already mixed by the side of the bed, addicts have spoken about how they had a "rig" (a hypodermic needle) loaded and ready for use so that they could inject the drug even before they got out of bed for the day.

Many physicians have boasted that the patients they worked with had no reason to lie to them. One physician declared that he knew a certain patient did not have prescriptions from other doctors because the patient "told me so!" The chemical dependency professional needs to remember at all times the twin realities that (a) for the person who is addicted, the chemical comes first, and (b) the addicted person centers his or her life around the chemical. For the physician to lose sight of this reality is to run the danger of being trapped in the addict's web of lies, half-truths, manipulations, or outright fabrications.

Recovering addicts will admit how manipulative they were, often saying they were their own worst enemy. For as they move along the road to recovery, addicted people will realize that they would also deceive themselves as part of the addiction process. One inmate said, "Before I can run a game on somebody else, I have to believe it myself." As the addiction progresses, addicts do not question their perception but come to believe what they need to believe in order to maintain the addiction.

False Pride: The Disease of the Spirit

Every addiction is, in the final analysis, a disease of the spirit. Edmeades (1987) tells that in 1931, Carl Jung was treating an American, Rowland H., for alcoholism. Immediately after treatment, Rowland H. relapsed but was not accepted back into analysis by Jung. His only hope of recovery, according to Jung, lay in a spiritual awakening, which he later found through a religious group in America.

Carl Jung identified alcoholism (and by implication all forms of addiction) as diseases of the spirit (Peluso & Peluso, 1988). The *Twelve Steps and Twelve Traditions of Alcoholics Anonymous* (1981) speaks of addiction as being a sickness of the soul. In support of this perspective, Kandel and Raveis (1989) found that a "lack of religiosity" (p. 113) was a significant predictor of continued use of cocaine or marijuana for young adults. For each addicted individual, a spiritual awakening appears to be an essential element of recovery.

In speaking with addicted people, one is impressed by how often they have suffered in their lives. It is almost as if a path can be traced from the emotional trauma to the addiction. Yet the addict's spirit is not crushed at birth, nor does the trauma that proceeds addiction come about overnight. The individual's spirit comes to be diseased over time, as the addict-to-be comes to lose his or her way in life.

Fromm (1968) observed that "we all start out with hope, faith and fortitude" (p. 20). However, the assorted insults of life often join forces to bring about disappointment and a loss of faith. The individual comes to feel an empty void within. It is at this point that if something is not found to fill the addict's "empty heart, he will fill his stomach with artificial stimulants and sedatives" (Graham, 1988, p. 14). An excellent example of this

process might be seen in the Poland of a decade ago. Many of that country's young adults saw no productive future for themselves, shaped by years of economic hardship and the martial law of the 1980s. Often they turned to heroin to ease their pain (Ross, 1991).

Few of us escape moments of extreme disappointment or awareness (Fromm, 1968). It is at these times that people are faced with a choice. They may "reduce their demands to what they can get and do not dream of that which seems to be out of their reach" (Fromm, 1968, p. 21). The Narcotics Anonymous pamphlet *The Triangle of Self-Obsession* (Narcotics Anonymous World Service Office, Inc., 1983) observed that this process is, for most, a natural part of growing up. But the person who is in danger of addiction refuses to reduce those expectations. Rather, the addicted person comes to demand "What *I* want when *I want* it!" *The Triangle of Self-Obsession* (Narcotics Anonymous World Service Office, Inc., 1983) noted that addicted people tend to "refuse to accept that we will not be given everything. We become self-obsessed; our wants and needs become demands. We reach a point where contentment and fulfillment are impossible" (p. 1).

Despair exists when people consider themselves powerless. Existentialists speak of the realization of ultimate powerlessness as awareness of one's nonexistence. In this sense, the individual is confronted with the utter futility of existence. Faced with the ultimate experience of powerlessness, people have a choice. They may either accept their true place in the universe, or they may continue to distort their perceptions and thoughts to maintain the illusion of self-importance. Only when they accept their true place in the universe, along with the pain and suffering that life might offer, are they capable of any degree of spiritual growth (Peck, 1978) . Their choice is to accept reality or to turn away from it. Many choose to turn away for it does not offer them what they think they are entitled to. In so doing, these people exhibit the characteristic false pride so frequently encountered in addiction.

People cannot accomplish the illusion of being more than they are without an increasingly large investment of time, energy, and emotional resources. This lack of humility, the denial of what one *is* in order to give an illusion of being better than this, plants the seeds of despair (Merton, 1961). Humility implies an honest, realistic view of self-worth. Despair rests upon a distorted view of one's place in the universe. This despair grows with each passing day, as reality threatens time and again to force upon the individual an awareness of the ultimate measure of his or her existence.

In time, external supports are necessary to maintain this false pride. Brown (1985) identified one characteristic of alcohol as being its ability to offer people an illusion of control over their feelings. This is a common characteristic of every drug of abuse. If life does not provide the pleasure drug users feel entitled to, at least they might find this comfort and pleasure in a drug, or combination of drugs, which frees them from life's pain and misery—at least for awhile. What they do not realize, often not until after the seeds of addiction have been planted, is that the chemical offers an illusion only. There is no substance to the self-selected feelings brought about by the chemical, only a mockery of peace. The deeper feelings made possible through the acceptance of one's lot in life (which is humility) seem to be a mystery to those who are addicted. "How can you be happy?" they ask; "you are nothing like me! You don't use!!!"

Humility is the honest acceptance of one's place in the universe (Merton, 1961). Included in this is the open acknowledgment of one's strengths and weaknesses. When people become aware of the reality of their existence, they may accept their lot in life or they might choose to struggle against existence itself. This struggle against acceptance ultimately leads to despair, the knowledge that one is lost (Fromm, 1968). This despair is often so all-inclusive that the "self" seems unable to withstand its attack. Addicts have described this despair as an empty, black void within. Then, as Graham (1988) noted, they have attempted to fill this void with the chemicals they find around them.

The *Twelve Steps and Twelve Traditions* (1981) viewed false pride as a sickness of the soul. In this light, chemical use might be viewed as a reaction against the ultimate despair of encountering one's lot in life—the false sense of being that says "not as it is, but as I want it!" in response to one's discovery of personal powerlessness. Surprisingly, in light of this self-centered approach to life, various authors have come to view the substance-abusing person as essentially seeking to join with a higher power. But in place of the spiritual struggle necessary to achieve inner peace, the addicted person

seems to take a shortcut through the use of chemicals (Chopra, 1997; Gilliam, 1998; Peck 1978, 1993, 1997b). Thus, May (1988) was able to view alcohol/drug addiction as side-tracking "our deepest, truest desire for love and goodness" (p. 14). In taking the shortcut through chemical abuse, people find that their lives are dominated by the drugs. They center their existence more and more around further chemical use, until at last they believe that they cannot live without it. Further spiritual growth is impossible when people see chemical use as their first priority.

In side-tracking their drive for truth and spiritual growth, addicts develop a sense of false pride, expressed almost as a form of narcissism. The clinical phenomenon of narcissism is a reaction against perceived worthlessness, loss of control, and an emotional pain so intense that it seems almost physical (Millon, 1981). In speaking of the Narcissistic Personality, Millon (1981) observed that such people view their own self-worth in such a way that "they rarely question whether it is valid" (p. 167); they "place few restraints on either their fantasies or rationalizations [and] their imagination is left to run free."

Drug-dependent people are not usually narcissistic personalities in the pure sense of the word, but significant narcissistic traits are present in addiction. One finds that false pride, which is based on the lack of humility, causes people to distort not only their perceptions of "self," but also of "other," in the service of their pride and their chemical use (Merton, 1961). People who are self-centered in this way "imagine that they can only find themselves by asserting their own desires and ambitions and appetites in a struggle with the rest of the world" (Merton, 1961, p. 47).

In Merton's words are found hints of the seeds of addiction, for the individual's chemical of choice allows the individual to impose his or her own desires and ambitions on the rest of the world. Brown (1985) speaks at length of the illusion of control over one's feelings that alcohol gives to the individual. May (1988) also speaks of how chemical addiction reflects a misguided attempt to achieve complete control over one's life. The drugs of abuse also give an illusion of control to users, a dangerous illusion that allows them to believe that they are imposing their own appetites onto the external world, whereas in reality they are losing their own wills to the chemical.

Addicted people sometimes talk with pride about their use, not realizing that other people see these descriptions as horrors the users have endured in the service of their addiction. This is known as "euphoric recall," a process in which addicts selectively recall mainly the pleasant aspects of their drug use, while selectively forgetting the pain and suffering they have experienced as a consequence (Gorski, 1993). In listening to the alcohol/drug-addicted person, one is almost left with the impression that they are speaking about the joys of a valued friendship rather than a drug of abuse (Byington, 1997). Addicted people, for example, have spoken at length of the quasi-sexual thrill that they achieved through cocaine or heroin, dismissing the fact that their abuse of this same drug cost them spouses, families, and perhaps several tens of thousands of dollars. There is a name for this distorted view of one's self and of one's world that comes about with chronic chemical use: It is called the insanity of addiction.

Denial, Rationalization, Projection, and Minimization: The Four Horsemen of Addiction

The traditional view of addiction is that all human behavior, including the addictive use of chemicals, rests on a foundation of characteristic psychological defenses. In the case of chemical dependency, the defense mechanisms that are thought to be involved are denial, rationalization, projection, and minimization. These, like all psychological defenses, are thought to operate unconsciously, in both the intrapersonal and interpersonal spheres. They exist in order to protect the individual from the conscious awareness of anxiety.

Often without knowing it, addicted individuals will utilize these defense mechanisms to avoid recognizing the reality of their addiction. For once the reality of the addiction is acknowledged, there is an implicit social expectation that the users will deal with their addiction. Thus, to understand addiction, one must also understand each of these characteristic defense mechanisms.

Denial. Clinical lore among substance-abuse rehabilitation professionals holds that the individual's substance use problem hides behind a wall of denial.

The characteristic denial of users' growing dependence on chemicals and the impact the drugs are having on their lives is thought to be the most common reason that individuals fail to seek help for alcoholism (Wing, 1995). Simply, denial is "a disregard for a disturbing reality" (Kaplan & Sadock, 1996, p. 20). It is a form of unconscious self-deception, used by people's unconscious to help them avoid anxiety and emotional distress (Shader, 1994). They accomplish this through a process of selective perception of the past and present so that painful and frightening elements of reality are not recognized or accepted. This has been called "tunnel vision" by the Alcoholics Anonymous program (to be discussed in a later section). Denial is classified as being a primitive form of unconscious defense, usually found in the person who is experiencing significant internal and interpersonal distress (Perry & Cooper, 1989).

Projection. This mechanism is an unconscious one, through which material that is emotionally unacceptable in oneself is unconsciously rejected and attributed to others (Kaplan & Sadock, 1996). Johnson (1980) defined projection differently, noting that the act of projection is the act of "unloading self-hatred onto others" (p. 31, italics in original deleted).

At times, the defense mechanism of projection will express itself through the behaviors of misinterpreting the motives or intentions of others (Kaplan & Sadock, 1996). Young children will often cry out "See what you made me do?!" when they have misbehaved in order to project responsibility for their action onto others. Individuals with substance-use problems will often do this as well, blaming their addiction or unacceptable aspects of their behavior on others.

Rationalization. The third common defense mechanism allows addicted individuals to justify feelings, motives, or behavior that they would otherwise find unreasonable, illogical, or intolerable (Kaplan & Sadock, 1996). Kaplan and Sadock later noted that rationalization may express itself through users' "invention of a convincing fallacy" (p. 184) through which their behavior might seemingly be justified. Some examples of rationalization used by addicts include blaming their spouse or family ("if you were married to _____ , you would drink, too!"), or medical problems (a 72-year-old alcoholic might blame his drinking on the fact that he had pneumonia when he was 12, for example).

Minimization. This mechanism operates in a different manner from the three reviewed earlier. In a sense, minimization operates like rationalization, but in a more specific way. By a variety of mechanisms, addicted individuals who use minimization as a defense will actively reduce the amount of chemicals that they admit to using, or deny the impact that their chemical use has had on their lives..

Alcohol-dependent individuals, for example, might pour their drinks into an oversized container, perhaps the size of three or four regular glasses, and then claim that they have "only three drinks a night!" (overlooking the fact that each drink is equal to three regular-sized drinks). Individuals with a substance-use problem might minimize their chemical use by claiming to "only drink four nights a week," and hope that the interviewer does not think to ask whether a "week" means a 5-day workweek or the full 7-day week. In such cases, it is not uncommon to find that such clients drink four nights out of five during the workweek and are intoxicated from Friday evening until they go to bed on Sunday night—with the final result being that they drink six nights out of each full week. Another expression of rationalization occurs when individuals claim time when they were in treatment, in jail, or hospitalized as "straight time" (i.e., time when they were not using chemicals), overlooking the fact that they were unable to get alcohol/drugs because they were incarcerated.[2]

Another common rationalization is that an individual might only become addicted to artificial chemicals, such as alcohol, amphetamines, or heroin. Obviously, as marijuana is an herb that grows naturally (it is rationalized), the individual could not possibly become addicted to it. Another popular rationalization is that it is "better to be an alcoholic than a needle freak. After all, alcohol is legal!"

Reactions to the Spiritual Disorder Theory of Addiction. Although the traditional view of substance abuse in the United States has been that the defense mechanisms of denial, rationalization, projection, and minimization are traditionally found in cases of chemical dependency,

this view is not universally accepted. There is a small, increasingly vocal minority that has offered alternative frameworks within which substance-abuse professionals might view the defense mechanisms that they encounter in their work with addicted individuals.

In the 1980s and 1990s, Stanton Peele proved to be a very vocal critic of the medical model of chemical dependency. In his (1989) work on the subject, he spoke at length of how treatment centers often utilize the individual's refusal to admit to his or her addiction as being a confirmation that the individual is addicted. The individual is automatically assumed to be "in denial" of his or her chemical abuse problem. However, a second possibility, all too often overlooked by treatment center staff, according to Peele, is that the individual might not be addicted to chemicals to begin with!!!

The automatic assumption that the client is "in denial" might blind treatment center staff to the possibility that the individual's refusal to admit to being addicted to chemicals might be a reflection of reality and not an expression of denial. This possibility underscores the need for an accurate assessment of the client's substance-use patterns to determine whether there is a need for active intervention or treatment. Miller and Rollnick (2002) offered a theory that radically departs from the belief that addicts typically utilize denial as a major defense against the admission of being "sick." The authors suggest that alcoholics, as a group, do not utilize denial more frequently than any other average group. Rather, the authors suggest that a combination of two factors has made it appear that addicts frequently utilize defense mechanisms such as denial, rationalization, and projection in the service of their dependency. First, the authors suggest that the process of selective perception on the part of treatment center staff makes it appear that substance-dependent people frequently use the defense mechanisms discussed earlier.

The authors point to the phenomenon known as the "illusion of correlation" to support this theory. According to the illusion of correlation, human beings tend to remember information that confirms their preconceptions and to forget or overlook information that fails to meet their conceptual model. Substance-abuse professionals would be more likely to remember clients who did use the defense mechanisms of denial, rationalization,

---

[2]This is often classified as "situational" abstinence by rehabilitation professionals, especially if the clients admit that they *would* have used chemicals during these "dry" periods if they could have done so without being caught.

projection, or minimization, according to the authors, because that is what they were trained to expect.

Second, Miller and Rollnick (2002) suggested that when substance-abuse rehabilitation professionals utilize the wrong treatment approach for the client's unique stage of growth, the resulting conflict is interpreted as evidence of denial, rationalization, projection, or minimization. On the basis of their work with addicted individuals, Berg and Miller (1992) also suggested that "denial" is found when the therapist utilizes the wrong treatment approach for the client that he or she is working with. Thus, both teams of clinicians have concluded that defense mechanisms such as "denial" are not a reflection of a pathological condition on the part of the client but the result of the wrong intervention being utilized by the professional who is working with the individual. These theories offer a challenging alternative to the traditional model that shows the addicted person using characteristic defense mechanisms such as those discussed in this chapter.

Summary

Many human service professionals who have had limited contact with addiction tend to have a distorted view of the nature of drug addiction. Having heard the term *disease* applied to chemical dependency, the inexperienced human service worker may think in terms of more traditional illnesses and may be rudely surprised at the deception that is inherent in drug addiction. Although chemical dependency is a disease, it is a disease like no other. It is, as noted in an earlier chapter, a disease that requires the active participation of the "victim." Further, self-help groups such as Alcoholics Anonymous or Narcotics Anonymous view addiction as a disease of the spirit and offer a spiritual program to help its members achieve and maintain their recovery.

Addiction is, in a sense, a form of insanity. The insanity of addiction rests upon a foundation of psychological defense mechanisms such as denial, rationalization, projection, and minimization. These mechanisms, plus self-deception, keep the person from becoming aware of the reality of his or her addiction until the disease process has progressed quite far. To combat self-deception, Alcoholics Anonymous places emphasis on honesty, openness, and a willingness to try to live without alcohol. Honesty, both with self and with others, is the central feature of the AA program, which is designed to foster spiritual growth to help the individual overcome his or her spiritual weaknesses.

An Introduction to Pharmacology[1]

Introduction

It is virtually impossible to discuss the effects of the various drugs of abuse without touching on a number of essential pharmacological concepts. In this chapter, some of the basic principles of pharmacology will be reviewed, and this should help you to better understand the impact that the different drugs of abuse may have on the user's body.[2]

There are many misconceptions about recreational chemicals. For example, some people believe that recreational chemicals are somehow unique. This is not true: They work the same way that other pharmaceuticals do. Alcohol and the drugs of abuse act by changing (strengthening/weakening) a potential that already exists within the cells of the body (Ciancio & Bourgault, 1989; Williams & Baer, 1994). In the case of the drugs of abuse, all of which exert their desired effects in the brain, they modify the normal function of the neurons of the brain.

The second misconception about the drugs of abuse is that they are somehow different from legitimate pharmaceuticals. This is also incorrect. Many of the drugs of abuse are—or were—once legitimate pharmaceuticals used by physicians to treat disease. Thus, the drugs of abuse obey the same laws of pharmacology that apply to the other medications in use today.

[1]This chapter is designed to provide the reader with a brief overview of some of the more important principles of pharmacology. It is not intended to serve as, nor should it be used for, a guide to patient care.

[2]Individuals interested in reading more on pharmacology might find several good selections in any medical or nursing school bookstore.

The Prime Effect and Side Effects of Chemicals

One rule of pharmacology is that whenever a chemical is introduced into the body, there is an element of risk (Laurence & Bennett, 1992). *Every* chemical agent presents the potential to cause harm to the individual, although the degree of risk varies as a result of a number of factors such as the specific chemical being used, the individual's state of health, and so on. The treatment of a localized infection caused by a fungus on the skin presents us with a localized site of action, that is, on the surface the body. This makes it easy to limit the impact that a medication used to treat the "athlete's foot" infection might have on the organism as a whole. The patient is unlikely to need more than a topical medication that can be applied directly to the infected region.

But consider for a moment the drugs of abuse. As mentioned in the last section, the site of action for each of the recreational chemicals lies deep within the central nervous system (CNS). There is increasing evidence that each of the various drugs of abuse ultimately will impact the limbic system of the brain. However, the drugs of abuse are very much like a blast of shotgun pellets: They will have an impact not only on the brain but also on many other organ systems in the body.

For example, as we will discuss in the chapter on cocaine, this drug causes the user to experience a sense of well-being, or euphoria. These sensations that might result from cocaine abuse are called the *primary effects* of the cocaine abuse. But the chemical has a number of side effects; one of these is causing the coronary arteries of the user's heart to constrict. Coronary artery constriction is hardly a desired effect, and, as will be discussed in Chapter 12, might appear to be the cause of heart attacks in cocaine users.[3] Such unwanted effects are often called *secondary effects*, or *side effects*. The side effects of a chemical might range from simply making the patient feel uncomfortable to being life threatening.

A second example is aspirin, which inhibits the production of chemicals known as prostaglandins at the site of an injury. This helps to reduce the individual's pain from an injury. But the body also produces prostaglandins in the kidneys and stomach, where these chemicals help control the function of these organs. Because aspirin tends to nonselectively block prostaglandin production *throughout* the body, including the stomach and kidneys, this unwanted effect of aspirin may put the user's life at risk as the aspirin interferes with the normal function of these organs.

A third example of the therapeutic effect/side effect phenomenon might be seen when a person with a bacterial infection of the middle ear (a condition known as *otitis media*) takes an antibiotic such as penicillin. The desired outcome is for the antibiotic to destroy the bacteria causing the infection in the middle ear. However, a side effect might be a case of drug-induced diarrhea, as the antibiotic interferes with normal bacteria growth patterns in the intestinal tract.

Thus, one needs to keep in mind that all pharmaceuticals, and the drugs of abuse, have both desired effects and numerous, possibly undesirable, side effects.

Drug Forms and How Drugs Are Administered

A drug is essentially a foreign chemical that is introduced into the individual's body to bring about a specific, desired response. Antihypertensive medications are used to control excessively high blood pressure, whereas antibiotics are used to eliminate unwanted bacterial infections. The recreational drugs are introduced into the body, as a general rule, to bring about feelings of euphoria, relaxation, and relief from stress. The specific

form in which a drug is administered will have a major effect on (a) the speed with which that chemical is able to work, and (b) the way the chemical is distributed throughout the body. In general, the drugs of abuse are administered by either the *enteral* or *parenteral* route.

Enteral Forms of Drug Administration

Medications that are administered by the enteral route are administered *orally, sublingually, or rectally* (Ciancio & Bourgault, 1989; Williams & Baer, 1994). The most common means by which a medication is administered orally is the *tablet*. Essentially, a tablet is "a compounded form in which the drug is mixed with a binding agent to hold the tablet together before administration. . . . Most tablets are designed to be swallowed whole" (Shannon, Wilson, & Stang, 1995, p. 8). A number of the drugs of abuse are often administered in tablet form, including aspirin, the hallucinogens LSD and MDMA, and on occasion, illicit forms of amphetamine. Amphetamine tablets are frequently made in illicit laboratories and are known on the street by a variety of names (e.g., "white cross" or "cartwheels").

A second common form that oral medication might take, according to the authors, is that of a *capsule*. Essentially, capsules are modified tablets, with the inside medication being surrounded by a gelatin capsule. The capsule is designed to be swallowed whole, and once it reaches the stomach the gelatin capsule breaks down, allowing the medication to be released into the gastrointestinal tract (Shannon, Wilson, & Stang, 1995).

Medications can take many other forms. For example, some medications are administered in liquid form, for oral use. Antibiotics and some over-the-counter analgesics often are administered in liquid forms, especially when the patient is a very young child. Liquid forms of a drug make it possible to tailor each dose to the patient's weight and are ideal for patients who have trouble taking pills or capsules by mouth. Of the drugs of abuse, alcohol is perhaps the best example of a chemical that is administered in liquid form.

Some medications, and a small number of the drugs of abuse, might be absorbed through the blood-rich tissues under the tongue. A chemical that enters the body by this method is said to be administered *sublingually*. The sublingual method of drug administration is considered a variation of the oral form of drug administration. Certain drugs, like nitroglycerin and fentanyl,

---

[3]Shannon, Wilson, and Stang (1995) refer to a chemical's *primary effects* as the drug's *therapeutic effects* (p. 21). However, their text is devoted to medications and their uses, not to the drugs of abuse. In order to maintain the differentiation between the use of a medication in the treatment of disease and the abuse of chemicals for recreational purposes, this text will use the term *primary effects*.

are well absorbed by the sublingual method of administration. However, for the most part, the drugs of abuse are not administered this way.

Parenteral Forms of Drug Administration

The parenteral method of drug administration essentially involves injecting the medication directly into the body. There are several forms of parenteral administration, which are commonly used in both the world of medicine and the world of drug abuse. First, there is the *subcutaneous* method. In this process, a chemical is injected just under the skin. This allows the drug to avoid the dangers of passing through the stomach and gastrointestinal tracts. However, drugs that are administered in a subcutaneous injection are absorbed more slowly than are chemicals injected into either muscle tissue or a vein. As we will see in the chapter on narcotics addiction, heroin addicts will often use subcutaneous injections, a process that they call "skin popping."

A second method of parenteral administration involves the *intramuscular* injection of a medication. Muscle tissues have a good supply of blood, and medications injected into muscle tissue will be absorbed into the general circulation more rapidly than when injected just under the skin. As we will discuss in the chapter on anabolic steroid abuse, it is quite common for individuals abusing anabolic steroids to inject them into the muscle tissue.

The third method of parenteral administration is the *intravenous* (IV) injection. Here the chemical is injected directly into a vein, going straight to the general circulation (Schwertz, 1991). Of the drugs of abuse, heroin, cocaine, and some forms of amphetamine are examples of chemicals administered by intravenous injection. Because of the speed with which the chemical reaches the general circulation when administered by intravenous injection, there is a very real potential for undesirable reactions. The very nature of intravenously administered drugs provides the body very little time to adapt to the arrival of the foreign chemical (Ciancio & Bourgault, 1989). This is one reason that users of intravenously administered chemicals, such as heroin, frequently experience a wide range of adverse effects in addition to the desired euphoria caused by the chemical being abused.

Just because a parenteral method of drug administration was utilized, the chemical in question will not have an instantaneous effect. The speed at which all forms of drugs administered by parenteral administration begin to work are influenced by a number of factors, which will be discussed in the section on drug distribution later in this chapter.

Other Forms of Drug Administration

A number of additional methods of drug administration at least need to be briefly identified. Some chemicals might be absorbed through the skin, a process that involves a *transdermal* method of drug administration. Eventually, chemicals absorbed transdermally reach the general circulation and are then distributed throughout the body. Physicians will often use transdermal drug administration to provide the patient with a low, steady, blood level of a chemical. A drawback of transdermal drug administration is that it is a very slow way to introduce a drug into the body. For certain agents, however, it is useful. An example is the skin patch used to administer nicotine to patients who are attempting to quit smoking. Some antihistamines are administered transdermally, especially when used for motion sickness. There also is a transdermal patch available for the narcotic analgesic fentanyl, although its success as a means of providing analgesia has been quite limited.

Occasionally, chemicals are administered *intranasally*. The intranasal administration of a chemical involves "snorting" the material in question so that it is deposited on the blood-rich tissues of the sinuses. From that point, it is possible for many chemicals to be absorbed into the general circulation. For example, both cocaine and heroin powders might be—and frequently are—"snorted."

The process of "snorting" is similar to the process of *inhalation*, which is used by both physicians and illicit drug users. Inhalation of a compound takes advantage of the fact that the blood is separated from exposure to the air by a layer of tissue that is less than 1/100,000ths of an inch (or 0.64 microns) thick (Garrett, 1994). Many chemical molecules are small enough to pass through the lungs into the general circulation, as is the case with surgical anesthetics. Some of the drugs of abuse, such as heroin and cocaine, might also be abused by inhalation when they are smoked. In another form of inhalation, the particles being inhaled are suspended in the smoke. These particles are small enough to reach the deep tissues of the lungs, where they are then deposited. In a brief period of time, the particles are broken down into smaller units until they are small enough to pass through the walls of the lungs and reach the general circulation. This is the process that takes place when tobacco products are smoked.

Each subform of inhalation takes advantage of the blood-rich, extremely large surface area of the lungs, through which chemical agents might be absorbed (Benet, Kroetz, & Sheiner, 1995). Further, depending on how fast the chemical being inhaled can cross over into the general circulation, chemicals can be introduced into the body relatively quickly. However, research has shown that the actual amount of a chemical absorbed through inhalation tends to be quite variable for a number of reasons. First, the individual must inhale at just the right time to allow the chemical to reach the desired region of the lungs. Second, some chemicals pass through the tissues of the lung very poorly and thus are not well absorbed by inhalation.

As we will see in the chapter on marijuana, the individual who smokes marijuana must use a different technique from that used in smoking tobacco in order to get the maximum effect from the chemical that is inhaled. The variability in the amount of chemical absorbed through the lungs limits the utility of inhalation as a means of administering medications. However, for some of the drugs of abuse, inhalation is the preferred method. Pharmaceuticals can be introduced into the body in other ways. For example, the chemical might be prepared in such a way that it might be administered rectally, or through enteral tubes. However, because the drugs of abuse are generally introduced into the body by injection, orally, intranasally, or through smoking, we will not discuss the more obscure methods of drug administration.

Bioavailability

In order to work, a drug being abused must enter the body in sufficient strength to achieve the desired effect. Pharmacists refer to this as the *bioavailability* of the chemical. Bioavailability is the *concentration of the unchanged chemical at the site of action* (Loebl, Spratto, & Woods, 1994; Sands, Knapp, & Ciraulo, 1993). The bioavability of a chemical in the body is influenced, in turn, by several factors (Benet, Kroetz, & Sheiner, 1995; Sands, Knapp, &

Ciraulo, 1993): (a) absorption, (b) distribution, (c) biotransformation, and (d) elimination. To understand the process of bioavailability, we will consider in more detail each of the factors that might influence the bioavailability of a chemical.

Absorption

Except for topical agents, which are deposited directly on the site of action, chemicals must be absorbed into the body. Ultimately, the concentration of a chemical in the serum and at the site of action is influenced by the process of absorption (Loebl, Spratto, & Woods, 1994). This process involves the movement of drug molecules from the site of entry, through various cell boundaries, to the site of action.

The human body is composed of layers of specialized cells that are organized into specific patterns in order to carry out certain functions. For example, the cells of the bladder are organized in such a way as to form a muscular reservoir in which waste products are stored and from which excretion takes place. The cells of the circulatory system are organized to form tubes (blood vessels) that contain the cells and fluids of the circulatory system.

As a general rule, each layer of cells the drug must pass through to reach the general circulation will slow the absorption down that much more. For example, just one layer of cells separates the air in our lungs from the general circulation. Drugs that are able to pass across this boundary may reach the circulation in just a few seconds. In contrast, a drug that is ingested orally must pass through several layers of cells before reaching the general circulation from the gastrointestinal tract. Thus, the oral method of drug administration is generally recognized as being one of the slowest methods by which a drug might be admitted into the body. Figure 6.1 demonstrates the process of drug absorption.

Drug molecules can take advantage of a number of specialized *cellular transport mechanisms* to pass through the walls of the cells at the point of entry. These cellular transport mechanisms are quite complex and function at the molecular level. Some drug molecules simply diffuse through the cell membrane, a process known as *passive diffusion* or *passive transport* across the cell boundary. This is the most common method of drug transport into the body's cells and operates on the principle that chemicals tend to diffuse from areas of

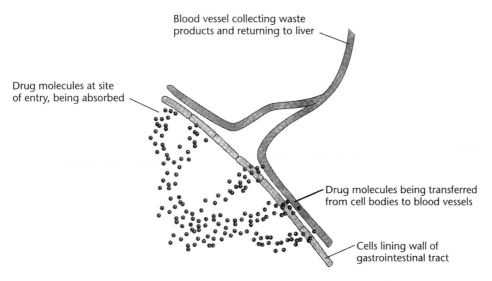

Blood vessel collecting waste
products and returning to liver

Drug molecules at site
of entry, being absorbed

Drug molecules being transferred
from cell bodies to blood vessels

Cells lining wall of
gastrointestinal tract

FIGURE 6.1   The process of drug absorption.

high concentration to areas of lower concentration. Other drug molecules take advantage of one of several molecular transport mechanisms that move various essential molecules into (and out of) cells. Collectively, these different molecular transport mechanisms provide a system of *active transport* across cell boundaries and into the interior of the body.

Several specialized absorption-modification variables influence the speed at which drugs might be absorbed from the site of entry. For example, there is the *rate of blood flow* at the site of entry and the *molecular characteristics of the drug molecule* being admitted to the body. However, for this text, simply remember that the process of absorption refers to the movement of drug molecules from the site of entry to the site of action. In the next section, we will discuss the second factor that influences how a chemical acts in the body—its distribution.

Distribution

The process of *distribution* refers to how the chemical molecules are moved about in the body. This includes both drug transport and the pattern of drug accumulation within the body at normal dosage levels. As a general rule, very little is known about drug distribution patterns in the overdose victim (Jenkins & Cone, 1998). As an example of drug distribution data, the hallucinogen PCP has been found to accumulate in the brain and in

adipose (fat) tissue. Drug distribution is highly variable between individuals and is affected by such factors as the individual's sex, muscle/adipose tissue ratio, blood flow patterns to various body organs, the amount of water in different parts of the body, the individual's genetic heritage, and his or her age (Jenkins & Cone, 1998).

Drug transport. Once a chemical has reached the general circulation, that substance can then be transported to the site of action. But the main purpose of the circulatory system is not to provide a distribution system for drugs! In reality, a drug molecule is a foreign substance in the circulatory system that takes advantage of the body's own chemical distribution system to move from the point of entry to the site of action. A chemical can use the circulatory system to reach the site of action in several different ways. Some chemicals are able to mix freely with the blood plasma. These are classified as *water-soluble* drugs. Because water is such a large part of the human body, the drug molecules from water-soluble chemicals are rapidly and easily distributed throughout the fluid in the body. Alcohol is an excellent example of a water-soluble chemical. Shortly after gaining admission into the body, alcohol is rapidly distributed throughout the body to *all* blood-rich organs, including the brain.

A different approach is utilized by other drugs. Their chemical structure allows them to "bind" to fat molecules known as *lipids* that are found floating in the general circulation. Chemicals that bind to these fat molecules are often called *lipid soluble*. Because fat molecules are used to build cell walls within the body, lipids have the ability to move rapidly out of the circulatory system into the body tissues. Indeed, one characteristic of blood lipids is that they are constantly passing out of the circulatory system and into the body tissues.

Thus, chemicals that are lipid soluble will be distributed throughout the body, especially to organs with a high concentration of lipids. In comparison to the other organ systems in the body, which are made up of 6% to 20% lipid molecules, fully 50% of the weight of the brain is made up of lipids (Cooper, Bloom, & Roth, 1986). Thus, chemicals that are highly lipid soluble will tend to concentrate rapidly within the tissues of the brain. The ultrashort and short-acting barbiturates are good examples of drugs that are lipid soluble. Although all the barbiturates are lipid soluble, there is a great deal of variability in the speed with which various barbiturates can bind to lipids. The speed at which a given barbiturate will begin to have an effect will depend, in part, on its ability to form bonds with lipid molecules. For the ultrashort-acting barbiturates, which are extremely lipid soluble, the effects might be felt within seconds of the time they are injected into a vein. This is one reason the ultrashort-duration barbiturates are so useful as surgical anesthetics.

Remember that drug molecules are foreign substances in the body. Their presence might be tolerated, but only until the body's natural defenses against chemical intruders are able to eliminate the foreign substance. The body will thus be working to detoxify (biotransform) and/or eliminate the foreign chemical molecules in the body almost from the moment they arrive. One way that drugs are able to avoid the danger of biotransformation and/or elimination before they have an effect is to join with protein molecules in the blood. These protein molecules are normally present in human blood, for reasons that need not be discussed further here. It is sufficient to understand that some protein molecules are normally present in the blood.

But by coincidence, the chemical structures of many drugs allow the individual molecules to bind with protein molecules in the general circulation. This most often involves a protein known as *albumin*. For this reason such chemicals are said to become "protein bound" (or if they bind to albumin, they might be said to be "albumin bound").[4] The advantage of protein binding is that while a drug molecule is protein bound, it is difficult for the body to either biotransform or excrete it. The strength of the chemical bond that forms between the chemical and the protein molecules will vary. Some drugs form stronger chemical bonds with protein molecules than do others. The strength of this chemical bond then determines how long the drug will remain in the body before elimination. The dilemma is that while they are protein bound, drug molecules are also unable to have any biological effect. Thus, to have an effect, the molecule must be free of chemical bonds (*unbound*).

Fortunately, although a chemical might be strongly protein bound, a certain percentage of the drug molecules will always be "unbound." For example, if 75% of a given drug's molecules are protein bound, then 25% of that drug's molecules are said to be unbound, or free. It is this unbound fraction of drug molecules that is able to have an effect on the bodily function, to be biologically active. The protein-bound molecules are unable to have any effect at the site of action and are biologically inactive while bound (Rasymas, 1992; Shannon, Wilson, & Stang, 1995). Thus, for chemicals that are largely protein bound, the unbound drug molecules must be extremely potent.

For example, the antidepressant amitriptyline is 95% protein bound. This means that only 5% of a given dose of this drug is actually biologically active at any time (Ciraulo, Shader, Greenblatt, & Barnhill, 1995). Another drug that is strongly protein bound is diazepam. Over 99% of the diazepam molecules that reach the general circulation will become protein bound. Thus, the sedative effects of diazepam (see Chapter 10) are actually caused by the small fraction (approximately 1%) of the diazepam molecules that remained unbound after the drug reaches the circulation.

As noted earlier, unbound drug molecules may easily be biotransformed and/or excreted (the process of drug biotransformation and excretion of chemicals will be discussed in a later section of this chapter). Thus, one advantage of protein binding is that the protein-bound

---

[4]In general, acidic drugs tend to bind to albumin, whereas basic drugs tend to bind to alpha$_1$-acid glycoprotein (Ciancio & Bourgault, 1989).

drug molecules form a "reservoir" of drug molecules that have not yet been biotransformed. These drug molecules are gradually released back into the general circulation as the chemical bond between the drug and the protein molecules weakens, or as other molecules compete with the drug for the binding site. The drug molecules that gradually are released back into the general circulation then replace those molecules that have been biotransformed and/or excreted.

It is the *proportion* of unbound to bound molecules that remains approximately the same. Thus, if 75% of the drug was protein bound and 25% was unbound when the drug was at its greatest concentration in the blood, then after some of that drug had been eliminated from the body the proportion of bound to unbound drug would continue to be approximately 75:25. Although, at first glance, the last sentence might seem to be in error, remember that as some drug molecules are being removed from the general circulation, some of the protein-bound molecules are also breaking the chemical bonds that held them to the protein molecule to once again become unbound. Thus, while the amount of chemical in the general circulation will gradually diminish as the body biotransforms or eliminates the unbound drug molecules, the proportion of bound:unbound drug molecules will remain essentially unchanged.

The characteristic of protein binding actually is related to another trait of a drug: the biological half-life of that chemical. This topic will be discussed in more detail later in this chapter. However, protein binding allows the drug in question to have a longer duration of effect. As the protein-bound molecules are gradually released back into the general circulation over an extended period of time, the total period of time in which that drug is present in sufficient quantities to remain biologically active is extended.

Biotransformation

Because a drug is a foreign substance, the natural defenses of the body try to eliminate the drug almost immediately. In some cases, the body is able to eliminate the drug without the need to modify its chemical structure. Penicillin is an example of a drug that is excreted unchanged from the body. Many inhalants and surgical anesthetics are also eliminated from the body without being metabolized to any significant

degree. But as a general rule, the chemical structure of most chemicals must be modified before they can be eliminated from the body.

This elimination is accomplished through what was once referred to as *detoxification*. However, as researchers have come to understand how the body prepares a drug molecule for elimination, the term *detoxification* has been replaced with the term *biotransformation*.[5] Drug biotransformation usually is carried out in the liver, although on occasion this process occurs in other tissues of the body. The *microsomal endoplasmic reticulum* of the liver produces a number of enzymes[6] that transform toxic molecules into a form that can be more easily eliminated from the body. Technically, the new compound that emerges from each step of the process of drug biotransformation is known as a *metabolite* of the chemical that was introduced into the body. The original chemical is occasionally called the *parent compound* of the metabolite that emerges from the process of biotransformation.

In general, metabolites are less biologically active than the parent compound. However, there are exceptions to this rule. Depending on the substance being biotransformed, the metabolite might actually have a psychoactive effect of its own. On rare occasions, a drug might actually have a metabolite that is actually more biologically active than the parent compound.[7] For this reason pharmacologists have come to use the term *biotransformation* rather than the older terms *detoxification* or *metabolism*.

Although it is easier to speak of drug biotransformation as if it were a single process, in reality there are four different subforms of this procedure known as (a) oxidation, (b) reduction, (c) hydrolysis, and (d) conjugation (Ciraulo, Shader, Greenblatt, & Barnhill, 1995). The specifics of each form of drug biotransformation are quite complex and are best reserved for pharmacology

[5]This process is inaccurately referred to as "metabolism" of a drug. Technically, the term drug *metabolism* refers to the total ordeal of a drug molecule in the body, including its absorption, distribution, biotransformation, and excretion.

[6]The most common of which is the P-450 metabolic pathway, or the microsomal P-450 pathway.

[7]For example, after Gamma-hydroxybutyrate (GHB) was banned by the Food and Drug Administration, illicit users switched to the compound gammabutyrolactone—a compound with reported health benefits such as improved sleep patterns—which is biotransformed into the banned substance GHB in the user's body.

texts. It is enough for the reader to remember that there are four different processes collectively called drug metabolism, or biotransformation. Many chemicals must go through more than one step in the biotransformation process before being ready for the next step: *elimination.*

One major goal of the process of metabolism is to transform the foreign chemical into a form that can be rapidly eliminated from the body (Clark, Bratler, & Johnson, 1991). But this process does not take place instantly. Rather, the process of biotransformation is accomplished through chemical reactions facilitated by enzymes produced in the body. The process is carried out over a period of time, and depending on the drug involved, a number of intermediate steps often occur before that chemical is ready for elimination from the body.

Simply stated, the goal of the drug biotransformation process is to change the chemical structure of the foreign substance in such a way that it would then be less lipid soluble and thus more easily eliminated from the body. There are two major forms of drug biotransformation. In the first subtype, a constant fraction of the drug is biotransformed in a given period of time, such as a single hour. This is called a *first order biotransformation* process. Certain antibiotics are metabolized in this manner, with a set percentage of the medication in the body being biotransformed each hour. Other chemicals are eliminated from the body by what is known as a *zero order biotransformation* process. Drugs that are biotransformed through a zero order biotransformation process are metabolized at a set rate, no matter how high the concentration of that chemical in the blood. Alcohol is a good example of a chemical that is biotransformed through a zero order biotransformation process.

As we will discuss in Chapter 7, alcohol is biotransformed at the rate of about what a person ingests if he or she were to drink one regular mixed drink or one can of beer per hour. It does not matter whether the person were to ingest just one can of beer or one regular mixed drink, or 20 cans of beer or regular mixed drinks in an hour. The body would still biotransform only the equivalent of one can of beer/mixed drink per hour, for alcohol is biotransformed through a zero order biotransformation process.

As a general rule, chemicals that are administered orally must pass through the stomach to the small intestine before they can be absorbed. However, the human circulatory system is designed in such a way that chemicals absorbed through the gastrointestinal system are carried first to the liver. This makes sense, as the liver is given the task of protecting the body from toxins. By taking chemicals absorbed from the gastrointestinal tract to the liver, the body is able to begin to break down any toxins in the substance that was introduced into the body before those toxins might damage other organ systems.

Unfortunately, one effect of this process is that the liver is often able to biotransform many medications that are administered orally before they have had a chance to reach the site of action. This is called *first pass metabolism.* First pass metabolism is one reason it is so hard to control pain through the use of orally administered narcotic analgesic medications. When taken by mouth, a significant part of the dose of an orally administered narcotic analgesic such as morphine will be metabolized by the liver into inactive forms, *before* reaching the site of action.

Elimination

In the human body, biotransformation and elimination are closely intertwined. Indeed, some authorities on pharmacology consider these to be a single process, as one goal of drug biotransformation is to change the foreign chemical into a water-soluble metabolite that can then be easily removed from the circulation (Clark, Bratler, & Johnson, 1991).

The most common method of drug elimination is by the kidneys (Benet, Kroetz, & Sheiner, 1995). However, the biliary tract, lungs, and sweat glands may also play a role (Shannon, Wilson, & Stang, 1995). For example, a small percentage of the alcohol that a person has ingested will be excreted when that person exhales. A small percentage of the alcohol in the system is also eliminated through the sweat glands. These characteristics of alcohol contribute to the characteristic smell of the intoxicated individual.

The Drug Half-Life

There are several different measures of *drug half-life*, all of which provide a *rough* estimate of the period of time that a drug remains active in the human body. The *distribution half-life* is the time that it takes for a drug to work its way from the general circulation into body tissues

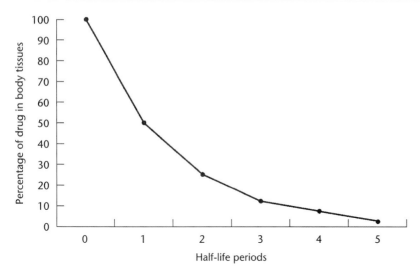

FIGURE 6.2 Drug elimination in half-life stages.

such as muscle and fat (Reiman, 1997). This is important information in overdose situations, for example, when the physician treating the patient has to estimate the amount of a compound in the patient's circulation. Another measure of drug activity in the body is the *therapeutic half-life*, or the period of time that it takes for the body to inactivate 50% of a single dose of a compound. The therapeutic half-life is intertwined with the concept of the *elimination half-life*. This is the time that it takes for 50% of a single dose to be *eliminated* from the body.

As an example, different chemicals might rapidly migrate from the general circulation into adipose or muscle tissues, with the result that that compound would have a short distribution half-life. THC, the active agent in marijuana, is such a compound. However, for heavy users, a reservoir of unmetabolized THC forms in the adipose tissue, and this is gradually released back into the user's circulation when the person stops using marijuana. As a result, THC has a long elimination half-life in the chronic user, although the therapeutic half-life of a single dose is quite short.

For this text, all of these different measures of half-life will be lumped together under the term of *biological half-life* (or *half-life*) of that chemical. Sometimes, the half-life is abbreviated by the symbol $t_{1/2}$. The half life of a chemical will be viewed as the period of time needed for the individual's body to reduce the amount of active drug in the circulation by one-half (Benet, Kroetz, & Sheiner, 1995). The concept of $t_{1/2}$ is based on the assumption that the individual ingested only one dose of the drug, and the reader should keep in mind that the dynamics of a drug following a single dose are often far different from those for the same drug when it is used on a continuing basis. Thus, although the $t_{1/2}$ concept is often a source of confusion even among health professionals, it does allow health care workers to roughly estimate how long a drug's effects will last when that chemical is used at normal dosage levels.

One popular misconception is that it takes only two half-lives for the body to totally eliminate a drug. In reality, 25% of the original dose remains at the end of the second half-life period, and 12% of the original dose is still in the body at the end of three half-life periods. As a general rule, five half-life periods are required before the body is able to eliminate virtually all of a single dose of a chemical (Williams & Baer, 1994). Figure 6.2 shows drug elimination in half-life stages.

Generally, drugs with long half-life periods tend to remain biologically active for longer periods of time. The reverse is also true: Chemicals with a short biological half-life tend to be active for shorter periods of time. Here is where the process of protein binding comes into play: Drugs with longer half-lives tend to become protein bound. As stated earlier, the process of protein binding allows a reservoir of an unmetabolized drug to be released gradually back into the general circulation as the drug molecules become unbound. This allows a chemical to remain in the circulation at a sufficient concentration to have an effect for an extended period of time.

The Effective Dose

The concept of the *effective dose* (ED) is based on dose-response calculations, in which pharmacologists calculate the percentage of a population that will respond to a given dose of a chemical. Scientists usually estimate the percentage of the population that is expected to experience an effect by a chemical at different dosage levels. For example, the ED_{10} is the dosage level at which 10% of the population will achieve the desired effects from the chemical being ingested.

The ED_{50} is the dosage level at which 50% of the population would be expected to respond to the drug's effects. Obviously, for medications, the goal is to find a dosage level at which the largest percentage of the population will respond to the medication. However, you cannot keep increasing the dose of a medication forever; sooner or later you will raise the dosage level to the point that it will become toxic and people may quite possibly die from the effects of the chemical.

The Lethal Dose Index

Drugs are, by their very nature, foreign to the body. When they are introduced into the body, drugs will disrupt the function of the body in one way or another. One common characteristic of both legitimate pharmaceuticals and the drugs of abuse is that the person who administered that chemical hopes to alter the body's function to bring about a desired effect. But chemicals that are introduced into the body hold the potential to disrupt the function of one or more organ systems to the point that it is no longer possible for them to function normally. At the extreme, chemicals may disrupt the body's activities sufficiently to put the life of the individual in danger.

Scientists express this continuum as a form of modified dose-response curve. In the typical dose-response curve scientists calculate the percentage of the population that would be expected to benefit from a certain exposure to a chemical; the calculation for a fatal exposure level, however, is slightly different. In such a dose-response curve, scientists calculate the percentage of the general population that would, in theory, die as a result of being exposed to a certain dose of a chemical or toxin.

This figure is then expressed in terms of a "lethal dose" (or LD) ratio. The percentage of the population that would die as a result of exposure to that chemical/toxin source is identified as a subscript to the LD heading. Thus, if a certain level of exposure to a chemical or toxin resulted in a 25% death rate, this would be abbreviated as the LD_{25} for that chemical or toxin. A level of exposure to a toxin or chemical that resulted in a 50% death rate would be abbreviated as the LD_{50} for that substance.

For example, as we will discuss in the next chapter, a person with a blood alcohol level of .350 mg/mL would stand a 1% chance of death without medical intervention. Thus, a blood alcohol level of .350 mg/mL is the LD_{01} for alcohol. It is possible to calculate the potential lethal exposure level for virtually every chemical. These figures provide scientists with a way to estimate the relative safety of different levels of exposure to chemicals or radiation, and a way to determine when medical intervention is necessary.

The Therapeutic Index

In addition to their potential to benefit the user, all drugs hold the potential for harm. Because they are foreign substances being introduced into the body, there is a danger that if used in amounts that are too large, the drugs might actually harm the individual rather than help him or her.

Scientists have devised what is known as the therapeutic index (TI) as a way to measure the relative safety of a chemical. Essentially, the TI is the ratio between the ED_{50} and the LD_{50}. In other words, the TI is a ratio between the effectiveness of a chemical and the potential for harm inherent in using that chemical. A smaller TI means that there is only a small margin between the dosage level needed to achieve the therapeutic effects and the dosage level at which the drug becomes toxic to the individual. A large TI suggests that there is a great deal of latitude between the normal therapeutic dosage range and the dosage level at which that chemical might become toxic to the user.

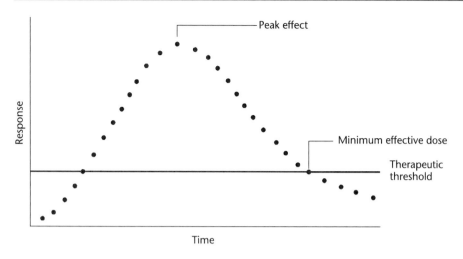

FIGURE 6.3 Hypothetical dose-response curve.

Unfortunately, as we will see in the next few chapters, many of the drugs of abuse have a small TI. These chemicals are potentially quite toxic to the user. For example, as we will discuss in the chapter on barbiturate abuse, the ratio between the normal dosage range and the toxic dosage range for the barbiturates is only about 1:3. In contrast to this, the ratio between the normal dosage range and the toxic dosage level for the benzodiazepines is estimated to be about 1:200. Thus, relatively speaking, the benzodiazepines are said to be much safer than the barbiturates.

Peak Effects

The effects of a chemical within the body develop over time until the drug reaches what is known as the *therapeutic threshold*. This is the point at which the concentration of a specific chemical in the body allows it to begin to have the desired effect on the user. The chemical's effects continue to become stronger and stronger until finally the strongest possible effects from a dose of that drug are reached. This is the period of *peak effects*. Then, gradually, the impact of the drug becomes less and less pronounced as the chemical is eliminated/biotransformed over a period of time. Eventually, the concentration of the chemical in the body falls below the therapeutic level. Scientists have learned to calculate dose-response curves in order to

estimate the potential for a chemical to have an effect at any given point in time after it was administered. Figure 6.3 shows a hypothetical dose-response curve.

The period of peak effects following a single dose of a drug varies from one chemical to another. For example, the peak effects of an ultrashort-acting barbiturate might be achieved in a matter of seconds following a single dose, while the long-term barbiturate phenobarbital might take hours to achieve its strongest effects. Thus, clinicians must remember that the period of peak effects following a single dose of a chemical will vary for each chemical.

The Site of Action

To illustrate the concept of the *site of action*, consider the case of a person with an "athlete's foot" infection. This condition is caused by a fungus that attacks the skin. Obviously, the individual who has such an infection will want to have it cured, and there are several excellent over-the-counter antifungal compounds available. In most cases, the individual need only select one, and then apply it to the proper area on his or her body to be cured of the infection.

At about this point, somebody is asking what antifungal compounds have to do with drug abuse. Admittedly, it is not the purpose of this chapter to sell antifungal compounds. But the example of the athlete's foot infection helps to illustrate the concept of the *site of action*. To put it simply, the site of action is where the drug being used will have its prime effect. In the case of the medication being used for the athlete's foot infection, the site of action is the infected skin on the person's foot. For the drugs of abuse, the central nervous system (or CNS) will be the primary site of action.

The Central Nervous System (CNS)

The CNS is, without question, the most complex organ system in the human body. At its most fundamental level, it comprises perhaps 100 billion neurons. These cells are designed to both send and receive messages from other neurons in a process known as information processing. To accomplish this task, each neuron may communicate with tens, hundreds, or thousands of its fellows through a system of perhaps 100 trillion synaptic junctions (Stahl, 2000).[8] To put this number into perspective, it has been estimated that the average human brain has more synaptic junctions than there are individual grains of sand on all of the beaches of the planet Earth.

Although most of the CNS is squeezed into the confines of the skull, the individual neurons do not actually touch. Rather, they are separated by microscopic spaces called *synapses*. To communicate across the sympatic void, one neuron will release a cloud of chemical molecules that function as *neurotransmitters*. When a sufficient number of these molecules contact a corresponding *receptor site* in the cell wall of the next neuron, a profound change is triggered in the postsynaptic neuron. Such changes may include the postsynaptic neuron "making, strengthening, or destroying synapses; urging axons to sprout; and synthesizing various proteins, enzymes, and receptors that regulate neurotransmission in the target cell" (Stahl, 2000, p. 21). Another change may be to force the postsynaptic neuron to release a cloud of neurotransmitter molecules in turn, passing the message that it just received on to the next neuron in that neural pathway.

[8]Although the CNS is, by itself, worthy of a lifetime of study, for the purpose of this text the beauty and complexities of the CNS must be compressed into just a few short paragraphs. The reader who wishes to learn more about the CNS should consult a good textbook on neuropsychology or neuroanatomy.

The Receptor Site

The receptor site is the exact spot either on the cell wall or within the cell itself where the chemical molecule carries out its main effects (Olson, 1992). To understand how receptor sites work, consider the analogy of a key slipping into the slot of a lock. The structure of the transmitter molecule fits into the receptor site in much the same way as a lock into a key, although on a greatly reduced scale. The receptor site is usually a pattern of molecules that allows a single molecule to attach itself to the target portion of the cell at that point. Under normal circumstances, receptor sites allow the molecules of naturally occurring compounds to attach to the cell walls in order to carry out normal biological functions.

By coincidence, however, many chemicals may be introduced into the body that also have the potential to bind to these receptor sites and possibly alter the normal biological function of the cell in a desirable way. Those bacteria susceptible to the antibiotic penicillin, for example, have a characteristic "receptor site," in this case, the enzyme transpeptidase. This enzyme carries out an essential role in bacterial reproduction. By blocking the action of transpeptidase, penicillin prevents the bacteria cells from reproducing. As the bacteria continue to grow, the pressure within the cell increases until the cell wall is no longer able to contain it, and the cell ruptures.

Neurotransmitter receptor sites are a specialized form of receptor site found in the walls of neurons at the synaptic junction. Their function is to receive the chemical messages from the presynaptic neuron in the form of neurotransmitter molecules at specific receptor sites. To prevent premature firing, a number of receptor sites must be occupied at the same instant before the electrical potential of the receiving (postsynpatic) neuron is changed, allowing it to pass the message on to the next cell in the nerve pathway. Essentially, all of the known chemicals that function as neurotransmitters within the CNS fall into two groups: those that stimulate the neuron to release a chemical "message" to the next cell, and those that inhibit the release of neurotransmitters. By altering the flow of these two classes of neurotransmitters, the drugs of abuse alter the way the CNS functions.

Co-transmission. When neurotransmitters were first identified, scientists thought that each neuron utilized just one form of neurotransmitter molecule. In recent

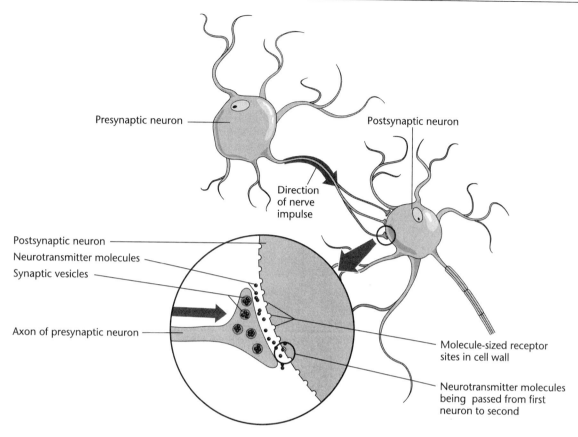

Presynaptic neuron

Postsynaptic neuron

Direction
of nerve
impulse

Postsynaptic neuron

Neurotransmitter molecules

Synaptic vesicles

Axon of presynaptic neuron

Molecule-sized receptor
sites in cell wall

Neurotransmitter molecules
being passed from first
neuron to second

FIGURE 6.4 Neurotransmitter diagram.

years, they have discovered that in addition to one "main" neurotransmitter, neurons often both receive and release "secondary" neurotransmitter molecules that are quite different from the main neurotransmitter (Stahl, 2000). The process of releasing secondary neurotransmitters is known as *co-transmission*, with opiate peptides most commonly being utilized as secondary neurotransmitters (Stahl, 2000). The process of co-transmission may explain why many drugs that affect the CNS have such wide-reaching secondary, or side effects.

Neurotransmitter reuptake/destruction. In many cases, neurotransmitter molecules are recycled. This does not always happen, however, and in some cases once a neurotransmitter is released it is destroyed by an enzyme designed to carry out this function. But

sometimes a neuron will activate a molecular "pump" that absorbs as many of a specific neurotransmitter molecules from the synaptic junction as possible for reuse. This process is known as "reuptake." In both cases, the neuron will also work to manufacture more of that neurotransmitter for future use, storing both the reabsorbed and newly manufactured neurotransmitter molecules in special sacs within the nerve cell, until needed. Figure 6.4 is a neurotransmitter diagram.

Upregulation and downregulation. The individual neurons of the CNS are not passive participants in the process of information transfer. Rather, each individual neuron is constantly adapting its sensitivity by either increasing or decreasing the number of neurotransmitter receptor sites on the cell wall. If a neuron is subjected to low levels of a given neurotransmitter, that nerve cell will respond by increasing (*upregulating*) the number of possible receptor sites in the cell wall to give the neurotransmitter molecules a greater number of potential receptor sites. An anology might be using a directional microphone to enhance faint sounds.

But if a neuron is exposed to a large number of neurotransmitter molecules, it will decrease the total number of possible receptor sites by absorbing/inactivating some of the receptor sites in the cell wall. This is *downregulation*, a process by which a neuron decreases the total number of receptor sites where the neurotransmitter (or drug) molecule can bind to that neuron. Again, an analogy would be turning down the volume of a sound amplification system so that it becomes less sensitive to distant sound sources.

Tolerance and cross-tolerance. The concept of drug "tolerance" was introduced in the last chapter. In brief, tolerance is a reflection of the body's ongoing struggle to maintain normal function. Because a drug is a foreign substance, the body will attempt to continue its normal function in spite of the presence of the chemical. Part of the process of adaptation in the CNS is the upregulation/downregulation of receptor sites as the neurons attempt to maintain a normal level of firing.

As the body adapts to the effects of the chemical, the individual will find that he or she no longer achieves the same effect from the original dose and must use larger and larger doses to maintain the original effect. When a chemical is used as a neuropharmaceutical—such as a drug that is intentionally introduced into the body by a physician to alter the function of the CNS in a desired manner—tolerance is often referred to as the process of *neuroadaptation*. If the drug being used is a recreational substance, the same process is usually called *tolerance*. However, neuroadaptation and tolerance are essentially the same biological adaptation. The only difference is that one involves a pharmaceutical and the other involves a recreational chemical.

The concepts of a drug agonist and antagonist. To understand how the drugs of abuse work, it is necessary to introduce the twin concepts of a drug *agonist* and the *antagonist*. These may be difficult concepts for students of drug abuse to understand. Essentially, a drug agonist mimics the effect(s) of a chemical that is naturally found in the body (Shannon, Wilson, & Stang, 1995). The agonist either tricks the body into reacting as if the endogeneous chemical were present,

or, it enhances the effect(s) of the naturally occurring chemical. For example, as we will discuss in the chapter on the abuse of opiates, there are morphine-like chemicals found in the human brain that help to control the level of pain that the individual is experiencing. Heroin, morphine, and the other narcotic analgesics mimic the actions of these chemicals, and for this reason might be classified as agonists of the naturally occurring painkilling chemicals.

The antagonist essentially blocks the effects of a chemical already working within the body. In a sense, aspirin might be classified as a prostaglandin antagonist because aspirin blocks the normal actions of the prostaglandins. Antagonists may also block the effects of certain chemicals introduced into the body for one reason or another. For example, the drug Narcan blocks the receptor sites in the CNS that opiates normally bind to in order to have their effect. Narcan thus is an antagonist for opiates and is of value in reversing the effects of an opiate overdose.

Because the drugs of abuse either simulate the effects of actual neurotransmitters or alter the action of existing neurotransmitters, they either enhance or retard the frequency with which the neurons of the brain "fire" (Ciancio & Bourgault, 1989). The constant use of any of the drugs of abuse force the neurons to go through the process of neuroadaptation, as they struggle to maintain normal function in spite of the artificial stimulation or inhibition caused by the drugs of abuse. In other words, depending on whether the drugs of abuse cause a surplus or a deficit of neurotransmitter molecules, the neurons in many regions of the brain will upregulate or downregulate the number of receptor sites in an attempt to maintain normal function. This will cause the individual's responsiveness to that drug to be different over time, a process that is part of the process of tolerance.

When the body begins to adapt to the presence of one chemical, it will often also become tolerant to the effects of other drugs that use the same mechanism of action. This is the process of *cross tolerance*. For example, a chronic alcohol user will often require higher doses of CNS depressants than a nondrinker in order to achieve a given level of sedation. Physicians have often noticed this effect in the surgical theater: Chronic alcohol users will require larger doses of anesthetics to achieve a given level of unconsciousness than nondrinkers. Anesthetics and alcohol are both classified as CNS depressants.

The individual's tolerance to the effects of alcohol will, through the development of *cross tolerance*, cause him or her to require a larger dose of many anesthetics in order to allow the surgery to proceed.

The Blood-Brain Barrier

The blood-brain barrier (BBB) is a unique structure in the human body. Its role is to function as a "gateway" to the brain. In this role, the BBB will admit only certain molecules needed by the brain. For example, oxygen and glucose, both essential to life, will pass easily through the BBB (Angier, 1990). But the BBB exists to try to protect the brain from toxins, or infectious organisms. To this end, endothelial cells that form the lining of the BBB have established tight seals, with overlapping cells.

Initially, students of neuroanatomy may be confused by the term *blood-brain barrier*, for when we usually speak of a barrier, we speak of a single structure. But the BBB actually is the result of a unique feature of the cells that form the capillaries through which cerebral blood flows. Unlike capillary walls throughout the rest of the body, those of the cerebral circulatory system are securely joined together. Each endothelial cell is tightly joined to its neighbors, forming a tight tube-like structure that protects the brain from direct contact with the general circulation. Thus, many chemicals in the general circulation are blocked from entering the CNS. However, the individual cells of the brain require nutritional support, and some of the very substances needed by the brain are those blocked by the endothelial cell boundary. Thus, water-soluble substances like glucose or iron, needed by the neurons of the brain for proper function, are blocked by the lining of the endothelial cells.

To overcome this problem specialized "transport systems," have evolved in the endothelial cells in the cerebral circulatory system. These transport systems selectively allow needed nutrients to pass through the

BBB to reach the brain (Angier, 1990). Each of these transport systems will selectively allow one specific type of water-soluble molecule, such as a glucose, to pass through the lining of the endothelial cell to reach the brain.

But lipids also pass through the lining of the endothelial cells and are able to reach the central nervous system beyond. Lipids are essentially molecules of fat. Lipids are essential elements of cell walls, which are made up of lipids, carbohydrates, and protein molecules, arranged in a specific order. As the lipid molecule reaches the endothelial cell wall, it gradually merges with the molecules of the cell wall and passes through into the interior of the endothelial cell. Later, it will also pass through the lining of the far side of the endothelial cell to reach the neurons beyond the lining of the BBB.

Summary

In this chapter, we have examined some of the basic components of pharmacology. It is not necessary for students in the field of substance abuse to have the same depth of knowledge possessed by pharmacists to begin to understand how the recreational chemicals achieve their effects. However, it is important for the reader to understand at least some of the basic concepts of pharmacology to understand the ways that the drugs of abuse achieve their primary and secondary effects. Basic information regarding drug forms, methods of drug administration, and biotransformation/elimination were discussed in this chapter.

Other concepts discussed include those of a drug's bioavailability, the therapeutic half-life of a chemical, the effective dose and lethal dose ratios, the therapeutic dose ratio, and how drugs need receptor sites in order to work. The student should have at least a basic understanding of these concepts before starting to review the different drugs of abuse covered in the next chapters.

CHAPTER SEVEN

Alcohol

Humans' Oldest Recreational Chemical

Introduction

Klatsky (2002) suggested that fermentation occurs naturally and that early humans discovered, but did not invent, alcohol-containing beverages such as wine and beer. Most certainly, this discovery occurred well before the development of writing, and scientists believe that man's use of alcohol dates back at least 10,000 to 15,000 years (Potter, 1997). Prehistoric humans probably learned about the intoxicating effects of fermented fruit by watching animals eat such fruit from the forest floor and then act strangely. Curiosity may have compelled one or two brave souls to try some of the fermented fruits that the animals seemed to enjoy, introducing prehistoric humans to the intoxicating effects of alcohol (R. Siegel, 1986). Having discovered alcohol's intoxicating action and desiring to repeat the use of fermented fruits, prehistoric humans started to experiment and eventually discovered how to produce alcohol-containing beverages at will.

It is not unrealistic to say that "alcohol, and the privilege of drinking have always been important to human beings" (Brown, 1995, p. 4). Indeed, it has been suggested that humans have an innate drive to alter their awareness through the use of chemical compounds, and one of the reasons that early hominids may have climbed out of the trees of Africa was to gain better access to mushrooms with a hallucinogenic potential that grew in the dung of savanna-dwelling grazing animals (Walton, 2002). Although this theory remains controversial, (a) virtually every known culture discovered or developed a form of alcohol production and (b) every substance that could be fermented has been made into a beverage at one time or another (Klatsky, 2002; Levin, 2002). Almost every culture discovered by anthropologists has advocated the use of certain compounds to

alter the individual's perception of reality (Glennon, 2004; Walton, 2002). In this context, alcohol is the prototype intoxicant.

Some anthropologists now believe that early civilization came about in response to the need for a stable home base from which to ferment a form of beer known as *mead* (Stone, 1991). Most certainly, the brewing and consumption of beer was a matter of considerable importance to the inhabitants of Sumer,[1] for many of the clay tablets that have been found there are devoted to the process of brewing beer (Cahill, 1998). If this theory is correct, it would seem that human civilization owes much to alcohol, which is also known as ethanol, or *ethyl alcohol*.[2]

A Brief History of Alcohol

The use of fermented beverages dates back before the invention of writing. Anthropologists believe that the process of making *mead*, a form of beer made from fermented honey, was discovered during the late paleolithic era, or what is commonly called the latter part of the stone age. Historical evidence suggests that mead was in common use around the year 8000 B.C.E.[3] (Ray & Ksir, 1993). This thick liquid was quite nutritious and provided both vitamins and amino acids to the drinker's diet. By comparison, modern beer is very thin and appears almost anemic. Both beer and

---

[1]See Glossary.

[2]Technically, at least 45 other forms of alcohol exist, but these are not normally used for human consumption and will not be discussed further in this text.

[3]Which stands for *before common era*. Remember that 8000 B.C.E. was actually 10,000 years ago.

wine are mentioned in Homer's epic stories the *Iliad* and the *Odyssey*, legends that date back thousands of years. Given the casual way these substances are mentioned in the epics, it is clear that their use was commonplace for an unknown period before the stories were developed.

Scientists have discovered that ethyl alcohol is an extraordinary source of energy. The human body is able to obtain almost as much energy from alcohol as it can from fat, and far more energy gram for gram than it can obtain from carbohydrates or proteins (Lieber, 1998). Although ancient people did not understand these facts, they did recognize that alcohol-containing beverages such as wine and beer were an essential part of the individual's diet, a belief that persisted until well into modern times.[4]

The earliest written record of wine making was found in an Egyptian tomb that dates back to around 3000 B.C.E. ("A Very Venerable Vintage," 1996), although scientists have uncovered evidence suggesting that ancient Sumerians might have used wine made from fermented grapes around 5400 B.C.E. ("A Very Venerable Vintage," 1996). The earliest written records of how beer is made date back to approximately 1800 B.C.E. (Stone, 1991). These findings suggest that alcohol played an important role in the daily life of early people, since only important information was recorded in early writing.

Ethyl alcohol, especially in the form of wine, was central to daily life in both ancient Greece and Rome[5] (Walton, 2002). Indeed, ancient Greek prayers for warriors suggested that they would enjoy continual intoxication in the afterlife, and in pre-Christian Rome intoxication was seen as a religious experience (Walton, 2002). When the Christian church began to play a major role in the Roman empire in the fourth century C.E., it began to stamp out the use of large amounts of alcohol for religious celebrations as reflecting pagan religions and began to force its own morality onto the

inhabitants of the Empire[6] (Walton, 2002). The Puritan ethic that evolved in England in the 14th and 15th centuries placed further restrictions on drinking, and by the start of the 19th century public intoxication was seen not as a sign of religious ecstasy as it had been in the pre-Christian Roman empire, but as a public disgrace.

How Alcohol Is Produced

As we saw in the last section, humans discovered early that if you crush certain forms of fruit and allow it to stand for a period of time in a container, alcohol will sometimes appear. We now know that unseen microorganisms called *yeast* settle on the crushed fruit, find that it is a suitable food source, and begin to digest the sugars in the fruit through a chemical process called *fermentation*. The yeast breaks down the carbon, hydrogen, and oxygen atoms it finds in the sugar for food and in the process produces molecules of ethyl alcohol and carbon dioxide as waste. Waste products are often toxic to the organism that produces them, and so it is with alcohol. When the concentration of alcohol in a container reaches about 15%, it becomes toxic to the yeast, and fermentation stops. Thus, the highest alcohol concentration that one might achieve by natural fermentation is about 15%.

Several thousand years elapsed before humans learned to obtain alcohol concentrations above this 15% limit. Although Plato had noted that a "strange water" would form when one boiled wine (Walton, 2002), it was not until around the year 800 C.E. that an unknown person thought to collect this fluid and explore its uses. This is the process of *distillation*, which historical evidence suggests was developed in the Middle East, and which had reached Europe by around 1100 C.E. (Walton, 2002). Because ethyl alcohol boils at a much lower temperature than water, when wine is boiled some of the alcohol content boils off as a vapor, or steam. This steam contains more ethyl alcohol than water vapor. If it is collected and allowed to cool down, the resulting liquid will have a higher concentration of alcohol and a lower concentration of water than did the original mixture. Over

---

[4]When the Puritans set sail for the new world, for example, they carried with them 14 tons of water and 42 tons of beer (Freeborn, 1996). The fact that they ran out of beer was one reason they decided to settle where they did (McAnalley, 1996).

[5]This is perhaps best reflected in the Roman proverb "Bathing, wine, and Venus exhaust the body, but are what life is about."

[6]Just 300 years later, around A.D. 700, the Qur'an was written, with an injunction against the use of alcohol by adherents of the Islamic faith, upon the threat of thrashing (Walton, 2002).

time, people discovered that the cooling process could take place in a metal coil, allowing the liquid to drip from the end of the coil into a container of some kind. This device is the famous "still" of lore and legend.

Around the year 1000 c.e. Italian wine growers had started using the distillation process to produce different beverages by mixing the obtained "spirits" that resulted from distillation with various herbs and spices. This produced various combinations of flavors for the resulting beverage, and physicians of the era were quick to draw on these new alcohol-containing fluids as potent medicines. The flavorful beverages also became popular for recreational consumption. Unfortunately, as a result of distillation, many of the vitamins and minerals in the original wine and beer are lost. It is for this reason that many dietitians refer to alcohol as a source of "empty" calories. Over time, the chronic ingestion of alcohol-containing beverages can contribute to a state of vitamin depletion called *avitaminosis*, which will be discussed in the next chapter.

Alcohol Today

Over the last nine hundred years since the development of the distillation process, assorted forms of fermented wines using various ingredients, different forms of beer, and distilled spirits combined with diverse flavorings have emerged. The widespread use of alcohol has resulted in multiple attempts to control or eliminate its use over the years, but these programs have had little success. Given the widespread, ongoing debate over the proper role of alcohol in society, it is surprising to learn there is no definition of what constitutes a "standard" drink or the alcohol concentrations that might be found in different alcoholic beverages (Dufour, 1999).

At this time in the United States most beer has an alcohol content of between 3.5% and 5% (Dufour, 1999; Herman, 1993). However, some brands of "light" beer might have less than 3% alcohol content, and "speciality" beers or malt liquors might contain up to 9% alcohol (Dufour, 1999). In the United States, wine continues to be made by allowing fermentation to take place in vats containing various grapes or other fruits. Occasionally, especially in other countries, the fermentation involves products other than grapes, such as the famous "rice wine" from Japan called *sake*. In the United States, wine usually has an alcohol content of

8% to 17% (Herman, 1993), although what are classified as "light" wines might be about 7% alcohol by content, and wine "coolers" contain 5% to 7% alcohol as a general rule (Duvour, 1999).

In addition to wine, there are the "fortified" wines. These are produced by a process in which distilled wine is mixed with fermented wine to raise the total alcohol content to 20% to 24% (Dufour, 1999). Examples of fortified wines include various brands of sherry and port (Herman, 1993). Finally, there are the "hard liquors," the distilled spirits, whose alcohol content generally contains 40% to 50% alcohol by volume (Dufour, 1999). However, there are exceptions to this rule, and some beverages contain 80% or higher alcohol concentrations, such as the famous "Everclear" distilled in the southern United States.

Scope of the Problem of Alcohol Use

Beverages that contain alcohol are moderately popular drinks. In the year 2001, 101 million adults (49% of the adult population) in the United States consumed alcohol at least once (Naimi et al., 2003). For much of the last quarter of the 20th century there was a gradual decline in the per capita amount of alcohol consumed until 1996. Since then, the annual per capita consumption of alcohol in the United States has gradually increased each year (Naimi et al., 2003). Currently, the average adult in the United States consumes 8.29 liters (or 2.189 gallons)[7] of pure alcohol a year, compared to 12.34 liters per year for adults in Greenland, 9.44 liters per year for the average adult in Finland, and 16.01 liters per year for the average adult in the Republic of Ireland (Schmid et al., 2003).

Note that these figures are *averages* and there is a significant inter-individual variation in the amount of alcohol consumed. For example, by some estimates just 10% of those who drink alcohol in the United States consume 60% of all the alcohol ingested, and the top 30% of drinkers consume 90% of all of the alcohol ingested (Kilbourne, 2002). Beer is the most common form of alcohol-containing beverage utilized in the United States (Naimi et al., 2003). Unfortunately, with an increase in the individual's frequency of alcohol

---

[7]See Glossary.

use and the amount of alcohol ingested, the person becomes more likely to develop some of the complications induced by excessive alcohol use. Some of these complications might be encountered after consuming a surprisingly small amount of alcohol, a matter of some concern as "binge" drinking seems to be on the increase (Motluk, 2004). The impact of excess alcohol use will be discussed more in the next chapter. In this chapter, we will focus on the casual, nonabusive, drinker.

Pharmacology of Alcohol

Ethyl alcohol, or simply alcohol, may be introduced into the body intravenously or inhaled as a vapor,[8] but the most common means is by oral ingestion as a liquid. The alcohol molecule is quite small and is soluble in both water and lipids, although it shows a preference for water (Jones, 1996). When consumed in sufficient quanities, alcohol molecules are rapidly distributed to all blood-rich tissues throughout the body including the brain. Indeed, because alcohol is so easily dissolved in lipids, high concentrations of alcohol in the brain are very rapidly achieved. Although alcohol does diffuse into adipose[9] and muscle tissues, it does not do so as easily as it does in water-rich tissues such as the brain. Thus, very obese or very muscular people achieve a slightly lower blood alcohol level than would a leaner person after ingesting a given dose of alcohol.

The main route of alcohol absorption is through the small intestine (Baselt, 1996). But when alcohol is ingested in the absence of food, about 10% (Kaplan, Sadock, & Grebb, 1994) to 25% (Baselt, 1996; Levin, 2002) of the alcohol is immediately absorbed through the stomach lining, with the first molecules of alcohol appearing in the drinker's blood in as little as one minute (Rose, 1988). Although the liver is the primary organ where alcohol is biotransformed in the human body, people produce an enzyme in the gastrointestinal tract known as *gastric alcohol dehydrogenase*, which

begins the process of alcohol biotransformation in the stomach (Frezza et al., 1990). The levels of gastric alcohol dehydrogenase are highest in rare social drinkers and are significantly lower in regular/chronic drinkers or people who ingested an aspirin tablet before drinking (Roine, Gentry, Hernandez-Munoz, Baraona, & Lieber, 1990).

Alcohol consumed with food is absorbed more slowly than that consumed on an empty stomach. When one consumes alcohol without food, he or she will experience peak blood levels in 30 to 120 minutes following a single drink (Baselt, 1996). When consumed with food, alcohol is absorbed more slowly, and peak blood levels will not be reached until 1–6 hours after a single drink was ingested (Baselt, 1996). However, all of the alcohol consumed will eventually be absorbed into the drinker's circulation. Researchers have long known that men tend to have lower blood alcohol levels than do women after consuming a given amount of alcohol for several reasons. First, males tend to produce more gastric alcohol dehydrogenase than do women (Frezza et al., 1990). Also, women tend to have lower body weights and lower muscle-to-body-mass ratios and have 10% less water volume in their bodies than do men (Zealberg & Brady, 1999).

In the early 20th century, alcohol's effects were thought to be caused by its ability to disrupt the structure and the function of the lipids in the cell wall of neurons (Tabakoff & Hoffman, 1992). This theory was known as the *membrane fluidization theory*, or the *membrane hypothesis*. This theory suggested that since alcohol was known to disrupt the structure of lipids, this might make it more difficult for neurons in the brain to maintain normal function. However, as scientists have come to better understand the molecular functioning of neurons, this theory has gradually fallen into disfavor.

Scientists now believe that the alcohol molecule "binds" to specific protein molecules located in the walls of neurons that act as receptor sites for neurotransmitter molecules, altering their sensitivity and function (Tabakoff & Hoffman, 2004). However, alcohol's effects are not limited to one neurotransmitter system or to neurons located in just one region of the brain. One of the neurotransmitter receptor sites in the brain that is affected by alcohol is utilized by the amino acid neurotransmitter *N-methyl-D-aspartate* (NMDA). NMDA functions as an excitatory amino acid within the brain

---

[8]One company actually has introduced this as a way for the individual to consume alcohol without the carbohydrates found in the typical alcohol-containing beverage. Fortunately, this practice remains virtually unknown in the United States.

[9]See Glossary.

(Hobbs, Rall, & Verdoorn, 1995;Valenzuela & Harris, 1997). Alcohol blocks the influx of calcium atoms through the ion channels normally activated when NMDA binds at those sites, slowing down the rate at which that neuron can "fire." It is for this reason that ethyl alcohol might be said to be an NMDA antagonist (Tsai, Gastfriend, & Coyle, 1995).

At the same time, alcohol enhances the influx of chloride atoms through one of the subtypes of the gamma-amino-butyric acid (GABA) receptor site, which is known as the $GABA_{a1}$ receptor sub-type (Tabakoff & Hoffman, 2004). This subform of the GABA receptor is found only in certain regions of the brain, which seems to explain why alcohol does not affect all neurons in the brain equally. GABA is the main inhibitory neurotransmitter in the brain, and approximately 20% of all neurotransmitter receptors in the brain utilize GABA (Mosier, 1999). Neurons that utilize GABA are found in the cortex,[10] the cerebellum, the hippocampus, the superior and inferior colliculi regions of the brain, the amygdala, and the nucleus accumbens. By blocking the effects of the excitatory amino acid NMDA while facilitating the inhibitory neurotransmitter GABA in these various regions of the brain, alcohol is able to depress the action of the central nervous system.

Scientists disagree on how alcohol is able to cause the drinker to feel a sense of euphoria. One theory suggests that the euphoria some drinkers experience after drinking alcohol is brought on by its ability to directly activate the endorphin reward system within the brain. Evidence *does* suggest that at moderate to high blood levels alcohol promotes the binding of opiate agonists[11] at the *Mu* opioid receptor site[12] (Tabakoff & Hoffman, 2004). However, other researchers believe that alcohol's euphoric effects are brought on by its ability to stimulate the release of the neurotransmitter dopamine. This theory is supported by evidence suggesting that alcohol ingestion forces the neurons to empty their stores of dopamine back into the synaptic junction (Heinz et al., 1998). When dopamine is released in the

[10]See Glossary.

[11]See Glossary.

[12]The various types of opiate receptor sites are discussed in Chapter 14.

nucleus accumbens region of the brain, the user experiences a sense of pleasure, or euphoria.

A third possibility is that alcohol's ability to potentiate the effects of the neurotransmitter *serotonin* at the 5-HT3 receptor site plays a role in the euphoric and intoxicating effects of alcohol (Hobbs, Rall, & Verdoorn, 1995; Tabakoff & Hoffman, 2004). This receptor site is located on certain neurons that inhibit behavioral impulses, and it is this action that seems to account at least in part for alcohol's disinhibitory effects. As is obvious from the above material, alcohol's effects on the function of the neurons of the central nervous system (CNS) is widespread and complex. It is thought that alcohol affects both the function of the primary neurotransmitters and various "secondary" messengers within the neurons affected by ethyl alcohol (Tabakoff & Hoffman, 2004).

The Biotransformation of Alcohol

In spite of its popularity as a recreational drink, ethyl alcohol is essentially a toxin, and after it has been ingested the body works to remove it from the circulation before it can cause widespread damage. Depending on the individual's blood alcohol level, between 2% and 10% of the alcohol ingested will be excreted unchanged through the lungs, skin, and urine, with higher percentages of alcohol being excreted unchanged in those individuals with greater blood alcohol levels (Sadock & Sadock, 2003; Schuckit, 1998).

But the liver is the primary site where foreign chemicals such as ethyl alcohol are broken down and removed from the blood (Brennan, Betzelos, Reed, & Falk, 1995). Alcohol biotransformation is accomplished in two steps. First, the liver produces an enzyme known as *alcohol dehydrogenase* (or ADH), which breaks the alcohol down into acetaldehyde. Evolution is thought to have equipped our ancestors with ADH to give them the ability to biotransform fermented fruits that might be ingested or the small amount of alcohol produced endogenously (Jones, 1996). In high concentrations, acetaldehyde is quite toxic to the body, although there is evidence to suggest that small amounts might function as a stimulant (Schuckit, 1998). Fortunately, many different parts of the body produce a second enzyme, *aldehyde dehydrogenase*, which breaks acetaldehyde down into acetic acid.[13] Ultimately, alcohol is bio-transformed into carbon dioxide, water, and fatty acids (carbohydrates).

The speed of alcohol biotransformation. There is some individual variation in the speed at which alcohol is biotransformed in the body (Garriott, 1996). However, a rule of thumb is that the liver can biotransform about one mixed drink of 80-proof alcohol, 4 ounces of wine, or one 12-ounce can of beer, every 60 to 90 minutes (Fleming, Mihic, & Harris, 2002; Renner, 2004). As was discussed in the last chapter, alcohol is biotransformed through a zero order biotransformation process, and the rate at which alcohol is biotransformd by the liver is relatively inde-pendent of the concentration of alcohol in the blood (Levin, 2002). Thus, if the person consumes *more* than one standard drink per hour, the alcohol concentration in the blood would increase, possibly to the point that the drinker would become intoxicated.

The alcohol-flush reaction. After drinking even a small amount of alcohol, 3% to 29% of people of European descent, and 47% to 85% of people of Asian descent experience what is known as the *alcohol-flush reaction* (Collins & McNair, 2002). This reaction is caused by a genetic mutation that is found predomi-nantly in people of Asian descent. Because of this genetic mutation, the liver is unable to manufacture sufficient aldehyde dehydrogenase for it to rapidly biotransform the acetaldehyde that is manufactured in the first stage of alcohol biotransformation.

People with this syndrome will experience symp-toms such as facial flushing, heart palpitations, dizzi-ness, and nausea as the blood levels of acetaldehyde climb to 20 times the level seen in normal individuals who have consumed the same amount of alcohol. Acetaldehyde is a toxin and the person with a signifi-cant amount of this chemical in his or her blood will become quite ill. This phenomenon is thought to be one reason that heavy drinking is so rare in persons of Asian descent.

---

[13]The medication Antabuse (disulfiram) works by blocking the enzyme aldehyde dehydrogenase. This allows acetaldehyde to build up in the individual's blood, causing the individual to become ill from the toxic effects of the acetaldehyde.

The Blood Alcohol Level

Because it is not yet possible to measure the alcohol level in the brain of a living person, physicians have to settle for a measurement of the amount of alcohol in a person's body known as the *blood alcohol level* (BAL).[14] The BAL is essentially a measure of the level of alcohol actually in a given person's bloodstream. It is reported in terms of milligrams of alcohol per 100 milliliters of blood (or mg/mL). A BAL of 0.10 is thus one-tenth of a mil-ligram of alcohol per 100 milliliters of blood.

The BAL provides a rough approximation of the individual's subjective level of intoxication. For reasons that are still not clear, the individual's subjective level of intoxication is highest when the BAL is still rising, a phenomenon known as the *Mellanby effect* (Drum-mer & Odell, 2001; Lehman, Pilich, & Andrews, 1994). Further, as will be discussed further in the next chapter, individuals who drink on a chronic basis become somewhat tolerant to the intoxicating effects of alcohol. For these reasons a person who is tolerant to the effects of alcohol might have a rather high BAL while appearing relatively normal.

The BAL that will be achieved by two people who consume a similar amount of alcohol will vary as a result of a number of different factors such as the individual's body size (or volume). To illustrate this confusing characteristic of alcohol, consider the hypothetical example of a person who weighs 100 pounds, who consumed two regular drinks in one hour's time. Blood tests would reveal that this individual had a BAL of 0.09 mg/mL (slightly above legal intoxication in most states) (Maguire, 1990). But an individual who weighs 200 pounds would, after consuming the same amount of alcohol, have a measured BAL of only 0.04 mg/mL. Each person would have consumed the same amount of alcohol, but it would be more concentrated in the smaller individual, resulting in a higher BAL.

A variety of other factors influence the speed with which alcohol enters the blood and the individual's blood alcohol level. However, Figure 7.1 provides a rough estimate of the blood alcohol levels that might be achieved through the consumption of different

---

[14]Occasionally, the term *blood alcohol concentration (BAC)* will be used in place of the blood alcohol level.

Weight (pounds)

	100	120	140	160	180	200	220
2	0.07	0.06	0.05	0.05*	0.04	0.04*	0.03
3	0.10	0.09	0.07	0.07*	0.06	0.05	0.05*
4	0.14	0.11	0.10	0.08	0.08*	0.07	0.06
5	0.18	0.14	0.12	0.11	0.10	0.08	0.08*
6	0.20	0.18	0.14	0.12	0.12*	0.10	0.09
7	0.25	0.20	0.18	0.16	0.12	0.12*	0.11
8	0.30	0.25	0.20	0.18	0.16	0.14	0.12

Number of drinks in one hour

← Level of legal intoxication with measured blood alcohol level of 0.08 mg/dl. Individuals at or below this line are legally too intoxicated to drive.

*Rounded off.

FIGURE 7.1   Approximate blood alchohol levels.

Note: This figure is intended only to illustrate the cumulative effects of alcohol ingestion. It is not intended to serve as a guide for alcohol use and should not be used for such a purpose.

amounts of alcohol. This chart is based on the assumption that one "drink" is either one can of standard beer or one regular mixed drink. It should be noted that although the BAL provides an estimate of the individual's current level of intoxication, it is of little value in screening individuals for alcohol abuse problems (Chung et al., 2000).

Subjective Effects of Alcohol on the Individual: At Normal Doses in the Average Drinker

Both as a toxin and as a psychoactive agent, alcohol is quite weak. To show the relative potency of alcohol compared to morphine, to achieve the same effects of a 10 mg intravenous dose of morphine, the individual must ingest 15,000–20,000 mg of alcohol (Jones, 1996).[15] However, when it is consumed in sufficient quantities, alcohol does have an effect on the user, and it is for its psychoactive effects that most people consume alcohol.

At low to moderate dosage levels, people's *expectations* play a role in both how they interpret the effects of alcohol and their drinking behavior (Brown, 1990; Smith, Goldman, Greenbaum, & Christiansen, 1995). These expectations about alcohol's effects begin to form early in life, perhaps as early as 3 years of age, and that such expectations solidify between the ages of 3 and 7 (Jones & McMahon, 1998). This is clearly seen in the observation that adolescents who abused alcohol were more likely to anticipate a positive experience when they drank than were their nondrinking counterparts (Brown, Creamer, & Stetson, 1987).

After a person has had one or two drinks, alcohol causes a second effect, known as the *disinhibition effect* on the individual. Researchers now believe that the disinhibition effect is caused when alcohol interferes with the normal function of inhibitory neurons in the cortex. This is the part of the brain most responsible for "higher" functions, such as abstract thinking, speech, and so on. The cortex is also the part of the brain where much of our voluntary behavior is planned. As the alcohol interferes with cortical nerve function, one tends to temporarily "forget" social inhibitions (Elliott, 1992; Julien, 1992). During periods of alcohol-induced

[15]This is the approximate amount of alcohol found in one standard drink.

disinhibition, the individual may engage in some behavior that, under normal conditions, he or she would never carry out. It is this disinhibition effect that may contribute to the relationship between alcohol use and aggressive behavior. For example, 40% to 50% of those who commit homicide (Parker, 1993) and up to two-thirds of those who engage in self-injurious acts (McClosky & Berman, 2003) used alcohol prior to or during the act itself. Individuals with either developmental or acquired brain damage are especially at risk for the disinhibition effects of alcohol (Elliott, 1992). This is not to say, however, that the disinhibition effect is seen *only* in individuals with some form of neurological trauma. Individuals without any known form of brain damage may also experience alcohol-induced disinhibition.

Effects of Alcohol at Intoxicating Doses: For the Average Drinker

For a 160-pound person, 2 drinks in an hour's time would result in a BAL of 0.05 mg/mL. At this level of intoxication, the individual's reaction time and depth perception become impaired (Hartman, 1995). The individual will feel a sense of exhilaration and a loss of inhibitions (Renner, 2004). Four drinks in an hour's time will cause a 160-pound person to have a BAL of 0.10 mg/mL or higher (Maguire, 1990). At about this level of intoxication, the individual's reaction time is approximately 200% longer than it is for the nondrinker (Garriott, 1996), and she or he will have problems coordinating muscle actions (a condition called *ataxia*). The drinker's speech will be slurred, and he or she will stagger rather than walk (Renner, 2004).

If our hypothetical 160-pound drinker were to drink *more* than four drinks in an hour's time, his or her blood alcohol level would be even higher. Research has shown that individuals with a BAL between 0.10 and 0.14 mg/mL are 48 times as likely as the nondrinker to be involved in a fatal car accident (*Alcohol Alert*, 1996). A person with a BAL of 0.15 mg/mL would be above the level of legal intoxication in every state and would definitely be experiencing some alcohol-induced physical problems. Also, because of alcohol's effects on reaction time, individuals with a BAL of 0.15 mg/mL are between 25 times (Hobbs et al., 1995) and 380 times (National Institute on Alcohol Abuse

and Alcoholism, 1996) as likely as a nondrinker to be involved in a fatal car accident. The person who has a BAL of 0.20 mg/mL will experience marked ataxia (Garriott, 1996; Renner, 2004). The person with a BAL of 0.25 mg/mL would stagger around and have difficulty making sense out of sensory data (Garriott, 1996; Kaminski, 1992). The person with a BAL of 0.30 mg/mL would be stuporous and confused (Renner, 2004). With a BAL of 0.35 mg/mL, the stage of surgical anesthesia is achieved (Matuschka, 1985). At higher concentrations, alcohol's effects are analogous to those seen with the anesthetic ether (Maguire, 1990).

Unfortunately, the amount of alcohol in the blood necessary to bring about a state of unconsciousness is only a little less than the level necessary for a fatal overdose. This is because alcohol has a therapeutic index (TI) of between 1:4 and 1:10 (Grinspoon & Bakalar, 1993). In other words, the minimal effective dose of alcohol (i.e., the dose at which the user becomes intoxicated) is a significant fraction of the lethal dose. Thus, when a person drinks to the point of losing consciousness she or he is dangerously close to the point of overdosing on alcohol. Because of alcohol's low TI, it is very easy to *die* from an alcohol overdose, or acute alcohol poisoning, something that happens 200 to 400 times a year in the United States (Garrett, 2000). Even experienced drinkers have been known to die from an overdose of alcohol. About 1% of drinkers who achieve a BAL of 0.35 mg/mL will die without medical treatment (Ray & Ksir, 1993).[16] At or above a BAL of 0.35 mg/mL, alcohol is thought to interfere with the activity of the nerves that control respiration (Lehman et al., 1994). Note that since a BAL of 0.35 mg/mL or above may result in death, *all cases of known or suspected alcohol overdose should be immediately treated by a physician*. A BAL of 0.40 mg/mL will cause the drinker to fall into a coma and has about a 50% death rate without medical intervention (Bohn, 1993). The LD50 is thus around 0.40 mg/mL.

Segal and Sisson (1985) reported that the approximate lethal BAL in human beings was 0.5 mg/mL, while Renner (2004) suggested that it is 0.60 mg/mL. In theory, the LD100 is reached when the drinker has a BAL between 0.5 and 0.8 mg/mL for the nontolerant drinker. However, there are cases on record in which an alcohol-tolerant person was still conscious and able to

---

[16]Thus, the LD01 dosage level for alcohol is about 0.35 mg/mL.

TABLE 7.1   Effects of Alcohol on the Infrequent Drinker

Blood alcohol level (BAL)	Behavioral and physical effects
0.02	Feeling of warmth, relaxation
0.02–0.09	Skin becomes flushed. Drinker is more talkative, feels euphoria. At this level, psychomotor skills are slightly to moderately impaired, and ataxia develops. Loss of inhibitions, increased reaction time, and visual field disturbances
0.10–0.19	Slurred speech, severe ataxia, mood instability, drowsiness, nausea, staggering gait, confusion
0.20–0.29	Lethargy, combativeness, stupor, incoherent speech, vomiting
0.30–0.39	Coma, respiratory depression
Above 0.40	Death

Sources: Based on material provided by Baselt (1996); Lehman, Pilich, & Andrews (1994), pp. 305–309; and Morrison, Rogers, & Thomas (1995), pp. 371–389.

talk with a BAL as high as 0.78 mg/mL (Bohn, 1993; Schuckit, 2000). The effects of alcohol on the rare drinker are summarized in Table 7.1.

At high doses, the stomach will begin to excrete higher levels of mucus than is normal and will also close the pyloric valve between the stomach and the small intestine to try to slow down the absorption of the alcohol that is still in the stomach (Kaplan et al., 1994). These actions contribute to feelings of nausea, which will reduce the drinker's desire to consume more alcohol and might also contribute to the urge to vomit that many drinkers report they experience at the higher levels of intoxication. Vomiting will allow the body to rid itself of the alcohol the drinker has ingested. But alcohol interferes with the normal vomit reflex and might even cause the drinker to attempt to vomit when unconscious, causing the person to run the risk of aspirating some of the material being regurgitated. This can contribute to the condition known as *aspirative pneumonia*,[17] or can cause death by blocking the airway with stomach contents.

[17]See Glossary.

Medical Complications of Alcohol Use in the Average Drinker

The hangover. Although there is evidence that humans have known about the alcohol-induced hangover for thousands of years, the exact mechanism by which alcohol is able to cause the drinker to suffer a hangover is still unknown (Swift & Davidson, 1998). Indeed, researchers are still divided over whether the condition is caused by the alcohol ingested by the drinker, a metabolite of alcohol (such as acetaldehyde), or some of the compounds found in the alcoholic beverage that give it flavor, aroma, and taste (called *congeners*) (Swift & Davidson, 1998). Some researchers believe that the hangover is a symptom of an early alcohol withdrawal syndrome (Ray & Ksir, 1993; Swift & Davidson, 1998). Other researchers suggest that the alcohol-induced hangover is caused by the lower levels of ß-endorphin that result during alcohol withdrawal (Mosier, 1999).

What *is* known about the alcohol-induced hangover is that 75% of individuals who drink to excess will experience a hangover at some point in their lives, although there is evidence that some drinkers are more prone to experience this alcohol-use aftereffect than are others (Swift & Davidson, 1998). Some of the physical manifestations of the alcohol-hangover include fatigue, malaise, sensitivity to light, thirst, tremor and nausea, dizziness, depression, and anxiety (Swift & Davidson, 1998). Although the hangover may, at least in severe cases, make the victim wish for death (O'Donnell, 1986), there usually is little physical risk for the individual, and in general the symptoms resolve in 8 to 24 hours (Swift & Davidson, 1998). Conservative treatment such as antacids, bed rest, solid foods, fruit juice, and over-the-counter analgesics are usually all that is required to treat an alcohol-induced hangover (Kaminski, 1992; Swift & Davidson, 1998).

The effects of alcohol on sleep. Alcohol, like the other CNS depressants, may induce a form of sleep, but it does not allow for a normal dream cycle. Alcohol-induced sleep disruption is strongest in the chronic drinker, but alcohol can disrupt the sleep of even the rare social drinker. The impact of chronic alcohol use on the normal sleep cycle will be discussed in the next chapter.

Even moderate amounts of alcohol consumed within 2 hours of going to sleep can contribute to episodes of sleep apnea.[18] The use of alcohol prior to going to sleep can weaken pharyngeal muscle tone, increasing the chances that the sleeper will experience increased snoring and sleep breathing problems (Qureshi & Lee-Chiong, 2004). Thus, people with a respiratory disorder, especially sleep apnea, should discuss their use of alcohol with their physician to avoid alcohol-related sleep breathing problems.

Alcohol use and cerebrovascular accidents. There is mixed evidence that alcohol use increases the individual's risk of a cerebrovascular accident (CVA, or, stroke). J. W. Smith (1997) concluded that even light alcohol use, defined as the individual's ingesting 1–14 ounces of pure alcohol per month, more than doubled the risk for hemorrhagic stroke. Note that the lower limit of this range of alcohol use, one ounce of pure alcohol per month, is less than the amount of alcohol found in just a single can of beer. Yet Jackson, Sesso, Buring, and Gaziano (2003) concluded that the moderate use of alcohol (defined as no more than 1 standard drink in 24 hours) reduced the individual's risk of both ischemic and hemorrhagic strokes in a sample of male physicians who had already suffered one CVA. The reason for these apparently contradictory findings is not known at this time.

Drug interactions involving alcohol.[19] There has been little research into the effects of moderate alcohol use (defined as 1–2 standard drinks per day) on the action of pharmaceutical agents (Weathermon & Crabb, 1999). It is known that alcohol functions as a CNS depressant, and thus it may potentiate the action of other CNS depressants such as antihistamines, opiates, barbiturates, anesthetic agents, and benzodiazepines and thus should not be used by patients using these agents (Weathermon & Crabb, 1999; Zernig & Battista, 2000). Patients who take nitroglycerin, a medication often used in the treatment of heart conditions, frequently develop significantly reduced blood pressure levels, possibly to the point of dizziness and loss of consciousness, if they drink while using this medication (Zernig & Battista, 2000). Patients

taking the antihypertensive medication propranolol should not drink, as the alcohol will decrease the effectiveness of this antihypertensive medication (Zernig & Battista, 2000). Further, patients taking the anticoagulant medication warfarin should not drink, as moderate to heavy alcohol use can cause the user's body to biotransform the warfarin more quickly than normal (*Alcohol Alert*, 1995a; Graedon & Graedon, 1995).

There is some evidence that the antidepressant amitriptyline might enhance alcohol-induced euphoria (Ciraulo, Creelman, Shader, & O'Sullivan, 1995). The mixture of alcohol and certain antidepressant medications such as amitriptyline, desimipramine, or doxepin might also cause the user to experience problems concentrating, as alcohol will potentiate the sedation caused by these medications, and the interaction between alcohol and the antidepressant might contribute to rapid blood pressure changes (Weathermon & Crabb, 1999). A person who drinks while under the influence of one of the selective serotonin reuptake inhibitors (SSRIs) may experience the *serotonin syndrome* as a result of the alcohol-induced release of serotonin within the brain and the blockade effect of the SSRIs (Brown & Stoudemire, 1998).

Surprisingly, there is some animal research to suggest that individuals who take beta carotene and who drink to excess on a chronic basis might experience a greater degree of liver damage than would the heavy drinker who did not take this vitamin supplement (Graedon & Graedon, 1995). When combined with aspirin, alcohol might contribute to bleeding in the stomach. This is because both alcohol and aspirin are irritants to the stomach lining, and when used together increase the chances of damage to the stomach lining (Sands, Knapp, & Ciraulo, 1993). Although acetaminophen does not irritate the stomach lining, the chronic use of alcohol causes the liver to release enzymes that transform the acetaminophen into a poison, even when the drug is used at recommended dosage levels (Zernig & Battista, 2000).

Patients taking oral medications for diabetes should not drink, as the antidiabetic medication may interfere with the body's ability to biotransform alcohol. This may possibly result in acute alcohol poisoning from even moderate amounts of alcohol for the individual who combines alcohol and oral antidiabetic medications. Further, because the antidiabetic medication prevents

---

[18]See Glossary.

[19]The list of potential alcohol-drug interactions is quite extensive. Patients who are taking either a prescription or over-the-counter medication should not consume alcohol without first checking with a physician or pharmacist to determine if there is a danger for an interaction between the two substances.

the body from being able to biotransform alcohol, the individual will remain intoxicated far longer than he or she would normally. In such a case, the individual might underestimate the time before which it would be safe to drive a motor vehicle.

Patients who are on the antidepressant medications known as monoamine oxidase inhibitors (MAO inhibitors, or MAOIs) should not consume alcohol under any circumstances. The fermentation process produces an amino acid, tyramine, along with the alcohol. Normally, this is not a problem. Indeed, tyramine is found in certain foods and it is a necessary nutrient. But tryamine interacts with the MAO inhibitors, causing dangerously high, and possibly fatal, blood pressure levels (Brown & Stoudemire, 1998). Patients who take MAO inhibitors are provided a list of foods that they should avoid while they are taking their medication, lists that usually include alcohol.

Researchers have found that the calcium channel blocker Verapamil inhibits the process of alcohol biotransformation, increasing the period of time in which alcohol might cause the user to be intoxicated (Brown & Stoudemire, 1998). Although early research studies suggested that the medications Zantac (ranitidine)[20] and Tagamet (cimetidine) interfered with the biotransformation of alcohol, subsequent research failed to support this hypothesis (Jones, 1996).

Patients who are taking the antibiotic medications chloramphenicol, furazolidone, metronidazole, or the antimalarial medication quinacrine should not drink alcohol. The combination of these antibiotics with alcohol may produce a painful reaction very similar to that seen when the patient on disulfiram (to be discussed in a later chapter) would consume alcohol (Meyers, 1992). Individuals taking the antibiotic erythromycin should not consume alcohol, as this medication can contribute to abnormally high blood alcohol levels due to enhanced gastric emptying (Zernig & Battista, 2000). Persons taking the antibiotic doxycycline should not drink, since alcohol can decrease the blood levels of this medication, possibly to the point that it will no longer be effective (Brown & Stoudemire, 1998). People who are taking the antitubercular drug

isoniazid (or, "INH" as it is often called) should also avoid the use of alcohol. The combination of these two chemicals will reduce the effectiveness of the isoniazid and may increase the individual's chances of developing hepatitis.

Although there has been little research into the possible interaction between alcohol and marijuana, as the latter substance is illegal, preliminary evidence does suggest that alcohol's depressant effects might exacerbate the CNS depressant effects of marijuana (Garriott, 1996). Alcohol is a very potent chemical, and it is not possible to list all of the potential interactions between alcohol and the various medications currently in use. Thus, before mixing alcohol with any medication, people should consult a physician or pharmacist in order to avoid potentially dangerous interactions between pharmaceutical agents and alcohol.

Alcohol Use and Accidental Injury or Death

Advertisements in the media proclaim the benefits of recreational alcohol use at parties, social encounters, or occasions to celebrate good news, but they rarely mention alcohol's role in accidental injury. The grim reality is that there is a known relationship between alcohol use and accidental injury. For example, in 2002, 17,970 people were killed on U.S. roads in alcohol-related motor vehicle accidents (41% of the total number of traffic-related deaths that year) ("National Traffic Death Toll," 2003). A BAL between 0.05 and 0.079, which is below the legal limit of 0.08, still increases the individual's risk of being involved in a motor vehicle accident by 546%, and a BAL above 0.08 increases the risk at least 1,500% above that of a nondrinking driver (Movig et al., 2004).

In addition to its role in motor vehicle deaths, alcohol use has been found to be a factor in 51% of all boating fatalities (Smith, Keyl, et al., 2001), and an estimated 70% of the motorcycle drivers who are killed in an accident are thought to have been drinking prior to the accident (Colburn, Meyer, Wrigley, & Bradley, 1993). Alcohol use is a factor in 17% to 53% of all falls, and 40% to 64% of all fatalities associated with fires (Lewis, 1997). Thirty-two percent of the adults who die

---

[20]The most common brand name is given first, with the generic name in parentheses.

in bicycling accidents were found to have alcohol in their systems (Li, Baker, Smialek, & Soderstrom, 2001). Indeed, 52% of those individuals treated at one major trauma center had alcohol in their blood at the time of admission (Cornwell et al., 1998). No matter how you look at it, even casual alcohol use carries with it a significantly increased risk of accidental injury or death. Indeed, the recommendation has been made that any patient involved in an alcohol-related accident, or who suffered an injury while under the influence of alcohol, should be examined to determine whether he or she has an alcohol use disorder (Reynaud, Schwan, Loiseaux-Meunier, Albuisson, & Deteix, 2001) (discussed in next chapter).

Summary

This chapter has briefly explored the history of alcohol, including its early history as humans' first recreational chemical. In this chapter, the process of distillation was discussed, as was the manner in which wine is obtained from fermented fruit. The use of distillation to achieve concentrations of alcohol above 15% was reviewed, and questions surrounding the use of alcohol were discussed. Alcohol's effects on the rare social drinker were reviewed as were some of the more significant interactions between alcohol and pharmaceutical agents. The history of alcohol consumption in the United States and the pattern of alcohol use in the United States were examined.

CHAPTER EIGHT

Chronic Alcohol Abuse and Addiction

Introduction

The focus of the last chapter was on the acute effects of alcohol on the "average" or rare social drinker. Unfortunately, alcohol abuse/addiction is the third leading preventable cause of death in the United States, causing between 85,000 and 175,000 premature deaths each year (Mokdad, Marks, Stroup, & Gerberding, 2004; Schuckit & Tapert, 2004). Alcohol abuse/addiction can also cause or exacerbate a wide range of physical, social, financial, and emotional problems for drinkers and their families. Indeed, given the potential of alcohol for harm, one could argue that if it were to be discovered only today, its use might never be legalized (Miller & Hester, 1995). In this chapter, some of the manifestations and consequences of alcohol addiction will be discussed.

Scope of the Problem

At some point in their lives, fully 90% of all adults in the United States will consume alcohol (Schuckit & Tapert, 2004). Most of those who consume alcohol do so in a responsible manner, but the alcohol-use disorders are still the most common psychiatric disorders encountered by mental health professionals (Gold & Miller, 1997b). Approximately 10% of people who consume alcohol develop an alcohol-use problem (Fleming, Mihic, & Harris, 2001). Alcohol abuse has been shown to impact the individual's social life, interpersonal relationships, and educational or vocational activities; it often causes or contributes to legal problems for the drinker. But not every person who experiences a *single* alcohol-related problem is *dependent* on this chemical. Indeed, 60% of the men and 30% of the women who consume

alcohol will demonstrate at least one transient alcohol-related problem (such as blackouts, which will be discussed later in this chapter) at some point in their lives (American Psychiatric Association, 2000; Sadock & Sadock, 2003).

The physical addiction to alcohol (alcohol dependence, or alcoholism) is the most extreme form of an alcohol-use disorder. Estimates of the scope of alcohol-use problems in the United States range from an estimated 9 million alcohol-dependent people to another 6 million alcohol abusers (Ordorica & Nace, 1998). In this country, alcoholism is predominantly a male disease, with alcohol-dependent males outnumbering alcohol-dependent females by a ratio of about 2:1 (Blume, 1994).

Clinicians who specialize in the area of substance abuse often hear clients deny that they are alcoholic, claiming that they are "only problem drinkers." Unfortunately, there is little evidence to suggest that "problem drinkers" are different from alcohol-dependent individuals (Prescott & Kendler, 1999; Schuckit, Zisook, & Mortola, 1985). At best, research data suggest that the so-called problem drinker differs from the alcohol-dependent individual only in the number and severity of the person's alcohol-related problems. There is little evidence supporting the theory that problem drinkers are significantly different from alcohol-dependent individuals (Schuckit, Zisook, & Mortola, 1985).

Alcohol dependence usually develops after 10 (Meyer, 1994) to 20 years (Alexander & Gwyther, 1995) of heavy drinking, and once established it can have lifelong implications for the individual. For example, once a person *does* become dependent upon alcohol, even if that person should stop drinking for a period of time, the physical addiction can reassert itself "in a matter of days to weeks" if he or she should resume drinking (Meyer, 1994, p. 165). Thus, once people become dependent upon alcohol, it would appear unlikely that they could return to nonabusive drinking.

Is There a "Typical" Alcohol-Dependent Person?

The "binge" drinker. A "binge" is defined as the consumption of five or more cans of beer or regular mixed drinks during a single episode of alcohol consumption by a person who is not a daily drinker (Naimi et al., 2003). The authors used this definition to determine that 14.3% of the adults in the United States had engaged in at least one period of binge drinking in any given 30-day period of the year 2001. Males accounted for the greatest percentage of binge drinking, involved in 81% of the estimated 1.5 *billion* annual episodes of binge drinking that take place in the United States (Naimi et al., 2003). Not surprisingly, heavy drinkers were more likely to engage in binge drinking and were more likely to consume more alcohol during a binge than were light to moderate drinkers.

Alcohol abusers/addicts are frequently "masters of denial" (Knapp, 1996, p. 19), able to offer a thousand and one rationalizations as to why *they* cannot possibly have an alcohol-use problem: They always go to work, never go to the bar to drink, know 10 people who drink as much as if not more than they do, and so on. One of the most common rationalizations offered by the person with an alcohol-use problem is that he or she has nothing in common with the stereotypical "skid row" derelict. In reality, only about 5% of those who are dependent on alcohol fit the image of the skid row alcoholic (Knapp, 1996). The majority of those with alcohol-use problems might best be described as "high functioning" (Knapp, 1996, p. 12) individuals, with jobs, responsibilities, families, and public images to protect. In many cases, individuals' growing dependence on alcohol is hidden from virtually everybody, including themselves. It is only in secret moments of introspection that the alcohol-dependent person wonders why he or she cannot drink "like a normal person."

Alcohol Tolerance, Dependence, and "Craving": Signposts of Alcoholism

Certain symptoms, when present, suggest that the drinker has moved past the point of simple social drinking to the place where there might be an alcohol-use problem or even physical dependence on alcohol and its effects. The first of these signs is known as *tolerance*.

As people repeatedly consume alcohol, their bodies will begin to make certain adaptations to try to maintain normal function in spite of their use of alcohol. One reflection of this process is when the individual's liver becomes more efficient at the biotransformation of alcohol. This improvement in the liver's ability to biotransform alcohol is seen in the earlier stages of the individual's drinking career and is known as *metabolic tolerance*. As the metabolic tolerance to alcohol develops drinkers notice that they must consume more alcohol to achieve a desired level of intoxication (Nelson, 2000). In clinical interviews, a drinker might admit that when he was 21, it "only" took 6 to 8 beers before he became intoxicated; now it takes 12 to 15 beers consumed over the same period of time before he is drunk.

Another expression of tolerance to alcohol's effects is known as *behavioral tolerance*. Where a novice drinker might appear quite intoxicated after five or six beers, the experienced drinker might show few outward signs of intoxication even after consuming a significant amount of alcohol. On occasion, even skilled law-enforcement or health care professionals are shocked to learn that the apparently sober person in their care has a BAL well into the range of legal intoxication, which is why objective test data are used to determine whether the individual is or is not legally intoxicated at the time he or she is stopped by the police.

Pharmacodynamic tolerance is the last subform of tolerance that will be discussed in this chapter. As the cells of the central nervous system attempt to carry out their normal function in spite of the continual presence of alcohol, they become less and less sensitive to the intoxicating effects of the chemical. Over time, the individual has to consume more and more alcohol to achieve the same effect on the CNS. As pharmacodynamic tolerance develops, the individual might switch

TABLE 8.1   Effects of Alcohol on the Chronic Drinker

Blood alcohol level (BAL)	Behavioral and physical effects
0.05–0.09	None to minimal effect
0.10–0.19	Mild ataxia, euphoria
0.20–0.29	Mild emotional changes, ataxia
0.30–0.39	Drowsiness, lethargy, stupor
Above 0.40	Coma, death

Sources: Based on material provided by Baselt (1996); Lehman, Pilich, & Andrews (1994), pp. 305–309; Morrison, Rogers, & Thomas (1995), pp. 371–389.

from beer to "hard" liquor, or increase the amount of beer ingested to achieve a desired state of intoxication.

If any of these subtypes of tolerance has developed, the patient will simply be said to be "tolerant" to the effects of alcohol. Compare the effects of alcohol for the chronic drinker in Table 8.1 with those of Table 7.1 (in the preceding chapter).

Tolerance requires great effort on the part of the individual's body, and eventually the different organs prove unequal to the task of maintaining normal function in the face of the constant presence of alcohol. When this happens, the individual actually becomes *less* tolerant to alcohol's effects. It is not uncommon for chronic drinkers to admit that in contrast to the past, they now can become intoxicated on just a few beers or mixed drinks. An assessor would say that this individual's tolerance is "on the downswing," a sign that the drinker has entered the later stages of alcohol dependence.

Another warning sign that suggests drinkers are addicted to alcohol is their growing *dependence* on alcohol. There are two subforms of alcohol dependence. First, there is *psychological dependence*. In psychological dependence, people repeatedly self-administer alcohol because they find it rewarding or because they believe that the alcohol is necessary to help them socialize, relax, sleep better, and so on. These people use alcohol as a "crutch," believing that they are unable to be sexual, to sleep, or to socialize without first using alcohol. Often, the alcohol-dependent person believes that he or she *deserves* to have a drink(s), for one reason or another.

The second form of dependence is known as *physical dependence*. Remember that the chronic use of alcohol

will force the body to attempt to adapt to the constant presence of the chemical. Indeed, in a very real sense the body might be said to now need the foreign chemical in order to maintain normal function. When the chemical is suddenly removed from the body, the body will go through a period of readjustment as it relearns how to function without the foreign chemical. This period of readjustment is known as the *withdrawal syndrome*.

Like many drugs of abuse, alcohol has a characteristic withdrawal syndrome. But unlike many of the other drugs of abuse, the alcohol withdrawal syndrome involves not only some degree of subjective discomfort for the individual but also the potential for life-threatening medical complications. It is for this reason that *all cases of alcohol withdrawal should be evaluated and treated by a physician*.

Several factors influence the severity of the alcohol withdrawal syndrome, including (a) how frequently and (b) in what amount, the individual consumed alcohol, and (c) his or her state of health. The longer the period of alcohol use and the greater the amount ingested, the more severe the alcohol withdrawal syndrome will be. The symptoms of alcohol withdrawal for the chronic alcoholic will be discussed in more detail in a later section of this chapter.

Often, the recovering alcoholic will speak of a "craving" for alcohol that continues long after drinking has stopped. Some individuals suggest that this is a feeling of being "thirsty" or they find themselves preoccupied with the possibility of drinking. At this point, it is not known why alcohol-dependent persons "crave" alcohol. However, the fact that the individual does become preoccupied with alcohol use or craves a drink is a sign that he or she has become dependent upon alcohol. The topic of "craving" will be discussed in more detail in the chapter on treatment problems.

The TIQ hypothesis. In the late 1980s Trachtenberg and Blum (1987) suggested that chronic alcohol use significantly reduces the brain's production of the endorphins, the enkephalins, and the dynorphins. These neurotransmitters function in the brain's pleasure center to help moderate an individual's emotions and behavior. They proposed that a byproduct of alcohol metabolism and neurotransmitters normally found within the brain combined to form the compound *tetrahydroisoquinoline* (or TIQ) (Blum, 1988). They also suggested that the TIQ was capable of binding to opiate-like receptor sites within the brain's pleasure center, causing the individual to experience a sense of well-being (Blum & Payne, 1991; Blum & Trachtenberg, 1988). However, TIQ's effects were thought to be short-lived, forcing the individual to drink more alcohol in order to regain or maintain the initial feeling of euphoria achieved through the use of alcohol.

Over time, it was thought that the individual's chronic use of alcohol would cause his or her brain to reduce its production of enkephalins, as the ever-present TIQ was substituted for these naturally produced opiate-like neurotransmitters (Blum & Payne, 1991; Blum & Trachtenberg, 1988). The cessation of alcohol intake was thought to result in a neurochemical deficit, which the individual would then attempt to relieve through further chemical use (Blum & Payne, 1991; Blum & Trachtenberg, 1988). Subjectively, this deficit was experienced as the "craving" for alcohol commonly reported by recovering alcoholics, according to the authors. While the TIQ theory had a number of strong adherents in the late 1980s and early 1990s, it has gradually fallen into disfavor. A number of research studies have failed to find evidence to support the TIQ hypothesis, and there are few researchers in the field of alcohol addiction who believe that TIQ plays a major role in the phenomenon of alcohol "craving."

Complications of Chronic Alcohol Use

Alcohol is a mild toxin, and over time its chronic use will often result in damage to one or more organ systems. It is important to recognize that chronic alcohol abuse includes both "weekend" and "binge" drinking. Repeated episodic alcohol abuse may bring about many of the same effects seen with chronic alcohol use. Unfortunately, there is no simple formula by which to calculate the risk of alcohol-related organ damage or which organs will be affected (Segal & Sisson, 1985). As the authors noted two decades ago:

> Some heavy drinkers of many years' duration appear to go relatively unscathed, while others develop complications early (e.g. after five years) in their drinking careers. Some develop brain damage; others liver disease; still others, both. The reasons for this are simply not known. (p. 145)

These observations remain true today. However, it is known that in different individuals, the chronic use of

alcohol will have an impact on virtually every body system. We will briefly discuss the effects of chronic alcohol use on various organ systems below.

The Effects of Chronic Alcoholism on the Digestive System

As was discussed in the last chapter, during distillation many of the vitamins and minerals that were in the original wine are lost. Thus, where the original wine might have contributed something to the nutritional requirements of the individual, even this modest contribution is lost through the distillation process. Further, when the body breaks down alcohol, it finds "empty calories." The body obtains carbohydrates from the alcohol it metabolizes, without the protein, vitamins, calcium, and other minerals needed by the body. Also, the frequent use of alcohol interferes with the absorption of needed nutrients from the gastrointestinal tract and may cause the drinker to experience chronic diarrhea (Fleming et al., 2001). These factors may contribute to a state of vitamin depletion called *avitaminosis*.

Although alcohol does not appear to *cause* cancer, it does seem to facilitate the development of some forms of cancer and thus can be classified as a *cocarcinogenic* agent (Bagnardi et al., 2001). The chronic use of alcohol is associated with higher rates of cancer of the upper digestive tract, the respiratory system, the mouth, pharynx, larynx, esophagus, and the liver (Bagnardi et al., 2001). Alcohol use is associated with 75% of all deaths due to cancer of the esophagus (Rice, 1993). Further, although the exact mechanism is not known, there is an apparent relationship between chronic alcohol use and cancer of the large bowel in both sexes, and cancer of the breast in women (Bagnardi et al., 2001).

The combination of cigarettes and alcohol is especially dangerous. Chronic alcoholics experience an almost sixfold increase in their risk of developing cancer of the mouth or pharynx (Garro, Espina, & Lieber, 1992, p. 83). For comparison, consider that cigarette smokers have slightly over a sevenfold increased risk of developing cancer of the mouth or pharynx. Surprisingly, however, alcoholics who also smoke have a *38-fold increased risk* of cancer in these regions, according to the authors.[1]

---

[1]The relationship between tobacco use and drinking is discussed in Chapter 19.

The body organ most heavily involved in the process of alcohol biotransformation is the liver, which bears the brunt of alcohol-induced organ damage (Sadock & Sadock, 2003). Unfortunately, scientists do not know how to determine the level of exposure necessary to cause liver damage for any given individual, but it is known that chronic exposure to even limited amounts of alcohol may result in liver damage (Frezza et al., 1990; Lieber, 1996; Schenker & Speeg, 1990). Indeed, chronic alcohol use is the most common cause of liver disease in both the United States (Hill & Kugelmas, 1998) and the United Kingdom (Walsh & Alexander, 2000). Approximately 80% to 90% (Ordorica & Nace, 1998; Walsh & Alexander, 2000) of heavy drinkers will develop the first manifestation of alcohol-related liver problems: a "fatty liver" (also called "steatosis"). This is a condition in which the liver becomes enlarged and does not function at full efficiency (Nace, 1987). There are few indications of a "fatty" liver that would be noticed without a physical examination, but blood tests would detect characteristic abnormalities in the patient's liver enzymes (Schuckit, 2000). This condition will reverse itself with abstinence (Walsh & Alexander, 2000).

Approximately 35% of individuals with alcohol-induced "fatty" liver who continue to drink go on to develop a more advanced form of liver disease: *alcoholic hepatitis*. In alcohol-induced hepatitis, the cells of the liver become inflamed as a result of the body's continual exposure to alcohol. Symptoms of alcoholic hepatitis may include a low grade fever, malaise, jaundice, an enlarged tender liver, and dark urine (Nace, 1987). Blood tests would also reveal characteristic changes in the blood chemistry (Schuckit, 2000), and the patient might complain of abdominal pain (Hill & Kugelmas, 1998). Even with the best of medical care, 20% to 65% of the individuals with alcohol-induced hepatitis will die (Bondesson & Sapperston, 1996).

Doctors do not know why some chronic drinkers develop alcohol-induced hepatitis and other do not, although the individual's genetic inheritance is thought to play a role in this process. Alcohol-induced liver damage usually develops after 15 to 20 years of heavy drinking (Walsh & Alexander, 2000). Individuals who have alcohol-induced hepatitis should avoid having surgery, if possible, as they are poor surgical risks. Unfortunately, if the patient were to be examined by a physician who was not aware of the patient's history of alcoholism, symptoms such as abdominal pain might be misinterpreted as being caused by other conditions such as appendicitis, pancreatitis, or an inflammation of the gall bladder. If the physician were to attempt surgical interventions, the patient's life might be placed at increased risk because of the complications caused by the undiagnosed alcoholism.

Alcoholic hepatitis is "a slow, smoldering process which may proceed or coexist with" (Nace, 1987, p. 25) another form of liver disease, known as *cirrhosis* of the liver. As a result of alcohol-induced hepatitis, the cells of the liver begin to die because of their chronic exposure to alcohol. Eventually, these dead liver cells are replaced by scar tissue. A physical examination of the patient with cirrhosis of the liver will reveal a hard, nodular liver, an enlarged spleen, "spider" angiomas on the skin, tremor, jaundice, mental confusion, signs of liver disease on various blood tests, and possibly a number of other symptoms such as testicular atrophy in males (Nace, 1987).

Although some researchers believe that alcoholic hepatitis precedes the development of cirrhosis of the liver, this has not been proven. Indeed, "alcoholics may progress to cirrhosis without passing through any visible stage resembling hepatitis" (National Institute on Alcohol Abuse and Alcoholism, 1993b, p. 1). Thus, many chronic alcoholics never appear to develop alcoholic hepatitis, and the first outward sign of serious liver disease is the development of cirrhosis of the liver. Statistically, only about 20% of alcohol-dependent persons develops cirrhosis, but this still means that there are about 3 million people in the United States with alcohol-related liver disease (Karsan, Rojter, & Saab, 2004). Cirrhosis can develop in people who consume as little as 2 to 4 drinks a day for just 10 years (Karsan et al., 2004).

A number of different theories have been advanced to explain the phenomenon of alcohol-induced liver disease. One theory suggests that "free radicals" that are generated during the process of alcohol biotransformation might contribute to the death of individual liver cells, initiating the development of alcohol-induced cirrhosis (Walsh & Alexander, 2000). It is known that as individual liver cells are destroyed, they are replaced by scar tissue. Over time, large areas of the liver may be replaced by scar tissue as significant numbers of liver cells die. Unfortunately, scar tissue is essentially nonfunctional. As more and more liver cells die the liver becomes unable to effectively cleanse the blood, allowing various toxins to accumulate in the circulation. Some toxins, like ammonia, are thought to then damage the cells of the CNS (Butterworth, 1995).

At one point, it was thought that malnutrition was a factor in the development of alcohol-induced liver disease. However, research has found that the individual's dietary habits do not seem to influence the development of alcohol-induced liver disease (Achord, 1995). Recently, scientists have developed blood tests capable of detecting one of the viruses known to infect the liver. The virus is known as the "Hepatitis Virus-C" (or Hepatitis-C, or HVC), and normally this virus is found in about 1.6% of the general population. But between 25% and 60% of chronic alcohol users have been found to be infected with HVC (Achord, 1995). This fact suggests that there may be a relationship between HVC infection, chronic alcohol use, and the development of liver disease.

Whatever its cause, cirrhosis itself can bring about severe complications, including liver cancer and sodium and water retention (Nace, 1987; Schuckit, 2000). As the liver becomes enlarged, it begins to squeeze the blood vessels that pass through it, causing the blood pressure to build up within the vessels, adding to the stress on the drinker's heart. This condition is known as *portal hypertension*, which can cause the blood vessels in the esophagus to swell from the back pressure. Weak spots form on the walls of the vessels much like weak spots form on an inner tube of a tire. These weak spots in the walls of the blood vessels of the esophagus are called *esophageal varices*, which may rupture. Ruptured esophageal varices is a medical emergency that, even with the most advanced forms of medical treatment, results in death for 20% to 30% of those who develop this disorder (Hegab & Luketic, 2001). Between 50% and 60% of those who survive will develop a second episode of bleeding, resulting in an additional 30% death rate. Ultimately, 60% of those afflicted with esophageal varices will die as a result of blood loss from a ruptured varix[2] (Giacchino & Houdek, 1998).

As if that were not enough, alcohol has been identified as the most common cause of a painful inflammation of the pancreas, known as *pancreatitis* (Fleming et al., 2001). Although pancreatitis can be caused by other things, such as exposure to a number of toxic agents such as the venom of scorpions or certain insecticides, the chronic exposure to ethyl alcohol is *the* most common cause of toxin-induced pancreatitis in this country, accounting for 66% to 75% of the cases of pancreatitis (McCrady & Langenbucher, 1996; Steinberg & Tenner, 1994). Pancreatitis develops slowly and usually requires "10 to 15 years of heavy drinking" (Nace, 1987, p. 26) before it can develop.

Even low concentrations of alcohol appear to inhibit the stomach's ability to produce sufficient levels of prostaglandins necessary to protect it from digestive fluids (Bode et al., 1996), and there is evidence that beverages containing just 5% to 10% alcohol can contribute to damage of the lining of the stomach (Bode et al., 1996). This process seems to explain why about 30% of chronic drinkers develop *gastritis*,[3] as well as bleeding from the stomach lining and the formation of gastric ulcers (McAnalley, 1996; Willoughby, 1984). If an ulcer forms over a major blood vessel, the stomach acid will eat through the stomach lining and blood vessel walls, causing a "bleeding ulcer." This is a severe medical emergency, which may be fatal. Physicians will try to "seal" a bleeding ulcer through the use of laser beams, but in extreme cases conventional surgery is necessary to save the patient's life. The surgeon may remove part of the stomach to stop the bleeding. This, in turn, will contribute to the body's difficulties in absorbing suitable amounts of vitamins from food that is ingested (Willoughby, 1984). This, either by itself or in combination with further alcohol use, helps to bring about a chronic state of malnutrition in the individual.

Unfortunately, the vitamin malabsorption syndrome that develops following the surgical removal of the majority of the individual's stomach will, in turn, make the drinker a prime candidate for the development of tuberculosis (or TB) if he or she continues to drink (Willoughby, 1984). The topic of TB is discussed in more detail in Chapter 33. However, at this point it should be pointed out that upwards of 95% of alcohol-dependent individuals who had a portion of their stomach removed secondary to bleeding ulcers and who continue to drink ultimately developed TB (Willoughby, 1984).

---

[2]Varix is the singular form of varicies.

[3]See Glossary.

The chronic use of alcohol can cause or contribute to a number of vitamin *malabsorption syndromes*, in which the individual's body is no longer able to absorb needed vitamins or minerals from food. Some of the minerals that might not be absorbed by the body of the chronic alcoholic include zinc (Marsano, 1994) as well as sodium, calcium, phosphorus, and magnesium (Lehman, Pilich, & Andrews, 1994). The chronic use of alcohol will also interfere with the body's ability to absorb or properly utilize vitamin A, vitamin D, vitamin B-6, thiamine, and folic acid (Marsano, 1994).

Chronic drinking is also a cause of a condition known as *glossitis*,[4] as well as possible stricture of the esophagus (Marsano, 1994). Each of these conditions can indirectly contribute to a failure on the part of the individual to ingest an adequate diet, further contributing to alcohol-related dietary deficiencies within the drinker's body. Further, as was noted in the last chapter, alcohol-containing beverages are a source of "empty" calories. Many chronic drinkers obtain up to one-half of their daily caloric intake from alcoholic beverages, rather than from more traditional food sources (Suter, Schultz, & Jequier, 1992). Alcohol-related dietary problems can contribute to a decline in the immune system's ability to protect the individual from various infectious diseases such as pneumonia and tuberculosis (TB). Alcohol-dependent individuals, for example, are three to seven times as likely to die from pneumonia as are nondrinkers (Schirmer, Wiedermann, & Konwalinka, 2000).

The chronic use of alcohol is a known risk factor in the development of a number of different metabolic disorders. For example, although there is mixed evidence to suggest that *limited* alcohol use[5] might serve a protective function against the development of Type 2 diabetes in women, *heavy chronic* alcohol use is a known risk factor for the development of Type 2 diabetes (National Institute on Alcohol Abuse and Alcoholism, 1993c; Wannamethee, Camargo, Manson, Willett, & Rimm, 2003). Between 45% and 70% of alcoholics with liver disease are also either glucose intolerant (a condition that suggests that the body is having trouble dealing with sugar in the blood) or diabetic (National Institute on Alcohol Abuse and

Alcoholism, 1994). Many chronic drinkers experience episodes of abnormally high (*hyperglycemic*) or abnormally low (*hypoglycemic*) blood sugar levels. These conditions are caused by alcohol-induced interference with the secretion of digestive enzymes from the pancreas (National Institute on Alcohol Abuse and Alcoholism, 1993c, 1994).

Further, chronic alcohol use may interfere with the way the drinker's body utilizes fats. When the individual reaches the point that he or she obtains 10% or more of the daily energy requirements from alcohol rather than more traditional foods, the individual's body will go through a series of changes (Suter et al., 1992). First, the chronic use of alcohol will slow down the body's energy expenditure (metabolism), which, in turn, causes the body to store the unused lipids as fatty tissue. This is the mechanism by which the so-called beer belly commonly seen in the heavy drinker is formed.

The Effects of Chronic Alcohol Use on the Cardiopulmonary System

Researchers have long been aware of what is known as the "French paradox," which is to say a lower-than-expected rate of heart disease in spite of a diet rich in the foods that supposedly are associated with an increased risk of heart disease (Goldberg, 2003).[6] For reasons that are not well understood, the *moderate* use of alcohol-containing beverages has been found to bring about a 10% to 40% reduction in the individual's risk of developing coronary heart disease (CHD) (Fleming et al., 2001; Klatsky, 2002, 2003). Mukamal et al. (2003) suggested that the actual form of the alcohol-containing beverage was not as important as the regular use of a moderate amount,[7] although there is no consensus on this issue (Klatsky, 2002). However, this effect was moderated by the individual's genetic heritage, with some drinkers gaining more benefit from moderate alcohol use than others (Hines et al., 2001).

---

[4]See Glossary.

[5]Defined as 1 standard drink or 4 ounces of wine in a 24-hour period.

[6]For reasons that are not well understood, advocates of the moderate use of alcohol point to the lower incidence of heart disease experienced by the French, who consume wine on a regular basis, but they overlook the significantly higher incidence of alcohol-related liver disease experienced by the French (Walton, 2003).

[7]"Moderate" alcohol use is defined as *no more than* 2 twelve-ounce cans of beer, 2 five-ounce glasses of wine, or 1.5 ounces of vodka, gin, or other "hard" liquor in a 24-hour period (Klatsky, 2003).

One theory for the reduced risk of CHD is that alcohol may function as an anticoagulant. Within the body, alcohol inhibits the ability of blood platelets to "bind" together (Klatsky, 2003; Renaud & DeLorgeril, 1992). This may be a result of alcohol's ability to facilitate the production of prostacyclin and reduce the fibrogen levels in the body when it is used at moderate levels (Klatsky, 2003, 2002). By inhibiting the action of blood platelets to start the clotting process, the moderate use of alcohol may result in a lower risk of heart attack and certain kinds of strokes by 30% to 40% (Stoschitzky, 2000). It is theorized that moderate alcohol consumption also "significantly and consistently raises the plasma levels of the antiatherogenic HDL cholesterol" (Klatsky, 2002, p. ix), making it more difficult for atherosclerotic plaque to build up.

However, physicians still hesitate to recommend that nondrinkers turn to alcohol as a way of reducing their risk of heart disease (Goldberg, 2003). Alcohol use to reduce one's risk of disease is a "double-edged sword" (Klatsky, 2002, p. ix). Although the moderate use of alcohol might provide a limited degree of protection against coronary artery disease, it also increases the individual's risk of developing alcohol-related brain damage (Karhunen, Erkinjuntti, & Laippala, 1994). There also is mixed evidence suggesting that consuming only one drink per day might be associated with a 10% increased risk of breast cancer for women for each drink they consume per day[8] (Ellison, 2002). Thus, the role of alcohol in reducing the risk of heart attack is limited at best and carries with it other forms of health risks.

When used to excess, alcohol not only loses its protective action but may actually harm the cardiovascular system. The excessive use of alcohol results in the suppression of normal red blood cell formation, and both blood clotting problems and anemia are common complications of alcoholism (Nace, 1987). Alcohol abuse is thought to be a factor in the development of cerebral vascular accidents (strokes, or CVAs). Light drinkers (2–3 drinks/day) have a twofold higher risk of a stroke, whereas heavy drinkers (4 + drinks/day) almost triple their risk of a CVA (Ordorica & Nace,

1998). Approximately 23,500 strokes each year in the United States are thought to be alcohol-related (Sacco, 1995).

In large amounts (defined as more than the 1–2 drink a day limit identified above), alcohol is known to be *cardiotoxic*. Animal research has shown that the chronic use of alcohol inhibits the process of muscle protein synthesis, especially the myobibrillar protein necessary for normal cardiac function (Ponnappa & Rubin, 2000). In humans, chronic alcohol use is considered the most common cause of heart muscle disease (Rubin & Doria, 1990). Prolonged exposure to alcohol (6 beers a day or a pint of whiskey a day for 10 years) may result in permanent damage to the heart muscle tissue, hypertension, inflammation of the heart muscle, and a general weakening of the heart muscle known as *alcohol-induced cardiomyopathy* (Figueredo, 1997). This condition appears to be a special example of a more generalized process in which chronic alcohol use results in damage to *all* striated muscle tissues, not just those in the heart muscle (Fernandez-Sola et al., 1994). The authors examined a number of men who were and were not alcohol dependent. They found that alcoholic men in general had less muscle strength and greater levels of muscle tissue damage than did the nonalcoholic men in this study. The authors concluded that alcohol is toxic to muscle tissue and that the chronic use of alcohol will result in a loss of muscle tissue throughout the body.

Cardiomyopathy itself develops in between 25% (Schuckit, 2000) and 40% of chronic alcohol users (Figueredo, 1997), and accounts for 20% to 50% of all cases of cardiomyopathy in the United States (Zakhari, 1997). But even this figure might not reflect the true scope of alcohol-induced heart disease. Rubin and Doria (1990) suggested that "the majority of alcoholics" (p. 279), which they defined as those individuals who obtained between 30% and 50% of their daily caloric requirement through alcohol, will ultimately develop "pre-clinical heart disease" (p. 279). Because of the body's compensatory mechanisms, many chronic alcoholics do not show evidence of heart disease except on special tests designed to detect this disorder (Figueredo, 1997; Rubin & Doria, 1990). However, 40% to 50% of those individuals with alcohol-induced cardiomyopathy will die within four years, if they continue to drink (Figueredo, 1997; Stoschitzky, 2000).

[8]Thus, a woman who consumed 2 glasses of wine per day would have a 20% higher risk of breast cancer than a nondrinking woman of the same age.

Although many individuals take comfort in the fact that they drink to excess only occasionally, even binge drinking is not without its dangers. Binge drinking may result in a condition known as the "holiday heart syndrome" (Figueredo, 1997; Klatsky, 2003; Stoschitzky, 2000; Zakhari, 1997). When used on an episodic basis, such as when the individual consumes larger-than-normal quanities of alcohol during a holiday break from work, alcohol can interfere with the normal flow of electrical signals within the heart. This might then contribute to an irregular heartbeat known as *atrial fibrillation*, which can be fatal if it is not diagnosed and properly treated. Thus, even episodic alcohol use is not without some degree of risk.

The Effects of Chronic Alcoholism on the Central Nervous System (CNS)

Alcohol is a neurotoxin, as evidenced by the fact that at least half of heavy drinkers show evidence of cognitive deficits (Schuckit & Tapert, 2004). A common example of the toxic effects of alcohol is seen in its ability to interfere with memory formation. Neuropsychological testing has revealed that alcohol may begin to affect memory formation after as little as one drink. Fortunately, one normally needs to consume more than five drinks in an hour's time before alcohol is able to significantly impact the process of memory formation (Browning, Hoffer, & Dunwiddie, 1993).

The extreme form of alcohol-induced memory dysfunction is the *blackout*.[9] A *blackout* is a period of alcohol-induced amnesia that may last from less than an hour to several days (White, 2003). During a blackout, the individual may *appear* to be conscious to others, be able to carry on a coherent conversation, and be able to carry out many complex tasks. However, afterward, the drinker will not have any memory of what she or he did during the blackout. In a sense, the alcohol-induced blackout is similar to another condition known as *transient global amnesia* (Kaplan, Sadock, & Grebb, 1994; Rubino, 1992).

[9]White (2003) suggested that alcohol-induced blackouts might be experienced by social drinkers as well as alcohol-dependent persons. However, as alcohol-induced memory impairment is seen after the blood alcohol level reaches 0.14 to 0.20, according to White, it is suggested in this text that *heavy* drinkers are most prone to alcohol-induced blackouts.

Scientists believe that alcohol prevents the individual from being able to form (encode) memories during the period of acute intoxication (Browning, Hoffer, & Dunwiddie, 1993). The alcohol-induced blackout is "an early and serious indicator of the development of alcoholism" (Rubino, 1992, p. 360). Current theory suggests that alcohol-induced blackouts are caused by alcohol in the brain blocking the normal function of the neurotransmitters gamma-amiobutyric acid (GABA) and N-methyl-D-Aspartate (NMDA) (Nelson et al., 2004). The individual's vulnerability to alcohol-induced memory disturbances is influenced by the manner in which she or he consumed alcohol and his or her genetic vulnerability (Nelson et al., 2004). A majority of heavy drinkers will admit to having alcohol-induced blackouts if they are asked about this experience (Schuckit, Smith, Anthenelli, & Irwin, 1993).

Although it has long been known that the chronic use of alcohol can result in brain damage, the exact mechanism by which alcohol causes damage to the brain remains unknown (Roehrs & Roth, 1995). Unfortuantely, for about 15% of heavy drinkers, the first organ to show damage from their drinking is not the liver but the brain (Berg, Franzen, & Wedding, 1994; Bowden, 1994; Volkow et al., 1992). Alcohol-induced dementia is the single most preventable cause of dementia in the United States (Beasley, 1987) and is the "second most common adult dementia after Alzheimer's disease" (Nace & Isbell, 1991, p. 56). Up to 75% of chronic alcohol drinkers show evidence of alcohol-induced cognitive impairment following detoxification (Butterworth, 1995; Hartman, 1995; Tarter, Ott, & Mezzich, 1991). This alcohol-induced brain damage might become so severe that institutionalization becomes necessary when the drinker is no longer able to care for himself or herself. It is estimated that between 15% and 30% of all nursing home patients are there because of permanent alcohol-induced brain damage (Schuckit, 2000).

A limited degree of improvement in cognitive function is possible in some alcohol-dependent persons who remain abstinent from alcohol for extended periods of time (Grant, 1987; Løberg, 1986). But research suggests that only 20% of chronic drinkers may return to their previous level of intellectual function after abstaining from alcohol for an extended period of time (Nace & Isbell, 1991). Some limited degree of recovery is possible in perhaps 60% of the cases, and virtually no recovery of lost intellectual function is seen in 20% of the cases, according to the authors.

The chronic use of alcohol is thought to be a cause of cerebellar atrophy, a condition in which the cerebellum withers away as individual cells in this region of the brain die as a result of chronic alcohol exposure. Fully 30% of alcohol-dependent individuals eventually develop this condition, which is marked by characteristic psychomotor dysfunction, gait disturbance, and loss of muscle control (Berger, 2000). Another central nervous system complication seen as a result of chronic alcohol abuse is *vitamin deficiency amblyopia*. This condition will cause blurred vision, a loss of visual perception in the center of the visual field known as central scotomata, and in extreme cases, atrophy of the optic nerve (Mirin, Weiss, & Greenfield, 1991). The alcohol-induced damage to the visual system may be permanent.

Wernicke-Korsakoff's syndrome. In 1881, Carl Wernicke first described a brain disorder that subsequently came to bear his name. *Wernicke's encephalopathy* is recognized as the most serious complication of chronic alcohol use (Day, Bentham, Callaghan, Kuruvilla, & George, 2004). If not treated, it can cause death in up to 20% of individuals who develop this disorder (Ciraulo, Shader, Ciraulo, Greenblatt, & von Moltke, 1994b; Day et al., 2004; Zubaran, Fernandes, & Rodnight, 1997). About 20% of chronic drinkers develop Wernicke's encephalopathy, which is thought to be caused by alcohol-induced avitaminosis (Bowden, 1994). As a result of the alcohol-related vitamin malabsorption, the reserves of thiamine (one of the "B" family of vitamins) in an individual's body will gradually be depleted, contributing to the development of various neurological problems such as Wernicke's encephalopathy. Between 30% and 80% of chronic drinkers show evidence of clinical/subclinical thiamine deficiency (Day et al., 2004).

Chronic thiamine deficiency results in characteristic patterns of brain damage, often detected on physical examination of the brain following death. The patient who is suffering from Wernicke's encephalopathy will often appear confused, possibly to the point of being delirious and disoriented. He or she would also be apathetic and unable to sustain physical or mental activities (Day et al., 2004; Victor, 1993). A physical examination would reveal a characteristic pattern of abnormal eye movements known as *nystagmus* and such symptoms of brain damage as gait disturbances and ataxia (Lehman et al., 1994).

Before physicians developed a method to treat Wernicke's encephalophy, up to 80% of the patients who developed this condition went on to develop a condition known as *Korsakoff's syndrome*. Another name for *Korsakoff's syndrome* is the *alcohol amnestic disorder* (Charness, Simon, & Greenberg, 1989; Day et al., 2004; Victor, 1993). Even when Wernicke's encephalophy is properly treated through the most aggressive thiamine replacement procedures known to modern medicine, fully 25% of the patients who develop Wernicke's disease will go on to develop Korsakoff's syndrome (Sagar, 1991).

For many years, scientists thought that Wernicke's encephalopathy and Korsakoff's syndrome were separate disorders. It is now known that Wernicke's encephalopathy is the acute phase of the Wernicke-Korsakoff syndrome. One of the most prominent symptoms of the Korsakoff phase of this syndrome is a memory disturbance, when the patient is unable to remember the past accurately. In addition to this, the individual will also have difficulty in learning new information. This should not be surprising, in that magnetic resonance imaging (MRI) studies of the brains of alcohol-dependent persons reveal atrophy far beyond what one would expect as a result of normal aging (Bjork, Grant, & Hommer, 2003). The observed loss of brain tissue is most conspicuous in the anterior superior temporal cortex region of the brain, which seems to correspond to the behavioral deficits observed in the Wernicke-Korsakoff syndrome (Pfefferbaum, Sullivan, Rosenbloom, Mathalon, & Kim, 1998). However, there are subtle differences between the pattern of brain damage seen in male and female alcohol abusers as compared to normal adults of the same age (Hommer, Momenan, Kaiser, & Rawlings, 2001; Pfefferbaum, Rosenbloom, Deshmukh, & Sullivan, 2001).

It is not unusual to observe that in spite of clear evidence of cognitive impairment, the patient frequently appears indifferent to his or her memory loss (Ciraulo et al., 1994b). In the earlier stages, the person might be confused by his or her inability to remember the past clearly and will often "fill in" these memory gaps by making up answers to questions. This process is called *confabulation*. Confabulation is not always found in cases of Korsakoff's syndrome, but when it is found, it is most common in the earlier stages of Korsakoff's syndrome (Parsons & Nixon, 1993; Victor, 1993). Later on, as the individual adjusts to the memory loss, he or she will not be as likely to use confabulation to cover up the memory problem (Blansjaar & Zwinderman, 1992; Brandt & Butters, 1986).

In rare cases, people will lose virtually all memories after a certain period of their lives and will almost be "frozen in time." For example, Sacks (1970) offered an example of a man who, when examined, was unable to recall anything that happened after the late 1940s. The patient was examined in the 1960s, but when asked, would answer questions as if he were still living in the 1940s. This example of confabulation, while extremely rare, can result from chronic alcoholism. More frequent are the less pronounced cases, in which significant portions of the memory are lost but the individual retains some ability to recall the past. Unfortunately, the exact mechanism of Wernicke-Korsakoff's syndrome is unknown at this time. The characteristic nystagmus seem to respond to massive doses of thiamine.[10] It is possible that victims of Wernicke-Korsakoff's syndrome possess a genetic susceptibility to the effects of the alcohol-induced thiamine deficiency (Parsons & Nixon, 1993). While this is an attractive theory, in that it explains why some chronic drinkers develop Wernicke-Korsakoff's syndrome and others do not, it remains just a theory.

Several different theories about how chronic drinking contributes to brain damage have been advanced over the years. Jensen and Pakkenberg (1993) suggested, after conducting post-mortem examinations of the brains of 55 individuals who were active alcoholics prior to their death, that alcohol causes a *disconnection syndrome* between neurons. This then prevents those nerve pathways from being activated. If not stimulated, neurons wither and die, a mechanism by which alcohol might cause damage to the brain, according to the authors. Another theory was offered by Pfefferbaum, Rosenbloom, Serventi, and Sullivan (2004) who suggested that the liver dysfunction found in chronic alcohol abusers, combined with the poor nutrition and chronic exposure to alcohol itself, all combined to cause the characteristic pattern of brain damage seen in alcohol-dependent individuals.

These are only theories that remain to be proven. It is known that once Wernicke-Korsakoff's syndrome has developed, only a minority of its victims will escape without lifelong neurological damage. It is estimated that even with the most aggressive of vitamin replacement therapy, only 20% (Nace & Isbell, 1991) to 25% (Brandt & Butters, 1986) of its victims will return to their previous level of intellectual function. The other 75% to 80% will experience greater or lesser degrees of neurological damage, and at least 10% of the patients with this disorder will be left with permanent memory impairment (Vik, Cellucci, Jarchow, & Hedt, 2004).

There is evidence to suggest that chronic alcohol abuse/addiction is a risk factor in the development of a movement disorder known as *tardive dyskinesia* (TD) (Lopez & Jeste, 1997). This condition may result from alcohol's neurotoxic effect, according to the authors. Although TD is a common complication in patients who have used neuroleptic drugs for the control of psychotic conditions for long periods of time, there are cases in which the alcohol-dependent individual has developed TD in spite of the fact that she or he had no prior exposure to neuroleptic agents (Lopez & Jeste, 1997). The exact mechanism by which alcohol causes the development of tardive dyskinesia remains to be identified, and scientists have no idea why some alcohol abusers develop TD while others do not. But TD usually develops in chronic alcohol users who have a history of drinking for 10 to 20 years, according to the authors.

Alcohol's effects on the sleep cycle. Although alcohol might induce a form of sleep, the chronic use of alcohol interferes with the normal sleep cycle (Karam-Hage, 2004). Chronic alcohol users tend to require more time to fall asleep[11] and as a group they report that their sleep is less sound and less restful than that of nondrinkers (Karam-Hage, 2004). Although the exact mechanism by which chronic alcohol use interferes with sleep is still unknown, scientists believe that the chronic use of alcohol suppresses melatonin production in the brain, which in turn interferes with the normal sleep cycle (Karam-Hage, 2004; Pettit, 2000).

Clinicians often encounter patients who complain of sleep problems without revealing their alcohol abuse. By some estimates, 17% to 30% of the general population might suffer from insomnia, but fully 60% of alcohol-dependent persons will experience symptoms of insomnia (Brower, Aldrich, Robinson, Zucker, & Greden, 2001). Indeed, insomnia symptoms might serve

---

[10]See Glossary.

[11]Known as *sleep latency*.

as a relapse trigger for the newly recovered alcohol-dependent person unless this problem is addressed through appropriate interventions. Karam-Hage (2004) suggested that gabapentin (sold under the brand name of *Neurontin*) is quite useful as a hypnotic agent in alcohol-dependent persons.

Chronic alcohol ingestion causes the drinker to experience a reduction in the amount of time spent in the rapid eye movement (or REM) phase of sleep. There is a relationship between REM sleep and dreaming. Scientists don't know why we dream, but they do know that we need to dream and that anything that reduces the amount of time spent in REM sleep will interfere with normal waking cognitive function. When chronic drinkers stop drinking, they will spend an abnormal amount of time in REM sleep, a phenomenon known as *REM rebound*. The dreams that former drinkers might experience during this period may be so frightening that they are tempted to return to the use of alcohol in order to "get a decent night's sleep." The phase of "REM rebound" can last for up to 6 months after the person has stopped drinking (Brower, 2001; Schuckit & Tapert, 2004).

Scientists know that the chronic use of alcohol interferes with the normal sleep process, but they do not know whether the individual's sleep will return to a more normal pattern with continued abstinence. The effects of alcohol can interfere with the normal sleep cycle for one to two years after detoxification (Brower, 2001; Karam-Hage, 2004). In addition to disrupting the normal sleep cycle, the chronic use of alcohol can trigger episodes of sleep apnea both during the period of heavy drinking and for weeks after the individual's last drink (Berger, 2000; Brower, 2001; Le Bon et al., 1997).

The Effects of Chronic Alcohol Use on the Peripheral Nervous System

The human nervous system is usually viewed as two interconnected systems. The brain and spinal cord make up the central nervous system; the nerves that are found in the outer regions of the body are classified as the peripheral nervous system. Unfortunately, the effects of alcohol-induced avitaminosis are sufficiently widespread to include the peripheral nerves, especially those in the hands and feet. This is a condition known as *peripheral neuropathy*. This condition is found in 10% (Schuckit, 1995a) to 33% of chronic alcohol users (Monforte et al.,

1995). Some of the symptoms of a peripheral neuropathy include feelings of weakness, pain, and a burning sensation in the afflicted region of the body (Lehman et al., 1994). Eventually, the person will lose all feeling in the affected region of the body. Approximately 30% of all cases of peripheral neuropathy is thought to be alcohol induced (Hartman, 1995).

At this point, the exact cause of alcohol-induced peripheral neuropathies is not known. Some researchers believe that peripheral neuropathy is the result of a deficiency of the "B" family of vitamins in the body (Charness et al., 1989; Levin, 2002; Nace, 1987). In contrast to this theory, Monforte et al. (1995) suggested that peripheral neuropathies might be the result of chronic exposure to either alcohol itself or its metabolites. Again, as was discussed in the last chapter, some of the metabolites of alcohol are themselves quite toxic to the body. The authors failed to find evidence of a nutritional deficit for those hospitalized alcoholics who had developed peripheral neuropathies. But they did find evidence of a dose-related relationship between the use of alcohol and the development of peripheral neuropathies.

Surprisingly, in light of alcohol's known neurotoxic effects, there is evidence to suggest that at some doses it might suppress some of the involuntary movements of Huntington's disease (Lopez & Jeste, 1997). This is not to suggest that alcohol is an acceptable treatment for this disorder, but this effect of alcohol might account for the finding that patients with movement disorders such as essential tremor, or Huntington's disease, tend to abuse alcohol more often than close relatives who do not have a movement disorder, according to the authors.

The Effects of Chronic Alcohol Use on the Person's Emotional State

The chronic use of alcohol can simulate the symptoms of virtually every form of neurosis, even those seen in psychotic conditions. These symptoms are thought to be secondary to the individual's malnutrition and the toxic effects of chronic alcohol use (Beasley, 1987). These symptoms might include depressive reactions (Blondell, Frierson, & Lippmann, 1996; Schuckit, 1995a), generalized anxiety disorders, and panic attacks (Beasley, 1987).

There is a complex relationship between anxiety symptoms and alcohol-use disorders. For example, without medical intervention, almost 80% of alcohol-dependent individuals will experience panic episodes during the acute phase of withdrawal from alcohol (Schuckit, 2000). The chronic use of alcohol causes a paradoxical stimulation of the autonomic nervous system (ANS). The drinker will often interpret this ANS stimulation as a sign of anxiety, and then turn to alcohol or antianxiety medications to control this apparent anxiety. A cycle is then started in which the chronic use of alcohol actually sets the stage for further anxiety-like symptoms, resulting in the perceived need for more alcohol/medication. Stockwell and Town (1989) discussed this aspect of chronic alcohol use and concluded: "Many clients who drink heavily or abuse other anixolytic drugs will experience substantial or complete recovery from extreme anxiety following successful detoxification" (p. 223). The authors recommend a drug-free period of *at least 2 weeks* in which to assess the need for pharmacological intervention for anxiety.

But this is not to discount the possibility that the individual has a concurrent anxiety disorder *and* an alcohol-use disorder. Indeed, researchers have discovered that 10% to 40% of those individuals who are alcohol dependent also have an anxiety disorder of some kind. Between 10% and 20% of those patients being treated for some form of an anxiety disorder also have some kind of alcohol-use disorder (Cox & Taylor, 1999). For these individuals, the anxiety co-exists with their alcohol-use disorder and does not reflect alcohol withdrawal as is often the case. The diagnostic dilemma for the clinician is to determine which patients have withdrawal-induced anxiety and which patients have a legitimate anxiety disorder in addition to their substance-use problem. This determination is made more difficult by the fact that chronic alcohol use can cause the drinker to experience feelings of anxiety for many months after he or she stops drinking (Schuckit, 1998).

The differentiation between "true" anxiety disorders, and alcohol-related anxiety-like disorders is thus quite complex. The team of Kushner, Sher, and Beitman (1990) concluded that alcohol withdrawal symptoms may be "indistinguishable" (p. 692) from the symptoms of panic attacks and generalized anxiety disorder (GAD). One diagnostic clue is found in the observation that in general, problems such as agoraphobia and social phobias usually predate alcohol use, according to the authors. Victims of these disorders usually attempt self-medication through the use of alcohol and only later develop alcohol-use problems. On the other hand, Kushner et al. (1990) concluded that the symptoms of simple panic attacks and generalized anxiety disorder are more likely to reflect the effects of alcohol withdrawal than a psychiatric disorder.

Another form of phobia that frequently coexists with alcoholism is the *social phobia* (Marshall, 1994). Individuals with social phobias fear situations in which they are exposed to other people and are twice as likely to have alcohol-use problems as people from the general population. However, social phobia usually precedes the development of alcohol abuse/addiction.

Unfortunately, it is not uncommon for alcohol-dependent individuals to complain of anxiety symptoms when they see their physician, who may then prescribe a benzodiazepine to control the anxiety. This, in turn, allows the chronic drinker to control his or her withdrawal symptoms during the day without having the smell of alcohol on the breath. (One alcohol-dependent individual explained, for example, that the effects of 10 mg of diazepam were similar to the effects of having had 3–4 quick drinks). Given this tendency for alcohol-dependent individuals to use benzodiazepines, it should not be surprising to learn that 25% to 50% of alcoholics are also addicted to these drugs (Sattar & Bhatia, 2003). If the physician fails to obtain an adequate history and physical (or if the patient lies about his or her alcohol use), there is also a risk that the alcohol-dependent person might combine the use of antianxiety medication, which is a CNS depressant, with alcohol (which is also a CNS depressant). There is a significant potential for an overdose when two different classes of CNS depressants are combined. Thus, the use of alcohol with CNS depressants such as the benzodiazepines or antihistamines presents a very real danger to the patient.

The interaction between benzodiazepines and alcohol has been implicated as one cause of the condition known as the *paradoxical rage reaction* (Beasley, 1987). This is a drug-induced reaction in which a CNS depressant brings about an unexpected period of rage in the individual. During the paradoxical rage reaction, these individuals might engage in assaultive or destructive behavior toward either themselves or others and would later have no conscious memory of what they had done during the paradoxical rage reaction (Lehman et al., 1994).

If antianxiety medication is needed for long-term anxiety control in recovering drinkers, buspirone should be used first (Kranzler et al., 1994). Buspirone is not a benzodiazepine and thus does not present the potential for abuse seen with the latter family of drugs. The authors found that those alcoholic subjects in their study who suffered from anxiety symptoms and who received buspirone were both more likely to remain in treatment and to consume less alcohol than those anxious subjects who did not receive buspirone. This suggests that buspirone might be an effective medication in treating alcohol-dependent persons with concurrent anxiety disorders.

Chronic alcohol use has been known to interfere with sexual performance for both men and women (Jersild, 2001; Schiavi, Stimmel, Mandeli, & White, 1995). Although the chronic use of alcohol has been shown to interfere with the erectile process for men, Schiavi et al. (1995) found that once the individual stopped drinking, the erectile dysfunction usually resolved itself. However, there is evidence that disulfiram (often used in the treatment of chronic alcoholism) itself may interfere with a man's ability to achieve an erection.

Although it was once thought that primary depression was rare in chronic drinkers, it is now believed that there is a relationship between alcohol-use disorders and depression. However, Hasin and Grant (2002) examined the history of 6,050 recovering alcohol abusers and found that former drinkers had a fourfold increased incidence of depression compared to nondrinkers. Further, depression was found to have a negative impact on the individual's ability to benefit from rehabilitation programs and might contribute to higher dropout rates from substance-use treatment (Charney, 2004; Mueller et al., 1994).

The individual's use of alcohol was found to interfere with the treatment of depressive disorder (Mueller et al., 1994). Even limited alcohol use has been found to exacerbate depression, with the depressing effects of even a 1–2 day alcohol binge lasting for several weeks after abstinence is achieved (Segal & Sisson, 1985). The potential is thus present for a cycle in which the alcohol abuse might ultimately cause more depression than

would be expected in a person with a depressive disorder, leading him or her to abuse alcohol even more.

Alcohol-induced depressive episodes will usually clear after 2–5 weeks of abstinence. Some researchers do not recommend formal treatment other than abstinence and recommend that antidepressant medication be used only if the symptoms of depression continue after that period of time (Decker & Ries, 1993; Miller, 1994; Satel, Kosten, Schuckit, & Fischman, 1993). However, Charney (2004) recommended that depressive disorders be aggressively treated with the appropriate medications as soon as they are detected.

There is a strong relationship between depression and suicide (Nemeroff, Compton, & Berger, 2001). Because alcohol-dependent people are vulnerable to the development of depression as a consequence of their drinking, it is logical to assume that as a group they are at high risk for suicide. Indeed, research has demonstrated that alcohol-dependent individuals are 58 to 85 times more likely to commit suicide than those who are not alcohol dependent (Frierson, Melikian, & Wadman, 2002). Various researchers have suggested that the suicide rate among alcohol-dependent people is 5% (Preuss et al., 2003), 7% (Conner, Li, Meldrum, Duberstein, & Conwell, 2003), or even as high as 18% (Bongar, 1997; Preuss & Wong, 2000). Each year, 25% of those who commit suicide in the United States are alcohol dependent (Harwitz & Ravizza, 2000). It has been suggested that alcohol-related suicide is most likely to occur late in middle adulthood, when the effects of the chronic use of alcohol begin to manifest as cirrhosis of the liver and other disorders (Nisbet, 2000).

The team of Preuss et al. (2003) followed a cohort of 1,237 alcohol-dependent people for 5 years, and found that individuals in their sample were more than twice as likely to commit suicide as were nonalcoholic individuals in the course of the study. Although the authors carried out an extensive evaluation of their subjects prior to the start of the study in an attempt to identify potential predictors of suicide, they concluded that they had failed to do so successfully. There was only a modest correlation between the identified risk factors and completed suicide, and the authors concluded that those factors that had the greatest impact on suicidality had not been identified.

Almost a decade earlier, the research team of Murphy, Wetzel, Robins, and McEvoy (1992) attempted to isolate the factors that seemed to predict suicide in the chronic male alcoholic. On the basis of their research, the authors identified seven different factors that appeared to be suggestive of a possible suicide risk in the male chronic drinker:

1. The victim was drinking heavily in the days and weeks just prior to the act of suicide.
2. The victim had talked about the possibility of committing suicide prior to the act.
3. The victim had little social support.
4. The victim suffered from a major depressive disorder.
5. The victim was unemployed at the time of the suicide.
6. The victim was living alone.
7. The victim was suffering from a major medical problem at the time of the act of suicide.

Although the authors failed to find any single factor that seemed to predict a possible suicide in the chronic male alcoholic, they did conclude that "as the number of risk factors increases, the likelihood of a suicidal outcome does likewise" (p. 461). Roy (1993) also identified several factors that seemed to be associated with an increased risk of suicide for adult alcoholics. Like Murphy et al. (1992), he failed to find a single factor that seemed to predict the possibility of suicide for the adult alcoholic. However, Roy (1993) did suggest that the following factors were potential indicators for an increased risk:

1. *Gender*: Men tend to commit suicide more often than women, and the ratio of male:female suicides for alcoholics may be about 4:1.
2. *Marital status*: Single/divorced/widowed adults are significantly more likely to attempt suicide than are married adults.
3. *Co-existing depressive disorder*: Depression is associated with an increased risk of suicide.
4. *Adverse life events*: The individual who has suffered an adverse life event such as the loss of a loved one, or a major illness, or legal problems is at increased risk for suicide.
5. *Recent discharge from treatment for alcoholism*: The first 4 years following treatment were found to be associated with a significantly higher risk for suicide, although the reason for this was not clear.
6. *A history of previous suicide attempts*: Approximately one-third of alcoholic suicide victims had attempted suicide at some point in the past.

7. *Biological factors*: Factors such as decreased levels of serotonin in the brain are thought to be associated with increased risk for violent behavior, including suicide.

One possible mechanism through which chronic drinking might cause or contribute to depressive disorders is that chronic alcohol use causes an increase in dopamine turnover in the brain and a down regulation in the number of dopamine receptors within the neurons (Heinz et al., 1998). The chronic use of alcohol has also been found to be associated with reduced serotonin turnover, with a 30% reduction in serotonin transporters being found in chronic drinkers by the authors. Low levels of both dopamine and serotonin have been implicated by researchers as causing depression, so that this mechanism might account for how chronic alcohol use contributes to increased levels of depression in heavy drinkers.

Alcohol Withdrawal for the Chronic Alcoholic

Each year in the United States up to 2 million people experience symptoms of the alcohol withdrawal syndrome, of which only 10% to 20% are hospitalized (Bayard, McIntyre, Hill, & Woodside, 2004). In most cases the symptoms of such alcohol withdrawal usually subside quickly without the need for medical intervention and they might not even be attributed by the individual to the use of alcohol. But the alcohol withdrawal syndrome (AWS) is potentially life threatening, and even with the best of medical care there is a significant risk of death from the AWS.

For reasons that are not known, chronic drinkers vary in terms of their risk for developing AWS (Saitz, 1998). However, there is evidence to suggest that repeated cycles of alcohol dependence and withdrawal might contribute to a pattern in which the AWS becomes progressively worse each time for the individual (Kelly & Saucier, 2004; Littleton, 2001). In 90% of the cases the symptoms of AWS develop within 4–12 hours after the individual's last drink, although in some cases the AWS develops simply because a chronic drinker significantly reduced his or her level of drinking (McKay, Koranda, & Axen, 2004; Saitz, 1998). In a small percentage of cases AWS symptoms do not appear until 96 hours after the last drink or reduction in alcohol intake (Lehman et al., 1994; Weiss & Mirin, 1988). In extreme cases, the person will not begin to experience the symptoms of AWS until 10 days after the last drink (Slaby, Lieb, & Tancredi, 1981).

The AWS is an acute brain syndrome that might, at first, be mistaken for such conditions as a subdural hematoma, pneumonia, meningitis, or an infection involving the CNS (Saitz, 1998). The severity of AWS depends on the (a) intensity with which that individual used alcohol, (b) the duration of time during which the individual drank, and (c) the individual's state of health. Symptoms of AWS include agitation, anxiety, tremor, diarrhea, hyperactivity, exaggerated reflexes, insomnia, vivid dreams, nausea, vomiting, loss of appitite, restlessness, sweating, tachycardia, headache, and vertigo (Kelly & Saucier, 2004; Lehman et al., 1994; Saitz, 1998).

One factor that might exacerbate the AWS is concurrent nicotine withdrawal (Littleton, 2001). The withdrawal process from nicotine is discussed in Chapter 19. Note, however, that concurrent withdrawal from nicotine *and* alcohol may result in a more intense AWS than withdrawal from alcohol alone (Littleton, 2001). For this reason, the author recommends that the patient's nicotine addiction be controlled through the use of transdermal nicotine patches until after he or she has completed the withdrawal process from alcohol.

In the hospital setting, the Clinical Institute Withdrawal Assessment for Alcohol Scale-Revised (CIWA-Ar) is *the* most common assessment tool used to determine the severity of the AWS (Kelly & Saucier, 2004; McKay et al., 2004). This noncopyrighted tool measures 15 symptoms of alcohol withdrawal such as anxiety, nausea, and visual hallucinations and it takes 3–5 minutes to administer. It has a maximum score of 67 points, with each symptom being weighted in terms of severity. A score of 0–4 points indicates minimal withdrawal discomfort, whereas a score of 5–12 points indicates mild alcohol withdrawal. Patients who earn a score of 13–19 points on the CISA-Ar are likely to be in moderately severe alcohol withdrawal, whereas 20 + points is indicative of severe alcohol withdrawal. The CISA-Ar might be repeatedly administered over time to provide a baseline measure of the patient's recovery from the acute effects of alcohol intoxication.

Patients who earn a score of 0–4 points on the CISA-Ar may experience few symptoms of alcohol withdrawal, and depending on their alcohol use history they might either remain at this level of withdrawal discomfort or progress to more severe levels of alcohol withdrawal. In more advanced cases, the above symptoms may become more intense over the first 6 to 24 hours following the individual's last use of alcohol. The patient may also begin to experience *alcoholic hallucinosis*. Alcoholic hallucinosis is seen in up to 10% of patients experiencing the AWS, and usually begins 1–2 days after the individual's last drink. In rare cases alcoholic hallucinosis may develop after drinkers cut back on their alcohol intake (Olmedo & Hoffman, 2000). The hallucinations may be visual, tactile, or auditory, and they occur when the patient is conscious (Kelly & Saucier, 2004).

The exact mechanism that causes alcoholic hallucinosis is not understood at this time, but it is known that in 10% to 20% of the cases, the individual enters a chronic psychotic stage (Soyka, 2000). Alcoholic hallucinosis can be quite frightening and may prompt the person experiencing it to attempt suicide or become violent in an attempt to escape from the hallucinations (Soyka, 2000).

In extreme cases of alcohol withdrawal, these symptoms will continue to become more intense over the next 24 to 48 hours, and by the 3rd day following the last drink the patient will start to experience fever, incontinence, and/or tremors in addition to the above noted symptoms. Approximately 10% to 16% of heavy drinkers will experience a seizure as part of the withdrawal syndrome (Berger, 2000; D'Onofrio, Rathlev, Ulrich, Fish, & Freedland, 1999; McRae, Brady, & Sonne, 2001). In 90% of such cases, the first seizure takes place within 48 hours after the last drink, although in 2% to 3% of the cases the seizure might occur as late as 5 to 20 days after the last drink (Renner, 2004; Trevisan, Boutros, Petrakis, & Krystal, 1998). Approximately 60% of adults who experience alcohol withdrawal seizures will have multiple seizures (D'Onofrio et al., 1999). Alcohol withdrawal seizures are seen in individuals who both do and do not experience alcoholic hallucinosis.

The most severe form of withdrawal, the *delirium tremens* (DTs), develop in 1% (McRae et al., 2001) to 10% (Weiss & Mirin, 1988) of chronic drinkers. Once the DTs develop, the condition is extremely difficult to control (Palmstierna, 2001). Some of the medical and behavioral symptoms of the DTs include delirium, hallucinations, delusional beliefs that one is being followed, fever, and tachycardia (Lieveld & Aruna,

1991). During the period the individual is going through the DTs she or he is vulnerable to the development of rhabdomyolsis[12] as a result of alcohol-induced muscle damage (Richards, 2000; Sauret, Marinides, & Wang, 2002).

Drawing upon the experiences of 334 patients in Stockholm, Palmstierna (2001) identified five symptoms that seemed to identify patients at risk for the development of the DTs: (a) concurrent infections such as pneumonia, (b) tachycardia, (c) signs of autonomic nervous system overactivity in spite of an alcohol concentration at or above 1 gram per liter of body fluid, (d) previous epileptic seizure, and (e) a history of a previous delirous episode. The author suggested that such patients receive aggressive treatment with benzodiazepines to minimize the risk that the full DTs will develop.

In some cases of DTs, the individual will experience a disruption of normal fluid levels in the brain (Trabert, Caspari, Bernhard, & Biro, 1992). This results when the mechanism in the drinker's body that regulates normal fluid levels is disrupted by the alcohol withdrawal process. The individual might become dehydrated or may retain *too much* fluid in the body. During alcohol withdrawal, some individuals become hypersensitive to the antidiuretic hormone (ADH). This hormone is normally secreted by the body to slow the rate of fluid loss through the kidneys when the person is somewhat dehydrated. This excess fluid may contribute to the damage that the alcohol has caused to the brain, possibly by bringing about a state of cerebral edema (Trabert et al., 1992). Researchers have found that only patients going through the DTs have the combination of higher levels of ADH and low body fluid levels. This finding suggests that a body fluid dysregulation process might somehow be involved in the development of the DTs (Trabert et al., 1992).

In the past, 5% to 25% of people who developed the DTs died from exhaustion (McKay et al., 2004; Schuckit, 2000). However, improved medical care has decreased the mortality from DTs to about 1% (Enoch & Goldman, 2002) to 5% (Kelly & Saucier, 2004; Weaver, Jarvis, & Schnoll, 1999; Yost, 1996). The main causes of death for people going through the DTs include sepsis, cardiac and/or respiratory arrest, cardiac

arrhythmias, hyperthermia, and cardiac and/or circulatory collapse (Kelly & Saucier, 2004; Lieveld & Aruna, 1991). These individuals are also a high risk group for suicide as they struggle to come to terms with the emotional pain and terror associated with this condition (Hirschfeld & Davidson, 1988).

Although a number of different chemicals have been suggested as being of value in controlling the symptoms of alcohol withdrawal, the benzodiazepines, especially chlordiazepoxide or diazepam, are considered the drugs of choice for treating the AWS (McKay et al., 2004). The use of pharmaceutical agents to control the alcohol withdrawal symptoms will be discussed in more detail in Chapter 32.

Other Complications From Chronic Alcohol Use

Either directly, or indirectly, alcohol contributes to more than half of the 500,000 head injuries that occur each year in the United States (Ashe & Mason, 2001). For example, it is not uncommon for the intoxicated individual to fall and strike his or her head on coffee tables, magazine stands, or whatever happens to be in the way. Unfortunately, the chronic use of alcohol contributes to the development of three different bone disorders (Griffiths, Parantainen, & Olson, 1994): (a) *osteoporosis* (loss of bone mass), (b) *osteomalacia*, (a condition in which new bone tissue fails to absorb minerals appropriately), and (c) *secondary hyperparathyroidism*.[13] Even limited regular alcohol use can double the speed at which the body excretes calcium (Jersild, 2001). These bone disorders in turn contribute to the higher than expected level of injury and death seen when alcoholics fall or when they are involved in automobile accidents.

Alcohol is also a factor in traumatic brain injury. Chronic alcohol use is thought to be the cause of 40% to 50% of deaths in motor vehicle accidents, up to 67% of home injuries, and 3%–5% of cancer related deaths (Miller, 1999). Chronic alcohol users are 10 times more likely to develop cancer than nondrinkers (Schuckit, 1998), and 4% of all cases of cancer in men and 1% of all cases of cancer in women are thought to be alcohol related (Ordorica & Nace, 1998). Approximately 5% of the total deaths that occur each year in

---

[12]See Glossary.

[13]See Glossary.

the United States are thought to be alcohol related (Miller, 1999). In addition, women who drink while pregnant run the risk of causing alcohol-induced birth defects, a condition known as the *fetal alcohol syndrome* (to be discussed later in Chapter 20).

Chronic alcoholism has been associated with a premature aging syndrome, in which the individual appears much older than he or she actually is (Brandt & Butters, 1986). In many cases, the overall physical and intellectual condition of the individual corresponds to that of a person between 15 and 20 years older than the person's chronological age. One such person, a man in his 50s, was told by his physician that he was in good health . . . for a man about to turn 70!

Admittedly, not every alcohol-dependent person will suffer from every consequence reviewed in this chapter. Some chronic alcohol users will never have stomach problems, for example, but they may suffer from advanced heart disease as a result of their drinking. However, Schuckit (1995a) noted that in one research study, 93% of alcohol-dependent individuals admitted to treatment had at least one important medical problem in addition to their alcohol use problem.

Research has demonstrated that in most cases, the first alcohol-related problems are experienced when drinkers are in their late 20s or early 30s. The team of Schuckit, Smith, Anthenelli, and Irwin (1993) outlined a progressive course for alcoholism, based on their study of 636 male alcoholics. The authors admitted that their subjects experienced wide differences in the specific problems caused by their drinking, but as a group the alcoholics began to experience severe alcohol-related problems in their late 20s. By their mid-30s, the individual was likely to have recognized that he had a drinking problem and to begin to experience more severe problems as a result of his continued drinking. However, as the authors pointed out, there is a wide variation in this pattern, and some subgroups of alcoholics might fail to follow it.

Summary

This chapter explored the many facets of alcoholism. The scope of alcohol abuse/addiction in this country was reviewed, as was the fact that alcoholism accounts for approximately 85% of the drug-addiction problem in the United States. In this chapter, the different forms of tolerance and the ways that the chronic use of alcohol can affect the body were discussed. The impact of chronic alcohol use on the central nervous system, the cardiopulmonary system, the digestive system, and the skeletal bone structure was reviewed. In addition, the relationship between chronic alcohol use and physical injuries and how chronic alcohol use can lead to premature death and premature aging were examined. Finally, the process of alcohol withdrawal for the alcohol-dependent person was discussed.

Abuse and Addiction to the Barbiturates and Barbiturate-like Drugs

Introduction

The anxiety disorders are, collectively, the most common form of mental illness found in the United States (Blair & Ramones, 1996). At any point in time, between 7% and 23% of the general population is thought to be suffering from anxiety in one form or another (Baughan, 1995), and over the course of their lives, approximately one-third of all adults will experience at least transient periods of anxiety intense enough to interfere with their daily lives (Spiegel, 1996). Further, at least 35% of the adults in the United States will experience at least transitory insomnia (Brower, Aldrich, Robinson, Zucker, & Greden, 2001; Lacks & Morin, 1992).

For thousands of years, alcohol was the only agent that could reduce people's anxiety level or help them fall asleep. However, as was discussed in the last chapter, the effectiveness of alcohol as an antianxiety[1] agent[2] is quite limited. Thus, for many hundreds of years, there has been a very real demand for effective antianxiety or hypnotic[3] medications. In this chapter, we will review the various medications that were used to control anxiety or promote sleep prior to the introduction of the benzodiazepines in the early 1960s. In the next chapter, we will focus on the benzodiazepine family of drugs and on medications that have been introduced since the benzodiazepines first appeared.

[1]Occasionally, mental health professionals will use the term *anxiolytic* rather than antianxiety. For the purpose of this section, however, the term *antianxiety* will be utilized.

[2]Such medications are often called sedatives.

[3]See Glossary.

Early Pharmacological Therapy of Anxiety Disorders and Insomnia

In the year 1870[4] *chloral hydrate* was introduced as a hypnotic. It was found that chloral hydrate was rapidly absorbed from the digestive tract, and that an oral dose of 1–2 grams would cause the typical person to fall asleep in less than an hour. The effects of chloral hydrate were found to usually last 8 to 11 hours, making it appear to be ideal for use as a hypnotic. However, physicians quickly discovered that chloral hydrate had several major drawbacks, not the least of which was that it was quite irritating to the stomach lining and the chronic use could result in significant damage to this lining. In addition, it was soon discovered that chloral hydrate is quite addictive and that at high doses it could exacerbate preexisting cardiac problems in patients with heart disease (Pagliaro & Pagliaro, 1998). Further, as physicians became familiar with its pharmacological properties, they discovered that chloral hydrate had a narrow therapeutic window of perhaps 1:2 or 1:3 (Brown & Stoudemire, 1998), making it quite toxic to the user. Finally, after it had been in use for awhile, physicians discovered that withdrawal from chloral hydrate after extended periods of use could result in life-threatening withdrawal seizures.

Technically, chloral hydrate is a *prodrug*.[5] After ingestion, it is rapidly biotransformed into *trichloroethanol*, which is the metabolite of chloral hydrate that causes the drug to be effective as a hypnotic. Surprisingly, in

[4]Pagliaro and Pagliaro (1998) said that this happened in 1869, not 1870.

[5]See Glossary.

spite of its known dangers, chloral hydrate continues to have a limited role in modern medicine. Its relatively short biological half-life makes it of value in treating some elderly patients who suffer from insomnia. Thus, even with all of the newer medications available to physicians, there are still patients who will receive chloral hydrate to help them sleep.

Paraldehyde was isolated in 1829 and first used as a hypnotic in 1882. As a hypnotic, paraldehyde is quite effective. It produces little respiratory or cardiac depression, making it a relatively safe drug to use with patients who have some forms of pulmonary or cardiac disease. However, it tends to have a very noxious taste, and users develop a strong odor on their breath after use. Paraldehyde is quite irritating to the mucous membranes of the mouth and throat and must be diluted in a liquid before use.

The half-life of paraldehyde ranges from 3.4 to 9.8 hours, and about 70% to 80% of a single dose is biotransformed by the liver prior to excretion. Between 11% and 28% of a single dose leaves the body unchanged, usually by being exhaled, causing the characteristic odor on the user's breath. Paraldehyde has an abuse/addiction potential similar to that of alcohol, and intoxication on paraldehyde resembles alcohol-induced intoxication. After the barbiturates were introduced, paraldehyde gradually fell into disfavor, and at the start of the 21st century it has virtually disappeared (Doble, Martin, & Nutt, 2004).

The *bromide salts* were first used for the treatment of insomnia in the mid-1800s. They were available without a prescription and were used well into the 20th century. Bromides are indeed capable of causing the user to fall asleep, but it was soon discovered that they tend to accumulate in the chronic user's body, causing a drug-induced depression after as little as just a few days continuous use. The bromide salts have been totally replaced by newer drugs, such as the barbiturates and the benzodiazepines.

Despite superficial differences in their chemical structure, the compounds discussed above are all central nervous system (CNS) depressants. The relative potency of the barbiturate-like drugs are reviewed in Table 9.1. These compounds share many common characteristics, in spite of the superficial differences

TABLE 9.1   Dosage Equivalency for Barbiturate-like Drugs

Generic name of drug of abuse	Dose equivalent to 30 mg of phenobarbital
Chloral hydrate	500 mg
Ethchlorvynol	350 mg
Meprobamate	400 mg
Methyprylon	300 mg
Glutethimide	250 mg

in their chemical structure, such as the ability to *potentiate* the effects of other CNS depressants. Another characteristic that these CNS depressants share is their significant potential for abuse. Still, in spite of these shortcomings, these agents were the treatment of choice for anxiety and insomnia until the barbiturates were introduced.

History and Current Medical Uses of the Barbiturates

Late in the 19th century, chemists discovered the barbiturates. Experimentation quickly revealed that depending upon the dose, the barbiturates were able to act either as a sedative or, at a higher dosage level, as a hypnotic. In addition, it was discovered that the barbiturates were safer and less noxious than the bromides, chloral hydrate, or paraldehyde (Greenberg, 1993). It was in 1903 that the first barbiturate—Veronal—was introduced for human use, and the barbiturates marketed as over-the-counter medications (Nelson, 2000; Peluso & Peluso, 1988). Since the time of their introduction, some 2,500 different barbiturates have been isolated by chemists. Most of these barbiturates were never marketed and they have remained only laboratory curiosities. Perhaps 50 barbiturates were marketed at one point or another in the United States, of which 20 are still in use (Charney, Mihis, & Harris, 2001; Nishino, Mignot & Dement, 1995). The relative potencies of the most common barbiturates are reviewed in Table 9.2. In the United States, the barbiturates have been classified as Category II

TABLE 9.2 Normal Dosage Levels of Commonly
Used Barbiturates

Barbiturate	Sedative dose*	Hypnotic dose**
Amobarbital	50–150 mg/day	65–200 mg
Aprobarbital	120 mg/day	40–60 mg
Butabarbital	45–120 mg/day	50–100 mg
Mephobarbital	96–400 mg/day	Not used as hypnotic
Pentobarbital	60–80 mg/day	100 mg
Phenobarbital	30–120 mg/day	100–320 mg
Secobarbital	90–200 mg/day	50–200 mg
Talbutal	30–120 mg/day	120 mg

Source: Table based on information provided in Uhde &
Trancer (1995).
*Administered in divided doses.
**Administered as a single dose at bedtime.

controlled substances[6] and are available only by
a physician's prescription. After the introduction of the
benzodiazepines in the 1960s, the barbiturates previously in use gradually fell into disfavor. At this point,
the barbiturates have no role in the routine treatment
of anxiety or insomnia (Uhde & Trancer, 1995).

In spite of the pharmacological revolution that took
place in the latter half of the 20th century, there are
still some areas of medicine where certain barbiturates
remain the pharmaceutical of choice. Some examples
of these specialized uses for a barbiturate include (but
are not limited to) certain surgical procedures and the
control of epilepsy.

As newer drugs have all but replaced the barbiturates in modern medicine, it is surprising to learn
that controversy still rages around the appropriate use
of many of these chemicals. For example, in the last
decade of the 20th century physicians thought that
the barbiturates could be used to control the fluid
pressure within the brain following trauma. Physicians now question the effectiveness of barbiturates
in the control of intracranial hypertension (Lund &
Papadakos, 1995). Another area of controversy

[6]See Appendix 4.

surrounding the barbiturates is the use of one barbiturate to execute criminals by lethal injection (Truog,
Berde, Mitchell, & Brier, 1992). Another equally
controversial use of the barbiturates is in the sedation
of terminally ill cancer patients who are in extreme
pain (Truog et al., 1992). Thus, although the barbiturates have been in use for more than a century, they
remain the agent of choice to treat certain medical
conditions, and controversy surrounds the use of
these pharmaceuticals.

The abuse potential of barbiturates. The barbiturates have a considerable abuse potential. Indeed,
between 1950 and 1970, the barbiturates were, as
a group, second only to alcohol as drugs of abuse
(Reinisch, Sanders, Mortensen, & Rubin, 1995).
Remarkably, the first years of the 21st century have
witnessed a minor resurgence in the popularity of
the barbiturates as drugs of abuse (Doble et al., 2004).
Indicative of this resurgence, 8.9% of the graduating
seniors of the class of 2002 admitted to abusing
barbiturates at least once (Johnston, O'Malley, &
Bachman, 2003a). A number of older people also, usually individuals over the age of 40, became addicted to
the barbiturates when they were younger. For people
of this generation, the barbiturates were the most effective treatment for anxiety and insomnia and many
users became—and remain—addicted (Kaplan,
Sadock, & Grebb, 1994). Finally, a small number of
physicians have turned to the barbiturates as antianxiety and hypnotic agents to avoid the extra paperwork
imposed on benzodiazepine prescriptions. Fortunately, the majority of physicians have not followed
this practice.

Pharmacology of the Barbiturates

Chemically, the barbiturates are remarkably similar.
The only major difference between the various
members of the barbiturate family of drugs is the length
of time it takes the individual's body to absorb, biotransform, and then excrete the specific form of barbiturate
that has been used. One factor that influences the
absorption of barbiturates is the drug's lipid solubility.
The different barbiturates vary in terms of their lipid
solubility, with those forms of barbiturate that are easily
soluble in lipids being rapidly distributed to all blood-
rich tissues such as the brain. Thus, pentobarbital,

which is very lipid soluble, may begin to have an effect in 10 to 15 minutes. In contrast, phenobarbital is poorly lipid soluble and does not begin to have an effect until 60 minutes or longer after the user has ingested the medication.

While neuropharmacologists understand why different forms of barbiturates might have a different duration of effect and speed of action, the exact mechanism by which barbiturates work is similar for these agents. Barbiturates have been found to inhibit the ability of the GABA$_A$ chloride channel to close, thus slowing the rate at which the cell can fire (Doble et al., 2004; Olmedo & Hoffman, 2000). However, the mechanism by which barbiturates accomplish this effect is different from that utilized by the benzodiazepines (Doble et al., 2004).

Barbiturates can be classified on the basis of their *duration of action.*[7] First, there are the *ultrashort*-acting barbiturates. When injected, the effects of the ultrashort-duration barbiturates begin in a matter of seconds and last for less than one-half hour. Examples of such ultrashort-duration barbiturates include Pentothal and Brevital. The ultrashort-duration barbiturates are extremely lipid soluble, pass through the blood-brain barrier quickly, and when injected into a vein have an effect on the brain in just a few seconds. These medications are often utilized in surgical procedures when a rapid onset of effects and a short duration of action are desirable.

Then there are the *short-acting* barbiturates. When injected, the short-acting barbiturates have an effect in a matter of minutes that lasts for 3–4 hours (Zevin & Benowitz, 1998). Nembutal is an example (Sadock & Sadock, 2003). In terms of lipid solubility, the short-acting barbiturates would fall between the ultrashort-acting barbiturates and the next group, the *intermediate-acting* barbiturates. The effects of the intermediate-acting barbiturates begin within an hour when the drug is ingested orally and last 6–8 hours (Zevin & Benowitz, 1998). Included in this group are Amytal (amobarbital) and Butisol (butabarbital) (Schuckit, 2000). Finally, there are the *long-acting*

barbiturates. These are absorbed slowly and their effects last for 6–12 hours (Zevin & Benowitz, 1998). Phenobarbital is perhaps the most commonly encountered drug in this class.

One point of confusion that must be addressed is that the short-acting barbiturates do *not* have extremely short half-lives. As was discussed in Chapter 3, the biological half-life of a drug provides only a *rough* estimate of the time a specific chemical will remain in the body. The shorter-acting barbiturates might have an effect on the user for only a few hours and still have a half-life of 8–12 hours, or even longer. This is because their effects are limited not by the speed at which they are biotransformed by the liver but by the speed with which they are removed from the blood and distributed to the various organs in the body. Significant levels of some shorter-acting barbiturates are stored in different body organs and are still present long after the drug has stopped having its desired effect. The barbiturate molecules stored in the different body organs will slowly be released back into the general circulation, possibly causing a barbiturate hangover (Uhde & Trancer, 1995).

Overall, the chemical structures of the various forms of barbiturates are quite similar, and once in the user's body, these drugs all tend to have similar effects. There are few significant differences in relative potency between various barbiturates. As a general rule, the shorter-term barbiturates are almost fully biotransformed by the liver before being excreted from the body (Nishino et al., 1995). In contrast, a significant proportion of the longer-term barbiturates are eliminated from the body essentially unchanged. Thus, for phenobarbital, which may have a half-life of 2–6 days, between 25% and 50% of the drug will be excreted by the kidneys virtually unchanged. Another barbiturate, methohexital, has a half-life of only 3–6 hours, and virtually all of it is biotransformed by the liver before it is excreted from the body (American Society of Health-System Pharmacists, 2002). An additional difference between the different barbiturates is the degree to which the drug molecules become protein bound. As a general rule, the longer the drug's half-life, the stronger the degree of protein binding for that form of barbiturate.

When used on an outpatient basis, the barbiturates are typically administered orally. On occasion,

[7]Other researchers might use classification systems different from the one that is used in this text. For example, some researchers use the chemical structure of the different forms of barbiturate as the defining criteria for classification. This text will follow the classification system suggested by Zevin & Benowitz (1998).

especially when used in a medical setting, an ultrashort-acting barbiturate might be administered intravenously, as when it is used as an anesthetic in surgery or for seizure control. On rare occasions, the barbiturates are administered rectally through suppositories. However, the typical patient will take barbiturates in oral form. When taken orally, the barbiturate molecule is rapidly and completely absorbed from the small intestine (Julien, 1992; Levin, 2002; Winchester, 1990). Once it reaches the blood, the barbiturate will be distributed throughout the body, but the concentrations will be highest in the liver and the brain (American Society of Health-System Pharmacists, 2002). The barbiturates are all lipid soluble, but they vary in their ability to form bonds with blood lipids. As a general rule, the more lipid soluble a barbiturate is, the more quickly it will pass through the blood-brain barrier (Levin, 2002).

The behavioral effects of the barbiturates are very similar to those of alcohol (Levin, 2002). Once the barbiturate reaches the bloodstream, it is distributed throughout the body just like alcohol, depressing not only the brain activity but also to a lesser degree the activity of the muscle tissues, the heart, and respiration (Matuschka, 1985). Although high concentrations of barbiturates are quickly achieved in the brain, the drug is rapidly redistributed to other body organs (Levin, 2002). The speed at which this redistribution process is carried out varies from one barbiturate to another, thus different barbiturates have different therapeutic half-lives. Following the redistribution process the barbiturate is metabolized by the liver and eventually excreted by the kidneys.

It is within the central nervous system (CNS) that the barbiturates have their strongest effect (Rall, 1990). In the brain, the barbiturates are thought to simulate the effects of the neurotransmitter gamma aminobutyric acid (GABA) (Carvey, 1998; Hobbs, Rall, & Verdoorn, 1995). At the same time, the barbiturates are thought to block the effects of the neurotransmitter *glutamate*. GABA is thought to be the most important "inhibitory" neurotransmitter in the brain, whereas glutamate functions as a stimulating neurotransmitter (Bohn, 1993; Nutt, 1996; Tabakoff & Hoffman, 1992). Within the

neuron, barbiturates reduce the frequency at which one of the GABA receptor sites, known as the $GABA_A$ site, is activated. At the same time they increase the time that the $GABA_A$ site remains activated, even in the absence of GABA itself (Carvey, 1998). This action reduces the electrochemical potential of the cell, reducing the frequency with which that neuron can fire (Cooper, Bloom, & Roth, 1996).

At the regional level within the brain, the barbiturates have their greatest impact on the cortex and the reticula activating system (RAS) (which is responsible for awareness) as well as the medulla oblongata (which controls respiration) (American Society of Health-System Pharmacists, 2002). At low dosage levels, the barbiturates will reduce the function of the nerve cells in these regions of the brain, bringing on a state of relaxation, and at slightly higher doses, a drug-induced sleep. At extremely high dosage levels, the barbiturates will interfere with the normal function of the neurons of the central nervous system to such a degree that death is possble.

The therapeutic dose of any barbiturate is very close to the lethal dose for that compound, and history has shown us that barbiturate-induced death is not uncommon. Some barbiturates have a therapeutic dosage to lethal dosage level ratio of only 1:3, reflecting the narrow therapeutic window of these agents. In the past, when barbiturate use was more common, a pattern of 118 deaths per one million prescriptions was noted for them (Drummer & Odell, 2001). This low safety margin and the significantly higher safety margin offered by the benzodiazepines is one reason the barbiturates have for the most part been replaced by newer medications in the treatment of anxiety and for inducing sleep.

Subjective Effects of the Barbiturates at Normal Dosage Levels

At low doses, the barbiturates reduce feelings of anxiety or possibly bring on a sense of euphoria. Some users also report a feeling of sedation or fatigue, possibly to the point of drowsiness, and a decrease in motor activity. This results in an increase in the individual's reaction time, and he or she might have trouble coordinating muscle movements, almost as if intoxicated by alcohol (Peluso & Peluso, 1988; "Sleeping Pills and Antianxiety Drugs," 1998). This is to be expected, as both alcohol and the barbiturates affect the cortex of the brain through a similar pharmacological mechanism. The disinhibition effects of the barbiturates, like alcohol, may cause a state of "paradoxical" excitement or possibly even a paradoxical rage reaction. Patients who have received barbiturates for medical reasons have reported unpleasant side effects such as nausea, dizziness, and a feeling of mental slowness. Anxious patients report that their anxiety is no longer as intense, whereas patients who are unable to sleep report that they are able to slip into a state of drug-induced sleep quickly.

Complications of the Barbiturates at Normal Dosage Levels

For almost 60 years, the barbiturates were the treatment of choice for insomnia. As they were so extensively prescribed to help people sleep, it is surprising to learn that tolerance rapidly develops to their hypnotic effects. Indeed, research suggests that they are not effective as hypnotics after just a few days of regular use (Drummer & Odell, 2001; Rall, 1990). In spite of their traditional use as a treatment for insomnia, the barbiturate-induced sleep is not the same as normal sleep. The barbiturates suppress a portion of the sleep cycle known as the rapid eye movement (REM) state of sleep (Peluso & Peluso, 1988). Scientists who study sleep believe that the individual needs to experience REM sleep for emotional well-being. To show the importance of REM sleep, about one-quarter of a young adult's total sleep time is normally spent in REM sleep (Kaplan et al., 1994). Barbiturate-assisted sleep results in a reduction in the total amount of time the individual spends in REM sleep (Rall, 1990). Thus, through the interference of the normal sleep pattern, barbiturate-induced sleep may impact the emotional and physical health of the individual.

After a period of continuous use, the user will experience "REM rebound" when he or she discontinues a barbiturate. In this condition, the person will dream more intensely and more vividly for a period of time as the body tries to catch up on lost REM sleep time. These dreams have been described by individuals as nightmares that were strong enough to tempt the individual to return to the use of drugs to get a "good night's sleep again." This rebound effect might last for 1 to 3 weeks, although in rare cases it has been known to last for up to 2 months (Tyrer, 1993).

Barbiturates can cause a drug-induced hangover the day after the person used the drug (Shannon, Wilson, & Stang, 1995). Subjectively, the individual who is going through a barbiturate hangover simply feels that he or she is "unable to get going" the next day. This is because barbiturates often require an extended period of time for the body to completely biotransform and excrete the drug. As was discussed in Chapter 3, in general, it takes five half-life periods to completely eliminate a single dose of a chemical from the blood. Because many of the barbiturates have extended biological half-life periods, some small amounts of a barbiturate might remain in the person's bloodstream for hours, or even days, after just a single dose. In some cases, the effects of the barbiturates on judgment, motor skills, and behavior might last for several days after a single dose of the drug (Kaminski, 1992).

If the person continually adds to this reservoir of unmetabolized drug by ingesting additional doses of the barbiturate, there is a greater chance of experiencing a drug hangover. However, whether from one single dose or repeated doses, the drug hangover is caused by the same mechanism: traces of unmetabolized barbiturates remaining in the individual's bloodstream for extended periods of time after he or she stops taking the medication. Subjectively, the individual might feel "not quite awake," or "drugged," the next day. The elderly or those with impaired liver function are especially likely to have difficulty with barbiturates. This is because the liver's ability to metabolize many drugs, such as the barbiturates, declines with age. Consequently, Sheridan, Patterson, and Gustafson (1982) advised that older individuals who receive barbiturates be started at one-half the usual adult dosage, and that the dosage level gradually be increased until the patient reaches the point that the medication is having the desired effect.

One side effect of long-term phenobarbital use is a possible loss in intelligence. Researchers have documented a drop of approximately 8 IQ points in patients who have been receiving phenobarbital for control of seizures for extended periods of time, although it is not clear whether this reflects a research artifact, a drug effect, or the cumulative impact of the seizure disorder (Breggin, 1998). It is also not clear whether this observed loss of 8 IQ. points on intelligence testing might be reversed or if a similar reduction in measured IQ develops as a result of the chronic use of other barbiturates. However, this observation does emphasize that the barbiturates are potential CNS agents that will affect the normal function of the brain.

Another consequence of barbiturate use, even when the drug is used in a medical setting, is that this class of pharmaceuticals can cause sexual performance problems such as decreased desire for either partner and both erectile problems and delayed ejaculation for the male (Finger, Lund, & Slagel, 1997). Also, hypersensitivity reactions have been reported with the barbiturates. Such hypersensitivity reactions are most common in (but not limited to) individuals with asthma. Other complications occasionally seen at normal dosage levels include nausea, vomiting, diarrhea, and in some cases, constipation. Some patients have developed skin rashes while receiving barbiturates, although the reason for this is not clear. Finally, some patients who take barbiturates develop an extreme sensitivity to sunlight known as *photosensitivity*. Thus, patients who receive barbiturates must take special precautions to avoid sunburn or even limited exposure to the sun's rays. Because of these problems and because medications are now available that do not share the dangers associated with barbiturate use, they are not considered to have any role in the treatment of anxiety or insomnia (Tyrer, 1993).

Children who suffer from attention deficit-hyperactivity disorder (ADHD) (or what was once called "hyperactivity") who also receive phenobarbital are likely to experience a resurgence of their ADHD symptoms. This effect would seem to reflect the ability of the barbiturates to suppress the action of the reticula activating system (RAS) in the brain. Currently, it is thought that the RAS of children with ADHD is underactive, so any medication that further reduces the effectiveness of this neurological system will contribute to the development of ADHD symptoms.

Drug Interactions Between the Barbiturates and Other Medications

Research has found that the barbiturates are capable of interacting with numerous other chemicals, increasing or decreasing the amount of these drugs in the blood through various mechanisms. Because of the potentiation effect, patients should not use barbiturates if they are using other CNS depressants such as alcohol, narcotic analgesics, phenothiazines, or benzodiazepines, except under a physician's supervision (Barnhill, Ciraulo, Ciraulo, & Greene, 1995). Another class of CNS depressants that might unexpectedly cause a potentiation effect with barbiturates is the antihistamines (Rall, 1990). Because many antihistamines are available without a prescription, there is a very real danger of an unintentional interaction between these two types of medications.

Patients who are taking barbiturates should not use antidepressants known as monoamine oxidase inhibitors (MAOIs, or MAO inhibitors) as the MAOI may inhibit the biotransformation of the barbiturates (Ciraulo, Creelman, Shader, & O'Sullivan, 1995). Patients using barbiturates should not take the antibiotic doxycycline except under a physician's supervision. The barbiturates will reduce the effectiveness of this antibiotic, which may have serious consequences for the patient (Meyers, 1992). If the patient is using barbiturates and tricyclic antidepressants concurrently, the barbiturate will cause the blood plasma levels of the tricyclic antidepressant to drop by as much as 60% (Barnhill et al., 1995). The barbiturates in such cases increase the speed with which the antidepressants are metabolized by activation of the liver's microsomal enzymes.

This is the same process through which the barbiturates will speed up the metabolism of many oral contraceptives, corticosteroids, and the antibiotic Flagyl (metronidazole) (Kaminski, 1992). Thus, when used concurrently, barbiturates will reduce the effectiveness of these medications, according to the author. Women who are taking both oral contraceptives and barbiturates should be aware of the potential for barbiturates to reduce the effectiveness of oral contraceptives (Graedon & Graedon, 1995, 1996).

Individuals who are taking the anticoagulant medication warfarin should not use a barbiturate except under a physician's supervision. Barbiturate use can interfere with the normal biotransformation of warfarin, resulting in abnormally low blood levels of this anticoagulant medication (Graedon & Graedon, 1995). Further, if the patient should stop taking barbiturates while on warfarin, it is possible for the individual's warfarin levels to rebound to dangerous levels. Thus, these two medications should not be mixed except under a physician's supervision.

When the barbiturates are biotransformed by the liver, they activate a region of the liver that also is involved in the biotransformation of the asthma drug theophylline (sold under a variety of brand names). Thus, patients who use a barbiturate while taking theophylline might experience abnormally low blood levels of the latter drug, a condition that might result in less than optimal control of the asthma. These two medications should not be used by the same patient at the same time except under a physician's supervision (Graedon & Graedon, 1995). Finally, in one research study, 5 of 7 patients on pentobarbital who smoked marijuana began to hallucinate (Barnhill et al., 1995). This would suggest that individuals who use barbiturates should not risk possible interactions between these medications and marijuana.

As is obvious from this list of potential interactions between barbiturates and other pharmaceuticals, the barbiturates are a family of powerful drugs. As in every case of concurrent chemical use, the individual should always consult a physician or pharmacist before taking different medications simultaneously.

Effects of the Barbiturates at Above-Normal Levels

When used above the normal dosage levels, barbiturates may cause a state of intoxication that is similar to that seen with alcohol intoxication. Patients who are intoxicated by barbiturates will demonstrate such behaviors as slurred speech and unsteady gait without the characteristic smell of alcohol (Jenike, 1991).

Chronic abusers are at risk for the development of bronchitis and/or pneumonia, as these medications interfere with the normal cough reflex. Individuals under the influence of a barbiturate will not test positive for alcohol on blood or urine toxicology tests (unless they also have alcohol in their systems). Specific blood or urine toxicology screens must be carried out to detect barbiturate intoxication if the patient has used these drugs.

Unfortunately, because barbiturates can cause a state of intoxication similar to that induced by alcohol, some barbiturate users will ingest more than the normal dose of the drug. The small "therapeutic window" of the barbiturates gives these drugs a significant overdose potential. The barbiturates cause a dose-dependent reduction in respiration as the increasing drug blood levels interfere with the normal function of the medulla oblongata (the part of the brain that maintains respiration and body temperature). Thus the barbiturates can cause both respiratory depression and hypothermia either when abused at higher than normal doses or when intermixed with other CNS depressants (Pagliaro & Pagliaro, 1998). Other complications of larger-than-normal doses include a progressive loss of reflex activity, and, if the dose is large enough, coma and ultimately, death (Jenike, 1991) (see Figure 9.1).

In past decades, prior to the introduction of the benzodiazepines, the barbiturates accounted for about three-fourths of all drug-related deaths in the United States (Peluso & Peluso, 1988). Even now, intentional or unintentional barbiturate overdoses are not unheard of. Mendelson and Rich (1993) found in their study of successful suicides in the San Diego, California, area that approximately 10% of those who committed suicide with a drug overdose used barbiturates either exclusively or as one of the chemicals that were ingested. Thus, the barbiturates present a danger of either intentional or unintentional overdose. Fortunately, the barbiturates do not directly cause any damage to the central nervous system. If the overdose victim reaches medical support before he or she develops shock or hypoxia, he or she may recover completely from a barbiturate overdose (Sagar, 1991). It is for this reason that *any suspected barbiturate overdose should be treated by a physician immediately.*

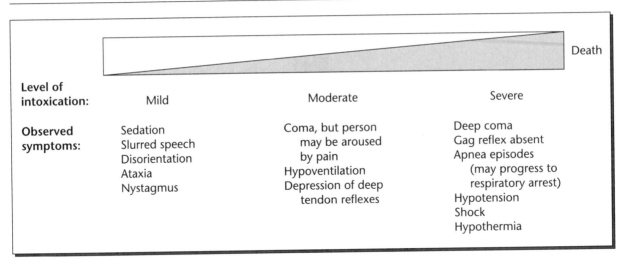

FIGURE 9.1   Symptoms observed at different levels of intoxication.

Neuroadaptation, Tolerance to, and Dependence on the Barbiturates

The primary use for barbiturates today is quite limited as newer, safer, and more effective drugs have been introduced that have replaced them for the most part. Even so, barbiturates continue to have a limited range of medical applications, including the control of epilepsy and the treatment of some forms of severe head injury (Julien, 1992).

Even when barbiturates are used in a medical setting, one unfortunate characteristic of them is that with regular use, neuroadaptation to many of their effects will develop quite rapidly. The process of barbiturate-induced neuroadaptation is not uniform, however. For example, when barbiturates are used for the control of seizures, tolerance may not be a significant problem. A patient who is taking phenobarbital for the control of seizures will eventually become somewhat tolerant to the sedative effect of the medication, but she or he will not develop a significant tolerance to the anticonvulsant effect of the phenobarbital. But if the patient were to take a barbiturate for its *sedating or hypnotic* effects, over time and with chronic use she or he would become less responsive to this drug-induced effect.

Patients have been known to try to overcome the process of neuroadaptation to the barbiturates by increasing their dosage of the drug without consulting their physician. Unfortunately, this attempt at self-medication has resulted in a large number of unintentional barbiturate overdoses, some of which have been fatal. This is because of a marked difference between the barbiturates and the narcotic family of drugs: While the individual taking barbiturates might experience some degree of neuroadaptation and become less responsive to the original dose, there is no concomitant increase in the lethal dose (Jenike, 1991).

Many barbiturate abusers report that the chemical can bring about a drug-induced feeling of euphoria. But as the user becomes tolerant of the euphoric effects of barbiturates following a period of chronic use, she or he will experience less and less euphoria from the drug. In such cases, it is not uncommon for the abuser to increase the dose in order to maintain the drug-induced euphoria. Unfortunately, as stated in the last paragraph, the lethal dose of barbiturates remains relatively stable in spite of the user's growing tolerance or neuroadaptation to the drug. Thus, as the barbiturate abuser increases the daily dosage level to continue to experience the drug-induced euphoria, she or he will come closer and closer to the lethal dose.

In addition to the phenomenon of tolerance to the barbiturate family of drugs, *cross tolerance* is also possible between barbiturates and similar chemical agents. With cross tolerance, once people have become tolerant of one family of chemicals, they will also become tolerant of the effects of other, similar drugs. Cross tolerance between alcohol and the barbiturates is common, as is some degree of cross tolerance between the barbiturates and the opiates, and barbiturates and the hallucinogen PCP (Kaplan et al., 1994).

Historically, the United States went through a wave of barbiturate abuse and addiction in the 1950s. Thus, physicians have long been aware that *once the person is addicted, withdrawal from barbiturates is potentially life threatening and should be attempted only under the supervision of a physician* (Jenike, 1991). The barbiturates should never be abruptly withdrawn, as to do so might bring about an organic brain syndrome that could include such symptoms as confusion, seizures, possible brain damage, and even death. Approximately 80% of barbiturate addicts who abruptly discontinue the drug will experience withdrawal seizures, according to the author.

Unfortunately, there is no set formula to estimate the danger period for barbiturate withdrawal problems. Indeed, the exact period during withdrawal when the barbiturate addict is most at risk for such problems as seizures depends on the specific barbiturate being abused (Jenike, 1991). As a general rule, however, the longer-lasting forms of barbiturates tend to have longer withdrawal periods. When an individual abruptly stops taking a short-acting to intermediate-acting barbiturate, one may normally expect withdrawal seizures to begin on the second or third day. Barbiturate-withdrawal seizures are rare after the 12th day following cessation of the drug. When the individual was abusing one of the longer-acting barbiturates, hs or she might not have a withdrawal seizure until as late as the 7th day after the last dose of the drug (Tyrer, 1993).

The person who is physically dependent on barbiturates will experience a number of symptoms as a result of the withdrawal process. Virtually every barbiturate-dependent patient will experience a feeling of apprehension, which will last for the first 3–14 days of withdrawal (Shader, Greenblatt, & Ciraulo,

1994). Other symptoms that the patient will experience during withdrawal include muscle weakness, tremors, anorexia, muscle twitches, and a possible state of delirium, according to the authors. All of these symptoms will pass after 3–14 days, depending on the individual. Physicians are able to utilize many other medications to minimize these withdrawal symptoms; however, the patient should be warned that there is no such thing as a symptom-free withdrawal.

Barbiturate-like Drugs

Because of the many adverse side effects of the barbiturates, pharmaceutical companies have long searched for substitutes that might be effective yet safe to use. During the 1950s, a number of new drugs were introduced to treat anxiety and insomnia in place of the barbiturates. These drugs included Miltown (meprobamate), Quaalude and Sopor (both brand names of methaqualone), Doriden (glutethimide), Placidyl (ethchlorvynol), and Noludar (methyprylon).

Although these drugs were thought to be nonaddicting when they were first introduced, research has shown that barbiturate-like drugs have an abuse potential very similar to that of barbiturates. This should not be surprising, as the chemical structures of some of the barbiturate-like drugs such as glutethimide and methyprylon are very similar to that of the barbiturates themselves (Julien, 1992). Like the barbiturates, glutethimide and methyprylon are metabolized mainly in the liver.

Both Placidyl (ethchlorvynol) and Doriden (glutethimide) are considered to be especially dangerous, and neither drug should be used except in rare, special circumstances (Schuckit, 2000). The prolonged use of ethchlorvynol may result in a drug-induced loss of vision known as *amblyopia*. Fortunately, this drug-induced amblyopia is not permanent but will gradually clear when the drug is discontinued (Michelson, Carroll, McLane, & Robin, 1988). Since its introduction, the drug glutethimide has become "notorious for its high mortality associated with overdose" (Sagar, 1991, p. 304). This overdose potential is a result of the drug's narrow therapeutic range. The lethal dose of glutethimide is only 10 grams, a dose only slightly above the normal dosage level (Sagar, 1991).

Meprobamate was a popular sedative in the 1950s, when it was sold under at least 32 different brand names, including Miltown or Equanil (Lingeman, 1974). However, it is considered obsolete by current standards (Rosenthal, 1992). Surprisingly, this medication is still quite popular in older patients, and older physicians often continue to prescribe it. An over-the-counter prodrug Soma (carisoprodol), which is sold in many states, is biotransformed into meprobamate after being ingested, and there have been reports of physical dependence on it just as there were on meprobamate in the 1950s and 1960s (Gitlow, 2001).

Fortunately, although meprobamate is quite addictive, it has generally not been used since the early 1970s. But some older patients have been using this medication continuously since that period, and quite a few remain addicted to it as a result of their initial prescriptions for the drug dating from the 1960s and 1970s (Rosenthal, 1992). Also, in spite of its reputation and history, meprobamate still has a minor role in medicine, especially for patients who are unable to take benzodiazepines (Cole & Yonkers, 1995). The peak blood levels of meprobamate following an oral dose are seen in 1–3 hours, and the half-life is 6–17 hours following a single dose. The chronic use of meprobamate may result in the half-life being extended to 24–48 hours (Cole & Yonkers, 1995). The LD50 of meprobamate is estimated to be about 28,000 mg. However, some deaths have been noted following overdoses of 12,000 mg, according to the authors. Physical dependence to this drug is common when patients take 3,200 mg/day or more.

Methaqualone was a drug that achieved significant popularity among illicit drug abusers in the late 1960s and early 1970s. It was originally intended as a nonaddicting substitute for the barbiturates in the mid-1960s. Depending on the dosage level being used, physicians prescribed it both as a sedative and a hypnotic (Lingeman, 1974). Illicit drug users quickly discovered that when they resisted the sedative or hypnotic effects of methaqualone, they would experience a sense of euphoria.

Methaqualone is rapidly absorbed from the gastrointestinal tract following an oral dose and the individual begins to feel its effects in 15–20 minutes. The usual dose for methaqualone, when used as a sedative, was 75 mg, and the hypnotic dose was between 150 and 300 mg. Tolerance to the sedating and hypnotic effects of methaqualone developed rapidly, and many abusers gradually increased their daily dosage levels in an attempt to reachieve the initial effect. Some individuals who abused methaqualone were known to use upward of 2,000 mg in a single day (Mirin, Weiss, & Greenfield, 1991), a dosage level that was quite dangerous. Indeed, the lethal dose of methaqualone was estimated to be approximately 8,000 mg for a typical 150-pound user (Lingeman, 1974).

Shortly after it was introduced, reports began to appear suggesting that methaqualone was being abused. It was purported to have aphrodisiac properties (which has never been proven) and to provide a mild sense of euphoria for the user (Mirin et al., 1991). People who have used methaqualone report feelings of euphoria, well-being, and behavioral disinhibition. As with the barbiturates, although tolerance of the drug's effects develop quickly, the lethal dosage of methaqualone remains the same. Death from methaqualone overdose was common, especially when the drug was taken with alcohol. The typical cause of death was heart failure, according to Lingeman (1974).

In the United States, methaqualone was withdrawn from the market in the mid-1980s, although it is still manufactured by pharmaceutical companies in other countries. It is often smuggled into this country or manufactured in illicit laboratories and sold on the street. Thus, the substance-abuse counselor must have a working knowledge of methaqualone and its effects.

Summary

For thousands of years, alcohol was the only chemical that was even marginally effective as an antianxiety or hypnotic agent. Although a number of chemicals with hypnotic action were introduced in the mid-1800s, each was of limited value in the fight against anxiety or insomnia. Then in the early 1900s, the barbiturates were introduced. The barbiturates, which have a mechanism of action very similar to that of alcohol, were found to have an antianxiety and a hypnotic effect. The barbiturates rapidly became popular and were widely used both for the control of anxiety and to help people fall asleep.

However, like alcohol, the barbiturates were found also to have a significant potential for addiction. This resulted in a search for nonaddictive medications that could replace them. In the post–World War II era, a number of synthetic drugs with chemical structures very similar to the barbiturates were introduced, often with the claim that these drugs were nonaddicting. However, they were ultimately found to have an addiction potential similar to that of the barbiturates. Since the introduction of the benzodiazepines (to be discussed in the next chapter), the barbiturates and similar drugs have fallen into disfavor. However, there is evidence to suggest that they might be making a comeback.

Abuse of and Addiction to Benzodiazepines and Similar Agents

Introduction

In 1960, the first of a new class of antianxiety[1] drugs, chlordiazepoxide, was introduced in the United States as a treatment for anxiety symptoms. Chlordiazepoxide is a member of a family of chemicals known as the *benzodiazepines*. Since its introduction, some 3,000 different benzodiazepines have been developed, of which about 50 have been marketed around the world and about 12 are used in the United States (Dupont & Dupont, 1998). Benzodiazepines have been found to be effective in treating a wide range of disorders, such as insomnia, muscle strains, and the control of anxiety symptoms, and seizures. Because they are far safer than the barbiturates, they have become *the* most frequently prescribed psychotropic medications in the world (Gitlow, 2001). Each year, approximately 10% to 20% of the adults in the Western world will use a benzodiazepine at least once (Jenkins & Cone, 1998). Legally, the benzodiazepines are a Category II controlled substance.[2]

The benzodiazepines were initially introduced as nonaddicting substitutes for the barbiturates or barbiturate-like drugs. However, in the time since their introduction, serious questions have been raised about their abuse potential. Indeed, misuse and abuse of benzodiazepines result in hundreds of millions of dollars in unnecessary medical costs each year in the United States (Benzer, 1995). In this chapter, the history of the benzodiazepines, their medical applications, and the problem of abuse/addiction to them and similar agents in the United States will be examined.

Medical Uses of the Benzodiazepines

Although the benzodiazepines were originally introduced as antianxiety agents, and they remain valuable aids to the control of specific anxiety disorders, the selective serotonin reuptake inhibitors (SSRIs) have become the "mainstay of drug treatment for anxiety disorders" (Shear, 2003, p. 28). The benzodiazepines, however, remain the treatment of choice for *acute* anxiety (such as panic attacks or short-term anxiety resulting from a specific stressor) and continue to have a role in the treatment of such conditions as generalized anxiety disorder (GAD).

Unfortunately, many physicians continue to view the benzodiazepines as the best medication to control anxiety in spite of the introduction of newer, safer, medications. Because the mechanism of action of the benzodiazepines is more selective than that of the barbiturates, they are able to reduce anxiety without causing the same degree of sedation and fatigue seen with the barbiturates. The most frequently prescribed benzodiazepines for the control of anxiety are shown in Table 10.1.

In addition to the control of anxiety, some benzodiazepines have been useful in the treatment of other medical problems such as seizure disorders and muscle strains (Ashton, 1994; Shader & Greenblatt, 1993). The benzodiazepine clonazepam (Clonopin),[3] is especially effective in the long-term control of seizures and is occasionally used as an antianxiety agent (Shader & Greenblatt, 1993).

Researchers estimate that 10% of the adults in the United States suffer from chronic insomnia (Report of the Institute of Medicine Committee on the Efficacy and Safety of Halcion, 1999). Some members

---

[1]Some authors use the term *anxioyltic* in place of the term *antianxiety*. For the purposes of this text, the term *antianxiety* will be used.

[2]See Appendix 4.

[3]Some authors spell the name of this medication Klonopin.

TABLE 10.1 Selected Pharmacological Characteristics of Some Benzodiazepines

Generic name	Equivalent dose	Average half-life (hours)
Alprazolam	0.5 mg	6–20
Chlordiazepoxide	25 mg	30–100
Clonazepam	0.25 mg	20–40
Clorazepate	7.5 mg	30–100
Diazepam	5 mg	30–100
Flurazepam	30 mg	50–100
Halazepam	20 mg	30–100
Lorazepam	1 mg	10–20
Oxazepam	15 mg	5–21
Prazepam	10 mg	30–100
Temazepam	30 mg	9.5–12.4
Triazolam	0.25 mg	1.7–3.0

Sources: Based on Hyman (1988) and Reiman (1997).

of the benzodiazepine family of drugs have been found useful as a *short-term* treatment for insomnia, including temazepam (Restoril), triazolam (Halcion), flurazepam (Dalmane), and quazepam (Doral) (Gillin, 1991; Hussar, 1990).

Two different benzodiazepines—alprazolam (Xanax) and adinazolam (Deracyn)—are reportedly of value in the treatment of depression. Although it does not have antidepressant effects, alprazolam is often used to treat the anxiety that frequently accompanies depression and thus would indirectly help the patient to feel better. It is also used to treat panic disorder, although there are rare case reports of alprazolam-induced panic attacks (Bashir & Swartz, 2002).

Unlike the other benzodiazepines, adinazolam (Deracyn) does seem to have a direct antidepressant effect. Researchers believe that adinazolam (Deracyn) works by increasing the sensitivity of certain neurons within the brain to serotonin (Cardoni, 1990). A deficit of or insensitivity to serotonin is thought to be the cause of at least some forms of depression. Thus, by increasing the sensitivity of the neurons of the brain

to serotonin, Deracyn (adinazolam) would seem to have a direct antidepressant effect, which is lacking in most benzodiazepines.

Benzodiazepines and suicide attempts. The possibility of suicide through a drug overdose is a very real concern for the physician, especially when the patient is depressed. Because of their high therapeutic index (discussed in Chapter 6), the benzodiazepines have traditionally held the reputation of being "safe" drugs to use with patients who were potentially suicidal. Unlike the barbiturates (see Chapter 9), the benzodiazepines have a therapeutic index estimated to be above 1:200 (Kaplan & Sadock, 1996) and possibly as high as 1:1,000 (Carvey, 1998). In terms of overdose potential, animal research suggests that the LD_{50} for diazepam is around 720 mg per kilogram of body weight for mice and 1240 mg/kg for rats (*Physicians' Desk Reference*, 2004). The LD_{50} for humans is not known, but these figures do suggest that diazepam is an exceptionally safe drug. However, other benzidoazepines have smaller therapeutic indexes than diazepam. Many physicians recommend the benzodiazepine Serax (oxazepam) for use in cases when the patient is at risk for an overdose because of its greater margin of safety (Buckley, Dawson, Whyte, & O'Connell, 1995).

Note, however, that the benzodiazepine margin of safety is drastically reduced when an individual ingests one or more additional CNS depressants in an attempt to end his or her life. This is because of the synergistic[4] effect that develops when different CNS depressants are intermixed—one reason that *any* known or suspected overdose should be evaluated and treated by medical professionals. If the attending physician suspects that the individual has ingested a benzodiazepine in an attempt to end his or her life, that physician might consider the use of Mazicon (flumazenil) to counteract the effects of the benzodiazepine in the brain. Mazicon occupies the benzodiazepine receptor site without activating that site, thus helping to protect the individual from the effects of a benzodiazepine overdose. Although this medication has provided physicians with a powerful new tool in treating the benzodiazepine overdose, it is effective for only 20 to 45 minutes and will block the effects of benzodiazepines only (Brust, 1998).

[4]See Glossary.

Pharmacology of the Benzodiazepines

The benzodiazepines are very similar in their effects, differing mainly in their duration of action ("Sleeping Pills and Antianxiety Drugs," 1988). Table 10.1 reviews the relative potency and biological half-lives of some of the benzodiazepines currently in use in the United States.

Like many pharmaceuticals, the benzodiazepines can be classified on the basis of their pharmacological characteristics. Tyrer (1993), for example, adopted a classification system based not on the duration of the effects of the benzodiazepines but on the basis of their elimination half-lives (discussed in Chapter 6), separating the benzodiazepines into four groups:[5] (a) *very short half-lives* (4 hours or less), (b) *short half-lives* (4–12 hours), (c) *intermediate half-life* (12–20 hours), and (d) *long half-life* (20 or more hours).

The various benzodiazepines currently in use range from moderately to highly lipid soluble (Ayd, 1994). Lipid solubility is important because the more lipid soluble a chemical is, the faster it is absorbed through the small intestine after being taken orally (Roberts & Tafure, 1990). Also, highly lipid soluble drugs can easily pass through the blood-brain barrier to enter the brain (Ballenger, 1995).

Once in the general circulation, the benzodiazepines are all protein bound. However, there is some degree of variation between the various forms of benzodiazepines as to what percentage of the medication will be protein bound. Diazepam, for example, is more than 99% protein bound (American Psychiatric Association, 1990) whereas 92% to 97% of chlordiazepoxide is protein bound (Ayd, Janicak, Davis, & Preskorn, 1996) and alprazolam is only about 80% protein bound (*Physicians' Desk Reference*, 2004). This variability in protein binding is one factor that influences the duration of effect for each benzodiazepine after a single dose (American Medical Association, 1994).

The benzodiazepines are poorly absorbed from intramuscular or subcutaneous injection sites (American Medical Association, 1994). This characteristic makes it difficult to predict in advance the degree of drug bioavailability when a benzodiazepine is injected. For

[5]To complicate matters, the *distribution half-life* for benzodiazepines is often far different from the *elimination half-life*, or the *therapeutic half-life*. For a discussion of these concepts, see Chapter 3.

this reason these medications are usually administered orally. One exception is when the patient is experiencing uncontrolled seizures. In such cases, intravenous injections of diazepam or a similar benzodiazepine might be used to help control the seizures.

Most benzodiazepines must be biotransformed before elimination can proceed, and in the process of biotransformation some benzodiazepines will produce metabolites that are biologically active. These biologically active metabolites may contribute to the duration of a drug's effects and may require extended periods of time before they are eliminated from the body. Thus, the *duration of effect* of many benzodiazepines is far different from the elimination half-life of the parent compound, a factor that physicians must keep in mind when prescribing these medications (Hobbs, Rall, & Verdoorn, 1995). For example, during the process of biotransformation, the benzodiazepine flurazepam will produce five different metabolites, each of which has a psychoactive effect of its own. Because of normal variation with which the individual's body can biotransform or eliminate flurazepam and its metabolites, this benzodiazepine might continue to have an effect on the user for *as long as 280 hours after a single dose*. Fortunately, the benzodiazepines lorazepam, oxazepam, and temazepam are either eliminated without biotransformation or produce metabolites that have minimal physical effects on the user. As will be discussed later in this chapter, these benzodiazepines are often preferred for older patients, who may experience over-sedation as a result of the long half-lives of some benzodiazepine metabolites.

Although the benzodiazepines are often compared with the barbiturates, they are actually far different from the barbiturates in the way they function in the brain. The barbiturates simulate the action of the neurotransmitter gamma aminobutyric acid (GABA), which is thought to be the most important "inhibitory" neurotransmitter in the brain (Bohn, 1993; Nutt, 1996; Tabakoff & Hoffman, 1992). This causes the barbiturates to nonselectively depress the activity of neurons in the cortex and many other parts of the brain. Subjectively, this effect is interpreted as a reduction in anxiety levels and possibly the ability to fall asleep (although benzodiazepines actually interfere with normal sleep, as discussed below).

In contrast to the barbiturates, the benzodiazepine molecule is thought to bind to one of the GABA receptor sites and also to a chloride channel on the neuron surface, making the cell more sensitive to the GABA that already exists. In support of this theory, in the absence of GABA the benzodiazepines have no apparent effect on the neuron (Charney, Mihis, & Harris, 2001; Hobbs et al., 1995; Pagliaro & Pagliaro, 1998). Neurons that utilize GABA are especially common in the *locus ceruleus* (Cardoni, 1990; Johnson & Lydiard, 1995). Nerve fibers from the locus ceruleus connect with other parts of the brain thought to be involved in fear and panic reactions. Animal research has suggested that stimulation of the locus ceruleus causes behaviors similar to those seen in humans who are having a panic attack (Johnson & Lydiard, 1995). By enhancing the effects of GABA, the benzodiazepines seem to reduce the level of neurological activity in the locus ceruleus, lowering the individual's anxiety level. Unfortunately, this theory does not provide any insight into the ability of the benzodiazepines to help muscle tissue relax or to stop seizures (Hobbs et al., 1995). Thus, there is still a lot to be discovered about how these drugs work.

Surprisingly, there is little information about the long-term effectiveness of these compounds as antianxiety agents (Ayd, 1994). Some researchers believe that the antianxiety effects of the benzodiazepines last about 1–2 months and that these drugs are not useful in treating anxiety continuously over a long period of time (Ashton, 1994; Ayd et al., 1996). One study found that after 4 weeks the subjects who received the medication had fewer panic attacks than did those patients who received the placebo. However, this same research study found that after 8 weeks of continuous use, patients who received Xanax had just as many panic attacks as the patients who received only a placebo, a finding that was not shared with the physicians (Leavitt, 2003; Walker, 1996).

On the other hand, some researchers do believe that the benzodiazepines are an effective agent in the long-term control of anxiety. For example, the *Harvard Medical School Mental Health Letter* ("Sleeping Pills and Antianxiety Drugs," 1988) suggested that while patients might develop some tolerance to the sedative effects of benzodiazepines, they did not become tolerant to the antianxiety effects of these medications. Thus, within the medical community, there is some degree of uncertainty as to the long-term effectiveness of benzodiazepines in the control of anxiety symptoms.

Side Effects of the Benzodiazepines When Used at Normal Dosage Levels

Some degree of sedation is common following the ingestion of a benzodiazepine (Ballenger, 1995); however, *excessive* sedation is uncommon unless the patient ingested a dose that was too large for him or her (Ayd et al., 1996). Advancing age is one factor that may make the individual more susceptible to the phenomenon of benzodiazepine-induced over-sedation (Ashton, 1994; Ayd, 1994). Because of an age-related decline in blood flow to the liver and kidneys, elderly patients often require more time to biotransform and/or excrete many drugs than do younger adults who receive the same medication (Bleidt & Moss, 1989). This contributes to over-sedation or in some cases a state of paradoxical excitement, as the bodies of older patients struggle to adjust to the effects of a benzodiazepine. To illustrate this process, an elderly patient might require *three times as long* to fully biotransform a dose of diazepam or chlordiazepoxide than would a young adult (Cohen, 1989). If a benzodiazepine is required in an older individual, physicians tend to rely on lorazepam or oxazepam (Ashton, 1994; Graedon & Graedon, 1991) because these compounds have a shorter "half-life" and are more easily biotransformed than diazepam and similar benzodiazepines.

Both Deracyn (adinazolam) and Doral (quazepam) are exceptions to the rule that the older patient is more likely to experience excessive sedation than a younger patient. It is not uncommon for patients to experience sedation from adinazolam. As many as *two-thirds* of those who receive this medication might experience some degree of drowsiness, at least until their bodies adapt to the drug's effects (Cardoni, 1990). Further, since the active metabolites of Doral (quazepam) have a half-life of 72 hours or more, a strong possibility exists that the user will experience a drug-induced hangover the next day (Hartmann, 1995).

Drug-induced hangovers are possible with benzodiazepine use, especially with some of the longer-lasting benzodiazepines (Ashton, 1992, 1994). If you will note, the data in Table 10.1 suggest that the *average* half-life of many benzodiazepines can be as long as 100 hours. In some cases, the half-life of some of the longer-acting benzodiazepines might be as much as 280 hours, depending on the user's biochemistry. Further, it usually requires 5 half-life periods before virtually all of a drug is biotransformed/eliminated from the body. If that patient were to take a second or even a third dose of the medication before the first dose were fully biotransformed, he or she would begin to accumulate the unmetabolized medication in body tissues. The unmetabolized medication would continue to have an effect on the individual's function well past the time that he or she thought the drug's effects had ended.

Even a single 10 mg dose of diazepam can result in visual motor disturbances for up to 7 hours after the medication was ingested (Gitlow, 2001), a finding that might account for the observation that younger adults who use a benzodiazepine are at increased risk for motor vehicle accidents (Barbone et al., 1998). Thus, even therapeutic doses of diazepam contribute to prolonged reaction times in users, increasing their risk for motor vehicle accidents by up to 500% (Gitlow, 2001).

Neuroadaptation to Benzodiazepines and Abuse/Addiction to These Agents

Within a few years of the time that the benzodiazepines were introduced, reports of abuse/addiction began to surface. Although these drugs were presented as nonaddicting agents, clinical evidence suggests that patients will experience a *discontinuance syndrome* after using them at recommended dosage levels for just a few months (Smith & Wesson, 2004). This effect occurs because patients experience a process of "neuroadaptation" (Sellers et al., 1993, p. 65) in which the CNS becomes tolerant to the drug's effects. If people using the medication were to suddenly discontinue it, they would experience rebound or "discontinuance" syndrome as their bodies adjusted to its sudden absence. Some researchers believe that this state of pharmacological tolerance to the benzodiazepines is evidence that the patient has become addicted to the medication.

The discontinuance syndrome may develop "within a few weeks, perhaps days" (Miller & Gold, 1991a, p. 28), and there is a great deal of disagreement as to whether this process reflects the patient's growing dependence on benzodiazepines. Some researchers view the rebound or discontinuance symptoms as a natural consequence of benzodiazepine use. For example, Sellers et al. (1993) argued that neuroadaptation "is not sufficient to define drug-taking behavior as dependent" (p. 65). Thus, while the patient might experience a discontinuance syndrome after using a benzodiazepine at recommended doses for an extended period of time, this is seen as a natural process. Advocates of this position note that the body must go through a period of adjustment whenever *any* medication is discontinued.

Researchers disagree as to the percentage of patients who will develop a discontinuance syndrome after using the benzodiazepines for an extended period of time. Ashton (1994) suggested that approximately 35% of patients who take a benzodiazepine continuously for 4 or more weeks will become physically dependent on the medication. These individuals will experience withdrawal symptoms when they stop taking it, according to the author. But in rare cases, pharmacological dependence on the benzodiazepines might develop in just days or weeks (American Psychiatric Association, 1990; Miller & Gold, 1991a). On the other hand, Blair and Ramones (1996) suggested that in most cases in which the benzodiazepines are used at normal dosage levels for less than 4 months, the risk of a patient's becoming dependent is virtually nonexistent. However, the Royal College of Psychiatrists in Great Britain now recommends that the benzodiazepines be used continuously for no longer than 4 weeks (Gitlow, 2001).

If the individual were using (or abusing) a benzodiazepine at high dosage levels and then were to discontinue the use of that compound, she or he would be at risk for the development of a *sedative-hypnotic withdrawal syndrome* (Smith & Wesson, 2004). This is an extreme form of the discontinuance syndrome and without timely medical intervention might include such symptoms as anxiety, tremors, anorexia, nightmares, vomiting, postural hypotension, seizures, delirium, and possibly death (Smith & Wesson, 2004).

Although the abuse potential of the benzodiazepines is viewed as being quite low, one group of patients for whom the benzodiazepines are known to be potentially addictive are those who struggle with other forms of chemical dependence (Fricchione, 2004; Sattar & Bhatia, 2003). There is only limited evidence that these drugs might be used safely with individuals with substance-use problems (Sattar & Bhatia, 2003). Clark, Xie, and Brunette (2004) found, for example, that while benzodiazepines are often used as an adjunct to the treatment of severe mental illness, "benzodiazepine treatment did not improve outcomes, and persons [with concurrent substance-use disorders and mental illness] were more likely to abuse them" (p. 151). For this reason, these medications should be used with individuals recovering from alcohol/drug addiction "only after safer alternative therapies have proved ineffective" (Ciraulo & Nace, 2000, p. 276) and physicians should attempt to use benzodiazepines such as Clonopin that are known to have lower abuse potentials when a benzodiazepine must be used by a patient with a substance-use problem.

Fully 80% of benzodiazepine abuse is seen in a pattern of polydrug abuse (Longo, Parran, Johnson, & Kinsey, 2000; Sattar & Bhatia, 2003). Such polydrug abuse seems to take place to (a) enhance the effects of other compounds, (b) control some of the unwanted side effects of the primary drug of abuse, or (c) help the individual withdraw from the primary drug of abuse (Longo et al., 2000). Finally, a small percentage of abusers will utilize the benzodiazepines to escape the feelings of dysphoria or anxiety that they face on a daily basis (Cole & Kando, 1993; Wesson & Ling, 1996).

Thus, while the benzodiazepines do not bring about a state of euphoria such as that induced by many of the other drugs of abuse, they retain a significant abuse potential in their own right (Spiegel, 1996; Walker, 1996). This abuse potential might best be seen in the observation that approximately 25% of recovering alcoholics relapse after receiving a prescription for a benzodiazepine (Gitlow, 2001). Abusers seem to prefer the shorter-acting benzodiazepines such as lorazepam or alprazolam (Longo & Johnson, 2000; Sellers et al., 1993; Walker, 1996), although there is evidence that the long-acting benzodiazepine clonazepam is also frequently abused by illicit drug users (Longo & Johnson, 2000).

Because of the potential for abuse of the benzodiazepines, it has been recommended that they *not* be routinely administered to people with known substance-use disorders (Minkoff, 2001). Further, physicians are warned that these drugs are contraindicated in patients with severe mental illness who also have substance-use disorders (Brunette, Noordsy, Xie, & Drake, 2003). These medications do not bring about a reduction in anxiety or depression levels in this population and place the patient at increased risk for either abusing or becoming addicted to the prescribed benzodiazepine, according to the authors.

Even in cases in which the medications were used as prescribed, withdrawal from the benzodiazepine can be quite difficult. Individuals who have been using or abusing benzodiazepines for months or years might require a gradual tapering in daily dosage levels over periods as long as 8 to 12 weeks (Miller & Gold, 1998). To complicate the withdrawal process, patients tend to experience an upsurge in anxiety symptoms when their daily dosage levels reach 10% to 25% of their original daily dose (Prater, Miller, & Zylstra, 1999). To combat these anxiety symptoms and increase the individual's chances of success, the authors recommended the use of "mood stabilizing" agents such as carbamazepine or valproic acid during the withdrawal process. Winegarden (2001) suggested that Seroquel (quetiapine fumarate) might provide adequate control of patients' anxiety while they are being withdrawn from benzodiazepines.

Factors influencing the benzodiazepine withdrawal process. The research team of Rickels, Schweizer, Case, and Greenblatt (1990) examined the phenomenon of benzodiazepine withdrawal and concluded that its severity was dependent on five different drug treatment factors, plus several patient factors. According to the authors, the drug treatment factors included (a) the total daily dose of benzodiazepines being used, (b) the total time during which benzodiazepines had been used, (c) the half-life of the benzodiazepine being used (short half-life benzodiazepines tend to produce more withdrawal symptoms than do long half-life benzodiazepines), (d) the potency of the benzodiazepine being used, and (e) the rate of withdrawal (gradual, tapered withdrawal, or abrupt stopping).

Some of the patient factors that influence the withdrawal from benzodiazepines include (a) the patient's premorbid personality structure, (b) expectations for the withdrawal process, and (c) individual differences in the neurobiological structures within the brain thought to be involved in the withdrawal process. Interactions between these two sets of factors were thought to determine the severity of the withdrawal process, according to Rickels et al. (1990). Thus, for the person who is addicted to these medications, withdrawal can be a complex, difficult process.

Complications Caused by Benzodiazepine Use at Normal Dosage Levels

The benzodiazepines are not perfect drugs. For example, because of tolerance to the anticonvulsant effects of benzodiazepines, they are of only limited value in the long-term control of epilepsy (Morton & Santos, 1989). Another shortcoming of the benzodiazepines is that they cause excessive sedation in rare cases even at normal dosage levels. This effect is most often noted in the older patient or in people with significant levels of liver damage. The fact that the elderly are most likely to experience excessive sedation is unfortunate, considering that two-thirds of those who receive prescriptions for benzodiazepines are above the age of 60 (Ayd, 1994).

Some of the known side effects attributed to benzodiazepines include hallucinations, a feeling of euphoria, irritability, tachycardia, sweating, and disinhibition (Hobbs et al., 1995). Even when used at normal dosage levels, the benzodiazepines may occasionally bring about a degree of irritability, hostility, rage, or outright aggression, which is called a *paradoxical rage reaction* (Drummer & Odell, 2001; Hobbs et al., 1995; Walker, 1996). This paradoxical rage reaction is thought to be the result of the benzidoazepine-induced disinhibition. A similar effect is often seen in people who drink alcohol, and the combination of alcohol and benzodiazepines is also thought to cause a paradoxical rage reaction in some individuals (Beasley, 1987). The combination of the two chemicals may lower the individual's inhibitions to the point that he or she is unable to control anger that had previously been repressed.

Although the benzodiazepines are very good at the *short-term* control of anxiety, evidence would suggest that antidepressant medications such as imipramine or paroxetine are more effective than benzodiazepines after 8 weeks of continual use (Fricchione, 2004). One benzodiazepine, alprazolam, is marketed as an antianxiety agent, but there is evidence to suggest that its duration of effect is too short to provide optimal control of anxiety (Bashir & Swartz, 2002). Further, there is evidence of

alprazolam-*induced* anxiety according to the authors, a previously unreported side effect that might contribute to long-term dependence on alprazolam as the patient takes more and more medication in an attempt to avoid what is, in effect, drug-induced anxiety.

One benzodiazepine, Dalmane (flurazepam), tends to cause confusion and over-sedation, especially in the elderly. This medication is often used as a treatment for insomnia. One of the metabolites of flurazepam is desalkyflurazepam, which, depending on the individual, might have a half-life of 40 to 280 hours (Doghramji, 2003). Thus, the effects of a single dose might last for *up to 12 days* in some patients. Obviously, with such an extended half-life, if the person should use flurazepam for even a few days he or she might continue to experience significant levels of CNS depression for some time after the last dose of the drug. Further, if a person should ingest alcohol or possibly even an over-the-counter cold remedy before the flurazepam is fully biotransformed, the unmetabolized drug could combine with the depressant effects of the alcohol or cold remedy to produce serious levels of CNS depression.

Cross tolerance between the benzodiazepines, alcohol, the barbiturates, and meprobamate is possible (Sands, Creelman, Ciraulo, Greenblatt, & Shader, 1995; Snyder, 1986). The benzodiazepines may also potentiate the effects of other CNS depressants such as antihistamines, alcohol, or narcotic analgesics, presenting a danger of over-sedation, or even death[6,7] (Barnhill, Ciraulo, Ciraulo, & Greene, 1995). Many of the benzodiazepines have been found to interfere with normal sexual function, even when used at normal dosage levels (Finger, Lund, & Slagel, 1997). The benzodiazepines interfere with normal rapid eye movement (REM) sleep at night, and when used for extended periods of time they may cause rebound insomnia when discontinued (Qureshi & Lee-Chiong, 2004). The phenomenon of rebound insomnia following treatment with a benzodiazepine has not been studied in detail (Doghramji, 2003). In theory, following an extended period of benzodiazepine use, patients

---

[6]When in doubt about whether two or more medications should be used together, *always* consult a physician, pharmacist, or the local poison control center.

[7]For example, the movie star Judy Garland reportedly died as a result of the combined effects of alcohol and the benzodiazepine diazepam (Snyder, 1986).

might experience symptoms on discontinuation that mimic the anxiety or sleep disorder for which they originally started to use the medication (Gitlow, 2001; Miller & Gold, 1991a). The danger is that the patient might begin to take benzodiazepines again in the mistaken belief that the withdrawal symptoms indicated that the original problem still existed.

Although it might be so slight as to escape notice by the patient, normal memory function is sometimes affected when benzodiazepines are used at normal dosage levels (Ayd, 1994; Gitlow, 2001; Juergens, 1993; O'Donovan & McGuffin, 1993). This drug-induced *anterograde amnesia*[8] is more pronounced when large doses of a benzodiazepine are ingested or when a benzodiazepine is used by an older person, and some benzodiazepines are more likely to produce this effect than others. Indeed, fully 10% of older patients referred for evaluation of a memory impairment suffer from drug-induced memory problems, with benzodiazepines being the most common cause of such problems in this population (Curran et al., 2003). Benzodiazepine-induced memory problems appear to be similar to the alcohol-induced blackout (Juergens, 1993) and they last for the duration of the drug's effects on the user (Drummer & Odell, 2001).

Even when used at normal dosage levels, the benzodiazepines might interfere with the normal psychomotor skills necessary to operate mechanical devices, such as power tools or motor vehicles. For example, the individual's risk of being involved in a motor vehicle accident was found to be 50% higher after a single dose of diazepam (Drummer & Odell, 2001). These drug-induced psychomotor coordination problems might persist for several days and are more common after the initial use of a benzodiazepine (Drummer & Odell, 2001; Woods, Katz, & Winger 1988). Further, the benzodiazepines occasionally will produce mild respiratory depression, even at normal therapeutic dosage levels, especially in people with pulmonary disease. Because of this, the benzodiazepines should be avoided in patients who suffer from sleep apnea, chronic lung disease, or other sleep-related breathing disorders in order to avoid serious, possibly fatal, respiratory depression (Charney et al., 2001; Drummer & Odell, 2001). Also, benzodiazepines should not be used

with patients who suffer from Alzheimer's disease as they might potentiate preexisting sleep apnea problems (Doghramji, 1989).

In rare cases, therapeutic doses of a benzodiazepine have induced a depressive reaction in the patient (Ashton, 1992, 1994; Drummer & Odell, 2001; Juergens, 1993). The exact mechanism by which the benzodiazepines might cause or at least contribute to depressive episodes is not clear at this time. To further complicate matters, there is evidence to suggest that benzodiazepine use might contribute to actual thoughts of suicide on the part of the user (Ashton, 1994; Drummer & Odell, 2001; Juergens, 1993). Although it is not possible to list every reported side effect of the benzodiazepines, the above list should clearly illustrate that these medications are both extremely potent and have a significant potential to cause harm to the user.

The trials of Halcion. Halcion (triazolam) was first introduced as a hypnotic, but it has generated a great deal of controversy. Within a short time of its introduction numerous reports of adverse reactions, as well as the admission by the manufacturer that there were "errors" in the original supporting research, resulted in triazolam's being banned in the United Kingdom and elsewhere (Charney et al., 2001). An independent review of the safety and effectiveness of triazolam was carried out by the Institute of Medicine, located in Washington, D.C., and the results were summarized in a report issued in April of 1999. The authors concluded that Halcion (triazolam) was "effective in achieving the defined end points in the general adult population with insomnia when used as directed (in the current labeling) at doses of 0.25 mg for as long as 7 to 10 days" (Report of the Institute of Medicine Committee on the Efficacy and Safety of Halcion, 1999, p. 350). However, this committee also suggested that further research be conducted into the long-term effects of current hypnotic agents, including Halcion (triazolam). Thus, it would appear that triazolam will be a controversial drug for many years to come.

Drug interactions involving the benzodiazepines. There have been a "few ancedotal case reports" (Sarid-Segal, Creelman, Ciraulo, & Shader, 1995, p. 193) of patients who have suffered adverse effects from the use of benzodiazepines while taking lithium. The authors reviewed a single case report of "profound hypothermia resulting from the combined use of lithium and

[8]See Glossary.

diazepam" (p. 194). In this case, lithium was implicated as the agent that caused the individual to suffer a progressive loss of body temperature. Further, the authors noted that diazepam and oxazepam appear to cause increased levels of depression in patients who are also taking lithium. The reason for this increased level of depression in patients who are using one of these benzodiazepines as well as lithium is not known at this time.

Patients who are on Antabuse (disulfiram) should use benzodiazepines with caution, as disulfiram reduces the speed at which the body can metabolize benzodiazepines such as diazepam and chlordiazepoxide (DeVane & Nemeroff, 2002). When a patient must use both medications concurrently, Zito (1994) recommended the use of a benzodiazepine such as oxazepam or lorazepam, which does not produce any biologically active metabolites. Surprisingly, grapefruit juice has been found to alter the P-450 metabolic pathway in the liver, slowing the rate of benzodiazepine biotransformation (Charney et al., 2001).

There is evidence that blood levels of Halcion (triazolam) might be as high as double when the patient also takes the antibiotic erythromycin (sold under a variety of brand names) (DeVane & Nemeroff, 2002; Graedon & Graedon, 1995). Further, probenecid might slow the biotransformation of the benzodiazepine lorazepam, thus causing excess sedation in some patients (Sands, Creelman, Ciraulo, Greenblatt, & Shader, 1995).

Patients who are taking a benzodiazepine should not use the antipsychotic medication clozapine (Zito, 1994). There have been reports of severe respiratory depression caused by the combination of these two medications, possibly resulting in several deaths. Patients with heart conditions who are taking the medication digoxin as well as a benzodiazepine should have frequent tests to check the digoxin level in their blood (Graedon & Graedon, 1995). There is some evidence that benzodiazepine use might cause the blood levels of digoxin to rise, possibly to the level of digoxin toxicity, according to the authors.

The use of benzodiazepines with anticonvulsant medications such as phenytoin, mephenytoin, and ethotoin, the antidepressant fluoxetine, or medications for the control of blood pressure such as propranolol and metoprolol might cause higher than normal blood levels of such benzodiazepines as diazepam (DeVane & Nemeroff, 2002; Graedon & Graedon, 1995). Patients

using St. John's wort may experience more anxiety, as this herbal medication lowers the blood level of alprazolam (DeVane & Nemeroff, 2002). Thus, it is unwise for a patient to use these medications at the same time.

Women who are using oral contraceptives should discuss their use of a benzodiazepines with a physician prior to taking one of these medications. Zito (1994) noted that oral contraceptives will reduce the rate at which the body will be able to metabolize some benzodiazepines, thus making it necessary to reduce the dose of these medications. Patients who are taking antitubercular medications such as isoniazid might need to adjust their benzodiazepine dosage (Zito, 1994). Further, patients who take antacids may have trouble absorbing chlordiazepoxide as quickly as they might normally if they had taken the chlordiazepoxide without an antacid (Ciraulo, Shader, Greenblatt, & Barnhill, 1995).

Because of the possibility of excessive sedation, the benzodiazepines should *never* be intermixed with other CNS depressants, except under the supervision of a physician. One medication that has emerged as being potentially dangerous when mixed with a benzodiazepine is buprenorphine (Smith & Wesson, 2004). This finding is consistent with the general prohibition against mixing benzodiazepines with CNS depressants such as alcohol, narcotic analgesics, and antihistamines (Graedon & Graedon, 1995). Individuals taking a benzodiazepine should discontinue their use of the herbal medicine kava (Cupp, 1999). The combined effects of these two classes of compounds may result in excessive, if not dangerous, levels of sedation. This list is not exhaustive, but it does illustrate that there is a potential for an interaction between the benzodiazepines and a number of other medications. People should consult a physician or pharmacist prior to taking two or more medications at the same time to rule out the possibility of an adverse interaction between the medications being used.

Subjective Experience of Benzodiazepine Use

When used as an antianxiety agent at normal dosage levels, benzodiazepines induce a gentle state of relaxation in the user. In addition to their effects on the cortex, the benzodiazepines have an effect on the spinal cord, which contributes to muscle relaxation through some unknown mechanism (Ballenger, 1995). When used in the treatment of insomnia, the benzodiazepines initially reduce the sleep latency period, and users report a sense of deep and refreshing sleep. However, the benzodiazepines interfere with the normal sleep cycle, almost suppressing stage III and IV/REM sleep for reasons that are not clear (Ballenger, 1995). When people use them for extended periods of time as hypnotics, they may experience REM rebound (Hobbs et al., 1995; Qureshi & Lee-Chiong, 2004).[9] There are cases on record of individuals who had used a benzodiazepine as a hypnotic for only 1–2 weeks, yet still experienced significant rebound symptoms when they tried to discontinue the medication ("Sleeping Pills and Antianxiety Drugs," 1988; Tyrer, 1993). To help the individual return to normal sleep, the hormone melatonin should be used during the period of benzodiazepine withdrawal (Garfinkel, Zisapel, Wainstein, & Laudon, 1999; Pettit, 2000).

In addition to REM rebound, patients who have used a benzodiazepine for daytime relief from anxiety have reported symptoms such as anxiety, agitation, tremor, fatigue, difficulty concentrating, headache, nausea, gastrointestinal upset, a sense of paranoia, depersonalization, and impaired memory after stopping the drug (Graedon & Graedon, 1991). There have been reports of people experiencing rebound insomnia for as long as 3 to 21 days after their last benzodiazepine use (Graedon & Graedon, 1991). The benzodiazepines with shorter half-lives are most likely to cause rebound symptoms (Ayd, 1994; O'Donovan & McGuffin, 1993; Rosenbaum, 1990). Such symptoms might be common when the patient experiences an abrupt drop in medication blood levels. For example, alprazolam has a short half-life, and the blood levels drop rather rapidly just before it is time for the next dose. It is during this period of time that the individual is most likely to experience an increase in anxiety levels. This process results in a phenomenon known as "clock watching" (Rosenbaum, 1990, p. 1302) by the patient, who waits with increasing anxiety until the time comes for the next dose.

To combat rebound anxiety, it has been suggested that a long-acting benzodiazepine such as clonazepam be substituted for the shorter-acting drug (Rosenbaum, 1990). The transition between alprazolam

and clonazepam takes about one week, after which time the patient should be taking only clonazepam. This medication may then be gradually withdrawn, resulting in a slower decline in blood levels. However, the patient still should be warned that there will be some rebound anxiety symptoms. Although the patient might believe otherwise, these symptoms are not a sign that the original anxiety is still present. Rather, as the author noted, these anxiety-like symptoms are simply a sign that the body is adjusting to the gradual reduction in clonazepam blood levels.

Long-Term Consequences of Chronic Benzodiazepine Use

Although introduced as safe and nonaddicting substitutes for the barbiturates, the benzodiazepines do indeed have a significant abuse potential. Benzodiazepine abuse/addiction is most common in people with preexisting substance-use disorders, and for this reason these medications "should rarely, if ever" be administered to patients with chemical-use disorders on a chronic basis (O'Brien, 2001, p. 629). Some of the signs of benzodiazepine abuse include (a) taking the drug after the medical/psychiatric need for its use has passed, (b) symptoms of physical or psychological dependence on one of the benzodiazepines, (c) taking the drug in amounts greater than the prescribed amount, (d) taking the drug to obtain an euphoriant effect, and (e) using the drug to decrease self-awareness, or the possibility of change (Dietch, 1983).

During withdrawal, the benzodiazepine-dependent individual might experience symptoms of anxiety, insomnia, dizziness, nausea and vomiting, muscle weakness, tremor, confusion, convulsions (seizures), irritability, sweating, and a drug-induced withdrawal psychosis (Brown & Stoudemire, 1998). There have been rare reports of depression, manic reactions, and obsessive-compulsive symptoms as a result of benzodiazepine withdrawal (Juergens, 1993). In extreme cases, patients have been known to experience transient feelings of depersonalization, muscle pain, and a hypersensitivity to light and noise during the benzodiazepine withdrawal process (Spiegel, 1996).

In addition to the problems of physical dependence, it is possible to become *psychologically* dependent on benzodiazepines (Dietch, 1983). Dietch (1983) noted

---

[9]See Glossary.

that "psychological dependence on benzodiazepines appears to be more common than physical dependence" (p. 1140). People with a psychological dependence might take the drug continuously or intermittently because of their *belief* that they need it in spite of their actual medical requirements.

When used as hypnotics, the benzodiazepines are useful for short periods of time. However, researchers believe that the process of neuroadaptation limits the effectiveness of the benzodiazepines as sleep-inducing (hypnotic) medications to just a few days (Ashton, 1994), to a week (Carvey, 1998), or to 2–4 weeks (American Psychiatric Association, 1990; Ayd, 1994) of continual use. Given this fact, it is recommended that the benzodiazepines be used for only the *short-term* treatment of insomnia (Taylor, McCracken, Wilson, & Copeland, 1998). Surprisingly, many users continue to use these benzodiazepines as a sleep aid for months or even years. This might indicate that these medications have become part of the psychological ritual that the individual follows to ensure proper sleep rather than evidence of the pharmacological effect of the medication (Carvey, 1998).

There is a tendency, at least among some users of the benzodiazepines, to increase their dosage levels above that prescribed by their physician. O'Brien (2001) noted that whereas 5–20 mg of diazepam might cause sedation in the typical person, some abusers have reached the point that they are taking more than 1,000 mg per day in divided doses in an attempt to overcome their tolerance to diazepam-induced euphoria.

All of the CNS depressants, including the benzodiazepines, are capable of producing a *toxic psychosis* especially in overdose situations. This condition is also called an *organic brain syndrome* by some professionals. Some of the symptoms seen with a benzodiazepine-related toxic psychosis include visual and auditory hallucinations and/or paranoid delusions, as well as hyperthermia, delirium, convulsions, a drug-induced psychosis, and possible death (Jenike, 1991). With proper treatment, this drug-induced psychosis will usually clear in 2 to 14 days (Miller & Gold, 1991a), but *withdrawal from benzodiazepines should be attempted only under the supervision of a physician.*

Benzodiazepines as a substitute for other drugs of abuse. There is little factual information available on the phenomenon of benzodiazepine abuse/addiction. It is known that because of the similarity between the effects of alcohol and those of the benzodiazepines, alcohol-dependent people often will substitute a benzodiazepine for alcohol in situations where they cannot drink. The author of this text has met a number of recovering alcoholics who reported that 10 mg of diazepam had the same subjective effect for them as 3–4 "stiff" drinks. Further, the long half-life of diazepam often is sufficient to allow the individual to work the entire day without starting to go into alcohol withdrawal, thus allowing the user to avoid the telltale smell of alcohol on the breath while at work.

Finally, research has shown that up to 90% of patients in methadone maintenace programs will abuse benzodiazepines, often doing so at high dosage levels (Sattar & Bhatia, 2003). Patients will take a single, massive dose of a benzodiazepine (the equivalent of 100–300 mg of diazepam) about 30 minutes after ingesting their methadone in order to boost the effect of the latter drug (Drummer & Odell, 2001; O'Brien, 2001). There is evidence that the experimental narcotic buprenorphine may, when mixed with benzodiazepines, offer the user less of a high, thus reducing the incentive for the narcotics user to try to mix the medications (Sellers et al., 1993).

Buspirone

In 1986, a new medication by the name of *BuSpar* (buspirone) was introduced. Buspirone is a member of a class of medications known as the *azapirones*, which are chemically different from the benzodiazepines. Buspirone was found as a result of a search by pharmaceutical companies for antipsychotic drugs that did not have the harsh side effects of the phenothiazines or similar chemicals (Sussman, 1994). Although the antipsychotic effect of buspirone was quite limited, researchers found that it was approximately as effective in controlling anxiety as were the benzodiazepines (Drummer & Odell, 2001). In addition, buspirone was found to only rarely cause sedation or fatigue for the user (Rosenbaum & Gelenberg, 1991; Sussman, 1994) and there was no evidence of potentiation between buspirone and select benzodiazepines, or alcohol and buspirone (Drummer & Odell, 2001; Feighner, 1987; Manfredi et al., 1991).[10]

---

[10]This is not, however, a suggestion that the user try to use alcohol and buspirone at the same time. The author does *not* recommend the use of alcohol with any prescription medication.

The advantages of buspirone over the benzodiazepines are more than outweighed by the fact that the patient must take this medication for up to 2 weeks before it becomes effective (Doble, Martin, & Nutt, 2004). Some of the more common side effects of buspirone include gastrointestinal problems, drowsiness, decreased concentration, dizziness, agitation, headache, feelings of lightheadedness, nervousness, diarrhea, excitement, sweating/clamminess, nausea, depression, nasal congestion, and rarely, feelings of fatigue (Cadieux, 1996; Cole & Yonkers, 1995; Feighner, 1987; Graedon & Graedon, 1991; Manfredi et al., 1991; Newton, Marunycz, Alderdice, & Napoliello, 1986; Pagliaro & Pagliaro, 1998). Buspirone has also been found to cause decreased sexual desire in some users as well as sexual performance problems in some men (Finger, Lund, & Slagel, 1997).

In contrast to the benzodiazepine family of drugs, buspirone has no significant anticonvulsant action. It also lacks the muscle relaxant effects of the benzodiazepines (Cadieux, 1996; Eison & Temple, 1987). Indeed, buspirone was been found to be of little value in cases of anxiety that involve insomnia, which is a significant proportion of anxiety cases (Manfredi et al., 1991). It has value in controlling the symptoms of general anxiety disorder, but it does not seem to control the discomfort of acute anxiety/panic attacks.

On the positive side, buspirone was found to be effective in treating many patients who suffered from an anxiety disorder with a depressive component (Cadieux, 1996; Cohn, Wilcox, Bowden, Fisher, & Rodos, 1992). Indeed, there is evidence that buspirone might be of value in the treatment of some forms of depression, both as the primary form of treatment and as an agent to potentiate the effects of other antidepressants (Sussman, 1994). In addition, buspirone is valuable in treating obsessive-compulsive disorder, social phobias, posttraumatic stress disorder, and possibly alcohol withdrawal symptoms (Sussman, 1994). Physicians who treat geriatric patients have found that buspirone is effective in controlling aggression in anxious, confused older adults without exacerbating psychomotor stability problems that can contribute to the patient's falling (Ayd et al., 1996). However, when used with older adults it should be used in smaller doses because of age-related changes in how fast the drug is removed from the circulation (Drummer

& Odell, 2001). It has also been found to reduce the frequency of self-abusive behaviors (SAB) in mentally retarded subjects (Ayd et al., 1996).

Researchers have found that the addition of buspirone to antidepressant medications seems to bring many resistant or nonresponsive cases of depression under control (Cadieux, 1996). There also is limited evidence to suggest that buspirone might be useful as an adjunct to cigarette cessation for smokers who have some form of an anxiety disorder (Covey et al., 2000).

The Pharmacology of Buspirone

The mechanism of action for buspirone is different from that of the benzodiazepines (Eison & Temple, 1987). Whereas the benzodiazepines tend to bind to receptor sites that utilize the neurotransmitter GABA, buspirone tends to bind to one of the many serotonin receptor sites known as the 5-HT$_{1A}$ site (Ayd et al., 1996; Cadieux, 1996; Sussman, 1994). Further, researchers have found that buspirone binds to dopamine and serotonin type 1 receptors in the hippocampus, a different portion of the brain than the site where the benzodiazepines exert their effect (Manfredi et al., 1991).

Within the brain, buspirone appears to function in a manner that moderates the level of serotonin (Cadieux, 1996). If there is a deficit of serotonin, as there is in depressive disorders, buspirone seems to stimulate its production (Anton, 1994; Sussman, 1994). If there is an excess of serotonin, as there appears to be in many forms of anxiety states, buspirone seems to lower the serotonin level (Cadieux, 1996). Unfortunately, when used with someone who has a history of addictive behavior, it may require 3–4 weeks before any significant improvement in the patient's status is noticed, and the user might have to take high doses of buspirone before achieving any relief from anxiety (Renner, 2001).

The half-life of buspirone is only 1–10 hours (Cole & Yonkers, 1995). This short half-life requires that the individual take 3–4 divided doses of buspirone each day, whereas the half-life of benzodiazepines like diazepam makes it possible for that drug to be used only 1–2 times a day (Schweizer & Rickels, 1994). Finally, unlike many other sedating chemicals, there does not appear to be any degree of cross tolerance between buspirone and the benzodiazepines, alcohol, the barbiturates, or meprobamate (Sussman, 1994).

Buspirone's abuse potential is quite limited (Smith & Wesson, 2004). There is no evidence of a significant withdrawal syndrome similar to that seen after protracted periods of benzodiazepine use or abuse (Anton, 1994; Sussman, 1994). Further, unlike benzodiazepines, buspirone does not seem to have an adverse impact on memory (Rickels, Giesecke, & Geller, 1987). Unfortunately, buspirone has not been shown to lessen the intensity of withdrawal symptoms experienced by patients who were addicted to benzodiazepines (Rickels, Schweizer, Csanalosi, Case, & Chung, 1988). Indeed, there is evidence that patients currently taking a benzodiazepine might be slightly *less* responsive to buspirone while they are taking both medications (Cadieux, 1996). But unlike the benzodiazepines, there is no evidence of tolerance to buspirone's effects, nor any evidence of physical dependence or a withdrawal syndrome from buspirone when the medication is used as directed for short periods of time (Cadieux, 1996; Rickels et al., 1988).

One very rare complication of buspirone use is the development of a drug-induced neurological condition known as the *serotonin syndrome*, especially when buspirone is used with the antidepressants bloxetine or fluvoxamine (Sternbach, 2003). Although the serotonin syndrome might develop as long as 24 hours after the patient ingests a medication that affects the serotonin neurotransmitter system, in 50% of the cases the patient develops the syndrome within 2 hours of starting the medication (Mills, 1995).

A limited number of cases have been reported in which patients who were taking buspirone and an antidepressant among the monoamine oxidase inhibitors (MAOIs or MAO inhibitors) developed abnormally high blood pressure (Ciraulo, Creelman, Shader, & O'Sullivan, 1995). However, at the same time there are countless other cases in which patients have taken these two medications at the same time without apparent ill effect. Thus, the possible role of either medication in the development of the observed hypertension is still unknown.

It is unfortunate, but the manufacturer's claim that buspirone offers many advantages over the benzodiazepines in the treatment of anxiety states has not been totally fulfilled. Indeed, Rosenbaum and Gelenberg (1991) cautioned that "many clinicians and patients have found buspirone to be a generally disappointing alternative to benzodiazepines" (p. 200). In spite of this note, however, the authors recommended a trial of buspirone for "persistently anxious patients" (p. 200). Further, at this point in time, buspirone would seem to be the drug of choice in the treatment of anxiety states in the addiction prone individual.

Zolpidem

The drug zolpidem was used as a sleep-inducing (hypnotic) drug in Europe for 5 years before it was introduced to the United States in 1993 (Hobbs et al., 1995). In the United States it is sold as an orally administered hypnotic by the brand name of Ambien, which is marketed as a short-term (defined as less than 4 weeks) treatment of insomnia available only by a physician's prescription.

Pharmacology of zolpidem. Technically, zolpidem is the first of a new family of sleep-inducing chemicals known as *imidazopryidines*. In contrast to the benzodiazepines, which bind to a number of receptor sites in the brain, zolpidem binds to just one of these receptor sites, which is also used by the benzodiazepines. Thus it is more selective than the benzodiazepines, a unique feature that also gives zolpidem only a minor anticonvulsant effect. Indeed, research has demonstrated that zolpidem's anticonvulsant action is seen only at doses significantly above those that bring about sleep in the user (Doble, Martin, & Nutt, 2004). The selective method of action is also the reason zolpidem has minimal to no effect on muscle injuries.

The biological half-life of a single dose of zolpidem is about 1.5–2.4 hours in the healthy adult, whereas in geriatric patients the half-life is approximately 2.5 hours (Charney et al., 2001; Doble et al., 2004; Folks & Burke, 1998; Kryger, Steljes, Pouliot, Neufeld, & Odynski, 1991). Most of a single dose of zolpidem is biotransformed by the liver into inactive metabolites before excretion by the kidneys. There is little evidence of neuroadaptation to zolpidem's hypnotic effects when the drug is used at normal dosage levels, even after the drug has been used for as long as one year (Folks & Burke, 1998; Holm & Goa, 2000). But there are rare reports of patients who have become tolerant to the hypnotic effects of zolpidem after using this medication at very high dosage levels for a period of several years (Holm & Goa, 2000).

Unlike the benzodiazepines or barbiturates, zolpidem causes only a minor reduction in REM sleep patterns at normal dosage levels (Hobbs et al., 1995). Further, it does not interfere with the other stages of sleep, allowing for a more natural and restful night's sleep by the patient (Doble, Martin, & Nutt, 2004; Hartmann, 1995). When used as prescribed, the most common adverse effects include nightmares, headaches, gastrointestinal upset, agitation, and some daytime drowsiness (Hartmann, 1995). There have also been a few isolated cases of a zolpidem-induced psychosis (Ayd, 1994; Ayd et al., 1996) and rebound insomnia when the medication is discontinued (Gitlow, 2001). Side effects are more often encountered at higher dosage levels, and it is for this reason that the recommended dosage level of zolpidem should not exceed 10 mg per day (Hold & Goa, 2000; Merlotti et al., 1989).

Zolpidem has been found to cause some cognitive performance problems similar to those seen with the benzodiazepines, although this medication appears less likely to cause memory impairment than the older hypnotics (Ayd et al., 1996). Further, alcohol enhances the effects of zolpidem and thus should not be used by patients on this medication because of the potentiation effect (Folks & Burke, 1998). Zolpidem is contraindicated in patients with obstructive sleep apnea as it increases the duration and frequency of apnea (Holm & Goa, 2000).

Effects of zolpidem at above-normal dosage leves. At dosage levels of 20 mg per day or above, zolpidem has been found to significantly reduce REM sleep. Also, at dosage levels of 20 mg per day or more, zolpidem was found to cause rebound insomnia when the drug is discontinued. At dosage levels of 50 mg per day, volunteers who received zolpidem reported such symptoms as visual perceptual disturbances, ataxia, dizziness, nausea, and vomiting. Patients who have ingested up to 40 times the maximum recommended dosage have recovered without significant aftereffects. It should be noted, however, that the effects of zolpidem will combine with those of other CNS depressants if the patient has ingested more than one medication in an overdose attempt, and such multiple-drug overdoses might prove fatal. As with all medications, *any suspected overdose of zolpidem either by itself or in combination with other medications should be treated by a physician.*

Abuse potential of zolpidem. There are only limited reports of zolpidem abuse, and such reports appear to be limited to individuals who have histories of sedative-hypnotic abuse (Gitlow, 2001; Holm & Goa, 2000). The abuse potential is rated as about the same as that of the benzodiazepine family of drugs (Charney et al., 2001). Thus, the prescribing physician must balance the potential for abuse against the potential benefit that this medication would bring to the patient. Because of zolpidem's sedating effects, this medication should not be used in people with substance-use problems, as its effects may trigger thoughts about returning to active chemical use again (Jones, Knutson, & Haines, 2003).

Zaleplon

The drug Sonata (zaleplon) is a member of the *pyrazolpyrimidine* class of chemicals and was introduced as the first of a new class of hypnotic agents intended for short-term symptomatic treatment of insomnia. Animal research suggests that zaleplon has some sedative and anticonvulsant effects, although it is approved for use only as a hypnotic in the United States (Danjou et al., 1999). When used to induce sleep it is administered orally in capsules containing 5 mg, 10 mg, or 20 mg of the drug. In most cases, the 10 mg dose was thought to be sufficient to induce sleep, although in individuals with low body weight, 5 mg might be more appropriate (Danjou et al., 1999).

Once in the body, approximately 30% of the dose of zaleplon is biotransformed by the liver, through the first pass metabolism process. Less than 1% of the total dose is excreted in the urine unchanged, with the majority of the medication being biotransformed by the liver into less active compounds that are eventually eliminated from the body either in the urine or the feces. The half-life of zaleplon is approximately one hour (Doble et al., 2004). In the brain, zaleplon binds at the same receptor site as zolepidem (Charney et al., 2001; Danjou et al., 1999; Walsh, Pollak, Scharf, Schweitzer, & Vogel, 2000). There is little evidence of a drug hangover effect, although it is recommended that the patient not attempt to operate machinery for 4 hours after taking the last dose (Danjou et al., 1999; Doble et al., 2004; Walsh et al., 2000).

As noted earlier, this medication is intended for the *short-term* treatment of insomnia, in part because of the rapid development of tolerance to the effects of it (or similar medication). Individuals who have used zaleplon nightly for extended periods of time have reported *rebound insomnia* upon discontinuation of this medication, although this might be more common when the drug is used at higher dosage levels than at the lowest dosage level of 5 mg per night. Because of the rapid onset of sleep, users are advised to take this medication just before going to sleep or after being unable to go to sleep naturally. Patients using zaleplon have reported such side effects as headache, rhinitis, nausea, myalgia, periods of amnesia while under the effects of this medication, dizziness, depersonalization, drug-induced hangover, constipation, dry mouth, gout, bronchitis, asthma attacks, nervousness, depression, problems in concentration, ataxia, and insomnia.

The abuse potential of zaleplon is similar to that of the benzodiazepines, especially triazolam (Smith & Wesson, 2004). When used for extended periods of time, which means periods possibly as short as 2 weeks of regular use, zaleplon has been implicated as causing withdrawal symptoms such as muscle cramps, tremor, vomiting, and in rare occasions, seizures. Because zaleplon is a sedating agent, Jones et al. (2003) do not recommend that it be used in persons with substance-use problems, as its effects may trigger thoughts about returning to active chemical use again.

Rohypnol

Rohypnol (flunitrazepam) was first identified as being abused in the United States in the mid 1990s. It is a member of the benzodiazepine family of pharmaceuticals, used in more than 60 other countries around the world as a presurgical medication, a muscle relaxant, and a hypnotic, but it is not manufactured or used as a pharmaceutical in the United States (Gahlinger, 2004; Klein & Kramer, 2004; Palmer & Edmunds, 2003).

Because it is not manufactured as a pharmaceutical in the United States, there was little abuse of flunitrazepam by U.S. citizens prior to the mid 1990s. Substance-abuse rehabilitation professionals in this country had virtually no experience with Rohypnol (flunitrazepam) when people first began to bring it into this country. Rohypnol was classified as an illegal

substance by the U.S. government in October 1996, and individuals convicted of trafficking in or distributing this drug may be incarcerated for up to 20 years ("Rohypnol and Date Rape," 1997).

Although it is used for medicinal purposes around the world, in the United States Rohypnol has gained a reputation as a "date-rape" drug (Gahlinger, 2004; Saum & Inciardi, 1997). This was because the pharmacological characteristics of flunitrazepam, especially when mixed with alcohol, could cause a state of drug-induced amnesia that lasts 8 to 24 hours. To combat its use as a date-rape drug, the manufacturer now includes a harmless compound in the tablet that will turn the drink blue if added to a liquid such as alcohol (Klein & Kramer, 2004). Because of this history of abuse and the fact that flunitrazepam is not detected on standard urine toxicology tests, the company that manufactures Rohypnol, Hoffmann-La Roche Pharmaceuticals, has instituted a program of free urine drug testing to provide law-enforcement officials with a means to detect flunitrazepam in the urine of suspected victims of date rape (Palmer & Edmunds, 2003).

In addition to its use in date-rape situations, there are reports of cocaine abusers ingesting flunitrazepam to counteract the unwanted effects of cocaine, and of heroin abusers mixing flunitrazepam with low-quality heroin to enhance its effect (Saum & Inciardi, 1997). Some drug abusers will mix Rohypnol (flunitrazepam) with other compounds to enhance the effect of these compounds. Illicit users may also use flunitrazepam while smoking marijuana and while using alcohol (Lively, 1996). The combination of Rohypnol (flunitrazepam) and marijuana is said to produce a sense of "floating" in the user. There are reports of abusers inhaling flunitrazepam powder and of physical addiction developing to this substance following periods of continuous use. There are also reports of adolescents abusing flunitrazepam as an alternative to marijuana or LSD (Greydanus & Patel, 2003).

Chemically, flunitrazepam is a derivative of the benzodiazepine chlordiazepoxide (Eidelberg, Neer, & Miller, 1965) and is reportedly 10 times as powerful as diazepam (Gahlinger, 2004; Klein & Kramer, 2004). When used as a medication, the usual method of administration is by mouth, in doses of 0.5–2 mg. Flunitrazepam is well absorbed from the gastrointestinal tract, with between 80% and 90% of a single 2 mg dose being absorbed by the user's body (Mattila & Larni, 1980). Following a single oral dose, the peak blood levels are reached in 30 minutes (Klein & Kramer, 2004) to 1–2 hours (Saum & Inciardi, 1997). Once in the blood, 80% to 90% of the flunitrazepam is briefly bound to plasma proteins, but the drug is rapidly transferred from the plasma to body tissues. Because of this characteristic, flunitrazepam has an elimination half-life that is significantly longer than its duration of effect. Indeed, depending upon the individual's metabolism, the elimination half-life can range from 15 to 66 hours (Woods & Winger, 1997) whereas the effects last only 8 to 10 hours (Klein & Kramer, 2004).

During the process of biotransformation, flunitrazepam produces a number of different metabolites, some of which are themselves biologically active (Mattila & Larni, 1980). Less than 1% of the drug is excreted unchanged. About 90% of a single dose is eliminated by the kidneys after biotransformation, whereas about 10% is eliminated in the feces. Because of this characteristic elimination pattern, patients in countries where flunitrazepam is legal and who have kidney disease require modification of their dosage level, as the main route of elimination is through the kidneys. Although the usual pharmaceutical dose of Rohypnol (flunitrazepam) is less than 2 mg, illicit users will often take 4 mg of the drug in one dose, which will begin to produce sedation in 20 to 30 minutes. The drug's effects normally last for 8 to 12 hours.

The effects of flunitrazepam are similar to those of the other benzodiazepines, including sedation, dizziness, memory problems and/or amnesia, ataxia, slurred speech, impaired judgement, nausea, and loss of sleep or consciousness (Klein & Kramer, 2004). Like the benzodiazepines used in the United States, flunitrazepam is capable of causing paradoxical rage reactions in the user (Klein & Kramer, 2004).

Flunitrazepam has an anticonvulstant effect (Eidelberg et al., 1965) and is capable of bringing about a state of pharmacological dependence. Side effects of flunitrazepam include excessive sedation, ataxia, mood swings, headaches, tremor, and drug-induced amnesia (Calhoun, Wesson, Galloway, & Smith, 1996). Although flunitrazepam has a wide safety margin, concurrent use with alcohol or other CNS depressants may increase the danger of overdose. Withdrawal from flunitrazepam is potentially serious for the chronic abuser, and there have been reports of withdrawal seizures taking place as late as 7 days after the last use of flunitrazepam ("Rohypnol Use Spreading," 1995). For this reason, patients should be withdrawn from flunitrazepam only under the supervision of a physician.

Summary

In the time since their introduction in the 1960s, the benzodiazepines have become some of the most frequently prescribed medications. As a class, the benzodiazepines are the treatment of choice for the control of anxiety and insomnia as well as many other conditions. They have also become a significant part of the drug-abuse problem. Even though many of the benzodiazepines were first introduced as "nonaddicting and safe" substitutes for the barbiturates, there is evidence to suggest that they have an abuse potential similar to that of the barbiturate family of drugs.

A new series of pharmaceuticals, including buspirone, which is sold under the brand name BuSpar, and zolpidem, have been introduced in the past decade. Buspirone is the first of a new class of antianxiety agents, which works through a different mechanism from that of the benzodiazepines. While buspirone was introduced as nonaddicting, this claim has been challenged by at least one team of researchers. Zolpidem has an admitted potential for abuse; however, research at this time suggests that its abuse potential is less than that of the benzodiazepine most commonly used as a hypnotic: triazolam. Researchers are actively discussing the potential benefits and liabilities of these new medications at this time.

Abuse of and Addiction to Amphetamines and CNS Stimulants

Introduction

The use of central nervous system (CNS) stimulants dates back several thousand years. There is historical evidence that gladiators in ancient Rome used CNS stimulants at least 2,000 years ago to help them overcome the effects of fatigue so that they could fight longer (Wadler, 1994). Not surprisingly, people *still* use chemicals that act as CNS stimulants to counter the effects of fatigue so they can work, or in times of conflict, fight longer.

Currently, there are several different families of chemicals that might be classified as CNS stimulants, including cocaine, the amphetamines, amphetamine-like drugs such as Ritalin (methylphenidate), and ephedrine. The behavioral effects of these drugs are remarkably similar (Gawin & Ellinwood, 1988). For this reason, the amphetamine-like drugs will be discussed only briefly; the amphetamines will be reviewed in greater detail in this chapter. Cocaine will be discussed in the next chapter. However, because the CNS stimulants are controversial and the source of much confusion, this chapter will be subdivided into two sections. In the first, the medical uses of the CNS stimulants, their effects, and complications from their use will be discussed. In the second subsection, the complications of CNS stimulant abuse will be explored.

I. THE CNS STIMULANTS AS USED IN MEDICAL PRACTICE

The Amphetamine-like Drugs

Ephedrine

Scientists have found ephedra plants at Neanderthal burial sites in Europe that are thought to be 60,000 years old (Karch, 2002). It is not known whether the plants were used for medicinal purposes in the paleolithic era, but it is known that by five thousand years ago, Chinese physicians were using *ephedra* plants for medicinal purposes (Ross & Chappel, 1998). The active agent of these plants, ephedrine, was not isolated by chemists until 1897 (Mann, 1992), and it remained nothing more than a curiosity until 1930. Then a report appeared in a medical journal suggesting that ephedrine was useful in treating asthma (Karch, 2002), and it quickly became the treatment of choice for this condition. In the 1930s the intense demand for ephedrine soon raised concern as to whether the demand might not exceed the supply of plants. The importance of this fear will be discussed in the section on "History of the Amphetamines" (below). In the United States, ephedrine continued to be sold as an over-the-counter agent marketed as a treatment for asthma, sinus problems, and headaches as well as a "food supplement" used to assist weight-loss programs and as an aid to athletic performance. In February 2004 the Food and Drug Administration (FDA) issued a ban on the over-the-counter sale of ephedrine that took effect on 12 April 2004 (Neergaard, 2004). After that time, ephedrine could only be prescribed by a physician.

Medical uses of ephedrine. Ephedrine's uses include the treatment of bronchial asthma and respiratory problems associated with bronchitis, emphysema, or chronic obstructive pulmonary disease (American Society of Health-System Pharmacists, 2002). Although ephedrine was once considered a valid treatment for nasal congestion, it is no longer used for this purpose after questions were raised as to its effectiveness. In hospitals it might also be used to control the symptoms of shock and in some surgical procedures where low blood pressure is a problem (Karch, 2002). Ephedrine might modify the cardiac rate; however, with the introduction of newer, more effective medications, it is rarely used in cardiac emergencies now (American Society of Health-System Pharmacists, 2002). Ephedrine may, in some situations, be used as an adjunct to the treatment of myasthenia gravis (Shannon, Wilson, & Stang, 1995).

Pharmacology of ephedrine. In the human body, ephedrine's primary effects are strongest in the peripheral regions of the body rather than the central nervous system (CNS), and it is known that ephedrine stimulates the sympathetic nervous system in a manner similar to that of adrenaline (Laurence & Bennett, 1992; Mann, 1992). This makes sense, as ephedrine blocks the reuptake of norepinephrine at the receptor sites in the body.

When used in the treatment of asthma, ephedrine improves pulmonary function by causing the smooth muscles surrounding the bronchial passages to relax (American Society of Health-System Pharmacists, 2002). It also alters the constriction and dilation of blood vessels by binding at the alpha-2 receptor sites in the body, which modulate blood vessel constriction and dilation (Rothman et al., 2003). When blood vessels constrict, the blood pressure increases as the heart compensates for the increased resistance by pumping with more force.

Depending on the patient's condition, ephedrine might be taken orally or be injected, and it can be smoked. This latter route of administration was the preferred method of ephedrine abuse in the Philippines for many years, but this practice is gradually declining (Karch, 2002). Oral, intramuscular, or subcutaneous doses are completely absorbed. Peak blood levels from a single oral dose are achieved in about one hour (Drummer & Odell, 2001). Surprisingly, given the fact that it has been in use for more than three-quarters of a century, there is very little research into the way that ephedrine is distributed within the body. The serum half-life has been estimated at between 2.7 and 3.6 hours (Samenuk et al., 2002). The drug is eliminated from the body virtually unchanged, with only a small percentage being biotransformed before ephedrine is eliminated from the body by the kidneys. The exact percentage that is eliminated unchanged depends on how acidic the urine is, with a greater percentage being eliminated without biotransformation when the urine is more acidic (American Society of Health-System Pharmacists, 2002).

Tolerance to its bronchodilator action develops rapidly, and because of this, physicians recommend that ephedrine be used as a treatment of asthma for only short periods of time. The chronic use of ephedrine may contribute to cardiac or respiratory problems in the user, and for this reason the medication is recommended for only short-term use except under a physician's supervision. As an over-the-counter diet aid, ephedrine appears to have a modest, short-term effect. Shekelle et al. (2003) found in their meta-analysis of the medical literature that ephedrine can help the user lose about 0.9 kilograms of weight over a short term. There is no information on its long-term effectiveness as an aid to weight loss, and there is no evidence to suggest that it is able to enhance athletic ability (Shekelle et al., 2003).

Side effects of ephedrine at normal dosage levels. The therapeutic index of ephedrine is quite small, which suggests that this chemical may cause toxic effects at relatively low doses. A meta-analysis of the efficacy and safety of ephedrine suggests that even users who take ephedrine at recommended doses are 200% to 300% more likely to experience psychiatric problems, autonomic nervous system problems, upper gastrointestinal irritation, and heart palpitations (Shekelle et al., 2003). Some of the side effects of ephedrine include anxiety, feelings of apprehension, insomnia, and urinary retention (Graedon & Graedon, 1991). The drug may also cause a throbbing headache, confusion, hallucinations, tremor, seizures, cardiac arrhythmias, stroke, euphoria, hypertension, coronary artery spasm, angina, intracranial hemorrhage, and death (American Society of Health-System Pharmacists, 2002; Cupp, 1999; Karch, 2002; Samenuk et al., 2002).

Complications of ephedrine use at above-normal dosage levels. When ephedrine is used at higher than normal dosage levels, the side effects can include those noted above as well as coronary artery vasoconstriction, myocardial infarction, cerebral vascular accidents (CVAs, or strokes), and death (Samenuk et al., 2002). Over-the-counter ephedrine use and abuse was linked to at least 155 deaths and "dozens of heart attacks and strokes" at the time its sale was restricted in February 2004 (Neergaard, 2004, p. 3).

Medication interactions involving ephedrine. It is recommended that patients using ephedrine not use any of the tricyclic antidepressants, as these medications will add to the stimulant effect of the ephedrine (DeVane & Nemeroff, 2002). Patients using ephedrine should check with a physician or pharmacist before the concurrent use of different medications.

Ritalin (Methylphenidate)

Ritalin (methylphenidate) is a controversial pharmaceutical agent, frequently prescribed for children who have been diagnosed as having attention deficit hyperactivity disorder (ADHD) (Breggin, 1998; Sinha, 2001). Fully 90% of the methylphenidate produced is consumed in the United States (Breggin, 1998; Diller, 1998). Although there are many advocates for the use of methylphenidate in the control of ADHD, there are also critics of this process. Indeed, there are serious questions about whether children are being turned into chemical "zombies" through the use of methylphenidate or similar agents in the name of behavioral control. Most certainly, the use of methylphenidate does not represent the best possible control of ADHD symptoms, as evidenced by the fact that about half of the prescriptions for this medication are never renewed (Breggin, 1998). Given the strident arguments for and against the use of methylphenidate, it is safe to say that this compound will remain quite controversial for many decades to come.

Medical uses of methylphenidate. Methylphenidate has been found to function as a CNS stimulant and is of value in the treatment of a rare neurological condition known as *narcolepsy*. In addition to its use with ADHD, it is also of occasional use as an adjunct to the treatment of depression (Fuller & Sajatovic, 1999).

Pharmacology of methylphenidate. Methylphenidate was originally developed by pharmaceutical companies looking for a nonaddicting substitute for the amphetamines (Diller, 1998). Chemically, it is a close cousin to the amphetamines, and some pharmacologists classify methylphenidate as a true amphetamine. In this text, it will be considered an amphetamine-like drug.

When methylphenidate is used in the treatment of attention deficit hyperactivity disorder, patients will take between 15 and 90 mg of the drug per day, in divided doses (Wender, 1995). Oral doses of methylphenidate are rapidly absorbed from the gastrointestinal tract, and the drug is thought to be approximately half as potent as D-amphetamine (Wender, 1995). Peak blood levels are achieved in 1.9 hours following a single dose, although

extended-release forms of the drug might not reach peak blood levels until 4–7 hours after the medication was ingested (Shannon et al., 1995). The half-life of methylphenidate is from 1 to 3 hours, and the effects of a single oral dose last for 3 to 6 hours. The effects of a single dose of an extended-release form of methylphenidate might continue for 8 hours. About 80% of a single oral dose is biotransformed to ritanic acid in the intestinal tract, which is then excreted by the kidneys (Karch, 2002).

Within the brain, methylphenidate blocks the action of the molecular "transporter" system by which free dopamine molecules are absorbed back into the neuron in a dose-dependent manner. This allows the dopamine to remain in the synapse longer and thus enhances its effect (Volkow & Swanson, 2003; Volkow et al., 1998). At normal therapeutic doses, methylphenidate is able to block 50% or more of the dopamine transporters, within 60 to 90 minutes of the time that the drug is administered (Volkow et al., 1998).

Side-effects of methylphenidate. Even though methylphenidate is identified as the treatment of choice for ADHD, very little is known about the long-term effects of this medication, and most follow-up studies designed to identify side effects of methylphenidate have continued for only a few weeks (Schachter, Pham, King, Langford, & Moher, 2002; Sinha, 2001). Surprisingly, the long-term effectiveness and safety of methylphenidate as a treatment for ADHD have not been established (Breggin, 1998; Diller, 1998; Schachter et al., 2002). Researchers do know that even when it is used at therapeutic dosage levels, methylphenidate can cause anorexia, insomnia, weight loss, failure to gain weight, nausea, heart palpitations, angina, anxiety, liver problems, dry mouth, hypertension, headache, upset stomach, enuresis, skin rashes, dizziness, or exacerbation of the symptoms of Tourette's syndrome (Fuller & Sajatovic, 1999). Other side effects of methylphenidate range from stomach pain, blurred vision, leukopenia, possible cerebral hemorrhages, hypersensitivity reactions, anemia, and perseveration, a condition in which the individual continues to engage in the same task long after it ceases to be a useful activity (Breggin, 1998).

Methylphenidate has been implicated as a cause of liver damage in some patients (Karch, 2002). It has the potential to lower the seizure threshold in patients with a seizure disorder, and the manufacturer recommends that if the patient has a seizure, the drug should be discontinued immediately. There are reports suggesting the possibility of methylphenidate-induced damage to the tissue of the heart, a frightening possibility in light of the frequency with which it is prescribed to children (Henderson & Fischer, 1994).

When used at recommended dosage levels, methylphenidate can rarely cause a drug-induced psychosis (Breggin, 1998). There are reports that methylphenidate can cause a reduction in cerebral blood flow patterns when used at therapeutic doses, an effect that may have long-term consequences for the individual taking this medication (Breggin, 1998). These findings suggest a need for further research into the long-term consequences of methylphenidate use or abuse.

Children who are taking methylphenidate at recommended dosage levels have experienced a "zombie" effect, in which the drug dampens personal initative on the part of the user (Breggin, 1998). This seems to be a common effect of methylphenidate, even when it is used by normal individuals, although in students with ADHD this effect is claimed to be beneficial (Diller, 1998). The zombie effect reported by Breggin (1998) and Diller (1998) was challenged by Pliszka (1998), who cited research to support his conclusion. Thus, the question of whether methylphenidate causes such a state in children has yet to be determined.

On rare occasions, methylphenidate has been implicated in the development of a drug-induced depression that might reach the level of suicide attempts (Breggin, 1998). Further, a long-term follow-up study of 5,000 adolescents with ADHD who were treated with methylphenidate found that in adulthood those adolescents who had received methylphenidate were three times as likely to have abused cocaine as were those whose ADHD was treated by other methods ("Ritalin May Increase Risk," 1998). However, the results of this study have been challenged (Stocker, 1999b) and the relationship between ADHD, pharmacological treatment of this disorder, and possible predisposition toward substance-use disorders has not been clearly identified.

Medication interactions involving methylphenidate. Individuals on methylphenidate should not use tricyclic antidepressants, as these medications can combine with the methylphenidate to cause potentially toxic blood levels of the antidepressant medications (DeVane & Nemeroff, 2002). Patients should not use any of the MAOI family of antidepressants while taking methylphenidate because of possible toxicity (DeVane & Nemeroff, 2002). The mixture of mythylphenidate and the selective serotonin reuptake inhibitor family of antidepressants has been identified as a cause of seizures and thus should be avoided (DeVane & Nemeroff, 2002). Patients who are using antihypertensive medications while taking methylphenidate may find that their blood pressure control is less than adequate, as the latter drug interferes with the effectiveness of the antihypertensives (DeVane & Nemeroff, 2002).

Challenges to the use of methylphenidate as a treatment for ADHD. A small, but vocal, group of clinicians has started to express concern about the use of methylphenidate as a treatment for ADHD (Breggin, 1998; Diller, 1998). Other researchers have noted that the long-term efficacy of methylphenidate in treating ADHD has never been demonstrated in the clinical literature (Schachter et al., 2002). Indeed, in spite of what is told to children or their parents by physicians, the professional literature is filled with research studies that failed to demonstrate any significant positive effect from methylphenidate on ADHD (Breggin, 1998). In contrast to this pattern of reports in the clinical literature, parents (and teachers) are assured that methylphenidate is *the* treatment of choice for ADHD, mainly because the "material on [methylphenidate's] lack of efficacy, while readily available in the professional literature, is not presented to the public" (Breggin, 1998, p. 111).

Breggin (1999) is a strong critic of the diagnosis of attention deficit hyperactivity disorder (ADHD), and although many clinicians dismiss his comments as being too extreme, some of his observations appear to have merit. For example, although the long-term benefits of methylphenidate use have never been demonstrated, the American Medical Association supports the long-term use of this medication to control the manifestations of ADHD. Research has also demonstrated that the child's ability to learn new material improves at a significantly lower dose of methylphenidate than is necessary to eliminate behaviors that are not accepted in the classroom (Pagliaro & Pagliaro, 1998). When the student is drugged to the point that these behaviors are eliminated or controlled, learning suffers, according to the authors. Further, two ongoing studies into the long-term effects of methylphenidate have found evidence of a progressive deterioration in the student's performance on standardized psychological tests, as compared to the performance of age-matched peers on these same tests (Sinha, 2001). These arguements present thought-provoking challenges to the current forms of pharmacological treatment of ADHD and suggest a need for further research in this area.

The Amphetamines

History of the amphetamines. Chemically, the amphetamines are *analogs*[1] of ephedrine (Lit, Wiviott-Tishler, Wong, & Hyman 1996). The amphetamines were first discovered in 1887, but it was not until 1927 that one of these compounds was found to have medicinal value (Kaplan & Sadock, 1996; Lingeman, 1974). Following the introduction of ephedrine for the treatment of asthma, questions began to be raised as to whether the demand for it might not exceed the supply. Pharmaceutical companies began to search for synthetic alternatives to ephedrine and found that the amphetamines had a similar effect as ephedrine on asthma patients. In 1932 an amphetamine product called Benzedrine was introduced for use in the treatment of asthma and rhinitis (Derlet & Heischober, 1990; Karch, 2002). The drug was contained in an inhaler similar to "smelling salts." The ampule, which could be purchased over the counter, would be broken, releasing the concentrated amphetamine liquid into the surrounding cloth. The Benzedrine ampule would then be held under the nose and the fumes inhaled, much like "smelling salts" are, to reduce the symptoms of asthma.

It was not long, however, before it was discovered that the Benzedrine ampules could be unwrapped, carefully broken open, and the concentrated Benzedrine injected,[2] causing effects similar to those of cocaine. The dangers of cocaine were well known to drug abusers and addicts of the era, but because the long-term effects of the amphetamines were not known they were viewed as a "safe" substitute for cocaine. Shortly afterward, the world was plunged into World War II and amphetamines were used by personnel in the American, British, German, and Japanese armed forces to counteract fatigue

and heighten endurance (Brecher, 1972). United States Army Air Corps crew members stationed in England alone took an estimated 180 million Benzedrine pills during World War II (Lovett, 1994), whereas British troops consumed an additional 72 million doses (Walton, 2002) to help them function longer in combat. It is rumored that Adolf Hitler was addicted to amphetamines (Witkin, 1995).

It is possible to excuse the use of amphetamines during World War II or Operation Desert Storm as being necessary to meet the demands of the war. But for reasons that are not well understood, there were waves of amphetamine abuse in both Sweden and Japan immediately following World War II (Snyder, 1986). The amphetamines were frequently prescribed to patients in the United States in the 1950s and 1960s, and President John F. Kennedy is rumored to have used methamphetamine, another member of the amphetamines, during his term in office in the early 1960s (Witkin, 1995). The amphetamines continued to gain popularity as drugs of abuse, and by 1970 their use had reached "epidemic proportions" (Kaplan & Sadock, 1996, p. 305) in the United States. Physicians would prescribe amphetamines for patients who wished to lose weight or who were depressed, whereas illicit amphetamine users would take the drug because it helped them to feel good. Many of the pills prescribed by physicians for patients were diverted to illicit markets, and there is no way of knowing how many of the 10 billion amphetamine tablets manufactured in the United States in 1970 were actually used as prescribed.

The amphetamines occupy a unique position in history, for medical historians now believe that the arrival of large amounts of amphetamines, especially methamphetamine, contributed to an outbreak of drug-related violence that ended San Francisco's "summer of love" of 1967 (Smith, 1997, 2001). Amphetamine abusers had also discovered that when used at high dosage levels the amphetamines would cause agitation and could induce death from cardiovascular collapse. They had also found that these compounds could induce a severe depressive state that might reach suicidal proportions, and this might last for days or weeks after the drug was discontinued. By the mid 1970s amphetamine abusers had come to understand that chronic amphetamine use would dominate the

---

[1]See Glossary and Chapter 35.

[2]Amphetamines are no longer sold over the counter without a prescription.

users' lives, slowly killing them. In San Francisco, physicians at the Haight-Ashbury free clinic coined the slogan "speed kills" by way of warning the general public of the dangers of amphetamine abuse (Smith, 1997, 2001).

By this time, physicians had discovered that the amphetamines were not as effective as once thought in the treatment of depressive states or obesity. This fact, plus the development of new medications for the treatment of depression, reduced the frequency with which physicians prescribed amphetamines. The amphetamines were classified as Schedule II substances by the U.S. government, which also limited their legitimate use. However, they continue to have a limited role in the control of human suffering. Further, although the dangers of amphetamine use are well known, during the Desert Storm campaign of 1991 some 65% of United States pilots in the combat theater admitted to having used an amphetamine compound at least once during combat operations (Emonson & Vanderbeek, 1995). Thus, the amphetamines have never entirely disappeared either from the illicit drug world or from the physician's handbag.

Medical uses of the amphetamines. The amphetamines improve the action of the smooth muscles of the body (Hoffman & Lefkowitz, 1990) and thus have a potential for improving athletic performance at least to some degree. However, these effects are not uniform and the overuse of the CNS stimulants can actually bring about a *decrease* in athletic abilities in some users. Regulatory agencies for different sports routinely test for evidence of amphetamine use among athletes. For these reasons, amphetamine abuse in this population is limited.

The amphetamines have an *anorexic* side effect,[3] and at one time this side effect was thought to be useful in the treatment of obesity. Unfortunately, subsequent research has demonstrated that the amphetamines are only minimally effective as a weight-control agent. Tolerance to the appetite suppressing side effect of the amphetamines develops in only 4 weeks (Snyder, 1986). After users have become tolerant to the anorexic effect of amphetamines, it is not uncommon for them to regain the weight that they initially lost. Indeed, research has demonstrated that after a 6-month period, there is no significant difference

in the amount of weight lost between patients using amphetamines and patients who simply dieted to lose weight (Maxmen & Ward, 1995).

Prior to the 1970s the amphetamines were thought to be antidepressants and were widely prescribed for the treatment of depression. However, research revealed that the antidepressant effect of the amphetamines was short-lived at best. With the introduction of more effective antidepressant agents the amphetamines fell into disfavor and are now used only rarely as an adjunct to the treatment of depression (Potter, Rudorfer, & Goodwin, 1987). However, they are the treatment of choice for a rare neurological condition known as *narcolepsy*.[4] Researchers believe that narcolepsy is caused by a chemical imbalance within the brain in which the neurotransmitted dopamine is not released in sufficient amounts to maintain wakefulness. By forcing the neurons in the brain to release their stores of dopamine, the amphetamines are thought to at least partially correct the dopamine imbalance that causes narcolepsy (Doghramji, 1989).

The first reported use of an amphetamine, Benzedrine, for the control of hyperactive children occurred in 1938 (Pliszka, 1998). Surprisingly, although the amphetamines are CNS *stimulants*, they appear to have a calming effect on individuals who have attention deficit hyperactivity disorder (ADHD). Research has revealed that the amphetamines are as effective in controlling the symptoms of ADHD as methylphenidate in about 50% of patients with this disorder and that 25% of the patients will experience better symptom control through the use of an amphetamine (Spencer et al., 2001). However, the use of amphetamines to treat ADHD is quite controversial. They are recognized as being of value in the control of ADHD symptoms by some, but research is needed into their long-term effects, and there are those who suggest that these medications may do more harm than good (Breggin, 1998; Spencer et al., 2001).

Pharmacology of the Amphetamines

The amphetamine family of chemicals consists of several different variations of the parent compound. Each of these variations yields a molecule that is similar to the others, except for minor variations in potency

---

[3]See Glossary.

[4]See Glossary.

and pharmacological characteristics. The most common form of amphetamine is dextroamphetamine (*d*-amphetamine sulfate), which is considered twice as potent as the other common form of amphetamine (Lingeman, 1974), methamphetamine (or *d*-desoxyephedrine hydrochloride). Because of its longer half-life and ability to cross the blood-brain barrier, methamphetamine seems to be preferred over dextroamphetamine by illicit amphetamine abusers (Albertson, Derlet, & Van Hoozen, 1999).

Methods of administration in medical practice. There are several methods by which physicians might administer an amphetamine to a patient. The drug molecule tends to be basic and when taken orally is easily absorbed through the lining of the small intestine (Laurence & Bennett, 1992). However, although the amphetamines have been used in medical practice for generations, very little is known about their absorption from the GI tract in humans beyond this fact (Jenkins & Cone, 1998). It is known that a single oral dose of amphetamine will begin to have an effect on the user in 20 (Siegel, 1991) to 30 minutes (Mirin, Weiss, & Greenfield, 1991). The amphetamine molecule is also easily absorbed into the body when injected either into muscle tissue or a vein.

In the normal patient who has received a single oral dose of an amphetamine, the peak plasma levels are achieved in 1 to 3 hours (Drummer & Odell, 2001). The biological half-life of the different forms of amphetamine vary as a result of the different chemical structures. For example, the biological half-life of a single oral dose of dextroamphetamine is between 10 and 34 hours whereas that of a single oral dose of methamphetamine is only 4 to 5 hours (Derlet & Heischober, 1990; Fuller & Sajatovic, 1999; *Physicians' Desk Reference*, 2004; Shannon et al., 1995). However, when injected, the half-life of methamphetamine can be as long as 12.2 hours (Karch, 2002).

The chemical structure of the basic amphetamine molecule is similar to that of norepinephrine and dopamine and thus might be classified as an agonist of these neurotransmitters (King & Ellinwood, 1997). The effects of amphetamines in the peripheral regions of the body are caused by its ability to stimulate norepinephrine release whereas its CNS effects are the result of its impact on the dopamine-using regions of the brain (Lit et al., 1996). Once in the brain, the amphetamine molecule is absorbed into those neurons that use dopamine as a neurotransmitter, and both stimulate those neurons to release their dopamine stores while simultaneously blocking the reuptake pump that normally would remove the dopamine from the synapse (Haney, 2004). The mesolimbic region of the brain is especially rich in dopamine-containing neurons and is thought to be part of the "pleasure center" of the brain. This fact seems to account for the ability of the amphetamines to cause a sense of euphoria in the user. Another region in the brain in which the amphetamines have an effect is the medulla (involved in the control of respiration), causing the individual to breathe more deeply and more rapidly. At normal dosage levels, the cortex is also stimulated, resulting in reduced feelings of fatigue and possibly increased concentration (Kaplan & Sadock, 1996).

There is considerable variation in the level of individual sensitivity to the effects of the amphetamines. The estimated lethal dose of amphetamines for a nontolerant individual is 20 to 25 mg per kg (Chan, Chen, Lee, & Deng, 1994); there is one clinical report of a case in which the person ingested a dose of only 1.5 mg per kg, which proved to be lethal, and rare reports of toxic reactions to amphetamines at dosage levels as low as 2 mg (Hoffman & Lefkowitz, 1990). There are also case reports of amphetamine-naive individuals[5] surviving a total single dose of 400–500 mg (or 7.5 mg/kg body weight for a 160-pound person). However the patients who ingested these dosage levels required medical support to overcome the toxic effects of the amphetamines. Individuals who are tolerant to the effects of the amphetamines may use massive doses "without apparent ill effect" (Hoffman & Lefkowitz, 1990, p. 212).

A part of each dose of amphetamine will be biotransformed by the liver, but a significant percentage of the amphetamines will be excreted from the body essentially unchanged. For example, under normal conditions 45% of a single dose of methamphetamine will be excreted by the body unchanged (Karch, 2002). During the process of amphetamine biotransformation, a number of metabolites are formed as the biotransformation process progresses from one step to the next.

[5]See Glossary.

The exact number of metabolites will vary, depending on the specific form of amphetamine being used. For example, during the process of methamphetamine biotransformation, seven different metabolites are formed at various stages in the process before the drug is finally eliminated from the body.

The percentage of a single dose of amphetamine that is eliminated from the body unchanged might be increased to as much as 75% if the users were to take steps to acidify their blood (Karch, 2002). However, if the individual's urine is extremely alkaline, perhaps as little as 5% of a dose of amphetamine will be filtered out of the blood by the kidneys and excreted unchanged, according to the author. This is because the drug molecules tend to be reabsorbed by the kidneys when the urine is more alkaline. Thus, the speed at which a dose of amphetamines is excreted from the body varies in response to how acidic the individual's urine is at the time that the drug passes through the kidneys.

At one point, physicians were trained to try to make a patient's urine more acidic in order to speed up the excretion of the amphetamine molecules following an overdose. However, in recent years it has been found that this treatment method increases the chances that the patient will develop cardiac arrhythmias or seizures, and physicians are less likely to utilize urine acidification as a treatment method for amphetamine overdose than they were 30 years ago (Albertson et al., 1999; Carvey, 1998).

Neuroadaptation/tolerance to amphetamines. The steady use of an amphetamine by a patient will result in an incomplete state of neuroadaptation. For example, when a physician prescribes an amphetamine to treat narcolepsy, it is possible for the patient to be maintained on the same dose for years without any loss of efficacy (Jaffe, 2000a). However, patients become tolerant to the anorexic effects of the amphetamines after only a few weeks, and the initial drug-induced state of well-being does not last beyond the first few doses when used at therapeutic dosage levels.

Interactions between the amphetamines and other medications. Patients who are taking amphetamines should avoid taking them with fruit juices or ascorbic acid as these substances will decrease the absorption of the amphetamine dose (Maxmen & Ward, 1995). Patients should avoid mixing amphetamines with opiates as these drugs will increase the anorexic and analgesic effects of narcotic analgesics. Further, patients who are taking a class of antidepressants known as monoamine oxidase inhibitors (MAOIs or MAO inhibitors) should avoid amphetamines as the combination of amphetamines and MAOIs can result in dangerous elevations in the person's blood pressure (Barnhill, Ciraulo, Ciraulo, & Greene, 1995). *You should always consult with a physician or pharmacist before taking two or more medications at the same time to make sure that there is no danger of harmful interactions between the chemicals being used.*

Subjective Experience of Amphetamine Use

The effects of the amphetamines on any given individual will depend upon that individual's mental state, the dosage level utilized, the relative potency of the specific form of amphetamine, and the manner in which the drug is used. The subjective effect of a single dose of amphetamines is to a large degree very similar to that seen with cocaine or adrenaline (Kaminski, 1992). However, there are some major differences: (a) the effects of cocaine might last from a few minutes to an hour at most, but the effects of the amphetamines last many hours; (b) unlike cocaine, the amphetamines are effective when used orally; and (c) unlike cocaine, the amphetamines have only a very small anesthetic effect (Ritz, 1999).

When used in medical practice, the usual oral dosage level is between 15 and 30 mg per day (Lingeman, 1974); however, this depends on the potency of the amphetamine or amphetamine-like drug being used (Julien, 1992). At low to moderate oral dosage levels, the individual will experience feelings of increased alertness, an elevation of mood, a sense of mild euphoria, less mental fatigue, and an improved level of concentration (Kaplan & Sadock, 1996). Like many drugs of abuse, the amphetamines will stimulate the "pleasure center" in the brain. Thus, both the amphetamines and cocaine produce "a neurochemical magnification of the pleasure experienced in most activities" (Gawin & Ellinwood, 1988, p. 1174) when initially used. The authors noted that the initial use of amphetamines or cocaine would "produce alertness and a sense of well-being . . . lower anxiety and social inhibitions, and heighten energy, self-esteem, and the emotions aroused by interpersonal experiences. Although they magnify pleasure, they do not distort it; hallucinations are usually absent" (p. 1174).

Side Effects of Amphetamine Use at Normal Dosage Levels

Patients who are taking amphetamines under a physician's supervision may experience such side effects as dryness of the mouth, nausea, anorexia, headache, insomnia, and periods of confusion (Fawcett & Busch, 1995). The patient's systolic and diastolic blood pressure will both increase, and the heart rate may reflexively slow down. More than 10% of the patients who take an amphetamine as prescribed will experience an amphetamine-induced tachycardia (Breggin, 1998; Fuller & Sajatovic, 1999). Amphetamine use, even at therapeutic dosage levels, has been known to cause or exacerbate the symptoms of Tourette's syndrome in some patients (Breggin, 1998; Fuller & Sajatovic, 1999). Other potential side effects at normal dosage levels include dizziness, agitation, a feeling of apprehension, flushing, pallor, muscle pains, excessive sweating, and delirium (Fawcett & Busch, 1995). Rarely, a patient will experience a drug-induced psychotic reaction when taking an amphetamine at recommended dosage levels (Breggin, 1998; Fuller & Sajatovic, 1999).

Surprisingly, in light of the fact that the amphetamines are CNS stimulants, almost 40% of patients on amphetamines experience drug-induced feelings of depression, which might become so severe that the individual attempts suicide (Breggin, 1998). Feelings of depression and a sense of fatigue, or lethargy, which last for a few hours or days are common when the amphetamines are discontinued by the patient.

II. CNS STIMULANT ABUSE

Scope of the Problem of CNS Stimulant Abuse and Addiction

Globally, amphetamines and amphetamine-like compounds are the second most commonly abused illicit chemical (cannabis is the first), with an estimated 34 to 35 million abusers around the world (Rawson, Gonzales, & Brethen, 2002; United Nations, 2003). In the United States, methamphetamine abuse is most popular among younger individuals, with the peak age of amphetamine abuse being the early 20s (Albertson et al., 1999; United Nations, 2003).

Methamphetamine continues to be a popular drug of abuse, especially by intravenous stimulant abusers. Orally administered methamphetamine is also a popular drug of abuse as well. It is estimated that about 800,000 people in the United States have abused some form of amphetamine at least once a month (Lemonick, Lafferty, Nash, & Park, 1997), and close to 5 million have abused methamphetamine at least once in their lives (Karch, 2002). Users typically use amphetamines manufactured in clandestine laboratories, the majority of which are in California. It is estimated that a single ounce of methamphetamine manufactured in an illicit laboratory can provide about 110 doses of the drug. Another major source of illicit amphetamines are Mexican drug dealers, who manufacture the drug in that country and then smuggle it into the United States (Lovett, 1994; Witkin, 1995).

Effects of the CNS Stimulants When Abused

Ephedrine

The frequency of ephedrine abuse in the United States is not known (Karch, 2002). This is because it was once available over the counter without restriction as a treatment for asthma and nasal congestion, and researchers have no way to determine how many people were legitimate users as opposed to abusers. Historically, ephedrine was abused by cross-country truckers, college students, and others who wanted to ward off the effects of fatigue. It was also occasionally sold in combination with other herbs under the label of "herbal ecstasy" (Schwartz & Miller, 1997), or sold either alone or in combination with other chemicals as a nutritional supplement to enhance athletic performance or aid weight-loss programs (Solotaroff, 2002). Also, ephedrine is used in the manufacture of illicit amphetamine compounds. All of these factors made it impossible to determine how much of the ephedrine produced in this country was being abused, or how much was being diverted to the manufacture of illicit drugs.

Effects of ephedrine when abused. Ephedrine is usually abused for its ability to stimulate the CNS. Alcohol abusers often will ingest ephedrine in order to continue to drink longer, using the ephedrine to conteract the sedative effects of the alcohol. At very high doses, ephedrine can cause the user to experience a sense of euphoria.

Methods of ephedrine abuse. The most common method of ephedrine abuse is for the user to ingest ephedrine pills purchased over the counter. On rare occasions, the pills will be crushed and the powder either "snorted" or even more infrequently injected. Ephedrine and its chemical cousin pseudoephedrine were also used in the illicit production of methamphetamine, a fact that may have contributed to the decision to outlaw the use of the former compound in 2004 (Office of National Drug Control Policy, 2004).

Consequences of ephedrine abuse. Ephedrine abuse produces effects that are essentially an exaggeration of the side effects of ephedrine seen at normal dosage levels. Although adverse effects *are* possible at very low doses, a rule of thumb is that the higher the dosage level being used, the more likely the user is to experience an adverse effect from ephedrine (Antonio, 1997). There is mixed evidence suggesting that ephedrine can contribute to cardiac dysfunctions, including arrhythmias, when used at high dosage levels (Karch, 2002). Theoretically, when used at high dosage levels ephedrine can increase the workload of the cardiac muscle and cause the muscle tissue to utilize higher levels of oxygen. This is potentially dangerous if the user should have some form of coronary artery disease.

Other complications from ephedrine abuse might include necrosis (death) of the tissues of the intestinal tract, potentially fatal arrhythmias, urinary retention, irritation of heart muscle tissue (especially in patients with damaged hearts), nausea, vomiting, stroke, drug-induced psychosis, formation of ephedrine kidney stones in rare cases, and possibly death (American Society of Health-System Pharmacists, 2002; Antonio, 1997; Karch, 2002; Solotaroff, 2002).

Ritalin (Methylphenidate)

Effects of methylphenidate when abused. There have been no case reports of methylphenidate from illegal laboratories, and thus it is logical to assume that illicit methylphenidate is obtained by diversion of legitimate sources (Karch, 2002). It is interesting to note that Volkow and Swanson (2003) believed that the clinical characteristics of methylphenidate when used as prescribed would constrain its abuse. The therapeutic use of methylphenidate was thought to cause slow, steady states of dopamine levels in the brain, which would mimic the tonic firing pattern of the cells that utilize dopamine in the brain, characteristics that would prohibit its abuse in the opinion of the authors.

Unfortunately, methylphenidate abusers do not follow recommended dosing patterns. It is rare for *orally* administered methylphenidate to be abused at normal dosage levels (Volkow & Swanson, 2003). But when the individual ingests a larger than normal dose, the abuser will experience a sense of mild euphoria (Diller, 1998). Students have also been known to abuse methylphenidate in order to help them study late before an exam ("Tip Sheet," 2004). In other common methods of abuse, users crush methylphenidate tablets and either inhale the powder or inject it into a vein (Karch, 2002; Volkow & Swanson, 2003). The strongest effects of methylphenidate abuse are thought to be achieved when it is injected intravenously. In contrast to the effects of methylphenidate when used at therapeutic doses, intravenously administered doses are able to bring about the blockage of more than 50% of the dopamine transporter system within a matter of seconds, causing the user to feel "high" (Volkow & Swanson, 2003; Volkow et al., 1998).

Consequences of methylphenidate abuse. The consequences of methylphenidate abuse are similar to those seen when its chemical cousin, the amphetamines, are abused. Even when used according to a physician's instructions, methylphenidate will occasionally trigger a toxic psychosis in the patient (Karch, 2002). Most certainly, when methylphenidate is abused it may trigger a toxic psychosis that is similar to paranoid schizophrenia. Unlike amphetamine abusers, methylphenidate abusers only rarely suffer CVAs, and cardiac problems associated with methylphenidate abuse are comparatively rare (Karch, 2002).

When drug abusers crush methylphenidate tablets then mix the resulting powder with water for intravenous use (Volkow et al., 1998), "fillers" in the tablet are injected directly into the circulation. These fillers are used to give the tablet bulk and form, and when the medication is used according to instructions they pass harmlessly through the digestive tract. When a tablet is crushed and injected, however, these fillers gain admission to the bloodstream and may accumulate in the retina of the eye, causing damage to that tissue (Karch, 2002).

The Amphetamines

Effects of the amphetamines when abused. Scientists are only now starting to understand how an amphetamine such as methamphetamine affects the brain (Rawson et al., 2002). It is known that when the amphetamines are abused, the effects will vary, depending on the specific compound being abused and the route by which it was administered. At low doses, such as those achieved through a single oral dose of amphetamines, the user experiences a sense of well-being, energy, and gentle euphoria. Some abusers claim that the amphetamines function as an aphrodisiac; however, there is little scientific evidence to support this claim.

When methamphetamine is either injected into a vein or smoked, users experience an intense sense of euphoria, which has been called a "rush" or a "flash." This sensation was described as "instant euphoria" by the author Truman Capote (quoted in Siegel, 1991, p. 72). Other users have compared the "flash" to sexual orgasm. Researchers have not studied the "rush" in depth, but it appears to last for only a short period of time and is limited to the initial period of amphetamine abuse (Jaffe, 2000a). Subsequent doses of amphetamine do not bring about the same intense euphoria seen with the first dose, and following the initial rush, the user may experience a warm glow or gentle euphoria that may last for several hours.

The chronic use of amphetamines at high dosage levels has been implicated as the cause of violent outbursts, possibly resulting in the death of bystanders (King & Ellinwood, 1997). Animal research suggests that following periods of chronic abuse at high dosage levels, norepinephrine levels are depleted throughout the brain, and the brain's norepinephrine might not return to normal even after 6 months of abstinence (King & Ellinwood, 1997). The effects of chronic amphetamine abuse on dopamine levels in the brain appear more limited to the region known as the *caudate putamen*; however, as with the norepinephrine economy within the brain, animal research suggests that the dopamine levels in the caudate putamen might not return to normal even after 6 months of abstinence (King & Ellinwood, 1997). Animal research

suggests that the chronic use of amphetamines at high dosage levels might be neurotoxic possibly through amphetamine-induced release of large amounts of the neurotransmitter glutamate (Batki, 2001; Haney, 2004; King & Ellinwood, 1997). Finally, although the mechanism by which this is accomplished is not clear, there have been documented changes in the vasculature of the brain in chronic amphetamine abusers, and researchers do not know whether these changes are permanent (Breggin, 1998).

Scope of amphetamine abuse. Globally the abuse of amphetamine or amphetamine-like compounds is estimated to be a $65 billion a year industry (United Nations, 2003). There are regional variations in the pattern of CNS stimulant abuse around the globe, but in the United States methamphetamine is the most commonly abused amphetamine compound (United Nations, 2003).

The abuse of amphetamines, especially methamphetamine, has increased dramatically in the last years of the 20th century and first few years of the 21st century (Milne, 2003). Information on how to manufacture methamphetamine is available on the Internet and there is evidence to suggest that organized crime cartels have started to manufacture and distribute methamphetamine in large quantities (Milne, 2003; United Nations, 2003). Unfortunately, there appear to be about as many formulas for producing methamphetamine as there are "chemists" who try to produce it, a matter that makes understanding the toxicology of illicit forms of methamphetamine quite difficult.

One measure of the popularity of amphetamines is seen in the increase in illegal laboratories manufacturing this substance that have been uncovered by law-enforcement officials in the past few years. Most illicit labs are "mom and pop" operations that produce relatively small amounts of amphetamine (usually methamphetamine) for local consumption, although a few "superlabs" have also been discovered by law-enforcement officials (United Nations, 2003). It is estimated that about 410 tons of amphetamine compounds (usually methamphetamine) were produced annually by such illicit laboratories around the globe (United Nations, 2003). The phenomenal growth of amphetamine abuse might be seen in the fact that in Iowa, only two small amphetamine production laboratories were uncovered in 1994; by 1999, there were 803 (Milne, 2003).

One method of methamphetamine production is known as "Nazi Meth," for the Nazi symbols that decorated the paper with the formula on it that was discovered by police officials ("Nazi Meth Is on the Rise," 2003). This method does not rely on the use of red phosphorus but uses compounds easily obtained from lithium batteries, ammonia, and other sources ("Nazi Meth Is on the Rise," 2003). A $200 investment into the required materials will yield methamphetamine that might sell for $2,500 on the street, although there is a danger that some of the contaminants contained in the compound might prove toxic to the user (apparently a matter of little concern to the abuser).

Methods of amphetamine abuse. The amphetamines are well absorbed when taken orally or when injected into muscle tissue or a vein; the powder might be snorted, and it may be smoked. When smoked, the amphetamine molecule is also absorbed through the lining of the lungs, and illicit drug chemists developed a smokable form of methamphetamine in the 1950s that is sold under the name of "Ice." When smoked, the amphetamines will be absorbed into the circulation through the lungs and will reach the brain in just a matter of seconds. In the United States, methamphetamine is commonly abused through the ingestion of tablets by mouth, by smoking it, or by intravenous injection (Karch, 2002). However, the amphetamine molecule is easily absorbed through the tissues of the naso-pharynx, and thus amphetamine powder might be snorted.

Subjective effects of amphetamine abuse. Because the amphetamines have a reputation for enhancing normal body functions (alertness, concentration, etc.), they have a reputation as being less dangerous than other illicit compounds (United Nations, 2003). The subjective effects of the amphetamines are dependent upon (a) whether tolerance to the drug has developed, and (b) the method by which the drug was used. Amphetamine abusers who are not tolerant to the drug's effects and who use oral forms of the drug, or who snort it, report experiencing a sense of euphoria that may last for several hours. Individuals who are not tolerant to the drug's effects and who inject amphetamines report an intense feeling of euphoria, followed by a less intense feeling of well-being that might last for several hours. It has been reported that the "high" produced by methamphetamine might last 8 to 24 hours, a feature of this drug

that seems to make it more addictive than cocaine (Castro, Barrington, Walton, & Rawson, 2000).

Tolerance to the amphetamines. Amphetamine abusers quickly become tolerant to some of the euphoric effects of the drug (Haney, 2004). In an attempt to recapture the initial drug-induced euphoria, amphetamine abusers try to overcome their tolerance to the drug in one of three ways. First, amphetamine *abusers* will try to limit their exposure to the drug to isolated periods of time, allowing their bodies to return to normal before the next exposure to an amphetamine. The development of tolerance requires *constant* exposure to the compound or the neuroadaptive changes that cause tolerance are reversed and the body returns to a normal state. Some individuals are able to abuse amphetamines for years by following a pattern of intermittent abuse followed by periods of abstinence (possibly by switching to other compounds that are then abused).

Another method by which amphetamine abusers attempt to recapture the initial feeling of euphoria induced by the drug is to embark on a cycle of using higher and higher doses of amphetamine each time the drug is used. This is done in an attempt to overcome tolerance to these chemicals (Peluso & Peluso, 1988). Other abusers "graduate" from oral or intranasal methods of amphetamine abuse to intravenous injections to provide a more concentrated dose. Finally, when this fails to provide abusers with sufficient pleasure, they might embark on a "speed run," injecting some more amphetamine every few minutes to try to overcome their tolerance to the drugs. Some amphetamine addicts might inject a cumulative dose of 5,000 to 15,000 mg in a 24-hour time span while on a "speed run" (Chan et al., 1994; Derlet & Heischober, 1990). Such dosage levels would be fatal to the "naive" (inexperienced) drug user and are well within the dosage range found to be neurotoxic in animal studies. Speed runs might last for hours or days and are a sign that the individual has progressed from amphetamine abuse to addiction to these compounds.

Consequences of Amphetamine Abuse

There is a wide variation in what might be considered a "toxic" dose of amphetamines (Julien, 1992). However, a general rule is that the higher the concentration of amphetamines in the blood, the more likely the individual is to experience one or more of the adverse effects.

Whereas adverse effects of an amphetamine dose are rarely encountered when the drugs are used at therapeutic doses under the supervision of a physician, *abusers* are more likely to experience one or more amphetamine-induced side effects as their dosage level increases to overcome their tolerance to the drug.

Central nervous system. Researchers have discovered that amphetamine abuse can cause damage in both a cellular and a regional level of the brain. At the cellular level, up to 50% of the dopamine-producing cells in the brain might be damaged after prolonged exposure to even low levels of methamphetamine (Leshner, 2001a, b). This methamphetamine-induced neurological damage might even be more widespread than just the dopamine-producing neurons. For example, Thompson et al. (2004) utilized high-resolution magnetic resonance imaging (MRI) studies to find significant reductions in gray matter in the brains of methamphetamine addicts as compared to normal subjects.

In addition, methamphetamine seems to be especially toxic to serotonin-producing neurons (Jaffe, 2000a; King & Ellinwood, 1997). There is evidence that methamphetamine-induced cellular damage might reflect the release of large amounts of glutamate within the brain. Eventually, the large levels of glutamate become toxic to the neurons, causing neuronal damage or even death (Fischman & Haney, 1999). Animal research suggests that methamphetamine-induced brain damage on the cellular level might persist for more than 3 years (Fischman & Haney, 1999).

It is thought that amphetamine-induced regional brain damage is caused by the ability of these compounds to bring about both temporary and permanent changes in cerebral blood flow patterns. Some of the more dangerous temporary change in cerebral blood flow caused by amphetamine abuse include the development of hypertensive episodes, cerebral vasculitis, and vasospasm in the blood vessels in the brain. All of these amphetamine-induced changes in cerebral blood flow can result in a cerebral vascular hemorrhage (CVA, stroke) which may or may not be fatal (Albertson et al., 1999; Brust, 1997; King & Ellinwood, 1997). Further, reductions in cerebral blood flow were found in 76% of amphetamine abusers, changes that could persist for years after the

individual had discontinued the use of these drugs (Buffenstein, Heaster, & Ko, 1999).

Chronic amphetamine abusers might experience sleep disturbances for up to 4 weeks after their last use of the drug (Satel, Kosten, Schuckit, & Fischman, 1993). The authors also cited evidence that chronic amphetamine users might have abnormal EEG tracings (a measure of the electrical activity in the brain) for up to 3 months after their last drug use. Another very rare complication of amphetamine use or abuse is the development of the neurological condition known as the *serotonin syndrome* (Mills, 1995).[6]

Consequences of amphetamine abuse on the person's emotions. Researchers have also found that the effects of chronic amphetamine abuse on the individual's emotions might last for an extended period of time after the last actual drug use. The amphetamines are capable of causing both new and chronic users to experience increased anxiety levels (Satel et al., 1993). Indeed, up to 75% of amphetamine abusers report significant degrees of anxiety when they started using amphetamines (Breggin, 1998). Amphetamine-related anxiety episodes might reach the proportions of actual panic attacks, which have been known to persist for months or even years after the last actual use of amphetamines (Satel et al., 1993). That amphetamine abuse should cause such effects is not surprising in light of the research by London et al. (2004). The authors utilized radioactive atoms and positron emission tomography (PET scan) technology to measure the activity level of various regions of the brain in abstinent methamphetamine abusers. They found that chronic methamphetamine abuse alters the metabolism of brain structures thought to be involved in the generation of anxiety and depression, helping researchers to better understand that these conditions can indeed be methamphetamine-induced effects.

It is not uncommon for illicit amphetamine users to try to counteract the drug-induced anxiety and tension through the use of agents such as alcohol, marijuana, or benzodiazepines. For example, Peluso and Peluso (1988) estimated that *half* of all regular amphetamine users may also be classified as heavy drinkers. These individuals attempt to control the side effects of the amphetamines through the use of CNS depressants

[6]See Glossary.

such as alcohol.[7] Amphetamine users also might experience periods of drug-induced confusion, irritability, fear, suspicion, drug-induced hallucinations, and a drug-induced delusional state (King & Ellinwood, 1997; Julien, 1992).

Other possible consequences of amphetamine abuse include assaultiveness, tremor, headache, irritability, weakness, insomnia, panic states, and suicidal and homicidal tendencies (Albertson et al., 1999; Derlet & Heischober, 1990). Physicians have found that the compounds haloperidol and diazepam are effective in helping the individual calm down from an amphetamine-induced agitation (Albertson et al., 1999). All amphetamine compounds are capable of inducing a toxic psychosis, although evidence suggests that methamphetamine is more likely to be involved in a drug-induced psychotic episode than other forms of amphetamine (Batki, 2001). This is because it is easier to achieve chronic high levels with methamphetamine than other CNS stimulants (Kosten & Sofuoglu, 2004). Using PET scan data, Sekine et al. (2001) were able to document long-lasting reductions in the number of dopamine transporter sites in methamphetamine abusers. The authors suggested that this reduction might be associated with the onset of the methamphetamine-induced psychosis in users who develop this complication of methamphetamine abuse.

In its early stages, this drug-induced psychosis is often indistinguishable from schizophrenia and might include such symptoms as confusion, suspiciousness, paranoia, auditory and visual hallucinations, delusional thinking (including delusions of being persecuted), anxiety, and periods of aggression (Beebe & Walley, 1995; Kaplan & Sadock, 1996; King & Ellinwood, 1997; United Nations, 2003). Less common symptoms of an amphetamine-induced psychotic episode include psychomotor retardation, incoherent speech, inappropriate or flattened affect, and depression (Srisurapanont, Marsden, Sunga, Wada, & Monterio, 2003). The ability of the amphetamines to induce a psychotic state is reflected in the fact that 46% of amphetamine abusers reported hallucinations and 52% experienced significant degrees of paranoia when they

first began to abuse amphetamines (Breggin, 1998). But where Kaplan and Sadock (1996) suggested that amphetamine-induced hallucinations tend to be mainly visual, which is not typical of a true schizophrenic condition, Srisurapanont et al. (2003) suggested that auditory hallucinations were more common in the amphetamine-induced psychosis.

Under normal conditions, this drug-induced psychosis clears up within days to weeks after the drug is discontinued (Haney, 2004). However, in some cases, this drug-induced psychosis may continue for several months (Karch, 2002). Researchers in Japan following World War II noted that in 15% of the cases of amphetamine-induced psychosis, it took up to 5 years following the last amphetamine use before the drug-induced psychotic condition eased (Flaum & Schultz, 1996). For reasons that are not well understood, occasionally the amphetamine-induced psychosis does not remit, and the individual develops a chronic psychosis. It was once thought that the amphetamine-induced psychosis reflected the activation of a latent schizophrenia in a person who was vulnerable to this condition. Chen et al. (2003) assessed 445 amphetamine abusers in Taipei (Taiwan) and found a tendency for those individuals who subsequently developed a methamphetamine-induced psychosis to have been younger at the time of their first drug use, to have used larger amounts of methamphetamine, and to have premorbid schizoid or schizotypal personalities. Further, the authors found a positive relationship between the degree of personality dysfunction and the duration of the methamphetamine-induced psychotic reaction.

Prolonged use of the amphetamines may also result in people's experiencing a condition known as *formication*. Victims have been known to scratch or burn the skin in an attempt to rid themselves of what they believe are unseen bugs. Also, following prolonged periods of amphetamine abuse, many individuals become fatigued or depressed. It is not uncommon for the individual's depression to reach suicidal proportions (Fawcett & Busch, 1995). The post-amphetamine depressive reaction can last for extended periods of time, possibly for *months* following cessation of amphetamine use.

The digestive system. Amphetamine abuse has been identified as causing such digestive system problems as diarrhea or constipation, nausea, and vomiting

---

[7]The reverse is also true: Alcohol abusers may ingest an amphetamine, or other CSN stimulant, in an attempt to counteract the sedation that results from heavy drinking.

(Albertson et al., 1999; Derlet & Heischober, 1990). There have been a few reports of liver damage associated with amphetamine abuse (Jones, Jarvie, McDermid, & Proudfoot, 1994). However, the exact mechanisms by which illicit amphetamines are able to cause damage to the liver are still not clear. The consequences of prolonged amphetamine use, like that of cocaine, include the various complications seen in people who have neglected their dietary requirements. Vitamin deficiencies are a common consequence of chronic amphetamine abuse (Gold & Verebey, 1984). Prolonged use of the amphetamines may result in the user vomiting, becoming anorexic, or developing diarrhea (Kaplan & Sadock, 1996).

The cardiovascular system. Overall, the amphetamines appear to have less potential for causing cardiovascular damage than does cocaine abuse (Karch, 2002). However, this does not mean that amphetamine abuse does not carry some risk of cardiovascular damage. In spite of its lower potential for cardiovascular damage, amphetamine abuse has been implicated as causing accelerated development of plaque in the coronary arteries, thus contributing to the development of coronary artery disease (CAD) in users (Karch, 2002). Amphetamine abuse can also result in hypertensive reactions, tachycardia, arrhythmias, and sudden cardiac death, especially when used at high dosage levels (Karch, 2002; Wender, 1995).

Amphetamine abusers have been known to suffer a number of serious, potentially fatal cardiac problems, including chest pain (angina), atrial and ventricular arrhythmias, congestive heart failure (Derlet & Horowitz, 1995), myocardial ischemia (Derlet & Heischober, 1990), cardiomyopathy (Brent, 1995; Fawcett & Busch, 1995), and myocardial infarction (Fawcett & Busch, 1995; Karch, 2002). The mechanism of an amphetamine-induced myocardial infarction is similar to that seen in cocaine-induced myocardial infarctions (Wijetunga, Bhan, Lindsay, & Karch, 2004). The amphetamines appear to induce a series of spasms in the coronary arteries at the same time that the heart's workload is increased by the drug's effects on the rest of the body (Hong, Matsuyama, & Nur, 1991). Amphetamine abuse has been identified as causing rhabodmyolysis in some users, although the exact mechanism by which the amphetamines might cause this disorder remains unclear (Richards, 2000).

Amphetamine abuse can also result in impotence in the male (Albertson et al., 1999; Derlet & Heischober, 1990).

On the pulmonary system. There has been very little research into the impact of amphetamine abuse and lung function (Albertson, Walby, & Derlet, 1995). As amphetamine smoking is a common method by which the drug is abused, it might be reasonable to expect that the side effects of smoked amphetamine would be similar to those found when the user smokes cocaine. Thus, amphetamine abuse might result in sinusitis, pulmonary infiltrates, pulmonary edema, exacerbation of asthma, pulmonary hypertension, and pulmonary hemorrhage or infarct (Albertson et al., 1995).

Other consequences of amphetamine abuse. One unintended consequence of *any* form of amphetamine abuse is that the amphetamine being abused might interact with surgical anesthetics if the abuser should be injured and require emergency surgery (Klein & Kramer, 2004). Further, there is evidence that amphetamine use or abuse might exacerbate some medical disorders such as Tourette's syndrome or tardive dyskinesia (Lopez & Jeste, 1997). Amphetamine abuse has also been implicated as a cause of sexual performance problems for both men and women (Finger, Lund, & Slagel, 1997). High doses or the chronic use of amphetamines can cause an inhibition of orgasm in the user, according to the authors, as well as delayed or inhibited ejaculation in men. The practice of smoking methamphetamine has resulted in the formation of ulcers on the cornea of the eyes of some users (Chuck, Williams, Goldberg, & Lubniewski, 1996).

The addictive potential of amphetamines. At present, there is no test that will identify those who are most at risk for amphetamine addiction, and if only for this reason, the abuse of these chemicals is not recommended. *Most* amphetamine abusers do not become addicted. But some abusers do become either emotionally or physically dependent on amphetamines (Gawin & Ellinwood, 1988). When abused, these compounds stimulate the brain's "reward system," possibly with greater effect than natural reinforcers such as food or sex (Haney, 2004). This effect, in turn, helps create "vivid, long-term memories" (Gawin & Ellinwood, 1988, p. 1175) of the drug experience for the user. These memories help sensitize the individual to drug-use cues, which cause the abuser to crave the drug when exposed to these cues.

"Ice"

In the late 1970s a smokable form of methamphetamine called "Ice" was introduced to the United States mainland (*The Economist*, 1989). Although it differs in appearance from methamphetamine tablets, on a molecular level it is simply methamphetamine (Wijetunga et al., 2004). Historical evidence would suggest that this form of methamphetamine was brought to Hawaii from Japan by U.S. army troops following World War II, and its use remained endemic to Hawaii for many years ("Drug Problems in Perspective," 1990). Smoking methamphetamine is also endemic in Asia, where it is known as "shabu" (United Nations, 2003). The practice has slowly spread across the United States, but by 2003 only 3.9% of the high school seniors surveyed admitted to having used Ice at least once (Johnston, O'Malley, & Bachman, 2003a).

How Ice is used. Ice is a colorless, odorless, form of concentrated crystal methamphetamine that resembles a chip of ice or clear rock candy. Some samples of Ice sold on the street have been up to 98%–100% pure amphetamine (Kaminski, 1992). Although injection or inhalation of methamphetamine is common, smoking Ice is also quite popular in some regions of the United States (Kaminski, 1992; Karch, 2002). Ice is smoked much like crack cocaine, crossing into the blood through the lungs and reaching the brain in a matter of seconds.

Subjective effects of Ice abuse. In contrast to cocaine, which induces a sense of euphoria that lasts perhaps 20 minutes, the high from Ice lasts for a significantly longer period of time. Estimates as to the duration of the effects of Ice vary from 8 hours ("Raw Data," 1990), 12 hours ("New Drug 'Ice,'" 1989; "Drug Problems in Perspective," 1990), 14 hours ("Ice Overdose," 1989), 18 hours (McEnroe, 1990), to 24 hours (Evanko, 1991). Kaminski (1992) suggested that the effects of Ice might last as long as 30 hours. The long duration of its effect, while obviously in some dispute, is consistent with the pharmacological properties of the amphetamines as compared with those of cocaine. The stimulant effects of the amphetamines in general last for hours, whereas cocaine's stimulant effects usually last for a shorter period of time.

The effects of Ice. In addition to the physical effects of the amphetamines, which were reviewed earlier in this chapter, users have found that Ice has several advantages over crack cocaine. First, although it is more expensive than crack, dose for dose Ice is actually cheaper than crack. Second, because of its duration of effect, it *seems* to be more potent than crack. Third, since Ice melts at a lower temperature than crack, it does not require as much heat to use. This means that Ice may be smoked without the elaborate equipment needed for crack smoking. Because it is odorless, Ice may be smoked in public without any characteristic smell alerting passersby that it is being used. Finally, another advantage of Ice is that if the user decides to stop smoking it for a moment or two, it will cool and reform as a crystal. This makes it highly transportable and offers an advantage over crack cocaine in that the user can use only a part of the piece of the drug at any given time, rather than having to use it all at once.

Complications of Ice abuse. Essentially, the complications of Ice abuse are the same as those seen with other forms of amphetamine abuse. This is understandable, since Ice is simply a different form of methamphetamine than the powder or pills sold on the street for oral or intravenous use. However, in contrast to the dosage level achieved when methamphetamine is used by a patient under a physician's care, the typical amount of methamphetamine admitted into the body when the user smokes Ice is between *150 and 1,000 times the maximum recommended therapeutic dosage* for methamphetamine (Hong et al., 1991). At such high dosage levels, abusers commonly experience one or more adverse effects from the drug.

In addition to the adverse effects of amphetamine abuse, which are also experienced by Ice users, there are many problems specifically associated with the use of Ice. Methamphetamine is a vasoconstrictor, which might be why some Ice users develop potentially dangerous elevations in body temperature (Beebe & Walley, 1995). When the body temperature passes above 104°F, the prognosis for recovery is quite poor. There have also been reports that female patients who have had anesthesia to prepare them for caesarean sections have suffered cardiovascular collapse because of the interaction between the anesthesia and Ice. Methamphetamine abuse has been known to cause kidney and lung damage as well as permanent damage to the structure of the brain itself, pulmonary edema, vascular spasm, cardiomyopathy, drug-induced psychotic reactions, acute myocardial infarctions (i.e., a "heart attack"), and cerebral arteritis (Albertson et al., 1995; Hong et al., 1991; Wijetunga et al., 2004). As these findings suggest, Ice is hardly safe.

"Kat"

In the late 1990s it appeared that methcathinone, or "Kat" (sometimes spelled "Cat," "qat," "Khat," or "miraa") might become a popular drug of abuse in the United States. Kat leaves contain norephedrine, and cathinone, which is biotransformed into norephedrine by the body. Kat is found naturally in several species of evergreen plants that are normally found in east Africa and southern Arabia (Community Anti-Drug Coalitions of America, 1997; Goldstone, 1993; Monroe, 1994). The plant grows to between 10 and 20 feet in height, and the leaves produce the alkaloids cathinone and cathine. Illicit producers began to produce an analog of cathinone, known as methcathinone, which has a chemical structure similar to that of the amphetamines and ephedrine (Karch, 2002).

The legal status of Kat. Kat was classified a Category I[8] controlled substance in 1992, and because of this classification the manufacture of this drug or its distribution is illegal (Monroe, 1994).

How Kat is produced. Kat is easily synthesized by illicit laboratories, using ephedrine and such compounds as drain cleaner, epsom salts, battery acid, acetone, tuolene, various dyes, and hydrochloric acid to alter the basic ephedrine molecule. The basic components from which Kat is produced are all legally available in the United States (Monroe, 1994). These chemicals are mixed in such a way as to add an oxygen molecule to the original ephedrine molecule ("Other AAFS Highlights," 1995c) to produce a compound with the chemical structure 2-methylamino-1-pheylpropan-l-one.

The scope of Kat use. After its introduction into the United States, Kat could be purchased in virtually any major city in the this country by the mid 1990s (Finkelstein, 1997). However, by the start of the 21st century, methcathinone has virtually disappeared from the drug scene, except for sub-Saharan immigrants who continue the practice of chewing the leaves even after arriving in the United States (Karch, 2002; "Khat Calls," 2004).

The effects of Kat. Users typically either inhale or smoke Kat, although it can be injected (Monroe, 1994). The drug's effects are similar to those of the amphetamines. Users report that the drug can cause a sense of euphoria (Community Anti-Drug Coalitions of America, 1997) as well as a more intense "high" than does cocaine ("'Cat' Poses National Threat," 1993). In contrast to cocaine, the effects of Kat can last from 24 hours (Community Anti-Drug Coalitions of America, 1997) up to 6 days (Goldstone, 1993; Monroe, 1994). Once in the body, Kat is biotransformed into ephedrine ("Other AAFS Highlights," 1995). Thus, its effects on the user are very similar to those seen with the chronic use of ephedrine at high dosage levels. Following the period of drug use, it is not uncommon for Kat users to fall into a deep sleep that might last for as long as several days (Monroe, 1994). Chronic users also have reported experiencing periods of depression following the use of Kat ("'Cat' Poses National Threat," 1993).

Adverse effects of Kat abuse. Because this is a relatively new drug, much remains to be discovered about the effects of Kat on the user. To date, some of the reported adverse effects include the development of drug-induced psychotic reactions; agitation; hyperactivity; a strong, offensive body odor; sores in the mouth and on the tongue; and depression. Death has been known to occur as a result of Kat use, although the exact mechanism of death has not been identified. Monroe (1994) suggested that Kat users are at increased risk for heart attack or stroke. Brent (1995) suggested that an overdose of Kat produces many of the same effects, and responds to the same treatment, as does an overdose of amphetamine. At this time, Kat seems to to be of less interest to the casual user of chemicals than to the occasional hardcore stimulant abuser (O'Brien, 2001).

Summary

Although they had been discovered in the 1880s the amphetamines were first introduced as a treatment for asthma some 50 years later, in the 1930s. The early forms of amphetamine were sold over the counter in cloth-covered ampules that were used in much the

[8]See Appendix 4.

same way as smelling salts are today. Within a short time, however, it was discovered that the ampules were a source of concentrated amphetamine, which could be injected. The resulting "high" was found to be similar to that of cocaine, which had gained a reputation as being a dangerous drug to use, but with the added "benefit" lasting much longer.

The amphetamines were used extensively both during and after World War II. Following the war, American physicians prescribed amphetamines for the treatment of depression and as an aid for weight loss. By the year 1970, amphetamines accounted for 8% of all prescriptions written. However, since then, physicians have come to understand that the amphetamines present a serious potential for abuse. The amphetamines have come under increasingly strict controls, which limit the amount of amphetamine manufactured and the reasons an amphetamine might be prescribed.

Unfortunately, the amphetamines are easily manufactured, and there has always been an underground manufacture and distribution system for these drugs. In the late 1970s and early 1980s street drug users drifted away from the amphetamines to the supposedly safe stimulant of the early 1900s: cocaine. In the late 1990s, the pendulum began to swing the other way, and illicit drug users began to use the amphetamines, especially methamphetamine, more and more frequently. This new generation of amphetamine addicts has not learned the dangers of amphetamine abuse so painfully discovered by amphetamine users of the late 1960s: "Speed" kills.

CHAPTER TWELVE

Cocaine

Introduction

Historically, the United States experienced a resurgence of interest in and abuse of cocaine in the early to mid 1980s. This wave of cocaine abuse peaked around 1986 and gradually declined in the mid to late 1990s; by the early years of the 21st century cocaine abuse levels in the United States were significantly lower than those seen 15 years earlier. However, cocaine abuse never entirely disappeared, and it remains a serious problem in this country. In this chapter, cocaine abuse and addiction will be discussed.

A Brief Overview of Cocaine

At some point in the distant past, a member of the plant species Erythroxylon coca began to produce a neurotoxin in its leaves that would destroy the nervous system of bugs that might try to ingest its leaves (Breiter, 1999). This neurotoxin, cocaine, was able to ward off most of the insects that would otherwise strip the coca plant of its leaves, allowing the coca plant to thrive in the higher elevations of Peru, Bolivia, and Java (DiGregorio, 1990). At least 5,000 years ago, it was discovered that chewing the leaves could ease feelings of fatigue, thirst, and hunger, enabling the individual to work for longer periods of time in the thin mountain air (Hahn & Hoffman, 2001). By the time the first European explorers arrived, the Inca empire was at its height, and the coca plant was used by the Incas not only in their religious ceremonies but as a medium of exchange (Ray & Ksir, 1993) and as part of the burial ritual (Byck, 1987).

Prior to the arrival of the first European explorers the coca plant's use was generally reserved for the upper classes (Mann, 1994). However, European explorers soon found that by giving native workers coca leaves to chew on, the workers would be more productive. The coca plant became associated with the exploitation of South America by European settlers, who encouraged its widespread use. Even today, the practice of chewing coca leaves, or drinking a form of tea brewed from the leaves, has continued. Modern natives of the mountain regions of Peru chew coca leaves mixed with lime, which is obtained from sea shells (White, 1989). The lime works with saliva to release the cocaine from the leaves and helps to reduce its bitter taste. Also, chewing coca leaves is thought to actually help the chewer absorb some of the phosphorus, vitamins, and calcium contained in the mixture (White, 1989). Thus, although its primary use is to help the natives work more efficiently at high altitudes, there might also be some small nutritional benefit obtained from the practice of chewing coca leaves.

As European scientists began to explore the biosphere of South America, they took a passing interest in the coca plant and attempted to isolate the compounds that made it so effective in warding off hunger and fatigue. In 1859, a chemist named Albert Neiman isolated a compound that was later called cocaine (Scaros, Westra, & Barone, 1990). This accomplishment then allowed researchers to first produce large amounts of relatively pure cocaine for research. One of these experiments involved the injection of concentrated cocaine directly into the bloodstream with another new invention: the hypodermic needle.

Before long researchers discovered that even orally administered cocaine made the user feel good. Extracts from the coca leaf were used to make a wide range of popular drinks, wines, and elixirs (Martensen, 1996). Physicians of the era, lacking effective pharmaceuticals for most human ills, experimented with cocaine concentrate as a possible agent to treat disease. No less a figure than Sigmund Freud experimented with cocaine, at first thinking it a cure for depression (Rome, 1984) and later as a possible "cure" for narcotic withdrawal symptoms (Byck, 1987; Lingeman, 1974). However, when Freud discovered the drug's previously unsuspected addictive potential, he discontinued his research on cocaine, as did many other scientists of the era.

Cocaine in Recent U.S. History

In response to the decision by the city of Atlanta to prohibit the use of alcohol, John Stith-Pemberton developed a new product that he thought would serve as a "temperance drink" (Martensen, 1996, p. 1615), which up until 1903 contained 60 mg of cocaine per 8 ounce serving (Gold, 1997). In time, the world would come to know Stith-Pemberton's product by another name: Coca-Cola. Although this is surprising to modern readers, one must remember that consumer protection laws were virtually nonexistent, and chemicals such as cocaine and morphine were readily available without a prescription. These compounds were widely used in a wide variety of products and medicines, usually as a hidden ingredient. This practice contributed to epidemics of cocaine abuse in Europe between the years 1886 and 1891, and in both Europe and the United States between 1894 and 1899, and again in the United States between 1921 and 1929.

These waves of cocaine abuse or addiction, the use of cocaine in so many patent medicines, combined with concern over its supposed "narcotic" qualities and the fear that cocaine was corrupting southern blacks, prompted both the passage of the Pure Food and Drug Act of 1906 (Mann, 1994) and the classification of cocaine as a "narcotic" in 1914 (Martensen, 1996). The Pure Food and Drug Act of 1906 required makers to list the ingredients of a patent medicine or elixir on the label. As a result of this law, cocaine was removed from many patent medicines. With the passage of the Harrison Narcotics Act of 1914, nonmedical cocaine use in the United States was prohibited (Derlet, 1989).

These regulations, the isolation of the United States during the First and Second World Wars, and introduction of the amphetamines in the 1930s, helped to virtually eliminate cocaine abuse in this country. It did not resurface as a major drug of abuse until the late 1960s. By then, cocaine had the reputation in this country of being the "champagne of drugs" (White, 1989, p. 34) for those who could afford it. It again became popular as a drug of abuse in the United States in the 1970s and early 1980s. There are many reasons for this resurgence in cocaine's popularity. First, cocaine had been all but forgotten since the Harrison Narcotics Act of 1914. Stories of cocaine abusers sneezing out long tubes of damaged or dead cartilage in the latter years of the 19th and early years of the 20th centuries were either forgotten or dismissed as "moralistic exaggerations" (Gawin & Ellinwood, 1988, p. 1173; Walton, 2002).

Also, there had been a growing disillusionment with the amphetamines as drugs of abuse that started in the mid 1960s. The amphetamines had acquired a reputation as known killers. Drug users would warn each other that "speed kills," a reference to the fact that the amphetamines could kill the user in a number of different ways. For better or worse, cocaine had the reputation of bringing about many of the same sensations caused by amphetamine use without the dangers associated with the abuse of other CNS stimulants. Cocaine's reputation as a special, glamorous drug combined with increasing government-sanctioned restrictions on amphetamine production by legitimate pharmaceutical companies helped focus attention on cocaine as a substitute by drug abusers in the late 1960s.

By the middle of the 1980s, cocaine had again become a popular drug of abuse in a number of countries around the world. The United States did not always lead in the area of cocaine abuse. For example, by the mid 1970s, the practice of smoking coca paste was popular in parts of South America but had only started to gain popularity in the United States. But as cocaine became more popular in this country, it attracted the attention of what is loosely called "organized crime." At the same time, cocaine dealers were eager to find new markets for their "product" in the United States, where the primary method of cocaine abuse was intranasal inhalation of the cocaine powder. Cocaine "freebase" (to be discussed below) was known to induce an intense feeling of euphoria when smoked, but it required the use of elaborate equipment by the user to separate the cocaine base from the powder then being sold on the street ("The Men Who Created Crack," 1991). After a period of experimentation, illicit drug manufacturers developed "crack," a form of cocaine that could be smoked without elaborate preparations or equipment, and crack started to become the preferred form of cocaine in this country in the early 1980s.

The epidemic of cocaine use/abuse that swept the United States in the 1980s and 1990s will not be discussed here; this topic is worthy of a book in its own right. But by the start of the 21st century, drug abusers had come full circle: The dangers of cocaine abuse were well known, and drug users were eager for an alternative to cocaine. Just as the then-new amphetamines replaced cocaine as the preferred stimulant of choice in the 1930s, it would appear that the amphetamines, especially methamphetamine, is again replacing cocaine as the CNS stimulant of choice for drug abusers. Cocaine use/abuse appears to have peaked sometime around 1986 in the United States, and casual cocaine use has been on the decline since then (Kleber, 1991). However, cocaine has by no means disappeared. Recreational cocaine use has leveled off, but it remains a significant part of the drug-abuse problem in the United States (Gold, 1997).

Cocaine Today

At the start of the 21st century, Erythroxylon coca continues to thrive in the high mountain regions of South America, and the majority of the coca plants grown in South America are harvested for the international cocaine trade and not for local use (Mann, 1994). Virtually 98% of the world's cocaine is produced in South America, with Colombia producing 75% of the total (Karch, 2002). People who live in the high mountain plateaus continue to chew coca leaves to help them work and live. Some researchers have pointed to this practice as evidence that cocaine is not as addictive as drug enforcement officials claim. For example, Jaffe (2000b) noted that while natives of Peru chew cocaine on a regular basis "few progress to excessive use or toxicity" (p. 1003). This was thought to be possible because chewing the leaves is a rather inefficient method of abusing cocaine, and much of the cocaine that is released by this method is destroyed by the acids of the digestive tract. As a result of these forces, the native who chewed cocaine was not thought to obtain a significant level of cocaine in the blood, according to Jaffe.

Other researchers have suggested that the natives of South America who chew coca leaves do indeed become addicted to the stimulant effect of the cocaine. These scientists point to studies that have revealed that the blood level of cocaine achieved when coca leaves are chewed barely enters the lower range of blood levels achieved by those who "snort" cocaine in the United States, and while this is barely enough to have a psychoactive effect, it is still a large enough dose to be addicting in the opinion of some scientists (Karch, 2002). Thus, the answer to the question of whether natives who chew coca leaves are or are not addicted to the cocaine that they might absorb has not been resolved.

Current Medical Uses of Cocaine

Cocaine was once a popular pharmaceutical agent that was used in the treatment of a wide range of conditions. By the 1880s, physicians had discovered that cocaine was an effective local anesthetic (Byck, 1987; Mann, 1994). Cocaine was found to block the movement of sodium ions into the neuron, thus altering its ability to carry pain signals to the brain (Drummer & Odell, 2001). Because of this effect, cocaine was once commonly used by physicians as a topical analgesic for procedures involving the ear, nose, throat, rectum, and vagina. When used as a local anesthetic, cocaine would begin to be effective in about 1 minute, and its effects would last as long as 2 hours (Shannon, Wilson, & Stang, 1995). Cocaine was also included in a mixture called Brompton's cocktail, which was used to control the pain of cancer. However, this mixture has fallen out of favor and is rarely, if ever, used today (Scaros et al., 1990).

As a pharmaceutical, cocaine's usefulness was limited by its often undesirable side effects. Because of these side effects, physicians have found a number of other chemicals that offer the advantages of cocaine without its side effects or potential for abuse. Today, cocaine "has virtually no clinical use" (House, 1990, p. 41), although on rare occasions it is still used by physicians to control pain.

Scope of the Problem of Cocaine Abuse and Addiction

Researchers believe that global cocaine production peaked in 1999, and that since that time it has ebbed and flowed in response to market pressure and intradiction efforts. An estimated 13.3 million people abuse cocaine around the world, of whom 48% (5.9 million) are thought to live in the United States (United Nations, 2004). An estimated 3.3 million cocaine abusers are in Europe, and 2.3 million in South America (United

Nations, 2004). The remaining 1.8 million cocaine abusers live in areas of the globe where cocaine abuse is not a major problem.

In the United States cocaine abusers consume 250 of the 700 metric tons of cocaine produced around the world each year (Office of National Drug Control Policy, 2004). Currently it is estimated that more than 30 million people in the United States have used cocaine at least once (Hahn & Hoffman, 2001), with 600,000 people trying it for the first time and an estimated 1.7 million people using cocaine each month (Craig, 2004). These people spend approximately $60 billion each year to purchase their illicit cocaine ("Cocaine Models," 2003).

Surprisingly, in spite of the fact that casual cocaine abuse in the United States peaked in the mid 1980s, the total amount of cocaine consumed each year in this country has remained at about the mid 1980 level (Karch, 2002). This apparent contradiction is explained by the fact that while there are fewer casual cocaine users, the number of regular cocaine abusers (those who use the drug once a week or more) has remained at about 640,000 persons for more than a decade (O'Brien, 2001). These individuals consume a disproportionate amount of all of the cocaine consumed in the United States.

Pharmacology of Cocaine

Cocaine is best absorbed into the body when it is administered as cocaine hydrochloride, a water-soluble compound. After entering the body, it quickly diffuses into the general circulation and is rapidly transported to the brain and other blood-rich organs such as the heart. In spite of its rapid distribution, the level of cocaine in the brain is usually higher than it is in the blood plasma, especially in the first 2 hours following use of the drug ("Cocaine in the Brain," 1994).

In the last decade of the 20th century, scientists began to unravel the mystery of cocaine's effects on the central nervous system (CNS). In part, cocaine seems to activate some of the same regions of the brain involved in sexual desire (Garavan et al., 2000). Cocaine also seems to activate the Mu and Kappa opioid receptors (Unterwald, 2001). These findings would help to account in part for the intensity of the craving that cocaine-dependent people report that they experience

when they abstain from the drug. According to Garavan et al. (2000), the regions of the brain that seem to be affected by cocaine include the nucleus accumbens, the amygdala, and the anterior cingulate. Given the importance of sexual desire and reproduction for the species, it is reasonable to expect that anything that activates the same regions of the brain would cause the same intense desire found in sexual lust. Perhaps it is for this reason that cocaine addicts refer to their drug as the "white lady" and speak of it almost as if it were a human lover.

Researchers have also discovered that unlike what was thought to be true in the late 1980s and early 1990s, cocaine does not cause the release of dopamine in the CNS. Rather, cocaine seems to block the reuptake of the dopamine that has already been released by the CNS (Haney, 2004). Further, researchers have found at least five different subtypes of dopamine receptors in the brain, and the reinforcing effects of cocaine seem to reflect its ability to stimulate some of these receptor subtypes more strongly than others. For example, Romach et al. (1999) found that when the dopamine D_1 receptor was blocked, their volunteers failed to experience the pleasure that cocaine usually induces when it is injected into the circulation. On the basis of this finding, the authors concluded that the dopamine D_1 receptor site was involved in the experience of euphoria reported by cocaine abusers.

In the human brain, the dopamine D_1 receptors are concentrated in the "mesolimbic" system of the brain, which includes structures such as the nucleus accumbens and the amygdala. These structures are known to be involved in the pleasure response induced by the drugs of abuse. Cocaine's effects come from its ability to cause a massive discharge of the neurotransmitter dopamine along the nerve pathways that connect the ventral tegmentum region of the brain with the nucleus accumbens, causing the abuser to experience intense pleasure (Beitner-Johnson & Nestler, 1992; Haney, 2004; Restak, 1994). Indeed, this drug-induced activation of the reward system of the brain might be more intense than rewards triggered by natural reinforcers such as food, drink, or sex (Haney, 2004).

But cocaine does not just cause the release of dopamine. It also blocks the process of reabsorption/reuptake of the neurotransmitters norepinephrine and serotonin (Reynolds & Bada, 2003; Unterwald, 2001). The significance of this cocaine-induced blockage of the norepinephrine and serotonin reuptake systems is not known at this time, although the noreadrenaline system is known to be involved in cardiac function among other things, and thus might account for cocaine's impact on the cardiovascular system.

On a cellular level, cocaine also alters the function of a protein known as postsynaptic density-95 (Sanna & Koob, 2004). Long-term changes in this protein, which is involved in helping the neuron adapt the synapse to changing neurotransmitter mixtures, are thought to be involved in the process of learning and memory formation, possibly accounting at least in part for cocaine's ability to cause the user to form strong memories of the drug's effects (Sanna & Koob, 2004). After periods of prolonged abuse, the neurons within the brain will have released virtually all their stores of the neurotransmitter dopamine without being able to reabsorb any of the dopamine, norepinephrine, or serotonin that has been released. Low levels of these neurotransmitters are thought to be involved in the development of depression. This pharmacological effect of cocaine might explain the observed relationship between cocaine abuse and depression, which has been known to reach suicidal proportions in some cocaine abusers.

Tolerance to cocaine's euphoric effect may develop within "hours or days" (Schuckit, 2000, p. 124). As tolerance develops, the individual will require more and more cocaine in order to experience a euphoric effect. This urge to increase the dosage and continue using the drug can reach the point that it "may become a way of life and users become totally preoccupied with drug-seeking and drug-taking behaviors" (Siegel, 1982, p. 731). Another of the brain subunits affected by cocaine is the diencephalon, which is the region of the brain responsible for temperature regulation. This will result in a higher than normal body temperature for the user. At the same time that cocaine is altering the brain's temperature regulation system, it will also cause the constriction of surface blood vessels. This combination of effects results in hyperthermia: excess body heat. The individual's body will conserve body heat at just the time it needs to release the excess thermal energy caused by the cocaine-induced dysregulation of body temperature, possibly with fatal results (Hall, Talbert, & Ereshefsky, 1990).

Cocaine's effects are very short-lived. When it is injected intravenously, the peak plasma levels are reached in just 5 minutes, and after 20–40 minutes the effects begin to diminish (Weddington, 1993). This is because the half-life of a single dose of intravenously administered cocaine is only 30 to 90 minutes (Jaffe, 2000b; Marzuk et al., 1995; Mendelson & Mello, 1996). Cocaine is biotransformed in the liver and produces about a dozen known metabolites (Karch, 2002). About 90% to 95% of a dose of intravenously administered cocaine is biotransformed into one of two primary metabolites: benzoylecgonine (BEG), or ecgonine methyl ester (Cone, 1993; Kerfoot, Sakoulas, & Hyman, 1996). The other metabolites are of minor importance and need not be considered further in this text. Only about 5% to 10% of a single dose of cocaine is excreted from the body unchanged. Neither of the major metabolites of cocaine has any known biological activity in the body. BEG has a half-life of 7.5 hours (Marzuk et al., 1995). Because the half-life of BEG is longer than that of the parent compound, and because it is stable in urine samples that have been frozen, this is the chemical that laboratories usually test for when they test a urine sample for evidence of cocaine use.

Cocaine is known to autometabolize following the user's death. This is to say that the body will continue to biotransform the cocaine in the blood even after the user has died. Thus, a post-mortem blood sample might not reveal any measurable amount of cocaine in the blood, even in cases where the user was known to have used cocaine prior to his or her death.

Drug interactions involving cocaine. There has been surprisingly little research into cocaine-drug interactions (Karch, 2002). It is known that cocaine has the potential to interact with a wide range of both pharmaceuticals and illicit drugs. Cross addiction is a common complication of chronic cocaine use. For example, between 20% and 50% of alcohol and heroin dependent individuals are also dependent on cocaine (Gold & Miller, 1997a), whereas more than 75% of cocaine abusers are dependent on alcohol (Zealberg & Brady, 1999).

There is a great deal of debate among clinical toxicologists about whether the combination of alcohol and cocaine is or is not inherently dangerous. When a person uses both cocaine and alcohol, a small amount (<10%) of the cocaine is biotransformed into cocaethylene (Gold & Miller, 1997a; Karch, 2002). Cocaethylene is so toxic to the user's body that when it is present in significant amounts, it is estimated to be 25 to 30 times as likely to induce death as cocaine itself (Karan, Haller, & Schnoll, 1998). Because its half-life is longer than cocaine's and because it functions as a powerful calcium channel blocker, clinicians suspected that cocaethylene is the cause of cocaine-induced heart problems or death (Hahn & Hoffman, 2001; Karch, 1996). As clinicians explored the relationship between concurrent alcohol and cocaine abuse and cocaethylene formation in the early years of the 21st century, they discovered that cocaethylene is formed only when high levels of alcohol are present in the user's body ("Is Cocaethylene Cardiotoxic?," 2002). Further, animal research found evidence of cocaethylene-related cardiotoxicity only when extremely high levels of cocaethylene were present (Wilson & French, 2002). Because (a) only a small amount of cocaine is biotransformed into cocaethylene, (b) this is accomplished only when the user has a high blood alcohol level, and (c) cardiotoxicity is seen only with high blood levels of cocaethylene, there is reason to doubt that it is a major cause of cocaine-related cardiac death.

Research also has suggested a possible relationship between the concurrent use of cocaine and alcohol, and death from pulmonary edema (Barnhill, Ciraulo, Ciraulo, & Greene, 1995). Unfortunately, cocaethylene may lengthen the period of cocaine-induced euphoria, making it more likely that the person will continue to use alcohol with cocaine in spite of the danger associated with this practice.

Some abusers will inject a combination of cocaine and an opiate, a process known as "speedballing." However, for reasons that are not well understood, cocaine will actually enhance the respiratory depressive effect of the opiates, possibly resulting in episodes of respiratory arrest in extreme cases (Kerfoot et al., 1996). As discussed later in this chapter, cocaine abuse often results in a feeling of irritation or anxiety. In order to control the cocaine-induced agitation and anxiety, users often ingest alcohol, tranquilizers, or marijuana. The combination of marijuana and cocaine appears capable of increasing heart rate levels by almost 50 beats per minute in individuals who are using both substances (Barnhill et al., 1995).

There is one case report of a patient who was abusing cocaine who took an over-the-counter cold medication that contained phenylpropanolamine. This person developed what seems to have been a drug-induced psychosis that included homicidal thoughts (Barnhill et al., 1995). It is not clear at this time if this was just an isolated incident or if the interaction between cocaine and phenylpropanolamine might precipitate a psychotic reaction, but the concurrent use of these chemicals is not recommended.

How Illicit Cocaine Is Produced

The process of cocaine production has changed little in the past generation. First, the cocaine leaves are harvested. In some parts of Bolivia, this may be done as often as once every 3 months, as the climate is well suited for the plant to grow. Second, the leaves are dried, usually by letting them sit in the open sunlight for a few hours or days, and although this process is illegal in many parts of South America, the local authorities are quite tolerant and do little to interfere with the drying of coca leaves.

In the next step, the dried leaves are put in a plastic lined pit, and mixed with water and sulfuric acid (White, 1989). The mixture is crushed by workers who wade into the pit in their bare feet. After the mixture has been crushed, diesel fuel and bicarbonate are added to the mixture. After a period of time, during which workers reenter the pit several times to continue to stomp through the mixture, the liquids are drained off. Lime is then mixed with the residue, forming a paste (Byrne, 1989), which is known as cocaine base. It takes 500 kilograms of leaves to produce one kilogram of cocaine base (White, 1989).

In step four, water, gasoline, acid, potassium permanganate, and ammonia are added to the cocaine paste. This forms a reddish brown liquid, which is then filtered. A few drops of ammonia, when added to the mixture, produce a milky solid that is filtered and dried. Then the dried cocaine base is dissolved in a solution of hydrochloric acid and acetone. A white solid forms, which settles to the bottom of the tank (Byrne, 1989; White, 1989). This solid material is the compound cocaine hydrochloride. Eventually, the cocaine hydrochloride is filtered and dried under heating lights. This will cause the mixture to form a white, crystalline powder that is gathered up, packed, and shipped, usually in kilogram packages. Before sale to the individual cocaine user, each kilogram is adulterated and the resulting compound is packaged in 1 gram units and sold to individual users.

How Cocaine Is Abused

Cocaine may be used in a number of ways. First, cocaine hydrocloride powder might be inhaled through the nose (intranasal use, also known as "snorting," or, more appropriately, insufflation). Second, it may be injected directly into a vein (an intravenous injection). Cocaine hydrochloride is a water soluble form of cocaine and thus is well adapted to either intranasal or intravenous use (Sbriglio & Millman, 1987). Third, cocaine base might be smoked. Fourth, cocaine may be used orally (sublingually). We will examine each of these methods of cocaine abuse in detail.

Insufflation. Historical evidence suggests that the practice of "snorting" cocaine began around 1903, which is the year that case reports of septal perforation began to appear in medical journals (Karch, 2002). When snorted, cocaine powder is usually arranged on a piece of glass such as a pocket mirror, in thin lines 3 to 5 cm long. Each of these lines contains between 25 and 100 mg of cocaine (Karch, 1996; Strang, Johns, & Caan, 1993). The powder is diced up, usually with a razor blade, on a piece of glass or a mirror, to make the particles as small as possible and enhance absorption. A gram of cocaine prepared in this manner might yield 25 to 30 lines (Karan et al., 1998). The powder is then inhaled through a drinking straw or rolled paper tube. This practice is quite common, and in the mid 1990s, 77% to 95% of cocaine abusers would snort it (Boyd, 1995; Hatsukami & Fischman, 1996).

When it reaches the nasal passages, which are richly supplied with blood vessels, the cocaine is quickly absorbed. This allows some of the cocaine to gain rapid access to the bloodstream, usually in 30 to 90 seconds (House, 1990), where it is carried to the brain. The peak effects of cocaine when it is snorted are reached within 15 to 30 minutes, and the effects wear off in about 45 to 60 minutes after a single dose (Kosten & Sofuoglu, 2004; Weiss, Greenfield, & Mirin, 1994), and between 2 and 3 hours for chronic use (Hoffman & Hollander, 1997).

Researchers disagree as to how much of the cocaine that is snorted will ultimately be absorbed into the user's body. Because cocaine functions as a vasoconstrictor it may limit its own absorption when it is snorted. Estimates of the amount of cocaine that is absorbed through the nasal passages when it is snorted range from 5% (Strang et al., 1993) to 25% to 94% (Hatsukami & Fischman, 1996). Karch (2002) took a middle-of-the-road position on this issue, suggesting that because of its vasoconstrictive effect, it takes longer for cocaine to be absorbed when it is snorted, but that it is virtually all eventually absorbed. Thus the question of whether intranasally administered cocaine might limit its own absorption rate and the degree to which it might do so has not been fully answered.

Intravenous cocaine abuse. It is possible to introduce cocaine directly into the body through intravenous injection. Cocaine hydrochloride powder is mixed with water, then injected into a vein. This method of cocaine abuse actually is the least common method by which cocaine is used, with only 7% of those individuals who use cocaine injecting it (Hatsukami & Fischman, 1996). Intravenously administered cocaine will reach the brain in just a matter of 3 to 5 seconds (Restak, 1994) or 30 seconds (Kosten & Sofuoglu, 2004). In contrast to the limited amount of cocaine that is absorbed when it is snorted, intravenous administration results in 20 times as much cocaine reaching the brain as in intranasal cocaine use (Strang et al., 1993).

Intravenous cocaine abusers have often reported a rapid, intense feeling of euphoria called the "rush" or "flash," which is similar to a sexual orgasm but feels different from the rush reported by opiate abusers (Brust, 1998). Following the rush, the user will experience a feeling of euphoria that lasts 10 to 15 minutes. Researchers believe that the rush is the subjective experience of cocaine-induced changes in the ventral tegmentum in the midbrain, and the basal forebrain. The rush will be discussed in more detail in the section on the subjective effects of cocaine (below). Intravenously administered cocaine is biotransformed quite quickly, which is one reason its effects last only about 15 minutes (Weiss et al., 1994).

Sublingual cocaine use. This form of cocaine abuse, the third method of administration discussed thus far, is becoming increasingly popular, especially when the hydrochloride salt of cocaine is utilized (Jones, 1987). The tissues in the mouth, especially under the tongue, are richly supplied with blood, allowing large amounts of the drug to enter the bloodstream quickly. After reaching the brain, the cocaine is transported to the brain, with results similar to those seen in the intranasal administration of cocaine.

Rectal cocaine use. The method of rectal cocaine administration has become increasingly popular, especially among male homosexuals (Karch, 2002). Cocaine's local anesthetic properties provide the desired effects for the user, allowing for participation in otherwise painful forms of sexual activity. Unfortunately, the anesthetic properties of cocaine might mask signs of physical trauma to the tissues in the rectal area, increasing the individual's risk of death from these activities (Karch, 2002).

Cocaine smoking. Historically, the practice of burning or smoking different parts of the coca plant dates back to at least 3000 B.C., when the Incas would burn coca leaves at religious festivals (Hahn & Hoffman, 2001). The practice of smoking cocaine resurfaced in the late 1800s, when coca cigarettes were used to treat hay fever and opiate addiction. By the year 1890, cocaine smoke was being used in the United States for the treatment of whooping cough, bronchitis, asthma, and a range of other conditions (Siegel, 1982). But in spite of this history of cocaine smoking for medicinal reasons, recreational cocaine smoking in the United States did not become popular until the early to mid 1980s.

This is because the medicinal uses of cocaine have gradually been reduced as other, more effective agents have been introduced for the control of various illnesses. When cocaine hydrochloride became a popular drug of abuse in the 1970s, users quickly discovered that it is not easily smoked. The high temperatures needed to vaporize cocaine hydrochloride also destroy it, making it of limited value to those who wish to smoke it. Although dedicated cocaine abusers of the 1970s and 1980s knew that it was possible to smoke the alkaloid base of cocaine, they also knew that the process of transforming cocaine hydrochloride into an alkaloid base that might be smoked was a long, dangerous process. This made the practice of smoking cocaine unpopular before around 1985.

To transform cocaine hydrochloride into an alkaloid base, cocaine powder had to be mixed with a solvent such as ether, and then a base compound such as ammonia (Warner, 1995). The cocaine will then form an alkaloid base that can be smoked. This form of cocaine is called "freebase" (or simply "base"). Then the precipitated cocaine freebase is passed through a filter,

which effectively removes some of the impurities and increases the concentration of the obtained powder. Unfortunately, the process of filtration does not remove all the impurities from the cocaine, and many of the impurities found in the original sample of cocaine will still remain in the alkaloid base that is produced through this process (Siegel, 1982).

The cocaine powder obtained through this process can then be smoked, but the process of transforming cocaine hydrochloride into this form is quite difficult. Further, the chemicals used to separate cocaine freebase from its hydrochloride salt are quite volatile, and there is a very real danger of fire or even an explosion from these compounds. As a result, smoking cocaine freebase never became popular in the United States. But when cocaine freebase was smoked, the fumes would reach the brain in just 7 seconds (Beebe & Walley, 1991; Hahn & Hoffman, 2001), with between 60% and 90% of the cocaine crossing over into the general circulation from the lungs (Beebe & Walley, 1991; Hatsukami & Fischman, 1996). Indeed, there is evidence that when it is smoked, cocaine reaches the brain more quickly than when it is injected (Hatsukami & Fischman, 1996) and has been called "the most addictive substance used by humankind" (Wright, 1999, p. 47).

This suggested to illicit drug producers that there would be a strong market for a form of cocaine that could easily be smoked, and by the mid 1980s such a product had reached the U.S. streets. Called crack, this product was essentially a solid chunk of cocaine base that was prepared for smoking before it was delivered for sale at the local level. This is done in illicit factories or laboratories where cocaine hydrochloride is mixed with baking soda and water and then heated until the cocaine crystals begin to precipitate at the bottom of the container (Warner, 1995). More than a generation ago, Breslin (1988) discussed how one crack factory worked:

> Curtis and his girlfriend dropped the cocaine and baking soda into the water, then hit the bottle with the blowtorch. The cocaine powder boiled down to its oily base. The baking soda soaked up the impurities in the cocaine. When cold water was added to the bottle, the cocaine base hardened into white balls. Curtis and Iris spooned them out, placed them on a table covered with paper, and began to measure the hard white cocaine. (p. 212)

The crack produced in such illicit factories is sold in small, ready-to-use pellets packaged in containers that allow the user one or two inhalations for a relatively low price (Beebe & Walley, 1991). Although at first glance crack seems less expensive than other forms of cocaine, research has demonstrated that it actually is about as expensive as cocaine used for intravenous injection (Karch, 2002). But since it is sold in smaller quanities, it is attractive to the under-18 crowd and in low-income neighborhoods (Bales, 1988; Taylor & Gold, 1990). Since the introduction of crack, the practice of smoking cocaine has arguably become the most widely recognized method of cocaine abuse. However, researchers believe that just over one-third of cocaine abusers in the United States smoke the drug (Hatsukami & Fischman, 1996).

In 1996, substance abuse rehabilitation professionals noted a disturbing new trend among some crack users in both England and isolated cities of the United States. In these areas, limited numbers of users would dissolve the pellets of crack in alcohol, lemon juice, vinegar, or water, and then inject it into their bodies through large-bore needles ("Crack Injecting in Chicago," 1996). Apparently, intravenous cocaine abusers were resorting to this practice when their traditional sources of cocaine hydrochloride were unable to provide them with the powder used for injection. It is not known how popular this practice will become, but it does represent a disturbing new twist to the ongoing saga of cocaine abuse/addiction.

Subjective Effects of Cocaine When It Is Abused

Two factors influence the individual's subjective experience from cocaine. First, the individual's expectations play a role in how he or she interprets the drug's effects. Second, there are the actual physiological effects of the drug. These two factors interact to shape the individual's experience from cocaine and how it is abused.

Experienced cocaine users tend to experience both positive (euphoric) and negative (depressive) effects from the drug (Schafer & Brown, 1991). The experienced cocaine abuser expects (a) a generalized feeling of arousal, (b) some feelings of anxiety, and (c) feelings of relaxation and a reduction in the level of tension as a result of the drug use.

Both intravenous injection and cocaine smoking can cause the user to experience a feeling of intense euphoria that has been compared to the sexual orgasm in intensity and pleasure. It is so intense for some users that "it alone can replace the sex partner of either sex" (Gold & Verebey, 1984, p. 719). Some male abusers have reported having a spontaneous ejaculation without direct genital stimulation after either injecting or smoking cocaine. There also appears to be a link between chronic cocaine use and compulsive acting-out behavior for both men and women (Washton, 1995). Within seconds, the initial rush is replaced by a period of excitation or euphoria that lasts for between 10 (Strang et al., 1993) and 20 minutes (Weiss et al., 1994). During this period, the individual will feel an increased sense of competence, energy (Gold & Verebey, 1984), or extreme self-confidence (Taylor & Gold, 1990). Some abusers report feeling powerful or "energized" while under the influence of cocaine, and the drug decreases the sense of fatigue and hunger, and increases awareness of sexual stimuli (Schuckit, 2000).

Snorting cocaine powder yields a less intense high than when it is smoked or injected. Still, intranasal cocaine will result in a sense of euphoria as well as many of the effects noted in the last paragraph. This sense of cocaine-induced euphoria might last only a few minutes for the individual who smokes cocaine (Byck, 1987), to an estimated 20 minutes to an hour for the individual who snorts cocaine powder. Then the effects begin to wane, and to regain the cocaine-induced pleasurable feelings, the user must again use cocaine.

Tolerance to the euphoric effects of cocaine develop quickly. To overcome their tolerance to the effects of cocaine, many users have been known to engage in a cycle of continuous cocaine use known as "coke runs." The usual cocaine run lasts about 12 hours, although there have been cases that have lasted up to 7 days (Gawin, Khalsa, & Ellinwood, 1994). During this time, the user is smoking or injecting additional cocaine every few minutes until the total cumulative dose might reach levels that would kill the inexperienced (naive) user. The coke run phenomenon is a similar pattern to that seen when animals are given unlimited access to cocaine. Rats that are given intravenous cocaine for pushing a bar set in the wall of their cage will do so repeatedly, ignoring food or even sex, until they die from convulsions or infection (Hall et al., 1990).

Complications of Cocaine Abuse/Addiction

Approximately 40% to 50% of people who die each year in the United States as a direct result of substance abuse do so because of their use of cocaine (Karch, 2002). In some cases death occurs so rapidly from a cocaine overdose that "the victim never receives medical attention other than from the coroner" (Estroff, 1987, p. 25). In addition, cocaine abuse might cause a wide range of other problems including addiction. In the 1960s and early 1970s there were those who believed that cocaine was not addictive. The belief that cocaine was not addictive was fueled by the observation that few users in the late 1960s could afford enough cocaine to allow them to use it long enough to become addicted. But, as has been discussed, cocaine has a very real potential to cause physical and psychological addiction.[1] About 15% of those who try cocaine will become addicted to it (Jaffe, Rawson, & Ling, 2005). The development of physical dependence varies among individuals, however, and there are reports of addiction developing in as little as 6 to 10 weeks (Lamar et al., 1986). There also appears to be a progression in the methods by which cocaine abusers utilize the drug, as their addiction to cocaine grows in intensity. As the user's need for the drug becomes more intense, he or she switches from the intranasal method of cocaine use to those methods that introduce greater concentrations of the drug into the body. For example, 79% to 90% of those who admitted to the use of crack cocaine started to use the drug intranasally (Hatsukami & Fischman, 1996).

Respiratory system dysfunctions. The cocaine smoker may experience chest pain, cough, and damage to the bronchioles of the lungs (O'Connor, Chang, & Shi, 1992). There have been reports that in some cases the alveoli of the user's lungs have ruptured, allowing the escape of air (and bacteria) into the surrounding tissues. This will establish the potential for infection to develop, while the escaping gas may contribute to the inability of the lung to fully inflate (a pneumothorax). Approximately one-third of chronic crack users develop

wheezing sounds when they breathe, for reasons that are still not clear (Tashkin, Kleerup, Koyal, Marques, & Goldman, 1996). Other potential complications of cocaine smoking include the development of an asthma-like condition known as chronic bronchiolitis (also known as "crack lung"), hemorrhage, pneumonia, and chronic inflammation of the throat (Albertson, Walby, & Derlet, 1995; House, 1990; Taylor & Gold, 1990). There is evidence that cocaine-induced lung damage may be irreversible.

There is also evidence that at least some of the observed increase in the incidence of fatal asthma cases might be caused by unsuspected cocaine abuse ("Asthma Deaths Blamed," 1997). Although cocaine abuse might not be the cause of all asthma-induced deaths, it is known that smoking crack cocaine can cause irritation to the air passages in the lungs, contributing to both fatal and nonfatal asthma attacks (Tashkin et al., 1996). The chronic intranasal use of cocaine can also cause sore throats, inflamed sinuses, hoarseness, and on occasion, a breakdown of the cartilage of the nose (Karch, 2002). Damage to the cartilage of the nose may develop after as little as 3 weeks' intranasal cocaine use (O'Connor et al., 1992). Other medical problems caused by intranasal cocaine use might include bleeding from the nasal passages and the formation of ulcers in the nasal passages, according to the authors.

Cardiovascular system damage. Cocaine abuse can result in damage to the cardiovascular system. Indeed, cocaine abuse is now thought to be the cause of approximately one-quarter of the nonfatal heart attacks in the 18 to 45 year-old- population ("Cocaine link to heart attack bolstered," 2001) and is the most common reason for chest pain in cocaine abusers (Hahn & Holffman, 2001). Cocaine abuse is also associated with such cardiovascular problems as severe hypertension, sudden dissection of the coronary arteries, cardiac ischemia, tachycardia, myocarditis, and sudden death (Altertson et al., 1995; Brent, 1995; Derlet & Horowitz, 1995; Hahn & Hoffman, 2001; Hollander, 1995; Jaffe, 2000b; Karch, 2002; O'Connor et al., 1992).

In addition to the above complications of cocaine use/abuse, it can cause, or at least speed up, the development of atherosclerotic plaques in the user (Hollander et al., 1997; Karch, 2002). Researchers still do not understand the exact mechanism by which cocaine

---

[1]While it is true that not everybody who uses cocaine will become addicted, it is not possible to determine at this time *who* will become addicted if they should try this drug. If only for this reason, cocaine abuse should be discouraged.

abuse can cause the development of atherosclerotic plaques in the coronary arteries of the user, but animal research has revealed that cocaine abuse can trick the body's immune system into attacking the tissue of the heart and endothelial cells that line the coronary arteries (Tanhehco, Yasojima, McGeer, & Lucchesi, 2000). Cocaine accomplishes this feat by triggering what is known as the "complement cascade," which is part of the immune system's response to invading microorganisms. This process causes protein molecules to form on the cell walls of invading microorganisms, eventually causing them to burst from internal pressure. The damaged cells are then attacked by the body's "scavenger" cells, the microphages. Some researchers believe that the microphages are also involved in the process of atherosclerotic plaque formation. They have suggested that atherosclerotic plaque is formed when the microphages mistakenly attack cholesterol molecules circulating in the blood, attaching these molecules to the endothelial cells of the coronary arteries, thus providing a possible avenue through which cocaine abuse might result in the development of atherosclerotic plaques in the coronary arteries of the user.

At one time, researchers believed that cocaine abuse could cause increased platelet aggregation, which is to say that cocaine would somehow cause the user's blood cells to form blood clots more easily. This possible side effect of cocaine seemed to account for clinical reports in which cocaine abusers were found to be at risk for many of the cardiovascular problems noted in the last paragraphs. However, research has failed to find support for this hypothesis (Heesch et al., 1996).

Researchers have found that cocaine can increase the heart rate, while reducing the blood flow to the heart (Karch, 2002; Moliterno et al., 1994). Unfortunately, cocaine seems to cause the coronary arteries to constrict at points where the endothelium is already damaged and the blood flow is already reduced by the buildup of plaque (Hahn & Hoffman, 2001). This effect is strongest in cigarette smokers, according to the authors, as evidenced by the 19% reduction in coronary artery blood flow in cigarette smoking cocaine users, as compared to the 7% decrease in coronary artery diameter after smoking cocaine experienced by nonsmokers (Moliterno et al., 1994). Cigarette smokers with no known coronary artery disease experience a temporary 9% reduction in coronary artery blood flow after smoking cocaine (Moliterno et al., 1994). This ability to reduce coronary artery blood flow at the moment of increased cardiac demand seems to be one mechanism by which cocaine abuse causes cardiac ischemia and myocardial injury (Hahn & Hoffman, 2001).

Cocaine has been implicated as causing a significant but transient increase in the individual's risk for a myocardial infarction (MI). Research has demonstrated that the risk of a MI is 23.7 times higher in the first hour after the individual began to use cocaine (Karch, 2002). Further, the individual may experience symptoms of cardiac ischemia up to 18 hours after the last use of cocaine because of the length of time it takes for the rupture of atheriosclerotic plaque to manifest as coronary artery blockages (Karch, 2002; Kerfoot, Sakoulas, & Hyman, 1996). It is important for physicians to be aware of possible cocaine abuse by the patient, since physicians use drugs known as beta-adrenergic antagonists to treat myocardial ischemia on many occasions. If the patient had recently used cocaine, these drugs can contribute to cocaine-induced constriction of the blood vessels surrounding the heart, making the condition worse (Shih & Hollander, 1996).

Cocaine abuse has been associated with a number of other cardiac problems, including atrial fibrillation (Hahn & Hoffman, 2001). However, researchers have not identified the exact mechanism by which cocaine is able to cause cardiac arrhythmias. Researchers once believed that cocaine would alter the effects of the catecholamines in the body. For example, the team of Beitner-Johnson and Nestler (1992) suggested that cocaine could block the reuptake of norepinephrine in the cardiac tissue, thus accounting for the increased risk of cardiac stress and distress in the user (Karch, 2002). The team of Tuncel et al. (2002) challenged these theories, noting that in rare cocaine abusers, a normal physiological response known as the baroreflex would block the release of excess norepinephrine, reducing the stress on the heart. Thus, the theory that the chronic use of cocaine causes increased levels of norepinephrine in the blood, placing an increased workload on the heart, especially the left ventricle, putting the individual at risk for sudden death remains only a theory, and the exact mechanism by which chronic cocaine abuse might contribute to increased risk of heart problems in humans remains unknown.

In addition to being a known cause of all of the above conditions, some scientists believe that cocaine abuse might also cause "microinfarcts," or microscopic areas of damage to the heart muscle (Gawin et al., 1994). These microinfarcts ultimately will reduce the heart's ability to function effectively and may lead to further heart problems later on. There is also evidence to suggest that cocaine abuse might cause "silent" episodes of cardiac ischemia while the individual is withdrawing from cocaine, leaving the person at risk for sudden cardiac death (Kerfoot et al., 1996).

Researchers have since found that in some settings fully 17% of the patients under the age of 60 seen in hospital emergency rooms for chest pain had cocaine metabolites in their urine (Hollander et al., 1995). There does not seem to be any pattern to cocaine-induced cardiovascular problems, and both first-time and long-term cocaine users have suffered cocaine-related cardiovascular problems. In a hospital setting, between 56% and 84% of those patients with cocaine-induced chest pain are found to have abnormal electrocardiograms (Hollander, 1995). Unfortunately, for those cocaine users who experience chest pain but do not seek medical help, there is a very real danger that these symptoms of potentially fatal cocaine-related cardiac problems might be ignored by the individual.

Another rare but potentially fatal complication of cocaine abuse is a condition known as acute aortic dissection (Brent, 1995; Karch, 2002). This condition develops when the main artery of the body, the aorta, suddenly develops a weak spot in its wall. The exact mechanism by which cocaine might cause an acute aortic dissection is not known, and it does occasionally develop in persons other than cocaine abusers. Acute aortic dissection is a medical emergency that may require emergency surgery in order to save the patient's life.

Male cocaine abusers run the risk of developing erectile dysfunctions, including a painful, potentially dangerous condition known as priapism (Finger, Lund, & Slagel, 1997; Karch, 2002). In contrast to patterns found with the intravenous injection of opiates, it is not common for intravenous cocaine abusers to develop scar tissue at the injection site. This is because the adulterants commonly found in powdered cocaine are mainly water soluble and are less irritating to the body than the adulterants found in opiates, and thus are less likely to cause scarring (Karch, 2002).

Cocaine abuse as a cause of liver damage. There is evidence that cocaine metabolites, especially cocaethylene, are toxic to the liver. However, the possibility that cocaine abuse can cause or contribute to liver disease remains controversial (Karch, 2002). Medical research has also discovered that a small percentage of the population simply cannot biotransform cocaine, no matter how small the dosage level used. In this pseudo-cholinesterase deficiency (Gold, 1989), the liver is unable to produce an essential enzyme necessary to break down cocaine. For people with this condition, the use of even a small amount of cocaine could be fatal.

Cocaine abuse as a cause of central nervous system damage. Research has now demonstrated that cocaine abuse causes a reduction in cerebral blood flow, and chronic cocaine abusers demonstrate cognitive deficits in the areas of verbal learning, memory, and attention (Kosten & Sofuoglu, 2004). This neurological damage has been classified as "moderate to severe" by Kaufman et al. (1998, p. 376). O'Malley, Adamse, Heaton, and Gawin (1992) found, for example, that 50% of the subjects who abused cocaine on a regular basis showed evidence of cognitive impairment on the neuropsychological tests used in their study, as compared to only 15% of the control subjects. The mechanism by which chronic cocaine use might cause cognitive dysfunction is thought to be another consequence of its vasoconstrictive effects on the blood vessels in the brain (Brust, 1997; Pearlson et al., 1993).

The reduction in blood flow to the brain is called a state of cerebral ischemia, and if this state continues for too long, the neurons deprived of blood will begin to die (Kaufman et al., 1998). This process is known as a cerebral vascular accident (CVA or stroke), of which there are two main types. Scientists have known since the mid 1980s that cocaine increases the user's risk for a CVA, especially a hemorrhagic CVA (Vega, Kwoon, & Lavine, 2002). In the hemorrhagic CVA, a weakened section of an artery in the brain ruptures, both depriving the neurons dependent on that blood vessel of blood and placing the patient's life at risk from the uncontrolled hemorrhage.

Cocaine-induced strokes might be microscopic in size (the "microstroke"), or they might involve major regions of the brain. Scientists have estimated that cocaine abusers are 14 times more likely to suffer a stroke than are nonabusers (Johnson, Devous, Ruiz, &

Ait-Daoud, 2001), and cocaine-induced strokes have reached "epidemic proportions" (Kaufman et al., 1998, p. 376) in recent years. The risk for a cocaine-induced CVA appears to be cumulative, with long-term users being at greater risk than newer users. However, a cocaine-induced CVA is possible even in a first-time user.

One possible mechanism by which cocaine might cause CVAs, especially in users without preexisting vascular disease, is through drug-induced periods of vasospasm and reperfusion between periods of drug use (Johnson et al., 2001; Karch, 2002). This cycle can induce damage to the blood vessels within the brain, contributing to the development of a CVA in the user. Cocaine-induced strokes have been documented to occur in the brain, retina, and spinal cord (Brust, 1997; Derlet, 1989; Derlet & Horowitz, 1995; Jaffe, 2000b; Mendoza & Miller, 1992). Cocaine abusers may also experience transient ischemic attacks (TIAs) as a result of their cocaine use, a phenomenon that could very well be caused by the cocaine-induced vasoconstriction identified by Kaufman et al. (1998).

Another very rare complication of cocaine use is the development of a drug-induced neurological condition known as the serotonin syndrome (Mills, 1995). Further, cocaine has been known to induce seizures in some users (Derlet, 1989; O'Connor et al., 1992). The mechanism by which cocaine contributes to or causes the development of seizures is not well understood, but the individual's potential for cocaine-induced seizures appears to be significantly higher for the first 12 hours after using cocaine (O'Connor et al., 1992). The development of seizures does not appear to be associated with past cocaine use, for seizures have been noted in first-time users as well as individuals who were using cocaine at doses that they had previously used without complications (Gold, 1997; Post et al., 1987). It is theorized that cocaine abuse might initiate a process of "kindling" through some unknown mechanism (Karch, 2002; Post et al., 1987).

Although cocaine might have a short half-life, "the sensitization effects are long lasting" (Post et al., 1987, p. 113). The authors believe that the sensitizing effects of cocaine might thus lower the seizure threshold, at least in some individuals, observing that "repeated administration of a given dose of cocaine without resulting seizures *would in no way assure the continued*

safety of this drug even for that given individual" (p. 159; italics added for emphasis).

The amygdala is known to be especially vulnerable to the kindling phemonenon (Taylor, 1993). Thus, cocaine's effects on the amygdala can make this region of the brain hypersensitive, causing the user to experience cocaine-induced seizures. In addition to all of the above, there is evidence that chronic cocaine abuse can cause, or at least significantly contribute to, a disruption in body temperature regulation known as malignant hyperthermia (Karch, 2002). Individuals who develop this condition suffer extremely high, possibly fatal, body temperatures as a result of CNS damage. In children, cocaine seems to lower the seizure threshold for those predisposed to seizures (Mott, Packer, & Soldin, 1994). The relationship between cocaine abuse and seizures in children was so strong that the authors recommended that all children/adolescents brought to the hospital for a previously undiagnosed seizure disorder be tested for cocaine abuse.

Cocaine's effects on the user's emotional state and perceptions. It has been suggested (Hamner, 1993) that cocaine abuse might exacerbate the symptoms of post-traumatic stress disorders (PTSD). The exact mechanism by which cocaine seems to be able to add to the emotional distress of PTSD is not clear at this time. However there does appear to be evidence that individuals who suffer from PTSD might find the distress made worse by the psychobiological interaction between the effects of the drug and their traumatic experiences.

There is evidence that cocaine use might cause an exacerbation of the symptoms of some medical disorders such as Tourette's syndrome and tardive dyskinesia (Lopez & Jeste, 1997). Further, after periods of extended use, some people have experienced the so-called cocaine bugs, a hallucinatory experience in which users feel as if bugs were crawling on or just under their skin. This is known as formication ("Amphetamines," 1990). Patients have been known to burn their arms or legs with matches or cigarettes, or scratch themselves repeatedly, in an attempt to rid themselves of these unseen bugs (Lingeman, 1974).

Cocaine has also been implicated as one cause of drug-induced anxiety or panic reactions (DiGregorio, 1990). One study in the early 1990s found that one-quarter of the patients seen at one panic disorder clinic eventually admitted to the use of cocaine (Louie, 1990).

Up to 64% of cocaine users experience some degree of anxiety as a side effect of the drug, according to the author. There is a tendency for cocaine users to try to self-medicate this side effect through the use of marijuana. Other chemicals often used by cocaine abusers in an attempt to control the drug-induced anxiety include the benzodiazepines, narcotics, barbiturates, and alcohol. These cocaine-induced anxiety and panic attacks might continue for months (Gold & Miller, 1997a) or even years (Satel, Kosten, Schuckit, & Fischman, 1993) after the individual's last use of cocaine.

Between 53% (Decker & Ries, 1993) and 65% (Beebe & Walley, 1991) of chronic cocaine abusers will develop a drug-induced psychosis very similar in appearance to paranoid schizophrenia. This condition is sometimes called "coke paranoia" by illicit cocaine users. Although it is very similar to paranoid schizophrenia, the symptoms of a cocaine-induced psychosis tend to include more suspiciousness and a strong fear of being discovered or of being harmed while under the influence of cocaine (Rosse et al., 1994). Further, the cocaine-induced psychosis is usually of relatively short duration, possibly a few hours (Haney, 2004; Karch, 2002) to a few days (Kerfoot et al., 1996; Schuckit, 2000) after the person stops using cocaine. The mechanism by which chronic cocaine abuse might contribute to the development of a drug-induced psychosis remains unknown. Gawin et al. (1994) suggested that the delusions found in a cocaine-induced psychotic reaction usually clear after the individual's sleep pattern has returned to normal, suggesting that cocaine-induced sleep disturbances might be one factor in the evolution of this drug-induced psychosis. Another theory suggests that individuals who develop a cocaine-induced paranoia might possess a biological vulnerability for schizophrenia, which is then activated by chronic cocaine abuse (Satel & Edell, 1991). Kosten and Sofuoglu (2004) disputed this theory however, stating that there was little evidence to suggest that cocaine-induced psychotic episodes are found mainly in people predisposed to these disorders.

Approximately 20% of the chronic users of crack cocaine in one study were reported to have experienced drug-induced periods of rage, or outbursts of anger and violent assaultive behavior (Beebe & Walley, 1991), which may be part of a cocaine-induced

delirium that precedes death (Karch, 2002). This cocaine-induced delirium might reflect the effects of cocaine on the synuclein family of proteins within the neuron. Under normal conditions, these protein molecules are thought to help regulate the transportation of dopamine within the neuron. But recent evidence (Mash et al., 2003) suggests that cocaine can alter synuclein production within the cell, causing or contributing to the death of the affected neurons, if not the individual. Indeed, cocaine-induced changes in synuclein production and utilization in the brain might cause cocaine-induced delirium, which is occasionally fatal to the user.

Finally, either a few hours after snorting the drug, or within 15 minutes if the person has injected it, the user slides into a state of depression. After periods of prolonged cocaine use, the individual's post-cocaine depression might reach suicidal proportions (Maranto, 1985). Cocaine-induced depression is thought to be the result of cocaine's depleting the nerve cells in the brain of the neurotransmitters norepinephrine and dopamine. After a period of abstinence, the neurotransmitter levels usually recover and the individual's emotions return to normal. But there is a very real danger that the cocaine abuser might attempt or complete suicide as a result of a drug-induced depression. One recent study in New York City found that one-fifth of all suicides involving a victim under the age of 60 were cocaine related (Roy, 2001).

Cocaine use as an indirect cause of death. In addition to its very real potential to cause death by a variety of mechanisms, cocaine use may indirectly cause, or at least contribute to, premature death of the user. For example, cocaine abuse is a known cause of rhabdomyolsis as a result of its toxic effects on muscle tissue and its vasoconstrictive effects, which can cause muscle ischemia (Karch, 2002; Richards, 2000). There is also evidence that cocaine abuse may alter the blood-brain barrier, facilitating the entry of the human immunodeficiency virus (HIV) into the brain (see Chapter 33).

Summary

Cocaine has a long history, which predates the present date by hundreds if not thousands of years. The active agent of the coca leaf, cocaine, was isolated only about 160 years ago, but people were using the coca leaf for a long time before that. Coincidentally, at just about the time that cocaine was isolated, the hypodermic needle was developed, which allowed users to inject large amounts of relatively pure cocaine directly into the circulatory system where it was rapidly transported to the brain. Users quickly discovered that intravenously administered cocaine brought on a sense of euphoria, which immediately made it a popular drug of abuse.

At the turn of the 20th century, government regulations limited the availability of cocaine, which was mistakenly classified as a narcotic at that time. The development of the amphetamine family of drugs in the 1930s, along with increasingly strict enforcement of the laws against cocaine use, allowed drug-addicted individuals to substitute amphetamines for the increasingly rare cocaine. In time, the dangers of cocaine use were forgotten by all but a few medical historians. But in the 1980s, cocaine again surfaced as a major drug of abuse in the United States as government regulations made it difficult for users to obtain amphetamines.

To entice users, new forms of cocaine were introduced, including concentrated "rocks" of cocaine, known as crack. To the cocaine user of the 1980s, cocaine seemed to be a harmless drug, although historical evidence suggested otherwise. Cocaine has been a major drug of abuse ever since.

In the 1980s, users rediscovered the dangers associated with cocaine abuse, and the drug gradually has fallen into disfavor. At this point it would appear that the most recent wave of cocaine addiction in the United States peaked around 1986 and that fewer and fewer people are becoming addicted to cocaine. Because of the threat of HIV-1 infection (see Chapter 33), and the increased popularity of heroin in the United States, many cocaine abusers are smoking a combination of crack cocaine and heroin. When cocaine is smoked, either alone, or in combination with heroin prepared for smoking, the danger of HIV transmission is effectively avoided, as intravenous needles are not involved.

In the past few years, the reported number of cocaine- and heroin-related emergency room visits has significantly increased in this country. This increase would seem to reflect the growing popularity of a mixture of both cocaine and heroin that is usually smoked. Thus, it would appear that cocaine will remain a part of the drug abuse problem well into the 21st century.

Schuckit (2000) reported that cocaine was isolated in 1857 rather than 1859. Surprisingly, recent research (Post et al., 1987) has cast doubt as to the antidepressant properties of cocaine. Although it is true that not everybody who uses cocaine will become addicted, it is not possible to determine at this time who will become addicted if they should try this drug. If only for this reason, cocaine abuse should be discouraged.

Marijuana Abuse and Addiction

Introduction

For many generations, marijuana has been a most controversial substance of abuse, and it is the subject of many misunderstandings. For example, people talk about marijuana as if it were a chemical in its own right, when in reality it is a plant, a member of the *Cannabis sativa* family of plants. The name *Cannabis sativa* is Latin for "cultivated hemp" (Green, 2002), reflecting the fact that some strains of Cannabis sativa have long been cultivated for the hemp fiber they produce, used to manufacture a number of substances.[1] Other strains of the Cannabis sativa family have been found to contain high levels of certain compounds found to have medicinal properties and a psychoactive effect.

Unfortunately, in the United States, the hysteria surrounding the use or abuse of Cannabis sativa has reached the point that *any* member of this plant family is automatically assumed to have an abuse potential (Williams, 2000). Indeed, to differentiate between forms of Cannabis sativa producing compounds that might be abused from members of this plant family that have low levels of these same compounds and are potentially useful plants for manufacturing and industry, Williams (2000) suggested that the term *hemp* be used for the latter. *Marijuana*, he suggested, should only be used to refer to those strains of Cannabis sativa that have an abuse potential. This is the pattern that will be followed in this text.

Unlike other substances such as alcohol, cocaine, or the amphetamines, marijuana is not in itself a drug of abuse. It is a plant that happens to contain some

chemicals that, when admitted to the body, alter the individual's perception of reality in a way some people find pleasurable. In this sense, marijuana is similar to the tobacco plant: They each contain compounds which, when introduced into the body, cause the user to experience certain effects that the individual deems desirable. In this chapter, the uses and abuses of marijuana will be discussed.

History of Marijuana Use in the United States

Almost 5,000 years ago, cannabis was in use by Chinese physicians as a treatment for malaria, constipation, the pain of childbirth, and when used with wine, a surgical anesthetic (Robson, 2001). Cannabis continued to be used for medicinal purposes throughout much of recorded history. As recently as the 19th century, physicians in the United States and Europe used marijuana as an analgesic, a hypnotic, a treatment for migraine headaches, and as an anticonvulsant (Grinspoon & Bakalar, 1993, 1995). The anticonvulsant properties of cannabis were illustrated by an incident that took place in 1838, when physicians were able to completely control the terror and "excitement" (Elliott, 1992, p. 600) of a patient who had contracted rabies through the use of hashish.

In the early years of the 20th century, cannabis came to be viewed with disfavor as a side effect of the hue-and-cry against opiate abuse (Walton, 2002). At the same time, researchers concluded that the chemicals in the marijuana plant were either ineffective or at least less effective than pharmaceuticals being introduced as part of the fight against disease. These two factors caused it to fall into disfavor as a pharmaceutical (Grinspoon & Bakalar, 1993,1995), and by the 1930s, marijuana was removed from the doctor's

---

[1]The Gutenberg and King James bibles were first printed on paper manufactured from hemp, and Rembrandt and Van Gogh both painted on canvas made from hemp (Williams, 2000). George Washington cultivated cannabis to obtain hemp, but there is no direct evidence that he smoked marijuana (Talty, 2003).

pharmacopoeia. By a historical coincidence, during the same period when medicinal marijuana use was being viewed with suspicion, *recreational* marijuana smoking was being introduced into the United States by immigrants and itinerant workers from Mexico who had come north to find work (Mann, 1994). Recreational marijuana smoking was quickly adopted by others, especially jazz musicians (Musto, 1991). With the start of Prohibition in 1920, many members of the working class turned to growing or importing marijuana as a substitute for alcohol (Gazzaniga, l988).

Recreational cannabis use declined with the end of Prohibition, when alcohol use once more became legal in the United States. But a small minority of the population continued to smoke marijuana, and this alarmed government officials. Various laws were passed in an attempt to eliminate the abuse of cannabis, including the Marijuana Tax Act of 1937.[2] But the "problem" of marijuana abuse in the United States never entirely disappeared, and by the 1960s use of marijuana again became popular. Indeed, by the start of the 21st century it is the most commonly abused illicit drug in the United States (Martin, 2004), with more than 50% of the entire population of the United States having used it at least once (Gold, Frost-Pineda, & Jacobs, 2004; Gruber & Pope, 2002).

Medicinal marijuana. Since the 1970s a growing number of physicians in the United States have again started to wonder if one or more of the chemicals found in the marijuana plant might continue to be of value in the fight against disease and suffering in spite of its legal status as a controlled substance. This interest was sparked by the reports from marijuana smokers being treated for cancer that they experienced less nausea if they smoked marijuana after receiving

chemotherapy treatments (Robson, 2001). Physicians began to follow up on these reports and found that marijuana, or selected chemicals found in the plant, might control the nausea sometimes caused by cancer chemotherapy. The drug Marinol (dronabinol) was introduced as a synthetic version of one of the chemicals found in marijuana, THC (to be discussed below), to control severe nausea. Marinol has met with mixed success, possibly because marijuana's antinausea effects are caused by a chemical other than THC (Smith, 1997).

Preliminary research conducted in the 1980s suggested that the practice of smoking marijuana might be helpful in treating certain forms of otherwise unmanageable glaucoma (Green, 2002; Grinspoon & Bakalar, 1993; Jaffe, 1990; Voelker, 1994). Unfortunately, the initial promise of marijuana in the control of glaucoma was not supported by follow-up studies (Watson, Benson, & Joy, 2000). Although marijuana smoking *does* cause a temporary reduction in the fluid pressure within the eye, only 60% to 65% of patients who smoke marijuana experience this effect (Green, 1998). Further, in order to achieve and maintain an adequate reduction in eye pressure levels, the individual would have to smoke 9 to 10 marijuana cigarettes per day—one every 2 to 3 hours (Green, 1998). Research into the possible use of marijuana in the treatment of glaucoma continues at this time.

There is evidence to suggest that marijuana can relieve at least some of the symptoms of amyotrophic lateral sclerosis (ALS) for short periods of time (Amtmann, Weydt, Johnson, Jensen, & Carter, 2004). Smoking marijuana also seems to help patients with multiple sclerosis, rheumatoid arthritis, and chronic pain conditions (Green, 2002; Grinspoon & Bakalar, 1997a; Robson, 2001; Watson, Benson, & Joy, 2000). An example of this is the work of the team of Karst et al. (2003), who utilized a synthetic analog of THC[3] known as CT-3[4] to explore whether this compound might be useful in the control of neuropathic pain. The authors found that CT-3 was not only effective in controlling neuropathic pain but also did not seem to have any adverse effects in the experimental subjects.

---

[2]Contrary to popular belief, the Marijuana Stamp Act of 1937 did not make *possession* of marijuana illegal but *did* impose a small tax on it. People who paid the tax would receive a stamp to show that they had paid the tax. Obviously, since the stamps would also alert authorities to the fact that the owners either had marijuana in their posession or planned to buy it, illegal users did not apply for the proper forms to pay the tax. The stamps are of interest to stamp collectors, however, and a few collectors have actually paid the tax in order to obtain the stamp for their collection. The Federal Marijuana Stamp Act was found to be unconstitutional by the U.S. Supreme Court in 1992. However, 17 states still have similar laws on the books ("Stamp Out Drugs," 2003).

[3]See "Pharmacology of Marijuana" section.

[4]Which is shorthand for 1',1'Dimethylheptyl-Δ 8 tetrahydro-cannabinol-11-oic acid.

Preliminary evidence suggests that it might help control the weight loss often seen in patients with late-stage AIDS or cancer (Green, 2002; Watson et al., 2000). There is also evidence, based on animal research, that a compound found in marijuana might function as a potent antioxidant, which might limit the amount of damage caused by cerebral vascular accidents (CVAs or strokes) (Hampson et al., 2002), and this is being actively explored by scientists eager to find a new tool for treating stroke victims.

There is also limited evidence suggesting that marijuana might be useful in controlling the symptoms of asthma, Crohn's disease, and anorexia as well as emphysema, epilepsy, and possibly hypertension (Green, 2002). One exciting possibility is that marijuana might also contain a compound that inhibits tumor growth (Martin, 2004), but research into possible medical applications of cannabis remains banned by the U.S. government (Green, 2002).

Claims that marijuana has a medicinal value are dismissed on the grounds that they are only anecdotal in nature (Marmor, 1998), although the Institute of Medicine concluded that there was enough evidence to warrant an in-depth study of the plant's medicinal value (Watson et al., 2000). Unfortunately, the Drug Enforcement Administration (DEA) has adopted the curious position that since it will recognize no legitimate medical use for marijuana, there is no need to look for any possible medical applications of this compound. For example, an administrative law judge ruled in 1988 that marijuana should be reclassified as a Schedule II substance (see Appendix IV). The DEA overruled its own judge and determined that marijuana would remain a Schedule I substance (Kassirer, 1997). Thus, in spite of evidence suggesting that at least some of the chemicals in marijuana might have medicinal value, all attempts at careful, systematic research into this area have been blocked by the DEA (Stimmel, 1997b).

In the late 1990s, a trend developed in which various state legislatures would debate the medicinal use of marijuana and put the matter to a vote. Several states, such as California, adopted measures approving the medicinal use of marijuana, often after a popular referendum on the subject had been approved by the voters. Unfortunately, the federal government continues to use bureaucratic mechanisms to block these efforts

(Sadock & Sadock, 2003). Thus, it would appear that marijuana will continue to remain a controversial recreational substance for many years to come.

A Question of Potency

Ever since the 1960s, marijuana abusers have sought ways to enhance the effects of the chemicals in the plant by adding other substances to the marijuana before smoking it, or by using strains with the highest possible concentrations of the compounds thought to cause marijuana's effects. To this end, users have taken to the process of growing strains of marijuana that have high concentrations of the compounds most often associated with pleasurable effects, and marijuana might be said to be *the* biggest cash crop in the United States at this time (Ross, 2002; Schlosser, 2003).[5]

There is strong evidence that much of the marijuana sold in the United States at this time is more potent than the marijuana commonly used in the 1960s and 1970s. The average marijuana sample seized by the police in the year 1992 had 3.08% THC, which had increased to 5.11% THC in the year 2002 (Compton, Grant, Colliver, Glantz, & Stinson, 2004).[6] There have been reports of marijuana with THC levels of 15% (Segal & Duffy, 1999) and even up to 20% for some Sinsemilla and Netherwood strains (Hall & Solowij, 1998; Weiss & Millman, 1998). One strain developed in British Columbia, Canada, reportedly has a THC content of 30% (Shannon, 2000).

A Technical Point

THC is found throughout the marijuana plant, but the highest concentrations are found in the small upper leaves and flowering tops of the plant (Hall & Solowij, 1998). Historically, the term *marijuana* is used to identify preparations of the cannabis plant that are used for smoking or eating. The term *hashish* is used to identify the thick resin that is obtained from the flowers of the

---

[5]This is to say the estimated retail value of the marijuana being raised in the United States, not the amount being cultivated, makes it the most valuable cash crop in this country at this time.

[6]Paradoxically, Schlosser (2003) suggested that the higher potency of the marijuana currently being sold might actually *increase* the safety of marijuana smoking as the user would need to smoke less to achieve a desired level of intoxication than with less potent preparations.

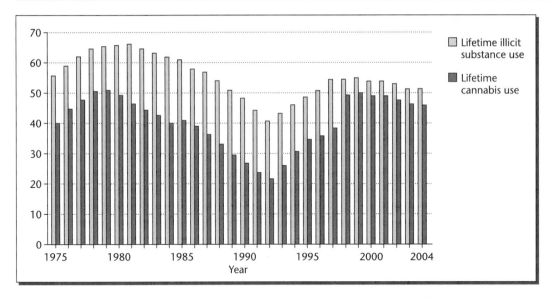

FIGURE 13.1   Comparison of marijuana abuse frequency with overall illicit drug abuse frequency: 1975–2004.
Source: Based on Johnston, O'Malley, Bachman, & Schulenberg (2004a).

marijuana plant. This resin is dried, forming a brown or black substance that has a high concentration of THC. This is subsequently either ingested orally (often mixed with some sweet substance) or smoked. *Hash oil* is a liquid extracted from the plant, which is 25% to 60% THC; this is added to marijuana or hashish to enhance its effect. However, in this chapter, the generic term *marijuana* is used for any part of the plant that is to be smoked or ingested.

Scope of the Problem of Marijuana Abuse

Estimates of the number of marijuana abusers around the world range from 146 million (United Nations, 2004) to 200–300 million people (Macfadden & Woody, 2000). Fully 30% of all marijuana abusers live in Asia, whereas North America (both the United States and Canada) and Africa each have about 24% of the world's marijuana abusers. Another 20% are found in Europe (United Nations, 2004).

In the United States, marijuana is the most frequently abused illicit substance, a status it has held for a number of decades (Compton et al., 2004; Hall & Degenhardt, 2005; Sussman & Westreich, 2003). Figure 13.1 provides an overview of the proportion of the illicit drug use

problem that is caused by marijuana abuse. It is estimated that more than 50% of the entire population of this country have used marijuana at least once (Gold et al., 2004). There have been no statistically significant changes in the overall rate of marijuana abuse in the adult population in the United States since 1991, although some subgroups have shown an increase in the frequency of marijuana abuse and the percentage of abusers who are addicted has increased in that period (Compton et al., 2004).

Marijuna use peaks in early adulthood and usually is discontinued by the time people are in their late 20s or early 30s (Gruber & Pope, 2002). About 46.1% of the seniors in the class of 2003 admitted to having used marijuana at least once (Johnston, O'Malley, & Bachman, 2003a), and the average age at which marijuana use begins is approximately 18 years (Hubbard, Franco, & Onaivi, 1999). Approximately 10% of those who use marijuana do so daily, and another 20% to 30% use it once a week (Hall & Solowij, 1998). Only a small percentage of marijuana abusers use more than 10 grams a month (about enough for 25–35 marijuana cigarettes) (MacCoun & Reuter, 2001). But marijuana is addictive, and it is estimated that 17% of those people who smoke marijuana more than five times will become addicted to it (Johns, 2001). Each year in the United States 100,000 people seek treatment for marijuana addiction (Hubbard et al., 1999).

Because of its popularity, the legal and the social sanctions against marijuana use have repeatedly changed in the past 30 years. In some states, possession of a small amount of marijuana was decriminalized, only to be *re*criminalized just a few years later (Macfadden & Woody, 2000). Currently, the legal status of marijuana varies from one state to another.

Pharmacology of Marijuana

In spite of its popularity as a drug of abuse, the mechanisms by which marijuana affects normal brain function remain poorly understood (Sussman & Westreich, 2003). The Cannabis sativa plant is known to contain at least 400 different compounds, of which an estimated 61 have some psychoactive effect (Gold et al., 2004; Sadock & Sadock, 2003; Weiss & Millman, 1998). The majority of marijuana's psychoactive effects are apparently the result of a single compound, Δ-9-tetrahydro-cannabinol[7] ("THC"), which was first identified in 1964 (Mirin, Weiss, & Greenfield, 1991; Restak, 1994; Sadock & Sadock, 2003). A second compound, *cannabidiol* (CBD), is also inhaled when marijuana is smoked, but researchers are not sure whether this compound has a psychoactive effect on humans or not (Nelson, 2000).

Once in the body, THC is biotransformed into the chemical 11-hydroxy-Δ 9-THC, a metabolite that actually is thought to cause its effects in the central nervous system (Sadock & Sadock, 2003). Only about 1% of the THC that is absorbed into the body is able to penetrate the blood-brain barrier to reach the brain, in part because the THC molecule is protein bound (Jenkins & Cone, 1998; Macfadden & Woody, 2000). Scientists have identified two receptor sites for THC in the body, the CB_1 and CB_2 receptors. Evidence also suggests the possibility that there are other THC receptor sites yet to be discovered (Karst et al., 2003). The CB_1 receptor sites are located in the hippocampus, cerebral cortex, basal ganglia, and cerebellum regions of the brain (Gruber & Pope, 2002; Martin, 2004; Watson et al., 2000; Zajicek et al., 2003). In general,

the THC that binds to the CB_1 receptor site seems to inhibit the release of excitatory neurotransmitters in these regions of the brain, possibly by opening the potassium ion channel in certain neurons while inhibiting the passage of calcium ions into the neurons, thus reducing the rate at which they might "fire" (Martin, 2004; Wingerchuk, 2004; Zajicek et al., 2003). The CB_2 receptor sites are found mainly in peripheral tissues that help mediate the body's immune response (Martin, 2004; Reynolds & Bada, 2003), which might explain why cannabis seems to have a mild immunosuppressant effect.

Scientists have also identified a pair of molecules within the brain that "bind" to the same receptor sites that THC occupies when the individual smokes marijuana. The first of these molecules is *anandamide* and the second is called *sn-2 arachidonyglycerol* (or 2-AG) (Martin, 2004). Scientists suspect that anandamide, which functions as a neurotransmitter in the brain, is involved in such activities as mood, memory, cognition, perception, muscle coordination, sleep, regulation of body temperature, and appetite; it possibly helps to regulate the immune system (Gruber & Pope, 2002; Nowak, 2004; Parrott, Morinan, Moss, & Scholey, 2004; Robson, 2001). Although THC uses this same receptor site, it seems to be 4–20 times as potent as anandamide, thus causing it to have a far stronger effect than this natural neurotransmitter (Martin, 2004).

Sn-2 arachidonyglycerol has not been studied in detail. It is thought to be manufactured in the hippocampus, a region of the brain known to be involved in the formation of memories (Parrott et al., 2004; Watson et al., 2000). Animal research would suggest that the brain uses these cannabinoid-type chemicals to help eliminate aversive memories (Marsicano et al., 2002; Martin, 2004). In addition, marijuana has been found to affect the synthesis and acetylcholine[8] turnover in the limbic system (Hartman, 1995) and the cerebellum (Fortgang, 1999). This might be the mechanism by which marijuana causes the user to feel sedated and relaxed.

Marijuana has a mild analgesic effect and is known to potentiate the analgesia induced by morphine (Martin, 2004). These effects appear to be caused by marijuana-induced inhibition of the enzyme *adenylate*

---

[7]Δ is the Greek letter for "delta."

[8]See Glossary.

cyclase, which is involved in the transmission of pain messages, although the exact mechanism by which this is accomplished remains to be identified. Marijuana is also able to inhibit the production of cyclooxygenase[9] which may play a role in its analgesic effects (Carvey, 1998). The analgesic effects of marijuana seem to peak at around 5 hours after it was used, and evidence suggests that marijuana is about as potent as codeine (Karst et al., 2003; Robson, 2001).

Once in the circulation, THC is rapidly distributed to blood-rich organs such as the heart, lungs, and brain. It then slowly works its way into tissues that receive less blood, such as the fat tissues of the body, where unmetabolized THC will be stored. Repeated episodes of marijuana use over a short period of time allow significant amounts of THC to be stored in the body's fat reserves. In between periods of active marijuana use, the fat-bound THC is slowly released back into the blood (Schwartz, 1987). In rare cases, this process results in heavy marijuana users testing positive for THC in urine toxicology screens for weeks after their last use of marijuana (Schwartz, 1987). However, this happens only with *very* heavy marijuana users, and casual users will usually have metabolites of THC in their urine for only about 3 days after the last use of marijuana.[10]

The primary site of THC biotransformation is in the liver, and more than 100 metabolites are produced during the process of THC biotransformation (Hart, 1997). The half-life of THC appears to vary as a result of whether metabolic tolerance has developed. However, the liver is not able to biotransform THC very quickly and in experienced users THC has a half-life of about 3 days (Schwartz, 1987) to a week for a single dose (Gruber & Pope, 2002). About 65% of the metabolites of THC are excreted in the feces, and the rest are excreted in the urine (Hubbard et al., 1999; Schwartz, 1987).

Tolerance to the subjective effects of THC will develop rapidly, and once tolerance has developed users must either wait a few days until their tolerance begins

to diminish or alter the manner in which they use the substance. For example, after tolerance to marijuana has developed the chronic marijuana smoker must use "more potent cannabis, deeper, more sustained inhalations, or larger amounts of the crude drug" (Schwartz, 1987, p. 307) in order to overcome tolerance.

Interactions between marijuana and other chemicals. There has been relatively little research into the possible interaction beween marijuana and other chemicals. It was suggested that when patients taking lithium used marijuana, their blood lithium levels would increase (Ciraulo, Shader, Greenblatt, & Barnhill, 1995). The reason for this increase in blood lithium level is not clear. However, because lithium is quite toxic and has only a narrow "therapeutic window," this interaction between marijuana and lithium is potentially dangerous to the person who uses both substances.

There has also been one case report of a patient who smoked marijuana while taking Antabuse (disulfiram). The patient developed a hypomanic episode that subsided when he stopped using marijuana (Barnhill, Ciraulo, Ciraulo, & Greene, 1995). When the patient again resumed the use of marijuana while taking Antabuse, he again became hypomanic, according to the authors, suggesting that the episode of mania was due to some unknown interaction between these two chemicals. For reasons that are not clear, adolescents who use marijuana while taking an antidepressant medication such as *Elavil* (amitriptyline) run the risk of developing a drug-induced delirium. Thus, individuals who are taking antidepressants should not use marijuana.

Cocaine users will often smoke marijuana concurrently with their use of cocaine because they believe that the sedating effects of marijuana will counteract the excessive stimulation caused by the cocaine. Unfortunately, cocaine is known to have a negative impact on cardiac function when it is abused. There has been no research into the combined effects of marijuana and cocaine on cardiac function in either healthy volunteers or patients with some form of preexisting cardiovascular disease.

Craig (2004) warned against the concurrent use of alcohol and marijuana. One of the body's natural defenses against poisons is vomiting. Marijuana inhibits nausea and vomiting. If the person were to ingest too much alcohol while using marijuana, Craig (2004) suggested that his or her body would be less likely to

---

[9]See Glossary.

[10]Some individuals have claimed that their urine samples tested positive for THC because they had used a form of beer made from the hemp plant. Unfortunately, test data fail to support the claim that one might ingest THC from this beer.

attempt to expel some of the alcohol through vomiting, raising the individual's chance of an overdose of the alcohol. There has been no research to test this hypothesis, but the concurrent use of alcohol and cannabis should be avoided on general principles.

Methods of Administration

In the United States, marijuana is occasionally ingested by mouth, usually after it has been baked into a product such as cookies or brownies. This process will allow the user to absorb about 4% to 12% of the available THC, with a large part of the THC being destroyed by the chemicals of the digestive tract (Drummer & Odell, 2001; Gold et al., 2004; Stimmel, 1997). In contrast to smoked marijuana, oral ingestion results in a slower absorption into the general circulation so that the user does not feel the effects of THC until 30–60 minutes (Mirin et al., 1991) or perhaps 2 hours (Schwartz, 1987) after ingesting it. The peak blood concentration of THC is usually seen 60–90 minutes after the person has ingested the cookie or brownie, although in rare cases this might be delayed for as long as 1 to 5 hours (Drummer & Odell, 2001). Estimates of the duration of marijuana's effects when ingested orally range from 3 to 5 hours (Mirin et al., 1991; Weiss & Mirin, 1988) to 8 to 24 hours (Gruber & Pope, 2002).

The most popular means by which marijuana is abused is by smoking (Gruber & Pope, 2002), a practice that can be traced back at least 5,000 years (Walton, 2002). It has been estimated that almost 60% of the available THC is admitted into the body when marijuana is smoked (Drummer & Odell, 2001; Gold et al., 2004). Marijuana can be smoked alone or mixed with other substances. Most commonly, the marijuana is smoked by itself in the form of cigarettes commonly called "joints." The typical marijuana cigarette usually contains between 500 mg and 750 mg of marijuana and provides an effective dose of approximately 2.5 mg to 20 mg of THC per cigarette (depending on potency). The amount of marijuana in the average joint weighs about 0.014 ounces (Abt Associates, Inc., 1995b). A variation on the marijuana cigarette is the "blunt." Blunts are made by removing one of the outer leaves of a cigar, unrolling it, filling it with high potency marijuana mixed with chopped cigar tobacco, and then rerolling the mixture into the cigar's outer leaves so that the mixture assumes the shape of the original cigar (Gruber & Pope, 2002). Users report some degree of stimulation, possibly from the nicotine in the cigar tobacco entering the lungs along with the marijuana smoke.

The technique by which marijuana is smoked is somewhat different from the normal smoking technique used for cigarettes or cigars (Schwartz, 1987). Users must inhale the smoke deeply into their lungs, then hold their breath for between 20 and 30 seconds in an attempt to get as much THC into the blood as possible (Schwartz, 1987). Because THC crosses through the lungs into the circulation very slowly, only 2% to 50% of the THC that is inhaled will actually be absorbed (Macfadden & Woody, 2000).

But the effects of this limited amount of THC begin within seconds (Weiss & Mirin, 1988) to perhaps 10 minutes (Bloodworth, 1987). It has been estimated that to produce a sense of euphoria the user must inhale approximately 25 to 50 micrograms per kilogram of body weight when marijuana is smoked, and between 50 to 200 micrograms per kilogram of body weight when ingested orally (Mann, 1994). Doses of 200 to 250 micrograms per kilogram when marijuana is smoked or 300 to 500 micrograms per kilogram when taken orally may cause the user to hallucinate, according to the author. As these figures suggest, it takes an extremely large dose of THC for this to occur. Marijuana users in other countries often have access to high potency sources of THC and thus may achieve hallucinatory doses. But it is extremely rare for marijuana users in this country to have access to such potent forms of the plant. Thus, for the most part, the marijuana being smoked in this country will not cause the individual to hallucinate. However, in many parts of the country, marijuana is classified as a hallucinogenic by law-enforcement officials.

The effects of smoked marijuana reach peak intensity within 30 minutes and begin to decline in an hour (Nelson, 2000). Estimates of the duration of the subjective effects of smoked marijuana range from 2–3 (O'Brien, 2001) to 4 hours (Grinspoon & Bakalar, 1997a; Sadock & Sadock, 2003) after a single dose. The individual might suffer some cognitive and psychomotor problems for as long as 5–12 hours after a single dose, however, suggesting that the effects of smoking marijuana might last longer than the euphoria (Sadock & Sadock, 2003).

Proponents of the legalization of marijuana point out that in terms of *immediate* lethality, marijuana appears to be a "safe" drug. Various researchers have estimated that the effective dose is 1/10,000th (Science and Technology Committee Publications, 1998) to 1/20,000th, or even 1/40,000th the lethal dose (Grinspoon & Bakalar, 1993, 1995; Kaplan, Sadock, & Grebb, 1994). It was reported that a 160-pound person would have to smoke 900 marijuana cigarettes simultaneously to achieve a fatal overdose (Cloud, 2002). An even higher estimate was offered by Schlosser (2003), who suggested that the average person would need to smoke *100 pounds of marijuana a minute for 15 minutes* to overdose on it. In contrast to the estimated 434,000 deaths each year in this country from tobacco use and the 125,000 yearly fatalities from alcohol use, only an estimated 75 marijuana-related deaths occur each year. Most marijuana-related deaths take place in accidents while the individual is under the influence of this substance rather than as a direct result of any toxic effects of THC (Crowley, 1988). As these data would suggest, there has never been a documented case of a marijuana overdose (Gruber & Pope, 2002; Schlosser, 2003). Indeed, in terms of its immediate toxicity, marijuana appears to be "among the least toxic drugs known to modern medicine" (Weil, 1986, p. 47).

Subjective Effects of Marijuana

At moderate dosage levels, marijuana will bring about a two-phase reaction (Brophy, 1993). The first phase begins shortly after the drug enters the bloodstream, when the individual will experience a period of mild anxiety; the second phase follows—a sense of well-being or euphoria as well as a sense of relaxation and friendliness (Kaplan et al., 1994). These subjective effects are consistent with the known physical effects of marijuana. Research has found that marijuana causes "a transient increase in the release of the neurotransmitter dopamine" (Friedman, 1987, p. 47), a neurochemical thought to be involved in the experience of euphoria.

The individual's *expectations* influence how he or she interprets the effects of marijuana. Marijuana users tend to anticipate that the drug will (a) impair cognitive function as well as the user's behavior, (b) help the user relax, (c) help the user interact socially and

enhance sexual function, (d) enhance creative abilities and alter perception, (e) bring some negative effects, and (f) bring about a sense of "craving" (Schafer & Brown, 1991). Individuals who are intoxicated on marijuana frequently report an altered sense of time as well as mood swings (Kaplan et al., 1994) and feelings of well-being and happiness. Marijuana also seems to bring about a splitting of consciousness, in which the user will possibly experience depersonalization and/or derealization while under its influence (Johns, 2001).

Marijuana users have often reported a sense of being on the threshold of a significant personal insight but not being able to put this insight into words. These reported drug-related insights seem to come about during the first phase of the marijuana reaction. The second phase of the marijuana experience begins when the individual becomes sleepy, which takes place following the acute intoxication caused by marijuana (Brophy, 1993).

Adverse Effects of Occasional Marijuana Use

More than 2,000 separate metabolites of the 400 chemicals in the marijuana plant may be found in the body after the individual has smoked marijuana (Jenike, 1991). Many of these metabolites may remain present in the body for weeks after a single episode of marijuana smoking. Unfortunately, scientists have not studied the long-term effects of these metabolites. Further, if the marijuana is adulterated (as it frequently is), the various adulterants add their own contribution to the flood of chemicals admitted to the body when the person uses marijuana. Again, there is little research into the long-term effects of these adulterants or their metabolites on the user.

Although advocates of marijuana use point to its safety record, it is not a benign substance. In addition to the famous "bloodshot eyes" seen in marijuana smokers, which is caused by marijuana making the small blood vessels in the eyes dilate and thus be more easily seen, approximately 40% to 60% of users will experience at least one other adverse drug-induced effect (Hubbard et al., 1999). About 15% of marijuana abusers experience episodes of drug-induced anxiety or even full-blown panic attacks (Johns, 2001; Kaplan et al., 1994; Millman

& Beeder, 1994). Factors that seem to influence the development of marijuana-related panic reactions are the use of more potent forms of marijuana, the individual's prior experience with marijuana, expectations for the drug, the dosage level being used, and the setting in which the drug is used. Such panic reactions are most often seen in the inexperienced marijuana user (Bloodworth, 1987; Gruber & Pope, 2002; Mirin et al., 1991). Usually the only treatment needed is simple reassurance that the drug-induced effects will soon pass (Millman & Beeder, 1994; Kaplan et al., 1994). Because smokers, more easily than oral users, are able to titrate the amount used, there is a tendency for panic reactions to occur more often after marijuana is ingested than when it is smoked (Gold et al., 2004).

Marijuana use also contributes to impaired reflexes for at least 24 hours after the individual's last use (Gruber & Pope, 2002; Hubbard et al., 1999; Meer, 1986). The team of Ramaekers, Berghaus, van Laar, and Drummer (2004) concluded that marijuana abuse caused a dose-related impairment of cognition and psychomotor function, with the risk of a motor vehicle accident being 300% to 700% higher in persons who had recently used marijuana. This finding was consistent with that of Schwartz (1987), who concluded that teenagers who smoked marijuana as often as six times a month "were 2.4 times more likely to be involved in traffic accidents" (p. 309) than were nonusers.

A more serious but quite rare adverse reaction is the development of a marijuana-induced psychotic reaction, often called a *toxic* or *drug-induced psychosis*. The effects of a marijuana-induced toxic psychosis are usually short-lived and will clear up in a few days to, at most, a week (Johns, 2001). Fortunately, researchers currently think that marijuana-induced psychotic reactions are only the result of extremely heavy marijuana use, making the danger of a marijuana-induced psychosis for the casual user quite low (Johns, 2001). However, research has also demonstrated that marijuana use can exacerbate preexisting psychotic disorders or initiate a psychotic reaction in an individual predisposed to this form of psychiatric dysfunction (Johns, 2001; Linszen, Dingemans, & Lenior, 1994; Mathers & Ghodse, 1992; O'Brien, 2001).

One possible mechanism through which marijuana might contribute to the emergence of schizophrenia was suggested by Linszen et al. (1994). The authors noted THC functions as a dopamine agonist in the nerve pathways of the region of the brain known as the *medial forebrain bundles*. Dysregulation of normal dopamine activity in this region of the brain has been suggested as one possible cause of schizophrenia, and this might be one mechanism through which marijuana might contribute to the emergence of psychotic symptoms in patients with schizophrenia.

Marijuana is known to reduce sexual desire in the user and for male users may contribute to erectile problems and delayed ejaculation (Finger, Lund, & Slagel, 1997). Finally, there is a relationship between cannabis abuse and depression, although researchers are not sure whether the depression is a result of the cannabis use (Bovasso, 2001). This marijuana-related depression is most common in the inexperienced user and may reflect the activation of an undetected depression in the user. The depressive episode is usually mild, is short-lived, and does not require professional intervention except in rare cases (Millman & Beeder, 1994).

Consequences of Chronic Marijuana Abuse

Researchers have found precancerous changes in the cells of the respiratory tract of chronic marijuana abusers similar to those seen in cigarette smokers (Gold et al., 2004). However, as many marijuana smokers also use tobacco cigarettes, it is not clear to what degree, if any, their marijuana abuse has caused or contributed to these cellular changes. It *has* been demonstrated that the chronic use of THC reduces the effectiveness of the respiratory system's defenses against infection (Gruber & Pope, 2002; Hubbard et al., 1999). Animal research also suggests the possibility of a drug-induced suppression of the immune system as a whole, although researchers do not know whether this effect is found in humans (Abrams et al., 2003; Gold et al., 2004). But given the relationship between HIV-1 virus infection and immune system impairment,[11] it would seem that marijuana abuse by patients with HIV-1 infection is potentially dangerous.

---

[11]This topic is discussed in more detail in Chapter 33.

With the exception of nicotine, which is not found in the cannabis plant, marijuana smokers are exposed to virtually all of the toxic compounds found in cigarettes, and if they smoke a blunt[12] their exposure to these compounds is even higher (Gruber & Pope, 2002). The typical marijuana cigarette has between 10 and 20 times as much "tar" as tobacco cigarettes (Nelson, 2000), and marijuana smokers are thought to absorb *four times* as much tar as cigarette smokers (Tashkin, 1993). In addition, the marijuana smoker will absorb *five times* as much carbon monoxide per joint as would a cigarette smoker who smoked a single regular cigarette (Oliwenstein, 1988; Polen, Sidney, Tekawa, Sadler, & Friedman, 1993; University of California, Berkeley, 1990b). Smoking just four marijuana joints appears to have the same negative impact on lung function as smoking 20 regular cigarettes (Tashkin, 1990).

Marijuana smoke has been found to contain 5 to 15 times the amount of a known carcinogen, benzpyrene, as does tobacco smoke (Bloodworth, 1987; Tashkin, 1993). Indeed, the heavy use of marijuana was suggested as a cause of cancer of the respiratory tract and the mouth (tongue, tonsils, etc.) in a number of younger individuals who would not be expected to have cancer (Gruber & Pope, 2002; Hall & Solowij, 1998; Tashkin, 1993). There are several reasons for the observed relationship between heavy marijuana use and lung disease. In terms of absolute numbers, marijuana smokers tend to smoke fewer joints than cigarette smokers do cigarettes. However, they also smoke unfiltered joints, a practice that allows more of the particles from smoked marijuana into the lungs than is the case for cigarette smokers. Marijuana smokers also smoke more of the joint than cigarette smokers do cigarettes. This increases the smoker's exposure to microscopic contaminants in the marijuana. Finally, marijuana smokers inhale more deeply than cigarette smokers and retain the smoke in the lungs for a longer period of time (Polen et al., 1993). Again, this increases the individual's exposure to the potential carcinogenic agents in marijuana smoke. These facts seem to account for the fact that like tobacco smokers, marijuana users have an increased frequency of bronchitis and other upper respiratory infections (Hall

& Solowij, 1998). The chronic use of marijuana also may contribute to the development of chronic obstructive pulmonary disease (COPD), similar to that seen in cigarette smokers (Gruber & Pope, 2002).

Marijuana abuse has been implicated as the cause of a number of reproductive system dysfunctions. For example, there is evidence that marijuana use contributes to reduced sperm counts (Brophy, 1993) and a reduction in testicular size (Hubbard et al., 1999) in men. Further, chronic male marijuana users have been found to have 50% lower blood testosterone levels than men who do not use marijuana (Bloodworth, 1987). Women who are chronic marijuana users have been found to experience menstrual abnormalities and/or a failure to ovulate (Gold et al., 2004; Hubbard et al., 1999). Researchers are still divided on whether chronic marijuana use could result in fertility problems in the woman. However, on the basis of the limited data that is available at this time, there is no evidence to suggest that chronic marijuana use results in fertility problems (Grinspoon & Bakalar 1997).

People who have previously used hallucinogenics may also experience marijuana-related "flashback" experiences (Jenike, 1991). Such flashbacks are usually limited to the 6-month period following the last marijuana use (Jeinke, 1991) and will eventually stop if the person does not use any further mood-altering chemicals (Weiss & Mirin, 1988). The flashback experience will be discussed in more detail in the chapter on the hallucinogenic drugs, as there is little evidence that cannabis alone can induce flashbacks (Sadock & Sadock, 2003).

There is little conclusive evidence that chronic cannabis use can cause brain damage (Grant, Gonzalez, Carey, Natarajan, & Wolfson, 2003) or permanent neurocognitive damage (Vik, Cellucci, Jarchow, & Hedt, 2004). At most, there seems to be a minor reduction in the user's ability to learn new information while using cannabis (Grant et al. 2003). Sussman and Westreich (2003) suggested that chronic marijuana abuse might result in a 20% to 30% reduction in the user's level of cognitive performance. It is possible to detect evidence of cognitive deficits in chronic cannabis abusers for up to 7 days after their last use of marijuana (Pope, Gruber, Hudson, Huestis, & Yurgelun-Todd, 2001; Pope

---

[12]Discussed earlier in this chapter.

& Yurgelun-Todd, 1996). Researchers have identified memory deficits associated with cannabis abuse that seem progressively worse in chronic users (Fletcher et al., 1996; Gruber, Pope, Hudson, & Yurgelun-Todd, 2003; Solowij et al., 2002). But these cognitive changes seem to reverse after 2 weeks of abstinence from marijuana (Vik et al., 2004).

Researchers have also found changes in the electrical activity of the brain, as measured by electroencephalographic (EEG) studies, in chronic marijuana abusers. These EEG changes seem to last for at least 3 months after the individual's last use of marijuana (Schuckit, 2000). However, the importance of these observed EEG changes is not known at this time, and neuropsychological testing of chronic marijuana users in countries such as Greece, Jamaica, and Costa Rica has failed to uncover evidence of permanent brain damage (Grinspoon & Bakalar, 1997). It is not known at this time whether these EEG changes are caused by the abuse of cannabis or the abuse of other recreational chemicals (Grant et al., 2003).

Hernig, Better, Tate, and Cadet (2001) used a technique known as transcranial Doppler sonography to determine the blood flow rates in the brains of 16 long-term marijuana abusers and 19 nonusers. The authors found evidence of increased blood flow resistance in the cerebral arteries of the marijuana abusers, suggesting that chronic marijuana abuse might increase the individual's risk of a cerebral vascular accident (stroke). Within 4 weeks of their last use of cannabis, the blood flow patterns of young marijuana abusers was comparable to that seen in normal 60-year-old adults, according to the authors, who were unable to predict whether the blood flow patterns would return to normal with continued abstinence from marijuana. This places cannabis in the paradoxical position of possibly contributing to the individual's risk for stroke and as possibly containing a compound that might limit the damage caused by a cerebrovascular accident after it occurs. While additional research is necessary to determine the degree to which chronic cannibis abuse might interfere with blood flow within the brain and the mechanism by which this might occur, the evidence suggesting that marijuana abuse might be a cause of permanent brain damage is mixed, at best, if not lacking at this time.

The "amotivational syndrome." Scientists have found conflicting evidence as to whether chronic marijuana use might bring about an "amotivational syndrome." The amotivational syndrome is thought to consist of decreased drive and ambition, short attention span, easy distractibility, and a tendency not to make plans beyond the present day (Mirin et al., 1991). Indirect evidence suggesting that the amotivational syndrome might exist was provided by Gruber et al. (2003). The authors compared psychological and demographic measures of 108 individuals who had smoked cannabis at least 5,000 times against 72 age-matched control subjects who admitted to having used marijuana no more than 50 times. The authors found that the heavier marijuana users reported significantly lower incomes and educational achievement than did the control group in spite of the fact that the two groups came from similar families of origin. While suggestive, this study does not answer the question of whether these findings reflect the effects of marijuana or if individuals prone to marijuana abuse tend to have less drive and initiative and are drawn to marijuana because its effects are similar to their personalities.

The "amotivational syndrome" has been challenged by many researchers in the field. Even chronic marijuana abusers demonstrate "remarkable energy and enthusiasm in the pursuit of their goals" (Weiss & Millman, 1998, p. 211). It has been suggested that the amotivational syndrome might reflect nothing more than the effects of marijuana intoxication in chronic users (Johns, 2001), and there is little evidence of "a specific and unique 'amotivational syndrome'" (Mendelson & Mello, 1998, p. 2514; Sadock & Sadock, 2003; Iverson, 2005).

Marijuana abuse as a cause of death. Although marijuana is, in terms of immediate lethality, quite safe, there is significant evidence that chronic marijuana use can contribute to or be the primary cause of a number of potentially serious medical problems. For example, some of the chemicals in marijuana might function as "dysregulators of cellular regulation" (Hart, 1997, p. 60) by slowing the process of cellular renewal within the body.

Marijuana users experience a 30% to 50% increase in heart rate that begins within a few minutes of use and can last for up to 3 hours (Craig, 2004; Hall & Solowij, 1998). For reasons that are unknown, marijuana also causes a reduction in the strength of the heart contractions and the amount of oxygen reaching the heart muscle, changes that are potentially serious for patients with heart disease (Barnhill et al., 1995; Schuckit, 2000). Although these changes are apparently insignificant for younger cannabis users, they may be the reason older users are at increased risk for heart attacks in the first hours following their use of marijuana ("Marijuana-related Deaths," 2002; Mittleman, Lewis, Maclure, Sherwood, & Muller, 2001). Thus, it would appear that marijuana use is not as benign as advocates of this substance would have us believe.

The myth of marijuana-induced violence. In the 1930s and 1940s, it was widely believed that marijuana use would cause the user to become violent. Researchers no longer believe that marijuana is likely to induce violence. Indeed, the sedating and euphoric effects of marijuana would be more likely to *reduce* the tendency toward violence while the user is intoxicated rather than bring it about (Husak, 2004). However, the chronic abuser, who is more tolerant of the effects, will experience less of the sedating effects and be more capable of violence than a rare user (Walton, 2002). Even so, currently few clinicians now believe that marijuana use is associated with an increased tendency for violent acting out.[13]

The Addiction Potential of Marijuana

Because marijuana does not cause the same dramatic withdrawal syndromes seen with alcohol or narcotic addiction, people tend to underestimate the addiction potential of cannabis. But tolerance, one of the hallmarks of addiction, does slowly develop to cannabis. Researchers believe that smoking as few as three marijuana cigarettes a week may result in tolerance to the effects of marijuana (Bloodworth, 1987). Further,

perhaps 9% of cannabis abusers will become addicted to marijuana (Cloud, 2002; Fortgang, 1999; Gruber & Pope, 2002). Gruber and Pope (2002) suggested that one-third of the adolescents who use marijuana daily are addicted to it. One characteristic that seems to identify individuals who are at risk for becoming addicted to marijuana is an early life (prior to age 16 years) positive experience with it (Fergusson, Horwood, Lynskey, & Madden, 2003).

The withdrawal syndrome from cannabis has not been examined in detail (Budney, Moore, Bandrey, & Hughes, 2003). A popular misconception is that there is no withdrawal syndrome from marijuana, but research has found that chronic marijuana abusers experience a withdrawal syndrome that includes such symptoms as irritability, aggressive behaviors, anxiety, insomnia, nausea, a loss of appetite, sweating, and vomiting (Gruber & Pope, 2002; Kouri, Pope, & Lukas, 1999; Nahas, 1986). The withdrawal symptoms begin anywhere from 1 to 3 days after the last use of cannabis, peak between the 2nd and 10th day, and can last up to 28 days or more (Budney et al., 2003; Sussman & Westreich, 2003) and has been classified as flu-like in terms of intensity (Martin, 2004). It would thus appear that despite claims to the contrary, marijuana meets the criteria necessary to be classified as an addictive compound.

Summary

Marijuana has been the subject of controversy for the past several generations. In spite of its popularity as a drug of abuse, surprisingly little is actually known about marijuana. After a 25-year search, researchers have identified what appears to be the specific receptor site, which the THC molecule uses to cause at least some of its effects on perception and memory.

In spite of the fact that very little is known about this drug, some groups have called for its complete decriminalization. Other groups maintain that marijuana is a serious drug of abuse with a high potential for harm. Even the experts differ as to the potential for marijuana to cause harm. For example, in contrast to Weil's (1986) assertion that marijuana was one of the safest drugs known, Oliwenstein (1988) classified it as a dangerous drug. In reality, the available evidence at this time would suggest that marijuana

---

[13]However, if the marijuana were adulterated with any other chemical(s), or if the abuser had used marijuana along with other chemicals, then the effects of that chemical(s) must be considered as a possible cause of drug-induced violent behaviors. For example, the hallucinogen PCP is known to trigger violent behaviors in some users, and it is a common adulterant in marijuana.

is not as benign as was once thought. Marijuana, either alone or in combination with cocaine, will increase heart rate, a matter of some significance to those with cardiac disease. There is evidence that chronic use of marijuana will cause physical changes in the brain, and the smoke from marijuana cigarettes has been found to be even more harmful than tobacco smoke. Marijuana remains such a controversial drug that the United States government refuses to sanction research into its effects on the grounds that they do not want to run the risk that researchers might find something about marijuana that proponents of its legalization might use to justify their demands (D. Smith, 1997).

CHAPTER FOURTEEN

Opiate Abuse and Addiction

Introduction

Pain is perhaps the oldest problem known to medicine (Meldrum, 2003). Each year in the United States more than 70% of adults will experience at least one episode of acute pain (Williams, 2004). In spite of all of the advances made by medical science in the past century, even now there is no objective measure of pain, and the physician must rely almost exclusively on the patient's assessment of his or her pain (Williams, 2004).

The phenomenon of pain is the outcome of a complex neurophysiological process that at best is only poorly understood by scientists (Chapman & Okifuji, 2004). With pain so poorly understood, it is not surprising to learn that the medications used to control pain, the narcotic analgesics, are a source of endless confusion not only for health care professionals but also for the general public. In spite of the relief that this family of medications offers for those in pain, the general public and physicians alike view them with distrust because of their history of abuse (Herrera, 1997; Vourakis, 1998). Over the years, myths and mistaken beliefs about narcotic analgesics and pain management have been repeated over and over from one health care professional to the next so often that they have been incorporated into professional journals and textbooks as medical "fact" and have then shaped patient care (Vourakis, 1998).

Much of the literature published about narcotic analgesics in the 20th century focused on the problem of *addiction* to these medications, making physicians hesitate to prescribe large doses of opioids out of a fear that they would cause or contribute to a substance-use problem (Antoin & Beasley, 2004). Physicians continue to *underprescribe* narcotic analgesics because of this fear, causing patients to suffer needlessly (Carvey, 1998; Kuhl, 2002). One study found that only slightly more than half of the 300 physicians surveyed were able to correctly estimate the dose of morphine needed to control cancer-related pain (Herrera, 1997). As many as 73% of patients in moderate to severe distress are thought to suffer unnecessarily because their physicians do not prescribe adequate doses of the appropriate analgesics (Stimmel, 1997b).

In addition, regulatory policies of the Drug Enforcement Administration (DEA) aimed at discouraging the diversion of prescribed narcotic analgesics[1] often intimidate or confuse physicians who wish to prescribe these medications for patients in pain. As a result of physicians' irrational fears of causing addiction coupled with federal supervisory edicts, only a minority of patients are thought to receive adequate doses of a narcotic analgesic to control pain (Herrera, 1997; Paris, 1996). This is unfortunate, for although the narcotic analgesics do have a significant abuse potential, they also remain potent and extremely useful medications. To try to clear up some of the confusion that surrounds the legitimate use of narcotic analgesics, this chapter will be divided into two sections. In the first section, the role and applications of narcotic analgesics as pharmaceutical agents will be examined. In the second section, the narcotic analgesics as drugs of abuse will be discussed.

I. THE MEDICAL USES OF NARCOTIC ANALGESICS

A Short History of the Narcotic Analgesics

There is anthropological evidence suggesting that opium was used in religious rituals 10,000 years ago (Restak, 1994; Walton, 2002). There is also archeological

---

[1]For many years, the issue of prescription diversion was not thought to be significant. Although the true scope of this problem is still unclear, it *has* become apparent that diversion of such compounds as Oxycontin is common (Meier, 2003).

evidence that the opium poppy was being cultivated as a crop in certain regions of Europe by the latter part of the Neolithic era (Booth, 1996; Spindler, 1994). Somehow, early humans had discovered that if you made an incision at the top of the *Papaver somniferum* plant during a brief period in its life cycle, the plant would extrude a thick resin. This resin is "an elaborate cocktail containing sugars, proteins, ammonia, latex, gums, plant wax, tats, sulphuric and lactic acids, water, meconic acid, and a wide range of alkaloids" (Booth, 1996, p. 4). Although the exact composition of this resin would not be determined for thousands of years, at some point early humans had discovered that it could be used for ritual and medicinal purposes.

Eventually, this resin was called *opium*. The English word *opium* can be traced to the Greek word *opion*, which means "poppy juice" (Stimmel, 1997b). In a document known as the Ebers Papyri, which dates back to approximately 7,000 B.C.E., there is a reference to the use of opium as a treatment for children who suffer from colic (Darton & Dilts, 1998). Historical evidence suggests that the widespread use of opium had developed by around 4200 B.C.E. (Walton, 2002). For the thousands of years when physicians could offer few truly effective treatments to the sick, opium came to be viewed as a gift from the gods (Ray & Ksir, 1993; Reisine & Pasternak, 1995). It could relieve virtually every form of pain, and it could control diarrhea, especially massive diarrhea such as that of dysentery.[2] Physicians also discovered that opium could control anxiety, and its limited antipsychotic potential made it marginally effective in controlling the symptoms of psychotic disorders in an era when physicians had no other effective treatment for psychosis (Beeder & Millman, 1995; Woody, McLellan, & Bedrick, 1995).

In 1803[3] a chemist named Friedrich W. A. Serturner first isolated a pure alkaloid base from opium that was recognized as being the active agent of opium. This chemical was later called *morphine* after the Greek god of dreams, Morphius. Surprisingly, morphine is a "nitrogenous waste product" (Hart, 1997, p. 59) produced by the opium poppy, and not the reason for the plant's existence. But by happy coincidence this waste product happens to control many of the manifestations of pain in humans. As chemists explored the various chemical compounds found in the sap of the opium poppy, they discovered a total of 20 distinct alkaloids in addition to morphine and including codeine, that could be obtained from that plant (Gold, 1993; Reisine & Pasternak, 1995). After these alkaloids were isolated, medical science found a use for many of them. Unfortunately, a number of these alkaloids can be abused.

In 1857, about half a century after morphine was first isolated from opium, Alexander Wood invented the hypodermic needle. This device made it possible to quickly and painlessly inject a substance into the body. The ready availability of relatively pure morphine, the intravenous needle, the mistaken belief that morphine was nonaddicting (it was an ingredient in patent medications that were used to treat every ailment imaginable), and the widespread use of morphine in military field hospitals of the era all combined to produce large epidemics of morphine addiction in both the United States and Europe in the last half of the 19th century.

The "patent medicine" phenonemon of the 19th century deserves special mention. In the latter half of this century, the average person placed little confidence in what medical science had to offer. Physicians were referred to as "croakers," and it was not unusual for the patient to rely on time-honored folk remedies, and patent medicines rather than to seek a physician's advice (Norris, 1994). Both cocaine and morphine were common ingredients in many of the patent medicines that were sold throughout the United States. Even if users of a patent medicine were aware of the contents of the bottle they had purchased, they were unlikely to believe that the "medicine" could hurt them. The idea of a medication as addictive was totally foreign to the average person, especially as the concept of "drug abuse" itself did not emerge until the latter years of the 19th century (Walton, 2002). As a result, large numbers of people unknowingly became addicted to one or more chemicals in the patent medicines they had come to rely on for every illness.

In other cases, people had started to use either opium or morphine for the control of pain or to treat diarrhea, only to become physically dependent on that chemical. When users tried to stop, they would begin to experience withdrawal symptoms. Like magic, these withdrawal symptoms would disappear when they

[2]See Glossary.
[3]Restak (1994) suggested that morphine was isolated in 1805, not 1803, whereas Antoin and Beasley (2004) suggested that this event took place in 1806.

resumed the use of the original medicine. As a result of these two phenomena—widespread availability of morphine for self-medication and its use in patent medicines—*more than 1% of the entire population of the United States* was addicted to opium or to narcotics at the start of the 20th century (Restak, 1994).

During this period, the practice of smoking opium had been introduced to the United States by Chinese immigrants, many of whom came to work on the railroad in the era following the Civil War. Opium smoking became somewhat popular, especially on the Pacific coast, and through this process many opium smokers became addicted to it. By 1900 fully a quarter of the opium imported into the United States was used not for medicine but for smoking (Jonnes, 1995; Ray & Ksir, 1993). Two-thirds to three-fourths of those individuals addicted to opiates in the United States were women (Kandall, Doberczak, Jantunen, & Stein, 1999). Faced with an epidemic of unrestrained opiate use, the United States Congress passed the Pure Food and Drug Act of 1906. This law required manufacturers to list the ingredients of their product on the label, revealing for the first time that many a trusted remedy contained narcotics. Other provisions in the law, especially the Harrison Narcotics Act of 1914, prohibited the use of narcotics without a prescription signed by a physician. Since then, the battle against narcotic abuse/addiction has waxed and waned, but it has never entirely disappeared.

The Classification of Narcotic Analgesics

Since morphine was first identified, medical researchers have either isolated or developed a wide variety of compounds that, in spite of differences in their chemical structure, have similar pharmacological effects to that of morphine. Segal and Duffy (1999) classified these compounds as falling into one of three groups:

1. *Natural opiates:* obtained directly from the opium, of which morphine and codeine are examples.
2. *Semisynthetic opiates:* chemically altered derivatives of natural opiates. Dihydromorphine and heroin are examples of this group of compounds.
3. *Synthetic opiates:* synthesized in laboratories and not derived from natural opiates at all. Methadone and propoxyphene are examples of these compounds.

Admittedly, there are significant differences in the chemical structures of different natural, semisynthetic, and synthetic opiates. However, for the sake of simplification, all of these compounds will be grouped together under the generic terms *opiates* or *narcotic analgesics* in this chapter, as they all have similar pharmacological effects.

The problem of pain is almost universal (Meldrum, 2003) and is poorly understood (Fishman & Carr, 1992). It is generally viewed as something to be avoided if possible, and the very word *pain* comes from the Latin word *poena*, which means a punishment or penalty (Stimmel, 1997). There are three basic types of pain (Holleran, 2002): acute, chronic, and cancer-induced pain. Acute pain is short, intense, and resolves when the cause of the pain (incision, broken bone, etc.) heals. Chronic pain[4] is associated with a nonmalignant pathological condition in the body, and cancer pain is the result of a tumor's growth or expansion (Holleran, 2002).

Because the experience of pain is so uncomfortable, there is a very real demand for medications that will control the individual's suffering. To meet this demand, researchers have developed a group of medications that are collectively known as *analgesics*. An analgesic is a chemical that is able to bring about the "relief of pain without producing general anesthesia" (Abel, 1982, p. 192). There are two different groups of analgesics. The first are agents that cause *local anesthesia*, of which cocaine was once the prototype. Local anesthetics block the transmission of nerve impulses from the site of the injury to the brain, preventing the brain from receiving the nerve impulses that would otherwise transmit the pain message.

The analgesics in the second group are more global in nature. These alter the individual's perception of pain within the central nervous system (CNS) itself. This group of analgesics was further divided into two subgroups by Abel (1982). The first consists of the *narcotics*, which have both a central nervous system (CNS) depressant capability as well as an analgesic effect. The second subgroup of global analgesics is drugs such as aspirin and acetaminophen, which will be discussed in Chapter 18.

---

[4]The treatment of an addicted person with chronic pain is addressed in Chapter 31.

TABLE 14.1   Some Common Narcotic Analgesics*

Generic name	Brand name	Approximate equianalgesic parenteral dose
Morphine	—	10 mg every 3–4 hours
Hydromorphone	Dilaudid	1.5 mg every 3–4 hours
Meperidine	Demerol	100 mg every 3 hours
Methadone	Dolophine	10 mg every 6–8 hours
Oxymorphone	Numorphan	1 mg every 3–4 hours
Fentanyl	Sublimaze	0.1 mg every 1–2 hours
Pentazocine	Talwin	60 mg every 3–4 hours
Buprenorphine	Buprenex	0.3–0.4 mg every 6–8 hours
Codeine	—	75–130 mg every 3–4 hours**
Oxycodone	Perdocet, Tylox	Not available in parenteral dosage forms

Source: Based on information contained in Medical Economics Company (2000) and Cherny & Foley (1996).
*This chart is for purposes of comparison only. It is not intended to serve as, nor should it be used for, a guide to patient care.
**It is not recommended that doses of codeine above 65 mg be used because doses above this level do not result in significantly increased analgesia and may result in increased risk of unwanted side effects.

Where Opium Is Produced

Surprisingly, the synthesis of morphine in the laboratory is extremely difficult, and most of the morphine used by physicians is still obtained from the opium poppy (Gutstein & Akil, 2001). Virtually the entire planet's need for legitimate opium might be met by the opium produced by just India. A single nation, Afghanistan, accounts for more than 75% of all of the illicit opium produced on this planet each year (United Nations, 2004). Virtually all of the opium produced beyond that needed for medicine finds its way to the illicit narcotics market, which is a thriving, multinational industry.

Current Medical Uses of the Narcotic Analgesics

Since the introduction of aspirin, narcotics are no longer used to control milder levels of pain. As a general rule, the opiates are most commonly utilized to control severe, acute pain (O'Brien, 2001) and some forms of chronic pain[5] (Belgrade, 1999; Marcus, 2003; Savage, 1999). In addition, they are of value in the control of severe diarrhea and the cough reflex in some diseases. A number of different opiate-based analgesics have been developed that have minor variations in potency, absorption characteristics, and duration of effects. The generic and brand names of some of the more commonly used narcotic analgesics are provided in Table 14.1.

Pharmacology of the Narcotic Analgesics

The resin that is collected from the *Papaver somniferum* plant contains 10% to 17% morphine (Jenkins & Cone, 1998). Chemists isolated the compound morphine from this resin almost 200 years ago and quickly discovered that it was the active agent of opium. In spite of the time that has passed since then, it is still the standard against which other analgesics are measured (Nelson, 2000). More surprisingly, only since the 1970s

[5]Although this use for narcotic analgesics is quite controversial (Antoin & Beasley, 2004).

have researchers been able to begin unraveling some of the mystery of how we experience pain.

In the brain, the narcotic analgesics mimic the actions of several families of endogenous opioid peptides, including the following (Jaffe & Jaffe, 2004):

enkephalin   prodynorphin

pro-opiomelanocortin   pro-OFQ/N

endorphin

These opioid peptides function as neurotransmitters in the brain and spinal cord (Hirsch, Paley, & Renner, 1996). Although these compounds function as neurotransmitters or modulate the action of other neurotransmitters in some manner, their exact mechanism of action remains unclear (Gutstein & Akil, 2001). It *is* known that opioid peptides are involved in such diverse functions in the CNS as the perception of pain, moderation of emotions, the perception of anxiety, the feeling of sedation, appetite suppression, anticonvulsant activity within the brain, smooth muscle motility, regulation of a number of body functions (such as temperature, heart rate, respiration, and blood pressure), and perhaps even the perception of pleasure (Hawkes, 1992; Restak, 1994; Simon, 1997). In the body, opioid peptides help to regulate the movement of food and fluid through the intestines (Pasternak, 1998).

As this list suggests, the opioid peptides are quite powerful chemicals. In contrast, morphine and its chemical cousins are only crude copies of them. For example, the opioid peptide known as *beta endorphin* (ß-endorphin) is thought to be 200 times as potent an analgesic as morphine. Currently, researchers believe that the narcotic analgesics function as opioid peptide agonists, occupying the receptor sites in the CNS normally utilized by the opioid peptides to simulate or enhance the action of these naturally occurring neurotransmitters.

In the last decade of the 20th century, researchers identified a number of receptor sites within the brain that are utilized by the opioid peptides (Carvey, 1998). There is some disagreement as to the exact number of receptor sites. However, the different sites are identified by letters from the Greek alphabet. Table 14.2 summarizes what is known about the different receptor sites in the central nervous system utilized by narcotic analgesics and the function controlled by each receptor subtype.

TABLE 14.2 Brain Receptor Sites Utilized by Narcotic Analgesics

Opioid receptor	Biological activity associated with opioid receptor
Mu	Analgesia, euphoria, respiratory depression, suppression of cough reflex
Delta	Analgesia, euphoria, endocrine effects, psychomotor functions
Kappa	Analgesia in spinal cord, sedation, miosis
Sigma	Dysphoria, hallucinations, increased psychomotor activity, respiratory activity
Epsilon	?
Lambda	?

Source: Based on information provided in Ashton (1992), Jaffe (1989), and Zevin & Benowitz (1998).

There is strong evidence that opioids will alter the blood flow pattern within the human brain. Using single photon emission computed tomography (SPECT) scans to examine the cerebral blood flow in the brains of nine nondependent volunteers, Schlaepfer et al. (1998) studied changes in the blood flow patterns of various regions of the brains of their subjects. The authors found statistically significant changes in the regional blood flow pattern, with significantly more blood being sent to the anterior cingulate cortex, the thalamus, and the amygdalae regions of the brain when a drug known to occupy the *Mu* receptor was administered. Although it was not clear whether the observed increase in blood flow was associated with the analgesic effect of the drug, it is known that these are areas of the brain with high concentrations of the *Mu* receptor, suggesting that they play a role in pain perception in humans.

Research has demonstrated that the region of the brain involved in pain perception is different from the area of the brain that is involved in the experience of euphoria. The thalamus seems to be involved in the perception of pain (Restak, 1994). On the other hand, the experience of euphoria often reported by narcotic abusers seems to be caused by the effects of the opioids on the ventral tegmental region of the brain (Kaplan, Sadock, & Grebb, 1994). This area uses dopamine as its major neurotransmitter and connects the cortex of the brain with the limbic system. Sklair-Tavron et al. (1996) found that the chronic administration of morphine to rats caused these same dopamine-utilizing neurons to shrink in volume by approximately 25%, suggesting that the morphine causes these neurons to alter their function in an as yet undetermined manner.

Another region of the brain rich in opioid peptide receptors is the *amygdalae* (singular: amygdala) (Reeves & Wedding, 1994). These regions of the brain function as a halfway point between the senses and the hypothalamus, which is the "emotion center" of the brain, according to the authors. It is thought that the amygdala will release opioid peptides in response to sensory data, thus influencing the formation of memory. For example, the sense of pleasure that one feels upon solving an intricate mathematics problem is caused by the amygdala's release of opioid peptides. This pleasure will make it more likely that the student will remember the solution to that problem if she or he should encounter it again.

When the *Mu* receptor site is occupied by a narcotic analgesic, the individual will experience a sense of well-being, an effect that might account for the reports that morphine and similar agents reduce the individual's awareness of pain without a significant loss of consciousness (Giannini, 2000). At first, narcotic analgesics also produce a sense of drowsiness, allowing a degree of sedation to be achieved in spite of the individual's pain (American Medical Association, 1994; Jaffe, 1992). Through these effects, narcotic analgesics are able to reduce the individual's anxiety level, promote drowsiness, and allow the person to sleep in spite of severe pain (Gutstein & Akil, 2001; Jaffe, Knapp, & Ciraulo, 1997). These effects seem to reflect the impact of the morphine molecule on the locus ceruleus region of the brain (Gold, 1993; Jaffe et al., 1997).

Codeine. Codeine is also an alkaloid found in the same milky sap from the plant papaver somniferum from which opium is obtained. It was first isolated in 1832 (Jaffe, 2000c; Melzack, 1990). Like its chemical cousin, morphine, codeine is able to suppress the cough reflex, and it has a mild analgesic potential.

As an analgesic, codeine is thought to be about one-fifth as potent as its chemical cousin, morphine (Karch, 2002). This is not surprising, as researchers have found that about 10% of a dose of codeine is biotransformed into morphine, which researchers believe is responsible for codeine's analgesic potential (Reisine & Pasternak, 1995). However, there is significant variability between individuals in the ability of their bodies to convert codeine into morphine, and thus there are differences between the amount of analgesia that different people might obtain from cocaine (Karch, 2002).

Following a single dose of codeine, peak blood levels are seen in 1 to 2 hours, and the half-life of codeine is between 2.4 and 3.6 hours (Karch, 2002). The analgesic potential of codeine is enhanced by over-the-counter (OTC) analgesics such as aspirin or acetaminophen (Gutstein & Akil, 2001). This is one reason it is commonly administered in combination with one of them (Cherny & Foley, 1996). Also, research has found that codeine is not as vulnerable to the first pass metabolism effect as is morphine, allowing better pain control from oral doses of codeine than can be achieved with oral doses of morphine (Gutstein & Akil, 2001).

Codeine, like many narcotic analgesics, is also quite effective in the control of cough. This is accomplished through codeine's ability to suppress the action of a portion of the brain known as the *medulla* that is responsible for the maintenance of the body's internal state (Jaffe et al., 1997; Jaffe & Martin 1990). Except in extreme cases, codeine is the drug of choice for cough control (American Medical Association, 1994).

Morphine. Morphine is well absorbed from the gastrointestinal tract, but for reasons discussed later in this chapter, orally administered morphine is of limited value in the control of pain. Morphine is also easily absorbed from injection sites and is often administered through intramuscular or intravenous injections. Finally, morphine is also easily absorbed through the mucous membranes of the body and it is occasionally administered in the form of rectal suppositories.

The peak effects of a single dose of morphine are seen about 60 minutes after an oral dose and between 30 and 60 minutes after the drug is administered through intravenous injection (Shannon, Wilson, & Stang, 1995). After absorption into the circulation, morphine will go through a two-phase process of distribution throughout the body (Karch, 1996). In the first phase, which lasts only a few minutes, the morphine is distributed to various blood-rich tissues, including muscle tissue, the kidneys, liver, lungs, spleen, and the brain. In the second phase, which proceeds quite rapidly, the majority of the morphine is then biotransformed into a metabolite known as *morphine-3-glucuronide* (M3G), with a smaller amount being transformed into the metabolite *morphine-6-glucuronide* (M6G) or one of a small number of additional metabolites (Karch, 2002).

The process of morphine biotransformation takes place in the liver, and within 6 minutes of an intravenous injection, the majority of a single dose of morphine has been biotransformed into one of the two metabolites discussed in the last paragraph. Scientists have only recently discovered that M6G has biologically active properties, and it has been suggested that this metabolite might be even more potent than the parent compound, morphine (Karch, 2002). About 90% of morphine metabolites are eventually eliminated from the body by the kidneys (Shannon et al., 1995); the other 10% will be excreted as unchanged morphine (Karch, 1996).

The biological half-life of morphine ranges from 1 to 8 hours, depending on the individual's biochemistry, with most textbooks giving an average figure of 2–3 hours (Drummer & Odell, 2001). Following a single dose, approximately one-third of the morphine becomes protein bound (Karch, 1996). The mechanism by which morphine is able to provide analgesic effects remains unclear, but it is known from experience that the effects of a single dose of morphine last for approximately 4 hours (Gutstein & Akil, 2001). Although it is well absorbed when administered through intramuscular or intravenous injection, morphine takes 20 to 30 minutes to cross through the blood-brain barrier to reach the target areas in the brain where it has its primary effect (Angier, 1990). Thus, there is a delay between the time the narcotic analgesic is injected and the moment the patient begins to experience some relief from pain.

Methadone. Methadone has been found quite useful in the control of severe, chronic pain and is sometimes prescribed by physicians for this purpose (O'Brien, 2001). When used this way, methadone begins to exert an analgesic effect within 30 minutes; its analgesic action peaks in 4 hours, and it may remain effective for 6 to 8 hours (Gutstein & Akil, 2001). The analgesic doses of methadone are significantly higher than those used when the drug is part of a detoxification or opiate maintenance program. These applications of methadone will be discussed in Chapter 32.

Oxycontin. Introduced in December 1995 as a time-release form of oxycodone, Oxycontin is designed for use by patients whose long-term pain can be controlled through the use of oral medications as opposed to intravenously administered narcotic analgesics (*Physicians' Desk Reference*, 2004). The time-release feature of Oxycontin allows the patient to achieve relatively stable blood levels of the medication after 24 to 36 hours of use, providing a better level of analgesia than could be achieved with shorter-acting agents. In theory, this feature would provide for fewer episodes of "breakthrough" pain, allowing the patient to experience better pain control. The abuse of Oxycontin will be discussed later in this chapter.

Heroin. Although it is used by physicians in other countries to treat severe levels of pain, heroin has no recognized medical use in the United States. Here, it is occasionally used in much the same manner as methadone: as an agonist replacement for illicit narcotics to control the patient's withdrawal symptoms and allow him or her to function in society. Surprisingly, both animal studies and autopsy-based human data suggest that opioids such as heroin have a cardioprotective potential (Mamer, Penn, Wildmer, Levin, & Maslansky, 2003; Peart & Gross, 2004). The exact mechanism by which heroin (and morphine) protect cardiac tissue from ischemia is not known at this time, and it is not clear whether this compound offers the promise of reducing the damage to the muscle tissues of the heart during myocardial infarction in humans.

Neuroadaptation to Narcotic Analgesics

Analgesia is not a static process but is influenced by a host of factors such as disease progression, an increase in physical activity, lack of compliance in taking analgesics, and medication interaction effects (Pappagallo, 1998). Another factor that influences the effectiveness of a narcotic analgesic is the process of neuroadaptation, which is occasionally misinterpreted as evidence that the patient is addicted to the narcotic analgesic being used.

The development of neuroadaptation is incomplete and uneven (Jaffe & Jaffe, 2004). Some patients have been known to develop a craving for opiates after having received intravenous injections of morphine every 2 hours for just a single day (Nelson, 2000). Other patients have become tolerant of the analgesic effect of a given dose of a narcotic analgesic in as little as 1 to 2 weeks of continual use (Fulton & Johnson, 1993; McCaffery & Ferrell, 1994; Tyler, 1994). However, in contrast to the development of tolerance to the analgesic effect of opiates, the patient may never become fully tolerant of the drug's ability to affect the size of the pupil of the eyes or of the drug-induced constipation brought on by this class of medications.

As the patient gradually becomes tolerant of the analgesic effects of lower doses of a narcotic, his or her daily dosage might be raised to levels that would literally kill a patient who had not had time to complete the process of neuroadaptation. To illustrate, a single intravenous dose of 60 mg of morphine is potentially fatal to the opiate-naive person (Kaplan et al., 1994). In contrast to this is the patient whose daily morphine levels gradually increased from 60 mg per day to 3,200 mg per day before that patient died of cancer (Fulton & Johnson, 1993).

When used in the control of pain, most dosage increases are made necessary by the progression of the disorder causing the patient to experience the pain (Savage, 1999). Only a minority of cases involve neuroadaptation to the analgesic effects of the opiate being prescribed. Clinical research has found that the concurrent administration of dextromethorphan, an NMDA receptor antagonist, with morphine slows the development of neuroadaptation and improves analgesia without the need for an increase in the morphine dose (O'Brien, 2001). Also, concurrent use of NSAIDs (non-steroidal anti-inflammatory drugs) such as aspirin or acetaminophen may potentiate the analgesic effect of narcotic analgesics through an unknown mechanism (Gutstein & Akil, 2001). Thus physicians may attempt to offset the development of neuroadaptation to the analgesic effects of narcotic analgesics or enhance their analgesic potential through the concurrent use of NSAID compounds.

Unfortunately, many physicians incorrectly interpret the process of neuroadaptation to an opiate as evidence of addiction rather than neuroadaptation, a mistake that results in the underutilization of opiates in patients experiencing severe pain (Herrera, 1997). Cherny (1996) termed the patient's repeated requests for additional narcotic analgesics in such cases

pseudoaddiction, noting that in contrast to true addiction the patient ceases to request additonal narcotics once his or her pain is controlled.

Drug interactions involving narcotic analgesics.[6] Even a partial list of potential medication interactions clearly underscores the potential for narcotic analgesics to cause harm to the individual if they are mixed with the wrong medication(s). The synthetic narcotic analgesic meperidine should not be used in patients who are taking or have recently used *monoamine oxidase inhibitors* (MAOIs, or MAO inhibitors) (Peterson, 1997). The combination of these two classes of medications might prove fatal to the patient, even if she or he had stopped using MAOIs within the last 14 days (Peterson, 1997). Patients who are taking narcotic analgesics should not use any other chemical classified as a CNS depressant except under a physician's supervision, as there is a danger of excessive sedation from the combination of two or more of these (Ciraulo, Shader, Greenblatt, & Barnhill, 1995).

There is evidence that the use of a selective serotonin reuptake inhibitor such as fluvoxamine might result in significantly increased blood levels of methadone, possibly to toxic levels (Drummer & Odell, 2001). Further, 21 of 30 methadone maintenance patients who started a course of antibiotic therapy with Rifampin experienced opiate withdrawal symptoms that were apparently caused by an unknown interaction between the methadone and the antibiotic (Barnhill, Ciraulo, Ciraulo, & Greene, 1995). The authors noted that the withdrawal symptoms did not manifest themselves until approximately the fifth day of Rifampin therapy, suggesting that the interaction between these two medications might require some time before the withdrawal symptoms develop.

Patients who are taking narcotic analgesics should not use other CNS depressants (antihistamines, benzodiazepines, barbiturates, etc.) except under a physician's supervision. The combination of opiates with other CNS depressants can result in a potentially fatal drug-induced reaction if certain medications are used at the same time. This list does not include every possible interaction between opiates and other

---

[6]The reader is advised to always consult a physician or pharmacist, before taking two different medications.

chemical agents, but it does underscore the potential for harm that might result if narcotic analgesics are mixed with the wrong medication(s).

Subjective Effects of Narcotic Analgesics When Used in Medical Practice

As stated earlier, the primary use of narcotic analgesics is to reduce the distress caused by pain (Darton & Dilts, 1998). To understand how this is achieved, one must understand that pain

> may be simplistically classified as acute or chronic. Acute pain implies sudden onset, often within minutes or hours. Usually, there is a clear-cut etiology, and the intensity of acute pain is severe, often reflecting the degree of pathology. Chronic pain is ongoing for weeks, months, or years; the original source of pain, if ever known, is often no longer apparent. This is particularly true of nonmalignant pain. (Katz, 2000, pp. 1–2)

Acute pain serves the function of warning the organism to rest until recovery from an acute injury can take place. Morphine is usually prescribed for the control of severe, acute forms of pain (Fulton & Johnson, 1993; Melzack, 1990).

Many factors affect the degree of analgesia achieved through the use of morphine. These factors include (a) the route by which the medication was administered, (b) the interval between doses, (c) the dosage level, and (d) the half-life of the specific medication being used (Fishman & Carr, 1992). Other factors that influence people's experience of pain are (e) their anxiety level, (f) their expectations for the narcotic, (g) the length of time they have been receiving narcotic analgesics, and (h) their general state of tension. The more tense, frightened, and anxious people are, the more likely they are to experience pain in response to a given stimulus. As discussed earlier in this chapter, between 80% and 95% of the patients who receive a dose of morphine experience a reduction in their level of fear, anxiety, and/or tension (Brown & Stoudemire, 1998), and they report that their pain becomes less intense or perhaps disappears entirely (Jaffe et al., 1997; Reisine & Pasternak, 1995).

Complications Caused by Narcotic Analgesics When Used in Medical Practice

Constriction of the pupils. When used at therapeutic dosage levels, the opiates will cause some degree of constriction of the pupils (miosis). Some patients will experience such constriction even in total darkness (Shannon et al., 1995). Although this is a diagnostic sign that physicians often use to identify the opioid abuser (discussed later in this chapter), it is not *automatically* a sign that the patient is abusing the medication. Rather, this is a side effect of opioids that the physician expects in the patient who is using a narcotic analgesic for legitimate medical reasons, and one that is unexpected in the patient who is not receiving such medication.

Respiratory depression. Another side effect seen at therapeutic dosage levels is some respiratory depression. Although the degree of this is not as significant when narcotics are given to a patient in pain (Bushnell & Justins, 1993), even following a single therapeutic dose of morphine (or a similar agent) respiration might be affected for up to 24 hours (Brown & Stoudemire, 1998). For this reason, many experts advise that narcotic analgesics be used with caution in individuals who suffer from respiratory problems such as asthma, emphysema, chronic bronchitis, and pulmonary heart disease.

Some experts in the field have challenged the belief that morphine has a significant effect on respiration when used properly (Barnett, 2001; Peterson, 1997). For example, Peterson (1997) concluded that severe respiratory depression is uncommon in patients with no previous history of breathing problems. As these different reports suggest, physicians are still not sure how much respiratory depression might be caused by narcotic analgesics or whether this is a problem only for patients with respiratory disorders. Thus, until a definitive answer arrives, health care workers should anticipate that narcotics will cause the respiratory center of the brain to become less sensitive to rising blood levels of carbon dioxide and thus should expect some degree of respiratory depression (Bushnell & Justins, 1993; Darton & Dilts, 1998).

Gastrointestinal side effects. When used at therapeutic dosage levels, narcotic analgesics can cause nausea and vomiting, especially in the first 48 hours after the patient starts the medication or receives a major dose increase (Barnett, 2001). At normal dosage levels, approximately 10% to 40% of ambulatory patients will experience some degree of nausea and approximately 15% will actually vomit as a result of receiving a narcotic analgesic (Brown & Stoudemire, 1998; Cherny & Foley, 1996). Ambulatory patients seem most likely to experience nausea or vomiting, and patients should rest for a period of time after receiving their medication to avoid this potential side effect. Whereas opiate-induced nausea is a dose-related side effect, some individuals who are quite sensitive to the opiates might experience drug-induced nausea and vomiting even at low dosage levels. This may reflect the individual's genetic predisposition toward sensitivity to opiate-induced side effects (Melzack, 1990). There is experimental evidence that *ultra-low* doses of the narcotic blocker naloxone might provide some relief from morphine-induced nausea in postsurgical patients without blocking the desired analgesic effect of the morphine (Cepeda, Alvarez, Morales, & Carr, 2004).

At therapeutic dosage levels, morphine and similar drugs have been found to affect the gastrointestinal tract in a number of ways. All of the narcotic analgesics decrease the secretion of hydrochloric acid in the stomach and slow the muscle contractions of peristalsis (which push food along the intestines) (Shannon et al., 1995). In extreme cases, narcotic analgesics may actually cause spasm in the muscles involved in peristalsis and possibly even constipation (Jaffe & Jaffe, 2004). This is the side effect that makes morphine so useful in the treatment of dysentery and severe diarrhea. But constipation is the most common adverse side effect encountered when narcotic analgesics are used for extended periods of time at therapeutic levels (Cherny & Foley, 1996; Herrera, 1997). This problem can usually can be corrected by using over-the-counter laxatives (Barnett, 2001; Herrera, 1997).

Blood pressure effects. Under normal conditions, narcotic analgesics will cause the patient to experience a mild degree of respiratory depression. In those patients who have experienced some form of head trauma, this might contribute to an increase in intracranial blood pressure as the body attempts to compensate for the increased levels of carbon dioxide in the blood by pumping more blood to the brain (Pagliaro & Pagliaro, 1998). Thus, narcotic analgesics should be

used with caution in patients with head injuries to avoid the potential complications caused by drug-induced intracranial blood pressure increase.

Other side effects. Another troublesome side effect of the narcotic analgesics is a stimulation of the smooth muscle tissue surrounding the bladder. This, plus a tendency for narcotic analgesics to reduce the voiding reflex, may cause the patient to experience some degree of urinary retention (Jaffe et al., 1997; Tyler, 1994). Twenty-five percent of the patients who receive a dose of morphine experience some degree of sedation, 4% to 35% experience some drug-induced irritability, and 4% to 25% experience some degree of depression as a side effect of the morphine they receive for pain control. An unknown percentage will experience morphine-induced nightmares.

The danger of addiction. Many health care workers admit to being afraid they will cause the patient to become addicted to narcotic analgesics by giving him or her too much medication.[7] In reality, the odds that a patient with no prior history of alcohol or drug addiction will become addicted to narcotic analgesics when these medications are used for the short-term control of severe pain has been estimated at only 1 of 12,000 to 14,000 (Roberts & Bush, 1996). Most patients who develop a psychological dependence on opiates after receiving them for pain control seem to have a preexisting addictive disorder (Paris, 1996). Further, as noted earlier in this chapter, neuroadaptation to the analgesic effects of opioids over time is a normal phenomenon and should not automatically be interpreted as a sign of developing addiction to these medications (Hirsch et al., 1996; McCaffery & Ferrell, 1994).

As the process of neuroadaptation progresses, some patients might require 10 to 50 times as much morphine as drug-naive individuals to experience the same degree of analgesia (Brown & Stoudemire, 1998). Unfortunately some physicians do not understand the process of neuroadaptation and consequently *under*-medicate the individual prior to and following surgery (Imhof, 1995). Few physicians realize that opiate-tolerant patients will require higher-than-normal doses of opiates to control their pain. Fearing that they will bring about

---

[7]This would, technically, be an *iatrogenic* addiction, as opposed to the usual form of addiction to narcotics that will be discussed later in this chapter.

an overdose or that they are contributing to the patient's abuse of medications, physicians often under-medicate patients, leaving them in needless pain just because they have become tolerant to the drug's effects.

Routes of administration for narcotic analgesics in medical practice. Although the narcotic analgesics are well absorbed from the gastrointestinal tract, orally administered narcotic analgesics are useful only in the control of mild to moderate levels of pain (Shannon et al., 1995). This is because the first pass metabolism effect severely limits the amount of the drug that is able to reach the brain. For example, the liver biotransforms 70% to 80% of the morphine that is absorbed through the gastrointestinal tract *before* it reaches the brain (Drummer & Odell, 2001). Thus, orally administered narcotics are of limited value in the control of severe levels of pain. A standard conversion formula is that 60 mg of orally administered morphine will give the same level of analgesia as 10 mg of injected morphine (Cherny & Foley, 1996).

The intravenous administration of narcotics actually allows for the greatest degree of control over the amount of drug that actually reaches the brain, so this is the primary method of administration for narcotic analgesics (Jaffe & Martin, 1990). However, there are exceptions. For example, there is a new transdermal patch, developed for the narcotic fentanyl. This will be discussed in more detail in the section on fentanyl.

Withdrawal from narcotic analgesics when used in medical practice. Most patients who receive narcotic analgesics for the control of pain, even when they do so for extended periods of time, are able to discontinue the medication without problems. A small number of patients will develop a "discontinuance syndrome" similar to that seen in patients who receive benzodiazepines for an extended period. This discontinuance syndrome is usually mild but may require the patient to gradually reduce daily intake of narcotic analgesics rather than to stop using the medication all at once. Thus, narcotic analgesics are relatively benign medications when used properly.

Fentanyl

In 1968, a new synthetic narcotic, fentanyl, was introduced. Because of its short duration of action, fentanyl has become an especially popular analgesic during and immediately after surgery (Shannon et al., 1995). It is well absorbed from muscle tissue, and a common method of administration is intramuscular injection. Because fentanyl can also be absorbed through the skin, a transdermal patch has been developed on the theory that by slowly absorbing small amounts of fentanyl through the skin the patient might experience some relief from chronic pain. Unfortunately, the medication is only slowly absorbed through the skin, and therapeutic blood levels of fentanyl are not achieved for up to 12 hours after the individual first starts to use the patch (Tyler, 1994).

Recently, a new dosage form, fentanyl-laced candy, has been introduced as a premedication for children about to undergo surgery ("Take Time to Smell," 1994). It is interesting that opium was once used in Rome to calm infants who were crying (Ray & Ksir, 1993). After thousands of years of medical progress, we have returned to the starting point of using opiates to calm the fears of children.

Pharmacology and subjective effects of fentanyl. Fentanyl is extremely potent, but there is some controversy over exactly how potent it is. It is estimated to be 50 to 100 times as potent as morphine (Drummer & Odell, 2001; Gutstein & Akil, 2001), although Ashton (1992) suggested that fentanyl was 1,000 times as potent as morphine. Kirsch (1986) concluded that fentanyl is "approximately 3,000 times stronger than morphine, (and) 1,000 times stronger than heroin" (p. 18). The active dose of fentanyl in the human is 1 microgram (Kirsch, 1986). As a basis of comparison, the average postage stamp weighs 60,000 micrograms. Thus, the average effective dose of fentanyl is 1/60,000th the weight of the typical postage stamp.

Fentanyl is highly lipid soluble and thus reaches the brain quickly after it is administered. This is a characteristic of value when the drug is used in surgical procedures. The biological half-life of a single intravenous dose of fentanyl is rather short, ranging between 1 and 6 hours depending on the individual's biochemistry[8] (Drummer & Odell, 2001). Laurence and Bennett (1992) offered a middle-of-the-road figure of 3 hours,

---

[8]Because of differences between individuals, different individuals biotransform and/or eliminate at different rates. Depending on the specific compound, there might be a difference in several orders of magnitude between those who are "fast metabolizers" of a specific drug and those whose bodies make them "slow metabolizers."

which is the average therapeutic half-life of fentanyl. Fentanyl's primary site of action is the *Mu* receptor site (Brown & Stoudemire, 1998), and the duration of fentanyl's analgesic effect is 30 to 120 minutes. The drug is rapidly biotransformed by the liver and excreted from the body in the urine (Karch, 1996).

The effects of fentanyl on the individual's respiration might last longer than the analgesia produced by the drug (Shannon et al., 1995). This is a characteristic that must be kept in mind when the patient requires long-term analgesia. The major reason fentanyl is so useful is that in a medical setting, fentanyl produces a more rapid analgesic response than does morphine. The analgesic effects of fentanyl are often seen in just minutes after injection. This is a decided advantage when physicians seek to control pain during and after surgery.

Side effects of fentanyl. About 10% of patients who receive a dose of fentanyl experience somnolence and/or confusion; 3% to 10% experience dizziness, drug-induced anxiety, hallucinations, and/or feelings of depression (Brown & Stoudemire, 1998). Approximately 1% of patients who receive a dose of fentanyl experience agitation and/or a drug-induced state of amnesia, and about 1% experience a drug-induced state of paranoia. Other side effects include blurred vision, a sense of euphoria, nausea, vomiting, dizziness, delirium, lowered blood pressure, constipation, and possible respiratory—and in extreme cases cardiac—arrest (Shannon et al., 1995). At high dosage levels, muscle rigidity is possible (Foley, 1993). Physicians have noted that when fentanyl is administered to a patient, the blood pressure might drop by as much as 20% and heart rate might drop by as much as 25% (Beebe & Walley, 1991). Thus, the physician must balance the potential benefits to be gained by using fentanyl against the drug's potential to cause adverse effects. Unfortunately, although fentanyl is an extremely useful pharmaceutical, it is also a popular drug of abuse. This aspect of fentanyl will be discussed in the next section.

Buprenorphine

Buprenorphine, a synthetic analgesic that was introduced in the 1960s, is estimated to be 25 to 50 times as potent as morphine (Karch, 2002). Medical researchers quickly discovered that orally administered doses of buprenorphine are extremely useful in treating postoperative and cancer pain. Further, as will be discussed in Chapter 32, researchers have discovered that when administered orally, buprenorphine appears to be at least as effective as methadone in blocking the effects of illicit narcotics.

Buprenorphine has a rather unique absorption pattern. The drug is well absorbed from intravenous and intramuscular injection sites as well as when administered sublingually (Lewis, 1995). These methods of drug administration offer the advantage of rapid access to the general circulation without the danger of first pass metabolism. Unfortunately, when administered orally, buprenorphine suffers extensive first pass metabolism, a characteristic that limits its effectiveness as an analgesic. Thus, when used for analgesia, buprenorphine is injected into the patient's body.

Upon reaching the general circulation, approximately 95% of buprenorphine becomes protein bound (Walter & Inturrisi, 1995). The drug is biotransformed by the liver, with 79% of the metabolites being excreted in the feces and only 3.9% being excreted in the urine (Walter & Inturrise, 1995). Surprisingly, animal research suggests that the various drug metabolites are unable to cross the blood-brain barrier (BBB). This suggests that the drug's analgesic effects are achieved by the buprenorphine molecules that cross the BBB to reach the brain rather than any drug metabolites that might be produced during the biotransformation process.

Once in the brain, buprenorphine binds to three of the same receptor sites in the brain that are utilized by morphine. Buprenorphine binds most strongly to the *Mu* and *Kappa* receptor sites, which is where narcotic analgesics tend to act to reduce the individual's perception of pain. However, buprenorphine does not cause the same degree of activation at the *Mu* receptor site that morphine does. For reasons that are still not clear, buprenorphine is able to cause clinically significant levels of analgesia with a lower level of activation of the *Mu* receptor site than morphine causes (Negus & Woods, 1995).

Buprenorphine also tends to form weak bonds with the *Sigma* receptor site (Lewis, 1995). However, just because a drug is able to *bind* at a receptor site does not mean that it is always able to activate the receptor site. Buprenorphine is an excellent example of a drug that might bind to different receptor sites in the brain without having the same potential to activate these different receptor sites in the brain. In the human brain, buprenorphine easily binds to both the *Mu* and *Kappa* receptor sites. However, the drug has relatively little effect on the *Kappa* receptor site, while more strongly affecting the activity of the *Mu* receptor site (Negus & Woods, 1995).

Virtually all of the drug's effects are achieved by buprenorphine's ability to bind at, and activate, the *Mu* opiate receptors in the brain (Lewis, 1995). Indeed, the drug effectively functions as a *Kappa* receptor site antagonist at the same dosage level that it activates the *Mu* opiate receptor sites in the brain to cause analgesia (Negus & Woods, 1995). Finally, buprenorphine molecules only slowly "disconnect" from their receptor sites, thus blocking large numbers of other buprenorphine molecules from reaching those same receptor sites. Thus, at high dosage levels, buprenorphine seems to act as its own antagonist, limiting its own effects.

Buprenorphine causes significant degrees of sedation for 40% to 70% of the patients who receive a dose of this medication. Between 5% and 40% will experience dizziness, and in rare instances (<1%) patients have reported drug-induced feelings of anxiety, euphoria, hallucinations, or depression (Brown & Stoudemire, 1998). As is obvious from this brief review of buprenorphine's pharmacology, it is a unique narcotic analgesic—more selective than morphine and more powerful than morphine. As will be discussed in the following section, however, it is slowly becoming popular as a drug of abuse.

II. OPIATES AS DRUGS OF ABUSE

Many of the opiates are popular as drugs of abuse. In this section, the opiate abuse/addiction will be discussed.

Why do people abuse opiates? Simply put, opiate-based analgesics are popular with illicit drug users because they make the user feel good. When they are used by people who are *not* experiencing any significant degree of pain, opioids are able to activate the brain's reward system, which normally is active when the individual is involved in life-enhancing activities such as eating or sex (Kosten & George, 2002). The abuser experiences a sensation of drug-induced euphoria that varies in intensity depending on how the abusers introduced the drug into their bodies.

When injected directly into the circulation, some opiates may cause the user to experience a rush or flash that is said to be similar to sexual orgasm (Bushnell & Justins, 1993; Hawkes, 1992; Jaffe, 1992, 2000c; Jaffe & Martin, 1990). This rush is different from the one reported by CNS stimulant abusers (Brust, 1998). Following the rush the user will experience a sense of euphoria, which usually lasts for 1–2 minutes (Jaffe, 2000c). Finally, the user often experiences a prolonged period of blissful drowsiness that may last several hours (Scaros, Westra, & Barone, 1990). These are characteristics that appeal to some drug users.

Neuropsychopharmacologists believe that they have identified the reasons that narcotic analgesics are able to bring about these effects. Narcotic analgesics seem to mimic the action of naturally occurring neurotransmitters. Two different regions of the limbic system of the brain, the *nucleus accumbens* and the *ventral tegmentum* seem to be associated with the pleasurable response that many users report when they use opioids (Kosten & George, 2002). When abused, opioids trigger the release of massive amounts of dopamine in the *nucleus accumbens*, which is experienced by the person as pleasure.

The Mystique of Heroin

There is widespread abuse of synthetic and semi-synthetic narcotic analgesics such as Vicodin and Oxycontin, with more than 1.5 million people abusing these for the first time each year (Kalb et al., 2001). But it is heroin that people think of when the topic of opioid abuse/addiction is raised. Globally, 9 million people are thought to be addicted to heroin (*diacetylmorphine*) (United Nations, 2000), and between 600,000 and 1 million people in the United States are heroin addicts (Kranzler, Amin, Modesto-Lowe, & Oncken, 1999; O'Brien, 2001). Olmedo and Hoffman (2000) suggested an even higher number of 1.5 million "chronic" heroin users in the United States but did not identify what percentage of these people were addicted. Each year, heroin-related deaths account for about half of all illicit drug-use deaths in this country (Epstein & Gfroerer, 1997; Karch, 1996).

A short history of heroin. Like aspirin, heroin was first developed by chemists at the Bayer pharmaceutical company of Germany, and it was first introduced in 1898. Like its chemical cousin morphine, heroin is obtained from raw opium. One ton of raw opium will, after processing, produce approximately 100 kilograms of heroin ("South American Drug Production," 1997). When the chemists who developed diacetylmorphine first tried it, they reported that the drug made them feel heroic. Thus, the drug was given the brand name Heroin (Mann & Plummer, 1991).

Following the Civil War in the United States, large numbers of men had become addicted to morphine. Because heroin at low doses was found to suppress the withdrawal symptoms of morphine addicts, physicians of the era thought it was nonaddicting, and it was initially sold as a cure for morphine addiction (Walton, 2002). Physicians were also impressed by the ability of morphine and its chemical cousin heroin to suppress the severe coughs seen in tuberculosis or pneumonia, both leading causes of death in the 19th century, and thus to comfort the patient. Not until 12 years after it was introduced, long after many morphine addicts had become addicted to heroin, was its true addiction potential finally recognized. However, by that time heroin abuse/addiction had become a fixture in the United States. During the 1920s, the term *junkie* was coined for the heroin addict who supported his or her drug use by collecting scrap metal from industrial dumps for resale to junk collectors (Scott, 1998).

Pharmacology of heroin. The heroin molecule is best visualized as a pair of morphine molecules that have been joined chemically. The result is an analgesic that is more potent than morphine, and a standard conversion formula is that 4 milligrams (mg) of heroin is as powerful as 10 mg of morphine (Brent, 1995; Lingeman, 1974). Estimates of the half-life of intravenous heroin range from less than 2 minutes (Drummer & Odell, 2001), through 3 minutes (Kreek, 1997), to a high estimate of 36 minutes (Karch, 2002). Surprisingly, research has shown that the heroin molecule does not bind to known opiate receptor sites in the brain, and researchers have suggested that it might more accurately be described as a *prodrug*[9] than as a biologically active compound in its own right (Jenkins & Cone, 1998). Once in the body, heroin is biotransformed into morphine, a process that gives heroin its analgesic potential (Drummer & Odell, 2002; Jaffe, 1992; Karch, 2002; Reisine & Pasternak,

1995). But because of differences in its chemical structure, heroin is much more lipid soluble than morphine. The difference in chemical structure allows heroin to cross the blood-brain barrier 100 times faster than morphine (Angier, 1990), a characteristic that makes it especially attractive as a drug of abuse.

Subjective effects of heroin when abused. A number of factors influence the subjective effects of heroin including (a) the individual's expectations for the drug and (b) the method of heroin abuse. For example, when it is used intranasally, only about 25% of the available heroin is absorbed by the user's body, and the rate of absorption is slower than if the drug is directly injected into the circulation.

In contrast to the slower rate of absorption and the limited amount that reaches the brain, virtually 100% of intravenously administered heroin reaches the circulation. In contrast to the gentle euphoria that intranasal users report, individuals who inject heroin directly into the circulation report that it produces a rush or a flash very similar to a sexual orgasm and that lasts for about 1 minute. Other sensations include a feeling of warmth under the skin, dry mouth, nausea, and a feeling of heaviness in the extremities. Users also report a sense of nasal congestion and itchy skin, both the result of heroin's ability to stimulate the release of histamine in the user's body. After this, the user will experience a sense of floating, or light sleep, that will last for about 2 hours, accompanied by clouded mental function.

Heroin in the United States today. In contrast to countries where heroin is a recognized therapeutic agent, heroin is *not* a recognized pharmaceutical in the United States, and its possession or manufacture is illegal. In spite of this fact, heroin use has been viewed by many as a sign of rebellion, perhaps reaching its pinnacle with the rise of the "heroin chic" culture in the late 1990s (Jonnes, 2002). Heroin abusers in the United States are estimated to consume between 13 and 18 metric *tons* of heroin each year (Office of National Drug Control Policy, 2004).

The average age of the individual at first use of heroin dropped from 27 in 1988 to 19 by the middle of the 1990s (Cohen et al., 1996; Hopfer, Mikulich, & Crowley, 2000). Adolescents (12–17 years of age) make up just under 22% of those who admit using heroin in the United States (Hopfer et al., 2000). One major reason for this increase in popularity among younger drug

[9]See Glossary.

abusers in the late 1990s was the availability of increasingly high potency heroin for relatively low prices. In the mid 1980s the average sample of heroin from the street was about 5% to 6% pure (Sabbag, 1994). By the start of the 21st century, heroin that was produced in South America and sold in the United States averaged 46% pure, and heroin produced in Mexico averaged 27% pure (Office of National Drug Control Policy, 2004). Heroin produced in Asia usually averaged about 29% pure when sold on the streets in the United States (Office of National Drug Control Policy, 2004).

These figures reflect the glut of heroin available to illicit users in the United States. To explain the oversupply, the entire world's need for pharmaceutical heroin[10] could be met by cultivation of 50 square miles of opium poppies; in contrast, an estimated *1,000* square miles of poppies are under cultivation at this time (Walton, 2002). The high purity of the heroin being sold, combined with its relatively low cost and the misperception that insufflated (snorted) heroin was nonaddicting, contributed to an increase in heroin use in the United States in the early 1990s (Ehrman, 1995). The level of heroin abuse/addiction in the United States reached a plateau in the early years of the 21st century and has remained at about this level (Office of National Drug Control Policy, 2001).

Other Narcotic Analgesics That Might Be Abused

Codeine. Surprisingly, codeine has emerged as a popular opiate of abuse, accounting for 12% of all drug-related deaths (Karch, 2002). There is little information available on codeine abuse, although it is possible that some of the codeine-related deaths are those of heroin addicts who miscalculate the amount of codeine they will need to block their withdrawal discomfort when they are unable to obtain their primary drug of choice.

Oxycontin. Oxycontin has been a drug of abuse since its introduction in 1995. A generic form of this substance was released in 2004. Abusers will often crush the time-release spheres within the capsule and inject the material into a vein. Other abusers will simply ingest

a larger than prescribed dose for the euphoric effect. In part because of a number of media reports, Oxycontin quickly gained a reputation as a "killer" drug. However, clinical research has suggested that the vast majority of those who died from drug overdoses had ingested multiple agents such as benzodiazepines, alcohol, cocaine, or other narcotic analgesics (Cone et al., 2003). The authors found that only about 3% of the drug-induced deaths reported only Oxycontin as the cause of death. Still, Oxycontin was heavily marketed by the pharmaceutical company that produced it, which also downplayed its abuse potential (Meier, 2003). But,

> while prescription-drug abusers may differ in their pharmaceutical choices, the dynamic of abuse shares a common theme: whatever a manufacturer's claims about a drug's "abuse liability," both hard-core addicts and recreational users will quickly find ways to make a drug their own. (Meier, 2003, p. 89, quotes in original)

It is estimated that Oxycontin is involved in approximately half of the estimated 4 million episodes of nonprescribed narcotic analgesic abuse that occurs each year in the United States (Office of National Drug Control Policy, 2004). Indeed, there is evidence that this medication may have unique dosing characteristics that make it especially attractive to drug abusers, which clouds the issue of whether it is a valuable tool in the fight against pain.

Buprenorphine. Another drug that is growing in popularity as an opiate of abuse is buprenorphine. As was noted earlier in this chapter, buprenorphine is a useful narcotic analgesic. Researchers are also considering oral doses of buprenorphine as an alternative to methadone (discussed in Chapter 32). Unfortunately, street addicts have discovered that *intravenously administered* buprenorphine has a significant abuse potential (Horgan, 1989; Moore, 1995). Buprenorphine is the most commonly abused opiate in Australia and New Zealand (Stimmel, 1997a), and there have been reports of its abuse from countries such as Ireland and India (Singh, Mattoo, Malhotra, & Varma, 1992) as well as in the United States (Torrens, San, & Cami, 1993). Researchers actually know very little about the abuse of buprenorphine (Fudala & Johnson, 1995). Apparently,

---

[10]This includes the medicinal use of heroin in countries where it is an accepted, and valuable, pharmaceutical agent.

the user will inject either buprenorphine alone or a mixture of buprenorphine and diazepam, cyclizine, or temazepam. It is not clear how significant buprenorphine will be as a drug of abuse, but the reader should be aware that there are limited reports of intravenous buprenorphine abuse in this country.

Fentanyl. A popular drug of abuse, in part because of its potency, fentanyl is thought to be 50 to 100 times as potent as morphine, It is used by physicians for the control of pain following surgery or for chronic pain (Drummer & Odell, 2001). When it is abused, fentanyl can be injected, smoked, or snorted; transdermal skin patches may be heated and the fumes inhaled (Karch, 2002). Some abusers also empty the transdermal patches by poking holes in the patch material and draining the reservoir. The drug that is obtained in this manner is used orally, injected, or possibly smoked. Because standard urine toxicology screens do not detect fentanyl, it is not clear how widespread the abuse of this pharmaceutical actually is at this time.

Methods of Opiate Abuse

When opiates are abused, they might be injected under the skin (a subcuteaneous injection, or "skin popping"), injected directly into a vein (mainlining), smoked, or used intranasally (technically, insufflation). As the potency of heroin sold on the streets has increased, skin popping has become less and less popular and insufflation has increased in popularity (Karch, 2002).

Opiates such as heroin are well absorbed through the lungs (as when it is smoked). Historically, the practice of smoking opium has not been common in the United States since the start of the 20th century. Supplies of opium are quite limited in the United States, and opium smoking wastes a great deal of the chemical. However, in parts of the world where supplies are more plentiful, the practice of smoking opium remains quite common.

The practice of snorting heroin powder and smoking heroin have become commonplace in the United States and are fueled by a popular myth that you cannot become addicted unless you *inject* heroin into your body (Drummer & Odell, 2001; Smith, 2001). By the time the person learns the grim truth, he or she has become dependent on heroin. The practice of snorting (insufflation) heroin is quite similar to the way that cocaine powder is inhaled. The user will use a razor

blade or knife to dice the powder until it has a fine, talcum-like consistency. The powder then is arranged in a small pile, or a line, and inhaled through a straw.

With the higher levels of potency that began to emerge in the middle to late 1990s, the practice of heroin smoking again became popular. However, the blood levels achieved when heroin is smoked are only 50% that of injected heroin at best (Drummer & Odell, 2001). This is because up to 80% of the heroin is destroyed by the heat of smoking (Drummer & Odell, 2001). Nonetheless, heroin smoking remains popular, spurred on in part by the mistaken belief that you cannot become addicted to heroin if you only smoke it.

One method by which heroin might be smoked is known as "chasing the dragon" (Strang, Griffiths, Powis, & Gossop, 1992). In this process, the user heats heroin powder in a piece of aluminum foil, using a cigarette lighter or match as the heat source. The resulting fumes are then inhaled, allowing the individual to get high without exposure to possibly contaminated needles (Karch, 2002). Another way heroin is abused is by smoking a combination of heroin and crack cocaine pellets called "speedball rock," "moon rock," or "parachute rock" (Dygert & Minelli, 1993). This combination of chemicals reportedly results in a longer high and a less severe post-cocaine use depression (Levy & Rutter, 1992). However, there is evidence that cocaine might exacerbate the respiratory depression produced by opiates.

The most common method of heroin abuse is the intravenous injection. In this process, the

> addict mixes heroin in the spoon with water, or glucose and water, in order to dissolve it. Lemon juice, citric acid or vitamin C may be added to aid dissolving. This cocktail is heated until it boils, drawn into the syringe through a piece of cotton wool or cigarette filter to remove solid impurities, and injected whilst still warm. (Booth, 1996, p 14)

Where do opioid addicts obtain their drugs? Opiate abusers obtain their daily supply of the drug from many sources. The usual practice for street addicts is to buy street opiates unless they have access to a "pharmaceutical."[11] Pharmaceuticals are obtained by either "making"

[11]See Glossary.

a doctor[12] or by diverting medication from a patient with a legitimate need for it to illicit abusers. Some opioid addicts have been known to befriend a person with a terminal illness, such as cancer, in order to steal narcotic analgesics from the suffering patient for their own use. This is how most users obtain their supplies of pharmaceuticals such Vicodin and Oxycontin.

Opiates such as heroin are obtained from supplies smuggled into the United States from other countries, especially Southeast Asia, Mexico, and South American countries such as Colombia (DEA, 1995). These are mixed with adulterants then distributed for sale on the local level. The opiates are usually sold in a powder form in small individual packets. The powder is mixed with water, then heated in a small container (usually a spoon) over a flame from a cigarette lighter or candle, and then injected by the user.

If users are health care professionals with access to pharmaceutical supplies, they might divert medications to themselves. This is difficult, however, because of the rigid controls on supplies of narcotics. Users will often inject the pharmaceutical, although some abusers will ingest an opioid. When users inject a pharmaceutical, they usually crush the tablet until it is a fine powder or take the capsule apart and mix the powder with water. The mixture is then heated in a small container (usually a spoon, but bottle caps or other small containers are also used for this purpose) over a small fire (usually a match, a candle, or a cigarette lighter), which helps mix the powder with the water. The resulting mixture is then injected, although the method of injection by intravenous opiate abusers is different from the way a physician or nurse injects medication into a vein. The process has changed little in the past 50 years, and Lingeman's (1974) description of the technique called "booting" remains as valid today as when it first appeared a quarter of a century ago. As the individual "boots" the drug, he or she injects it

> a little at a time, letting it back up into the eye dropper, injecting a little more, letting the blood-heroin mixture back up, and so on. The addict believes that this technique prolongs the initial pleasurable sensation of the heroin as it first takes effect—a feeling of warmth in the abdomen, euphoria, and sometimes a sensation similar to an orgasm. (p. 32)

In the process, however, the hypodermic needle and the syringe (or the eye dropper attached to a hypodermic needle, a common substitute for a hypodermic needle) become contaminated with the individual's blood. When other intravenous drug abusers share the same needle, which is a common practice, contaminated blood from one individual is passed to the next, and the next, and the next.

Sometimes, the opiate abuser will attempt to inject a pharmaceutical tablet or capsule originally intended for oral ingestion. Unfortunately, this practice inserts starch or other fillers[13] not intended for intravenous use directly into the bloodstream (Wetli, 1987). When tablets or capsules are used for intravenous injection, the fillers cannot be inactivated by the body's defenses. Further, repeated exposure to the compounds used as fillers or the adulterants often found in street drugs can cause extensive scarring at the point of injection. These scars form the famous tracks caused by repeated injections of illicit opiates.

The development of tolerance. Over time, opiate abusers become tolerant to the euphoric effects of narcotics. As a result of their growing tolerance they do not experience the rush or flash with the same intensity as when they first started to use. To reacquire the rush experience, narcotics addicts will often increase the dosage level of the drugs being abused, possibly to phenomenal levels. Heroin addicts have been known to increase their daily dosage level 100-fold over extended periods of time in their attempt to overcome their developing tolerance to the euphoric effects of the drug (O'Brien, 2001).

One reason for the loss of drug-induced euphoria in opiate addicts may be that with the chronic administration of narcotics, the brain reduces the amount of endorphins it produces (Klein & Miller, 1986). Over time, the brain substitutes the chemical opiates for natural endorphins, and the effect of the narcotics on the person becomes less intense. Further, there appears to be a "threshold effect" (Parry, 1992, p. 350) or a level after which the user will experience a "stable genial state" (p. 350) without becoming high on the opiate he or she is using. When chronic opioid abusers reach this state, they are no longer using the drug to get high. At this point, they are taking narcotics just

---

[12]See Glossary.

[13]See Glossary.

to function in a normal state ("to maintain," as many people say when they reach this point).

As when narcotic analgesics are used in a medical setting, the illicit user will develop tolerance to each of the various effects of the opiates at different rates (Jaffe & Jaffe, 2004). Where, for example, individuals might develop some degree of tolerance to the respiratory depression induced by narcotic analgesics, they are unlikely to become tolerant to the constipating side effect of this class of drugs (Zevin & Benowitz, 1998). For this reason the chronic abuse of narcotics can (and often does) cause significant constipation problems for illicit users (Karch, 2002; Reisine & Pasternak, 1995). Opiate abusers also never develop tolerance to the pupillary constriction induced by this class of medications (Nestler, Hyman, & Malenka, 2001).

Scope of the Problem of Opiate Abuse and Addiction

Opiate abuse around the world. Although heroin is the drug that comes to mind when people think about the abuse of opiates, it is not the most common form of narcotic to be abused in the world. The United Nations (2004) estimated that there are 15 million opiate abusers worldwide, of which half live in Asia. Another 25% live in Europe, and only 2.5 million (or 16.67% of the total) live in the United States (United Nations, 2004).

The abuse of prescribed narcotic analgesics. Each year, approximately 1.6 million people are thought to abuse a prescribed narcotic analgesic for the first time in just the United States alone (Zickler, 2001). Reynolds and Bada (2003) gave an even higher estimate, noting that each year 1.1 million women between the ages of 14 and 55 took a nonprescribed narcotic analgesic. The United Nations (2004) gave a lower estimate of 1.1 million prescription narcotic abusers in the United States.

Prescription drug abuse might take many different forms. For example, a man who had received a prescription for a narcotic analgesic after breaking a bone might share a leftover pill or two with a family member who had the misfortune to sprain his or her ankle and be in severe pain. With the best of intent, this person has provided another with medications that are, technically, being abused, in the sense that the second person did not receive a prescription for the narcotic analgesic that she or he ingested. Nationally, an estimated

11 million people have abused opioid medications not prescribed for them at some point in their lives (Kreek, 2000). Fully 13% of the high school seniors of the class of 2003 admitted to having abused an opiate other than heroin at least once, and 1.5% admitted to the use of heroin at least once (Johnston, O'Malley, & Bachman, 2003a).

Most people who abuse narcotic analgesics on a regular basis try to avoid being identified as medication abusers, or as "drug seeking." It is not uncommon for patients to visit different physicians or different hospital emergency rooms to obtain multiple prescriptions for the same disorder. Patients have also been known to manufacture symptoms (after doing a bit of research) to allow them to simulate the signs of a disorder virtually guaranteed to result in a prescription for a narcotic analgesic. Finally, patients with actual disorders have been known to exaggerate their distress in the hope of being able to obtain a prescription for a narcotic analgesic from an overworked physician. Thus, one of the warning signs that a physician will look for in a medication-seeking patient is that he or she has had multiple consultations for the same problem.

Heroin abuse/addiction. The reputation of heroin is that it is the most potent and most commonly abused narcotic analgesic. During the latter part of the 20th century heroin was reputed to enslave any person foolish enough to abuse it, as evidenced by Lingeman's statement that "the majority [of heroin abusers] go on to mainlining" (1974, p. 106).

However, much of its reputation has been exaggerated at best or is wildly inaccurate. Clinical research suggests that as an analgesic it is no more potent than hydromorphone (O'Brien, 2001). Further, researchers have concluded that only a fraction of those who *briefly* abuse opiates, perhaps one of every four people, will become addicted (O'Brien, 2001).[14] But one should remember that heroin remains a potentially addictive substance, and that approximately half of those who *repeatedly* abuse an opioid such as heroin will go on to become addicted (Jenike, 1991).

The most realistic estimates suggest that 3 million people in the United States have used heroin at least

[14]However, because it is not possible to predict in advance who will become addicted, and who will not, the abuse of narcotic analgesics is *not* recommended.

once (O'Connor, 2000) and that there are about 980,000 current users (including those who are addicted to it) (D'Aunno & Pollack, 2002). The United Nations (2004) estimated that there are 1.4 million heroin abusers/addicts in the United States. It is not known what percentage of this number are addicted to heroin. Actually, scientists know very little about the natural history of heroin abuse/addiction. Users are presumed to take approximately 2 years between the initiation of heroin abuse and the development of physical dependence on this chemical (Hoegerman & Schnoll, 1991). Further, there is a wide variation in individual opiate abuse patterns. This is clearly seen in a subpopulation of narcotic abusers who engage in occasional abuse without becoming addicted (Shiffman, Fischer, Zettler-Segal, & Benowitz, 1990). These people are called "chippers." Chippers seem to use opiates more in response to social stimuli or because of transient states of internal distress than because they are addicted to one of these compounds. They also seem to have no trouble abstaining from opiates when they wish to do so. But because research in this area is prohibited, scientists know virtually nothing about heroin chipping or what percentage of those who start out as chippers progress to a more addictive pattern of heroin use.

Researchers generally agree that the typical heroin addict is estimated to spend about $250 a week to support his or her habit (Abt Associates, Inc., 1995a). They also agree that males make up about three-fourths of the total of those who are addicted to heroin in the United States (Kaplan & Sadock, 1996). But this ratio also suggests that of the estimated 900,000 heroin addicts in this country, perhaps 675,000 are males and 225,000 are female. If the higher estimate of 1 million active heroin addicts is used, then some 250,000 women are addicted to heroin in the United States. Geographically, heroin-addicted persons are thought to be concentrated on the coasts, with New York City and California accounting for the vast majority of heroin addicted people in this country.

Complications Caused by Chronic Opiate Abuse

Withdrawal from opioids for the addicted person. The hallmark sign of an addiction to opiates is the existence of the classic pattern of opioid withdrawal symptoms.

The symptoms of withdrawal from narcotics will vary in intensity as a result of several different factors: (a) the dose of the opiate that was abused, (b) the length of time the person has used the drug,[15] (c) the speed with which withdrawal is attempted (Jaffe & Jaffe, 2004), and (d) the half-life of the opioid being abused (Jaffe & Jaffe, 2004; Kosten & O'Connor, 2003). Heroin withdrawal symptoms peak 36 to 72 hours after the last dose, and the acute withdrawal discomfort lasts for 7 to 10 days; the acute phase of methadone withdrawal peaks 4 to 6 days after the last dose and continues for approximately 14 to 21 days (Collins & Kleber, 2004; Kosten & O'Connor, 2003).

As a general rule, an opiate-addicted person who has been using the equivalent of 50 mg of morphine a day for 3 weeks will have an easier detoxification than would someone who has been using the equivalent of 50 mg of morphine a day for 3 months. Also, an opiate addict who is gradually withdrawn from opiates at the equivalent of 10 mg of morphine a day will have an easier detoxification than would the opiate-dependent person who just suddenly stops using the drug ("cold turkey").

A number of aspects to the phemonenon of withdrawal from narcotics makes it unique. First, in many patients, the symptoms of narcotics withdrawal can be managed through the use of hypnotic suggestion (Erlich, 2001). Second, the individual's perception of and response to the withdrawal process is influenced to a large degree by his or her cognitive "set." This set is, in turn, influenced by such factors as the individual's knowledge, attention, motivation, and degree of suggestibility. Opiate withdrawal discomfort is a learned phenomenon. This seems to be confirmed in real-life settings where narcotics addicts are forced to go through the withdrawal process cold turkey. For example, when the individual is in a therapeutic community that actively discourages reports of withdrawal discomfort, opiate-dependent individuals do not go through the dramatic withdrawal displays so often noted in methadone detoxification programs (Peele, 1985). Further, when narcotics addicts are incarcerated and denied further access to the drug, they are often able to go through withdrawal without the dramatic symptoms seen at a detoxification center.

---

[15]However, after 2–3 months of continuous use, there is generally no increase in the severity of the withdrawal symptoms.

Acute withdrawal. To avoid withdrawal-related symptoms, opiate-dependent individuals must either inject another dose of their drug of choice or substitute another drug. Withdrawal symptoms include a craving for more narcotics, tearing of the eyes, running nose, repeated yawning, sweating, restless sleep, dilated pupils, anxiety, anorexia, irritability, insomnia, weakness, abdominal pain, nausea, vomiting, GI upset, chills, diarrhea, muscle spasms and muscle aches, irritability, and in males, possible ejaculation (Collins & Kleber, 2004; Gold, 1993; Hoegerman & Schnoll, 1991; Kosten & O'Connor, 2003). It has been suggested that 600 to 800 mg of ibuprofen can provide significant relief from the muscle pain experienced in opiate withdrawal (Collins & Kleber, 2004). Constipation is a potential complication of narcotics withdrawal and in rare cases can result in fecal impaction and intestinal obstruction (Jaffe, 1990; Jaffe & Jaffe, 2004). On very rare occasions, withdrawal can cause or contribute to seizures, especially if the opiate being abused was one that could precipitate seizures (Collins & Kleber, 2004).

Anxiety is a common withdrawal-induced emotion and might make the person so uncomfortable as to reinforce the tendency toward continued drug use (Bauman, 1988; Collins & Kleber, 2004). Indeed, the individual's fear of withdrawal-induced distress might almost reach phobic proportions (Collins & Kleber, 2004). Rather than the use of a benzodiazepine to control this anxiety, Seroquel (quetiapine fumarate) has been suggested as a means to control opiate withdrawal-related anxiety (Winegarden, 2001).

In a medical setting, opiate-dependent individuals will often emphasize their physical distress during withdrawal in an attempt to obtain additional drugs. Such displays are often quite dramatic but are hardly a reflection of reality. Withdrawal from narcotics may be uncomfortable but it is not fatal if the patient is in good health, and it is rarely a medical emergency (Henry, 1996; Mattick & Hall, 1996; O'Brien, 1998, 2001; Sadock & Sadock, 2003).[16] The subjective experience

has been compared to a bad case of influenza (Brust, 1998; Kosten & O'Connor, 2003; Mattick & Hall, 1996; Weaver, Jarvis, & Schnoll, 1999).[17] The acute symptoms of the opiate withdrawal syndrome will eventually abate in the healthy individual, even in the absence of treatment.

Extended withdrawal symptoms. There is evidence of a second phase of withdrawal from narcotics that lasts beyond the period of acute withdrawal. During this time, which may last for several months, the individual may experience feelings of fatigue, heart palpitations, and a general sense of restlessness (Satel, Kosten, Schuckit, & Fischman, 1993). There is evidence that this phase of protracted abstinence might extend for up to 30 weeks after acute withdrawal (O'Brien, 1996; Satel et al., 1993). During this stage of protracted abstinence, the physical functioning of the individual slowly returns to normal. The authors support this hypothetical phase of protracted abstinence by citing research studies that have found significant changes in respiration rate, size of the pupils of the eyes, blood pressure changes, and body temperature changes in recovering narcotics addicts for more than 17 weeks after the last dose of narcotics. However, Mattick and Hall (1996) suggested that the case for the existence of a protracted phase of withdrawal was quite weak and that this phenomenon is not an accepted part of the recovery process from opiate addiction.

Although opiate-dependent persons often attempt to taper or withdraw from opiates on their own, little is known about this phenomenon (Collins & Kleber, 2004; Gossop, Battersby, & Strang, 1991). Some individuals will simply go cold turkey and stop using opioids; others will attempt to control their withdrawal distress through the use of benzodiazepines or other pharmaceuticals.

Organ damage. Scientists have long known that patients in extreme pain (such as found in some forms of cancer, for example) who receive massive doses of narcotic analgesics for extended periods of time fail to show evidence of opiate-induced damage to any of the body's organ systems. This is consistent with historical evidence from early in the 20th century, before the strict safeguards imposed by the government were

---

[16]This assumes that the patient is using *only* opioids and that the individual has no concurrent medical problems such as a seizure disorder or cardiac disease. A physician should supervise *any* drug withdrawal program in order to reduce potential danger to life that might exist if the patient is a polydrug user.

[17]The problem of opiate withdrawal in the infant will be discussed in Chapter 20.

instituted, where cases would come to light in which a physician (or less often a nurse) had been addicted to morphine for years or even decades. The health care professional involved would take care to utilize proper sterile technique, thus avoiding the danger of infections inherent in using contaminated needles. With the exception of the opiate addiction, the addicted physician or nurse would appear to be in good health. For example, the famed surgeon William Halsted was addicted to morphine for 50 years without suffering any apparent physical problems (Smith, 1994).

However, health care professionals have access to pharmaceutical-quality narcotic analgesics, not street drugs. The typical opiate addict must inject drugs purchased from illicit sources and of questionable purity. In addition to this, the lifestyle of the opioid addict carries with it serious health risks. For example, morphine abuse has been implicated as a cause of decreased sexual desire for both men and women as well as causing erectile problems in men (Finger, Lung, & Slagel, 1997). Other common health complications found in heroin abusers include cerebral vascular accidents (strokes), cerebral vasospasms, infectious endocarditis, liver failure, disorders of the body's blood clot formation mechanisms, malignant hypertension, heroin-related nephropathy, and uremia (Brust, 1993, 1997; Karch, 2002).

Heroin addicts have been known to die from pulmonary edema, but the mechanism by which heroin may induce this condition is not clear (Karch, 2002). Also, chronic opiate abuse is known to be associated with a reduction in the effectiveness of the immune system, although the reasons are not known (Karch, 2002). The chronic abuse of opiates has also been identified as a cause of renal disease and rhabdomyolysis[18] (Karch, 2002). Researchers did find evidence suggesting an autoimmune syndrome in which the kidneys are damaged in chronic heroin abusers for reasons that were not well understood. This is perhaps most clearly seen in chronic oxycodone abusers, who suffer from a drug-induced autoimmune syndrome resulting in damage to the kidneys (Hill, Dwyer, Kay, & Murphy, 2002). At this point it is not clear whether the heroin-induced kidney failure was caused by the same mechanism as that induced by oxycodone addiction. It is also not clear

whether these effects are due directly to the abuse of heroin or if they are due to the adulterants that are added to illicit opiates (for more information on drug fillers, see Chapter 36).

However, one complication of intravenous heroin abuse/addiction that occasionally develops in some users is what is known as *cotton fever* (Brent, 1995; Karch, 2002). The heroin abuser/addict will try to purify the heroin by using wads of cotton as a crude filter. During times of hardship, when heroin supplies are scarce, some users will try to use the residual heroin found in old cotton filters. When they inject the mixture, they will inject microscopic cotton particles as well as the impurities filtered out by the cotton; this can often cause pulmonary arteritis (a serious medical condition in which the pulmonary artery becomes inflamed).

There is much debate in the medical community as to whether prolonged exposure to narcotic analgesics alters the function of the nervous system. Studies involving rats, for example, have found that the chronic use of heroin seems to cause the shrinkage of dopamine-utilizing neurons in the brain's "reward system" (Nestler, 1997). Further, there appears to be an associational learning process at work through which specific sights/sounds/smells/activities are associated with the impending use of opiates (Schroeder, Holahan, Landry, & Kelly, 2000). These microscopic neurological changes then contribute to the phenomenon of relapse in patients who are exposed to specific sights/sounds/smells/activities formerly associated with the use of the desired substance. These findings are consistent with the theories suggesting that chronic exposure to opiates can result in physical changes within the brain (Dole, 1988, 1989; Dole & Nyswander, 1965).

This theory, however, has been challenged. Hartman (1995) stated that opiates, including heroin, do not appear to have neurotoxic effects on human cognition. There is also evidence that the heroin-induced shrinkage in the dopamine-using neurons of the rat brain will reverse with abstinence (Nestler, 1997). These findings raise questions about whether the observed opiate-induced neurological changes are permanent.

Generally, the complications seen when narcotics are abused at above-normal dosage levels are an exaggeration of the side effects observed when these medications

---

[18]See Glossary.

are used in medical practice. Thus, where morphine can cause constipation when used by physicians, morphine abusers/addicts experience pronounced constipation that can reach the levels of intestinal obstruction. Further, when abused at high dosage levels, many narcotics are capable of causing seizures (Foley, 1993). This rare complication of narcotics use is apparently caused by the high dosage level of the opioid being administered and usually responds to the effects of a narcotics blocker such as Narcan (naloxone), according to the author.

One exception to this rule are seizures caused by the drug meperidine. Naloxone may actually reduce the patient's seizure threshold, making it more likely that he or she will continue to experience meperidine-induced seizures (Foley, 1993). Thus, the physician must identify the specific narcotics being abused in order to initiate the proper intervention for opioid-induced seizures.

There is research evidence suggesting that heroin abuse might be the cause of neurological damage, at least in isolated cases. In rare cases, this practice has resulted in a progressive spongiform leukoencephalophy, a condition similar to the "mad cow" disease in English cattle in the mid 1990s (Karch, 2002; Kriegstein et al., 1999). At this point very little is known about how inhaling heroin fumes might lead to a case of progressive spongiform leukoencephalophy, and there is a chance that this is caused by one or more chemicals added to the heroin to dilute it rather than by the heroin itself ("Heroin Encephalophy," 2002; Kriegstein et al., 1999). There was an outbreak of heroin-induced progressive spongiform leukoencephalophy in the Netherlands in the 1990s, with the first cases in the United States being identified in 1996. At first these cases were thought to be associated with the practice of "chasing the dragon," but at least one case has been identified in an intravenous drug abuser ("Heroin Encephalophy," 2002). There also has been one case report of a possible heroin-induced inflammation of the nerves in the spinal cord in a man from Holland who resumed the practice of smoking heroin after 2 months of abstinence (Nuffeler, Stabba, & Sturzenegger, 2003). However, the etiology of the inflammatory process in this patient's spinal cord was not clear, and it is possible that heroin was not a factor in the development of this disorder.

Overdose of Illicit Opiates

A given opiate abuser might overdose on narcotics for many reasons. For example, it is difficult to estimate the potency of illicit narcotics, and the user might miscalculate the amount of heroin that he or she had purchased or might safely inject, bringing on an overdose. Some of these individuals die before they reach the hospital, but others survive long enough for health care professionals to intervene and rescue them from the effects of the drug overdose.

An overdose of narcotics will produce a characteristic pattern of reduced consciousness, pinpoint pupils, and respiratory depression, with death occurring from respiratory arrest (Carvey, 1998; Drummer & Odell, 2001; Henry, 1996). Without medical intervention, death usually occurs 5 to 10 minutes following an intravenous injection of an opiate overdose, and 30 to 90 minutes following an intramuscular injection of an overdose of narcotic analgesics (Hirsch et al., 1996). However, these data apply only for cases of overdose with pharmaceutical opiates. Medical experts are still not sure whether deaths from illicit narcotics are caused by the drugs themselves, by the various combinations of substances commonly abused by illicit drug users, or by the multitude of other chemicals commonly added to street narcotics to dilute them. For example, there is evidence that the concurrent use of heroin and cannabis might increase the individual's chances of a heroin overdose, although the exact mechanism for this is not known (Drummer & Odell, 2001).

Illicit drugs are commonly adulterated before sale. In the early 1990s a typical sample of street heroin usually contained between 68 and 314 mg of the common adulterant quinine (Scaros, Westra, & Barone, 1990). If the addict were to inject the heroin over a 10-second period, he or she would be injecting between 10 and 131 mg of quinine per second. This is *up to 182 times the maximum recommended rate of injection of quinine*. This rate of quinine injection is in itself capable of causing a fatal reaction in many individuals. Thus, some question exists as to whether deaths by "narcotics overdoses" are indeed caused by the narcotics or by other substances that are mixed in with narcotics sold on the streets.

Street myths and narcotics overdose. There are several street myths about the treatment of opiate overdose.

First, there is the myth that cocaine (or another CNS stimulant) will help in the control of an opiate overdose. Another myth is that it is possible to control the symptoms of an overdose by putting ice packs under the arms and on the groin of the overdose victim. A third myth is that the person who had the overdose should be kept awake and walking around until the drug wears off.

Unfortunately, the treatment of an opiate overdose is a complicated matter and does not lend itself to such easy solutions. Even in the best-equipped hospital, a narcotics overdose may result in death. The current treatment of choice for a narcotics overdose is a combination of respiratory and cardiac support as well as a trial dose of *Narcan* (naloxone hydrochloride) (Henry, 1996). Naloxone hydrochloride is thought to bind at the receptor sites within the brain occupied by opiate molecules, displacing them from the receptors and reversing the effects of the opiate overdose.

Unfortunately, naloxone has a therapeutic half-life of only 60 to 90 minutes. Its effects are thus quite short-lived and it might be necessary for the patient to receive several doses before he or she has fully recovered from the opiate overdose (Roberts, 1995). Although naloxone-induced complications are rare, they do occasionally develop when this drug is used to treat opiate overdoses (Henry, 1996). Finally, the patient might have ingested or injected a number of different chemicals, each of which has its own toxicological profile. For these reasons, remember that *known or suspected opiate overdoses are life-threatening emergencies that always require immediate medical support and treatment.*

Summary

The narcotic family of drugs has been effectively utilized by physicians for several thousand years. After alcohol, the narcotics might be thought of as man's oldest drug. Various members of the narcotic family have been found effective in the control of severe pain, severe cough, and severe diarrhea. The only factor that limits their application in the control of less grave conditions is the addiction potential that this family of drugs represents. The addiction potential of narcotics has been known for hundreds if not thousands of years. For example, opiate addiction was a common complication of military service in the last century and was called the "soldier's disease."

But it was not until the advent of the chemical revolution, when synthetic narcotics were first developed, that new forms of narcotic analgesics became available to drug users. Fentanyl and its chemical cousins are products of the pharmacological revolution that began in the late 1800s and which continues to this day. This chemical is estimated to be several hundred, to several thousand, times as powerful as morphine and promises to remain a part of the drug abuse problem for generations to come.

Hallucinogen Abuse and Addiction

Introduction

It has been estimated that about 6,000 different species of plants might be used for their psychoactive properties (Brophy, 1993), including several species of mushrooms that will, when ingested, produce hallucinations (Rold, 1993). Many of these plants and mushrooms have been used for centuries in religious ceremonies, healing rituals, for predicting the future (Berger & Dunn, 1982; Metzner, 2002), and on occasion to prepare warriors for battle (Rold, 1993). Even today, certain religious groups use mushrooms with hallucinogenic properties as part of their worship, although their use is illegal in the United States (Karch, 2002). There are those who advocate the use of hallucinogenic substances as a way to explore alernative realities or gain knowledge about one's self (Metzner, 2002). Hallucinogens are also popular drugs of abuse. In this chapter, the hallucinogens will be examined.

History of Hallucinogens in the United States

Over the years, researchers have identified approximately 100 different hallucinogenic compounds that might be found in various plants or mushrooms. In some cases, the active agent(s) has been isolated and studied by scientists. Psilocybin is an example of such a compound; it was isolated from certain mushrooms that are found in the southwestern region of the United States. However, many potential hallucinogens have not been subjected to systematic research, and much remains to be discovered about their mechanism of action in humans (Glennon, 2004).

One family of organic compounds that has been subjected to the greatest level of scientific scrutiny are those produced by the ergot fungus, which grows in various forms of grain. Historical evidence long suggested that this fungus could produce exceptionally strong compounds. For example, the ingestion of grain products infected by ergot fungus can cause vasoconstriction so severe that entire limbs have been known to auto-amputate, and sometimes the individual will die from gangrene (Walton, 2002). It was thought that the ingestion of ergot fungus-infected bread caused the death of 40,000 people in the French district of Aquitaine around the year 1000 C.E. (Walton, 2002).

Compounds produced by the ergot fungus were of interest to scientists eager to isolate chemicals that might have a use in the fight against disease. In 1943, during a clinical research project exploring the characteristics of one compound obtained from the rye ergot fungus *Claviceps purpurea* (Lingeman, 1974), Lyergic acid diethylamide-25 (LSD-25, or LSD) was identified as a hallucinogen. Actually, this discovery was made by accident, as the purpose of the research was to find a cure for headaches (Monroe, 1994). But a scientist accidentally ingested a small amount of LSD-25 while conducting an experiment, and later that day began to experience LSD-induced hallucinations. After he recovered, the scientist correctly concluded that the source of the hallucinations was the specimen of *Claviceps purpurea* on which he had been working. He again ingested a small amount of the fungus and experienced hallucinations for the second time, confirming his original conclusion.

Following World War II, there was a great deal of scientific interest in the various hallucinogenics, especially in light of the similarities between the subjective effects of these chemicals and various forms of mental illness. Further, because they were so potent, certain agencies of the United States government, such as the

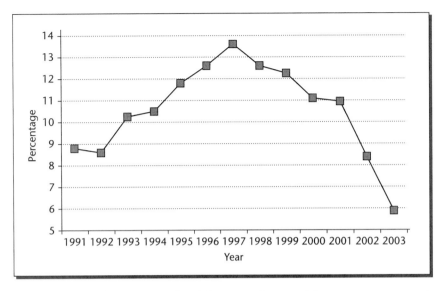

FIGURE 15.1   Lifetime LSD use by adolescents and young adults.
Source: Johnston, O'Malley, Bachman, & Schulenburg (2004b).

Department of Defense and the Central Intelligence Agency, experimented with various chemical agents, including LSD, as possible chemical warfare weapons (Budiansky, Goode, & Gest, 1994). There is strong evidence that the United States Army administered doses of LSD to soldiers without their knowledge or permission between 1955 and 1975 as part of its research into possible uses for the compound (Talty, 2003).

In the 1950s, the term *psychedelic* was coined to identify this class of compounds (Callaway & McKenna, 1998). By the 1960s these chemicals had moved from the laboratory into the streets where they quickly became popular drugs of abuse (Brown & Braden, 1987). The popularity and widespread abuse of LSD in the 1960s prompted the classification of this chemical as a controlled substance in 1970 (Jaffe, 1990), but the classification did not solve the problem of its abuse. Over the years, LSD abuse has waxed and waned, reaching a low point in the late 1970s and then increasing until it was again popular in the early 1990s. The abuse of LSD in the United States peaked in 1996, and it has gradually been declining since then (Markel, 2000). Whereas 12% of high school seniors in the class of 2000 admitted to having used LSD once and 8% reported that they had used it within the past year

(Markel, 2000), only 5.9% reported having ever used LSD in 2002 (Johnston, O'Malley, & Bachman, 2003a). The incidence of reported LSD abuse by young adults in recent years is reviewed in Figure 15.1.

The hallucinogen *Phencyclidine* (PCP) deserves special mention. Because of its toxicity, PCP fell into disfavor in the early 1970s (Jaffe, 1989), but in the 1980s, a form of PCP that could be smoked was introduced and it again became popular with illicit drug users in part because smokers could more closely control how much of the drug they used. PCP remained a common drug of abuse until the middle to late 1990s, when it declined in popularity (Karch, 2002). PCP is still occasionally seen, especially in the big cities on the east and west coasts (Drummer & Odell, 2001), and it is often sold to unsuspecting users in the guise of other, more desired, substances. It is also sold on the streets as part of the compound called "dip dope" or "dip"; cigarettes or marijuana cigarettes are dipped into this compound, a mixture of PCP, formaldehyde, and methanol, before being smoked (Mendyk & Fields, 2002). Another drug, N, alpha-dimethyl-1,3-benzodioxole-t-ethanamine (MDMA), became quite popular as a chemical of abuse in the late 1970s and early 1980s and continued to be a drug of abuse in the 1990s and the first part of the 21st century. Both PCP and MDMA will be discussed in later sections of this chapter.

Scope of the Problem

It is difficult to estimate the number of casual hallucinogenic abusers in the United States, but evidence suggests that the number has fallen over the past 5 to 10 years. In contrast to the 12.6% of 12th grade students in 1998 who admitted using LSD at least once, only 5.9% of the seniors of the class of 2003 said they had used it at least once (Johnston, O'Malley, & Bachman 2003a). In years past, the majority of those who used the hallucinogens such as LSD were those who experimented with it, then either totally avoided further hallucinogen use or only abused it on an episodic basis (Jaffe, 1989). LSD was repackaged and reformulated in the mid 1990s so that the typical dose contained lower amounts than were seen in the 1960s and 1970s (Gold, Schuchard, & Gleaton 1994), which may have contributed to the resurgence in interest in LSD in the early to mid 1990s.

Pharmacology of the Hallucinogens

To comprehend how the hallucinogenic compounds affect the user, it is necessary to understand that normal consciousness rests on a delicate balance of neurological function. Compounds such as serotonin and dopamine, although classified as neurotransmitters, might better be viewed as *neuromodulators* that shift the balance of brain function from normal waking states to the pattern of neurological activity seen in sleep or various abnormal brain states (Hobson, 2001).

The commonly abused hallucinogenics can be divided into two major groups, the indolealkylamines,[1] and the phenylalkylamines (Glennon, 2004).[2] The "classic" hallucinogens such as LSD seem to act as agonists to the 5-HT serotonin receptor site, and their effects are blocked by experimental 5-HT antagonists (Drummer & Odell, 2001; Glennon, 2004). In spite of the differences between hallucinogens in chemistry

and potency, illicit drug abusers tend to adjust their intake of the drugs being abused to produce similar effects (Schuckit, 2000).

The "classic" hallucinogens all produce hallucinations, or hallucinatory-like experiences, by alterning the normal function of serotonin in the raphe nuclei of the brain. This has the effect of allowing acetylcholine neurons that normally are most active during dream states to express themselves during the waking state. In other words, the user begins to dream while remaining in an altered state of waking, a condition interpreted as hallucinations by the individual (Hobson, 2001). One exception to this rule is DMT. The effects of DMT last only about 20 minutes and for this reason DMT is often called a "businessman's high." The drug experience may fit into a typical half-hour lunch break, making it a popular drug of abuse for some of the business community. With this one exception, however, DMT is very similar to the other hallucinogens to be discussed in this chapter.

It is common for a person under the influence of one of the hallucinogens to believe that he or she has a new insight into reality. But these drugs do not generate new thoughts so much as alter one's perception of existing sensory stimuli (Snyder, 1986). The waking-dreams that are called hallucinations are usually recognized by the user as being drug induced (Lingeman, 1974). Thus, the terms *hallucinogen* or *hallucinogenic* are usually applied to this class of drugs. As LSD is the most popular hallucinogen, this chapter will focus on LSD as the prototypical hallucinogenic, and other drugs in this class will be discussed only as needed.

The Pharmacology of LSD

There is much to be discovered about how LSD affects the human brain (Sadock & Sadock, 2003). LSD is one of the most potent chemicals known to man. Researchers have compared it to hallucinogenic chemicals naturally found in plants, such as psilocybin and peyote, and found that LSD is between 100 and 1,000 times as powerful as these "natural" hallucinogens (Schwartz, 1995). It has been estimated to be 3,000 times as potent as mescaline (O'Brien, 2001) but is also weaker than synthetic chemicals such as the hallucinogenic DOM/STP (Schuckit, 2000).

[1]LSD is a member of this group of hallucinogens.

[2]Subcategories of each major group exist, but will not be discussed further in this text. See Glennon (2004) for more information about these subcategories of hallucinogenic compounds.

For the casual user, LSD might be effective at doses as low as 50 micrograms, although the classic LSD "trip" usually requires twice that amount of the drug (Schwartz, 1995). Users in the 1960s might have ingested a single 100–200 microgram dose, but current LSD doses on the street seem to fall in the 20–80 microgram range, possibly to make it more appealing to first-time users (Gold & Miller, 1997c). Although it is possible to inject LSD directly into a vein, the most common method of abuse is through oral doses (Henderson, 1994a).

The LSD molecule is water soluble and simular in structure to the neurotransmitter serotonin (Klein & Kramer, 2004). Indeed, it seems to bind to the 5-HT2a receptor site in the human brain (Glennon, 2004). Although many drug abusers claim to have absorbed LSD through the skin after it was detected by urine toxicology testing, this is not possible (Henderson, 1994a). It is usually administered orally but can be taken intranasally, intravenously, and by inhalation (Klein & Kramer, 2004). LSD is rapidly absorbed from the gastrointestinal tract after oral ingestion and is distributed to all body tissues (Mirin, Weiss, & Greenfield, 1991). Only about 0.01% of the original dose actually reaches the brain (Lingeman, 1974).

Although much remains to be discovered about how LSD affects the brain, it is known that LSD functions as a serotonin agonist. Classified as a hallucinogenic compound, LSD actually causes misinterpretations of reality that are better called *illusions* for the most part, with actual hallucinations being seen only when very high doses of LSD are taken (Pechnick & Ungerleider, 2004). The majority of the serotonin-based neurons in the brain are located in the region known as the *midbrain raphe nuclei*, which is also known as the dorsal midbrain raphe (Hobson, 2001; Mirin et al., 1991). Evidence emerging from sleep research suggests that one function of the raphe nuclei of the brain is to suppress neurons that are most active during rapid eye movement (REM) sleep. By blocking the action of this region of the brain, acetylcholine-induced REM sleep begins to slip over into the waking state, causing perceptual and emotional changes normally seen only when the individual is asleep (Henderson, 1994a; Hobson, 2001; Lemonick, Lafferty, Nash, Park, & Thompson, 1997).

Tolerance to the effects of LSD develop quickly, often within 2 to 4 days of continual use (Henderson, 1994a; Mirin et al., 1991; Schwartz, 1995). If the user has become tolerant to the effects of LSD, increasing the dosage level will have little effect (Henderson, 1994a). However, the individual's tolerance to LSD will also abate after 2 to 4 days of abstinence (Henderson, 1994a; Jaffe, 1989). Cross tolerance between the different hallucinogens is also common (Callaway & McKenna, 1998). Thus, most abusers alternate between periods of active hallucinogen use and times during which they abstain from further use of these compounds

In terms of direct physical mortality, LSD is perhaps the safest compound known to modern medicine, and scientists have yet to identify a lethal LSD dosage level (Pechnick & Ungerleider, 2004). Some abusers have survived doses up to 100 times those normally used without apparent ill effect (Pechnick & Ungerleider, 2004). Reports of LSD-induced death are exceptionally rare and usually reflect accidental death caused by the individual's misperception of sensory data rather than the direct effects of the compound (Drummer & Odell, 2001; Pechnick & Ungerleider, 2004). But this is not to say that LSD is entirely safe. The LSD currently available through illicit markets is much more potent than that used in the 1960s, and it is capable of inducing seizures in the user for more than 60 days after it was last used (Klein & Kramer, 2004).

The biological half-life of LSD has not been determined accurately. It is known that the drug is rapidly biotransformed by the liver and that it is rapidly eliminated from the body. Indeed, so rapid is the process of LSD biotransformation and elimination that traces of the major metabolite of LSD, 2-oxy-LSD, will remain in the user's urine for only 12 to 36 hours after the last use of the drug (Schwartz, 1995). The estimates of the biological half-life of LSD range from 2–3 hours (Jaffe, 1989, 1990; Karch, 1996; Shepherd & Jagoda, 1990; Weiss, Greenfield, & Mirin, 1994) to 5 hours (Henderson, 1994a). The subjective effects of a single dose of LSD appear to last between 8 and 12 hours (Kaplan & Sadock, 1996; Klein & Kramer, 2004), although Mendelson and Mello (1998) suggested that the drug's effects might last 18 hours.

The duration of an LSD-induced "trip" are apparently dose related, with larger doses having a longer effect on the person's perception (Drummer & Odell, 2001). Only about 1% to 3% of a single dose of LSD is excreted unchanged, with the rest being biotransformed by the liver and excreted in the bile (Drummer & Odell, 2001). LSD continues to challenge researchers, who struggle with such questions as how, when the person ingests such a small dose of the original compound and when such a small portion of the total ingested dose actually reaches the brain, can LSD have such a profound impact on the user's state of mind? Obviously, there is much to learn about the hallucinogens.

Subjective Effects of Hallucinogens

Subjectively, users will begin to feel the first effects of a dose of LSD in 5 to 10 minutes. These initial effects include such symptoms as anxiety, gastric distress, and tachycardia (Schwartz, 1995). In addition, users might also experience increased blood pressure, increased body temperature, dilation of the pupils, nausea, and muscle weakness after ingesting the drug (Jaffe, 1989). Other side effects include an exaggeration of normal reflexes (a condition known as hyperreflexia), dizziness, and some degree of muscle tremor (Jaffe, 1989). Lingeman (1974) characterized these changes as "relatively minor" (p. 133), although for the inexperienced user they might cause some degree of anxiety.

The hallucinogenic effects of LSD usually begin 30 minutes to an hour after the user first ingests the drug, peak 2–4 hours later, and gradually wane after 8–12 hours (Pechnick & Ungerleider, 2004). Scientists believe that the effects of a hallucinogen such as LSD will vary depending on a range of factors including (a) the individual's personality makeup, (b) the user's expectations for the drug, (c) the environment in which the drugs are used, and (d) the dose of the compounds used (Callaway & McKenna, 1998).

Users often refer to the effects of LSD as a *trip*, during which they might experience such effects as a loss of psychological boundaries, a feeling of enhanced insight, a heightened awareness of sensory data, enhanced recall of past events, a feeling of contentment, and a sense of being "one" with the universe (Callaway & McKenna, 1998). The LSD trip is made up of several distinct phases (Brophy, 1993). First, within a few minutes of taking LSD there is a release of inner tension. This stage, which will last 1–2 hours (Brophy, 1993), is characterized by either laughing or crying as well as a feeling of euphoria (Jaffe, 1989). The second stage usually begins between 30–90 minutes (Brown & Braden, 1987) and 2–3 hours (Brophy, 1993) following the ingestion of the drug. During this portion of the LSD trip the individual will have perceptual distortions such as visual illusions and synesthesia[3] that are the hallmark of the hallucinogenic experience (Pechnick & Ungerleider, 2004).

The third phase of the hallucinogenic experience will begin 3–4 hours after the drug is ingested (Brophy, 1993). During this phase of the LSD trip users will experience a distortion of the sense of time. They may also have marked mood swings and a feeling of ego disintegration. Feelings of panic are often experienced during this phase, as are occasional feelings of depression (Lingeman, 1974). These LSD-related anxiety reactions will be discussed in the next section. It is during the third stage of the LSD trip that individuals express a belief that they possess quasi-magical powers or that they are magically in control of events around them (Jaffe, 1989). This loss of contact with reality is potentially fatal, and individuals have been known to jump from windows or attempt to drive motor vehicles during this phase of the LSD trip. Shea (2002) warned that on rare occasions LSD might induce suicidal thoughts or acts in the individual who has ingested it.

The effects of LSD normally start to wane 4–12 hours after ingestion (Pechnick & Ungerleider, 2004). As the individual begins to recover, he or she will experience "waves of normalcy" (Mirin et al., 1991, p. 290; Schwartz, 1995), which gradually blend into the waking state of awareness. Within 12 hours, the acute effects of LSD have cleared, although users might experience a "sense of psychic numbness, [that] may last for days" (Mirin et al., 1991, p. 290).

The LSD "bad trips." As noted earlier, it is not uncommon for the individual who has ingested LSD to experience significant levels of anxiety, which may reach the levels of panic reactions. This is known as a "bad trip" or the "bummer." Scientists used to believe that a bad trip was more likely with novice users, but

[3]See Glossary.

now it is believed that even experienced LSD abusers might have a bad trip. The likelihood of a bad trip seems to be determined by three factors: (a) the individual's expectations for the drug (which is known as the "set"), (b) the setting in which the drug is used, and (c) the psychological health of the user (Mirin et al., 1991). If the person does develop a panic reaction to the LSD experience, he or she will often respond to calm, gentle reminders from others that these feelings are caused by the drug and that they will pass. This is known as "talking down" the LSD user.

In extreme cases, the individual might require pharmacological intervention for the LSD-induced panic attack. There is some evidence that the newer, atypical antipsychotic medications clozapine and risperidone bind to the same receptor sites as LSD and that they can abort the LSD trip within about 30 minutes of the time the medication was administered (Walton, 2002). This recommendation has not been replicated by researchers, however, and it is somewhat controversial. The use of diazepam to control anxiety and haloperidol to treat psychotic symptoms has been suggested by some physicians (Jenike, 1991; Kaplan & Sadock, 1996; Schwartz, 1995); others (Jenike, 1991) have advised against the use of diazepam in controlling LSD-induced anxiety. In the latter case the theory is that diazepam distorts the individual's perception, which might contribute to even more anxiety. Normally, this distortion is so slight as to be unnoticed, but when combined with the effects of LSD, the benzodiazepine-induced sensory distortion may cause the patient to have even more anxiety than before (Jenike, 1991).

Many samples of hallucinogens sold on the street are adulterated with belladonna or other anticholinergics (Henderson, 1994a). These substances, when mixed with phenothiazines, may bring about coma and death through cardiorespiratory failure. Thus, it is imperative that the physician treating a bad trip know what drug(s) have been used and if possible be provided with a sample of the drugs ingested to determine what medication is best in treating each patient.

The LSD-induced bad trip normally lasts only a few hours and typically will resolve itself as the drug's effects wear off (Henderson, 1994b). However, in rare cases LSD is capable of activating a latent psychosis (Henderson, 1994b). Carvey (1998) noted that

various Indian tribes who have used the hallucinogen *mescaline* for centures fail to have significantly higher rates of psychosis than the general population, suggesting that the psychosis seen in the occasional LSD user is not a drug effect, but the final answer to this question has not been identified as of this time.

One reason it is so difficult to identify LSD's relationship to the development of psychiatric disorders such as a psychosis is that the "LSD experience is so exceptional that there is a tendency for observers to attribute *any* later psychiatric illness to the use of LSD" (Henderson, 1994b, p. 65, italics added for emphasis). Thus, as the author points out, psychotic reactions that develop weeks, months, or even years after the last use of LSD have been attributed to the individual's use of this hallucinogen rather than to nondrug factors. At this time, it has been suggested that LSD is capable of causing long-term complications such as a drug-induced psychosis. However, this theory has also been challenged by other researchers.

One extremely rare complication of LSD use is the overdose (Schuckit, 2000). Some symptoms of an LSD overdose include convulsions and hyperthermia. Medical care is necessary in any suspected drug overdose to reduce the risk of death. In a hospital setting, the physician can take appropriate steps to monitor the patient's cardiac status and to counter drug-induced elevation in body temperature, cardiac arrhythmias, seizures, and other such effects.

The LSD flashback. The "flashback" is a spontaneous recurrence of the LSD experience, now classified as the *hallucinogen persisting perceptual disorder* by the American Psychiatric Association (2000) (Pechnick & Ungerleider, 2004). The exact mechanism by which flashbacks occur remains unknown (Drummer & Odell, 2001). They might develop days, weeks, or months after the individual's last use of LSD, and even first-time abusers have been known to have them (Batzer, Ditzler, & Brown, 1999; Pechnick & Ungerleider, 2004). Flashbacks have been classified as being (a) perceptual, (b) somatic, or (c) emotional (Weiss & Millman, 1998). The majority of flashbacks involve visual sensory distortion, according to the authors. Somatic flashbacks consist of feelings of depersonalization, and emotional flashbacks involve periods when the individual reexperiences distressing emotions felt during the period of active LSD use (Weiss & Millman, 1998).

The "majority" (Schwartz, 1995, p. 409) of those who use LSD at least 10 times can expect to experience at least one flashback. Flashbacks might be triggered by stress, fatigue, marijuana use, emerging from a dark room, illness, the use of certain forms of antidepressant medications, and occasionally by intentional effort on the part of the individual. The use of sedating agents such as alcohol might also trigger LSD-induced flashbacks, although the reasons for this are not understood (Batzer et al., 1999). They usually last a few seconds to a few minutes, although occasionally to 24–48 hours or even longer (Kaplan & Sadock, 1996). Approximately 50% of those who develop flashbacks will do so in the first 6 months following their last use of LSD. In about 50% of the cases, the individual will continue to experience flashbacks for longer than 6 months and possibly for as long as 5 years (Schwartz, 1995; Weiss, Greenfield, & Mirin, 1994).

Flashback experiences often are occasionally frightening to the inexperienced user; however, for the most part they seem to be accepted by seasoned LSD users in much the same way that chronic alcohol users accept some physical discomfort as being part of the price they must pay for their chemical use. LSD abusers might not report flashbacks unless specifically questioned about these experiences (Batzer et al., 1999). People's reactions to LSD flashbacks vary from one individual to another. Some LSD abusers enjoy the visual hallucinations, "flashes" of color, halos around different objects, the perception that things are growing smaller, the perception that things are growing larger, and feelings of depersonalization that are common in an LSD flashback (Pechnick & Ungerleider, 2004). Other individuals have been known to become depressed, develop a panic disorder, or even become suicidal after an LSD-related flashback (Kaplan & Sadock, 1996). The only treatment needed for the typical patient is reassurance that the episode will end. On rare occasions a benzodiazepine might be used to control the flashback-induced anxiety that might develop.

Post-hallucinogen perceptual disorder. Post-hallucinogen perceptual disorder is a rare, poorly understood complication of LSD use/abuse (Hartman, 1995). Some chronic users of LSD will experience a disturbance in their visual perceptual system that may or may not become permanent. Victims of this disorder report seeing afterimages or distorted "trails" following behind objects in the environment for extended periods after their last use of LSD (Hartman, 1995). The exact mechanism by which LSD might cause these effects is not known at this time.

Although LSD has been studied by researchers for the past 50 years, much remains to be discovered about this elusive chemical. For example, there is one case report of a patient who developed grand mal seizures after taking LSD while taking the antidepressant fluoxetine (Ciraulo, Creelman, Shader, & O'Sullivan, 1995). The reason for this interaction between these two chemicals is not known. Unfortunately, even before scientists were able to learn all that there was to learn about LSD, another popular hallucinogen appeared. This is called PCP.

Phencyclidine (PCP)

The drug *Phencyclidine* (PCP) was first introduced in 1957 as an experimental intravenously administered surgical anesthetic (Milhorn, 1991). By the mid 1960s, researchers had discovered that 10% to 20% of the patients who had received PCP experienced a drug-induced delirium as well as a drug-induced psychosis that lasted up to 10 days in some patients, so the decision was made to discontinue using the drug with humans (McDowell, 2004; Milhorn, 1991). However, phencyclidine continued to be used in veterinary medicine in the United States until 1978, when all legal production of PCP in the United States was discontinued. The compound was classified a controlled substance under the Comprehensive Drug Abuse Prevention and Control Act of 1970 (Slaby, Lieb, & Tancredi, 1981). PCP continues to be used as a veterinary anesthetic in other parts of the world and is legally manufactured by pharmaceutical companies outside of the United States (Kaplan, Sadock, & Grebb, 1994). As a drug of abuse in this country, PCP's popularity has waxed and waned. Currently it is not a popular drug of abuse, although it is still encountered from time to time. Only 2.5% of the class of 2003 admitted to having ever used PCP (Johnston et al., 2003a). It is occasionally used as a component of "dip dope," discussed earlier (Mendyk & Fields, 2002).

Although *intentional* PCP abuse is rare, unintentional PCP use remains a very real problem. PCP is easily manufactured in illicit laboratories by people with minimal training in chemistry. Because of this, it is often mixed into other street drugs to enhance the effects of low-quality illicit substances. Further, misrepresentation is common, with PCP being substituted for other compounds that are not as easily obtained. When it is intentionally abused, it usually is smoked. The practice of smoking PCP, either alone or with compounds such as marijuana, allows abusers to titrate the dose to suit their taste or needs. If the individual finds the drug experience too harsh and aversive, he or she can simply stop smoking the PCP-laced cigarette for awhile.

Methods of PCP administration. PCP can be smoked, used intranasally, taken by mouth, injected into the muscle tissue, or injected intravenously (Karch, 2002; Weaver, Jarvis, & Schnoll, 1999). The most common method is by smoking it either alone or mixed with other compounds.

Subjective experience of PCP abuse. Phencyclidine's effects might last for several days, during which time users will experience rapid fluctuations in their level of consciousness (Weaver et al., 1999). The main experience for users is a sense of dissociation in which reality appears distorted or distant. Parts of their bodies might feel numb or as if they were no longer attached. These experiences might prove frightening, especially to novice users, resulting in panic reactions. Some of the other desired effects of PCP intoxication include a sense of euphoria, decreased inhibitions, a feeling of immense power, a reduction in the level of pain, and altered perception of time, space, and the user's body image (Milhorn, 1991).

Not all of the drug's effects are desired by the user. Indeed, "most regular users report unwanted effects" (Mirin et al., 1991, p. 295) caused by PCP. Some of the more common negative effects include feelings of anxiety, restlessness, and disorientation. In some cases, the user retains no memory of the period of intoxication, a reflection of the anesthetic action of the drug (Ashton, 1992). Other negative effects of PCP include disorientation, mental confusion, assaultiveness, anxiety, irritability, and paranoia (Weiss & Mirin, 1988). Indeed, so many people have experienced so many different undesired effects from PCP that researchers remain at a loss to explain why the drug was ever a popular drug of abuse (Newell & Cosgrove, 1988). PCP can cause users to experience a drug-induced depressive state, which in extreme cases might reach suicidal proportions (Jenike, 1991; Weiss & Mirin, 1988). This is consistent with the observations of Berger and Dunn (1982), who, drawing upon the wave of PCP abuse that took place in the 1970s, reported that the drug would bring the user either to "the heights, or the depths" (p. 100) of emotional experience.

Scope of PCP use/abuse. Researchers have found that approximately 2.5% of high school seniors who graduated in 2002 admitted to having used PCP at least once, a figure that has remained relatively stable for the past decade (Johnston et al., 2003a).

Pharmacology of PCP

Chemically, phencyclidine is a weak base, soluble in both water and lipids. When ingested orally, because it is a weak base it will be absorbed mainly through the small intestine rather than through the stomach lining (Zukin & Zukin, 1992). This will slow the absorption of the drug into the body, for the drug molecules must pass through the stomach to reach the small intestine. But the effects of an oral dose of PCP are still generally seen in just 20 to 30 minutes, and last for between 3 and 8 hours ("Consequences of PCP Abuses Are Up," 1994).

When smoked, PCP is rapidly absorbed through the lungs. The user will begin to experience symptoms of PCP intoxication within about 2–3 minutes after smoking the drug (Schnoll & Weaver, 2004). When smoked, much of the PCP will be converted into the chemical *phenylcyclohexene* by the heat of the smoking process (Shepherd & Jagoda, 1990) and only about 30% to 50% of the PCP in the cigarette will actually be absorbed (Crowley, 1995). When injected or ingested orally, 70% to 75% of the available PCP will reach the circulation (Crowley, 1995). The effects of injected PCP last for about 3–5 hours.

PCP is very lipid soluble; because of this it tends to accumulate in fatty tissues and in the tissues of the brain (Schnoll & Weaver, 2004). Indeed, the level of PCP in the brain might be 31 to 113 times as high as blood plasma levels (Shepherd & Jagoda, 1990). Further, animal research data suggest that PCP remains in the brain for up to 48 hours after it is no longer detectable in the blood (Hartman, 1995). Once in the brain, PCP tends to act at a number of different receptor sites, including blocking those utilized by a neurotransmitter known as N-methyl-D-aspartic acid

(NMDA) (Drummer & Odell, 2001; Zukin, Sloboda, & Javitt, 1997). PCP functions as an NMDA channel blocker, preventing NMDA from being able to carry out its normal function (Zukin et al., 1997). PCP also binds to the sigma opioid receptor site, which is how it causes many of its less pleasant effects (Daghestani & Schnoll, 1994; Drummer & Odell, 2001); it is found at some of the same cannabinoid receptor sites occupied by THC, which might explain its hallucinogenic effects (Glennon, 2004).

One of the factors that influences the subjective effect of PCP is the dosage level and the route of administration utilized by the individual. Another is the specific neurotransmitter system(s) being influenced by the dose of PCP (Roberts, 1995). Thus, PCP might function as an anesthetic, a stimulant, a depressant, or a hallucinogenic (Brown & Braden, 1987; Weiss & Mirin, 1988). PCP is biotransformed by the liver into a number of inactive metabolites, which are then excreted mainly by the kidneys (Zukin et al., 1997; Zukin & Zukin, 1992). Following a single dose of PCP, only about 10% (Karch, 2002) to 20% (Crowley, 1995) of the drug will be excreted unchanged. Unfortunately, one characteristic of PCP is that it takes the body an extended period of time to biotransform/excrete the drug. The half-life of PCP following an overdose may be as long as 20 (Kaplan et al., 1994) to 72 hours (Jaffe, 1989), and in extreme cases it might be several weeks (Grinspoon & Bakalar, 1990).

One reason for the extended half-life of PCP is that it tends to accumulate in the body's adipose (fat) tissues, where in chronic use it can remain for days or even weeks following the last dose of the drug. There have even been cases of a chronic PCP user losing weight, either because of intentional attempts to lose weight or because of trauma, causing the adipose tissue to release unmetabolized PCP back into the general circulation, triggering flashback-type experiences long after the last use of the drug (Zunkin & Zunkin, 1992).

In the past, physicians believed it was possible to reduce the half-life of PCP in the body by making the urine more acidic. This was done by having the patient ingest large amounts of ascorbic acid or cranberry juice (Grinspoon & Bakalar, 1990; Kaplan & Sadock, 1996). However, patients receiving this treatment were discovered to be vulnerable to developing a condition known as myoglobinuria, which may cause the kidneys to fail

(Brust, 1993). Because of this potential complication, many physicians do not recommend the acidification of the patient's urine for any reason.

There is virtually no research data on the possibility that the user might become tolerant to the effects of PCP. However, clinical evidence with burn patients who have received repeated doses of the anesthetic agent ketamine, which is similar in chemical structure to PCP, suggests that some degree of tolerance to its effects are possible (Zukin et al., 1997). There is no evidence of physical dependence on PCP (Weiss et al., 1994; Zevin & Benowitz, 1998).

Symptoms of mild levels of PCP intoxication. Small doses of PCP, usually less than 1 mg, do not seem to have an effect on the user (Crowley, 1995). At dosage levels of about 5 mg, the individual will experience a state resembling that seen in alcohol intoxication (Crowley, 1995; Mirin et al., 1991). The individual will experience muscle coordination problems, staggering gait, slurred speech, and numbness of the extremities (Jaffe, 1989). Other effects of mild doses of PCP include agitation, some feelings of anxiety, flushing of the skin, visual hallucinations, irritability, possible sudden outbursts of rage, and feelings of euphoria, nystagmus, changes in the body image, and depression (Beebe & Walley, 1991; Crowley, 1995; Milhorn, 1991).

The acute effects of a small dose of about 5 mg of PCP last between 4 and 6 hours. Following the period of acute effects is a post-PCP recovery period that can last 24 to 48 hours (Beebe & Walley, 1991; Milhorn, 1991). During the post-PCP recovery period the user will gradually "come down," or return to normal.

Symptoms of moderate levels of PCP intoxication. As the dosage level increases to the 5–10 mg range, many users will experience a range of symptoms, including a disturbance of body image in which different parts of their bodies will no longer seem "real" (Brophy, 1993). The user may also experience slurred speech, nystagmus, dizziness, ataxia, tachycardia, and an increase in muscle tone (Brophy, 1993; Weiss & Mirin, 1988). Other symptoms of moderate levels of PCP intoxication might include paranoia, severe anxiety, belligerence, and assaultiveness (Grinspoon & Bakalar, 1990) as well as demonstration of unusual feats of strength (Brophy, 1993; Jaffe, 1989) and extreme salivation (Brendel, West, & Hyman, 1996). Some people have exhibited drug-induced fever, drug-induced psychosis, and violence.

Symptoms of severe levels of PCP intoxication. As the dosage level reaches the 10–25 mg level or higher, the individual's life is in extreme danger. At this dosage level the PCP user might experience vomiting or seizures; even if the user is still conscious, his or her reaction time would be seriously impaired. The user who has ingested more than 10 mg of PCP might experience hypertension and severe psychotic reactions similar to schizophrenia (Grinspoon & Bakalar, 1990; Kaplan & Sadock, 1996; Weiss & Mirin, 1988). Estimates of the period of time that the PCP-induced coma might last range from up to 10 days (Mirin et al., 1991) to several weeks (Zevin & Benowitz, 1998). Further, because of the absorption/distribution characteristics of the drug, the individual might slip into, and apparently recover from, a PCP-induced coma several times before the drug is eliminated from the body (Carvey, 1998). Other symptoms of severe PCP intoxication might include cardiac arrhythmias, encopresis, visual and tactile hallucinations, and a drug-induced paranoid state. PCP overdoses have caused death from respiratory arrest, convulsions, and hypertension (Brophy, 1993).

Complications of PCP Abuse

It is difficult to understand why people would be drawn to PCP as the subjective experience of PCP abuse is positive only about half the time and is decidedly unpleasant or adverse the rest of the time. Paradoxically, the very fact that it is not possible to predict in advance which experience the user will have adds a measure of excitement and attractiveness to PCP abuse for many people (Schnoll & Weaver, 2004).

One of the more uncomfortable consequences of PCP abuse is a drug-induced psychosis, which might not abate for days, weeks (Jaffe, 1989; Jenike, 1991; Weiss & Mirin, 1988), or months (Ashton, 1992). It is theorized that a history of a previous psychotic episode or a preexisting vulnerability to psychosis may exist in those individuals who develop this complication of PCP abuse (Mirin et al., 1991; Weiss & Millman, 1998). But this is only a theory, and it is possible that PCP can induce a psychotic episode even in individuals who normally would lack the genetic predisposition for such a reaction. It is known that PCP can cause "a long

lasting syndrome marked by neuropsychological deficits, social withdrawal, and affective blunting as well as hallucinations, formal thought disorder, paranoia and delusions" (Jentsch et al., 1997, p. 954). Thus, the effects of PCP abuse can be both profound and devasting for the individual.

It *is* known that the PCP psychosis usually will progress through three different stages, each of which lasts approximately 5 days (Mirin et al., 1991; Weiss & Mirin, 1988). The first stage is usually the most severe and is characterized by paranoid delusions, anorexia, insomnia, and unpredictable assaultiveness. During this phase, the individual is extremely sensitive to external stimuli (Jaffe, 1989; Mirin et al., 1991), and the "talking down" techniques that might work with an LSD bad trip do not often work with PCP (Brust, 1993; Jaffe, 1990).

The middle phase is marked by continued paranoia and restlessness, but users are usually calmer and in intermittent control of their behavior (Mirin et al., 1991; Weiss & Mirin, 1988). This phase will again usually last 5 days and will gradually blend into the final phase of the PCP psychosis recovery process. This final phase is marked by a gradual recovery over 7 to 14 days; however, in some patients the PCP psychosis may last for months (Mirin et al., 1991; Slaby et al., 1981; Weiss & Mirin, 1988). Social withdrawal and severe depression are also common following chronic use of PCP (Jaffe, 1990).

There would appear to be some minor withdrawal symptoms following prolonged periods of hallucinogen use. Chronic PCP users have reported memory problems, which seem to clear when they stopped using the drug (Jaffe, 1990; Newell and Cosgrove, 1988). Recent evidence would suggest that chronic PCP users demonstrate the same pattern of neuropsychological deficits found in other forms of chronic drug use, suggesting that PCP might cause chronic brain damage (Grinspoon & Bakalar, 1990; Jentsch et al., 1997; Newell & Cosgrove, 1988).

Research has also revealed that PCP can, at high dosage levels, cause hypertensive episodes (Lange, White, & Robinson, 1992) that in extreme cases might last as long as 3 days after the drug was ingested (Weiss & Millman, 1998). These periods of unusually high blood pressure may then cause the individual to experience a cerebral vascular accident (CVA or stroke) (Brust,

1993; Daghestani & Schnoll, 1994). Although research into this area is lacking, the possibility does exist that this is the mechanism through which PCP is able to bring about brain damage in the user.

The majority of PCP users who die do so because of traumatic injuries that they suffer while under the drug's effects ("Consequences of PCP Abuse," 1994). For example, because of the assaultiveness frequently induced by PCP, many users end up as either the victim or the perpetrator of a homicide while under the drug's effects (Ashton, 1992). In spite of its extremely deleterious effects, at the start of the 21st century PCP continues to lurk in the shadows and may again become a popular drug of abuse, just as it has been in the past.

Ecstasy: Evolution of a New Drug of Abuse

History of ecstasy. The hallucinogen N, alpha-dimethyl-1,3 benzo-dioxole-t-ethanamine (MDMA) was first isolated in 1914.[4] It was thought that MDMA would function as an appetite suppressant, but when the initial animal studies did not suggest that the compound was worth developing, researchers quickly lost interest in it. In the mid 1960s some psychiatrists suggested that MDMA might be useful as an aid in psychotherapy (Batki, 2001; Gahlinger, 2004; Rochester & Kirchner, 1999). MDMA also briefly surfaced as a drug of abuse during the 1960s but was eclipsed by LSD, which was more potent and did not cause the nausea or vomiting often experienced by MDMA users. The compound was considered unworthy of classification as an illegal substance when the drug classification system currently in use was set up in the early 1970s.

Partially because it was not classified as an illicit substance, illicit drug producers became interested in MDMA in the mid 1970s. The marketing process behind MDMA was impressive and numerous possible product names were discussed before "ecstasy" was

selected (Kirsch, 1986; McDowell, 2004), a demand for the "product" was generated, and supply/distribution networks evolved to meet this demand. The original samples of ecstasy included a "package insert" (Kirsch, 1986, p. 81) that "included unverified scientific research and an abundance of 1960s mumbo-jumbo" (p. 81) about how the drug should be used and its purported benefits. The package inserts also warned the user not to mix ecstasy with alcohol or other chemicals, to use it only occasionally, and to take care to ensure a proper "set" in which to use it.

Within the span of a few years, MDMA had become a popular drug of abuse in both the United States and Europe. The Drug Enforcement Administration (DEA) classified MDMA as a controlled substance with no recognized medical use in 1985 (McDowell, 2004). As of that date, "trafficking in MDMA [was made] punishable by fifteen years in prison and a $125,000 fine" (Kirsch, 1986, p. 84). Unfortunately, it has remained a popular drug of abuse, in part because of its reputation as a safe hallucinogen that helps the user feel closer to others. At the start of the 21st century MDMA has not only remained a popular drug of abuse but has actually become *the* most commonly abused stimulant in dance clubs (Gahlinger, 2004). Although there are reports of MDMA being produced in the United States, the majority is manufactured in Europe and smuggled into this country (United Nations, 2003).

Scope of the problem of MDMA abuse. Globally, 8 million people are thought to have abused MDMA in 2003, a number that is greater than the combined number of heroin and cocaine abusers around the world (United Nations, 2003, 2004). In the United States, MDMA abuse seems to have peaked around the year 2000 and has dropped by about 50% since then (Office of National Drug Control Policy, 2004). Still, the total worldwide annual production of MDMA is estimated to be about 113 tons, and there is evidence that MDMA abuse continues to increase globally (United Nations, 2003, 2004).

Much of the early abuse of MDMA was fueled by the belief that it was harmless (Ramcharan et al., 1998). It found wide acceptance in a subculture devoted to loud music and parties centered around the use of MDMA and dancing, a pattern similar to that of the LSD parties of the 1960s (Randall, 1992). Such parties, known as "raves," began in Spain, spread to England in

---

[4]Cook (1995) said that MDMA was patented in 1913, and Rochester and Kirchner (1999) suggested that the patent was issued in 1912 in Germany. Schuckit (2000) suggested that MDMA was first synthesized in 1912 and that the patent was for this compound was issued in 1914. There obiously is some disagreement over the exact date that the patent for this chemical was issued.

the early 1980s, and from there to the United States (McDowell, 2004; Rochester & Kirchner, 1999). Such parties remain popular, and each weekend an estimated 20 million MDMA tablets are thought to be consumed in the United Kingdom alone (Rogers et al., 2003). These parties have been described as the modern equivalent of the Dionysian religious festivals of ancient Rome (Walton, 2002). MDMA is viewed by many as a "dance making drug" because users feel the urge to dance for extended periods of time ("The Agony of 'Ecstasy,'" 1994).

As one measure of its early popularity, between 10% and 40% of older adolescents and young adults admit to having used MDMA at least once (Schuckit, 2000). Researchers have found that 8.3% of the high school seniors who were surveyed in 2002 admitted to having used MDMA at least once (Johnston et al., 2003a).

Pharmacology of MDMA

The chemical structure of MDMA is so similar to that of the amphetamines that it was classified as a "semisynthetic hallucinogenic amphetamine" by Klein and Kramer (2004, p. 61). The chemical structure of MDMA is also similar to that of the hallucinogens, MDA, and mescaline (Creighton, Black, & Hyde, 1991; Gahlinger, 2004; Kirsch, 1986; Schuckit, 2000).

MDMA is well absorbed from the gastrointestinal tract, and the most common method of MDMA use is through oral ingestion (McDowell, 2004). The effects of a dose of MDMA usually begin in about 20 minutes and peak within an hour (Gahlinger, 2004; McDowell, 2004) to an hour and a half (Schwartz & Miller, 1997). Peak blood levels are usually seen in 1–3 hours after a single dose is ingested (Ramcharan et al., 1998). Maximum blood levels of MDMA are achieved about 2–4 hours following a single dose, and the estimated half-life of a single dose is estimated to be between 4 and 7 (Karch, 2002) to 8 hours or more (Gahlinger, 2004; Klein & Kramer, 2004; Schwartz & Miller, 1997). MDMA is biotransformed in the liver, and its elimination half-life[5] is estimated to be approximately 8 hours. One major metabolite of MDMA is a compound that is itself a hallucinogen: MDA. However, one study, which used a single volunteer subject, found that almost

three-fourths of the MDMA ingested was excreted unchanged in the urine within 72 hours of ingestion.

Because it is so highly lipid soluble, MDMA is able to cross the blood-brain barrier into the brain itself without significant delay. Within the brain, MDMA functions as an indirect serotonin agonist (McDowell, 2004). It first forces the release of, and then inhibits the reabsorption of, serotonin, with a smaller effect on norepinephrine and dopamine (Gahlinger, 2004; Parrott, Morinan, Moss, & Scholey, 2004). Scientists think that MDMA's main effects involve the serotonin neurotransmitter system, but there is very little objective research into its effects on users, and virtually all that is known about the drug's effects is based on studies done on illicit drug abusers.

Patterns of MDMA abuse. MDMA users tend to have drug-use patterns that are different from those in other chemicals of abuse. First, the typical MDMA abuser tends to be a polydrug user (Karch, 2002; McDowell, 2004; Schwartz & Miller, 1997). When MDMA is used by itself, the typical abuser will ingest 1–2 tablets of the drug, each of which contains 100–140 mg of the drug, and then abstain from further MDMA use for at least a week (Gouzoulis-Mayfrank et al., 2000). This rather unusual drug use pattern reflects the pharmacology of MDMA in the brain. By blocking the reuptake of serotonin, MDMA contributes to a tendency for subsequent doses not to cause the euphoria that is the goal of abusers but many side effects mediated by other neurotransmitter systems. Further, taking a double dose of the drug does not increase the desired effects of MDMA but makes the individual more likely to experience unpleasant side effects (Bravo, 2001; Peroutka, 1989) and increases the chances of MDMA-induced brain damage (McGuire & Fahy, 1991). The typical dosage levels ingested by abusers seem to be between 60 and 250 mg (Gouzoulis-Mayfrank et al., 2000).

Subjective and objective effects of MDMA abuse. Currently, at least six different methods of making MDMA are known to exist, and specific instructions on how to make the drug are available on the Internet (Rochester & Kirchner, 1999). Specialized equipment and training in organic chemistry are required to avoid the danger of contaminating the MDMA by toxins, but beyond these requirements the drug is easily synthesized. In past decades MDMA was usually produced in Europe

[5]See Chapter 3 and Glossary.

and then shipped to the United States, but it is increasingly being made in this country. Virtually all that is known about MDMA's effects are based on observations of illicit drug users, as there has been little objective research into the subjective, pharmacological, or toxicological effects of this drug (Bravo, 2001; Karch, 2002).

The subjective effects of MDMA are, to a large degree, dependent on the "set" and the individual's expectations for the drug (Bravo, 2001). At dosage levels of 75–100 mg, users report experiencing a sense of euphoria, a sense of closeness to others, and improved self-esteem (Beebe & Walley, 1991; Bravo, 2001). At this dosage level, the user might also possibly experience mild visual hallucinations (Evanko, 1991). After the period of acute drug intoxication, some users will experience a degree of confusion, anxiety, headache, feelings of derealization and/or depersonalization, as well as depression and paranoia during or following their use of MDMA (Bravo, 2001; Buia, Gulton, Park, Shannon, & Thompson, 2000; Cohen, 1998). Many of these feelings may persist for several hours to several days following the last use of the drug.

Some of the subjective effects of MDMA include "tachycardia, an occasional 'wired' feeling, jaw clenching, nystagmus, a nervous desire to be in motion, transient anorexia, panic attacks, nausea and vomiting, ataxia, urinary urgency, . . . insomnia, tremors, inhibition of ejaculation, and rarely, transient hallucinations" (Climko, Roehrich, Sweeney, & Al-Razi, 1987, p. 365). The user's tendency to clench the teeth while under the effects of MDMA is also known as bruxism (grinding of teeth) and has been linked to excessive wear on the teeth (McDowell, 2004; Redfearn, Agrawl, & Mair, 1998). Many abusers will attempt to control this effect by using baby pacifiers or candy to suck on after ingesting the drug (Gahlinger, 2004; Klein & Kramer, 2004). Other effects of a "typical" dose of MDMA include increase in heart rate, muscle tremor, tightness in jaw muscles, nausea, insomnia, headache, difficulty concentrating, vertigo, dry mouth, a decrease in appetite, ataxia, and sweating (Bravo, 2001). People who are sensitive to the effects of MDMA might experience numbness and tingling in extremities of the body, vomiting, increased sensitivity to cold, visual hallucinations, crying, blurred vision, nystagmus, and the experience of having the floor appear to shake.

MDMA has been implicated as the cause of decreased sexual desire and in men, inhibition of the ejaculatory reflex and erectile problems (Finger, Lund, & Slagel, 1997; McDowell, 2004). However, males are often sexually aroused when the effects of MDMA begin to wear off (Buia et al., 2000).

Complications of MDMA Use

There is a significant overlap between the therapeutic and toxic levels of MDMA (Karch, 2002). Research using animals suggests that the LD50 following a single intravenous dose of MDMA is approximately 8–23 mg/kg in dogs, and 17–28 mg/kg in Rhesus monkeys (Karch, 1996). In the early 1950s, the United States Army conducted a series of secret research projects to explore MDMA's possible military applications, and the data from these studies suggest that just 14 of the more potent MDMA pills being produced in illicit laboratories might prove fatal to the user if ingested together (Buia et al., 2000).

MDMA-related cardiac problems. There is growing evidence that MDMA has a negative effect on cardiac function, a discovery that has profound implications for people who abuse this compound. Although the mechanism by which MDMA is able to cause death is not known at this time, it *is* known that the majority of deaths in MDMA abusers are the result of cardiac arrhythmias (Beebe & Walley, 1991; Schwartz & Miller, 1997). It is thought that MDMA, like its chemical cousins the amphetamines, shares the ability to alter cardiac function (Gahlinger, 2004; Karch, 2002; Klein & Kramer, 2004).

Further, there is experimenal evidence that MDMA functions as a cardiotoxin[6] causing inflammation of the heart muscle (Badon et al., 2002). Some chronic abusers have been found to suffer from cardiomyopathy (Klein & Kramer, 2004). Further, other abusers had altered cardiac function when they were admitted to the hospital. MDMA is able to cause tachycardia (Gahlinger, 2004), and one study of the records of 48 patients admitted to a hospital accident and trauma center following MDMA use found that two-thirds had heart rates above 100 beats per minute (Williams, Dratcu, Taylor, Roberts, & Oyefeso, 1998). It was

[6]See Glossary.

recommended that MDMA overdoses be treated with the same protocols used to treat amphetamine overdoses, with special emphasis placed on assessing and protecting cardiac function (Gahlinger, 2004; Rochester & Kirchner, 1999).

There is also evidence suggesting that the chronic use of MDMA might result in damage to the valves of the heart (Setola et al., 2003). The authors examined the impact of MDMA on tissue samples in laboratories and found that MDMA caused many of the same changes to the cardiac tissue samples that were found when tissue samples were exposed to the now-banned weight-loss medication fenfluramine.[7] Given the widespread popularity of MDMA, these research findings hint at a possible future epidemic of MDMA-induced cardiac problems in chronic abusers.

MDMA-related neurological problems. There is preliminary evidence that for reasons not understood women might be more vulnerable to MDMA-induced brain damage than men (Greenfield, 2003). Researchers have found that MDMA impacts the system of blood vessels that serves the brain, as evidenced by reports of intracranial hemorrhage in some abusers (Sternbach & Varon, 1992) and nonhemorrhagic cerebrovascular accidents.[8] There is one case report of a young woman who developed a condition known as cerebral venous sinus thrombosis (a blood clot) after ingesting MDMA at a rave party (Rothwell & Grant, 1993). The authors speculated that dehydration may have been a factor in the development of the cerebral venous sinus thrombosis in this case and warned of the need to maintain adequate fluid intake while exercising under the influence of MDMA.

Unfortunately, animal research has demonstrated that MDMA causes the body to secrete abnormal amounts of the antidiuretic hormone (ADH) (Gahlinger, 2004; Henry & Rella, 2001). This hormone then promotes water reabsorption by the kidneys, reducing urine production and forcing the water back into the body. If the user ingests a great deal of water in an attempt to avoid dehydration, he or she might be vulnerable to

developing abnormally low blood sodium levels (hyponatemia), which could cause or contribute to arrhythmias, seizures, or other problems (Henry & Rella, 2001; Parrott et al., 2004). Thus, the problem of how to deal with MDMA-related dehydration is far more complex than simply having the user ingest fluids.

Preliminary evidence suggests that MDMA might induce, or at least exacerbate, memory problems (Rogers et al., 2003). The authors found that the regular MDMA abusers in their sample achieved scores on memory function tests that were more than 20% lower than those of their control group. The methodology utilized by this study (volunteers solicited over the Internet) was unique, and it is not known whether these results will generalize to the population of MDMA abusers, but the initial findings do suggest that MDMA might interfere with normal memory function long after the drug's desired effects have ended.

MDMA has also been implicated as the cause of the serotonin syndrome[9] (Henry & Rella, 2001; Karch, 2002; Sternbach, 2003). Because temperature dysregulation is one effect of the serotonin syndrome, this process might explain why some abusers develop severe hyperthermia following MDMA ingestion (Klein & Kramer, 2004). MDMA has also been implicated as the cause of increased seizure activity in users, for reasons that are not well understood (Karch, 2002). On occasion, these MDMA-related seizures have been fatal (Henry, 1996; Henry & Rella, 2001).

The available evidence suggests that MDMA is a neurotoxin[10] in both humans and animals. This might explain the observed relationship between MDMA abuse and Parkinson's disease (Gahlinger, 2004). Animal studies suggest that MDMA functions as a neurotoxin for both dopaminergic neurons and serotonergic neurons. Earlier research studies had discovered evidence that MDMA functioned as a selective neurotoxin in humans that destroyed serotonergic neurons alone (Batki, 2001; Gouzoulis-Mayfrank et al., 2000; Marston, Reid, Lawrence, Olverman, & Butcher, 1999; McCann, Szabo, Scheffel, Dannals, & Ricaurte, 1998; Morgan, 1999; Reneman, Booij, Schmand, van den Brink, & Gunning, 2000; Ritz,

---

[7]This medication was called "Fen-Phen" and was withdrawn from the market after reports suggested that patients who were taking it developed potentially life-threatening damage to their heart valves.

[8]See Glossary.

[9]See Glossary.

[10]See Glossary.

1999; Vik, Cellucci, Jarchow, & Hedt, 2004; Wareing, Risk, & Murphy, 2000).

MDMA-induced brain damage has been found to be dose-related, with higher levels of impairment in individuals who had ingested greater amounts of MDMA. The frequency of use is not thought to be correlated with the degree of brain damage (Croft, Klugman, Baldeweg, & Gruzelier, 2001). Researchers disagree as to whether this MDMA-induced brain damage is permanent (Walton, 2002) or if some limited degree of recovery is possible (Buchert et al., 2003; Buchert et al., 2004; Gouzoulis-Mayfrank et al., 2000; Renerman et al., 2001; Ritz, 1999).

Although at one point it was suspected that the neurotoxic effects of MDMA were possibly due to contaminants in the MDMA rather than the drug itself (Rochester & Kirchner, 1999), positive emission tomographic (PET) studies have uncovered significant evidence suggesting global, dose-related decreases in brain 5-HT transporter, a structural element of neurons that utilize serotonin (Buchert et al., 2004; McCann et al., 1998). Even limited MDMA use has been associated with a 35% reduction in 5-HT metabolism (an indirect measure of serotonin activity in the brain) for men and almost a 50% reduction in 5-HT metabolism in women (Hartman, 1995), findings that are highly suggestive of organic brain damage at a cellular level. However, there is preliminary evidence to suggest that a single dose of the selective serotonin reuptake inhibitor Prozac (fluoxotine) might protect neurons from MDMA-induced damage if it is ingested within 24 hours of the MDMA (Walton, 2002).

MDMA-related emotional problems. The MDMA user might experience flashbacks very similar to those seen with LSD use (Creighton et al., 1991). These MDMA flashbacks usually develop in the first few days following the use of the drug (Cook, 1995). In another interesting drug effect seen at normal dosage levels, the user will occasionally "relive" past memories. The memories that are experienced anew are often ones that were suppressed because of the pain associated with the experience (Hayner & McKinney, 1986). Thus, users might find themselves reliving an experience they did not want to remember. This effect, which many psychotherapists thought might prove of benefit in the therapeutic

relationship, may seem so frightening to the user as to be "detrimental to the the individual's mental health" (p. 343). Long-time use has contributed to episodes of violence and also to suicide ("The Agony of 'Ecstasy,'" 1994).

MDMA abuse might also result in such residual effects as anxiety attacks, persistent insomnia, irritability, rage reactions, and a drug-induced psychosis (Gahlinger, 2004; Hayner & McKinney, 1986; Karch, 2002; McGuire & Fahy, 1991). The exact mechanism by which MDMA might cause a paranoid psychosis is not clear at this time (Karch, 2002). It is theorized that MDMA is able to activate a psychotic reaction in a person who has a biological predisposition for this disorder (McGuire & Fahy, 1991). As the effects wane, users typically experience a depressive reaction that might be quite severe and last 48 hours or more (Gahlinger, 2004).

MDMA-related gastrointestinal problems. In Europe, where MDMA abuse is common, there have been a number of reports of liver toxicity and hepatitis in MDMA abusers. The exact relationship between the MDMA abuse and the development of liver problems is not clear at this time, and it is possible that these were idiosyncratic reactions in isolated individuals (Karch, 2002). Another possibility is that the liver problems were induced by one or more contaminants in the MDMA dose consumed by the user (Cook, 1995; Henry, Jeffreys, & Dawling, 1992; Henry & Rella, 2001; Jones, Jarvie, McDermid, & Proudfoot, 1994).

Other MDMA-related physical problems. MDMA abuse has been identified as a cause of rhabdomyolysis,[11] which appears to be a consequence of the motor activity induced by or associated with the abuse of this compound (Gahlinger, 2004; Karch, 2002; Klein & Kramer, 2004; Sauret, Marinides, & Wang, 2002).

MDMA overdose. Symptoms of an MDMA overdose include restlessness, agitation, sweating, tachycardia, hypertension, hypotension, heart palpitations, renal failure, muscle rigidity, and visual hallucinations (Jaffe, 2000a; Williams et al., 1998). There have been rare reports of fatalities as a result of MDMA abuse. Many experienced MDMA users eventually have one or more of the complications noted above, suggesting that the

---

[11]See Glossary.

possibilty for an adverse reaction continues throughout the period of MDMA use (Williams et al., 1998). While fatalities involving MDMA alone are rare, the potential danger for abusers is increased if multiple agents are ingested (McDowell, 2004). *The Economist* ("Better than Well," 1996) estimated that MDMA causes one death for each 3 million doses. Although the use of *ß*-blocking agents (Beta blockers, or Beta adrenergic blockers) were recommended early in the 1990s (Ames, Wirshing, & Friedman, 1993), the team of Rochester and Kirchner (1999) advised against the use of these agents as this might make control of blood pressure more difficult since the *a*-adrenergic system would remain unaffected.

Drug interactions involving MDMA. Little research has been done on the possible interactions between illicit drugs, such as MDMA, and pharmaceuticals (Concar, 1997). There have been case reports of interactions between the anti-HIV agent Ritonavir and MDMA (Concar, 1997; "Ecstasy-using HIV Patients," 1997; Harrington, Woodward, Hooton, & Horn, 1999). Each agent affects the serotonin level in the blood, and the combination of these two chemicals results in a threefold higher level of MDMA than normal; some fatalities have been reported in users who have mixed these compounds (Concar, 1997).

Summary

Weil (1986) suggested that people initially use chemicals to alter the normal state of consciousness. Hallucinogen use in this country, at least in the last generation, has followed a series of waves, as first one drug and then another becomes the current drug of choice for achieving this altered state of consciousness. In the sixties, LSD was the major hallucinogen, and in the seventies and early eighties, it was PCP. Currently, MDMA seems to be gaining in popularity as the hallucinogen of choice, although research suggests that MDMA may cause permanent brain damage, especially to those portions of the brain that utilize serotonin as a primary neurotransmitter.

If we accept Weil's (1986) hypothesis as correct, it is logical to expect that other hallucinogens will emerge over the years as people look for a more effective way to alter their state of consciousness. One might expect that these drugs in turn will slowly fade as they are replaced by newer hallucinogenics. Just as cocaine faded from the drug scene in the 1930s and was replaced for a period of time by the amphetamines, so one might expect wave after wave of hallucinogen abuse as new drugs become available. Thus, chemical dependency counselors will have to maintain a working knowledge of an ever-growing range of hallucinogens in the years to come .

CHAPTER SIXTEEN

Abuse of and Addiction to the Inhalants and Aerosols

Introduction

The inhalants are unlike the other chemicals of abuse. They are toxic substances that include various cleaning agents, herbicides, pesticides, gasoline, kerosene, certain forms of glue, lacquer thinner, and chemicals used in felt-tipped pens. These agents are not primarily intended to function as recreational substances.

When inhaled, many of the chemicals in these compounds will alter the manner in which the brain functions. At low doses, inhalants may cause the user to experience a sense of euphoria. It is often possible for adolescents and even children to purchase many agents that have the potential to be abused by inhalation. For these reasons, children, adolescents, or even the rare adult will occasionally abuse chemical fumes. Because these chemicals are inhaled, they are often called *inhalants*, or *volatile substances* (Esmail, Meyer, Pottier, & Wright, 1993). For the purpose of this text, the term *inhalants* will be used.

The inhalation of volatile substances, or inhalants, has become a major concern in the European Union, where 1 in every 7 adolescents in the 15- to 16-year age group abuses inhalants ("Solvent Abuse Puts Teens at Risk," 2003). Because they are so easily accessible to children and adolescents, inhalants continue to be a major substance for chemical abuse among adolescents in the United States as well. In this chapter, the problem of inhalant abuse will be discussed.

History of Inhalant Abuse

The first episodes of inhalant abuse in modern history involve anesthetics, dating back to the 19th century. Indeed, the earliest documented use of the anesthetic gases appears to have been for recreation, and historical records from the 1800s document the use of such agents as nitrous oxide for parties. The use of gasoline fumes to get high is thought to have started prior to World War II (Morton, 1987), with the first documentation of this practice being found in the early 1950s (Blum, 1984). By the mid 1950s and early 1960s, the popular press was reporting "glue sniffing" (Morton, 1987; Westermeyer, 1987). In this practice the individual will use model airplane glue as an inhalant. The active agent of model glue in the 1950s was often toluene. Nobody knows how the practice of glue sniffing first started, but there is evidence that it began in California, when teenagers accidentally discovered the intoxicating powers of toluene-containing model glue (Berger & Dunn 1982).

The first known reference to this practice appeared in 1959, in the magazine section of a Denver newspaper (Brecher, 1972). Local newspapers soon began to carry stories on the dangers of inhalant abuse, in the process explaining just how to use airplane glue to become intoxicated and what effects to expect. Within a short time, a "Nationwide Drug Menace" (Brecher, 1972, p. 321) emerged in the United States. Currently, inhalant abuse is thought to be a worldwide problem (Brust, 1993) and is especially common in Japan and Europe (Karch, 2002).

Brecher (1972) suggested that the inhalant abuse "problem" was essentially manufactured through distorted media reports. The author said that in response to media reports of deaths due to glue sniffing, one newspaper tracked down several stories and found only nine deaths that could be attributed to this practice. Of this number, six deaths were due to asphyxiation: Each victim had used an airtight plastic bag and had suffocated. In another case, there was evidence that asphyxiation was also the cause of death, and in the eighth case there was no evidence that the victim had been using inhalants. Finally, in the ninth case, the individual had been using gasoline* as an inhalant but was reported to be in poor health prior to this incident. Brecher (1972) noted that "among tens of thousands of glue-sniffers prior to 1964, no death due unequivocally to glue vapor had as yet been reported. The lifesaving advice children needed was not to sniff glue with their heads in plastic bags" (p. 331).

Since these words were written, research has shown that the use of inhalants may introduce potentially toxic chemicals into the user's body (Brunswick, 1989; Jaffe, 1989). Some of the consequences of inhalant abuse include cardiac arrhythmias, anoxia, damage to the visual perceptual system through increased intraocular pressure, and neuropathies (Greydanus & Patel, 2003). Thus, while the media might have played a role in the development of this crisis back in the late 1950s and early 1960s, by the 1990s it had become a legitimate health concern.

Pharmacology of the Inhalants

Many chemical agents reach the brain more rapidly and efficiently when they are inhaled rather than ingested by mouth or injected. When a chemical is inhaled, it is able to enter the bloodstream without its chemical structure being altered in any way by the liver. Once in the blood, one factor that influences how fast that chemical might reach the brain is whether the molecules are able to form chemical bonds with the lipids in the blood. As a general rule, inhalants are quite lipid soluble (Crowley & Sakai, 2004; Henretig, 1996). Further, inhalants share the characteristic of being able to rapidly cross the blood-brain barrier to reach the brain itself in an extremely short period of time, usually within seconds (Blum, 1984; Crowley & Sakai, 2004; Hartman, 1995; Heath, 1994; Watson, 1984).

Cone (1993) grouped all of the inhalants into two broad classifications: (a) anesthetic gases and (b) volatile hydrocarbons. In contrast to this classification scheme, Monroe (1995) suggested three classes of chemicals that might be inhaled:

1. The *solvents*, such as glues, paint, paint thinner, gasoline, kerosene, lighter fluid, fingernail polish, fingernail polish remover, correction fluids for use in the office, felt tip markers.

2. Various *gases*, such as butane in cigarette lighters, propane gas, the propellant in whipping cream cans, cooking sprays.
3. The *nitrites*, such as butyl nitrite and amyl nitrite.

However, Espeland (1997)[1] suggested four classes of inhalants:

1. Volatile organic solvents such as those found in paint and fuel[2]
2. Aerosols, such as hair sprays, spray paints, and deodorants
3. Volatile nitrites (such as amyl nitrite or its close chemical cousin, butyl nitrite)
4. General anesthetic agents such as nitrous oxide

As these different classification systems suggest, there are many chemicals, with a multitude of uses, that produce fumes; when inhaled, many of these will alter the user's sense of reality. Of the different classes of inhalants commonly abused, children and adolescents will most often abuse the first two classes. Children or adolescents have limited access to the third category of inhalants, and extremely limited access to general anesthetics, the final class of inhalants.

Because so many different compounds might be abused, it is virtually impossible to speak of a "pharmacology" of inhalants. Many of the more common inhalants are biotransformed by the liver before being elimated from the circulation by the kidneys, but some are exhaled without extensive biotransformation taking place (Brooks, Leung, & Shannon, 1996; Crowley & Sakai, 2004). Further, many of the compounds that are abused were never intended for introduction into the human body but were designed as industrial solvents or for household use. Even in research into the effects of a specific compound on the human body, it has only rarely involved the concentrations of these agents at the levels commonly used by inhalant abusers (Blum, 1984;

---

[1]Children and adolescents have only limited access to volatile nitrites, although butyl nitrite is sometimes sold without a prescription in some states. Except in rare cases, the abuse of surgical anesthetics is usually limited to a small percentage of health care workers, because access to anesthetic gases is carefully controlled.

[2]Technically, alcohol might be classified as a solvent. However, since the most common method of alcohol use/abuse is through oral ingestion, ethyl alcohol will not be discussed in this chapter.

Fornazzazri, 1988; Morton, 1987). For example, the maximum permitted exposure to toluene fumes in the workplace is 50–100 parts per million (ppm) (Crowley, 2000). But when toluene is used as an inhalant, the users may willingly expose themselves to levels 100 times as high as the maximum permitted industrial exposure level.

Once in the brain, the inhalants are thought to alter the normal function of the membranes of the neurons. There is preliminary evidence that the inhalants affect the gamma-amino-butyric acid (GABA) and/or N-methyl-D-aspartate (NMDA) neurotransmitter systems (Crowley & Sakai, 2004). However, the effect of a specific inhalant on neuron function is dependent on the exact compounds being abused. There is no standard formula by which to estimate the biological half-life of an inhalant, since so many different chemicals are abused. It should be noted, however, that the half-life of most solvents tends to be longer in obese users than in thin ones (Hartman, 1995). As a general rule, the half-life of the various compounds commonly abused through inhalation might range from hours to days, depending on the exact chemicals being abused (Brooks et al., 1996).

Either directly or indirectly, the compounds that are inhaled for recreational purposes are *all* toxic to the human body to one degree or another (Blum, 1984; Fornazzazri, 1988; Morton, 1987). But most of what is known about the effects of these chemicals is based on the short-term impact on the individual. There is very little research into the effects of chronic exposure to many of the compounds abused by inhalant users. For these reasons, it is difficult to talk about the pharmacology of the inhalants.[3] Ultimately, the material devoted to this topic would be many tens of thousands of pages long, as there are literally thousands of compounds that might be abused by inhalation. But behavioral observations of animals who have been exposed to inhalants suggest that many inhalants act like alcohol or barbiturates on the brain. Indeed, alcohol and the benzodiazepines have been found to potentiate the effects of many inhalants such as toluene. However, ultimately, the pharmacology of a given inhalant will depend on the various chemicals found in the specific

compound being abused. Such compounds often contain dozens or scores of different chemicals.

Scope of the Problem

Although the mass media most often focus on inhalant abuse in the United States, in reality it is a worldwide problem (Spiller & Krenzelok, 1997). Inhalant abuse is growing in popularity, increasing by 44% in sixth graders in recent years ("Huffing Can Kill Your Child," 2004). In the United States, the group most likely to abuse inhalants is children and adolescents, especially boys in their early teens, who live in poor or rural areas where more expensive drugs of abuse are not easily available (Drummer & Odell, 2001; Henretig, 1996; Jaffe, 1989; Spiller & Krenzelok, 1997).

Just under 16% of eighth graders surveyed in 2003 admitted to having abused an inhalant at least once, a percentage lower than the 21.6% of eighth graders who admitted to having abused an inhalant in 1996 (Anderson & Loomis, 2003; Johnston, O'Malley, & Bachman, 2003a). There is mixed evidence that inhalants are becoming increasingly popular with younger teens (Anderson & Loomis, 2003; Greydanus & Patel, 2003). Behaviorally, most adolescents who abuse inhalants will do so only a few times and then stop without going on to develop other drug-use problems (Crowley, 2000). The mean age for first-time inhalant abuse is about 13 years (Anderson & Loomis, 2003), and the mean age of inhalant abusers is about 16.6 years (with a standard deviation of 7.3 years) (Spiller & Krenzelok, 1997).

Inhalant abuse is most popular among 11- to 13-year-olds, after which it becomes less and less common (Brooks et al., 1996). However, there are reports of children as young as 7 or 8 years of age abusing inhalants (Henretig, 1996). Physical dependence on inhalants is quite rare, with only about 4% of those who abuse inhalants becoming dependent on them (Crowley & Sakai, 2004). But it is believed that for children and adolescents, inhalants are the most commonly abused substance after alcohol and tobacco (Wilson-Tucker & Dash, 1995). The practice of abusing inhalants appears to involve boys more often than girls by a ratio of about 3:1 (Crowley, 2000). Inhalant users are usually between 10 and 15 years of age (Miller & Gold, 1991b). In England, 3% to 10% of the adolescents asked admitted to the use of inhalants at least once, and about 1%

[3]Hartman (1995) provides an excellent technical summary of the neuropsychological effects of chronic exposure to some of the more common industrial solvents.

were thought to be current users (Esmail et al., 1993). The most commonly abused compounds appear to be spray paint and gasoline, which collectively accounted for 61% of the compounds abused by subjects in a study by Spiller and Krenzelok (1997).

Unfortunately, for a minority of those who abuse them, the inhalants appear to function as a "gateway" chemical, setting the stage for further drug use in later years. Approximately one-third of the children/adolescents who abuse inhalants go on to abuse one or more of the traditional drugs of abuse within 4 years (Brunswick, 1989). Crowley (2000) reported, for example, that people who admitted to the use of inhalants were 45 times as likely to have used self-injected drugs, whereas individuals who admitted to the use of both inhalants and marijuana were 89 times as likely to have injected drugs as the general population.

Why Are Inhalants So Popular?

The inhalants are utilized by children/adolescents for several reasons. First, these chemicals have a rapid onset of action, usually a few seconds. Second, inhalant users report pleasurable effects, including a sense of euphoria, when they use these chemicals. Third, and perhaps most important, the inhalants are relatively inexpensive and are easily available to children or adolescents (Cohen, 1977). Virtually all of the commonly used inhalants may be easily purchased, without legal restrictions being placed on their sale to teenagers. An additional advantage for the user is that the inhalants are usually available in small, easily hidden packages.

Unfortunately, as we will discuss in the next section, many of the inhalants are capable of causing harm and even death to the user. The inhalant abuser thus runs a serious risk whenever he or she begins to "huff."[4]

Method of Administration

Inhalants can be abused in a number of ways depending on the specific chemical involved. Some compounds may be inhaled directly from the container, a practice called "sniffing" or "snorting" (Anderson & Loomis, 2003). Other compounds, such as glue and adhesives,

[4]See Glossary.

may be poured into a plastic bag, which is then placed over the mouth and nose so that the individual can inhale the fumes, a practice called "bagging" (Anderson & Loomis, 2003; Esmail et al., 1993; Nelson, 2000). Sometimes, the compound is poured into a rag that is then placed over the individual's mouth and nose, a practice called "huffing" (Anderson & Loomis, 2003; Nelson, 2000).

Fumes from aerosol cans may also be inhaled directly or sprayed into the mouth, according to Esmail et al. (1993). Finally, some users have attempted to boil the substance to be abused, so that they might inhale the fumes (Nelson, 2000). Obviously, if the substance being boiled is flammable, there is a significant risk of fire if the compound should ignite.

Subjective Effects of Inhalants

The initial effects of the fumes on the individual might include a feeling of hazy euphoria, somewhat like the feeling of intoxication caused by alcohol, although nausea and vomiting may also occur (Anderson & Loomis, 2003; Crowley, 2000; Henretig, 1996; McHugh, 1987). Inhalant-induced feelings of euphoria usually last less than 30 minutes (McHugh, 1987). Other reported effects include a floating sensation, decreased inhibitions, amnesia, slurred speech, excitement, double vision, ringing in the ears, and hallucinations (Blum, 1984; Kaminski, 1992; Morton, 1987; Schuckit, 2000). Occasionally, the individual will feel as if he or she is omnipotent, and episodes of violence have been reported (Morton, 1987). These effects are usually short-lived, lasting around 45 minutes (Mirin et al., 1991; Schuckit, 2000). After the initial euphoria, depression of the central nervous system (CNS) develops. The stages of inhalant intoxication are summarized in Figure 16.1.

The inhalant-induced euphoria is not achieved without some aftereffects. Some inhalant abusers experience an inhalant-induced hangover, which usually will clear "in minutes to a few hours" (Westermeyer, 1987, p. 903). Abusers also report a residual sense of drowsiness and/or stupor, which will last for several hours after the last use of inhalants (Kaplan, Sadock, & Grebb, 1994; Miller & Gold, 1991b). Further, there have been reports of the inhalant-induced headache reported by many users and lasting for several days after the last use (Heath, 1994).

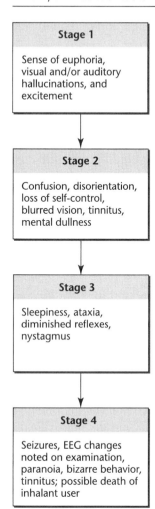

FIGURE 16.1 The stages of inhalant abuse.

Complications From Inhalant Abuse

When the practice of abusing the inhalants first surfaced, most health care professionals did not think it could cause many serious complications. However, in the last quarter of the 20th century, researchers uncovered evidence that inhalant abuse might cause a wide range of physical problems. Depending on the concentration and the compound being abused, even a single episode of abuse might result in the user's developing symptoms of solvent toxicity (Hartman, 1995).

A partial list of the possible consequences of inhalant abuse includes the following: (Anderson & Loomis, 2003; Brunswick, 1989; Crowley & Sakai, 2004; Hartman, 1995; Henretig, 1996; Karch, 1996; Monroe, 1995; Morton, 1987; Weaver, Jarvis, & Schnoll, 1999):

Liver damage

Cardiac arrhythmias[5]

Kidney damage or failure, which may become permanent

Transient changes in lung function

Anoxia and/or respiratory depression possibly to the point of respiratory arrest

Reduction in blood cell production possibly to the point of aplastic anemia

Possible permanent organic brain damage (including dementia, and inhalant-induced organic psychosis)

Permanent muscle damage secondary to the development of rhabdomyolysis[6]

Vomiting, with the possibility of the user aspirating some of the material being vomited, resulting in death

In addition to the effects listed above, inhalant abuse might also cause damage to the bone marrow, sinusitis (irritation of the sinus membranes), erosion of the nasal mucosal tissues, and laryngitis (Crowley & Sakai, 2004; Henretig, 1996; Westermeyer, 1987). The individual might develop a cough or wheezing, and inhalant abuse can exacerbate asthma in individuals prone to this disorder (Anderson & Loomis, 2003). There also may be chemical burns on the skin (Anderson & Loomis, 2003).

The impact of the inhalants on the central nervous system (CNS) are perhaps the most profound, if only because inhalant abusers are usually so young. Many of the inhalants have been shown to cause damage to the central nervous system, resulting in such problems as cerebellar ataxia,[7] tremor, peripheral neuropathies,

[5]See Glossary.

[6]See Glossary.

[7]A loss of coordination caused by physical damage to a region of the brain that is involved in motor coordination.

memory problems, coma, optic neuropathy, and deafness (Anderson & Loomis, 2003; Brooks et al., 1996; Fornazzazri, 1988; Maas, Ashe, Spiegel, Zee, & Leigh, 1991). One study found that 44% of chronic inhalant abusers had abnormal magnetic resonance imaging (MRI) results, compared with just 25% of chronic cocaine abusers (Mathias, 2002).

Inhalant abuse has been classified as "one of the leading causes of death in those under 18" (Esmail et al., 1993, p. 359). Death might occur the first time the individual uses one of these compounds or the 200th time ("Huffing Can Kill Your Child," 2004). Each year, between 100 and 1,000 deaths in the United States are directly attributable to inhalant abuse (Hartman, 1995; Wisneiwski, 1994).

Depending on the compound being used, there is a very real danger that the individual using an inhalant might be exposed to toxic levels of various heavy metals such as copper or lead (Crowley, 2000). For example, gasoline sniffing by children is a major cause of lead poisoning (Henretig, 1996; Monroe, 1995; Parras, Patier, & Ezpeleta, 1988). Exposure to lead is a serious condition that may have long-term consequences for the child's physical and emotional growth. Further, although the standard neurological examination is often unable to detect signs of solvent-induced organic brain damage until it is quite advanced, sensitive neuropsychological tests often find signs of significant neurological dysfunction in workers who are exposed to solvent fumes on a regular basis (Hartman, 1995).

Toluene is found in many forms of glue and is the solvent most commonly abused (Hartman, 1995). Researchers have found that chronic toluene exposure can result in intellectual impairment (Crowley & Sakai, 2004; Maas et al., 1991; Rosenberg, 1989). Finally, researchers have identified what appears to be a withdrawal syndrome that develops following extended periods of inhalant abuse and is very similar to alcohol-induced "delirium tremens" (DTs) (Blum, 1984; Mirin et al., 1991). But the exact withdrawal syndrome that develops after episodes of inhalant abuse depends on the specific chemicals being abused, the duration of inhalant abuse, and the dosage levels (Miller & Gold, 1991b). Some of the symptoms of inhalant withdrawal include muscle tremors, irritability, anxiety, insomnia,

muscle cramps, hallucinations, sweating, nausea, and possible seizures (Crowley, 2000).

Inhalant abuse and suicide. Espeland (1997) suggested a disturbing relationship between inhalant abuse and adolescent suicide. Some suicidal adolescents put inhalant into a plastic bag and then put the bag over their heads. The plastic bag is then closed about the head/neck area, allowing the inhalant to cause the individual to lose consciousness. The person will quickly suffocate as the oxygen in the bag is used up, and unless found, will die. In such cases, it is quite difficult to determine whether the individual *intended* to end his or her own life or if the death was an unintended side effect of the inhalant-abuse method.

Anesthetic Misuse

Berger and Dunn (1982) reported that nitrous oxide and ether, the first two anesthetic gases to be used, were first introduced as recreational drugs rather than as surgical anesthetics. Indeed, these gases were routinely utilized as intoxicants for quite some time before they were utilized by medicine. Horace Wells, who introduced medicine to nitrous oxide, noted the pain-killing properties of this gas when he observed a person under its influence trip and gash his leg, without any apparent pain (Brecher, 1972). As medical historians know, the first planned demonstration of nitrous oxide as an anesthetic was something less than a success. Because nitrous oxide has a duration of effect of about 2 minutes following a single dose and thus must be continuously administered, the patient returned to consciousness in the middle of the operation and started to scream in pain. However, in spite of this rather frightening beginning, physicians began to understand how to use nitrous oxide properly to bring about surgical anesthesia, and it is now an important anesthetic agent (Brecher, 1972).

Julien (1992) noted that the pharmacological effects observed with the general anesthetics are the same as those observed with the barbiturates. There is a dose-related range of effects from the anesthetic ranging from an initial period of sedation and relief from anxiety on through sleep and analgesia. At extremely high dosage levels, the anesthetic gases can cause death.

Below is a discussion of one of the most commonly abused anesthetic gases: nitrous oxide.

Nitrous oxide. This gas presents a special danger as precautions must be observed to maintain a proper oxygen supply to the individual's brain. Room air alone will not provide sufficient oxygen to the brain when nitrous oxide is used (Julien, 1992), and oxygen must be supplied under pressure to avoid the danger of hypoxia (a decreased oxygen level in the blood that can result in permanent brain damage if not corrected immediately). In surgery, the anesthesiologist takes special care to ensure that the patient has an adequate oxygen supply. However, few nitrous oxide abusers have access to supplemental oxygen sources and thus they run the risk of serious injury, or even death, when they use this compound.

It is possible to achieve a state of hypoxia from virtually any of the inhalants, including nitrous oxide (McHugh, 1987). In spite of this danger, nitrous oxide is a popular drug of abuse in some circles (Schwartz, 1989). Nitrous oxide abusers report that the gas is able to bring about a feeling of euphoria, giddiness, hallucinations, and a loss of inhibitions (Lingeman, 1974). Dental students, dentists, medical school students, and anesthesiologists, all of whom have access to surgical anesthetics through their professions, will occasionally abuse agents such as nitrous oxide as well as ether, chloroform, trichlorothylene and halothane. Also, children and adolescents will occasionally abuse the nitrous oxide used as a propellant in certain commercial products by finding ways to release the gas from the container. In rare cases, abusers might even make their own nitrous oxide, risking possible death from impurities in the compound they produce (Brooks et al., 1996).

The volatile anesthetics are not biotransformed by the body to any significant degree but enter and leave unchanged (Glowa, 1986). Once the source of the gas is removed, the concentration of the gas in the brain begins to drop and normal circulation brings the brain to a normal state of consciousness within moments. While the person is under the influence of the anesthetic gas, however, the ability of the brain cells to react to painful stimuli seems to be reduced.

The medicinal use of nitrous oxide, chloroform, and ether are confined for the most part to dental or general surgery. Very rarely, however, one will encounter a person who has abused or is currently abusing these agents. Little information is available concerning the dangers of this practice, nor is there much information about the side effects of prolonged use.

Abuse of Nitrites

Two different forms of nitrites are commonly abused: *amyl nitrite* and its close chemical cousins *butyl nitrite* and *isabutyl nitrite*. When inhaled, these substances function as coronary vasodilators, allowing more blood to flow to the heart. This effect made amyl nitrite useful in the control of angina pectoris. The drug was administered in small glass containers, embedded in cloth layers. The user would "snap" or "pop" the container with his or her fingers and inhale the fumes in order to control the chest pain of angina pectoris.[8]

With the introduction of nitroglycerine preparations, which are as effective as amyl nitrite but lack many of its disadvantages, amyl nitrite fell into disfavor and few people now use it for medical purposes (Schwartz, 1989). It does continue to have a limited role in diagnostic medicine and the medical treatment of cyanide poisoning.

Amyl nitrite is available only by prescription, but butyl nitrite and isabutyl nitrite are often sold legally by mail order houses or in speciality stores, depending on specific state regulations. In many areas, butyl nitrite is sold as a room deodorizer, packaged in small bottles that may be purchased for under 10 dollars. Both chemicals are thought to cause the user to experience a prolonged, more intense orgasm when they are inhaled just before the individual reaches orgasm. However, amyl nitrite is also known to be a cause of delayed orgasm and ejaculation in the male user (Finger, Lund, & Slagel, 1997). Aftereffects include an intense, sudden headache, increased pressure of the fluid in the eyes (a danger for those with glaucoma), possible weakness, nausea, and possible cerebral hemorrhage (Schwartz, 1989).

---

[8]It was from the distinctive sound of the glass breaking within the cloth ampule that both amyl nitrite and butyl nitrite have come to be known as "poppers" or "snappers" by those who abuse these chemicals.

When abused, both amyl nitrite and butyl nitrite will cause a brief (90 second) rush that includes dizziness, giddiness, and the rapid dilation of blood vessels in the head (Schwartz, 1989), which in turn causes an increase in intracranial pressure ("Research on Nitrites," 1989). It is this increase in intracranial pressure that may on occasion contribute to the rupture of unsuspected aneurysms, causing the individual to suffer a cerebral hemorrhage (stroke).

The use of nitrites is common among male homosexuals and may contribute to the spread of the virus that causes AIDS ("Research on Nitrites," 1989; Schwartz, 1989). By causing the dilation of blood vessels in the body, including the anus, the use of either amyl or butyl nitrite during anal intercourse (a common practice for male homosexuals) may actually aid the transmission of HIV from the active to the passive member of the sexual unit ("Research on Nitrites," 1989). Given the multitude of adverse effects, one questions why the use of these substances is popular during sexual intercourse.

Summary

For many individuals, the inhalants are the first chemicals abused. For the most part, inhalant abuse seems to be a phase that mainly involves teenagers, although occasionally children will abuse an inhalant. The abuse of these chemicals appears to be a phase, during which the individual will engage in the abuse of them on an episodic basis.

Individuals who use these inhalants do not usually do so for more than 1 or 2 years. But some will continue to inhale the fumes of gasoline, solvents, certain forms of glue, or other substances for many years. The effects of these chemicals on the individual seem to be rather short-lived. There is evidence, however, that prolonged use of certain agents can result in permanent damage to the kidneys, brain, and liver. Death, either through hypoxia or through prolonged exposure to inhalants, is possible. Very little is known about the the effects of prolonged use of this class of chemicals.

CHAPTER SEVENTEEN

The Unrecognized Problem of Steroid Abuse and Addiction

Introduction

The problem of steroid abuse/addiction might be viewed as a social disease. Society places much emphasis on appearances and winning. To achieve the goal of victory, athletes look for something—anything—that will give them an edge over the competition. This might include the use of a certain coaching technique or special equipment, or the use of a chemical substance designed to enhance performace. A whole industry has evolved to help people modify their appearance so they might better approximate the social ideal of size, shape, and appearance.

For decades persistent rumors have circulated that anabolic steroids are able to significantly enhance athletic performance or physical appearance (Dickensheets, 2001). These rumors are fueled by real or suspected use of a steroid by different athletes or teams of athletes. Rather than risk failure, others have initiated the unsupervised use of anabolic steroids, with disastrous results. In response to an ever-growing number of adverse reactions to the steroids, federal and state officials placed rigid controls on their use in the 1990s.[1] However the rumors and the problem still persist. In reality, very little is known about anabolic steroid abuse (Karch, 2002). This is unfortunate, because in spite of their considerable potential to harm the user, these substances are viewed by many as a means to increase muscle mass or improve physical appearance (Pope & Brower, 2004). Recognition of the problem of anabolic steroid abuse is slowly growing,

[1]In response to these controls, a $4 billion a year industry in what are known as "nutritional" supplements, which are composed of various combinations of amino acids, vitamins, proteins, and naturally occurring simulants such as ephedrine, has developed (Solotaroff, 2002). As is true of the anabolic steroids, the consequences of long-term use of many of these compounds at high dosage levels are not known.

however, and mental health and chemical dependency professionals should have a working knowledge of the effects of this class of medications.

An Introduction to the Anabolic Steroids

The term *anabolic* refers to the action of this family of drugs to increase the speed of growth of body tissues (Redman, 1990) or to their ability to force body cells to retain nitrogen (and thus indirectly enhance tissue growth) (Bagatell & Bremner, 1996). The term *steroids* indicates that the steroids are chemically similar to testosterone, the male sex hormone. Because of the chemical similarity with testosterone, steroids have a masculinizing (androgenic) effect upon the user (Landry & Primos, 1990). At times, the anabolic steroids are referred to as the *anabolic-androgenic* steroids.

Athletes abuse steroids because they are thought to (a) increase lean muscle mass, (b) increase muscle strength, (c) increase aggressiveness, and (d) reduce the period of time necessary for recovery between exercise periods (Karch, 2002). On occasion, they may be abused because of their ability to bring about a sense of euphoria (Johnson, 1990; Kashkin, 1992; Lipkin, 1989; Schrof, 1992). However, this is not the primary reason most people abuse the anabolic steroids. Repeated, heavy physical exercise can actually result in damage to muscle tissues. The anabolic steroids have been found to stimulate protein synthesis, a process that indirectly may help muscle tissue development, possibly increase muscle strength, and limit the amount of damage done to muscle tissues through heavy physical exercise (Congeni & Miller, 2002; Gottesman, 1992; Pettine, 1991; Pope & Katz, 1990).

Athletes are not the only people vulnerable to steroid abuse. Many nonathletic users believe that steroid use will help them look more physically attractive (Bahrke,

1990; Brower, 1993; Corrigan, 1996; Johnson, 1990; Pettine, 1991; Pope & Brower, 2004; Schrof, 1992). In addition, there is a subgroup of people, especially some law-enforcement/security officers, who abuse steroids because of their belief that these substances will increase their strength and aggressiveness (Corrigan, 1996; Galloway, 1997; Schrof, 1992).

Medical Uses of Anabolic Steroids

Although the anabolic steroids have been in use since the mid 1950s, there still is no clear consensus on how they work (Wadler, 1994). There are few approved uses for these compounds (Dobs, 1999; Sturmi & Diorio, 1998). It is thought that the steroids force the body to increase protein synthesis and inhibit the action of chemicals known as the glucocorticoids, which cause tissue break down. In a medical setting, the anabolic steroids might be used to promote tissue growth and help damaged tissue recover from injury (Shannon, Wilson, & Stang, 1995).

Physicians may also use a steroid to treat certain forms of anemia, help patients regain weight after periods of severe illness, treat endometriosis, treat delayed puberty in adolescents, and as an adjunct to the treatment of certain forms of breast cancer in women (Bagatell & Bremner, 1996; Congeni & Miller, 2002). The steroids may also promote the growth of bone tissue following injuries to the bone in certain cases and might be useful in the treatment of certain forms of osteoporosis (Congeni & Miller, 2002). There is evidence that the steroids might be of value in treating AIDS-related weight loss (the so-called wasting syndrome) and certain forms of chronic kidney failure (Dobs, 1999).

The anabolic steroids can be broken down into two classes: (a) those that are active when used orally and (b) those that are active only when injected into muscle tissue. Anabolic steroids intended for oral use tend to be more easily administered but have a shorter half-life and are also more toxic to the liver than parenteral forms of steroids (Bagatell & Bremner, 1996; Tanner, 1995).

The Legal Status of Anabolic Steroids

Since 1990, anabolic steroids have been classified as a Category III[2] controlled substance, available with

[2]See Appendix 4.

a doctor's prescription for certain medical purposes. The law identified 28 different anabolic steroids as being illegal for nonmedical purposes, and their sale by individuals who are not licensed to sell medications was made a crime punishable by a prison term of up to 5 years (10 years if the steroids are sold to minors) (Fultz, 1991).

Scope of the Problem of Steroid Abuse

The true scope of anabolic steroid abuse in the United States is not known (Karch, 2002). It is thought that males are more likely to abuse steroids than females, possibly by as much as a 13:1 ratio, in part because few adolescent girls are interested in adding muscle mass (Pope & Brower, 2004). Estimates of the total number of steroid abusers in the United States range from more than 1 million people who either are abusing or have abused steroids to as many as 3 million current users (Dickensheets, 2001). In Canada, some 83,000 people between the ages of 11 and 18 admitted to having used a steroid at least once in the past year (Peters, Copeland, & Dillon, 1999). Steroid abuse is not unknown in high school, with 3.5% of the high school seniors of the class of 2003 admitting to the use of steroids (Johnston, O'Malley, & Bachman, 2003a). In contrast to use of the other recreational chemicals, most users do not use steroids as drugs of abuse until early adulthood. The median age for anabolic steroid abusers is 18 (Karch, 2002). Most college-age steroid users did not begin to use these compounds until just before starting or after they entered college (Brower, 1993; Dickensheets, 2001).

Sources and Methods of Steroid Abuse

Because of their illegal status and strict controls on their being prescribed by physicians, most anabolic steroids are obtained from illicit sources (Galloway, 1997). These sources include drugs smuggled into the United States or legitimate pharmaceuticals that are diverted to the black market. There is a thriving market for what are known as "designer" (Knight, 2003, p. 114) steroids, which are not detected by standard laboratory tests utilized by sports regulatory agencies. Another common source of steroids is veterinary products, which are sold on the street for use by humans. These compounds are distributed through an informal network that frequently is centered around health clubs or gyms (Johnson, 1990; Schrof, 1992).

If a physician suspects that a patient has been abusing anabolic steroids, he or she might confront the individual and force a confession that the person has been using anabolic steroids for personal reasons. Some physicians will attempt to limit their patients' use of anabolic steroids, promising to prescribe medications for them if they will promise to use *only* the medications prescribed by the physician (Breo, 1990). This misguided attempt at "harm reduction"[3] is made by the physician on the grounds that he or she would then be able to monitor and control the individual's steroid use. However, in most cases the user supplements the prescribed medications with steroids from other sources. Thus, this method of harm reduction is not recommended for physicians (Breo, 1990).

Rarely, users will obtain their steroids by diverting[4] prescribed medications or by obtaining multiple prescriptions for steroids from different physicians. But between 80% (Bahrke, 1990) and 90% (Tanner, 1995) of the steroids used by athletes comes from the black market,[5] with many of the steroids smuggled into the United States coming from the former Soviet Union (Karch, 2002). Various estimates of the scope of the illicit steroid market in the United States range from a $100 million (DuRant, Rickert, Ashworth, Newman, & Slavens, 1993; Middleman & DuRant, 1996) to a $300–500 million (Fultz, 1991; Wadler, 1994) to a $1 billion dollar a year industry (Hoberman & Yesalis, 1995).

There are more than 1,000 known derivatives of the testosterone molecule (Sturmi & Diorio, 1998). Because performance-enhancing drugs are prohibited in many sports, chemists will attempt to alter the basic testosterone molecule to develop a designer steroid that might be invisible to the current tests used to detect such compounds. An example of such a designer steroid is tetrahydrogestrinone (THG). This compound appears to have "all the hallmarks of an anabolic steroid, crafted to escape detection in urinanalysis

tests" (Kondro, 2003, p. 1466). THG was undetectable by standard urine tests until late 2003. Acting on an anonymous tip and a syringe, the Olympic Analytical Laboratory in Los Angeles developed a test that would expose this steroid in the urine of athletes. Armed with the new test, various regulatory agencies have conducted urine toxicology tests on samples provided by athletes in various fields, prompting a flurry of reports that various athletes had tested positive for this substance, were suspected of having abused it, or were about to be suspended for having submitted a urine sample that had traces of THG in it ("Athletes Caught," 2003; Knight, 2003).

Anabolic steroids may be injected into muscle tissue, taken orally, or used both ways at once. Anabolic steroid abusers have developed a vocabulary of their own to describe many aspects of steroid abuse, the most common of which are summarized in Table 17.1.

Many of the practices described in Table 17.1 are quite common among steroid abusers. For example, fully 61% of steroid-abusing weight lifters were found to have engaged in the practice of "stacking" steroids (Brower, Blow, Young, & Hill, 1991; Pope & Brower, 2004; Porcerelli & Sandler, 1998). Some steroid abusers who engage in the process of "pyramiding" are, at the midpoint of the cycle, using massive amounts of steroids. Episodes of pyramiding are interspaced with periods of abstinence from anabolic steroid use that may last several weeks, months (Landry & Primos, 1990), or even as long as a year (Kashkin, 1992). Unfortunately, during the periods of abstinence, much of the muscle mass gained by the use of steroids will be lost, sometimes quite rapidly. When this happens, anabolic steroid abusers often become frightened into prematurely starting another cycle of steroid abuse in order to recapture the muscle mass that has disappeared (Corrigan, 1996; Schrof, 1992; Tanner, 1995).

Problems Associated With Anabolic Steroid Abuse

Numerous adverse effects of anabolic steroids have been documented at relatively low doses when these medications were used to treat medical conditions (Hough & Kovan, 1990). The potential consequences of long-term steroid abuse are not known (Kashkin, 1992; Porcerelli & Sandler, 1998; Schrof, 1992; Wadler, 1994). One reason

[3]See Glossary.

[4]See Glossary.

[5]As used here, *black market* is a term that is applied to any steroid obtained from illicit sources and then sold for human consumption.

TABLE 17.1   Some Terms Associated With Steroid Abuse

Term	Definition
Blending	Mixing different compounds for use at the same time.
Bulking up	Increasing muscle mass through steroid use. Nonusers also use the term to refer to the process of eating special diets and exercising in order to add muscle mass before a sporting event such as a football game or race.
Cycling	Taking multiple doses of a steroid(s) over a period of time, according to a schedule, with drug holidays built into the schedule.
Doping	Using drugs to improve performance.
Injectables	Steroids that are designed for injection.
Megadosing	Taking massive amounts of steroids, usually by injection or a combination of injection and oral administration.
Orals	Steroids designed for oral use.
Pyramiding	Taking anabolic steroids according to a schedule that calls for larger and larger doses each day for a period of time, followed by a pattern of smaller doses each day.
Shotgunning	Taking steroids on an inconsistent basis.
Tapering	Slowly decreasing the dosage level of a steroid being abused.

for this lack of information is that many steroid abusers utilize dosage levels that are often 10 (Hough & Kovan, 1990), 40–100 (Congeni & Miller, 2002), or even 1,000 times the maximum recommended therapeutic dosage level for these compounds (Council on Scientific Affairs, 1990a; Wadler, 1994).

In one study, the dosage range of steroids being used by a sample of weight lifters was between 2 and 26 times the recommended dosage level for these agents (Brower, Blow, Young, & Hill, 1991). Another study found that the *lowest* dose of anabolic steroids being used by a group of weight lifters was still 350% above the usual therapeutic dose when the same drug was used by physicians (Landry & Primos, 1990). There is very little information available on the effects of the anabolic steroids on the user at these dosage levels (Johnson, 1990; Kashkin, 1992). It is known that the effects of the anabolic steroids on muscle tissue last for several weeks after the drugs are discontinued (Pope & Katz, 1991). This characteristic is known to muscle builders, who often discontinue their use of steroids before competition in order to avoid having

their steroid use detected by urine toxicological screens (Knight, 2003).

The adverse effects of anabolic steroids depend on the (a) route of administration used, (b) the specific drugs taken, (c) the dose utilized, (d) the frequency of use, (e) the health of the individual, and (f) the age of the individual (Johnson, 1990). However, even at recommended dosage levels, steroids are capable of causing sore throat or fever, vomiting (with or without blood being mixed into the vomit), dark-colored urine, bone pain, nausea, unusual weight gain or headache, and a range of other side effects (Congeni & Miller, 2002).

Although physicians and sports officials will often conduct blood/urine tests in an attempt to detect illicit steroid abuse, there is an ongoing "arms race" between the steroid abusers and regulatory agencies. The former search for anabolic steroids or similar compounds that cannot be detected by urine/blood toxicology testing, whereas the latter search for new methods by which unauthorized steroid use might be detected. A good example of this is the controversy over tetrahydrogestrinone (THG) that erupted in late

2003, discussed above. Thus, a "clean" urine sample does not rule out steroid use in modern sporting events or the possibility that the individual is at risk for any of a wide range of complications.

Complications of Steroid Abuse

The reproductive system. Males who utilize steroids at the recommended dosage levels might experience enlargement of breasts[6] (to the point that breast formation is similar to that seen in adolescent girls). The male steroid abuser might also experience increased frequency of erections or continual erections (a condition known as priapism, which is a medical emergency), unnatural hair growth/hair loss, reduced sperm production, and a frequent urge to urinate. In men, steroid abuse may cause the degeneration of the testicles, enlargement of the prostate gland, difficulty in urination, impotence, and sterility (Blue & Lombardo, 1999; Galloway, 1997; Kashkin, 1992; Pope & Brower, 2004; Pope & Katz, 1994; Sturmi & Diorio, 1998). On rare occasions steroid abuse has resulted in carcinoma (cancer) of the prostate (Johnson, 1990; Landry & Primos, 1990; Tanner, 1995) and urinary obstruction (Council on Scientific Affairs, 1990a). Both men and women might experience infertility and changes in libido as a result of steroid abuse (Sturmi & Diorio, 1998).

Women who use steroids at recommended dosage levels may experience an abnormal enlargement of the clitoris, irregular menstrual periods, unnatural hair growth and/or hair loss, a deepening of the voice, and a possible reduction in the size of the breasts (Galloway, 1997; Pope & Brower, 2004; Pope & Katz, 1988; Redman, 1990; Tanner, 1995). The menstrual irregularities caused by steroid use will often disappear after the steroids are discontinued (Johnson, 1990). The Council on Scientific Affairs (1990a) suggested that women who use steroids may experience beard growth, which is one example of the unnatural hair growth pattern anabolic steroids might cause. Another possible outcome is for the woman who is using anabolic steroids to develop "male pattern" baldness. Often, steroid-induced baldness in a woman is irreversible (Tanner, 1995).

The liver, kidneys, and digestive system. Steroid abusers may experience altered liver function, which may be detected through blood tests such as the serum glautamic-oxaloacetic transaminase (SGOT) and the serum glautamic-pyruvic transaminase (SGPT) (Johnson, 1990; Karch, 2002; Sturmi & Diorio, 1998). Oral forms of anabolic steroids might be more likely to result in liver problems than injected forms (Tanner, 1995). Anabolic steroid abuse has been implicated as a cause of hepatoxicity[7] (Pope & Brower, 2004; Stimac, Milic, Dintinjana, Kovac, & Ristic, 2002). In addition, there is evidence that steriods, when used for periods of time at excessive doses, might contribute to the formation of both cancerous and benign liver tumors (Karch, 1996; Sturmi & Diorio, 1998; Tanner, 1995).

The cardiovascular system. Anabolic steroids are mainly abused by those who wish to increase muscle size. Unfortunately the heart is itself a muscle and it is affected by steroid use ("Steroids and Growth Hormones," 2003). Anabolic steroid abuse may cause hypertension, cardiomyopathy, and heart disease for some abusers. One mechanism for these effects is a steroid-induced reduction in high-density lipoprotein levels and a concurrent increase in the low-density lipoprotein levels by up to 36%, contributing to accelerated atherosclerosis of the heart and its surrounding blood vessels (Blue & Lombardo, 1999; Fultz, 1991; Johnson, 1990; Tanner, 1995).

Anabolic steroid abuse might also result in the user's experiencing a thrombotic stroke—a stroke caused by a blood clot in the brain (Karch, 2002; Tanner, 1995). Such strokes are a side effect of high doses of the anabolic steroids, which cause blood platelets to clump together, forming clots. Researchers have also found evidence that steroids have a direct, dose-related cardiotoxic effect (Slovut, 1992). Indeed, there is evidence of physical changes in the structure of the heart of some steroid users, although the mechanism by which steroids cause this effect is not known (Middleman & DuRant, 1996).

The central nervous system. Although it was disputed in the latter part of the 20th century, researchers now accept the fact that anabolic steroids cause behavioral changes in the user. The massive doses of steroids utilized by some athletes has been identified as the trigger of a drug-induced psychosis in some

---

[6]Technically, this is called *gynecomastia*.

[7]See Glossary.

cases (Johnson, 1990; Kashkin, 1992; Pope & Brower, 2004; Pope & Katz, 1994; Pope, Katz, & Champoux, 1986). Kashkin (1992) reported that about 50% of steroid abusers will abuse other substances in an effort to control the side effects of the anabolic steroids. Some of the drugs that might be abused included diuretics (to counteract steroid-induced bloating) and antibiotics (to control steroid-induced acne).

Although most abusers reported minimal impact on measured aggression levels, Pope, Kouri, and Hudson (2000) found that 2% to 10% of male abusers became manic and/or developed other neuropsychiatric problems after abusing steroids. The authors found no significant premorbid sign that might identify those steroid abusers who would develop such problems as a result of their steroid use, raising questions as to why they responded so strongly to the chemicals they injected. Other responses noted in some of their subjects included depressive reactions or drug-induced psychotic reactions (Pope & Brower, 2004; Pope & Katz, 1987, 1988). Sometimes, the individual becomes violent after using steroids, a condition known by abusers as the "roid rage" (Fultz, 1991; Galloway, 1997; Johnson, 1990). In rare cases, steroid-induced violence has resulted in the death of the user or a victim who became the target of the abuser's anger (Pope, Phillips, & Olivardia, 2000), and it has been recommended that large, muscular, perpetrators of interpersonal violence be screened for steroid abuse (Pope & Brower, 2004).

In 1994, Pope and Katz carried out an investigation into the psychiatric side effects of anabolic steroid abuse. Their research sample was 88 steroid-abusing athletes and 68 individuals who were not abusing steroids. Twenty-three percent of the steroid-abusing athletes were found to have experienced a major mood disturbance, such as mania or depression, and an increased level of aggressiveness, which was attributed to their steroid use. This was illustrated by an incident in which one member of the sample of steroid abusers reportedly started to smash three different automobiles out of frustration over a traffic delay (Pope & Katz, 1994). Another individual was implicated in a murder plot, while yet a third beat his dog to death. Still another individual in the research sample rammed his head through a wooden door, and several others were expelled from their homes because of their threatening behavior ("The Back Letter," 1994). Other psychiatric effects of anabolic steroid abuse include loss of inhibition, lack of judgment, irritability, a "strange edgy feeling" (Corrigan, 1996, p. 222), impulsiveness, and antisocial behavior (Corrigan, 1996).

In the early 1990s a number of researchers challenged the suspected relationship between anabolic steroid abuse and increased violent tendencies. Yesalis, Kennedy, Kopstein, and Bahrke (1993) suggested that for some unknown reason, anabolic steroid abusers might have exaggerated their self-report of violent behavior noted in earlier studies. A second possibility, according to the authors, was that violent individuals are prone to abuse steroids for some unknown reason, giving the illusion of a causal relationship. However, by the start of the 21st century, the evidence suggesting a relationship between aggressive behavior and steroid abuse for at least a minority of steroid abusers has been clearly identified (Pope, Kouri, & Hudson, 2000; Pope, Phillips, & Olivardia, 2000).

Steroids have been identified as the cause of depressive reactions, especially during the withdrawal phase (Pope & Brower, 2004). Such depressive reactions seem to respond well to simple discontinuation of the offending substance(s) (Schuckit, 2000) or the selective serotonin reuptake inhibitors (SSRIs) (Pope & Brower, 2004). On occasion, steroid abusers have developed a form of body dysmorphic disorder, especially following their decision to discontinue steroid use (Pope & Brower, 2004). This condition responds well to psychotherapy combined with the use of the appropriate SSRI, according to the authors.

Other complications. Patients with medical conditions such as certain forms of breast cancer; diabetes mellitus; diseases of the blood vessels, kidney, liver, or heart; or males who suffer from prostate problems should not utilize steroids unless the physician is aware that the patient has these problems (United States Pharmacopeial Convention, 1990). The anabolic steroids are thought to be possibly carcinogenic (Johnson, 1990), and their use is not recommended for patients with either active tumors or a history of tumors except under a physician's supervision.

Other side effects caused by steroid use include severe acne (especially across the back) and possibly a foul odor on the breath (Redman, 1990). There has been one isolated case of unnatural bone degeneration that was attributed to the long-term use of steroids by a weight lifter (Pettine, 1991). Also, animal research suggests that anabolic steroids may contribute to the degeneration of tendons, a finding that is consistent with clinical case reports of athletes who are using anabolic steroids having tendons rupture under stress (Karch, 1996).

Surprisingly, although anabolic steroids are often abused to improve athletic performance, the evidence that steroids actually do improve the user's athletic abilities is mixed (Tanner, 1995). One factor that complicates research into athletic performance is the individual's belief that these drugs will improve his or her abilities. The authors suggested that the athlete's expectation of improved performance might contribute, at least in part, to the observed performance on the part of the user.

There is evidence that anabolic steroid abuse might prove to be a "gateway" to the abuse of other compounds such as narcotic analgesics (Kanayama, Cohane, Weiss, & Pope, 2003). The authors suggested that the abuse of anabolic steroids might be one avenue through which some individuals began to abuse opiates, especially as eight of their subjects first purchased opiates from the same source that sold them anabolic steroids. The authors proposed that a history of anabolic steroid abuse might be an under-recognized problem among those admitted to treatment for more traditional substance-use problems.

Growth patterns in the adolescent. Adolescents who use steroids run the risk of stunted growth, as these drugs may permanently stop bone growth (Johnson, 1990; Schrof, 1992). A further complication of steroid abuse by adolescents is that the tendons do not grow at the same accelerated rate as the bone tissues, producing increased strain on the tendons and a higher risk of injury to them (Galloway, 1997; Johnson, 1990).

Anabolic steroid abuse and blood infections. In addition to the complications of steroid abuse itself, individuals who abuse steroids through intramuscular or intravenous injection often share needles. These individuals run the same risk of contracting infections transmitted by contaminated needles as seen in heroin or cocaine addicts. Indeed, there have been cases of athletes contracting AIDS when they used a needle that had been used by another athlete who was infected (Kashkin, 1992).

Drug interactions between steroids and other chemicals. The anabolic steroids interact with a wide range of medications, including several drugs of abuse. Potentially serious drug interactions have been noted in cases where the individual has utilized acetaminophen in high doses while on steroids. The combination of these two drugs—steroids and acetaminophen—should be avoided except when the individual is being supervised by a physician. Patients who utilize Antabuse (disulfiram) should not take steroids, nor should individuals who are taking Trexan (naltrexone) anticonvulsant medications such as Dilantin (phenytoin), Depakene (valproic acid), or any of the phenothiazines (United States Pharmacopeial Convention, 1990).

Are Anabolic Steroids Addictive?

Surprisingly, when used for periods of time at high dosage levels, the anabolic steroids have an addictive potential. Some users have reported preoccupation with the use of these chemicals and a craving when they were not using steroids (Middleman & DuRant, 1996). Further, anabolic steroids have been known to bring about a sense of euphoria both when used for medical purposes and when abused (Fultz, 1991; Middleman & DuRant, 1996). This may explain why steroid use is so attractive to at least some of those who abuse this family of drugs.

There also is evidence to suggest that the user might become either physically or psychologically dependent on the anabolic steroids (Johnson, 1990). It has been estimated that 14%–69% of abusers will ultimately become addicted to anabolic steroids (Pope & Brower, 2005). Withdrawal from steroid addiction is very similar to cocaine withdrawal. Symptoms of withdrawal from steroids include depressive reactions, possibly to the point of suicide attempts (Pope & Brower, 2005), as well as sleep and appetite disturbances (Bower, 1991). Additional symptoms of the steroid withdrawal syndrome include fatigue, restlessness, anorexia, insomnia, and decreased libido (Brower, Blow, Young, & Hill, 1991).

Like their drug-using counterparts, many steroid abusers require gradual detoxification from the drugs over time as well as intensive psychiatric support to both limit the impact of withdrawal on the individual's life and to try to prevent a return to steroid use (Bower, 1991; Hough & Kovan, 1990; Kashkin & Kleber, 1989).

Robert Dimeff, Donald Malone, and John Lombardo (cited in Bower, 1991) listed some of the symptoms of steroid addiction:

1. The use of higher doses than originally intended.
2. A loss of control over the amount of steroids used.
3. A preoccupation with further steroid use.
4. The continued use of steroids in spite of the individual's awareness of the problems caused by their use.
5. The development of tolerance to steroids, and the need for larger doses to achieve the same effects as once brought on by lower doses.
6. The disruption of normal daily activities by steroid use.
7. The continued use of steroids to control or avoid withdrawal symptoms.

The authors suggested that three or more of these symptoms would identify those individuals who were dependent on steroids. Kashkin (1992) suggested that people who had gone through five or more cycles of steroid use were very likely to be heavy steroid users.

Summary

The anabolic steroids emerged as drugs of abuse in the latter part of the 20th century. But their popularity as drugs of abuse rest on different dynamics from those of the more traditional recreational substances. Adolescents and young adults abuse steroids because of a belief that these substances will increase aggressiveness and athletic ability, and improve personal appearances. Little is known about the effects of these drugs at the dosage levels utilized by individuals who abuse steroids. The identification and treatment of steroid abusers is primarily a medical issue, but substance abuse counselors should have a working knowledge of the effects and the complications of steroid abuse.

The Over-the-Counter Analgesics

Unexpected Agents of Abuse

Introduction

As was discussed earlier, the narcotic analgesics are not the only class of pharmaceuticals available to physicians for pain control. A second variety of medications with analgesic potential are available without the need for a physician's prescription and thus are collectively known as the over-the-counter (OTC) analgesics.[1] The OTC analgesics have a different mechanism of action from that of the narcotic analgesics, and these medications have unique side-effect profiles. Examples of non-narcotic analgesics include aspirin,[2] ibuprofen, ketoprofen, naproxen,[3] and acetaminophen. Collectively these chemicals are classified as over-the-counter medications. Although not considered drugs of abuse in the traditional sense, the OTC analgesics still have a significant potential for harm to the user, as evidenced by the 103,000 people hospitalizatized for complications and the 16,500 deaths caused by the OTC analgesics known as NSAIDs each year in just the United States (Graumlich, 2001). In this chapter we will focus on the OCT analgesics.

A Short History of the OTC Analgesics

Plants that contain chemical cousins of aspirin have long been used to control pain and fever. For example, willow bark, which contains salicin (from *Salix*, the Latin name for willow) has been recommended for the relief of pain and fever for 2,000 years (Stimmel, 1997b). Around the year 400 B.C.E. the Greek physician Hippocrates recommended that patients chew the bark of the willow tree for such conditions as headache, fever, and labor pain. But although willow bark was recognized as an herbal remedy for pain, the bitter taste, limited availability of the bark, and inconsistent effect forced physicians to utilize narcotic analgesics for even mild levels of pain. But because narcotic analgesics are both addictive and have a depressant effect on the central nervous system, they are a poor choice for the control of anything less than severe pain (Giacona, Dahl, & Hare, 1987).

Then, in the 1880s, the active agent of willow bark was isolated and ways were found to synthesize large amounts of this compound for commercial use. Aspirin, or *acetylsalicylic acid*, was first developed from salicin, which is found in the bark of certain willow trees. In the 1800s chemists learned to produce a chemical cousin of salicin known as salicylic acid, which had the same properties as salicin but was easier to produce. However, salicylic acid, like salicin, was found to cause a great deal of gastric distress when ingested, and so chemists continued to search for a compound with the advantages of salicin but which produced less intense side effects. Chemists in Germany introduced the compound acetylsalicylic acid in the year 1898, and Bayer pharmaceuticals marketed this compound under the brand name "Aspirin."

The term *aspirin* is a historical accident. Aspirin (with a capital "A") was introduced by the Bayer pharmaceuticals company as the brand name for their form of acetylsalicylic acid. Over time, however, the word aspirin (with a small "a") has come to mean *any* preparation of acetylsalicylic acid sold for human

---

[1]See Glossary.

[2]Aspirin is one of a family of related compounds, many of which have some analgesic, anti-inflammatory, antipyretic (anti-fever) action. However, since none of these aspirin-like chemical compounds is as powerful as aspirin, they will not be discussed.

[3]These agents were available only by prescription until the 1990s when they were approved by the Food and Drug Administration for use as over-the-counter drugs, in modified dosage levels.

use.[4] Like its chemical cousin salicin, aspirin is effective in controlling mild to moderate levels of pain while avoiding the danger of addiction found with the narcotic family of analgesics. It also produces less gastric distress than its chemical cousins salicylic acid and salicin. Further, aspirin is able to control inflammation and reduce fever. Because of its multiple uses, aspirin has become the most frequently used drug in the world (Mann & Plummer, 1991). An estimated 50 billion doses of aspirin are consumed around the world each year (Begley, 1997), of which 12.5 billion doses are ingested by Americans (Page, 2001).

Although aspirin's side effects are less intense than those of salicylic acid or salicin, it still has a significant potential to cause harm to the user. This was one of the reasons that pharmaceutical companies embarked on a search for pharmaceuticals with the analgesic antipyretic[5] and anti-inflammatory actions of aspirin, but which were safer to use. This search resulted in the discovery of a class of chemicals known as the *propionic acids*, from which the pharmaceutical agents now known as naproxen, ketoprofen, and ibuprofen were developed (Yost & Morgan, 1994). All of these agents were initially available in the United States only by prescription, but in the past two decades these three were approved for over-the-counter use in modified dosage form.

Acetaminophen was introduced as an OTC analgesic in this country in the 1950s. The term *acetaminophen* is based on a form of chemical shorthand. The true name of this chemical is *N-acetyl-para-aminophenol*, from which the word acetaminophen is obtained. This compound was first isolated in 1878, and its ability to reduce fever was identified shortly after its discovery. But at the time it was thought that acetaminophen would share the dangerous side effects found in a close chemical cousin, para-aminophenol, so it was set aside, and chemists did not pay much attention to this chemical until the early 1950s (Mann & Plummer, 1991).

By the early 1950s, sufficient evidence had accumulated to show that acetaminophen was much safer than para-aminophenol, and that it did not have the same potential for harm found in aspirin. A massive advertising campaign followed the introduction of acetaminophen, playing on the fact that aspirin might irritate the stomach whereas acetaminophen does not. This advertising campaign was successful, and by the start of the 21st century acetaminophen was the most common compound used for the control of fever on the planet (Sharma, 2003). However, aspirin still remains a popular OTC analgesic, and it still accounts for 28% of the OTC analgesic sales in this country ("Take 2 Aspirins," 1994).

Aspirin has been called "the most cost-effective drug available today" (Elwood, Hughes, & O'Brien, 1998, p. 587). It is such a potent drug that were it to be discovered today rather than a century ago, its use would be closely regulated and would be available only by prescription (Graedon & Ferguson, 1993). Indeed, since the early 1990s physicians have discovered that all of the OTC analgesics are far more toxic to the user, even at normal dosage levels, than had been thought earlier ("Strong Medicine," 1995).

The origin of the term NSAID. As will be discussed below, aspirin and the propionic acid derivatives have an anti-inflammatory effect. Another class of chemicals that have an anti-inflammatory effect is the adrenocortical steroids, potent agents whose function lies beyond the scope of this text. However, because aspirin and the propionic acid derivatives have a different chemical structure from that of the adrenocortical steroids, they are often called non-steroidal anti-inflammatory drugs (NSAIDs). There are approximately 20 NSAIDs currently in use in the United States, although most are available only by prescription. The exceptions to this rule are aspirin and the propionic acid derivatives ibuprofen, ketoprofen, and naproxen. The new COX-2 inhibitors, which are available only by prescription, are also classified as NSAIDs (Jackson & Hawkey, 2000).

Medical Uses of the OTC Analgesics

Aspirin. Aspirin was first introduced in 1897, and in spite of its age scientists are still discovering new uses for it. The most common application for aspirin is the control of mild to moderate levels of pain from such conditions as common headaches, neuralgia, the pain associated

---

[4]The manner in which this happened lies beyond the scope of this chapter but is reviewed in excellent detail by Mann and Plummer (1991).

[5]See Glossary.

with oral surgery, toothache, dysmenorrhea, and various forms of musculosketal pain (Giacona et al., 1987; Supernaw, 1991). Further, just one aspirin tablet every other day has been found to reduce the frequency of migraine headaches by 20% in a small subgroup of migraine sufferers (Gilman, 1992; Graedon & Ferguson, 1993; Graedon & Graedon, 1991).

Aspirin continues to be a popular treatment for the control of fever (Payan & Katzung, 1995). This effect is brought on, in part, by aspirin's ability to cause peripheral vasodilation and sweating in the patient, as well as its ability to interfere with prostaglandin production in the hypothalamus[6] (Laurence & Bennett, 1992; Shannon, Wilson, & Stang, 1995). These effects help to reduce fever but do not lower the body temperature below normal.

By the start of the 21st century, physicians were still discovering uses for aspirin. It has been discovered that aspirin reduces the incidence of myocardial infarctions (Eidelman, Hebert, Weisman, & Henneckens, 2003; Elwood et al., 1998) and is of value in the treatment of a myocardial infarction once it develops (Hung, 2003). There are several mechanisms by which aspirin is able to reduce the risk of myocardial infarction. Aspirin has been found to reduce the *C-reactive protein* level in the blood (Ridker, Cushman, Stampfer, Tracy, & Hennekens 1997). Higher levels of *C-reactive protein* in the individual's blood are associated with a greater risk of either a myocardial infarction, an occlusive stroke (CVA),[7] or a blood clot that might block another vessel (a *venous thrombosis*). However, this beneficial effect of aspirin was noted only for individuals older than 50 years of age and was strongest for those individuals with lower blood cholesterol levels.

Another mechanism by which aspirin is able to reduce the individual's risk for cardiovascular disease is its ability to inhibit the formation of blood clots by blood platelets. There is a great deal of variation in people's sensitivity to aspirin's ability to destroy the compound *thromboxane A2* in platelets, but inhibition of this blood component makes it more difficult for blood clots to form (Hutchison, 2004; Page, 2001). Since platelets have a normal lifetime of 8–10 days,

the body is constantly replacing old blood platelets with new ones. These new blood platelets will have unaltered thromboxane A2, incrementally restoring blood clot formation proficiency. To avoid this danger, the patient must take a dose of aspirin every day, or at least every other day, to provide optimal inhibition of blood clot formation. It is necessary for a physician to determine how much aspirin each patient needs for optimal clot inhibition, as some patients are resistive to low doses of aspirin (Halushka & Halushka, 2002).

Aspirin's effects are not limited to the cardiovascular system. Aspirin has been shown to be of value in the treatment of a rare neurological disorder known as *transient ischemic attacks* (TIAs). It is also an effective anti-inflammmatory agent, making it of value in the treatment of such disorders as rheumatoid arthritis and osteoarthritis (Giacona et al., 1987; Graedon & Graedon, 1991; McGuire, 1990). There is an impressive body of evidence suggesting that regular aspirin use interferes with the development of some forms of cancer (Page, 2001; Terry et al., 2004; Wright, 2001). It appears that there is a relationship between the COX-2 enzyme (discussed later in this chapter) and some forms of cancer (Kreeger, 2003). Aspirin's ability to inhibit the formation of cyclooxygenase, of which COX-2 is a subtype, appears to be the mechanism through which it inhibits the development and growth of colorectal cancer (Adler & Underwood, 2002; Baron et al., 2003; DuBois, Sheng, Shao, Williams, & Beauchamp, 1998). Patients with a previous history of colorectal cancer were found to have a lower rate of recurrence if they used one 325 mg aspirin tablet per day (Sandler et al., 2003).

In addition to its effect on colon cancer, preliminary evidence suggests that regular aspirin use might reduce the incidence of esophageal cancer by 80% or more and of ovarian cancer by 25% (Page, 2001). Evidence also suggests that regular use of aspirin or another NSAID might reduce a man's risk of prostate cancer and improve blood flow to capillaries that feed the retina, inhibiting the development of diabetic retinopathy[8] (Adler & Underwood, 2002; Roberts et al., 2002). Further, evidence suggests that regular aspirin use is

[6]See Glossary.

[7]See Glossary.

[8]See Glossary.

associated with a reduced risk of breast cancer in women, especially the subtype of breast cancer known as hormone receptor-positive cancers (Terry et al., 2004). There is also evidence that aspirin might slow the development of cataracts (Payan & Katzung, 1995) and interfere with the formation of gallstones (Elwood et al., 1998). There are even data suggesting that aspirin might interfere with the ability of the virus that causes AIDS to replicate (Stolberg, 1994).

Acetaminophen. Because acetaminophen has no significant anti-inflammatory effect, it is not usually classified as an NSAID (Supernaw, 1991). In spite of this, however, acetaminophen is not without its uses. Acetaminophen has been found to be as effective in the control of fever as is aspirin (American Society of Health-System Pharmacists, 2002). Further, as an OTC analgesic, acetaminophen is as potent as aspirin and might be used for pain control in virtually the same situations as aspirin is used.

The propionic acids. As a class, the propionic acids are used to control fever, inflammation, and mild to moderate levels of pain. The anti-inflammatory effect of these compounds makes them useful in treating such condtions as rheumatoid arthritis, dysmenorrhea, gout, tendinitis, and bursitis, as well as headaches, the aches of the common cold, backache and muscle aches, arthritis, the discomfort of menstrual cramps, and the control of fever (Gannon, 1994). Physicians have found that when used in combination with narcotic analgesics, some NSAIDs are of value in controlling the pain associated with certain forms of cancer. There is mixed evidence suggesting that the regular use of NSAIDs (including aspirin) might slow the development of Alzheimer's disease (Launer, 2003). But there is no evidence suggesting that the NSAIDs would slow the development of vascular dementia (Adler & Underwood, 2002; Veld et al., 2001). In addition to these general applications, researchers have identified specific applications for each of these compounds.

Ibuprofen. In addition to its use as an OTC analgesic and anti-inflammatory agent, there is evidence that ibuprofen might help to control the tissue inflammation caused by cystic fibrosis (CF) (Konstan, Byard, Hoppel, & Davis, 1995; Konstan, Hoppel, Chai, & Davis, 1991).

Naproxen. In addition to its uses as an anti-inflammatory and analgesic, physicians have discovered that when used in combination with the antibiotic ampicillin, naproxen seems to reduce the distress felt by children with respiratory infections caused by bacteria.

Pharmacology of the OTC Analgesics

Aspirin. Aspirin is usually administered by mouth. In the body, acetylsalicylic acid is biotransformed into salicylic acid, which is the active agent for aspirin's effects (Peterson, 1997). In contrast to the 15 minute half-life of aspirin, the half-life of its primary metabolite, salicylic acid, is between 2 and 3 hours (Katz, 2000), accounting for its duration of effect. It is rapidly absorbed, and when it is taken on an empty stomach, aspirin begins to reach the bloodstream in as little as 1 minute (Rose, 1988). However, its primary site of absorption is the small intestine, so while it is possible to detect the first atoms of aspirin in the blood in approximately 1 minute, it usually takes about 1 hour before aspirin is able to bring about any significant degree of analgesia (Stimmel, 1997b).

After a single dose, peak blood levels of aspirin are achieved in between 15 (Shannon, Wilson & Stang, 1995) and 60–120 minutes (McGuire, 1990; Stimmel, 1997b). Once in the blood, between 80% and 90% of aspirin is bound to plasma proteins (Stimmel, 1997b). Aspirin is rapidly biotransformed by the liver into water-soluble metabolites, which are then promptly removed from the blood by the kidneys (Payan & Katzung, 1995). Only about 1% of a single dose of aspirin is excreted unchanged from the body. In contrast to its 2–3 hour half-life following a single dose, when aspirin is used at high dosage levels for longer than a week, the half-life of aspirin might be extended to between 8 (Kacso & Terezhalmy, 1994) and 15 hours (Payan & Katzung, 1995). It is rare for tolerance to the analgesic effects of aspirin to develop (Stimmel, 1997b).

Unlike the narcotic analgesics, which seem to work mainly within the brain, aspirin seems to have a different mechanism of action. First, aspirin does not seem to work within the cortex of the brain (Kacso & Terezhalmy, 1994). Rather, aspirin appears to work at the site of the injury, in the hypothalamic region of the brain, and although scientists are not sure how, it also appears to work through unidentified sites in the spinal cord (Fishman & Carr, 1992; Graedon & Ferguson, 1993; Kacso & Terezhalmy, 1994).

To understand how aspirin works at the site of the injury, it is necessary to investigate the body's response to injury. Each cell in the human body contains several chemicals that are released when that cell is damaged to warn neighboring cells of the damage and to activate the body's repair mechanisms. Some of these chemicals include *histamine, bradykinin* and a group of chemicals collectively known as the *prostaglandins*. The inflammation and pain that result when these chemicals are released serves both to warn the individual that he or she has been injured and to activate the body's repair mechanisms.

Aspirin's analgesic effect at the site of the injury might be attributed to its power to inhibit the production of the prostaglandins (American Society of Health-System Pharmacists, 2002; Bushnell & Justins, 1993). Aspirin does this by inhibiting the production of two known subtypes of the enzyme *cyclooxygenase*, the COX-1 and COX-2 varieties, which were discovered in the early 1990s. In 2002 scientists discovered a third subform, which has been identified as COX-3 (Greener, 2003). COX-1 is predominantly involved in essential prostaglandin production in body organs where the prostaglandins carry out a protective function. Its chemical cousin, COX-2, is produced mainly by body tissues when they are damaged, contributing to the inflammation response (Pairet et al., 1998; Rehman & Sack, 1999). On a molecular level, COX-1 and COX-2 share about 60% of their chemical structure, and it is through the shared elements that NSAIDs interfere with the production of both COX-1 and COX-2 (Rehman & Sack, 1999). In other words, it is through their nonselective action on both COX-1 and COX-2 that NSAIDs such as aspirin are able to block injury-induced prostaglandin production, lower pain levels, and reduce inflammation. One consequence of this nonselective inhibition of both forms of cyclooxygenase is the unwanted reduction of COX-1 levels in the body, increasing the risk of NSAID-induced tissue damage.

Acetaminophen. Acetaminophen is usually administered orally, although it may also be administered as a rectal suppository. Oral preparations include tablet, capsule, or liquid forms, and virtually 100% of the medication is absorbed through the gastrointestinal tract (Shannon et al., 1995). The peak effects are seen in 30 minutes to 2 hours after a single dose, and acetaminophen is metabolized in the liver. Virtually 100% of the drug is eliminated in the urine, although some acetaminophen might also be found in breast milk of nursing mothers.

Scientists speculate that acetaminophen might block the synthesis of only the recently discovered COX-3 enzyme, which may account for its ability to reduce fever and pain without interfering with inflammation (Greener, 2003). In terms of its analgesic and fever-reducing potential, acetaminophen is thought to be as powerful as aspirin (Supernaw, 1991). Indeed, in terms of its analgesic or anti-fever effects, acetaminophen might be substituted for aspirin on a milligram-for-milligram basis. As will be discussed later in this chapter, when used at dosage levels above those recommended by the manufacturer, there is a danger of acetaminophen toxicity. However, liver toxicity or damage from acetaminophen is rare, as long as the user does not ingest more than 4,000 mg of acetaminophen per day (Cherny & Foley, 1996), or use the drug for more than 10 days (Peterson, 1997).

Clinical evidence would suggest that COX-3 synthesis is limited to the central nervous system (CNS), which is where acetaminophen seems to have its main effect. In the future, research may reveal a relationship between COX-3 synthesis and the fever response, which would explain why acetaminophen is able to reduce fever in patients without the anti-inflammatory effects of NSAIDs. Unlike aspirin, acetaminophen does not interfere with the normal clotting mechanisms of the blood (Shannon et al., 1995). Finally, individuals who are allergic to aspirin do not usually suffer from adverse reactions when they take acetaminophen according to label instructions. These are features that often make acetaminophen an ideal substitute for individuals who are unable to take aspirin due to any of the following conditions—being allergic to it, being prone to bleeding disorders, or taking another medication with which aspirin might interfere.

Ibuprofen. Ibuprofen is a member of the propionic acid family of chemicals, and it is most commonly administered orally. About 80% of a single dose of ibuprofen is absorbed from the gastrointestinal tract. The primary site of ibuprofen biotransformation is the liver, and its half-life is between 2 and 4 hours (Shannon et al., 1995). About 99% of the ibuprofen molecules will become protein bound following absorption into the general circulation (Olson, 1992). The therapeutic half-life of a single dose of ibuprofen is between 1.8 and 2.6 hours (American Medical Association, 1994). Peak plasma levels following a single oral dose are achieved in between 30 minutes and 1.5 hours. Ibuprofen and its metabolites are mainly eliminated by the kidneys, although a small amount of ibuprofen is eliminated through the bile.

Although ibuprofen inhibits the action of the enzyme cyclooxygenase, this does not mean that ibuprofen might automatically be substituted for aspirin to control inflammation. Indeed, there is disagreement as to ibuprofen's effectiveness as an anti-inflammatory agent. Payan and Katzung (1995) stated that when used at a dosage level of 2,400 mg/day,[9] ibuprofen is as effective as aspirin in the control of inflammation in the average adult. However, when used at a dosage level lower than 2,400 mg per day, ibuprofen is far less effective as an anti-inflammatory agent than is aspirin (Payan & Katzung, 1995). Mann (1994), on the other hand, suggested that when used at effective dosage levels, ibuprofen is 30 times as effective in fighting inflammation as aspirin. One factor that affects the anti-inflammatory effect of ibuprofen is the period of time during which it is used. As a general rule, the longer the therapeutic half-life of the NSAID, the longer it takes for that compound to have an anti-inflammatory effect (Blackburn, 1999). While researchers still disagree as to the exact anti-inflammatory potential of ibuprofen, the greater part of the evidence to date suggests that it does function as an anti-inflammatory if it is used at effective dosage levels for an appropriate period of time.

There is strong evidence suggesting that when ibuprofen is taken concurrently with aspirin, these two chemicals interfere with the anti-inflammatory action of each other (Payan & Katzung, 1995). Thus, ibuprofen should not be used by a patient taking aspirin except under a physician's orders. Unfortunately, ibuprofen's anti-inflammatory effects are seen only after 2 to 4 weeks of continuous use (Fischer, 1989). This might suggest that one would do better to utilize aspirin for the control of inflammation, but one must remember that aspirin

is quite irritating to the stomach. Ibuprofen, on the other hand, is about one-fifth to one-half as irritating to the stomach as aspirin (Giacona et al., 1987). Thus, ibuprofen is often utilized when the individual is unable to tolerate the gastrointestinal irritation caused by aspirin. But while ibuprofen is less irritating to the stomach, 4% to 14% of those who use ibuprofen may still experience some degree of gastrointestinal irritation (Graedon & Graedon, 1996).

When ibuprofen is used for prolonged periods of time, approximately 3 out of every 1,000 users will also experience some degree of drug-induced gastrointestinal bleeding (Carlson et al., 1987). The team of Taha, Dahill, Sturrock, Lee, and Russell (1994) found that 27% of their sample who had used ibuprofen for an extended period of time had evidence of ulcer formation in the gastrointestinal tract. However, the number of ibuprofen-using subjects in their sample was quite small, and it was not clear how representative these findings were of the ability of ibuprofen to contribute to gastrointestinal ulcer formation.

Naproxen. This analgesic may be more effective as an anti-inflammatory agent than aspirin (American Medical Association, 1994; American Society of Health-System Pharmacists, 2002; Graedon & Graedon, 1991). Like aspirin, naproxen has an antipyretic effect. Researchers are not sure of the exact mechanism through which naproxen reduces fever. However, at this time naproxen is thought to suppress the synthesis of prostaglandins in the hypothalamus (American Society of Health-System Pharmacists, 2002). Researchers have found that naproxen has an antiplatelet effect similar to that seen in aspirin, but this effect lasts for only the half-life of naproxen and it is not clear at this time whether this compound will find a role in the treatment of myocardial infarctions (Hutchison, 2004; Solomon, Glynn, Levin, & Avorn, 2002).

When used as an analgesic, naproxen will begin to have an effect in 1 hour, and its effects will last for 7–8 hours (American Medical Association, 1994). The biological half-life of naproxen in the healthy adult is approximately 10–20 hours. About 30% of a given dose of naproxen is metabolized by the liver into the inactive metabolite *6-desmethylnaproxen* (American Society of Health-System Pharmacists, 2002), and only 5% (American Medical Association,

---

[9]The 2,400 mg is taken in divided doses, not all at once.

1994) to 10% (American Society of Health-System Pharmacists, 2002) of a standard dose of naproxen is excreted unchanged. The majority of the drug is excreted in the urine as either metabolized or unmetabolized drug.

As stated earlier, naproxen binds to proteins in the blood plasma, which can absorb only so much of the medication before reaching a saturation point. Research suggests that the concentration of naproxen reaches a plateau if the patient takes 500 mg twice daily for 2–3 days (American Society of Health-System Pharmacists, 2002).[10] Thus, even under a physician's direction the typical dosage level does not exceed 500 mg twice daily.

Ketoprofen. When ketoprofen was sold as a prescription drug, patients were advised to take *no more* than 300 mg per day and to take it with food to minimize irritation to the gastrointestinal tract. Ketoprofen is well absorbed from the gastrointestinal tract, with peak blood levels appearing in 30 minutes to 2 hours after a single dose taken on an empty stomach (American Medical Association, 1994). It is more slowly absorbed when taken with food, but eventually all of the ketoprofen will be absorbed even when taken with a meal. Ketoprofen is extensively bound to plasma proteins, with 99% of the drug molecules being protein bound. There are no known active metabolites of ketoprofen.

In young adults the half-life of a single dose of ketoprofen is 3 hours; in the elderly, this might be increased to 5 hours. Because of this characteristic, older patients or patients with impaired kidney function should consult their physician before taking this medication.

Although all of the OTC analgesics are usful in the control of mild to moderate levels of pain or fever, a common danger inherent in the use of these agents is that they might mask the development of a serious medical condition. For example, although the OTC analgesics are effective in controlling fever, the cause of the fever must still be identified and treated to ensure adequate medical care for the patient (Fishman & Carr, 1992).

---

[10]It should be noted that a patient should not take 500 mg of naproxen twice a day, except under a physician's supervision.

Normal Dosage Levels of OTC Analgesics

Aspirin. McGuire (1990) reported that 650 mg of aspirin or acetaminophen, a standard dose of two regular-strength tablets of either medication, provided an analgesic effect equal to that of 50 mg of the narcotic painkiller meperidine (Demerol). It has been estimated that 325–650 mg of aspirin has the same analgesic potential as 32 mg of codeine or 65 mg of Darvon (propoxyphene) or a 50 mg oral dose of Talwin (pentazocine) (Gutstein & Akil, 2001; Kaplan & Sadock, 1996). Thus, although it is an over-the-counter analgesic, aspirin would seem to be rather potent.

Even after more than a century of use, physicians still debate the optimum dosage level for aspirin use. Kacso and Terezhalmy (1994) reported that a single 1,300 mg dose of aspirin seemed to provide a greater degree of relief from pain than did a single 600 mg dose. However, dosage levels above 1,300 mg in a single dose did not provide a greater degree of analgesia and actually put the user at risk for a toxic reaction from the aspirin, according to the authors. These findings were consistent with the conclusions of Aronoff, Wagner, and Spangler (1986), who found a "ceiling effect" of "approximately 1,000 mg every 4 hr" (p. 769) for aspirin. Dosage levels higher than this did not provide greater pain relief, and "only increases the threat of a toxic reaction" (McGuire, 1990, p. 30).

The American Society of Health-System Pharmacists (2002) recommends a normal adult oral dosage level of aspirin of 325 to 650 mg every 4 hours, as needed for the control of pain. Furthermore, this text warns that aspirin should not be continuously used for longer than 10 days by an adult or longer than 5 days for a child under the age of 12 except under a doctor's orders.[11]

When taken by mouth, aspirin is rapidly and completely absorbed from the gastrointestinal tract and is distributed by the blood to virtually every body tissue

---

[11]A physician may, when using aspirin in the treatment of arthritis, for example, elect to have the patient take it at higher-than-normal dosage levels for extended periods of time. This represents a special application of aspirin's anti-inflammatory effect, and the physician will weigh the advantages of using aspirin at such high dosage levels against the potential for harm to the patient. Because this is a special application of aspirin, however, it will not be discussed in this chapter.

and fluid. The actual speed at which aspirin is absorbed by the user depends on the acidity of the stomach contents (Sheridan, Patterson, & Gustafson, 1982). When taken on an empty stomach, the rate at which aspirin is absorbed depends on how quickly the tablet may crumble after reaching the stomach (Rose, 1988). After the tablet crumbles, the individual aspirin molecules will pass through the stomach lining into the general circulatory system.

When the individual takes aspirin with food it may take 5 to 10 times longer to reach the individual's bloodstream (Pappas, 1990). Ultimately, however, *all* of the aspirin will be absorbed from the gastrointestinal tract. Because of this, Rodman (1993) suggested that patients take aspirin with meals or at least a snack to limit aspirin-induced irritation to the stomach lining. However, in some cases, it is desirable to achieve as high a blood level of aspirin as possible. Patients should discuss with their physicians or pharmacists whether they should take aspirin on an empty stomach or with a meal before using this technique to limit stomach irritation.

Aspirin is sold both alone and in combination with various agents designed to reduce the irritation that it might cause to the stomach. In theory, timed-released and enteric coated tablets have the potential for reducing the irritation to the gastrointestinal tract. However, both forms of aspirin have been known to bring about erratic absorption rates, making it harder to achieve the desired effect (Shannon et al., 1995). Some patients will take aspirin with antacids in order to reduce irritation to the stomach. When antacids are mixed with aspirin, the patient's blood level of aspirin will be 30% to 70% lower than when aspirin is used alone (Graedon & Graedon, 1996; Rodman, 1993). This is a matter of some concern for individuals who are taking the drug for the control of inflammation or pain, as lower blood levels of aspirin mean that less of the drug is available to help control the pain.

Acetaminophen. The usual adult dose of acetaminophen is also 325 to 650 mg every 4 hours as needed for the control of pain (American Society of Health-System Pharmacists, 2002). In many ways, dosage recommendations for aspirin and acetaminophen are very similar. Aronoff, Wagner, and Spangler (1986) observed that acetaminophen's antipyretic and analgesic effects are equal to those of aspirin, and that the ceiling level of acetaminophen is the same for these two drugs.

Peak blood concentrations are achieved in 30 minutes to 2 hours after an oral dose of acetaminophen (Shannon et al., 1995). The half-life of an oral dose of acetaminophen is normally from 1 to 4 hours. However, because this chemical is biotransformed in the liver, people with significant liver damage might experience a longer acetaminophen half-life than normal and should avoid the use of acetaminophen except when under the supervision of a physician.

Ibuprofen. When used as an OTC analgesic, the recommended dose of ibuprofen is 200–400 mg every 4 hours (Dionne & Gordon, 1994). As a prescription medication, individual dosage levels of 400–800 mg are often utilized, depending on the specific condition being treated. Shannon et al. (1995) recommended that 400–800 mg of ibuprofen be used 3–4 times a day by adults who suffer from inflammatory diseases. The authors suggest that 400 mg every 4–6 hours be utilized in the control of mild to moderate pain. However, there is some disagreement as to the analgesic potential of ibuprofen. Dionne and Gordon (1994) noted that the greatest degree of relief from pain is achieved with doses of 400–600 mg, and that additional ibuprofen above this level is unlikely to result in greater levels of analgesia. In contrast, however, Rosenblum (1992) stated that 800 mg of ibuprofen provided greater control of postoperative pain than did therapeutic doses of the narcotic fentanyl in a small sample of women who had laparoscopic surgery.

Remember that the OTC dosage levels of ibuprofen are limited to 200–400 mg every 4 hours. A physician who prescribes this medication might elect to use a higher dosage level. However, even when it is used as a prescription medication, the total daily dosage level is not recommended to exceed 3,200 mg per day in divided doses (Dionne & Gordon, 1994; Shannon et al., 1995). Ibuprofen is rapidly absorbed when used orally, and the drug is rapidly distributed throughout the body. About 80% of a single oral dose is absorbed from the intestinal tract. Following a single oral dose, peak blood plasma levels are achieved in 1–2 hours (American Society of Health-System Pharmacists, 2002). The drug's half-life is between 1.8 and 2.6 hours, and the effects of a single dose of ibuprofen last for about 6–8 hours following a single oral dose (Shannon et al., 1995).

Naproxen. When using naproxen as an OTC analgesic, users are advised to take up to three tablets, twice a day. The medication is well absorbed from the intestinal tract, with 100% of a single dose being absorbed. Absorption is somewhat delayed when naproxen is ingested with food, but eventually all the medication will be absorbed. Peak blood concentrations are found 2 to 4 hours after a single dose, and 99% of the medication is bound to proteins in the blood after absorption. Although this compound will cross the placenta, it does so with difficulty, and fetal plasma levels will be approximately 1% of those in the mother's blood (American Society of Health-System Pharmacists, 2002).

About 30% of a single dose of naproxen is biotransformed by the liver into the inactive metabolite 6-desmethylnaproxen (American Society of Health-System Pharmacists, 2002). The rest is biotransformed into other metabolites, and less than 1% is excreted unchanged by the kidneys. Only 5% of the drug is excreted in the feces, and 95% is excreted in the urine, mainly as one of the many metabolites formed when naproxen is biotransformed by the liver, as discussed above.

Ketoprofen. As a prescription medication, ketoprofen was available in 25, 50, and 75 milligram (mg) capsules. Recommended dosage levels were 50–75 mg every 8 hours, up to a maximum of 300 mg per day. There is no evidence that dosage levels above 300 mg per day are more effective than lower doses, and the manufacturer does not recommend that ketoprofen be used in dosage levels higher than this (*Physicians' Desk Reference*, 2004). In the modified OTC analgesic form, it is sold in 25 mg tablets.

Complications Caused by Use of OTC Analgesics

The OTC analgesics are hardly "safe" medications. As a group, the NSAIDs account for nearly 25% of the adverse drug reactions reported to the Food and Drug Administration (FDA) (Noble, King, & Olutade, 2000) and cause 103,000 people each year to be hospitalized for NSAID-induced problems. Of this number, 16,500 will die from their NSAID-induced medical problem (Graumlich, 2001). Thus, although these medications are available without a prescription, the OTC analgesics pose a significant potential for harm, a fact that many people tend to forget.

Aspirin. Aspirin is the most commonly used drug in this country. The popularity of aspirin is shown in the statistics: An estimated 35,000 kilograms of aspirin are consumed each day in the United States and 6,000 kilograms are consumed each day in the United Kingdom (Halushka & Halushka, 2002). Steele and Morton (1986) gave another measure of aspirin use in this country, stating that between 30 and 74 million *pounds* of aspirin are consumed in the United States each year. These figures reflect the popularity of aspirin as a home remedy. But because it is such a common agent for self-medication of pain, many people underestimate both its usefulness and its potential for causing serious side effects (Jaffe & Martin, 1990). Even occasional use of aspirin at recommended doses will result in up to 15% of the users having at least one significant, potentially fatal, adverse side effect (Rapoport, 1993). For example, even a single dose of aspirin can reduce the level of melatonin in the brain by as much as 75%, possibly contributing to insomnia (Pettit, 2000). At recommended dosage levels, aspirin will cause a minor amount of bleeding in the gastrointestinal tract. The chronic use of aspirin can cause the patient to become anemic (Pappas, 1990; Talley, 1993), and between 500 and 1,000 people die each year in the United States from massive aspirin-induced hemorrhage (Grinspoon & Bakalar, 1993).

Of patients who use an NSAID for an extended period of time, 4% will develop gastric ulcers (Marcus, 2003). Aspirin shares the ability to cause or contribute to gastric ulcers with the other NSAIDs, as evidenced by the fact that up to 40% of those individuals who use aspirin at recommended doses on a chronic basis will experience an erosion in their stomach lining, and between 17% (Kitridou, 1993) and 30% (Taha et al., 1994) will actually develop aspirin-induced stomach ulcers. Researchers believe aspirin is a factor in the formation of between 20% (Talley, 1993) and 41% (Wilcox, Shalek, & Cotsonis, 1994) of all cases of "bleeding" ulcers. Even dosage levels as low as 75 mg per day have been found to significantly increase the individual's risk for damage to the lining of the gastrointestinal system (Guslandi, 1997).

Many of the gastrointestinal ulcers that form as a result of aspirin use fail to produce major warning symptoms usually associated with ulcer formation (Taha et al., 1994). Aspirin's ability to cause gastric irritation is thought to be a side effect of its nonselective ability to interfere with production of both the COX-1 as well as the COX-2 subtypes of cyclooxygenase. This may also be why, when used at recommended dosage levels for extended periods of time, aspirin can cause breathing problems in up to 33% of users (Kitridou, 1993).

For these reasons aspirin should not be used by people with a history of ulcers, bleeding disorders, or other gastrointestinal disorders (American Society of Health-System Pharmacists, 2002). Further, people should not take aspirin with acidic foods such as coffee, fruit juices, or alcohol, which might further irritate the gastrointestinal system (Pappas, 1990).

Aspirin can also cause allergic reactions in some users. Approximately 0.2% of the general population is allergic to aspirin. However, of those individuals with a history of *any* kind of allergic disorder, approximately 20% will be allergic to aspirin. Patients who are sensitive to aspirin are likely also to be sensitive to ibuprofen or naproxen, as cross-sensitivity between these drugs is common (Fischer, 1989; Shannon et al., 1995). Symptoms of an allergic reaction to aspirin might include rash and breathing problems (Zuger, 1994). Patients with symptoms of the "aspirin triad," which is to say those individuals with a history of nasal polyps, asthma, and sensitivity to aspirin, should not use any NSAID except under the supervision of a physician (Craig, 1996).

Aspirin has been known to trigger fatal asthma attacks in patients with this disorder (Zuger, 1994). Indeed, all of the NSAIDs are capable of causing an exacerbation of the symptoms of asthma as a result of their ability to inhibit prostaglandin production (Craig, 1996; McFadden & Hejal, 2000). People with a history of chronic rhinitis should not use aspirin except under a physician's supervision (Shannon et al., 1995). These conditions are warning signals for individuals at risk for an allergic reaction to aspirin or similar agents. About 5% to 15% of people who suffer from asthma will experience an adverse reaction if they use an NSAID (Craig, 1996). If the asthma patient also has a history of nasal polyps, the possibility of an adverse reaction to

an NSAID might be as high as 40%, according to the authors.

Aspirin can cause a number of other side effects, including anorexia, nausea, and vomiting (Sheridan et al., 1982). Because of their effects on blood clotting, aspirin, naproxen, or ibuprofen should not be utilized by people with a bleeding disorder such as hemophilia (American Society of Health-System Pharmacists, 2002; Shannon et al., 1995). People who are undergoing anticoagulant therapy involving such drugs as heparin or warfarin should not use aspirin except when directed by a physician (Rodman, 1993). The combined effects of aspirin and the anticoagulant may result in significant, unintended blood loss for the patient, especially if he or she were to have an accident. Further, the anticoagulent effect of aspirin can contribute to the development of a hemorrhagic stroke (He, Whelton, Vu, & Klag, 1998). Thus, the physician must weigh the advantages of aspirin use in treating heart disease against its potential to cause or contribute to a potentially fatal hemorrhagic stroke.

As stated earlier in this chapter, patients taking other NSAIDs such as ibuprofen or naproxin should not take aspirin, except under a physician's supervision. The combined effects of these medications, in addition to interfering with each other, can cause significant gastrointestinal tract irritation (Rodman, 1993). Aspirin, naproxen, and ibuprofen may all cause a condition known as tinnitus (loss of hearing and a persistent "ringing" in the ears). The patient's hearing will usually return to normal when the offending medication is discontinued. Also, aspirin use may result in a very rare side effect known as *hepatotoxicity* (Gay, 1990). In such cases, aspirin prevents the liver from filtering the blood effectively (Gay, 1990). Another rare complication from aspirin use is a drug-induced depression (Mortensen & Rennebohm, 1989).

For reasons not entirely clear, the elderly are especially susceptible to toxicity from aspirin and similar agents. This might be because they are unable to metabolize and excrete this family of drugs as effectively as younger adults. Bleidt and Moss (1989) suggested that this was due at least in part to the fact that as people grow older, there is a reduction in blood flow to the liver and kidneys. This results in difficulties for the elderly in metabolizing and excreting many drugs, including aspirin. About 1% of patients who use NSAIDs for extended periods of time experience drug-induced kidney failure (Marcus, 2003). There is also preliminary evidence that regular aspirin use is associated with an increased risk for end stage renal disease (ESRD) (Fored et al., 2001).

Another complication of aspirin use in the elderly is the development of drug-induced anxiety states (Sussman, 1988). Aspirin or related compounds should not be used with children who are suffering from a viral infection, except when directed by a physician. Research strongly suggests that aspirin might increase the possibility of the child's developing Reye's syndrome as a complication of the viral infection (Graedon & Graedon, 1996; Sagar, 1991; Stimmel, 1997b). Surprisingly, in light of the frequency with which it is used to treat the symptoms of a common cold, aspirin has been found to actually suppress the body's immune response to the invading virus (Bartlett, 1999).

Aspirin has been implicated in the failure of intrauterine devices (IUDs) to prevent pregnancy. The anti-inflammatory action of aspirin is thought to be the cause of this. Aspirin has also been implicated in fertility problems for couples who wish to have children. The use of aspirin at therapeutic dosages may reduce the ability of sperm to move (sperm motility) by up to 50%, a side effect that may reduce the chances of successful conception for at least some couples. While this is not to say that aspirin might serve as a method of birth control, the reduction in sperm motility might interfere with the couple's ability to conceive when they wish to do so.

Medication interactions involving aspirin.[12] Individuals being treated for hyperuricemia (a buildup of uric acid in the blood often found in gout as well as other conditions) should not use aspirin except under a physician's direction. At normal dosage levels, aspirin reduces the body's ability to excrete uric acid, contributing to the problem of uric acid buildup. Further, if the individual is taking the prescription medication probenecid, one of the drugs used to treat hyperuricemia, he or she should

not take aspirin. At therapeutic doses, aspirin inhibits the action of probenecid, allowing uric acid levels to build up in the blood. Acetaminophen has been advanced as a suitable substitute for patients who suffer from gout and who need a mild analgesic (Shannon et al., 1995).

Aspirin also should not be used by patients who are receiving medications for control of their blood pressure or anticoagulants such as warfarin, except under a physician's supervision. Aspirin or the other NSAIDs might interfere with the effectiveness of some antihypertensive medications (Fischer, 1989). The exact mechanism by which this happens is unclear; however, it may reflect the impact of aspirin use on prostaglandin production within the kidneys, resulting in fluid retention ("Strong Medicine," 1995). Individuals who are taking aspirin for its anticoagulation effect should avoid the use of vitamin E, which also has an anticoagulation effect, except under a physician's direction (Harkness & Bratman, 2003). The combined effects of aspirin and vitamin E increase the individual's risk of abnormal bleeding, according to the authors.

Patients using *any* of the NSAIDs should be aware that these compounds can interfere with folate metabolism (Harkness & Bratman, 2003). High folate levels pose a health risk for the individual, and the concurrent use of these compounds should be avoided except under a physician's direction, according to the authors. There is also a danger that patients using aspirin and valproate at the same time will experience higher-than-normal blood levels of the valproate because the aspirin molecules will bind to the albumin sites that the latter medication normally would occupy (DeVane & Nemeroff, 2002). Patients on valproate should discuss their use of aspirin with their physician before mixing these two medications.

Individuals who plan to consume alcohol should not use aspirin immediately prior to or while they are actively drinking. There is evidence that the use of aspirin prior to the ingestion of alcohol decreases the activity of gastric alcohol dehydrogenase, an enzyme produced by the stomach that starts to metabolize alcohol even before it reaches the bloodstream (Roine, Gentry, Hernandez-Munoz, Baraona, & Lieber, 1990). Even the rare social drinker who ingests aspirin shortly before drinking alcohol will experience a higher-than-normal blood alcohol level. Finally, patients who are using aspirin

[12]It is not possible to list every possible medication interaction involving aspirin and other compounds. The reader is advised to consult a physician or pharmacist with any questions about possible interactions between a given drug and aspirin.

should not use the herbal medicine ginko biloba because this compound might contribute to excessive bleeding (Cupp, 1999).

Ibuprofen. Ibuprofen has been implicated as the cause of blurred vision of patients (Nicastro, 1989). Graedon and Graedon (1996) suggested that people using ibuprofen who experience some change in their vision discontinue the medication and consult with their physician immediately. In addition to producing skin rashes or hives as a side effect in 3% to 9% of patients, ibuprofen has been implicated in the formation of cataracts (Graedon & Graedon, 1996) and as the cause of migraine headaches in both men and women (Nicastro, 1989).

When ibuprofen was first introduced as a prescription medication in 1974, it was manufactured by the Upjohn Company and sold under the brand name *Motrin*. The Upjohn Company warned that ibuprofen has been found to cause a number of side effects, including heartburn, nausea, diarrhea, vomiting, nervousness, hearing loss, congestive heart failure in persons who had marginal cardiac function, changes in vision, and elevation of blood pressure (*Physicians' Desk Reference*, 2004).

Recent research has also suggested that ibuprofen can cause or contribute to kidney failure in people with high blood pressure, kidney disease, or other health problems (Squires, 1990). This may be a side effect of ibuprofen's ability to block the production of prostaglandin. Research has shown that by blocking the body's production of prostaglandin, ibuprofen also reduces the blood flow throughout the body, especially to the kidneys. If the individual is already suffering from a reduction in blood flow to the kidneys for any reason, including "normal aging, liver or cardiovascular disease or simply dehydration from vomiting, diarrhea and fever accompanying the flu" (Squires, 1990, p. 4E), ibuprofen might either cause or at least contribute to acute kidney failure.

Patients who are suffering from systemic lupus erythematosus (often simply called "lupus" or SLE) should not use ibuprofen, except under a physician's supervision. Occasionally, ibuprofen has caused the development of a condition known as *aseptic meningitis* within hours of the time that a patient with SLE ingested it. Aseptic meningitis will also be a complication in extremely rare cases in which a patient who does

not have SLE ingests ibuprofen (Zuger, 1994). However, there have been fewer than 40 reported cases of this side effect in patients who do not have SLE or some other autoimmune disorder.

When used by a client who is also taking lithium, ibuprofen may also increase the blood levels of lithium by 25% to 60% (DeVane & Nemeroff, 2002; Rodman, 1993). This effect is most pronounced in the older individual and may contribute to lithium toxicity in some, according to the author. Close monitoring of blood lithium levels would be necessary in patients who use both lithium and ibuprofen concurrently to avoid the danger of lithium toxicity. Patients who are on lithium should discuss their use of ibuprofen and other over-the-counter preparations with their physician to avoid the danger of lithium toxicity.

Patients taking the prescription medication methotrexate should not use ibuprofen as this drug reduces the rate at which methotrexate is excreted from the body (Rodman, 1993). Reduced excretion rates may result in toxic levels of methotrexate building up in the patient, according to the author. If an OTC analgesic should be required, Rodman (1993) recommended the use of acetaminophen. The combined effects of NSAIDs may result in excessive irritation to the gastrointestinal tract and possibly severe bleeding. Further, the use of ibuprofen has been found to block the antiplatelet effects of aspirin, a matter of some concern for patients who use aspirin for reasons of cardiovascular health (Catella-Lawson et al., 2001; Hutchison, 2004). For this and other reasons, ibuprofen should not be used in conjunction with other NSAIDs, including aspirin, except under a physician's supervision (Rodman, 1993).

Acetaminophen. Acetaminophen has been called "the safest of all analgesics" (Katz, 2000, p. 100) when used as directed. Still, this medication has the potential for significant adverse effects. Individuals with alcohol-related liver damage or individuals who are actively drinking should totally avoid the use of acetaminophen (Draganov, Durrence, Cox, & Reuben, 2000; Johnston & Pelletier, 1997; Peterson, 1997; Sands, Knapp, & Ciraulo, 1993). The combined effects of alcohol and acetaminophen can produce toxic levels of the latter compound in the individual's body. When acetaminophen is ingested, about 4% to 5% of the drug is biotransformed into a toxic metabolite known as N-acetyl-*p*-benzoquinoneimine

(Peterson, 1997). Normally, this metabolite of acetaminophen poses no danger to the user, and it is rapidly biotransformed into other substances by the liver enzyme glutathione. However, when the user is actively drinking or has alcohol-induced liver damage, the body's supply of glutathione is rapidly depleted even when the drug is used at recommended dosage levels, setting the stage for acetaminophen toxicity.

Individuals who ingest very large doses of vitamin C should not use acetaminophen except under a doctor's supervision (Harkness & Bratman, 2003). Doses greater than 3 grams of vitamin C per day appear to interfere with acetaminophen biotransformation, increasing the risk that the individual's blood level of the latter chemical might reach toxic levels, according to the authors.

Because of its cumulative toxic effects on the liver, acetaminophen should *not* be used for longer than 10 days *at any dosage level* (Kacso & Terezhalmy, 1994). Another rare but not unknown complication of acetaminophen use is the development of anaphylactic reactions on the part of the user. Acetaminophen has also been found to be *nephrotoxic*, that is, if used too often or at too high a dosage, it may be toxic to the cells of the kidneys. A controversial research finding is that acetaminophen use is associated with end state renal disease (ESRD) (Perneger, Whelton, & Klag, 1994). However, these results have been challenged (Fored et al., 2001; Rexrode et al., 2001). Until a definitive conclusion is reached, it must be assumed that acetaminophen should be used only when the advantages outweigh the potential for ESRD from this analgesic.

Naproxen. Much of the information available on naproxen and its effects is based on experience obtained with prescription forms of this chemical. Naproxen has been related to potentially fatal allergic reactions in some users. Patients with the "aspirin triad" (discussed earlier) should not use naproxen except under a physician's supervision. This medication may also contribute to the formation of peptic ulcers and gastrointestinal bleeding. In rare cases, male users have experienced naproxen-induced problems achieving an erection and the loss of the ability to ejaculate (Finger, Lund, & Slagel, 1997).

On occasion, naproxen has contributed to drowsiness, dizziness, feelings of depression, and vertigo (Qureshi & Lee-Chiong, 2004). Patients have been known to experience diarrhea, heartburn, constipation, and vomiting while taking naproxen. Indeed, between 3% and 9% of the patients who used prescription strength naproxen experienced such side effects as constipation, heartburn, abdominal pain, and nausea. Taha et el. (1994) found that 44% of their sample who had used naproxen for extended periods of time had evidence of gastrointestinal ulcers. Although it was not clear how representative these findings were of naproxen's ability to contribute to the formation of ulcers, it was recommended that naproxen not be utilized by patients with a history of peptic ulcer disease (Dionne & Gordon, 1994).

As is true with acetaminophen, NSAIDs such as naproxen, but not aspirin itself, have been implicated as one cause of ESRD (Perneger et al., 1994). There have been rare reports of patients who developed side effects such as a skin rash, diarrhea, headache, insomnia, problems with their hearing, and/or tinnitus after using naproxen. There have also been reports of potentially fatal liver dysfunctions that seem to have been caused by naproxen. Thus, as with all medications, naproxen should be used only when the benefits of this drug outweigh the potential dangers caused by its use. Animal research has suggested the possibility of damage to the eyes as a result of naproxen use, although it is not clear at this time whether the medication may cause damage to the visual system of a human being.

Ketoprofen. The side effects of ketoprofen are essentially the same as those seen with naproxen or other NSAID agents.

Overdose of OTC Analgesics

Acetaminophen. Unfortunately, in spite of its value as an OTC analgesic, acetaminophen is also the drug most commonly ingested in an overdose attempt, accounting for 5% to 10% of all hospital admissions and 94% of all intentional drug overdoses (Sharma, 2003). Each year in the United States an estimated 100,000 intentional cases of acetaminophen overdose occur (Cetaruk, Dart, Horowitz, & Hurilbut, 1996; Sporer & Khayam-Bashi, 1996). The mortality from acetaminophen overdoses is only 0.03% overall and <2% for those patients admitted to the hospital (Sharma, 2003), a reflection of the skill with which physicians have been able to treat acetaminophen overdoses. However, some of those who survived an acetaminophen overdose required a liver transplant in order to live (Cetaruk et al., 1996).

Acetaminophen is often ingested by individuals, especially adolescents, who want to make a suicide gesture. The individual who makes this gesture rarely intends to kill himself or herself, but the relatively low dose necessary to produce a toxic reaction to acetaminophen makes it a poor choice for a gesture. Because the first evidence of acetaminophen toxicity might not appear until 12 to 24 hours after the drug was ingested, the individual might falsely conclude that he or she is not at risk for adverse effects from the suicide gesture and not seek medical assistance until several hours or even days after the overdose was ingested.

The untreated acetaminophen overdose will progress through four different stages if the patient lives. Within 30 minutes of the time the individual ingests the overdose, he or she will experience anorexia, nausea, and vomiting in response to the effects of the acetaminophen on the gastrointestinal tract (McDonough, 1998). In the second phase, which begins about 24 hours after the overdose was ingested, the individual will experience abdominal pain, oliguria,[13] and pain over the liver (McDonough, 1998). During this phase, blood tests will reveal abnormal liver function. In phase three, which begins 72 to 96 hours after the overdose was ingested, the individual will experience nausea, vomiting, jaundice, and symptoms of liver failure (McDonough, 1998). Other possible complications that might emerge during the third phase include hemorrhage, hypoglycemia, renal failure, and hypotensive episodes. It is during phase three that the indivudal might die if she or he ingested a sufficient amount of acetaminophen to be fatal.

However, if the person (a) did not ingest a fatal overdose or (b) was treated for the overdose in time, she or he will proceed to the final phase: recovery. During the fourth phase, the liver gradually repairs itself, with recovery taking 2 to 4 weeks after the overdose was ingested (McDonough, 1998). It is unfortunate that the symptoms of an acetaminophen overdose can take so long to develop; an antidote to acetaminophen overdose is available, but it must be administered *within 12 hours of the time the overdose was ingested* to be fully effective.

This antidote is a chemical known as *N-acetylcysteine* (NAC). When it is administered within several hours of the initial overdose, N-acetylcysteine is quite effective in the treatment of acetaminophen poisoning (American Medical Association, 1994). But if, as all too often happens, the individual waits until the symptoms of acetaminophen toxicity develop before seeking help, it may be too late to prevent permanent liver damage or even death.

When it is taken in large doses, acetaminophen will destroy the liver enzyme *glutathione*. Glutathione is a chemical produced by the liver to protect itself from various toxins (Anker & Smilkstein, 1994). Taking more than 4,000 mg per day (just 8 "extra-strength" tablets), or even less if the person is also drinking alcohol, can result in serious, potentially fatal liver damage ("Scientists Call for," 2002). A dose of just 7.5 to 15 grams of acetaminophen (just 15–30 "extra-strength" tablets) in a single dose, or 5–8 grains (650–975 mg) per day for several weeks, is enough to cause a toxic reaction in the healthy adult (McDonough, 1998; Supernaw, 1991; Whitcomb & Block, 1994). For children, the toxic level is approximately 140 mg per kilogram of body weight.[14]

One factor that seems to contribute to liver damage in at least some cases is whether the individual ingested the acetaminophen on an empty stomach (Schiødt, Rochling, Casey, & Lee, 1997; Whitcomb & Block, 1994). Even otherwise normal patients who were attempting to control their weight through semi-starvation or fasting seem to be especially at risk for an unintentional acetaminophen toxic reaction (Schiødt et al., 1997). The authors pointed out that the enzyme glutathione is depleted by starvation diets, placing the individual at risk for a toxic reaction to even normal dosage levels of acetaminophen. Thus, the individual's diet is an important factor to consider when he or she is using acetaminophen for the control of mild to moderate levels of pain. These studies suggest that at least for certain individuals, acetaminophen has the potential to cause toxic reactions at dosage levels just above the normal therapeutic dosage range.

Aspirin. Aspirin is commonly ingested in suicide gestures or attempts (Sporer & Khayam-Bashi, 1996). Unfortunately, although scientists have learned a great

---

[13]See Glossary.

[14]Any suspected chemical overdose should be evaluated by a physician.

deal in the past 40 years about how an aspirin overdose effects the body (Yip, Dart, & Gabow, 1994), aspirin remains a potentially dangerous chemical. For example, in 1990 aspirin caused approximately as many deaths in the United States as did heroin overdoses ("Forum," 1991).

The average dosage level necessary to produce a toxic reaction to aspirin is about 10 grams for an adult, and about 150 mg of aspirin for every kilogram of body weight for children. A dose of 500 mg of aspirin per kilogram of body weight is potentially fatal to the individual. Symptoms of aspirin toxicity include headache, dizziness, tinnitus, mental confusion, increased sweating, thirst, dimming of sight, and hearing impairment (Shannon et al., 1995). Other symptoms of aspirin toxicity include restlessness, excitement, apprehension, tremor, delirium, hallucinations, convulsions, stupor, coma, hypotension, and at higher dosage levels, possible death (Sporer & Khayam-Bashi, 1996). These symptoms are most often seen in the person who has ingested a large dose of aspirin, but even small doses might result in toxicity for the individual who is aspirin sensitive.

Ibuprofen. Ibuprofen's popularity as an OTC analgesic has resulted in an increasing number of overdose attempts involving this drug (Lipscomb, 1989). Symptoms of overdose include seizures, acute renal failure, abdominal pain, nausea, vomiting, drowsiness, and metabolic acidosis (Lipscomb, 1989). There is no specific antidote for a toxic dose of ibuprofen, and medical care is often aimed at supportive treatment only.

Naproxen. The *2004 Physicians' Desk Reference* reported that the life-threatening dose of naproxen in humans is not known. Animal research involving dogs suggests that a dose of 1,000 mg/kg is potentially fatal, although in hamsters the estimated LD100 was estimated to be 4,100 mg/kg. No specific antidote is known for an overdose of naproxen, and medical care is limited to supportive treatment only. There are no symptoms specific to a naproxen overdose. Symptoms of an NSAID overdose include lethargy, drowsiness, nausea, vomiting, epigastric pain, respiratory depression, coma, and convulsions. The NSAIDs are capable of causing gastrointestinal bleeding in overdose situations and may cause either hypotension or hypertension (*Physicians' Desk Reference*, 2004). An overdose of

naproxen is considered a medical emergency, and the overdose victim should be evaluated by a physician.

Ketoprofen. There is limited information about ketoprofen overdoses. The *Physicians' Desk Reference* identified 26 overdoses for the prescription form of ketoprofen known as Orudis (*Physicians' Desk Reference*, 2004). No fatalities were noted, although these overdoses reflect cases in which the patient received immediate medical care. There are no symptoms specific to a ketoprofen overdose. Symptoms of an NSAID overdose include lethargy, drowsiness, nausea, vomiting, epigastric pain, respiratory depression, coma, and convulsions. The NSAIDs are capable of causing gastrointestinal bleeding in overdose situations and may cause either hypotension or hypertension (*Physicians' Desk Reference*, 2004). An overdose of naproxen or ketoprofen is considered a medical emergency and the overdose victim should be evaluated by a physician. The basic treatment procedures involve supportive treatment, as well as special interventions designed to treat the individual's specific problems as they emerge (*Physicians' Desk Reference*, 2004).

Summary

Over-the-counter analgesics are often discounted by many as not being "real" medications. But although it is often discounted by the average user as being something less than a real pharmaceutical, aspirin is America's most popular "drug." Each year, more than 20,000 tons of aspirin are manufactured and consumed in this country alone, and aspirin accounts for only about 28% of the OTC analgesic sales.

Aspirin, acetaminophen, naproxen, and ibuprofen are all quite effective in the control of mild to moderate levels of pain without exposing the patient to the side effects found with narcotic analgesics. Some of the OTC analgesics are useful in controlling the inflammation of autoimmune disorders and in helping to control postsurgical pain. Researchers have discovered that the OTC analgesics are of value in controlling the pain associated with cancer. Surprisingly, research has suggested that aspirin might even contribute to the early detection of some forms of cancer. Although the oldest OTC analgesic, aspirin, was introduced more than a century ago, medical researchers are still discovering new applications for this potent medication and its chemical cousins.

In spite of the fact that they are available over the counter, the OTC analgesics do carry significant potential for harm. Acetaminophen has been implicated in toxic reactions in chronic alcohol users at near-normal dosage levels. It also has been implicated as the cause of death in people who have taken acetaminiphen overdoses. Aspirin and ibuprofen have been implicated in fatal allergic reactions, especially in those who suffer from asthma. The use of aspirin in children with viral infections is not recommended.

CHAPTER NINETEEN

Tobacco Products and Nicotine Addiction

Introduction

Historians believe that the natives of the New World had used tobacco for many hundreds, if not thousands, of years before the arrival of the first European explorers. Tobacco was used in various religious ceremonies and for recreational purposes by the natives of North America. Following the discovery of the New World, the art of smoking was carried back across the Atlantic to Europe by early explorers, many of whom had themselves adopted the habit of smoking tobacco during their time in the Americas.

In Europe, the use of tobacco for smoking was received with some skepticism if not outright hostility. For example, in Germany, public smoking was once punishable by death; in Russia, castration was the sentence for the same crime (Berger & Dunn, 1982). In Asia, the early Chinese rulers made the use or distribution of tobacco a crime punishable by death, and smokers were executed as infidels in Turkey. In spite of these harsh measures, the practice of smoking became quite popular in Europe. Within a few decades of its introduction, the use of tobacco had spread across Europe and moved into Asia (Schuckit, 2000).

Even though there was a strong initial response against smoking in Europe, the practice soon became at least moderately acceptable in European society. Indeed, tobacco was thought to be a medicine by many European physicians, and its use was encouraged as a cure for numerous conditions. Smoking tobacco was interpreted as a mark of sophistication in both Europe and North America in the 19th and 20th centuries, but in the last half of the 20th century, tobacco use began to be criticized, especially after medical research began to find an association between cigarette smoking and various diseases. In the first years of the 21st century, tobacco use is both widespread and the subject of much controversy. In this chapter, the history of tobacco use and the complications caused by using tobacco will be reviewed.

History of Tobacco Use in the United States

Anthropological evidence suggests that tobacco was cultivated in South America as early as 8,000 years ago (Walton, 2002). Note that today's tobacco is much different from that used centuries earlier. The tobacco that was used in the New World when the first European explorers arrived was possibly more potent and may have contained hallucinatory substances not found in the tobacco now in use (Schuckit, 2000; Walton, 2002). This is because European tobacco growers learned to grow the milder, more acceptable *Nicotiana tabacum* rather than the potent *Nicotina rustica* used by the Native Americans for their religious ceremonies (Hilts, 1996).

Several different forces combined in the mid 19th century to change the shape of tobacco use. First, new varieties of tobacco were planted, allowing for a greater yield than in previous years. Second, new methods of curing the leaf of the tobacco plant were found, speeding up the process by which the leaf could be prepared for use. Third, the manner in which tobacco was used changed. The advent of the industrial age brought with it machinery capable of manufacturing the cigarette, a smaller, less expensive, neater way than cigars to smoke. Prior to this time, cigars were manufactured by hand, a slow, expensive process. However, just one machine, invented by James A. Bonsack, could produce 120,000 cigarettes a day. Such machines greatly increased the number of cigarettes that could be produced, expanding supply while reducing price. This made it possible for less affluent groups to afford tobacco products, and cigarettes soon became a favorite of the poor (Tate, 1989). By the year 1890, the price of domestic cigarettes had fallen to a nickel for a pack of 20 (Tate, 1989), making them affordable to all but the poorest smoker. But this rapid acceptance of cigarettes was not always automatic. Indeed, by 1909, no fewer than 10 different states had laws that prohibited their use.

Prior to the introduction of the cigarette, the major method of tobacco use was chewing. The practice of chewing tobacco, then spitting into the ever-present cuspidor, contributed to the spread of tuberculosis and other diseases (Brecher, 1972). Because of this, public health officials began to campaign against the practice of chewing tobacco after the year 1910. The new cigarette, manufactured in large numbers by the latest machines, provided a more sanitary and relatively inexpensive alternative to chewing tobacco. Cigarette smokers soon discovered that unlike cigars or pipes, the new cigarette had smoke that was so mild it could be inhaled (Burns, 1991). The smoke from pipes or cigars is much more bitter, making it unlikely that the smoker will inhale deeply. For many, cigarette smoking became the preferred method through which their nicotine addiction might be serviced. The world has never been the same since.

Scope of the Problem

Cigarettes became popular after these changes in the tobacco industry. In the year 1900, the per capita cigarette consumption in the United States was just 54 cigarettes per person (United States Department of Health & Human Services, 1999). The use of cigarettes grew in popularity during and immediately after World War I, and this growth in cigarette smoking continued until its peak in the mid 1960s (Schuckit, 2000). The social climate was one of "total social acceptance" (Jaffe, 1989, p. 680) of tobacco use, and until "quite recently, tobacco use was so common and socially acceptable . . . [that] . . . almost everyone tried smoking" (p. 680). At the peak of its popularity, approximately 52% of adult American males and 32% of adult American females were cigarette smokers (Schuckit, 2000).

Then, in 1964, the Surgeon General of the United States released a report stating that cigarette smoking was a danger to the smoker's health and outlining the various problems thought to be caused by smoking. At

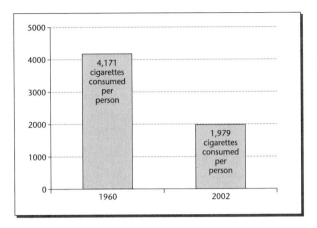

FIGURE 19.1 Comparison of per capita cigarette consumption in the United States: 1960 and 2002.
Source: Data from "40th Anniversary," 2004.

the time, the per capita daily consumption of cigarettes was 4,345 per adult per year ("40th Anniversary," 2004). In the wake of this report, the number of adults who continued to smoke in this country began to decline slowly until cigarette consumption reached 1,979 per adult per year in the United States in 2002 ("40th Anniversary," 2004). (See Figure 19.1.)

It is estimated that there are almost 1 billion cigarette smokers worldwide (Rose et al., 2003). In the United States, approximately three-quarters of people between 15 and 54 have smoked at least one cigarette (Anthony, Arria, & Johnson, 1995). The majority of those who smoke one cigarette probably do so out of curiosity. However, the authors suggested that one in every three individuals who smoke that first cigarette will continue to smoke until they become addicted. For them, the interval between experimental cigarette use and the start of daily smoking is 2 to 3 years (Schwartz, 1996). Of the estimated 265 million people in the United States, approximately 46.5 million are thought to currently smoke cigarettes (Fiore, Hatsukami, & Baker, 2002).

Only a small minority of cigarette smokers abuse other chemicals, but it is not uncommon for substance abusers to be heavy smokers also. The prevalence rates for cigarette smoking among alcohol- and drug-dependent people range from 71% to 100% (el-Guebaly, Cathcart, Currie, Brown, & Gloster, 2002). These figures suggest that cigarette use is a significant problem for those who are addicted to other chemicals.

Researchers have found that experimentation with cigarette smoking begins early in life. In the United States, the median age for individuals to begin experimenting with cigarette smoking is 15 (Patkar, Vergare, Batra, Weinstein, & Leone, 2003). But the individual's attitudes toward smoking are established even before using that first cigarette—in childhood or at the latest by early adolescence. This is true even for individuals who do not *begin* to smoke until late adolescence or early adulthood.

Pharmacology of Cigarette Smoking

The primary method by which tobacco is used is by smoking cigarettes (Schuckit, 2000), although chewing tobacco and cigar smoking have again become popular in recent years. Chemically, cigar smoke is very similar to cigarette smoke, although it does contain a higher concentration of ammonia (Jacobs, Thun, & Apicella, 1999). For these reasons, the terms *smoking*, *cigarette*, and *tobacco* will be used interchangeably in this chapter, except when other forms of tobacco (such as tobacco prepared for chewing) are discussed.

Tobacco smoke is influenced by such variables as (a) the exact composition of the tobacco being used, (b) how densely the tobacco is packed in the cigarette, (c) the length of the column of tobacco (for cigarette or cigar smokers), (d) the characteristics of the filter being used (if any), (e) the paper being used (for cigarette smokers), and (f) the temperature at which the tobacco is burned (Jaffe, 1990). To further complicate matters, the cigarette of today is far different from the cigarette of 1900 or even 1950, with up to 40% of today's typical cigarette being composed of "leftover stems, scraps and dust" (Hilts, 1996, p. 44). In 1955, it took 2.6 pounds of tobacco leaves to produce a thousand cigarettes; now, the use of fillers has reduced this amount of tobacco to 1.7 pounds (Hilts, 1996). This explains why a pack of "Marlboro" cigarettes that sells for $3.15 yields a $1.40 profit for the manufacturer, the Phillip Morris Tobacco company, a profit margin of 44% per pack (Fonda, 2001).

Cigarette tobacco smoke is known to contain some 4,000 different compounds, of which 2,550 come from the unprocessed tobacco itself (Burns, 1991; Stitzer, 2003). The other compounds found in cigarette smoke come from additives, pesticides, and other organic or metallic compounds that either intentionally or unintentionally find their way into the cigarette tobacco. A partial list of the compounds found in tobacco smoke would include

> acetaldehyde, acetone, aceturitrile, acrolein, acrylonitrile, ammonia, arsenic, benzeye, butylamine, carbon monoxide, carbon dioxide, cresols, crotononitrile, DDT, dimethylamine, endrin, ethylamine, formaldehyde, furfural hydroquinone, hydrogen cyanide (used in the gas chamber), hydrogen sulfide, lead, methacrolein, methyl alcohol, methylamine, nickel compounds, nicotine, nitric oxide, nitrogen dioxide, phenol, polonium-210 (radioactive), pyridine, [and] "tar" (burned plant resins). (Shipley & Rose, 2003, p. 83, heavy print in original deleted)

In addition to all these compounds, various perfumes are added to the tobacco leaves to give the cigarette a distinctive aroma (Hilts, 1996). Other compounds found in cigarettes or the paper wrapper include various forms of sugar, insecticides, herbicides, fungicides, rodenticides, pesticides, and various manufacturing machine lubricants (which come into contact with the tobacco leaves or paper as these products move through machines used in the manufacturing process) (Glantz, Slade, Bero, Hanauer, & Barnes, 1996). Although smokers inhale these products when they smoke a cigarette, there has been virtually no research into the effects of these chemicals on the human body when they are smoked.

The concentrations of many of the chemicals found in cigarette smoke, such as carbon monoxide, are such that "uninterrupted exposure" (Burns, 1991, p. 633) would result in death. For example, the concentration of carbon monoxide found in cigarettes is "similar to that found in automobile exhaust" (p. 633), a known source of potentially dangerous concentrations of this chemical. Cigarette smoke also contains radioactive compounds such as polonium 210 (Evans, 1993; Jaffe, 1990) and lead 210 (Brownson, Novotny, & Perry, 1993). These compounds for the most part are in the soil where tobacco is grown and are absorbed into the tobacco plant. When the individual smokes, these radioactive compounds are carried into the lungs along with the smoke. Over a year, the cumulative radiation exposure for a two pack a day smoker is equal to what a person would receive from 250 to 300 chest x-rays (Evans, 1993).

Cigarette smoke is known to contain a small amount of arsenic (Banerjee, 1990). Some of the chemicals found in tobacco smoke, like benzene, are documented carcinogens.[1] This smoke contains at least 43 known or suspected carcinogens, and smokers introduce these compounds into their bodies when they smoke (Burns, 1991; Hilts, 1996).

Nicotine. Nicotine was first isolated in 1828. As early as 1889 scientists knew that nicotine had an effect on nervous tissue, but not until almost a century later was the mechanism by which nicotine affected neurons identified (Stitzer, 2003). As a result of legal action against tobacco companies in the last years of the 20th century, it has come to light that for many years these companies were well aware that nicotine was the major psychoactive agent in cigarettes. The process of smoking delivers nicotine to the brain faster than any other known method of drug delivery (Fogarty, 2003). As various lawsuits against the tobacco industry have unfolded over the last years of the 20th century and the first decade of the 21st, it became clear that many major tobacco companies viewed cigarettes as little more than a single-dose nicotine administration mechanism that was able to deliver this drug quickly to the smoker's brain (Benowitz & Henningfield, 1994; Glantz et al., 1995; Glantz, Slade, Bero, Hanauer, & Barnes, 1996; Hilts, 1996). Further, in spite of strident denials to the contrary, there is strong evidence that tobacco companies selectively grew more potent strains of tobacco for use in producing cigarettes for smoking ("How He Won the War," 1996). In the settlement of a class action lawsuit against the tobacco industry by 40 of the 50 states, the industry agreed to allow the Food and Drug Administration to gradually lower the acceptable nicotine level in cigarettes over the next 12 years (Smolowe, 1997).

Although nicotine is well absorbed through the gastrointestinal tract, much orally administered nicotine is biotransformed by the liver as a result of the first pass metabolism effect (see Chapter 6). This characteristic limits the impact of orally administered nicotine. To circumvent this problem, tobacco companies encourage the use of cigarettes over the oral use of tobacco products, as smoking is the ideal method of introducing nicotine into the body. With each "puff" on a cigarettes, a small dose of nicotine gains admission to the circulation, from where it will reach the brain in 7 (Fiore, Jorenby, Baker, & Kenford, 1992) to 8 (Hilts, 1996; Jaffe, 1990) seconds. As a result of this process, a typical one pack a day smoker will self-administer between 60,000 and 80,000 doses of nicotine each day without the problem of first pass metabolism (Jorenby, 1997; Parrott, 1999). At the same time, smokers "overlearn" the nicotine self-administration through repetition as they self-administer another dose of nicotine with each puff.

The lethal dose of nicotine for the average adult is estimated to be approximately 60 mg (Stitzer, 2003). Atlhough the average cigarette contains between 6 and 11 milligrams (mg) of nicotine (Henningfield, 1995), the bioavailability of nicotine from cigarette smoking is only 3% to 40% (Benowitz & Henningfield, 1994). Nicotine is not able to cross over from the lungs to the blood very easily, and so the typical smoker absorbs only 1–3 mg of nicotine from each cigarette (Henningfield, 1995; Stitzer, 2003). In terms of absolute toxicity, the typical smoker will receive between 1/60th and 1/24th of the estimated lethal dose of nicotine with each cigarette. Over the course of the typical day, the average smoker absorbs a cumulative dose of 20–40 mg of nicotine, a dosage level that, if not lethal to the smoker, is still quite toxic to the body (Henningfield, 1995).

Once in the body, nicotine will be rapidly distributed to virtually every blood-rich tissue, including the lungs, the spleen, and the brain (Henningfield & Nemeth-Coslett, 1988). Nicotine is both water soluble and lipid soluble, and its lipid solubility allows it to cross over the blood-brain barrier very rapidly. Indeed, the brain is one of the organs where the highest levels of nicotine accumulate, with measured levels of nicotine in the brain being twice as high as the level found in the blood (Fiore et al., 1992). It has been estimated that only 0.05 to 2.5 mg of the nicotine from each cigarette actually reaches the brain (Ashton, 1992; Lee & D'Alonzo, 1993). But once in the brain, nicotine's effects are "similar to those of cocaine and amphetamine" (Rustin, 1988, p. 18). Nicotine stimulates the release of dopamine in the nucleus accumbens, possibly through the stimulation of acetylcholine receptor sites in the brain (Patkar et al., 2003).

In the body, the peak nicotine concentration is reached in the first minutes after the cigarette is smoked, and then it drops. The biological half-life of nicotine is between 100 minutes (Rustin, 1992) and 2 hours,

[1]See Glossary.

(Stitzer, 2003). Because only 50% of the nicotine from one cigarette is biotransformed during the first half-life period, over the course of a day a reservoir of unmetabolized nicotine is established in the smoker's body. A limited degree of tolerance to nicotine's effects develops each day, but this acquired tolerance is lost just as rapidly during the night hours when the typical smoker abstains from cigarette use (Bhandari, Sylvester, & Rigotti, 1996). This is why many smokers find that the first cigarette of the day has such a strong effect.

Only 5% to 10% of the nicotine that enters the body is excreted unchanged. The rest is biotransformed by the liver. About 90% of the nicotine that is biotransformed will be turned into *cotinine*, a metabolite of nicotine that has no known psychoactive properties. The other 10% of the nicotine is biotransformed into *nicotine-n-oxide*. These chemicals are then excreted from the body in the urine. Although it was once thought that cigarette smokers were able to biotransform nicotine more rapidly than nonsmokers, research has failed to support this belief (Benowitz & Jacob, 1993).

Acetaldehyde. In addition to nicotine, tobacco smoke also includes a small amount of acetaldehyde. By coincidence, this is also the first metabolite produced by the liver when the body biotransforms alcohol. In terms of its psychoactive potential, acetaldehyde is thought to be more potent than alcohol. Also, like alcohol, acetaldehyde has a sedative effect on the user, possibly accounting for the effect reported by smokers that cigarette smoking helps them to relax (Rustin, 1988).

Cigarette smoking and Alzheimer's disease. In the early 1990s, researchers found a "negative association" (Brenner et al., 1993, p. 293) between cigarette smoking and the later development of Alzheimer's disease. However, subsequent research failed to support this association (Riggs, 1996). Indeed, cigarette smokers were found to be at *increased* risk for developing some form of dementia in later life (Ott et al., 1998).

Drug interactions between nicotine and other chemicals. Drug interactions between nicotine and various other therapeutic agents are well documented. Cigarette smokers, for example, will require more morphine for the control of pain (Bond, 1989; Jaffe, 1990). Tobacco smokers may experience less sedation from benzodiazepines than do nonsmokers (Barnhill, Ciraulo, Ciraulo, & Greene, 1995). Thus, the physician treating the patient who smokes might need to adjust the individual's daily benzodiazepine dose in order to achieve the desired level of sedation. Surprisingly, cigarette smokers seem to be able to biotransform THC faster than nonsmokers, and thus the effects of marijuana do not last quite as long in the cigarette smoker as in the nonsmoker (Nelson, 2000).

Scientists have discovered that between 70% (Enoch & Goldman, 2002) and 95% (Hughes, Rose, & Callas, 2000) of heavy drinkers also smoke, possibly because nicotine is more reinforcing for alcohol users than for nondrinkers.[2] Cigarette smoking interacts with alcohol in a number of ways. First, cigarette smoking slows the process of gastric emptying and thus the process of alcohol absorption (Nelson, 2000). Further, the nicotine absorbed by the smoker seems to counteract some of the sedation seen with alcohol use. Tobacco also interacts with many anticoagulants as well as the beta blocker propranol and caffeine (Bond, 1989). Women who use oral contraceptives and who smoke are more likely to experience strokes, myocardial infarction, and thromboembolism than their nonsmoking counterparts, according to the author.

After a cigarette smoker who uses the medication theophylline stops smoking, he or she will experience a 36% rise in theophylline blood levels over the first week of abstinence. This seems to be caused by the effects of such chemicals as benzopyrene, which are found in the tobacco smoke (Henningfield, 1995). Also, the concentration of caffeine in the blood might increase by as much as 250% following smoking cessation, causing caffeine-induced anxiety symptoms. Anxiety is an early symptom of nicotine withdrawal, and smokers quickly learn to avoid this unpleasant experience by smoking another cigarette (Little, 2000). The result of this process is that former smokers might interpret caffeine-related anxiety symptoms as a sign that they should have a cigarette.

Nicotine use has been found to decrease the blood levels of clozapine and the antipsychotic medication haloperidol by as much as 30% to 50% (American Psychiatric Association, 1996; Kavanagh, McGrath, Saunders, Dore, & Clark, 2002). It has also been found to *increase* the blood levels of medications such as clomipramine, and antidepressant medications such as desipramine, doxepin, and nortriptyline (American

---

[2]The author of this text has met many alcohol abusers who report, for example, that they smoke cigarettes *only* while they are drinking.

Psychiatric Association, 1996). The list of potential inter-actions between nicotine and various pharmaceuticals reviewed in the last few paragraphs does not list every possible chemical that might interact with nicotine, but it does highlight nicotine's very strong effect on how other chemicals work in the body.[3]

The Effects of Nicotine Use

In the brain, nicotine mimics the actions of the neuro-transmitter acetylcholine, binding to what are called the nicotinic-acetylcholine[4] receptor sites. These receptor sites are located throughout the brain, especially in the thalamus and midbrain regions. It is thought that nicotine can bring about a dose-dependent, biphasic response at the level of the individual neuron, especially those that utilize the neurotransmitter acetylcholine (Ashton, 1992; Benowitz, 1992; Restak, 1991; Ritz, 1999; Rose et al., 2003). Initially, nicotine stimulates these neu-rons, possibly contributing to the smoker's feeling of increased alertness as the brain responds to the nicotine molecules as if they were acetylcholine itself. However, over longer periods of time the nicotine blocks the acetyl-choline receptor site, reducing the rate at which those neurons fire.

This theory would seem to account for the observed effects of cigarette smoking. Smokers are known to expe-rience stimulation of the brain (Schuckit, 2000) as well as decreased muscle tone (Jaffe, 1990). The first-time smoker will report a sense of nausea and may possibly even vomit (Restak, 1991). However, if the individual persists in his or her attempts to smoke, the stimulation of the neurotransmitter systems outlined above will eventually result in an association between smoking and the nicotine-induced pleasurable sensations, as the smoker "over-learns" the association between smok-ing and the drug-induced subjective experience of pleasure as the neurotransmitters norepinephrine and dopamine are released within the brain.

For much of the latter part of the 20th century, tobacco companies argued that because nicotine does not produce the pattern of intoxication seen with alcohol or barbiturate abuse it was not "addicting" in the tradi-tional sense of the word (Stitzer, 2003). However, as the criteria for addiction were more clearly defined, it became evident that nicotine was indeed an addictive substance in every sense of the word (Stitzer, 2003). Unfortunately, scientists are still attempting to under-stand the mechanism by which nicotine is able to cause the smoker to become dependent on it (Rose et al., 2003).

Once nicotine reaches the brain, it stimulates the release of several different neurotransmitters includ-ing GABA, serotonin, norepinephrine, glutamate, and dopamine (Fogarty, 2003). In the brain nicotine appears to reduce the levels of monoamine oxidase β, which is involved in the breakdown of dopamine molecules, while increasing the effects of nitric oxide, which has the effect of slowing the reuptake of dopamine molecules (Fogarty, 2003). Thus, nicotine stimulates the release of dopamine in such regions of the brain as the limbic system while interfering with other chemicals that normally destroy or control the reuptake of dopamine that has already been released. Nicotine also stimulates the release of β-endorphin in the limbic system. β-endorphin is a member of the endorphin family of neurotransmit-ters and it is thought to be about 200 times as potent as morphine (Jorenby, 1997).

The net effect of all of these individual effects is that nicotine is able to activate the dopamine reward system within the brain, especially the mesolimbic region, and increase dopamine levels in this region of the brain for several hours after the last cigarette (Fogarty, 2003; Mansvelder, Keath, & McGehee, 2002). Another region of the brain where nicotine exerts a major effect is the medulla, which is responsible for such functions as swallowing, vomiting, respiration, and the control of blood pressure (Restak, 1984). This is also why many first-time smokers experience both nausea and vomit-ing (Jaffe, 1990). However, with repeated exposure to tobacco chewing or smoking, the smoker will become tolerant to nicotine-induced nausea.

Outside of the brain, nicotine stimulates the release of acetylcholine, which is involved in controlling many of the body's muscle functions. Nicotine-induced acetylcholine release in the body seems to account, at least in part, for nicotine's immediate effects on the

---

[3]In order to avoid potentially dangerous interaction effects between a pharmaceutical and a compound found in cigarettes, you should ask a physician or a pharmacist if there is any danger in taking that medicine while smoking.

[4]These are a subset of the known acetylcholine receptor sites in the brain and are identified by their ability to allow either acetylcholine or nicotine to bind at the receptor site.

cardiovascular system, such as an increase in heart rate and blood pressure, as well as an increase in the strength of heart contractions (Jorenby, 1997). At the same time that the heart rate is increased, nicotine causes the blood vessels in the outer regions of the body to constrict, causing a reduction in peripheral blood flow (Schuckit, 2000). In addition to its effects on the brain, nicotine causes a decrease in the strength of stomach contractions (Schuckit, 2000), and cigarette smoke itself can cause irritation of the tissues of the lungs and pulmonary system. The process of smoking deposits potentially harmful chemicals in the lungs and causes a decrease in the motion of the cilia[5] in the lungs. These features of cigarette smoking are thought to contribute to the development of pulmonary problems in long-term smokers.

Nicotine Addiction

Sometime in the early 1960s, researchers for various tobacco companies discovered that nicotine, which is the chemical in cigarettes that makes smoking rewarding, was also highly addictive. This research was apparently suppressed by the tobacco industry for many years (Hurt & Robertson, 1998; Slade, Bero, Hanauer, Barnes, & Glantz, 1995). Indeed, one memo from 1963, cited by Slade et al. (1995) illustrates that the tobacco industry knew that it was "in the business of selling nicotine, an addictive drug" (p. 228) to smokers. However, it was not until 1997 that a major tobacco company in the United States, the Liggett Group, admitted in court that tobacco was addictive (Solomon, Rogers, Katel, & Lach 1997).

The addictive potential of cigarettes would seem to be significantly greater than that of cocaine, as illustrated by the observation that only 3% to 20% of those who try cocaine once go on to become addicted to it (Musto, 1991), but between 33% and 50% of those who experiment with smoking will become addicted (Henningfield, 1995; Pomerleau, Collins, Shiffman, & Pomerleau, 1993). Further, like the other drugs of abuse, the greater the individual's level of exposure to cigarette smoking, the greater the chances are of becoming addicted. Jaffe (1989) concluded that "a very high percentage" (p. 680) of those who smoke 100 cigarettes will go on to become daily smokers.

[5]See Glossary.

As another reflection of the strength of nicotine addiction, scientists have discovered neurochemical changes in the brain after just a few cigarettes, suggesting that even a limited exposure to nicotine may initiate the addiction process (Mansvelder, Keath, & McGehee, 2002). This might explain why children who smoke just four or more cigarettes stand a 94% chance of continuing to smoke (Walker, 1993).

Although nicotine appears to be significantly more likely to bring about physical addiction than is cocaine, not everybody who begins to smoke will go on to become addicted to nicotine (Henningfield & Nemeth-Coslett, 1988). A small minority (perhaps 5% to 10%) of those who smoke cigarettes are not addicted to nicotine (Jarvik & Schneider, 1992; Shiffman, Fischer, Zettler-Segal, & Benowitz, 1990). These individuals, who demonstrate an episodic pattern of nicotine use, are classified as cigarette "chippers." As a group, chippers do not appear to smoke in response to social pressures, and they do not seem to smoke to avoid the symptoms of withdrawal (Shiffman et al., 1990). Unfortunately, very little is known about the phenomenon of tobacco "chipping," and researchers still do not understand what personality or biological characteristics separate those who "chip" from those who go on to become addicted to cigarette smoking.

But it is known that 90% to 95% of those who smoke are addicted to nicotine. These individuals demonstrate all of the characteristics typically seen in necessary drug addiction: (a) tolerance, (b) withdrawal symptoms, and (c) drug-seeking behaviors (Rustin, 1988, 1992). Further, like drug abusers, tobacco users develop highly individual drug-using rituals that seem to provide them with a sense of security and contribute to their tendency to engage in smoking behaviors when anxious.

Cigarette smokers tend to smoke in such a way as to regulate the nicotine level in their blood (Djordjevic, Hoffmann, & Hoffmann, 1997). When given cigarettes of a high nicotine content, smokers will use fewer cigarettes; the reverse is true with low-nicotine cigarettes (Benowitz, 1992; Djordjevic et al., 1997; Jaffe, 1990). Smokers of "low-tar" brands also have been found to inhale more deeply and to hold the smoke in their lungs longer than do smokers of cigarette brands with higher levels of tar (Djordjevic et al., 1997). This difference in smoking pattern may account for the increase in the frequency with which certain forms of cancer develop in the lungs of some smokers. Obviously, there is a need for more research into how the tar content of a cigarette affects the manner in which the smoker engages in the habit of cigarette smoking.

Nicotine withdrawal. Withdrawal symptoms usually begin within 2 hours of the last use of tobacco, peak within 24 hours (Kaplan & Sadock, 1996), then gradually decline over the next 10 days to several weeks (Hughes, 1992; Jaffe, 1989). The exact nature of the withdrawal symptoms varies from person to person. Surprisingly, in light of the horror stories often heard about the agony of giving up cigarette smoking, research has found that approximately one-quarter of those who quit cigarettes report no significant withdrawal symptoms at all (Benowitz, 1992).

Some symptoms of nicotine withdrawal include sleep disturbance, irritability, impatience, difficulties in concentration, restlessness, a craving for tobacco, hunger, gastrointestinal upset, headache, and drowsiness (Fiore et al., 1992; Hughes, 1992). Other possible symptoms include depression, hostility, fatigue, lightheadedness, headaches, a tingling sensation in the limbs, constipation, and increased coughing (Jarvik & Schneider, 1992). Although many cigarette smokers report that the act of smoking a cigarette helps to calm them down, evidence now suggests that nicotine can induce or exacerbate anxiety symptoms in people with panic disorder (Isensee, Hans-Ulrich, Stein, Hofler, & Lieb, 2003; Parrott, 1999; West & Hajek, 1997). The subjective distress caused by the cigarette withdrawal syndrome will gradually decrease in frequency and intensity in the first 2 weeks after the individual's last cigarette. However, some withdrawal discomfort and craving for cigarettes will continue for at least 6 months (Hughes, Gust, Skoog, Keenan, & Fenwick, 1991).

There is evidence that people who smoke more frequently experience stronger withdrawal symptoms than light or moderate smokers (Jaffe, 1990). However, there has been little research into what smoking patterns or biochemical markers might be associated with more severe withdrawal symptoms after the individual stops smoking. It *is* known that within 2 weeks of the last cigarette, smokers' heart rate and blood pressure begin to drop, and they will begin to experience an improvement in peripheral blood flow patterns (Hughes, 1992; Jarvik & Schneider, 1992).

Complications of the Chronic Use of Tobacco

The impact of smoking on any given individual is quite difficult to determine. For example, consider the manner in which the exact amount of nicotine, tar, and carbon monoxide obtained from a specific brand of cigarette is determined: The cigarette is "smoked" by a test machine, and the composition of the smoke is then analyzed (Hilts, 1994). Because this is a mechanical process, the test data obtained through this method have little rrelationship to the chemicals the average smoker will inhale.[6] This is because the machine does not hold the cigarette with fingers that might block the microscopic holes in the filter region of the cigarette, or inhale the cigarette smoke deeply into the lungs in order to savor the flavor of the smoke. These smoker-specific behaviors all influence exactly which chemicals—and in what concentration—gain admission to the body when a person smokes a cigarette.

By the middle of the 20th century, researchers at the Mayo Clinic had found a relationship between smoking and coronary artery disease (Bartecchi, MacKenzie, & Schrier, 1994). In the next half century, thousands of research studies identified a relationship between cigarette smoking and other forms of illness. Scientists now believe that tobacco use is the cause of 19% of the annual deaths in the United States, responsible for an estimated 435,000 to 440,000 premature deaths in the this country alone (Carmona, 2004; Mokdad, Marks, Stroup, & Gerberding, 2004). This number includes 15,000 nonsmokers who are estimated to die each year in the United States from what is known as "passive," smoke, "environmental tobacco smoke" (ETS), or "secondhand" smoke (which will be discussed, below).

It is difficult to put the risks associated with cigarette smoking into strong enough terms. Statistically, male smokers die 13.2 years earlier than their nonsmoking counterparts; female smokers lose an estimated 14.5 years of their lives as a result of their smoking (Carmona, 2004). This was clearly seen in the study

---

[6] The Federal Trade Commission is aware of this fact but continues to rely on data provided by the tobacco industry itself to determine the content of cigarette smoke, according to Hilts (1994) and Cotton (1993).

TABLE 19.1 Tobacco-Related Causes of Death

Condition	Percentage of smoking-related deaths	If annual death toll from smoking is 430,000 people a year in the U.S.	If annual death toll from smoking is 450,000 people a year in the U.S.
Smoking-induced lung cancer	28%	120,000	126,000
Smoking-induced coronary heart disease	23%	98,900	103,500
Smoking-induced chronic lung diseases other than lung cancer	17%	73,100	76,500
Other forms of smoking-induced cancer	7%	30,100	31,500
Smoking-related strokes	6%	25,800	27,000
All other forms of smoking-induced illness	19%	81,700	85,500

conducted by Phillips, Wannamethee, Thomson, and Smith (1996), based on data from the ongoing British Regional Heart Study. The authors found that 78% of the nonsmokers who began this study survived to the age of 73, whereas only 44% of lifelong smokers survived to that age. Table 19.1 identifies the various causes of death associated with cigarette smoking.

One of the mechanisms by which cigarette smoking is thought to cause death is by aiding, if not causing, the development of cancer in the smoker's body. Indeed, tobacco products are the only products sold in this country that are "unequivocally carcinogenic when used as directed" (MacKenzie, Bartecchi, & Schrier, 1994b, p. 977). Cigarette smokers are estimated to have 1,100% to 2,400% greater chances of developing some form of cancer than nonsmokers of the same age (Pappas, 1995). Thirty percent of *all* cancer deaths are caused by smoking (Bartecchi, MacKenzie, & Schrier, 1994; Fiore, Epps, & Manley, 1994). Cigarette smoking is thought to cause more than 75% of all cases of esophageal cancer, 30% to 40% of all bladder cancers, and 30% of the cases of cancer of the pancreas (Sherman 1991), making cigarette smoking *the* single largest cause of preventable death in the United States (Bartecchi, MacKenzie, & Schrier, 1994).

Each year in the United States, cigarette smoking is thought to cause

- 17% to 30% of the deaths from cardiovascular disease
- 90% of the deaths from lung cancer
- 24% of the deaths from pneumonia and/or influenza
- 10% of infant deaths (Hughes, 2000; Miller, 1999)

The direct annual cost of health care problems caused by cigarette smoking is estimated at $75 billion in the United States alone, with an additional $82 billion a year in lost productivity from smoking-related illness (Carmona, 2004). For each person who dies from smoking-related illness, 20 people are thought to be living with a smoking-related disorder (Carmona, 2004). The cost of cigarette smoking to society (in terms of lost productivity, medical care, and premature death) is estimated at $3,000 per smoker per year (Centers for Disease Control, 2004).[7] One indirect consequence of

[7]Many smokers point out that they pay state and federal taxes when they purchase a pack of cigarettes. The taxes are added to the cost of the cigarettes prior to purchase. However, even the most passionate does not pay $3,000 worth of taxes per year in cigarette purchases, so this rationalization is not supported by the facts.

cigarette smoking is the relationship between smoking and accidental fires. Each year in the United States there are an estimated 187,000 smoking-related fires, resulting in an additional loss of $550 million in property damage (Bhandari, Sylvester, & Rigotti, 1996).

There is hardly a body system that is not affected by cigarette smoking. What follows is just a short list of the various conditions known or strongly suspected to be a result of cigarette smoking.

The mouth, throat, and pulmonary system. Chronic cigarette smokers are at increased risk for sleep-related respiratory problems (Wetter, Young, Bidwell, Badr, & Palta, 1994). The authors reviewed data from 811 adults who were examined at the sleep disorders program at the University of Wisconsin-Madison medical center and found that current smokers were at greater risk for such disorders as snoring and sleep apnea than were nonsmokers. The relationship between smoking and sleep disorders is so strong that Wetter et al. (1994) suggested smoking cessation as one of the treatment interventions for a patient with a sleep-related breathing disorder.

In spite of the tobacco industry's refusal to accept the evidence, the research data are viewed as supporting a firm link between smoking and lung cancer (Carmona, 2004). Reserchers believe that cigarette smokers are 10 to 15 times (1,000% to 1,500%) more likely to develop lung cancer than are nonsmokers (Kuper, Boffetta, & Adami, 2002). Indeed, 90% of all cases of lung cancer and 35% of *all* cases of cancer might be traced to cigarette smoking (Anczak & Nogler, 2003; Hughes, 2000). Cigarette smokers are also 10 to 15 times more likely to develop laryngeal cancer than nonsmokers, with the degree of risk increasing with greater cigarette consumption (Kuper et al., 2002). In addition to the increased risk for cancer, cigarette smokers have higher rates for chronic bronchitis, pneumonia, and chronic obstructive pulmonary disease (COPD) such as emphysema compared to nonsmokers (Carmona, 2004). Indeed, it has been estimated that 90% of all deaths from COPD might be traced to cigarette smoking (Anczak & Nogler, 2003). Finally, although nonsmokers also develop respiratory disease, research has shown that smokers are more likely to die from a lung disorder if one develops than are nonsmokers (Burns, 1991; Jaffe, 1990; Lee & D'Alonzo, 1993; Schuckit, 2000).

The digestive tract. Cigarette smoking is the cause of approximately half of all cases of tooth loss and gum disease (Centers for Disease Control, 2004). Smokers are also at greater risk for oral cancers than nonsmokers (Carmona, 2004). This risk is compounded by the effects of alcohol if the smoker is also an alcohol abuser (Garro, Espin, & Lieber, 1992). Heavy drinkers have almost a 6-fold greater chance of developing cancer in the mouth and pharynx than nondrinkers, whereas cigarette smokers have been found to have a 7-fold greater risk of mouth or pharynx cancer than nonsmokers. However, alcoholics who *also* smoke have a 38-fold greater risk for cancer of the mouth or pharynx than do nonsmoking nondrinkers (National Institute on Alcohol Abuse and Alcoholism, 1998).

For reasons that are not entirely clear, the use of tobacco products is thought to contribute to the formation of peptic ulcers (Carmona, 2004; Jarvik & Schneider, 1992; Lee & D'Alonzo, 1993) and cancer of the stomach (Carmona, 2004), and contributes to the development of cancer of the pancreas (Carmona, 2004). For reasons that are not clear, regular smoking also places the smoker at increased risk for developing diabetes (Rimm, Chan, Stampfer, Colditz, & Willett, 1995).

The cardiovascular system. Smoking is a known risk factor in the formation of aortic aneurysms and for the development of coronary heart disease, hypertension, and atherosclerotic peripheral vascular disease. Cigarette smoking has been identified as the "single most important preventable risk factor for cardiovascular disease" (Tresch & Aronow, 1996, p. 24), causing 30% of the annual deaths from coronary heart disease in this country. It is a known risk factor for leukemia (Carmona, 2004), with approximately 14% of all cases of adult onset leukemia in the United States thought to be caused by cigarette smoking (Brownson et al., 1993). Cigarette smokers are at increased risk for cerebrovascular diseases such as cerebral infarction or a cerebral hemorrhage (Carmona, 2004; Robbins, Manson, Lee, Satterfield, & Hennekens, 1994; Sherman, 1991). Cigarette smoking is thought to be the cause of 60,000 strokes per year in the United States alone (Sacco, 1995), of which an estimated 26,000 are fatal (Carpenter, 2001).

Another way that cigarette smoking impacts the cardiovascular system is by causing the coronary arteries to briefly constrict. Moliterno et al. (1994) measured the diameters of the coronary arteries of 42 cigarette smokers who were being evaluated for complaints of chest pain. For those who had recently smoked a cigarette but who did not have coronary artery disease, the authors found a *7% decrease* in coronary artery diameter. Because the coronary arteries are the primary source of blood for the heart, anything that causes a reduction in the amount of blood flow through the coronary arteries, even if for a short period of time, holds the potential to cause damage to the heart itself. Thus, the short-term reduction in coronary artery diameter brought on by cigarette smoking may ultimately contribute to cardiovascular problems for the smoker.

In addition to causing a reduction in coronary artery diameter, cigarette smoking introduces large amounts of carbon monoxide into the circulation. The blood of a cigarette smoker might lose as much as 15% of its oxygen-carrying capacity, as the carbon monoxide binds to the hemoglobin in the blood and blocks the transportation of oxygen to the body's cells (Tresch & Aronow, 1996).

The visual system. In addition to cigarette-induced cancer, smokers may experience other, nonfatal forms of illness as well. Cigarette smoking appears to be associated with a higher risk of cataract formation (Centers for Disease Control, 2004; Christensen et al., 1992; Hankinson et al., 1992). Although the exact mechanism for cataract formation was not clear, male smokers who used 20 or more cigarettes a day were found to be twice as likely to form cataracts as were nonsmokers (Christensen et al., 1992). Former female smokers were found to be at increased risk for cataract formation even if they had quit smoking a decade earlier (Hankinson et al., 1992). The findings from these two studies reveal that cigarette-induced disease is far more involved than had previously been thought and suggest that at least some of the physical damage caused by cigarette smoking does not reverse itself if the smoker quits.

The reproductive system. The chemicals introduced into the body by smoking reach every body system that receives blood, including the reproductive system. Smoking has been identified as a cause of reduced fertility in women, and as a causal factor for fetal death or stillbirth (Carmona, 2004). Cigarette smoking has been identified as a risk factor for the development of cervical cancer (Carmona, 2004), and researchers estimate that between 20%–25% (Simons, Phillips, & Coleman, 1993) and 30% (Bartecchi et al., 1994) of all cases of cervical cancer can be related to smoking. Fortunately, evidence suggests that when a woman stops smoking, her risk of cervical cancer slowly declines; stopping smoking might even contribute to a reduction in the size of the cancerous growth (Szarewski et al., 1996).

Male smokers are also at increased risk for reproductive system dysfunctions as a result of cigarette smoking. There is a significant body of evidence that cigarette smoking is a cause of erectile dysfunction for men, possibly through smoking-induced circulatory damage to blood vessels involved in the erectile response (Bach, Wincze, & Barlow, 2001). Surprisingly, men who smoke do not appear to be at increased risk for cancer of the prostate, although they suffer from a higher mortality rate than nonsmokers when this form of cancer develops (Carmona, 2004).

Other complications caused by cigarette smoking. For reasons that remain unclear, cigarette smoking is thought to be a risk factor for the development of psoriasis (Baughman, 1993). Cigarette smokers are known to suffer from higher rates of cancer of the kidneys than do nonsmokers, and there appears to be a relationship between cigarette smoking and a thyroid condition known as *Graves' disease* (Carmona, 2004). There is a relationship between cigarette smoking and bone density reduction in postmenopausal women (Carmona, 2004). Further, as a group, older women who smoke were found to be physically weaker and had less coordination than did nonsmoking women of the same age (Nelson, Nevitt, Scott, Stone, & Cummings, 1994). The authors administered a battery of physical and neuromuscular function tests to 9,704 women who were at least 65 years of age and were living independently. The results suggested that "women who are current smokers, and to a lesser extent former smokers, are weaker, have poorer balance, and have impaired neuromuscular performance compared with those who have never smoked" (p. 1829). However, the authors did not identify a mechanism by which cigarette smoking might interfere with neuromuscular performance in women who did smoke cigarettes. Further, they admitted that their study was limited to volunteers who were able to come in to the research center, and thus these women might, in some manner, be different from women who were unable to participate in the research study because of ill health, lack of transportation, or other reasons.

Finally, there is evidence that smoking can cause changes in brain function that may persist for many years after the individual stops (Sherman, 1994). There is a measurable decline in mental abilities that begins about 4 hours after the last cigarette. It is not known how long former smokers will need before they return to their normal level of intellectual function. However, some former smokers report that they have never felt "right" for as long as 9 *years* after their last cigarette. There has been no research into the long-term effects of cigarette abstinence on cognitive function (Sherman, 1994), but these reports are quite suggestive.

Smoking and gender. An estimated 240,000 women are thought to die each year in the United States alone as a result of smoking-related illness (Peto, Lopez, Boreham, Thun, & Heath, 1992). This figure represents approximately half of the estimated 440,000 annual deaths attributable to cigarette smoking.

The degrees of risk. There is no such thing as a "safe" cigarette, and smoking cessation is the only proven way to reduce or avoid these known smoking-related problems (Carmona, 2004). Low-tar cigarettes were found to present the same degree of risk as regular cigarettes (Carmona, 2004). There is a dose-related risk of premature death caused by cigarette smoking for some conditions, such as cerebrovascular disease (Robbins et al., 1994).

The passive smoker. Many nonsmokers are exposed to the toxins found in cigarette smoke by inhaling cigarette smoke exhaled by others. This is called "environmental tobacco smoke," or "secondhand smoke," or "passive smoking" by researchers, and it would appear to be a common problem. For example, research has shown that almost 88% of *nonsmokers* have cotinine in their blood, suggesting that passive exposure to cigarette smoke in the United States is quite common (Pirkle et al., 1996).

One might expect, given the toxins found in cigarettes, that nonsmokers also suffer from the toxic effects of cigarette smoke. This has indeed been found true. Researchers now believe that 100 people a day die from the effects of secondhand cigarette smoke in just the United States (Shipley & Rose, 2003). The coronary arteries of nonsmokers who are exposed to secondhand

smoke become constricted, just as happens in cigarette smokers, reducing the blood flow to the individual's heart (Otsuka et al., 2001). Fully 70% of the people who die from secondhand smoke in the United States each year do so from coronary heart disease caused by passive smoking (Kritz, Schmid, & Sinzinger, 1995; Tresch & Aronow, 1996). Exposure to ETS (environmental tobacco smoke) is now thought to increase the speed at which atherosclerotic plaque forms by 20%, compared to 50% faster for the smoker (Howard et al., 1998). As a result of this process, secondhand cigarette smoke is now thought to cause 30,000 to 60,000 fatal heart attacks and three times this number of nonfatal heart attacks each year in the United States alone (Glantz & Parmley, 1995; Tresch & Aronow, 1996).

Children are especially affected by secondhand tobacco smoke, which is frightening in light of the finding by Mannino, Moorman, Kingsley, Rose, and Repace (2001) that 85% of the children studied were exposed to it at least once in the 6 days preceding their study. Environmental tobacco smoke exposure has been identified as the cause of approximately 6,100 childhood deaths per year in the United States and thousands of nonfatal bouts with such conditions as acute otitis media (Aligne & Stoddard, 1997). In addition, ETS is thought to be a factor in 300,000 cases of respiratory disease each year in this country (Bartecchi et al., 1994). There is evidence that children who are exposed to secondhand tobacco smoke are at increased risk for asthma (Guilbert & Krawiec, 2003), and it has been estimated that secondhand smoke causes between 150,000 and 300,00 respiratory infections in just the 5.5 million children in this country who are under the age of 18 months (Pappas, 1995).

In spite of the different opinions as to the scope of the problem, it is clear that ETS remains the third most common preventable cause of death in the United States, and only active smoking and alcohol use result in a greater number of preventable deaths in this country (Werner & Pearson, 1998). Even so, what is loosely called "the tobacco industry" attempts to dispute research findings suggesting that secondhand cigarette smoke is dangerous (Glantz & Parmley, 2001, p. 452), possibly to limit the movement to allow cigarette smoking only in designated areas.

The initiative to limit cigarette smoking to specific areas is supported by research findings such as the apparent precancerous changes in the lung tissue of nonsmokers who live with smokers (Trichopoulos et al., 1992) and the finding that nonsmoking women who were exposed to secondhand smoke have a 30% greater chance of developing lung cancer than nonsmokers who do not live with a smoker (Fontham et al., 1994). Nonsmoking women who are exposed to cigarette smoke have also been found to have a higher incidence of breast cancer (Morabia, Bernstein, Heritier, & Khatchatrian, 1996), and there is evidence of a relationship between secondhand smoke and sudden infant death syndrome (SIDS) (Klonoff-Cohen et al., 1995).

It is interesting to discover that in response to these studies and the EPA's decision to classify environmental smoke as a carcinogen, several scientists were paid by the tobacco industry to write letters or papers challenging these conclusions (Hanners, 1998). The tobacco industry paid $156,000 to 13 scientists to dispute the EPA's ruling and reviewed their work before it was submitted for editorial review for possible publication; in some cases the letters or articles were written by the staff of law firms that represented the tobacco industry and only signed by the scientists (Hanners, 1998). Most certainly, these actions underscore how far the tobacco industry is willing to go to keep its product on the market with as few restrictions as possible.

Complications caused by chewing tobacco. There are three types of smokeless tobacco: moist snuff, dry snuff, and chewing tobacco (Westman, 1995). The last is also known as "spit tobacco" (Bell, Spangler, & Quandt, 2000). Of these three, chewing tobacco is the most common. Some 17% of the seniors of the class of 2003 admit to having used smokeless tobacco at least once (Johnston, O'Malley, & Bachman, 2003a), but this figure includes those who have tried it out of curiosity. Only 5.6% of men, and 0.6% of the adult women in the United States use smokeless tobacco, although there are regional variations in the frequency with which people use chewing tobacco (Bell, Spangler, & Quandt, 2000).

Many of those who use chewing tobacco mistakenly believe that it is safer than cigarette smoking or that it will expose them to lower levels of nicotine. Research has shown that using smokeless tobacco 8 to 10 times a day will expose users to as much nicotine as if they had smoked 30–40 cigarettes (Shipley & Rose, 2003). Further, at least three compounds in smokeless

tobacco are capable of causing hypertension: nicotine, sodium, and licorice (Westman, 1995). There are 28 different chemical compounds in smokeless tobacco capable of causing the growth of tumors (Bartecchi et al., 1994). Thus, it would be natural to expect that individuals who use oral forms of tobacco would be at increased risk for cancer of the mouth and throat. This assumption has been proven correct. Indeed, in one study cited by Spangler and Salisbury (1995), 93% of the patients with oral cancer reported using snuff and 6% admitted to the use of chewing tobacco. Other possible consequences that seem to be caused by the use of smokeless tobacco include damage to the tissues of the gums, and staining and damage to the teeth (Spangler & Salisbury, 1995).

It is not clear whether tobacco chewers experience the same degree of risk for coronary artery disease as do cigarette smokers, but they are known to have a greater incidence of coronary artery disease than individuals who neither chew nor smoke tobacco. Further, smokeless tobacco can contribute to problems with the control of the individual's blood pressure (Westman, 1995). Thus, while smokeless tobacco is often viewed as "the lesser of two evils," it is certainly not without an element of risk.

The cost of cigarette smoking around the world. Each day, 9,000 people around the world die from smoking-related illness, with approximately 1,300 of these deaths taking place in the United States (Shipley & Rose, 2003). If present trends continue, it is estimated that 1 in every 10 deaths on this planet will be caused by tobacco-related illness by the year 2020 ("Health Spending Criticized," 1996). It is also anticipated that by the year 2025 cigarette smoking will cause 10 million premature deaths around the world each year, or 27,300 deaths each day from cigarette-related illness (Peto, Chen, & Boreham, 1996). Seventy percent of these premature deaths will take place in the so-called Third World or developing world (Phillips, Savigny, & Law, 1995). As these figures suggest, cigarette smoking is a most dangerous pastime.

Recovery from risk. When cigarette smokers stop, their bodies will begin the process of recovery from the damage caused by smoking. It has been estimated, for example, that the impact of smoking cessation is *at least* as powerful a treatment for coronary artery disease as are the effects of the cholesterol-lowering agents,

TABLE 19.2   The Stages of Smoking Cessation

Precontemplation phase	*Contemplation phase*	*Action phase*	*Maintenance phase*
Smoker is not considering an attempt to stop smoking. Smoker is still actively smoking.	Smoker is now seriously thinking about trying to give up smoking in the next 6 months.	Day to stop smoking is selected. The individual initiates his or her program to stop smoking.	Having been smoke free for 6 months, the ex-smoker works to remain smoke free.

aspirin, or angiotenin converting enzyme inhibitors (ACE) *combined* (Critchley & Capewell, 2003). The Centers for Disease Control (2004) have suggested a number of benefits of quitting smoking:

> *Stroke/CVA*: Within 5 to 15 years of the last cigarette, the former smoker's risk of a CVA is about that of a person who never smoked.
>
> *Cancer of mouth, throat, and esophagus*: These diseases are 50% less likely to develop after 5 years of abstinence from smoking.
>
> *Coronary Artery Disease (CAD)*: The former smoker's risk of CAD is cut in half after 1 year of abstinence and is virtually the same as that of a person who never smoked after 15 years of abstinence.
>
> *Lung cancer*: This disease is 50% less likely to develop in the former smoker who abstains for 10 years.

Other improvements in the ex-smoker's health include a slowing of peripheral vascular disease and an improved sense of taste and smell, according to Lee and D'Alonzo (1993). Grover, Gray-Donald, Joseph, Abrahamowicz, and Coupal (1994) found that former cigarette smokers as a group added between 2.5 and 4.5 years to their life expectancy when they stopped smoking. The authors found that cessation of cigarette use was several times as powerful a force in prolonging life as was changing one's dietary habits. Finally, as a group, former smokers show less cardiac impairment and lower rates of reinfarction than do smokers who continue to smoke after having a heart attack. As these findings suggest, there are very real benefits to giving up cigarette smoking.

Smoking cessation. In spite of the health advantages noted in the last section, it is difficult to quit. The Centers for Disease Control (2004) noted that only 19% of

cigarette smokers have *never* tried to quit, which means that more than 80% of cigarette smokers will try to quit smoking at least once. Each year in the United States at least 15 million smokers quit for at least 24 hours, but most of these people relapse back to cigarette use (Centers for Disease Control, 2004). However, it is not impossible to quit smoking, as evidenced by the number of adults in the United States who have quit smoking: 45.7 million; this is just slightly lower than the number of adults who are still smoking: 46.5 million (Fiore et al., 2002). Thus, there is cause for hopeful optimism: It is difficult, but possible, to stop smoking cigarettes (see Table 19.2).

The least effective method of smoking cessation is the one that is most common: going "cold turkey" (Patkar et al., 2003). The sudden discontinuation of cigarettes results in the highest relapse rates; methods that utilize a nicotine replacement therapy combined with psychosocial support have higher success rates (Patkar et al., 2003). The various methods of nicotine replacement are discussed in Chapter 32.

People who wish to quit smoking need to know that a major relapse trigger is being around people who are still smoking. Exposure to smoking "cues" in the form of smoke from other people and watching them smoke seems to be a factor in more than 50% of the relapses of a former smoker (Ciraulo, Piechniczek-Buczek, & Iscan, 2003). As with other forms of drug addiction, smokers who wish to quit will have to avoid contact with friends who continue to smoke if they want to have a chance at giving up this addiction.

There is a poorly understood relationship between cigarette smoking and depression. Evidence exists to suggest that individuals who are depressed experience more reinforcement from cigarette smoking than non-depressed individuals, whereas people with a history of depression seem vulnerable to a recurrence of this disorder after giving up cigarette use (Patkar et al., 2003). Cigarette smoking seems to precede the development of depression in teenagers (Goodman & Capitman, 2000). These findings suggest that cigarette smoking and depression are separate conditions that may be influenced by the same genetic factors (Breslau et al., 1993; Glassman, 1993). For this reason, individuals who wish to quit smoking and who have experienced past depressive episodes should be warned that depression might trigger thoughts of returning to cigarette smoking.

In addition to depression, some smokers have come to rely on cigarette smoking as a way to deal with such negative emotional states as anxiety, boredom, and sadness (Sherman, 1994). Because nicotine becomes an easily administered, quick method for coping with these feelings, smokers soon learn that they can control such negative emotional states through the use of cigarettes. However, unless they learn alternative methods for coping with painful emotional states, they are unlikely to be able to give up their reliance on cigarette smoking as a way to deal with the emotional stresses of everyday life.

Cigarette cessation and weight gain. Many cigarette smokers justify their continued use of cigarettes because they have heard that former smokers tend to gain weight after they quit smoking. Admittedly, about 80% of former smokers will gain *some* weight after they quit smoking, but 57% of cigarette smokers also gain weight during the same period of life (Centers for Disease Control, 2004). Following smoking cessation, the average smoker increases his or her daily caloric intake by 200 calories a day, which contributes to weight gain (Stitzer, 2003). Also, the regular use of nicotine raises the individual's metabolism by about 10%, which means that he or she "burns" off weight faster when smoking (Stitzer, 2003). Finally, most smokers are underweight for their sex/age/body frame, so postcessation weight gain reflects the body's attempt to attain its normal weight level (Stitzer, 2003). However, a smoker also tends to retain less fluid than a nonsmoker, and some of the weight gain noted after a person stops smoking might reflect fluid weight gain.

Following smoking cessation, the average individual gains about 5 pounds (Centers for Disease Control, 2004). Ten percent of men and 13% of women who stop smoking experience a larger weight gain of 13 kilograms (28.6 pounds) following their last cigarette. On the positive side, those who do gain weight seem more likely to remain abstinent following their last cigarette (Hughes et al., 1991; Shipley & Rose, 2003). Klesges et al. (1997) found that former smokers who remained abstinent for an entire year averaged a 13-pound (5.90 kg) weight gain whereas smokers who had "slipped" during the initial year had a smaller average weight gain of 6.7 pounds (3.04 kg). Although the initial weight gain is often distressing to the former smoker, there is strong evidence that the individual's weight will return "to precessation levels at 6 months [following the last cigarette]" (Hughes et al., 1991, p. 57).

Obesity is a known risk factor for cardiovascular disease, but the health benefits of giving up cigarette use far outweigh the potential risks associated with post-cigarette weight gain (Eisen, Lyons, Goldberg, & True, 1993). To illustrate, a former smoker would have to gain 50 to 100 pounds after giving up cigarettes before the health risks of the extra weight came close to those inherent in cigarette smoking (Brunton, Henningfield, & Solberg, 1994).

Summary

Tobacco use, once limited to the New World, was first introduced to Europe by Columbus's men. Once the practice of smoking or chewing tobacco reached Europe, tobacco use spread rapidly. Following the introduction of the cigarette around the turn of the century, smoking became more common, rapidly replacing tobacco chewing as the accepted method of tobacco use.

The active psychoactive agent of tobacco, nicotine, has an addiction potential similar to that of cocaine or narcotics. Each year, 34% of smokers attempt to quit, but only 2.5% are ultimately successful (McRae, Brady, & Sonne, 2001). More comprehensive treatment programs have been suggested for nicotine addiction and smoking cessation. These are patterned after alcohol addiction treatment programs but have not demonstrated a significantly improved cure rate for cigarette smoking. It has been suggested that such formal treatment programs might be of value for those whose tobacco use has placed them at risk for tobacco-related illness.

CHAPTER TWENTY

Chemicals and the Neonate

The Consequences of Drug Abuse During Pregnancy

Introduction

Science has long known that the drug molecules of many pharmaceuticals, and most of the drugs of abuse, are able to cross from the mother's blood into that of the fetus, usually in just a matter of minutes (Bolnick & Rayburn, 2003). But the problem of interuterine exposure to recreational drugs has received scant attention from health care researchers (Kandall, 1999). Unfortunately, recreational drug abuse is *most* prevalent in the same age group that is actively involved in reproduction (Bolnick & Rayburn, 2003). In spite of this, there has been very limited research into the impact of maternal chemical abuse on fetal growth and development or which biological or environmental forces might intervene to mitigate against this potential damage. In this chapter, the topic of prenatal exposure to the drugs of abuse will be explored.

Scope of the Problem

A *period of special vulnerability*. Women who have abused alcohol or illicit drugs during pregnancy should be classified as having a high-risk pregnancy (Finnegan & Kandall, 2004). The very nature of prenatal growth makes the period of pregnancy, especially the first trimester, one of special vulnerability for the rapidly developing fetus (Barki, Kravitz, & Berki, 1998). Unfortunately, many women will not even attempt to alter their chemical abuse pattern until their pregnancy has been confirmed or until relatively late in the pregnancy (Bolnick & Rayburn, 2003). This has profound consequences for the developing fetus. For example, the process of organ differentiation takes place during the third to eighth week following conception, often before the mother-to-be is aware that she is pregnant.

Maternal exposure to certain agents that might interfere with normal fetal development during this period could prove disastrous for the developing fetus and possibly the mother.

Another reason that exposure to toxic compounds is potentially so devastating to the developing fetus is that only 60% of the blood that the fetus receives from the umbilical cord is processed by the liver before it proceeds on to the rest of the body. The other 40% of the fetal venous blood and any toxins found in that blood directly enters the general circulation (Barki et al., 1998). The fetal liver and excretory systems are still quite immature, so compounds that *are* routed to the liver by the fetal circulation are not biotransformed at the same rate as in the mother's body. This contributes to the buildup of potential toxins within the fetal circulatory system.

To further compound the problem, the blood-brain barrier of the fetus is still immature, allowing many compounds to enter the fetal central nervous system more easily than that same compound could later in life (Barki et al., 1998). Finally, the fetal circulatory system has lower blood protein levels than an adult's blood, allowing a greater concentration of "unbound" drug molecules to circulate in the fetal blood system than would be possible in an adult's blood system. All of these factors combine to magnify the effects of a toxin on the body of the fetus, possibly with lifelong consequences.

Thus, there are sound reasons that maternal chemical abuse might place the fetus at risk. To illustrate the scope of the problem, in the United States an estimated 19% of women will use alcohol, 20% smoke cigarettes, and 5.5% use illicit drugs at some point during pregnancy (Mathias, 1995; Raut, Stephen, & Kosopsky 1996). In terms of absolute numbers, it has been estimated that 140,000 pregnant women drink potentially dangerous levels of alcohol each year in this country (Cohen, 2000) and that 221,000 infants are born each year in this country who were exposed to an illicit drug at least once during gestation (Chasnoff et al., 1998; Kandall, 1999).

In the 20th century, physicians expected to find a direct relationship between prenatal drug exposure and infant development. What they found was that the effects of prenatal drug exposure were not so clear-cut. One reason for this is that the "perinatal effects [of drugs] may therefore reflect pharmacological effects of individual agents or the combined effects of multiple drugs" (Finnegan & Kandall, 2004, p. 547). Thus, it is difficult to isolate the effects of one specific drug in an era when polydrug abuse is common. Further, perinatal drug exposure is just one of the risk factors that collectively would alter normal fetal or infant development to a greater or lesser degree (Moe & Slinning, 2001). Other potential risk factors include the quality of prenatal medical care, poor postnatal caregiving, malnutrition, and adverse social environment. It is difficult, if not impossible, to separate the effects of these other risk factors from those of prenatal drug exposure.

The effects of the drugs of abuse on neonatal growth are not limited to the prenatal period. Maternal preoccupation with drug use, the effects of poverty, the impact of maternal depression on the parent-child relationship, and/or competing demands for the mother's attention by siblings, combined with the intense needs of the drug-exposed infant, can result in a "serious mismatch between the mother's limited emotional resources and the infant's intense caregiving needs" (Johnson, Nusbaum, Bejarano, & Rosen, 1999, p. 450). Indeed, Werner (1989) concluded that the impact of such adverse social factors as those noted were 10 times as likely as perinatal complications to cause poor development in childhood, adolescence, and young adulthood.

Because all these forces impact fetal growth and development, scientists have consistently failed to find a pattern or syndrome unique to prenatal drug exposure. Many of the consequences attributed to maternal drug use are similar to those reported in the literature for such conditions as maternal depression, stress, poverty, and limited social support, all conditions commonly found in both normal and drug-abusing homes (Johnson, Nusbaum, et al., 1999). Yet in spite of the large number of variables that can impact fetal growth, scientists have been able to determine that the drugs of abuse have the potential to deflect normal development in a number of ways. The definitive example of this is the impact of maternal alcohol use on prenatal growth and development.

The Fetal Alcohol Spectrum Disorder

It has been estimated that up to 10% of pregnant women use alcohol on a regular basis during pregnancy (Cunniff, 2003). Each year in the United States an estimated 140,000 pregnant women are thought to consume enough alcohol to present a danger to the health of the fetus (Cohen, 2000). When an expectant mother drinks, the alcohol will quickly cross the placenta into the fetal bloodstream, reaching *the same level as the mother's in only 15 minutes* (Rose, 1988). In effect, the fetus becomes an unwilling participant in the mother's alcohol use. If the mother has been drinking shortly prior to childbirth, the smell of alcohol might be detected on the breath of the infant following birth (Rose, 1988). If the mother is alcohol dependent, the infant will also be alcohol dependent and will begin to go through alcohol withdrawal 3 to 12 hours after delivery (American Academy of Pediatrics, 1998).

By the early 1970s, it had become clear that women who consumed alcohol while pregnant ran the risk of causing alcohol-induced birth defects in their children. The longer and the more severe the fetal exposure to alcohol might be, the greater the odds that the child would exhibit any of a number of alcohol-related problems following birth, and the greater the chance that he or she would require special support as a child and adolescent (Autti-Ramo, 2000). The most severe of the problems brought on by maternal alcohol use during pregnancy was the fetal alcohol syndrome (FAS), which was first described in a medical journal in 1973 (Sokol, Delaney-Black, & Nordstrom, 2003). FAS is now accepted as the third most common cause of birth defects in the United States (North, 1996; Sadock & Sadock, 2003) and the most common preventable cause of mental retardation in developed countries (Cunniff, 2003; Glasser, 2002).

But FAS is actually the most extreme outcome brought on by maternal alcohol use during pregnancy.

Physicians now recognize that many children who were exposed to alcohol in utero will have some but not necessarily *all* of the symptoms of FAS (Cunniff, 2003; Sokol et al., 2003). In the 1990s these children were said to have *fetal alcohol effects* (FAE) (Charness, Simon, & Greenberg, 1989; Streissguth et al., 1991). Although FAS and FAE are still used in clinical reports, physicians are increasingly using the term *fetal alcohol spectrum disorder* (FASD) to identify children whose prenatal growth was affected in any way by maternal alcohol use during pregnancy (Sokol et al., 2003).

Scope of the problem. There are no biological markers that can identify children with FASD, and researchers are forced to rely on maternal self-report to confirm fetal alcohol exposure during pregnancy (Warren & Foudin, 2001). Because of this, the full prevalence of alcohol-related birth defects remains unknown (Cunniff, 2003). Current estimates suggest that in the United States just under 1 in every 100 live births involves a child with FASD of greater or lesser severity (Sokol et al., 2003). In some isolated communities in the United States where maternal alcohol use is exceptionally common, this figure might be as high as 19% (Hartman, 1995). In South Africa, the nation with the highest rate of FAS in the world, 6.66% of the children, or 1 in every 15 live births, is a child with severe FASD (Glasser, 2002). In addition to these numbers are the 3 to 5 of every 1,000 children in the United States thought to suffer from less severe FADS, or what was once called FAE (Spohr, Williams, & Steinhausen, 1993).

How does maternal alcohol use impact fetal development? Maternal alcohol use during pregnancy is thought to inhibit the production (biosynthesis) of chemicals known as *gangliosides* within the developing fetal brain (Rosenberg, 1996). These chemicals play a role in the formation of the brain in the earliest stages of development. Gangliosides in the fetal brain are thought to be most active during the first trimester, and alcohol's effects can be especially disruptive on fetal neurological growth during this phase of growth (Pirozzolo & Bonnefil, 1995). Pregnant women who ingest greater amounts of alcohol or who drink more frequently are thought to put the fetus at greater risk, as the more frequent and intense the fetal exposure to alcohol, the greater its impact on fetal ganglioside biosynthesis.

At this time, research suggests that there is no safe dose of alcohol during pregnancy (Cunniff, 2003; Gottlieb, 1994; Sokol et al., 2003). Although few heavy drinkers would consider four to six drinks a day a significant amount of alcohol, research has shown that this amount for the typical woman during pregnancy will result in 66% of the children having some form of FASD (Raut et al., 1996).

Characteristics of severe fetal alcohol spectrum disorder children. Infants who develop severe FASD usually have a lower than normal birth weight, a characteristic pattern of facial abnormalities, and a smaller brain size at birth. In the 1990s these children were said to have fetal alcohol syndrome (FAS). Noninvasive neurodiagnostic imaging examination of the brains of children who were exposed to alcohol prior to birth reveals damage to such structures of the infant's brain as the cerebral cortex, cerebellum, basal ganglia, hippocampus, and the corpus callosum (Cunniff, 2003; Mattson & Riley, 1995). In later life these children often demonstrate behavioral problems such as hyperactivity, a short attention span, impulsiveness, poor coordination, and numerous other developmental delays (Charness et al., 1989; Committee on Substance Abuse and Committee on Children With Disabilities, 1993; Gilbertson & Weinberg, 1992).

Seventeen percent of the infants with fetal alcohol syndrome are either stillborn or die shortly after birth (Renner, 2004). Of those infants who survive, 1:5 has a birth defect (Renner, 2004). Less than 6% of the FAS infants who begin school are able to function without special support, and many are mildly to moderately retarded. Indeed, the average IQ of 61 children with FAS was found to be 68[1] (Chasnoff, 1988; Renner, 2004; Streissguth et al., 1991). Seventy two percent of FAS children were found to suffer from a major psychiatric disorder (Renner, 2004).

Characteristics of children with mild to moderate fetal alcohol spectrum disorder. Unfortunately, scientists have yet to identify a test that will reliably identify children with FASD, and children with less severe forms of this disorder are often not identified (Sokol et al., 2003). Children with less severe forms of FASD will have

---

[1] An IQ of 68 falls in the mildly retarded range of intellectual function. The average IQ is 100, with a standard deviation of 15 points. An IQ of 68 is thus more than 2 standard deviations below the mean.

a greater or lesser number of the signs of severe FASD, and these signs may not be as clear as in the most severe forms.

Unfortunately, even when children who suffered from FASD were identified at birth and were enrolled in special rehabilitative programs, they still failed to achieve normal growth or intelligence (Mirin, Weiss, & Greenfield, 1991; Spohr et al., 1993). Children with severe FASD have been found to grow at only 60% the normal rate for height and 33% the normal rate for weight gain (Aase, 1994). Only 6% of students with FAS were able to function in regular school classes without special help (Streissguth et al., 1991). Further, "major psychosocial problems and lifelong adjustment problems were characteristic of most of these patients" (Streissguth et al., 1991, pp. 1965–1966). Surprisingly, the low birth weight characteristic of FAS seemed to at least partially resolve itself by adolescence, according to the authors. Even so, "none of these [adolescent or young adult] patients were known to be independent in terms of both housing and income" (p. 1966) at the time of the study. These findings again underscore the lifelong impact on the child of maternal alcohol use during pregnancy.

Breast feeding and alcohol use. Alcohol in the mother's circulation passes freely into her breast milk in concentrations similar to her blood alcohol level (BAL) (Heil & Subramanian, 1998). Fortunately, even if the infant were to nurse while the mother was quite intoxicated, the amount of alcohol ingested by the infant along with the mother's milk would be diluted throughout his or her system, resulting in a lower BAL for the infant (Heil & Subramanian, 1998).

Unfortunately, even this limited exposure to alcohol has been shown to cause abnormal gross motor development for the infant, with higher levels of maternal alcohol consumption resulting in greater developmental delays for the infant (Little, Anderson, Ervin, Worthington-Roberts, & Clarren, 1989). In addition to this direct effect on infant growth, it is hypothesized that maternal alcohol use might interfere with the development of the child's immune system (Gilbertson & Weinberg, 1992). These results would strongly suggest that alcohol use by the mother who is breast feeding is indeed a risk factor for the infant and should be avoided.

Cocaine Use During Pregnancy

As recently as 1982 some medical textbooks claimed that maternal cocaine use did not have a harmful effect on the fetus (Revkin, 1989). Then, when the last wave of cocaine abuse in the United States began in the late 1970s and early 1980s, questions were raised as to the possibility that maternal cocaine abuse might affect the growth and development of the fetus. A series of research studies were carried out, which warned of impaired children born to cocaine-abusing mothers. The mass media, either by accident or design, seized upon this first generation of studies and based on this research provided the general public with ever-larger estimates of the number of infants whose lives were supposedly forever damaged by maternal cocaine abuse during pregnancy.

A wave of near hysteria developed in the middle to late 1980s as states passed laws allowing the legal prosecution of pregnant women for child abuse if evidence of maternal cocaine abuse was found during prenatal testing. Women were prosecuted for child abuse under these new laws and in many cases were incarcerated at least until the birth of the child who was supposedly put at risk by the mother's cocaine abuse. This resulted in some pregnant cocaine-abusing women avoiding medical care until the onset of labor to avoid possible prosecution under the new laws designed to protect unborn infants from cocaine's effects (Lester et al., 2001).

Then a strange thing happened: The anticipated wave of brain damaged "crack [cocaine] babies" simply failed to materialize (Garrett, 2000; Gray, 1998). Further, virtually every prenatal complication initially attributed to prenatal cocaine abuse was later found to have been caused by such factors as a lack of prenatal care, maternal use of toxic compounds such as tobacco and/or alcohol during pregnancy, or poor nutrition. Researchers suspect that maternal cocaine abuse can cause placentia previa. But most cocaine abusers smoke cigarettes, and cigarette smokers have a 2.3 times greater incidence of placentia previa than nonsmokers, so the actual incidence of cocaine-induced placentia previa is not known (Karch, 2002). Research has also found that half of the women who abused cocaine during pregnancy also consumed alcohol, a known toxin. This makes it difficult to identify the role that cocaine might have had in causing the observed developmental problems (Sexson, 1994).

This did not prevent the mass media from presenting the public with a picture of cocaine-damaged children who were "inevitably and permanently damaged" (Zuckerman, Frank, & Mayes, 2002, p. 1991) by their mother's abuse of cocaine. But researchers were finding other factors besides prenatal cocaine abuse that seemed to be associated with neonatal risk for cocaine-abusing mothers. For example, for many cocaine-abusing pregnant women, the first "prenatal care" they received was when they arrived at a hospital emergency room in labor (Sexson, 1994). Even limited prenatal care was found to significantly reduce the possibility of abnormal fetal growth and to improve the chances of a healthy baby at birth (Racine, Joyce, & Anderson, 1993). The baby's status was not a direct consequence of the mother's cocaine abuse so much as whether she had received adequate prenatal care, a finding that was not dramatic enough to make newspaper headlines.

Scope of the problem of maternal cocaine abuse during pregnancy. In spite of the popular image of a tidal wave of cocaine-abusing women, researchers now admit that the prevalence of maternal cocaine abuse during pregnancy is simply not known (Karch, 2002). Maternal self-report, a popular method by which substance abusers are identified, tends to underestimate the prevalence not only of prenatal cocaine abuse but of all forms of maternal drug use during pregnancy (Lester et al., 2001). But the National Institute on Drug Abuse (NIDA) provided a working estimate of about 1.1% of the 4 million pregnant women in the United States, or just 45,000 women, having abused cocaine during their pregnancy (Chasnoff et al., 1998; Kandall, 1999).

What do we really know about the effects of maternal cocaine use? Researchers now believe that many of the effects attributed to maternal cocaine abuse in the past are better explained by the use of tobacco, alcohol, and/or marijuana during pregnancy (Frank, Augustyn, Knight, Pell, & Zuckerman, 2001). Myers et al. (2003) attempted to learn whether prenatal cocaine exposure might be detected with the Brazelton Neonatal Behavioral Assessment Scale after birth and failed to find significant differences between the cocaine-exposed and cocaine-naive babies examined. It is assumed that there were no differences between the two groups of babies.

There have been few cocaine-induced effects observed in children 6 years old and younger exposed to cocaine in utero (Frank et. al., 2001; Keller & Snyder-Keller, 2000). Thus, in spite of often dramatic reports in the popular media about a wave of drug-impaired "crack" babies about to descend upon society in the 1980s and early 1990s, "few effects of prenatal cocaine exposure on children's cognitive, motor, play, language and socioemotional development during early childhood have been found" (Tronick & Beeghly, 1999, p. 152). When researchers *have* found differences between infants who were and were not exposed to cocaine prenatally, such findings have been small in magnitude. For example, researchers at Brown University have concluded that the intelligence quotient (IQ) of infants exposed to cocaine in utero averages 3.3 points lower than that of nonexposed infants from the same socioeconomic level (Leshner, 1999; Tronick & Beeghly, 1999). This is a modest difference, and Singer et al. (2004) failed to find evidence of a lower verbal, performance, or full-scale IQ score for cocaine-exposed infants than for normal infants. Other researchers have found evidence that prenatal cocaine use can result in developmental delays for the infant in such areas as psychomotor skills (Zickler, 1999) and mental development (Singer et al., 2002).

Laboratory evidence suggests that cocaine can cause strong contractions in the uterus and thus might initiate or speed up labor (Karch, 2002). This research suggests that maternal cocaine abuse could cause a late stage abortion (Burkett, Yasin, Palow, LaVoie, & Martinez, 1994; Sexson, 1994). For this reason some physicians advocated routine urine toxicology testing for women who experienced preterm labor (Peters & Theorell, 1991). However, this recommendation has not resulted in a formal treatment guideline that all women who experience preterm labor be tested for possible cocaine abuse, and thus researchers still do not know what percentage of premature births are initiated by maternal cocaine use or abuse. Women who abuse cocaine during pregnancy are at increased risk for hypertensive crises, cardiac problems, and cerebrovascular accidents (CVA) (Finnegan & Kandall, 2004).

The current theories. In spite of all of the rhetoric, there has been little empirical research into the long-term effects of prenatal cocaine exposure on the infant

(Finnegan & Kandall, 2004; Tronick & Beeghly, 1999). One empirical research study examined brain metabolism of children exposed to cocaine through maternal cocaine abuse 8 years earlier and found evidence of altered function in the frontal cortex of these children (Smith, Chang, Yonekura, Gilbride, et al., 2001). These findings were similar to others that showed evidence of altered frontal cortex function in men (former cocaine abusers) who were abstinent from cocaine abuse, although it is not clear if the same mechanism was responsible for the similarity in the effects of cocaine on the children exposed to it prior to birth and the men who had abused cocaine.

Researchers have failed to identify a specific pattern of deficits that might be attributed to maternal cocaine abuse during pregnancy. Biologists have found that the concentration of cocaine in the amniotic fluid might be higher than that in the maternal blood system (Woods, 1998). This finding is of importance when one considers that the skin of the fetus does not develop an ability to block passive absorption of cocaine from the amniotic fluid until the 24th week of pregnancy (Woods, 1998), and the long-term consequences of fetal cocaine exposure are simply not known (Keller & Snyder-Keller, 2000).

The most common consequences of maternal cocaine abuse on the fetus are thought to be lower birth weight, premature birth, increased frequency of respiratory distress syndrome following birth, malformations of the genitourinary tract, infarctions of the bowels, cerebral infarctions, reduced head circumference, and increased chance of cerebral infarctions (Keller & Keller-Snyder, 2000). Some researchers have suggested an association between maternal cocaine abuse during pregnancy and the later development of sudden infant death syndrome (SIDS) in the infant (Bell & Lau, 1995; Peters & Theorell, 1991). However, this possibility has been challenged by other researchers (Karch, 2002; Ostrea, Ostrea, & Simpson, 1997; Plessinger & Woods, 1993; Weathers, Crane, Sauvian, & Blackhurst, 1993). Thus, the possible relationship between SIDS and prenatal cocaine exposure remains unknown.

Unanswered questions. Animal research has revealed that at least some of the cocaine in the mother's blood will cross the placenta and enter the fetal circulation. However, it is still not clear that fetal cocaine levels are the same as or significantly different from those of the mother's blood. In some animal species, the placenta appears to be able to biotransform limited amounts of cocaine before it enters the fetal circulatory system. But it is not known whether humans share this ability with other animals (Plessinger & Woods, 1993).

Animal research has also demonstrated that maternal cocaine use during pregnancy can cause constriction of the blood vessels in the placenta and uterine bed, reducing the blood flow to the fetus for a period of time. This cocaine-induced reduction in uterine blood flow is postulated to be a possible cause of poor intrauterine growth for the infant exposed to cocaine prenatally. The same mechanism has been suggested as the cause of premature labor and birth in pregnant cocaine-abusing women (Behnke & Eyler, 1993; Chasnoff, 1991b; Glantz & Woods, 1993; Plessinger & Woods, 1993). However, there has not been any research to determine whether this is indeed the case with human infants born to cocaine-abusing mothers.

Cocaine's vasoconstrictive effects may also be the mechanism by which maternal cocaine abuse may result in injury to the developing bowel of the fetus (Cotton, 1994; Plessinger & Woods, 1993). Animal research suggests that maternal cocaine use causes damage to the mesenteric artery that provides blood to the intestines, according to the authors. An alternative hypothesis is that cocaine is able to cause a reduction in blood flow to nonvital organ systems of the developing fetus, including the bowel and kidneys. This would explain why the team of Mitra, Ganesh, and Apuzzio (1994) found evidence that the renal artery in the cocaine-exposed fetus did not function normally, reducing the blood flow to the kidneys for extended periods of time.

There is also evidence suggesting that infants born to mothers who use cocaine during pregnancy might suffer from small strokes prior to birth (Kandall, 1999; Volpe, 1995). One research study found that 6% of cocaine-exposed infants showed evidence of having had at least one cerebral infarction (stroke, or CVA) (Volpe, 1995). Another study found evidence of CVAs in 35% of infants exposed to cocaine or amphetamines in utero (Kandall, 1999). These strokes are thought to be a result of the rapid changes in the mother's blood pressure brought on by the maternal cocaine use. Chasnoff (1988) postulated that such strokes are similar to those occasionally seen in adults who use cocaine and noted that cocaine use during pregnancy may result in cardiac and central nervous system abnormalities in the fetus.

Cocaine and breast feeding. Cocaine, because it is highly lipid-soluble, may be stored in breast milk. Thus some of the drug may be passed on to the infant by the mother through breast feeding (Peters & Theorell, 1991; Revkin, 1989). But the level of cocaine exposure for the infant might be far higher than it was for the mother. Research has shown that cocaine levels in the maternal milk might be *eight times* as high as the level of cocaine in the mother's blood (Revkin, 1989). If the cocaine-using mother were to breast feed her infant, that child might be exposed to extremely high levels of cocaine through the mother's breast milk. For this reason, maternal cocaine use during the time when the mother breast feeds her infant should be discouraged.

Amphetamine Use During Pregnancy

Women who abuse amphetamines, especially methamphetamine, during pregnancy will frequently deny the abuse of these chemicals, even when confronted with urine toxicology test results to the contrary (Catanzarite & Stein, 1995). This is unfortunate, as the effects of amphetamines on the developing human fetus or on the mother have not been studied in detail (Bell & Lau, 1995).

Clinically, the effects of the amphetamines are very similar to those of cocaine; therefore, it might be assumed that the impact of maternal use of amphetamines during pregnancy could produce the same effects as maternal cocaine use during pregnancy (Pirozzolo & Bonnefil 1995). Researchers have found that infants who were exposed to amphetamines during pregnancy tend to be born with a decreased head circumference, length, and body weight (Bell & Lau, 1995). The authors also suggested that maternal amphetamine use during pregnancy was associated with a higher rate of premature births and congenital brain lesions. There is a possibility that maternal amphetamine abuse during pregnancy might increase the mother's risk for fatal complications of the pregnancy, although there is a lack of definitive research in this area that would identify these potential risks (Catanzarite & Stein, 1995).

Researchers have found that infants who were exposed to methamphetamine prior to birth seem to have altered neurological function in the frontal cortex, as evidenced by creatine levels in this region of the brain (Smith, Chang, Yonekura, Grob, et al., 2001). This would suggest possible damage to the neurons in this critical brain area, although the significance of these findings has not been determined. Research studies using animal subjects suggest that prenatal exposure to methamphetamine seems to predispose the fetus to the neurotoxic effects of this compound later in life through some unknown mechanism (Heller, Bubula, Lew, Heller, & Won, 2001). It is not known if humans also experience vulnerability to the neurotoxic effects of methamphetamine following prenatal exposure to this drug.

There is also evidence that maternal use of methamphetamine may result in premature birth, poor intrauterine growth, and, a tendency for the placenta to separate from the wall of the uterus (Catanzarite & Stein, 1995). Other possible complications of maternal amphetamine use during pregnancy include meconium aspiration, placental hemorrhage, and neonatal anemia (Beebe & Walley, 1995).

Following birth, there is evidence to suggest that children born to mothers who abused amphetamines during pregnancy might experience abnormal psychosocial development (Bell & Lau, 1995) or frontal lobe dysfunction (Beebe & Walley, 1995). However, most normal developmental milestones are achieved on time, and there is little firm evidence of long-term damage to the fetus or neonate (Pirozzolo & Bonnefil 1995).[2] Thus, it is difficult to predict what long-term effects maternal amphetamine use during pregnancy will have on the child following birth.

Opiate Abuse During Pregnancy

Because of the ability of narcotic analgesics to cross over from the mother's circulation to that of the fetus, it is estimated that each year approximately 300,000 children are exposed to narcotics in utero in this country (Glantz & Woods, 1993). Not all of these children are

[2] Of course, there also is no evidence that suggests that amphetamine use during pregnancy is safe, either. If only for this reason, amphetamine abuse by the pregnant woman should be discouraged.

exposed to illicit narcotics. Each year, it is estimated that between 1% to 21% of expectant mothers will use a narcotic analgesic at least once during pregnancy (Behnke & Eyler, 1993). Most of these women are using narcotic pharmaceuticals under a physician's supervision, for medically necessary reasons, and their use of the narcotic analgesic is limited to periods of medical necessity. But an estimated 650,000 women have used heroin at least once, and approximately 88,000 women use heroin on a regular basis (Bell & Lau, 1995). Some of these women will be of childbearing age, and a significant percentage of those women who use heroin on a regular basis will do so while they are pregnant. In the United States, maternal heroin abuse accounts for almost a quarter of all cases of fetal exposure to illegal drugs (American Academy of Family Physicians, 1990). Each year in this country some 9,000 (Bell & Lau, 1995; Glantz & Woods, 1993) to 10,000 (Zuckerman & Bresnahan, 1991) children are born to women who are addicted to narcotics.

Unfortunately, many of the early symptoms of pregnancy, feelings of fatigue, nausea, vomiting, pelvic cramps, and hot sweats might be interpreted by the narcotics-addicted woman as early withdrawal symptoms rather than possible pregnancy (Levy & Rutter, 1992). Even physicians experienced in the treatment of narcotics addiction find it quite difficult to diagnose pregnancy in narcotics-addicted women, according to the authors. All too often, rather than seek prenatal care for her unborn child, the woman will initally try to self-medicate what she believes is withdrawal by using even higher doses of narcotics. This results in the fetus being exposed to significant levels of narcotic analgesics (and the chemicals that are used to cut street narcotics) by a woman who is not yet aware that she is pregnant.

Maternal narcotics abuse during pregnancy carries with it a number of serious consequences for both the mother and the developing fetus. Pregnant women who abuse opiates are at risk for such problems as septic thrombophlebitis, postpartum hemorrhage, depression, gestational diabetes, eclampsia, and death.

Physical complications associated with narcotic abuse during pregnancy include stillbirth, breech presentation during childbirth, placental insufficiency, spontaneous abortions, premature delivery, neonatal meconium aspiration syndrome (which may be fatal), neonatal infections acquired through the mother, lower birth weight, and neonatal narcotic addiction (Chasnoff, 1988; Glantz & Woods, 1993; Hoegerman & Schnoll, 1991; Levy & Rutter, 1992).

In addition to all these potential complications in pregnancy, children born to women who are addicted to narcotics have a two to three times higher risk of suffering from SIDS than children whose mothers have never used illicit chemicals (Kandall, Gaines, Habel, Davidson, & Jessop, 1993; Pirozzolo & Bonnefil 1995). Volpe (1995) suggested that the risk of SIDS increased with the severity of the infant's withdrawal from narcotics.

Chronic use of narcotics during pregnancy results in a state of chronic exposure to opiates for the fetus. Such infants are physically dependent on narcotics at birth because of their passive exposure to the drug. Following birth, the infant will no longer be able to absorb drugs from the mother's blood and will go through drug withdrawal starting within 24 to 72 hours of birth. Depending on the specific narcotics being abused by the mother, the withdrawal process may last for weeks or even months in the newborn (Hoegerman & Schnoll, 1991; Levy & Rutter, 1992; Volpe, 1995). Pirozzolo and Bonnefil (1995) suggested that the *acute* stage of the neonatal withdrawal syndrome subsides in 3 to 6 weeks, but that a *subacute* stage marked by such symptoms as restlessness, agitation, tremors, and sleep disturbance might continue for 4 to 6 months after the acute stage of withdrawal ends.

Some of the most immediate symptoms of neonatal narcotic withdrawal include muscle tremors, hyperactivity, hyperirritability, a unique, high-pitched cry, frantic efforts to find comfort, sleep problems, vomiting, loose stools, increased deep muscle reflexes, frequent yawning, sneezing, seizures, increased sweating, dehydration, constant sucking movements, fever, and rapid breathing (American Academy of Pediatrics, 1998). In years past, neonatal narcotics withdrawal resulted in almost a 90% mortality rate (Mirin, Weiss, & Greenfield, 1991). The mortality rate has dropped significantly in recent years in response to increased medical awareness of the special needs of the addicted infant and improved withdrawal programs for such children (Mirin, Weiss, & Greenfield 1991).

Surprisingly, in light of the dangers of maternal narcotics abuse to the fetus, it is *not* recommended that the mother be withdrawn from opioids during pregnancy if she is addicted. Except in special cases, the danger to the fetus seems higher if the mother is withdrawn from narcotic analgesics during the gestation period (Hoegerman & Schnoll, 1991).

The authors recognize that infants born to mothers who are addicted to narcotics present special needs and require specialized care in order to survive the first few days of life and beyond. One element of this specialized care is the judicious use of methadone (Vincenzo et al., 2003). The authors found that when stabilized on an appropriate dose of methadone, the women in their study were less likely to abuse illicit drugs. Further, there is evidence that children born to mothers whose opiate addiction has been stabilized on methadone tend to have longer gestation periods and to weigh more at the time of birth than children whose mothers were not using methadone (Kaltenbach, 1997). There is also research to suggest that it is better for the fetus if the mother's methadone dose is administered in two smaller units, one in the morning and the other in the late afternoon or early evening (Kandall, Doberczak, Jantunen, & Stein, 1999). This split dosing schedule has been found to result in lower daily dosage levels of methadone for the mother and seems to lower the danger of drug-induced suppression of fetal activity (Kandall et al., 1999). Following delivery, both the mother and child can then be detoxified from narcotics through the use of methadone (Hoegerman & Schnoll, 1991; Miller, 1994).

There are many nondrug factors that might contribute to later developmental problems for the child, including poverty and/or indifferent caregivers (Hawley, Halle, Drasin, & Thomas, 1995). Indeed, after following a sample of 330 children children, 120 of whom were raised by heroin-dependent parents, researchers at the Hebrew University Medical School in Israel concluded that except for a small percentage of infants with neurological problems, the developmental delays noted in children born to heroin-dependent mothers were more the result of environmental deprivation than the effects of prenatal heroin exposure (Fishman, 1996). Thus, with the proper childhood environment, it appears possible for the child to outgrow most, if not all, of the negative effects of prenatal exposure to narcotic analgesics.

Narcotics and breast feeding. The woman using narcotics who is breast feeding her child will pass some of the drug on to the infant through the milk (Lourwood & Riedlinger, 1989). In theory, prolonged use of narcotics by a breast-feeding mother might cause the child to become sleepy, eat poorly, and possibly develop respiratory depression. Because of the infant's "immature liver metabolizing functions" (Lourwood & Riedlinger, 1989, p. 85), there is a danger that narcotics will accumulate in the child's body if the mother is using a narcotic analgesic during breast feeding.

Research has shown, however, that breast-feeding mothers who are taking morphine can do so safely under a physician's supervision, as only minimal levels of morphine are found in breast milk and only a small portion of that actually reaches the infant's circulation (Hale, 2003). A similar situation exists for women who are placed on codeine or who are on methadone maintenance programs and who are breast feeding an infant. Research has shown that the methadone level in the mother's milk is usually less than 5% of the maternal dosage level, and only minimal levels of codeine are ingested through maternal milk by the infant if the mother is on low to moderate dosage levels (Hale, 2003; Kaltenbach, 1997). However, physicians recommend against the use of the narcotic meperidine by breast-feeding women as this medication causes the infant to become sedated after ingesting the medication through the mother's milk (Hale, 2003).

Marijuana Use During Pregnancy

After more than a quarter century of study, the effects of THC on fetal growth and development are still unclear (Finnegan & Kandall, 2004). This is surprising, as some researchers believe that marijuana is the illicit substance most commonly abused by women of child-bearing years (Kandall, 1999). Nationally, it has been estimated that between 2.9% (Kandall, 1999) and 12% (Pirozzolo & Bonnefil, 1995) of the women who are pregnant in non-ghetto urban areas use marijuana at least once during their pregnancy. The estimate of 2.9% of pregnant women would translate into approximately 119,000 women who use marijuana at least once while they are pregnant (Mathias, 1995).

Scientists have discovered that the placenta is able to provide the fetus with *some* protection from marijuana smoke, with fetal blood levels of THC reaching only one-sixth those of the mother (Nelson, 2000). But there remains a great deal to discover about the effects of marijuana use on either the pregnant mother or the fetus (Dreher, Nugent, & Hudgins, 1994).

Unfortunately, it is difficult to isolate the effects of maternal marijuana use from confounding variables such as the effects of poor nutrition, use of other drugs, poor prenatal care, or maternal health. Other variables that would affect such research include the frequency of marijuana use, the potency of the marijuana being used, and the amount of marijuana smoke the user inhaled. It is thus not surprising that research into the possible effects of maternal marijuana use on fetal growth and development has resulted in conflicting or inconclusive results. There are simply too many variables to allow for an easy answer to the question of how maternal marijuana use affects the growing fetus.

A number of research studies, summarized by Eyler and Behnke (1999), have uncovered abnormal tremors, startle reflexes, and eye problems in children exposed to marijuana in utero. Women who used marijuana at least once a month during pregnancy were also found to have a higher risk of premature delivery, lowered birth weight, and children who were smaller than normal for their gestational age (Bays, 1992).

In contrast to the studies that identified a clear effect of maternal marijuana use on fetal growth and development is the study conducted by Dreher et al. (1994). The authors examined 24 babies born in rural Jamaica, where heavy marijuana use is common; the infants were known to have been exposed to marijuana in utero. The development of these infants was contrasted with that of 20 other infants known not to have been exposed to marijuana. The authors failed to find *any* developmental differences in the two groups that could be attributed to maternal marijuana use. Where significant differences between the two groups of infants were found, the authors were able to attribute them to the mother's social status. Marijuana-using mothers were also found to have a greater number of adults living within the household and to have fewer children within the home. These factors allowed for more care to be given to the newborn than was the case in the homes where the mother did not use marijuana, according to the authors. These findings are suggestive, but too little is known about either the short-term or long-term effects of maternal marijuana use during pregnancy to allow researchers to reach any definite conclusions (Day & Richardson, 1991).

One possibility that has been overlooked in the research efforts to date is that it might take several years for the effects of maternal marijuana use to manifest in the child. Fried (1995) examined this possibility and found that in older children whose mothers used marijuana during pregnancy, subtle neuropsychological testing found deficits in the "executive functioning" regions of the brain (Fried, 1995 p. 2159). This was evidence of problems in prefrontal lobe brain function, in children whose mothers used marijuana during pregnancy, that did not manifest itself until the child was 6 to 9 years of age.

Admittedly, many variables might confound the conclusions reached by Fried (1995), including the quality of the child's environment, parental interactions with the child, and other factors. While there is little conclusive evidence that marijuana use during pregnancy has an adverse effect on fetal growth and development (Science and Technology Committee Publications, 1998), given the lifelong consequences for the child if such effects exist, marijuana use during pregnancy should be discouraged.

Marijuana and breast feeding. THC, the active agent of marijuana, will be concentrated in human milk and be passed on to the infant during breast feeding. The THC level in breast milk has been found to be six times (Nelson, 2000) to eight times (Hartman, 1995) as high as the mother's blood plasma level. This would suggest that maternal marijuana use might have some impact on the infant if the mother breast feeds her child. Breast feeding by mothers who smoke marijuana is thought to result in slower motor development for the child in the first year of life (Frank, Bauchner, Zuckerman, & Fried, 1992; "Marijuana and Breast Feeding," 1990). Admittedly, this is based on a preliminary study of the effects of the mother's use of marijuana on the infant's development, but it does suggest a potential hazard that should be avoided if at all possible.

Benzodiazepine Use During Pregnancy

The question of whether pregnant women, especially those in their first trimester of pregnancy, should use any of the benzodiazepines remains controversial.

Some studies have suggested that the use of benzodiazepines during the first trimester of pregnancy is associated with an increased risk of facial abnormalities; other studies have failed to find such a relationship (Barki et al., 1998; Iqbal, Sobhan, & Ryals, 2002). Although the possibility that benzodiazepine use during pregnancy might contribute to cleft palate is not clear, Iqbal et al. (2002) suggested that these medications be used at the lowest possible dose for the shortest possible period of time during pregnancy, with every effort being taken to avoid their use in the first trimester of pregnancy. Further, the benzodiazepines should be used only when the anticipated benefits to the mother outweigh the potential danger to the fetus (Barki et al., 1998; Iqbal et al., 2002).

Benzodiazepine use during breast feeding. All of the benzodiazepines will cross from the nursing mother's circulation to her milk. In spite of this fact, Hale (2003) concluded that the short-term use of a benzodiazepine by a breast-feeding mother (e.g., 1–2 weeks) was "not problematic" (p. 344). However, long-term use of a benzodiazepine such as diazepam has been identified as the cause of fetal sedation and lethargy (Iqbal et al., 2002), and this is one reason that nursing mothers have been advised not use benzodiazepines (Graedon & Graedon, 1996). Because these drugs are metabolized mainly by the liver, an organ that is not fully developed in the infant, nursing mothers should not use any of the benzodiazepines unless the potential benefits to the mother outweigh the risk to the baby in the opinion of the attending physician (Lourwood & Riedlinger, 1989).

Hallucinogen Use During Pregnancy

There is only limited research into the effects of maternal hallucinogen abuse on fetal growth and development (Kandall, 1999). Because of the lack of information on the pharmacokinetics of the hallucinogens in the breast-feeding mother, the use of these compounds is not recommended (Hale, 2003).

PCP abuse during pregnancy. Tabor, Smith-Wallace, and Yonekura (1990) examined the birth records of 37 children born between 1982 and 1987 whose medical records indicated that the mothers had used PCP during pregnancy. The authors then compared these birth records to those of infants born to mothers who had

abused cocaine during pregnancy. They concluded that the majority of the women in both groups had minimal prenatal care, a factor that might influence the growth and development of the fetus, and most of the women in the study were polydrug users. However, on the basis of their study, the authors concluded that infants who were exposed to PCP in utero had a high incidence of intrauterine growth retardation and their mothers a higher incidence of premature labor; also, the infants often required extended hospitalization following birth. Infants born to women who had used PCP during pregnancy also seemed to experience abrupt changes in the level of consciousness, fine tremors, sweating, and irritability, according to Tabor et al. (1990).

MDMA/ecstasy use in pregnancy. Because widespread abuse of ecstasy is a relatively recent phenomenon, there has been little time to conduct systematic research into the effects of this compound on fetal growth and development. Preliminary research suggests, however, that congenital growth problems are five times more prevalent for women who used MDMA during pregnancy than is normal (McElhatton, Bateman, Evans, Pughe, & Thomas, 1999). The authors reported on the outcome of 136 pregnancies in the United Kingdom, 74 of which involved women who had abused only MDMA during their pregnancy, and found that 15% of the infants born to women who had abused MDMA at some point in their pregnancy had a congenital abnormality, a rate five times higher than the normal rate of 2% to 3%.

Buspirone Use During Pregnancy

Buspirone has not been studied in sufficient detail to determine whether there is a potential for harm to the human fetus (Barki et al., 1998). Animal research involving rats found an increased risk for stillbirth when buspirone was used at high dosage levels, but there did not appear to be any effect on the speed with which newborn rats were able to learn, their level of motor activity, or their emotional development (Miller, 1994).

Bupropion Use During Pregnancy

The effects of bupropion on the developing fetus have not been studied in detail (Miller, 1994).

Disulfiram Use During Pregnancy

Disulfiram is not recommended for use in pregnant women (Miller, 1994). Animal research suggests that the combination of alcohol with disulfiram is potentially dangerous for the fetus, according to the author. Further, there is evidence, based on animal research, suggesting that a metabolite of disulfiram, diethyldithiocarbamate, may bind to lead, allowing this metal to cross the blood-brain barrier and reach the central nervous system. Lead is a known toxin, which may cause neurological disorders and mental retardation. There is a need for further research into this potential danger to determine whether disulfiram use may contribute to higher lead levels in humans.

Cigarette Use During Pregnancy

Approximately 820,000 women, or about 20% of the estimated 4 million women who give birth in this country each year, smoke during their pregnancy (Finnegan & Kandal, 2004). Byrd and Howard (1995) give an even higher estimate of 29% of the infants born in the United States each year, or 1 million infants, who are exposed to cigarette smoke prenatally. An additional 22% of all infants are exposed to secondhand or environmental cigarette smoke after birth, in spite of the fact that their mothers did not themselves smoke cigarettes (Byrd & Howard, 1995).

Many of the compounds in cigarette smoke, including nicotine, are able to cross the placental barrier and reach the fetus throughout pregnancy (Buka, Shenassa, & Niaura, 2003). In terms of fetal development, maternal cigarette use during pregnancy might be *worse than maternal cocaine use* (Cotton, 1994). The nicotine that the mother inhales when she smokes causes the blood vessels in the placenta to constrict for a period of time, reducing maternal blood flow to the fetus (Lee & D'Alonzo, 1993). This, in turn, contributes to a tendency for babies of cigarette smokers to be born with lower than normal birth weights (Centers for Disease Control, 2004). Infants born to mothers who smoke cigarettes during pregnancy are likely to weigh an average of 200 grams less at birth than children born to nonsmoking mothers (Bell & Lau, 1995; Byrd & Howard, 1995; Eyler & Behnke, 1999). Low birth weight is a potential cause of neonatal death, claiming 300,000 infants in the United States each year (Centers for Disease Control, 2004). The American Medical Association (AMA) (1993) estimated that 20% to 30% of low birth weight in children can be traced to maternal tobacco use.

Further, nicotine use during pregnancy seems to be associated with such problems as premature labor and delivery. Pregnant women who smoke have a 30% higher risk of stillbirth. Indeed, even after the child is born there is a 26% higher risk that he or she will die within the first few days if the mother smoked during pregnancy (Bell & Lau, 1995). Women who smoke (or who are exposed to cigarette smoke) during pregnancy are more likely to suffer spontaneous abortion and an increased chance of vaginal bleeding (Centers for Disease Control, 2004; Lee & D'Alonzo, 1993). Women who smoke during pregnancy are also at risk for a premature rupture of uterine membranes; their infants may exhibit delayed crying time and decreased fetal breathing time following birth (Graedon & Graedon, 1996).

There is a strong association between maternal cigarette use during pregnancy and the later development of asthma in the young child (Guilbert & Krawiec, 2003). There is also evidence that maternal cigarette smoking during pregnancy may contribute to neurological problems for the developing fetus, and, following birth, to cognitive developmental problems for the child (Olds, Henderson, & Tatelbaum, 1994). The authors found in their study that children born to mothers who smoked 10 or more cigarettes a day during pregnancy scored an average of 4.35 points lower on a standardized intelligence test at ages 3 to 4 than did children born to nonsmoking mothers. The authors concluded that the observed effects were due to maternal cigarette use during pregnancy.

There is also a growing body of literature that suggests that maternal cigarette use during pregnancy is one risk factor for the development of attention deficit hyperactivity disorder (ADHD) (Milberger, Biederman, Faraone, Chen, & Jones, 1996). Maternal cigarette use during pregnancy has also been linked to such neurodevelopmental problems as impulsiveness, although it is not clear what role cigarette smoking plays in the development of these problems (Day & Richardson, 1994). Finally, after examining the records of some 1.57 million births in Hungary over a 10-year period,

Czeizel, Kodaj, and Lenz (1994) concluded that maternal cigarette smoking was a risk factor for the condition known as *congenital limb deficiency* (a failure for the limbs of the fetus to develop properly). The authors hypothesized that nicotine's ability to disrupt blood flow patterns to the uterus might be the cause of this developmental abnormality.

Infants born to smoking mothers appear to suffer from reduced lung capacity, with such infants experiencing an average of a 10% reduction in lung function (Byrd & Howard, 1995). Infants born to women who smoke a pack a day or more were found to be twice as likely to grow up to become cigarette smokers as children born to nonsmokers (Buka et al., 2003). Finally, infants who are exposed to cigarette smoke suffer a significantly higher rate of SIDS than infants who are not exposed to this environmental hazard. Research suggests that the risk that a newborn infant will die from SIDS increases 300% to 400% if the mother smokes (Centers for Disease Control, 2004). Thus, as these various studies suggest, maternal cigarette use during pregnancy carries with it a number of risks for the developing fetus.

Cigarette smoking during breast feeding. Medical research would suggest that the mother abstain from cigarette use during the period that she is breast feeding the infant. Nicotine tends to concentrate in breast milk, with a half-life in breast milk of 1.5 hours (Byrd & Howard, 1995). The total concentration of nicotine in the woman's breast milk is dependent on the number of cigarettes she smokes and the time between the last cigarette and the time she breast feeds the infant, according to the authors. Nicotine itself has been shown to interfere with the process of breast feeding, reducing the amount of milk produced and the process of milk ejection (the "let down" reflex) (Byrd & Howard, 1995). Infants who are breast fed by cigarette smoking mothers tend to put on weight more slowly than breast-fed infants whose mothers do not smoke.

Nicotine replacement therapy during pregnancy. Given the fact that nicotine and its primary metabolite, continine, are thought to be harmful to the fetus, one would expect that nicotine replacement therapies would be contraindicated for the pregnant woman. However, as the other 4,000 chemicals in cigarette smoke are also at least potentially harmful to the fetus, the use of nicotine replacement devices is appropriate

if, in the physician's opinion, the potential benefits outweigh the risks (Black & Hill, 2003).

Over-the-Counter Analgesic Use During Pregnancy

Aspirin. Women who are or who suspect that they might be pregnant should not use aspirin except under the supervision of a physician (Black & Hill, 2003; Shannon, Wilson, & Stang, 1995). Aspirin has been implicated as a cause of decreased birth weight in children born to women who used it during pregnancy. There is also evidence that aspirin may be a cause of stillbirth and increased perinatal mortality (United States Pharmacopeial Convention, 1990).

Briggs, Freeman, and Yaffe (1986) explored the impact of maternal aspirin use on the fetus and concluded that the use of aspirin by the mother during pregnancy might produce "anemia, antepartum and/or postpartum hemorrhage, prolonged gestation and prolonged labor" (p. 26a). Aspirin has also been implicated in significantly higher perinatal mortality and retardation of intrauterine growth when used at high doses by pregnant women (Briggs et al., 1986). The authors noted that maternal use of aspirin in the week before delivery might interfere with the infant's ability to form blood clots following birth. The United States Pharmacopeial Convention (1990a) went further than this, warning that women should not use aspirin in the last 2 weeks of pregnancy. Aspirin has been found to cross the placenta, and research has suggested that maternal aspirin use during pregnancy might result in higher levels of aspirin in the fetus than in the mother (Briggs et al., 1986).

Acetaminophen. Acetaminophen is viewed as the OTC analgesic of choice for women who are pregnant (Black & Hill, 2003). There have been no reports of serious problems in women who have used acetaminophen during pregnancy. The reported death of one infant from kidney disease shortly after birth was later attributed to the mother's continuous use of acetaminophen at high dosage levels during pregnancy (Briggs et al., 1986). However, there are no reports of harmful effects on the fetus if the drug is used as directed.

Although acetaminophen is excreted in low concentrations in the mother's breast milk, Briggs et al. (1986)

found no evidence suggesting that this had adverse effects on the infant. Lourwood and Riedlinger (1989) suggested, however, that since acetaminophen is metabolized mainly by the liver, which is still quite immature in the newborn child, the mother who breast feeds during the immediate postpartum period should not use this drug. However, the authors did not warn against the occasional use of acetaminophen in women who are breast feeding their children after the postpartum period.

Ibuprofen. There has been limited research into the effects on the fetus of maternal ibuprofen use during pregnancy (Black & Hill, 2003). However, similar drugs have been known to inhibit labor, prolong pregnancy, and potentially cause other problems for the developing child. Because of the limited research into the potential dangers of ibuprofen use during pregnancy, it is recommended that it be used only under a doctor's supervision at this time (Black & Hill, 2003).

Research would suggest that ibuprofen does not enter into human milk in significant quantities when used at normal dosage levels (Briggs et al., 1986; Hale, 2003) and is considered "compatible with breast feeding" (p 217i). Indeed, Lourwood and Riedlinger (1989) reported that ibuprofen was "felt to be the safest" of the nonsteroidal anti-inflammatory drugs for the woman who was breast feeding her child.

Inhalant Abuse During Pregnancy

Virtually nothing is known about the effects of the various inhalants on the developing fetus. Although only a small percentage of those who experiment with inhalants go on to abuse these chemicals on a chronic basis, more than 50% of people who chronically abuse inhalants are women "in their prime childbearing years" (Pearson, Hoyme, Seaver, & Rimsza, 1994, p. 211). It is thus safe to assume that some children are being exposed to one or more of the inhalants during gestation.

Researchers have just started to study the effects of toluene inhalation on the developing fetus. Toluene is found in many forms of paint and solvents. It is known to cross the placenta into the fetal circulation when the mother inhales toluene fumes. In adults, about 50% of the toluene inhaled is biotransformed into hippuric acid, and the remainder is excreted unchanged (Pearson et al., 1994). But neither the fetus nor the newborn child has the ability to metabolize toluene. There is thus some question as to whether the effects of toluene exposure for the fetus or newborn would be the same as it would be for the adult who inhaled toluene fumes.

To attempt to answer this question, Pearson, Hoyme, Seaver, and Rimsza (1994) examined 18 infants who were exposed to toluene through maternal paint sniffing during pregnancy. They found that there were several similarities between the effects of toluene and the effects of alcohol on the fetus. The authors found that toluene exposure during pregnancy may cause a wide range of problems, similar to those of FAS, including premature birth, crainofacial abnormalities (abnormal ears, thin upper lip, small nose, etc.), abnormal muscle tone, renal abnormalities, developmental delays, abnormal scalp hair patterns, and retarded physical growth.

To explain the similarity between the effects of toluene abuse and alcohol abuse on the developing fetus, the authors hypothesized that toluene and alcohol might both result in a state of maternal toxicity. This state of maternal toxicity would, in turn, contribute to the fetal malformations seen in cases of toluene and alcohol exposure during pregnancy. While the authors' work is only preliminary, it would appear that toluene exposure during pregnancy may have lifelong consequences for the developing fetus. Until proven otherwise, it would be safe to assume that maternal abuse of the other inhalants would have similar destructive effects on the growing fetus.

Summary

If a substance-abusing woman is pregnant, the fetus that she carries will become an unwilling participant in the mother's chemical use/abuse. However, the impact of the chemical use is often much greater on the growing fetus than it is on the mother. Because of this, infants born to women who have used chemicals of abuse during pregnancy represent a special subpopulation of alcohol/drug users. The child who was exposed to recreational chemicals did not willingly participate in the process of chemical use, yet his or her life might be profoundly affected by the effects of alcohol or drugs.

An extreme example of the unwilling participation of infants in maternal alcohol or drug use is a child who is born already addicted to the chemicals the mother used during pregnancy. Other fetal complications of maternal chemical abuse might include stroke, retardation, or lower weight at birth as well as a number of other drug-specific complications. The over-the-counter analgesics present a special area of risk, for the effects of these medications on fetal growth and development are not well understood. However, available research suggests that the OTC analgesics should be used with caution by pregnant or nursing women.

CHAPTER TWENTY-ONE

Hidden Faces of Chemical Dependency

Introduction

Chemical dependency has many faces. Some of these images are familiar. For example, there is the stereotype of the "typical skid row" alcoholic, drinking a bottle of cheap wine that is wrapped in a plain brown paper bag. Another popular image is that of the young male heroin addict, with a belt wrapped around his arm, pushing a needle into a vein. A popular stereotype of the chemically addicted woman is that of the "fallen" woman: immoral, a poor parent, and most certainly nothing like "us." These popular stereotypes are quite persistent and grossly inaccurate (Schneiderman, 1990). As popular as they are, few people recognize that they serve only to limit our vision. If the addicted person deviates from our expectation, we may not recognize the chemical dependency hiding behind the social facade. For example, how many of us would expect to meet a white, middle-class, well-groomed heroin addict at work? How many people would recognize the benzodiazepine dependency behind the smiling face of a day care worker?

It is the purpose of this chapter to explore some of the hidden faces of chemical dependency so that the reader might be more sensitive to the many forms that substance abuse might take.

Women and Addiction: An Often Unrecognized Problem

All too often, the lessons of history are discovered through hindsight. Only rarely is such a lesson acknowledged *before* a crisis develops so that the problem might be circumvented. For example, during the epidemic of chemical abuse that took place in the last years of the 19th century, the ratio of men to women who were addicted to chemicals was only 1:2 (Lawson, 1994). Significant numbers of women were addicted to various mail-order medicines that were freely available without prescription at the time. Then laws were passed that limited the availability of compounds containing addictive substances and the epidemic of drug addiction gradually waned.

Yet when the current epidemic of alcohol/drug abuse began in the second half of the 20th century, society tended to focus on *men* who had chemical-use problems and virtually ignored the possibility that significant numbers of *women* might also be struggling with alcohol or drug abuse. A double standard evolved, in which a substance abusing/addicted woman was subjected to greater levels of social disapproval than was true for alcohol- or drug-dependent man (Chang, 2001), and women's addiction to alcohol or drugs was viewed as less important than that of men (Cohen, 2000; Jersild, 2001; Ramlow, White, Watson, & Leukefeld, 1997).

As a group, substance-abusing women tend to be: hidden, protected, and/or abandoned (Cohen, 2000). Possibly because of this social response to the problem of alcohol or drug misuse by women, it was not until the early 1980s that mental health professionals became aware that "gender plays a role in differential use of various substances by men and women, in their physiological reactions to the substances, in familial and societal reactions to their problems, in their help-seeking behavior, and in their interactions with clinicians" (Lala & Straussner, 1997, p. 3). Deplorably, there is still much to learn about the impact of chemical use or abuse on women. It is not possible to do full justice to the interplay between gender and chemical abuse, but this section will provide an overview of some of the issues and controversies surrounding alcohol or drug abuse by women.

Statement of the problem. Currently, one of every three alcohol-dependent individuals is believed to be a woman (Sinha, 2000). An estimated 4.4 million women in the United States either abuse or are addicted to alcohol, and an additional 2 million women in this country abuse or are addicted to illicit drugs (Greenfield, 2003). The implications of substance abuse in women might be seen in the statistic that alcohol-dependent women are up to 23 times as likely as women who are not dependent on alcohol to commit suicide (Markarian & Franklin, 1998). Yet in spite of the awareness that women make up such a large percentage of those who are addicted to chemicals, there has been little systematic research into the need for or the effectiveness of gender-specific treatment programs (Brady & Randall, 1999; Greenfield, 2003) and there is a "paucity of female-only support groups" (Coughey, Feighan, Cheney, & Klein, 1998, p. 929).

Obviously, there are inadequate resources to offer rehabilitation programs for women who abuse or are addicted to chemicals. This situation is so dismal that the development of gender-specific treatment programs is still in its infancy, even though the need for such programs has been known for a generation (Sinha, 2000).

The "convergence" theory. In the last decade of the 20th century, as substance-abuse rehabilitation professionals began to recognize that large numbers of women were abusing or addicted to recreational chemicals, they began to speak of a "convergence" in the incidence of substance-abuse problems among men and women. It was thought that as ever-growing numbers of women became addicted to chemicals the time was rapidly drawing near when approximately equal numbers of men and women would struggle with substance-use problems. The convergence theory for adults did not develop as predicted, but there is growing evidence that adolescents are abusing alcohol or drugs in ways suggesting that their generation might experience approximately equal rates of addiction.

How Does Gender Affect the Rehabilitation Process?

Gender impacts the process of rehabilitation in a number of ways. First, there are different pathways for men and women who become addicted to chemicals. Second, women present special needs in a rehabilitation setting (Kauffman, Dore, & Nelson-Zlupko, 1995). For example,

women who are addicted to chemicals are also more likely to present a history of having been exposed to some form of interpersonal violence than are male substance abusers, and they will have to come to terms with these victimization issues as part of their recovery program (Byington, 1997; Cohen, 2000; Del Boca & Hesselbrock, 1996; Miller & Downs, 1995; Sinha, 2000).

Another difference was found in the way the individual perceived the causes of his or her chemical addiction: Men tend to externalize the responsibility for their alcohol- or drug-use problem; women tend to blame themselves (Lala & Straussner, 1997). For this reason, alcohol-dependent women tend to suffer more from poor self-esteem than do alcoholic men (Alexander, 1996; Cohen, 2000; Coughey et al., 1998; North, 1996; Sinha, 2000). Indeed, some evidence suggests that drug abuse represents an attempt on the part of the woman to medicate feelings of low self-worth (Alexander, 1996).

Women with alcohol- or drug-use problems generally experience greater demands on their time than their male counterparts (Kauffman et al., 1995; O'Dell, Turner, & Weaver, 1998; Sinha, 2000). For example, it is not uncommon for the woman to be granted custody of the children following divorce on the grounds that the children should live with their mother. If that mother should also have a substance-use problem, she would find few rehabilitation programs that have provisions for taking care of the children while she is in treatment. In such cases, child custody often becomes a barrier to the mother's ability to participate in treatment for substance-use problems (Beckman, 1994; Blume & Zilberman, 2004; Kauffman et al., 1995; Raskin, 1994).

Substance-abusing women also tend to enter the rehabilitation system in a far different manner from that of their male counterparts (Alexander, 1996; Blume & Zilberman, 2004; Brady & Randall, 1999; Weisner & Schmidt, 1992). Compared to men with substance-use problems, women tend to enter treatment programs through advertisements in the media or on the referral of a friend, whereas men are more likely to enter treatment on referral from a physician, employer, or the court system (Beckman, 1994).

Research has also found that alcohol-addicted women are far more likely to suffer from a primary depression than are alcohol-dependent men (Dixit & Crum, 2000), but the depressed alcohol-dependent woman usually has a better prognosis than would a depressed male who is dependent on alcohol (Hill, 1995; Schutte, Moos, & Brennan, 1995). For women, the symptoms of depression are likely to serve as a drinking cue, triggering further alcohol use as the depressed woman attempts to self-medicate her depression. In contrast, men appear less likely to try self-medicating a depressive disorder through alcohol use and might even reduce their alcohol use when they become depressed (Schutte et al., 1995).

This difference in the pathway that men and women typically follow toward alcohol dependence would seem to account for the observation that women initially tend to seek help from mental health providers rather than substance-abuse rehabilitation professionals (Weisner & Schmidt, 1992). Men who are addicted to chemicals, on the other hand, are less likely to be attempting to self-medicate emotional distress and thus tend to become involved with substance-abuse treatment professionals immediately, according to the authors.

Women who enter treatment usually present a different constellation of problems from those of men. For example, although not every woman with a substance-use problem engages in prostitution, as a general rule men tend to engage in the sale of drugs to support their addiction whereas women are more likely to sell their bodies (Lala & Straussner, 1997). Women who enter treatment also have different interpersonal and intra-personal resources than do men at the beginning of the rehabilitation process. There is evidence that being married is a protective factor against relapse for men following treatment but a possible risk factor for women (Sinha, 2000). This finding suggests that as a group, husbands of alcohol-dependent women may be less supportive than wives of men with a substance-abuse problem.

Some of the barriers that women face when they wish to enter a substance-abuse rehabilitation treatment include funding problems, child care or custody issues, transportation problems, lack of support from partners, and the stigmatization that often surrounds those who have a substance-abuse problem. Many treatment programs will accept neither a pregnant woman nor a woman with dependent children (Blume & Zilberman, 2004; Ringwald, 2002). As a general rule women have smaller social support circles and receive less emotional support from their friends at the time of

admission to treatment than do their male counterparts (O'Dell, Turner, & Weaver, 1998).

Alcohol-dependent women are often four times more likely to be living with a partner who also has an alcohol-use problem than is the male alcoholic (Miller & Cervantes, 1997). Men whose partner is alcoholic are more likely to turn to divorce as a way of resolving this marital problem than are women (Byington, 1997). For these reasons, many women report that they receive less support from their partner for their efforts to abstain from chemical use than do recovering men (Kauffman et al., 1995; O'Dell et al., 1998).

Work, gender, and chemical abuse. There is little evidence to support the popular stereotype that working outside the home increases the chance that the woman will abuse alcohol (Jersild, 2001). However, there is a complex relationship between work status and alcohol-use patterns. For example, women who are less satisfied with their work status tend to abuse alcohol more often (Jersild, 2001), a significant problem when one stops to consider that many women in the workforce are working below their potential work capacity, often in low-status high-frustration positions.

For some women, the increased social status, social support, and improved self-esteem that go with full-time paid employment seem to help reduce the chances of developing a substance-use problem (Brady & Randall, 1999; Wilsnack & Wilsnack, 1995; Wilsnack, Wilsnack, & Hiller-Sturmhoffel, 1994). Yet for reasons that are not well understood, employment can also facilitate the development of a chemical-use problem in other women (Brady & Randall, 1999). For example, women working in nontraditional, male-dominated professions where more than 50% of their coworkers are males tend to report higher levels of alcohol-use problems (Wilsnack & Wilsnack, 1995; Wilsnack et al., 1994).

Unfortunately, it is often more difficult to detect problem chemical use in working women who do have a substance-use problem (Jersild, 2001). Being underemployed, their chemical use is less likely to cause unacceptable job performance than it is for men (Blume & Zilberman, 2004). The low-paying jobs that many women hold usually do not allow for easy access to employee assistance program counselors, thus making the referral process more difficult for the woman than it is for many men. Also, the threat of job loss if the addicted woman does not seek treatment is not as effective as it is for men, as the majority of women work only to supplement their husbands' incomes. It is often easier for such a women to simply quit her job than to give in to a threatened loss of employment if she does not seek treatment (Pape, 1988).

Victimization histories and substance-use patterns. Research has shown that women who are addicted to alcohol are 2.5 times as likely to report having been sexually abused in childhood than nonalcoholic women (Byington, 1997; Miller & Downs, 1995). Some studies have found that as many as 85% of the women in treatment for alcohol dependence give a history of having been an incest victim (Beckman, 1994). As these statistics suggest, there appears to be a tendency for those women who are treated for a substance-use problem to have been the victim of some form of sexual violence (Alexander, 1996; Blume, 1998). However, alcohol or drug misuse is not *automatically* a result of having been abused by a significant other (Holloway, 1998; Jersild, 2001). The assumption that such an abuse history will result in a chemical-use problem is "not only damaging but also antitherapeutic and disempowering" (p. 35) to women in treatment. Thus, staff must be careful in drawing conclusions about the role of victimization in the development of a substance-use disorder.

Although the woman with a substance-use problem is often referred to a mixed-sex group as part of her treatment program, research has found that many women fail to benefit from this format (Greenfield, 2003; Lala & Straussner, 1997). Many women feel inhibited in mixed groups, especially if they have been victimized by a male at some point in life (Alexander, 1996; Lala & Straussner, 1997). Often, the language used by many men in the therapeutic setting is intimidating to women and in some cases may even revictimize them as memories of past abuse surface. This contributes to the increased dropout rate for women from mixed groups as opposed to unisex groups.

Gender and substance use patterns. Within the past generation, researchers have discovered that women usually obtain their drug of choice in different ways than do men. Unlike male substance abusers, women drug abusers tend to obtain their drugs from their own physician. More than a decade ago it was suggested that sedatives and "diet pills" had become "women's drugs" (Peluso & Peluso, 1988, p. 10), a distinction that

continues to be true. This trend could be seen in the fact that nearly 70% of all prescriptions for psychotropic medications are written for women (Cohen et al., 1996). But because these women obtain their drugs through prescriptions and the local pharmacy, their drug-abuse problem all too often has "been rendered invisible" (Peluso & Peluso, 1988, p. 9).

Another way that substance use by women might be rendered invisible is found in the observation that many women were initially introduced to illicit drugs by their male partner, who then serves as a source of supply (Blume, 1998). In this manner, the woman's need for chemicals is met by a male partner, possibly in return for sexual favors, and she does not have to actively seek out illicit drugs on her own.

Differing Effects of Common Drugs of Abuse on Men and Women

As medical researchers learn more about the effects of various drugs on men and women, they are starting to uncover significant differences in how each gender responds to different chemicals. Not surprisingly, there are also differences in how men and women react when they use one or more of the popular drugs of abuse.

Narcotics abuse and gender. Griffin, Weiss, Mirin, and Lang (1989) found that the woman who was addicted to narcotics was likely to have started using opiates at a significantly older age than her male counterparts. But the typical narcotics-dependent woman will, as a general rule, have a history of heavier drug use than male addicts, and women addicted to narcotics tend to be approximately the same age as men at the time of their first admission into drug treatment, according to the authors.

At the same time, there appear to be differences in how opiate-dependent men and women use their drug of choice. In England, Gossop, Battersby, and Strang (1991) found that male narcotics addicts were more likely to inject their drug whereas female narcotics addicts were more likely to inhale narcotic powder. Female addicts were also more likely to be involved in a sexual relationship with another drug user than were male narcotics addicts. Finally, just under half of the female narcotics addicts studied by the authors had received drugs as a present from a sexual partner, confirming that for women, narcotics addiction follows a different course than the one for men.

Cocaine abuse and gender. Women make up approximately 50% of those addicted to cocaine (Lawson, 1994). However, research has revealed that cocaine-use patterns differ between men and women. Female cocaine abusers tend to start their drug use at an earlier age and to reach the stage of addiction more rapidly than male cocaine users (Kender & Prescott, 1998). Cocaine-addicted women are likely to be significantly younger at the time of their first admission to a drug treatment program than their male counterparts and to have followed a different pathway to cocaine addiction (Griffin et al., 1989). Yet in spite of this growing awareness that men and women might become addicted to cocaine for different reasons, little research has been conducted into how treatment programs should be modified to be more effective with cocaine abusers of either sex.

Alcohol abuse and gender. Because of differences in body mass, fluid content, and levels of gastric alcohol dehydrogenase found in the woman's body, women require up to 40% less alcohol than men to achieve the same blood alcohol level (Blume, 1998; Collins & McNair, 2002; North, 1996). Further, the monthly variations in estrogen levels can affect the speed with which the woman's body absorbs alcohol, and oral contraceptive medications used by women can slow the biotransformation of the alcohol already in the body (North, 1996; Reynolds & Bada, 2003).

These are some of the reasons women tend to experience alcohol-related problems at an earlier point in life than do men. For example, one begins to see alcohol-related physical problems in female alcohol abusers at just one-third the level of alcohol intake necessary for the typical male alcohol abuser to experience similar problems (North, 1996). Further, women appear to be more sensitive to the toxic effects of alcohol on striated muscle tissues such as the tissues of the heart than are male alcohol users (Urbano-Marquez et al., 1995).

Researchers have also found that when women first enter treatment for alcoholism their addiction, and the medical consequences of that addiction, are usually more severe than would be expected for a man with the same drinking history (Sinha, 2000). Thus, the typical alcoholic woman will develop cirrhosis of the liver after about 13 years of addictive drinking whereas it might take the typical male alcoholic

22 years to develop the same disorder (Blume, 1994; Hennessey, 1992). In a sense, the woman's experience of alcohol-related consequences is often "telescoped" into a shorter time frame than that found for the typical male alcoholic (Blume & Zilberman, 2004; Greenfield, 2003; Schuckit, Daeppen, Tipp, Hellelbrock, & Bucholz, 1998).

In addition, there is a known association between alcohol abuse and infertility, miscarriage, amenorrhea, uterine bleeding, dysmenorrhea, abnormal menstruation, osteoporosis, and possibly breast cancer (Emanuele, Wezeman, & Emanuele, 2002; Kovalesky, 2004; Sampson, 2002). Unfortunately, in spite of this known association between alcohol abuse/addiction and illness, physicians are very poor at recognizing the signs of alcohol addiction in their female patients (Kitchens, 1994; North, 1996).

Gender group membership is now considered one of the major variables that helps to define the developmental pathway of different subtypes of alcohol abuse or addiction (Del Boca & Hesselbrock, 1996). Research has uncovered at least two subforms of alcohol dependence in women (Hill, 1995). The first group, which is composed of only a minority of women drinkers, appears to include those whose alcoholism finds full expression between the ages of 18 and 24 years of age. These women might be said to have "early-onset" (Hill, 1995, p. 11) alcohol dependence, and their drinking pattern tends to be atypical. In contrast to this group, however, is the larger group of alcohol-dependent women. These women are classified as the "later-onset" (Hill, 1995, p. 11) drinkers, whose drinking seems to reach its peak between the ages of 35 and 49 years of age. However, the relationship between the two subtypes of female alcoholics identified by Hill, and the Type I/Type II typology of alcoholism in males (discussed elsewhere in this text) is still not clear.

In their examination of the subtypes of alcoholism, Del Boca and Hesselbrock (1996) concluded that at least two of the four subtypes of alcoholism that they identified were strongly influenced by the individual's gender. On the basis of their data, the authors concluded that there were a number of possible developmental pathways that could result in alcoholism for men and women. Although the authors' data do not explore possible etiologies of these different subforms of alcoholism, their data *do* suggest that the expression of alcoholism for men and women follows traditional gender role expectations in the United States.

However, Miller and Cervantes (1997) suggested a positive note in that women with alcohol-use problems were more likely to respond positively to minimal interventions. One reason is that women "are often first to recognize their drinking problem, while men are more likely to have confrontations, especially with authorities, that bring them involuntarily into contact with treatment caregivers" (Beckman, 1993, p. 236). Thus, according to the author, women are more accepting of the treatment process and the need for treatment. There is evidence that one catalyst that helps to bring the substance-abusing woman in for treatment is her responsibility for her children (Kline, 1996).

Unfortunately, there are significant social barriers between the recovering woman and community resources such as Alcoholics Anonymous (AA). One such barrier is the "subtle but significant form of sexism" (Coker, 1997, p. 268) that serves to help make women who join AA feel unwelcome. Indeed, the AA program, "which confronts the false pride of the alcoholic, may not be helpful to a woman who needs to build her self-esteem from the ground up" (Jersild, 2001, p. 6).

Because of the differences in how men and women perceive the "self" when they are addicted to chemicals, as well as because of past victimization experiences, women tend to feel more shame than do men when they enter AA. It is for this reason that women are more likely to to be solitary drinkers than men with alcohol-use problems. AA's heavy emphasis on uncovering sources of shame might make women feel unwanted or unwelcome in AA (Blume & Zilberman, 2004; Coker, 1997; Jersild, 2001). To complicate matters, there is strong evidence that the face of alcoholism in women is changing. It would appear that women are starting to drink alcohol at an earlier age and in far greater quantities than did their older counterparts (Greenfield, 2003; Sinha, 2000). Thus, the challenge that faces AA is the need to both eliminate the subtle sexism inherent in its 12-Step program and to make the program relevant to different age cohorts of women with different forms of alcoholism.

In the last quarter of the 20th century, many of the traditional social values that limited the exposure of women to alcohol or drug use have weakened or disappeared entirely (Blume & Zilberman, 2004). One example is how Madison Avenue has targeted women as a group, in order to make alcohol use more acceptable to the average woman (Blume, 1994). One might only hope that society will learn to face the problem of drug addiction in both men and women with openness, compassion, and unrestricted access to proven treatment methods.

Addiction and the Homeless

There has been a limited amount of research into substance-use problems among the homeless. Researchers have found that 45% to 78% of those who are homeless have a substance-use disorder (Arehart-Treichel, 2004; Smith, Meyers, & Delaney, 1998). Surprisingly, the incidence of substance abuse does not seem to increase after the person becomes homeless, and in some cases losing one's home seems to serve as an incentive for the individual to stop using alcohol or drugs (Arehart-Treichel, 2004). The role of the individual's substance use in the loss of his or her home is not always clear, and there is not always a causal relationship. Rather, substance abuse and loss of housing may reflect co-existing issues indicative of a third factor, such as loss of employment or mental illness.

Substance Use Problems and the Elderly

Research into addictive disorders in older age groups has progressed very slowly (Zisserson & Oslin, 2004). One reason might have been the myth that alcoholism was a self-limiting disorder, in the sense that alcohol-dependent individuals rarely lived long enough to reach old age (Mundle, 2000). This myth rests on research failing to consider that as aging occurs in the cohort of those born in the period between 1950 and 1960—raised in an atmosphere in which recreational drug use was viewed as normal—the problem of substance abuse or addiction in older age groups is becoming more common (Gomberg, 2004; Zisserson & Oslin, 2004).

Scope of the problem. The elderly make up approximately 12% of the population of the United States and use approximately one-third of all prescription medications and half of all over-the-counter medications (Gomberg, 2004; Reid & Anderson, 1997). Many of these prescriptions are for medications designed to control the symptoms of nonpsychiatric disorders such as coronary artery disease, gout, and arthritis. If an older individual were to consume alcohol, it is possible that the alcohol would interfere with many of the medications that are used to treat these conditions (Goldstein, Pataki, & Webb, 1996; Rigler, 2000). The reverse is also true: The use of medications by an older person might alter the way his or her body responds to alcohol, even if the person were not drinking to excess (J. W. Smith, 1997).

Alcohol-use problems in older people are not insignificant. It has been estimated that 1% of the elderly have used an illicit drug in the past 30 days, and that 13% of the men and 2% of the women over the age of 60 and living in the community have alcohol-use problems (Gomberg, 2004; Mundle, 2000; Rigler, 2000). Other researchers have suggested that between 10% and 15% of individuals over the age of 65 have a substance-use disorder (Mosier, 1999; Prater, Miller, & Zylstra, 1999; Zimberg, 1996; Zisserson & Oslin, 2004). Alcohol abuse is the third most common form of psychiatric problem seen in the elderly, surpassed only by the various forms of dementia and anxiety disorders in terms of frequency (Abrams & Alexopoulos, 1998).

Elderly alcohol abusers are overrepresented in the population of those who are seeking health care for one reason or another. Researchers estimate that between 5%–15% (Dunne, 1994; Vandeputte, 1989) and 49% (Blake, 1990) of elderly patients seeking medical treatment have an alcohol- or drug-related problem. These estimates are consistent with those of Dunlop, Manghelli, and Tolson (1989) who suggested that 25% of the elderly population might be suffering from alcohol-related problems. Zimberg (1995) suggested that 10% of the men and 20% of the women might be classified as "escape drinkers" (p. 413) who have an alcohol-use problem. Unfortunately, only about 20% of alcohol abusers/addicts in this age group are correctly identified as such (Mundle, 2000).

Older adults do not experience just alcohol-use problems. They also experience problems caused by the abuse of other chemicals besides alcohol. Abrams and Alexopoulos (1987) suggested that "more than 20 percent of patients over 65 years old admitted to a psychiatric hospital in one year could be considered drug dependent" (p. 1286). Up to 15% of older adults might be classified as having a drug-abuse problem (Cohen et al., 1996). The vast majority of these individuals

either abuse or have become dependent on prescribed medications. Yet illicit drug abuse continues to be a problem for older people, as evidenced by the fact that 2% of illicit drug abusers are older than the age of 50 (Rosenberg, 1997). Rigler (2000) warned that about 15% of the elderly patients who are alcohol dependent also abuse or are dependent on other psychoactive agents. In spite of this information, however, virtually nothing is known about the older drug abuser.

Researchers have found that older alcoholics take up a disproportional part of the health care resources in the United States. For example, after an examination of discharge diagnosis statistics from across the United States, Adams, Yuan, Barboriak, and Rimm (1993) found that between 19 and 77 of every 10,000 elderly patients admitted to acute care hospitals had an alcohol-use disorder. The authors also found that the number of elderly patients being treated for myocardial infarction was between 17 and 44 per 10,000 patient admissions in the same age group. Their figures suggest that the rates of hospital admission for alcohol-related health problems in the elderly was "similar to those for myocardial infarction" (p. 1224) and may even have exceeded that for this form of heart disease in the elderly. This finding is consistent with data that families with an alcoholic member have health care costs 21 times as high as similar families without an alcoholic member. Nor is the problem of substance abuse in the older population limited only to alcohol. If these figures are accurate, it would appear that chemical-use problems are commonly found in the elderly.

A definition of abusive alcohol use in the elderly. Medical researchers now believe that one standard alcohol-containing beverage per day is the upper limit of "moderate" alcohol use for those over the age of 60 (Rigler, 2000; Zisserson & Oslin, 2004). The consequences for older individuals who consume *more* than the recommended one drink per day limit are all too evident. Fully 14% of the elderly patients seen in emergency rooms, 23% to 44% of elderly patients seen in an inpatient psychiatric treatment center, 18% of the patients hospitalized for general medical problems, and 11% of the elderly patients admitted to a nursing home are thought to have alcohol-use problems (Goldstein et al., 1996).

Why is the detection of substance-use disorders in the elderly so difficult? Alcohol- or drug-use problems are often unrecognized among older individuals (Beullens & Aertgeerts, 2004; Dunne, 1994; Kitchens, 1994; Rains, 1990). This is unfortunate, because although older adults tend to have more medical problems than do younger adults, physicians are ill-prepared to recognize the signs of substance abuse or addiction in the elderly. First, few physicians are adequately trained in the area of addiction medicine. But the issue is more complicated than just a lack of physician training. For reasons that are not well understood, older alcoholics appear to be less likely to visit their physician than their nondrinking peers (Rice & Duncan, 1995).

There are many possible reasons that older adults with alcohol-use disorders are less likely to go to a physician on a regular basis. It is possible that the older drinker tends to avoid seeing a physician to escape the danger of having the alcohol-use disorder discovered. Also, older drinkers, like their physicians, tend to attribute physical complications caused by their drinking to the aging process rather than to alcohol use. Thus, older drinkers might avoid going to see a physician because they do not understand the true cause of their medical problems. Also, older drinkers do not demonstrate such traditional symptoms of excessive drinking as consuming a large number of drinks or missing work, because older drinkers are more vulnerable to the negative effects of alcohol at dosage levels that rarely cause problems in younger drinkers and frequently are retired and thus do not need to go to work (Baselt, 1996; Gambert, 1997; Gomberg, 2004; Zisserson & Oslin, 2004).

Older drinkers are more vulnerable to alcohol's negative effects for a number of reasons. First, as a result of the aging process, the bodies of older individuals contain lower levels of different body fluids than those of young adults. This contributes to a tendency for older drinkers to achieve higher blood alcohol levels than young adults after consuming a given amount of alcohol (Lieber, 1998; Zimberg, 1996). As a result of the normal aging process, just three beers or mixed drinks consumed by a 60-year-old may have the same effect on the drinker as 12 beers or mixed drinks consumed at the age of 21 (Anderson, 1989). Second, the brain of an older drinker is more sensitive to the toxic effects of alcohol than it was decades earlier (Goldstein et al., 1996). Even social drinking might contribute to cognitive deterioration in the older drinker (Abrams & Alexopoulos, 1987; Rains, 1990). Given this fact, it should not be surprising to discover a "high association between alcoholism and dementia" (Goldstein et al., 1996, p. 941; Smith, 1997).

Although alcohol use or abuse is a known risk factor for the development of a wide range of psychosocial impairments, these problems are not as obvious in the older alcohol abusing or dependent person as they are in the young adult (Abrams & Alexopoulos, 1998). All too often, alcohol-induced problems in the older individual such as blackouts, financial problems, or job loss are attributed to medical or age-related psychosocial problems, not a possible alcohol-use problem (Szwabo, 1993). Many of alcohol's effects on the cognitive abilities of older adults mimic changes associated with normal aging. Even trained physicians find it difficult to differentiate between late-onset Korsakoff's syndrome and many forms of senile dementia, such as Alzheimer's disease or multi-infarct dementia (Blake, 1990; Rains, 1990).

Alcohol use in older persons is often hidden from family and friends (Peluso & Peluso, 1989; Vandeputte, 1989). To illustrate this point, just imagine the family's reaction if grandmother or grandfather were to announce at the dinner table that "I'm going out tonight to get wasted!" Shame also contributes to this process of avoidance, as the individual's family and friends often feel hurt or guilty about the possibility that an older family member has an alcohol-use problem. These feelings of shame prevent family or friends from reporting their suspicions to the individual's physician or from confronting the individual with their concerns (Goldstein et al., 1996; Gomberg, 2004; Peluso & Peluso, 1989; Vandeputte, 1989).

What are the consequences of alcohol/drug addiction in the elderly? Alcohol use or abuse may cause or contribute to accidental falls, bone fractures, depression, memory problems, liver disease, cardiovascular disorders, and sleep problems (Rigler, 2000; Zisserson & Oslin, 2004). Older drinkers also seem to have an increased risk for motor vehicle accidents. Higgins, Wright, and Wrenn (1996) found that 14% of the elderly patients seen for injuries suffered in motor vehicle accidents had a positive blood alcohol screen.

Alcohol use may either complicate the treatment of other diseases or even cause the individual to develop various new medical problems that may become life threatening (Vandeputte, 1989). Alcohol use in the elderly may either influence the development of or actually cause such medical problems as myopathy, cerebrovascular disease, gastritis, diarrhea, pancreatitis, cardiomyopathy, and various sleep disorders (Liberto, Oslin, & Ruskin, 1992). Other disorders that might be caused by alcohol use by older individuals include hypertension, diminished resistance to infections, peripheral muscle weakness, electrolyte and metabolic disturbances, and orthostatic hypotension (Szwabo, 1993).

Unfortunately, as noted earlier, older drinkers are less likely to seek medical attention for their distress, at least until the complications caused by their drinking become severe enough to require hospitalization. Further, even when their drinking is identified, few elderly alcoholics receive treatment for their drug addiction (Vandeputte, 1989). This results in increased medical costs for both the individual and ultimately society to treat these alcohol-induced problems.

Although few people stop to consider the possible impact of an alcohol or drug-use problem on the mental health of older individuals, substance abuse extracts a terrible toll on the older user's peace of mind. For example, depression is a common problem in old age. Unfortunately, depression is also a common consequence of alcohol or drug abuse, and it has been estimated that 25% to 50% of all elderly suicide victims have used alcohol prior to their suicide attempt (Abrams & Alexopoulos, 1998). For reasons that are not clear, there is evidence of a relationship between alcohol-abuse problems in early or middle adulthood and the development of depression in the elderly, even if the individual's alcohol use was not problematic in later adulthood (Abrams & Alexopoulos, 1998). Unrecognized substance-induced depressive episodes can result in both misdiagnosis and mistreatment of the individual's mental health problem, adding urgency to the need for an accurate diagnosis of the causes of depression in the elderly.

Different patterns of alcohol/drug abuse in the elderly. Many older individuals develop alcohol-use problems only in their later years (Zimberg, 1996). This phenomenon has been termed *"late onset alcoholism"* (Mundle, 2000; Rigler, 2000) or "reactive alcoholism" (Peluso & Peluso, 1989). Perhaps as many as 30% to 50% of the elderly alcoholic population actually began to have problems with alcohol only in either middle or late life (Brennan & Moos, 1996; Liberto et al., 1992).

Zimberg (1995) suggested that there were three subgroups of older alcoholics. The first group was made up of individuals who had no drinking problem in young or middle adulthood but who developed late-life alcoholism. These individuals could be said to have *late-onset alcoholism*, according to the author. The second subgroup of older alcoholics had a history of intermittent problem drinking over the years but developed a more chronic alcohol problem only in late adulthood. This group of individuals could be said to have *late-onset exacerbation* drinking, according to Zimberg (1995). Finally, there were those individuals whose alcohol problems started in young adulthood and continued into the later part of the individual's life, a pattern known as "early-onset" alcoholism (Mundle, 2000; Zimberg, 1995).

Medication misuse is another problem area for the elderly. Campbell (1992) estimated that 10% of the elderly misuse prescription medications. Drug misuse takes several forms, including (a) intentional overuse of a medication, (b) underuse of a medication, (c) erratic use of a prescribed medication, or (d) the failure of the physician to obtain a complete drug history, including use of over-the-counter medications, resulting in dangerous medication combinations (Abrams & Alexopoulos, 1998). The intentional misuse of prescribed medications is the largest category of drug abuse in the elderly. Surprisingly, however, the elderly are far more likely to engage in the *under*utilization as opposed to the overutilization of prescription medications, most commonly because of financial problems (Abrams & Alexopoulos, 1987, 1998; Piette, Heisler, & Wagner, 2004).

The treatment of the older alcohol/drug abuser. Unfortunately, as a group, the elderly substance abuser is (a) rarely identified as such, (b) rarely referred to treatment, and (c) often overlooked by treatment agencies, who are often overwhelmed with the task of dealing with younger alcohol or drug abusers. Even when the the older alcoholic/drug abusing patient is referred to treatment, he or she will present special treatment needs rarely found in younger addicts, which few treatment centers are prepared to meet (Goldstein et al., 1996). To meet these special treatment needs, Dunlop et al. (1989) recommended that treatment programs working with the elderly include several different components, including the following:

1. A primary prevention program to warn about the dangers of using alcohol as a coping mechanism for life's problems.
2. An outreach program to identify and serve older alcoholics who might be overlooked by more traditional treatment services.
3. Detoxification service workers trained and experienced in working with the elderly, who frequently require longer detoxification periods than younger addicted persons.
4. Protective environments for the elderly, such as structured living environments that would allow them to take part in treatment while being protected from the temptation of further alcohol use.
5. Primary treatment programs for those who could benefit from either inpatient or outpatient short-term primary treatment programs.
6. Aftercare programs to help the older alcoholic with the transition between primary care and independent living.
7. Long-term residential care for those who suffered from severe medical and/or psychiatric complications from alcoholism.
8. Access to social work support services.

In working with the older alcoholic or drug-abusing patient, it is wise to keep in mind that he or she might require an extended period of time just to fully detoxify from alcohol or drugs (Gomberg, 2004; Mundle, 2000). Rains (1990) suggested that older alcoholics might require up to 18 months of abstinence in order to fully recover from the effects of drinking. Thus, the standard 21- to 28-day inpatient treatment program might fail to meet the needs of an elderly client, as he or she would hardly have completed the detoxification process before being discharged as "cured." Further, older adults might require more help than younger clients to build a nonalcoholic support structure (Anderson, 1989). The older client often has a slower physical and mental pace than younger individuals, presents a range of sensory deficits rarely found in younger clients, and very often dislikes the profanity commonly encountered with younger individuals in treatment (Dunlop et al., 1989).

Unless these special needs are addressed, the older individual is unlikely to be motivated to participate in treatment. Treatment professionals must help the older addict deal with more than the direct effects of chemical addiction. For example, health care professionals need to be aware of the possibility that in addition to the drinking problem, the older alcoholic is also experiencing age-specific stressors such as retirement, bereavement, loneliness, and the effects of physical illness (Dunlop et al., 1989; Zimberg, 1996). On a positive note, however, there is evidence suggesting that late-onset drinkers respond better to treatment than do younger alcohol abusers (Brennan & Moos, 1996; Mundle, 2000). Group therapy approaches that included a problem-solving and social-support component were thought to be useful in working with the older alcoholic, especially if such programs included exposure to the Alcoholics Anonymous 12-Step program (Dunlop et al., 1989; Rains, 1990; Zimberg, 1978).

The Homosexual and Substance Abuse

In spite of social changes in the 1980s and 1990s, the homosexual (gay) man or (lesbian) woman continues to be part of a "hidden minority" (Fassinger, 1991, p. 157) within society. Estimates as to the percentage of the population that is bisexual, gay, or lesbian vary. Seidman and Rieder (1994) estimated that 20% of the men in the United States have had at least one homosexual experience at some point in their lives, and between 1% and 6% of the male population have had a homosexual encounter in the last year. In spite of the fact that, statistically, homoerotic relationships appear to be common, society's response to individuals who engage in a nontraditional form of sexuality is less than supportive. Many gay/lesbian individuals feel ostracized by a culture that neither understands nor encourages a homosexual lifestyle, and they go to great lengths to hide their sexual orientation.

Research suggests that homosexuals/lesbians tend to abuse chemicals more often than the general public (King et al., 2003). Such individuals constitute a special needs population for substance-abuse rehabilitation professionals (Cabaj, 1997; Rathbone-McCuan & Stokke, 1997). It is estimated that 28% to 35% of gay men/lesbians have engaged in some form of recreational drug use that did not involve some form of injection, compared to 10% to 12% of the heterosexual population (Ungvarski & Grossman, 1999). Further, it has been hypothesized that gay/lesbian clients are at risk for alcohol-use problems because of the central role that the "gay" bar plays in the homosexual lifestyle. To understand this special area of risk, it is necessary for the average person to understand that because homosexuals live on the fringes of society, opportunities for socialization within the gay community are limited. It is for this reason that the gay bar assumes a role of central importance as a place where one might socialize without fear of ridicule, meet potential partners, or simply escape from society in general (Paul, Stall, & Bloomfield, 1991). Further, the homosexual bar continues to play a role of central importance in the process of discovering one's sexuality for both gay men and lesbian women.

There has been very little research into the frequency of alcohol-use problems (Cabaj, 1997; Hughes & Wilsnack, 1997; Rathbone-McCuan, & Stokke, 1997) or drug-abuse problems (Warn, 1997) among gay/lesbian individuals. The limited data that are available suggest that there is a significantly higher alcoholism rate for gay/lesbian people than for the general population. It has been estimated that 25% to 35% of the homosexual population meets the diagnostic criteria for a formal diagnosis of alcohol/drug dependency (Klinger & Cabaj, 1993). Indeed, there is evidence that more than half of all lesbians have alcohol-use problems, a rate 5–7 times higher than that seen in nongay women (Blume, 1998; North, 1996).

There are a number of reasons for the apparent association between homosexuality and alcohol abuse. Some individuals, uncomfortable with their sexual orientation or anticipating rejection once their sexual preference becomes known, may use alcohol or drugs to self-medicate shame or guilt feelings (Paul et al., 1991). The authors noted, for example, that individuals who experienced negative feelings surrounding their sexual orientation tended to use alcohol to reduce internal tension. Also, the homosexual bar plays an important role within the gay community, often providing the only safe environment within which the individual might explore his or her sexuality.

The use of alcohol or drugs might also be involved with the process of exploring or accepting one's sexual identity in a society that rarely accepts deviation from the self-proclaimed "norm" (Cabaj, 1997). This process would serve to strengthen the association between bisexuality/homosexuality and substance-use problems. Finally, some researchers have suggested that alcohol or drugs might be abused by male homosexuals to deaden the pain of receptive anal intercourse (Ungvarski & Grossman, 1999).

Thus, there is ample evidence to suggest that alcohol- or drug-use problems might be more common in the homosexual community than in the heterosexual population. However, to complicate matters, the role of the gay bar as a source of recruiting research subjects has been challenged by researchers. It has been suggested that research samples drawn from this scene might *inflate* estimates of alcohol- or drug-use disorders among the bisexual/gay/lesbian population (Cabaj, 1997; Friedman & Downey, 1994). Statistically, those people who are most likely to frequent the bar are the ones who are more likely to have alcohol- or drug-use problems. As a result of this selection bias, individuals who were not alcohol or drug users tend to be underrepresented in research samples drawn from homosexual bars. As a result, research samples drawn from such settings might overestimate the prevalence of alcohol- or drug-use problems among bisexual/gay/lesbian individuals.

In contrast to this theory, Hughes and Wilsnack (1997) concluded that lesbians may indeed have higher rates of alcohol-use problems than their heterosexual counterparts. However, because of the lack of adequate research studies, and the fact that many of the estimates of alcohol-use problems among lesbians are extrapolated from studies done on male homosexuals, the authors call for more research into alcohol- or drug-use patterns among homosexual women. Thus, at this time, it is virtually impossible to determine the actual prevalence of these problems among the gay/lesbian population (Friedman & Downey, 1994). There also is little research into the special health care needs of the bisexual/gay/lesbian client, and virtually no research into what treatment methods are effective for the substance abusing gay/lesbian client (Cabaj, 1997). However, with some estimates stating that gay/lesbian individuals make up 10% to 15% of the population (Fassinger, 1991), and the estimate that approximately one-third of gays/lesbians abuse chemicals, it would appear that a significant percentage of those in treatment for substance-abuse problems live a nontraditional lifestyle.

Unfortunately, the development of specialized treatment services for gay/lesbian clients has been "slow" (Hughes & Wilsnack, 1997, p. 31). There are few treatment programs dedicated to working with homosexual adults, and such programs are usually located in major cities where there is a significant homosexual population. There is no program known that is devoted entirely to the treatment of lesbians (Rathbone-McCuan & Stokke, 1997). A significant percentage of substance abuse professionals were deficient in their ability to work with the homosexual client, and in almost 40% of the cases substance-abuse counselors received no formal training in how to effectively work with the gay/lesbian person (Hellman, Stanton, Lee, Tytun, & Vachon, 1989).

There has been a movement for creation of special AA groups oriented toward the specific needs of bisexual/gay/lesbian members (Paul et al., 1991), but these groups are usually located in the same major metropolitan areas where there are significant numbers of gay/lesbian individuals. Needless to say, in spite of the progress that society has made toward accepting homosexual/lesbian persons, there remains a significant need for substance-abuse counselors to become aware of the unique needs presented by these clients and for the treatment professional to arrange for the specialized training necessary to effectively meet these needs.

Substance Abuse and the Disabled

It is unfortunate that within this society individuals who are physically challenged are often viewed as being "damaged" or different. These stereotypes may have contributed to the limited amount of research addressing the problem of substance abuse among the disabled (Tyas & Rush, 1993). Unfortunately, the limited research that does address this topic suggests that substance abuse is a significant problem among those who are physically challenged. For example, Nelipovich and Buss (1991) suggested that between 15% and 30% of the 33 to 45 million Americans with disabilities abuse alcohol or drugs, a rate that is generally between one and a half and three times higher for the disabled as compared to the physically able.

Although substance-use problems are thus common for those who have a disability, the treatment resources are quite limited. Indeed, it is safe to conclude that as a group "this is a highly underserved population" (Nelipovich & Buss, 1991, p. 344). For example, Cavaliere (1995) noted that although many treatment programs have videotapes of lectures with closed-captions and utilize sign language interpreters during group therapy sessions for the hearing-impaired client, few programs utilize sign language interpreters outside of group/individual therapy sessions. This prevents the hearing-impaired client from participation in the informal give-and-take discussions outside .of group that are so much a part of the rehabilitation program. Thus, within the treatment setting, the hearing-impaired client continues to be isolated and treated as if he or she were "different."

In a very real sense, rather than being identified as a special needs subgroup the disabled are often "perceived as isolated occasional cases, only remembered because of the difficulty and frustration they present to the professionals trying to serve them" (Nelipovich & Buss, 1991, p. 344). The authors call for "creativity" (p. 345) on the part of rehabilitation staff who are attempting to meet the needs of the disabled, substance-abusing client.

Unfortunately, only a minority of treatment programs have the special resources necessary for working with the disabled (wheelchair ramps, etc.). Indeed, many programs would rather not serve this subpopulation (Tyas & Rush, 1993). In contrast, drug *dealers* are only too happy to offer their services to the disabled. There are hints that at least some drug dealers are specifically targeting hearing-impaired individuals, going so far as to learn sign language or recruit assistants who know sign language in order to sell drugs to the hearing impaired (Associated Press, 1993).

To further complicate the problem, family members often believe that the disabled person is "entitled" to use recreational chemicals, even if she or he does so to excess. A common attitude among family members of a hearing-impaired person is that he or she should be allowed to use chemicals because of the disability (Cavaliere, 1995). Family and friends often rationalize the substance abuse by the hearing-impaired individual on the grounds that "I'd drink to, if I were deaf." In this manner, the significant others of the hearing-impaired person might overlook signs that substance use was starting to interfere with the individual's life.

Thus, the physically disabled form an invisible subgroup of those who abuse or are addicted to chemicals in the United States. As such, they are hidden victims of the world of drug abuse or addiction.

Substance Abuse and Ethnic Minorities

One factor that must be considered in the issue of substance-use patterns among members of minority groups is the length of time that the individual has been living in this country (Collins & McNair, 2002). There is strong evidence that each successive generation tends to move closer to the social norms of the country as a whole and further away from the cultural identity of the previous generation (Collins & McNair, 2002). There are thus intergenerational differences in the use or abuse of alcohol and/or illicit drugs for different minority groups. What follows is a brief summary of the substance-abuse patterns of some of the larger ethnic groups found in the United States.

Native Americans. It is estimated that there are approximately 2 million individuals in the United States who might be classified as Native Americans (Beauvais, 1998). These individuals are members of the estimated 300 (Beauvais, 1998) to 500 (Caetano, Clark, & Tam, 1998; Collins & McNair, 2002) tribes in the United States who speak more than 200 distinct languages and who each have their own cultural and social histories. Only about one-third of these individuals live on identified reservations; the majority live in traditional residential areas outside of established reservation lands (Beauvais, 1998).

Collectively, these individuals are called Native Americans, or (less politically correct) Indians, or American Indians. They are often viewed as if they form a single group, although as the statistics in the last paragraph demonstrate Native Americans are a heterogeneous group. To further complicate matters, some studies have grouped American Indians with Alaska natives (National Institute on Alcohol Abuse and Alcoholism, 2002, p. 1) as if these diverse groups might be classified together. This makes it quite difficult to understand the alcohol-use patterns of this diverse, geographically dispersed group of people.

Collectively, alcohol use is thought to be quite widespread among the Native American population. The alcohol-related death rate for Native Americans is 440% higher than it is for the general population, and alcohol is a factor in just under one-fifth of all deaths for Native Americans (Ringwald, 2002). It is known that drug- or alcohol-use patterns and expectations for recreational chemical use vary from tribe to tribe (Beauvais, 1998; Caetano et al., 1998; Collins & McNair, 2002). This is clearly seen in the drinking patterns of the Navaho and Hopi tribes of the Southwest. Both tribes live in the same geographic region of Nevada, yet the Navaho tolerate alcohol use whereas the Hopi view drinking as a sign of irresponsibility (Caetano et al., 1998).

As a general rule, alcohol-use problems are about twice as common among the male members as the women members of different tribes (Beauvais, 1998; National Institute on Alcohol Abuse and Alcoholism, 2002), but there are exceptions. For example, the rate of heavy drinking is about the same for male and female members of the Sioux nation (Collins & McNair, 2002). There is also significant variation in alcohol-use patterns between different tribal units, with 111 of every 1,000 members of some tribes in the northern United States being diagnosed as having alcohol-use problems whereas some tribes in the southwestern part of the country have alcohol-use problems diagnosed in only 11 people per 1,000 (Beauvais, 1998). There is also evidence of marked intergenerational differences in alcohol-use rates within tribal units, with the younger individuals tending to use alcohol more often than their elders (Beauvais, 1998).

Thus, there are few specific facts that might help clinicians work with clients from Native American cultures. Markarian and Franklin (1998) suggested that Native American clients in substance-abuse rehabilitation programs might withdraw into themselves if exposed to high levels of confrontation similar to those found in many traditional treatment programs, reinforcing the observation that individuals working with these subpopulations must be sensitive to cultural differences and beliefs.

Although one popular misconception is that Native Americans are more sensitive to the effects of alcohol, there is little evidence to support this belief (Garcia-Andrade, Wall, & Ehlers, 1997). There is little evidence to suggest that Native Americans are especially vulnerable to alcohol's effects for either physical or psychological reasons (Caetano et al., 1998). Further, although popular belief is that European traders introduced the Native American population to alcohol, there is historical evidence that at least some Native American tribes used alcohol for religious purposes, as a medicine, or as part of the preparation for warfare prior to the arrival of European settlers (Collins & McNair, 2002).

Hispanic. In the United States, approximately 11% of the entire population is Hispanic American (Randolph, Stroup-Benham, Black, & Markides, 1998). Although sociologists tend to speak of the Hispanic subpopulation as if this were a single entity, in reality a multitude of cultures occur under the heading of Hispanic, each with different attitudes and expectations for alcohol or drugs (Caetano et al., 1998). About 60% of Hispanic Americans in the United States trace their national heritage through Mexico, another 15% originally were from Puerto Rico, 5% are Cuban Americans, and the remainder from one or another Spanish-speaking nation in this hemisphere (Randolph et al., 1998). As these statistics suggest, there is no standard model of drinking for the Hispanic population in the United States because there is no single dominant Hispanic culture within this country.

In general, drinking, especially heavy drinking, tends to be a male activity. Women tend either to be light drinkers or to abstain from alcohol use entirely within Hispanic cultures in the United States (Collins & McNair, 2002; Randolph et al., 1998). But there are significant variations within the Hispanic community, depending on the nation of origin. For example, 18% of Mexican American males were considered heavy drinkers whereas only 5% of Cuban American males met the criteria for heavy alcohol use. In each culture, 2% or less of the women met the criteria for heavy drinking, and 10% to 11% were light drinkers, compared with 4% of the Mexican American and 38% of the Cuban American males (Randolph et al., 1998). In each Hispanic subgroup, only a small minority of women drink alcohol, and an even smaller minority abuse it (Collins & McNair, 2002).

Asian Americans. As with other cultures within the United States, there is no single "Asian American" model for recreational chemical use or abuse because

there is no dominant Asian American culture. Rather, disparate cultural groups have widely different patterns of alcohol or drug use, based on the nation of origin for that specific culture (Caetano et al., 1998). Individuals who came to this country from Vietnam or Cambodia must be considered separately from individuals whose national heritage can be traced back to Japan or Korea, although all four groups are classified as Asian American. To complicate matters, some researchers also include persons from the various island groups of the Pacific in the subgroup of Asian Americans (National Institute on Alcohol Abuse and Alcoholism, 2002).

In general, women from Asian American cultures are more likely than their male partners to abstain or drink only on social occasions (Caetano et al., 1998). But even this generalization must be tempered with the observation that women in different Asian American subgroups have widely disparate alcohol-use patterns. For example, only 20% of Korean American women reported that they consumed alcohol, whereas 67% of Japanese American women admitted to using alcohol in one survey (Caetano et al., 1998).

African Americans. Franklin (1989) found that of 16,000 articles on alcoholism published between 1934 and 1974, only 11 "were specifically studies of blacks" (p. 1120). In the decade since Franklin's original study, a small number of research studies have addressed the issue of alcohol-use problems among African Americans. One such study was conducted by Markarian and Franklin (1998), who found that African American males are more likely to initiate heavy drinking later in life than European males, and that their drinking rates peak at an age when that of European male alcoholics is declining. Further, the authors found that in comparison to alcoholics of European descent, Blacks "have a higher incidence of medical complications from alcoholism" (Franklin, 1989, p. 1120), possibly as much as 10 times as high as would be seen from a similar group of White alcoholics.

National surveys designed to explore alcohol-use patterns among different groups of people have found that as a group, African Americans are more likely to abstain from alcohool use than are individuals of European descent (Jones-Webb, 1998). Fifty one percent of Black women and 35% of African American men reported complete abstinence from alcohol at the time of their inclusion in the study, as compared with 36% of White women and 28% of White men (Jones-Webb, 1998). In spite of this fact, however, African Americans were found to be as likely to engage in heavy, abusive drinking as were Whites, possibly because of the tendency for Blacks in the lower socioeconomic groups to abuse alcohol (Jones-Webb, 1998). Although it was founded by a group of mostly White, middle-class individuals, Alcoholics Anonymous (AA) has become a significant part of the treatment and recovery process within the Black community (Franklin, 1989).

Summary

We all have, within our minds, a picture of what the "typical" addict looks like. For some, this is the picture of the "skid row" alcoholic; for others the picture that is associated with addiction is that of a heroin addict, hidden in the ruins of an abandoned building with a belt around his or her arm, ready to inject the drug into a vein. These images of addiction are correct, yet each image fails to accurately reflect the many hidden faces of addiction.

There is a grandfather who is quietly drinking himself to death, or the mother who exposes her unborn child to staggering amounts of cocaine, heroin, or alcohol. There is the working woman whose chemical addiction is hidden behind a veil of productivity or who is an addict whose drug use is sanctioned by the unsuspecting physicians trying to help her cope with feelings of depression or anxiety. There are faces of addiction so well hidden that even today they are not recognized. As professionals, we must learn to look for and recognize the hidden forms of addiction.

CHAPTER TWENTY-TWO

The Dual-Diagnosis Client

Chemical Addiction and Mental Illness

Introduction

In spite of the growing awareness that alcohol or drug abuse frequently co-exists with various forms of mental illness, mental health professionals lack the knowledge of what forces initiate or maintain substance abuse in those who have a form of mental illness (Sharp & Getz, 1998). Indeed, researchers have yet to develop a universally accepted definition of the *dual-diagnosis* client (Patrick, 2003), and there has been only limited research into what treatment methods might work best with this population (Petrakis, Gonzalez, Rosenheck, & Krystal, 2002). This is a frightening state of affairs, in that mental health professionals have finally recognized chemical abuse/addiction among the mentally ill as a serious problem. Although psychiatric textbooks of even the mid 1970s suggested that substance-use problems among the mentally ill population were rare, mental health workers now understand that patients with co-existing substance-use problems and mental health issues are not just a small minority of the patients they see but actually comprise the majority of individuals in substance abuse rehabilitation settings (Minkoff, 2001). In this chapter, the problem of substance abuse in people with some form of mental illness will be explored.

Definitions

Patients who suffer from a form of mental illness and who also abuse chemicals are often said to be dual-diagnosis clients. Unfortunately, the term *dual-diagnosis* has been applied to a wide range of co-existing problems, including combinations of substance abuse/addiction and (a) anorexia, (b) bulimia, (c) gambling, (d) spouse abuse, (e) AIDS, and others. To further complicate matters, mental health professionals have used a wide variety of terms to describe the substance-abusing psychiatric patient. For the purpose of this text, the terms *dual-diagnosis* or *MI/CD* (mentally ill/chemically dependent) will be used to denote individuals with a *co-existing* psychiatric disorder and a substance-abuse problem.

Recreational chemical use can magnify preexisting psychiatric disorders or bring about a drug-induced disorder that simulates any of a wide range of psychiatric problems (S. J. Cohen, 1995; Schuckit & Tapert, 2004; Washton, 1995). But these drug-induced complications will usually diminish or entirely disappear shortly after the patient stops abusing recreational drugs. As such, these conditions might be said to be "substance induced" (Fals-Stewart & Lucente, 1994; Woody, McLellan, & Bedrick, 1995). Dual diagnosis refers to disorders that are (a) *equally important*, (b) *independent disorders* that (c) *co-exist* in the same patient at the same time (Minkoff, 2001).

The concept of co-existing disorders is not really difficult to understand. Consider, for example, an alcohol-dependent person who also suffers from a concurrent medical problem. Perhaps the alcohol-dependent individual has a kidney dysfunction or a genetic disorder of some kind. The patient's medical condition did not *cause* him or her to become alcohol dependent, nor did the alcohol dependence bring about the medical condition. Yet each disorder, once it develops, is intertwined with the other. The prudent physician treating this hypothetical patient would need to consider the impact of the patient's alcohol-use problem on the possible treatment methods under consideration for the kidney disorder because once each condition is established, it becomes intertwined with the other. In much the same way, MI/CD clients have separate disorders that are intertwined, and each is able to influence the progression of the other (Drake et al., 2001; Woody et al., 1995).

Dual-Diagnosis Clients: A Diagnostic Challenge

In assessing the dual-diagnosis client, the assessor must have "the ability to distinguish the signs and symptoms of the primary psychiatric illness from those caused or exacerbated by a primary SUD [substance-use disorder]" (Geppert & Minkoff, 2004, p. 105). This is a daunting task. Up to two-thirds of patients admitted to substance-abuse treatment programs have symptoms of psychiatric problems at the time of admission (Fals-Stewart & Lucente, 1994). But many of these psychiatric problems remit after the individual is alcohol or drug free for a period of time, suggesting that the presenting symptoms are substance induced rather than an expression of mental illness. To identify individuals with a true dual-diagnosis disorder, the assessor might have to wait for as long as 8 *weeks* for the diagnostic picture to clear (Jones, Knutson, & Haines, 2003).

There are three basic subgroups of alcohol-abusing psychiatric patients (Shivani, Goldsmith, & Anthenelli, 2002): (a) individuals with alcohol-related psychiatric symptoms, (b) individuals with alcohol-induced psychiatric syndromes, and (c) individuals with comorbid alcohol and psychiatric disorders. In the first group, the individual's heavy use of alcohol results in a disruption in normal brain function, causing him or her to experience symptoms of a psychiatric disorder. In the second group, the individual suffers from any of a range of alcohol-induced psychiatric problems. Admittedly there is a fine line between these two groups of people and the distinction between the two groups is made even more difficult by the fact that in each case the psychiatric symptoms clear after a period of abstinence. However, in the third group, there is clear evidence of a co-occurring psychiatric disorder and an alcohol-use disorder, according to the authors.

Accurate diagnosis of either a substance-use disorder or a form of mental illness is complicated by the fact that each condition is viewed as a stigmatizing disorder in this culture (Pies, 2003). Just like their "normal" counterparts, dual-diagnosis patients are motivated by the stigma associated with substance-abuse problems to utilize the defense mechanisms of denial and minimization to try to hide their chemical-abuse problems (Carey, Cocco, & Simons, 1996; Shivani et al., 2002). But these attempts to hide their addiction are complicated by many factors: (a) they have ongoing psychiatric problems (Kanwischer & Hundley, 1990), (b) direct questions about alcohol or drug use contribute to their feelings of shame (Pristach & Smith, 1990), (c) they fear that admitting to having a substance-use problem may cause them to lose entitlements (such as Social Security payments), or (d) such admissions may cause them to be denied access to psychiatric treatment (Mueser, Bellack, & Blanchard, 1992). Further, (e) many dual-diagnosis patients have little motivation to stop using a drug of abuse because they view their situation as hopeless (Ziedonis & Brady, 1997).

Why Worry About the Dual-Diagnosis Client?

Perhaps the most eloquent answer to this question was provided by Geppert and Minkoff (2004):

> As a whole, this population has worse treatment outcomes; higher health care utilization; increased risk of violence, trauma, suicide, child abuse and neglect, and involvement in the criminal justice system; more medical comorbidity, particularly of infectious diseases; and higher health care costs than people with a single disorder. (p. 103)

The risk of suicide in alcohol-dependent persons has been found to be 60–120-fold higher if they also have some form of mental illness (Nielson et al., 1998). As a group, dual-diagnosis clients are at increased risk of incarceration, are less likely to be able to handle personal finances, and are more prone to depression and/or feelings of hopelessness (Drake et al., 1998). These feelings of hopelessness and the other symptoms of psychiatric disorders can be exacerbated by the individual's abuse of recreational chemicals (Cohen & Levy, 1992; Evans & Sullivan, 2001; Pristach & Smith, 1990; Ries & Ellingson, 1990; Rubinstein, Campbell, & Daley, 1990; Sharp & Getz, 1998).

Researchers have also found that "patients with mental disorders have such fragile brain chemistry that even 'social' use of alcohol or drugs can destabilize them and cause psychotic episodes" (Patrick, 2003, pp. 68–69). Given this information, it is not surprising to learn that even drinking in amounts clearly not abusive by traditional standards has been found to predict which alcohol-consuming patients with schizophrenia would require rehospitalization within a year (Hopko, Lachar, Bailley, & Varner, 2001; RachBeisel, Scott, & Dixon, 1999;). Almost a generation ago, researchers discovered that psychiatric patients who abused chemicals on a regular basis had hospitalization rates 250% higher than those who rarely or never abused chemicals (Kanwischer & Hundley, 1990). They also are at significantly higher risk of becoming victims of violent assault than their nondrinking counterparts (Brekke, Prindle, Woo Bae, & Long, 2001).

For these reasons, mental health professionals now see alcohol or drug abuse as one reason that MI/CD patients tend to make less progress in therapy and to suffer a greater number of problems while in treatment (Drake et al., 1998; Kivlahan, Heiman, Wright, Mundt, & Shupe, 1991; Osher & Drake, 1996; Osher et al., 1994; Rubinstein et al., 1990; Sharp & Getz, 1998; Woody et al., 1995). One such problem is that the individual's concurrent mental illness and chemical-dependency problems place a financial strain on the family's resources (Clark, 1994). When one stops to consider the emotional pain experienced by the mentally ill; the cost of lost productivity; the cost of hospitalization and treatment; and the added financial, social, and personal cost brought on by substance abuse, the need to address this problem becomes undeniable.

The Scope of the Problem

The true scope of the problem of dual-diagnosis clients is dependent on which problems are or are not identified as reflecting a form of mental illness. Some researchers, for example, classify individuals with attention deficit hyperactivity disorder (ADHD) as having a developmental disorder rather than a form of mental illness. From this perspective, substance-abusing individuals with a co-existing ADHD diagnosis might not be classified as a dual-diagnosis client as much as a substance abuser with a developmental disorder.

In the United States, "mental illness" is usually defined by the criteria established by the American Psychiatric Association in the *Diagnostic and Statistical Manual of Mental Disorders (4th ed-text revision) (DSM-IV-TR)* (American Psychiatric Association,

TABLE 22.1 The Overlap Between Substance Use Disorders and Various Psychiatric Disorders

Lifetime prevalence of psychiatric diagnosis	Substance-use disorder
Depression	32%
Bipolar affective disorder (or manic depression)	64%
Anxiety disorder	36%
Antisocial personality disorder	84%
Attention deficit hyperactivity disorder (ADHD)	23%
Eating disorders	28%
Schizophrenia	50%
Somatoform disorders	Unknown, but suspected to be related

Source: This chart is based on Ziedonis & Brady (1997).

2000). Researchers disagree on the percentage of individuals who suffer from both a form of mental illness and a co-existing substance-use disorder. Svikis, Zarin, Tanielian, and Pincus (2000) found that only 12% of patients under psychiatric care qualified for an alcohol abuse/addiction diagnosis. In contrast to this low estimate, Ries et al. (2000) concluded that people with schizophrenia were three times as likely to abuse alcohol and six times as likely to abuse drugs as was the general population. Overall, it has been suggested that between 40% and 75% of people who struggle with mental illness have a separate substance-use disorder (Appleby, Dyson, Luchins, & Cohen, 1997; Leshner, 1997b; Patrick, 2003; Watkins, Burnam, Kung, & Paddock, 2001). Table 22.1 summarizes the overlap between substance-use disorders and various psychiatric disorders.

In the early 21st century, it has become generally accepted that about 50% of patients with a form of mental illness will have a concurrent substance-abuse problem (Patrick, 2003; RachBeisel et al., 1999). There is evidence that the more serious the individual's psychiatric diagnosis, the more difficult it is for him or her to abstain from drugs of abuse (Ritsher, Moos, & Finney, 2002).

Unfortunately, mental health professionals, lacking a pattern to look for, are often ill-equipped to detect substance-abuse problems, especially in people with a psychiatric problem (Cohen & Levy, 1992; Peyser, 1989).

Characteristics of Dual-Diagnosis Clients

Researchers often speak of substance-abusing mentally ill clients as if they were all the same. In reality, because of the interplay between various combinations of mental illness and substance-use disorders, the dual-diagnosis population is "not a uniform clinical entity, but a heterogeneous group who differ in psychiatric disorder, level of functioning, social support, and capacity for independent living" (Director, 1995, p. 377). In spite of this observation, different researchers have examined the MI/CD subpopulation and concluded the following:

- As a group, dual-diagnosis patients are more likely to have multiple problems than just two intertwined illnesses (Drake et al., 2001).
- Schizophrenic patients who abused alcohol were found to have poor social adjustment; be more delusional, disruptive, and assaultive; be less compliant with psychiatric treatment; have more housing instability and homelessness; experience higher rates of rehospitalization; and be more depressed than nonabusing patients with mental illnesses (Osher et al., 1994; RachBeisel et al., 1999).
- MI/CD patients were found to be at higher risk for suicide in comparison with mentally ill patients who do not abuse alcohol or drugs (Drake et al., 1998; Osher & Drake, 1996; Osher et al., 1994).
- Psychiatric clients who also have substance-use disorders seem to have more trouble abstaining from alcohol than patients who do not have a psychiatric disorder (Osher & Drake, 1996).
- MI/CD clients are less likely to be able to use alcohol on a social/recreational basis for extended periods of time as compared with normal social drinkers (Drake & Wallach, 1993).
- Dual-diagnosis clients tend to be "binge" users of recreational chemicals (Osher & Drake, 1996; Riley, 1994).
- MI/CD clients tend to be more manipulative than traditional psychiatric patients (Mueser et al., 1992).

- MI/CD clients tend to have trouble accepting the need for abstinence as a treatment goal (Drake, Mueser, Clark, & Wallach, 1996; Drake et al., 2001).

Essentially, although all of the characteristics reviewed above must be assumed to be true, *they are true for only certain subgroups of patients*. There is still a great deal to be discovered about the dual-diagnosis patient population. For example, although the severely depressed patient who drinks alcohol to excess and the patient with a severe form of schizophrenia who also drinks heavily might both be said to be dual-diagnosis patients, researchers are not sure of the degree to which they are or are not similar.

Psychopathology and Drug of Choice

For many years, clinical lore has maintained that dual-diagnosis clients are attempting to self-medicate their emotional pain through chemical abuse (Caton, Gralnick, Bender, & Simon, 1989; Rubinstein et al., 1990). This hypothesis, although it remains popular, has received only limited support from clinical research studies (Drake & Mueser, 2002). Indeed, research has found that the individual's alcohol abuse frequently precedes clinical manifestations of the person's psychiatric condition.

Another example of the self-medication hypothesis might be seen in those patients who suffer from post-traumatic stress disorder (PTSD) (Khantzian, 2003b; Preuss & Wong, 2000; Volpicelli, Balaraman, Hahn, Wallace, & Bux, 1999). But to understand the role of substance-use disorders as self-treatment for PTSD, it is necessary to understand that the individual experiences a biphasic response to emotional trauma. First, these individuals experience various symptoms of emotional *flooding*, which may threaten to overwhelm their defenses. During such times, substances that help to sedate them may seem attractive. However, during periods of emotional *numbing*, they struggle to feel emotions that are "safe" while controlling feelings that threaten to reawaken memories of the original trauma. Thus, their goal in self-medication will vary, depending on whether they are struggling with intrusive memories or thoughts of the trauma, or the emptiness of emotional numbing (Khantzian, 2003b). Although chemical abuse might be successful at first, after a period of time the early symptoms of withdrawal might become associated with the symptoms of PTSD, triggering additional distress on the part of the individual and the desire for further chemical abuse to avoid the anticipated resurgence of PTSD symptoms.

However, the theory that MI/CD clients are attempting to self-medicate their emotional pain has been challenged (Dervaux et al., 2001). Some dual-diagnosis clients may be drawn to recreational chemical use for the same reason that other people are: because it is considered "cool" (Sharp & Getz, 1998, p. 642). Chemical abuse is also thought to facilitate the development of a social network and even offer an identity of sorts (Drake & Mueser, 2002). Finally the social stigma associated with substance use or abuse is far less severe than the stigma that continues to be associated with mental illness, serving as a source of motivation for some dual-diagnosis patients to substitute the less severe stigma of being an alcohol or drug abuser for that associated with their mental illness (Sharp & Getz, 1998).

Another challenge to the self-medication hypothesis of drug abuse in this population came from Dervaux et al. (2001). On the basis of their research, the authors suggested that substance-abusing schizophrenic patients, like their drug-abusing counterparts in the general population, were more impulsive and interested in new sensations. But they found little evidence to suggest that the patients in their sample were motivated to use alcohol or drugs in an attempt to self-medicate anhedonia.[1]

One variable has often been overlooked by those who believe in the self-medication hypothesis: the impact of the *availability* of alcohol or drugs on the individual's substance-use behavior (Mueser et al., 1992). For years, research studies have attempted to discover whether people with a certain diagnosis might be prone to abuse one chemical over the others without considering how the issue of availability might influence the substance-use behavior of their research sample. This might explain why alcohol is one of the most commonly abused substances by dual-diagnosis clients: It is a legal substance and is easily available.

At this time there does not appear to be a strong relationship between the various forms of psychopathology and the individual's drug(s) of choice (Bellack & DiClemente, 1999; Miles et al., 2003). Miles et al. (2003) did find a positive relationship between the abuse of CNS stimulants and violence, but it was not clear on the basis of their study whether the CNS stimulant abuse was the *cause* of or a *marker for* the violent tendencies of the individuals in this subgroup of drug abusers. In the sections that follow, the literature exploring some specific forms of mental illness and alcohol- or drug-use problems will be explored.

Attention deficit hyperactivity disorder (ADHD). It has been estimated that between 20% and 50% of adults and an unknown percentage of adolescents (Diller, 1998; Milin, Loh, Chow, & Wilson, 1997; Renner, 2001) with ADHD will also have an alcohol- or drug-use disorder (Smith, Molina, & Pelham, 2002). Researchers know that ADHD precedes the development of these disorders but are not sure whether ADHD *causes* the subsequent development of substance-use disorders or if these two problems might reflect the influence of a third factor. The available evidence suggests that the latter is the case, with both ADHD and substance-use disorders reflecting a suspected dysfunction in the dopamine neurotransmission system of the medial forebrain region of the brain.

In spite of the popular myth that adolescents with ADHD are at increased risk for CNS stimulant abuse, there is little evidence to suggest that children with ADHD are at increased risk for drug abuse or addiction later in life *if* their ADHD is adequately controlled through the use of pharmaceuticals (Wilens, 2004b; Zickler, 2001). Indeed, proper treatment of ADHD serves a *protective* function, reducing the chances that the individual will later develop a substance abuse problem, although it is recommended that a parent control the child's access to his or her medication (Knight, 2005). This apparent relationship between ADHD and substance-use disorders appears to reflect an illusion. It has been suggested that individuals with ADHD are not at increased risk for a substance-use disorder *unless* they also have a condition known as a *conduct disorder*[2] (Disney, Elkins, McGue, & Iacono, 1999; Lynskey & Hall, 2001).[3] Between 33% and 50% of children with ADHD *also* have a conduct disorder (Smucker & Hedayat, 2001), which may explain why

[1]See Glossary.

[2]See Glossary.

[3]Discussed in the next chapter.

early investigations into the relationship between ADHD and later substance-use problems found a relationship between these two disorders. The child's physician should determine whether he or she has a concurrent conduct disorder in addition to the attention deficit disorder.

The treatment of ADHD is complicated and controversial. It has been suggested that highly addictive substances such as methylphenidate *not* be used with patients who have concurrent ADHD *and* substance-use problems, especially since compounds such as bupropion, pemoline, and atomoxetine have been found to be both safe and effective for use with adolescents with periodic monitoring of liver function. These compounds also lack the high abuse potential of CNS stimulants such as methylphenidate or the amphetamines (Riggs, 2003).

A complicating factor is that clinicians lack standard guidelines for the assessment of ADHD either in children or adults (Diller, 1998; Milin et al., 1997). Further, as with other MI/CD disorders, it is necessary for the individual to be alcohol/drug free before the ADHD can be assessed. However, researchers have yet to agree on how long the individual must be alcohol/drug free before an evaluation for ADHD might be carried out. Indeed, the entire concept of attention deficit hyperactive disorder has been challenged (Breggin, 1998; Diller, 1998), raising questions as to the validity of this theoretical construct.

Schizophrenia. It has been suggested that over 40% of the patients who suffer from schizophrenia will have a comorbid substance-use disorder (Kavanagh, McGrath, Saunders, Dore, & Clark, 2002). There is no apparent relationship between psychiatric diagnosis and the individual's drug of choice, but there is an interesting interaction between the dynamics of schizophrenia and the experience of cocaine withdrawal. Central to the disease of schizophrenia is a disruption of the normal function of the dopamine neurotransmission system within the brain. As cocaine impacts the dopamine systems, one would expect that individuals who suffer from schizophrenia and also abuse cocaine might experience different effects from those experienced by non-schizophrenic patients who abuse cocaine (Carol, Smelson, Losonczy, & Ziedonis, 2001). The cocaine-abusing schizophrenic research subjects examined by Carol et al. (2001) seemed to experience more intense craving for cocaine during the first 3 months of abstinence than did non-schizophrenic cocaine abusers, suggesting the need for more intense treatment efforts for cocaine-abusing schizophrenic patients to help them achieve abstinence.

Anxiety disorders. As a general rule, anxiety disorders seem to predate the development of alcohol-use disorders (Cheng, Gau, Chen, Chang, & Chang, 2004). But a case-by-case assessment is necessary to determine the relationship between the individual's anxiety disorder and his or her substance use. For example, alcohol-dependent individuals tend to experience significant anxiety during the detoxification process and in the first few weeks of abstinence (Driessen et al., 2001). This anxiety usually subsides in the first days and weeks following alcohol cessation, and if the individual continues to experience moderate to severe levels of anxiety or depression after 3 weeks of abstinence, the possibility that he or she has a concurrent anxiety disorder that should be treated must be considered (Driessen et al., 2001). But during that first 3 weeks the person's anxiety might be withdrawal related.

The CNS depressants such as alcohol, benzodiazepines, or (on rare occasions) the increasingly rare barbiturates offer these individuals temporary relief from their defensiveness, helping them to feel less isolated, lonely, and empty (Khantzian, 2003b). This would help to explain why up to 20% of individuals with a primary anxiety disorder will have a concurrent alcohol- or drug-abuse problem (Preuss & Wong, 2000). There is also evidence that about 15% of people in treatment for an alcohol-use disorder have *social* anxiety whereas 20% of individuals in treatment for social anxiety also have an alcohol-use disorder (Book & Randall, 2002).

A number of effective pharmacological and psychological treatments for social anxiety are available as well as some medications that are contraindicated for use with substance-abusing patients with anxiety disorders. For example, although the monoamine oxidase inhibitors (MAOIs) have been found quite effective in controlling the symptoms of social anxiety disorder, these medications should *not* be used in alcohol-abusing social phobia patients because of the danger inherent in mixing MAOIs with alcohol (Book & Randall, 2002). Some of the common chemicals in many alcoholic beverages can combine with MAOIs to cause a potentially fatal hypertensive crisis.

Because of the "well known abuse potential" (Riggs, 2003, p. 24) of the benzodiazepines, these medications should not be used in the treatment of social phobia in patients with concurrent alcohol-use disorders (Book & Randall, 2002; Jones et al., 2003; Riggs, 2003). The selective serotonin reuptake inhibitors (SSRIs) were seen as a more appropriate choice for this subgroup of patients (Book & Randall, 2002; Jones et al., 2003).

Dissociative disorders. The team of Dunn, Paolo, Ryan, and Van Fleet (1993) found evidence that *over 41%* of the patients in treatment settings for alcohol- or drug-use disorders might also experience some form of a dissociative disorder. The dissociative disorders are marked by episodes in which the individual loses touch with reality. In its most extreme form, the individual might develop more than one personality, a condition known as *dissociative personality disorder* (DPD, once called multiple personality disorder or MPD).

Although the diagnosis of a dissociative disorder is quite complex, Kolodner and Frances (1993) found two diagnostic signs that might suggest that the patient being examined had co-existing substance-abuse and dissociative disorders. First, the authors suggested that, unlike "regular" patients who were addicted to chemicals, patients with dissociative disorders did not feel better after completing the detoxification stage of treatment. Rather, patients with dissociative disorders tended to experience significant levels of emotional pain after detoxification from chemicals. Second, patients who suffered from dissociative disorders tended to relapse at times of "relative comfort and clinical stability" (p. 1042), in contrast to "regular" substance-abusing patients who are thought to relapse most often when under stress (see Chapter 27). The authors suggested that these situations might alert the clinician to the possibility that the patient suffered from a dissociative disorder, which might then be addressed in treatment.

As mentioned earlier, the most serious form of a dissociative disorder is the dissociative personality disorder. Perhaps one-third of those who suffer from DPD are thought to also abuse chemicals (Putnam, 1989). These individuals tend to utilize CNS depressants and alcohol, although stimulants are also frequently abused by DPD patients, according to the author. Hallucinogenics, possibly because of the nature of DPD, did not seem to be a popular drug of abuse for this subgroup (Putnam, 1989). The exact reason that chemicals are so popular with those who suffered from DPD is not clear. However, clients who suffer from dissociative disorders or DPD might be using chemicals in an attempt to medicate their internal distress (Putnam, 1989).

Obsessive-compulsive disorder (OCD). Obsessive-compulsive disorder is the fourth most common psychiatric disorder found in the United States (Fals-Stewart & Lucente, 1994). The authors suggested that OCD is four to five times as common among substance abusers as in the general population, although the reason for this is not clear.

The bipolar affective disorders. Acute alcohol intoxication can induce some of the symptoms of mania, elevated mood, grandiosity, irritability, and aggressiveness that are hallmarks of the bipolar affective disorder (Sonne & Brady, 2002). Thus, it is necessary for the individual to be observed both during and after alcohol withdrawal before a definitive diagnosis is possible (Modesto-Lowe & Kranzler, 1999).

What is now called a bipolar affective disorder (or bipolar disorder) was once called manic depression. Research has suggested that up to 61% of patients with a bipolar affective disorder will also have a substance-use disorder at some point in their lives (Sonne & Brady, 2002). The importance of this finding might be seen in the observation that while drug-induced mania usually resolves when the drug wears off, physicians must wait until 2 to 4 weeks after the patient's last use of a drug before attempting to determine whether his or her depressive symptoms were drug induced (Sonne & Brady, 1999). Further, many of the symptoms of alcohol or drug withdrawal may mimic the symptoms of a bipolar affective disorder (Sonne & Brady, 1999). The authors noted the similarity between mixed mania, where the symptoms of both mania and depression co-exist, and cycles of cocaine abuse/withdrawal.

As with many cases where substance abuse co-exists with psychiatric problems, substance abuse by patients with an affective disorder complicates the treatment of their psychiatric illness, resulting in more frequent hospitalizations and less effective symptom control (Sonne & Brady, 1999, 2002). This process contributes to higher hospitalization costs for society and needless emotional suffering for the individual. Unfortunately, the reasons that patients with bipolar affective disorder also abuse recreational chemicals is not understood (Sonne & Brady, 2002). A number of theories have been advanced to account for this phenomenon, however, one of which is the theory that some patients with bipolar affective disorders actively abuse drugs to cause some of the symptoms of this disorder. Behavioral health professionals now believe that some individuals with manic depression might use cocaine to artifically induce or prolong the sense of power and invulnerability often experienced in the earlier stages of mania (Jamison, 1999). There is also evidence that individuals with bipolar disorder tend to be most prone to alcohol- or drug-use problems during the manic phase of their illness, although they might also drink alcohol to relieve their depression (Modesto-Lowe & Kranzler, 1999).

Depression. Depression can range in intensity from simply feeling "blue" through what is now called dysthymia[4] to the agony of a major depression with psychotic features. In one form or another, depression is one of the most common forms of mental illness encountered within the population of alcohol or substance abusers (Monti, Kadden, Rohsenow, Cooney, & Abrams, 2002). Substance abuse frequently complicates the treatment of the different forms of depression. One study found, for example, that the amount of money spent for treating patients with comorbid dysthymia and substance-use disorders was *almost five times as great* as the amount of money spent on patients with only a chemical-abuse diagnosis (Westermeyer, Eames, & Nugent, 1998). The importance of this finding is underscored by the observation that 31% of those patients with dysthymia will also have a substance-use disorder at some point in their lives (Evans & Sullivan, 2001; Sonne & Brady, 1999). Twenty seven percent of patients with a major depressive disorder will also have a chemical-use problem at some point in their lives (Sonne & Brady, 1999; Jamison, 1999). Untreated depression is one factor that increases the patient's risk of relapse following detoxification (Driessen et al., 2001).

Posttraumatic stress disorder (PTSD). Posttraumatic stress disorder was discussed earlier in this chapter to illustrate the self-medication hypothesis of substance abuse during mental illness. It should be recognized that anxiety is a significant problem for people with PTSD. The judicious use of pharmaceuticals by mental health professionals trained to help the patient with PTSD may be a valuable asset in the treatment of this disorder. If pharmacological therapy is necessary for a patient who has PTSD, evidence would suggest that the SSRIs and/or beta-blocking (β-blocking) agents are more effective than benzodiazepines for the control of PTSD-induced anxiety.

Compulsive gambling. As a behavior, gambling is defined as "placing something of value at risk with the hope of gaining something of greater value" (Potenza, Kosten, & Rounsaville, 2001, p. 141). Such behavior is unique in that it is seen only in humans. The act of gambling is not in itself a sign of mental illness. But about 2% of the general population will gamble compulsively and in a manner inconsistent with the maintenance of proper health (Grant, Kushner, & Kim, 2002; Potenza, Fiellin, Heninger, Rounsaville, & Mazure, 2002). Further, the individual who gambles in spite of past negative experiences with gambling is at risk for developing a compulsive gambling problem.

Pathological or compulsive[5] gambling frequently co-exists with alcohol and/or drug abuse. Researchers have found that up to 44% of those individuals who have a compulsive gambling problem will also have an alcohol-use disorder at some point in their lives (Grant et al., 2002). Individuals with compulsive gambling problems are thought to be two to four times as likely to develop an alcohol-use disorder as are persons without the compulsion to gamble (Grant, Kushner, & Kim, 2002). This shared vulnerability seems to reflect the fact that both behaviors activate the brain's reward circuitry.

There is also a relationship between depression and gambling. In spite of popular belief, however, there is little correlation between the amount of money lost and the depth of the individual's depression (Unwin, Davis, & De Leeuw, 2000). Suicidal thinking is possible, especially if the gambler is losing or has lost a significant amount of money. Long-term rehabilitation involves confronting the individual's irrational beliefs and helping the compulsive gambler develop a coping system to prevent him or her from gambling any more. Although self-help groups such as Gambler's Anonymous (GA) are modeled after similar groups for alcohol- and drug-abuse problems, they are not associated with substance-based self-help groups. Treatment for gambling problems should specifically address *gambling*-related issues, and the two disorders should be treated as co-existing but equally important disorders for the substance abusing compulsive gambler.

---

[4]Or what was once called depressive neurosis.

[5]These two terms will be used interchangeably.

TABLE 22.2 Summary of Subgroups of Antisocial Personality Disordered (ASPD) Clients

Group	Percentage of research sample	Conduct disorder in childhood?	Characteristics of members of this group
Early onset/strong ASPD features	10%	Yes	Meet *DSM-IV* criteria for formal diagnosis of antisocial personality disorder
Late onset/strong ASPD features	12%	Yes, but not as often as subgroup 1	Antisocial personality disorder behaviors do not appear until adulthood, with minor conduct problems as child or adolescent
Emotionally unstable ASPD subgroup	18%	Moderately strong history of conduct disorder in childhood	Hostility, guilt, dependency, and avoidant personality features are all part of clinical picture with this subgroup when they become adults
Non-ASPD/drug induced-behaviors	17%	Rarely had a formal diagnosis of conduct disorder in childhood	Antisocial behaviors found in these people can be traced back to their substance abuse
Moderate substance abuse/moderate ASPD	15%	Rarely had a formal diagnosis of conduct disorder in childhood	Strong ASPD features, intermixed with low levels of guilt/depression, and moderate levels of alcohol- or drug-related distress
Low ASPD	28%	Rare reports of conduct disorder in childhood	Rare reports of antisocial behavior in adulthood

Source: Alterman et al. (1998).

The antisocial personality disorder. Just under 6% of men and 1.2% of women, will meet the diagnostic criteria for the antisocial personality disorder (ASPD) during their lifetime (Daghestani, Dinwiddie, & Hardy, 2001). The individual with ASPD does not, as the name would seem to suggest, dislike people. Rather, the individual with ASPD has trouble living within society's limits. Such individuals view their own needs and desires as being of supreme importance while the rights of others are seen as insignificant. The presence of ASPD is viewed as a negative influence on the rehabilitation process, and individuals with this personality pattern tend to do poorly in and after treatment (Compton, Cottler, Jacobs, Ben-Abdallah, & Spitznagel, 2003).

Unfortunately, given the association between ASPD and negative treatment outcomes, individuals with ASPD are exceptionally vulnerable to alcohol-use problems.

Some researchers have estimated that the person with ASPD is *21 times as* likely to have an alcohol-use disorder as are similar individuals who do not have this personality pattern (Moeller & Dougherty, 2001). Between 15% and 50% (McCrady, 2001) of alcohol-dependent males and 10% of alcohol-dependent women are thought to have ASPD (Shivani et al., 2002). Other studies suggest that 35% to 60% of individuals with a substance-use problem also meet the diagnostic criteria for ASPD (Sadock & Sadock, 2003).

The diagnostic category of antisocial personality disorder is quite broad, and there are various subtypes of this personality pattern. Alterman et al. (1998) found *six* subgroups of individuals in a research sample of 252 people in a methadone maintenance program, all of whom met the criteria for ASPD, as shown in Table 22.2.

In working with the substance-abusing antisocial personality disordered person, it is imperative to keep in mind the possibility that his or her apparent ASPD is an artifact of the substance-use disorder rather than a reflection of an actual personality disorder (Evans & Sullivan, 2001). Chronic alcohol/drug abuse can block normal personality development, causing the development of an "acquired" (Shea, 2002, p. 44) personality disorder. Thus, part of the assessment process should include a determination of whether the personality disorder preceded or followed the onset of the substance-use disorder.[6]

The concept of an "acquired" personality disorder might explain why individuals with ASPD and comorbid substance-use disorders *who are able to experience psychiatric distress* in the form of anxiety and/or depression might be able to benefit from treatment for their alcohol- or drug use-problem (Evans & Sullivan, 2001; Modesto-Lowe, & Kranzler, 1999). Their ability to experience psychiatric distress might suggest that they have an acquired rather than primary personality disorder; on the other hand, individuals with histories of violence resulting in serious injury to a victim, who rationalize away antisocial behavior, who use fear to control others, and who are unable to form deep emotional attachments to others, are poor candidates for traditional rehabilitation programs because they have a more primary personality disorder.

A note on other forms of personality disorder and substance abuse. There has been virtually no research into the relationship between the majority of the *DSM-IV* personality disorder categories and substance abuse. Thus, nothing is known about the relationship between, for example, the schizotypal personality pattern and substance abuse, or the dependent personality disorder and alcohol/drug abuse. This area remains to be examined in the future.

Problems in Working With Dual-Diagnosis Clients

The most effective approach to working with a dual-diagnosis client is the medical model (Patrick, 2003). The therapist should be nonconfrontational, optimistic, and empathetic, and should avoid making

moralistic judgments about the client's behavior (Patrick, 2003). Unfortunately, at this time residential treatment beds for substance abuse rehabilitation, especially for MI/CD clients, are "woefully scarce" (Pepper, 2004, p. 343).

A major problem for dual-diagnosis clients is the fragile nature of their support systems. Although the recovering community is slowly coming to accept the need for some patients to use psychotropic medications, it is still not uncommon for older members of the recovering community to view the use of prescribed medication as an indication that the patient is substituting one addiction for another (Evans & Sullivan, 2001; Fariello & Scheidt, 1989; Penick et al., 1990; Riley, 1994). Mental health/substance abuse professionals may also fall into this trap and should examine their attitudes toward prescribed use of psychotropic medications by substance abusers. If they are uncomfortable with the idea, they should not work with MI/CD clients.

One of the problems that substance abuse rehabilitation/medical staff will encounter in working with dual-diagnosis clients is the significant level of *denial* seen in such clients. Co-existing "thought or affective disorders may exacerbate denial of substance abuse" (Kofoed, Kania, Walsh, & Atkinson, 1986, p. 1209) in dual-diagnosis clients. The added dimension of a psychiatric disorder means that denial might potentially be expressed in different ways. Some clients, for example, will focus almost exclusively on their psychiatric disorder when talking to an alcohol/drug counselor and focus entirely on their chemical-abuse problem when talking to a mental health professional. This is the process of "interchangable" or "free-floating" denial. In a sense, the client is using one disorder as a shield against intervention for the other disorder. One example of this process might be seen when individuals who suffer from multiple personality disorder attribute the loss of memory (experienced when one personality is forced out of consciousness and another takes over) to the use of chemicals rather than to the process of dissociation.

To complicate matters, dual-diagnosis patients are often viewed as being primarily psychiatric patients by chemical-dependency professionals and as primarily substance-abuse cases by mental health professionals. This is a legacy of the federal drug treatment initiatives of the 1970s and 1980s, which resulted in the establishment

---

[6]The topic of assessment is discussed in Chapter 26.

of a number of agencies devoted to the identification and rehabilitation of the substance user (Osher & Drake, 1996). Responsibility for substance-abusing psychiatric patients was assigned to a different series of federal agencies. Interdepartmental communication/cooperation between these two groups was virtually nonexistent even though they were all funded by the same taxpayers. As a result of this political (Layne, 1990, p. 176) atmosphere, the treatment of substance-abuse cases became separated from traditional psychiatric care.

When the MI/CD client does come into contact with a treatment center, the staff frequently views the patient as "not our problem" and will refer the patient elsewhere. The deplorable outcome of this refusal-to-treat philosophy is that clients are bounced between psychiatric and chemical-dependency treatment programs, much like a Ping-Pong ball is bounced between players (Osher & Kofoed, 1989; Wallen & Weiner, 1989). This process is both a cause and a consequence of the fact that the mentally ill, chemically dependent client is often only a "crisis user" (Rubinstein et al., 1990, p. 99) of medical and chemical-dependency services. This makes it hard for treatment staff to become motivated to invest a great deal of time and energy in working with MI/CD clients. It is often far easier to refer them elsewhere, contributing to the tendency for such clients to bounce between treatment settings.

Unfortunately, staff psychiatrists in traditional psychiatric hospitals usually lack training and experience in working with the addicted individual (Howland, 1990; Riley, 1994). So when such patients are admitted to a psychiatric facility, they may receive potentially addictive substances as part of their psychiatric care, prescribed by the psychiatrist who is more experienced in working with the "traditional" client (Drake et al., 1996).

The MI/CD client and medication compliance. Another reason that dual-diagnosis clients are unpopular is that they are often noncompliant with prescribed medications (Bellack & DiClemente, 1999; Drake et. al., 1998; Owen, Fischer, Booth, & Cuffel, 1996). As a group, MI/CD patients are 8.1 times more likely not to take medications as prescribed as are non-drug-abusing psychiatric patients (RachBeisel et al., 1999). Medication noncompliance might be expressed in a variey of ways such as (a) refusing to take prescribed medications or (b) continuing to use drugs of abuse even after admission to inpatient psychiatric treatment (Alterman, Erdlen,

La Porte, & Erdlen, 1982). Some MI/CD clients will even stop taking prescribed medication in anticipation of recreational drug use in order to avoid potentially dangerous chemical interactions (Ryglewicz & Pepper, 1996). The most common reason for these behaviors is simply the patient's desire to get high, not an attempt to self-medicate psychiatric distress (Bellack & DiClemente, 1999).

Prescribed medications offer another avenue through which medication noncompliance might express itself. Many psychiatric medications have a significant abuse potential of their own. For example, anticholinergic medications, which are often prescribed to help control the side effects of antipsychotic agents, have been abused by patients for recreational purposes (Buhrich, Weller, & Kevans, 2000). The anticholinergics may potentiate the effects of alcohol or the amphetamines (Land, Pinsky, & Salzman, 1991). Even when used alone, anticholinergic medications produce a "buzz" that is often substituted for the effects of other chemicals when supplies run short. Thus, treatment center staff must remember that the MI/CD client might even resort to abusing his or her psychiatric medications.

Urine toxicology testing is a useful tool to help determine whether the patient is taking his or her antipsychotic medications as prescribed. Urine toxicology testing is also valuable to detect illicit chemical use as MI/CD clients often test positive for recreational drugs even when they openly deny the use of such agents (Drake et al., 1996). Another approach to the problem of noncompliance is the use of long-term injectable forms of some phenothiazines currently available rather than the more traditional short-term preparations for control of the thought disorder and agitation often found in dual-diagnosis clients (Fariello & Scheidt, 1989).

Treatment Approaches

Although treatment professionals have recognized the benefits of integrated treatment programs for substance-abusing psychiatric patients (Bellack & DiClemente, 1999), such programs are still virtually nonexistent (Patrick, 2003). In place of this ideal approach is one in which staff will address the client's mental illness first, and after psychiatric stabilization has been achieved, begin to explore the client's chemical-use pattern (Rado, 1988). Usually, different professionals work with the client in turn, first to achieve a reduction in the patient's psychiatric symptoms and then to address the substance-use problem. This approach is an example of the *serial treatment model* (Miller, 1994).

The decision of whether to treat the psychiatric condition or the drug dependency first is often quite arbitrary (Howland, 1990; Kofoed et al., 1986) and there is little research data to offer direction in this decision. To further complicate matters, the managed care initiatives of the late 1990s have significantly complicated the treatment environment (Evans & Sullivan, 2001; Patrick, 2003).

One alternative to the serial treatment model was suggested by Layne (1990). In this model, both disorders are treated *concurrently*. Miller (1994) identified two subtypes of concurrent treatment models. In the first, which he termed the *parallel treatment model*, the patient "shuttles" between treatment facilities, dealing with his or her mental health concerns on one unit and substance-use issues in another unit. Unfortunately, this treatment approach makes it imperative that the staff in each unit communicate freely with their counterparts in the other; this is often a problem, especially if the psychiatric rehabilitation staff is not accustomed to working with substance abuse rehabilitation professionals. Second, the need to move physically from one unit to another might prove to be a source of stress to vulnerable patients, resulting in an exacerbation of their psychiatric problems. Finally, parallel treatment facilities tend to experience significant problems of patient attrition (Drake et al., 1996).

The second subtype of concurrent treatment, which Miller (1994) termed the *integrated treatment model*, is clearly the most efficient. In an integrated treatment setting, there are both mental health and substance abuse rehabilitation professionals on the same staff. By coordinating their treatment goals, staff are able to address both the psychiatric and chemical-use issues at the same time and in the same treatment facility. In such a treatment model, interstaff communications and cooperation are essential, according to the author. This treatment approach offers the advantage of dealing with the client's substance-use and psychiatric issues simultaneously while reducing the potential for conflict between different treatment professionals. Ries et al. (2000) found that the substance-abusing patients with schizophrenia in their sample seemed to recover more quickly than did patients with schizophrenia alone; they attributed this result to the availability of an integrated treatment program for the dual-diagnosis patients studied.

In the models discussed above, one basic requirement is the team approach. The rehabilitation team provides a forum in which the different treatment philosophies of psychiatric and chemical-dependency professionals can be synthesized into a unified approach for working with the substance-abusing mentally ill client (Evans & Sullivan, 2001; Osher & Kofoed, 1989; Riley, 1994). Chemical detoxification is a necessary first step in treating a dual-diagnosis client (Layne, 1990; Wallen & Weiner, 1989). This requires psychiatric support from professionals who are knowledgeable in the fields of both psychiatry and chemical dependency (Evans & Sullivan, 2001). Once detoxification has been achieved, the treatment team would be in a position to identify which problems are a result of the client's chemical use, which ones are manifestations of the client's psychiatric disorder, and in what order the problems need to be addressed.

The treatment setting. The general psychiatric unit is usually unsuited to meeting the needs of a dual-diagnosis client (Howland, 1990; Kofoed & Keys, 1988). Kofoed and Keys (1988) suggested that traditional psychiatric units might do best if treatment goals were limited to (a) detoxification from drugs of abuse, (b) psychiatric stabilization, and (c) persuasion of the client to enter chemical-dependency treatment. The clinician must be patient, often waiting years until conditions are right to finally persuade a dual-diagnosis client to enter treatment. The ideal program for a dual-diagnosis client would have facilities for working with both the psychiatric and the chemical-use problems. This would allow the staff to utilize the treatment resources most needed by the dual-diagnosis patient at that moment. This would obviously be easier in a facility that used the integrated treatment model discussed earlier. Such a program might work on either an outpatient (Kofoed et al., 1986) or inpatient (Pursch, 1987) basis, depending on (a) the client's needs and (b) the available resources. However, in more difficult cases, long-term inpatient treatment may be the only option for effectively working with the MI/CD client (Caton et al., 1989).

The stages of treatment. Director (1995) called this first phase of treatment *initial assessment/engagement*; it is also called *acute treatment and stabilization* (Lehman,

Myers, & Corty, 1989, p. 1020) or *acute stabilization* (Geppert & Minkoff, 2004; Minkoff, 1989). The goal during this phase is for the professional staff to establish a therapeutic relationship and arrive at an accurate diagnosis. The possibility that the stage of acute stabilization might be subdivided into early and late phases has been suggested (Bellack & DiClemente, 1999). In the early stage of acute stabilization the individual is assessed and his or her psychiatric problems are addressed. If the symptoms of a psychiatric disorder completely clear during detoxification, then the possibility that the client is not a dual-diagnosis patient should be considered (Layne, 1990). However, if the symptoms persist after detoxification, then the possibility of a dual-diagnosis client becomes more likely (Lehman et al., 1989). During the second half of this phase, the emphasis shifts to establishing a firm therapeutic relationship based on mutual trust between the client and the therapist (Drake & Mueser, 2002).

During the second phase of treatment, that of *persuasion* (Drake & Mueser, 2002), treatment staff focus on helping clients to understand the relationship between their substance use and psychiatric problems. Staff will try to break "the cycle of substance abuse, non-compliance, decompensation, and rehospitalization once the patient is sober and psychiatrically stable" (Fariello & Scheidt, 1989, p. 1066). It is during this stage that treatment staff attempt to convince clients that abstinence is a goal that is worth their effort, not only because substance use complicates their psychiatric condition but because substance-use problems are destructive in their own right. Motivational interviewing skills are of value in this process (Patrick, 2003).

The second stage of treatment has also been called *engagement* (Osher & Kofoed, 1989; Minkoff, 1989) or *motivational enhancement/engagement* (Geppert & Minkoff, 2004). During this phase staff attempt to break through clients' denial system that surrounds both the mental illness and the addiction. Staff members should attempt to work with family members or legal representatives during this period to bring clients into treatment on an involuntary basis if this should become necessary. This is the same process that Fariello and Scheidt (1989) identified as *breaking the cycle of addiction*. Osher and Kofoed (1989) called this phase of treatment *persuasion*. The therapeutic goals are (a) to persuade clients to accept the reality of their drug dependency and (b) to persuade them to seek continued treatment for their substance-abuse problem (Kofoed & Keys, 1988).

The third stage of treatment, that of *active treatment*, involves teaching clients the skills and helping them find the sources of support to manage their illness (Drake & Mueser, 2002; Osher & Kofoed, 1989). This has been called the stage of *prolonged stabilization: active treatment/relapse prevention* (Geppert & Minkoff, 2004) or *continuing care* (Director, 1995). During this phase group therapy might be the most effective treatment modality for working with the dual-diagnosis client (Kofoed & Keys, 1988). Because of the stigma associated with mental illness, it is usually more effective for these groups to be held in the psychiatric unit rather than in the substance abuse unit (Kofoed & Keys, 1988; Layne, 1990).

The final phase of treatment is *relapse prevention* (Drake & Mueser, 2002). During this phase the client and clinical team work together to identify potential problems that might cause or contribute to a relapse of either the psychiatric or substance-use disorder and develop techniques to minimize the impact of these problems. During this stage, staff might need to teach specific life skills to help the individual client learn how to function in society without the use of alcohol or drugs in spite of ongoing psychiatric problems (Layne, 1990).

Many of the same techniques utilized in general drug addiction treatment groups are useful in working with dual-diagnosis clients. But there is no single intervention for MI/CD clients that is equally effective with each individual patient in this population (Geppert & Minkoff, 2004). Rather, the treatment team must tailor each treatment intervention to the individual patient's phase of recovery, stage of treatment, and stage of change (Geppert & Minkoff, 2004). As a general rule, the confrontational model often used with traditional substance-abusing clients is counterproductive with MI/CD clients, especially those with schizophrenia (Bellack & DiClemente, 1999). When confrontational approaches *are* deemed to be appropriate, the confrontation should be less intense than when confronting more traditional personality disordered clients (Carey, 1989; Penick et al., 1990; Riley, 1994).

Unfortunately, once the patient's psychiatric condition is controlled, the client's drug-related defenses again begin to operate (Kofoed & Keys, 1988). Dual-diagnosis clients will often express a belief that once their psychiatric symptoms are controlled they are no longer in danger of being addicted to chemicals. These clients are often unable to see the relationship between their chemical abuse and the psychiatric symptoms they experience. This is a form of denial, but one that is not unique to the MI/CD client. For example, the patient who has financial problems and an addictive disorder might express a similar belief that once the financial problem is resolved he or she will no longer be in danger of relapse. Another common form of denial is evident when the client informs the drug rehabilitation specialist that he or she has discontinued all drug/alcohol use and thus further treatment is not necessary. In effect, the client enters into a period where he or she will try to "tell the counselor what he wants to hear" in order to avoid confrontation.

Although substance abuse rehabilitation professionals place great emphasis on social support systems for the recovering person, dual-diagnosis clients are often unable to utilize traditional support systems such as Alcoholics Anonymous or Narcotics Anonymous. This is because MI/CD clients tend to feel out of place in traditional self-help group meetings (Petrakis et al., 2002), especially in the earlier states of rehabilitation (Drake et al., 1996). It is for this reason that a group of peers is most effective in working with the dual-diagnosis client, as group members who have dropped out of treatment in the past can now share their own experiences with the group (Kofoed & Keys, 1988).

Therapy groups provide an avenue through which clients may share their experiences with even limited recreational drug use, discuss the need for the support of a Twelve Step group, and talk about problems in utilizing such groups (Fariello & Scheidt, 1989; Kofoed & Keys, 1988; Rado, 1988). When the group is effective, dual-diagnosis clients tend to achieve a lower rehospitalization rate (Kofoed & Keys, 1988) and function better in society. However, the few limited follow-up studies suggest that MI/CD clients tend to continue to abuse alcohol and/or drugs in spite of the best efforts of staff (Drake et al., 1996).

Summary

The dual-diagnosis client presents a difficult challenge to mental health and chemical-dependency professionals. Many of the syndromes that may result from the chronic use of chemicals are virtually indistinguishable from organic or psychiatric problems. This makes it most difficult to arrive at an accurate diagnosis. Further, MI/CD clients often use defenses, such as an interchangeable system of denial, and this further complicates the diagnostic process.

Dual-diagnosis clients are also difficult to work with in the rehabilitation setting. When they are in treatment, they will often talk about their psychiatric problem with drug-addiction counselors, and talk about their drug abuse or addiction with mental health professionals. Because of these characteristics, it has been found necessary to modify some of the traditional treatment methods used when working with the chemically dependent client. For example, the degree of confrontation useful in working with a personality disordered client is far too strong for working with a dual-diagnosis client who suffers from schizophrenia or other form of mental illness. However, gentle confrontation will often work with the mentally ill and drug-dependent client who is not personality disordered.

CHAPTER TWENTY-THREE

Chemical Abuse by Children and Adolescents

Introduction

Scientists have long known that the childhood and adolescent years are critical transitional periods, which build the foundation on which adulthood rests. Unfortunately, these are also periods in which the individual might initiate substance-use habits. Research has demonstrated that (a) midadolescence is the most common period in life when individuals begin to use recreational chemicals (Flanagan & Kokotailo, 1999) and (b) substance use/abuse is most prevalent among 18- to 25-year-olds (Greydanus & Patel, 2003). In spite of this fact, medical researchers do not understand how substance abuse during these critical periods of growth might impact the still maturing body of the adolescent abuser.

Substance use/abuse by adolescents did not emerge in the last quarter of the 20th century. During the early 1800s, for example, alcoholism was rampant among the youth of England (Wheeler & Malmquist, 1987). Child/adolescent alcohol use in the 19th century was one of the reasons that the child welfare movement started at that time. The social reforms brought about by this movement helped to drive child/adolescent recreational chemical use underground. However, children and adolescents have always wondered about and experimented with recreational chemicals, as evidenced by the fact that 50 years ago almost half the adolescents entering high school had already used alcohol at least once (Takanishi, 1993).

Although it appears that the rate of substance use problems has reached a plateau (Kaminer & Tarter, 2004), the possibility that substance-use problems in the childhood or adolescent years have lifelong consequences requires substance-abuse rehabilitation professionals to have a working knowledge of the problem and its treatment.

The Importance of Childhood and Adolescence in the Evolution of Substance-Use Problems

Currently, substance use/abuse is most common among 18- to 25-year-olds (Greydanus & Patel, 2003). It has been found that 80% of 18-year-olds have used alcohol at least once, and 4% use it on a regular basis (Kaminer & Tarter, 2004). Sixty-six percent of 18-year-olds have tried cigarettes, and 13% smoke at least half a pack per day. Eight percent of 18-year-olds have used cocaine at least once, and 15% have used an inhalant, hallucinogen, or stimulant at least once, according to Kaminer and Tarter (2004). These figures suggest that substance use continues to be a problem in the adolescent years.

Researchers also believe that adolescence is a period of special vulnerability. Substance use in early adolescence is associated with a higher risk of alcohol/drug addiction, for example. This is seen in the fact that 16% of those children who begin to experiment with marijuana before the age of 12 will go on to use heroin, compared to only 8% of those whose first marijuana exposure is after the age of 12 (Kandel, 1997). On a similar note, adolescents who begin to use alcohol before the age of 15 are more likely to have an alcohol-use problem than are those whose first exposure to alcohol occurs after the age of 15.

As social scientists have identified the factors that predispose individuals to or protect them from a substance-use problem during adolescence, they have discovered that substance use or resilience have deep roots in childhood. For example, it has been suggested that the quality of a child's *attachment bonds* with the parents helps to protect them from substance-use problems in childhood or adolescence (Bell, Forthun, & Sun, 2000; Hogan, 2000). Infants with positive attachment bonding experiences tend to become adolescents who have positive relationships with their parents, have more positive peer relationships, are more socially competent, and exhibit better coping skills, all characteristics found in nonabusing adolescents. The fact that the roots of child/adolescent substance abuse are found in the early childhood years might explain why antidrug programs developed for students in grade school have been ineffective. These discoveries, combined with the awareness that significant numbers of children and adolescents are abusing recreational chemicals, have made the childhood and adolescent periods of life of special interest to substance-abuse rehabilitation professionals.

Child and adolescent drug-use patterns: What do we know? Substance abuse in childhood and adolescence is quite controversial. Some believe that *any* recreational substance use in the childhood or adolescent years is a sign of a serious problem, whereas others argue that *experimental* use might be just one aspect of adolescence (Bell, 1996; Kaminer & Tarter, 2004). But research into substance-use trends in the pre-adult years is limited and accurate estimates of the scope of the problem are difficult to develop (Committee on Child Health Care Financing and Committee on Substance Abuse, 2001; Evans & Sullivan, 2001).

The literature on adolescent substance abuse is quite limited (Bukstein, 1995; Evans & Sullivan, 2001; Newcomb & Bentler, 1989), and many of the estimates of childhood/adolescent substance abuse are little more than watered-down versions of the assumptions made about adults who abuse chemicals (Bukstein, 1995; Knight, 2000). Finally, even under the best of circumstances, the distinction between adolescent substance use, abuse, and dependence are blurred and arbituary, and it is becoming clear that substance *abuse*, while a risk factor for later addiction, does not automatically lead to the addictive use of chemicals (Hogan, 2000; Kaminer & Tarter, 2004).

Much of what researchers believe is true about adolescent drug-use patterns is based on studies that use school students as research subjects. Unfortunately, many high-risk adolescents do not attend school on a regular basis and thus are unlikely to participate in a study based on students (Committee on Child Health Care Financing and Committee on Substance Abuse, 2001; O'Brien, 2001). Further, childhood/adolescent drug-use patterns may exhibit regional variation, as evidenced by the fact that the percentage of adolescents thought to have a substance-use problem ranges from 3% to 10% (Kaminer & Tarter, 2004). Childhood/adolescent substance-abuse patterns are affected by a wide range of variables, including the individual's geographic location, peer group, the current drug use "trends," and availability. The phenomenon of inhalant abuse is one such drug use "fad," which rapidly waxes and wanes in a given geographic area as individuals embrace and then discard the use of these substances.

Scope of the Problem

Childhood chemical-abuse patterns. Nationally, an estimated 800,000 adolescents between the ages of 12 and 17 are thought to be addicted to an illicit drug (Office of National Drug Control Policy, 2001). Nine percent of these admit to having abused an illicit drug in the past 12 months.

Alcohol remains a popular substance of abuse for adolescents. Surprisingly, alcohol use during childhood seems to be more common than most parents are willing to admit. This is clearly seen in the statistic that 45% of the children/adolescents older than 12 years of age admit to having used alcohol at least once in the preceding 30 days (Johnston, O'Malley, & Bachman, 2003a). Fetro, Coyle, and Pham (2001) found that just under half of the 11- to 14-year-old students in their sample admitted to the use of alcohol, with half of these students doing so before the age of 9. Boys tend to begin drinking earlier than girls, with an average age for the first drink of alcohol being 11.9 years for boys, compared with 12.7 years for girls (Alexander & Gwyther, 1995; Morrison, Rogers, & Thomas, 1995). This observed age difference may reflect different patterns of alcohol *availability* (Van Etten, Neumark, & Anthony, 1999). Although boys are more likely than girls to have access to alcohol/drugs, boys and girls are equally likely to abuse chemicals if their access to recreational

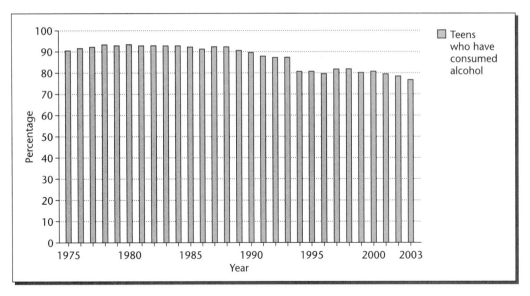

FIGURE 23.1   Trends in adolescent alcohol use: 1975–2003.
Source: Based on information in Johnston, O'Malley, & Bachman (2003a).

substances is equal. Trends in adolescent alcohol use for 1975 through 2003 are shown in Figure 23.1.

Why worry about child/adolescent substance abuse? There is evidence that the brain of the adolescent who consumes alcohol reacts to it differently from the brain of the adult. For example, adolescents who drink do not seem to develop the same sense of sedation that adults do after consuming a similar amount of alcohol (Strauch, 2003). Also, because the adolescent brain is still developing, it is more vulnerable to the alcohol-induced damage than is the adult brain. Adolescence is a period of life when the region of the brain known as the *hippocampus* matures, and researchers have found evidence to suggest that alcohol use during this period of life can impact hippocampal development (DeBellis et al., 2000). On the basis of animal research, developmental neurologists now believe that the still-developing adolescent brain might be four to five times as vulnerable to alcohol-induced brain damage as the adult brain (Wuethrich, 2001). This brain damage might not become evident until after the individual has stopped drinking, when a small (7% to 10%) but marked decline in psychological test performance is noted (Strauch, 2003). This decline in cognitive abilities appears to be permanent, suggesting that adolescent binge drinking can have lifelong consequences.

However, alcohol is not the only recreational chemical that children or adolescents are likely to experiment with. Many children use inhalants as their first mood-altering chemical (Hogan, 2000). As discussed in Chapter 16, adolescent inhalant abuse is a serious problem, and while it might not be the norm for childhood, it is still quite common. For example, 15.8% of the eighth graders surveyed in 2003 had used an inhalant at least once (Johnston et al., 2003a). Fortunately for most children/adolescents, inhalant abuse is usually only a transient process and thus the potential for inhalant-induced brain damage is limited. Most adolescents will engage in rare, episodic inhalant abuse over a 1–2-year span of time, after which they will abandon this practice.

The "gateway" drug theory. Some researchers have suggested that certain drugs of abuse such as the inhalants (Brunswick, 1989) and marijuana (Millman & Beeder, 1994) serve as an introduction to the abuse of more destructive compounds. One investigation of 1,160 subjects from the ages of 15 to 35 did find evidence of such a progression from the gateway chemicals to other, more serious, forms of substance use (Kandel, Yamaguchi, & Chen, 1992). Others dispute the "gateway" theory. It has been suggested that marijuana's role as a gateway chemical may be simply an illusion and that "most drug users begin with alcohol and nicotine before marijuana" (Watson, Benson, & Joy, 2000, p. 551). Personality characteristics such as the antisocial personality disorder or conduct disorder in adolescence may be more predictive of subsequent substance-use disorders than simple marijuana abuse (Clark, Vanyukrov, & Cornelius, 2002; Watson et al., 2000).

Kandel and Chen (2000) examined the marijuana use patterns of a community-based sample of 708 marijuana abusers (364 male and 304 females) who were followed from adolescence until the age of 34–35 years. The marijuana abusers fell into four groups: (a) early-onset/heavy use group, (b) early-onset/light use group, (c) midadolescence-onset/heavy use group, and (d) midadolescence-onset, light use group. By itself, the early use of marijuana was not found by Kandel and Chen (2000) to be predictive of later problems or a progression to the abuse of other chemicals. This is not surprising, given that just under 50% of individuals 13 to 24 years of age will use cannabis at least once (Knight, 2002). However, Kandel and Chen (2000) found that the individual's *motivation* for using marijuana and the presence of other dysfunctional behaviors were associated with later drug abuse/dependence problems, casting doubt on the gateway theory as it applied to marijuana abuse. Thus, whether there are certain gateway substances that predispose the individual to the abuse of other compounds remains a theory that has not been proven.

Adolescent chemical-abuse patterns. Adolescent substance abuse peaked sometime around the year 1981 and then slowly declined for about a decade until it reached a plateau in the early 1990s. After years of relative stability, there were modest declines in the level of adolescent substance abuse in the early years of the 21st century (Doyle, 2001a; Johnston et al., 2003a). Currently, it is estimated that 10% of older adolescents in the United States meet the diagnostic criteria for an alcohol-use disorder (De Bellis et al., 2000) and 7% to 10% of adolescents are thought to need some form of treatment for a substance-use disorder other than alcoholism (Kaminer, 2001). Knight (2002) suggested that approximately 25% of adolescents would qualify for a substance-use disorder diagnosis, whereas a similar proportion of adolescents engage in rare, social use of chemicals. On a positive note, however, 50% of

adolescents abstain from all recreational chemical use, according to the author.

Not surprisingly, adolescent drug-use patterns tend to mirror those of society (Callahan, 1993). Indeed, Ross (2002) spoke of adolescent alcohol- and drug-abuse issues as an *adult* problem, projected onto children and adolescents. Thus, in a society where alcohol is the most popular recreational chemical, it should not be surprising to learn that alcohol is by far the most popular chemical of choice for adolescents (Hogan, 2000; Komro & Toomey, 2002). Of the estimated 27 million teenagers, just under a million had become intoxicated in the past month, and 50,000 drank to intoxication on a daily basis (Doyle, 2001a). The percentage of high school seniors who have experimented with alcohol has remained relatively stable over the past decade (Knight, 2000). For example, 76.6% of the class of 2003 admitted to the use of alcohol at least once (Johnston et al., 2003a). There also is evidence that the percentage of high school seniors who use alcohol heavily has remained stable over the past decade, with approximately 30% to 40% of adolescents being classified as heavy drinkers (Knight, 2000).

The most popular form of alcohol for the adolescents surveyed is beer, followed by wine "coolers" (Novello & Shosky, 1992). Few adolescents seem to be drawn to "hard" liquor. Indeed, so rare is adolescent use of hard liquor that even occasional experimentation with vodka, gin, whiskey, or bourbon should be considered a sign of an alcohol-abuse problem (Rogers, Harris, & Jarmuskewicz, 1987). Surprisingly, although many parents worry about possible alcohol use by their adolescent children, they are poor sources of information about their teenagers' use of this chemical. Parents tend to underestimate their teenagers' alcohol consumption by a factor of at least 10 to 1 (Morrison et al., 1995; Rogers et al., 1987; Zarek, Hawkins, & Rogers, 1987). More distressing, 40% of parents surveyed think that they have no influence over their teenagers' decision to use alcohol/drugs (Comerci, Fuller, & Morrison, 1997).

In spite of its popularity, alcohol is not the only recreational chemical used by adolescents. By the time of graduation, 51% of the seniors from the class of 2003 admitted to the use of an illicit chemical at least once (Johnston et al., 2003a). The most popular illicit drug for adolescents appears to be marijuana, which accounts for 75% of illicit drug use by teens (Hogan, 2000). Some 49.7% of the seniors of the class of 2003 admitted to having used marijuana at least once, according to the authors (Johnston et al., 2003a). For eighth graders, alcohol is the most commonly used mood altering chemical, with 52% of the students surveyed in 1999 admitting to having used alcohol at least once (Johnston et al., 2003a). Marijuana is the most frequently used illicit mood-altering chemical, with inhalants a close second. Fully 17% of eighth graders surveyed in 2003 admitted to the use of marijuana at least once, as compared with 15.8% admitting to the use of inhalants at least once (Johnson et al., 2003a). Hallucinogenics are unpopular, with 5.9% of the high school seniors surveyed in 2003 admitting to the use of LSD and 9% admitting to the use of a hallucinogen other than LSD (Johnston et al., 2003a).

It has been suggested that adolescents who develop substance-use problems seem to show a definite progression in their substance use (Kandel & Davies, 1996). In the first stage, the adolescent will engage in the use of a chemical normally reserved for adults (e.g., tobacco and/or alcohol). Most adolescents do not progress beyond this stage (Newcomb, 1996). But for those who do, the next step is the use of an illicit chemical. This substance is usually marijuana (Kandel & Davies, 1996). Again, of those adolescents who reach this stage, most do not proceed further. However, the use of marijuana usually precedes the use of "hard" drugs such as cocaine, according to the authors. Thus, the progression of substance abuse first identified in the 1970s seems to continue to apply to adolescent chemical-use patterns at the start of the 21st century.

College students form a unique subpopulation. Traditionally, college is viewed as spanning the period from late adolescence to early adulthood, a period in life when risk-taking behaviors reach their peak (Arnett, 2000). Neurologically, the individual's brain is in a state of transition during the college years, a process that might actually predispose adolescents in this age group to alcohol's reinforcing effects in spite of the potential for substance-induced neurological damage (Spear, 2002).

Legally, most college students are considered adults at the age of 18, although the age at which an individual can legally purchase alcohol in most states is 21. Thus, the majority of college students are below the age at which they are able to purchase alcohol legally. In spite of this little detail, more than 90% of college students view drinking as a central part of their social lives (Saffer, 2002) and "spend more on alcohol than they spend on books, soda, coffee, juice and milk combined" (Jersild, 2001, p. 99). As a group, college students drink more heavily than their noncollege peers (Coombs, 1997; Demers-Gendreau, 1998). Nationally, 500,000 college students are injured while under the influence of alcohol each year, and approximately 1,300 (Wechsler, 2002) to 1,400 college students die each year as a result of alcohol-related accidents (1,100 of which are motor vehicle accidents) (Hingson, 2003).

The prohibition against underage drinking may have caused adolescents to become obsessed with alcohol use, leading them to engage in a binge pattern of overuse when they do drink (Barr, 1999). Most certainly, there is a trend for advertisers to stress alcohol use in college newspapers (Saffer, 2002), a fact that may contribute to the high levels of alcohol use/abuse in this age group. Research suggests that college students typically engage in binge drinking rather than steady drinking on a daily basis (Weingardt et al., 1998). Fully 44% of college students engage in binge drinking with the goal of getting drunk (Demers-Gendreau, 1998).[1]

Wechsler (2002) reported that most college students whose drinking patterns were examined followed the same drinking pattern established in their high school years. Thus, the roots of college binge drinking appear to be set before the student begins college. However, binge drinking becomes less common after the age of 23, as the student begins to face the demands of adult life (Marlatt et al., 1998; Wechsler, 2002). Only a minority (5% to 19% of those students surveyed) continued to drink abusively over extended periods of time (Weingardt et al., 1998).

One reason that many college students might abuse alcohol is their misperception of the amount of alcohol ingested by their peers. As a group, college students tend to overestimate both their peers' acceptance of their drunken behavior and the number of their peers who are drinking heavily (DeAngelis, 1994). This is unfortunate; by the time the student arrives at college, the influence of his or her peer group is one of the strongest factors in shaping individual drinking

[1]A "binge" was defined as a period in which an individual consumed five or more drinks at a time.

patterns (Marlatt et al., 1998). Further, there is a tendency among heavy drug/alcohol users to equate substance use with fun (DeAngelis, 1994).

These observations would suggest that alcohol/drug abuse by the majority of college students is only part of a phase, but they do not negate the fact that for some college-age drinkers their alcohol use is indicative of a substance-use disorder that will be present in later life. Unfortunately, researchers have not isolated the diagnostic signs that suggest which individuals are at risk for a substance-use disorder later in adulthood.

The 1997 Tobacco Lawsuit Settlement and Tobacco Use by Children/Adolescents

Cigarettes and other tobacco products occupy a unique place within this society. These substances are known to be addictive and are terribly destructive, and yet they may be legally purchased by adults. Unfortunately, tobacco-use problems are also a very real part of childhood and adolescence. In the United States, the *average* age at which a smoker begins is about 12, and most of those who begin to smoke at this stage of life are regular smokers by the age of 14 (Hogan, 2000). This may be a reflection that the adolescent brain, which is still growing, seems especially vulnerable to the addictive effects of tobacco (Strauch, 2003).

In the United States an average of 6,000 adolescents start smoking every day, and half of these individuals will become daily smokers (Committee on Substance Abuse, 2001b; Dickinson, 2000). In the late 1990s, a number of states filed lawsuits against cigarette manufacturers. During the course of these lawsuits, it was discovered that cigarette manufacturers had targeted the adolescent population. At least one major tobacco company conducted research into the phases of adolescent cigarette smoking, apparently in order to better understand how to induce young people to make the transition to regular cigarette smoking (Hilts, 1996). Another major tobacco company referred to adolescents in an internal memo as an "up and coming new generation of smokers" (Phelps, 1996, p. A1). The R. J. Reynolds Tobacco Co., a major cigarette producer, went so far as to classify 12-year-old children as "younger adult" smokers ("Big Tobacco's Secret," 1998).

In 1997, what has variously been called "Big Tobacco" or "The Tobacco Industry" offered to settle a lawsuit brought against it by representatives of 40 of the 50 states. Without admission of wrongdoing, the major tobacco producers offered a financial settlement of $368.5 billion and agreed to discontinue a number of advertising tactics, including the development of advertising aimed at children/adolescents (Smolowe, 1997). Included in this legal settlement was a provision that if the number of underage smokers was not reduced by 50% within 7 years of the settlement, the tobacco industry would be fined additional penalities. A force that helped to bring about this settlement was an admission by one of the smaller tobacco companies that the industry had specifically targeted children and adolescents for years (Smolowe, 1997).

Because of the nature of the neurological growth process in adolescence, it is difficult for the individual to perceive the risk associated with such acts as smoking (Strauch, 2003). Further, the natural rebelliousness of adolescents makes them especially vulnerable to the message, encouraged by many tobacco companies' advertising, that cigarette smoking is a way to rebel against parental authority (Dickinson, 2000; Hilts, 1996). The same appears to be true of the estimated 1.5 million people under the age of 19 who use "smokeless tobacco" (Kessler, 1995). Just under three-quarters of this group started their use by the time they were in the ninth grade (Barker, 1994). Further, 90% of cigarette smokers are already *addicted* to nicotine by the age of 20 (Walker, 1993). These figures underscore the need to address the use of tobacco products during childhood or adolescence.

In support of this observation, by the time of graduation from high school, just 53.7% of the seniors surveyed in 2003 had used cigarettes at least once (Johnston et al., 2003a). An estimated 100,000 of the adolescents who smoke are thought to be below the age of 13 (Bhandari, Sylvester, & Rigotti, 1996).

Although advertising by the tobacco industry aimed at children/adolescents is a major factor in the initiation of smoking, parental cigarette use is a strong shaper of the adolescent's tobacco-use patterns. Males (1992) observed that 75% of all teenagers who smoke had parents who also smoked and suggested that "teenage smoking is largely the active continuation of a childhood of passive smoking" (p. 3282). This theory is certainly consistent with research suggesting that the transition from a nonsmoker to smoker in childhood or adolescence passes through several stages (Holland & Fitzsimons, 1991):

1. *Preparatory phase:* Forming attitudes accepting of cigarette smoking
2. *Initiation phase:* Smoking for the first time
3. *Experimentation phase:* Learning how to smoke
4. *Transition:* Smoking regularly

Hints for successful intervention. Given the progression from forming attitudes accepting of smoking through the addictive use of tobacco, it would seem that attempts at intervention need to be aimed at children who have not yet started to form pro-smoking attitudes (Holland & Fitzsimons, 1991). Attempts at intervention should focus on helping children learn social skills that will enable them to resist smoking on the grounds that if the adolescent reaches the age of 16 to 18 without having initiated smoking, he or she is unlikely to do so. For example, fully 90% of those who *begin* to smoke cigarettes after the age of 21 are unlikely to continue the habit, according to Hilts (1996).

However, successful intervention will require further investigation of the refusal skills utilized by boys and girls who are offered the opportunity to smoke/use alcohol/drugs (Moon, Hecht, Jackson, & Spellers, 1999). The authors have found that boys are less likely to "just say 'no' " as a result of the socialization process and that they tend to explain their reasons for why they do not want to use. This makes them vulnerable to counterexplanations and raises their risk of ultimately giving in and accepting tobacco/drugs when offered. Thus, a successful intervention program would need to enhance the refusal skills of both boys and girls given the opportunity to smoke or abuse chemicals.

Why Do Adolescents Use Chemicals?

Hogan (2000) suggested five reasons that adolescents used/abused chemicals: (a) to feel grown-up, (b) to take risks/rebel against authority, (c) to fit into a specific peer group, (d) to relax and feel good, and (e) to satisify curiosity about the drug's effects. To this list might be added self-medication: Some adolescents self-medicate negative feelings such as depression or interpersonal stress by the use of alcohol/drugs (Joshi & Scott, 1988; Morrison et al., 1995; Wills, Sandy, Yaeger, Cleary, &

Shinar, 2001). For some adolescents, the use of alcohol/drugs is a way to prove sexual prowess (Barr, 1999; Morrison et al., 1995). The mass media also influence adolescent behavior. So pervasive is their influence in defining what is or is not expected of the individual socially that Hogan (2000) referred to them collectively as a "superpeer" (p. 937).

As this list of potential contributing factors illustrates, there is no simple reason to explain why adolescents use recreational chemicals. One factor that seems to be related to adolescents' abstinence or use of recreational chemicals is their cognitive level. Because adolescents view themselves as immortal, many have trouble seeing themselves as being vulnerable to the negative effects of alcohol/drugs (Hogan, 2000). In the section that follows, the relationship between these factors and adolescent substance use/abuse will be examined in more detail.

Adolescent affective disorders. Depression, especially severe depression, has been found to be a risk factor for adolescent substance use/abuse (Kriechbaum & Zernig, 2000). In such cases, the adolescent might abuse chemicals in an attempt to self-medicate emotional distress (Jorgensen, 2001). Adolescents who suffer from an affective disorder such as anxiety or depression should be viewed as being at high risk for substance-abuse problems because of the association between emotional distress and substance abuse (Burke, Burke, & Rae, 1994, p. 454).

Extremes of behavior (i.e., total abstinence or serious drug abuse) were found in adolescents who were most maladjusted, whereas the healthiest were those who would only occasionally experiment with chemicals (Lundeen, 2002; Shedler & Block, 1990). The crucial factor is the individual's emotional health, as the emotionally healthy adolescent might experiment with recreational drugs but ultimately has the interpersonal and intrapersonal skills necessary to cope with life without using chemicals to self-medicate emotional distress. In contrast, adolescents who frequently abuse drugs tend to have poor impulse control, be socially alienated, and experience high levels of emotional distress, all signs that they lack the emotional resources of the first group. Adolescents who totally abstain from chemical use tend to be anxious, emotionally constricted, and lacking in self-confidence and social skills. Thus, adolescents' pattern of substance abuse can be understood only within the context of their emotional adjustment.

Conduct/oppositional defiant disorder. The *conduct disorder* (CD) and the *oppositional defiant disorder* (ODD) are two forms of mental illness that first appear in childhood and adolescence. The diagnostic criteria for both conditions are outside the scope of this text but are listed in the American Psychiatric Association's *Diagnostic and Statistical Manual of Mental Disorders (4th edition–text revision)* (American Psychiatric Association, 2000). Both these conditions reflect a behavioral control disorder during childhood/adolescence, which seems to increase that individual's risk for developing a substance-use disorder (Clark et al., 2002). These signposts of behavioral dyscontrol seem to precede the development of substance-use disorders, and both the behavioral control disorders and the development of alcohol/drug use disorders might reflect a common neurological or genetic basis (Clark et al., 2002).

Researchers have found evidence on neurological tests that the prefrontal cortex region of the brain is actively involved in behavioral control. Preliminary evidence suggests that individuals with severe forms of antisocial behavior (including CD and ODD) have abnormal brain function in this region, suggesting that this might be one cause of the behavioral control disorders (Clark et al., 2002). Researchers have found that when the substance-abusing child/adolescent has either CD or ODD, it complicates the treatment process and reduces the chances of success. For treatment to be at all effective, the therapist must include a program to help develop behavioral control in addition to the treatment of the substance-use disorder (Clark et al., 2002).

Peer group influences on adolescent substance-use patterns. For adolescents, peer groups may serve as either a protective or a negative influence (Ross, 2002; Simkin, 2002). Although genetic factors influence whether a substance-use disorder is likely to develop, peers were found to strongly influence the *initiation* of chemical abuse in adolescents (Rhee et al., 2003). There is also a strong relationship between the peer group membership and substance-use patterns of the individual (Adger & Werner, 1994; Bukstein, 1995; Farrell & White, 1998; Kaminer & Bukstein, 1998; Simkin, 2002). For example, exposure to alcohol-using social models such as peers is one factor that predicts

the development of positive expectations for alcohol in children/adolescents in the fifth to seventh grades (Cumsille, Sayer, & Graham, 2000).

Surprisingly, peer group selection is the *last step* in the chain of events that ultimately results in the adolescent's use of alcohol/drugs (Kumpfer, 1997). Adolescents actively seek out a peer group consistent with their values, expectations and demands, including the area of substance-use patterns (Oetting, Deffenbacher, & Donnermeyer, 1998; Strauch, 2003). Thus, peer group selection often precedes active chemical use, as the individual's perception of approval from peers precedes his or her first use of marijuana. Thus, the actual use of a chemical is often the last step in a chain of events that began with the selection of a specific peer group, moved to the anticipation of approval from members of that group for chemical-use behvior, and finally included the actual use of the substance itself.

The peer-group influence model has been challenged by other scientists, however (Bauman & Ennett, 1994; Novello & Shosky, 1992). Novello and Shosky (1992) noted that of the 10.6 million adolescents who consume alcohol, almost one-third do so when alone rather than in groups. The authors interpreted these data as suggesting that the theory that adolescents use chemicals in response to peer pressure may not be true in all cases.

A factor that might distort the apparent relationship between substance-use patterns and peer group membership was the possibility of *projection* on the part of the research subjects. When asked about their friends' substance use, drug-using adolescents are more likely to respond on the basis of *their own* drug-use behavior rather than on what they know about their friends' chemical use. In support of this theory, Bauman and Ennett (1994) pointed out that adolescents who do not use chemicals were more likely to be judged as using recreational drugs by their drug-using friends than they were by their non-drug-using friends. On the basis of their research, Bauman and Ennett (1994) suggested that the factor of adolescent peer use on substance-abuse patterns was "overestimated" (p. 820).

Personal values and their influence on adolescent chemical-use patterns. One factor that *does* seem to protect the child/adolescent from pressure to use alcohol/drugs is personal values. There is a negative correlation between such forces as scholastic performance, church attendance, the individual's beliefs about the importance of academic achievement, and his or her substance-use behaviors (Kaminer & Bukstein, 1998). However, it is not clear whether these forces help to protect the adolescent from becoming ensnared in substance use as correlation does not imply causality.

The impact of parent-child relationships on adolescent chemical-use patterns. Research has shown that during the childhood years, parental influence on values development and subsequent drug use is the strongest. Parents' behaviors such as spending time with their children, their own substance-use patterns, and the degree of their emotional involvement or neglect of their children have all been found to influence the individual's substance use in childhood and adolescence (Kaminer & Bukstein, 1998). Children who reported that their parents spent more time with them and who made greater efforts to communicate with them have lower rates of alcohol/tobacco use than children who experience less parental involvement (Cohen, Richardson, & LaBree, 1994; Griffin, Botvin, Scheier, Diaz, & Miller, 2000). Children/adolescents are also very aware of parental modeling behaviors (Cohen et al., 1994; Rogers et al., 1987; Shalala, 1997). Thus, what the parents *do* often has a stronger influence on the child than what they *say* about chemical abuse (Alexander & Gwyther, 1995; Chassin, Curran, Hussong, & Colder, 1996).

As children move into adolescence, parental leverage on their behavior is muted by social and peer influences but it does not entirely disappear. Parental impact on such emerging facets of the adolescent's personality as his or her values and the quality of the family's affectional interactions also help shape the individual's tendency to use recreational chemicals (Cohen et al., 1994). Children whose parents spent more time interacting with them were less likely to abuse chemicals; adolescents who came from intact families or who felt that their parents were emotionally supportive were also found to be less likely to engage in alcohol/drug abuse than adolescents from less secure family situations (Farrell & White, 1998; Griffin et al., 2000).

Parental control seems to be another factor that shapes the individual's chemical-use pattern (Chassin et al., 1996). When parents made the time and effort to monitor their children's behavior, the children exhibited lower rates of delinquency, one form of which may

be substance abuse (Griffin et al., 2000). In contrast, parents who abused recreational chemicals tended to engage in fewer "parental control practices" (Chassin et al., 1996, p. 70) with their adolescents, allowing them greater opportunities to join social groups likely to engage in recreational drug/alcohol use, according to the authors.[2]

Victimization history. Another factor that consistently seems to identify adolescents who are at risk for substance use problems is whether the individual had ever been the victim of some form of physical/sexual abuse (Fuller & Cabanaugh, 1995) or had witnessed violence within the family (Kilpatrick et al., 2000). It is thought that adolescents might turn to alcohol/drugs as a way of self-medicating their feelings of shame and fear as a result of having been victimized. Another group of adolescents who are vulnerable to the effects of recreational chemicals are those who become aware of homosexual urges within themselves. According to Fuller and Cabanaugh (1995), the homosexual adolescent might use alcohol and/or drugs in an attempt to self-medicate feelings of guilt, inadequacy, or self-depreciation.

Rebellion. A number of researchers have suggested that the very fact that adolescents are prohibited from using alcohol makes drinking a goal for many (Barr, 1999). Indeed, because *any* use of alcohol by the adolescent is considered illegal by authorities, individuals who indulge in heavy alcohol use are viewed as being especially daring in the eyes of their peers (Barr, 1999). As will be discussed in Chapter 35, many other countries allow adolescents to drink alcoholic beverages *with their families* and do not seem to suffer from the problem of alcohol misuse by adolescents.

Section summary statement. Ultimately, the research data do not support a simplistic unidirectional model such as the individual's peer group membership as a cause of chemical-use patterns (Curran, Stice, & Chassin, 1997). Rather, it is the interplay between such factors as the quality of parent-child relationships, whether the adolescent is depressed, and his or her age-specific struggle for autonomy that all might play

---

[2]An interesting question to consider is which came first: Do the parents not engage in adequate supervisory behaviors because they are using chemicals, or do they use recreational chemicals because they are less well adjusted and are unable to fulfill their parental roles?

a role in the development of substance use or abstinence in the teenager. The early adolescent years appear to be a time of special vulnerability for later drug-use problems.

The Adolescent Abuse/Addiction Dilemma: How Much Is Too Much?

Adolescent substance use/abuse/addiction falls along a continuum with total abstinence on one end and severe dependency on the other. Between these two extremes are the conditions of experimental chemical use, occasional chemical use, and regular use of recreational chemicals (Tweed, 1998). Unfortunately, researchers still do not have a proven method to determine which adolescents require treatment for substance-use problems (Knight, 2000; Rohde, Lewinsohn, Kahler, Seeley, & Brown, 2001), how to measure the adolescent's motivation to participate in such treatment (Melnick, De Leon, Hawke, Jainchill, & Kressel, 1997), or the effectiveness of adolescent treatment programs (Kaminer, 2001). These may be some of the reasons that 50% of adolescents admitted to substance-abuse treatment programs return to the abuse of recreational chemicals within 90 days of their discharge (Latimer, Newcomb, Winters, & Stinchfield, 2000).

There is a very real need for diagnostic criteria by which to identify adolescents who are abusing alcohol/drugs. For example, chest pain is the third most common reason that adolescents seek medical care, and research has found that 17% of the adolescents tested in a hospital setting had evidence of ephedrine in their urine in spite of their denial that they had used this compound (James et al., 1998). Thus, physicians need diagnostic tools to rule out *both* cocaine and/or ephedrine abuse as a possible cause of chest pain in adolescents who are seen in the emergency room setting.

Tweed (1998) suggested several symptoms that might indicate an adolescent with an alcohol/substance-use problem: (a) unexplained weight loss, (b) nasal irritation, (c) frequent "colds" or "allergies" (brought on by intranasal use of drugs or inhalants), (d) hoarseness, (e) chronic cough, (f) unexplained injuries, (g) needle tracks, (h) social withdrawal, (i) promiscuity, (j) fights (with family or individuals outside the family), (k) hiding bottles/drug paraphernalia, (l) selling possessions, or (m) legal problems. Another possible warning sign according

to the author was a drastic change in the individual's sleep pattern without apparent reason.

Most certainly, if adolescents are abusing alcohol/drugs, their chemical abuse must be considered in terms of their psychosocial development (Bukstein, 1995; Cattarello, Clayton, & Leukefeld, 1995; Kriechbaum & Zernig, 2000). Heavy use of alcohol/drugs to the point of intoxication in early adolescence appears to indicate adolescents who are at risk for later drug-use problems (Bukstein, 1995). If experimental substance use is initiated after the age of 15, it might not be a reflection of serious problems so much as a parallel to society's more liberal attitude toward recreational substance use, according to the author.

Problems in diagnosis and treatment of adolescent drug abuse. In spite of the attention that has been paid to the problem of adolescent substance use/abuse since the mid 1980s, "the standards guiding diagnosis and treatment decisions specifically related to adolescents are relatively primitive and often lack empirical support" (Bruner & Fishman, 1998, p. 598). For the most part, diagnostic criteria used for adolescents are based on standards developed for use with adults, and these may not be applicable to this special population (Kaminer, 1999; Monti, 2003; Pollock & Martin, 1999; Rohde et al., 2001). Further, even when a substance-abusing adolescent *is* correctly identified, there are few effective treatment programs available for referral (Ross, 2002).

One way to improve accuracy in assessing an adolescent's chemical-use pattern is to establish an extensive data base about the individual and his or her substance-use patterns (Evans & Sullivan, 2001; Juhnke, 2002). For example, the occasional use of alcohol or marijuana at a party—say, once every 6 months—is not automatically a sign of a problem; it may reflect only curiosity about the effects of these chemicals (Hogan, 2000).

Referrals for a chemical dependency evaluation of an adolescent will come from many potential sources. The juvenile court system, especially the emerging "drug courts," will frequently refer an offender for an evaluation, especially when that individual was under the influence of chemicals at the time of his or her arrest. School officials may request an evaluation of a student suspected of abusing chemicals. Treatment center admissions officers will frequently recommend an evaluation, although this is usually referred to

TABLE 23.1   Two Theories of the Stages of Adolescent Substance Abuse

Stages of adolescent substance use/abuse according to Jones (1990)	*Stages of adolescent substance use/abuse according to Chatlos (1996)*
Learning the mood swing: The adolescent is exposed to substance use and learns from more experienced users what to expect from the use of recreational substances.	*Initiation:* Individual begins the use of mood-altering chemicals.
Seeking the mood swing: The young substance user's life begins to revolve around chemical use, and his or her use of recreational chemicals increases.	*Learning the mood swing:* The new substance user learns what effects to expect from his or her chemical use and why these effects are to be desired.
Preoccupied with the mood swing: The young person ends relationships with non-using friends; may lose job or be expelled from school; uses mood-altering drugs daily; may lie to friends and family to protect his or her continued use of drugs.	*Regular use/seeking the mood swing:* The adolescent continues to seek what she or he has come to view as the positive effects of recreational chemical use.
Using just to feel normal: Drug/alcohol use has reached the point that the individual must use chemicals just to feel normal and to function. The person experiences some consequences of chronic chemical abuse; may become paranoid, have memory loss, or experience flashbacks.	*Abuse/harmful consequences:* The negative effects of recreational chemical use begin to make themselves felt on the user's life (poor academic performance, etc.), but the individual continues to use recreational chemicals.
	Substance dependency/compulsive use: The adolescent is now physically addicted to chemicals, or at least is trapped in a cycle of compulsive use, in spite of the serious consequences of this behavior.

in-house staff rather than to an independent professional. Some parents, especially those with "religious, restrictive families" (Farrow, 1990, p. 1268), will also request an evaluation and/or treatment after the first known episode of alcohol or drug use.

As a group, adolescents tend to have a rather immature view of life and the consequences of their decisions. Unfortunately, this simplistic outlook on life, and possible continued chemical use, may mistakenly be interpreted by treatment staff as a sign of denial or resistance rather than emotional immaturity. Another common problem is for treatment center staff to interpret "acting out" behaviors as a sign of rebellion rather than an attempt by the adolescent to overcome emotional trauma (Jorgensen, 2001). A multidisciplinary team approach to assessment in cases of suspected adolescent substance abuse will allow the accurate identification of the client's strengths, weaknesses, level of maturity, and adaptive style so that staff can understand what role resistance and acting out behaviors play in the individual's coping style.

The stages of adolescent chemical use. For adolescents who abuse chemicals, there is a progression that leads ultimately to more serious substance-use problems. The

individual's progression from experimental substance use to a substance use-problem might be viewed as passing through four different stages. Chatlos (1996), on the other hand, suggested a five-stage model of adolescent substance use/abuse. These two different models are contrasted in Table 23.1.

Each model suggests that adolescent substance users must first be exposed to the chemicals they will abuse and learn what to expect from the use of that substance. Each model suggests that for adolescents who continue to engage in recreational chemical use there is a change in friendship patterns as they begin to drift away from their former peer group toward a new peer group that is more accepting of chemical use. Other new behaviors that might develop during this stage include erratic school performance, unpredictable mood swings, and manipulative behaviors, all in the service of continued substance abuse.

When the individual becomes preoccupied "with the mood swing" (Jones, 1990, p. 680), non-drug-using friends are avoided and family fights and confrontations develop; there is often a loss of employment, expulsion from school, consistent lying, and daily use of mood-altering chemicals. The individual's daily activities center around the use of chemicals (Tweed, 1998). Ultimately, some individuals will progress to the final stage of substance use, in which they must use drugs just "to feel normal" (Jones, 1990, p. 680). Tweed (1998) refers to this as the "burnout" stage (p. 33) of adolescent chemical abuse. During this stage the individual will experience physical complications from the drug use, memory loss and/or flashback experiences, paranoia, anger, and drug/ alcohol overdoses. Feelings of guilt, shame, depression, remorse, and possible suicidal thinking are all possible during this phase (Tweed, 1998).

Adolescence and addiction to chemicals. It was once thought that adolescents were unlikely to have the opportunity to use a drug long enough to develop physical dependence on that chemical (Kaminer & Frances, 1991). It is now known that this theory is incorrect. For example, whereas a history of alcohol-withdrawal symptoms is one of the major landmarks used to identify an adult with an alcohol-use disorder, only 23% of adolescents diagnosed as being dependent on alcohol had ever experienced any symptoms of alcohol withdrawal (Martin & Winters, 1998).

Adolescents who *are* physically dependent on alcohol/drugs tend to have fewer, and less severe, symptoms of their addiction than do adults (Evans & Sullivan, 2001; Kriechbaum & Zernig, 2000). However, adolescent heavy drinkers were found to typically continue a pattern of heavy alcohol use in the early adult years, suggesting that adolescent heavy drinkers do not "mature out of" their substance-use problem (Rohde et al., 2001). One of the most frequently encountered symptoms of alcohol/drug dependence in the adolescent is the development of physical tolerance to the effects of their drug of choice (Martin & Winters, 1998). Hoffmann, Belille, and Harrison (1987) found, for example, that more than three-fourths of their sample of 1,000 adolescents, all of whom were in treatment at the time, reported having developed tolerance to alcohol or other drugs. But because adolescents usually do not have an extensive history of substance abuse, they are less likely to have experienced any major organ damage as a result of their alcohol/drug abuse (Kriechbaum & Zernig, 2000). Thus, "physical health problems associated with substance abuse [are] infrequent in adolescents" (Harrison, Fulkerson, & Beebe, 1998, p. 491), although it is still possible for adolescents to suffer substance-induced organ damage in rare cases (Chassin & DeLucia, 1996).

Although there are mental health professionals who question the possibility that adolescents can become addicted to alcohol/drugs, they are in a distinct minority. Farrow (1990) was one researcher who challenged the concept of adolescent addiction, stating that "the number of teenagers who are truly chemically dependent is less than 1% of all users" (p. 1268). Another 10% to 15% might meet the diagnostic criteria for drug or alcohol abuse whereas a full 10% to 15% of all teens have little or no experience with either alcohol or drugs. The remainder are occasional users of alcohol/drugs and will likely adjust "their use in non-problematic ways as they grow older" (p. 1268). However, even Farrow's (1990) conclusions support the possibility of adolescent addiction and certainly accept the possibility that adolescents might develop disorders of alcohol/drug use.

Adolescent substance use: A cause for optimism? There is strong evidence that even if the adolescent *has* developed an alcohol-use disorder, the prognosis is better than it is for an adult (Kriechbaum & Zernig, 2000). This is because the adolescent's personality is still evolving, allowing the potential for growth. In many cases, the trauma that prompted the adolescent to use chemicals is easier to access and address through therapy than it is in older clients (Jorgensen, 2001). Also, only a minority of adolescents who abuse chemicals go on to develop a drug-dependency problem (Chatlos, 1996; Kaminer, 1994, 1999; Kriechbaum & Zernig, 2000; Larimer & Kilmer, 2000). Heavy alcohol/drug use is often "adolescence limited" (Kaminer, 1999, p. 277). For most adolescents, recreational substances might be viewed as reflecting no more than a phase of experimentation (Miller, Westerberg, & Waldron, 1995). During this phase of experimentation, the individual is exploring new forms of behavior that are commonly found in the culture in which he or she lives. Only a small percentage of adolescents continues to have problems with chemicals later in life.

The financial incentive for overdiagnosis. The admissions officers of many treatment centers hold that the use of chemicals by adolescents automatically means that there is a drug-abuse problem present. Such treatment professionals, perhaps with an eye more on the balance sheet than on the individual's needs, frequently recommend treatment at the first sign of drug abuse by an adolescent. Harold Swift, president of the world-famous Hazelden Foundation, was quoted by Iggers (1990) as asking "what harm has been done?" if a teenager was mistakenly told that he or she was addicted to chemicals. This question ignores the reality that an unknown percentage of intervention programs actually harm the adolescent (Dishion, McCord, & Poulin, 1999) and assumes that *any* treatment exposure for the adolescent would be a positive experience for that individual.

Because it is against the law for adolescents to buy/use alcohol or recreational chemicals, in many treatment centers "the term substance 'use' has been largely abandoned in favor of substance 'abuse', reflecting the ideology that *any* use among minors constitutes abuse, since it violates the law" (Harrison, Fulkerson, & Beebe, 1998, p. 486, italics added for emphasis). Unfortunately, financial considerations often influence the decision to admit an adolescent to a substance-abuse treatment probram. Such programs became a "lucrative industry" (Bell, 1996, p. 12) in the 1980s, and in order to maximize profits many treatment centers blur the lines between use, abuse, and addiction for adolescents, offering a "one size fits all" type of treatment (Weiner, Abraham, & Lyons, 2001).

Forcing the individual—even if this person is "only" an adolescent—into treatment when he or she does not have a chemical addiction may have lifelong consequences (Peele, 1989). Such action may violate the rights of the individual, and in some states, it is illegal to force an adolescent into treatment against his or her will, even with parental permission (Evans & Sullivan, 2001). Further, even though diagnostic criteria to identify adolescents with substance-use problems have not been developed, many drug rehabilitation programs continue to try to convince the patient that he or she is permenently impaired because of alcohol/drug abuse in their adolescent years and that they will never be "whole" emotionally (Peele, 1989).

Lamentably, there is no research into how this treatment approach will affect the individual's subsequent emotional growth. Nor is there research to determine whether there might be a negative consequence in telling the adolescent at such a young age that he or she is forever an addict, especially when the literature does not support this extreme view.

Statistically, the peak period for substance-use problems is between the ages of 18 and 22, after which the average individual tends to return to a more appropriate pattern of chemical use (Bukstein, 1995). Of those adolescents identified as heavy drinkers at age 18, half were not judged to be heavy drinkers 12 years later (Bukstein, 1994). Thus, the adolescent who might have abused chemicals on a regular basis may or may not go on to develop a problem with chemicals in young adulthood.

The risks of underdiagnosis. Although significant risks are associated with failing to treat adolescents for whom drug use is a serious problem (Evans & Sullivan, 2001), health care providers often fail to identify the majority of adolescent substance abusers (Lee, Garnick, Miller, & Horgan, 2004). The implications of this failure are staggering. Protracted chemical abuse might interfere with the adolescent's ability to develop age-specific coping mechanisms (Kaminer, 1994). Further, adolescent substance abuse holds the potential to cause permanent injuries or expose the individual to chronic, potentially fatal, blood infections.

The last half of the 20th century saw a phenomenal increase in the rate of adolescent suicide, caused at least in part by adolescent drug/alcohol abuse (Bukstein, 1995; Simkin, 2002; Weiner et al., 2001). The exact nature of this relationship is not clear, but researchers do know that chemical abuse is a factor in 70% of all adolescent suicides (Bukstein et al., 1993). Other risk factors include the individual's (a) suffering from a major depression, (b) having thoughts of suicide within the past week, (c) having a family history of suicide and/or depression, (d) facing legal problems, and (e) having access to a handgun within the home (Bukstein et al., 1993; Simkin, 2002).

Substance abuse is a common factor in accidental injuries to adolescents (Chassin & DeLucia, 1996; Loiselle, Baker, Templeton, Schwartz, & Drott, 1994). Of injured adolescents on whom parents gave permission for urine toxicology tests to be conducted, fully 34% tested positive for alcohol and/or drugs (Loiselle et al., 1994). Because alcohol/drug use is frequently associated with traumatic injuries, the authors suggested that urine toxicology tests be a standard part of the treatment protocol for such cases. Indeed, a serious injury might be the first sign of an adolescent substance-use problem (Morrison, 1990).

Thus, the chemical-dependency treatment professional who works with adolescents must attempt to find the middle ground between the underdiagnosis, with all the dangers associated with teenaged drug/

alcohol abuse, and overdiagnosis, which may leave the individual with a false lifelong diagnosis of chemical dependency.

Possible Diagnostic Criteria for Adolescent Drug/Alcohol Problems

Each adolescent will present the assessor with a complex, constantly evolving pattern of strengths and needs (Weiner et al., 2001). Problems such as preexisting mood/anxiety disorders, conduct disorders, or an evolving personality disorder may identify many adolescents who are at high risk for a substance-use problem (Clark et al., 2002; Evans & Sullivan, 2001). Fortunately, a number of possible diagnostic criteria, listed below, are available to help the clinician identify the child/adolescent with a possible substance-use problem (Adger & Werner, 1994; Alexander & Gwyther, 1995; Fuller & Cabanaugh, 1995; Johnson, Hoffmann, & Gerstein, 1996; Jones, 1990; Kriechbaum & Zernig, 2000; Miller, Davies, & Greenwald, 2000; Nunes & Parson, 1995; Simkin, 2002; Tweed, 1998; Wills, McNamara, Vaccaro, & Hirky, 1996; Wills et al., 2001):

- Family history of alcoholism or drug abuse.
- Depression or other psychiatric illness.
- A history of suicide attempt(s).
- Loss of loved one(s).
- Low self-esteem.
- High levels of stress.
- Poor social skills/maladaptive coping mechanisms.
- Problems in relationship with parents (parents are either too permissive or too authoritarian) resulting in lower levels of parental support.
- Living in a single parent/blended family.
- Feelings of alienation/running away from home.
- School problems, or limited commitment to school
- Low expectations for school.
- Family tolerance for deviant behavior.
- Peer tolerance for deviant behavior.
- Attitude accepting of drug use.
- Early cigarette use.
- High levels of engagement with drug-using peers.
- Antisocial behavior/poor self-control.
- Early sexual experience.
- Early experimental drug use.

- Legal problems during adolescence.
- Absence of strong religious beliefs.
- Tendency to seek novel experiences/take risks.
- Unsuccessful attempts to cut back on frequency/intensity of chemical abuse.
- Having experienced alcohol/drug withdrawal symptoms.
- Continued alcohol/drug use in spite of social, physical, or legal consequences.
- Having experienced one or more alcohol-induced blackouts.

Nunes and Parson (1995) suggested that the adolescent who had five or more of the risk factors they suggested (all of which are included in the above list) was virtually guaranteed to have a substance-use problem.

An instrument that has shown some promise as a screening tool is the CRAFFT. A "yes" answer to two or more of the six questions on this instrument suggests a need for a more complete substance-abuse assessment. Three or more "yes" answers were found to identify approximately two-thirds of adolescent substance abusers (Knight, 2005).

Chung et al. (2000) attempted to identify brief screening tools that would be effective in detecting alcohol-abuse problems in adolescents. The authors administered modified versions of the CAGE, the TWEAK and the AUDIT (see Chapter 26) to a sample of 415 adolescents who failed to have a detectable blood alcohol level (BAL) at the time of their admission to a hospital emergency room for treatment of an injury. Eighteen percent of the adolescents were found to have an alcohol-use problem, according to the authors, who recommended that a cut-off score of 4 points be used when the AUDIT is administered to an adolescent. The TWEAK performed best when the cut-off score was only 2 points (Chung et al., 2000). The CAGE was found to be inappropriate for use with most adolescents as it is relatively insensitive to the types of alcohol-related problems that most adolescents will encounter (Monti, 2003).

Age at the onset of alcohol use was found to be one significant factor, with the individual's risk of developing a lifelong alcohol-use problem declining 8% to 14% per year for each year that the individual delayed the initiation of alcohol abuse beyond the age of 12 (Larimer & Kilmer, 2000). Individuals who began to drink before the age of 15 were four times as likely to become alcohol dependent later in life as were those who waited until after the age of 21 to begin to use alcohol (Komro & Toomey, 2002). However, even those who began to use alcohol at an early age were not doomed to remain alcohol dependent. Research has found that only 40% of 12-year-old alcohol abusers would meet the diagnostic criteria for alcohol dependence for the rest of their lives (Larimer & Kilmer, 2000). These conclusions were similar to those of DeWit, Adlaf, Offord, and Obborne (2000) who found that 40% of those individuals with an alcohol-use disorder began to drink before the age of 14, whereas only 10% of those who began to drink after the age of 20 went on to develop such a problem.

According to Martin and Winters (1998), the signs of an individual who is experiencing a substance-use disorder include (a) use of alcohol/drugs under hazardous conditions (driving while under the influence of chemicals, for example), (b) use of alcohol/drugs in a manner that allows *tolerance* to the effects of that chemical to develop, (c) reduction of activities that are not alcohol/drug related, (d) blackouts, (e) loss of consciousness due to chemical abuse, (f) engaging in risky sexual behavior while under the influence of chemicals, (g) the development of craving for the drugs of choice between periods of active use, (h) unsuccessful attempts by the individual to quit on his or her own, and (i) a drop in academic performance due to substance use.

As the adolescent becomes more and more preoccupied with chemical use or demonstrates an interest in an expanding variety of chemicals, she or he might be said to have developed the adolescent equivalent to the progression of chemical use often seen in adults (Evans & Sullivan, 2001). Loss of control for adolescent substance abusers is expressed through the violation of personal rules about drug use (e.g., "I will not use marijuana, tonight," or "I will only drink on weekend parties," or "I will only drink three beers at the party tonight").

Even when the legitimate need for treatment is identified, several factors might interfere with the treatment process, including (a) unrealistic parental expectations for treatment, (b) hidden agendas for treatment by both the adolescent and the parents, (c) parental psychopathology, and (d) parental drug or alcohol abuse (Kaminer & Frances, 1991). Another factor is parental refusal to provide consent for treatment even when the individual has been identified as an alcohol/drug abuser (Kaminer, 1994).

The Special Needs of the Adolescent in a Substance-Abuse Rehabilitation Program

The adolescent who is in need of rehabilitation because of a substance-use problem presents special needs to treatment staff. First, staff should be sufficiently aware of the developmental process that is taking place during adolescence to be able to understand the adolescent's cognitive abilities, strengths, and defensive style. Second, the treatment center should be able to offer a wide variety of services, including the ability to work with the student's educational needs, recreational needs, and possible co-existing psychiatric disorders (Bukstein, 1994). The staff should also address issues peripheral to the adolescent's substance abuse, such as AIDS, birth control, and the individual's vocational needs.

Treatment center staff should be sensitive to the adolescent's cultural heritage and the social status of the adolescent and his or her family (Bukstein, 1994, 1995). A diverse staff helps to ensure that the adolescent is able to find at least one member of the staff to identify with during the treatment program. Also, rehabilitation center staff should attempt to engage family members in the treatment process (Bukstein, 1994). Some of the goals that might be addressed with family members include improving communications among family members, the development of problem-resolution skills, resolution of discipline problems, and identification of problems within the family unit that might undermine the efforts of the treatment center staff (such as undiagnosed substance use by one or both of the parents). Next, the treatment process should also be of sufficient duration to ensure a meaningful change in how the adolescent and the family cope with life's problems (Bukstein, 1995). Adolescents who had a signficant nonusing peer and who remained in treatment/aftercare for approximately a year were found to be less likely to relapse (Latimer et al., 2000). These findings indicate that behavioral change takes time. Thus, the treatment process should be sufficiently long and intense to allow for these necessary components of recovery to take place.

The next component of an adolescent treatment program should be a wide range of specialized social service agencies that is available to the treatment center staff. In addition to their own work with the adolescent, treatment center staff might need to make referrals to juvenile justice, child welfare, and social support agencies (Bukstein, 1994, 1995). As part of the rehabilitation process, involvement in Alcoholics Anonymous or Narcotics Anonymous might be useful for the adolescent, especially if a young person's group is available. Al-anon might be a valuable support for the family members who question their role in the adolescent's substance use. Finally, the goal of the rehabilitation effort should be for the adolescent to achieve a chemically free lifestyle (Bukstein, 1995, 1994).

Adolescents offer treatment center staff unique challenges, but there are also rewards in effectively working with a younger substance abuser. Adolescents are less entrenched in their pathology and thus more responsive to rehabilitation efforts in many cases. Thus, when substance abuse does become an issue for adolescents, rehabilitation offers the opportunity to help them turn their lives around.

Summary

Clearly, children and adolescents are often hidden victims of drug addiction. Yet there is a serious lack of research into the problem of child or adolescent drug use/abuse. Mental health professionals acknowledge that peer pressure and family environment influence the adolescent's chemical-use pattern, but the exact role these forces (or the media) play in shaping the adolescent's behavior is still not known. There are many unanswered questions surrounding the issue of child and adolescent drug use, and in the years to come one might expect to see significant breakthroughs in our understanding of the forces that shape chemical-use beliefs and patterns of use in the young. In the face of this dearth of clinical research, the treatment professional must steer a cautious path between the underdiagnosis of chemical dependency in the younger client and overdiagnosis. Just as surgery carried out on the individual during childhood or adolescence will have lifelong consequences, so will the traumatic experience of being forced into treatment for a problem that may or may not exist. As with surgery, the treatment professional should carefully weigh the potential benefits from such a procedure against the potential for harm to the individual.

During the phase of experimentation, an adolescent might demonstrate repeated and regular use of one or more chemicals, only to settle down in young adulthood to a more acceptable pattern of chemical use (Peele, 1989). One recent study, for example, found that of identified "problem drinkers" during adolescence, fully 53% of the men and 70% of the women were not judged to be problem drinkers 7 years later (Zarek et al., 1987). Thus, the adolescent who might have abused chemicals on a regular basis may or may not develop a problem with chemicals in young adulthood.

Although treatment professionals understand that chemical use during adolescence is a factor in a wide range of emotional and physical problems that develop during this phase of life, the diagnostic criteria needed to identify those adolescents at risk for subsequent problems are still evolving. Thus, treatment professionals have no firm guidelines as to what symptoms might differentiate the adolescent who is passing through a phase of experimental chemical use from the adolescent whose chemical use reflects a more serious problem.

CHAPTER TWENTY-FOUR

Codependency and Enabling

Introduction

Scientists who specialize in the behavioral sciences are often faced with a bewildering array of behaviors that they must both categorize and try to understand. To help with this task, behavioral scientists utilize *constructs* to allow them to express complex ideas to others more easily. An example of a construct is the symbol of a weather front on a meteorological map: In reality there are no lines between different weather cells or firm boundaries between different bodies of air. But by using the analogy of battle lines from World War I, it is possible for meteorologists to quickly summarize data and communicate that information to others.

As substance-abuse rehabilitation professionals began to explore the interpersonal dynamics within the family with a substance abuser, they developed a number of new constructs to help them explain the impact of alcoholism or drug addiction on the family. Two of these constructs were *codependency* and *enabling,* topics that were quite popular in the 1980s and early 1990s but have drifted out of the public spotlight in the past few years. In this chapter, these constructs will be examined.

Enabling

Essentially, to *enable* someone means to *knowingly* behave in such a way as to make it possible for another person to continue to use chemicals without having to pay the natural consequences for that behavior. The concept of enabling emerged in the early 1980s, when some therapists suggested that within some families there seemed almost to be a conspiracy in which at least certain family members supported the continued use of chemicals by the individual with a substance-use

problem. This belief rests in part on the observation that some family members confuse caretaking with the expression of love and thus continue to foster the dysfunctional behavior (Ruben, 2001). Through this process, the behavior of at least certain family members became part of the problem, not the solution. The enabler came to be viewed as doing something that prevented the person with a chemical-use problem from taking advantage of the many opportunities to discover firsthand the cost and consequences of his or her chemical abuse. The spouse, for example, might call the partner's workplace with the excuse that the substance-abusing partner was "sick," when he or she was actually under the influence of chemicals.

A popular misconception is that only family members can enable a substance abuser, but this is not so. An enabler can be a parent, sibling, coworker, neighbor, or even a supervisor. Other potential enablers could be a well-meaning friend, a trusted adviser, a teacher, a therapist, or even a drug rehabilitation worker. Any person who *knowingly* acts in such a way as to protect the alcohol/drug abuser from the natural consequences of his or her behavior might be called an enabler (Johnson Institute, 1987). The same criteria can be applied to those who enable people who are addicted to other drugs of abuse: The *enabler* is any person who knowingly shields the alcohol/drug abusing person from the harmful consequences of her or his behavior.

One does not need to be involved in an ongoing relationship with a person who abuses or is addicted to chemicals to enable that person. People who refuse to provide testimony about a crime they witnessed out of fear or because they do not wish to become involved have enabled the perpetrator of that crime to escape. But the clinical theory suggests that the

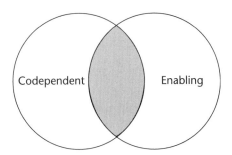

FIGURE 24.1 Relationship between codependency and enabling behaviors.

enabler is usually involved in an ongoing relationship with a person with a substance-use problem.

The relationship between enabling and codependency. The key concept to remember is that an enabler *knowingly* behaves in such a manner as to protect the addicted person from the consequences of his or her behavior. We all behave in ways that, in retrospect, may have enabled someone to avoid consequences that he or she would otherwise have suffered as a result of drug use. This is a point that is often quite confusing to the student of addiction. Codependency and enabling may be and often are found in the same person. However, one may also enable an addicted person without being codependent on that person. *Enabling refers to specific behaviors; codependency refers to a relationship pattern.* Thus, one may enable addiction without being codependent. But the codependent individual, because he or she is in an ongoing relationship with the addict, will also frequently enable the alcohol/drug abusing person. Enabling does not require an ongoing relationship. A tourist who gives a street beggar a gift of money, knowing that the beggar is likely addicted and in need of drugs, might be said to have enabled the beggar, although the tourist is hardly in a meaningful relationship with the beggar.

The issues of codependency and enabling may be thought of as *overlapping* issues. A diagram of such a relationship is shown in Figure 24.1. This diagram illustrates how these two forms of behavior might overlap. But it is most important to remember that enabling and codependency are two different patterns of behavior that are not automatically found in the same person.

Codependency

The concept of codependency emerged in the latter part of the 20th century to become one of the cornerstones of rehabilitation. Surprisingly, codependency is *only* a theoretical construct, and in spite of its popularity in clinical circles there is no standard definition of this term (Heimel, 1990; Sadock & Sadock, 2003; Tavris, 1990). Indeed, mental health professionals have long disagreed on such a basic issue as whether the word was hyphenated (i.e., *co-dependency*) or not (*codependency*) (Beattie, 1989), although the latter spelling eventually won out. But while the professionals debated the spelling of codependency, families began to talk about how they had suffered and often continued to suffer as a result of having "a relationship with a dysfunctional person" (Beattie, 1989, p.7).

Codependency defined. Codependency can be viewed as a condition "characterized by preoccupation and extreme dependence (emotionally, socially, and sometimes physically) on a person or object. Eventually, this dependence . . . becomes a pathological condition that affects the co-dependent in all other relationships" (Wegscheider-Cruse, 1985, p. 2).

A different conceptualization of codependency suggests that it is a relationship in which

> the needs of two people are met in dysfunctional ways. The chemical dependent's need for a care taker, caused by an increasing inability to meet basic survival needs as the drug becomes increasingly intrusive . . . is met by the codependent's need to control the behavior of others who have difficulty caring for themselves. (O'Brien & Gaborit, 1992, p. 129)

In contrast, Gorski (1992) defined codependency as "describing a cluster of symptoms or maladaptive behavior changes associated with living in a committed relationship with either a chemically dependent person or a chronically dysfunctional person either as children or adults" (p. 15). Perhaps the most inclusive definition of the term *codependency* is offered by Zelvin (1997), who suggested that "codependency [is a] problematic or maladaptive seeking of identity, self worth, and fulfillment outside the self" (p. 50).

All these definitions seek to identify different core aspects of codependency: (a) the *overinvolvement* with the dysfunctional family member, (b) the *obsessive* attempts by the codependent person to control the dysfunctional family member's behavior, (c) the extreme tendency to use *external sources of self-worth* (e.g., approval from others, including the dysfunctional person in the relationship), and (d) the *tendency to make personal sacrifices* in an attempt to "cure" the dysfunctional family member of his or her problem behavior.

The dynamics of codependency. In an early work on the subject, Beattie (1987) spoke of codependency as a process in which the individual's life had become unmanageable because she or he is involved in a committed relationship with a person who is addicted to chemicals (Beattie, 1987). Codependent people interpret the commitment as prohibiting them from leaving the addicted person or confronting this person about his or her behavior. In many cases, codependents come to believe that somehow the addicted person's behavior is a reflection upon the codependent. This process of extreme involvement in the life of another person illustrates the boundary violations often seen in codependency; it is called *enmeshment.*

As a result of enmeshment, the codependent person believes that "*your* behavior is a reflection on *me*" and thus will view inappropriate behavior by the significant other as a threat to the codependent's self-esteem. To avoid this threat to self-worth, the codependent person often becomes obsessed with the need to control the behavior of the person who is addicted to chemicals, assuming responsibility for decisions or events not normally under his or her control (Beattie, 1987). An extreme example of this process is the codependent person who will assume responsibility for the significant other's recreational chemical use, as when the codependent person takes the blame for "causing" the alcoholic spouse to go out on a binge after a fight. "It's all my fault that he or she went out drinking" is a common belief of the codependent partner.

Thus, the codependent person is often *preoccupied* (Wegscheider-Cruse, 1985) or *obsessed* (Beattie, 1989) with controlling the behavior of the significant other. This obsession can extend to the point that the codependent will try to control the addict's drug use or all of the partner's life. An excellent example of this obsessive attempt to control the significant other's behavior took place several years ago. A staff psychologist at a maximum security penitentiary for men in the Midwest

received a telephone call from the elderly mother of an inmate. She asked the psychologist to "make sure that the man who shares my son's cell is a good influence" on her son, because "there are a lot of bad men in that prison, and I don't want him falling in with a bad crowd!"

The woman in this case overlooked the grim reality that her son was not in prison simply for singing off-key in choir practice and that he had been to prison on several different occasions for various crimes. Rather than let him live his life and try to get on with hers, she continued to worry about how to "cure" him of his behavior problem. She continued to treat him as a child, was overly involved in his life, and was quite upset at the suggestion that it might be time to let her son learn to *suffer* (and perhaps learn from) *the consequences of his own behavior.* This woman had yet to learn how to *detach* from her son's behavior. *Detachment* is one of the cornerstones of the recovery process (Brown & Lewis, 1995). By learning to detach and separate from her dysfunctional son, this woman could learn to let go and cease in her attempt to control *his* life. But with the best of intentions, she remains overinvolved in her son's life.

The rules of codependency. Although the codependent person often feels as if he or she is going crazy, an outside observer will notice that there are certain patterns or "rules" to codependent behavior. Beattie (1989) identified several of these:

1. It's not okay for me to feel.
2. It's not okay for me to have problems.
3. It's not okay for me to have fun.
4. I'm not lovable.
5. I'm not good enough.
6. If people act bad or crazy, I'm responsible.

These rules are actively transmitted from one partner in the relationship to the other, setting the pattern for codependency. "If you weren't so unreasonable, I would never have gone out drinking last night!" is a common example of rule "6." "You shouldn't have tried in the first place!" might enforce rules 2, 3, 4, and 5.

Are codependents born or made? Proponents of the concept suggest that codependency is a *learned behavior,* often as a result of the codependent individual's having been physically or sexually abused in childhood (Knauer, 2002). In dysfunctional homes, caretaking behaviors are often learned as a way to avoid conflict (Ruben, 2001). As a result of childhood abuse experiences, the codependent individual becomes exceptionally tolerant of boundary violations, and attempts to achieve a sense of control over his or her personal life by attempting to "fix" the dysfunctional partner (Knauer, 2002; Ruben, 2001).

Zelvin (1997) identified three routes to codependency: (a) being in a close relationship with an alcohol/drug abuser, (b) growing up in a dysfunctional family, and (c) being socialized into accepting a codependent role. Each of these routes allows codependent behaviors to be passed from one generation to another. The first two routes reflect the impact of a chaotic life on the individual. A very good example of the third route might be seen in the parent who screams at a child who wants to go to college with the taunt, "You're too dumb to go to college! The best that you can hope for is that somebody is stupid enough to marry you and take care of you!" Through this and a multitude of other boundary violations, the codependent individual comes to learn that he or she is "less than" others and not worthy of ordinary levels of respect or achievement (Knauer, 2002).

Clinicians have long recognized that people frequently try to resolve "unfinished business" from their childhood by recreating significant early relationships in their adult lives (Scarf, 1980). Feeling as if their lives were out of control, with feelings of low self-esteem and worthlessness, the codependent person almost becomes addicted to a significant other. This pseudo-addiction may reflect the individual's fear of abandonment or other unresolved issues from childhood (Knauer, 2002).

As the dysfunctional elements of a relationship develop, the codependent person may feel imprisoned in the relationship. The codependent person becomes obsessed with "fixing" what is wrong with the marriage or the family. Communications, if they ever existed in the relationship, grind to a stop. In contrast to the healthy relationship, where partners confront unhealthy elements of their relationship and work on resolving them, in the codependent relationship this "working through" process is stalled. If one partner does express some concern over a possible problem, the other partner will move to prevent the problem from being clearly identified, or if it is identified, resolved. Stability is seen as being of critical importance.

One way this drive to maintain stability is seen is in the avoidance of any discussion of the diseased individual's substance-use problem. The codependent individual might become afraid to say the "wrong" thing, talk to the "wrong people," or even to assert selfhood in any way, lest he or she displease the addicted partner. The codependent person comes to feel trapped: unable to leave the sick partner but also unable to feel fulfilled in the relationship.

Codependency and self-esteem. In an attempt to live up to the unspoken rules of codependency, the codependent experiences a great deal of emotional pain. One core trait of codependent people is low self-esteem (Craig, 2004; Zerwekh & Michaels, 1989). Unfortunately, "co-dependents frequently appear normal, which in our culture is associated with a healthy ego. Nevertheless, they also describe themselves as 'dying on the inside,' which is indicative of low self-worth or esteem" (p. 111). Because of low self-esteem, the codependent person often comes to measure personal worth by how well she or he can take care of/please/fix the dysfunctional partner. Another way that codependent individuals measure self-worth is through the sacrifices they make for significant others (Miller, 1988). In this way, codependents substitute an external measure of personal worth for their inability to generate *self*-worth.

Another core characteristic of codependent people is their intense desire to *control* the behavior of the addicted person (Craig, 2004). They have difficulty recognizing *boundaries*, often tolerating role reversals within the relationship and accepting responsibility for issues beyond their control (Craig, 2004). Codependent people also utilize *denial* to avoid facing truths that threaten their sense of security; they are often prone to *depression* as well as feelings of *hopelessness* and *helplessness* (Craig, 2004). They often demonstrate *emotional constriction* to avoid facing such negative emotions, living rigid, compulsive lifestyles that are externally focused on the other person's behavior (Craig, 2004).

It is surprising to see that in spite of all of their emotional pain many codependent persons do not *want* to end their pain. Rather, they seem to be locked into their codependency, often resisting efforts by friends or mental health professionals to help them escape from their unhappy lifestyles. For the

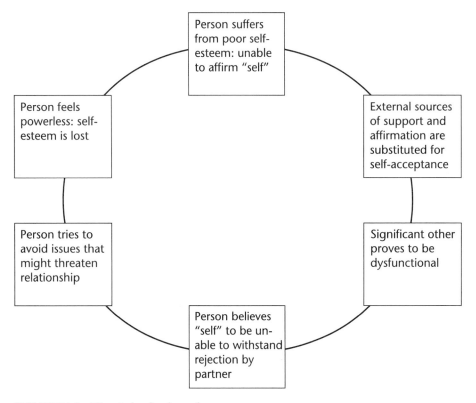

FIGURE 24.2   The circle of codependency.

codependent person, there is a reward for enduring their pain! Many people feel a sense of moral victory through suffering at the hands of another (Shapiro, 1981). By suffering at the hands of a dysfunctional spouse, the codependent individual is able to accuse "the offender by pointing at his victim; it keeps alive in the mind's record an injustice committed, a score unsettled" (p. 115). For such a person, this suffering is "a necessity, a principled act of will, from which he cannot release himself without losing his self-respect and feeling more deeply and finally defeated, humiliated, and powerless" (Shapiro, 1981, p. 115). Through this process, the trials and suffering imposed on the codependent person become almost a badge of honor, a defense against the admission of personal powerlessness or worthlessness. In such cases, it is not uncommon for the codependent person to affirm personal worth by being willing to "carry the cross" of another person's addiction or dysfunctional behavior.

The cycle of codependency. Once the cycle of codependency has started, it takes on a life of its own. A graphic representation of this cycle is shown in Figure 24.2. Notice that in the figure there are two necessary components. First, one partner, the codependent, suffers from low self-esteem. If one partner *does not* suffer from low self-esteem, he or she would be able to affirm "self." Such a person would back away from a dysfunctional partner or at the very least find a way to cope without depending on the dysfunctional partner's approval. In such a case, it is unlikely that a codependent relationship pattern would evolve. Second, the significant other must be dysfunctional. If the partner were to be emotionally healthy, he or she would affirm the codependent, breaking the cycle.

Patterns of codependency. In the last quarter of the 20th century, substance-abuse rehabilitation professionals attempted to identify common behavioral styles that might identify the codependent person. They found a number of such roles (Craig, 2004; Ellis, McInerney, DiGiuseppe, & Yeager, 1988):

Apathetic person: Has simply stopped caring (might also be called a "silent sufferer").

Approval seeker: Constantly seeks the approval/acceptance of the partner.

Caretaker: Devotes his or her life to taking care of the addicted person.

Coconspirator: Will undermine the efforts of the addicted person to change his or her lifestyle, helping to continue the dysfunctional behaviors (also called a *Joiner*).

Controller: Engages in controlling behaviors in an attempt to control every aspect of their lives, which they feel (often with justification) are out of control.

Martyr: Comes to measure self-worth by the sacrifices he or she makes in life with the addicted individual.

Messiah: Fights against the addict's chemical use but does so in such a way that the addict is never forced to experience the consequences of his or her behavior.

Persecutor: Blames everybody *but* the addicted person for any problems, expressing anger and bitterness that the Martyr is unable to express.

Mental health and substance-abuse rehabilitation professionals often encounter family members of an addicted person who exhibit some or all of the behaviors of these patterns. A common example of a coconspirator is the woman who might seek marital counseling because her husband would not limit his cocaine use to the $100 a week that she set aside in the family budget for his drug use, or the couple who requests marital counseling for one partner's angry outbursts but who do not continue once the subject of substance abuse on the part of one or both partners is broached.

Another all too common example of the coconspirator is the spouse who drinks or who uses chemicals along with the addicted person in the hope of somehow controlling his or her chemical use. For example, substance-abuse rehabilitation professionals know that it is quite common for a spouse to go to a bar with the alcohol abusing/dependent partner in the hope that he or she might teach the partner how to drink in a "responsible" manner. Such efforts to join with the spouse with the substance-use problem and change him or her from within are usually doomed to failure. After all, if the addicted spouse were capable of drinking or using chemicals responsibly, he or she wouldn't be addicted in the first place.

A very good example of the *messiah* might be seen in the father of an opiate-dependent young adult woman who was in a mixed group of family members and other opiate-addicted patients during "family day" at a treatment center. The father admitted tearfully that he had taken out a personal loan more than once to pay off his daughter's drug debts, which he viewed as a measure of how much he loved his daughter. Another group member asked why the father would do this. After all, the second person said, if the father pays off her debts, she will not have to worry about having to pay her drug debts herself. The father responded that if he did not, his daughter "might leave us!" Several group members then suggested to this parent that that would not be a bad thing as his daughter might need to suffer some consequences on her own in order to "hit bottom" and accept the need to address her addiction to chemicals. The father was silent for a moment, then said "Oh, I couldn't do that! She's not ready to assume responsibility for herself yet!"

The relationship between codependency and emotional health. There is a very real tendency for some to *over-identify* with the codependency concept. As Beattie (quoted in Tavris, 1992), pointed out, there are those who believe that codependency is "anything, and everyone is codependent" (p. 194). This is an extreme position that overlooks the fact that many of the same characteristics that define codependency are also found in healthy human relationships. Only a few "saints and hermits" (Tavris, 1990, p. A21) fail to demonstrate at least some of the characteristics of the so-called codependent individual.

Even Wegscheider-Cruse and Cruse (1990), strong advocates of the codependency movement, admitted that "codependency is an exaggeration of normal personality traits" (p. 28). But in some cases these traits become so pronounced that the individual "becomes disabled (disease of codependency)" (p. 28). To further

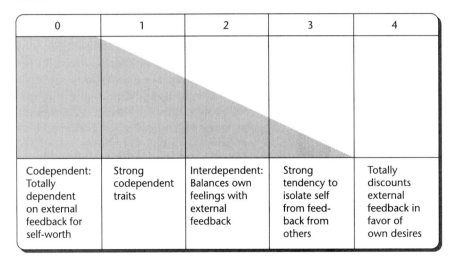

0	1	2	3	4
Codependent: Totally dependent on external feedback for self-worth	Strong codependent traits	Interdependent: Balances own feelings with external feedback	Strong tendency to isolate self from feed-back from others	Totally discounts external feedback in favor of own desires

FIGURE 24.3   The continuum between isolation and dependency.

complicate matters, because of the way that love is viewed within this society, there is a strong relationship between love and codependency (Zelvin, 1997). This is because society places much emphasis on the blending of identities or the loss of ego boundaries in love relationships, making the individual vulnerable to codependency (Zelvin, 1997). This is in sharp contrast to many personality patterns, where the individual's ego boundaries are so intensely defended that he or she is virtually isolated from interpersonal feedback. Between these two extremes is an *interdependency* that is the hallmark of healthy relationships. The continuum that includes the endpoints of codependency on one end and the total affirmation of the ego's boundaries on the other end is shown in Figure 24.3.

There are degrees of codependency, just as there are degrees of ego affirmation and isolation from interpersonal feedback. Few of us are at either extreme, and the majority of people fall somewhere in the middle, exhibiting tendencies both to behave in codependent ways and to be overly isolated from feedback from others.

Reactions to the Concept of Codependency

The roots of the concept of *codependency* can be traced to M. L. Lewis's (1937) hypothesis that the spouse of the alcohol-dependent person (usually the wife) has

a disturbed personality and that she tries to resolve her own neurotic conflicts through marriage to an alcohol-dependent partner. Through these efforts, the partner of the alcohol-dependent person is now identified as herself being dysfunctional. From the time that Lewis presented his hypothesis to the present, mental health professionals have struggled to determine whether codependency is a legitimate form of psychopathology. Most certainly, given the fact that it has been characterized as "an addiction, a personality disorder, a psychsocial condition, and an interpersonal style" (Hurcom, Copello, & Orford, 2000, p. 487), one could argue that it is little more than a "garbage can" diagnosis, which communicates little useful information about the patient.

Many professionals believe that codependency is a *pseudo*-problem more than a legitimate mental health concern. This position would seem to be correct as research into codependency and enabling all but disappeared from the professional journals by the first few years of the 21st century. If it were a legitimate problem in the 1980s and the 1990s, like coronary artery or kidney disease in the realm of physical medicine, what happened to it in the early years of the 21st century? Coronary artery disease remains the focus of a significant percentage of research articles in the medical literature, and entire journals are devoted to the subject of heart disease and kidney disorders.

In sharp contrast, the topic of codependency has virtually disappeared from professional journals.

One very real challenge to the concept of codependency is that it *disempowers* the individual and makes relationship problems a medical problem (Hurcom et al., 2000). In contrast to most effective forms of psychotherapy, codependency *reduces the individual's power base*. The concept of codependency is based on traditional 12-Step program beliefs that the "disease" of codependency is progressive and that people can come to terms with their codependency only through the aid of the appropriate "self-help" group (Randle, Estes, & Cone, 1999).

Proponents of the concept of codependency point out that individuals diagnosed as having this disorder tend to have similar life experiences and similar personality traits. However, such uniformity in patient histories and presenting symptoms might be an artifact introduced into the therapeutic relationship by therapist expectations, selective attention to symptoms that confirm rather than dispute the diagnosis, and self-fulfilling vague diagnostic criteria that guarantee that virtually everybody will qualify for the condition of codependency (Randle et al., 1999). The very nature of the defining characteristics of the codependent person virtually guarantees that any given individual will meet at least one of the defining "criteria" (Tarvis, 1992; Walker, 1996).

One reason for the uniformity of codependency is the basic assumption that up to 99% of all people are raised in a "dysfunctional" home. Building on this foundation, much of the codependency literature strives to convince the reader that she or he is "doomed to suffer as a result of the trauma of childhood travails" (Japenga, 1991, p. 174). People are "encouraged to see themselves as victims of family life rather than self-determining participants" (Kaminer, 1992, p. 13). Those who challenge the concept of codependency point out that the family is viewed as nothing more than an "incubator of disease" (Kaminer, 1992, p. 12). Within this incubator, the helpless child is infected with one or more dread conditions that he or she will have to struggle with forever unless salvation is achieved through the appropriate 12-Step group.

Yet little research evidence suggests that a child raised in a "dysfunctional" home is automatically doomed. Indeed, many, perhaps a majority, of those who are exposed to even extreme conditions in childhood find a way to adjust, survive, and fulfill their life goals (Garbarino, Dubrow, Kostelny, & Pardo, 1992). Admittedly, some children will suffer deep emotional scars as a result of childhood trauma, but the evidence does not suggest children are *automatically* doomed to suffer if their home life is less than perfect. One reason for this is that children are naturally resilient (Masten, 2001; Wolin & Wolin, 1993, 1995). Far from being rare, resilience appears to be common in children (Bonanno, 2004). This natural resilience helps them not only weather the emotional storms of childhood but of later adult life as well. Indeed, the very fact that the child's environment *is* dysfunctional might serve as an impetus toward the development of positive emotional growth in many cases (Garbarino et al., 1992; Wolin & Wolin, 1993, 1995). Proponents of codependency do not appear to accept the possibility of individual resilience. Rather, they suggest that *all* children raised in a dysfunctional environment have emotional scars that must be addressed.

Another objection to the concept of codependency is that self-help groups that are supposed to help the individual actually tend to "promote dependency under the guise of recovery" (Katz & Liu, 1991, p. xii). To maintain membership and the identity as a group member, the individual is expected to produce material that is consistent with the expectations of the group, which is to say to continue to behave (and think) in a "codependent" manner (Randle et al., 1999). The codependency model presents the individual with a subtle demand that she or he not grow and achieve a sense of autonomy but conform to a standard recipe for salvation and grace (Kaminer, 1992). According to the codependency model, no matter how trivial or serious the trauma, there is just one model for recovery. If the individual resists the various "insights" offered by different books on codependency, that person is automatically viewed as being in "denial" (Kaminer, 1992; Katz & Liu, 1991). There is no room for individuality in the codependency model as it is applied to therapeutic situations.

Another challenge to the codependency movement was based on the theory (frequently advanced in different books on the subject) that all suffering is relative. In reality, it is virtually impossible to equate degrees of suffering (Kaminer, 1992). To illustrate, consider two hypothetical children in two different families. Both were the oldest boys in a family of three children with an alcoholic father. In the first family, the father was a "happy" drunk who would drink each evening after work, tell a few "funny" jokes, watch television, and fall asleep in his favorite chair. In the second family, the father would drink each evening after work and become violently angry. He would physically abuse his wife and children and on occasion fire a rifle at family members. The impact of these two father on their respective families would be quite different. Yet in the literature on codependency, both events are treated as being of equal importance.

Critics of the codependency movement have pointed out that the theory of codependency seems to excuse the addicted individual from all responsibility for his or her behavior (Roehling, Koelbel, & Rutgers, 1994; Tavris, 1990). In effect, through the "disease" of codependency, blame is shifted from the individual with the substance-use problem to his or her significant other, who is said to "enable" the unhealthy behaviors of the afflicted person to continue. Further, the codependency model pathologizes the spouse for engaging in behaviors that might very well be role specific, simply because the partner is addicted to alcohol (Hurcom et al., 2000). The foundation of the codependency movement rests on the *family disease model* of family therapy, which holds that "the solution is for each family member to recognize that he or she has a disease" (Fals-Stewart, O'Farrell, & Birchler, 2003, p. 148) either of addiction or codependency.

Within this model, family members are judged not on their own accomplishments but on whether the addicted family member is able to abstain from chemicals. This is an apparent extension of Lewis's (1937) research, cited earlier in this chapter. Family members are thus guilty of "addiction by association" (Katz & Liu, 1991, p. 13). An illustration of this concept might be seen in the observation that entire communities, states, and even nations might be described as codependent (Hurcom et al., 2000). Through the application of the concept of codependency, the problem becomes not that one parent is alcohol dependent, physically or sexually abusive of the family members, or possibly both emotionally inappropriate and absent. Rather, the problem is that the *family* members suffer from the disease of codependency!

Although Lewis's (1937) work was advanced almost three-quarters of a century ago, it was recycled and refor-

mulated as a theory (popular in the 1950s) that the spouse of the alcoholic is a "co-alcoholic" (Sher, 1991; Simmons, 1991). This theory assumed that the co-alcoholic is as much in need of treatment as is the alcoholic, on the assumption that he or she (a) helped to bring about the other's alcoholism, (b) currently continues to support it, and (c) must accordingly be quite disturbed. These beliefs reflect the historical fact that spouses of alcoholics have "been blamed and pathologized for their partner's drinking" (Hurcom et al., 2000, p. 473). This theory continues to survive even though researchers have failed to find any evidence that the spouse of the alcoholic has any predictable form of psychopathology (Tavris, 1992). But the discredited theory of co-alcoholism has been resurrected in the guise of "codependency."

Nor is codependency limited to the world of addiction. It has even been suggested (O'Brien & Gaborit, 1992) that codependency is a separate condition, or even an addiction in its own right (Knauer, 2002). However, there is little evidence to support the contention that codependency activates the pleasure center of the brain, as is the case with substance-use disorders. Another challenge to the concept of codependency rests on the lack of firm parameters. The term is vague, without foundation. Consider M. Scott Peck's definition of codependency as "a relationship in which the partners cater to—and thereby encourage—each other's weaknesses" (1997b, p. 180). This would certainly seem to be an apt definition of virtually all relationships, not just those that are "codependent," as we all tend to encourage others to behave in unhealthy ways from time to time.

Many critics of the concept of codependency point out that it rests on little more than a foundation of "new age" rhetoric. For example, the husband and wife team of Wegecheder-Cruse and Cruse (1990) speak knowingly of how codependency results from the "interaction between one's own manufactured 'brain chemicals' (having to do with our reinforcement center) and one's behavior that stimulates the brain to establish compulsive and addictive behavior processes" (p. 12). The authors conclude that codependency is a disease of the brain, on the grounds that "we have a brain that gives us an excessive rush [and] we get into self-defeating behaviors that keep the rush coming (codependency)" (pp. 12–13).

What the authors overlook is that there is no scientific evidence to support this theory. Science has failed, to date, to find evidence of "an excessive rush."[1] Nor have scientists found evidence to suggest that people tend to "get into self-defeating behaviors that keep the rush coming." Indeed, such a position tends to be a contradiction: If human beings as a species engaged in self-defeating behaviors simply for the "rush," how would *homo sapiens* ever have survived?

In considering the construct of codependency, there is a need for a sense of balance. Admittedly, there are those people who experience significant hardships because of their involvement in an ongoing relationship with an addict. But not every person who is in such a relationship is codependent. Indeed, there is little evidence to support the concept of codependency, according to its detractors. Further, according to the codependency model, the victim must somehow come to terms with his or her emotional pain without blaming the substance abuser for virtually anything the abuser might have done. In other words,

> according to adherents of this theory, families of alcoholics cannot . . . hold them responsible for the abuse. Somehow the victim must get well by dint of pure self-analysis, meditation and prayer, without reference to the social, economic, legal and psychological forces that create dysfunctional

families in the first place. (University of California, Berkeley, 1990a, p. 7)

For many people, this is an impossible task.

Summary

In the late 1970s, substance abuse professionals were introduced to a new way of viewing the substance-abusing person and his or her support system. The constructs of "codependency" and "enabling" were introduced as a way of explaining how the members of the substance abuser's support system behaved. However, since these constructs were introduced, the fact that they are just theoretical constructs has been forgotten. Proponents have seized upon them and suggested that they are real manifestations of a new "disease"—that of "codependency." In the last decade, a battle has raged over whether these constructs are indeed real and how to apply this new disorder to the problem of substance-related interpersonal dysfunctions.

That the partner of the alcohol-dependent person might play a role in the development or maintenance of the alcohol dependence was first suggested in 1937 by M. L. Lewis. Another version of this theory surfaced in the 1950s, when it was suggested that the alcoholic spouse was a "co-alcoholic." These theories were last discredited in the 1960s, but seem to have found new life under the guise of codependency. Ultimately, these constructs might be said to still be evolving, and the role that they will play in the understanding and rehabilitation of substance abusers remains to be determined.

[1]Out of curiosity, answer this: What would be a "sufficient" rush? If something exists to excess, does this not imply that there is a middle ground where there is a sufficient supply of this thing, without it being present in excess?

CHAPTER TWENTY-FIVE

Addiction and the Family

Outside of residence in a concentration camp, there are very few sustained human experiences that make one the recipient of as much sadism as does being a close family member of an alcoholic. (Vaillant, 1995, p. 22)

Introduction

As Vaillant (1995) observed, the experience of living in a family with an alcohol-dependent person has a profound impact on the spouse and the children. Unfortunately, this experience is quite common, with an estimated 25% of the children in the United States being exposed to alcohol abuse or dependence at some point in their lives (Anda et al., 2002). In spite of this fact, there has been very little research into the impact of alcohol on the marital unit (Leonard & Roberts, 1996) and virtually none on the impact of drug abuse/addiction on the marital partner or the children of that couple (Merikangas, Dierker, & Szatmari, 1998). In this chapter, what is known and what is suspected about the impact of chemical abuse on the family will be explored.

Scope of the Problem

Researchers believe that 11 million children or adolescents are being raised in a home where there is at least one parent who is dependent on alcohol or drugs (Black, 2003). Twenty percent of these children are in homes where both parents have substance-use problems (Black, 2003). It is believed that *one of every six individuals* in the United States is or was raised in a home with at least one alcohol-dependent parent (Kelly & Myers, 1996).

Addiction and Marriage

Unfortunately, the relationship between alcohol/drug abuse and family dynamics is both extremely complex and poorly understood. For example, it was found that marriages in which there were wide discrepancies in the alcohol-use patterns of the partners tended to demonstrate lower levels of intimacy than marriages in which the alcohol-use patterns of the partners were similar (Roberts & Leonard, 1998). To further complicate matters, it is virtually impossible to identify a specific area of a marriage/family that is affected *only* by the alcohol abuse of one or both partners (McCrady & Epstein, 1995). Problems within the marital unit become intertwined, with parental alcoholism impacting virtually every other aspect of the family's life. But while it is almost impossible to determine which part of the problem is due to the parental alcoholism, it is known that there is a reciprocal relationship between alcohol/drug use and marital problems (O'Farrell, 1995).

Clinicians are often confronted by the spouse of the addicted person who wonders why the partner has a substance-use problem when he or she seemed so normal during the courtship period. The answer to this dilemma is that during the courtship phase and the first year of marriage, alcohol abusers commonly reduce their alcohol intake (Leonard & Mudar, 2003; Leonard & Roberts, 1996). There is also a shift in relationship patterns following marriage, as evidenced by the observation that husbands tend to drop friends whose alcohol use does not correspond with their own and to spend less time in social activities (or more time with the partner, depending on how you look at it) in the first year of marriage (Leonard & Mudar, 2003; Leonard & Roberts, 1996).

Researchers have found that the individual's drinking preference seems to play a role in the choice of a marital partner. In many cases people select a partner whose alcohol use is very similar to their own. When there is a discrepancy in the alcohol-use pattern of the partners, there are several possible adjustments: First, in the pattern that is seen in the majority of cases, each individual will adjust his or her alcohol use until it is more consistent with that of the partner. However, in a minority of cases, a wide discrepancy in the alcohol-use pattern of the partners evolves, and there is a negative impact on the marriage or the family (Roberts & Leonard, 1998).

The family system's perspective. As a general rule, people tend to marry those who have achieved similar levels of "differentiation of self" (Bowen, 1985, p. 263). The concept of differentiation is "roughly equivalent to the concept of emotional maturity" (Bowen, 1985, p. 263).

A primary developmental task is for the individual to separate from his or her parents (*individuate*) and to resolve the various emotional attachments to the parents that evolved during childhood. Through this process, the relationship between the parent and the child should evolve as the child becomes more and more independent. In the healthy family, this process is encouraged. But in unhealthy families, adult children are often encouraged to put the family's needs before their own (Knauer, 2002). Rather than progress through the various stages of *individuation* (Bowen, 1985), the normal growth process is subverted to meet the needs of significant others.

For the first few years following birth, children are almost totally dependent on their parents. As they mature, they become less and and less dependent on their parents, communicating their growing independence by a variety of means. In healthy families, the parents gradually withdraw their control as children become more capable of independent living. But just as the parents may encourage children's emotional growth, they might also inhibit it. If the parents teach their children that they must take care of others, the children may mistakenly come to believe that if they cannot provide the service for which they are valued (e.g., caretaking, being a sexual object), others will not care for them (Knauer, 2002). This is often the outcome of the home where there is an alcohol-dependent parent.

Communication patterns within the alcohol-impacted home are often quite poor (McCrady & Epstein, 1995). One reason for this is parental psychopathology. Because of their own lack of emotional maturity, parents are unable to provide the proper guidance and support to the maturing children. In many cases, these parents interpret the children's natural predilection to mature and become less dependent on them as a threat. The parents may then respond by smothering the children's independence under layers of parental control to ensure that the family environment does not change. As boundaries are violated and children are threatened with parental abandonment (physical, emotional, or both), they learn to interpret as something negative their natural desire to explore and to become self-reliant. Autonomy becomes a source of shame, and if this shame is experienced for too long or too intensely, it becomes so painful for the children that they begin to detach the "self" from an awareness of their feelings in order to cope.

In this manner, children come to view their natural inclination to individuate not as a source of pride but as a threat to familial stability. Rather than learning autonomy, they learn to view themselves as being weak, incompetent, unable to stand alone, and shameful. For some individuals, this shame becomes a central feature of the self-concept, and the person comes to believe that "I am not worthy—I am spoiled—damaged—unable to cope on my own." Being unable to "nuture" the "self," the individual becomes dependent on external sources of feedback and support, which might be provided either by continued dependency on the parents or a parental substitute. Because we look for a marital partner with a similar level of individuation as our own (Bowen, 1985), we then replace the emotionally damaged parent with a partner who is also emotionally damaged, allowing us to relive the same conflicts in our marriage that we had with our parents. If neither partner has achieved a significant degree of individuation, each would look to the partner to meet his or her emotional needs (Bowen, 1985). Within this marriage further emotional growth of either partner is viewed as a threat to the stability of the marital unit, especially if such growth threatens to break through the layers of denial that each partner has used to insulate the "self" from the partners' respective shame-based identities. In response, they both turn away from the potential for growth and accept a form of pseudo-intimacy and the illusion of control offered by alcohol or chemicals.

Characteristics of the alcohol-abusing marriage. Remember that the individual's first priority is the service of his or her addiction. Within the marriage where one member is an alcohol abuser or addict, issues of control become important as each person struggles to achieve some sense of order within the unstable marital unit. Control often becomes a central theme within the marriage, and *conditional* love becomes one of the avenues through which each tries to control the other. Conditional love finds expression in a number of demands, such as (a) you must behave in a certain way if you want to be loved by me, supported by me, and so on; (b) if you don't meet my demands, I will leave you, withdraw my love from you, not give you money, go out and get drunk, or abuse you physically.

The alcohol-dependent person strives to build a support system that will enable him or her to continue to use alcohol (Brown, 1985). A significant part of this support system is the individual's marriage, which the alcohol-dependent person struggles to control and manage. At the same time, the partner struggles to cope with the spouse's addiction to alcohol. One tool that is frequently utilized by the partner of an alcohol-dependent person is *emotional withdrawal.* Almost 50% of those married to an alcohol-abusing spouse use this tactic to cope at least occasionally (Hurcom, Copello, & Orford, 2000). Emotional withdrawal is more a *means of control* than the more active process of *detachment.* The nonabusing spouse may withdraw from the partner hoping that this will reduce or stop the substance abuse, but more often than not it has the opposite effect.

In contrast to withdrawal, detachment is an active process that reflects *unconditional love* while affirming the separate identities of the marital partners. In effect, the nondrinking spouse affirms that "your behavior is *not* a reflection of me." As part of the process of detachment, the individual must learn appropriate interpersonal *boundaries.* Boundary violations are rife in the home with an alcohol-dependent member (Black, 2003). As a result of the lack of boundaries, each family member develops an unnatural involvement in the life of the other family members. In the natural growth process that results in individuation, the child must learn to establish boundaries between "self" and "other"; in the alcoholic home, however, the child learns to become *enmeshed* in the lives of others. Each person has been trained to believe that he or she is responsible for every other member of the family. The circle of shame is then complete, insulating the alcoholic from responsibility for his or her addiction and behavior.

Addiction and the Family

From the family system's perspective, the treatment of an addictive disorder involves the identification and ultimately the modification of whatever dysfunctional family system allowed the development and maintenance of the addiction in the first place (Bowen, 1985). In the alcoholic marriage, the alcoholism becomes a "secret partner" first of the marriage and ultimately of the family. Within the framework of this "family secret," the individual's addiction becomes the dominating force around which the family's rules and rituals are centered (Brown, 1985). Parental injunctions then serve to transmit the "secret" to the children, allowing the dysfunctional communication system to be passed from one generation to the next. Such parental injunctions might include "There is no alcoholism in this home," and "Don't you dare talk about it!" The child being raised in this web of contradictory injunctions is taught that his or her perception of what is going on is never (or at best only rarely) correct, a situation that fosters overdependence on others for guidance to what is "correct" thinking in a given situation (Linehan, 1993).

One of the developmental tasks facing a new child is learning to adapt to the environment into which he or she was born. In addition to the normal adaptations that the child faces, in the home where one or both parents is alcohol dependent, the whole family must learn to cope with the parental alcoholism (Ackerman, 1983). One way is for the family to structure itself so that the alcoholic parent is actually allowed to continue drinking. Although this is often surprising to an outside observer, keep in mind that there are rewards for this behavior. For example, in some families, one partner's alcohol abuse could be viewed as a stabilizing influence within the family unit (Hurcom et al., 2000). In such cases, the alcohol use of one parent might help the marital/family unit cope with other problems that suddenly spring to life (Heath & Stanton, 1998).

For the person with an alcohol-use problem, the act of marriage provides the individual with an opportunity to form a "drinking partnership" (Leonard & Roberts, 1996, p. 194) with the partner. A reflection of this partnership might be seen in the role reversal (Ackerman, 1983) that develops in such families. The alcohol-dependent member will give up some of the power and roles she or he would normally hold within the marital/family unit in return for opportunities to drink. In time, this role reversal might span two or even three generations as an unhealthy state of interlocking dependency patterns evolves within that family. Often marital partners or family members find themselves holding unusually powerful positions within the new family constellation, as the family adapts itself to the individual's alcoholism.

The process of adaptation to familial rules, values, and beliefs is a normal part of family life (Bradshaw, 1988a). However, when these guides are warped by a dysfunctional partner, the entire family must struggle to adapt to the resulting unhealthy family themes. This adjusting to the addiction of one member takes place without external guidance or support. Members are left on their own as they struggle to come to terms with the problems within the family, and they often come to use the very same defense mechanisms so characteristic of addicted individuals: denial, rationalization, and projection.[1]

As the other family members assume responsibilities formerly held by the addicted member of the family, the addicted individual becomes less and less responsible for his or her family duties and less involved in the family life. An older brother assumes the responsibility for discipline of the children, or a daughter makes sure that the children are fed each night before they go to bed. In each case, one of the children has assumed a parental responsibility left vacant, perhaps because of alcoholism.

The alcohol-dependent parent is hardly a passive participant in teaching the family to accommodate his or her alcohol dependence. One of the weapons that is often employed to shape the family is fear, either alone or in combination with guilt and threats (both real and imagined). "If you don't do what I want, I will go out drinking again, and it will be *your* fault!" is a common refrain. So effective are the threats and assaults of the addicted partner that within some families it is possible to find "chaos (covert or overt), inconsistency, unpredictability, blurring of boundaries, unclear roles, arbitrariness, changing logic, and perhaps violence and incest" (Brown & Lewis, 1995, p. 285). It is within this atmosphere that the family as a unit, and each individual member, must attempt to achieve some degree of stability.

Within such a marital/family unit a form of *pseudo-stability* might be unconsciously accepted by the family members. Although the members are uncomfortable with the alcohol/drug addiction of one member, they might be quite happy with the current distribution of power, responsibility, and the temporary peace and quiet that results from this state of pseudo-stability. *Peace at any cost* becomes the central theme of the family, and in service of this goal the family members turn a blind eye toward the continued use of alcohol/drugs by the dysfunctional member. If the members lose sight of the origins of this state of pseudo-stability or forget that it evolved out of an attempt by the family to accommodate itself to the dysfunctional behavior of one member, they may defend it as the status quo and even enable the individual's dysfunctional behavior to continue.

The state of familial pseudo-stability is accomplished in an atmosphere of real and unspoken fear and guilt that is passed from one generation to another (Beattie, 1989; Stein, Newcomb, & Bentler, 1993). For this reason, many professionals view addiction as a multigenerational, family-centered disorder in which parental alcohol/drug addiction becomes "a governing agent affecting the development of the family as a whole and the individuals within" (Brown & Lewis, 1995, p. 281). Without professional intervention, it is difficult for the individual members of the family to learn how to detach from the member who is addicted to chemicals, and family members are unlikely to learn how to let the addicted individual suffer the natural consequences of his or her behavior (Johnson Institute, 1987). Rather, the life of the entire family centers on the pathology of a single member, and the family members live their lives in an attempt to somehow "cure" that one of the addiction.

The cost of parental addiction. As scientists learn more about how extreme abuse affects the developmental

---

[1]The Johnson Institute (1987), instead of *denial*, used the term *avoiding*.

process, they are gaining new insights into the long-term impact of physical, sexual, and emotional abuse on children. Extreme abuse in childhood is of special importance because the child's brain is still growing in response to his or her genetic predisposition and life experiences (Teicher, 2002). Extreme abuse/neglect may predispose the child to depression, anxiety states, suicide attempts or thoughts, or the development of post-traumatic stress disorder as well as impulse control disorders and substance abuse (Teicher, 2002). In their study of the impact of parental alcoholism on 9,346 adults, Anda et al. (2002) found that parental alcoholism was strongly associated with the later development of depression in the child raised in such a home. However, the parental alcoholism was not causal to this later depression. Rather, the child raised by an alcoholic parent was found to be at higher risk for adverse events such as physical/emotional/sexual abuse than were children raised by nonalcoholic parents, and these events seemed to be the root cause of the depressive disorders seen later in life, according to the authors. Further, Dube et al. (2001) identified growing up in a home where there was substance abuse as one factor associated with later suicidal behavior.

One theory suggested the possibility that some children raised in an alcoholic home would become "addicted" to excitement (Ruben, 2001; Webb, 1989). Such children might engage in fire-setting behaviors or be attracted to a partner who struggles with substance-use problems in later life. Such children might also become super-responsible, assuming roles far beyond their abilities or maturity, such as spending "an inordinate amount of time worrying about the safety of the whole (family) system" (Webb, 1989, p. 47). Further, as adolescents these children will stay awake while the alcoholic parent is out drinking, check on the safety of sleeping siblings, and develop elaborate fire escape plans that might involve returning time and time again to the burning house to rescue siblings, pets, and valuables. Such adolescents might become overly mature, serious, and well organized, behaviors that are likely to be viewed as signs of emotional maturity and stability (Ruben, 2001; Webb, 1989).

Adolescents raised in an alcoholic home are forced to spend so much time and energy meeting basic survival needs that they are unlikely to have the opportunity to establish a strong self-concept (Webb, 1989).

Because of the atmosphere of "chronic trauma" (Brown & Lewis, 1995, p. 285), a significant percentage of these children were thought to develop long-lasting emotional injuries. These observations are consistent with clinical experience, which suggests that children raised in an alcoholic home do indeed seem to suffer some form of psychological harm.

But since the 1980s, researchers have discovered that parental alcohol- or drug-use problems do not *automatically* result in problems for the growing child. A number of factors shape the impact of parental alcoholism on the developing children in the family (Ackerman, 1983). For example, there is the sex of the substance-abusing parent. Each parent plays a different role within the family. An alcoholic mother will have a far different impact on the family from that of an alcoholic father. A second factor is the length of time the parent has actively been abusing or addicted to chemicals. For example, an alcoholic father who has used chemicals for "only" 3 years will have a far different impact on the family than an alcoholic father who has been physically dependent on alcohol for 15 or 16 years.

A third factor is the sex of the child. For example, a daughter will be affected differently than a son by an alcohol-dependent father (Ackerman, 1983). Also, the specific family constellation will play a role in how parental alcoholism will impact each individual child. This is a difficult point for many people to understand. Consider, for example, two different families. In the first family, the father has a 3-month relapse when the third boy in a family of six children is 9 years old. Contrast this child's experience with that of the oldest child in a family of six children whose father relapsed for 3 months when the child was 9 years old. These children would experience far different family constellations than would the only child, a girl, whose father relapsed for 3 months when she was 9 years old. And all three children would have quite different experiences from those of the third boy in a family of six children whose mother was constantly drinking until he turned 14.

Finally, as Ackerman (1983) observed, it is possible for the child to escape the brunt of parental alcoholism if he or she is able to find a *parental surrogate*. A parental substitute (uncle, neighbor, real or imagined hero, etc.), may help the child find a way to avoid the worst of the father's alcoholic parenting (Ackerman, 1983).

The Adult Child of Alcoholics (ACOA) Movement

In the latter part of the 20th century, a number of adults stepped forward to claim that they were suffering from emotional dysfunctions that could be traced in large part to the impact of their parents' alcoholism. These individuals came to be known as "adult children of alcoholics" (ACOA). At its height, the number of such individuals was estimated to be from 22 million (Collette, 1990) to 34 million adults (Mathew, Wilson, Blazer, & George, 1993). Although the therapeutic focus has since shifted away from the ACOA model, treatment professionals and lay persons alike still hear the occasional hint that the ACOA movement is still alive.

There was never a single definition of the "adult child," but Ruben (2001) suggested that the term "adult children of alcoholics carries a double meaning: an adult who is trapped in the fears and reactions of a child, and the child who was forced to be an adult without going through the natural stages that result in a healthy adult" (p. 8). Proponents of the ACOA model claim that the alcoholic home is dysfunctional and that children raised in such a home are emotionally scarred for life (Ruben, 2001). Because of the parents' abusive drinking, these children would grow into adults who would

1. Have to "guess" at what normal adult behavior is like.
2. Have trouble in intimate relationships.
3. Have difficulty following a project through from beginning to end.
4. Have a tendency to lie in situations when it is just as easy to tell the truth.
5. Often be unable to relax, but always be ready to judge themselves harshly and feel the need to keep busy.
6. Tend not to feel comfortable with "self" but constantly seek affirmation from significant others.
7. Try to avoid conflict situations, or handle them poorly.
8. Be loyal to others, even when the other has abused them or failed to respect their loyality. (Ruben, 2001; Woititz, 1983).

The "adult child" might also have a tendency to self-sabotage (Ruben, 2001) and to be more self-critical and self-deprecating than adult children of nonalcoholic parents (Berkowitz & Perkins, 1988).

It has been argued that the traditional view of the adult child of alcoholic parents is too narrow (Hunter & Kellogg, 1989; Ruben, 2001). The authors suggested that in addition to the expected forms of psychopathology, ACOAs might also develop personality characteristics that are the *opposite of those expected of a child raised in a dysfunctional home*. For example, rather than having trouble completing a project, as noted above, some ACOAs become workaholics and come to assume great responsibility in their family (Ruben, 2001).

In the early 1990s, Sher, Walitzer, Wood, and Brent (1991) explored the differences between young adults who had and had not been raised by alcoholic parents. The authors used a volunteer sample of college students whose parental drinking status was confirmed by extensive interviews. Their findings are listed below:

1. College freshmen with an alcoholic father tended to drink more and to have more symptoms of alcoholism than freshmen who were not raised by an alcoholic father.
2. Women who were raised by an alcoholic parent or parents reported a greater number of alcohol-related consequences than their nondrinking counterparts.
3. Children of alcoholic parents showed an increased risk of using not only alcohol but other drugs of abuse as well.
4. Adolescent children of alcoholic parents had more positive expectancies for alcohol than did adolescent children of nonalcoholic parents.
5. As adults, children raised by alcoholic parents tended to have higher scores on test items suggesting "behavioral under-control" (p. 444) than did those who were not raised by alcoholic parents.
6. As college students, children raised by alcoholic parents tended to score lower on academic achievement tests than did their non-ACOA counterparts.

Although this research study produced suggestive findings, it failed to answer many questions about the assumed relationship between the parental drinking pattern and the student's academic performance. However, it *did* suggest that parental alcoholism had a strong impact on the subsequent growth and adjustment of the children raised in that family, providing support for the ACOA model.

Hart and Fiissel (2003) explored the impact of having an alcohol-dependent parent during childhood on the later adjustment of the individual and found that the children of alcohol-dependent parents might be vulnerable to later illness as an adult for reasons that were not entirely clear. These self-reported medical problems did not seem to reflect neuroticism as much as an increased incidence of actual medical problems in the ACOA sample examined. Earlier research has suggested that being raised in such an environment might predispose the child to later mental health problems such as dysthymia, phobias, and anxiety disorders (Mathew et al., 1993). These studies suggest that being raised in a home with an alcohol-dependent parent might predispose the child to later stress-related medical and psychiatric problems.

There are other ways in which adult children of alcoholic parents suffer beyond the development of psychiatric problems. They might learn to blame themselves for their parents' drinking (Collette, 1988, 1990; Freiberg, 1991), live in fear that their parents might separate/divorce (Sanders, 1990), or learn not to excel beyond the level that their parents achieved (Ruben, 2001). Not surprisingly, a number of research studies have revealed higher levels of psychiatric problems in adult children of alcoholic parents, providing some support for the ACOA model.

The growth of ACOA groups. Obviously, in a survey text such as this book, it is not possible to examine the self-help movement for Adult Children of Alcoholic parents in great detail. However, the reader should be aware that the historical growth and later decline of ACOA groups was phenomenal. At one point, 40% of the adults in this country were thought to belong to some kind of a 12-Step self-help group such as the groups for Adult Children of Alcoholics (Garry, 1995). This number was a reflection of many different factors. First, it seemed to reflect how many people had been hurt by a parent's alcoholism. Second, the growth of the ACOA groups indicated that these hidden victims of parental addiction were trying to find peace by working through the shame and guilt left over from their childhood years (Collette, 1990).

Criticism of the ACOA movement. The ultimate goal of the ACOA movement was to provide a self-help group format for those who believed that their emotional growth had been hurt because they had been raised in a dysfunctional environment. However, others were critical of the ACOA movement, and some researchers questioned whether being raised in such a home automatically resulted in psychological distress for the child (Kaminer & Bukstein, 1998). Still others challenge the ACOA concept on philosophical grounds:

> We all want to feel like victims. [But] if you identify yourself as a survivor of incest or abuse, you are making an existential and self-hypnotic statement that defines you by the most destructive thing that ever happened to you. In the short term, it's important to say it, but you can get stuck there. (Elkin, quoted in Collette, 1990, p. 30)

Some critics of the ACOA movement pointed out that therapies focusing on traumatic events such as childhood abuse or rape tend to keep the focus on the trauma, not on the individual's strengths and potential for further growth (Walker, 1996). This seems to explain why individuals became dependent on the ACOA program, almost as if they were "addicted" to being in an ACOA recovery group (May, 1991).

Other critics of the ACOA movement noted that the process of attaching a label to the "adult child" simply perpetuated "the process of blaming in a new language" (Treadway, 1990, p. 40). In other words, the format of the ACOA movement allows the "adult child" to continue to blame his or her parents for whatever problems he or she might have encountered in life. Thus, the ACOA group might help meet the ever-present need within this culture for "a sense of community, empowerment, and spiritual renewal" (Treadway, 1990, p. 40), but at what price?

Critics argued further that the concept of ACOA limited individual growth by *keeping the focus on the previous generation* (Peele, Brodsky, & Arnold, 1991). Admittedly, some children are raised in terrible, abusive environments. But the central thesis of the ACOA movement rests on the impact of past parental behavior (often, years past!) on the individual's *current* life problems. In a very real sense, the ACOA movement tends to encourage the individuals to define "self" on the basis of their parents' problems and choices, according to Peele et al.

The validity of one of the cornerstones of the ACOA movement was never even examined. In spite of repeated statements that being raised in a dysfunctional home hurt the child, nobody ever explored the possibility that the "healthy," conflict-free, family is a myth. Members of ACOA groups frequently bemoan the fact that their families did not meet the stereotypical standard of the American family, but historians "have been unable to identify a period in America's past when family life was untroubled" (Furstenberg, 1990, p. 148). In other words, familial conflict has been the norm within this culture, not the exception.

Another criticism of the ACOA model is that it rests on an assumption that Wolin and Wolin (1995, 1993) term the *damage model*. This model holds that children raised in a dysfunctional environment *automatically* suffer psychological harm. Black, a proponent of the model, said, "All children are affected" (1982, p. 27) if they were raised in an alcoholic home, an observation supported by other research (Anderson, 1995; Black, 2003; Brown & Lewis, 1995). Children raised by an alcoholic parent were viewed as never having the chance to express their "anger or outrage in a healthy manner" (Anderson, 1995, p. ex4), causing them everlasting emotional pain.

The damage model assumes that people are simply "passive vessels whose dysfunctional histories inhabit and control them like so many malignant spirits" (Garry, 1995, p. A10). Yet the this model has never been established as actually being applicable to situations in which the child is raised in a disturbed home. Indeed, research studies have generally failed to support it. In their study, Tweed and Ryff (1991) found no clear differences between the emotional adjustment of the adults raised in an alcoholic home and the adjustment of those raised in nonalcoholic homes.

Senchak, Leonard, Greene, and Carroll (1995) examined 82 adult children of alcoholic parents, 80 adult children of divorced parents, and 82 control subjects whose parents were neither divorced nor alcoholic to determine the impact being raised in a dysfunctional home might have on later adjustment. The authors concluded that "negative outcomes among adult children of alcoholics are neither pervasive nor specific to paternal alcoholism" (p. 152). Indeed, after controlling for confounding variables such as parental depression and the effects of low socioeconomic status, a number of studies have failed to find any significant form of psychopathology specific to the adult children of alcoholic parents (D'Andrea, Fisher, & Harrison, 1994; Giunta & Compas, 1994).

Finally, Kelly and Myers (1996) administered the Beck Depression Inventory (BDI) to a sample of 20 volunteer ACOA female undergraduate college students and a control group of 20 female undergraduate college students whose parents were not alcohol dependent. Although there was a statistically significant difference in the measured levels of depression between these two groups, according to the authors, the average BDI score for both subgroups fell within the normal range. In other words, as a group, neither the ACOA sample nor the control sample seemed to be significantly depressed. These findings cast doubt on the damage model, which serves as the foundation of the ACOA movement. Indeed, in contrast, it appears that many individuals are able to avoid significant emotional scars in spite of being raised in a "dysfunctional" environment (Wolin & Wolin, 1995).

Perhaps a more appropriate model for how children respond to the problem of having an alcoholic parent might be called the "*challenge model*" (Wolin & Wolin, 1993). This model takes into account the possibility of individual resiliency, something the damage model fails to do. *Resiliency* does *not* mean that people are invulnerable to the trials and tribulations of life (Blum, 1998), but during the natural course of growth in childhood, adaptive systems have evolved that seem to help them become resilient to life's trials (Masten, 2001). Only when these protective systems are shattered by extreme stress is normal growth threatened. This reslience allows the individual to learn from life's experiences without being overcome by trauma encountered along the way (Masten, 2001). Some signs of resilience include finding surrogate parents to replace natural parents who are unavailable due to accident or illness during childhood or developing support systems in adulthood to help the person cope during times of trial (Blum, 1998). Other characteristics include a tendency to look for things to change in the future and to set goals in the future, as well as to recognize personal strengths in spite of adverse situations.

The damage model suggests that emotional trauma in childhood causes problems in later life. But research has found that "childhood adversity is *not* always associated with a poor outcome" (Parker, Barrett, & Hickie, 1992, p. 883, italics added for emphasis). The quality of interpersonal relationships formed in later life may moderate or overcome the impact of adverse life events such as poor parenting (Parker et al., 1992; Werner, 1989). These studies provide at least partial support for Ackerman's (1983) assertion that if children find a suitable parental substitute, they may escape the full consequences of parental alcoholism. At the same time, the studies raise questions about the validity of the ACOA model.

There is "a danger in assuming . . . that growing up in an alcoholic home inevitably leads to dysfunction in adulthood" (D'Andrea et al., 1994, p. 580), a warning that proponents of the damage model overlooked. Being raised in a dysfunctional home does not automatically result in some lasting form of psychological distress (Garbarino, Dubrow, Kostelny, & Pardo, 1992). The team of Domenico and Windle (1993) examined the intrapersonal and interpersonal functioning of 616 middle-age women and also failed to find evidence to support the theory of ACOA psychopathology. The authors compared the adjustment of women who were adult children of an alcoholic parent with that of women who were not raised by an alcoholic parent. Although they found that the ACOA women seemed to have higher levels of depression and lower levels of self-esteem, as a group the ACOA women scored in the normal range on the tests used in this study. These findings were consistent with those of Seilhamer, Jacob, and Dunn (1993), who failed to find any consistent impact, either positive or negative, of parental alcoholism on parent-child interactions.

In the absence of hard research data, the literature on which the ACOA movement is based seems to rest on a foundation of nothing more than "assertions, generalizations and anecdotes" (University of California, Berkeley, 1990a, p. 7). Indeed, a very real shortcoming of the ACOA literature is that it is "long on rhetoric and short on empirical data" (Levy & Rutter, 1992, p. 12). In support of this, although research into characteristics of the ACOA population was popular for a few years, little research has been conducted in this area for almost a decade.

Another criticism of the ACOA movement is that the clinical theories claiming that parental alcoholism impacts the emotional well-being of children have been oversimplified (Zweig & Wolf, 1997). Proponents have ignored the impact of parental alcoholism (or parental abuse) on the development of the child's unconscious mind, according to the authors. Further, in the process of simplifying the basic theory, many less skilled proponents of the ACOA rehabilitation model have overlooked the fact that simply to name a process does not mean that the individual understands it on all levels. Thus, the authors claim that the reconstructive model is often left unfinished because it did not proceed to the deeper levels of the victim's personality.

In the United States, the self-help movement, of which the ACOA movement is a part, has been a growth industry ever since its inception (Blau, 1990; Boyd, 1992). Some have suggested that the publishing industry, knowing that the majority of those who purchase self-help books are women, slant their titles and design their covers to attract and activate the insecurities of women (Boyd, 1992). One could very well argue that the ACOA movement is the stepchild of the publishing industry, which then used the movement to develop a market for a new line of self-help books. This idea explains the observed phenomenon that the original ACOA movement, which focused upon survivors of extreme abuse, has expanded to blame virtually *all* parents for what they did or did not do. By the 1980s and 1990s, blaming one's parents had become "a national obsession—and big business" (Blau, 1990 p. 61; Kaminer, 1992).

Allthough psychology as a science is more than a century old, it has produced very little research about what constitutes a "normal" family or the limits of the unhealthy behaviors (which we all have) that might be tolerated in an otherwise "normal" family. There has been even less valid scientific research into the psychodynamics of families of alcohol- or drug-addicted individuals (D'Andrea et al., 1994; Goodwin & Warnock, 1991; Sher, 1991, 1997; University of California, Berkeley, 1990a). On this nonexistent foundation, proponents of the ACOA model claim that *96% of the population was raised in a "dysfunctional" family* (Garry, 1995; Peele et al., 1991).

There has never been any research to suggest that this 96% figure is accurate (Hughes, 1993), but proponents of the ACOA movement quote it as if it were gospel truth. They point to studies in which a high percentage of the ACOA adults participating claim to have one or more of the characteristics often attributed to ACOAs. However, such studies are flawed because the language used to describe the typical Adult Child of Alcoholic Parents is so vague that Sher (1997) suggested it has a P.T. Barnum-like quality to it: "a little something in it for everybody" (p. 252). Both ACOA and non-ACOA adults tend to agree that these descriptors apply to them (Sher, 1997). Given these findings, one must wonder whether the characteristics identified by the proponents of the ACOA movement reflect not some form of pathology but simply common problems in living in today's society. But now, thanks to an overabundance of self-help books, we have the "language" for which to blame our parents or grandparents for all of our current problems.

Blau (1990) challenged the ACOA concept on the grounds that the "adult child" is simply a reflection of the "baby-boomers'" resistance to accepting that they are now adults who are themselves entering middle adulthood. Developmentally, the adults of the baby-boomer generation are no longer the children of their parents, at least in the same sense that they were four decades ago. They are now middle-age adults who are discovering that they will not fulfill all their dreams of young adulthood. Perhaps, as Blau (1990) suggested, the ACOA movement is simply a reaction by the baby-boomers against growing older, a possibility that is supported by the fact that the focus of baby-boomers has finally shifted from ACOA issues to those of impending retirement, health care, and other factors in aging.

The ACOA movement places great emphasis on the so-called inner child. However, the inner child concept is not a part of any single therapeutic theory. Rather, the theory behind the ACOA concept of the inner child is a complex blend of "[Carl] Jung, New Age mysticism, holy child mythology, pop psychology, and psychoanalytic theories about narcissism and the creation of a false self" (Kaminer, 1992, p. 17). However "just at the moment when Americans ought to be figuring out where their Inner *Adult* is, and how that disregarded oldster got buried under the rubble of pop psychology and short-term gratification" (Hughes, 1993, p. 29, italics added for emphasis), along comes the ACOA movement to focus not on the problems of adulthood but on what should have happened one or more generations ago. In reality, the inner child concept is based on a phase of life when the individual

was developmentally, socially, psychologically, and neurologically immature, and one must wonder to what degree this construct is able to meet the demands of adult life.

Finally, as Levy and Rutter (1992) point out, the ACOA movement is essentially a white, middle-class invention. We don't know whether this model applies to inner-city children, whose parents might be addicted to heroin or cocaine, where the child might come from a single-parent family, and so on. As the authors note, children of heroin and cocaine addicts are "primarily nonwhite, minority members who live in poverty. They have no national movement . . . do not write books and make the rounds of the talk shows" (p. 5). Thus, virtually nothing is known about them. However, as the authors remind us, many children are raised by parents who are addicted to chemicals other than alcohol, in environments other than the white, middle-class world. There is no research as to whether the ACOA model applies to these other children of addiction.

Summary

This chapter explored the family of the addicted individual and the impact that one individual's addiction to chemicals is thought to have on the rest of the family. Unfortunately, few research studies have actually explored this. Much of what is assumed to be true about the family in which one or more persons is addicted to alcohol/drugs is based on theory, not established fact.

The theory of codependency assumes that the codependent individual is "trained" by a series of adverse life events to become dependent on the feedback and support of others. Further, it is assumed that family members come to assume new roles, as the addicted person gives up the power and responsibility that he or she would normally hold within the family. In this manner, the family comes to "accommodate" or adapt to the individual's chemical addiction.

From the perspective of the codependency model, the individual's substance abuse is viewed as a family-centered disorder, passed on from one generation to the next. The self-help group movement of "adult children" of alcoholics is viewed as a logical response to the pain and suffering that the family members experienced because of their participation in a "dysfunctional" family. However, the "adult child" concept has met with some criticism. Certain health care professionals stress that the theory behind the adult children movement places too much emphasis on past suffering at the expense of possible resilience on the part of the individual or the person's future growth.

Further criticism of this movement is that it automatically assumes the individual has experienced some lasting psychological trauma as a result of parental alcoholism or drug addiction. This theory has never been tested; thus, much of the ACOA self-help movement rests on unproven assumptions. Research is needed if we are to begin to understand how chemical addiction impacts the growth and development of both the individual family members and the family unit.

CHAPTER TWENTY-SIX

The Evaluation of Substance-Use Problems

Assessment procedures and diagnostic categories are not helpful if merely used to label . . . while ignoring the strengths, coping capacities and desire for growth and development inherent in most people. Rather, systems of classification are useful in identifying symptoms, challenges, and abilities, necessary for planning and implementing effective treatment and . . . interventions. (Levy & Orlans, 1998, p. 81)

Introduction

In this era of managed care, program cutbacks, and increased accountability, health care professionals are being required to justify each procedure in advance, to ensure the maximum return for each dollar spent on health care. This is accomplished in part through the process of assessment. The assessment serves as the foundation of the rehabilitation process, a gatekeeping process, and serves the more traditional role of identifying people who require some form of professional intervention to help them deal with their substance-use problems (Juhnke, 2002). In this chapter, the evaluation of a client's drug- or alcohol-use pattern and the relation of assessment to rehabilitation will be dicussed.

The Theory Behind Alcohol-
and Drug-Use Evaluations

Substance-abuse assessment is "more than a one-time paperwork procedure conducted at the onset of treatment to simply gather minimal facts and secure a . . . diagnosis" (Juhnke, 2002, p. vii). It is the first step in the rehabilitation process (Miller, Westerberg, & Waldron, 1995).

Unfortunately, in spite of decades of effort, scientists have yet to develop a "Holy Grail" (Fleming, 2001, p. 321) for the detection of alcohol- or drug-use problems. Behavioral scientists have not agreed on a universally accepted definition of *addiction* (Erlich, 2001). Thus the substance-abuse rehabilitation professional, using imperfect tools, must determine whether an individual requires assistance for a chemical-use problem, a decision that might have lifelong implications for the person. For example, a person's eligibility for health care insurance at age 50 might be affected by a diagnosis of alcohol dependence made 30 years earlier, when he or she was only 20 years old.

The assessment process is quite complicated. Simply *screening* a patient (to determine whether indications of a specific condition are present) is *not* the same as making a formal *diagnosis* (Miller et al., 1995). After the appropriate diagnosis has been made, the criteria supporting that diagnosis need to be indicated and the appropriate type and level of care identified. The assessor must determine (a) whether there is evidence of a substance-use disorder, (b) the severity of this disorder if present, and (c) the most appropriate form of treatment for each individual.

An aid to this process are the "four C's" suggested by Rustin (2000):

1. The individual has a *compulsion* to use chemicals.
2. The individual has struggled to *control* his or her chemical use (or can no longer control it).
3. The individual has tried to *cut down* on his or her chemical use.
4. The individual has suffered *consequences* of his or her alcohol or drug use.

If substance abusers were all alike, the assessment process could stop with determining whether the individual has a chemical-use problem. However, all substance abusers are not alike, and there is no "one size fits all" form of treatment for alcohol/drug dependence problems (Leshner, 2001a, b). Effective treatment must be (a) individualized, (b) continually evaluated for effectiveness, and (c) modified where necessary, according to the author.

For this reason, the assessment process is viewed as the first step toward rehabilitation. On the basis of the information uncovered during a careful evaluation, the substance-abuse rehabilitation professional is able to identify the appropriate goals and treatment strategies for each client. The opposite is also true: Without a careful evaluation of the client's strengths, experiences, and needs, it will be difficult to identify appropriate goals for him or her or to effectively intervene. The evaluation process consists of three interrelated phases: Screening, Assessment, and Diagnosis.

Screening

The first step in the assessment process is to identify individuals who might have a chemical abuse/addiction problem and might benefit from treatment. The screening process can be relatively simple and straightforward, or quite complicated and time-consuming. For example, the screening process for the individual who arrives in a hospital emergency room with alcohol-induced liver disease, alcohol-induced gastritis, a history of five prior admissions for alcohol-related disorders, and a current blood alcohol level of .230 would present few questions that he or she has an alcohol-use disorder. However, every case is not as simple and easy to screen as this hypothetical example.

To aid in the screening process, researchers have devised a number of paper-and-pencil tests, or questionnaires, to help detect substance-use problems. Note that a test score by itself does *not* establish whether the individual has a substance-abuse problem (Vanable, King, & de Wit, 2000). The test results are one part of the overall assessment process, which is designed to provide an overview of each individual's substance-use pattern. These instruments are either filled out by the client (and as such are known as *self-report* instruments) or by the assessor as he or she asks questions of the person being evaluated. Self-report instruments offer the advantages of being inexpensive and possibly less

threatening to the client than a face-to-face interview (Cooney, Zweben, & Fleming, 1995; Juhnke, 2002).

One of the most popular self-report instruments for alcohol-use problems is the Michigan Alcoholism Screening Test (MAST) (Selzer, 1971). The MAST is composed of 24 questions that may be answered either "yes" or "no" by the respondent. Test items are weighted with a value of 1, 2, or in some cases 5 points. A score of 7 or more suggests an alcohol-use problem (Craig, 2004). The effectiveness of this screening instrument has been demonstrated in clinical literature (Miller, 1976). But the MAST has some drawbacks: (a) It can be used only in cases of alcohol dependence (Vanable et al., 2000), (b) it provides only a "crude general screen" (Miller et al., 1995, p. 62) for alcohol-use problems, (c) it does not detect binge drinking, (d) it does not shed light on the individual's drinking pattern (Smith, Touquet, Wright, & Das Gupta 1996), and (e) it does not differentiate between current and past drinking (Schorling & Buchsbaum, 1997). Thus, although the MAST is suited to the detection of individuals with severe alcohol dependence (Saunders, Aasland, Babor, de la Fuente, & Grant, 1993), it is of limited value in cases of polydrug use or for patients who are "problem" drinkers but not alcohol dependent.

Another screening tool for alcoholism that is growing in popularity is the "CAGE" questionnaire (Ewing, 1984). CAGE is an acronym for the key words in this test:

- Have you ever felt you ought to CUT DOWN on your drinking?
- Have people ANNOYED you by being critical of your drinking?
- Have you ever felt bad or GUILTY about your drinking?
- Have you ever had a drink first thing in the morning to steady your nerves or to get rid of a hangover (EYE-OPENER)?

A "yes" response to one of these four questions suggests the need for a more detailed inquiry by the assessor. Affirmative answers to two or more items suggests that the client has an alcohol-use problem. The CAGE questionnaire has been found to have an accuracy of 80% to 90% in detecting alcoholism when the client answers "yes" to two or more questions. But, like the MAST, the CAGE is most effective in detecting alcohol-*dependent* individuals rather than alcohol *abusers* or people at risk for developing an alcohol-use problem (Saunders et al., 1993; Vanable et al., 2000). It is insensitive to binge drinking (Smith et al., 1996), adolescent drinkers (Knight, 2002), or alcoholism in women and minority populations (Bradley, Boyd-Wickizer, Powell, & Burman, 1998; "Screening for Alcohol Problems," 2002). By some estimates, up to 50% of at-risk drinkers (Fleming, 1997, p. 345) might be missed by the CAGE because of these flaws.

Another paper-and-pencil screening tool that has grown in popularity in the past decade is the Alcohol Use Disorders Identification Test (AUDIT) (Saunders et al., 1993). Research has suggested that the AUDIT is over 90% effective in detecting alcohol-use disorders (Brown, Leonard, Saunders, & Papasoulioutis 1997), and it appears to be effective in detecting women with drinking problems (Bradley et al., 2003). However, the AUDIT tends to miss active drinkers above the age of 65 (Isaacson & Schorling, 1999), and it is not appropriate for use with adolescent drinkers (Knight, 2002).

Other instruments have been developed for the detection of alternate forms of chemical abuse. Brown et al. (1997) suggested the use of two simple questions to detect possible substance-use disorders:

1. In the last year, have you ever drunk or used drugs more than you meant to?
2. Have you felt you wanted or needed to cut down on your drinking or drug use in the last year?

Despite the assessment's brevity, the authors claimed that a "yes" answer to one item indicated a 45% chance that the individual had a substance-use disorder and a "yes" response to both items indicated a 75% chance (Brown et al., 1997). The authors pointed out that their two-item test can result in false-positive results in some cases and that their initial findings needed to be replicated in follow-up studies. However, this two-item test shows promise as a screening tool for health care workers.

One instrument that is often mistakenly considered a screening/assessment tool is the Minnesota Multiphasic Personality Inventory (MMPI). The original MMPI was introduced almost 65 years ago. To aid in the utility of the MMPI in working with addicted persons, the MacAndrew Alcoholism Scale (also known as the "Mac" Scale) was introduced in 1965,

after an item analysis suggested that alcohol-dependent individuals tended to answer 49 of the 566 items of the MMPI differently from nonalcoholics. A cut-off score of 24 items out of 49 answered in the "scorable" direction correctly identified 82% of the alcohol-dependent clients in a sample of 400 male psychiatric patients (Graham, 1990). In 1989 an updated version of the MMPI, the Minnesota Multiphasic Personality Inventory-2 (MMPI-2) was introduced. The Mac scale was modified slightly but was essentially retained in its original form. Craig (2004) suggested that the Mac scale is 85% accurate in the detection of substance abuse.

Although this is an impressive figure, the Mac scale is not perfect. It has been discovered, for example, that Black clients tend to score higher on the Mac scale than White clients. Further, rather than being specific for alcohol-use problems, the Mac scale might best be viewed as detecting personality patterns commonly associated with substance-use problems (Rouse, Butcher, & Miller, 1999). Also, clients who are extroverted, are exhibitionistic, experience blackouts for *any* reason (such as a seizure disorder), are assertive, or enjoy risk-taking behaviors tend to score higher on the Mac scale, even if they are not addicted to chemicals (Graham, 1990).

In their work with the original MMPI, Otto, Lang, Megargee, and Rosenblatt (1989) discovered that alcohol-dependent people might be able to "conceal their drinking problems even when the relatively subtle special alcohol scales of the MMPI are applied" (p 7). This is because personality inventories such as the MMPI/MMPI-2 are vulnerable to both conscious and unconscious attempts at denial, self-deception, and distortion (Isenhart & Silversmith, 1996). Thus, although the MMPI Mac scale was designed as a subtle test for alcoholism, it can yield either false positive or false negative results. Until proven otherwise, counselors should assume that the revised Mac scale on the MMPI-2 shares this weakness with the original Mac scale.

Unlike many of the other assessment tools, the MMPI offers an advantage of having five "truth" scales built into it. These scales offer insight into how truthful the test taker may have been; they are discussed in more detail by Graham (1990). A major disadvantage of the MMPI is the length of time the typical client needs to complete the test items. This makes the MMPI/MMPI-2 a test that might better be employed in the *diagnosis* phase of assessment (discussed later in this chapter) than during the screening phase.

Assessment

During the assessment phase of the evaluation process, the assessor attempts to measure the severity of the individual's substance-use problem. One of the most useful tools of the assessment phase is the clinical interview, which forms the cornerstone of the drug- or alcohol-use evaluation. Juhnke (2002) identified four benefits of the clinical interview:

1. It is more flexible than paper-and-pencil or computer-based assessment procedures.
2. It allows the assessor/therapist to establish a basic level of rapport with the client.
3. The confused/distressed client might respond better to a living person than to a computer screen or written test.
4. The therapist/assessor can watch the client's nonverbal behavior in response to questions to identify areas for further exploration.

Client information provides an important source of data about current and previous chemical use. Remember, however, that clients may either consciously or unconsciously distort the information they provide. This underscores the need for collateral information sources (discussed below).

The first part of the interview process is an introduction by the assessor who explains that he or she will be asking questions about the client's possible chemical-use patterns and that *specific* responses are most helpful. The assessor will tell the client that although many of these questions may have been asked by others in the past, this information is important. The client is asked if he or she has any questions, after which the interview begins. The assessor should attempt to review the diagnostic criteria for chemical-use problems in the *Diagnostic and Statistical Manual of Mental Disorders (4th edition-Text Revision) (DSM-IV-TR)* (American Psychiatric Association, 2000). This manual provides a framework within which the diagnosis of chemical dependency can be made and provides

a standard language that is understood by most treatment professionals. The *DSM-IV-TR* criteria for alcohol- or drug-abuse problems will be discussed in more detail in the next section.

Many of the questions utilized in the clinical interview are designed to explore the same information from different perspectives. For example, at one point in the interview process the client might be asked, "In the average week, how often do you use drugs/alcohol?" At a later point this same client might be asked, "How much would you say, on the average, that you spend for drugs/alcohol in a week?" The purpose of this redundancy is not to trap the client so much as to provide different perspectives on the client's chemical-use pattern. For example, it is often wise to consider the *percentage of the client's income spent on recreational chemicals* (Washton, 1995). Consider the case of a client who claimed to use alcohol one or two nights a week, spending 60 dollars per week on beer. This person's alcohol use would be seen as excessive in anybody's eyes. But if the client's only source of income was an unemployment check for $120 each week, this person is devoting fully 50% of his or her income to buy alcohol. This information reveals more about the individual's chemical-use pattern, helping the evaluator better understand the client.

In addition to the clinical interview, Juhnke (2002) suggests that the assessor use a standardized test to aid in the assessment process. The test results will then become part of the database the assessor will use to make his or her conclusions. A number of assessment instruments are available to professionals conducting an alcohol use evaluation.[1,2] One popular instrument for individuals over the age of 16 is the Alcohol Use Inventory (AUI). The AUI is a copyrighted instrument made up of 228 items and takes 30 to 60 minutes to complete. The answers to the test items provide data for 24 subscales the assessor can use to better understand the client's alcohol-use pattern. But the AUI is limited to alcohol-use problems.

[1]There are many assessment instruments currently in use. It is not possible to review them all, especially since new tools are constantly being introduced. This section will discuss only some of the more popular instruments currently in use.

[2]There is no single instrument for the assessment of drug use that is widely accepted, nor is it expected that such a screening tool will be developed (Connors, Donovan, & DiClemente, 2001).

A popular research instrument, which is gaining popularity as an assessment tool, is the Addiction Severity Index (ASI). The ASI is administered to adult clients during a semistructured interview. The fifth edition contains 161 items and requires approximately 1 hour to complete. The administrator asks the questions of the client and records his or her answers on the answer form. The ASI is in the public domain, which is to say that it is not copyrighted, and it provides a severity rating score based on the impressions of the person who administers the test. Unlike the AUI, the ASI can be used for evaluating the severity of abuse of other drugs such as cocaine and opiates. In spite of its many advantages, the ASI has been found to have limited effectiveness with dual-diagnosis clients (see Chapter 22) (Monti, Kadden, Rohsenow, Cooney, & Abrams, 2002).

Two other instruments that are gaining widespread acceptance are the Substance Abuse Subtle Screening Inventory-3 (SASSI-3) and the version of the SASSI-3 designed for use with adolescents (Juhnke, 2002). This copyrighted instrument can be used with individuals 16 years or older with fourth-grade reading skills. The client needs about 15 minutes to complete the SASSI-3, and it can be scored by hand or by computer. The SASSI-3 provides the user with scores on 10 different scales such as the Symptoms Scale and the Obvious Attribute Scale. Some of the scales use face-valid measures of alcohol/drug-use problems, whereas other scales attempt to measure the effects of the individual's substance use through subtle questions that do not reveal their intent to the reader. The Defensiveness and Supplemental Addiction Measure scales attempt to measure the degree to which the client has attempted to hide his or her addiction (Juhnke, 2002).

Diagnosis

The final stage in the evaluation process is diagnosis. Abel (1982) identified four elements as being necessary for the diagnosis of alcohol/drug addiction. These were the interrelated elements of (a) a compulsion to continue use of the chemical(s) in question, (b) the development of tolerance, (c) major withdrawal symptoms following withdrawal from the drug, and (d) adverse effects from drug use for both the individual and society. A more standardized conceptual model was presented by the American Psychiatric Association (2000). In its *Diagnostic and Statistical Manual of Mental Disorders* the American Psychiatric Association suggested that some of the signs of alcohol/drug addiction include the following:

1. *Preoccupation* with use of the chemical between periods of use.
2. *Using more of the chemical* than had been anticipated.
3. *The development of tolerance* to the chemical in question.
4. A *characteristic withdrawal syndrome* when the person stops using the chemical.
5. *Use of the chemical to avoid or control withdrawal symptoms.*
6. *Repeated efforts to cut back or stop* the drug use.
7. *Intoxication at inappropriate times* (such as at work) or when *withdrawal interferes with daily functioning* (hangover makes person too sick to go to work, for example).
8. A *reduction in social, occupational, or recreational activities* in favor of further substance use.
9. *Continuation of chemical use* in spite of having suffered social, emotional, or physical problems related to drug use.

Any combination of three or more of these signs indicates the individual may be suffering from an addiction to one or more recreational chemicals.

Chapter 2 introduced the concept of a substance-use continuum. The chart in Figure 26.1 was used to illustrate the continuum of drug use/abuse, with the different points on the continuum ranging from total abstinence from chemicals to chronic addiction. If the *DSM-IV-TR* criteria are applied to this continuum, the individual who meets four or more would fall in level 3 or 4.

Of these various diagnostic systems, the one offered by the American Psychiatric Association in its *DSM-IV-TR* (2000) provides a standardized framework within which a professional can make a diagnosis of substance dependence. It is through the evaluation process that the professional gathers the data on which to make such a diagnosis, that is, an opinion of where on a continuum the individual being assessed might fall. A second part of the evaluation process is the

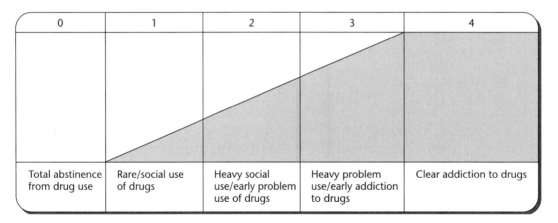

0	1	2	3	4
Total abstinence from drug use	Rare/social use of drugs	Heavy social use/early problem use of drugs	Heavy problem use/early addiction to drugs	Clear addiction to drugs

FIGURE 26.1   The continuum of recreational chemical use.

determination, to the degree that this is possible, of the client's motivation. A willingness to enter treatment does not automatically translate into a willingness to change one's chemical-use pattern (Connors et al., 2001). Some clients enter treatment mainly for the purposes of *impression management* (Wild, Cunningham, & Hobdon, 1998), not for rehabilitation. These are the clients who want to "get into treatment so that I will look good to the judge." Although the vast majority of people who are abusing or addicted to chemicals are unready or unwilling to pursue abstinence (Miller et al., 1995), the client who enters "treatment" for the sole purpose of attempting to manipulate the court wastes valuable treatment resources better used to treat other patients.

The Assessor and Data Privacy

The issue of confidentiality has always been quite complicated, and with recent changes in the federal regulations that govern data privacy, it has become even more confusing. In situations where the clinician is not clear about his or her responsibility under the data privacy regulations, it is wise to consult an attorney. However, as a general rule, information about the client is always considered privileged or confidential. There are exceptions, however. If a client were to indicate that he or she were seriously thinking about suicide or committing a homicide, it might be necessary for the assessor to break confidentiality to protect the client from the impulse to end his or her life or to protect another person from the client's anger.[3]

Because of data privacy regulations, the assessor might not have immediate access to privileged information from such sources as treatment centers clients attended earlier or their past medical/psychiatric history. Also, clients can refuse to provide a specific item of information or even to talk to the assessor if they do not want to do so.[4] If information is obtained from people other than the client, *the professional should always first obtain written permission* from the client giving authorization to contact *specific* individuals to obtain the desired information about the client, his or her chemical use, and other information. This written permission is recorded on a form known as a *release-of-information authorization* (ROI) form. The ROI should identify the specific information being requested, the person/agency from which this information is to be released, and the specific individual/agency that is to receive it.

When the client is being referred for an evaluation by the court system, the court will often provide referral information about the client's previous legal history. The courts will often also include a detailed social history of the client, which was part of the pre-sentencing investigation. If asked, the evaluator should acknowledge

[3]The reader is advised to become familiar with the data privacy and duty-to-report regulations that are applicable in his or her home community.

[4]The problem of the uncooperative client is reviewed in Chapter 31.

having read this information but should not discuss the contents of the referral information provided by the courts. Such discussions are to be avoided because (a) the purpose of the clinical interview is to assess the client's *chemical-use patterns*. A discussion of what information was or was not provided by the court does nothing to further this evaluation. Also, (b) the client has access to this information through his or her attorney. Thus, if the client wishes to have a chance to review the information provided by the court, he or she may do so at another time through established legal channels.

Clients will occasionally ask to see the records provided by the court during the clinical interview. Frequently, they are checking to see what information has been provided by the courts so they can decide how much and what they should admit to during the interview. This often reflects the philosophy of "let me know how much *you* know about me so that I will know how 'honest' I should be!" The solution to this dilemma is a simple statement that the client may obtain a copy of the court record through the established legal channels. Those persistent clients who demand to see their court records on the grounds that "it is about me, anyway" are to be reminded that the purpose of the interview is to explore the client's drug- and alcohol-use patterns, not to review court records. However, under no circumstances should the chemical dependency/mental health professional let the client read the referral records. To do so would be a violation of the data privacy laws, as the referral information was released to the professional, *not* the client.

When the final evaluation is written, the evaluator should identify the source of the information summarized in it. Collateral information sources should be advised that the client or his or her attorney has a right to request a copy of the final report before the interview. It is *extremely* rare for clients to request a copy of the final report, although technically they have the right to do so after the proper release-of-information authorization forms have been signed.

Diagnostic Rules

Many, perhaps most, clients will initially resist a diagnosis of chemical dependency (Washton, 1990). Because of this, assessors should follow two diagnostic rules as closely as possible in the evaluation and diagnosis of a possible drug addiction. Occasionally, it is not possible to adhere to each of these diagnostic rules, but one should always attempt to evaluate each individual case carefully in light of these guidelines, even in special cases. Then, even if the rule is not followed, the professional making the diagnosis should explain why one or another guideline could not be met in a given situation, to avoid missing important information.

Rule 1: Gather collateral information.[5] As a group, alcohol-dependent individuals will, when sober, be reasonably accurate as to the amount and frequency of their alcohol use. But there are exceptions to this rule, as when the individual is facing some kind of legal problem (Donovan, 1992; McCrady, 2001). Further, individuals who have both a mental illness problem and a substance-use problem tend to underreport the extent of their substance-use problems (Carey, Cocco, & Simons, 1996).

Because of the importance of the diagnostic process, the assessor should *utilize as many sources of information as possible* (Evans & Sullivan, 2001; Juhnke, 2002). This means using sources of information other than the client's self-report (McCrady, 2001). To illustrate the importance of collateral information, every chemical dependency professional has encountered cases in which the individual being evaluated has claimed to drink "once a week . . . no more than a couple of beers after work." The spouse of the person being evaluated often reports, however, that the client was intoxicated "5 to 7 nights a week."

Collateral information sources might include patients' families, friends, employers or coworkers, clergy members, local law-enforcement authorities, primary care physicians, and psychotherapists (if any) (Slaby, Lieb, & Tancredi, 1981). Obviously, time restrictions might prevent the use of some of these collateral resources. If the assessment must be completed by the end of the week and the professional is unable to contact the client's mother, it may be necessary to write the final report without benefit of her input. In addition, the other people involved may simply refuse to provide any information. It is the assessor's responsibility, however, to *attempt* to contact as many of these individuals as possible and to include their views in the final evaluation report.

---

[5]Morgan (2003) advises the assessor to obtain release-of-information authorizations before contacting collateral information sources.

Rule 2: Always *assume deception until proven otherwise*. Patients being assessed might consciously try to deceive the assessor. It is more likely that they will offer the assessor what they believe is the truth, *based on their pattern of distorted thinking* (Ross, 2002). Thus, the individual who drinks eight beers in a bar with friends 5 to 7 nights a week might say that he or she was an "infrequent" drinker not because of a conscious attempt at deception but because he or she literally believes that 5 to 7 nights a week *is* "infrequent" alcohol consumption, compared to the person who drinks a minimum of 12–15 beers every night of the week, plus more at home.

This is not to say that some individuals will not attempt to deceive the assessor. Rather, the wise assessor will simply remember that even cooperative patients will answer questions based on their beliefs and defense systems. For example, one individual reported that he was spending "$20 a week" on alcohol, consumed with friends. The assessor multiplied the $20 per week times 52 to arrive at the figure of $1,040 that this individual spent on alcohol each year. Yet, confronted with this figure, the client became slightly angry and repeated that, no, he was spending *only* $20 a week of alcohol. His denial system would not allow him to admit to the higher figure of more than $1,000 a year.

It is not uncommon for people addicted to alcohol to admit to drinking only "once or twice a week" until reminded that their medical problems were unlikely to have been caused by such moderate drinking levels. The individuals might be attempting to deceive the assessor or they might literally not remember drinking more often than this. However, even when confronted with evidence of serious, continual alcohol use, many alcoholics will deny the reality of their alcoholism. Clients have been known to admit to "one" arrest for driving under the influence of alcohol or possession of a controlled substance when records provided by the court have often revealed that these people had been arrested in two or three different states for similar charges. When confronted, these clients might respond that they thought the evaluator "only meant in *this* state." Thus, to avoid the danger of deception or distorted recall, the assessor *must utilize as many different sources of information as possible*.

The Assessment Format

Often, the assessor's diagnosis is recorded on a standardized record form, which is often titled an "Alcohol & Drug Use Evaluation Summary." Although, ultimately, each individual is unique, there is a general assessment format that may be used by professionals for record keeping. This format is modified as necessary to take into account the differences between individuals and provides a useful framework within which to evaluate the individual and his or her chemical-use pattern. This format will be utilized for this chapter.

Area 1: Circumstances of Referral

The first step in the diagnostic process is to examine the circumstances under which the individual is seen. People with a substance-use disorder will only rarely come in for help on a voluntary basis and are usually forced into the assessment process through external pressure (Craig, 2004).

The manner in which the client responds to the question "What brings you here today?" can provide valuable information about how willing a participant the individual will be in the evaluation process. If the person responds with words like "I don't know, they told me to come here," or "You should know, you've read the report" obviously is being less than fully cooperative. The rare client who responds "I think I have a drug problem" is demonstrating some degree of cooperativeness with the assessor. In each case, the manner in which the client identifies the circumstances surrounding the referral for evaluation provides valuable information to the assessor.

Area 2: Drug- and Alcohol-Use Patterns

The next step is for the evaluator to explore the individual's drug- and alcohol-use patterns *both past and present*. All too often, clients will claim to drink "only once a week now," or to have had "nothing to drink in the last 6 months." Treatment center staff are not surprised to find that this drinking pattern has been the rule *only* since the person's last arrest for an alcohol-related offense.

From time to time, one will encounter a person who proudly claims not to have had a drink or to have used chemicals in perhaps the last 6–12 months, or perhaps even longer. This person may forget to report that he or she was locked up in the county jail awaiting trial during that time or was under strict supervision after being released from jail on bail and had little or no access to chemicals. This is a far different situation from the client who reports that he or she has not had a drink or used chemicals in the last year, is not on probation or parole, and has no charges pending.

Thus, the evaluator should explore the client's living situation to determine whether there were any environmental restrictions on the individual's drug use. Obviously, a person who is incarcerated, in treatment, or on probation requiring frequent and unannounced supervised urine screens to detect drug/alcohol use will be under environmental restrictions. In such a case, a report of having "not used drugs in 6 months" may be the literal truth but will fail to identify the situational constraints that prohibit substance misuse. Also, the individual's chemical-use pattern and *beliefs about his or her drug use* should then be compared with the circumstances surrounding referral. For example, there is the person who states that he or she does not have a problem with chemicals. Earlier in the interview, he or she may also have admitted to a recent arrest on the charge of possession of a controlled substance for the second time in 4 years. In this situation, the client has provided two important but quite discrepant pieces of information to the evaluator.

Several important areas should be explored at this point in the evaluation process. The evaluator needs to consider whether the client has ever been in a treatment program for chemical dependency; whether the individual's drug or alcohol use has ever resulted in legal, family, financial, social, or medical problems; and whether there is evidence of either psychological dependency or physical addiction to drugs or alcohol.

To understand this point, one need only contrast the case of two hypothetical clients who were seen following their recent arrest for driving a motor vehicle while under the influence of alcohol/drugs. The first person might claim (and have collateral information sources support the claim) that she or he only drank in moderation once every few weeks. Furthermore, a background check conducted by the court might reveal that this client never had any previous legal problems of any kind. The evaluation might reveal that after receiving a long-awaited promotion, the client celebrated with some friends. The client was a rare drinker, who uncharacteristically drank heavily with friends to celebrate the promotion and apparently misjudged the amount of alcohol that she or he had consumed.

In contrast is the client who also was seen following an arrest for driving a motor vehicle under the influence of chemicals. This individual's collateral information sources suggest a more extensive chemical-use pattern to the evaluator than admitted during the interview. A background check conducted by the police at the time of the individual's arrest revealed several prior arrests for the same offense.

In the first case, one might argue that the client simply made a mistake. Admittedly, the person in question was driving under the influence of alcohol. However, he or she had *never* done so in the past and does not fit the criteria for a diagnosis of even heavy social drinking. The report to the court would outline the sources of data examined and in this case provides a firm foundation for the conclusion that this individual made a mistake in driving after drinking.

But in the second case, the individual's drunk driving arrest was the tip of a larger problem, which was outlined in the report to the court. The assessor would detail the sources of information that supported this conclusion, including information provided by family members, the individual's physician, the patient, the county sheriff's department, and friends of the client. The final report in this case would conclude that the client had a significant addiction problem, requiring treatment in a chemical-dependency treatment program.

Area 3: Legal History

Part of the assessment process should include an examination of the client's legal history. This information might be based on the individual's self-report or on a review of the client's police record as provided by the court, the probation/parole officer, or other source. *It is important to identify the source of the information on which the report is based.* The following questions should be answered:

- What charges have been brought against the client in the past by the local authorities, and what was their disposition?
- What charges have been brought against the client in the past by authorities in other localities, and what was their disposition?
- What is the nature of current charges (if any) against the individual?

There are many cases on record when the individual was finally convicted of a misdemeanor charge for possession of less than an ounce of marijuana. However, all too often, a review of the client's police record reveals that the individual was *arrested* for felony drug possession and the charges were reduced through a plea bargain agreement. The assessor needs to be aware of *both the initial charge and the ultimate disposition* by the court of these charges. The assessor should also inquire as to whether the client has had charges brought against him or her in other states or by federal authorities. Individuals may admit to *one* charge for possession of a controlled substance only for the staff to later find that this same client has had several arrests and convictions for the same charge in other states. Or the client may have admitted to having been *arrested* for possession charges in other states but may not mention that he or she had left the state before the charges were brought to trial.

Many clients will reason that since they were never *convicted* of the charges, they will not have to mention them during the assessment. The fact that the charges were never proven in court because the person was a fugitive from justice (as well as the fact that interstate flight to avoid prosecution is a possible federal offense) may well be overlooked by the client.

Past military record. One important and often overlooked source of information is the client's *military history, if any.* Many clients with military history will report only on their civilian legal history unless specifically asked about their military legal record. Clients who may have denied any drug/alcohol legal charges whatsoever may upon inquiry admit to having been reprimanded or brought before a superior officer on charges because of chemical use while in the military.

The assessor must specifically inquire whether the individual has ever been in the service. If the client denies military service, it might be useful to inquire *why* the client has never been in the service. Often, this question will elicit a response to the effect that "I wanted to join the Navy, but I had a felony arrest record," or "I had a DWI (driving while under the influence of alcohol) on my record, and couldn't join." These responses provide valuable information to the assessor and open new areas for investigation. If the client has been in the military, was he or she released with an honorable discharge, a general discharge under honorable

conditions, a general discharge under dishonorable conditions, or a dishonorable discharge? Was the client ever brought up on charges while in the service? If so, what was the disposition of these charges? Was the client ever referred for drug treatment while in the service? Was the client ever denied a transfer or promotion because of drug/alcohol use? Finally, was the client ever transferred because of drug/alcohol use?

The client's legal history should be verified, if possible, by contacting the court or probation/parole officer, especially if the client was referred for evaluation for an alcohol/drug related offense. The legal history will often provide significant information about the client's lifestyle and the extent to which drug use has (or has not) resulted in conflict with social rules and expectations.

Area 4: Educational/Vocational History

The next step in the assessment process is to determine the individual's educational and vocational history. This information, which might be based on the person's self-report or school and employment records, provides information on the client's level of function and on whether chemical use has interfered with his or her education or vocation. As before, the evaluator should identify the source of this information. For example, the client who says that she dropped out of school in the tenth grade "because I was into drugs" presents a different picture from the client who completed a bachelor of science degree from a well-known university. The individual who has had five jobs in the last 2 years might present a far different picture from the individual who has held a series of responsible positions and received regular promotions in the same company for the last 10 years. Thus, the assessor should attempt to learn the client's educational/vocational history to determine the individual's educational level, potential, and the degree to which chemical use has started to interfere with the client's educational or work life.

Area 5: Developmental/Family History

The assessor can often uncover significant material through an examination of the client's developmental and family history. The client might reveal a father who was "a problem drinker" in response to the question "Were either of your parents chemically dependent?" but hesitate to call that parent an alcoholic. How the client describes parental or sibling chemical use might reveal how the client thinks about his or her own chemical use.

For example, the client who reports a mother who "had a problem with alcohol" might be far different from the client who says "My mother was an alcoholic." Clients who hesitate to call a sibling alcoholic but are comfortable with the words "problem drinker" might be hinting that they are also uncomfortable with the term *alcoholic* as it applies to themselves. But they may also have rationalized that they are not "problem drinkers," just as their brother or sister was not. Information about either parental or sibling chemical use is important for another reason. As will be recalled from the chapter on alcohol, there is significant evidence suggesting a genetic predisposition toward alcoholism. By extension, one might expect that future research will uncover a genetic link toward the other forms of drug addiction. Thus, a statement by the individual being assessed about a sibling who is perceived as being addicted to alcohol/drugs *hints* at the possibility of a familial predisposition toward substance-use disorders.

In addition, the reviewer will be able to explore clients' attitudes about parental alcohol/drug use in the home where they grew up. Did they view this chemical use as normal? Were they angry or ashamed about their parents' chemical use? Do they view chemical use as being a problem for the family? Thus, it is important for the assessor to examine the possibility of either parental or sibling chemical use either while clients were growing up or at the present time. Such information will offer insights into clients' possible genetic inheritance, especially as to whether they might be at risk to develop an addiction. Furthermore, an overview of the family environment provides clues as to how clients view drug or alcohol use.

As discussed in Chapter 25, family environments differ. Clients whose parents were rare social drinkers would have been raised in a far different environment from that of clients whose parents were drug addicts. A client who reports never knowing his or her mother because she was a heroin addict who put the children up for adoption when they were young might view drugs far differently from clients who reported that they were raised to believe that hard work would see a person through troubled times and whose parents never consumed alcohol.

Area 6: Psychiatric History

Often, chemical use will result in either outpatient or inpatient psychiatric treatment. A natural part of the assessment process should be to discuss with clients whether they have ever been treated for psychiatric problems on either an inpatient or an outpatient basis, including the possible role that their alcohol- and drug-use patterns might have played in the need for hospitalization (Beeder & Millman, 1995).

For example, clients have been known to admit to having been hospitalized for observation because they were hallucinating, had attempted suicide, were violent, or were depressed. On admission to chemical dependency treatment, perhaps months or years later, they might reveal that they were using drugs at the time of their hospitalization for a "psychiatric" disorder and that they failed to mention their substance abuse to the staff of the psychiatric hospital. This might happen because clients lied to the hospital staff or because the staff may simply not have asked the appropriate questions. For these reasons, the assessor should always ask whether clients (a) have *ever* been hospitalized for psychiatric treatment, (b) have ever had outpatient psychiatric treatment, and (c) if so, had revealed to the mental health professional the truth about their drug use.

If possible, the assessor should obtain a release-of-information form from the client and request the treatment records and discharge summary from the treatment center where the client was previously hospitalized. The possibility that drugs contributed to the psychiatric hospitalization or outpatient treatment should either be confirmed or ruled out if possible. This information then will allow the assessor to determine whether the client's drug use has resulted in psychiatric problems serious enough for professional help to be necessary.

Area 7: Medical History

The assessor needs to explore clients' medical history, especially as it relates to their chemical-use history. Questions about whether the client has ever been hospitalized, and if so, for what reasons are of special relevance when working with alcohol- or drug-abusing clients. The hospitalization might have been for drug-related injuries—one client reported having been hospitalized many times after rival drug dealers tried to kill him—or for the treatment of an infection acquired through the use of illicit chemicals. When in doubt, the assessor should attempt to obtain copies of admission/discharge summaries from hospitals where clients have been treated, after obtaining the proper written authorization from the clients. The assessor should also inquire about *current* medical problems, whether clients are taking one or more prescription medications, and possible over-the-counter medication use. An attempt should be made to identify clients' regular physicians and try to learn whether the clients have been "doctor shopping" to try to obtain prescriptions.

Area 8: Previous Treatment History

In working with people who may be addicted to chemicals, it is helpful for the evaluator to determine whether they have ever been in a treatment program for chemical dependency. This information, which may be based on client self-report or information provided by the court system, sheds light on clients' past and their potential to benefit from treatment.

People who have been hospitalized three times for a heart condition and who continue to deny having any heart problems are denying the reality of their condition. The same is true for clients who say they do not think they have a problem with chemicals but who have been in drug treatment three times; they may not have accepted the reality of their drug problem. The problem then becomes one of making a recommendation for such clients in light of their previous treatment history and current status.

The assessor should pay attention to the discharge status from previous treatment programs and how long after treatment the person maintained abstinence. More than one client has proclaimed that he or she was "alcohol-free" for a given period, only to admit to having used marijuana during that time. Further, the client may admit that he or she started to use drugs shortly after discharge, if not before. Deplorably, the situation of a client who reports using chemicals on the way home following treatment is well known to chemical dependency treatment professionals. A client who admits to using chemicals throughout the time that he or she was in treatment is providing valuable information about his or her possible attitude toward *this* treatment exposure as well. This client would have a different prognosis from that of a client who had

maintained total sobriety for 3 years following the last treatment exposure, and who then relapsed.

The evaluator should pay attention to the individual's past treatment history, the discharge status from these treatment programs, and the total period of time the individual was sober after completing treatment. Specific questions should be asked about when clients entered treatment, how long they were there, and when they started to use chemicals following treatment.

Other Sources of Information

Medical Test Data

Laboratory test data are of only limited value in the assessment of a person who is suspected of being addicted to chemicals. There are no blood or urine tests specific for alcohol/drug addiction that a physician might use for general screening purposes. However, elevations in certain blood tests such as liver function tests might serve as "alerting factors" (Hoeksema & de Bock, 1993, p. 268) to the physician for possible alcohol dependence, thus providing important hints about a person's chemical-use status. For example, if a patient being assessed admitted that his or her personal physician had warned about alcohol-related liver damage 3 years ago, this would suggest that the problems caused by the patient's alcohol use date back at least that long and provide strong evidence that the client is alcohol dependent.

Medical test data can often shed light on the client's chemical-use pattern at the time of the evaluation by detecting actual traces of alcohol/illicit drugs in the patient's body. For this reason, Washton (1995) recommended that urine toxicology testing be a routine part of a drug- or alcohol-use assessment. Consider the client who claimed never to have used marijuana, only to have a supervised blood or urine toxicology test be positive for THC. This would strongly suggest that the patient was using marijuana in addition to whatever other drugs of abuse might be suspected.

Medical tests can often

- Confirm the presence of certain chemicals in the client's blood or urine samples.
- Identify the *amount* of certain chemicals present in a person's blood/urine sample (example, the BAL).

- Determine whether the drug levels in the blood or urine sample have increased (suggesting further drug use), remained the same (which also might suggest further drug use), or declined (suggesting no further drug use since the last test).
- Offer hints as to how long the patient has been using chemicals.

The detection of chemical use by laboratory testing is very technical and is affected by many different variables (Verebey, Buchan, & Turner, 1998). Although urine toxicology testing is less intrusive than blood tests, it still involves an element of intrusiveness (Cone, 1993). At the very least, urine toxicology testing involves an invasion of privacy, and the process of obtaining a blood sample for toxicology screening is physically invasive. However, medical test data are often quite useful to the assessor. It is not uncommon, for example, for a client who was involved in an automobile accident to claim to have "only had two beers" prior to when he or she started to drive. A blood alcohol (BAL) test conducted within an hour of the accident may reveal, however, that the client's BAL was far higher than what would be achieved from "only" two beers. This information would suggest some distortion on the client's part.

Clients who had tested negative for marijuana on one occasion may very well test positive for this same chemical only a few days later. Subsequent inquiry might reveal that they used drugs sometime after the first test, thinking that it was "safe." Such deception might be detected by *frequent* and *unannounced* urine tests that are *closely supervised* to detect illicit drug use.[6] It is for these reasons that the assessor should always attempt to utilize medical test information when possible to further establish a foundation for the diagnosis of a chemical-use problem.

Psychological Test Data

Several psychological tests may be of use in the diagnosis of chemical dependency either directly or indirectly. A major disadvantage of paper-and-pencil tests is that they are best suited to situations when the client is unlikely to fake (the technical term is *positively dissimulate*) his

or her answers on the test in order to appear less disturbed (Evans & Sullivan, 2001). A common problem, well known to chemical-dependency rehabilitation professionals, is that these instruments are subject to the same problems of denial, distortion, and outright misrepresentation often encountered in the clinical interview setting.

A technique that may be useful in detecting intentional dissimulation is to review the test results with not only the client but the client's spouse or significant other also present. The assessor then reviews the test item by item, stating the client's response. Often, the spouse or significant other will contradict the client's response to one or more test items, providing valuable new data for the assessment process. For example, on the Michigan Alcoholism Screening Test (MAST), clients often answer "no" to the question of whether they had ever been involved in an alcohol-related accident. The client's wife, if present, may speak up at this point, asking about "that time when you drove off the road into the ditch a couple of years ago." When, in this hypothetical example, the client pointed out that the police had ruled the cause of the accident as being ice on the road, the wife may have responded "but you told me that you had been drinking earlier that night."

Another technique to detect dissimilation is to administer the same test or ask the same questions twice during the assessment process. For example, the MAST may be administered during the initial interview and again at the follow-up interview a week or so later. If there are significant discrepancies, these are explored with the client to determine why there are so many differences between the two sets of test data. Obviously, if a client scored 13 points when he or she first took the MAST but scored only 9 points on the same test just a week later, the assessor would have reason to conduct further inquiry and might suspect some level of deception until this is disproven.

Psychological test data can often provide valuable insights into the client's personality pattern and chemical use. Many such tests require a trained professional to administer and interpret the test to the client. The accuracy of psychological test data in the detection of alcohol/drug abusers has been disputed ("California Judges Get Toughter," 1997). However, when used properly, psychological test data can add an important dimension to the diagnostic process.

---

[6]The use of urine, hair, and saliva samples for toxicology testing is discussed in more detail in Chapter 31.

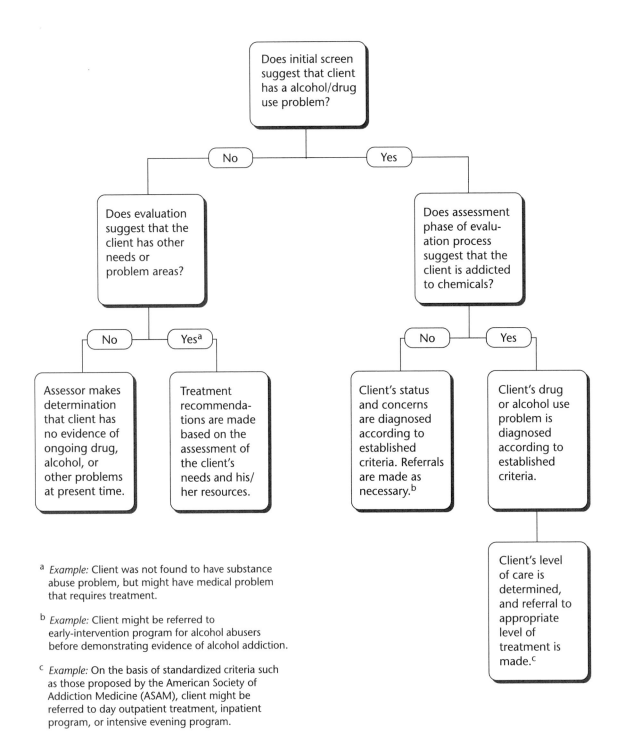

Does initial screen suggest that client has a alcohol/drug use problem?

No

Yes

Does evaluation suggest that the client has other needs or problem areas?

Does assessment phase of evaluation process suggest that the client is addicted to chemicals?

No

Yes[a]

No

Yes

Assessor makes determination that client has no evidence of ongoing drug, alcohol, or other problems at present time.

Treatment recommendations are made based on the assessment of the client's needs and his/her resources.

Client's status and concerns are diagnosed according to established criteria. Referrals are made as necessary.[b]

Client's drug or alcohol use problem is diagnosed according to established criteria.

Client's level of care is determined, and referral to appropriate level of treatment is made.[c]

[a] *Example:* Client was not found to have substance abuse problem, but might have medical problem that requires treatment.

[b] *Example:* Client might be referred to early-intervention program for alcohol abusers before demonstrating evidence of alcohol addiction.

[c] *Example:* On the basis of standardized criteria such as those proposed by the American Society of Addiction Medicine (ASAM), client might be referred to day outpatient treatment, inpatient program, or intensive evening program.

FIGURE 26.2 A flowchart of the assessment process.

The Outcome of the Evaluation Process

At the end of the assessment, the chemical dependency professional should be in a position to answer four interrelated questions: (a) Does the client seem to have a substance-use problem? (b) How *severe* is the individual's substance-use problem? (c) What is the individual's *motivation to change?* (d) What *factors seem to contribute to further substance use* by the individual? (Connors et al., 2001; McCrady, 2001). Based on the assessment, the professional should also be able to determine the level of care that appears necessary to help the client and to make some recommendations as to the disposition of the client's case. Figure 26.2 shows a flowchart outlining the assessment process.

Obviously, if the client is found to be addicted to one or more chemicals, a recommendation that he or she enter treatment would be appropriate. The detection of a substance-use problem is of little value if there is no recommendation for treatment (Appleby, Dyson, Luchins, & Cohen, 1997; Paton, 1996). The form of treatment, however, would be determined by the assessor's opinion as to the *appropriate level of care*. Treatment programs are ranked by the *intensity* of the treatment program. For example, a medical inpatient treatment program is considered more intense than a day outpatient treatment that meets on a 5-day a week basis, and both of these programs are considered more intense than an evening outpatient treatment program that meets once a week. The deciding factor is the client's need for treatment.

Summary

The evaluation process involves three phases: screening, assessment, and diagnosis. Each of these phases was reviewed. The application of various tools such as the Addiction Severity Index, the Minnesota Multiphasic Personality Inventory (MMPI), and the Michigan Alcoholism Screening Test (MAST) were discussed as aids to the evaluation process. The goal of each phase was examined, as was the need for a wide database in order to provide the most comprehensive picture possible of the client's chemical-use pattern. Data sources discussed include the client and collateral information providers as well as the application of medical test data as possibly providing information that would aid the evaluation process.

Information from medical personnel, who would be in a position to evaluate the client's physical status, can often prove valuable in understanding a client and the role that drugs have had on his or her life. Finally, psychological test data may reveal much about the client's personality profile and drug-use pattern. However, psychological test data suffer from the drawback that they are easily manipulated by a client who wishes to dissimulate.

The outcome of the assessment process should be a formal report outlining the evidence that the client is or is not abusing or is dependent on chemicals. The recommendations from the evaluation process might include suggestions for further treatment, even if the client is found not to be addicted to chemicals.

CHAPTER TWENTY-SEVEN

The Process of Intervention

Introduction

The benefit of treating individuals who are abusing or addicted to recreational chemicals is that each dollar invested in treatment brings a return of $10 (Lowe, 2004). Part of these savings is in the reduced cost of health care for these individuals. The average monthly medical cost for a drug abuser is estimated at $750 per month (Rosenbloom, 2000). Following treatment, those same costs drop to $200 per month, compared with the typical monthly medical care cost of $100 a month for a person who has never abused recreational chemicals. These figures demonstrate that the attempt to rehabilitate substance abusers/addicts is cost-effective and could bring about a marked reduction in the annual expenditure for health care in this country if adequate treatment could be provided for this population.

Surprisingly, although alcohol/drug use is a factor in so many accidents and diseases, the cost of insurance benefits for substance-abuse rehabilitation was found to be only 13% of the total expenditure for behavioral health care and less than 1% of the expenditure for overall health care (Schoenbaum, Zhang, & Strum, 1998). These data suggest that substance abuse/addiction causes an inordinate drain on the health care resources of this country. Even so, substance-abuse rehabilitation professionals encounter resistance from both substance abusers and health insurance providers when they attempt to intervene in such cases. In this chapter, the process of intervention with substance abusers will be discussed.

A Definition of Intervention

It was once thought that for addicts to accept the need for help, they had to "hit bottom," as it is called in Alcoholics Anonymous. "Bottom" is the point at which the individual has to admit absolute, total defeat. When the alcohol- or drug-dependent individual reached this point, he or she would have no question about the need to stop using chemicals. But this passive approach to treatment meant that many alcohol/drug abusers died before reaching bottom, and many others never accepted the need to stop abusing chemicals.

Vernon Johnson (1980), a pioneer in the intervention process, challenged the belief that it was necessary for the addict to hit bottom before accepting help. He suggested that the alcohol-dependent person could learn to comprehend the reality of his or her addiction *if this information was presented in language that the person could understand.* Even the substance-abusing client who is functioning poorly (McCrady, 2001), or the person who is "not in touch with reality" (Johnson, 1980, p. 49) because of chemical abuse, is "capable of accepting some useful portion of reality, *if that reality is presented in forms they can receive*" (p. 49, italics in original). Further, because of the physical and emotional damage that uncontrolled addiction could cause, Johnson (1980) did not recommend that concerned family/friends wait until the addicted person hit bottom. Rather, he advocated *early intervention* in cases of alcohol/drug addiction.

In a later work, Johnson identified intervention as being a

> process by which the harmful, progressive and destructive effects of chemical dependency are interrupted and the chemically dependent person is helped to stop using mood-altering chemicals, and to develop new, healthier ways of coping with his or her needs and problems. (1987, p. 61)

In the eyes of Twerski (1983), an early advocate of the intervention process, intervention was "a collective, guided effort by the significant persons in the patient's environment to precipitate a crisis through confrontation, and thereby to remove the patient's defensive obstructions to recovery" (p. 1028).

A final definition. Drawing on these three definitions, it is possible to define an intervention project as being (a) an *organized* effort on the part of (b)*significant others* in the addict's environment to (c) *break through the wall of denial, rationalization, and projection* by which the addict seeks to protect his or her addiction. The purpose of this collective effort, which is (d) *usually supervised* by a chemical-dependency professional, is to (e) secure an agreement to *immediately* seek treatment.

A consequence of early intervention projects. Unfortunately, substance abusers might not view their chemical abuse as being problematic (McCrady, 2001). Because they have not hit bottom, they might not have come to understand or accept the relationship between the problems they have encountered and their chemical use. Thus, they might resist efforts by concerned others to intervene in an area where they do not see a need for corrective action. There is a very real potential for a negative outcome from poorly planned and executed intervention projects, especially if agreed-upon sanctions are imposed on the individual (Fals-Stewart, O'Farrell, & Birchler, 2003). Thus, intervention techniques are not to be utilized lightly or by inexperienced practitioners.

Characteristics of the Intervention Process

Pressure from family and loved ones to address a person's substance-use problem is second only to legal pressure as a way to force the individual to seek treatment (Fals-Stewart et al., 2003). Such pressure is applied *without malice.* This is not a session to allow people to vent their pent-up frustration but is a "profound act of caring" (Johnson Institute, 1987, p. 65) through which significant others in the addict's social circle break the rule of silence surrounding his or her addiction. Effective intervention sessions are *planned in advance* and are repeatedly *rehearsed* by the individual participants to ensure that the information presented is appropriate for an intervention session.

Further, participants must agree *in advance* about the goal of the intervention effort. This goal is to help the addicted person accept the need to enter treatment *immediately.* To do this, each person involved confronts the addicted person with specific evidence that he or she has lost control of his or her drug use, in language that the individual can understand. The participants also express their desire for the addict to seek professional help for the drug problem (Williams, 1989). In the process, all members affirm their concern for the addict, but each participant will offer hard data showing that the addicted person is no longer in control of his or her life. The collective hope is that those involved will be able to break through the addicted person's system of denial.

Although the intervention process has been an accepted tool for more than a generation, there has been little research into which types of families might benefit most from intervention training or the type of client who would benefit most from the intervention process (Edwards & Steinglass, 1995). In a very real sense, the process of intervention is based on a clinical theory that has not been subjected to research studies designed to identify its utility or the optimum conditions under which it might be utilized.

The Mechanics of Intervention

The intervention process, as noted above, is *planned* and should be rehearsed beforehand by the participants. Usually, three to four sessions are held prior to the formal intervention session so participants can learn more about the process and practice what they are going to say (O'Farrell, 1995). The intervention process should involve *everyone* in the addicted person's life who might possibly have something to add, including the spouse, siblings, children, possibly friends, supervisor/employer, minister, coworkers, or others. The Johnson Institute (1987) suggested that the supervisor be included because addicts often will use their perception of their job performance as an excuse not to listen to the others in the intervention project. All participants are advised to bring forward *specific incidents* in which the addicted person's behavior, especially the chemical use, interfered with their lives in some manner.

Individually confronting an addicted person is difficult at best, and in most cases it is an exercise in futility (Johnson Institute, 1987). Anyone who has tried to talk to an addicted person knows that the addict will use denial, rationalization, or threats or simply try to avoid any confrontation that threatens her or his continued drug use. If the spouse questions whether the alcoholic was physically able to drive the car home last night, he or she might meet with the response, "No, but my friend Joe drove the car home for me, then walked home after he parked the car in the driveway."

However, if Joe *also* is present, he might then confront the alcoholic by saying he did *not* drive the car home last night, or any other night for that matter! The alcoholic's wife might be surprised to hear this, as the excuse "Joe drove me home last night" could very well have been a common one. But quite likely, nobody ever asked Joe whether he drove the car home. Before everybody was brought together for an intervention session, probably no one checked out the isolated lies, rationalizations, or episodes of denial. The addicted individual's denial, projection, and rationalization will often crumble when he or she is confronted with all the significant people in his or her environment. This is why a collective intervention session is most powerful in working with the alcohol/drug addicted person.

Twerski (1983) observed that it is common for the person for whom the intervention session was called to make promises to change his or her behavior. These promises might be made in good faith or they might be made simply as a means of avoiding further confrontation. But because the disease of addiction "responds to treatment and not to manipulation, it is unlikely that any of these promises will work, and the counselor must recommend treatment as the optimum course" (Twerski, 1983, p. 1029).

If a substance abuser refuses to acknowledge the addiction, or acknowledges the addiction but refuses to enter treatment, each participant in the intervention session should be prepared to detach from the addict. This is *not* an attempt to manipulate the addict through empty threats. Rather, all involved should be willing to follow through with a specific action to help themselves begin the detachment should the person refuse to enter treatment. For example, if the individual's employer/supervisor has decided to participate, he or she needs to state clearly that if the addicted individual does not seek treatment, his or her employment will be terminated. Then, if the addicted person refuses treatment, the employer/supervisor should follow through with this action.

Family members should also have thought about and discussed possible options through which they might begin to detach from the addict. This should be done prior to the start of the intervention session, and if the addicted person refuses treatment (possibly by leaving the session before it ends) they should follow through with their alternative plan. The options should be discussed with the other participants of the intervention project, and during the rehearsal each participant should practice informing the addicted person what he or she will do if the person does not accept treatment.

Again, there is no malice in the intervention process. There is a very real danger that without proper guidance the intervention session might become little more than a weapon that is used by some family members to control the behavior of another (Claunch, 1994). The participants in the intervention process do not engage in threats to force the addicted person into treatment. Having the addicted person see and accept the need for treatment is one goal of the intervention process, but it is not the only goal. An even more important goal is for participants to begin to break the conspiracy of silence that surrounds the subject of the addicted person's behavior.

In the intervention process, all participants will learn that they have the right to *choose* how they will respond should the addict decide to continue to use chemicals. The addicted person is still able to exercise his or her own freedom of choice, by either accepting the need for treatment or not, as he or she sees fit. But now the involuntary support system of friends and family members will not be as secure: People will be talking to each other and drawing strength from each other. Along with the goal of having the addict either accept the need for treatment or gain a clear understanding of the consequences of not going into treatment, an equally important goal is that all members of the family be *heard* when they voice their concerns (Claunch, 1994).

Family Intervention

Family intervention is a specialized intervention process by which *all* concerned family members, under the supervision of a trained professional, will gather together and plan a joint confrontation of the individual. The family intervention session, like all other forms of intervention, is carried out to break through the addict's denial, allow the family members to begin to voice their concerns, and possibly, obtain a commitment from the addict to enter treatment. The focus is on the individual's drug-using behaviors and on the concern the participants have for the addicted family member.

An advantage of the intervention session is that through confrontation family members of the addicted person may begin to detach from the addict. The conspiracy of silence that existed within the family is broken, and family members may begin to communicate more openly and more effectively. Meyer (1988) identified the intervention process as an "opportunity for healing" (p. 7) for this reason. The participants in the intervention session can express their love and concern for the addicted person while rejecting his or her drug-induced behaviors.

It is often helpful during the stress of the moment for the participants in the intervention process to have written notes they can refer to. These notes should include information about the specific episodes of drug use, dates, and the addict's response to these episodes. Sometimes, family members will bring in a personal diary to use as a reference in the intervention session. One advantage of the written notes is that they help to focus the participant on the specific information that he or she wishes to bring to the intervention session.

During the rehearsal, the professional who will coordinate the intervention session decides who will present such information and in which order. As much as possible, this planned sequence is followed during the intervention session itself. The participants do not threaten the addict. Rather, they present specific concerns and information that highlight the need for the addicted person to enter treatment. The Johnson Institute's (1987) work provides a good overview of the intervention process.

An example of a family intervention session. In this hypothetical intervention session, the central character is a patient named Jim. Also involved are his parents as well as two sisters and a chemical dependency counselor. The intervention session was held at his parents' home, where Jim has been living. During the early part of the session, Jim asserted that he had

never drunk to the point of passing out. He also claimed that he always drank at home so that he wouldn't be out on the roads while intoxicated. For these reasons, he did not believe that his drinking was as bad as everybody said it was and he could see no reason why everybody was so concerned.

One of Jim's siblings, Sara, also lives at home with their parents. She immediately pointed out that just 3 weeks ago, Jim had run out of vodka early in the evening after having four or five mixed drinks. Sara remembered that he got into the car to drive down to the liquor store to buy more vodka. Sara concluded that she was not calling Jim a liar, but that she *knew* he had driven a car after drinking, at least on this one occasion. She was concerned that he might have had an accident and still felt uncomfortable about this incident. She was afraid that he might do it again, and that the next time he might not be so lucky as to make it back home again in one piece.

Jim's mother then spoke. She noted that she had found her son unconscious on the living room floor twice in the past month. She identified the exact dates that this had happened and said she felt uncomfortable with his sleeping on the floor, surrounded by empty beer bottles. She had picked up the empty bottles to keep them from being broken by accident and covered Jim with a blanket while he slept. But she also was concerned, and she believed that her son was drinking more than he thought.

As Jim's mother finished, his other sister Gloria, began to present her information and concerns. She said that she had had to ask Jim to leave her house last week, which was news to the rest of the family. She took this step, she explained, because Jim was intoxicated, loud, and abusive toward his nephew. She said that everybody who was present, including her son's friend who happened to be visiting at the time, smelled the alcohol on his breath and was repulsed by his behavior. Gloria concluded by stating that Jim was no longer welcome in her home unless he (a) went through treatment and (b) abstained from alcohol use in the future.

At this point, the chemical dependency counselor spoke, pointing out to Jim that his behavior was not so very different from that of many thousands of other addicts. The counselor noted that this was about the time in the intervention session when the addict begins to make promises to cut back or totally eliminate the drug use, a prediction that caught Jim by surprise because it was true. His protests and promises died in his throat, even before he opened his mouth.

Before Jim could think of something else to say, the counselor pointed out that Jim gave every sign of having a significant alcohol problem. The counselor listed the symptoms of alcohol addiction one by one and noted that Jim's family had identified different symptoms of addiction in their presentations. "So now," the counselor concluded, "we have reached a point where you must make a decision. Will you accept help for your alcohol problem?" If Jim says "yes," family members will explain that they have contacted the admissions officer of two or three nearby treatment centers who have agreed to hold a bed for him until after the intervention session ends. Jim will be given a choice of which treatment center to enter and will be told that travel arrangements have been taken care of. His luggage is packed in the car, waiting, and if he wishes, the family will escort him to the treatment center as a show of support.

If Jim says "no," the family members then will confront him about the steps they are prepared to take to separate from his addiction. His parents may inform him that they have arranged for a restraining order from the court and present him with papers from the court informing him that if he should come within a quarter of a mile of his parents' home, he will be arrested. The other family members might inform Jim that until he seeks professional assistance for his drinking, he is not welcome to live with them, either. If his employer is present, Jim may be told that his job is no longer there for him if he does not enter treatment.[1]

Jim may be told that no matter what he may think, these steps are not being taken as punishment. Each person will inform him that because of his drug addiction, they find it necessary to detach from him until such time as he chooses to get his life in order. Each person there will affirm concern for Jim but will also start the process of no longer protecting him from his addiction to chemicals. These decisions have all been made in advance of the intervention session. Which option the participants will take depends in large part

on Jim's response to the question: "Will you accept help for your alcohol problem?" Through the process of intervention, the family members have been helped to identify boundaries, which are limits that they can enforce for their own well-being (Claunch, 1994).

Criticism of the Johnson Institute model. Many detractors point out that the "surprise party intervention" model is not the best way to intervene in cases where the individual has a substance-use problem. In the 1980s a new approach, motivational interviewing, was presented as an alternative to the intervention process suggested by the Johnson Institute (Miller, 2003). The motivational interviewing approach attempts to help the client to explore and resolve resistance and ambivalence, to enhance treatment retention and to help the client make a personal choice to abstain from chemical abuse.

A final word. There are strong advocates of the family intervention model presented here. In spite of these advocates, however, there is limited research into its effectiveness (Connors, Donovan, & DiClemente, 2001). The professional coordinating the intervention session should be familiar with this and alternative models of intervention in order to best meet the client's needs. Rather than utilizing a "one size fits all" approach, the therapist should attempt to match a specific form of intervention with the needs of the addicted person and the family.

Intervention With Other Forms of Chemical Addiction

The Johnson Institute (1987) addressed the issue of intervention when the person's drug-of-choice was not alcohol but any of a wide range of other chemicals. The same techniques used in alcoholism also apply when the person is using cocaine, benzodiazepines, marijuana, amphetamines, or virtually any other drug of abuse. Significant others will gather, discuss the problem, and review their data about the addict's behavior. Practice intervention sessions are held, and the problems are addressed during the practice sessions as they are uncovered.

Finally, when everything is ready, the formal intervention session is held with the addicted person. The person might need to be tricked into attending the intervention session, but there is no malice in the attempt to

---

[1]The employee has certain legal rights, and it is necessary for the employer to consult with an attorney to ensure that he or she does not violate the employee's rights by this process. See Kermani and Castaneda (1996) for a discussion of this issue.

help him or her see how serious the drug problem has become. Rather, there is a calm, caring, review of the facts by person after person until the individual is unable to defend the chemical use and recognizes that he or she is in need of professional help.

The goal of the intervention session is, again, to secure an agreement from the individual to enter treatment immediately. During the pre-intervention practice sessions, arrangements are made to find a time when the addicted person would be able to participate. A family reunion might be an opportunity to carry out an intervention session, for example. Although this might, at first glance, seem disruptive to a family holiday, would the intervention session be any more painful than the family's unspoken anger and frustration at the addicted member's behavior? Indeed, the intervention project might serve as a catalyst for change within the family constellation, opening the door for changes in other areas. However, the point is that the intervention project must be timed so that the person who is the focus can participate for as long as the session lasts.

Arrangements are made in advance for the individual's admission into treatment. This may be accomplished by a simple telephone call to the admissions officer of the treatment center. The caller may then explain the situation and ask if the treatment center would accept the target person as a client. Usually, treatment center staff will want to carry out their own chemical dependency evaluation to confirm that the person is an appropriate referral to treatment. But most should be more than willing to consider a referral from a family intervention project.

The Ethics of Intervention

The process of intervention is fraught with ethical dilemmas. The "judgement that a person constitutes a sufficiently significant danger to himself or others such that some intervention is justified is often highly speculative" (Kleinig, 2004, p. 381). Thus, the case for intervention needs to be *firmly* established before the process is allowed to proceed (Rothenberg, 1988). The process of intervention rests on the assumption that through treatment, the substance-abusing individual can be saved from the negative consequences of his or her behavior. However, as Kleinig (2004) pointed out, the success rates of existing treatment modalities

does not offer much of a guarantee that this assumption will be met. At the very least, a thoughtful and honest assessment of the risks, benefits, and alternatives to treatment as the goal of the intervention project should be carried out (Kleinig, 2004).

Another concern is that the patient's *informed consent* is a necessary component of the intervention project (Kleinig, 2004). In the past, the authoritative assertion of the health care professional that the intervention was necessary was deemed sufficient; now, however, the legal environment holds that the patient must offer informed consent before participating in *any* form of treatment, including intervention (Kleinig, 2004). One of the tenets of informed consent is that the individual is free to refuse the proposed treatment at any point. But to complicate matters, there are exceptions. Kleinig (2004) suggested that one exception is in such cases where harm will occur to one individual because of the chemical-abuse problem of a second person. This is the basis on which pregnant substance abusers are remanded to treatment in many parts of the country, as a protection for their unborn children (Kleinig, 2004).

Another issue that must be addressed in the intervention project is data privacy (Kleinig, 2004). Information can not be indiscriminately revealed to others, even if the goal is to help the client who is the center of the intervention. The individual's substance-use problems are viewed in many districts as matters of private concern and thus protected by data privacy regulations. This is of particular concern in teaching hospitals or professional training programs, where students/trainees might be exposed to information about clients that the clients would prefer to keep hidden.

A common ethical problem that emerges in the intervention project is the potential for a *conflict of interest* to arise if the substance-abuse counselor coordinating the intervention process refers the client *only* to himself or herself, or to the facility where the counselor works (Fals-Stewart et al., 2003). The counselor/therapist who coordinates the intervention project should have no vested economic interest in *where* the client goes for treatment. Ideally, the client should be offered a number of treatment options, although economic and geographic realities limit the available options.

Finally, other aspects of the intervention project, such as the counselor's qualifications and adherence to professional ethical codes, must also be considered when planning the intervention project (Kleinig, 2004). Obviously, legal counsel is necessary to guide the chemical-dependency professional through the legal quagmire that surrounds intervention, and such professionals are advised to consult an attorney about the specific laws that apply to intervention in their state.

Intervention via the Court System

Court-ordered treatment reflects the theory that although internal motivation is necessary for people to change their substance-use behavior, *external* motivation can promote abstinence during the critical early stages of recovery while the drug user develops the internal motivation to sustain a recovery program (DiClemente, Bellino, & Neavins, 1999; Satel, 2000). Individuals who participate in a rehabilitation program at the invitation of the court may do so after having been convicted for driving while under the influence of alcohol, for possession of chemicals, or for some other drug-related charge. In court-ordered treatment, the judge offers the offender an alternative to incarceration: *Either* you successfully complete a drug-treatment program *or* you will be incarcerated.

The exact length of time the individual might spend in jail depends on the specific nature of the charge for which he or she was convicted. However, either/or treatment situations are unique in that the individual is offered a choice. Some people might select incarceration to fulfill the obligation to the courts; others might accept completion of a treatment program. In many ways, such "either/or" treatment admissions are easier to work with than voluntary admissions to treatment. Court-sponsored intervention is a powerful incentive for individuals to complete the treatment program they select, and research suggests that people in treatment at the invitation of the court system work harder on treatment goals than those who volunteered to enter treatment (Moylan, 1990; Satel, 2000).

When there is a legal hold on drug abusers, they cannot leave treatment when their denial system is confronted. Also, the nature of their admission can be used to confront them about the severity of their chemical-use problem. After all, it is difficult for a person who has been arrested for a second or third substance-related offense to

deny having a chemical-use problem, although this has been known to happen.

The theory behind court-mandated treatment is that

> proactive approaches involving persons with addictive behaviors, in contrast to the more traditional reactive approaches of waiting until motivation for treatment is fully developed, can be helpful in reaching individuals who are not currently interested in changing the addictive behavior. (DiClemente & Prochaska, 1998, p. 7)

This theory was tested by a pair of research studies in which individuals who were "legally induced to seek treatment" (Collins & Allison, 1983, p. 1145) were compared with those who entered treatment voluntarily. In each study, there were no significant differences in outcome (Collins & Allison, 1983; Ouimette, Finney, & Moos, 1997). But those who were in treatment at the court's invitation were more likely to stay in treatment longer than those who had no restrictions placed on them. On the basis of their research, Collins and Allison (1983) concluded that

> the use of legal threat to pressure individuals into drug treatment is a valid approach for dealing with drug abusers and their undesirable behaviors. Legal threat apparently helps keep these individuals constructively involved in treatment and does not adversely affect long-term treatment goals. (p. 1148)

In her review of the effectiveness of court-mandated treatment, Wells-Parker (1994) concluded that individuals who were mandated to treatment after conviction of driving a motor vehicle while under the influence of alcohol/drugs were 8% to 9% less likely to have a subsequent DWI offense than were untreated offenders. Further, the author concluded that DWI offenders who were mandated to treatment had a 30% lower mortality rate than untreated offenders, although the exact mechanism through which treatment might reduce mortality is still not clear.

A naive clinician might conclude that court-mandated treatment is the answer to the problem of substance abuse in this country, but remember that individuals who are court-ordered into treatment do *only* about as well as those who were self-referred (Kleber, 1997; Miller, 1995). Court-mandated treatment is not a guarantee of success for a number of reasons. Three of these reasons were identified by Howard and McCaughrin (1996). The authors examined 330 treatment programs that accepted court-mandated patients but did not utilize methadone. The authors found that (a) treatment programs whose staff did not view as a hindrance the fact that the client was court-ordered into treatment had better client outcomes; (b) programs with more than 75% court-mandated referrals had poor client outcomes; and (c) treatment programs that allowed the court-mandated client some input into the length of stay, the treatment goals, and treatment methods as well as whether the employer was to be notified that the individual was in treatment seemed to have better client outcomes than programs that did not grant court-mandated clients these rights.

These findings, while suggestive, do not find universal support among clinicians. Peele (1989) viewed such either/or referrals as intrusive and counterproductive. He pointed out that individuals convicted of driving a motor vehicle while under the influence of chemicals responded better to legal sanctions (i.e., jail, probation) than to being forced into treatment. In place of treatment, Peele (1989) argued that the individual be held responsible for his or her actions, *including the initial decision to use chemicals*, and that chemical use or abuse should not excuse the individual from responsibility for his or her behavior. Thus there is not yet a definitive answer for the question of whether using legal sanctions in the treatment of chemical abuse is productive.

Drug court. The concept of drug court was first tried in 1989 (Taylor, 2004). Since then, at least 1,180 drug court programs have been established in at least 40 different states (Huddleston, Freeman-Wilson, & Boone, 2004; Taylor, 2004). The drug court model will

> quickly identify substance abusing offenders and place them under strict court monitoring and community supervision, coupled with effective, long-term treatment services . . . the drug court participant undergoes an intense regimen of substance abuse and mental health treatment, case management, drug testing, and probation supervision while reporting to

regularly scheduled status hearings before a judge with specialized expertise in the drug court model. (Huddleston et al., 2004, p. 1)

Such programs are most effective with first-time offenders (Goldkamp, White, & Robinson, 2002), breaking the revolving door cycle of repeated offenses for those who might turn aside from their current life direction. The drug court program includes frequent urine toxicology testing conducted at least weekly, if not more often. Consequences for "dirty" urine or failure to participate in agreed-upon treatment programs are immediate, but rewards for participation and progress are equally swift. Such programs have shown a lower recidivism rate than traditional legal sanctions and are quite cost-effective (Huddleston et al., 2004; Taylor, 2004). New York State, for example, found that drug court saved $250 million in a year's time, whereas St. Louis, Missouri, found that every dollar invested in drug court resulted in a savings of $6.32 in welfare, medical, and law-enforcement expenses (Taylor, 2004).

Court-ordered involuntary commitment. In more than 30 states, people can be committed to treatment against their will if the courts have sufficient evidence to believe they are in imminent danger of harming themselves or others (Olson et al., 1997). The exact provisions of such a court-ordered commitment vary from state to state but are usually imposed when the individual has failed to respond to less-intensive sanctions (Olson et al., 1997). In spite of the frequency with which these laws are used to commit individuals to treatment for substance-use problems, there is little research into the effectiveness of this form of intervention (Olson et al., 1997). Wild, Cunningham, and Hobdon (1998) suggested that clients who enter treatment because of such external motivation might comply with treatment expectations for a short period of time without making any permanent changes in attitude or behavior.

Occasionally, the individual will demonstrate *autonomous motivation*, that is, enter treatment on a voluntary basis (Wild et al., 1998). As the Johnson Institute (1987) observed, this is unusual, although it does happen. It is more common, however, for the substance-abusing person to continue to use chemicals if he or she could do so. For this reason, external pressure of some kind, be it family, legal, medical, or professional penalties, is often necessary to help the addicted person see the need to enter treatment.

Other Forms of Intervention

Morgan (2003) suggested that *contingency management* techniques are often effective when working with individuals who have substance-use problems. Another way to view contingency management is that the client is confronted with an "either/or" situation: "*Either* you stop drinking, *or* I will _____." Clients who enter treatment under such circumstances might be said to demonstrate *controlled motivation* (Wild et al., 1998). A common source of such external motivation is for a physician to threaten to file commitment papers for individuals with a substance-use problem unless they enter treatment. Also, with the advent of worksite-mandated urine toxicology testing, it is not uncommon for employees to be referred to a specific form of treatment after failing a worksite urine toxicology test. Another source of external motivation might be supplied by the spouse who promises that "either you stop using chemicals, or I will leave/seek a divorce!"

Employer-mandated treatment. With urine toxicology testing at workplaces increasing, coupled with growing sensitivity in industry to the economic losses incurred through employee substance abuse, employer-mandated treatment referrals are becoming more and more common. But there is relatively little research data to show which forms of intervention are most effective in the workplace (Roman & Blum, 1996). It has been found that employees who had to be coerced into treatment under threat of job loss tend to have more serious substance-use problems, but they also tend to benefit more from treatment (Adelman & Weiss, 1989; Lawental, McLellan, Grissom, Brill, & O'Brien, 1996). Employer-mandated treatment has been justified from an economic

standpoint. A company with just 500 employees will typically pay $132,881 in health care costs for alcohol-related problems each year (Brink, 2004). Further, individuals who are abusing/dependent on alcohol typically use twice as many "sick" days and are five times as likely to file a workman's compensation claim as nondrinkers (Brink, 2004). Thus, "constructive coercion" (Adelman & Weiss, 1989, p. 515) might actually provide a positive service to employees with substance-use problems. However, a great deal of research is needed to determine which forms of intervention are most effective in the workplace (Roman & Blum, 1996).

Summary

The intervention process is an organized effort by significant others in the addicted person's social environment to break through the defenses that protect the individual from the realization that his or her life is out of control. Intervention projects are usually supervised by a substance-abuse rehabilitation professional and are held with the goal of securing an agreement for the individual to enter treatment immediately.

In this chapter, we discussed the mechanics of the intervention project and some of the more common forms that intervention might take. It was pointed out that the individual retains the right to choose or refuse to enter treatment. People who participate in the intervention project must be prepared for either choice and to have alternate plans in case the addicted individual does not accept the need for treatment.

Also in this chapter, we discussed the fact that the individual retains certain rights, even during the intervention process. Indeed, the drug user cannot be detained if he or she expresses the wish to leave the intervention session. Finally, the question of when legal sanctions should be imposed or when treatment might be substituted for these legal sanctions was discussed.

CHAPTER TWENTY-EIGHT

The Treatment of Chemical Dependency

Introduction

Questions about the effectiveness of substance-abuse treatment no longer spark fierce debate among health care professionals. As they have examined the impact of chemical abuse/addiction on society, they have seen clearly that alcohol- and drug-use problems constitute a serious drain on the health care resources of this country. Breithaupt (2001) estimated that the cost of treating medical problems caused or exacerbated by addiction in the United States was $300 billion a year, a substantial fraction of the total expenditure for health care in this country. Note that the cost of medical care for each drug-addicted person is $1,000 more per year than for individuals who do not abuse chemicals (Laine et al., 2001).

Substance-abuse rehabilitation is not perfect, but its success rate compares very well with that of other chronic relapsing diseases such as diabetes, hypertension, or multiple sclerosis (Frances & Miller, 1998; McLellan, 2001). For every dollar invested in rehabilitation efforts, the estimated return ranges from $4–$12 (Breithaupt, 2001; Carroll, 1997; Frances & Miller, 1998; Mee-Lee, 2002) to as much as $50 (Garrett, 2000). In the late 1990s, a research study conducted in California showed that an investment of $209 million for drug treatment resulted in a savings of $1.5 *billion* in reduced criminal activity and health care costs (Craig, 2004). To explain the reduction in health care costs, the typical alcohol-dependent individual requires *10 times* the health care expenditure as the nonalcoholic, and family members of alcoholics utilize five times the health care resources required for family members of nonalcoholics (McLellan, 2001).

Unfortunately, in the United States, treatment programs for individuals with substance-use problems

developed in a haphazard manner, and for the most part the evolution of treatment formats was not guided by scientific feedback (Miller & Brown, 1997). As a result, treatment methods that are least effective seem to be the most deeply entrenched (Miller, Andrews, Wilbourne, & Bennett, 1998; Miller & Brown, 1997). Fierce debates have raged in the professional literature as to which form of treatment is most effective for individuals with chemical-use problems. In this chapter, some of the basic elements of traditional substance-abuse treatment in the United States are explored. The specific treatment components utilized may vary from one program to another. For example, a treatment program that specializes in working with alcohol-dependent businessmen would have little use for a methadone maintenance component. Yet there are also many common elements in the various treatment processes, and this is the focus of the chapter.

Characteristics of the Substance-Abuse Rehabilitation Professional

The relationship between the client and the counselor is of such critical importance to the rehabilitation process that it has been compared to the individual's initial relationship with his or her parents (Bell, Montoya, & Atkinson, 1997). To provide effective help to people with substance-use disorders, the helper should have certain characteristics. For example, individuals who are dealing with chemical dependency or psychological issues of their own should be discouraged from actively working with clients in treatment, at least until they have resolved their own problems. This injunction makes sense: If the counselor is preoccupied with personal problems, including those of chemical addiction, he or she would be unlikely to be able to help the client advance further in terms of personal growth.

In his work on the characteristics of the effective mental health counselor, Rogers (1961) suggested a number of characteristics he thought were essential: (a) warmth, (b) dependability, (c) consistency, (d) the ability to care for and respect the client, (e) the ability to be separate from the client (which is to say the ability not to try to "live through" a client), (f) the ability not to be perceived as a threat by the client, (g) the ability to free one's self from the urge to judge or evaluate the client, and (h) the ability to see the client as a person capable of growth

In a sense, people who enter a rehabilitation program are admitting that they have been unable to change on their own (Bell et al., 1997). As such people need professional assistance, it would make sense that the therapist with the strongest interpersonal skills would be best equipped to help them change. It is thus not surprising that the therapeutic alliance that evolves between the client and the therapist is one important factor in a positive outcome of the treatment process (Adelman & Weiss, 1989; Connors, Carroll, DiClemente, Longabaugh, & Donovan, 1997; Joe, Simpson, Dansereau, & RowanSzal, 2001).

The client's acceptance of the therapist's efforts is one of the most essential characteristics of a successful therapeutic relationship (Bell et al., 1997). The other characteristics that most strongly influence a client's efforts to change are his or her ability to trust the therapist, to depend on the therapist, to be open with the professional, and to accept external help. Miller (2003) identified several factors that seem to facilitate or inhibit recovery from a substance-use problem, shown in Table 28.1.

One common trap that many beginning therapists fall into is attempting to "buy" client approval through permissiveness. *Caring for clients does not mean protecting them from the natural consequences of their behavior.*

Confrontation and other treatment techniques. For a number of years, substance-abuse rehabilitation in the United States has used a "hard-hitting, directive, exhortational style" (Miller, Genefield, & Tonigan, 1993, p. 455) designed to overwhelm the client's defenses against acceptance and understanding of the disease. Confrontation has been a central feature of many rehabilitation programs and in theory is used to help the client begin to understand the impact that substance use has had on his

TABLE 28.1   Factors That Facilitate or Inhibit Recovery From Substance-Use Problems

Factors that facilitate abstinence	Factors that inhibit abstinence
Empowerment	Disempowerment
Active interest in client as person	Hostility, disinterest
Empathy	Confrontation
Making client feel responsible for change	Making client feel that she or he is not responsible for change
Advice about how to change	Ordering client to change
Helping client find a sense of hope	Hopelessness or powerlessness
Involving client in change process	Giving client a passive role
Environment will support recovery	Environment does not support the client's recovery

Source: Based on Miller (2003).

or her life. But there is little evidence that such confrontation actually helps to bring about behavior change (Hester, 1994; Miller, 1995; Miller & Rollnick, 2002; Miller et al., 1993; Washton, 1995; Zoldan, 2000).

It has been found that harsh, confrontational treatment approaches are counterproductive when applied to substance abusers (Miller, 2003; Miller et al., 1993; Miller et al., 1998). This makes clinical sense, as one factor that predicts successful treatment outcomes is the client's satisfaction with the rehabilitation process (Hser, Evans, Huang, & Anglin, 2004). Few people would enjoy the levels of confrontation once thought necessary by substance-abuse rehabilitation professionals. Indeed, as the therapist's level of confrontation increases, the client's level of resistance increases proportionally (Miller et al., 1993).

To counter this resistance, *empathy* combined with a "supportive-reflective" (Miller et al., 1993, p. 455) style of therapy seems to be effective (Miller, 1998; Miller et al., 1998). Ramsay and Newman (2000) suggested that when confrontation is necessary, it should be infused with caring and concern for the client. The client should not be shamed into conformity but should be allowed to save face, with the therapist initially placing emphasis on the client's distress and slowly assisting the client as he or she learns how the chemical abuse contributed to those problems. Such a therapeutic style places emphasis on the client's ability and responsibility to change, combined with therapist advice, the development of behavioral alternatives, and attempts to help the client achieve a sense of self-efficacy.

The Minnesota Model of Chemical-Dependency Treatment

To say that the Minnesota Model of chemical-dependency treatment has been a success is something of an understatement. Within a short time of its inception, it became and has remained the dominant model for rehabilitation programs in the United States (Ringwald, 2002; Washton & Rawson, 1999). With the changes in insurance program reinbursement policies in the late 1990s, the basic model has been revised, but it still remains a strong influence on both inpatient and outpatient rehabilitation program formats (Ringwald, 2002).

The Minnesota Model was designed in the 1950s by Dr. Dan Anderson. In order to earn money to finish his college education, Dr. Anderson worked as an attendant at the state hospital in Willmar, Minnesota (Larson, 1982). Following graduation, he returned to the state hospital as a recreational therapist. He was assigned to work with the alcoholics who were in treatment there, the least desirable position at that time. Anderson was himself influenced by the work of Ralph Rossen, who was later to become the Minnesota State Commissioner of Health. At the same time, the growing influence of Alcoholics Anonymous (AA) was utilized by Dan Anderson and a staff psychologist, Dr. Jean Rossi, as a means of understanding and working with the alcoholic. They were supported in this approach by the medical director of the hospital, Dr. Nelson Bradley (Larson, 1982).

These individuals joined together in an effort to understand and treat the patients who were sent to the state hospital for treatment of alcoholism. Coming from different professions, each person contributed a different perspective on the patients' needs and addiction. To this team was added the Reverend John Keller, who had been sent to Willmar to learn about alcoholism in 1955. The staff then had "knowledge of medicine, psychology, AA and theology together under one roof to develop a new and innovative alcohol treatment program" (Larson, 1982, p. 35)

This new treatment approach, since called the Minnesota Model of treatment, was designed to work with dependency on alcohol ("ONDCP Gives Rundown," 1990). In the time since its introduction, it has also been used as a model for treating other forms of chemical addiction. The Minnesota Model utilizes a *treatment team* of chemical-dependency counselors familiar with AA, psychologists, physicians, nurses, recreational therapists, and clergy, all of whom will work with the client during the treatment program.

In Stage 1 of the Minnesota Model treatment approach, the evaluation phase, each member of the treatment team meets with the client to assess his or her needs from the professional's own area of expertise. Each professional then makes recommendations for the client's *treatment plan*. In Stage 2, goal setting, the professionals meet *as a team* to discuss the areas they feel should be the focus of treatment. The treatment team meeting is chaired by the individual who is ultimately responsible for the execution of the treatment process, the *case manager*. This is usually the chemical-dependency counselor. Each of the assessments and the recommendations that come from these assessments is reviewed and discussed by the treatment team. The team then selects the recommendations that in their training and experience are most appropriate to help the client achieve and maintain recovery. Interested people such as the client, his or her parole or probation officer, and family members are invited to participate in the treatment plan meeting.

On the basis of this meeting, the case manager and client enter Stage 3 of the treatment process. In this phase, the client and the case manager develop a formal *treatment plan*. The treatment plan that emerges as a result of this process is multimodal and offers a wide variety of potential treatment goals and recommendations. It identifies specific problem areas, behavioral objectives, methods to measure progress toward these objectives, and a target date for each goal. The treatment plan will be discussed in more detail in the next section of this chapter. A flowchart of the treatment plan process appears in Figure 28.1.

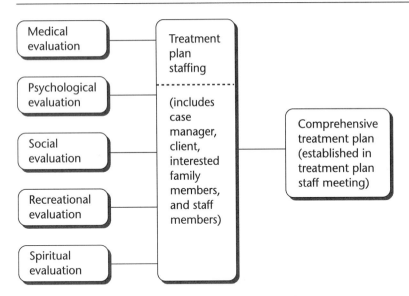

FIGURE 28.1   Flowchart of the evolution of a treatment plan.

The strength of the Minnesota Model of treatment lies in its redundancy and its multimember concept. The information provided by the client is reviewed by many different professionals, each with different training; this allows any one of them to identify a potential treatment problem that others may have overlooked, providing for the greatest possible evaluation of the client's needs, strengths, and priorities. Also, the Minnesota Model allows different professionals to work together in the rehabilitation of the client, addressing that client's specific needs. Under such a system, the chemical-dependency counselor does not need to be a "jack of all trades, master of none." This feature has helped to make the Minnesota Model one of the dominant treatment program models in the field of chemical-dependency rehabilitation for more than 40 years, although under managed care it has been modified or replaced by other treatment formats.

The Treatment Plan

No matter what treatment approach the therapist elects, he or she should develop a *treatment plan* with the client. This plan is based on information obtained during the assessment process and "serves as the plan of action for pursuing the identified goals of treatment"

(Connors, Donovan, & DiClemente, 2001, p. 82). It is a highly specific form, which in some states might be viewed as a legal document. Different treatment centers use different formats, depending on the specific licensure requirements in that state and the treatment methods being utilized.

However, all treatment plans have several similarities. First, the plan should provide a brief summary of the problems that brought the client into treatment. Another section might provide a brief summary of the client's physical and emotional state of health. A third section might contain the individual's own input into the treatment process—what he or she thinks should be included in the plan. The fourth section identifies the specific goals of treatment, the heart of the treatment plan. Following this are discharge criteria, the steps that must be accomplished for the client to be discharged from treatment. Finally, there is a brief summary of the steps that are to be part of the client's *aftercare* program.

Treatment goals should include (a) a brief statement of the *problem*, (b) *long-term goals*, (c) *short-term objectives*, (d) *measurement criteria*, and (e) a *target date*. The problem statement is short, usually a sentence or two, identifying a *specific problem* to be addressed in treatment. The *long-term goal* is the ultimate objective, a general statement of a hoped-for outcome. The long-term goal statement is usually also only one or two sentences long. Next is a *short-term objective*. The objective is *a very specific behavior that can be measured*. The objective statement is usually between one and three sentences long and identifies the measurement criteria by which both the client and staff will be able to assess whether progress toward this objective is being made. Finally, there is the *target date*, usually a simple sentence identifying a specific date by which this goal will be achieved.

An example of a treatment goal for a 24-year-old male who is polydrug addicted (cocaine, alcohol, marijuana, and occasionally benzodiazepines) and has abused alcohol/drugs daily for the last 27 months might appear as follows:

> *Problem:* Client has used chemicals daily for at least the past 2 years and has been unable to abstain from drug use on his own.
>
> *Long-term Goal:* That the client abstain from further chemical abuse.
>
> *Short-term Objective:* That the client not use mood-altering chemicals for 90 days.
>
> *Method of Measurement:* Random supervised urine toxicology screens to detect possible drug use. Patient self-report.
>
> *Target Date:* Scheduled discharge date.

The typical treatment plan might identify as many as five or six different problem areas. Each of these goals can be modified as the treatment program progresses, and each provides a yardstick of the client's progress. Obviously, if the client is not making progress on *any* of the goals, it is time to question whether the client is serious about treatment. The goals become the heart of the treatment program.

Although the Minnesota Model of treatment was long considered the gold standard against which other programs were compared, it was not without its critics. In the next section some of the criticism of the Minnesota Model will be examined.

Reaction to the Minnesota Model. The Minnesota Model has been challenged for a number of reasons. First, it was designed to work with cases of alcoholism.

There has been no research into its applicability to other forms of substance addiction. Even so, this model has been used to treat virtually every known form of substance abuse ("ONDCP Gives Rundown," 1990).

The Minnesota Model draws heavily on the philosophy of Alcoholics Anonymous (AA), and participation in AA is often required. Yet AA itself is not a form of treatment (Clark, 1995). Further, as will be discussed in Chapter 34, there is no clear evidence that AA is effective in cases where the individual is coerced into joining. Thus, there is an inherent contradiction involved in the Minnesota Model, in that one of the central tenets of the model is mandatory participation in AA.

Another challenge to the Minnesota Model involves its length. When it was developed, the client's length of stay at Willmar State Hospital was often arbitrarily set at 28 days. However, there is little research data supporting a need for a 28-day inpatient treatment stay (Turbo 1989). Indeed, the optimal length for inpatient treatment programs has yet to be defined (McCusker, Stoddard, Frost, & Zorn, 1996). Unfortunately, the 28-day treatment program became something of an industry standard for Minnesota Model programs for several decades (Turbo, 1989) and at one time served as a guide for insurance reimbursement (Berg & Dubin, 1990). Surprisingly, in spite of its popularity, there is little evidence that the Minnesota Model was actually effective in helping people deal with their chemical-use problems (Hester & Squires, 2004; McCrady, 2001). Fortunately, it has become almost extinct except at a few private treatment centers where clients can afford to pay for extended substance-abuse rehabilitation programs (Monti, Kadden, Rohsenow, Cooney, & Abrams, 2002).

Other Treatment Formats for Chemical Dependency

In the last years of the 20th century, rehabilitation professionals explored a number of different treatment approaches to alcoholism rehabilitation that differed from the Minnesota Model. While it is not possible to do full justice to each treatment philosophy, we will briefly examine some of the more promising models that have emerged in the past three decades.

Detoxification programs. Technically, the term *detoxification* refers to the process of removing toxins from the body. A second related definition is the medical management of the patient's withdrawal from a drug or drugs of abuse (Haack, 1998). The process of detoxification from alcohol/drugs is not viewed as a form of treatment in itself but is a prelude to the individual's rehabilitation (Leshner, 2001a, b; Mattick & Hall, 1996; Tinsley, Finlayson, & Morse, 1998). Research has shown that up to 95% of people who complete "detox" will relapse without further treatment (Craig, 2004). Thus detox is only the first step in the rehabilitation of individuals with substance-abuse problems.

The goal of the detoxification process is to offer the patient a safe, humane withdrawal from alcohol/drugs of abuse (Mattick & Hall, 1996). The patient's safety is assured, to the degree that this is possible, by having the detoxification process carried out under the supervision of a physician who is both trained and has experience in this area of medicine (Miller, Frances, & Holmes, 1988). The physician will evaluate the patient's needs and resources, and then recommend that the process of detoxification be carried out either on an inpatient or an outpatient basis.

Although detoxification from alcohol/drugs has traditionally been carried out in a hospital setting, the practice of automatically admitting alcohol-dependent people into a hospital for detoxification might not be cost-effective (Berg & Dubin, 1990; Mattick & Hall, 1996). Under certain circumstances, detoxification can be done on an outpatient basis. With careful screening, more than 90% of alcohol-dependent patients can be detoxified as outpatients (Abbott, Quinn, & Knox (1995). One recent study from Australia found that less than 0.5% of the alcohol-dependent patients *required* hospitalization for detoxification (Mattick & Hall, 1996).

Patients who are selected for outpatient detoxification, called "ambulatory detox" (National Academy of Sciences, 1990, p. 175) or "social detox" (Mattick & Hall, 1996), are first evaluated by a physician. Then, depending on their medical status, the patient might be sent home with instructions on how to complete the detoxification process or referred to a special detoxification setting. In either case, the patient's progress after this point is monitored either by a physician, nurse, or other trained personnel. When the patient is sent home, a nurse might stop by to check on his or her progress once or twice a day, or the patient could be instructed to see his or her physician on a daily basis (Prater, Miller, & Zylstra, 1999). In the detoxification center, the patient's progress and vital signs are monitored as often as necessary.

As long as the patient's physical status does not indicate that he or she is in danger of experiencing severe withdrawal-related distress, there is no need for referral to a more manpower-intensive setting such as a general hospital. If, on the other hand, the patient begins to have significant withdrawal-related distress or is unable to complete detoxification on an outpatient basis, then he or she would be transferred to a more suitable setting.

One of the factors in the decision to refer the patient to an inpatient or outpatient detoxification program is the drug of choice. Some of the drugs of abuse, when the patient is addicted to them, can cause severe or even life-threatening problems during detoxification. Withdrawal from either the barbiturates or the benzodiazepines can produce life-threatening seizures for physically dependent patients. There is little evidence that detoxification from opiates can cause any significant physical danger to the patient, but there is strong evidence that opiate-dependent patients are more likely to complete the detoxification process when they are inpatients (Mattick & Hall, 1996).

There is some debate as to whether detoxification programs should be a "funnel" for guiding patients into the rehabilitation process. When detoxification is done at a free-standing clinic, many patients fail to go on to participate in rehabilitation programs (Miller & Rollnick, 2002). On the other hand, some have charged that detoxification programs housed in treatment settings are often little more than recruitment centers for the treatment program. To avoid a possible conflict of interest, staff should advise the patient of treatment options, including the possibility of seeking treatment elsewhere.

Whether undergoing detoxification as an inpatient or an outpatient, the patient being withdrawn from chemicals should be closely monitored by staff to detect signs of drug overdose or seizures, to monitor medication compliance, and to ensure abstinence from recreational chemical use (Miller et al., 1988). Unfortunately, it is not uncommon for patients to take additional drugs when they are supposedly being withdrawn from chemicals.

The process of detoxification is vulnerable to being abused in other ways besides having the patient self-administer alcohol/drugs. For example, some individuals who are addicted to alcohol/drugs will go through detoxification dozens or perhaps even hundreds of times to give themselves a place to live (Whitman, Friedman, & Thomas, 1990). Other individuals will "check into detox" as a place to hide because of drug debts or to try to escape from the police. Individuals who are addicted to opiates have been known to enter a detox program when they are unable to obtain drugs or when they want to lower their daily drug requirement to more affordable levels. At other times, the authorities might create a panic for users by arresting a major drug supplier or by breaking up a major drug supply source. In such cases, it is not uncommon for large numbers of opiate-dependent patients to seek admission to detox in order to have a source of drugs while they wait for new supplies of opiates to become available through illicit avenues. Thus, while detoxification programs provide a valuable service, they are also vulnerable to abuses.

Videotape/self-confrontation. Videotape has long been viewed as a useful means for showing clients what they looked like and how they behaved while intoxicated. There is little data to support this form of confrontation, and some data suggest that it might contribute to higher than anticipated client dropout from treatment (Hester & Squires, 2004).

Acupuncture. Acupuncture is a form of alternative medicine that is occasionally used in the treatment of the addictive disorders. Individual case reports have suggested that it may have a calming effect on some individuals and that may reduce craving for chemicals. The theory behind acupuncture is beyond the scope of this text. In brief, small sterile needles are inserted into specific locations on the individual's body in an attempt to liberate or block the body's energy.

At this time, there is limited evidence that acupuncture is effective in the rehabilitation of substance abusers (Hester & Squires, 2004). Margolin et al. (2002) concluded that acupuncture is not effective by itself as a treatment for cocaine addiction. Ernst (2002) stated that the "complementary therapies" such as acupuncture were about as effective as placebos in treating addictive disorders (p. 1491).

Family and marital therapy. Although once looked upon with some disdain, family and marital therapy have become valuable components of alcohol/drug rehabilitation programs and are now considered an integral part of treatment except in unusual circumstances (Fals-Stewart, O'Farrell, & Birchler, 2004).

The best known and most common form of family therapy is the *family disease approach*, which holds that substance misuse is an illness of the *family*, not just the person with the substance-use problem (Fals-Stewart et al., 2003). Within this framework, the therapist and family members work to identify the role that substance abuse plays within the family and to correct dysfunctional interaction patterns such as communication problems. In many marriages or families where one partner has a substance-use problem, communication patterns tend to be unhealthy, and this in turn helps support the individual's addiction (Alter, 2001). For this reason marriage/family therapy approaches that stress communication skills training are four to five times as effective as rehabilitation programs that focus only on the individual (Alexander & Gwyther, 1995).

Such therapy is quite difficult. It is not uncommon for the defense system of the addicted member and those of the other family members to be *inter*-reinforcing (Williams, 1989). As a result of these interlocking defense systems, the family will, *as a unit*, resist any change in the addicted person's behavior. Also, boundaries are often fluid or nonexistent within the dysfunctional family. These and a multitude of other issues can be addressed within the context of family/marital therapy.

The effectiveness of marital therapy as a treatment modality for chemical dependency has repeatedly been demonstrated in the clinical literature (Edwards & Steinglass, 1995). It is a specialized area of expertise with a vast, evolving literature of its own (Bowen, 1985).

Group therapy approaches. Group psychotherapy offers a number of advantages over individual therapy (Connors et al., 2001; Yalom, 1985). First, therapy groups allow one professional to work with a number of different individuals at once. Second, in the therapy group, group members can learn from and offer feedback to each other. Third, group members provide behavioral models for each other, and this is useful for clients who do not trust the therapist. The group format provides an opportunity for clients to work on many of the interpersonal deficits that contribute to their own addiction within the safety of the group setting. Finally, because of the nature of the therapy group, each individual would find within the group members a reflection of his or her family of origin, allowing him or her to work through problems from earlier stages of growth.

For these reasons, the majority of substance abuse rehabilitation programs use therapy groups as the primary method of working with clients. Individual sessions might be used for special problems too sensitive to discuss in a therapy group situation, but the client is usually encouraged to bring his or her concerns to group, which may meet every other day, daily, or more often than once a day, depending on the pace of the program. Unfortunately, there is limited evidence that group psychotherapy approaches are at all effective in the rehabilitation of substance abusers (Hester & Squires, 2004). Group therapy formats that utilize cognitive-behavioral approaches to identify and help the client learn to deal with painful affective states that might contribute to the urge to use chemicals seem to be effective with personality disordered substance abusers (Fisher & Bentley, 1996).

McCrady (2001) pointed out that women who have substance-use problems seem to be somewhat inhibited in group settings, possibly because of shame-based issues. Further, the elderly might feel overwhelmed by the complex pattern of interactions within the group setting. In such cases the individual might respond more favorably if she or he were seen on an individual basis. Thus, while group therapy is a common treatment modality, there is limited evidence at best as to its effectiveness.

Assertiveness/social skills training. Many individuals with substance-use problems began to abuse alcohol/drugs while they were adolescents, and this interfered with their developing interpersonal skills necessary for adulthood (Monti et al., 2002). There is evidence that assertiveness training is useful as an adjunct to rehabilitation in such cases, helping to build clients' self-esteem and self-confidence and aiding the development of interpersonal relationship skills (Monti et al., 2002). Such social skills training might include *substance use refusal skills* as well as helping the recovering individual learn to increase non-drug-related pleasant activities and communication training (Morgan, 2003). Social skills training is not the primary focus of the rehabilitation program, but it does seem to provide a useful tool for those who turn to alcohol/drugs as a way of coping with their perceived weak interpersonal coping skills (Morgan, 2003).

Self-help groups. The topic of self-help, or 12-Step groups will be discussed in Chapter 34. However, the reader should be aware that participation in self-help or 12-Step groups is often a valuable adjunct to substance-abuse rehabilitation programs.

Biofeedback training. A number of plans use biofeedback training in treating addictive disorders. The technique of biofeedback involves monitoring select body functions, such as skin temperature or muscle tension, and providing information to the individual as to how his or her body is doing. Depending on the parameter selected (e.g., tension of a certain muscle group, skin temperature, brain wave patterns) and the training provided, the individual can sometimes learn how to modify his or her body function at will. This skill, in turn, is thought to allow the individual to learn how to change these body functions in a desired direction, such as being able to relax without the use of drugs.

Peniston and Kulkosky (1990) attempted to teach a small number of patients in an alcoholic treatment program to change the frequency with which their brain could produce two specific electrical patterns, known as *alpha* and *theta* waves. These patterns of electrical activity in the brain are thought to reflect the relaxation and stress-coping responses of the individual. The authors found that their sample had significant changes on standard psychological tests used to measure personality patterns and that these changes continued over an extended follow-up period. The authors suggested that biofeedback training, especially alpha and theta brain wave training, might offer a new, possibly more effective treatment approach for working with the chronic alcoholic.

Ochs (1992) examined the application of biofeedback training techniques to the treatment of addictive disorders and concluded that the term *biofeedback training* for the addictions was a bit misleading, as different clinicians employed a wide range of techniques and body functions for biofeedback training. Yet, in spite of the variations in techniques, the author found that biofeedback training for the treatment of addictive disorders did seem to have value, especially when it was integrated into a larger treatment format designed to address social, economic, vocational, psychological, and familial problems. Thus, there is evidence that biofeedback training may play an increasing role in the treatment of addictive disorders.

Harm reduction model. The *harm reduction* model of substance-abuse rehabilitation is quite different from the Minnesota Model or the other models of treatment discussed in this chapter; it is based on the assumption that the behavior of alcohol/drug abusers can change over time, including the ways they use chemicals, so that they will gradually come to behave in ways that reduce the consequences of their substance abuse (MacCoun & Reuter, 1998). This model is in sharp contrast to "zero tolerance" (Marlatt, 1994) or supply reduction (MacCoun & Reuter, 1998) models of chemical-use intervention.

The use of nicotine skin patches and nicotine gum are examples of the harm reduction philosophy as they reduce the individual's risk of negative consequences from cigarette smoking (Marlatt, 1994). From this perspective, formal detoxification from chemicals in a medical setting might also be viewed as a form of harm reduction as the individual is protected from many of the dangers of withdrawal during the detoxification program. Another example of the harm reduction philosophy is the needle exchange programs in place in several cities around the country. Because the virus that causes AIDS is often transmitted through contaminated intravenous needles, some cities allow intravenous drug abusers to exchange dirty needles for new, uncontaminated ones. Citing reasons of cost-effectiveness, Baltimore Mayor Kurt Schmoke authorized a needle exchange program in that city to limit the damage done by HIV:

> This program costs $160,000 a year. The cost to the state of Maryland of taking care of just one adult AIDS patient infected through the sharing of a syringe is $102,000 to $120,000. In other words, if just two addicts are protected from HIV through the city's needle exchange, the program will have paid for itself. (Schmoke, 1996, p. 40)

With a needle exchange program, the transmission of the virus that causes AIDS is slowed or perhaps even stopped. Further, although critics were afraid that this type of program would encourage intravenous drug use, there is little evidence of increased drug use in communities with needle exchange programs (MacCoun & Reuter, 1998). Unfortunately, in spite of its apparent advantages, fewer than 100 communities in the United States have needle exchange programs as of 1998, and resistance to such programs is strong (MacCoun & Reuter, 1998).

Aftercare Programs

Research suggests that participation in a *continuing care* or *aftercare* program significantly contributes to abstinence from drugs (Ritsher, Moos, & Finney, 2002). The goals of the aftercare program should include (a) maintaining gains made in treatment and (b) helping to prevent relapse to active use/abuse of chemicals (McKay et al., 1998). Included in the concept of aftercare programs is the identification and correction of mistaken beliefs that might contribute to a possible relapse as well as helping the client establish and monitor "the habit of sobriety" (Downing, 1990, p. 22).

Participation in self-help groups such as Alcoholics Anonymous or Narcotics Anonymous is often part of the aftercare program, especially those based on the Minnesota Model of treatment (Clark, 1995). Medical problems identified earlier in the rehabilitation process are also addressed in aftercare program, as are needs for transitional living facilities or other special needs. The aftercare program is designed and carried out on the assumption that treatment does not end with the individual's discharge from a formal rehabilitation program. Rather, treatment is the first part of a recovery program that should continue for the rest of the individual's life.

Summary

This chapter reviewed the Minnesota Model of treatment, one of the primary treatment models found in this country. The concept of a comprehensive treatment plan, which serves as the heart of the treatment process, was also discussed. Various pharmacological supports for people in the early stages of sobriety and those going through detoxification from chemicals were explored.

The role of assertiveness training, biofeedback, and marital and family therapy as a component of a larger treatment program were examined. The use of blood and urine samples for toxicology screening to detect medication compliance and illicit drug use was also reviewed.

CHAPTER TWENTY-NINE

Treatment Formats
for Chemical-Dependency Rehabilitation

Introduction

For many years, researchers and clinicians have debated the relative merits of *outpatient* versus *inpatient* rehabilitation programs. This debate, which continued through much of the past 20 years, has been spirited. To date, neither side has scored a decisive victory, and both inpatient and outpatient treatment programs have vocal proponents. In this chapter, some of the characteristics of an average outpatient treatment program, the typical inpatient program, and some of the issues that have been raised about the relative advantages and disadvantages of each will be discussed.

Outpatient Treatment Programs

Outpatient treatment—a working definition. Outpatient chemical-dependency treatment may best be defined as a formal treatment program (a) involving one or more professionals who are trained to work with individuals addicted to a chemical(s), (b) designed specifically to work with the addicted person to help him or her achieve and maintain a recovery program, (c) utilizing a number of different treatment modalities (e.g., psychoeducational approaches; family, marital, individual and/or group therapies) to help the addicted person come to terms with his or her chemical abuse problem, and (d) working with the patient on an outpatient basis. Such programs are extremely popular at the start of the 21st century, with an estimated 85% of all patients in substance-abuse treatment receiving their care in an outpatient rehabilitation program (Fuller & Hiller-Sturmhofel, 1999; Tinsley, Finlayson, & Morse, 1998). In spite of their popularity, however, the effectiveness of outpatient treatment programs has not been established.

Components of Outpatient Treatment Programs

Outpatient treatment programs will utilize many of the components of treatment discussed in Chapter 28. Such programs will usually offer individual and group therapy formats as well as possibly marital and family therapy in working with the addicted person. Most such programs will follow a 12 Step philosophy, usually either Alcoholics Anonymous (AA) or Narcotics Anonymous (NA), and the individual is expected to attend regular self-help group meetings as part of the treatment format. The individual's treatment program is usually coordinated by a certified chemical-dependency counselor (sometimes called an addictions, AODA [alcohol- or drug-abuse], or substance-abuse counselor).

During the rehabilitation process, a formal treatment plan will be established, review sessions will be scheduled on a regular basis, and the client's progress toward the agreed-on goals will be monitored by staff. Individual and group therapy sessions are utilized to help the individual work through his or her system of denial and identify and address the problems of daily living *without* the use of chemicals. Psychoeducational lectures might also be used to present the client with factual information about the disease of chemical addiction and its treatment.

Referrals to vocational counseling centers or community mental health centers for individual, family, or marital counseling are made as necessary. Some programs provide a "family night," with family members encouraged to participate once a week or once a month to discuss their concerns. Other programs feature a "family group" orientation in which couples participate together on a day-to-day basis as part of the program. In such a format, the spouse of the addicted person will sit in on the group sessions and participate as an equal with the addicted person in the group therapy.

Whatever the general approach, the goal of any outpatient treatment program is to enhance the highest level of functioning while providing support for the alcoholic. Some programs require that the detoxification phase of treatment, when the individual is withdrawn from chemicals, be carried out either at a detoxification center or in a general hospital. However, the individual is generally expected to have stopped all chemical use before starting a treatment program. Abstinence from alcohol/drug use is expected. Many treatment programs will require the use of Antabuse (disulfiram) or will carry out random breath or urine tests to detect alcohol/drug use by the patient. One advantage of using urine testing is that this procedure allows the staff to check on the individual's compliance in taking Antabuse (disulfiram), if this is a part of the treatment program.

Outpatient treatment programs allow the individual to live at home, continue to work, and participate in family activities while participating in the rehabilitation program designed to help him or her achieve and maintain abstinence (Youngstrom, 1990a). Unfortunately, research suggests that in spite of their advantages, outpatient treatment programs experience high dropout rates.

Varieties of Outpatient Treatment Programs for Substance-Abuse Rehabilitation

DWI school. Outpatient rehabilitation programs differ mainly in terms of how often the individual meets with treatment professionals and the specific methods staff use in working with the client. For example, the psychoeducational approach is often the mainstay of the "DWI school" or DWI class. The DWI school is usually limited to the first-time offender, who is assumed to have simply made a mistake by driving under the influence of chemicals. Participants in the DWI school are not addicted to alcohol/drugs in the opinion of the assessor. They are exposed to 8–12 hours of educational lectures designed to help them better understand the dangers inherent in driving while under the influence of chemicals. This is done with the expectation that the person might learn from his or her mistake.

Short-term outpatient programs (STOP). STOP programs are usually time limited. Some STOP programs

utilize only individual therapy sessions; others combine individual and group therapy formats for individuals whose substance-use problem is, in the opinion of the assessor, mild to moderate in severity. The individual may be required to attend Alcoholics Anonymous or similar self-help group meetings in addition to sessions with the therapist that are held at least once a week. Clients in STOP programs are often assigned material to read between sessions with the therapist, and psychoeducational lectures might be utilized to provide program participants with factual information about the effects of the drugs of abuse. The individual client participates in program activities 1–2 nights a week, usually for less than 2 months.

The goal of STOP programs is to (a) break through the individual's denial about his or her substance use, (b) achieve a commitment to abstinence from the client, and (c) make appropriate referrals for those who appear to require more in-depth help. Such programs are usually utilized for patients with lower severity substance-use problems. In spite of the promise of STOP programs for patients who have limited substance-use experience, short-term rehabilitation programs seem to be ineffective for individuals who do not have extensive substance-abuse problems (Shepard, Larson, & Hoffmann, 1999). The reason for this apparent paradox is not clear.

Intensive short-term outpatient programs (I-STOP). Programs at the I-STOP level are aimed at the patient with a moderate to severe substance-use problem. Program participants are usually seen in both individual and group therapy sessions for up to 5 nights a week. These programs are time limited, but in addition to having a level of treatment that is more intense than those on the previous level (4–5 times a week versus 1–2 times a week) they usually last longer (up to 6 months). Program participants are often required to attend self-help group meetings, such as AA, in addition to participating in scheduled treatment activities. Additional sessions for family/marital counseling are scheduled outside scheduled treatment hours for those whose recovery requires additional forms of intervention or support.

Patients assigned to I-STOP intervention programs usually have middle-severity substance-use problems. The goal of I-STOP programs is to (a) break through the individual's denial about his or her substance use,

(b) achieve a commitment to abstinence from the client who is unlikely to respond to less intense forms of treatment, and (c) to make appropriate referrals for those who appear to require more in-depth help. Shepard, Larson, and Hoffmann (1999) concluded that programs at this level of intensity were most effective when applied to the target population of individuals with mid-severity substance-use problems.

Intensive long-term outpatient treatment (ILTOT). ILTOT programs are usually open-ended outpatient treatment programs, which are designed for the individual whose substance-use problem is moderate to severe in intensity but for whom less radical treatment would hold little chance of success. ILTOT programs usually last for a minimum of 6 months and often for as long as 12–18 months. Program participants are involved in a series of individual and group therapy sessions for a specified number of days each week, with the exact timing and sequence of individual and/group sessions determined by the individual's treatment plan.

ILTOT programs were designed for patients with moderate to severe substance-use problems. The goal is to (a) break through the individual's denial about his or her substance use, (b) achieve a commitment to abstinence from the client who either has not been able to benefit from less intense forms of treatment or whose substance-use pattern suggests that less intense treatment is likely to fail, (c) support the individual during the early stages of recovery from drug/alcohol use problems, and (d) make appropriate referrals for individuals who appear to require more in-depth help. Surprisingly, such programs were found to be less effective than short-term intervention programs for people with moderate to severe substance-use problems (Shepard et al., 1999).

Advantages of Outpatient Treatment Programs

Outpatient treatment programs are popular. For example, it has been reported that perhaps as many as 88% of those who are treated for alcohol abuse or addiction are treated on an outpatient basis (McCaul & Furst, 1994). Outpatient treatment programs are significantly less expensive than inpatient treatment programs. Outpatient treatment programs also avoid the need to remove the patient from his or her environment. In many cases, the individual is able to continue to work and thus remains self-supporting during

treatment. Unlike inpatient treatment programs, there is no community reorientation period needed after outpatient treatment (Youngstrom, 1990a). In addition, outpatient treatment programs tend to last longer than do inpatient rehabilitation programs. Nace (1987) suggested that the ideal outpatient treatment program would last one full year. A treatment program one year in duration would offer long-term follow-up for the crucial first year of recovery, a time when the client is most likely to relapse.

Berg and Dubin (1990) outlined an intensive outpatient treatment program that was divided into four phases. Each of the first three phases—intensive, intermediate, and moderate treatment—was designed to last for 2 weeks. The individual's placement was determined by "the severity of the patient's addiction, progress in treatment, financial resources, and ability to attend the program" (Berg & Dubin, 1990, p. 1175). The final phase of treatment, the extended phase, involved an aftercare meeting once a week for an indefinite period of time. Because outpatient treatment programs last longer than inpatient programs they offer the counselor a longer time to help the client achieve the goals outlined in the treatment plan (Lewis, Dana, & Blevins, 1988). The client also has an extended period of time in which to practice and perfect new behaviors that will support his or her recovery from substance abuse/addiction.

Outpatient treatment programs offer yet another advantage over inpatient treatment programs: *flexibility* (Turbo, 1989). Program participation may be through an *outpatient day treatment* program, where treatment activities are scheduled during normal working hours, or through an *outpatient evening treatment* program with rehabilitation activities offered in the evening. Finally, outpatient treatment programs offer the client the opportunity to practice sobriety while still living in the community. This is a significant advantage over traditional inpatient treatment programs in which the client is removed from his or her home community for the duration of treatment.

Disadvantages of Outpatient Treatment Programs

Surprisingly, although inpatient treatment might cost more, because of available insurance coverage, many clients actually pay *less* for inpatient treatment than they would for outpatient treatment. This is because outpatient treatment programs traditionally are not reimbursed at the same rate as the more expensive inpatient substance-abuse program by health insurance carriers. This factor often drives a tendency for health care providers to recommend inpatient over outpatient treatment programs (Berg & Dubin, 1990).

Although statistical research has found no significant difference in the percentage of outpatient treatment program "graduates" who remain abstinent compared to those who complete inpatient treatment programs, this is not to say that outpatient treatment is as effective as inpatient treatment. Rather, inpatient treatment programs tend to deal more effectively with a different class of client from those in outpatient treatment programs. This difference makes comparisons between inpatient and outpatient treatment difficult.

Outpatient treatment programs typically do not offer the same degree of structure and support found in the inpatient treatment setting. Further, outpatient treatment programs offer less control over the client's environment, as he or she continues to live at home, and thus is of limited value for some patients who require a great deal of support during the early stages of recovery. Outpatient treatment of substance abuse seems to work for many clients, but it does not seem to be the ultimate answer to the problem of chemical dependency.

Inpatient Treatment Programs

Definition of inpatient treatment. The inpatient treatment program might best be defined as a residential treatment facility where the client lives while he or she participates in treatment. Such programs usually deal with the hard-core, the seriously ill, or the "difficult" patient. These are individuals for whom outpatient treatment either has not been successful or has been ruled out. Residential treatment programs usually have strong emphasis on a 12-Step philosophy and utilize individual and group therapy extensively. The client's length of stay in treatment depends on such factors as his or her motivation, support system, and other variables that the treatment team considers.

In response to the challenge presented by clients, residential treatment programs have evolved to provide the greatest degree of support and help. Inpatient treatment also is "the most restrictive, structured, and protective of treatment settings" (Klar, 1987, p. 340). It combines the greatest potential for positive change with high financial cost and the possibility of branding the patient for life (Klar, 1987). The decision to utilize inpatient treatment is one that should not be made lightly.

Many general hospitals offered inpatient rehabilitation programs for drug/alcohol abuse in the 1990s but have since either scaled back the number of available beds or closed their doors entirely. In the mid 1990s, 21% of the hospitals surveyed offered inpatient treatment for substance abuse (Bell, 1995). Other non-hospital programs such as *therapeutic communities* or *halfway houses* also were available in many geographic areas. But by the first decade of the 21st century, many of these programs had closed, victims of the economic realities and shift in priorities that took place at the start of the new millennium. Not all inpatient/residential programs closed, however, and many varieties of inpatient treatment programs are available in the United States today.

Varieties of Inpatient Treatment

Hospital/program-based inpatient treatment. Traditional inpatient drug rehabilitation is often carried out either in a center that specializes in chemical-dependency treatment or in a traditional hospital setting as part of a specialized drug treatment unit. Some of these programs utilize the Minnesota Model, explored in detail in Chapter 28, although this is becoming less and less common as managed care providers demand shorter treatment stays for their clients.

Inpatient rehabilitation programs, especially those in a hospital setting, will often begin with detoxification. One advantage of having a detoxification component is that it allows a patient to begin treatment in the last stages of withdrawal from chemicals. This blending of withdrawal and treatment might aid in patient retention. Patients live in the treatment unit and participate in a program of daily lectures and individual and group therapy sessions. Each patient will be assigned some form of "homework," which might include assignments to read certain material that rehabilitation staff believe would support the individual's recovery. In most programs, the client is also expected to follow the 12-Step program of AA or a similar self-help group, and attendance in self-help group meetings is required.

Therapeutic communities. One controversial form of inpatient treatment is the therapeutic community (TC). At the start of the 21st century the TC movement has evolved away from the harsh confrontational format that marked its inception, and although the original TC concept was quite resistant to the use of 12-Step programs, there is a growing trend to integrate them into the TC program (Ringwald, 2002).

At the start of the 21st century, the TC concept has become a generic term for a wide variety of short- and long-term residential treatment programs as well as for some outpatient day programs that have evolved from the residential TCs of the 1960s and 1970s (DeLeon, 2004). In general, the traditional TC program operates on the theory that drug abuse is a deviant behavior reflecting impeded personality development or chronic deficits in a person's social, educational, and economic skills (DeLeon, 2004). To correct the deficit(s), the TC attempts to help the individual through a global lifestyle change, including abstinence from illicit drugs, elimination of antisocial activity, and development of prosocial attitudes and behaviors (DeLeon, 2004). In spite of differences in treatment philosophies or methods, the effective TC helps individuals to understand and cope with their specific life circumstances without the use of recreational chemicals (Moos, 2003).

In terms of length of stay, the traditional TC programs usually require a commitment between 6 months and 3 years (DeLeon, 2004; Ringwald, 2002). This extended length of stay is thought to be necessary to help the individual learn how to live without reliance on chemicals. The TC program originated in the United States and was designed for individuals addicted to opiates. Now the TC format has evolved to the point that it is being integrated into some penal institutions to help substance-dependent criminals (Ringwald, 2002) and is also being used with other people addicted to substances besides opiates (DeLeon, 2004).

All therapeutic communities share the characteristic of a single treatment philosophy. One central tenet of the TC model is that "drug abuse [is viewed as] a whole person disorder" (DeLeon, Melnick, & Kressel, 1997). Further, the *community* is viewed as the treatment modality by which the individual changes (DeLeon, 2004). This adherence to a single vision seems to contribute to the effectiveness of the TC.

Other characteristics of the TC include social and physical isolation, a structured living environment, a firm system of rewards and punishments, and an emphasis on self-examination and the confession of past wrongdoing. Clients are expected to work, either outside the TC in an approved job or within the TC itself as part of the housekeeping or kitchen staff. In many TCs there is some potential mobility from the status of client to that of a paraprofessional staff member (National Academy of Sciences, 1990).

Although many TCs utilize the services of mental health professionals, much of the treatment is carried out by paraprofessional staff members who are often former residents of the TC. This is done on the theory that only a person "who has been there" can understand and help the addicted person. Such paraprofessional counselors are thought to be effective in breaking through the client's denial and manipulation on the basis of personal experience. The TC might offer an extended family for the individual. Indeed, the original members of Synanon (one of the early therapeutic communities) were expected to remain there on a permanent basis, as part of the "family" (Lewis et al., 1988).

About two-thirds of those admitted to TCs are under the supervision of a probation or parole agent and thus are involved in the criminal justice system (Hiller, Knight, Rao, & Simpson, 2002). In spite of this and the "family" orientation found in TCs, these programs suffer from significant dropout rates (DeLeon et al., 1997). DeLeon (2004) suggested that 30% to 40% of those admitted to a TC will drop out in the first 30 days, and that only 10% to 15% complete the typical 2-year program. A significant percentage of those who do not leave on their own are asked to leave or are discharged from treatment for various rules infractions (Gelman, Underwood, King, Hager, & Gordon, 1990).

A great deal of controversy continues to surround the therapeutic community phenomenon. Many have objected to the use of harsh methods such as ego stripping and unquestioned submission to the rules of the program. However, others (DeLeon, 1989, 1994; Peele, 1989; Yablonsky, 1967) have argued that the TC was effective in cases where more traditional treatment methods had failed. Proponents of the therapeutic community model point to the high abstinence rates *of those who complete the program.* Of those who complete treatment, 90% remain drug free for at least 2 years after their graduation from treatment.

But only 10% to 15% of those admitted to TCs actually graduate (DeLeon, 2004), and the picture is not quite so bright for those who fail to complete the program. Approximately 50% of those who remain in the program for 1 year before dropping out are able to abstain from drugs for at least 2 years, but only 25% of those who remained in the TC for less than 1 year are able to abstain from drugs for at least 2 years following their decision to leave (DeLeon, 2004). However, 3 years following discharge from a TC in Scandinavia, almost half of those who were still alive were either working full time or were in training for eventual entry into the workforce (Berg, 2003). Three years after discharge from a therapeutic community in Europe, 25% of residents were found still to be abusing drugs, 14% were in a methadone maintenance program, and 13% were either in treatment or prison (Berg, 2003). These results do not show TCs as a panacea for the field of substance-abuse rehabilitation, but they do suggest that these programs play a valuable role in the rehabilitation of some chronic drug abusers.

Is There a Legitimate Need for Inpatient Treatment?

In the mid 1980s, a flurry of research studies concluded that "the relative merits of residential treatment are less than clear" (Miller & Hester, 1986, p. 794). Many critics of inpatient treatment point to the Project MATCH Research Group study of the mid 1990s as providing evidence that inpatient treatment is not automatically superior to less intense methods of treatment. The Project MATCH Research Group tried to isolate what patient characteristics predicted a better response to inpatient versus outpatient treatment for alcoholism. The project failed to find evidence that matching patients to one form of treatment or another yielded any additional benefit or that there were specific patient characteristics suggesting that one treatment setting was more advantageous than the other (Rychtarik et al., 2000). As a result of such studies, the "advantages of inpatient versus outpatient care . . . have been difficult to show" (Chick, 1993, p. 1374). However, the Project MATCH Research Group study also failed to provide for a control group in their experiment, making comparisons between groups quite difficult (Moos, 2003).

Miller and Hester (1986) were also quite critical of inpatient treatment programs. However, they did not advocate the complete abolition of these programs, noting that "there may be subpopulations for whom more intensive treatment is justifiable. From the limited matching data available at present, it appears that intensive treatment may be better for severely addicted and socially unstable individuals" (Miller & Hester, 1986, p. 1246).

In response to Miller and Hester's original (1986) work, Adelman and Weiss (1989) conducted their own research into the merits of inpatient treatment. They found that 77% of individuals treated for alcoholism eventually required some form of inpatient treatment. Further, the authors concluded that there was a treatment duration effect, with those who were discharged from shorter programs having a higher relapse rate than people who had remained in treatment longer.

In 1991, the treatment team of Walsh et al. reported the results of a research project in which 227 workers at a large factory who were known to be abusing alcohol were randomly assigned to one of three treatment programs: compulsory attendance in Alcoholics Anonymous, compulsory inpatient treatment, or a choice between these two alternatives. The authors were surprised to find that although the referral to compulsory AA meetings was *initially* more cost-effective, in the long run inpatient treatment resulted in higher abstinence rates.

How does one determine whether inpatient or outpatient rehabilitation was successful? One of the traditional measures is whether the former patient would take part in follow-up care. However, Berg (2003) identified a subgroup of former drug abusers who were (a) stable at the time of follow-up but (b) refused to take part in follow-up studies or treatment because they did not wish to reawaken memories of their past life as an addicted person. This is not to say that *every* former patient who refuses to take part in follow-up care or research is recovering, but it is possible that a percentage of those who do not participate in posttreatment research (including effectiveness-of-treatment studies) might simply not wish to call attention to their former addiction.

In spite of the problems associated with determining which form of treatment might be best, the emerging consensus seems to be that individuals most likely to benefit from inpatient rehabilitation programs are those who have the most severe alcohol/drug addiction problems or the ones with substance-use and mental illness issues (Moos, King, & Patterson, 1996; Rychtarik et al., 2000; Shepard et al., 1999). Some researchers have found evidence of a "threshold effect" for the treatment process, with stronger results being achieved after 14 days of inpatient treatment for those who require inpatient treatment (Moos et al., 1996). Other researchers have found that lower functioning alcohol abusers/addicts appear to benefit more from inpatient than outpatient treatment (Rychtarik et al., 2000).

The benefits of inpatient treatment do not appear to be limited to alcohol abusers alone, for inpatient treatment also appears to be a cost-effective approach to the rehabilitation of heroin addicts. Swan (1994) noted that the cost of a 6-month inpatient treatment program for a person addicted to heroin would be about $8,250, whereas the cost to society for not treating the heroin-addicted person in terms of criminal activity, social support services, and health care services would be approximately $21,500 for the same period. Although a residential treatment program was four times as expensive as simply placing the heroin addict in a methadone maintenance program, it was still only 40% as expensive as not providing any form of treatment for the individual. Thus, one could argue, residential treatment programs appear to be a cost-effective way to deal with individuals who are addicted to heroin.

The Advantages of Inpatient Treatment

In some ways, it is a mistake to compare patients who enter an outpatient rehabilitation program with those who enter an inpatient treatment programs. Inpatient substance abuse treatment programs tend to work with individuals who have encountered a greater number and severity of problems than those referred to outpatient treatment.

If the individual should require a residential treatment program, this is because she or he requires *more comprehensive treatment programming* than is possible in an outpatient treatment setting (Klar, 1987). Because environmental factors play a significant role in long-term recovery from substance-use problems (Moos, 2003), it is logical to assume that a well-designed residential treatment program would allow the individual to assess and address those environmental forces that might contribute to the substance-use problem. For example, research has found that chemically dependent individuals often live alone or lack close interpersonal supports. The inpatient "community" can function as a pseudo-family in the critical early stages of recovery when the individual is learning to "let go" of the support system that helped to sustain his or her chemical use.

Further, patients who require inpatient treatment tend to have a greater number of medical problems than do patients who might better be referred to an outpatient rehabilitation program. Inpatient treatment settings allow for the early identification and treatment of these ongoing medical problems. Malnutrition is a common problem for people with a chronic substance-use disorder, for example, and inpatient treatment settings allow medical professionals to address the effects of the client's malnutrition through diet modification and vitamin supplments.

Because inpatient rehabilitation provides for almost total control over the client's environment, staff members can help to discourage continued drug use in what should be the early stages of recovery. It is not unknown, for example, for clients to attempt to "help out" the detoxification process by taking a few additional drugs or drinks during detoxification. When detected, these individuals often try to defend their continued substance use on the grounds that they were in distress and *needed* the drugs or alcohol that they had ingested. In such cases, the medical staff can address the client's continued substance use and outstanding medical issues.

Another advantage offered by the inpatient rehabilitation setting is the opportunity for a structured environment where individual and group therapy sessions, meals, recreational opportunities, self-help group meetings, and spiritual counseling are available (Berg & Dubin, 1990). Many clients will attend their first Alcoholics Anonymous meeting while in an inpatient setting. In some cases, the client will often affirm that he or she would never have attended the AA or NA meeting if not required to by treatment staff.

The observation that outpatient treatment might become a "revolving door" (Nace, 1987, p. 130) is quite old. Such charges reflect, in part, the treatment bias of many health care professionals who believe that, unlike the treatment for cancer, heart disease, or diabetes, the individual should require *just one* residential treatment program in order to address his or her substance-use disorder. While there *is* a danger that inpatient treatment will become a revolving door, an effective, well-designed treatment program should offer the individual the same chances of recovery as a well-designed cancer or cardiac treatment center.

Disadvantages of Inpatient Treatment

Residential/inpatient treatment is quite disruptive to the individual's social, vocational, and family life (Morey, 1996). The person is forced to leave the normal environment to participate in the rehabilitation program at the expense of the time necessary to work, take part in family life, or otherwise engage in activities outside the treatment center setting. The economic cost of inpatient treatment is also significantly higher than that of outpatient rehabilitation programs. Inpatient treatment programs tend to address severe and chronic substance-use problems and thus are out of step with individuals with less intense chemical-abuse issues (Larimer & Kilmer, 2000). Finally, the treatment center setting might be quite isolated, preventing easy contact between the patient and family or friends. All of these factors are disadvantages of the inpatient rehabilitation program.

Inpatient or Outpatient Treatment?

The decision of whether to utilize inpatient or outpatient treatment for a client is perhaps one of the most important decisions that a treatment professional will make (Washton, Stone, & Hendrickson, 1988). Fortunately, in the last decade several organizations have published referral guidelines to assist in referring the substance abuser to the proper rehabilitation program. For example, the Group for the Advancement of Psychiatry (1991) identified several criteria that could be used to identify who would best benefit from inpatient as opposed to outpatient treatment programs:

1. Whether the client's condition was associated with significant *medical* or *psychiatric* conditions or complications.
2. The *severity of actual or anticipated withdrawal* from the drugs being used.

3. *Multiple failed attempts at outpatient treatment.*
4. The strength of the client's *social support systems.*
5. The *severity of the client's addiction* and the *possibility of polysubstance abuse.*

Since the time of their introduction, the patient placement criteria suggested by the American Society of Addiction Medicine (ASAM) have become the most commonly used guides for determining the level of care that will best meet the patient's needs (Gastfriend, 2004b). The ASAM placement criteria system requires the assessor to determine the patient's strengths and needs in each of six areas or dimensions, such as the individual's potential for serious medical problems during detoxification from drugs, the strength of the individual's abstinence support system, and so on. Depending on the patient's requirements in each area, she or he might be placed in one of four levels of care ranging from outpatient treatment through intensive outpatient treatment and on to medically supervised inpatient treatment. The ASAM original placement criteria might be thought of as forming a 4×6 grid, on which each individual's needs might be plotted, as shown in Table 29.1.

Since their introduction, the ASAM placement criteria have been found to be effective by research studies designed to address criticism of the system raised by managed care[1] programs (Gastfriend, 2004a, b). But the original criteria were relatively inflexible, grouping treatment options together and forcing restrictions on patient placement (Gastfriend, 2004a). The 1996 revision added sublevels for different treatment options as outpatient or evening day treatment, partial hospitalization, and halfway house placement. These new sublevels do complicate the original 4×6 grid, but they do allow for more comprehensive treatment placement for individuals addicted to chemicals.

For example, in terms of total cost, outpatient treatment programs are usually less expensive than inpatient programs. Outpatient rehabilitation programs are best suited to clients who do not have an extensive treatment history (Nace, 1987). The individual's motivation for treatment and treatment history offer hints to whether an inpatient or outpatient program would be most effective in his or her recovery. Further, as noted

---

[1]Discussed in Chapter 31.

TABLE 29.1   The ASAM Placement Criteria*

Dimension \ Level of care	*Level I* Outpatient treatment	*Level II* Intensive outpatient treatment/partial hospitalization program	*Level III* Medically monitored inpatient treatment (residential treatment)	*Level IV* Medically managed inpatient treatment (traditional medical treatment)
Acute intoxication/ withdrawal potential**	None	Minimal	Severe risk, but does not require hospitalization	Severe risk that requires hospitalization
Biomedical conditions or complications**	None/stable	Minimal: can be managed in outpatient setting	Serious: requires medical monitoring	Severe: requires inpatient hospitalization
Emotional/behavioral conditions or complications	None/stable	Mild: but can be managed in outpatient setting	Serious: requires patient to be monitored 24 hours/day	Severe: requires inpatient psychiatric care
Treatment acceptance or resistance	Cooperative: needs guidance and monitoring	Some resistance: intensive treatment needed	Resistance is severe: requires intensive treatment	N/A
Relapse potential	Minimal risk of relapse: needs monitoring and guidance only	High risk of relapse without close monitoring and support by staff	Patient is unable to control use without being in inpatient setting	N/A
Recovery environment	Patient has skills and support to abstain on own	Patient lacks environmental support but has skills to cope, given some structure	Environment is dangerous to patient, and she or he must be removed from it	N/A

*This table is designed to illustrate the ASAM placement criteria and should not be utilized as a guide to patient placement.
**As determined by a licensed physician.

in the ASAM criteria, the patient's need for inpatient detoxification from chemicals should weigh in the referring physician's recommendation of inpatient or outpatient treatment.

A sad, rarely discussed fact is that restrictions on funding will play a role in deciding which treatment options are available for the individual. The person whose insurance will pay only for inpatient chemical-dependency treatment will have certain financial restrictions placed on his or her treatment options. Thus, availability of funding is one factor that influences the decision of whether to seek inpatient or outpatient treatment for substance abuse. Finally, the

individual's psychiatric status and availability of social support should be evaluated when considering outpatient treatment as an option (Group for the Advancement of Psychiatry, 1991; Nace, 1987). Obviously, a deeply depressed individual who is recovering from an extended period of cocaine use might benefit more from the greater support offered by an inpatient treatment program, at least during the initial recovery period when the depression is most severe.

Turbo (1989) identified several criteria suggesting that an inpatient treatment program might be better for the client than the outpatient setting. These criteria included (a) clients showing repeated failure to maintain sobriety in outpatient treatment, (b) the acutely suicidal client, (c) clients with seriously disturbed home environments, (d) clients with serious medical problems, and (e) clients with serious psychiatric problems. In addition, Allen and Phillips (1993) suggested that the patient's legal status also be considered in deciding whether to refer him or her to inpatient or outpatient treatment. Those who have been arrested for drug possession charges or for driving while under the influence of chemicals might do better in an outpatient treatment program, according to the authors. Patients who had achieved periods of sobriety but had then relapsed might be treated briefly on an inpatient basis, according to the authors. But following a brief stabilization stay in the hospital, these patients might be switched to an outpatient treatment program, according to Allen and Phillips.

The final decision on whether to suggest an inpatient or an outpatient treatment program ultimately centers around this: *Given the client's resources and needs, what is the least restrictive treatment alternative?* (American Psychiatric Association, 1995). The treatment referral criteria advanced by ASAM (Morey, 1996) are useful guides to the selection of the least restrictive alternative that will meet the client's needs. Although some will argue that the inpatient treatment program sounds very similar to a concentration camp experience, remember that the dysfunction caused by drug addiction often requires drastic forms of intervention.

Partial Hospitalization Options

In recent years, several new treatment formats have been explored that combine elements of inpatient and outpatient rehabilitation programs. In terms of effectiveness, partial hospitalization programs offer success rates that are equal to, or possibly even superior to, inpatient treatment, yet are only one-third to one-half as expensive as inpatient treatment (Gastfriend & McLellan, 1997). Each of these rehabilitation formats offers advantages and disadvantages, yet each should be considered a viable treatment option. Depending on the client's needs, some of the new treatment formats might be quite beneficial.

Two by four programs. One proposed solution to the treatment dilemma of whether to utilize inpatient or outpatient treatment is the so called two by four program. This format borrows from both inpatient and outpatient treatment programs to establish a biphasic rehabilitation system that seems to have some promise. The patient is first hospitalized for a short period of time, usually 2 weeks, in order to achieve total detoxification from chemicals. Depending on the individual's needs, the initial period of hospitalization might be somewhat shorter or longer than 2 weeks. However, the goal is to help the client reach a point where he or she can participate in outpatient treatment as soon as possible. If, as will occasionally happen, the client is unable to function in the less restrictive outpatient rehabilitation program, he or she may be returned to the inpatient treatment format. Later, when additional progress has been made, the client may again return to an outpatient setting to complete the treatment program there.

Turbo (1989) discussed an interesting variation on the 2×4 program developed for the Schick Shadel chain of hospitals, located in California, Texas, and Washington. These programs admit the individual for 10 days of inpatient treatment, followed by 2 additional inpatient "reinforcement" days later. The first "reinforcement" day of hospitalization occurs 1 month after discharge, and another 2 days of inpatient treatment are scheduled for 2 months following the initial admission. One disadvantage of inpatient treatment is that admission to such a level of care, even if only for short periods of time, appeared to result in "a lower probability of complying with outpatient aftercare" (Berg & Dubin, 1990, p. 1177) by the client. The authors found a 60% dropout rate for those who were initially hospitalized for a brief period of time and then were referred to an intensive outpatient treatment program.

Day hospitalization. The day hospitalization format is also known as *partial day hospitalization*. Such programs typically provide 3–12 hours a day of treatment for 3–7 days of the week. After detoxification has been accomplished, the client is allowed to live at home but will come to the treatment center during scheduled treatment hours to participate in the rehabilitation program.

Partial hospital programs for substance-abuse rehabilitation have a number of advantages, including their provision of "an intensive and structured treatment experience for patients with substance dependence who require more services than those generally available in traditional outpatient settings" (American Psychiatric Association, 1995, p. 23). Further, day hospitalization programs are generally approximately half as expensive as traditional inpatient treatment programs (French, 1995). They are designed to provide for a greater intensity of therapeutic intervention than is available through traditional outpatient treatment while still avoiding the need for inpatient treatment where possible (Guydish et al., 1998).

An essential requirement for day hospitalization is that the client have a supportive, stable family. Obviously, if the client's spouse (or other family member) also has a chemical-abuse problem, day hospitalization may not be a viable treatment option. If the client's spouse is severely codependent and continues to enable the client's chemical use, day hospitalization should not be the treatment of choice. But if the client has a stable home environment, day hospitalization can combine intensive programming with the opportunities for growth possible by having the client spend the morning/evening hours at home. Such programs are of value for clients who need to rebuild family relationships after a protracted period of chemical use, and they have been found to be as effective as inpatient treatment programs in the rehabilitation of clients (Guydish et al., 1998).

Halfway houses. The halfway house concept emerged in the 1950s in response to the need for an an intermediate step between the inpatient treatment format and independent living (Miller & Hester, 1980). For clients who lack a stable social support system, the period of time following treatment is often most difficult. Even if strongly motivated to remain sober, clients must struggle against the urge to return to chemical use unless they have the social support necessary to aid in this struggle. The halfway house provides a transitional living facility for such clients during the time immediately following treatment.

Miller and Hester (1980) identified several common characteristics of halfway houses: (a) small patient population (usually fewer than 25 individuals), (b) a brief patient stay (less than a few months), (c) emphasis on Alcoholics Anonymous or similar Twelve Step philosophy, (d) minimal rules, and (e) small number of professional staff members. Many halfway houses hold in-house self-help group meetings such as Alcoholics

Anonymous; others require residents to attend a specified number of community self-help group meetings a week. Each individual is expected to find work within a specified period of time (usually 2–3 weeks) or is assigned a job within the halfway house.

The degree of structure found in the traditional halfway house setting is somewhere between an inpatient treatment program setting and a traditional household. This gives clients enough support to function during the transitional period between treatment and self-sufficiency, but allows them to make choices about their lives. As Miller and Hester (1980) pointed out, halfway houses usually have fewer rules than an inpatient treatment center. Halfway house participation is usually time limited, usually 3–6 months, after which clients are ready to assume their responsibilities again.

Miller and Hester (1980) concluded that there was little evidence suggesting that the halfway house concept was a useful adjunct to treatment, but a number of subsequent studies have failed to support this conclusion. Moos and Moos (1995) followed a sample of 1,070 subjects who had been treated for substance-abuse problems at one of 77 Veterans Administration medical centers across the United States and had been referred to community residential living facilities following completion of their primary treatment program. The authors found that patients who had remained in the community residential living facility were significantly less likely to have been readmitted for substance use in the 4 years following discharge from the community living unit. In other words, those patients who remained in the halfway house longer were less likely to require additional treatment for substance-use problems in the 4 years following discharge from treatment.

These findings were consistent with those of Hitchcock, Stainback, and Roque (1995), who compared the relapse rates of 82 patients who elected not to enter a halfway house setting and 42 patients who were admitted to a halfway house setting. The authors found that patients discharged to a community setting (e.g., to live at home, in an apartment, or with friends/relatives) were significantly more likely to drop out of treatment in the first 60 days following discharge from an inpatient substance abuse rehabilitation program. On the basis of their findings, the authors concluded that halfway house placement can significantly enhance patient retention in aftercare programs, thus improving treatment outcome.

Two variables that seem to impact patient outcome after placement in a halfway house setting were (a) length of stay in the halfway house and (b) whether the individual continues to be involved in a rehabilitation program (Moos, Moos, & Andrassy, 1999). Moos et al. (1999) examined the outcome for 2,376 patients admitted to halfway house settings after completing primary treatment in Veterans Administration Hospital units. The authors found that patients who remained in the halfway house longer abstained from alcohol/drug use longer than those who were not in the halfway house. Further, individuals assigned to halfway houses that continued rehabilitation by expecting clients to participate in programming designed to help them abstain from chemicals did better than those who were referred to "undifferentiated" halfway houses, where there was no attempt at continued treatment.

The findings of the team of Moos et al. (1999) would seem to explain the often contradictory findings of earlier researchers who examined whether halfway house placement is useful for substance-abusing clients. They showed that it is necessary to examine the treatment philosophy of the different halfway houses utilized in previous research studies to determine whether they attempted to involve the resident in some form of continued treatment. Thus, although early research failed to support the halfway house concept, subsequent investigations have revealed that halfway houses do indeed seem to be an effective adjunct to the rehabilitation process of chemical abusers.

Summary

There is significant evidence that for at least some addicted individuals, outpatient treatment is an option that should be considered by treatment professionals. For clients with the proper social support and for whom there is no co-existing psychiatric illness or need for inpatient hospitalization, outpatient therapy for drug addiction may offer the chance to participate in treatment while still living at home. This avoids the need for a reorientation period following treatment, as is often seen in patients who have been hospitalized in an inpatient rehabilitation facility.

Outpatient treatment also allows for long-term therapeutic support that is often not available from shorter term inpatient programs. Within an outpatient drug-addiction program, random urine toxicology screening may be utilized to check on medication compliance and to identify individuals who have engaged in illicit drug use. Research evidence suggests that for many patients, outpatient drug-addiction treatment is as effective as inpatient chemical-dependency programs. There is a significant dropout rate from outpatient treatment programs, however, and much is yet to be learned about how to make outpatient addiction treatment more effective.

Inpatient treatment is often viewed as a drastic step. Yet for a minority of those who are addicted to chemicals, such a drastic step is necessary if the client is ever to regain control of his or her life. The inpatient rehabilitation program offers many advantages over less restrictive treatment options, including a depth of support services unavailable in outpatient treatment. For many of those in the advanced stages of addiction, inpatient treatment offers the only realistic hope of recovery.

In recent years, questions have been raised concerning the need for inpatient treatment programs or halfway house placement following treatment. It has been suggested that inpatient treatment does not offer any advantage over outpatient treatment, or that a longer stay was any more effective than short-term treatment. However, others have concluded that length of stay was inversely related to the probability of relapse following treatment.

CHAPTER THIRTY

The Process of Recovery

Introduction

It is common for substance-abuse rehabilitation professionals to speak of the process of recovering from a drug/alcohol use problem as if this were a single step. Even the language of recovery seems to imply that abstinence is a single entity rather than a *process*, which has a definite beginning but no definite end-point. In this chapter, the process of recovering from an alcohol/drug abuse problems will be discussed.

The Decision to Seek Treatment

Researchers have discovered that a number of factors impact the individual's decision to seek treatment for a substance-use disorder, including the severity of the problem (abuse versus dependence) and the severity of the consequences of that chemical abuse on the individual (Kessler et al., 2001). People who seek formal treatment tend to be more impaired and have more severe life problems than those who are able to abstain without formal intervention (Moos, 2003). On average, people with substance-use disorders seek professional treatment after about 5–8 years of dependence on a chemical or 10–19 years of heavy abuse (Kessler et al., 2001). Substances that result in greater levels of impairment (cocaine or heroin, for example) will precipitate a decision to enter treatment earlier than chemicals such as alcohol (Kessler et al., 2001).

The Stages of Recovery

In the last decade of the 20th century, the first theoretical models of the change process began to emerge. The most detailed of these was developed by James Prochaska (Prochaska, 2002; Prochaska, DiClemente, &

Norcross, 1992). This model is based on the assumption that the person recovering from drug abuse/addiction passes through definite stages, and that individuals at each different point have different characteristics (Connors, Donovan, & DiClemente, 2001; Sadock & Sadock, 2003) (see Figure 30.1).

The first stage of recovery is *precontemplation* (Connors et al., 2001; DiClemente, Bellino, & Neavins, 1999; Prochaska, 1998, 2002; Prochaska et al., 1992). About 40% of the population is thought to be in this stage (DiClemente & Prochaska, 1998; Prochaska, 2002) during which the individual is actively abusing chemicals and has no thought of trying to abstain from them. This phase can continue for years or decades. It is during this phase of chemical use that *denial* and *rationalization* are most prominent (Ramsay & Newman, 2000). Clients in this stage will overestimate the problems inherent in quitting and underestimate their available resources for change (Prochaska, 2002).

The challenge for the therapist faced with clients in the first stage is (a) to teach them the effects of the drugs of abuse, (b) to make them aware of the dangers associated with continued substance use/abuse, (c) to help awaken within them a desire for a different lifestyle, (d) to help them identify barriers to their recovery, and (e) to help them identify routes by which they might enhance their self-esteem. One goal for the therapist working with such clients is to address their ambivalence about change (Ramsay & Newman, 2000; Rose, 2001).

It is only during the second stage, the *contemplation* stage, that clients begin to entertain vague thoughts about possibly stopping the alcohol/drug use "one of these days." About 40% of the population of alcohol/drug abusers might be found in the contemplation stage at any given time (DiClemente & Prochaska,

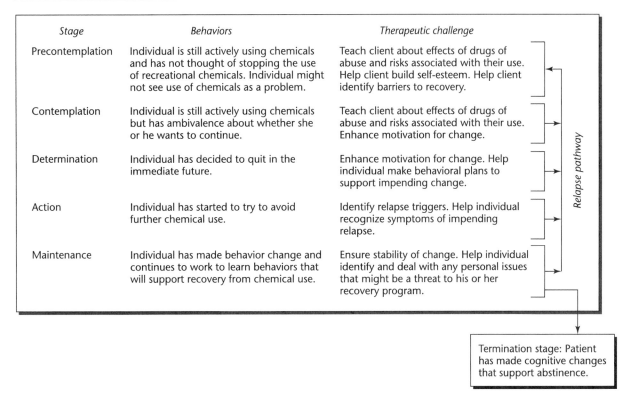

Stage	Behaviors	Therapeutic challenge
Precontemplation	Individual is still actively using chemicals and has not thought of stopping the use of recreational chemicals. Individual might not see use of chemicals as a problem.	Teach client about effects of drugs of abuse and risks associated with their use. Help client build self-esteem. Help client identify barriers to recovery.
Contemplation	Individual is still actively using chemicals but has ambivalence about whether she or he wants to continue.	Teach client about effects of drugs of abuse and risks associated with their use. Enhance motivation for change.
Determination	Individual has decided to quit in the immediate future.	Enhance motivation for change. Help individual make behavioral plans to support impending change.
Action	Individual has started to try to avoid further chemical use.	Identify relapse triggers. Help individual recognize symptoms of impending relapse.
Maintenance	Individual has made behavior change and continues to work to learn behaviors that will support recovery from chemical use.	Ensure stability of change. Help individual identify and deal with any personal issues that might be a threat to his or her recovery program.

Relapse pathway

Termination stage: Patient has made cognitive changes that support abstinence.

FIGURE 30.1   The stages of recovery
Source: Based on Prochaska, DiClemente, & Norcross (1992); Prochaska (1998).

1998). During this phase, users remain ambivalent about the possibility of change but have a growing sense of dissatisfaction with their present (alcohol/drug centered) lifestyle. Individuals might remain in this phase for months or even years while they continue to engage in active chemical use. For the therapist who is confronted with clients at this stage in the recovery process, the challenge is to (a) enhance the motivation to change, (b) awaken a desire for spiritual growth (see Chapter 34), and (c) help them learn how the chemical use has impacted their lives.

Brown (1997) suggested that this process takes place not in the contemplation stage of treatment, as advocated by Prochaska et al. (1992), but rather in the *determination* stage of treatment. According to Brown, during the determination stage the individual begins to make the cognitive changes necessary to support his or her recovery. It is the therapist's goal to nurture this process, offering encouragement, support, feedback, gentle confrontation, humor, and external validation for the client's struggles and successes.

The recovery process is difficult, as evidenced by the fact that only 20% of all addicted persons can be found in the last three stages of the recovery model suggested by Prochaska (DiClemente & Prochaska, 1998). Thus, most of those clients seen will be in the earlier stages of the Prochaska model (Connors et al., 2001; DiClemente & Prochaska, 1998; Prochaska et al, 1992). Few clients reach the actual initiation of abstinence, which the Prochaska model identifies as the *action* stage (Brown, 1997; Connors et al., 2001; DiClemente et al., 1999; Prochaska et al., 1992). During this phase the individual actively engages in the process of changing his or her addictive behaviors. Therapeutic goals during this stage include (a) optimizing opportunities for growth, (b) being alert to signs that clients are unable to handle the perceived level of stress, (c) encouraging them to begin the process of building a substance-free support system, (d) helping them handle the emotional "roller coaster" they might experience, (e) helping them to be realistic about their progress (for clients often overestimate their growth and progress), and (f) serving as a parent-substitute, mentor, cheering section, and guide.

Relapse is a very real danger during this stage of recovery. In the past, this was viewed as a signal of treatment failure, although this view has been challenged (Burge & Schneider, 1999). Recovery is a dynamic process that will proceed through the various stages of change in a cyclical rather than a linear manner (DiClemente & Prochaska, 1998). An example is the struggle many people face to give up cigarette smoking. In the first 3–4 weeks following cessation of cigarette smoking, people are especially vulnerable to smoking "cues," such as being around other smokers (Bliss, Garvey, Heinold, & Hitchcock, 1989). At such times, they are less likely to cope effectively with the urge to smoke and are in danger of a relapse into active cigarette smoking again. This is one reason that smokers who want to quit typically require an average of 3–4 attempts (Prochaska et al., 1992) to perhaps as many as 5–7 "serious attempts" (Brunton, Henningfield, & Solberg, 1994, p. 105; Sherman, 1994) before being able to stop smoking cigarettes. Thus, one task that will face clients during the action stage of recovery is to learn about their relapse "triggers" (discussed in Chapter 31).

After individuals have abstained from recreational chemical use for at least 6 months, they will enter the fifth or *maintenance* stage of recovery (Brown, 1997; Prochaska et al., 1992), during which they work on learning the behaviors that will enable them to continue to abstain from chemical use, including possibly addressing employment issues that have been ignored while they were actively abusing chemicals. Also, during this stage they might have to confront personal issues that contributed to or at least supported their use of chemicals. The *maintenance* stage blends into the *termination* stage at around 5 years (Prochaska, 2002). Only about 20% of people who begin the recovery process will reach this stage, which is marked by cognitive changes that free them from such things as dreaming about using the drug of choice and preoccupation with chemical use (Prochaska, 2002). During these periods the therapist must work to assure the stability of

change and help clients both identify and then address issues that might threaten their recovery.

One of the more frustrating aspects of substance-abuse rehabilitation is that it *does* proceed in a cyclical rather than a linear manner. Because of this, relapse *must* be acknowledged as a possible outcome for any given attempt at abstinence. The process of smoking cessation provides an excellent example, as periods of abstinence are mixed with periods of relapse. Indeed, "The return to smoking . . . occurs so frequently that it should be thought of as a part of the process of quitting and not as a failure in quitting" (Lee & D'Alonzo, 1993, p. 39). This is not to say that rehabilitation professionals should *accept* continued chemical use/abuse as being unavoidable. Rather, it is an acknowledgment that the process of recovery is difficult and ongoing, and relapsing back to active chemical use is a constant danger.

One interesting observation was offered by Cunningham, Sobell, Gavin, Sobell, and Breslin (1997), who suggested that the individual with a substance-use problem would subjectively evaluate the benefit/cost of quitting far differently at each of the discrete stages in the recovery process. A person in the precontemplation stage of recovery would view the benefits/costs of stopping the use of alcohol far differently than would someone in the maintenance stage. For the substance-abuse rehabilitation professional working with a client who wishes to stop using chemicals, it is necessary to help him or her reassess the potential benefits of abstinence and the discomfort associated with gaining this state at each stage of recovery.

Surprisingly, the model developed by Prochaska et al. (1992) seems to apply to those who recover from substance-use problems both with and without professional intervention. This makes sense, as "natural" recovery from substance-use problems is the norm rather than the exception (DiClemente & Prochaska, 1998; Walters, Rotgers, Saunders, Wilkinson, & Towers, 2003).

Another model of recovery was suggested by Nowinski (2003), who sees the first stage of recovery as *acceptance*. But there appear to be several pathways: (a) Users could decide that the consequences of further use of the chemical are not worth the anticipated benefits and cut back or discontinue the use of that chemical (or possibly any recreational drug) on their own. (b) They might turn to a self-help group such as Alcoholics Anonymous (AA) to help them learn how to abstain from chemical use. (c) They might seek outpatient therapy to help them learn how to abstain from chemical use. Finally, (d) people might seek inpatient treatment to help them learn how to abstain from further chemical use.

During this stage, individuals struggle to understand why willpower alone is not sufficient to guarantee abstinence and recovery. It is only after they have reached the second stage, *surrender*, that they become willing to make the changes in their lifestyle necessary to support their recovery, according to Nowinski (1996). As will be discussed in a later section of this chapter, the goal of the substance-abuse rehabilitation professional is to facilitate individuals' movement through the different stages of recovery.

Reactions against stage models of recovery. It is often surprising to the student of substance-abuse rehabilitation to learn that stage models of change are not universally accepted. However, few theoretical models of any kind are accepted without challenge, modification, or extensive revision. In psychology, stage models tend to pass through several periods, starting with the uncritical acceptance that follows introduction of a new theoretical model (Davidson, 1998). After a time, the model is subjected to guarded and sympathetic commentary, and cautious cricitism is offered suggesting that the model might not be totally accurate. This upswelling of criticism grows until the theoretical model is awash in a sea of downright hostility, after which time it is relegated to the archives as being good only for illustrative purposes as not every person follows each stage in the predicted order (Davidson, 1998).

In terms of recovery from substance-abuse problems, it is not clear what percentage of clients do so by progressing from one stage to the next (Davidson, 1998). Further, because of individual variation, one person might progress rapidly from one stage to the next, whereas another might remain in the same stage for up to 2 years or more (Davidson, 1998). The author suggested that stage models of recovery such as those discussed in this text are "at best descriptive rather than explanatory" (p. 32). Thus, they illustrate a general process and are not an outline of specific stages that each individual must pass through.

Then what works in predicting substance abuse and recovery? Although there is a great deal to be discovered about how recovery from substance-use problems

occurs, research suggests that "ongoing environmental factors can augment or nullify the short-term influence of an intervention" (Moos, 2003, p. 3). This is not to say that the treatment process is ineffective. Rather, "relatively stable factors in people's lives, such as informal help and ongoing social resources, tend to play a more enduring role" (Moos, 2003, p. 3) than the effects of formal treatment. Thus, the treatment process might best be envisioned as the foundation of a recovery program, not an end unto itself.

Research has also suggested that this foundation might be most effective when psychosocial factors are addressed as part of the individual's recovery program. Humphreys, Moos, and Finney (1995) identified a number of the most important factors that should be addressed:

Interpersonal relationships. People who drink more have fewer interpersonal relationships to draw on as sources of support. Those who drink less seem to have stronger interpersonal support systems.

Cognitive reappraisals. Many former drinkers can identify a point when they realized that their alcohol use was causing physical and emotional damage, and this realization was critical to their recovery.

Demographic variables. There is a tendency for those who drink more to come from lower socioeconomic groups.

Severity of drinking problems. Alcohol-related problems such as blackouts, difficulties on the job, and legal problems may serve as warning signs to some people that their drinking has started to reach uncontrollable levels.

Health problems. Adverse effects on health may serve as a warning that alcohol use has started to reach problematic levels.

Involvement in AA and/or religious groups. These associations may help people realize that their drinking has started to cause problems.

Individual expectations and self-evaluations. These can help to shape people's beliefs about themselves and their behavior.

Humphreys et al. (1995) followed a sample of 135 individuals classified as problem drinkers who either went through an alcohol detoxification program or contacted an alcoholism information and referral center to determine what steps they went through in their recovery. Although the members of this sample did not enter formal treatment for their alcohol-use problems, the authors found that there were still two pathways away from problem drinking: (1) going through a detoxification program and (2) practicing abstinence without entering a program. The authors found that the sample members fell into three subgroups at the end of 3 years. The first subgroup was made up of people who reported that they had achieved stable abstinence and were apparently able to abstain from further alcohol use during the 3-year follow-up period. The second subgroup had achieved a moderate drinking pattern, consuming no more than five beers or mixed drinks within any given 24 hours during the 3-year follow-up period. The final group continued to abuse alcohol in a problematic manner.

Humphreys et al. (1995) then examined the histories of the individuals in these three groups to determine what factors seemed relevant to the observed outcome. They found that problem drinkers who became controlled drinkers had consumed less alcohol at the start of the study and tended to be members of higher socioeconomic groups for the most part. As a group, they viewed their drinking as being less of a problem than did other drinkers, had higher self-esteem, and were more confident that they could resist the temptation to return to abusive drinking. The authors found that those who adopted an alcohol-free lifestyle tended to be from lower socioeconomic groups. These individuals tended to suffer a greater number of lost jobs and economic problems related to their drinking. As a group, the alcohol-free members were less sure of their ability to control their drinking and tended to turn to social support groups such as the church and AA in their quest for recovery.

Overall, the model that is emerging from clinical experience and research is that recovery from an alcohol/drug use problem is a dynamic process in which the individual must proceed through a series of specific stages before being able to make any meaningful changes in his or her chemical-use patterns. Some of the variables that will affect attempts at alcohol/drug rehabilitation are reviewed in Table 30.1.

Should abstinence be the goal of treatment? One issue that substance-abuse rehabilitation professionals fiercely debate is whether the goal of treatment should be to help people learn to *control* their chemical use or to learn how to abstain from all recreational alcohol/drug use. Although most treatment programs believe that abstinence is the only viable goal of rehabilitation, the truth is that following treatment the majority of those with alcohol-use disorders continue to use alcohol at least occasionally (Peele, 1985; Peele, Brodsky, & Arnold, 1991). George Vaillant (1983, 1996) did follow-up studies on identified alcohol-dependent individuals and found that over the course of their alcohol use they tended to alternate between periods of more and less problematic drinking.

This raises an interesting problem, as treatment centers advocate that the individual abstain from *all* chemical use, an outcome achieved by a very small minority of those who are "treated" for alcohol/drug use problems. For example, in the treatment of marijuana addiction, total abstinence from *all* psychoactive drugs is considered essential if treatment is to be effective (Bloodworth, 1987). Although the ultimate answer to this problem has not been found, it does suggest that there is still a great deal to learn about the natural history of alcohol/drug use problems and their treatment. At the same time, successful intervention for the substance-use disorders requires the therapist to address more than just the individual's chemical use, as such problems are best thought of as reflecting a *problem in living* that allows alcohol/drugs to be part of the individual's life. Some of the domains that must be addressed by the treatment professional and the possible outcome of the treatment process are reviewed in Table 30.2.

Specific Points to Address in the Treatment of Addiction to Common Drugs of Abuse

Although the process of recovering from any substance-use problem would tend to reflect the steps identified by Prochaska et al. (1992), there are specific issues that must be considered and addressed in working with individuals who have been abusing or are addicted to the various chemicals of abuse. In this section, some of those issues associated with abstinence from different drugs will be addressed.

TABLE 30.1   Variables That Affect Rehabilitation

Variable	Reason
Age	Older clients are more likely to have a successful treatment outcome. Research suggests that clients younger than 30 are more likely to become readdicted to narcotics following treatment, for example.
Employment	Clients with a stable employment history seem to do better in treatment than those with a history of employment problems.
Motivation	Clients who acknowledge that their substance use is causing them problems and who seek help on their own seem to be more likely to benefit from treatment.
Consequences or sanctions brought on by substance use/abuse	Clients who understand that continued substance use will result in sanctions of some kind (health problems, loss of employment, legal problems) seem to do better in treatment and afterward.
Physical/social environment	Clients who make a break with past associates and avoid going to places where they used to use alcohol/drugs (bars, homes of friends who use drugs, etc.) are less likely to resume using chemicals.
Legal status or peer criminal activity	Clients with fewer arrests have a higher success rate than clients with a long legal history. Clients who restrict or avoid contact with friends who are still using alcohol/drugs have higher success rates.
Social support	If clients' interpersonal support systems are strained, they are more likely to relapse. For example, if there is a lot of family conflict, the family will be unable to provide much support for the recovering individual.
History of drug use	Clients who use a greater variety of chemicals, who use chemicals more often, who began to use at a younger age, and who have been addicted for longer periods of time seem to relapse more often. Length of previous sobriety also seems to predict level of success; clients with long periods of sobriety in their past are more likely to benefit from treatment.
Treatment history	Clients who are "treatment wise" as a result of having been enrolled in many treatment programs in the past are more likely to return to the use of chemicals than are those individuals who haven't been in treatment before.
Concurrent psychiatric problems	Clients with concurrent psychiatric diagnoses are more likely to return to the use of chemicals. (Dual-diagnosis clients are discussed in Chapter 22.)
Anger	Clients with a great deal of anger (a history of fighting, etc.) are more likely to have trouble handling stress—and thus more likely to use chemicals to help them deal with their frustration. They are less likely to be able to abstain without help in learning how to deal with their anger/frustration.
History of victimization in interpersonal relationships	Clients who have been physically, sexually, and/or emotionally abused in the past have trouble dealing with the intense feelings of anger/shame that surface during treatment and are a high risk for return to chemical use.
Chronic illness	Clients who have concurrent chronic illness (chronic back pain, cancer, arthritis, asthma, HIV infection, etc.) are at high risk for return to chemical use as a way of dealing with the pain of their disease and/or the emotional frustration caused by their disorder.

Source: Chart based on Alemi, Stephens, Llorens, & Orris (1995).

TABLE 30.2   Summary of Possible Treatment Outcomes

Domain	Possible outcome
Substance use	• Abstinence • Reduced consumption of chemical(s) • Fewer days intoxicated by a chemical(s) • Substitution of illicit drug by authorized medication (as in methadone maintenance programs)
Medical/physical health	• Individual more likely to meet his or her basic food and shelter needs • Improved overall health, resulting in reduced use of health care resources • Fewer medical problems • Reduced use of health care resources by spouse or significant other • Reduced incidence of high-risk sexual behavior • Reduced sharing of needles
Psychosocial functioning	• Individual introduced to substance-free lifestyle • Improved quality of interpersonal relationships • Reduced level of conflict within family • Reduced danger of neglect/abuse within family • Improved psychological function for individual • Emotional disorders identified and treated • Psychiatric disorders identified and treated • Parenting skills improved
Employment history	• Increased chances of finding suitable work • Increased job retention • Improved job performance in present position • Reduced number of potential accidents • Reduced absenteeism
Criminal justice	• Reduced involvement with criminal justice system • Reduction in number of subsequent DWI or drug-related arrests • Reduced involvement in number of criminal activities • Reduced violent behavior
Relapse prevention	• Reduced possibility of subsequent substance use • Individual learns how to prepare for possibility of relapse • Individual learns how to minimize adverse effects of possible relapse for self/family.

Source: Based on information provided in Landry (1997).

Opiate Addiction: Is Treatment Worthwhile?

The man-on-the-street seems to believe that once an opiate addict, always an addict, and is quite pessimistic about treatment for narcotic addiction. Indeed, there *does* seem to be some basis for this pessimism, as research has found that 90% of opiate-dependent individuals who successfully are withdrawn from narcotics will return to chemical use within 6 months (Schuckit, 2000).

A pair of research studies have provided a rather gloomy view of the evolution of narcotics addiction (Hser, Anglin, & Powers, 1993; Hser, Hoffman, Grella, & Anglin, 2001). In 1986, 24 years after being identified as opiate addicts by the criminal justice system, only 22% of the original sample of 581 narcotics addicts were opiate free (Hser et al., 1993). Some 7% of the original sample was involved in a methadone maintenance program, and 10% reported engaging in only occasional narcotics use.

Almost 28% of the original sample had died, with the main causes of death being homicide, suicide, and accidents, in that order.

A decade later, in 1996–97, researchers contacted the original subjects and found that almost half of the subjects (284 of the original 581) were dead. Almost 56% of those who were still alive were opiate free, as confirmed by urine toxicology testing; another 10% refused to provide a urine sample for testing. About the same percentage of opiate-dependent individuals had died as had achieved lasting abstinence (Hser et al., 2001). The authors concluded on the basis of their data that heroin-use patterns were "remarkably stable" (p. 503) for the group as a whole, with returns to alcohol/drug use taking place even after some subjects had been drug free for 15 years. They concluded that heroin addiction was a lifelong condition, with severe social and medical consequences for those who were addicted to this chemical. However, there are also studies that have concluded that more than one-third of all opiate-dependent people will ultimately be able to stop using drugs. For those who survive their addiction to opiates and establish a recovery program, abstinence from opiate use is finally achieved in 6 (Smith, 1994) to 9 (Jaffe, 1989; Jenike, 1991) years after their addiction to opiates first developed.

CNS Stimulant Abuse: Withdrawal and Recovery Issues

Even though a great deal is known about the manifestations of CNS stimulant abuse/addiction, very little is known about the natural history of dependence on these agents (Jaffe, 1990). A great deal remains to be discovered about the abuse of and addiction to cocaine, the amphetamines, and similar drugs. For example, although cocaine has a reputation of being exceptionally addictive, not everybody who abuses cocaine will become addicted. Researchers disagree as to the exact percentage of those who use cocaine and then become addicted. The National Institute on Drug Abuse (quoted in Kotulak, 1992) suggested that only about 10% of those who use cocaine actually go on to become heavy users. Restak (1994) gave a higher estimate of between 25% and 33% of those who used cocaine ultimately becoming addicted.

Unfortunately, there is virtually no research into the factors contributing to the development of CNS

stimulant addiction. In contrast to the research into the genetics of alcoholism, "research on genetic factors in stimulant abuse has not been pursued" (Gawin & Ellinwood, 1988, p. 1177). Thus, there is virtually no information into possible genetic markers that might identify the person who is vulnerable to cocaine or amphetamine addiction. The point here is that not all CNS stimulant users are or will become addicted to that chemical. It is only through the process of *assessment* (discussed in Chapter 26) that the individual's need for treatment for a cocaine-use problem and the appropriate level of care for that person can be determined. Fortunately, people with only CNS stimulant-abuse problems rarely require hospital-based detoxification services ("Amphetamines," 1990). This is because physical withdrawal from the CNS stimulants is rarely life threatening.

One major exception to this rule is that CNS stimulant abuse/addiction can result in suicidal thinking. If the individual is suffering from a post-stimulant depression that has reached suicidal proportions, hospital-based observation and treatment may be necessary to protect him or her from self-destructive impulses. The decision to hospitalize or not hospitalize a CNS stimulant abuser should be made on a case-by-case basis by qualified physicians. Some of the factors that must be considered in making the decision include the individual's current state of mind, his or her medical status, and the presence or absence of adequate resources and social support to help the person deal with the withdrawal process on an outpatient basis.

Although the physical withdrawal from CNS stimulants is achieved quite rapidly, protracted cocaine abuse may result in an extended withdrawal syndrome (Satel et al., 1991). The cocaine withdrawal syndrome does not include the severe physical withdrawal distress seen in opiate withdrawal, but it does include such symptoms as paranoia, depression, fatigue, craving for cocaine, agitation, chills, insomnia, nausea, changes in the individual's sleep patterns, ravenous hunger, muscle tremors, headache, and vomiting (DiGregorio, 1990). These symptoms begin within 24 to 48 hours after the last dose of cocaine and persist for 7 to 10 days, according to the author. A similar process is seen with amphetamine withdrawal.

Stages of recovery from CNS stimulant abuse/addiction. A triphasic model for the post-cocaine binge recovery process has been proposed (Gawin, Khalsa, & Ellinwood, 1994; Gawin & Kleber, 1986). In the early part of the first stage, which lasts from 1 to 4 days, people experience feelings of agitation, depression, and anorexia (loss of desire to eat) as well as a strong craving for cocaine. As they progress through the second half of the first stage, they lose the craving for cocaine but experience insomnia and exhaustion, combined with a strong desire for sleep. The authors suggested that the second half of the first stage would last from the fourth until the seventh day of abstinence.

After the seventh day of abstinence, people experiencing withdrawal would return to a normal sleep pattern but would gradually experience stronger cravings for cocaine or stimulants and higher levels of anxiety. Conditioned cues would exacerbate the craving for stimulants, drawing them back to chemical abuse. If the person can withstand the environmental and intrapersonal cues for further drug use, they would move into the "extinction" stage, in which they would gradually return to a more normal level of functioning.

The extinction stage begins after 10 weeks of abstinence. If people relapse, the cycle will repeat itself. But if they can withstand the craving, there is a good chance that they might achieve lasting recovery. Hall, Havassy, and Wasserman (1991) concluded that approximately 80% of cocaine addicts who were able to abstain from cocaine use for 12 weeks after treatment were still drug free after 6 months. However, this does not mean that they have fully recovered from their CNS stimulant addiction. Cocaine and amphetamine addicts might suddenly experience craving for these drugs "months or years after its last appearance" (Gawin & Ellinwood, 1988, p. 1176), and long after the last period of chemical use.

The research team of Satel et al. (1991), examined the cocaine withdrawal process and concluded that their data failed to support the model advanced by Gawin and Kleber (1986). These authors found that for their sample, the cocaine withdrawal process was marked by mild withdrawal symptoms that declined over the first 3 weeks of inpatient treatment. However, the withdrawal symptoms they noted were much milder than had been anticipated and failed to follow the triphasic model suggested by earlier research.

The treatment of stimulant addiction involves more than just helping the user discontinue drug use. One common complication of stimulant addiction is that the individual has often forgotten what a drug-free life is like (Siegel, 1982). Further, prolonged stimulant abuse may have interfered with the user's dietary habits, resulting in vitamin deficiencies, especially of the B complex and C vitamins (Gold & Verebey, 1984). Because the stimulant effects of the amphetamines are so similar to that of cocaine, one would expect that the amphetamines would also lead to the vitamin deficiencies seen in chronic cocaine abuse. To test this hypothesis, the authors examined a number of cocaine abusers and found that 73% had at least one vitamin deficiency. To combat this, Gold and Verebey (1984) recommended that vitamin replacement therapy be a routine part of the treatment for cocaine abusers.

Total abstinence from recreational chemicals is thought to be essential if the individual wants to avoid further CNS stimulant-use problems. Hall et al. (1991) found that cocaine-dependent people who made a commitment to full abstinence following treatment were more likely to avoid further cocaine use than were addicts who did not desire abstinence as a treatment goal. Follow-up treatment should include behavior modification and psychotherapy to help individuals learn the skills they will need to continue to abstain from chemicals (Gold & Verebey, 1984). Social support and self-help group support in the form of Alcoholics Anonymous (AA), Narcotics Anonymous (NA), or Cocaine Anonymous (CA) are often of great help. As with the other forms of drug addiction, the recovering individual is at risk for cross-addiction to other chemicals and needs to avoid all recreational drug use for the rest of his or her life.

Issues Surrounding Recovery From Marijuana Abuse

Although marijuana use has been popular in this country since the Prohibition era, and most certainly after the "hippie" generation "discovered" marijuana in the 1960s, virtually nothing is known about the treatment of marijuana abuse/dependence (Stevens, Roffman, & Simpson, 1994; "Treatment Protocols for Marijuana," 1995). It is known that the short-term, acute reaction to marijuana does not require any special intervention (Brophy, 1993). Thus, marijuana-induced feelings of anxiety or panic usually respond to "firm reassurance in a non-threatening environment" (Mirin, Weiss, &

Greenfield, 1991, p. 304). However, the patient should be watched to ensure that no harm comes to either the marijuana user or others.

A number of problems are associated with working with marijuana abusers, First, it is rare for a person to be abusing *only* marijuana. Thus, treatment usually must focus on the abuse of a number of chemicals rather than marijuana alone. Second, marijuana users rarely present themselves for treatment unless there is some form of coercion. One reason for this is that in spite of their chemical use, marijuana abusers rarely view themselves as being addicted to cannabis ("Treatment Protocols for Marijuana," 1995).

Specific therapeutic methods for working with the chronic marijuana user are not well developed (Mirin et al., 1991). Total abstinence from *all* recreational chemical use is thought to be imperative (Smith, 2001). Because marijuana smokers often use the drug as a way to cope with negative feelings such as anger ("Treatment Protocols for Marijuana," 1995), rehabilitation professionals must help clients identify specific problem areas in their lives, then help them identify non-drug-related coping mechanisms for these "trigger" situations.

A treatment program that identifies the individual's reasons for continued drug use and helps the individual find alternatives to further drug use is thought to be most effective. Auxiliary groups that focus on vocational rehabilitation and socialization skills are also of value in treating the chronic marijuana user (Mirin et al., 1991). Jenike (1991) reported that treatment efforts should focus on understanding the abuser's disturbed psychosocial relationships. Bloodworth (1987) concluded that "family therapy is almost a necessity" (p. 183). Group therapy as a means of dealing with peer pressure to use chemicals was necessary in this author's opinion, and self-help support groups such as AA or NA[1] "cannot be overemphasized" (Bloodworth, 1987, p. 183).

Issues Surrounding the Treatment of Nicotine Addiction

When one asks a cigarette smoker why he or she continues to smoke in spite of the dangers associated with this habit, the response is often "I can't help myself. I'm addicted." Indeed, the addictive power of nicotine is believed to be the reason that 90% to 98% of those who

attempt to quit smoking in any given year will ultimately fail (Benowitz & Henningfield, 1994; Henningfield, 1995; Sherman, 1994).

Although health care workers have tried for many years to identify the factors that contribute to a person's successful attempt to quit smoking, they have met with little success (Kenford et al., 1994). Thus, cigarette cessation programs are something of a hit-or-miss affair, in which neither the leaders nor the participants have much knowledge of what *really* works. Smoking cessation training programs usually help between 70% and 80% of the participants to stop smoking on a short-term basis. But of those who attempt to stop smoking, two-thirds may stop for a very few days but only 2% to 3% will be tobacco free a year later (Henningfield, 1995). Hughes, Gust, Skoong, Keenan, and Fenwick (1991) found that 65% of their experimental sample relapsed within the first month of quitting, suggesting that the first month is especially difficult for the recent ex-smoker.

There appears to be a relationship between the frequency with which a given individual smokes and his or her success in giving up tobacco use. Cohen et al. (1989) reviewed data from 10 different research projects that involved a total of 5,000 subjects who were attempting to stop smoking cigarettes. The authors found that light smokers, defined as those who smoked fewer than 20 cigarettes each day, were significantly more likely to be able to stop smoking on their own than were heavy smokers. Cohen et al. (1989) also found that the number of previous attempts to quit smoking was not an indication of hopelessness. Rather, the authors found that the number of unsuccessful previous attempts was unrelated to the question of whether the smoker would be able to quit this time. They concluded that "most people who fail a single attempt [to quit smoking] will try again and again and eventually quit" (p. 1361).

Another factor that seems to be associated with the difficulty a smoker experiences when attempting to quit is his or her *expectancies* for the nicotine withdrawal process. Tate et al. (1994) divided their research sample of 62 cigarette smokers into four subgroups, each of which was given a different description of smoking cessation. The former smokers who were led to believe that they would not experience any significant distress during the nicotine withdrawal process reported significantly fewer physical or emotional complaints

[1]Discussed in detail in Chapter 34.

than did the other research groups. It appeared to the authors that people's expectations for the nicotine withdrawal process might play a role in how they interpret and respond to the symptoms they might experience during early abstinence.

There is other evidence that the individual's expectations for recovery can influence his or her experience of abstinence. Kviz, Clark, Crittenden, Warnecke, and Freels (1995) found that for smokers over the age of 50, the perceived degree of difficulty in quitting was negatively associated with the individual's actual attempts to quit smoking. In other words, the authors found that the harder the individual expected the task of quitting to be, the less likely he or she was to do so. Thus, people's expectations for quitting were found to play a significant role in whether they actually stopped smoking cigarettes.

Smokers who wish to quit should be warned that the struggle against cigarette smoking is a lifelong one, and that their mind-set will play a major role in whether they are successful in breaking the habit. Further, former smokers should be warned that they will be vulnerable to relapsing back to cigarette smoking for the rest of their lives.

Although there has been a great deal of emphasis on formal cigarette cessation treatment programs, perhaps as many as 90% (Brunton et al., 1994; Fiore et al., 1990) to 95% (Hughes, 1992; Kozlowski et al., 1989; Peele, 1989) of cigarette smokers who quit do so without participating in a formal treatment program. Of those who do quit, it seems that the individual's motivation to quit smoking is most "critical" (Jaffe, 1989, p. 682) to the success of his or her efforts. These conclusions raise serious questions as to whether extensive treatment programs are necessary for tobacco dependence. But formal treatment programs might be of value to heavy smokers or those at risk for tobacco-related illness.

Issues Associated With the Treatment of Anabolic Steroid Abusers

The first step in the treatment of steroid abusers is identification of those who are indeed abusing anabolic steroids. On the basis of clinical history, blood, and/or urine tests, the physician may be the first person to suspect that a patient is abusing steroids and is in the best position to confront the user. At this time, the addictions counselor is not thought to have a significant role to play in the treatment of anabolic steroid users, at least in the earliest stages, unless they are also abusing other chemicals.

Once the steroid abuser has been identified, he or she needs close medical supervision so that potential complications of steroid abuse can be identified and treated. The attending physician may need to consider a gradual detoxification program for the steroid abuser. Most medical complications caused by steroid abuse will usually clear up after the individual stops using the substances (Hough & Kovan, 1990); however, some of the complications (e.g., heart tissue damage) may be permanent. Surgical intervention may be able to correct some of the side effects of steroid use (Hough & Kovan, 1990), but this is not always possible.

Following the detoxification from anabolic steroids, the patient, with the help of staff, should try to identify why he or she started using steroids to begin with. Self-concept problems should be identified and the proper therapy initiated to help the steroid user learn self-acceptance without needing an artificial underpinning such as chemicals. Proper nutritional counseling may be necessary to help the athlete learn how to enhance body strength without using potentially harmful substances such as anabolic steroids. Group and individual support programs should also be considered as possible treatment modalities, depending on the client's needs.

Summary

In this chapter, two different models of the recovery process were discussed. The most popular model, introduced by Prochaska et al. (1992), suggested that clients who wish to make behavioral changes proceed from a *precontemplation* period, in which no specific change is being contemplated, through a stage in which the individual is thinking about possibly making some changes (*contemplation*), and on to a time when he or she actively considers making the change (*determination* stage).

Clients next enter the *action* stage, in which they attempt to make the desired behavioral changes, and if successful, enter the *maintenance* stage, where the new behavior becomes entrenched. Also discussed in this chapter were some specific points that should be addressed in treating clients who are abusing drugs.

CHAPTER THIRTY-ONE

Problems Frequently Encountered in the Treatment of Chemical Dependency

Introduction

Research has consistently demonstrated that treatment is more effective than criminal justice sanctions as a way of dealing with the problem of drug abuse (Scheer, 1994b). But no matter which treatment approach the therapist chooses, he or she will probably experience any of a number of problems in working with the substance-abusing person. In this chapter, we will examine some of the more common and more serious problems encountered by treatment professionals working with recovering addicts in different settings.

Limit Testing by Clients in Treatment

Clients in therapeutic relationships, which includes addicted clients in a treatment setting, will often "test the limits." This is done either consciously or unconsciously by the client, to determine whether the professional will be consistent in his or her treatment of the client. This limit-testing can take a number of different forms—from missed appointments to the use of chemicals while the client is in treatment.

The chemical-dependency professional should be aware that dependability and consistency are also important in the enforcement of program rules. For instance, patients in a methadone maintenance program were informed that if their urine toxicology tests detected evidence of illicit drug use four times in a year they would be removed from the program; these patients did better than those who did not have this expectation placed on them (McCarthy & Borders, 1985).

The counselor and treatment "secrets." One common situation is for the client to ask for an individual conference with a staff member and then confess to a rules infraction. Often, this admission of guilt is made to a student or intern at the agency rather than to a regular staff member. The confession might be having used chemicals while in treatment or some other rule infraction. After making the admission, the client will ask the staff member not to bring this information to the group, other staff members, or the program director so that he or she will not be discharged from treatment.

For the chemical-dependency professional to honor the request not to tell other staff members would be to enter into a partnership with the addicted person— a partnership that, because it was set up by the addicted person, would make the professional an enabler. In some situations, not to report the rule violation might make the professional vulnerable to later extortion by the client, who would be in the position of reporting the professional to his or her superiors for not passing on the information as required.

The proper response to this situation is to properly document the material discussed *immediately*, in writing and through proper channels. This might be a memo or an entry in the client's progress notes, as well as a discussion of the material revealed by the client with the professional's immediate supervisor. This reporting is done without malice, to ensure both uniform enforcement of the rules for all clients and to protect the professional's reputation.

Treatment Noncompliance

In no other sphere of medicine is the social stigma surrounding substance use as apparent as in the arguments that because substance-abuse rehabilitation programs suffer from high dropout and relapse rates they are not effective. These assertions are not applied

TABLE 31.1   Approximate Rates of Treatment
Noncompliance

Class of medications	Percentage of patients who fail to follow dosing instructions
Antiepileptics	30–50%
Antihypertensives	30–60
Blood-lipid-lowering agents	25–30
Antiarrhythmics	20
Antidepressants	30–40
Immunosuppressive agents	18
Antidiabetics	30–50
Anticoagulants	30
Antiasthmatics	20–60

Sources: Based on Lacombe, Bicente, Pages, & Morselli (1996);
McLellan, Lewis, O'Brien, & Kleber (2000).

to the other specialities in medicine, where patient noncompliance is also a problem, but exclusively to the field of addiction medicine. To illustrate, a patient who is repeatedly hospitalized for diabetes-related problems might be termed a "brittle" diabetic by physicians, whereas the alcohol-dependent individual who is repeatedly hospitalized for alcohol-related problems is called "a treatment failure." Proponents of the public health model of addictions point out that each of these patients has a chronic, relapsing disorder, yet only in the field of substance-abuse rehabilitation is rehospitalization referred to as a treatment failure.

Patient noncompliance is a problem for every speciality in medicine, not just substance-abuse rehabilitation. For example, 40% to 60% of patients with Type 1 diabetes, hypertension, or asthma do not take the medications prescribed for these conditions as instructed (Marlowe & DeMatteo, 2003).[1] Even for mild bacterial infections, it is the rare patient who completes the prescribed 10-day course of antibiotics (Markel, 2004). Table 31.1 provides a summary of different medical conditions and the percentage of

patients who do not follow treatment recommendations for that disorder.

Thus, although treatment noncompliance is not limited to substance-abuse rehabilitation programs, it *is* a significant problem. For example, many patients request "detoxification" from alcohol/drugs, only to fail to complete the detoxification process initiated at their own request because of factors such as the severity of medical disease and severity of drug use (Franken & Hendriks, 1999). Other studies have found that only 10% to 30% of those who are deemed to be at risk for an alcohol-use disorder actually follow through with treatment recommendations after being referred to treatment (Cooney, Zweben, & Fleming, 1995).

Unfortunately, there are no personality traits that seem to function as predictors of patient dropout (Miller, 2003). A complicating factor is that the individual's commitment to *treatment* is not the same as making the commitment to *change* (Connors, Donovan, & DiClemente, 2001). People might agree to enter a rehabilitation program for many different reasons without ever making a commitment to change or discontinue their substance abuse (Connors et al., 2001). Others, usually those who have been mandated to treatment, may go through the motions of following a treatment program without having any internal desire to stop or reduce their chemical abuse (Connors et al., 2001).

It is well known that substance-abuse rehabilitation programs suffer significant levels of patient attrition, possibly because entering treatment is not automatically a sign that one wants to change. Up to 50% of those admitted to substance-abuse rehabilitation programs will drop out of treatment before the 90th day, and 66% will drop out by the end of 6 months (McCusker, Stoddard, Frost, & Zorn, 1996). Israel, Rabinowitz, and Marjefsky (1998) examined the issue of premature termination from treatment through a retrospective analysis of the records of 764 male patients. They found that social isolation was a major predictor of patient dropout. Behaviors such as solitary drinking, not being married, having no children, and being unemployed were associated with a greater chance of treatment failure. These indicators could serve as possible warning signals for male patients who are at risk for premature termination from treatment, possibly alerting staff to the need for special efforts to help these individuals remain in and benefit from treatment.

---

[1]Pirisi & Sims (1997) suggested that this percentage might be as high as 86% for some conditions.

Relapse and Relapse Prevention

Unfortunately, although 99% of substance-abuse treatment programs aspire to the goal of total abstinence (Leavitt, 2003), only a minority of those who complete a rehabilitation program will continue to abstain from chemical abuse. Fully 90% of those treated for alcohol dependence will have consumed alcohol at least once within the first 90 days following discharge, and 45% to 50% will have returned to pretreatment drinking levels within a year (Polivy & Herman, 2002). Only 25% of alcohol-dependent individuals who completed an abstinence-based treatment program were found to be alcohol free a year after discharge (Miller, Walters, & Bennett, 2001). These findings indicate that "as many as 90% of individuals do not achieve behavior change on their first attempt" (Witkiewitz & Marlatt, 2004, p. 226). Behavioral lapses for the individual hold the potential to become full-blown relapses back to active substance abuse/addiction (Witkiewitz & Marlatt, 2004).

The first 90 days following discharge from treatment is a period of special vulnerability for the individual's potential relapse back to drug use (DeJong, 1994; Dimeff & Marlatt, 1995). However, this is not a sign that rehabilitation is a waste of effort. Rather, the grim fact that relapse follows efforts at treatment reinforces the basic message that the disease of addiction can be *arrested* but never *cured*.

To combat the tendency for the former patient to return to the use of chemicals, treatment professionals began to place emphasis on *relapse prevention* skills the patient could develop while in treatment and use after completing the rehabilitation program. Several factors contribute to the tendency to relapse (Witkiewitz & Marlatt, 2004):

1. Self-efficacy: The individual's confidence in his or her ability to cope with the high-risk situation.
2. Outcome expectancies: The individual's expectations about the effects of a substance if he or she should use it.
3. Craving: Although "craving" itself is a poor predictor of relapse, it may be triggered by drug-use cues (smells, the sight of the drug, sounds, etc.) and trigger moods and memories that predispose the individual to substance use. For example, the sight of a cigarette ashtray may reawaken memories of past cigarette smoking, causing the individual to crave a cigarette at that time.
4. Motivation: The individual's motivation to change his or her behavior or to return to past behaviors has been found to play an important role in successfully coping with drug-use cues.
5. Coping: This poorly understood determinant of relapse seems to reflect the individual's ability to call on learned coping resources (behavioral, cognitive, etc.) when confronted with drug-use cues.
6. Emotional states: Research suggests a strong association between negative affect states and relapse.
7. Interpersonal support: The individual's access to strong social support systems during times of craving seems to contribute to continued abstinence.

In his analysis of the problem of relapse, Chiauzzi (1990, 1991) suggested four elements common to those who relapse. First, there are *personality traits* that predispose some people to relapse. Such relapse-prone personality traits include a tendency toward compulsive behaviors, as such individuals do not adjust well to even minor changes in routine. Another personality trait that interfered with recovery was a tendency toward dependency, as such individuals had trouble asserting their wish to maintain a recovery program when confronted with drug-use cues or opportunities (Chiauzzi, 1990, 1991). Passive-aggressive personality traits also place individuals at risk for relapse because of a tendency to blame others for their own behavior. The narcissistic traits often found in addicted people prevent many from admitting the need for help during a weak moment, and antisocial personality traits underscore a tendency toward impulsiveness and a desire not to follow the road taken by others (Chiauzzi, 1990, 1991).

A second factor is a tendency for such individuals to *substitute addictions* for the chemicals they once abused (Chiauzzi, 1990, 1991). Examples of such substitute addictions include compulsive work, relationships, food, or switching from one drug of abuse to another. Third, a *narrow view of recovery* often predicts relapse (Chiauzzi, 1990, 1991). An example is equating abstinence with recovery. Such a view of recovery places people at risk for relapse because they are not working to change the personality structure or the interpersonal problems that contributed to the development of the addiction in the first place. Such individuals do not develop the self-awareness necessary to see the personal drift toward relapse.

People in early recovery are remarkably insensitive to what Chiauzzi (1990, 1991) termed warning signals of impending relapse. Through a series of seemingly *irrelevant decisions,* the fourth factor, the newly recovered individuals will often place themselves in a high-risk situation (discussed below), possibly without being aware of more than the last decision in a chain of choices that ultimately results in their relapse (Keller, 2003). The minidecisions that contribute to a relapse can be either conscious or unconscious (Chiauzzi, 1991). A central characteristic of minidecisions is that they do *not* involve a decision to actively use chemicals. Rather, these irrelevant decisions will collectively set the stage for a relapse. Examples might be for the recovering person to continue a friendship with an active drug addict or for the recovering alcoholic to go to the local bar to socialize or "just to play pool." A common minidecision is to reduce the frequency with which a person attends a support group. Often, there appears to be a valid reason for the individual to do so at the time, but only after a relapse does the impact of these minidecisions on recovery become apparent. When the decision chain that ultimately resulted in the individual's relapse is outlined, the person is able to see that it was not a random event but the result of a chain of seemingly innocent individual minidecisions (Cummings, Gordon, & Marlatt, 1980; Keller, 2003).

Another potential threat to the individual's recovery program is *maladaptive thoughts*[2] (Beck, 2004; Keller, 2003). Examples of maladaptive thoughts include "I can control it now," or "Just *one* won't hurt," or the ever-popular "I *deserve* a drink after all that I've done/been through/suffered." Another common maladaptive thought is the desire to "test" one's recovery, often rationalized as a desire to return to the bar to see "friends." Such maladaptive thoughts may allow the individual to (a) convert ordinary stress into a source of excessive distress (example: "I cannot *stand* feeling this way!"), (b) transform distress into a craving (example: "I need to use ___ in order to cope with this!"), and (c) rationalize the relapse (example: "I *deserve* this," or "Just *one* won't hurt")

(Beck, 2004). Such maladaptive thoughts, or cognitive distortions, need to be addressed if the individual is to successfully abstain from chemicals.

High-risk situations contribute to the possibility of relapse by exposing the individual to chemical-use cues or opportunities. Such situations often arise without warning (Witkiewitz & Marlatt, 2004). Dimeff and Marlatt (1995) reported that fully 75% of all relapses involved the failure to deal successfully with a high-risk situation. Given this fact, it is not surprising that techniques that help individuals anticipate potential high-risk situations and develop coping skills for these situations increase their chances of abstaining from chemicals (Annis & Davis, 1991). They must learn to monitor internal mood states, aided by treatment center staff and the results of such psychological tests as the Inventory of Drinking Situations (IDS-100).[3] The test data would be utilized to develop a hierarchy of drinking situations, which staff would use to help identify clients' strengths, resources, and environmental supports that they could call on to deal with the potential relapse situation. Clients then could rehearse how they might deal with a high-risk situation to develop skills to help them avoid the risk of relapse. Clients could carry a reminder card in the wallet or purse with written instructions on the steps to take to limit the relapse. These steps help individuals enhance their coping skills and self-efficacy.

High-risk situations fall into two categories (Cummings et al., 1980). The first category consists of the acute period of drug withdrawal, when people are likely to be motivated to avoid further withdrawal discomfort through the ingestion of chemicals. The second category includes the social, environmental, and emotional states individuals perceive as stressful and for which they used drugs as a coping mechanism in the past (Cummings et al., 1980; Keller, 2003). In this second group of high-risk situations, cognitive evaluations of the social, environmental, or emotional stimuli mediate whether the individual considers the possibility of drug use. Such cognitive evaluations may then be interpreted by the individual as an *urge* or *craving* to use a substance.

A number of "stimulus factors" (Shiffman, 1992, p. 9) can also contribute to a relapse situation. It is important to remember that a process of conditioned learning

---

[2]Members of AA would call these thoughts "stinkin' thinking" (Keller, 2003).

[3]See Glossary.

TABLE 31.2 Common Relapse Situations

Category of relapse	Description of situation that contributed to or caused relapse	Percentage of cases
Negative emotional states	Feelings of frustration, anger, anxiety, depression, or boredom	35%
Peer pressure	Pressure from either a single person (such as a close friend) or a group of people (co-workers, for example) to use chemicals	20
Interpersonal conflict	Conflict between patient and a friend, employer, employee, family member, or dating partner	16
"Craving" for drugs/alcohol	Person becoming preoccupied with use of alcohol and/or drugs, in spite of abstinence	9
Testing personal control	Person exposing self to "high risk" situation, in order to see whether he or she is able to resist urges to use chemicals	5
Negative physical states	Person experiencing a negative physical state such as illness, postsurgical distress, or injury	3

Source: Chart based on material provided by Dimeff and Marlatt (1995).

takes place during the time people are using alcohol/drugs. Following cessation, sights/sounds/smells/affect states associated with chemical use can trigger "using" thoughts. This process of associative learning is clearly seen in the observation that 58% of recovering alcohol-dependent people say that they smoke cigarettes to cope with the "urge" to use alcohol (Monti, Kadden, Rohsenow, Cooney, & Abrams, 2002). Given the strong association between alcohol use and cigarette smoking, resorting to cigarette use to cope with an urge to drink might be viewed as the individual's engaging in a "half measure." Another way to view it is that by smoking, the individual is trying to cope with the urge to drink by engaging in a behavior associated with drinking without actually using alcohol itself.

It has also been found that recovering opiate-dependent individuals might suddenly experience a craving for narcotics even after being drug free for months or even years, if they return to the neighborhood where they once used chemicals (Galanter, 1993). The mechanism through which this takes place might be based in the unconscious, for "most of a person's everyday life is determined not by their conscious intentions and deliberate choices but by mental processes that are put into motion by features of the environment and that operate outside of conscious awareness" (Bargh & Chartrand, 1999, p. 462). It is for this reason that Shiffman (1992) advocated

behavioral rehearsal procedures to help clients learn relapse prevention skills. Such behavioral training might include exposure to the smells, sights, and sounds once associated with chemical use so that people might learn to anticipate how these things might trigger thoughts/urges to use chemicals and develop coping mechanisms. These behavioral rehearsals can be viewed as fostering self-efficacy in Witkiewitz and Marlatt's (2004) model of relapse prevention.

It is necessary to identify and address clients' feelings of demoralization and self-blame during the early phases of recovery (Shiffman, 1992). These negative mood states are powerful determinants of behavior and may be so intense that people return to the abuse of chemicals to escape or cope. Cognitive-behavioral therapies are especially useful in this area.

DeJong (1994) also explored the problem of relapse and identified a number of antecedents that seemed to predict increased risk of relapse: (a) stress, (b) negative emotional states, (c) interpersonal conflict, (d) social pressure, (e) positive emotional states, (f) use of other substances, and (g) presence of drug-related cues. Some of the more common triggers for relapse are summarized in Table 31.2.

One factor that contributes to relapse is for individuals to take a very *short-term view of recovery*. Researchers have found that after the individual has abstained for 6 years he or she is unlikely to relapse to active drinking (Vaillant, 1996). Treatment staff must thus help recovering patients learn not to let down their guard before abstinence becomes a new lifestyle. During this interim period the newly abstinent people will continue to think in much the same way they did when actively addicted. They must learn not to rush the recovery in the first months or years after that last drink or use of a drug.

Research has found mixed evidence supporting the concept of relapse prevention training (Hester & Squires, 2004; Irvin, Bowers, Dunn, & Wang, 1999). Such programs may very well combat the sense of demoralization, anger, and depression that seem to identify individuals who are most prone to relapse (Miller & Harris, 2000). Successful relapse prevention training programs include an element of support for people in the earliest stages of recovery, when they are most vulnerable.

"Cravings" and "Urges"

Although researchers agree that *craving* and *urges* are important concepts in the treatment of people with substance-use disorders, there is no universally accepted definition of either term, nor a way to measure these constructs (Anton, 1999; Ciraulo, Piechniczek-Buczek, & Iscan, 2003; Merikle, 1999; Weiss et al., 2003). Different researchers have used each term in widely disparate ways, resulting in confusion not only in the professional literature but also the popular media about their meaning and definition.

For the purpose of this text, the concept of craving will be viewed as an intense *subjective* emotional and physical experience that varies in intensity from one individual to another (Merikle, 1999). Because it is a subjective experience the same symptoms of craving might be interpreted as intense by one individual and as quite weak by another (Weiss et al., 2003). The experience of craving has been reported to wax and wane in intensity during the first 12 months of abstinence, and the strongest craving for chemicals seems to occur during the first 90 days (Carol, Smelson, Losonczy, & Ziedonis, 2001).

Symptoms of craving include obsessive thoughts about obtaining chemicals, and physical symptoms of arousal such as sweating palms, rapid heartbeat, and salivation (Anton, 1999; Merikle. 1999). The experience of

craving might best be understood as a "pathological motivational state" (Wexler et al., 2001, p. 86) in which the individual becomes fixated upon his or her drug of choice. During this altered motivational state, the individual feels compelled to obtain and use that chemical. Researchers have identified altered blood flow patterns in the regions of the brain associated with pleasure and reward during periods of craving, even in alcohol-abusing adolescents whose alcohol-use history is limited (Tapert et al., 2003). This study suggests that there are neurological aspects to craving that contribute to the subjective experience of wanting to use chemicals again. As part of the cognitive preoccupation with the chemical of choice, the individual might engage in euphoric recall about past chemical use (Anton, 1999; Beck, Wright, Newman, & Liese, 1993).

Euphoric recall takes place when the individual frames his or her drug-use experience as being desirable and pleasurable (Johnson, 1980). This process seems to reflect the pattern of activation in the brain that develops after repeated periods of drug/alcohol use, which may then become activated in response to drug-use cues that the individual encounters in the environment (Wexler et al., 2001).

Urges are of less intensity than the experience of craving and were viewed as more of a cognitive experience than the whole-body episode of craving (Merikle, 1999). In contrast to this definition, Beck et al. (1993) suggested that urges were behavioral impulses to find and use one's drug of choice. As behavioral scientists come to understand better the forces that sustain human motivation, they are discovering that many of the triggers for decision making are based on unconscious perceptions and motivations that are only later rationalized by the conscious mind (Bargh & Chartrand, 1999), opening up new avenues to discover the sources of urges and craving for chemicals and why people respond to these sensations the way they do.

Beck et al. (1993) identified four different situations that contributed to urges to use chemicals: The first was the individual's learned *response to the discomfort of withdrawal*. As has been discussed earlier in this text, the use of many of the recreational chemicals can result in a characteristic pattern of withdrawal symptoms. To avoid this withdrawal syndrome, the individual will engage in additional substance use. For example, the nicotine-dependent individual will smoke a cigarette and the alcohol-dependent individual will have another drink when they experience the earliest symptoms of withdrawal.

Next, many people tend to use chemicals when they are unhappy or uncomfortable (Beck et al., 1993). These chemical-use urges are triggered by some of the antecedents of relapse identified by DeJong (1994) (see preceding section). These antecedent situations then cause the individual to crave chemicals as a way of coping with the negative situation. Over time, the individual gives in to these cravings by beginning to make specific behavioral plans to use chemicals: the urge to use alcohol/drugs.

The third sources of drug-use urges were external drug-use cues, including the perceived opportunity to engage in drug-use behaviors (Beck et al., 1993; Wertz & Sayette, 2001). Such chemical-use cues might include cleaning out one's apartment and finding a stash of alcohol or drugs. Other cues might be a chance (or intentional) encounter with a former using/drinking partner, the return to the same environment where the individual had once used chemicals, or experiencing the many sights, sounds, or smells associated with chemical use (Monti et al., 2002). For example, some recovering heroin addicts will begin to think about using heroin again if they happen to smell the smoke of a burning match.

Finally, the fourth source of chemical use urges is the individual's desire to enhance positive experiences (Beck et al., 1993). Many recovering alcohol/drug dependent individuals find that they associate chemical use with feelings of pleasure. Especially in the earlier stages of recovery, when they find themselves starting to feel good, they begin to fear losing this feeling. The urge is to return to the use of chemicals in order to extend or enhance the positive experience so it will last longer. This category of urge was discussed by DeJong (1994) under the heading of "positive emotional states."

Both urges and periods of craving are normal in the early stages of abstinence, and existing psychosocial treatment modalities appear to help people deal with these experiences (Monti et al., 2002; Weiss et al., 2003). In spite of the frequency with which they are encountered, however, behavioral scientists have yet to identify the mechanisms by which urges and periods of craving are generated. Further, there is only limited evidence that urges and/or craving for chemicals are

significant predictors of relapse (Anton, 1999; Spanagel & Hoelter, 2000). However, because most individuals in the earliest stages of recovery experience craving and urges, it is important for them to learn how to cope with these experiences. The alternative is that their recovery will be threatened or destroyed by their urges to return to the use of chemicals in the earliest stages of recovery.

The "Using" Dream

A phenomenon that is both frequently encountered and little understood is the "using" dream. These experiences may be quite distressing to newly abstinent individuals, who dream that they had just used alcohol/drugs—a dream that was so intense and seemed so real they actually thought they were under the influence of chemicals for the first few seconds after awakening. Such dreams then become relapse triggers because of their intensity, especially if clients had not been informed they would have such dreams in the early stages of recovery.

Research into the dream state is still in its infancy, and there has been no research into the "using" dream. It is known that dreams that take place during rapid eye movement (REM) sleep are noted for bizarre, intense imagery (Doweiko, 2002). A second element of the dream state is a neuromuscular blockade that prevents the brain from acting on the movement commands generated by the motor cortex in the dream state; this also seems to contribute to the "using" dream. The final piece to the puzzle is the brain's formation of the dream memory in the transitional stage between the dream state and full waking. In these few moments, the individual must come to terms with trace memories of the dream experience and make sense out of what seemed like a bizarre, unusual situation in which the brain did not function normally. This is also a pretty good capsule summary of the subjective experience of intoxication: The brain experiences a bizarre, atypical state, often marked by intense, vivid imagery, in which the individual is unable to properly coordinate muscle activity because of substance-induced ataxia. Thus, the "using" dream seems to result when the mind attempts to make sense of the recently terminated dream state by comparing it to a waking experience when it experienced a similar state of being: when the individual was under the influence of chemicals.

Fortunately, anticipatory guidance[4] and reassurance seem to be the best tools to help clients through this stage. As the association between the dream state experience and substance abuse becomes weaker with the passage of time, the "using" dream seems to become less intense and less frequent. It is rare for a client to report such a dream after the first 3 months of abstinence.

Controlled Drinking

In contrast to England, where 75% of all alcohol-rehabilitation programs offer patients training to help them moderate their drinking (Barr, 1999), in the United States the theory that the alcoholic might return to "social" or "controlled" drinking has met with skepticism (Hester, 1995; Vaillant & Hiller-Sturmhofel, 1996). Unfortunately, ever since the first preliminary reports that it *might* be possible to help a small number of people with alcohol-use problems return to a state of "controlled" drinking, many alcohol-dependent individuals have seized on the concept as a justification for their continued drinking.

The effectiveness of controlled drinking has been challenged in the research literature. Miller, Walters, and Bennett (2001) suggested that only 10% of test subjects were able to remain controlled drinkers during the first 12 months after treatment. Other studies have found that less than 2% of individuals who are dependent on alcohol might return to a state of social drinking again (Helzer et al., 1985; Vaillant, 1996; Vaillant & Hiller-Sturmhofel, 1996). Controlled drinking is a viable goal only for those individuals who are not addicted to alcohol and who have not experienced significant problems associated with alcoholism (Hester, 1995). It might be possible to teach a large percentage of those who *abuse* alcohol to control their drinking, but research has shown that "stable moderate drinking [is] a rare outcome among treated alcoholics" (Wallace, 2003, p. 19). Typically, individuals who are moderately to severely addicted to alcohol do not remain controlled drinkers but quickly return to the abusive drinking pattern of the past (Watson, Hancock, Malovrh, Gearhart, &

Raden, 1996). Those who attempt to return to controlled alcohol use following treatment were four times as likely to return to abusive drinking as those who focus on abstinence (Watson et al., 1996).

Unfortunately, many alcohol-dependent individuals cling to the hope that they can somehow find their way into the 1% to 10% of alcohol-dependent people who can be trained to return a controlled or social pattern of alcohol use. Levin (2002) warned that the longer people have been drinking, the less likely it is that they will be able to return to social drinking, and Morgan (2003) advised that controlled drinking not be accepted as a viable treatment goal for alcohol-dependent persons. However, Hester (1995) suggested that alcohol-dependent individuals who wish to attempt to learn how to drink in a social manner be allowed to try. An attempt at controlled drinking may help the individual realize the need for total abstinence (Hester, 1995). Further, many individuals who start out working to become social drinkers switch to total abstinence as they encounter problems controlling their alcohol intake (Hester, 1995). Once the individual fails in this task, he or she might be more willing to accept alcoholism as a disease "that can be arrested with abstinence but never cured in a way that will permit the person to drink again" (Brown, 1995, p. 11).

But the mental health or substance-abuse professional needs to weigh the potential benefits from this trial against the potential risks. Confirmed alcoholics who believe they can learn social drinking behaviors once again *and maintain* a pattern of social drinking for the rest of their lives are taking a bet where the odds are at best 49:1, if not 99:1, against them. There are very few of us who would be willing to chance an operation where the odds were 50 to 1 against us. Few would be willing to consent to a surgical procedure with only a 1% or 2% chance of recovery. Yet many alcoholics have voiced the secret wish that they could win this bet and land in what more than one alcoholic has called "the lucky 2%."

The Uncooperative Client

Clients who are being assessed or are in treatment for an alcohol- or drug-abuse problem often have little incentive to cooperate with treatment staff. A client might be less than fully cooperative with the assessor

---

[4]A therapeutic technique in which the therapist warns the client what to expect in certain settings, so that he or she might anticipate feeling anxious or afraid and thus not be overwhelmed by these feelings.

or the treatment staff in many ways. In this section, some of the more common forms of client resistance are discussed.

Appearing for sessions under the influence of chemicals. It is not uncommon for the substance-abuse rehabilitation worker to suspect that a client is under the influence of chemicals because of the client's behavior. Perhaps it is how the client slurs words, the look in his or her eyes, or the pungent smell of a chemical such as alcohol or cannabis. The assessor might, for example, wonder why clients who are being seen for a court-ordered alcohol/drug use assessment have such a huge wad of chewing gum in their mouths during the interview or why they use breath mints so frequently. For these or other reasons, the counselor might suspect that the client either (a) is under the influence of chemicals or (b) has recently abused alcohol/drugs.

In such cases, the treatment professional might (a) confront the client with the suspicion that the client is under the influence of chemicals and/or (b) request the client to provide a urine sample under appropriate supervision for toxicology testing. It should be explained that addictions are diseases that often are both cunning and deceptive, and that the hard evidence of a breath analysis or urine toxicology test report would help to shed light on the counselor's suspicion and the client's possible chemical use. The counselor should then listen very carefully to the client's response, especially protests that he or she has certainly not used alcohol or drugs, and how could the counselor *think* such a thing? Such protests are often an attempt to hide chemical use, for the experience of the author has been that if the person is "clean," he or she will welcome a chance to demonstrate this to the counselor.

If the counselor's suspicion is confirmed, either by the test results or an admission from the client, two different issues are raised. First, there is a clinical issue of the client's abuse of chemicals prior to his or her assessment or counseling session. This reflects a serious substance-use problem and interferes with the assessment or counseling process. It is impossible to conduct a therapy session or complete an accurate assessment of the client's substance-use pattern when she or he is under the influence of recreational chemicals (Washton, 1995). Thus, meeting with a client who is intoxicated is a waste of time, and the appointment should be rescheduled for a later date.

But the client's use of recreational chemicals prior to a therapy session also raises a number of liability issues for client and therapist. If the counselor allows the client to go home, he or she could be liable if that person were to be injured or were to harm somebody else. Imagine, for example, that a client appeared for an appointment smelling of alcohol and obviously intoxicated. If the therapist recommended that the client "go home and sleep it off" and that person were to have an accident while driving home, the therapist might be held liable on the grounds of knowing that the client had used alcohol but not providing medical supervision while the person's body recovered from the effects of drinking.[5] To protect themselves from potential liability for injuries to either the client or another person, mental health workers might be required to intervene in cases of substance use, possibly to the point of initiating an involuntary commitment to a hospital for detoxification from chemicals or even calling the authorities to report that the client is attempting to drive home and that the caller has reason to suspect that he or she is under the influence of alcohol/drugs.

The threatening client.[6] On occasions, a client will behave in a threatening manner. The therapist should not hesitate to call the police any time there is reason to believe that clients are a danger to themselves or others. The therapist should *carefully document* the reasons he or she believed the client was a danger as soon as possible after calling the authorities. For example, a client who says during a session that he or she was "so mad I could have killed him" might just be venting anger and not presenting a real danger to another person. However, if during a session the client says, "I want to take my shotgun from the closet and shoot my ex-wife and her boyfriend," he has identified (a) specific victims (ex-wife and her current boyfriend) and a (b) specific method (shotgun blast) of harm. *Careful* assessment of

---

[5]Readers are advised to check with an attorney about what their responsibility might be if they should suspect that a client is intoxicated, and for guidance as to how they should handle this or similar situations.

[6]Prudent therapists will consult with an attorney about what their duty-to-report responsibilities are when they have reason to suspect that a client is a potential danger to self or others. The fact that the consultation took place and the attorney's recommendations should also be documented in the client's chart.

the client's potential for harm and appropriate action to reduce the danger should be taken. Documentation is also necessary to justify the steps taken, and if necessary the authorities should be called to intervene.

On occasions, the client might begin to behave in a threatening manner during the session. The therapist must (a) not tolerate threats and (b) must maintain control of the session. This might be accomplished by gently confronting the client with the observation that he or she seems to be making a threat or by suggesting that the client seems to be overly upset. If the person does not show signs of becoming less agitated, the therapist should call for assistance (including the police). A good rule of thumb is that if you think about whether you should call for help, the time has come to call immediately.

The resistant client. It is not unusual for some clients to be less than cooperative. For example, a client might deny having *any* significant others that the assessor might contact (Juhnke, 2002). This refusal in itself might say a great deal about how open and honest the client has been with the assessor, especially if the evaluator has explained to the client exactly what information will be requested. One possible solution to this problem, which some professionals advocate, is to have the client sit in on the collateral interview. One drawback is that the client's presence might inhibit the collateral information source from being free to discuss his or her perception of the client. If this were to happen, a potentially valuable source of information about the client would be unavailable to the assessor. Thus, it is rarely productive to have the client or the client's representative present at collateral interviews.

Another approach is to suggest to the client that since the therapist must complete *some* kind of an assessment, this is the client's chance to tell his or her version of the incident. Otherwise, the counselor can say that he or she will be forced to rely on the official version of the incidents alone, which might put the client in a negative light. Reminding the client that the therapist is in charge of the session and will determine what issues should or should not be included in the report might be enough to help the client become more cooperative. Skilled therapists might ask a client to help them understand why the client does not wish to cooperate in order to explore the source of this lack of cooperation.

Toxicology Testing

Urine

Because of the ease with which it is collected and the large quantities of urine available for testing, urine toxicology testing is the preferred method for detecting illicit drug abuse (Bolnick & Rayburn, 2003). Even so, realize that urine toxicology testing is still somewhat intrusive and may involve an invasion of the patient's right to privacy (Cone, 1993). It is for this reason that written consent for urine toxicology testing is required prior to the collection of urine samples. Such written consent should note that staff may collect a urine sample at their discretion as part of the treatment process and outline the procedures that will be employed.

One misconception about urine toxicology testing is that a positive urine sample is indicative of *impairment* ("Predicting Drug-related Impairment," 2004). When urine testing is used by industry, employers argue that even the smallest trace of a drug of abuse in an employee's urine after an accident is evidence of impairment, an argument that is both unfounded and widely believed ("Predicting Drug-related Impairment," 2004). It it unfortunate that employers choose to judge employees on the basis of this myth without regard to the lives that might be affected by inaccurate evidence of or by trace amounts of a drug of abuse.

In spite of the disadvantages of urine toxicology testing, when used in the rehabilitation setting urine toxicology tests are potentially valuable as a means to (a) break through the resistant individual's denial, (b) check patient compliance with program expectations, and (c) determine whether the individual is truly abstaining from illicit chemical use (Verebey & Buchan, 1997).

Although substance-abuse and mental health professionals speak of "urine toxicology testing" as if it were a single, uniform procedure, in reality there are a number of different forms of urine toxicology testing. *Thin-layer chromatography* (TLC) is the most commonly used procedure, especially when large numbers of urine samples must be screened for illicit drugs (Craig, 2004). The results are often available in less than 2 hours. Unfortunately, the results of a TLC test are reported only in terms of positive or negative, and this test is best suited for initial screening of urine samples (Craig, 2004).

Gas liquid chromotography (GC) is a more expensive and more labor-intensive procedure; it is often used to confirm positive TLC tests (Craig, 2004). The equipment necessary for GC testing is quite expensive, and the technicians who carry out the tests must receive special training in this procedure. However GC tends to have fewer false positive results than TLC testing and provides quantitative levels of chemicals detected in the individual's urine (Craig, 2004; Woolf & Shannon, 1995).

Another form of urine toxicology testing is the *immunoassay* family of tests. Such tests have the advantage of being sensitive and may be used to test large numbers of urine samples for initial screening (Craig, 2004; Woolf & Shannon, 1995). There are also many *spectometric* tests that have various advantages and disadvantages. The *mass spectrometric* procedure provides the greatest sensitivity and specificity at this time but is labor intensive as well as expensive and can be used on only a small number of urine samples at a time (Craig, 2004). It is most often used to confirm drugs detected by another, less expensive, less labor intensive procedure.

It is important to recognize that as a therapeutic tool urine toxicology testing is not perfect. There are "detection windows" for various recreational chemicals, after which it is unlikely that urine toxicology tests will detect a drug of abuse. Also, most commercial drug screens do *not* test for every possible drug of abuse (Verebey & Buchan, 1997). Compounds such as LSD, fentanyl, Dilaudid, MDMA, Rohypnol, and many designer drugs are not routinely included in standard urine drug screens and may require special, very expensive, tests to be detected ("Dilaudid Users May Be," 1995; Verebey, Buchan, & Turner, 1998). Further, urine toxicology tests usually do not not detect illicit chemicals used in the last 6 hours, as the body needs to begin the biotransformation and elimination process before urine toxicology testing can detect evidence of substance use (Juhnke, 2002).

False positive test results are a significant problem, especially with the growing popularity of on-site testing by employers, law-enforcement officials, and others. On-site tests have a high false positive rate—that is, the test results frequently indicate possible illicit drug use when the individual has not used chemicals ("Why Confirmatory Testing Is," 1997). Some over-the-counter medications such as non-steroidal anti-inflammatory drugs (NSAIDS)—examples are aspirin, ibuprofen, and Tolmetin—might interfere with some of the urine

toxicology test procedures currently in use; the non-narcotic cough suppressant dextromethorphan might register as a metabolite of a narcotic or the hallucinogen PCP on some of the urine toxicology test procedures currently in use. Antibiotics such as the quinolone family of chemicals might register as opiate metabolites on some tests ("Quinolones May Cause," 2002), and many herbal products can cause false positive results. An example is the false positive results for methamphetamine abuse caused by ephedra (Levisky et al., 2003).

For this reason, on-site test results should *always* be confirmed by independent toxicology testing in a certified laboratory, which will be able to confirm the results if there was evidence of illicit drug use. Also, because there are so many different urine toxicology test procedures currently in use, the substance-abuse rehabilitation professional should request a written summary from the laboratory concerning the following:

1. The methods the laboratory uses to attempt to detect illicit chemical use.
2. The accuracy of this method.
3. The specific chemicals that can be detected by the laboratory.
4. The period of time after the person has used chemicals when the urine test may reveal such drug use.
5. Other drugs (including over-the-counter medications and antibiotics) that might yield false positive results.

This statement should be updated on a regular basis to ensure that the treatment center staff are familiar with the strengths and weaknesses of the test procedures of the laboratory.

Attempts at deception. Clients will often attempt to influence urine toxicology test results. A number of products are purported to remove "toxins" from the urine by "flushing" one's body with massive amounts of water (Coleman & Baselt, 1997). Such products appear to be effective *only* when the level of illicit chemicals in the user's urine is close to the cut-off level used by laboratories to detect drug abuse (Coleman & Baselt, 1997).

In another common method of deception, the client attempts to "flush" his or her body with large amounts of fluid in the hours or days before giving the urine sample for toxicology testing. Some illicit drug users ingest up to a gallon of water at once in an attempt to flush drug metabolites from their bodies, or at least dilute them so much that they cannot be detected by the urine test. Staff (or the laboratory conducting the toxicology test) should test the urine sample's specific gravity, acidity level, and creatinine levels as part of the test procedure. Abnormally low results should alert staff that the urine sample has been altered in some way and is thus of questionable value (Coleman & Baselt, 1997).

Another method to manipulate the urine test results is through various urine *substitution* methods. This is accomplished by having a "clean" (i.e., drug-free) urine sample on hand, possibly hidden in a balloon or small bottle, that can be substituted for the individual's own urine when he or she is asked to submit a sample for urine toxicology testing. This method is most effective (a) if the urine sample being substituted did not come from another drug abuser, and (b) staff do not closely supervise the urine collection process.

Clients asked to provide a urine sample for toxicology testing have been known to "accidentally" dip the bottle into the toilet water in the hope that the laboratory or staff do not detect the attempted deception. This will dilute their urine so much that the laboratory is unlikely to detect any urine, never mind possible chemical use. Again, testing the specific gravity and level of acidity of the urine sample will reveal this form of deception, since toilet water has a different specific gravity and acid level than does urine. Also, toilet water is unlikely to be as warm as the human body. A fresh urine sample *is always within 1–2 degrees of the core body temperature* if the temperature of the urine sample is measured within 4 minutes of the time it is produced. Immediately testing the temperature of the urine sample will detect abnormally cool samples and alert staff to possible deception. Some treatment centers color the toilet water with a dye so that it cannot be substituted for urine, but this procedure is not carried out at every test collection facility.

Yet another way some clients attempt to defeat the urine toxicology screen is to substitute another substance for the urine sample. The list of compounds submitted as "urine" by various individuals includes apple juice, citrus-flavored soda, diluted tea, ginger ale, lemonade, salt water, plain tap water, and white grape juice (Winecker & Goldberger, 1998). Again, testing the temperature, specific gravity, and acidity of the liquid submitted for testing will reveal many of these substitutions.

Finally, some drug users will try to hide evidence of chemical use in a urine sample by adding foreign substances that they believe will defeat the chemical tests conducted on the urine. There are various substances that might, or at least are thought to be able to, hide evidence of recent illicit drug use. There are also some commercial products that supposedly will eliminate evidence of illicit drug use from urine samples. A partial list of these adulterants is given below (Winecker & Goldberger, 1998):

ammonia	bleach	blood
Drano	ethanol	gasoline
kerosene	lemon juice	liquid soap
peroxide	sodium bicarbonate	table salt
vinegar		

Depending on the test procedure used, bleach or table salt added to the urine sample might hide evidence of recent cocaine use (Warner, 1995; Winecker & Goldberger, 1998) and small amounts of table salt, liquid soap, or the commercial drain cleaner Drano might alter the chemical properties of the urine sample so that the test will not reveal evidence of illicit cannabis abuse (Jenkins, Tinsley, & Van Loon, 2001). But the addition of one or more adulterants to a urine sample is not without its dangers. For example, when Drano is added to a "clean" urine sample, it makes the urine more alkaline than would be possible if it were a real urine sample (Jenkins et al., 2001). A small amount of the metal salt alum might hide evidence of methamphetamine use, but it will alter the acidity of the urine sample, a characteristic that can easily be detected if staff perform a simple acidity test ("Tolmetin Foils EMIT Assay," 1995).

Because clients may attempt to manipulate the outcome of urine toxicology testing, they should be closely supervised during the urine collection process. But this is controversial. Some rehabilitation professionals argue that as long as the temperature of the urine sample is above 90° F., the urine sample is probably valid. Others note that given the various ways patients attempt to deceive urine toxicology test results, *extremely close supervision of both male and female clients who are giving a urine sample for detection of illicit drug use* is necessary.

This means that the person supervising the collection of the urine sample *must actually see the urine enter the bottle* and not just stand outside the men's room or lady's room or the toilet stall while the client is inside.

Urine toxicology testing should not be routine or predictable. Surprise is one way to avoid the problem of adulterant use or substitution (Juhnke, 2002). Staff might wait until the client is about to enter the lavatory, then say that he or she has been selected for urine drug testing. It is unlikely that the client will carry around a bottle of substitute urine all the time on the off chance of being asked for a urine sample. This surprise procedure is likely to force the client to give a sample of his or her own urine, especially if the client is observed providing the sample. If the counselor announces, at the beginning of a group session or other supervised activity, that the client has 2 hours in which to provide a supervised urine sample for toxicology screen, he or she will be unable to leave the group to pick up a urine sample stashed away without staff being aware that he or she has left the group. The client should have access to water, coffee, or soda to stimulate the production of urine that can be collected for toxicology testing without leaving the group room until he or she is escorted to the bathroom for collection of the urine sample.

In spite of all the shortcomings and problems associated with urine toxicology testing, it remains the most commonly used type of testing for illicit drug use. The following is a summary of the "detection window" for some of the more popular recreational chemicals, *if* proper urine toxicology test procedures are utilized.

Marijuana. Surprisingly, there has been little research into how long THC might be detected in the urine of a marijuana user ("Not Enough Data," 1995). Urine from a person who is a rare to occasional cannabis abuser might test positive for THC for 5 days at a cut-off level of 20 ng/ml (nanograms per milliliter) of urine (Woolf & Shannon, 1995). However, because the body stores THC in various body tissues and gradually releases it back into the blood, chronic marijuana users will test positive at the 20 ng/ml level for 10 to 20 days. The journal *Forensic Drug Abuse Advisor* ("CPPD in Puerto Rico," 1996) suggested that urine samples will test positive for THC for "at least four days" (p. 42) following the use of a single marijuana cigarette, and Jenkins, Tinsley, and Van Loon (2001) suggested that THC could be detected for 10 to 45 days following the last use of marijuana,

depending on the potency of the marijuana and the frequency with which it was used.

To avoid controversy about whether the individual did or did not use marijuana recently, Ravel (1989) advocated urine toxicology testing every 4–5 days for chronic users. If there has been no additional marijuana use between urine sample collection dates, such serial urine samples should show "a progressive downward trend in the values" (p. 629). The *Forensic Drug Abuse Advisor* ("Secondhand Crack Smoke," 1995) recommended daily urine toxicology tests until the user had tested negative for 3 days in a row to ensure that any residual THC had been eliminated from the body.

One potential problem for drug testing companies and employers alike is that the synthetic THC compound Marinol has been classified as a Schedule III compound, allowing physicians to prescribe it for a wide range of conditions. Unfortunately, every urine toxicology test available today will detect Marinol and report that the person has used THC (McWilliams, 1999). To avoid this problem, testers will have to determine whether the individual being tested has been placed on this medication by a physician, and confirm this claim by examination of the original prescription or a conversation with the prescribing physician.

Occasionally, people whose urine tested positive for THC might claim to have passively inhaled marijuana smoke because they were in a room where other people were smoking it. The *Forensic Drug Abuse Advisor* ("Not Enough Data," 1995) did suggest that under special conditions it was possible for a nonusing individual to be exposed to concentrations of secondhand marijuana smoke high enough to cause a positive urine test for THC. However, in one study where this was attempted, the volunteers had to sit in a chamber so filled with smoke from the marijuana cigarettes that they had to wear special eye protection. Thus, under normal circumstances, it is unlikely that an individual would test positive for THC because of exposure to secondhand smoke from marijuana cigarettes.

Cocaine. Depending on the route of administration and the amount of cocaine utilized, metabolites of cocaine can be detected in urine samples for about 72–96 hours after the last drug use (Craig, 2004; Jenkins et al., 2001). There is evidence, however, that in heavy abusers cocaine might be stored in the body tissues, especially in body fat, and released back into the general circulation after it was last used (Preston et al., 2002). This process might even cause heavy abusers to test negative for the drug on one day and then positive on the next day after they discontinue cocaine use. Serial quantitative urine toxicology tests should shed light on whether the cocaine being detected is residual or the result of new cocaine use, as recent use will result in higher levels of cocaine metabolites than residual cocaine could produce. Nelson (2000) suggested that individuals with liver damage might continue to test positive for cocaine for up to 8 days after their last use of this substance, and Preston et al. (2002) said that chronic cocaine abusers might continue to produce cocaine metabolites in their urine for at least 2 days after their last use.

Researchers have found evidence that unlike cannabis, cocaine can be absorbed through the fumes of cocaine smoke by a nonuser. However, the blood levels of cocaine in nonusers was not high enough to cause any physiological reaction, and the concentration of cocaine metabolites in the nonuser's urine would not result in a positive toxicology test at the cut-off levels recommended by the National Institute on Drug Abuse (NIDA).

LSD. LSD can be detected in a person's urine for up to 8 hours after it was ingested *if* the laboratory conducts special tests for this substance (Craig, 2004).

PCP. The hallucinogen PCP or its metabolites can be detected for 2–3 days following use by a casual user (Jenkins et al., 2001). Craig (2004) offered a detection window of 2–8 days for PCP, but chronic abusers might continue to show evidence of PCP in their urine for up to 21 days after the last use of this substance (Woolf & Shannon, 1995). The speed at which PCP is excreted from the body depends on the acidity of the urine. Thus, there will be some variation in the speed at which PCP is eliminated from the body. Cone (1993) suggested that PCP might be detected in body fluids for 5 to 8 days in the casual user and for as long as 30 days in the chronic user.

MDMA. MDMA can be detected for 24–48 hours after it was used if the proper urine toxicology test procedures are employed (Craig, 2004).

Amphetamines. The amphetamines may be detected for only 24 to 48 hours after last use (Bolnick & Rayburn, 2003; Jenkins et al., 2001). Because high doses of ephedrine or pseudoephedrine might cause false positive urine test results, federal guidelines require that amphetamine molecules be identified along with methamphetamine to rule that urine sample positive for the latter substance. In the body, methamphetamine is biotransformed into amphetamine, but ephedrine or pseudoephedrine does not produce amphetamine molecules when biotransformed, allowing the presence or abscence of amphetamine to determine whether that urine sample contains evidence of methamphetamine abuse.

Narcotics. The detection window for narcotics depends on the specific compound being abused and the test employed. Propoxyphene is a popular drug of abuse and its window of detection is just 8 hours if the laboratory is testing for the drug itself. But metabolites of this compound may be detectable for up to 48 hours following use (Jenkins et al., 2001). Thus the window of detection for propoxyphene depends on whether the laboratory is testing for the drug itself or for metabolites of this compound.

Other narcotic analgesics such as heroin, morphine, codeine, or Dilaudid (hydromophone) might be detected for 1–2 days following the last use of this class of drugs (Jenkins et al., 2001). It might be necessary to conduct special tests to detect some of the semisynthetic and synthetic narcotics. Methadone may be detected for 96 hours following the last dose (Bolnick & Rayburn, 2003).

Benzodiazepines. The benzodiazepines currently in use in the United States might be detected by urine toxicology tests for 1 to 4 weeks after their last use (Craig, 2004). Although Rohypnol (flunitrazepam) is technically a benzodiazepine, it is illegal in this country. Routine urine toxicology testing will not detect flunitrazepam, and special test procedures must be done to detect it in urine samples within 60 hours of the time that it was ingested (Lively, 1996).

Hair Samples

When a person ingests a chemical, molecules of that substance are circulated throughout the body. Depending on the pharmacokinetics of the chemical, molecules will enter various types of cells. If the cell dies and is ejected from the body before the drug molecule is released back into the general circulation, the drug molecules would remain attached to the cell wall and thus could be detected through specific test procedures designed to detect these molecules. This characteristic makes it possible to detect evidence of illicit drug use in hair samples of patients. This is because the roots of hair remain alive, but the hair itself is composed of long strands of dead cells pushed outward from the root by the pressure of new hair cells forming at the root.[7]

Scientists have developed the technology to detect metabolites of many illicit drugs in the hair of the user, and some people have suggested this as a less intrusive alternative to urine or blood toxicology testing (Brady, 1997). Hair samples also offer a window of detection that is usually between 7 and 100 days (Dolan, Rouen, & Kimber, 2004). This detection window is far longer than that offered by urine toxicology tests, thus eliminating the danger that a drug abuser might abstain for a few days prior to a urine toxicology test in order to hide the chemical abuse (Craig, 2004). There are no known methods by which hair samples might be adulterated or diluted to hide evidence of illicit drug use, and substitution is virtually impossible as the hair samples are removed from the individual's body by the collecting technician. Although some people think that shaving their heads defeats the process of hair toxicology testing, *any* body hair can be used for such tests (Brady, 1997).

Advocates of hair follicle testing point out that this procedure is far less intrusive than urine toxicology testing. However, it is hardly conclusive. The Food and Drug Administration (FDA) has advised several companies that produce hair-testing test kits to include the warning that false positive results are possible ("FDA Revised Guidelines," 2004). Indeed, in 60 out of 100 cases of hair testing, the preliminary positive results for opiate abuse were found to be inaccurate when further testing was carried out ("FDA Revised Guidelines," 2004). Fully 50% of the preliminary positive results for amphetamine abuse, 10% of the preliminary positive results for marijuana abuse, and 2% of the initial positive results for cocaine abuse were found to be false positive[8] results upon further testing.

In the case of hair testing for marijuana abuse, Uhl and Sachs (2004) suggested that researchers look for metabolites other than THC, such as 11-nor-delta-9-tetra-hydrocannabinol-9-carboxylic acid (THCA), in order to differentiate between actual marijuana use and passive exposure to marijuana smoke. The authors point out that hair samples from nonsmokers exposed to marijuana smoke failed to show evidence of THCA, whereas hair samples from marijuana smokers had both THC and THCA. This discovery might allow identification of actual marijuana smokers and negate the defense that any hair sample was contaminated by marijuana smoke in the environment.

For hair testing, a number of hairs must be removed (Craig, 2004, suggested 40–60 strands) and it is virtually impossible to determine *when* the individual indulged in illicit drug use by hair sample testing, according to detractors. In theory, by measuring the distance of the drug molecules from the root and then estimating the time needed for hair to grow that distance at a standard rate of growth of 1 centimeter (cm) per month, one could estimate the time since that person had used an illicit chemical. Unfortunately, the accuracy of hair testing has not been proven in clinical practice (Harrell & Kleiman, 2002). There also are questions of whether racial differences affect the absorption rate at which the drug molecules are incorporated into body hair. At any given time, 15% of the hairs are either in resting phase or are ready to fall out, factors that would influence the accuracy of hair samples in the detection of drug abuse (McPhillips, Strang, & Barnes, 1998). Finally, hair toxicology tests do not detect substance abuse in the 7 days preceding the test (Juhnke, 2002), and there is a danger that the hair sample might be contaminated by drug molecules in the air (such as marijuana smoke) (McPhillips et al., 1998).

Even if there is evidence of alcohol/drug use detected, hair testing does not provide information on the level of *impairment* caused by exposure to the chemical (Juhnke, 2002). The fact that hair toxicology testing requires the removal of hair from the body, as opposed to the collection of urine, a waste product expelled from the body, makes it of limited value for serial toxicology tests such as those utilized in correctional or rehabilitation facilities (Craig, 2004). Thus, while toxicological testing of hair samples is of possible value, its applicability in the detection of illicit drug use remains uncertain at this time.

Saliva

Another emerging technology is the use of saliva to test for residual traces of alcohol (Wilson & Kunsman,

---

[7]This is why it is possible to have your hair cut without feeling pain: The hair is dead and thus does not have functional nerve endings.

[8]See Glossary.

1997). Although laboratories have been able to use saliva samples to test for alcohol traces since the 1950s, new techniques are making this procedure attractive for workplace screening programs, according to the authors. The individual will place a cotton swab in his or her mouth, allowing it to become moistened by saliva. The cotton swab is then tested by exposing it to chemicals that will react to the presence of alcohol. The use of saliva allows for a simple, short (less than 20 minutes) test that is just as accurate as breath testing but can be carried out in the workplace. As with any screening procedure, there is a need for follow-up testing to rule out false positive results.

The Addicted Patient With Chronic Pain Issues

One of the most complicated and frustrating patients to work with is the one with a history of chemical dependency who presents with chronic pain. Physicians often hesitate to prescribe adequate doses of narcotic analgesics for the average patient following an accident or surgery because of an exaggerated fear that they will contribute to the development of an addiction.[9] If the patient has a past or current history of substance abuse or addiction, the physician becomes even more concerned about prescribing narcotic analgesics. Yet this class of medications is being recognized as having a role in the treatment of chronic pain. The problem arises when a patient with an addictive disorder presents with a chronic pain disorder (Compton & Athanasos, 2003).

Physicians tend to fear that patients with both addictive disorders and chronic pain should not receive narcotic analgesics because such medications are thought to increase their risk for relapse or abuse (Compton & Athanasos, 2003). Most certainly some will attempt to manipulate physicians into prescribing narcotic analgesics for personal pleasure. But there are also patients who suffer legitimate pain issues even if they have a concurrent addictive disorder. The diagnostic dilemma is whether patients are seeking narcotic analgesics to control pain or as a reflection of their addictive disorder. Compton and Athanasos (2003) suggested that the latter group of patients tend to use narcotic analgesics to self-medicate non-pain issues such as insomnia,

depression, loneliness, and anxiety as they lack such supports as family and 12-Step groups. Addictive patients are also less likely to respond to pain management programs, less likely to consider non-opioid-based pain management techniques (such as biofeedback), and present histories of chronic opioid therapy, according to the authors.

Note, however, that patients' requests for additional medication are *not* automatically signs that they are addicted to chemicals. Unrelieved or only partially controlled pain might lead patients to request additional medications. To complicate matters, patients with addictive disorders tend to be less tolerant of pain than nonaddicted patients (Compton & Athanasos, 2003). There is no evidence to suggest that withholding narcotic analgesics from patients with an addictive disorder and chronic pain is at all effective, but some physicians continue to believe this therapeutic myth. An essential question seems to be whether the patient would require narcotic analgesics (or an increase in medication dosage) to control the pain if he or she were not addicted.

The treatment of a drug-addicted person with concurrent pain problems is a complex demanding task that is best addressed by a treatment team working together closely and utilizing frequent intra-staff communication. The patient should be required to sign a treatment contract stating that he or she will use only one pharmacy and the services of only one physician (except in emergencies). The treatment contract should also specify that the staff will utilize urine toxicology testing both to check treatment compliance and to discourage the use of nonprescribed substances. Further, staff should utilize non-opioid treatments where indicated.

Insurance Reimbursement Policies

Between 1988 and 1998, the "value of employer-provided mental health care [insurance] benefits . . . declined by 55%" (Wu & Schlenger, 2004, p. 182), with many health care providers now providing funding for less than half the recommended length of treatment for substance-use problems. The issue of health care insurance is quite confusing. Some proponents of health care insist that it is a right; others hold that health care is a commodity (Kluge, 2000). To complicate the debate,

[9]The technical term for this fear is *opiophobia*. See Glossary.

medical advances result in the need for greater expenditures for health care (Levant, 2000). For example, as treatment advances reduce the death rate from myocardial infarction, a pool of heart attack survivors requiring aggressive medical management is established, placing an unanticipated drain on health care resouces. Thus, the increase in health care costs over the past decades appears to reflect, in part, the impact of successful medical interventions in earlier decades, not evidence of inefficiency on the part of health care providers.

But insurance companies have adopted the positions that (a) health care is a commodity and (b) increased costs reflect inefficiency, not increased effectiveness. Given this perception on the part of health care insurers, it was only natural that they institute programs designed to reduce costs. These programs, known as managed care (MC) initiatives, became popular in the 1990s with the purported goal to control the rising cost of providing health care. Since such programs were introduced, it has become clear that managed care is a system designed to ration health care services for people covered by such health care insurance programs (Sanchez & Turner, 2003). Managed care has also been found to cut *costs* while doing little, if anything, to change long-term health risk (Ceren, 2003; Prochaska, 2002).

In theory, MC is designed to provide the most appropriate care for the patient at the best possible price to the insurance company. In reality, the MC system "wasn't meant to care for sick people; it was meant to make and manage money" for the insurance company (Glasser, 1998, p. 36). The danger is that while many MC systems have a legitimate interest in helping people find the appropriate medical care at an affordable price,

> there are great potential profits for the unscrupulous managed care companies that will maximize their profits without concern for the well-being of the patient. Ethics do not seem dependent on the size of the company and unethical companies appear from among the largest as well as the smallest companies. (Frances & Miller, 1998, p. 11)

Indeed, many health care providers have come to call managed care "managed profits" because of the way this process has come to limit the amount of care that an insurance company was liable for under its policy

with the individual. For example, in the decade from 1989 to 1999, the value of benefits paid out by managed care companies *fell* by 54%, a process that has "translated into big money for these largely for-profit companies" ("Magellan Slashes Fees," 1999, p. 5). During this same period, the cost of health care was increasing by approximately 8.3% per year (Teich, 2000).

The impact of the MC initiative on substance-abuse treatment has not been studied in detail (Olmstead, White, & Sindelar, 2004). One of the few studies to examine this issue found that substance-abuse treatment programs funded by managed care companies generally offered a smaller number of core services and was less likely to fund aftercare therapy services than programs that do not rely on MC-based companies as their major source of funding (Olmstead et al., 2004). These findings are consistent with earlier research showing that the impact of MC on substance-abuse treatment programs has been to restrict the emphasis of treatment to the short-term needs of the client population while simultaneously reducing accessibility to treatment (Ceren, 2003; Yeager & Gregoire, 2000). The alcohol/drug treatment delivery system has been virtually stripped of flexibility and forced to conform to a strict set of guidelines in order to earn limited reinbursement for treatment services provided (Marinelli-Casey, Domier, & Rawson, 2002).

A point often overlooked by health care providers is that insurance companies *do not exist to provide funding for health care procedures*. They exist to make money for the owners of the company (stockholders), and one method by which they do this is by selling health insurance. A health insurance policy is, in effect, a gamble by the insurance company that the policyholder will not become ill for the period of time that the policy is in effect. The company charges a "premium," which the company will then keep if the policyholder does not become ill with any of the conditions identified by the company as reflecting "illness." If the policyholder *does* become ill, the insurance company is then required to provide a certain level of care, as identified in the policy, if it is "medically necessary" (Ford, 2000).

Needless to say, the insurance company will attempt to control costs and maximize profit. This is accomplished, in part, through a process known as "prior authorization," in which an insurance company representative whose credentials are often "questionable and whose role is to cut costs" (Ceren, 2003, p. 77) must be consulted prior to the initiation of any but emergency care. Depending on the company, up to half the individual's insurance fee might be applied to administrative fees and company profit (Gottlieb, 1997). The money an insurance company spends providing health care coverage for those who had purchased a policy from that company is considered a financial loss to the company. The insurance company thus attempts to maximize the inflow of money while reducing or eliminating the need to pay money to policyholders. Some ways to accomplish this are excluding as many conditions as possible from the health insurance coverage and excluding individuals with known medical problems from participation in the policy on the grounds of a "preexisting condition."

A third way that insurance companies attempt to limit their losses is to adopt a very conservative definition of disease. Thus, it is uncommon for health insurance companies to provide substantial benefits for substance-abuse rehabilitation even though the cost of providing unlimited benefits for such programs was estimated to cost program members only about $5 per year per member (Breithaupt, 2001). Even when insurance companies *have* provided benefits for substance-abuse rehabilitation, they have substituted *symptom reduction* for the "treatment" or "cure" of the addictive disorder (Kaiser, 1996; Sanchez & Turner, 2003). In the area of alcohol/drug use problems, insurance companies utilize a very conservative definition of "recovery" to determine when benefits should be terminated. The outcome of this process is that many health insurance providers now provide coverage that funds less than half the recommended treatment period for substance-use problems (Wu & Schlenger, 2004).

This is true even though a large number of studies have found that the longer that the individual is involved in a rehabilitation program, the better the chance of a successful outcome (Brochu, Landry, Bergeron, & Chiocchio, 1997). For example, Sadock and Sadock (2003) observed that treatment for the addiction to substances such as cocaine and heroin must last "at least 3 months" (p. 389) for maximum effectiveness, and Ringwald (2002) suggested that the typical alcoholic might require 30 days of abstinence in order to "clear" from the effects of chronic alcohol use. Unfortunately,

few health care insurance policies would fund such an extended period of "detox," and all too often insurance benefits are limited to just 5–7 days of inpatient treatment. Although such programs are more cost effective by some measures, one sad consequence of this process is that many clients are being referred to aftercare programs without having completed treatment (Coughey, Feighan, Cheney, & Klein, 1998).

The apparent contradiction is easy to understand if one accepts that insurance companies are able to present *symptom resolution* as a substitute for long-term treatment. In other words, health insurance companies have come to view the stabilization of the immediate crisis as being an acceptable goal for inpatient treatment, and in the case of the addictive disorders, *not* long-term rehabilitation. Unfortunately, symptom reduction does not *automatically* mean that the condition that caused the symptoms has been resolved. For example, patients who suffer a ruptured appendix frequently report a significant reduction in pain after their appendix has burst. The fact that a patient is no longer in imminent danger of acute alcohol withdrawal does not mean that his or her substance abuse/addiction has been adequately resolved. Adequate treatment of the addictive disorders requires time for meaningful change.

Few health care providers are willing to accept symptom resolution, which in this case means the immediate cessation of chemical use, as adequate "treatment." In contrast, the health care insurance companies interpret "adequate" treatment as just that: the stabilization of the immediate crisis. But managed care companies often view substance-abuse rehabilitation treatment as imperfect at best, reflecting their "deep suspicion of anything unquantifiable, unprovable, or lingering as probably being poor technique on the therapist's part, self-indulgence on the patient's, and a waste of money by both" (Gottlieb, 1997, p. 47).

D.A.R.E. and Psychoeducational Intervention Programs

The Drug Abuse Resistance Education (D.A.R.E.) and similar programs are established on the theory that teaching children about the harmful effects of alcohol and drugs while helping them build self-esteem would somehow inoculate them against the desire to abuse chemicals later in life. The D.A.R.E. program is typically coordinated by a local police officer and taught in the classroom setting. Similar programs are coordinated by a variety of mental health or school guidance professionals. There is a great deal of testmonial support for such programs, but virtually no evidence that they are effective in reducing adolescent/young adult substance abuse (Gorman, 2003; Lynam et al., 1999; Rowe, 1998).

Supporters of the program acknowledge that it has not lived up to its promise, but after revamping the program they have appealed for ever-increasing levels of funding and larger amounts of student classroom time on the theory that the changes will improve the effectiveness of D.A.R.E. and similar programs. Critics of these programs suggest that they consist of negative propaganda (Leavitt, 2003; Walton, 2002). They claim that such programs continue in spite of their proven lack of effectiveness because they give the illusion of doing *something* effective in the face of rising levels of substance abuse in childhood and adolescence (Leavitt, 2003).

Summary

Even after a client has been identified as needing substance-abuse rehabilitation services, the course of treatment is often difficult. Clients will test the limits imposed on them by the therapist or the treatment center. Some will, with greater or lesser degrees of justification, challenge the accuracy of urine toxicology test results. Clients will occasionally come to treatment sessions under the influence of chemicals. Virtually every client will experience urges and craving to use chemicals after beginning a recovery program. Some of these individuals will relapse and return to active chemical abuse, especially if they fail to respond appropriately to relapse triggers that are encountered in everyday life. Finally, insurance company policies often place severe constraints on the length of time a client might be in either an inpatient or an outpatient rehabilitation program.

This chapter cannot possibly discuss every problem that clients might encounter in a rehabilitation program, but it does touch on some of the more common situations that might interfere with recovery from alcohol/drug use problems.

CHAPTER THIRTY-TWO

Pharmacological Intervention Tactics and Substance Abuse[1]

Introduction

The pharmacological treatment of substance abuse is, in a very real sense, a logical extension of the medical model. In spite of this, pharmaceutical companies have not been interested in developing agents that might be useful in the fight against drug abuse, in part because they view this market as too limited (Ciraulo, 2004). Thus, the pharmaceutical agents currently used to treat substance-use problems are usually those that were originally developed for other purposes and were then found to be of value in treating drug abuse/addiction (Ciraulo, 2004). These agents are used in the hope that through the utilization of various biochemicals, the individual's substance-use problem might be controlled or totally eliminated.

In this chapter we will review the commonly used pharmaceutical components of treatment so that readers might become familiar with how pharmacological agents may assist or detract from the rehabilitation of substance abusers.

Pharmacological Treatment of Alcohol Abuse and Dependence

Medications used in the treatment of the alcohol withdrawal syndrome (AWS). The benzodiazepines are accepted as the treatment of choice for the alcohol with-

drawal syndrome (Bayard, McIntyre, Hill, & Woodside, 2004; Daeppen et al., 2002; McKay, Koranda, & Axen, 2004). Long-acting or intermediate duration benzodiazepines are preferred over shorter acting compounds, as they reduce the risk of rebound withdrawal symptoms (Bayard et al., 2004). The judicious use of chlordiazepoxide (20–100 mg every 6 hours) or diazepam (5–20 mg every 6 hours) has been found to control the tremor, hyperactivity, convulsions, and anxiety associated with alcohol withdrawal (Milhorn, 1992; Miller, Frances, & Holmes, 1989; Yost, 1996). However, in very rare cases exceptionally high doses of up to 2,000 mg per day of diazepam have been necessary to control the symptoms of the AWS (Bayard et al., 2004).

For many years, physicians advocated the use of "standing orders/fixed schedule" for the administration of benzodiazepines whenever a patient goes into alcohol withdrawal. Such a program might involve the patient's receiving an oral dose of 50–100 mg of chlordiazepoxide every 6 hours, with an additional dose of 25–100 mg of chlordiazepoxide by mouth administered at 1 hour intervals until the withdrawal symptoms are controlled (Saitz & O'Malley, 1997). Then, the daily dosage level of benzodiazepines should be reduced by 10% to 20% each day until the medication is finally discontinued (Miller et al., 1989).

Physicians now advocate the use of a symptom-driven approach to the AWS (McKay et al., 2004). Depending on the patient's withdrawal symptoms, a benzodiazepine such as chlordiazepoxide or diazepam would be administered to the patient to control his or her alcohol withdrawal symptoms. Symptom-driven alcohol withdrawal programs allow the symptoms of AWS to be controlled with significantly lower total dosage levels of benzodiazepines being administered to the patient and shorter hospital stays (Bayard et al., 2004; Daeppen et al., 2002).

---

[1]Pharmacological support of alcohol or drug withdrawal or as part of the treatment of an ongoing substance-abuse problem should be supervised by a licensed physician who is skilled and experienced in working with substance-abuse cases. The information in this chapter is for information purposes only. It is not intended to encourage self-treatment of substance-abuse problems, nor should it be interpreted as a standard of care for patients who are abusing/ addicted to chemicals.

If the patient should begin to experience significant levels of agitation or hallucinations, a low dose of an antipsychotic medication such as haloperidol can be added to the patient's medication regimen as an adjunct to the benzodiazepines being used (Bayard et al., 2004).

There has been one research study in the United States that utilized an anticonvulsant medication, carbamazepine, as an alternative to benzodiazepines in mild to moderate AWS. This medication has frequently been used to control the symptoms of AWS in Europe with great success (Bayard et al., 2004). Dosage levels are usually 800 mg on the first day of alcohol withdrawal and are gradually reduced to 200 mg on the fifth day of the alcohol withdrawal process (Bayard et al., 2004). Carbamazepine appears to be nonsedating and to reduce the individual's craving for alcohol following acute detoxification.

Medications used in the treatment of alcohol dependence. Frances and Miller (1991) struck a rather pessimistic note when they observed that even after a century of searching for an antidipsotrophic[2] medication, "at this writing there is no proven biological treatment for alcoholism. Each promising drug that has been tested in the hope it would reduce relapse by intervening in the basic disease process has failed" (p. 13). However, the authors noted, Antabuse (disulfiram) continues to provide one avenue for the symptomatic treatment of alcoholism.

Antabuse (disulfiram). At the 1949 annual meeting of the American Psychiatric Association, Barrera, Osinski, and Davidoff (1949/1994) presented a paper in which they reported the outcome of their research into the possible use of Antabuse (disulfiram) as an antidipsotrophic[3] medication. Antabuse reflects an attempt to apply aversive conditioning principles to the treatment of alcoholism, as the combination of alcohol and Antabuse produces "unpleasant effects" for the drinker, thus reducing the reward value of the alcohol.

These "unpleasant effects" were first discovered by workers in rubber factories, who had experimented with the use of disulfiram to vulcanize rubber. After work, many of the workers stopped off for a drink or two, only to find themselves becoming ill from the interaction of the alcohol and the disulfiram they had absorbed through their skin (Bohn, 2001). A few years later, researchers administered disulfiram to animals in an attempt to cure worm infestations, and afterward they went out for a few drinks only to rediscover the uncomfortable effects of the alcohol–disulfiram interaction. A veterinarian, observing the interaction in coworkers, suggested that this compound might be useful in the treatment of alcoholism (Bohn, 2001).

Since it was first suggested as a way to combat chronic alcoholism, researchers have discovered that disulfiram is a potentially dangerous drug that should not be used with patients who have serious medical disorders (Schuckit, 1996a). Prior to 1970, when dosage levels of 1–2 grams per dose were used (compared to the present dosage level of 250–500 mg per dose), disulfiram was noted to cause delerium, depression, anxiety, and manic and psychotic reactions. However, it is not known whether these same contraindications apply now that the standard dose is only 250–500 mg per dose (Petrakis, Gonzalez, Rosenheck, & Krystal, 2002). Other known or suspected side effects of disulfiram include skin rash, fatigue, halitosis, a rare and potentially fatal form of hepatitis, peripheral neuropathies, and potential optic nerve damage (Schuckit, 1996a).

Surprisingly, in spite of its popularity within the rehabilitation community, research studies have found only limited evidence that it is effective in helping alcohol-dependent individuals abstain from alcohol (Bohn, 2001; Carroll, 2003; Kick, 1999; Tinsley, Finlayson, & Morse, 1998). There is some evidence that people who take disulfiram tend to drink less frequently than those who do not (Tinsley et al., 1998), but medication noncompliance is a major problem with disulfiram use (Bohn, 2001; Carroll, 2003; Petrakis et al., 2002; Tinsley et al., 1998). To sidestep the problem of medication compliance, researchers have experimented with disulfiram implants designed to release a steady supply of the medication into the user's circulatory system. However, subsequent research failed to demonstrate any significant advantage in abstinence rates over the oral preparations of disulfiram currently in use (Bohn, 2001; Tinsley et al., 1998).

For patients who *do* use Antabuse (disulfiram) appropriately, it can provide an additional source of

---

[2]This term is a carryover from the 19th century, when alcoholics were said to suffer from "dipsomania." A medication that was antidipsotrophic would thus be against dipsomania.

[3]See Glossary.

support in a weak moment. Because people know that they cannot drink alcohol until the medication is entirely out of their bodies, a process that can take as long as 10–14 days, disulfiram can provide time for "second thoughts" about drinking. But this does not mean that Antabuse (disulfiram) will reduce the frequency or intensity of the individual's craving for alcohol. It can only interfere with the biotransformation of alcohol after it enters the individual's body, causing a number of unpleasant—*potentially fatal*—effects.

Clinically, disulfiram interferes with the body's ability to biotransform alcohol by destroying the enzyme aldehyde dehydrogenase in the drinker's body. This will allow the alcohol metabolite acetaldehyde to build up in the blood. Acetaldehyde is a toxin, and even small amounts of alcohol will cause the disulfiram-treated patient to experience symptoms of acetaldehyde poisoning such as facial flushing, heart palpitations, a rapid heart rate, difficulty in breathing, nausea, vomiting, and possibly a serious drop in blood pressure (Schuckit, 2000).

Under normal conditions, it takes 3 to 12 hours after the first dose of disulfiram before it can begin to interfere with the metabolism of alcohol. But the individual who has been using disulfiram for several days and then ingests alcohol will experience the alcohol–disulfiram reaction within about 30 minutes. Typically, this interaction lasts for 30 to 180 minutes, although there are case reports of its lasting longer than this. The strength of these side effects depends on several factors: (a) how much alcohol has been ingested, (b) the amount of disulfiram being used each day, and (c) the period of time since the last dose of disulfiram was ingested. The time since the last dose is important because the body will biotransform the disulfiram starting almost immediately, and over time, the effects of any given dose become less and less powerful unless the patient ingests more medication.

To make sure the user understands the consequences of mixing alcohol with disulfiram, patients are repeatedly warned about the danger of drinking while under the influence of disulfiram. Some treatment centers advocate a learning process in which patients take disulfiram for a short period of time (usually a few days) after which they are allowed to drink a small amount of alcohol under controlled conditions. The hope is that this experience will make them less likely to drink a large amount of alcohol later.

On occasion, the spouse of an alcohol abuser will inquire about the possibility of obtaining disulfiram to "teach him (her) a lesson." Inquiry usually reveals that the spouse wants a sample of disulfiram to place in the alcoholic's coffee, or "eye opener" with the intent that the next time the alcoholic drinks, he or she will experience the alcohol–disulfiram interaction without expecting it. Needless to say, *disulfiram should never be given to an individual without his or her knowledge and consent* (American Psychiatric Association, 1995). *The interaction between disulfiram and alcohol is potentially serious, and may be fatal.*

Disulfiram is not a perfect solution to the problem of alcohol dependence. For example, it is not an effective aversive conditioning agent. Theoretically, an effective behavior modification program for alcohol dependence would involve an immediate negative consequence to shape the drinker's behavior. But the 30-minute delay between the ingestion of alcohol and the disulfiram–alcohol reaction is far too long for it to serve as an *immediate* consequence for the drinker. This makes it difficult for the person to associate the use of alcohol with the delayed discomfort caused by the reaction.

Another disadvantage of disulfiram is that its *full* effects last only about 24 to 48 hours. There have been rare reports of alcohol–disulfiram interactions up to 2 weeks after the last dose of disulfiram. But in most cases, the individual's body ceases to react to alcohol on the sixth or seventh day after his or her last dose of disulfiram. Because of the body's biotransformation of disulfiram, most patients take the drug every day or perhaps every other day for optimal effectiveness. Thus, it is up to the individual to take the medication according to the schedule worked out with his or her physician to ensure that there is an adequate supply of the drug in the body at all times.

Further, depending on the individual's biochemistry, disulfiram might react to the small amounts of alcohol found in many over-the-counter medications or a wide range of other products. The individual using disulfiram should be warned by his or her physician to avoid certain products to keep from having an unintentional reaction caused by the alcohol in these products. Most treatment centers or physicians who utilize disulfiram have lists of such products and foods that they will give to patients on disulfiram.

Research has suggested that disulfiram interacts with the neurotransmitter serotonin to boost brain levels of a by-product of serotonin known as 5-hydrooxy-tryptophol (5-HTOL) (Cowen, 1990). Animal research suggests that increased levels of 5-HTOL result in greater alcohol consumption. Although research with human subjects has yet to be completed, preliminary data suggest that there is a need for alcoholics to avoid serotonin-rich foods such as bananas and walnuts to avoid increasing the craving for alcohol experienced by many recovering alcoholics.

Disulfiram is *not* recommended for individuals who have a history of cardiovascular and cerebrovascular disease, kidney failure, depression, or liver disease, or for women who might be pregnant (Fuller, 1995). It is not recommended for use in elderly patients because of the potential danger that it might cause or contribute to hypotension, myocardial infarction, and stroke in the older individual (Goldstein, Pataki, & Webb, 1996). This medication has also been implicated as a possible cause of peripheral neuropathies and has been found to lower the seizure threshold for individuals with idiopathic seizure disorders (Fuller, 1995; Schuckit, 1996a). Further, there are reports that disulfiram has caused exacerbation of the symptoms of schizophrenia in patients with this disorder (Fuller, 1995).

Drug interactions have been reported between disulfiram and phenytoin (sold under the brand name of Dilantin), warfarin, isoniazid (used in the treatment of tuberculosis), diazepam (Valium), chlordiazepoxide (Librium), and several commonly used antidepressants (Fuller, 1995). Patients who are taking the anti-tubercular drug isoniazid (or "INH" as it is also called) should not take disulfiram. These drugs may, when used together, bring on a toxic psychosis or cause other neurological problems in the patient (Meyer, 1992).

There are reports that disulfiram may interfere with male sexual performance. Schiavi, Stimmel, Mandeli, and White (1995) noted that one-half of the males in their sample who reported having trouble achieving an erection claimed that this problem began only when they started to take disulfiram. Obviously, this may prove to be a somewhat frightening side effect for some users, especially if they are not warned of this possibility before starting the medication. Further, patients who use disulfiram should do so only under the supervision of a physician who has a *complete* medication-use history on the patient. Because of the danger of disulfiram–medication interactions, the use of multiple prescriptions from different doctors should be most strongly discouraged.

Admittedly, some individuals will drink in spite of the disulfiram in their system, a behavior known as trying to "drink through" the disulfiram. Other individuals will drink in spite of having ingested disulfiram in the recent past because they believe they know how to neutralize the drug while it is in their body. Many alcohol abusers/addicts will stop taking the drug several days before a "spontaneous" relapse, and only about 20% of those individuals who start the drug actually take it for a full year. Still, in spite of these disadvantages, for the majority of those who use disulfiram as intended, the drug provides an extra bit of support during a weak moment.

Lithium. In the late 1980s and early 1990s there was a great deal of interest in the possible use of lithium in the treatment of alcoholism. Lithium is an element that is useful in treating bipolar affective disorders (formerly called the manic-depressive disorder). Early research suggested that lithium was also able to reduce the number of relapses that chronic alcoholics experienced, reduce the apparent level of intoxication, and reduce the desire of chronic alcohol users to drink (Judd & Huey, 1984; Miller et al., 1989). Unfortunately, subsequent research failed to support these early findings. An obvious exception is the patient who has a bipolar affective disorder in addition to alcohol abuse/dependence, for lithium has been found to be quite effective in controlling the mood swings in manic depression.

Topiramate. Topiramate was found to contribute to long-term abstinence in chronic alcohol users when compared with a placebo (Johnson, Ait-Daoud, Akhtar, & Ma, 2004; Johnson et al., 2003). Research suggests that when alcohol-dependent individuals are placed on topiramate, an anticonvulsant medication, they are six times as likely to abstain as are people who do not receive the medication. These findings suggest that this medication might be at least as effective as other pharmaceuticals being examined as possible aids in the treatment of alcoholism (Johnson et al., 2004).

Ondansetron. Ondansetron has been used to treat early-onset alcoholism with some success (B. A. Johnson et al., 2000). Drawing on the knowledge that early-onset alcoholism might reflect a serotonergic system dysfunction, the authors utilized a serotonin blocking agent that focused its effects on the 5-HT3 receptor subtype, which has been found to be involved in the subjective experience of alcohol-induced pleasure for the drinker. They found that the use of ondansetron reduced the individual's desire to drink and the subjective experience of pleasure if the individual did drink. However, this medication is still experimental, and research suggests that it works best when taken twice per day. Whether ondansetron has a role in the treatment of alcoholism remains to be seen.

Naltrexone hydrochloride. As discussed earlier in this text, when an individual consumes alcohol, his or her brain is thought to release endogenous opioids, neurotransmitters involved in the "pleasure center" of the brain. In recent years, researchers have discovered that drugs that function as antagonists for one of the neurotransmitter binding sites for endogeneous opioids, the receptor site known as the *mu* opioid receptor site, seem to reduce alcohol consumption in both animals and man (Swift, Whelihan, Kuznetsov, Buongiorno, & Hsuing, 1994).

In January 1995 the generic agent naltrexone hydrochloride was approved by the Food and Drug Administration (FDA) for the treatment of alcohol dependence (Litten, 2001). This medication is not a "magic bullet" against alcohol dependence, as research into its effectiveness in controlling craving for alcohol is mixed. One study found that 50% of patients treated with naltrexone relapsed within 12 weeks (Kiefer et al., 2003), and at least one study failed to find any significant effect for naltrexone in preventing relapse (Krystal, Cramer, Krol, Kirk, & Rosenheck, 2001). However, the consensus is that individuals who take 50 mg per day of naltrexone seem to derive less pleasure from their use of alcohol, to crave it less, and have a lower relapse rate following treatment (Mason, Salvato, Williams, Ritvo, & Cutler, 1999). However, even in studies in which naltrexone was found to have an effect, medication noncompliance was a significant problem, with 40% of the patients who started on naltrexone discontinuing the medication within 30 days, and 60% within 90 days (Carroll, 2003).

Naltrexone hydrochloride is thought to reduce alcohol's reward value and and limit the craving for alcohol that so often complicates rehabilitation efforts (American Psychiatric Association, 1995; Holloway, 1991; Meza & Kranzler, 1996; Swift et al., 1994). Unfortunately, this medication has a dose-dependent toxic effect on the liver, limiting its use to those who have not suffered significant levels of liver damage (Mason et al., 1999).

Acamprosate (calcium acetylhomotaurinate). Acamprosate was approved by the Food and Drug Administration for treating alcohol dependence in July 2004. It is also utilized in 37 other countries for this purpose (Litten, 2001). In spite of its widespread acceptance in Europe and Asia as an adjunctive treatment for alcohol dependence, the exact mechanism by which Acamprosate works remains unknown (Carroll, 2003; Kiefer et al., 2003; Overman, Teter, & Guthrie, 2003). Further, information about the pharmacological actions in humans is very limited (Overman et al., 2003). The available literature *does* suggest that Acamprosate does not have a "rebound" effect when it is discontinued, and there are no published reports suggesting that it has an abuse potential (Overman et al., 2003). There are no reports of interactions with commonly used pharmaceutical agents, including disulfiram (Overman et al., 2003; Sherman, 2000a), and the most serious known side effect is diarrhea (Litten, 2001).

Calcium acetylhomotaurinate has a chemical structure similar to that of the neurotransmitter GABA. Unlike the disulfiram–alcohol interaction, Acamprosate stimulates the production of GABA. This, in turn, inhibits the effects of neurotransmitters such as glutamate that stimulate the CNS (Whitworth et al., 1996). The apparent effect is that the individual feels less *need* to ingest alcohol. The limited information available at this time does not suggest that Acamprosate is extensively biotransformed prior to excretion, and its primary route of excretion is thought to be through the kidneys (Overman et al., 2003; Sherman, 2000a).

Other pharmacological treatments for chronic alcohol dependence. Over the years, researchers have experimented with a number of compounds that seemed to be potential antidipsotrophic medications. In the 1970s, the antibiotic compound Flagyl (metronidazole) was examined as a possible adjunct to the treatment of alcoholism, as this medication will cause discomfort when mixed with alcohol. But this research was discontinued when little evidence emerged to suggest it was effective (Hester & Squires, 2004).

Another compound considered for possible use with alcohol-dependent individuals is nalmefene, an opioid antagonist that is similar to naltrexone in its chemical structure (Mason et al., 1999). The medication has a longer half-life than naltrexone, and it binds more effectively at the *mu, kappa,* and *sigma* opioid receptor sites (which are thought to be most involved in the pleasurable effects caused by drinking) than naltrexone, suggesting that nalmefene might be at least of equal value to naltrexone in the treatment of alcoholism. However, there has been little interest in developing this compound for use with alcohol-dependent people.

Buspirone. Research studies have suggested a possible benefit from the use of buspirone in controlling the symptoms of anxiety and excessive worry associated with protracted abstinence (Meza & Kranzler, 1996; Schuckit, 1996a). Unfortunately, the first research studies to examine the effectiveness of buspirone in the treatment of alcohol dependence were poorly designed. Thus, there is a need for further research into its possible effectiveness as an adjunct to the treatment of alcohol dependence.

Selective serotonin reuptake inhibitors (SSRIs). In the late 1980s, psychiatrists began to use a new class of medications known as *selective serotonin reuptake inhibitors (SSRIs)* in the treatment of depression. Members of this class of antidepressants include Prozac (fluoxetine). Subsequent research has failed to support the theory that the SSRIs should reduce alcohol abuse/addiction, except when the drinker has a concurrent depressive disorder (Bohn, 2001).

Pharmacological Treatment of Opiate Addiction

Naltrexone hydrochloride. Although it has been found to have some value in treating alcohol dependence (discussed earlier in this chapter), naltrexone hydrochloride is primarily used in the treatment of opioid addiction. Naltrexone is an opioid antagonist with no significant agonist effect (Kranzler, Amin, Modesto-Lowe, & Oncken, 1999). The drug is well absorbed when taken orally, with peak blood levels achieved within an hour, according to Kranzler et al. (1999). In spite of its elimination half-life of 3.9 to 10.3 hours, the drug has an extended action within the brain, and depending on the dosage level being used, naltrexone can block the euphoric effects of injected opiates for up to 72 hours.

The theory behind the use of naltrexone hydrochloride is that if the person taking this medication does not experience any feelings of euphoria from opiates, he or she is less likely to use opiates again. But a number of dangers are associated with naltrexone use. First, to avoid initiating an undesired opiate withdrawal syndrome, this medication should be used only after the person is *completely* detoxified from opiates. The patient must also be warned not to attempt to "shoot through" a narcotic antagonist such as naltrexone, to avoid the danger of overdose. This warning is necessary because on rare occasions individuals have been known to inject a large dose of narcotics in an attempt to overcome the antagonist, in spite of the risk of narcotic overdose (Callahan, 1980). Further, when the individual stops using naltrexone, she or he will then begin to reexperience a craving for narcotics. There is no extinction of the craving for the drug during the time the narcotics addict is usually maintained on a narcotics blocker, and the patient must be warned about this to minimize the danger of relapse.

Jenike (1991) reported that a 50 mg dose of naltrexone hydrochloride will block the euphoria of an injection of narcotics for 24 hours, and a 100 mg dose will work for about 48 hours. Further, a 150 mg dose of naltrexone hydrochloride will block the euphoria from injected narcotics for 72 hours. According to Jenike, the usual dosage schedule is three times per week, with 100 mg being administered on Monday and Wednesday, and 150 mg being administered on Friday to provide a longer term dose for the weekend.

To date, no research has demonstrated an *unequivocal* benefit from this medication in the treatment of narcotics addiction (*Physicians' Desk Reference,* 2004). Indeed, naltrexone seems to be most effective for the subgroup of opiate-dependent people who are most likely to follow treatment recommendations (Carroll, 2003). One early study found that *only* 2% of opiate-dependent patients continued to take this drug for 9 months (Youngstrom, 1990a).

Obviously, naltrexone hydrochloride is not the "magic pill" for treating opiate addiction.

Ibogaine. Ibogaine is an alkaloid obtained from the root bark of the shrub *Tabernanthe iboga*, which grows in some regions of Africa. It has some hallucinogenic properties (Abrams, 2003). In spite of this characteristic, a growing number of researchers are studying ibogaine, which seems to be able to eliminate the individual's craving for narcotics such as heroin in the early phases of abstinence (Glick & Maisonneuve, 2000). Scientists are uncomfortable with the use of ibogaine itself, as research has demonstrated that high doses can result in cellular damage to certain regions of the brain, thus limiting its applicability to humans (Glick & Maisonneuve, 2000). Further, ibogaine has side effects that are unpleasant for many users.

The major metabolite of ibogaine is a compound called *noribogaine*. This metabolite has a biological half-life of several weeks and a chemical structure that lends itself to chemical manipulation by scientists who hope to find a chemical cousin to ibogaine that is effective yet lacking the potentially destructive side effects of the parent compound (Glick & Maisonneuve, 2000). These efforts have resulted in the development of a derivative of igobaine known as 18-MC, which seems to block the craving for narcotics in animal test subjects without the harsh side effects of the parent compound (Abrams, 2003). Unfortunately, there are still many misconceptions and government bureaucratic hurdles that must be overcome before a controversial compound such as 18-MC can be approved for human use, even if subsequent studies prove that it is effective in humans.

Methadone maintenance. Methadone is classified as an opioid agonist. While opioid agonist therapy is the most effective treatment for dependence on narcotics (Schottenfeld, 2004), this treatment modality is quite controversial (Khantzian, 2003a). To understand the concept of methadone maintenance, it is necessary to (a) explore a little bit of history, (b) review the theory behind methadone maintenance programs, and (c) learn how methadone maintenance programs function in the United States at this time.

Methadone is a synthetic narcotic analgesic developed by German chemists during World War II. It is an effective analgesic that continues to be used in treating severe, chronic pain such as that caused by certain forms of cancer. In the 1960s researchers discovered that used in doses far lower than the analgesic dose, orally administered methadone would block the narcotic withdrawal process and the individual's craving for narcotics for at least 24 hours (Kreek, 2000). This action reflects methadone's half-life, which might range from 13 to 58 hours depending on the individual's metabolism and the acidity of his or her urine (Karch, 2002). If the patient's urine is very acidic, the half-life of methadone can be 50% shorter than if the urine is not acidic (Drummer & Odell, 2001).

The theory behind the use of methadone in the rehabilitation of opiate-dependent individuals is that when certain individuals abuse an opiate, permanent changes in brain function occur at the cellular level (Dole, 1988; Dole & Nyswander, 1965). It was hypothesized that *even a single dose* of a narcotic analgesic might be enough to change the structure of the brain on a cellular level, causing the individual to begin to crave narcotics as soon as the blood levels began to drop. Such craving was thought to continue for months or possibly even years after the individual's last dose of a narcotic, motivating him or her to return to the use of narcotics again in order to feel "normal" and stop the drug craving (Dole & Nyswander, 1965).

Based on this theory, researchers thought that if a compound could eliminate the individual's almost constant craving for drugs, he or she would be able to begin a program of psychosocial rehabilitation (Dole & Nyswander, 1965). The patient does not experience significant euphoria at these dosage levels, as only 25% to 35% of the opiate receptor sites in the brain must be occupied by methadone to block the development of withdrawal symptoms or drug craving (Kreek, 2000). Thus, the theory was advanced that oral doses of methadone were "corrective, but not curative" (Dole, 1988, p. 3025) for the hypothesized neurological dysfunction that causes the compulsive use of narcotics. Once the patient has been stabilized on a therapeutically indicated level of methadone and "has been normalized, the ex-addict, supported by counseling and social services, can begin the long process of social rehabilitation" (Dole, 1988, p. 3025).

Since the time of its inception, research has repeatedly demonstrated that when sufficiently high dosage levels of methadone are combined with a range of psychosocial support services (e.g., psychotherapy, vocational counseling, social services), a significant number of opiate-dependent individuals are able to remain drug free for extended periods of time (J. F. Kauffman, 2003; McLellan, Arndt, Metzger, Woody, & O'Brien, 1993). Indeed, once a patient is stabilized on a sufficiently high dose, his or her daily dosage requirement would remain stable for years (J. F. Kauffman, 2003).

Research has demonstrated that the *minimum* effective level of methadone when used in maintenance programs is 80 mg per day. There is a great deal of variability in the methadone blood levels achieved at this dosage level, however, as interindividual variation in drug absorption, distribution biotransformation, and elimination cause a 17-fold variation in blood methadone levels between different patients ("Methadone Dose Debate Continues," 2003). Once a steady dosage level has been achieved, blood studies usually reveal a peak methadone blood level that is two to four times as high as the individual's lowest blood level (the "trough") (Schottenfeld, 2004).

Unfortunately, in spite of the promise of methadone maintenance programs, fewer than 15% of known opioid-dependent people are involved in them (Fiellin, Rosenheck, & Kosten, 2001). Of the estimated 600,000 to 800,000 people who are thought to be dependent on heroin in the United States, only about 179,000 are enrolled in a methadone maintenance program (Kreek, 2000). Because of political and philosophical constraints, more than one-third of patients in a methadone maintenance program receive less than 60 mg per day (D'Aunno & Pollack, 2002), even though Dole and Nyswander (1965) indicated that the *lowest* effective dose was 80 mg per day. This suggests that many people in these programs will experience some form of subclinical withdrawal because they are being undertreated.

Kraft, Rothbard, Hadley, McLellan, and Asch (1997) found that in addition to the need for therapeutic doses of methadone, three counseling sessions per week seemed to be most cost effective in terms of the total number of clients who were able to abstain from heroin use. Such counseling sessions are labor intensive, and few programs come close to providing this level of support for the individual on methadone maintenance. Thus, in spite of the promise of the methadone maintenance program concept, the reality is that by the start of the 21st century many methadone maintenance clinics have become little more than drug distribution centers that provide subtherapeutic doses of methadone to opiate-dependent clients while making no effort at actual rehabilitation (J. F. Kauffman, 2003).

This sad state of affairs is further complicated by lack of understanding of many physicians about the pharmacokinetics[4] of methadone or the theory behind methadone maintenance (DeVane & Nemeroff, 2002). This is clearly seen in the confusion that arises when a patient on a methadone maintenance program requires analgesia following surgery or a traumatic injury. Health care providers typically do not understand that the dosage level of methadone utilized in maintenance programs is usually *not* sufficient to block significant levels of pain. Thus, special provisions for pain control must be made for patients on methadone maintenance (Krambeer, von McKnelly, Gabrielli, & Penick, 2001). Even so, patients have been forced to suffer needless pain because of the mistaken perception by a health care provider that they did not need additional medications for pain control since they were taking methadone.

Another area of potential misunderstanding for patients on methadone maintenance lies in the potential for interactions between methadone and other pharmaceutical agents. There are *at least* 100 different pharmaceutical compounds in use in the United States that might interact with methadone in some way (Schottenfeld, 2004; "Taming Drug Interactions," 2003).[5] Some medications, such as carbamazepine, phenytoin, risperidone, Ritonavir, and the herbal medicine St. John's Wort, may reduce the blood levels of methadone (Schottenfeld, 2004). Other medications, such as the antidepressants fluoxetine and fluvoximine, as well as sanquinavir, cimetidine, and the antibiotics erythromycin and ciprofloxacin, may slow the rate of methadone biotransformation, thus increasing the blood plasma levels of this medication possibly to fatal levels (Drummer & Odell, 2001; "Methadone-Cipro Interactions," 2002; Schottenfeld, 2004). There also is evidence that methadone is able to block the antithrombotic action of aspirin, allowing

---

[4]See Glossary.

[5]If different medications are to be used concurrently, a physician or pharmacist should be consulted first to avoid the possibility of a potentially fatal drug interaction.

the body to form blood clots more easily when the patient is taking both aspirin and methadone concurrently, a matter of some concern for patients who rely on aspirin to help them avoid a myocardial infarction (Malinin, Callahan, & Serebruany, 2001).

Methadone's safety record when used as an agonist agent is quite good, and even after extended periods of use there is no evidence of methadone-related damage to the heart, lungs, kidneys, liver, brain, or other body organs (Schottenfeld, 2004). One common side effect is excessive sweating (Jaffe & Jaffe, 2004). A rare but potentially fatal complication of methadone treatment is the possible development of a heart rhythm disturbance known as *torsade de pointes* (Roden, 2004). This is a form of ventricular tachycardia in which the normal cycle of electrical discharge/repolarization of the heart is disrupted, setting the stage for possible sudden cardiac death. It is estimated that 5% to 10% of people who develop this disorder have a subclinical form of ventricular tachycardia that is exacerbated by the medications they are taking (Roden, 2004). Although the exact percentage of methadone patients who develop torsade de pointes is not known, less than 1% of patients on methadone are believed to develop this potentially fatal disorder (Roden, 2004).

Methadone can be fatal when an overdose is ingested, with doses as low as 5 to 10 mg proving fatal to children who accidentally ingested it (Schottenfeld, 2004). The lethal dose is higher in adults, and the recommendation is that adults not be started on doses greater than 40 to 50 mg per day at the start of methadone agonist therapy, and daily doses should be increased only slowly (Schottenfeld, 2004). If the overdose is treated with a narcotic blocker such as naloxone, it is necessary to continue the administration of the narcotic blocker for extended periods of time because of methadone's extended half-life (Schottenfeld, 2004). Death has occurred up to 24 hours after the overdose was ingested or naloxone was discontinued, according to the author.

Methadone is usually administered in a single dose, traditionally in the morning, although some of the more progressive programs allow for split dosing to allow the patient to take the medication in two or three equal doses. Whether administered in a single dose or in smaller quantities, methadone is administered as a liquid that can be mixed with a fruit juice to make it easier to swallow. Depending on program rules and patient compliance, the individual might be permitted take-home dosing privileges, with federal guidelines allowing for up to 30 take-home doses in a month for patients who adhere to program rules.

The potential benefits of methadone maintenance programs are clear and include a $4 to $7 return to society for every $1 invested in such treatment in the form of shorter hospital stays, reduction in HIV infection rates, reduced relapse to intraveneous drug abuse, and reduced criminal activity by program participants (J. Kauffman, 2003). The annual cost of the methadone itself has been estimated to be approximately $4,500 per patient (Krambeer et al., 2001), much of which might be paid for by private insurance or Medicaid, according to the authors.

In May 2001, administration control of methadone maintenance programs was transferred from the Food and Drug Administration (FDA) to the Substance Abuse and Mental Health Service Administration (SAMHSA), a move that reflected the growing emphasis on rehabilitation rather than incarceration as the treatment of choice for working with opiate-dependent people. Minimum standards of treatment were established by SAMHSA to enhance the rehabilitation potential of methadone maintenance programs (Jackson, 2002). It remains to be seen whether funding for these enhanced services is provided and what impact such program requirements will have on the traditional "warehousing" of opiate-dependent people.

There continues to be a stigma associated with methadone maintenance (Joseph, 2004), strong resistance to the concept of methadone maintenance in general, and even stronger resistance to the higher dosage levels that research suggests are most effective (D'Aunno & Pollack, 2002). Critics of methadone maintenance programs have challenged the basic assumptions on which these programs rest. For example, Dole used a theoretical model of narcotics addiction that assumed the opiate being abused played a role similar to that of insulin in diabetes (Kleber, 2002). However, Marlowe and DeMatteo (2003, 2004) suggest that this analogy, while useful, does not *make* chemical dependency a true disease. Their challenge to the disease model is also a challenge to the foundation of methadone maintenance programs.

Critics also argue that providing methadone for narcotic-dependent people is simply switching addictions (Joseph, 2004; Kleber, 2002). Methadone is not the magic bullet for addiction, as 50% to 90% of the patients in methadone maintenance programs will abuse other compounds (Glantz & Woods, 1993). Patients have also found weak spots in the methadone maintenance program concept. For example, it has been discovered that other recreational drugs, especially alcohol and cocaine, will speed up the process of methadone biotransformation. This will cause the patient to experience earlier withdrawal symptoms which, if the program staff did not detect the concurrent substance abuse, might cause them to administer higher doses of methadone to avoid opiate withdrawal (Karch, 2002; Kreek, 2000). Some patients on methadone will try to obtain the drug propoxyphene, which enhances the effects of the methadone and produces a sense of euphoria (DeMaria & Weinstein, 1995). These drug-seeking behaviors raise serious questions in the eyes of some critics as to the individual's motivation for using methadone.

Dole (1989) acknowledged that methadone is "highly specific for the treatment of opiate addiction" (p. 1880) and that it will not block the euphoric effects of other drugs of abuse. Further, methadone "diversion" is a significant problem (Dole, 1995), although the abuse potential of methadone is quite limited. The dropout rate from methadone maintenance programs is greater than 50% in the first year (Schottenfeld, Pakes, Oliveto, Ziedonis, & Kosten, 1997), suggesting that such programs are not the final answer to the problem of narcotics addiction.

Buprenorphine: Buprenorphine is a chemical cousin to morphine with the unique property of acting as both an agonist and an antagonist, depending on the dosage level being used. At low doses it behaves as an opioid agonist; at high doses it demonstrates antagonist properties (Kosten & George, 2002). Because of this characteristic, buprenorphine tends to be self-limiting in that doses above a certain level force the body to respond to the drug as if it were an antagonist (O'Connor, 2000).

Low oral doses (2–4 mg/day) of buprenorphine function as a narcotic agonist, and in this capacity buprenorphine is used in a manner similar to that of methadone (Kosten & George, 2002; Schottenfeld, 2004). Like methadone, buprenorphine needs to be administered only once a day. Oral doses of 2–8 mg

per day of buprenorphine are thought to be as effective as up to 65 mg of methadone in blocking the euphoric effects of illicit narcotics (Stein & Kosten, 1994; Strain, Stitzer, Liebson, & Bigelow, 1994). Buprenorphine offers another advantage over methadone: Whereas withdrawal from methadone may last up to 2 weeks and is moderately uncomfortable, withdrawal from buprenorphine lasts only a few days and has fewer symptoms (O'Connor, 2000).

To date, buprenorphine also has not proven to be the final answer for the problem of illicit opiate addiction, and physicians have been slow to embrace it to treat opiate-dependent people (Vastag, 2003). Even when used at high doses, it is at best *only as effective as methadone* and is more expensive (Doran et al., 2003; Schottenfeld et al., 1997). Further, *intravenously* administered buprenorphine has a significant abuse potential and has been implicated as at least contributing to, if not causing, the death of a number of intravenous drug addicts in France (Kintz, 2002). For this reason, the form of buprenorphine used in treating narcotic-dependent patients has been modified to contain naloxone as well. The nalaxone will, in theory, cause the user to go into opiate withdrawal if she or he should attempt to inject a dose of buprenorphine intended for oral use, but it is harmless if the compound is used orally as intended (Leinwand, 2000).

Dosage levels of buprenorphine above 8 mg per day might be necessary to suppress illicit opiate use (Fudala & Johnson, 1995). There have been reports of fatal overdoses of buprenorphine and benzodiazepines, and this medication is known to interact with nifedipine, imipramine, and the protease inhibitors used to treat HIV-1 infection (Fiellin et al., 2001).

An interesting application of a modified form of buprenorphine was reported by Bai-Fang et al. (2004) who used an experimental polymer microencapsulated long-acting form of buprenorphine for intravenous injection in a small group of volunteers who were opiate dependent. This new process allowed for a single injection to release small amounts of buprenorphine into the individual's blood over a 4- to 6-week period, gradually allowing the volunteer to withdraw from narcotics without significant distress. The medication also appeared to block narcotic-induced euphoria while it was in the patient's system. It is too soon to determine whether this process will be of more than experimental interest to researchers, but this application of a modified form of buprenorphine does seem promising.

LAAM. Another chemical that was initially approved for the treatment of opiate addicts was L-alpha-acetylmethadol, sold in the United States under the brand name of Orlaam. Like methadone, orally administered LAAM is able to prevent opiate-addicted individuals from going into withdrawal. LAAM's biological half-life of more than 48 hours (compared with methadone's 24-hour half-life) allowed for a dosing schedule of once every 2 to 3 days for patients who were placed on this compound (Leinwand, 2000). This dosing schedule holds the advantage of virtually eliminating the need for take-home doses, vastly reducing the problem of drug diversion to the illicit market.

Initial research suggested that LAAM was potentially useful in the fight against opiate dependence. Unfortunately, follow-up studies have suggested that LAAM can cause serious cardiac arrhythmias, and the medication production of LAAM in the United States was discontinued in late 2004.

Opiate withdrawal. Physician-supervised withdrawal from narcotic analgesics can be done either on an inpatient or outpatient basis (Collins & Kleber, 2004). Research has found that only 17% of opiate-dependent individuals will successfully complete an outpatient withdrawal program, however, in contrast to the 80% retention rate seen in inpatient withdrawal programs (Collins & Kleber, 2004). For both outpatient and inpatient programs, methadone is the drug of choice for opiate withdrawal (Karch, 2002), although other compounds are occasionally utilized in addition to it or in its place.

Initially, the individual will receive 10 mg per hour of methadone until the withdrawal symptoms are brought under control (Collins & Kleber, 2004). Once the withdrawal symptoms have been controlled, the total dose of methadone administered becomes the starting dose for withdrawal. On day 2 of withdrawal, the patient receives this same dose as a single dose. From this point on, there are two variations on the methadone withdrawal process (Collins & Kleber, 2004). In the most common variant, the individual's daily dose is reduced by 5 to 10 mg per day until she or he is completely off narcotic analgesics. An alternative program is to reduce the individual's daily dose by 5 to 10 mg per day until the daily dose reaches just 10 mg per day, after which it is reduced by 2 mg per

day until the person is drug free (Collins & Kleber, 2004). There are no data comparing the efficacy of these two methods, however.

Patients should be warned that when their daily dosage levels drop to the 15 or 20 mg per day range, they will experience some withdrawal distress (Mirin, Weiss, & Greenfield, 1991). It is at this point that many individuals drop out of detoxification programs. At one point rehabilitation professionals hoped that by drawing out the withdrawal process over a 180-day span rather than the traditional 5- to 21-day period it would be possible to improve on the retention/abstinence rates. However, such programs have failed to demonstrate a significant improvement over the more traditional short-term withdrawal process (O'Connor, 2000).

Clonidine. Clonidine is an antihypertensive that has shown value in controlling the symptoms of opiate withdrawal. As noted in Chapter 14, narcotic analgesics suppress the action of the locus coeruleus region of the brain. During the withdrawal process, the locus coeruleus becomes hyperactive, contributing to the individual's subjective sense of discomfort. Clonidine, which is technically an alpha-2 adrenergic agonist, helps to suppress the activity of the locus coeruleus, easing the individual's withdrawal-related discomfort.

In contrast to methadone-based withdrawal, where patients tend to drop out of treatment when their daily dose drops to lower levels, the highest dropout rate for clonidine-based withdrawal is usually seen at the start of treatment (Collins & Kleber, 2004). The reasons for this phenomenon are not known. Some programs utilize both clonidine and an opiate blocker such as naltrexone hydrochloride in a 4- to 5-day opiate withdrawal program (Stein & Kosten, 1992). The combination of naltrexone hydrochloride and clonidine is not a standard treatment for narcotics withdrawal (Weiss, Greenfield, & Mirin, 1994). However, the authors noted that this approach "holds promise" (p. 281) as a method of withdrawal from opiates. When used appropriately, the combination of clonidine and naltrexone hydrochloride appears to be as effective as a 20-day methadone withdrawal program for opiate addicts (Stein & Kosten, 1992). The combined effects of naltrexone hydrochloride (which blocks the opiate receptors in the brain) and the clonidine (which serves to control the individual's craving for narcotics, and the severity of the withdrawal symptoms) thus allows for rapid detoxification from opiates with minimal discomfort.

The authors found that over 95% of their sample were completely withdrawn from narcotics at the end of 5 days. Although there is some degree of discomfort for the addicted person, Stein and Kosten (1992) suggested that individuals report about the same level of discomfort from withdrawal using a combination of clonidine and naltrexone hydrochloride as they experienced during a methadone taper. Milhorn (1992) suggested that withdrawal discomfort might be further reduced through the use of transdermal clonidine patches, which would provide a steady supply of the drug while the patch was in place. However, because of the delay in absorption, the author advocated the use of an oral "loading" dose of 02 mg of clonidine at the beginning of the withdrawal process.

Although clonidine has been proven to be an effective tool in controlling the withdrawal symptoms in opiate-dependent individuals, some individuals have learned to combine clonidine with methadone, alcohol, benzodiazepines, or other drugs in order to experience a sense of euphoria (Jenike, 1991). Health care professionals must carefully monitor the patient's medication use to avoid the danger of medication misuse through such patient-directed pharmacotherapy.

Experimental methods of opiate withdrawal. One exciting, although unproven, method of opiate withdrawal that is slowly gaining acceptance is the ultra-rapid method. Developed at the Center for Investigation and Treatment of Addiction (CITA) in Israel, ultra-rapid opiate detoxification is carried out while the patient is in a state of general anesthesia. Both clonidine and opiate antagonists are administered to the patient while he or she is unconscious, and the entire withdrawal process is completed within a single day (Rabinowitz, Cohen, & Kotler, 1998). The program has been found to be safe when proper procedures are followed, and it allows the patient to avoid much of the discomfort associated with opiate withdrawal (Kaye et al., 2003).

Proponents of this detoxification protocol suggest that following complete withdrawal, the individual should participate in a 6-month follow-up course of naltrexone and individual counseling. The former is to block the euphoric effects of narcotics that the individual might attempt to use following detoxification; the latter is to help identify and resolve issues that might

contribute to the individual's relapse. Proponents claim that up to 80% of clients remain abstinent for 6 months, although Rabinowitz et al. (1998) claimed that only 57% of their sample of 113 opiate-dependent males had not relapsed in the 6 months following ultra-rapid detoxification from opiates.

Detractors of this approach note that the long-term abstinence rates for such ultra-rapid detoxification programs do not support the claims that these programs are effective (Collins & Kleber, 2004; Kosten & O'Connor, 2003). Thus, the utility of this experimental method of opiate withdrawal remains unclear at the present time.

Pharmacological Treatment of Cocaine Addiction

In spite of an extensive search for a pharmacological treatment for cocaine addiction, researchers have failed to identify a compound that effectively treats cocaine abuse or dependence (Carroll, 2003; McRae, Brady, & Sonne, 2001; O'Brien, 2001), but the search continues ("Addiction Treatment Might Be Old Drugs," 2004).

There have been many false alarms in the search for a pharmacological treatment for cocaine addiction. At one point researchers hoped that bromocriptine (sold in this country under the brand name *Parlodel*) might control postwithdrawal craving for cocaine (DiGregorio, 1990). However, subsequent research did not support this theory (Kosten & O'Connor, 2003). Another compound, *flupenthixol*, has not only demonstrated some initial promise in the treatment of cocaine-use problems but has also continued to appear effective in controlling cocaine use or abuse by reducing postwithdrawal craving (Mendelson & Mello, 1996). Flupenthixol is currently available in Europe, the Far East, and the Caribbean, but not in the United States. When cocaine-addicted research participants were administered flupenthixol, "some" (Holloway, 1991, p. 100) subjects reported that their craving for cocaine was "manageable but is not eliminated" (p. 100). Thus, at this time, flupenthixol appears to hold some promise as a possible pharmacological agent in the treatment of cocaine-use problems, but it remains to be seen whether it will live up to its initial promise as a potential agent in the war against cocaine use and abuse.

One surprising agent that is proving useful in treating cocaine addiction is disulfiram (el-Kashen, 2001). When administered in therapeutic doses, disulfiram inhibits the enzyme dopamine beta hydroxylase in the patient's body and functions indirectly as a dopamine agonist (Kosten & Sofuoglu, 2004). When the patient mixes cocaine and disulfiram, he or she will experience a sense of *dysphoria* rather than cocaine-induced pleasure ("Addiction Treatment Might Be Old Drugs," 2004; el-Kashen, 2001; Leshner, 2001b). Disulfiram does not eliminate the problem of cocaine abuse, but it does appear to hold promise in the treatment of cocaine addiction.

Researchers have attempted to develop compounds that block the action of the dopamine reuptake pump in order to treat cocaine abuse or addiction (Stocker, 1997). Such compounds include chemicals identified as GBR 12909, a long-acting form of GBR 12909 known as "Compound 5," and another chemical known as "PTT" (Stocker, 1997). But to date these approaches have failed to be remarkably effective against cocaine-use problems. Other researchers have tried to teach the body to use the immune system against cocaine molecules (Wright, 1999). In theory, it is possible to develop a "vaccine" against cocaine, which would target an immune response against certain elements of the cocaine molecule so that the body would attack and destroy any molecule that had the same chemical structure (Wright, 1999). However, to date, researchers have not developed such a vaccine for general use.

Even if such an anti-cocaine vaccine could be developed, it would be specific only to cocaine and thus not interfere with the use of other recreational drugs (Wright, 1999). The long-term consequences of such a vaccine are not known, and it is difficult to imagine that cocaine abusers would volunteer to be injected with such a vaccine without strong external pressure.

There was experimental evidence that carbamazepine, a compound used to control seizures in patients with seizure disorders, might also be useful both during the cocaine withdrawal phase of cocaine addiction treatment and the earliest stages of abstinence (Sherman, 2000b). However, the need for pharmacological support following cocaine withdrawal has been challenged (Satel et al., 1991). The authors concluded that their data "failed to demonstrate the emergence" (p. 1715) of severe withdrawal symptoms following the initiation of abstinence, and that while there were reports of craving for cocaine, their subjects experienced a marked decline in the strength and frequency of such craving over the first 3 weeks of abstinence. For these reasons, the authors concluded that there did not seem to be a need for routine pharmacological support of cocaine addicts during the early stages of recovery.

Pharmacological Treatment of Amphetamine Abuse/Dependence

At this time there are no known, reliable, treatments for amphetamine abuse/dependence (Kosten, quoted in Milne, 2003).

Pharmacological Treatment of Nicotine Dependence

Nicotine replacement therapies. Because nicotine is the chemical that is thought to cause most, if not all, of the addiction to smoking, one therapeutic approach has been to provide the individual with a steady blood level of nicotine without the other 4,000 compounds found in cigarettes that seem to cause the undesired health consequences associated with smoking. In theory, after the individual had achieved a stable blood level of nicotine, he or she could gradually be tapered from nicotine and be free of the addiction to cigarettes.

Nicotine-containing gum was first introduced to U.S. consumers as a prescription-only medication in 1984 and became an over-the-counter aid to smoking cessation in 1996 (Anczak & Nogler, 2003). The principle behind nicotine-containing gum is that by chewing the gum, the smoker would slowly absorb the nicotine through the soft tissues in the mouth. However, it was quickly discovered that the use of nicotine-containing gum requires some patient training. Nicotine-containing gum is chewed differently from traditional chewing gum. With nicotine containing gum, the individual must adopt a "chew-park-chew-park" (Fiore, Jorenby, Baker, & Kenford, 1992, p. 2691) system of chewing the gum. When used properly, about 90% of the nicotine in the gum is released in the first 30 minutes that the gum is chewed.

Unfortunately, researchers soon discovered that the use of nicotine-containing gum resulted in a lower blood level of nicotine than that achieved by cigarette smoking. Nicotine-containing gum with 2 mg of nicotine was found to bring about a blood level of nicotine only about one-third as high as that achieved through cigarette use, and a piece of gum with 4 mg of nicotine brought about a blood level only about two-thirds that achieved through smoking (American Psychiatric Association, 1996). Further, the use of nicotine-containing gum itself could cause side effects such as sore gums, excessive salivation, nausea, anorexia, headache, and the formation of ulcers on the gums (Lee & D'Alonzo, 1993). Also, beverages with a high acid content, such as orange juice or coffee, were found to block the absorption of the nicotine from the gum.

Although nicotine-containing gum was initially promoted with great enthusiasm, subsequent research has shown that its success rate was about the same as that of a placebo. Several factors were found to impact its effectiveness as an aid to cigarette cessation. First, smoking-cessation counseling was found to increase the individual's chance of successfully quitting when the individual used nicotine-containing gum (Fiore, Smith, Jorenby, & Baker, 1994). Another factor that affected the individual's chances of successfully quitting was his or her expections for the nicotine-containing gum (Gottlieb, Killen, Marlatt, & Taylor, 1987). At this time, nicotine-containing gum is thought to have little value in cigarette cessation programs (Fiore et al., 1992).

By 1991, several companies had introduced transdermal nicotine patches designed to supply a constant blood level of nicotine to the user without the need to smoke cigarettes. It was hypothesized that the smoker might find it easier to break the habit of smoking if he or she did not actually have to smoke to obtain a moderately high blood level of nicotine. Later (usually 2–8 weeks) after the individual no longer engaged in the physical motions of smoking, the dosage levels of nicotine in the patches would be reduced, providing a gradual taper in blood nicotine levels.

Researchers found that transdermal nicotine patches were moderately effective adjuncts to cigarette cessation programs (Fiore et al., 1992; Fiore, Smith et al., 1994). Of those individuals who had used the "patch," approximately 22% to 42% were still smoke free 6 months after treatment, whereas only 5% to 28% of those who used a placebo transdermal patch were still smoke free 6 months after treatment. Further, transdermal nicotine replacement systems reduce some of the more troublesome side effects of cigarette

cessation, such as the insomnia that many people experience as they try to quit smoking.

But transdermal nicotine patches have several drawbacks. First, they do not provide the rapid rise in blood nicotine levels achieved when the individual smokes a cigarette. In contrast to the nearly instantaneous rise in blood nicotine levels achieved when a person smokes a cigarette, the transdermal nicotine patch requires approximately 1 hour for blood nicotine levels to reach their peak (Nelson, 2000). Another problem is that individuals who smoke while using the patch or within an hour of removing it run the risk of nicotine toxicity and even possible cardiovascular problems. The transdermal nicotine patch was shown to reduce levels of nicotine craving, but the nicotine blood levels achieved from the patch often were lower than those achieved by cigarette smoking, resulting in some degree of craving for cigarettes on the part of the user (Henningfield, 1995).[6] Also, the patch can cause skin irritation as well as abnormal or disturbing dreams, insomnia, diarrhea, and a burning sensation where the patch is resting on the skin.

Even with the use of the transdermal nicotine patch, a significant number of smokers returned to smoking. Kenford et al. (1994) attempted to identify factors that would predict which individuals would succeed in giving up cigarette smoking while using a transdermal nicotine patch. Study participants also received group counseling. The authors found that individuals who were able to abstain from cigarette smoking during the first 2 weeks of treatment, especially during the second week, were most likely to give up their cigarette use. However, 90% of those who smoked during the second week of treatment while using a transdermal nicotine patch were still smoking cigarettes 6 months later, according to the authors.

The results of the study by Kenford et al. (1994) are consistent with earlier studies that suggest the first month of cigarette cessation is especially difficult for the ex-smoker. Results of this study also suggest that the transdermal nicotine patch, although useful as an adjunct to cigarette cessation programs, is not totally

---

[6]To try to eliminate this problem, the American Psychiatric Association (1996) recommended that the user try supplementary doses of nicotine-containing gum, if he or she should find that the transdermal skin patch did not provide sufficiently high levels of nicotine to block this craving.

effective in helping smokers quit. Indeed, some evidence suggests that some former smokers will require transdermal nicotine patches for years in order to abstain from cigarette use (Sherman, 1994). These individuals will still be putting nicotine into their systems, but at least they will not be exposing themselves to the multitude of known or suspected toxins in cigarette smoke.

A nicotine-containing nasal spray was approved by the Food and Drug Administration as an aid to smoking cessation in March 1996. This spray is sold in the United States under the brand name of *Nicotrol NS*, and the user administers one spray in each nostril up to 40 times a day (Pagliaro & Pagliaro, 1998). Within 10 minutes of using the spray, the nicotine blood level will reach two-thirds (Anczak & Nogler, 2003) to about the same level (Pagliaro & Pagliaro, 1998) as that achieved by smoking one tobacco cigarette. It is suggested that this spray be used for less than 6 months, but while there was initial concern that the user might become addicted to the nicotine in the nasal spray, there is little evidence that this occurs (Anczak & Nogler, 2003).

Sutherland et al. (1992) found that the nasal spray utilized in their investigation was rapidly absorbed through the nasal membranes, and that with the exception of some sinus irritation, it has no serious side effects. According to the authors, only 2 subjects of the 116 in the treatment group had to discontinue use of the nicotine nasal spray because of adverse side effects, suggesting that this method of nicotine replacement therapy is quite safe. Heavy smokers seemed to be the most likely to benefit from the use of the nasal spray (Sutherland et al., 1992). Smokers who used the spray had less weight gain than subjects who received a placebo nasal spray, and 26% of the smokers using the nasal spray had remained smoke free for a full year, whereas only 10% of the group that received the placebo was able to abstain from cigarette smoking.

In 1998, McNeil Pharmaceuticals introduced a nicotine inhalation system for use by smokers who were trying to quit (Korberly, 1998, personal communication). This device is used in place of cigarettes, delivering about 4 mg of nicotine to the user out of the 10 mg contained in the cartridge. The device is designed for short-term use only, and the individual should not use more than 16 cartridges per day, but 20% of smokers who used this system in preliminary studies were able to abstain from smoking for 6 months (Korberly, 1998, personal communication).

Clonidine. A number of researchers have attempted to use an antihypertensive drug, clonidine, to control the craving for nicotine often reported by former cigarette smokers. Although the initial research studies were promising, subsequent research suggested that the side effects of clonidine were so severe that it was not useful as an initial approach to cigarette cessation (Anczak & Nogler, 2003). At this time, scientists believe that clonidine might be most effective only in smokers who experience high levels of agitation when they try to quit smoking (Covey et al., 2000). The American Psychiatric Association (1996) recommended that clonidine be used only with those who had attempted nicotine replacement therapy without success.

Silver acetate. Silver acetate is a chemical that when used by a cigarette smoker will produce a disulfiram-like reaction for the smoker (Hymowitz, Feuerman, Hollander, & Frances, 1993). Chewing gum and lozenges with silver acetate have been used in Europe for more than a decade, although this medication is not available in the United States. When the individual has recently used the gum or lozenge and then attempts to smoke, a "noxious metallic taste" results (Hymowitz et al., 1993, p. 113). This unpleasant taste causes the smoker to discard the cigarette and replaces the nicotine-based pharmacological reward with an aversive experience.

Silver acetate is quite dangerous, and overuse may result in *permanent* discoloration of the skin and body organs. However, this side effect is quite rare and is usually seen only after "massive overuse and abuse" (Hymowitz et al., 1993, p. 113). Another drawback of silver acetate is that its effectiveness in smoking cessation has not been fully tested. However, preliminary research has suggested a possible role for silver acetate lozenges and gum as an aid in smoking cessation.

Buspar. Buspar (buspirone), discussed in Chapter 10, was initially thought to be potentially useful in cigarette cessation programs. Theoretically, the ability of buspirone to counteract the agitation and anxiety often experienced when the individual tried to quit smoking made this medication appear useful to researchers. However, subsequent research failed to support its use in cigarette cessation programs unless the individual experienced high levels of anxiety when he or she tried to quit smoking (Covey et al., 2000).

Bupropion. Scientists do not understand the exact mechanism by which bupropion is able to help smokers give up their addiction to nicotine (Fogarty, 2003), but this treatment is apparently able to achieve abstinence rates comparable to those seen with nicotine-replacement therapies (Anczak & Nogler, 2003). It is believed that because nicotine facilitates the release of dopamine within the brain's "pleasure center," agents that stimulate the release of dopamine are potentially useful in controlling the craving that many smokers experience (Nelson, 2000). Bupropion has a weak ability to stimulate the release of dopamine within the brain and for this reason has been found useful in helping people stop smoking (Benowitz, 1997b). However, even with bupropion, smokers find it difficult to stop. Continued use of this antidepressant will increase the individual's chances of abstaining from smoking after successfully quitting, but there still is a high relapse rate in the first year following cessation (Hays et al., 2001).

Inversine (mecamylamine). Inversine is an antihypertensive agent that impedes the effects of the neurotransmitter acetylcholine by blocking the receptor site. This has the advantage of blocking the individual's desire to smoke cigarettes, as many of the acetylcholine receptor sites are also utilized by nicotine. This medication is moderately successful in helping the individual quit smoking cigarettes.

Other agents. A number of other agents have been utilized in the treatment of nicotine withdrawal over the years including the tricyclic antidepressants and lobeline (a drug derived from a variety of tobacco) (Lee &

D'Alonzo, 1993). The combination of nicotine-replacement therapies and bupropion has also been suggested but has not been tested (Benowitz, 1997b). In spite of extensive research, however, no single substance has proven effective in treating the symptoms of nicotine withdrawal beyond any reasonable doubt.

Summary

The pharmacological treatment of substance abuse involves the use of selected chemicals to aid the recovering addict in his or her attempt to maintain sobriety. These agents might be classified as falling into one of five different groups (Bailey, 2004): (a) agents that ameliorate withdrawal-related distress; (b) agents that decrease the effect of a drug of abuse, thus reducing its reinforcing effects; (c) agents that cause an aversive reaction when a drug of abuse is ingested; (d) drug agonists that promote abstinence from more dangerous drugs of abuse; and (e) compounds used to treat comorbid medical/psychiatric conditions.[7] In addition, a number of experimental compounds are being examined to determine whether they might be able to prevent the effects of various drugs of abuse, possibly by activating the body's immune system so that it will attack drug molecules as foreign substances. However, to date, pharmacological treatment of the addictions has met with only limited success.

---

[7]This latter group of pharmaceuticals lies outside of the scope of this book.

CHAPTER THIRTY-THREE

Substance Abuse/Addiction and Infectious Disease[1]

Introduction

As a group, illicit drug abusers are twice as likely as nonusers to use the services of a hospital emergency room and seven times as likely to require hospitalization (Laine et al., 2001). Further, when they are hospitalized, illicit drug users tend to require longer stays before they are ready for discharge, according to the authors. One reason for the higher need for inpatient medical treatment is the higher frequency of infection found among intravenous drug abusers.

Infectious diseases are, collectively, one of the more serious medical complications of intravenous drug abuse (Mathew et al., 1995; Passaro, Werner, McGee, MacKenzie, & Vugia, 1998). These infections gain admission into the individual's body in a variety of ways: by being "punched through" the skin by intraveneous drug abusers, by being inhaled by individuals who smoke a drug of abuse, or by passive exposure in an environment that predisposes the individual to infection. Some of the infections commonly found in intravenous drug addicts include peripheral cellulitis, skin abscesses, pneumonia, lung abscesses, and tetanus. In this chapter, we will discuss some of the infections more commonly associated with recreational chemical abuse.

Why Is Infectious Disease Such a Common Complication of Alcohol/Drug Abuse?

Chronic substance abuse is a prime cause of malnutrition, which in turn lowers the individual's resistance to infection. For example, alcohol-related malnutrition or vitamin malabsorption syndromes, can both compromise the effectiveness of the immune system. Finally, alcohol use by itself can impair the effectiveness of the body's immune system (Szabo, 1997). All of these factors contribute to the higher rate of infectious disease seen in alcohol abusers/addicts.

Sterile technique. The conditions under which intravenous drug abusers inject chemicals also make infection almost a guaranteed complication. This is because intravenous drug abusers rarely use proper sterile technique when injecting a chemical into their bodies. In a hospital setting, staff will sterilize the injection site with alcohol or an antiseptic solution and then inject a sterile solution containing the pharmaceutical into the patient's body. In contrast, intravenous drug addicts usually will simply find a vein and insert the needle directly into it without washing the injection site with any kind of an antiseptic. In so doing, the intravenous drug addict will push microscopic organisms on the surface of the skin directly into his or her body, bypassing the protective layers of skin that usually keep such microorganisms from the blood-rich tissues inside the body.

Another reason that IV drug users are prone to infections is that intravenous street drugs are often contaminated with various microscopic pathogens. When users inject the compound into their bodies, they also inject whatever microscopic pathogens are in the mixture. Another common characteristic of intravenous drug abusers is sharing needles. It is not uncommon for several people to use the same needle and syringe without sterilizing them. This practice exposes each subsequent user of that needle to infectious agents in the blood of previous users (Garrett, 1994). Admittedly, some intravenous drug users will try to clean the needle before use, perhaps by licking the needle clean before use. This will transfer microorganisms such as *Neisseria*

[1]The author would like to express his appreciation to John P. Doweiko, M.D., for his kindness in reviewing this chapter for technical accuracy.

sicca and *Streptococcus viridans*, bacteria normally limited to the mouth, to the intravenous needle that is about to be inserted under the user's skin, contributing to infection (Dewitt & Paauw, 1996). Some IV drug abusers will wash the "rig"[2] with water. But ordinary tap water may also contain microorganisms that are harmless to the individual when the water is ingested but which can cause infection if injected into the user's circulation (Dewitt & Paauw, 1996).

Among the infections that might be transmitted from one person to another through contaminated needles are any of the viruses that cause hepatitis (discussed later in this chapter). Occasionally, malaria and syphilis are transmitted in this way (Cherubin & Sapira, 1993; Garrett, 1994). Some of the more common forms of infection will be discussed below.

Endocarditis. Endocarditis is a condition that develops when bacteria infect the valves of the heart. Approximately 1 in every 20,000 people in the general population will develop this condition, which can be life threatening. However, about 1 in every 500 intravenous drug abusers will eventually develop endocarditis (Robinson, Lazo, Davis, & Kufera, 2000). The chronic use of irritating chemicals such as those often used to adulterate illicit narcotics is one cause of endocarditis (Mathew et al., 1995). Another cause of endocarditis is thought to be the bacteria normally found on the skin, which are punched into the subdermal tissues when an intravenous drug abuser fails to sterilize the injection site. Finally, shared, unsterilized needles allow bacterial infections to be rapidly transmitted from one individual to another.

Necrotizing fasciitis. Necrotizing fasciitis is an infection in which subcutaneous tissues are attacked by bacteria normally found on the surface of the skin (Karch, 1996). There are clinical indications that cocaine users are especially vulnerable to this infection, but it can develop in any intravenous drug abuser who fails to use an antiseptic to prepare the skin before injection, thus pushing bacteria on the skin into the blood-rich tissues of the body. As the bacteria destroy the tissues under the skin, the infection can spread to internal organs or deeper tissues. The surface of the skin appears normal until late in the course of the infection, making diagnosis difficult. This condition can be fatal.

[2]See Glossary.

Skin abscesses. Skin abscesses are a common complication of intravenous drug abuse. Adulterants mixed with heroin or cocaine probably cause or contribute to skin abscesses. Because the adulterants are usually not water soluble, they cause the body to react to their presence at the injection site. Further, most intravenous drug abusers do not utilize proper antiseptic techniques, setting the stage for bacterial infection. The result of these factors is the formation of abscesses under the surface of the skin, which may develop into a life-treating infection.

The Pneumonias

Technically, the term *pneumonia* refers to an acute infection of the lung tissue, usually caused by bacteria. Pneumonia is generally diagnosed by x-ray examination of the lungs. Numerous conditions contribute to the development of pneumonia, including alcohol dependence, immune system disorders, cigarette smoking, extreme age, vitamin malabsorption syndromes, and exposure to infective agents. Alcohol/drug abuse can predispose the individual to one or more forms of pneumonia. For example, as a group, alcoholics have at least twice the rate of bacterial pneumonia as nonalcoholics (Nace, 1987).

Fungal pneumonia. Fungal pneumonia is a common complication of HIV-1 infection (discussed below) and of heroin abuse (Karch, 1996). There are two primary reasons for this. First, chronic heroin abuse interferes with the effectiveness of the immune system. Second, many samples of street heroin are contaminated by fungi. When the user injects fungi-contaminated heroin, the fungi are able to evade the defensive barriers of the skin or the respiratory tract. The fungi are often deposited within the lungs by the circulatory system, helping to cause a fungal pneumonia.

Aspirative pneumonia. In addition to providing a holding site for undigested food, the stomach allows bacteria essential to the digestive process access to the food that has been ingested so they can begin their work transforming essential nutrients into forms that can be absorbed by the body. By blocking the normal function of the upper digestive tract, especially the vomiting and gag reflexes, alcohol can cause the drinker to inhale (aspirate) some of the stomach contents being passed up the esophagus during the act of vomiting. As a result, (a) bacteria normally found only in the digestive tract are able to gain access to the respiratory tract, which has few defenses specific to the bacteria found in the digestive system, and (b) undigested food particles might also be aspirated into the lungs, where they decay, fueling bacterial growth. The chronic use of alcohol also (c) alters the normal pattern of bacterial growth in the mouth and throat. These factors, along with alcohol's ability to interfere with the normal cough/gag reflex, combine to make it more likely that the chronic drinker will (e) aspirate in the process of vomiting and (f) expose himself or herself to bacteria not normally found in the lungs, which then infect the lung tissues (Mandell & Niederman, 1999; Marik, 2001; Saitz, Ghali, & Moskowitz, 1997).

All these factors can contribute to a condition known as *aspiration pneumonia*. The true incidence of aspiration pneumonia is not known as many cases are misdiagnosed as either community-acquired or nosocomial pneumonias (Johnson & Hirsch, 2003). When the amount of aspirated material is sufficient, the individual may develop hypoxemia and may die if unable to reestablish adequate airflow to the respiratory tract (Johnson & Hirsch, 2003). Aspiration pneumonia is a serious medical condition that can be caused by the abuse of alcohol or other CNS depressants and which has the potential to be fatal if not treated adequately.

Community-acquired pneumonia. Intravenous heroin abusers, cigarette smokers, and alcohol-dependent people are all known to be at increased risk for a condition known as community-acquired pneumonia (CAP) (Karch, 1996).[3] CAP affects an estimated 2 million to 4 million people in the United States each year. There are 10 different microorganisms that can cause a form of community-acquired pneumonia (Finch & Woodhead, 1998). Mild cases can be treated on an outpatient basis, but fully 20% of individuals with CAP will eventually require hospitalization (Campbell, 1994; Rubins & Janoff, 1997). People who are most likely to require hospitalization for CAP are those with comorbid conditions in addition to the lung infection, and this includes alcohol/drug abusers. Depending on the patient's age and health status, approximately 45,000 people die of CAP each year in spite of the best possible medical care

(Campbell, 1994; Finch & Woodhead, 1998; Leeper & Torres, 1995; Mandell & Niederman, 1999).

As early as the 1890s pneumonia was recognized as a significant cause of death for alcohol-dependent individuals, although doctors did not know how alcohol contributed to its development (Leeper & Torres, 1995). Since then, researchers have found that chronic alcohol use interferes with the lung's ability to defend itself against infectious microorganisms, thus contributing to the possible development of CAP (Nelson, Mason, Kolls, & Summer, 1995). Researchers have also discovered that intravenous drug abuse can indirectly impair the effectiveness of the immune system, contributing to the development of CAP in drug abusers. Finally, cigarette smoking both reduces the effectiveness of the lungs' defenses and causes changes within the lungs, making smokers vulnerable to CAP, especially the form caused by the bacteria *H. influenzae* (Finch & Woodhead, 1998; Leeper & Torres, 1995; Rubins & Janoff, 1997).

Acquired Immune Deficiency Syndrome (AIDS)

In 1981, it became clear to medical researchers that a previously unknown disease had started to spread through the population of the United States. Initially, the disease seemed to be isolated to the homosexual male population. In afflicted people, the immune system would rapidly fail, leaving them vulnerable to rare opportunistic infections virtually never encountered in the patient with a normal immune system. Medical researchers termed this process the *acquired immune deficiency syndrome* (AIDS).

Shortly after it was identified, physicians began to uncover cases of AIDS in some intravenous drug abusers and in individuals whose only apparent risk factor was that they had received a blood transfusion in the past. These facts indicated that AIDS was caused by some kind of blood-borne infection, and within a short period of time researchers had isolated a virus they named the *human immunodeficiency virus* (HIV) (McCutchan, 1990). As other members of the same virus family have been identified, it has become necessary to identify each by a number. The virus that is thought to cause AIDS is now known to medicine as HIV-1.

---

[3]As opposed to pneumonia acquired in a hospital setting, aspirative pneumonia, or pneumonia secondary to some form of lung trauma.

What is AIDS? Technically, AIDS is not a disease in its own right but a *constellation* of symptoms, the most important of which is the destruction of the individual's immune system (Welsby, 1997). AIDS is the end stage of a viral infection caused by HIV-1. As the HIV-1 infection progresses, the untreated patient eventually will die from an infection, or neoplasm, or other condition that the immune system was once able to control easily. By the start of the 21st century, AIDS has become the fourth most common cause of death around the world, with 95% of all new infections being in the so-called developing nations (Markel, 2004, p. 176).

Where did HIV-1 come from? In the latter part of the 20th century, scientists confirmed the suspicion that a virus might "jump" between host species, including from animals to humans. When this happened, the virus might cause a far more serious illness in humans than in the original animal host (David Baltimore, quoted in Svitil, 2003). Some examples of viral infections that were passed to humans by animals include West Nile virus, hantavirus, Ebola, and HIV-1 (David Baltimore, quoted in Svitil, 2003).[4] This is known as a trans-species jump. The virus changes during the course of a jump, adapting to its new host. The trans-species jump is the virus's most important means of long-term survival. "Species go extinct; viruses move on" (Preston, 1999, p. 54). It is thought that HIV-1 originally infected chimpanzees and that it may have jumped to a human host when a person with an open cut on his or her hands butchered a chimpanzee for human consumption, possibly sometime in the 1930s (Cantor, 2001; Fauci, 1999; Park, 2000). However, until the advent of modern transportation systems, HIV-1 infection remained isolated in remote Africa and was not a major threat to population centers. There is little, if any, credible evidence that HIV-1 was intentionally released into the population to target homosexual males or other minority group members, or that it is divine retribution for past sins (Karlen, 1995).

How does AIDS kill? In brief, every species of bacterium, virus, or fungus has a characteristic pattern of protein molecules in the wall of its cells. When the human body is invaded by a bacterium, fungus, or virus, the immune system learns to recognize the specific pattern of proteins that make up the cell wall of the invader and attack those with foreign protein patterns. The first time the body is exposed to a new organism, it must rely on more generalized disease-fighting cells, known as *lymphocytes*. These generalists roam through the body, seeking out and attacking microscopic invaders with a foreign protein pattern in the cell wall. These generalist cells are the ones that mount the initial attack against a new invader while the body learns to produce disease-specific antibodies. Unfortunately, the process of producing the disease-specific cells necessary to fight off a new invader may take hours, days, weeks, or in some cases, years.

After it has been exposed to a virus, fungus, or species of bacterium, the body "tailor-makes" some immune cells (antibodies) for each different form of microorganism it encounters. These pathogen-specific antibodies are designed to recognize the individual protein pattern on the surface of each species of bacterium, fungus, or virus and drift in the individual's blood searching for each specific species. This is the mechanism through which a person who once had an infection becomes immune to that disease. After recovering from the infection, the individual will have in reserve a number of white blood cells from the previous exposure to the invader, patiently waiting until the next time the same microorganism might try to enter his or her body. The person is now immune to that disease.

In the body, HIV-1 is able to infect cells with the CD4 protein group in the cell wall (Markel, 2004). This protein group is known as the *virus receptor site*, a term that identifies where the virus first gains entry into the cells that it ultimately infects. Unfortunately, the receptor site is commonly found in the cells of the immune system, especially the type of lymphocytes known as the CD4 or T4-helper cells (Markel, 2004). These cells serve to activate the body's immune response. Between 93% and 99% of the HIV-1 virus particles in a person's body might be found in the CD4 cells (Pomerantz, 1998). Thus, in the infected individual, the greatest concentration of the virus will be hiding in the very cells designed to destroy an invader such as HIV-1. Small concentrations of the virus invade other regions of the body, such as the cells of the retina, the brain, the testes, and other sites in the body (Pomerantz, 1998, 2003), providing reservoirs

[4]Glasser (2004) stated that there are more than 1,400 *known* microorganisms that can infect humans, of which half initially caused diseases in animals. As of this time, scientists have identified about 1% of the bacteria and 4% of the viruses thought to exist, according to Glasser (2004).

of virus particles that can reinfect a person whose body has been otherwise cleansed of the virus (Pomerantz, 1998, 2003).

In the early 1980s, researchers believed that the virus passed through a period of latency in which there was little viral activity (Weiner, 1997). However, they now know that the virus begins to replicate almost immediately after it gains admission to the human body. The apparent latency period was actually an illusion, resulting from the type of early blood test used to detect HIV-1. The earliest blood tests to determine whether a person was infected were designed to detect the lymphocytes manufactured by the body in an attempt to fight off the virus. Because a given person's body might need 9 months to begin to manufacture lymphocytes specific to the AIDS virus, scientists were left with the impression that the virus went through a period of latency (Markel, 2004). But after the development of special HIV-1 viral load tests, scientists discovered that this was only an illusion (Henry, Stiffman, & Feldman, 1997).

Each time the HIV-1 virus replicates in a person's body, it produces slightly different copies of itself. The specific mechanism is quite technical and well beyond the scope of a text such as this. However, in brief, HIV-1 tends to be sloppy during replication, allowing subtle "mistakes" to slip into the genetic code of each new generation of virus particles. These new "daughter" virus particles are called mutations or variants (Forstein, 2002). The HIV-1 variations are eventually released back into the general circulation. Because of the altered genetic code of each new generation of HIV-1, the body responds to them as if they were new viral invaders (Nowak & McMichael, 1995; Terwilliger, 1995). As a result of the replication process, by the later stages of HIV-1 infection a single individual might have as many as *one billion* different forms of the HIV-1 virus in his or her body (Richardson, 1995). Further, research suggests that up to 10 *billion* new virus particles will be produced each day in an infected person's body (Henry et al., 1997; Saag, 1997). Toward the end of the infectious process, the individual's body is host to, and ultimately overwhelmed by, a swarm of viruses (Barre-Sinoussi, 1996; Beardsley, 1994; Terwilliger, 1995).

As the immune system becomes weaker, various opportunistic infections begin to develop; these are caused by microorganisms that were once easily controlled by the immune system. When the person develops AIDS, the body's weakened defenses are overwhelmed by these invading microbes and eventually the patient dies.

The chain of HIV-1 infection. HIV-1 is a fragile virus, not easily transmitted from one person to another (Langone, 1989). The virus must be passed *directly* from the body fluids of one individual to another. The use of another person's intravenous needle is "a particularly effective means of transmitting the virus" (Steinbrook, 2004, p. 115). However, Sax (2003) estimated the odds of contracting HIV-1 infection after sharing a contaminated needle with an HIV-1 infected person as only 1:150. In contrast to this, the odds of contracting HIV-1 infection after a single episode of unprotected vaginal intercourse were estimated at 1:500 to 1:1,250 (Sax, 2003). The odds of contracting HIV-1 infection after a single episode of receptive anal intercourse with an infected male were estimated at 1:300 to 1:1,000 (Sax, 2003). As these statistics demonstrate, the most common means of HIV-1 transmission in the United States is by sharing intravenous needles. But there is a great deal of variation in how HIV-1 is transmitted around the world and even within different countries, with heterosexual and homosexual activities being the most common method of HIV-1 transmission in Africa and Asia (Steinbrook, 2004).

A rare method of HIV-1 transmission is known as vertical transmission, which occurs when a woman infected with HIV-1 passes the virus on to the fetus. Each year in the United States, 7,000 infants are born with HIV-1 infection (Klirsfeld, 1998). Another rare method of HIV-1 transmission is through the use of contaminated blood products for blood transfusion. At this time, the typical patient receiving a blood transfusion consisting of one unit of contaminated blood[5] has approximately 1 in 2,000,000 chances of being infected (Goodnough, Brecher, Kanter, & AuBuchon, 1999).

In the United States, approximately 70% of new cases of HIV-1 infection occur in men (Work Group on HIV/AIDS, 2000). The avenue by which the individual becomes infected varies between men and women. For men, 60% of those who contract HIV-1 do so as a result of homosexual activity, 25% through the sharing of contaminated intravenous needles, and 15% as a result of

---

[5]Usually 1,000 cubic centimeters, or just under one pint of blood.

heterosexual activity. It has been estimated that approximately 6% of homosexual males contract HIV-1 each year (Garrett, 2000). In contrast to this pattern, however, is the one for women who contract HIV-1: 75% do so as a result of heterosexual activity with an infected partner, and 25% become infected because of intravenous drug abuse with shared needles (Work Group on HIV/AIDS, 2000). Unfortunately, only a minority of those infected with HIV-1 tell their partners of this fact, which helps to spread the virus to unsuspecting partners (Stein et al., 1998).

Research into the genetics of the virus has revealed three basic families of HIV-1: the M (Main) group, the O (Outlier, and the N (New). There are no known subtypes of the O or the N forms of HIV-1, but there are 10 known subtypes of the M form, identified by the letters A–H, J, and K (Kuiken, Thakallapalli, Eskild, & de Ronde, 2000). Different substrains of HIV-1 are found in different regions of the world, suggesting that the virus has been moving in waves as infected individuals have carried one or another strain of the virus to different parts of the globe. At this time, the B is the most common strain of HIV-1 in the United States, Europe, South America, and Australia (Kuiken et al., 2000).

The E subtype, which is found mainly in Asia and Africa, is more easily passed from an infected male to his female partner. This is the reason that heterosexual transmission of HIV-1 is *the* most common means by which the virus is passed from one person to another in Asia and Africa. But the B subtype of the HIV-1 virus is not able to easily pass into the mucous membranes of the woman, thus making heterosexual transmission of the B subtype more difficult (R. Anderson, 1993).

The scope of the problem. With the advent of better statistical databases, in 2003 the number of people around the world estimated to be infected with HIV-1 was revised down to between 34 million and 42 million (Steinbrook, 2004). Still, this means that 1.1% of *all* people between 15 and 49 worldwide are infected with a virus that 25 years ago was unknown to medical science. Each day, another 15,000 people are infected with HIV-1 (Markel, 2004; Schmitt & Stuckey, 2004). The global annual death toll from HIV-1 infection is 3 million people, a number that is expected to increase significantly in the next 25 years (Will, 2002). By the year 2012, possibly as many as 150 million people will be infected with HIV-1 globally (Forstein, 2002), a number that might increase to 500 million people by the year 2020 unless effective, inexpensive treatments are found before then (Garrett, 2000).

The continent of Africa has been especially hard-hit; there, an estimated 28 million people are currently infected with HIV-1 and 20 million people have died from AIDS (Will, 2002). The rate of infection varies from country to country, but in some regions of Africa, 80% of the adults between 20 and 49 years of age are thought to be infected with HIV-1 (Bowers, 2000). In the United States, approximately 950,000 people are currently infected with HIV-1, with about 44,000 new infections each year (Steinbrook, 2004). Unfortunately, HIV-1 infection is most often a disease of youth, for more than half of those who contract the infection each year in the United States are under the age of 25 (Malow, Devius, & Rosenberg, 2001).

The stages of HIV-1 infection. Sax (2003) identified six stages of HIV-1 infection in humans: (a) viral transmission, (b) acute HIV-1 infection, (c) seroconversion, (d) asymptomatic HIV infection, (e) symptomatic HIV infection, and (f) acquired immune deficiency syndrome (AIDS).

1. *Viral transmission:* This is the point when a previously noninfected individual becomes infected with the virus. (See "Chain of HIV-1 Infection" above.)
2. *Acute HIV-1 infection:* Within 1 to 4 weeks, 50% to 90% of newly infected individuals develop a mild, flu-like syndrome that might be dismissed by the individual as inconsequential. Because the initial symptoms are so vague and nonspecific, HIV-1 infection is often misdiagnosed at this stage (Khan & Walker, 1998; Yu & Daar, 2000). If the physician is suspicious, he or she might order a viral load test that *might* detect the presence of HIV-1 in the patient's blood a few days after infection, although in most cases it takes 2 to 6 weeks before such blood tests are effective (Sax, 2003; Yu & Daar, 2000). The current viral load test procedures can detect as few as 20 virus particles in a cubic milliliter of blood (Mylonakis, Paliou, & Rich, 2001; Work Group on HIV/AIDS, 2000). Although the individual's body has not yet started to produce an immune response specific to HIV-1 during this state, the virus itself is actively replicating throughout the body and the individual can pass the infection on to others.

3. *Seroconversion:* This occurs within 6 months of the date of infection and marks the point when the individual's body has started to mount an immune response to the HIV-1 virus. At this time HIV-1 specific antibodies can be detected in the individual's blood. Such individuals are said to be *seropositive* or HIV-positive. *Seronegative* individuals are those whose blood test results failed to detect evidence of HIV-1 specific antibodies. There are two possible explanations for a negative finding: (a) The individual in question has never been exposed to HIV-1, or (b) he or she has been exposed to the virus but it is still too early for the tests to detect the virus in the person's blood. In either case, the individual should be tested again at a later date, usually 3 months after the initial blood test or last high-risk behavior, to rule out the second possibility.[6]

HIV-1 specific antibodies are detected in the patient's blood through blood tests such as the enzyme-linked immunosorbent assay (ELISA); if this is positive, it should be confirmed through such blood tests as the Western blot test (Sax, 2003; Tantisiriwat & Tebas, 2001). The Western blot assay screens for three specific protein markers indicative of HIV-1 infection. Once the person is known to be infected, the more detailed viral load test can be performed. This measures the approximate number of HIV-1 virus particles per cubic milliliter of the individual's blood to assess the patient's status once HIV-1 infection has been diagnosed (Henry et al., 1997; Mylonakis et al., 2001).

4. *Asymptomatic infection:* Individuals in this stage might remain stable for many years, and the HIV-1 infection would be detectable only through the use of the appropriate blood tests. However, even though the individual is asymptomatic, he or she might pass the infection on to others through needle sharing or unprotected sex.

5. *Symptomatic HIV infection:* When the infection reaches this stage, the immune system has been weakened to the point that opportunistic infections begin to develop. These are infections rarely seen except in patients whose immune systems have been compromised in some manner. Such disorders include thrush infections, cervical dysplasia/carcinomas, constant low-grade fevers, unexplained weight loss, and the development of peripheral neuropathy (Sax, 2003). Blood tests for the HIV antibody are positive, and viral load tests show large numbers of virus particles per cubic milliliter of blood.

6. *AIDS:* Normally, there are between 1,000 and 1,200 CD4+T cells for every cubic milliliter of a person's blood (Lisanti & Zwolski, 1997). These cells help the body fight off infections caused by microscopic organisms. When the number of CD4+ T cells falls below 200 per cubic milliliter (mm3) of blood, the individual becomes vulnerable to one or more opportunistic infections, such as *Pneumocystis carinii pneumonia* (*P. carinii*, or "PCP") and various tumors, and bacterial and fungal infections. One bacterial infection that is commonly encountered in the HIV-1 positive patient is tuberculosis, which is 100 times more common in individuals infected with HIV-1 than in the general population (Bartlett, 1999). Thus, if a physician were to encounter a patient who had developed TB, he or she would automatically consider the possibility that the patient has AIDS.

The median survival time is 1 year when the CD4+ T cell count falls below 50 cells per cubic milliliter, although some individuals have been known to survive as long as 3 years with a CD4+ T cell count this low (Sax, 2003). Death usually occurs from one or more opportunistic infections easily controlled by an intact immune system.

The natural history of HIV-1 infection. Untreated, it usually will take 9 to 11 years before the HIV-1 infection is able to progress to AIDS in the patient (Steinbrook, 2004). About 10% of those infected are thought to be rapid progressors, who develop AIDS within about 5 years of infection; a similar proportion of those infected do not seem to progress to the stage of AIDS at all (Hogan & Hammer, 2001; Sax, 2003). Without effective antiviral treatment, HIV-1 infection is "chronic and usually fatal" (Sax, 2003, p. 227).

The treatment of HIV-1 infection. In the time since HIV-1 was first identified as the virus that causes AIDS, a number of antiviral drugs have been developed to help fight the infection. These antiviral agents have changed the clinical picture of HIV-1 infection in the United

---

[6]Screening tests to detect exposure to HIV-1 are not perfect. Kleinman et al. (1998) found a false positive rate of 1 in every 379,000 samples of blood tested at one of five blood banks. An initial positive screen should be verified through further testing.

TABLE 33.1 Antiviral Agents Currently Used to Treat HIV-1 Infection

Class of antiviral agent	Mechanism of action
Nucleoside/nucleotide analogs	Compounds act as DNS chain termination agents, inhibiting the transcription of viral RNA into DNA in cells infected with HIV-1, thus inhibiting viral replication.
Nonnucleoside reverse transcriptase inhibitors	Chemicals that bind to and inhibit the actions of the enzyme reverse transcriptase, which is essential for viral replication.
Protease inhibitors	Chemicals that block the action of a protein known as viral protease, which is necessary for viral replication.
Fusion inhibitors	Chemicals that block the protein complex on the host cell that HIV-1 grabs onto to "bind" to the cell wall. This is the first step by which HIV-1 then invades the cell, forcing the cell to make copies of itself to go out and invade other cells.

States from an automatic death sentence to a chronic condition, such as diabetes or heart disease (Kuhl, 2002). Unfortunately, the high cost of effective treatment for HIV-1 infection, estimated at $100,000 per patient per year, limits the accessibility to treatment (Craig, 2004).

Currently, four classes of antiviral agents are used to fight HIV-1: *Nucleoside/nucleotide analogs*, the *protease inhibitors*, the *nonnucleoside reverse transcriptase inhibitors*, and the *fusion inhibitors* (Clavel & Hance, 2004; Godwin, 2004). The method by which each class of drugs interferes with viral replication is quite complex, but a brief summary of the different classes of antiviral agents and their mechanism of action is found in Table 33.1.

Following the introduction of the protease inhibitors, AIDS-related deaths dropped from 29.4 per 100 patient-years[7] in 1995 to just 8.8 per 100 patient-years in 1997 (Palella et al., 1998). These figures are impressive, but they still mean that almost 9 of every 100 individuals infected die of AIDS each year in spite of the most aggressive treatment with the most advanced medications available.

Unfortunately, the HIV-1 virus is adept at finding ways to resist the effects of these antiviral compounds, and as many as 50% of individuals being treated for HIV-1 have strains of HIV-1 in their bodies that are resistant to at least one antiviral compound currently in use (Clavel & Hance, 2004). The current treatment methodology calls for the patient to take a complex

mixture of two, three, or possibly even all four varieties of antiviral medications, as it is unlikely that the different strains of HIV-1 are resistant to all the medications in the different classes of antiviral medications at once (Clavel & Hance, 2004). These antiviral agents slow the progression of HIV-1, but they do not prevent the ultimate progression to AIDS (Garrett, 2000).

The antiviral agents are effective in significantly slowing the HIV-1 infection, but thus far there has not been one proven cure of an HIV-1 infected person (Schmitt & Stuckey, 2004). The virus is known to persist in areas of the body not affected by the current generation of antiviral agents, making eradication of the virus in the individual's body virtually impossible (Fauci, 1999). Further, the high cost of treating HIV-1 makes its treatment prohibitive in much of the developing world, and the side effects of the current antiviral medications may be quite debilitating, making it difficult for many patients to continue to take these medications (Farber, 2000).

Scientists remain hopeful that they can eventually develop a treatment program that will completely arrest the progression of HIV-1. However, to cure the individual it will be necessary to *eliminate every single virus particle* from the person's body. To understand this task, remember that up to *one trillion* copies of the HIV-1 virus might nestle in the body of an infected person, and the virus might hide in the body for up to 10 years after antiviral treatment has been initiated (Doweiko, J., 2004, personal communication). If it is assumed that there are 10^8 virus particles in just the lymph tissue of an infected individual, a treatment that was 99.99% effective in eliminating the

[7]See Glossary.

virus from the body would still leave 9,999,000 virus particles in the lymphoid tissues, any one of which could emerge and restart the infection cycle. Science has no idea how to elimate *every* virus particle from the body of a living person, and the cost of antiviral therapy is such that many infected people cannot afford the medications currently available without government assistance. Given these facts, it is clear that the ultimate treatment for AIDS at this time lies in prevention.

AIDS and suicide. There is a great deal of controversy about whether those who are infected with HIV-1 are prone to suicide. Research *does* suggest that individuals who have been infected with the virus are between 7 and 36 times as likely to end their own lives as are uninfected persons of the same age (Kalichman, Heckman, Kochman, Sikkema, & Bergholte, 2000; Roy, 2003; Treisman, Angelino, & Hutton, 2001). The period of greatest risk appears to be right after the individual learns that he or she is infected with HIV-1 (Kalichman et al., 2000; Treisman et al., 2001). However, suicide risk must be assessed on a case-by-case basis, as a multitude of factors can contribute to or inhibit a person's desire to end his or her life.

AIDS and Kaposi's sarcoma. When AIDS was first identified in the early 1980s, physicians thought that a rare form of cancer known as *Kaposi's sarcoma* was a manifestation of AIDS. This misunderstanding was because 40% of individuals who had AIDS in 1981 also developed Kaposi's sarcoma and because doctors still had not isolated the cause of AIDS itself (Antman & Chang, 2000). However, by the early 1990s researchers had identified the cause of both AIDS and Kaposi's sarcoma. AIDS was found to be the result of infection with HIV-1, and Kaposi's sarcoma was found to be caused by a member of the herpes virus family known as the Kaposi's sarcoma-associated herpesvirus (KSHV, or human herpesvirus 8) (Antman & Chang, 2000).

As researchers have come to better understand KSHV, they realized that Kaposi's sarcoma was usually found in patients whose immune systems were compromised by HIV-1 infection, or individuals whose immune systems were suppressed by physicians following organ transplant procedures (Antman & Chang, 2000), or people who had been exposed to radiation (Miles, 1996). The virus was also found to be endemic in certain regions of Africa (Antman & Chang, 2000) and is the most common

AIDS-related cancer in the United States—but it is a separate disorder from HIV-1 (Antman & Chang, 2000; Miles, 1996).

Tuberculosis (TB)

In the United States, people tend to underestimate the damage tuberculosis (TB) causes around the world. Fully 2 billion of the world's estimated population of 6 billion people have been infected with TB, although for the most part the infection lies latent within their bodies (Markel, 2004). But for 10% of those who are infected, TB does not remain latent but rather explodes within the body, speeding if not actively causing death. Further, each victim is thought to infect 20 others before being treated or succumbing to the infection (Markel, 2004).

Without proper treatment, the prognosis for active tuberculosis is quite grim. An estimated 7 to 8 million new cases of active TB appear around the globe each year, and 2 to 3 million people die annually from this disease (Hopewell, 1996; Seymour, 1997). This makes TB the leading cause of death from infectious disease on earth (Markel, 2004; Szabo, 1997; Wilkinson et al., 2000), with 500 million new cases expected globally in the next 50 years (Savitch, 1998).

Tuberculosis itself is an opportunistic disease: It preys mainly on those whose immune systems have been weakened by illness or malnutrition. There is preliminary evidence that either dietary or metabolic conditions that limit the body's absorption of vitamin D place the individual at increased risk for contracting tuberculosis (Wilkinson et al., 2000). Because individuals who abuse drugs/alcohol on a chronic basis tend also to be malnourished, the vitamin D hypothesis might help to explain why this subgroup of people tends to be at risk for developing TB. So strong is the relationship between chronic alcohol use and TB that Cunha (1998) recommended that the attending physician specifically rule out tuberculosis in alcohol-abusing patients who present with symptoms of pneumonia. Further, individuals whose immune systems are compromised by infection, such as HIV-1, are also at high risk for contracting TB (Garrett, 1994). Indeed, the first outward sign that an individual is infected with HIV-1 might be when she or he develops TB (Karlen, 1995). It is for this reason that alcohol/drug rehabilitation counselors need to have an awareness of the relationship between substance misuse and tuberculosis infections.

What is tuberculosis? Tuberculosis (TB) is an infectious disease, caused by the bacterium *Mycobacterium tuberculosis* (Markel, 2004). Physicians have struggled against TB for hundreds of generations. With the advent of effective treatments, public health officials and physicians in the United States became complacent, and treatment efforts were scaled back or eliminated entirely. The late 1980s and 1990s saw a resurgence of new cases in this country, although the vast majority were later determined to be reactivation of formerly latent infections rather than new ones (Markel, 2004). Several factors contributed to the return of TB, but the most important of these was treatment noncompliance (Markel, 2004).

Unlike other bacterial infections, tuberculosis must be treated with antituberculosis medications for 6 months or more in order to eradicate the infection (Markel, 2004). This makes medication compliance difficult in an era when most people fail to complete even a 10-day course of medication for a minor bacterial infection. The lifestyle of the typical alcohol/drug abuser often makes treatment compliance for TB even more difficult. Treatment noncompliance, professional nonchalance, plus the rise of AIDS contributed to the rise of the antibiotic-resistant strains of TB that began to be identified in the early 1990s. For example, 90% of antibiotic-resistant TB infections occur in people whose immune systems are already struggling with HIV-1 infection (Savitch, 1998; Telenti & Iseman, 2000). Multidrug resistant strains of TB are important because they are fatal in 80% to 90% of the cases.

How does TB kill? TB most often invades the pulmonary system, although it is possible for TB to infect virtually every organ system in the body. The bacteria seem to prefer oxygen-rich body tissues, such as those found in the lungs, central nervous system, and kidneys (Markel, 2004). If the infection becomes established in the lungs, whenever the infected person sings, talks, coughs, or sneezes, he or she will release microscopic droplets of moisture from the lungs that will remain suspended in the air for extended periods of time and that harbor *Mycobacterium tuberculosis* cells. These moisture droplets carry the bacteria into the surrounding air, waiting for another person to breath them in (Markel, 2004).

Once the *Mycobacterium tuberculosis* cells gain admission to the victim's body, his or her immune system begins to mount a counterattack to rid the body of the invader. The immune system's initial response begins when the *macrophages* engulf the invading bacteria and wall them inside little pockets known as granulomas. This action prevents the infection from proceeding further. However, *Mycobacterium tuberculosis* is difficult for the body to destroy, and the bacteria might continue to survive in a dormant stage within the granulomas for years or decades.

If the individual's immune system becomes weakened by another infection, disease, or malnutrition, the body loses its ability to isolate the TB bacteria in the granulomas. Eventually, the TB bacteria might burst out and again invade the surrounding body tissue. This is known as reactivation TB, which accounts for virtually all the new cases of TB in the United States (Markel, 2004). At this point the body attempts a different approach to the invading bacteria. Another part of the immune system, the lymphocytes, attempt to destroy the bacteria that cause TB. Unfortunately, during this process, they release a toxin that destroys surrounding lung tissue. Eventually, as less and less of the lung is able to function properly, the patient dies of pulmonary failure.

The treatment of TB. Although a great deal has been written about treatment resistant TB in the past few years, physicians still have a wide range of medications they can call on to treat this infection. Unfortunately, the treatment process might take as long as 24 months, with the patient being expected to take the proper medications as often as 3 or 4 times a day for up to 24 months in cases of drug-resistant strains (Markel, 2004). Even this intensity of treatment is not always effective, and with the best of medical care TB remains potentially fatal to those people who are infected.

Viral Hepatitis

There are at least seven different viruses that can infect the liver. Each form of viral infection results in inflammation of the liver, a condition known as *hepatitis*.[8] Physicians often refer to each different virus simply by a letter, such as Hepatitis A, B, and so on. At least four

[8]See Glossary.

different forms of viral hepatitis are known to affect alcohol/drug users. In this section these disorders will be discussed.

A brief orientation to viral hepatitis. Physicians have long known that if people were exposed to water or food contaminated by fecal matter they might become ill. In the 20th century, researchers discovered that in addition to the various strains of bacteria that might be contracted in this manner, a person could also contract a virus that attacked the liver. This virus was identified as the Hepatitis type A (HVA) virus.

Each year in the United States, an estimated 200,000 new cases of HVA infection appear (Shute, Licking, & Schultz, 1998). Although the usual route of transmission is food or water that has become contaminated with fecal matter from a person infected with HVA, on occasions HVA will also be passed between intravenous drug abusers (discussed below).

Although physicians have long been aware of HVA, they also knew that some patients who had received blood transfusions developed symptoms of liver disease other than HVA. These patients were said to have developed serum hepatitis. In 1966, a virus that was later classified as Hepatitis type B (HVB) was identified (Lee, 1997). Unfortunately, scientists soon realized that the virus that causes HVB was responsible for only 28% (Bondesson & Saperston, 1996) to 43% (Vail, 1997) of all new cases of viral hepatitis in the United States (Hoffnagle & Di Bisceglie, 1997). There was evidence of at least one other virus capable of causing hepatitis, which for many years was classified simply as Non A-Non B hepatitis. In 1988,[9] the cause of Non A-Non B hepatitis was identified as being the result of an infection by one of five previously unidentified viral agents; they have since been classified as Hepatitis virus type C (HVC), type D (HVD), type E (HVE), type F (HVF), and type G (HVG) (Sjogren, 1996). Surprisingly, there is genetic evidence to suggest that HVG is a distant cousin to HVC.

Relationship between viral hepatitis and intravenous drug abuse. Although exposure to food or water that was contaminated with fecal material is the most common route of HVA infection, HVA might also be passed

from one person to another through the sharing of intravenous needles. It is estimated that 40% to 70% of intravenous drug abusers will contract HVA at some point in their drug-abuse careers (Sorensen, Masson, & Perlman, 2002). However, because the body usually overcomes HVA infection without serious complications, this infection will not be discussed in detail.

The most common route of transmission for the other forms of viral hepatitis discussed here is contaminated intravenous needles shared by drug abusers. Each IV drug abuser leaves a small amount of fluid in the needle that he or she uses. If another person uses that same needle, he or she is exposed to whatever bacteria or viral agents are in the previous user's blood (Becherer, 1995; Vail, 1997). However, IV drug abusers rarely worry about possible exposure to blood-borne infections in their haste to use the first available needle to inject their drugs. In some communities, 60% to 90% of IV drug abusers contract HVB and/or HVC (Krambeer, von McKnelly, Gabrielli, & Penick, 2001; Pearlman, 2004; Sorensen et al., 2002). In the late 1990s a theory was advanced that snorting cocaine might be one way that people contracted HVC. However, it is now thought that unreported intravenous cocaine use was the most likely reason that those who reported that they snorted cocaine actually contracted this viral infection (Willenbring, 2004). It is estimated that 78% of new intravenous drug abusers will contract HVC within a year, 83% within 5 years, and 94% after 10 years if they share needles (Parini, 2003).

Prevalence of HVB. The virus that causes HVB is a member of the *Hepadnaviridae* family of viruses, which show a preference for infecting liver cells (Ganem & Prince, 2004). Globally, 5% of the world's population, or about 350 million (Lee, 1997) to 400–500 million people (Bondesson & Saperston, 1996) are thought to be infected with HVB. In the United States an estimated 12.5 million people have been exposed to HVB (Krain, Wisnivesky, Garland, & McGinn, 2004). Of the six subforms of HVB identified at this time, it is not known if all subforms, or *genotypes*, carry the same potential for liver damage, or if some genotypes are less likely to cause HVB-induced liver disease than others (Russo, 2004).

Prevalence of HVC. HVC was first isolated in 1988 (Kirchner, 1999). Since that time, researchers have discovered that up to 300 million people around the globe are infected with this virus, a number five times as large

---

[9]Pearlman (2004) stated that the virus that causes HVC was first isolated in 1989, not 1988.

as the number of people infected with HIV-1 (Hines, 2002; Woods & Herrera, 2002). There are six known subtypes of HVC (Bonkovsky & Mehta, 2001; Karch, 2002; Parini, 2003; Seymour, 1997). The prevalence of HVC infection varies from region to region around the globe. Between 9% and 14.6% of the population in north Africa has been exposed to HVC; elsewhere the percentage of the population that is infected with HVC is much lower (Dieperink, Willenbring, & Ho, 2000).

In the United States, HVC has become *the* most common chronic blood-borne infection, and it is the most common cause for liver transplant surgery, a trend that is likely to increase as more of those infected in the 1970s and 1980s begin to develop long-term consequences of HVC infection (Parini, 2003; Pearlman, 2004; Willenbring, 2004). Four million people in the United States (1.8% of the population) are believed to be infected with HVC (Karsan, Rojter & Saab, 2004; Patel & McHutchison, 2003), with approximately 30,000 new cases of HVC infection occurring each year (Dieperink et al., 2000).

Prevalence of HVD and HVE. Fortunately, the HVD and HVE viruses are rarely found in the United States. An estimated 15 million people are infected with HVD worldwide, of whom 70,000 live in this country (Najm, 1997). Each year in the United States an estimated 5,000 new cases of HVD appear (Karsan et al., 2004). HVE is not commonly found in this country (Shute et al., 1998).

Routes of transmission for HVB. HVB is *extremely* contagious, possibly 100 times as contagious as HIV-1. Physicians have identified cases of individuals contracting HVB by such activities as sharing a toothbrush or a razor, or even simply by kissing an infected person (Brody, 1991). HVB may also be transmitted through blood transfusions. This fact has resulted in the development of new blood tests to screen out blood donors who might carry the virus. In the early 1970s, the rate of infection with the hepatitis B virus was 1 per 100 units of blood transfused in the United States (Edelson, 1993). However, new blood tests for screening potential blood donors (and ways of storing blood prior to use) have reduced the rate of transfusion-related HVB infection in the United States to about 1 in 250,000 units of blood (Goodnough et al., 1999).

Intravenous drug abuse is a common method of HVB transmission in the United States. Research has shown that between 75% and 98% of intravenous drug abusers have been exposed to HVB in this country (Michelson, Carroll, McLane, & Robin, 1988). However, HVB infection is also transmitted through sexual contact, and in the United States sexual transmission of HVB infection is the most common cause of new cases of HVB (Russo, 2004). Thus, like HIV-1, HVB is now classified both as a blood borne and as a *sexually transmitted disease* (STD).

Routes of transmission for HVC. One of the risk factors for HVC infection is having received a blood transfusion prior to 1990, when new blood tests designed to test for HVC in blood supplies were introduced. Since the advent of these blood tests, the risk of contracting HVC from a blood transfusion has dropped to around 1 for every 103,000 units of blood used (Dieperink et al., 2000; Goodnough et al., 1999).

The most common method by which a patient contracts HVC infection is through contaminated intravenous needles (Pearlman, 2004). Approximately 75% of intravenous drug addicts have been exposed to HVC (Pearlman, 2004). HVC is found in almost every body fluid, although it is not thought to be active in bile acids and the stool and is most concentrated in the blood (Woods & Herrera, 2002). Both HVC and HIV-1 are transmitted through contaminated intravenous needles, and at least 33% of patients with HIV-1 are also infected with HVC (Parini, 2003). On rare occasions, HVC is transmitted sexually. The transmission rate in monogamous, sexually active couples is estimated to be 0.3% per year, but sexual promiscuity increases the odds of sexual transmission of HVC (Pearlman, 2004). Other known or suspected routes of HVC transmission include contaminated needles used in tattooing, organ transplant procedures when the donor had been infected with HVC, and hemodialysis (DiBisceglie & Bacon, 1999; Hager & Reibstein, 1998; Sharara, Hunt, & Hamilton, 1996).

Routes of transmission for HVD. HVD is a bloodborne virus, and it requires some of the enzymes produced by the HVB virus in order to replicate (Russo, 2004). It is for this reason that HVD is sometimes referred to as being "incomplete" or "defective" (Sjogren, 1996, p. 948). By itself, HVD is unable to replicate, and if the patient has not been exposed to HVB, it cannot infect the individual. Researchers have discovered that 20% to 80% of intravenous drug abusers (Vail, 1997) and 10% of individuals with *chronic* HVB infection also test positive for exposure to HVD (Di Bisceglie, 1995).

Routes of transmission for HVE. Although HVE might be transmitted by exposure to body fluids, the most common method of transmission is exposure to water contaminated by humans who were infected (Shute, Licking, & Schultz, 1998).

What are the consequences of HVB infection? HVB infection is the most common cause of liver disease on the face of the earth (Vail, 1997). The vast majority of HVB infections in normal, healthy adults are self-limited and the immune system is able to eventually eliminate the virus from the body (Ganem & Prince, 2004). However, in about 5% to 10% of the cases the individual develops a chronic HVB infection (Ganem & Prince, 2004; Hines, 2002; Russo, 2004). Unfortunately, between 15% anpd 20% of those people who are chronically infected will ultimately die as a result of HVB-induced complications (Vail, 1997).

About 40% of individuals infected with HVB will experience HVB-induced liver problems, and a significant percentage of these people will die (Purow & Jacobson, 2003). Although it was once thought that the virus caused significant damage to the liver, mounting evidence suggests that in cases of chronic HVB infection, it is the body's reaction to the HVB infection that causes damage to the victim's liver (Ganem & Prince, 2004). About 20% of people with chronic HVB infections develop cirrhosis (Ganem & Prince, 2004), and each year in the United States between 3,500 (Lee, 1997) and 5,000 (Karlen, 1995) die as a result of HVB-induced cirrhosis. However, hepatitis B may kill in another way. For reasons that are not known at this time, the person who has been infected with the hepatitis B virus is *10 to 390 times* as likely to develop liver cancer as is a noninfected person (Bondesson & Saperston, 1996; Ganem & Prince, 2004; Gordon, 2000). Liver cancer is quite difficult to detect or treat and is usually fatal. Each year, there are roughly 1,200 new cases of HVB-related liver cancer in the United States (Karlen, 1995).

What are the consequences of HVC infection? It is thought that HVC infection is the primary cause of death in 10,000 to 12,000 people each year in the United States alone (Parini, 2003; Schiff & Ozden, 2003). Between 15% and 25% of those who are infected are able to fight off the HVC infection without serious complications, usually in the first 6 months after exposure to the virus

(Dieperink et al., 2000; Hines, 2002; Lieber, 2001; Woods & Herrera, 2002). Physicians used to think that in 20% to 25% of those who were infected with HVC, the body would be able to contain the infection. Now it seems that the infectious process just proceeds more slowly in these individuals, and that the infection will progress at markedly different rates for different people (Parini, 2003).

There are no outward manifestations of HVC infection, and only a blood test can determine whether the individual has been exposed to HVC (Najm, 1997). In about 20% of the cases, HVC is able to cause progressive liver damage, cirrhosis, end-stage liver disease, cancer of the liver, or various combinations of these conditions, usually after a period of 20–40 years (Patel & McHutchison, 2003). If a person with HVC infection should also be a chronic alcohol user, the destruction of the liver is accelerated (Karsan et al.,, 2004; Lieber, 2001; Parini, 2003; Schiff & Ozden, 2003; Willenbring, 2004).

What are the consequences of HVD infection? Early evidence suggests that the combination of HVB and HBD infections results in a more severe syndrome than seen in HVB alone (Karsan et al., 2004). Approximately 60% to 70% of people infected with HVD will develop cirrhosis of the liver, usually in 2 to 15 years after being infected (Najm, 1997).

What are the consequences of HVE infection? Scientists are still exploring the impact of HVE infection on the individual. The virus can cause loss of appetite, nausea, and vomiting as a result of liver inflammation as well as fever, fatigue, and abdominal pain (Shute et al., 1998). It is known that up to 20% of the pregnant women who contract HVE will die as a result of the infection (Gorbach, Mensa, & Gatell, 1997).

The treatment of HVB. The most effective treatment for HVB is prevention. A vaccine against HVB was developed in the early 1980s and individuals who are likely to be exposed to the body fluids of an infected individual should be vaccinated against possible HVB infection (Vail, 1997). In some states, vaccination against HVB is required before a child is admitted to public school (Vail, 1997). Other examples of individuals who should be immunized against HVB are health care workers, the spouse of an individual who is infected, and children/adolescents.

For the past 20 years, the search for effective pharmacological treatments for HVB infection has been ongoing, and this research is starting to show results. Interferon has been found to suppress HVB viral replication during treatment, and in many cases there has been no evidence of viral activity for up to 8 years afterward (Purow & Jacobson, 2003). Another medication, lamivudine, has been approved by the Food and Drug Administration (FDA) for the treatment of both HIV-1 and HVB infections. In September 2002 the FDA also approved adefovir to treat HVB infection. To date, there have been no identified resistant mutations of the HVB virus to this medication, making it an important adjunct to the treatment of chronic HVB infection (Purow & Jacobson, 2003).

The treatment of HVC. The current treatment for HVC infection is a combination of interferon and ribavirin.[10] This combination is effective in about 50% to 60% of the patients treated (Patel & McHutchison, 2003). The individual's adherence to the therapeutic program is a strong indicator of his or her response to treatment, so patients must be encouraged to complete the course of treatments in spite of side effects such as fever, chills, headache, anxiety, and problems concentrating in the hours and days after the medications are injected.

The treatment of HVD. Preliminary evidence suggests that since co-infection with HVB is necessary for HVD

---

[10]Which, if you must know, is a nucleoside analog compond that is taken orally.

infection to develop, immunization against HVB will provide protection against HVD (Vail, 1997). Immunization against HVB blocks the chain of infection, preventing HVD co-infection if an individual should be exposed to this virus (Najm, 1997).

The treatment of HVE, HVF, and HVG. Very little is know about how these viral infections might be treated. Like HVB, the most effective treatment for these viral infections is prevention, by avoiding exposure to body fluids of other individuals who are known or suspected to have a form of viral hepatitis.

Summary

It is impossible to identify in advance every potential infectious disease that substance abusers are exposed to as a result of their chemical use. In this chapter, a few of the more common forms of infection that might arise as a result of alcohol/drug abuse have been reviewed. Although this chapter is not intended as a guide for the treatment of these infections, substance-abuse rehabilitation professionals need to understand some of the risk factors associated with infectious diseases frequently found in alcohol/drug abusing individuals. These include the hepatitis family of viral infections, HIV-1, and tuberculosis (TB). Knowing about these diseases will help rehabilitation professionals understand the needs of their patients and their own potential for being exposed to these disorders as a result of their work with infected individuals.

CHAPTER THIRTY-FOUR

Self-Help Groups

The Twelve Steps of Alcoholics Anonymous[1]

Step One: We admitted that we were powerless over alcohol—that our lives had become unmanageable.

Step Two: Came to believe that a Power greater than ourselves could restore us to sanity.

Step Three: Made a decision to turn our will and our lives over to the care of God *as we understood Him.*

Step Four: Made a searching and fearless moral inventory of ourselves.

Step Five: Admitted to God, to ourselves, and to another human being the exact nature of our wrongs.

Step Six: Were entirely ready to have God remove all these defects of character.

Step Seven: Humbly asked Him to remove our shortcomings.

Step Eight: Made a list of all persons we had harmed, and became willing to make amends to them all.

Step Nine: Made direct amends to such people wherever possible, except when to do so would injure them or others.

Step Ten: Continued to take personal inventory and when we were wrong, promptly admitted it.

Step Eleven: Sought through prayer and meditation to improve our conscious contact with God *as we understood Him,* praying only for knowledge of His will for us, and the power to carry that out.

Step Twelve: Having had a spiritual awakening as the result of these steps, we tried to carry this message to alcoholics, and to practice these principles in all our affairs.

[1]The Twelve Steps are reprinted by permission of Alcoholics Anonymous World Services, Inc. Permission to reprint this material does not mean that AA has reviewed or approved the contents of this publication, nor that AA agrees with the views expressed herein. AA is a program of recovery from alcoholism—use of the Twelve Steps in connection with programs and activities that are patterned after AA, but which address other problems, does not imply otherwise.

Introduction

Alcoholics Anonymous (AA) is the "most frequently consulted source of help for drinking problems" (Miller & McCrady, 1993, p. 3). Approximately 1 in every 10 adults in the United States has attended an AA meeting at least once (Miller & McCrady, 1993; Tonigan & Toscova, 1998; Zweben, 1995). This is not to say that all of these people had alcohol-use problems of their own, however. Perhaps two-thirds of those who have attended at least one AA meeting, have done so out of concern about another person's drinking (Zweben, 1995). However, this still means that one-third of those who have attended AA, or 3.1% of the adults in the United States, have done so because they thought they might have an alcohol-use problem (Godlaski, Leukefeld, & Cloud, 1997).

In spite of its popularity, AA is perhaps the least rigorously studied element in the spectrum of rehabilitation programs (Meza & Kranzler, 1996). Even though the organization has existed for over 60 years, "the empirical research on the efficacy of Alcoholics Anonymous is sparse and inconclusive" (Watson et al., 1997, p. 209). AA remains something of a mystery not only to nonmembers but all too often even to active members, a fact that makes AA or similar self-help groups rather controversial. Supporters claim that AA is the most effective means of treating alcoholism. Critics of AA or similar programs challenge this claim. In this chapter, the self-help group phenomenon patterned after the Alcoholics Anonymous program will be examined.

The History of AA

Among the diverse forces that were to blend together to form Alcoholics Anonymous (AA) was the American temperance movement of the late 1800s (Peele, 1989);

a nondenominational religious group known as the Oxford Group, which was popular in the 1930s (Bufe, 1998; Nace, 1987); and the psychoanalysis of an American alcoholic by Carl Jung in the year 1931 (Edmeades, 1987). The religious group was especially influential, imparting to the AA program a strong belief in free will and personal responsibility (Committee on Addictions of the Group for the Advancement of Psychiatry, 2002).

Historically, AA is thought to have been founded on June 10, 1935, the day an alcoholic physician had his last drink (Nace, 1997). Earlier, following a meeting between a stockbroker, William Griffith Wilson, and the surgeon, Dr. Robert Holbrook Smith, the foundation of AA was set down. William "Bill" Wilson was struggling to protect his new-found sobriety while on a business trip in a strange city. After making several telephone calls to try to find support in his struggle, Wilson was asked to talk to Dr. Smith, who was drinking at the time that Wilson called.

Rather than looking out for his own needs, Wilson choose a different approach. He carried a message of sobriety to another alcoholic. The self-help philosophy of AA was born from this moment. In the half-century since then, it has grown to a fellowship of 97,000 "clubs" or AA groups, that includes chapters in 150 countries, with a total membership estimated at more than 2 million people (Humphreys, 1997; Nace, 2003). Of this number, 1.2 million members are from the United States or Canada (Marvel, 1995). Thus, 68% of the entire world membership of AA is found just in North America.

During its early years, AA struggled to find a method that would support its members in their struggle to achieve and maintain sobriety. Within 3 years of its founding, three different AA groups were in existence, but even with three groups "it was hard to find two score of sure recoveries" (*Twelve Steps and Twelve Traditions*, 1981, p. 17). But the fledgling group continued to grow slowly, until by the fourth year following its inception, there were about 100 members in isolated AA groups (Nace, 1997). In spite of this rather limited beginning, the early members decided to write of their struggle to achieve sobriety in order to share their discoveries with others. The book that was published as a result of this process was the first edition of *Alcoholics Anonymous* in 1939. The organization took its name from the title of this book, which has since come to be known as the "Big Book" of AA (*Twelve Steps and Twelve Traditions*, 1981).

Elements of AA

There are several factors that help to shape an effective self-help group (Rootes & Aanes, 1992):

1. Members have *shared experience*, in this case their inability to control their drug or alcohol use.
2. *Education*, not psychotherapy, is the primary goal of AA membership.
3. Self-help groups are *self-governing*.
4. The group places emphasis on *accepting responsibility for one's behavior.*
5. There is but a *single purpose* to the group.
6. Membership is *voluntary*.
7. The individual member must make a *commitment to personal change*.
8. The group places emphasis on *anonymity and confidentiality*.

George Vaillant (2000) identified four factors that were common to recovery programs from substance-use disorders: (a) compulsory supervision, (b) introduction and use of competing behavior to replace the chemical-use pattern, (c) new love relationships, and (d) increased spirituality and religiosity. Many of these elements are contained in the list of helpful elements of AA advanced by Rootes and Aanes (1992).

Most researchers recognize the core characteristics of AA as very much a product of society in the United States in the late 1930s, especially the Oxford Group's movement (Bufe, 1998). Americans have always had a strong belief in the process of public confession, contrition, and salvation through spirituality, which are all elements of the AA program. Further, as the *Twelve Steps and Twelve Traditions* (1981) acknowledged, the early members of AA also freely borrowed from the fields of medicine and religion to establish a program that worked for them. The program that emerged is the famous "12 Steps" of AA, which form the core of the recovery program that AA offers.

A breakdown of the 12 Steps. The core of the recovery program for AA are the 12 Steps, which are suggested not as the *only* way to recovery, but as *a* way that might work for the individual (Beazley, 1998). The 12 Steps fall into three groups. The first three steps are viewed as necessary for the acceptance of one's limitations. Through these steps, the individual is able to come to accept that his or her own resources are insufficient for dealing with the problems of life, especially the addiction to alcohol. In the final step of this first group, the individual is called on to make a profound choice: that of surrender and of turning one's life over to God (Cole & Pargament, 1999).

Steps Four through Nine are a series of change-oriented activities. These steps are designed to help the individual identify, confront, and ultimately overcome character shortcomings that were so much a part of the individual's addicted lifestyle. Through these steps, one may work through the guilt associated with past behaviors and learn to recognize the limits of personal responsibility. These steps allow the person to learn the tools of non-drug-centered living, something which at first is often alien to both the alcohol-dependent person and his or her family.

Finally, Steps Ten through Twelve challenge the individual to continue to build on the foundation established in Steps Four through Nine. The individual is asked to continue to search out personal shortcomings and to confront them. The person also is challenged to continue the spiritual growth initiated during the earlier steps and to carry the message of hope to others.

In a sense, AA might be viewed as functioning as a form of psychotherapy that aids personal growth (Alibrandi, 1978; Peck, 1993; Tobin, 1992), or a series of successive approximations toward a better way of life (McCrady & Delaney, 1995). The guiding philosophy behind AA is that whereas the individual's resources are inadequate for controlling his or her addiction to alcohol, through a lifelong commitment to the group the individual is able to achieve some measure of control over the incurable disease of addiction (Davison, Pennebaker, & Dickerson, 2000). As a self-help growth program, the AA program has five different phases (Alibrandi, 1978). The first stage starts on the first day of membership in AA and lasts for the next week. During this phase, the individual's goal is simply to stay away from his or her first drink (or episode of chemical use).

The second phase of recovery starts at the end of the first week and lasts until the end of the second month of AA membership (Alibrandi, 1978). Major steps during this part of the recovery process include the recovering addict's acceptance of the disease concept of addiction and learning to accept help with his or her addiction. During this phase, the individual struggles

to replace old drug-centered behavioral habits with new, sobriety-oriented habits. The third stage of recovery spans the interval from the second to the sixth month of recovery, according to Alibrandi (1978). During this stage, the individual is to use the 12 Steps as a guide and to try to let go of old ideas. Guilt feelings about past chemical use are to be replaced with gratitude for sobriety, wherever possible, and the member is to stand available for service to other individuals who are addicted to alcohol.

The fourth stage begins at around the sixth month of recovery and lasts until the first year of abstinence (Alibrandi, 1978). During this stage, the individual is encouraged to take a searching and fearless moral inventory of himself or herself and to share this with another person. At the same time, if the individual is still shaky, he or she is encouraged to work with another member. Emphasis during this phase of recovery is on acceptance of responsibility and the resolution of the anger and resentments on which addiction is so often established. Finally, after the first year of recovery, the rehabilitation process has reached what Brown (1985) termed *ongoing sobriety*. Alibrandi (1978) identified the goal during this phase of recovery as being the maintenance of a "spiritual condition." The person is warned not to dwell on the shortcomings of others, to suspend judgment of self and others, and to beware of the false pride that could bring him or her back to chemical use.

Although the AA program is designed to aid spiritual growth, this process is not rapid. The process of correcting the spiritual defects on which alcoholism rests takes many years. Beazley (1998), for example, suggested that the member must be actively involved in AA for at least 5 years before the process of spiritual growth might proceed. But once this process of spiritual renewal is initiated,

> there is no going back. You develop a knowledge that is so powerful that you will wonder how you could have lived any other way. The awakened life begins to own you, and then you simply know within that you are on the right path. (Dyer, 1989, p. 17)

Whether the 12 Steps are effective, or why they are effective, is often disputed. But within the AA community, there are those who believe that the 12 Steps offer a program within which personality transformation might be accomplished (DiClemente, 1993). Surprisingly, the Steps are not required for AA membership. But they are viewed within AA as a proven method of behavioral change that offers the individual a chance to rebuild his or her life. There are many who believe that these Steps were instrumental in saving their lives.

AA and Religion

The discussion of spiritual matters in the United States is frequently complicated by the fact that the words *faith*, *religion*, and *spirituality* are mistakenly used interchangeably. But there are very real differences in these terms. Religion is an *organized set of beliefs* that are encoded in certain texts (considered sacred by believers) and are viewed as providing some of the answers to life's questions for those who belong to that community of believers (Ameling & Povilonis, 2001). Through religious belief the individual's search for meaning is raised to the level of the community of believers, where spirituality is a reflection of the individual's search for answers.

There is a strong positive relationship between spirituality and abstinence, with those individuals who have the strongest spiritual beliefs being least likely to abuse alcohol (Nace, 2003). The difference between spirituality and religion was best summarized by McDargh (2000), who observed that "religion is for those who are afraid of going to hell . . . spirituality is for those who have already been there [as a result of their substance-use problems]." Within this context, it is possible to view alcohol-dependent people as having a "higher power": alcohol. In effect, they have placed alcohol (or drugs) in the role of being their "god" (Ringwald, 2002). Twelve-step programs seek to help individuals switch from their addiction to a more benign higher power (Wallace, 2003). It is through this process that AA presents itself as a program for *spiritual* growth but not as a religious movement (Berenson, 1987; McGowan, 1998; Vaillant, 2000; Wallace, 2003).

To better understand the distinction between spirituality and belief, it is helpful to view religion as the *form* and spirituality as the *content* of belief (McGowan, 1998). To counter the addiction, the newcomer is asked to "let go," something that he or she might find impossible to understand. But "having faith is not a question of clinging to a particular set of beliefs, a particular set of . . . practices or psychotherapeutic techniques. Having faith . . . requires that we let go of what we are clinging to" (Rosenbaum, 1999, p. xii). For the individual to recover, AA requires that he or she *be receptive to the possibility that there is more than "self,"* and to stop clinging to unhealthy doubts, resentments, demands, and eventually, alcohol. An example of this process is Step Three of the AA 12-Step program. This step "doesn't demand an immediate conversion experience . . . but . . . does call for a decision" (Jensen, 1987a, p. 22) from the alcohol-dependent person to turn his or her will over to his or her God.

The emphasis on spiritual growth in the AA program rests on the dual assumptions that (a) each individual seems to desire a relationship with the infinite (higher power), and (b) it is the individual's distorted perception of "self" as the center of the universe rather than his or her higher power that helps to make the person vulnerable to alcoholism (McCrady, 1994; McDargh, 2000; Ringwald, 2002).

Note that the Third Step of the AA program does not name God, or His "true" religion. It "simply assumes that there is a God to understand and that we each have a God of our own understanding" (Jensen, 1987a, p. 23). In this manner, AA sidesteps the question of religion while still addressing the spiritual disease it views as forming the foundation for the addiction. In turning one's will over to a higher power, the individual comes to accept that his or her own will is not strong enough to maintain recovery and that the disease has affected the individual's perception of reality. The individual learns how his or her resentments from the past contribute to the spiritual sickness that is so essential to alcoholism and how to resolve or renounce these resentments.

To further the process of spiritual growth, the individual is encouraged to carry out a daily self-examination similar to that of the *Examen* or *Conscious Examen* proposed by Ignatius as one of the rules of the Jesuit order. This is done by the individual to better understand the will of the higher power and how it applies to the individual's life. In a similar manner, AA offers a spiritual program that ties the individual's will to that of a "higher power," without offering a specific religious dogma that might offend members.

One "A" Is for Anonymous

Anonymity is central to the AA program (*Understanding Anonymity*, 1981) This is one major reason that most meetings are "closed." There are three types of closed meetings. In the first, when there is a designated speaker, one individual will talk at length about his or her life, substance use, and how he or she came to join AA and benefit from the program (Nowinski, 2003). In the second form of closed AA meeting, the discussion meeting, a theme or problem of interest to the members of the AA group is identified and each member of the group is offered the chance to talk about how this problem affects him or her. Finally, in the last type of closed meeting, the "Step" meeting, the group will focus on one of the 12 Steps for a month at a time, with each member offered the chance to talk about his or her understanding of the step and how that person attempts to put that step into practice in his or her recovery program. Closed meetings are limited to members of AA only. In contrast to the closed meeting, there are also open AA meetings. In the open meeting, which any interested person may attend, one or two volunteers will speak, and visitors are encouraged to ask questions about AA and how it works.

Anonymity is a central concept of AA. For this reason, many AA members believe that court-ordered or employer-mandated attendance of AA runs counter to the central philosophy of anonymity: In order to verify his or her attendance, the individual must ask a member of AA to break anonymity to confirm that the person indeed did attend the meetings he or she was ordered to attend. The AA program places emphasis on anonymity to protect the identities of members and to ensure that no identified spokesperson emerges who claims to "speak" for AA (*Understanding Anonymity*, 1981). Through this policy, the members of AA strive for humility, each knowing that he or she is equal to the other members. The concept of anonymity is so important that it is said to serve "as the spiritual foundation of the Fellowship" (*Understanding Anonymity*, 1981, p. 5) of AA.

The concept of equality of the members underlies the AA tradition that no "directors" are nominated or voted on. Rather, "service boards" or special committees are created from the membership as needed. These boards always remain responsible to the group *as a whole* and must answer to the entire AA group. As is noted in Tradition Two of AA "our leaders are but trusted servants; they do not govern" (*Twelve Steps and Twelve Traditions*, 1981, p. 10). Because of this emphasis on equality, the structure of AA has evolved into one in which the "interpersonal conflicts and the petty jealousy, greed or self-importance that could create havoc among fellowship members" (DiClemente, 1993, p. 85) is minimized, if not almost totally avoided.

AA and Outside Organizations

Each Alcoholics Anonymous group is both self-supporting and not-for-profit. Each individual group is autonomous and must support itself only through the contributions of its members. Further, each individual member is prohibited from contributing more than $1,000 per year to AA. Outside donations are discouraged to avoid the problem of having to decide how to deal with these gifts. Outside commitments are also discouraged for AA groups. As stated in the text *Twelve Steps and Twelve Traditions* (1981), AA groups will not "endorse, finance, or lend the AA name to any related facility or outside enterprise, lest problems of money, property and prestige divert us from our primary purpose" (p. 11).

The relationship between different autonomous AA groups, and between different AA groups and other organizations, is governed by the Twelve Traditions of AA The Traditions are a set of guidelines or a framework within which different groups may interact and through which AA units as a whole may work together. They will not be reviewed in this chapter; however, interested readers might wish to read *The Twelve Steps and Twelve Traditions* (1981) to learn more about the Traditions.

The Primary Purpose of AA

This primary purpose of AA is twofold. First, the members strive to "carry the message to the addict who still suffers" (Narcotics Anonymous World Service Office, Inc., 1976, p. 1). Second, AA seeks to provide its members a program for living without chemicals. This is done not by preaching to the alcohol/drug addicted individual but by presenting to the individual a simple, truthful, realistic picture of the disease of addiction. This is accomplished by confronting the alcohol/drug addicted person in language that he or she can understand. The manner in which this confrontation is carried out is somewhat different from the usual methods of confrontation. In AA, speakers share their own life stories, a public confession of sorts when each individual tells of the lies, the distortions, the self-deceptions, and the denial that supported his or her own chemical use. In so doing, the speaker hopes to break through the defensiveness of the alcohol-addicted person by showing that others have walked the same road and yet found a way to recovery.

> Helping others is a central theme of AA, in part because: Even the newest of newcomers finds undreamed rewards as he tries to help his brother alcoholic, the one who is even blinder than he. . . . And then he discovers that by the divine paradox of this kind of giving he has found his own reward, whether his brother has yet received anything or not. (*Twelve Steps and Twelve Traditions*, 1981, p. 109)

In this, one finds a therapeutic paradox (not the only one) in AA. For the speaker seeks first of all to help himself or herself through the public admission of powerlessness over chemicals. This is not to say that the individual is *helpless*, but only that he or she is *powerless* over the addiction (Wallace, 2003). Through the public admission of weakness, the speaker seeks to gain strength from the group. It is almost as if by owning the reality of his or her own addiction, the speaker says "This is what *my* life was like, and by having shared it with you, I am reminded again of the reason I will not return to alcohol again."

This is the method pioneered by Bill Wilson in his first meeting with Bob Smith. In that meeting, Bill Wilson spoke at length of his own addiction to alcohol, of the pain and suffering that he had caused others and that he had suffered in the service of his addiction. He did not preach but simply shared with Dr. Smith the history of his own alcoholism. Bill Wilson concluded with the statement: "So thanks a lot for hearing me out. I know now that I'm not going to take a drink, and I'm grateful to you" (Kurtz, 1979, p. 29).

Earlier, it was noted that the methods of AA present a paradox in that by helping others the speaker comes to receive help for his or her own addiction to alcohol/drugs. At the same time, he or she confronts the defenses of the new member by saying, in effect, "I am a mirror of you, and just as you cannot look into a mirror without seeing your own image, you cannot look at me without seeing a part of yourself."

As mentioned above, Alcoholics Anonymous is a spiritual program that is at the same time not religious. Within the AA program, alcoholism is viewed as a "spiritual illness, and drinking as a symptom of that illness. The central spiritual 'defect' of alcoholics is described as an excessive preoccupation with self. . . . Treatment of the preoccupation with self is at the core of AA's approach" (McCrady & Irvine, 1989, p. 153). Within this framework, compulsive alcohol use is viewed as the diametric opposite of spiritual growth (Martin & Booth, 1999). Thus, by engaging in activities that enhance spiritual growth such as a 12-Step program like AA, the individual turns away from the temptation of alcohol use (McCrady, 1994; Miller & Hester, 1995).

Proponents of 12-Step groups note that in alcoholism the individual lives a self-centered lifestyle. To combat this excessive preoccupation with "self," AA offers the 12 Steps as a guide for spiritual growth and for living. But the individual is not *required* to follow the 12 Steps to participate in AA. Rather, "*the program* does not issue orders; it merely *suggests* Twelve Steps to recovery" (Jensen, 1987b, p. 15, italics in original). Thus, the individual is offered a choice between the way of life that preceded AA, or acceptance of a program that others have used to begin their journey toward recovery. But the individual does not *passively* accept the 12 Steps. The emphasis is on *using* the 12-Step program the person has joined, a process that requires *active participation* at meetings, not just passive attendance, and an intentional application of the lessons learned from the 12-Step work to the individual's problems in living (Nowinski, 2003).

The 12 Steps offer the promise and the tools necessary for daily abstinence. One of these tools is that the member of AA is not encouraged to look for the "cause" of his or her addiction to alcohol. Rather, the individual's alcoholism is accepted as a given fact. "It is not so much *how* you came to this place as what you are going to do now that you are here," as one member said to a newcomer. Neither is the member admonished for being unable to live without chemicals. Members of AA know from bitter experience that relapse is possible and common (McCrady & Irvine, 1989). Chemical addiction is assumed in membership: "If chemicals were not a problem for you, you would not be here!" In place of the chemical-centered lifestyle, new members are offered a step-by-step program for living that allows them to achieve, and maintain, recovery.

To take advantage of this program, members need only accept *the program*. Admittedly, in doing so they are asked to accept yet another therapeutic paradox, known as Step One. The First Step, which is the only step that specifically mentions alcohol by name, asks that the individual accept that she or he is powerless over this chemical. The individual is asked to do so not on the most superficial of levels necessary to speak the words "I am powerless over chemicals," but on the deepest level of his or her being. In so doing, the person is forced to accept a measure of humility and to cast doubt on his or her ability to face life alone (Norris, 1998). This is a difficult step. The individual must learn that she or he is not God, a lesson that must be learned time and time again (Yancey, 2000). The essence of the First Step is the acceptance in the deepest level of the individual's soul that he or she is *addicted to and totally powerless over* alcohol.

At first, the newcomer might view alcohol as the problem. But at some point he or she will be forced to accept that "it is we ourselves, not the pills or alcohol, who cause most of our problems. Chemicals will not bring destruction upon a person until that person learns how to justify continual use and abuse of those chemicals" (Springborn, 1987, p. 8). In other words, the individual is helped to see that while she or he is not responsible for having the bio/psycho/spiritual/genetic predisposition for alcoholism, she or he *is* responsible for working toward his or her recovery (Wallace, 2003).

Hitting bottom. The process of "hitting bottom" has been challenged by some theorists but remains a central component of the AA program. When people reach the point that they learn how completely alcohol/drugs have come to dominate their lives they are said to have hit bottom. At that moment, they accept the painful, bitter, frightening reality that their lives have been spent in the service of the addiction. At this moment, they recognize that *nothing* they might do will allow them to control the chemical, for they are *addicted* to it. This is a moment of extreme despair, when the addicted person might turn to another and say: "I need help." It is at this point that the individual becomes receptive to the possibility of living without the chemicals.

Of AA and Recovery

Alcoholics Anonymous does not speak of a "cure" for the disease of alcoholism. Rarely do members of AA speak of themselves as having "recovered," for the process of recovery is viewed as a lifelong process of growth (Wallace, 2003). A good illustration of this growth process is that there is often a period of several months between the time a new member first begins to attend AA meetings and when the person stops drinking. Research has shown that a new member might attend AA for 20 months before he or she will even admit to being a member, and 8 more months before he or she stops drinking (Zweben, 1995). During this 2-year period, the individual is taking the first steps of a lifelong process of growth.

Alcoholics Anonymous also does not speak of itself as an ultimate cure for alcoholism because it views the recovering person as being only a moment away from the next slip. The 25-year veteran may, in a weak moment, relapse into active drinking. Affiliation with AA does not guarantee abstinence from alcohol/drugs (McCrady & Irvine, 1989). Each member faces a personal struggle to abstain from alcohol/drugs, a struggle that members are advised to face "one day at a time." If "today" is too long to think about, the individual is encouraged to think about abstaining for the next hour, or the next minute, or just the next second.

Once the addicted person accepts *the program*, he or she finds a way of living that provides support for recovery 24 hours a day for the rest of his or her life (DiClemente, 1993). In accepting the program, the addicted person may discover a second chance that he or she thought was forever lost.

Sponsorship

To help each person on the spiritual odyssey that will hopefully result in sobriety, new members of AA are encouraged to find a sponsor. The sponsor is a key element to the AA program (McCrady & Delaney, 1995; Zweben, 1995), a person who has worked his or her way through the step program and has achieved a basic understanding of his or her own addiction. The sponsor acts as a spiritual (but not a religious) guide, offering confrontation, insight, and support in equal amounts to the new member.

It is the duty of the sponsor to take an interest in the newcomer's progress, but *not to take responsibility for it* (Alibrandi, 1978; McCrady & Irvine, 1989). Each new AA member is expected to have daily contact with the sponsor either by telephone or in person at least at first (Nowinski, 2003). In spite of frequent communications between the new member and the sponsor, the responsibility for recovery remains with the individual. In a sense, the sponsor says to the client, "I can be concerned for you, but I am not responsible for you." In today's terminology, the sponsor is a living example of what might be called "tough love." In a sense, one might view the sponsor's role as being similar to that of a skilled folk psychotherapist (Peck, 1993).

The sponsor should not try to control the newcomer's life. Ideally, the sponsor should be the same sex as the new AA member being sponsored; the sponsor should also recognize his or her personal limitations (McCrady & Delaney, 1995; Nowinski, 2003). The sponsor should possess many, if not all, of the same characteristics of the healthy human services professional identified by Rogers (1961).

In a very real sense, the sponsor, acting as an extension of AA, is a tool. But while the sponsor is a tool, it is up to the newcomer to grasp and use this tool to achieve sobriety. There are no guarantees, and the sponsor often struggles with many of the same issues that face the newcomer. The newcomer must assume the responsibility for reaching out and using the tools that are offered. Sponsorship is, in essence, an expression of the second mission of AA, which is to "carry the message" to other addicts who are still actively using chemicals. This is a reflection of Step Twelve, and one will often hear the sponsor speak of having participated in a Twelfth Step visit, or of having been involved in Twelfth Step work. The sponsor is, in a sense, a guide, friend, peer-counselor, fellow traveler, conscience, and devil's advocate all rolled into one.

AA and Psychological Theory

The psychiatrist and popular writer M. Scott Peck (1993) advanced the theory that AA offers a form of folk psychology. But the AA/NA (Narcotics Anonymous) step programs are different from other therapeutic programs that the addict may have been exposed to, in the sense that the Steps are "reports of action taken rather than rules not to be broken" (Alibrandi, 1978, p. 166). Each Step is a public (or private) demonstration of action taken in the struggle to achieve and maintain sobriety rather than a rule that might be broken.

Brown (1985) speaks of the AA steps as serving another purpose as well. For Brown (1985), the Twelve Steps serve to keep the recovering addict focused on his or her addiction. Just as the alcohol was an "axis" around which the individual centered his or her life while drinking, through the Twelve Steps the addict continues to center his or her life around alcohol, but in a different way: a way without chemicals. During the period of active chemical use the individual learned to center his or her life around the drug of choice (Brown, 1985). In order to avoid the danger of being deceived, the individual needs to learn a new way to openly relate to his or her addiction. But the addict must learn to do so in a way that allows him or her to achieve and maintain sobriety. According to Brown (1985), the Twelve Steps accomplish this by providing a structured program by which the individual continues to relate to his or her addiction while still being able to draw on the group for support and strength.

How Does AA Work?

One of the tenets on which AA rests is the belief that alcohol dependence is a spiritual disorder. "What was once called 'idolatry,' enlightened Westerners call addictions" (Yancey, 2003, p. 33). Within this context, the "idolater chooses things that may be good in themselves and grants to them a power they were never meant to have" (p. 33). Eventually, however, the object of the idolatry—in this case, alcohol—takes control of the individual's life.

In light of the fact that AA has been a social force in the United States for three-quarters of a century, there has been surprisingly little research into what elements of the 12-Step program are effective (Emrick, Tonigan, Montgomery, & Little, 1993). Charles Bufe (1988) offered three reasons he thought AA was effective, "at least for some people" (p. 55). First, AA provides a social outlet for its members. "Loneliness," as Bufe (1988) observed, "is a terrible problem in our society, and people will flock to almost *anything* that relieves it— even AA meetings" (p. 55, italics in original).

Second, AA allows its members to recognize that their problems are not unique (Alibrandi, 1978; Bufe, 1988). Through AA participation, the individual member is able to restore identity and self-esteem through AA's unconditional acceptance of its members, all of whom suffer from the same disease (Nace, 1997). Through this, each member of AA is able to discover a relatedness to others. Finally, AA can offer a proven path to follow that can "look awfully attractive when your world has turned upside down and you no longer have your best friend—alcohol—to lean on" (Bufe, 1988, p. 55). Thus, the AA program is able to offer the individual *hope*, at a time when he or she feels that there is nobody to turn to (Bean-Bayog, 1993; Nace, 1997). Even though hope is an essential part of recovery, one must wonder if, as Bufe (1988) concluded, "These things, especially the first two, are all that is really needed" (p. 55). Bufe's (1988) view, although perhaps accurate, would also appear to be rather limited. For AA seems to offer more than just a way to deal with loneliness or a way of relating to others.

Herman (1988) observed that 12-Step programs such as AA offer at least one more feature to the recovering addict: *predictability*. Consistency was one of the characteristics identified by Rogers (1974) as being of value in the helping relationship, and one must wonder if the predictability of AA is not one of the curative forces of this self-help group. However, this remains only a hypothesis.

The AA 12-Step program provides a format for "a planned spontaneous remission" (Berenson, 1987, p. 29) that is "designed so that a person can stop drinking by either education, therapeutic change, or transformation" (p. 30). Berenson (1987) speculated that as part of the therapeutic transformation inherent in AA participation, people would "bond to the group and use it as a social support and as a refuge to explore and release their suppressed and repressed feelings" (p. 30). Most certainly, these things are possible in the typical AA meeting, which is "generally characterized by warmth, openness, honesty, and humor" (Nace, 1987, p. 242), attributes that may promote personal growth. AA is thought to be "the treatment of choice" (Berenson, 1987, p. 27) for active alcoholics, although Brodsky (1993) disputed this claim. Brodsky's challenge to the AA 12-Step recovery model will be discussed later in this chapter.

Outcome Studies: The Effectiveness of AA

Many substance-abuse rehabilitation professionals view AA as being the single most important component of a person's recovery program. Indeed, at least one study found that AA participation was the *only* significant predictor of long-term recovery (McCaul & Furst, 1994). But in spite of this fact, AA is not without its critics (Brodsky, 1993; Marvel, 1995; Ogborne & Glaser, 1985; Uva, 1991). Indeed, virtually everything about AA has been challenged and/or defended. For example, there are those who suggest that AA "should be used only as a supportive adjunct to treatment" (Lewis, Dana, & Blevins, 1988, p. 151) and not considered "treatment" of alcoholism by itself. At the same time, there are those who argue that AA has many similarities to a therapeutic program of change and thus should be viewed as a form of treatment in its own right (Tobin, 1992).

It is surprising, in light of the controversy that surrounds AA, that there has been very little empirical research into its effectiveness (Watson et al., 1997) or for what types of people it might be most useful (Galanter, Castaneda, & Franco, 1991; George & Tucker, 1996; McCaul & Furst, 1994; Tonigan & Hiller-Sturmhofel, 1994). Unfortunately, the very nature of AA makes it virtually impossible to carry out a well-designed outcome study that might help isolate the effective elements of the AA program (Gernstein, 2003). Within the recovering community, questions have been raised as to whether AA is necessary for every individual with an alcohol- or drug-use problem (Peele, 1989; Peele, Brodsky, & Arnold, 1991). However, even critics of AA seem to accept that it might be helpful at least to some, but not necessarily all, of those who have a problem with chemicals (Brodsky, 1993; Ogborne & Glaser, 1985).

It has been pointed out that those who join and who remain in AA are *not* a representative sample of all who are dependent on alcohol (Galanter et al., 1991). Only certain people elect to join and remain in AA of their own free will. Thus, the members of AA are different from alcohol-dependent individuals who choose not to join AA, or those who join but do not remain active.[2] Further, member retention is a significant problem. *At least half* of those who join stop going to meetings

---

[2]Yet, as the reader will recall, it was on data obtained from members of AA that Jellinek (1960) based his model of alcoholism.

within 3 months, and at the end of 1 year, 95% of the new members will have dropped out (Dorsman, 1996; Nace, 2003). Proponents point out that 70% of those who abstain from alcohol for 1 year will still be alcohol free at the end of their second year, whereas 90% of those who abstained from alcohol for 2 full years were still alcohol free at the end of their third year of AA participation. But these statistics belie the fact that only 2% of those individuals who initially join AA will be alcohol free at the end of 2 years (Dorsman, 1996). However, abstinence rates for those individuals who begin and maintain their involvement in AA over an 8-year period were found to be very similar to those obtained with a sample of alcohol-dependent individuals who entered formal treatment programs (Timko, Moos, Finney, & Lesar, 2000). Nace (2003) referred to national surveys showing that the average AA member has 84 months of recovery, and that 18% have been alcohol free for more than 5 years whereas 30% have less than 1 year of recovery to their credit.

One factor that seems to predict relapse is not *participating* in 12-Step program meetings, with those who are less active in meetings being most likely to relapse (Chappel & DuPont, 1999; Gitlow, 2001). Unfortunately, it is not uncommon to learn that although a given individual claims to have "attended" several 12-Step group meetings, she or he "sat in the back of the room, arrived late, left early, never spoke with anyone, and didn't have a sponsor" (Gitlow, 2001, p. 172). Thus, involvement in AA meetings must be measured by a standard other than simple attendance.

In spite of the limitations of research to date, Humphreys and Moos (1996) concluded that "alcohol self-help organizations may promote positive outcomes in alcohol-dependent individuals and may also take a significant burden off the public and private health care sectors" (p. 712).

Another factor closely related to active involvement is the *frequency* with which a person attends AA meetings (Watson et al., 1997). There is a positive relationship between AA attendance following discharge from inpatient treatment and continued abstinence from chemicals (Brigham, 2003; Morgenstern, Labouvie, McCrady, Kahler, & Frey, 1997; Nace, 2003; Watson et al., 1997). AA involvement appears to reflect some of the same forces that predicted the individual's efforts to make meaningful personality changes, such as

attempting to learn more effective ways to cope with stress (Morgenstern et al., 1997).

One popular belief is that life stressors trigger increased alcohol use. Although suggestive, this theory actually is misleading. Miller and Harris (2000) found that a sense of general depression and demoralization seemed to be predictive of relapse in those individuals who had successfully completed treatment. If people feel overwhelmed by the stressors they face, they are more likely to engage in increased alcohol use or abuse. Further, increased alcohol use seems to *predate the development of many stressors*, which then set the stage for even more alcohol use (Humphreys, Moos, & Finney, 1996). Active involvement in AA seems to allow the individual to begin to develop a support system that is both nondrinking and seeks to help the individual cope with his or her problems without encouraging him or her to drink, thus breaking the cycle of drinking and ineffectual coping.

The results of these studies are suggestive, but there is still insufficient evidence to conclude that AA is effective in the treatment of alcoholism at this time (Hester, 1994; Holder, Longabaugh, Miller, & Rubonis, 1991). Even if future research proves that AA is an effective tool in the rehabilitation of the problem drinker, the majority of alcohol-dependent individuals never join an AA group (Bean-Bayog, 1993). This may be because AA "is not effective for *all* kinds of persons with alcohol problems" (Ogborne & Glaser, 1985, p. 188). At best, it would appear that AA is most effective with a subset of problem drinkers: those socially stable white males, over 40 years of age, who are physically dependent on alcohol, prone to guilt, and the firstborn or only child.

But this picture of the person who is most likely to benefit from AA membership is only the first preliminary effort to identify the "typical" AA member. Research does suggest that individuals with stronger religious beliefs and/or a severe addiction to alcohol are more likely to attend AA meetings (Weiss et al., 2000). Research also indicates that approximately 35% of the members of AA are women, and among members under the age of 30, 43% are women (Coker, 1997).

Surprisingly, in light of how often individuals are required to attend AA meetings by the courts, there is little evidence that this approach is effective (Clark, 1995; Hester & Squires, 2004; Humphreys & Moos,

1996; Miller, Andrews, Wilbourne, & Bennett, 1998). The practice of requiring the individual to attend AA meetings has been cited as one factor that has changed the AA movement itself (Humphreys & Moos, 1996). Further, there is evidence that individuals who face legal consequences as a result of driving while intoxicated (i.e., were sent to jail or were placed on probation) seem to have better subsequent driving records (i.e., fewer accidents or further arrests) than those "sentenced" to treatment (Bufe, 1998; Peele et al., 1991). These findings raise questions about the effectiveness of court-ordered participation in AA or similar 12-Step groups for individuals who are convicted of driving while under the influence of alcohol.

Ultimately, the issue of whether AA is effective is far too complex to be measured by a single research study (Glaser & Ogborne, 1982; Ogborne, 1993). The very nature of AA ensures that there will be vast differences between different AA groups, even though they all share the same name (Ogborne, 1993). There continues to be a need for well-controlled research studies designed to identify all the variables that might influence the outcome of AA participation (McCrady & Irvine, 1989). Thus, the very nature of the question "Is AA effective?" makes it unanswerable. For example, would the chronic alcoholic who, as a result of participation in AA, stopped drinking on a daily basis, but then began a pattern of binge drinking, be measured as a successful outcome or as a failure? Would the chronic alcohol user who entered AA, stopped drinking, but died of alcohol-induced liver disease 6 weeks later, be a successful or unsuccessful outcome? These examples illustrate how the question "Is AA effective?" is unlikely to generate a meaningful answer (Ogborne & Glaser, 1985). A more meaningful approach would be to attempt to identify which types of people are most likely to benefit from 12-Step programs such as AA.

Narcotics Anonymous

In 1953, another self-help group patterned after AA was founded called Narcotics Anonymous (NA). This group honors its debt to Alcoholics Anonymous while recognizing differences:

> We follow the same path with only a single exception. Our identification as addicts is all-inclusive in respect to any mood-changing, mind-altering substance.

> "Alcoholism" is too limited a term for us; our problem is not a specific substance, it is a disease called "addiction." (Narcotics Anonymous World Service Office, 1982, p. x)

To the members of NA the problem is the disease of addiction. This self-help group emerged for those whose only "common denominator is that we failed to come to terms with our addiction" (Narcotics Anonymous World Service Office, 1982, p. x). Many outsiders, however, view the major difference between AA and NA as being one of emphasis. Alcoholics Anonymous addresses only alcoholism; NA addresses addiction to chemicals in addition to alcohol.

The growth of NA has been phenomenal, with a 600% increase in the number of NA groups from 1983 to 1988 (Coleman, 1989). There are more than 25,000 chapters of NA in the United States with about 250,000 active members (Ringwald, 2002). Alcoholics Anonymous and Narcotics Anonymous are not affiliated with each other, although there is an element of cooperation between these organizations (M. Jordan, personal communication, February 27, 1989). Each follows a similar 12-Step program offering the addicted person a day-by-day program for recovery. This is understandable, as NA is essentially an outgrowth of AA.

There are no inherent advantages of one program over the other. The most important point is this: Which group works best for the individual? Some people feel quite comfortable going to AA for their addiction to alcohol. Other people feel that NA offers them what they need to deal with their addiction. In the end, the name of the group does not matter as much as the fact that it offers the recovering person the support and understanding that he or she needs to abstain for today.

Al-Anon and Alateen

The book *Al-Anon's Twelve Steps & Twelve Traditions* (1985) provides a short history of Al-Anon in its introduction. According to this history, while their husbands were at the early AA meetings, the wives would often meet to wait for them. As they waited, they would talk over their problems. At some point, they decided to try applying the same Twelve Steps that their husbands had found so helpful to their own lives, and the group known as *Al-Anon* was born.

In the beginning, each isolated group made whatever changes it felt necessary in the Twelve Steps. However, by 1948 the wife of one of the co-founders of AA became involved in the growing organization, and in time a uniform family support program emerged. This program, known as the Al-Anon Family Group, borrowed and modified the AA Twelve Steps and Twelve Traditions to make them applicable to the needs of families of alcoholics. Unfortunately, although joining Al-Anon is the most common recommendation for spouses of alcohol-abusing individuals, there is limited research into its effectiveness (O'Farrell, 1995). Little is known about the characteristics of an effective Al-Anon group or the successful Al-Anon member. Thus, although Al-Anon is viewed as a resource for the spouse of the alcohol-abusing individual, its effectiveness is still not proven.

By 1957, in response to the recognition that teenagers presented special needs and concerns, Al-Anon itself gave birth to a modified Al-Anon group for teens known as *Alateen*. Alateen members follow the same Twelve Steps outlined in the Al-Anon program. The goal of the Alateen program, however, is to provide the opportunity for teenagers to come together to share their experiences, discuss current problems, learn how to cope more effectively with their various concerns, and provide encouragement to each other (*Facts About Alateen*, 1969).

Through Alateen, teenagers learn that alcoholism is a disease; they are helped to detach emotionally from the alcoholic's behavior while still loving the individual. The goal of Alateen is also to help the teen members learn that they did not cause the alcoholic to drink and to see that they can build a rewarding life in spite of the alcoholic's continued drinking (*Facts About Alateen*, 1969).

Support Groups Other Than AA

Criticism has been aimed at the AA program for its emphasis on spiritual growth, its failure to empower women, and its basic philosophy. Several new self-help groups have emerged since 1986 to offer alternatives to AA.

Self Management and Recovery Training (SMART):[3] SMART was founded in 1985 and initially was part of the Rational Recovery (RR) movement. But SMART is a splinter group that broke away from RR in 1994 (Chappel & DuPont, 1999; Horvath, 2000). Currently, it is estimated that SMART has more than 350 groups around the United States meeting each week, and it offers 15 online meetings and a 24-hour-a-day online support group for members with access to the Internet (Bishop, 2002; Gernstein, 2003; Horvath, 2000).

The SMART program is an abstinence-oriented program that draws heavily on the cognitive-behavioral school of psychotherapy and stresses four points: (a) enhancing and maintaining the individual's recovery to abstain, (b) coping with thoughts/cravings about chemicals, (c), solving old problem behaviors through cognitive-behavioral techniques, and (d) developing a balance in one's lifestyle (Gernstein, 2003; Horvath, 2000). Within this perspective, alcoholism (or other drug abuse) is viewed as reflecting the impact of negative, self-defeating thought patterns (Ouimette, Finney, & Moos, 1997; Tonigan & Toscova, 1998). For example, members are encouraged to stop drinking as a sign of self-respect, as opposed to drinking in order to feel good about themselves. Groups are advised by mental health professionals and strive to help the individual addict identify and correct self-defeating ways of viewing "self" and the world.

Gorski (1993) identified two general irrational thought patterns that contribute to the individual's substance use. The first of these was termed *addictive thinking* (p. 26), defined as the individual's use of irrational thoughts to support a claim that he or she has a "right" to use chemicals and that his or her chemical use is not the cause of the problems facing the person. The second set of irrational thoughts used to support substance use were *relapse justifications* (p. 26). These were specific thoughts used by the individual to justify his or her return to chemical use. Examples of this kind of thinking are "I *can't cope* with the stress without having a drink!," or "I *should* be able to drink, just like everybody else."

SMART groups assume that virtually any approach to rehabilitation will be of some value to the individual and thus encourage participation in traditional 12-Step groups (Horvath, 2000). In a comparison of the effectiveness of traditional 12-Step programs and cognitive-behavioral (CB) treatment approaches, Ouimette et al. (1997) discussed the results of a multicenter experiment involving 3,018 patients who were being treated for

---

[3]Steinberger (2001) gave the Internet address for this organization as: www.smartrecovery.org.

substance-use problems at one of 15 selected Veterans Administration Hospitals in the United States. Participants in this study were assigned to one of three treatment conditions: "pure" 12-Step treatment, "pure" CB treatment, or a mixed CB/12-Step format. Participants were interviewed after 1 year's time to determine their employment and substance-use status. The authors concluded that "pure" cognitive-behavioral and 12-Step programs were equally effective in helping people address substance-use problems. This study thus supported treatment approaches such as the SMART program for persons with substance-use problems.

In terms of those who seem to be best suited to SMART groups, research suggests that they are people with an internal locus of control (Gernstein, 2003). Such people tend to avoid passive recovery programs, although 10% of SMART program members also attend more traditional 12-Step programs such as AA (Gernstein, 2003). The program is not used for treating adolescents but is intended mainly for adults, but there are efforts under way to determine whether the SMART group approach might be used with adolescents with substance-use problems in its current or a modified form.

Secular Organizations of Sobriety (SOS):[4] SOS was founded in 1986. By the late 1990s an estimated 2,000 SOS groups were meeting each week, and total membership was about 100,000 people (Chappel & DuPont, 1999; Ringwald, 2002), but the program was struggling in the eyes of some (Gernstein, 2003).

SOS was founded as a self-help group in reaction to the heavy emphasis on spirituality in AA and NA (Ringwald, 2002). SOS draws heavily from cognitive-behavioral psychotherapies, and its guiding philosophy stresses personal responsibility, the role of critical thinking in recovery, and the identification of the individual's specific "cycle of addiction" (Tonigan & Toscova, 1998). In contrast to the AA model, in which the individual must call on a higher power to achieve abstinence, SOS teaches that the individual has the potential within to learn how to live without alcohol (Ringwald, 2002). The program is neutral toward traditional 12-Step groups, and a significant portion of the members have attended a 12-step group (or are currently doing so).

Women for Sobriety (WFS):[5] WFS was founded in 1976 (Chappel & DuPont, 1999). There are approximately 300 WFS groups and about 5,000 active members in the United States (Ringwald, 2002). It is an organization specifically for women and was founded on the theory that the AA program failed to address the very real differences between the meaning of alcoholism for men and women. There are 13 core statements or beliefs aimed at providing the members with a new perspective on themselves. WFS places a great deal of emphasis on self-esteem and on building self-esteem for the member. Research suggests that about one-third of the members continue their involvement in AA, and that approximately the same percentage of members of WFS groups as AA groups learn to abstain from chemicals (Chappel & DuPont, 1999).

Unlike participants in traditional 12-Step groups, WFS members are encouraged to leave the group to live on their own when they feel they have recovered from their alcohol dependency (Ringwald, 2002). Thus, assessing the organization on only the basis of its small number of active members does not do it justice, as the program claims that an additional 36,000 individuals were members at one time or another. The program attempts to address stumbling blocks to recovery, such as guilt, shame, powerlessness, and depression, from the woman's perspective, and many members note that traditional 12-Step groups were designed to help *male* members or that they are male oriented.

Alcoholics Anonymous for Atheists and Agnostics (Quad A): Quad A is a 12-Step program that draws heavily from traditional AA (Rand, 1995). However, it tends to downplay the emphasis on religion found in traditional AA and thus is attractive to those whose beliefs do not include the possibility of a Supreme Being. The Quad A format places less emphasis on "letting go" of one's personal will and ego, features that make it attractive to many women (Rand, 1995). Further, in place of the emphasis on the "Power Greater than Ourselves" found in traditional AA meetings, Quad A stresses the forces in the individual's life that support recovery (Rand, 1995).

Quad A is found mainly in the Chicago area and had an estimated 400–500 members in the mid 1990s (Rand,

---

[4]Steinberger (2001) gave the Internet address for this organization as www.secularsobriety.org.

[5]Steinberger (2001) gave the Internet address for this organization as www.womenforsobriety.org.

1995). Whereas traditional AA meetings usually last about an hour, Quad A meetings might last for several hours, especially when members become involved in a heated discussion of a topic of interest to a number of those present. Only time will tell whether the Quad A format will spread across this country or remain a local phenomenon. For those in the Chicago area, it *does* offer an interesting alternative to traditional AA meetings.

Moderation Management (MM): MM was founded in 1993 (Chappel & DuPont, 1999) and has been quite controversial since its beginning. MM evolved out of the frustration of its founder, Shirley Kishline, with traditional alcohol-rehabilitation programs. Kishline felt that although she was referred to a traditional inpatient treatment program that placed great emphasis on 12-Step program involvement, her addiction to alcohol was apparently never firmly established in her mind. She initially recommended *moderation* as the most appropriate goal for her, on the grounds that she was a "problem drinker" (Kishline, 1996, p. 53) but not an "alcoholic." Ms. Kishline defined a problem drinker as a person who consumes no more than 35 drinks per week and has experienced only mild to moderate alcohol-related problems (Kishline, 1996). She rationalized in her book *Moderation Management*, published in 1994, that the chronic drinker was a person who was physically dependent on alcohol and who would, in the majority of cases, experience severe withdrawal symptoms when he or she stopped drinking (Shute & Tangley, 1997).

The goal of MM was to "provide a supportive environment in which people who have made the decision to reduce their drinking can come together to help each other change" (Shute & Tangley, 1997, p. 55). MM drew heavily on behavior modification principles used by professionals to help individuals learn how to change their behavior. The MM movement initially gained some acceptance in the United States and eventually meetings were held in 25 states. Critics of the MM movement suggested that members with actual alcohol-dependence problems would use the group as an excuse to continue trying to achieve "controlled" drinking. Note that the founder of MM, Shirley Kishline, renounced her objections to traditional 12-Step groups and accepted total abstinence as the treatment method of choice for her alcohol-use disorder (Vaillant, 2000). Shortly after taking this step, Ms. Kishline was involved in an alcohol-related motor vehicle accident in which a man and his 12-year-old daughter were killed when her truck struck theirs on an interstate highway (Noxon, 2002). Ms. Kishline's measured BAL was 0.260, more than three times the legal limit for the state of Washington. She was charged with and convicted of the crime of vehicular homicide.

Surprisingly, many of the goals of MM are consistent with the teaching of Alcoholics Anonymous (Humphreys, 2003). Further, research suggests that the vast majority of those who are drawn to MM have alcohol-related problems that are low in severity, have strong social supports, and show little interest in a program such as AA that advocates total abstinence as its goal (Humphreys, 2003). The program seems to be of some value to those who are indeed not dependent on alcohol, in the opinion of the author.

Criticism of the AA/12-Step Movement

Although the 12-Step movement has achieved an almost irreproachable status in the addictions recovery community, it is not without a small, vocal group of critics. Fletcher (2003) observed that although it is an article of faith that the alcohol-dependent person might be *recovering* but could never be fully *recovered* from alcoholism, the AA "Big Book" actually speaks several times of people having "recovered" from alcohol dependency. Indeed, it indicates that the individual might reach a point when he or she no longer needs to depend on AA.

Another criticism of the AA 12-Step program is that it is potentially "damaging, violative and ineffective" (Brodsky, 1993, p. 21) for many individuals. The author notes that while it might be a useful tool for some, AA is based on "a 19th century fundamentalist tradition" (p. 21) that is essentially conservative Protestant in nature. Such a program, when forced on many people, might prove more destructive than helpful (Brodsky, 1993). Further, the courts have ruled that AA is a religious movement and that, as such, attendance cannot be forced on the individual as this violates federal law (Peele, 2004a). Based on these rulings, programs cannot *require* participants to attend AA meetings.

It has also been suggested that the AA program is based on fear, demands conformity, and fails to affirm the individual (Gilliam, 1998). Although the AA 12-Step program has helped thousands of people, it was established in the 1930s. It might not meet the needs of addicted people of the next century because AA "was founded on the experiences of one hundred men and one token woman. All these men were white, privileged, and in Bill Wilson's own words, suffered from 'self-will run riot' " (p. 29). These individuals are hardly representative of all the different forms of alcoholism, and thus the program is not a "one size fits all" process. Originally, the AA program was designed to "completely deflate the [individual's] ego," on the assumption that false pride was a common characteristic of those who were addicted to alcohol. But this assumption might make AA inappropriate for many of those who struggle with chemical-use disorders at the start of the 21st century, as it is not clear that this core assumption continues to be common among those who have chemical-use disorders (Gilliam, 1998).

Other critics of the 12-Step movement note that the spiritual "awakening" of one of the founders of AA, William ("Bill") Griffith Wilson, was possibly based on his having received belladonna in helping him recover from the acute effects of alcohol intoxication under his physician's supervision (Bufe, 1998; Lemanski, 1997; Peck, 1993). Others object to the heavy emphasis that such programs place on a "higher power" (Marvel, 1995; Wallace, 2003). Because it was an outgrowth of an early 20th century religious movement, the 12-Step model accepts the necessity of an external, supernatural, "higher power" to which the individual must "surrender" if she or he is to learn how to abstain from drugs or alcohol (Gernstein, 2003).

It is interesting to note that what might be viewed as one of the more destructive elements of the 12-Step program, the need for spiritual desperation, is only rarely acknowledged as a possible problem (Gilliam, 1998; Lemanski, 1997). Yet any other form of psychological or psychiatric treatment that required the individual to experience the depths of despair and defeat, as is required in the experience of hitting bottom, would be branded as abusive by the mental health community. Indeed, the need to hit bottom has been challenged by Fletcher (2003).

Stanton Peele (1989, 1998) has pointed out a number of problems with the AA/12-Step model as it is currently used in the United States. For example, the program is based on an unproven theory about the cause of alcoholism first suggested by the physician Benjamin Rush in the 17th century. Another problem with the AA/12-Step model, according to Peele, is that

it points to those individuals who were *least* successful in dealing with their addiction on their own, the members who were able to recover through the use of the 12-Step program, as role models for new members. Yet these role models often are people who have had extended periods of failure and relapse before their ultimate recovery, behaviors that are hardly acceptable in most role models. It should also be noted that the goal of AA/12-Step programs, total abstinence, is only rarely achieved: Most alcohol-dependent individuals merely cut back on the amount of their alcohol use, and few achieve total abstinence (Peele, 1998).

Critics point out that many of the basic tenets of AA, such as the twin beliefs that (a) alcoholism will *always* grow worse without treatment and (b) people cannot cut back or quit drinking on their own are not supported by research data. Alcohol-dependent people rarely follow the downward spiral thought to be inescapable by AA. Further, the majority of those with alcohol-use problems often learn to control or discontinue drinking without formal intervention (Peele, 1989; Vaillant, 1983).

The manner in which the AA program is implemented has been characterized as a form of "indoctrination" (Bufe, 1998, p. 6). This theory is supported by the observation that up to 95% of inpatient treatment programs utilize some kind of 12-Step approach and that recovering staff are quite uninterested in treatment programs that do not utilize such an approach (Brigham, 2003).

Finally, many critics of AA have observed that the AA/12-Step model does not embrace the possibility of a cure (Fletcher, 2003; Gilliam, 1998; Lemanski, 1997). Indeed, the AA/12-Step model does not even incorporate the concept of *health*, according to Gilliam (1998). The only way for the program to be effective is for the individual to continue to attend meetings forever, although few people actually maintain their involvement in the organization for extended periods of time.

Summary

The self-help group Alcoholics Anonymous (AA) has emerged as one of the predominant forces in the field of drug-abuse treatment. Drawing on the experience and knowledge of its members, AA has developed a program for living that is spiritual without being religious and confrontive without using confrontation in the traditional sense of the word; it relies on no outside support, and many of its members believe it is effective in helping them stay sober on a daily basis.

The program for living established by AA is based on those factors that early members believed were important to their own sobriety. This program for living is known as the Twelve Steps. The Steps are suggested as a guide to new members. Emphasis is placed on the equality of all members, and there is no board of directors within the AA group.

Questions continue to arise as to whether AA is effective. Researchers agree that it seems to be effective for some people, but not for all of those who join. The problem of how to measure the effectiveness of AA is quite complex. A series of well-designed research projects to identify the multitude of variables that make AA effective for some people is needed.

In spite of these unanswered questions, AA has served as a model for many other self-help groups, including Narcotics Anonymous (NA). One of the central tenets of Narcotics Anonymous is that the alcohol focus of AA is too narrow for people who have become addicted to other chemicals, either alone or in combination with alcohol. Narcotics Anonymous sets forth the belief that addiction is a common disease that may express itself through many different forms of drug dependency. NA has established a Twelve-Step program based on the Twelve Steps offered by Alcoholics Anonymous and draws heavily from its parent, AA. But NA seeks to reach out to those whose addiction involves chemicals other than alcohol, and thus it avoids the strict alcohol focus of AA.

Other self-help groups that have emerged as a result of the AA experience have included Al-Anon and Alateen. Al-Anon emerged from informal encounters between the spouses of early AA members and strives to help the families of those who are addicted to alcohol. Alateen emerged from Al-Anon, in response to the recognition that adolescents have special needs. Both groups seek to help the member learn how to be supportive without being dependent on the alcoholic, and to learn how to detach from the alcoholic and his or her behavior.

CHAPTER THIRTY-FIVE

The Debate Around Legalization

Introduction

When the United States is not invading some sovereign nation—or setting it on fire from the air, which is more fun for our simple-minded pilots—we're usually busy "declaring war" on something here at home.

Anything we don't like about ourselves, we declare war on it. We don't do anything about it, we just declare war. "Declaring war" is our only public metaphor for problem solving. We have a war on crime, a war on poverty, a war on hate, a war on litter, a war on cancer, a war on violence, and Ronald Reagan's ultimate joke, the war on drugs. More accurately, the war on the Constitution. (Carlin, 2001, p. 109)

The comedian George Carlin is, in the opinion of many, at his best when he is poking fun at social trends. However, in a very real sense, the quotation at the beginning of this chapter is more of a joke on the general public than most people realize—for it is the truth. The "war" on drugs is almost 100 years old (Shenk, 1999). In terms of effectiveness, it has been compared to the Vietnam conflict of the 1960s and 1970s, in which the observation was made that to save a village from the enemy, one had to be prepared to destroy it (Simon & Burns, 1997). In much the same manner, the United States government seems to have adopted a policy of arresting and prosecuting its own citizens in order to protect them from the scourge of using compounds that it deems inappropriate. The goal of this process, the "war on drugs," is to stop illicit drug use, and it has been affirmed by every president for the past 60 years. Yet at the start of the 21st century, illicit drugs are more plentiful than they have ever been, and people are spending more for illicit drugs in this country than they do for cigarettes (Schlosser, 2003).

Future historians will look back on this most curious "war" and see that the form of the "enemy" is shaped by religious, social, and political forces that are only poorly understood; this war is fought with weapons proven to be ineffective, in which the rights of the majority have been trampled so that society can impose its will on those who are, in reality, only a small minority of the population. The most destructive chemicals, alcohol and tobacco, are for the most part exempt from attack, whereas relatively benign chemicals with high social disapproval ratings are subjected to multipronged assaults. Entire books have been devoted to the subject of the war on drugs and how it has manufactured "criminals" in this country. In this chapter, the debate over whether the time has come to legalize drugs will be discussed.

The Debate Over Medicalization

Although opponents of the medicalization of certain recreational drugs speak of this suggestion as if it were the *legalization* of these substances, in reality medicalization and legalization are two different concepts, which might best be viewed as shown in Figure 35.1.

If a physician were entitled to prescribe certain substances, such as marijuana, this would simply give that substance the same status as other prescription medications. It is not the full legalization of that substance but simply the use of a selected compound in the treatment of specific disease states. But the federal government's policy is that even conducting basic scientific research into possible medical benefits from compounds such as cannabis could be grounds for arrest. In effect, the

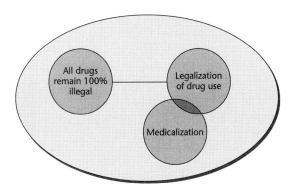

FIGURE 35.1 Medicalization and legalization as two different concepts.

government has adopted a policy affirming that (a) there are no proven uses for cannabis, and (b) you cannot do research into possible benefits from any compounds found in cannabis because of (a).

But the issue has become more complicated than this, for a federal judge has ruled that the Drug Enforcement Administration's threat to suspend a physician's license to write prescriptions was a violation of his or her First Amendment rights under the U.S. Constitution ("Medical Reprieve," 2003). Thus, the issue of whether some substances might be medicalized has become confused indeed.

The "War on Drugs": The Making of a National Disaster

What history could teach us. In the 1930s, the United States carried out an experiment in social reform known as Prohibition in which the nonmedicinal use of alcohol was prohibited by law.[1] Criminal elements, sensing a huge profit in meeting the demand for alcohol from those who desired it for personal recreational use, moved in to take control of the emerging supply and distribution network (Gray, 1998). Their motive was personal profit: At its height the alcohol black

market made up 5% of the entire gross national product of the United States during Prohibition (Schlosser, 2003). But business practices were often difficult in this era. Contract negotiations were frequently marked by gunfire, with those who resisted often receiving the benefit of a decent burial. Other marketing techniques included bribing officials to look the other way or to leave the bootleggers alone, and fighting between various distribution networks for control of markets.

One totally unanticipated change brought by Prohibition was that it forced people to switch from drinking beer to drinking hard liquor (Gray, 1998). In comparison to the bulk, low alcohol content, and short shelf life of beer, hard liquor had a high alcohol content, less bulk, and did not spoil. Before the start of Prohibition, alcohol users would "sip" alcoholic beverages throughout the day, or drink beer, without evidence of widespread intoxication (Barr, 1999; Gray, 1998). Following the start of Prohibition, drinkers shifted to a "binge" pattern of alcohol use: periods of heavy drinking interspaced with periods of abstinence, with intoxication being the goal of drinking (Barr, 1999; Gray, 1998). At the same time, alcohol users switched from beer to hard liquor, which produced the highest levels of intoxication in the least amount of time (Gray, 1998). In this manner, the "noble experiment" of Prohibition helped to shape the drinking habits of people for generations to come.

A similar process took place in the 1970s, although the parallels with the Prohibition era were not discovered until much later. Researchers now believe that the interdiction efforts against marijuana may have caused drug smugglers to switch from transporting marijuana to importing cocaine (Scheer, 1994a). This theory is based on the fact that pound for pound, cocaine is "less bulky, less smelly, more compact, and more lucrative" (Nadelmann, Kleiman, & Earls, 1990, p. 45) than marijuana. The prohibition against recreational cocaine use has also contributed to the wave of violence that spread across the United States in the late 1980s, as drug pushers fought over potential markets in a manner very similar to the way gang members during the Prohibition era fought for the right to distribute alcohol in city after city (Hatsukami & Fischman, 1996).

Another lesson from history can be drawn from the aftermath of the 1950s era efforts to deal with the drug-use problem. In the 1950s in the fight against narcotics abuse, Congress passed a series of mandatory

[1]One must question this nation's commitment to the experiment of Prohibition, in light of the fact that then-President Warren G. Harding, and the U.S. Senate both flouted the law by maintaining well-stocked supplies of liquor, which was supplemented by new shipments seized by customs agents (Walton, 2002).

minimum-sentence laws loosely called the Boggs Act (Schlosser, 1994). These laws imposed minimum prison sentences for the illicit use of narcotics in this country, and they met with almost universal acceptance.

In contrast to the general acceptance of the Boggs Act laws, then-director of the United States Bureau of Prisons James V. Bennett expressed strong reservations about the effectiveness of these laws. Although he had not personally broken any laws, Mr. Bennett, himself a federal employee, was subsequently followed by agents of the Federal Bureau of Narcotics, who submitted regular reports to their superiors on the content of speeches he gave (Schlosser, 1994). By the late 1960s, it was clear that Mr. Bennett was right: Mandatory sentencing did little to reduce the scope of narcotics use/abuse in this country. In 1970, the Boggs Act was replaced by a more sensible set of sentencing guidelines, which allowed a judge to assign appropriate sentences to defendants based on the merits of each individual case.

However, in one of the great reversals of all time, just 14 years later Congress again imposed mandatory prison sentences for drug-related offenses. The lessons of the past were once more forgotten. Through the Sentencing Reform Act of 1984, Congress mandated minimum prison terms. Even first-time offenders were sent to prison for extended periods without the hope of parole. One result of the Sentencing Reform Act of 1984 is that the prison system soon became filled with people serving lengthy mandatory sentences. In 1970, only 16% of all federal prisoners were incarcerated because of drug-related convictions; by 1994, fully 62% of those incarcerated in federal penitentiaries were there because of drug-related convictions ("The Drug Index," 1995; Nadelmann & Wener, 1994; Schlosser, 1994).

By the year 2001, the largest category of offenders, 21% of the estimated 1.32 million people in state prisons, were there because of drug-related convictions as opposed to the 13% incarcerated in various state prisons because of a conviction for murder or manslaughter (Doyle, 2001b). If those arrested and awaiting trial, who are under the supervision of the criminal justice system (CJS), are also counted, the CJS now holds more people with substance-use problems than are found in all the public and private treatment programs in the United States combined (DuPont, 2002). The total number of people arrested just for marijuana-related crimes (possession, etc.) in 2001 exceeds the total arrested for murder, manslaughter, forcible rape, robbery, and aggravated assault combined ("Marijuana Arrests," 2003).

In retrospect, like the Boggs Act, the Sentencing Reform Act of 1984 has been a dismal failure. Many of those incarcerated for drug-related crimes are first-time offenders who have never had a prior conviction for *any* offense, who are sentenced to serve terms that are not proportional to the offense. Consider, for example, that although the offender who is convicted of intentional homicide is usually sentenced to life in prison, "the average sentence *served* for murder in the U.S. is six and a half years, while eight years with no possibility of parole is *mandatory* for the possession of 700 marijuana plants" (Potterton, 1992, p. 47, italics added for emphasis). As another example of the unfair nature of the sentences imposed on first-time drug offenders, an employee caught embezzling between $10 million and $20 million from a bank would be sentenced to prison for 5 years. This is the same sentence a person would receive for possession of 5 grams of crack cocaine (Bovard, 1997).

If only we listened. Historians may very well conclude that the reason the war on drugs raged for much of the 20th century lies not in the destructive potential of the chemicals being abused but on the irrational beliefs of those in command, beliefs that are often blindly applied to the problems of society. In spite of the lessons from the Prohibition era, the process of drug interdiction has become one of the most enduring features of the war on drugs. The modern war on drugs was shaped by President Richard Nixon in the early 1970s and reflects his personal beliefs that (a) people who drink do not consume alcohol for its intoxicating effects but only for fun, and (b) people who used marijuana were mainly those who were against the then-current Vietnam conflict and thus were interested in the spread of communism (Zeese, 2002). The antidrug efforts of the Nixon administration also had covert racial undertones that have only recently been discovered by historians (Zeese, 2002).

But even this knowledge has not influenced the onward march toward stupidity. For example, a centerpiece of the current war on drugs is interdiction. The possibility that drug interdiction could be an effective response to the problem of drug abuse/addiction overlooks the fact that on a worldwide level the production and distribution of illicit drugs is a $400 billion a year industry (United Nations, 1997). The criminal groups involved use both bribery and violence to make sure their drugs reach willing buyers (Gray, 1998). Only a very small percentage of the illicit drugs sent to the United States are ever confiscated by law-enforcement officials; drug interdiction results in only short-term, local reductions in the supply of certain chemicals, and these are rapidly corrected by market pressures.

The policy toward interdiction of drugs ignores the fact that

> the more "effective" police activity is, the more [drug] prices rise, increasing the profits of smuggling, and the more likely it will be that drug purity and concentration will also increase, to make importation more cost-effective and detection more difficult. (Manderson, 1998, p. 589)

This was a lesson that law-enforcement officials could have learned from the Prohibition era if only they had bothered to study its history and its effects. *If* drug interdiction were to prove effective, it would only increase the profit margin of those who engaged in providing recreational chemicals for people who desire them.

As a result of the prohibition against recreational drugs, their production, distribution, and sale are for the most part carried out by people who are, by definition, criminals. As was the case with alcohol during the Prohibition era, a black market has evolved to ensure that these chemicals are available to potential users for a price (Buckley, 1996; McWilliams, 1993; Nadelmann, 1989; Nadelmann & Wenner, 1994; Walton, 2002). In a process quite similar to alcohol distribution in the Prohibition era, the price for drugs is rigidly controlled by the operators of the supply and distribution network in return for risking criminal prosecution for bringing the drugs into this country, usually to a major city, from where they are funneled to outlying regions (Furst, Herrmann, Leung, Galea, & Hunt, 2004). For this, the modern drug supplier at each level demands a significant profit margin. In the mid 1990s, the supply and distribution network was estimated to generate $50 to $60 billion in *profits* each year in the United States alone (Nadelmann & Wenner, 1994).

The profit margin for illicit drugs is illustrated by the fact that a patch of ground the size of a pool table can yield $250,000 worth of cannabis in a year at current market prices (Walton, 2002). Another measure of the effectiveness of the war on drugs in the latter part of the 20th century is the drop in the cost of a gram of cocaine or heroin on the streets (see Figure 35.2). As these graphs illustrate, the cost of both cocaine and heroin declined significantly from 1981 to 2000. At the same time, however, the *potency* of the substances being sold increased significantly (see Figure 35.3).

The information summarized in the two figures suggests that the war on drugs has been a dismal failure, given that the price for heroin or cocaine in 2000 was only a fraction of what it was 20 years earlier, whereas the potency per gram of each substance was many orders of magnitude greater than in 1981. Another, admittedly unintended consequence of the prohibition against illicit drug use is that law-enforcement agencies have become "addicted" to the money invested in the "war on drugs" (Leavitt, 2003). Further, the war contributes to the problem of police corruption.

The forfeiture fiasco. During the administration of President Reagan in the 1980s, Congress enacted a law that allows authorities to confiscate property purchased with money made from the illicit drug trade. It was not necessary for the authorities to *prove* that drug money had been used to purchase the property in question or that any money confiscated was the result of illicit drug trade activities. To justify the seizure, the authorities just had to voice their *suspicion* that the individual had gained the money or property from illegal drug sales. The goal was to prevent drug dealers from being able to profit from their illegal activities.

Since taking effect, the "forfeiture" laws have been widely abused. Some police departments now *depend* on money and property seized under federal drug forfeiture provisions of the antidrug laws for at least part of their operating budget. To show the level of abuse, up to 80% of the money seized by federal authorities comes from people who are *never* indicted for criminal acts, much less convicted (Leavitt, 2003). Police officials in at least two states (Florida and Louisiana) have been known to use minor traffic offenses as a pretense to confiscate money from motorists who had committed no illegal act other than the traffic rules violation (Leavitt, 2003).

The forfeiture laws do contain a simple provision that allows the citizen whose property was seized to seek its return. The individual must file a lawsuit against the police agency that seized the money or property and

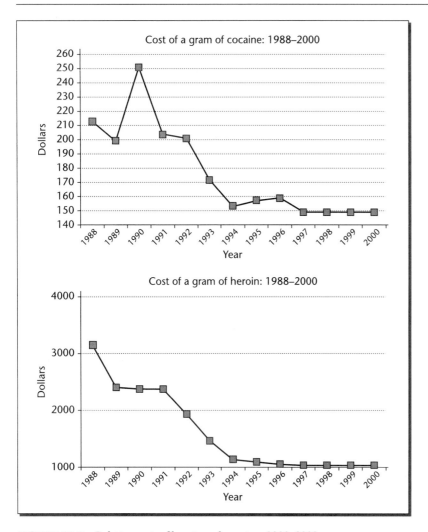

FIGURE 35.2   Relative costs of heroin and cocaine: 1988–2000.
Source: Based on information provided by Office of National Drug Control Policy (2002).

then *prove* in a court of law that the seized items were not obtained as a result of participation in illegal drug-related activities. This process is expensive and time-consuming, and the final cost might be several times that of the property or money seized by the authorities, who are not required to pay any kind of interest to claimants who can prove to the court that they are the rightful owners. Few people are willing to pay $4,000 in legal fees, for example, to prove that the $1,000 seized by police was rightfully theirs, and thus many people who have had money or property seized by the authorities do not attempt to get it back.

The war on drugs as political nonsense. The irrational nature of the "war" against drug use is such that politicians can now score political points by simply making the claim that their opponent is "soft" on drugs (Maher, 2002). This claim does not have to be proven correct; one politician simply has to hint that the opponent does not have a strong stand on drugs to undermine that person's campaign for office.

Another example of the irrational nature of the war on drugs is the federal government's program to spray defoliants on Colombian crop land where cocaine is being grown. This is done with the blessing of the

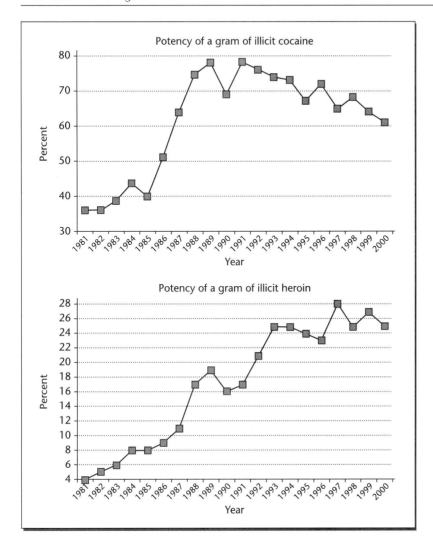

FIGURE 35.3 Relative potencies of heroin and cocaine: 1981–2000.
Source: Based on information provided by Office of National Drug Control Policy (2002).

Colombian government, after appropriate bribes and contributions are made to the ruling party. But

it's got to be done, because some of the plants that grow in the southern hemisphere are just plain evil. We know that because they're not stamped with labels like Bristol-Meyers Squibb, Eli Lilly or Pfizer. And it's vital that we understand that these southern hemisphere plants and their cultivators are to blame because the alternative is to believe that our national appetite for drugs is our own problem. And that's just plan crazy talk. (Maher, 2002, p. 49)

So, rather than for politicans to admit that it is our *demand* for drugs such as cocaine that is the problem, we spray defoliants on hundreds of thousands of acres of land in far-off Colombia, destroying entire ecospheres in the process. But the demand for cocaine is still there, so the farmers just move over into the next valley to plant a new crop of coca for next year's harvest. They are, after all, just trying to grow a cash crop that they can sell to feed their children and buy the basic necessities of life—which obviously is a good reason to spray poisons on them, at least in the eyes of some.

Manufacturing criminals. Some have argued that the war on drugs reflects the tactics and philosophy of World War I being applied to the issue of drug abuse in the 21st century (Walton, 2002). Just as the generals of that long-ago conflict kept sending wave after wave of soldiers into the killing fields created by recently invented machine guns, so do the modern generals of public order send greater and greater numbers of citizens to jail or prison in the name of the public good. Indeed, the analogy is quite apt, for the generals of public order often call their struggle a "war" on drugs, while sending not the drugs to prison, but those who abuse them.

Another example of drug-related irrationality is the controversy surrounding urine toxicology testing in the workplace. Employers often argue that even the smallest trace of a drug of abuse in an employee's urine after an accident is evidence of drug-induced impairment, an argument that is both unfounded and widely believed ("Predicting Drug-related Impairment," 2004). In such a case, the *employee* would be blamed for the accident, not unsafe working conditions. But imagine a situation in which two different employees had the same accident at work on successive days. One, who is being treated for attention deficit hyperactivity disorder (ADHD), had a prescription for an amphetamine compound, which was detected in his urine but not viewed as evidence of impairment because it was a prescribed pharmaceutical. The second employee might have traces of the same amphetamine compound in his urine because of a false positive test resulting from use of pseudoephedrine to control the symptoms of an allergy. The latter employee might lose his job in this hypothetical example because the initial positive test result was not confirmed with more expensive follow-up testing, whereas the first employee might have no action taken against him even though the urine test does not reveal that he was abusing the prescribed medication by taking more than the prescribed amount for the "buzz."

The war on drugs is thus quite complicated. As the number and type of intoxicants available to the general public has grown, the "repertoire of sanctions against them has grown more invasive and prohibitive" (Walton, 2002, p. 225). Those who engage in recreational drug use are, as a result of the war, classified as criminals, an action that effectively turns what had been a medical problem into a legal issue. Because these compounds have been stamped illegal, individuals who indulge in

their use become, by definition, criminals who face sanctions from the legal system. This general policy, in effect since the 1930s, has proven to be ineffective in the battle against recreational chemical use (Gray, 1998; Nadlemann, 2002; Walton, 2002), yet it remains a centerpiece of the government's efforts to eliminate drug use and abuse in the 21st century.

Some political observers have suggested that personal, recreational drug use (as opposed to distribution of illicit chemicals to others) is simply a consensual crime, on the grounds that the individual who is using a recreational chemical has made a conscious choice to do so in a manner that does not hurt others (McWilliams, 1993; Royko, 1990; Walton, 2002). By classifying individual drug use a consensual crime, it might be possible to avoid the "gun battles, the corruption and the wasted money and effort trying to save the brains and noses of those who don't want them saved" (Royko, 1990, p. 46).

One possible solution to the drug-use problem is to legalize recreational drugs, possibly with restrictions by the authorities as to who might dispense the compounds. This would allow some measure of control over who has access to drugs and at what age they might be allowed to use them, in much the same manner that access to alcohol is restricted by law. A benefit of this approach is that the compounds would at least be available to the person who wished to "sniff away his nose or addle his brain" (Royko, 1990, p. 46), without branding as criminals large numbers of citizens who engage in this consensual act.

But such commonsense suggestions are drowned by the strident cry that we *must* protect the public from their own impulse to engage in recreational drug use. To obtain the money necessary to buy the drugs to feed their addiction, many people are forced to steal, engage in burglary, armed robbery, prostitution (heterosexual and homosexual), car theft, forgery, drug sales (itself a crime), and a range of other crimes.

People who support their drug use through theft will receive only a fraction of the stolen material's worth when they sell it; they must steal more and more so that the pittance they receive for the stolen property will meet their drug needs. It has been estimated that the typical heroin addict in an average city would need to steal some $200,000 worth of goods annually to support a drug habit (Kreek, 1997). In this way, the national prohibition against the drugs of abuse might be said to have contributed to the wave of crime that plagues this nation.

The reason so many otherwise unremarkable citizens have been classified as criminals is quite complex and certainly does not reflect the pharmacological potential for harm inherent in the recreational chemicals. For example, in the 1980s President Ronald Reagan was quite frustrated with the apparent widespread flouting of civil authority inherent in recreational drug use. Ignoring the lessons learned during the reign of the "Boggs age" (discussed earlier in this chapter), he called for a "zero tolerance" program in the early 1980s. Just a few years later, in 1988, Congress passed a resolution calling for a "drug-free" America by 1995 (Nadlemann, 2002). Legal sanctions and incarceration were immediately imposed on those who were convicted of a drug-related criminal offense, even if the crime was the possession of only a single seed of a marijuana plant. Mandatory sentencing provisions were also applied in cases where the individual had used a controlled substance. The goal of such zero tolerance programs is to make substance use "as dreadful as possible in order to discourage others from engaging in drug experimentation" (Husak, 2004, p. 427). Unfortunately, such programs have proven to be dismal failures: By 1995 this nation enjoyed a greater quantity and quality of illicit drugs than had existed at any point before the passage of the "zero-tolerance" laws.

But it should be noted that President Reagan's stance on recreational drug abuse was not motivated by the potential for harm found in the compounds being abused. If this were true, alcohol and tobacco products would have been the target of his wrath as well. These substances were noticeably absent from his zero-tolerance program, and the fact that it has been a dismal failure has been quietly ignored by historians. To illustrate, one need only examine the arrest statistics in the last 20 years of the 20th century compared with the problem of heroin and cocaine abuse. In that period, "imprisonment for drug dealing . . . increased about tenfold, but the prices of cocaine and heroin [fell to] about 25% of 1980 levels" (Harrell & Kleiman, 2002, p. 150). There is such a glut of cocaine flowing into the United States at the start of the 21st century, compared with the amount smuggled into this country in the early 1980s, that even if law-enforcement officials

were to seize 50% of it, the price of illicit cocaine on the street would probably increase by only about 5% (Walton, 2002). This was promptly demonstrated by the U.S.-funded coca plant eradication program in Colombia (discussed earlier), which by 2003 had resulted in a 38% reduction in the number of coca plants available for harvest. Yet the price of cocaine in the United States remained unchanged ("Coca Leaf Production Decreases in Colombia," 2003).

The mandatory sentencing of drug offenders and the whole war on drugs has become an abject example of how the lessons of history are ignored in order to continue the war. In the years following World War II, some heroin dealers in this country were actually executed in an attempt to stem the tide of narcotics abuse (Walton, 2002). The number of abusers continued to increase, however, and the practice of execution was soon discontinued. But by the 1980s lawmakers were discussing the possibility of reintroducing the death penalty for drug dealers as a deterrent, in spite of its proven lack of effectiveness.

Mandatory sentencing is based on the assumption that it is possible to "arrest your way out of the [drug abuse] problem" (Simon & Burns, 1997, p. 164). Unfortunately, this policy ignores the truism that it is impossible to punish an undesirable behavior out of existence (Husak, 2004; Lundeen, 2002). Mandatory sentencing has resulted in the need for habitual and violent prisoners to be released from prison in order to make room for *first-time* offenders convicted and sentenced under mandatory drug-enforcement laws (Asseo, 1993; Potterton, 1992). If the existing federal laws against drug possession or use were to be fully implemented, the U.S. government would have to build a new 650-bed prison *every month* just to house those convicted of violating only the *federal* antidrug laws ("Ibogaine and Minimum Sentencing," 1994).

Other critics of the mandatory sentencing laws for possession of illegal substances point out that the small-time user is usually the victim of a lengthy mandatory prison term (Steinberg, 1994).[2] In spite of the intent of the law (which was intended to punish those involved

---

[2]This is not always the case, however. When the son of Indiana Congressman Dan Burton was arrested and found to have 8 pounds of marijuana in the trunk of his car and 30 marijuana plants in his apartment, he was simply placed on probation.

in drug distribution), mid-level and upper-level suppliers are frequently able to bargain their knowledge of who is buying drugs from them for lighter prison sentences. Thus, the

> former hippie with 1,000 marijuana plants growing in his basement and no drug ring to rat on gets the full decade in prison, while the savvy dealer bringing in boatloads of pot from south of the border can finger a few friends and be out in half the time. (Steinberg, 1994, p. 33)

In 2003, the U.S. prison population reached a staggering 2.17 million people (Mailer, 2004). As a result of the mandatory sentencing requirements, fully 52% of this number are drug users or those who "deal" on the streets, whereas only 11% might be classified as major suppliers (Dwyer 2000; Petersen, 1999).

The war on drugs' racial bias. The Sentencing Reform Act of 1984 had a racial/class bias built into it. Cocaine hydrochloride, which is usually sold as a *powder*, is abused mainly by middle-class users whereas crack is found most often in the ghetto areas. Federal sentencing guidelines require that a first-time offender with 5 grams of crack be sentenced to prison for 5 years; a first-time offender would need to have *500* grams of cocaine hydrochloride on his or her possession to receive a similar sentence (Hatsukami & Fischman, 1996). This distinction has contributed to inequities in prosecution and sentencing. For example, fully 90% of all those incarcerated in state and federal prisons for substance-related offenses during the administration of the first President Bush were either African American or Latino (Garrett, 2000).

The war on drugs as a drain on national resources. To underscore the cost of incarcerating individuals for drug-use related offenses, consider the following statistics: In 1972, the entire United States had an estimated 200,000 jail and prison cells. Currently, there are more than *two million* jail and prison cells in this country (Pepper, 2004). More than 400,000 people are incarcerated in state and federal prisons for violating one of the antidrug laws, a number that is 24% of the total number of people incarcerated in this country (MacCoun & Reuter, 1998; Nadelmann, 2002). At the start of the 21st century, many states are spending more for the construction of prison cells than they are for building college classrooms (Taylor, 2004).

It is expensive to keep a person in prison. The cost of incarcerating one individual for 1 year has been estimated as $35,000 to $70,000, depending on the inmate's status and the location of the prison (Kreek, 1997). If a median figure of $60,000 a year is used, assuming there are about 800,000 people in prison for drug-related offenses, then *$48 billion a year* is being spent just to keep already convicted drug offenders behind bars. Substance-abuse treatment programs are required to demonstrate their effectiveness in order to obtain funding; prisons, however, are not required to do so (MacCoun & Reuter, 1998; Smith, 2001). One consequence of not requiring prisons to demonstrate any form of effectiveness is that although 80% of those who are incarcerated have some form of a chemical-use problem, only 5% receive some form of substance-abuse treatment while in prison (Smith, 2001).

If it is such a failure, why does the war on drugs continue? This is a very difficult question to answer. It has been suggested that the war on drugs continues

> because it suits politicians to blame drug abusers for many of the social problems that currently beset America; by sounding tough on drugs they can sound tough on crime without having to address the real problems confronting the urban poor. (Barr, 1999, p. 304)

From this perspective, the war on drugs has continued as a form of political smokescreen, allowing those in power to use moral insecurities and false images of what is right to fool the population into spending money to protect itself from mythical dangers while avoiding the real problems facing society (Barr, 1999; Gray, 1998; Leavitt, 2003). As support for this hypothesis, the original draft of the Federal Omnibus Crime Bill called for criticism of the government's antidrug policies to be classified as *treason*, which would then become grounds for criminal prosecution (Leavitt, 2003).

Another reason the federal government might not really be interested in "winning" the war against drug use is that it provides money to fund covert activities by government agencies. History has repeatedly demonstrated that the Central Intelligence Agency (CIA) has allowed, and in some cases actually encouraged and supported, the drug trade in order to finance insurrections or armed conflict in various regions of the world (Leavitt, 2003). The heroin and cocaine grown in such places as Afghanistan and Central America eventually find their way to the United States, sometimes on aircraft supplied by the CIA (Leavitt, 2003). That one agency of the federal government has taken such action should not be surprising, as the United States government often holds itself exempt from laws passed to control the general population. During the Prohibition era, both Congress and the White House maintained their own bars, using supplies of alcohol seized by the Coast Guard to quench the thirst of its members (Walton, 2002).

Summary: The war on drugs. The war on drugs has continued through most of the 20th century, reaffirmed by every president, and although it has been a dismal failure, it has cost each man, woman, and child in the United States approximately $133 each year (Buckley, 1997). A *minimal* estimate of $150 billion was spent "fighting" the war on drugs at the federal level[3] in the last decade of the 20th century, with an additional $17.8 billion additional being devoted to this "war" in 2000 (Dwyer, 2000). Yet in spite of all this expenditure of time, energy, and resources, in many regions of the country it is now easier for high school students to buy marijuana than it is to buy beer (Bovard, 2001).

In return for this investment, the past 20 years have seen an erosion of traditional constitutional rights, and we are yet to become drug free (Elders, 1997). Indeed, there is a greater variety, and greater quantity, of illicit drugs available now than at any time in history (Bovard, 2001; Nadlemann, 2002).

As should be obvious by now, the social program to solve the drug-abuse problem through law enforcement and interdiction has been a failure. However, this does not stop law-enforcement officials from trumpeting the successes of the past year, or from hinting that, for just a few billion dollars more, it might be possible to eliminate the problem of recreational drug use in the United

States. Yet those who are openly calling the war on drugs a failure and are looking for alternatives to this social policy are ignored or called unrealistic.

The debate over legalization. It is in the environment outlined in the first part of this chapter that some citizens and political observers have suggested that perhaps at least some of the chemicals now deemed illegal should be legalized. But it is impossible to enter the debate to legalize some or all the drugs of abuse without becoming ensnared in the minefield of political agendas. The problem of drug abuse in the United States has reached the point that the military has been recruited to help law-enforcement authorities stem the flow of illicit drugs that are being purchased by citizens of this country. In effect, the military is now at war with the citizens (Walton, 2002), a sign that the issue of legalization is exceptionally complex.

Some have suggested, for example, that federal and state law-enforcement agencies *need* to keep marijuana classified as an illicit substance because marijuana abusers make up the bulk of those classified as "drug abusers" in the United States (Gray, 1998; Walton, 2002). If this group of people were to be reclassified as nonoffenders by the decision to legalize marijuana, then the number of illegal drug abusers in the United States would instantly drop from 13 million to just 3 or 4 million, a number that makes it difficult to justify the expenditure of so many billions of dollars on enforcement and interdiction (Dwyer, 2000; Gray, 1998; Walton, 2002).

Given the fact that some federal and state law-enforcement agencies justify their continued existence on the basis of a drug "problem," it should not be surprising to learn that some of these same law-enforcement agencies have been known to simply manufacture data for their official reports (Gray, 1998). In other instances, they have utilized questionable statistical methods to prove the need for their existence. In 1994, for example, "the Center on Addiction and Substance Abuse at Columbia University made the shocking announcement that marijuana smokers were eighty-five times more likely to go on to cocaine than nonsmokers" (Gray, 1998, p. 177). This figure has since been frequently cited as evidence that marijauna is a "gateway" drug, the use of which will place the user on a "slippery slope" to further drug abuse. Yet few people understand that this "fact" was uncovered

[3]Plus an unknown but sizable amount of money spent on the state and local level.

by "taking the estimated number of cocaine users who had smoked reefer first, and dividing it by the estimated number who hadn't (almost nobody)" (Gray, 1998, p. 177). Using such quasi-statistical methods, the author pointed out, it would be possible to "prove" that coffee, alcohol, tobacco, and apple pie were also "gateway" chemicals placing the individual on a slippery slope to further drug abuse.

Advocates of drug legalization point out that through legalization an important source of revenue for what is loosely called organized crime would be removed because the manufacture and transport of illicit drugs is an important source of income for criminal groups. Further, there is evidence that drugs would lose their appeal to adolescents and young adults if they were legal, as many of these individuals are drawn to substance use as a form of rebellion (Barr, 1999).

The theory that decriminalization of a substance such as cannabis would reduce substance abuse is based on the theory that "if the appeal of drugs lies in their prohibited status, then we must expect that cannabis will soon be as fascinating as a new set of tax guidelines [if decriminalized]" (Walton, 2002, p. 137). Partial evidence for this theory is found in the Netherlands, Spain, and Italy, countries that have decriminalized marijuana; in these countries the cannabis abuse pattern is virtually the same as in neighboring countries where it is prohibited (MacCoun & Reuter, 2001). In 2001 Portugal decriminalized the possession of all drugs, and there is evidence that Canada and England will decriminalize possession of marijuana (Schlosser, 2003). Many other countries in the European Union are following the Dutch example of allowing individuals to possess small amounts of marijuana for personal use (McAllister et al., 2001).

Another example of what might happen if drugs were legalized can be seen in New Zealand where there are no laws that prohibit minors from buying or consuming alcohol in public if they are with their parents. There is no minimum age requirement for the purchase of alcohol in Portugal and Belgium, and in France, Spain England, Austria, and Italy an adolescent might legally purchase alcohol at the age of 16 (Barr, 1999). In these countries, adults believe that adolescents should learn to drink within the context of their families in order to learn moderate, social drinking skills. In spite of this rather liberal pattern of

alcohol use, these countries have rates of child and adolescent alcohol abuse similar to those seen in the United States.

One alternative to the free-market legalization program envisioned by Frances (1991) would be that recreational drugs be made available through a physician's prescription (Lessard, 1989; Schmoke, 1997). This is a very similar approach to that adopted by England, where physicians who hold a special license may prescribe heroin to individuals proven to be addicted to it ("Rx Drugs," 1992). As a compromise for those who fear the impact of legalized marijuana, the medical journal *The Lancet* ("Deglamorising Cannabis," 1995) suggested the legalization of marijuana, with controls similar to those on the sale of tobacco, on the grounds that the criminal sanctions currently in place against marijuana only add a degree of glamor to its use.

Admittedly, chemical users might experience health problems. However, Curley (1995) suggested that insurance companies might be permitted to charge higher health insurance premiums for drug users, as they do now for cigarette smokers. These higher health care premiums would be to cover the expense of providing health care to people who engage in such high-risk behaviors as abusing recreational chemicals. In this way, access to the drugs could be limited while the profit incentive for organized crime would be removed. What Lessard (1989) suggested, in other words, is that the problem of drug abuse be approached from a health perspective as it is in the Netherlands and England.

In contrast to these positions, however, Walton (2002) suggested that one immediate consequence of legalization would be that the number of drug abusers might increase. The reduction in legal sanctions might encourage greater numbers of individuals to engage in the abuse of chemicals now prohibited by various laws. But even this price would not be unreasonable as large segments of society currently being criminalized for nothing more than attempting to fulfill their desire to become intoxicated would no longer run afoul of the legal system (Walton, 2002).

Other consequences of the prohibition against drug abuse. Medical sociologists have observed that because of the prohibition against drugs, the individual must use the limited supply of drugs under hazardous conditions. Various researchers have suggested that between 1%–3% (Drummer & Odell, 2001) and 2%–4% (Anthony, Arria, & Johnson, 1995) of heroin abusers die each year from violence or infection. This death rate is 6 to 20 times higher than that seen in nonusers (Drummer & Odell, 2001). The causes of death for intravenous drug abusers include drug overdose, infections (including AIDS), malnutrition, accidents, and violence. A likely consequence of legalization would be a decrease in such deaths, as people would stop engaging in the dangerous practices associated with illegal drug use.

Summary

Although legalization might not be the answer to the problem of alcohol/drug abuse in this country, it is clear that the current policy of interdiction and punishment of those who choose to violate the substance-use laws in the United States also has failed. There are no clear answers for how to address this problem, but it is clear that new social policies addressing substance use/abuse should be developed with the lessons from the past in mind.

CHAPTER THIRTY-SIX

Crime and Drug Use

Introduction

Social scientists have long known that there is a strong correlation between substance misuse and criminal activity. Unfortunately, correlation does *not* imply causality, and researchers continue to debate whether the drug use precedes criminal activity, or follows it, or if both criminal behavior and substance misuse might not reflect a third, unknown factor (McCollister & French, 2002; Moore, 1991; Newcomb, Galaif, & Carmona, 2001). The last theory suggests that individuals who are predisposed to crime might also be predisposed to the use of alcohol and/or drugs. This position is supported by research findings suggesting that 60% to 80% of those who break the law have abused recreational drugs at some point in their lives (Hartwell, 2004; McCollister & French, 2002). The debate over the relationship between criminal activity and substance abuse has been the subject of numerous books and learned essays on the subject. The argument over how much substance misuse contributes to criminal behavior raged through much of the 20th century and shows no sign of being resolved. In this chapter, the relationship between these two social phenomena—drug use and criminal activity—will be very briefly examined.

Criminal Activity and Drug Use: Partners in a Dance?

The problems of substance misuse and criminal behavior are hardly insignificant. It has been estimated that the economic impact of drug-related criminal activity in the United States alone is about $59.1 billion a year (Craig, 2004). The topic is thus quite controversial, with different schools of thought competing for attention. Depending on which facts one chooses to embrace, it is possible to argue that substance use is or is not a causal factor in criminal activity. Those who suggest that substance abuse *causes* crime overlook certain facts—for example, longitudinal studies have repeatedly found that deliquency usually *precedes* the development of substance-use problems, and whereas the individual might outgrow delinquent behaviors in the young adult years, she or he is less likely to outgrow the substance-use problems (Husak, 2004).

A different perspective on the relationship between criminal activity and chemical abuse was offered by Elliott (1992), who suggested that chemical abuse and criminal activity both reflect the "decline in the power of cultural restraints" (p. 599) taking place in this country. He supported his argument with the observation that Europe had experienced "tidal waves of crime" (Elliott, 1992, p. 599) every few decades since the 14th century. According to Elliott, a similar pattern has emerged here in the United States over the past 200 years. A common thread connecting these waves of crime is that in each successive period of social unrest, one could observe "an erosion of personal integrity, widespread dehumanization, a contempt for life, material greed, corruption in high places, sexual promiscuity, *and increased recourse to drugs and alcohol*" (p. 599, italics added for emphasis).

It is the contention of this text that there are multiple pathways between substance abuse and criminal activity, with drug-use problems both resulting from and predicting criminal behavior (Newcomb et al., 2001). Early drug abuse was found to predict later criminal activity in a community sample, and substance use was found to impair impulse control, contributing to the tendency for the individual to engage in socially inappropriate behavior. The authors found evidence that "a proneness toward criminality" (p. 190) was associated with substance-use problems, whereas limited support was found for the theory that both drug use and criminal activity reflected the impact of a third factor called "social conformity" (p. 191). Thus, there is no single pathway between substance abuse and criminality.

For those who point to the relationship between substance abuse and criminal behavior, the one substance that is legal, alcohol, is the substance most commonly involved in criminal activity (Husak, 2004). Twenty-one percent of individuals incarcerated for violent crimes were under the influence of alcohol alone at the time they committed the crime; only 3% were under the influence of cocaine alone, and 1% were under the influence of heroin alone (Husak, 2004). This fact is overlooked by those who wish to use the link between substance misuse and criminal behavior as justification for the harsh prison sentences awarded to those convicted of substance-related criminal activity.

Criminal activity and personal responsibility. The issue of personal responsibility in cases when the individual might have been under the influence of chemicals at the time of the offense is a difficult one. Unfortunately, it is a very real issue considering that between 51% and 76% of adult males and 39% and 85% of adult females who are arrested test positive for at least one illicit substance at the time of their arrest (Farabee, Prendergast, & Cartier, 2002; Makkai, 2003).[1]

The issue of responsibility for criminal behavior is often sidestepped through the use of the social fiction that the drugs somehow interfered with the individual's ability to think coherently. This is an extreme position based on the unproven assumption that substance abuse obliterates free choice (Husak, 2004). As was observed 30 years ago, any "perceived correlation between the use of a drug and the unwanted consequences is attributed to the drug, removing the individual from any and all responsibility" (National Commission on Marihuana and Drug Abuse, 1973, p. 4). This position was echoed by Walton (2002), who, speaking of alcohol, noted, "If intoxication is wrong, it is in large part these days because it is perceived to be guilty of inciting criminality and other antisocial activities in too many of those who regularly take intoxicants" (p. 75).

[1]One should not automatically assume that these individuals were under the influence of chemicals at the time they committed the crime for which they were arrested, as there is often a delay of hours, days, weeks, or sometimes even months between the time of the offense and the individual's arrest.

These views are extensions of the "demon rum" philosophy of the late 1800s (Peele, 1989; Walton, 2002). According to that belief, once the person ingests even one drink, the alcohol totally overwhelms his or her self-control. From that point on, the person has no control over his or her behavior: It is controlled by the demon of alcohol. The modern version of this belief is that when a crime is committed by a person under the influence of chemicals, the responsibility for that crime is attributed not to the person but to the chemical used. The individual's role in the commission of the crime is overlooked, or at least minimized, and the person is viewed as a helpless victim of the drug's effects. The outcome of this process is that whereas drug use in itself is not an excuse for criminal behavior, *extreme* drug use often derails the legal system by blurring the issue of the individual's responsibility.

This is not to say that substance abuse/addiction can be used to justify criminal activity. The courts have ruled that the use of recreational chemicals involves some element of choice (Husak, 2004; Kermani & Castaneda 1996) and thus the individual is still held responsible for the acts he or she committed while under the influence of chemicals. Unfortunately, the criminal justice system is often unable to determine whether the individual actually *intended* to commit a crime while under the influence of chemicals. In such cases, as a way of clearing a difficult case from the court schedule, the system often simply accepts the compromise that the individual suffered a "diminished capacity" as a result of his or her use of chemicals. Because of this social and legal fiction, it is not unusual for defense attorneys to negotiate a reduced sentence, based on the claim that the defendant was under the influence of chemicals at the time of the offense (Graham, 1989).

The law and morality: Where to draw the line? In the modern "war on drugs," federal and state authorities have instituted legal sanctions against those who would engage in recreational drug use, effectively turning what had been a medical problem into a legal issue. But the legal system is selective: Only certain substances, only certain euphoric states, are deemed inappropriate (Husak, 2004). Caffeine users achieve a certain drug-induced psychological state without fear of arrest or incarceration, for example, and long-distance runners still experience the "runner's high" without fear of legal consequences (Husak, 2004). When the use of select compounds is made illegal, individuals who indulge in these substances become, by definition, criminals and thus must fear the wrath of the legal system. This general policy, in effect since the 1930s, has proven to be ineffective in the battle against recreational chemical use (Gray, 1998). Further, the moral foundation of this position is suspect (Husak, 2004), yet it remains entrenched as the centerpost of the government's efforts to eliminate drug use/abuse in the United States.

The decision to bring the weight of the legal system to bear on substance abusers demands that clear decisions be made about what is or is not acceptable behavior, a moral dilemma in that there are no clear-cut standards of behavior. The

> person to be blamed must have done something wrongful; no one can merit blame for conduct that is permissible. But whether and to what extent someone should be blamed is not simply a function of the wrongfulness of his conduct. We must also decide whether the wrongful act is fairly attributed to him, that is, whether he is responsible for it. (Husak, 2004, p. 405)

Whereas recreational drug use for euphoric purposes is prohibited and judged as immoral, the line between legitimate medical purposes and recreational drug use has become quite vague (Husak, 2004). It has been argued that personal, recreational drug use (as opposed to distribution of illicit chemicals to others) is simply a consensual crime, in the sense that the individual who is using a recreational chemical has made the choice to do so in a manner that does not hurt others (McWilliams, 1993; Royko, 1990). Are euphoric states grounds for legal constraints? At what point does medical necessity blend into recreational drug use? Nobody would fault a man for using a drug such as Viagra if he suffered from a clear case of erectile dysfunction. But what about the businessman who ingests Viagra only to enhance sexual performance? Each individual would have obtained the same drug from a physician, but where is the line between legitimate medical use and recreational use of that same chemical compound?

Would either of these hypothetical cases be different from that of a businessman who smokes marijuana in the belief that it would enhance his sexual performance? Is the case of the businessman who takes diazepam to help him relax after a hard day's work that different from the businessman who drinks a martini or the individual who smokes marijuana to relax after a hard day's work? Where does one draw the line between appropriate and inappropriate substance use? The legal system tends to be extraordinarily selective about where it draws this line, often failing to provide any rationale for its actions.

Manufactured criminals. The national prohibition against drug use has served mainly to prohibit access to certain chemicals except through illicit channels. The drugs are controlled by those who are willing to break the law by selling them, and people wishing to buy them must pay the price asked, often obtaining the money to do so by illegal means.

Urine Toxicology Testing in the Workplace

Estimates of drug-related lost productivity in the United States range from $14.2 billion (Craig, 2004) to $30 billion a year (May, 1999). In the mid 1980s, prior to the initiation of widespread urine toxicology testing for workers, it was thought that perhaps as many as 20% of workers were abusing illicit drugs at work (Goldberg, 2002). With the encouragement of the federal government and insurance companies, an increasing number of employers now require urine toxicology testing at the time an employee is hired and on a random basis during the workweek.

The widespread testing of employees for signs of illicit drug use is controversial. Proponents of the concept of drug testing in the workplace point to research findings suggesting that during 1987–1994, the number of workers testing positive for an illicit drug dropped by 57%. Detractors of this movement point out that (a) urine drug testing does not include testing for alcohol, which is thought to be consumed on the job site by 8% of the hourly workers and 23% of the managers; (b) members of Congress are exempt from the mandatory drug testing laws they have imposed on everybody else; (c) drug testing does not tell *when* the worker used the chemicals detected, just that there were signs of an illicit chemical in his or her urine (Schlosser, 2003); and (d) a positive test does not determine impairment (Husak, 2004). To illustrate, a urine sample drawn on a Tuesday morning detected THC in the worker's urine. But what does that mean? It might suggest that the person had used marijuana prior to coming to or at work. But the same results might be obtained if the individual had used marijuana the preceding weekend, in the privacy of his or her home (Schlosser, 2003).

Random toxicology testing on the job, at schools, and in other places has been challenged on various legal grounds, but the courts have supported it, even though such testing is viewed by many as an erosion of personal liberties. Critics of drug testing in the workplace point to the episode in the early 1990s when 38 different federal agencies tested 29,000 employees at a cost of $12 million, to find only 155 individuals whose urine samples were positive for illicit drugs (mostly cannabis) (Leavitt, 2003; Petersen, 2000). The cost of this exercise was $77,000 per positive sample, hardly a cost-effective approach to the perceived problem of workers engaging in illicit drug use (Petersen, 2000).

In the past, agencies such as the National Institute on Drug Abuse (NIDA) have argued that if *every* worker in the United States were to be tested for alcohol/drug use at once, between 14% and 25% would test positive for a controlled substance (Vereby, Buchan, & Turner, 1998). Such figures are used by proponents of urine toxicology testings to justify the use of this procedure. However, Leavitt (2003) has challenged the foundation on which this (and similar) estimates rest, pointing out that these are *assumptions*, not research study results, and thus it is possible that only a small proportion of those tested would show evidence of illicit drug use in their urine.

Unseen Victims of Street Drug Chemistry

Because their use is illegal, many of the drugs of abuse are produced in illicit laboratories. Product reliability is hardly a strong emphasis in these clandestine drug laboratories, providing stark reminders of the problems from the Prohibition era. During these years, a very real danger was that the "bathtub gin" or "home brew" (beverages containing alcohol) might contain methanol—a form of alcohol that could blind people or even kill them—rather than the desired ethanol. Indeed, victims of methanol poisoning during Prohibition were thought to number in the "tens of thousands" (Nadelmann, Kleiman, & Earls, 1990, p. 46). This was one reason that smuggled alcohol was so popular during Prohibition: People could trust a legitimate alcoholic beverage not to blind or kill them.

Nor were the problems associated with illegally manufactured alcohol limited to the Prohibition era. Even today, whiskey produced by illegal stills, known in many parts of the country as "moonshine," is frequently contaminated with high levels of lead (Morgan, Barnes, Parramore, & Kaufmann, 2003). The lead contamination is caused by the practice of many producers of filtering the brew through old automobile radiators, where it comes into contact with lead from soldered joints. So common is this problem that the authors considered illegal whiskey "an important and unappreciated source of lead poisoning" (p. 1501) in some parts of this country.

In today's world, contaminants are commonly found in the drugs sold on the street. If the drug was manufactured in an illegal laboratory, a simple mistake in the production process might produce a dangerous or even a lethal chemical combination. For example, the illicit production of methamphetamine requires only a few common chemicals and only a basic knowledge of chemistry. But the use of lead acetate in one of the more common production processes for illicit methamphetamine can contaminate the drug with high levels of lead if the "chemist" makes a mistake (Norton, Burton, & McGirr, 1996).

In the mid 1970s, heroin addicts in California were sold a compound they were told was synthetic heroin. These addicts injected the drug and quickly developed a drug-induced condition very similar to advanced cases of Parkinson's disease (Kirsch, 1986). Legitimate chemists discovered that a mistake in the production process had produced not 1-methyl-4–4-phenyl-4-pro-pionoxy-piperidine (a synthetic narcotic known as MPPP), but the chemical 1-methyl-4-phenyl-1,2,3, 6-tetrahydropyridine (known as MPTP).[2] Unfortunately,

---

[2]The very names of these chemicals gives the reader some idea as to how easy it would be for chemists to make mistakes in their manufacture.

once in the body, the enzyme monoamine oxidase biotransforms MPTP into a neurotoxin known as 1-methyl-4-phenylpyridinium (MPP+), which kills the dopamine-producing brain cells in the nigrostriatal region of the brain (Langston & Palfreman, 1995; Lopez & Jeste, 1997). Subsequent research revealed that the loss of these same neurons is implicated in Parkinson's disease. Thus, indirectly, this mistake in the manufacture of illicit narcotics allowed researchers to make an important discovery about the cause of Parkinson's disease. Unfortunately, because the MPTP was sold on the street, many opiate abusers died from this manufacturing mistake or suffered a lifelong disorder similar to Parkinson's.

There is no way to determine how many people have suffered or died because of other impurities in illicit drugs. But it is known that addicts have been and still are being poisoned because of mistakes made in the production of street drugs. Heroin contaminated with lead has been sold to abusers (Parras, Patier, & Ezpeleta, 1988). Cases have been reported of amphetamine users who have also been exposed to toxic levels of lead or any number of possible carcinogenic compounds as a result of impure manufacture (Centers for Disease Control, 1990; Evanko, 1991). In France, samples of heroin were found to be contaminated with the heavy metal thallium, which killed at least one individual ("Bald Is Not Beautiful," 1996).

Nor is the problem of contaminated drugs limited to narcotics or cocaine. Most of the drugs "intended for popular recreational use are most often produced in clandestine laboratories with little or no quality control, so generally speaking users cannot be sure of the purity of what they are ingesting" (Hayner & McKinney, 1986, p. 341). Where illicit drugs are concerned, "misrepresentation is the rule" (Brown & Braden, 1987, p. 341). One survey of the pills being sold as MDMA in Europe and the United States found that only 30% actually contained this compound, with other compounds such as "PCP, ketamine, paramethoxyamphetamine, methamphetamine, dog worm pills and prescription meds" ("Dance Safe," 2001, p. 157; Walton, 2002) also being sold as MDMA. When average users buy a street drug, they cannot, without a detailed chemical analysis, be sure what the substance actually is, whether it is contaminated, or how potent it might be. Thus, one should not automatically accept any illicit drug as

what it is represented to be. Indeed, one should not even assume that the chemical is safe for human consumption without a chemical analysis. In the world of illicit drug use, it is indeed a case of "let the buyer beware."

Drug Analogs: The "Designer" Drugs

When a pharmaceutical company develops a new compound for use in the fight against disease, the company applies for a patent. To do so, the pharmaceutical company must identify and record the exact location of each atom in relation to every other atom in the chemical chain of that drug molecule. After review by the Food and Drug Administration, the pharmaceutical company may then be granted a patent on that drug molecule for a specific period of time.

When law-enforcement agencies wish to classify a drug as an illicit substance, they must go through much the same process. Chemists must identify and record the chemical structure of the new drug molecule and the exact location of each atom in relation to every other atom in the molecule's chemical chain. This process can take several months but will yield a chemical formula that can then be used to identify that specific compound as an illicit substance.

Because drug molecules are very complex, it is often possible to add, rearrange, or remove some atoms from the parent drug molecule without having much impact on the original drug's psychoactive effect. Depending on the exact chemical structure of the parent drug, it is possible to develop dozens, or even hundreds, of variations of the original drug molecule. For example, there are 184 known potential variations on the parent drug from which the hallucinogen MDMA was developed ("Market Update," 1993). These variations are called drug analogs, or analogs. Many of the drug analogs will have no psychoactive effect and thus are of little interest to the illicit chemists who produce chemicals for sale on the street. Some drug analogs will be abusable and thus would be of interest to illicit drug producers. A drug analog might be less potent than the parent compound, equally potent, or even in some cases more potent than the original chemical. For example, as will be discussed in the next section, some of the analogs of the pharmaceutical fentanyl are more powerful than the original drug.

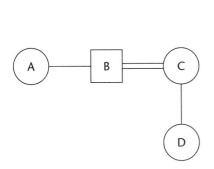

FIGURE 36.1 Parent molecule.

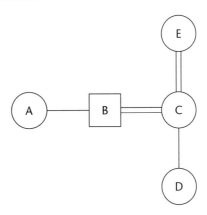

FIGURE 36.2 First analog.

The main point is that even if just one atom has been added or moved around on the chemical chain, the chemical structure of the drug analog will be different from that of the parent drug. If the parent drug has been classified as an illegal substance, it is possible, by removing just one atom from the chemical chain of the original drug, to create a "new" drug that has not yet been outlawed. For the sake of discussion, assume that the simplified drug molecule shown in Figure 36.1 has been outlawed as an illegal hallucinogen.[3]

Notice that in this simplified example, the parent drug molecule only has four atoms, not the thousands of atoms found in some actual chemical molecules. However, a drug with the chemical structure shown in Figure 36.2 would technically be a different drug, as its molecular structure is not *exactly* the same as that of the first chemical.

The chemical in Figure 36.2 would be a drug analog of the parent drug shown in Figure 36.1. There is an obvious difference in the chemical structure of these two drugs. The new atom that was added to the chemical structure in the second one might not make the analog more potent than the parent compound but it will change the chemical structure just enough that it is not covered by the law that made the original, parent drug illegal. For this analog to be declared illegal, researchers would have to identify the location of every atom in the second compound and the nature of the chemical bond that holds that atom in place. Then, law-enforcement

officials would have to present their findings to the appropriate agency for the drug analog to be outlawed. This process could take months or longer. When the analog is declared illegal, it would be a simple matter to again change the chemical structure a little, build a new analog, and start the whole cycle over again. The new analog might look like the diagram in Figure 36.3.

Notice that there is a very subtle difference in the chemical structure of the last two hypothetical drug molecules. In each case, however, in the eyes of the law, they are different drugs. Technically, the one shown in Figure 36.3 is a new drug, which is not covered by the law that prohibited the parent drug. If this drug molecule *were* to be outlawed, the street chemist might again change the drug into something like the molecule shown in Figure 36.4.

The drug molecule used in this example was very simple, with only five atoms. However, even with this simplistic example, it was possible to produce several different analogs of the original parent molecule. When you consider that many of the psychoactive drugs have molecules with many hundreds or thousands of atoms, the number of potential combinations is impressive.

Some Existing Drug Analogs

It should be no surprise that street chemists manipulate the chemical structure of known drugs of abuse, hoping to produce a new drug not yet outlawed. Some of the following drug analogs have been outlawed by government agencies; action against some of the other compounds discussed below is still pending.

[3]Figure 36.1 is a simplified drawing; real drug molecules are much more complex than this.

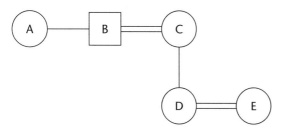

FIGURE 36.3   Second analog.

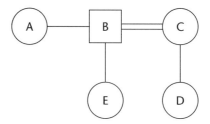

FIGURE 36.4   Third analog.

Analogs of the amphetamines. The amphetamine molecule lends itself to experimentation, and several analogs of the original amphetamine molecule have been identified by law-enforcement agencies. Some known analogs include 2,5-dimethoxy-4-methylamphetamine, or the hallucinogenic DOM (Scaros, Westra, & Barone, 1990). MDMA, also known as Ecstacy, is a drug analog of the amphetamine family of chemicals. There are 184 known analogs of the parent drug of MDMA, some of which have a psychoactive effect on the user.

The drug 3,4-methylenedioxyamphetamine, or MDEA, is another analog of the amphetamine family. When the hallucinogen Ecstasy (MDMA) was classified as a controlled substance in 1985, many street chemists simply began producing MDEA. The chemical structure and effects of MDEA are very similar to those of MDMA (Mirin, Weiss, & Greenfield, 1991). This substance is often sold under the name of "Eve." There have been isolated reports of death associated with MDEA use, and it is not known what role, if any, MDEA had in these deaths. Further, the long-term effects of MDEA are still unknown.

A recent addition to the list of illicit stimulants being produced by street chemists in this country is methcathinone, or "Kat." This compound was discussed in Chapter 11. However, the reader should be aware that Kat is also a designer drug.

Another derivative of the amphetamines is a compound known as "Ya ba," (crazy medicine), which is used in southeast Asia, especially in Thailand where up to 5% of the population is reported to use it (Hilditch, 2000; Kurutz, 2003). It has recently been imported into the United States and is occasionally found on the West Coast. This compound, which includes ephedrine, caffeine, methamphetamine, lithium (obtained from extended-use batteries), and chemicals from household cleaning products, among others, provides an extended (8–12 hour) high. The compound can be inhaled, smoked, or used transdermally in the form of a skin patch, but it is usually taken orally. Long-term use seems to contribute to suicidal or homicidal impulses, and so most abusers follow a pattern of taking the drug for 2–3 days, followed by a day or two of sleep. Very little is known about the toxicology of Ya ba, which has not been subjected to controlled research by physicians.

Analogs of PCP. PCP is a popular parent drug molecule for illicit chemists to experiment with. To date, at least 30 drug analogs of PCP have been identified, many of which are actually more potent than PCP itself (Crowley, 1995; Weiss, Greenfield, & Mirin, 1994). These are the drugs N-ethyl-1-phenylcyclohexylamine (also known as PCE), (1-(1–2-thienylcyclohexyl) piperidine) (TCP), (1-(1-phenylcyclohexyl)-pyrrolidine (PHP), (1-piperidinocyclohexanecarbonitrile) (PCC), and Eu4ia (pronounced "euphoria"), an amphetamine-like drug synthesized from legally purchased, over-the-counter chemicals (Scaros et al., 1990).

Ketamine. The compound (2-o-chlorophenyl)-2-methylamine cyclohexanone is a chemical cousin to PCP, which was classified as a Schedule III compound[4] in 1999. Ketamine itself is a surgical anesthetic of value when other anesthetics cannot be used because it does not cause respiratory or cardiac depression (Walton, 2002). Although ketamine can be manufactured in illicit laboratories, doing so is quite difficult, and so most of the ketamine found on the streets is diverted from human or veterinary supplies (Gahlinger, 2004).

Neuropharmacologists believe that ketamine binds at an NMDA receptor on the neuron, forcing

[4]See Appendix 4.

a calcium ion channel to close (McDowell, 2004). This reduces the rate at which that neuron can fire, thus suppressing its action. It is believed that the typical abuser will ingest a dose about half as strong as that needed to cause anesthesia, or about 1/60th the LD50 for this compound, thus giving ketamine a fairly large therapeutic window (McDowell, 2004). Because it does not suppress cardiac or respiratory function, ketamine is potentially useful in combat, post-earthquake, or other situations when an emergency anesthetic is necessary (Schultz, 2002). When used as a surgical anesthetic, ketamine may be introduced into the body by intravenous injection, intramuscular injection, or in oral form. Abusers may ingest ketamine in oral form or use a powdered form of the compound to mix with tobacco or marijuana for smoking (Gahlinger, 2004). On rare occasions the powder is also used intranasally, which abusers refer to as a "bump" (Gahlinger, 2004).

The effects of ketamine begin in 30–45 minutes after ingestion and are dose dependent (Freese, Miotto, & Reback, 2002; Gahlinger, 2004). Lower doses, such as those typically used by illicit drug users, produce a feeling of euphoria, visual hallucinations, a sense of unreality, depersonalization, and vivid dreams (Freese et al., 2002; Gahlinger, 2004). Some of the side effects of ketamine abuse include a sense of psychological dissociation and/or a trancelike state that appears similar to catatonia, panic states, and at higher doses hallucinations, hypertension, tachycardia, respiratory depression, and apnea (Gahlinger, 2004; Jansen, 1993; McDowell, 2004; Walton, 2002). Some users report that they have had experiences like flashbacks for days or even weeks after their last use of the drug (Gahlinger, 2004).

The half-life of ketamine is between 3 and 4 hours. The drug is extensively biotransformed prior to excretion from the body, and only 3% of a single dose is excreted unchanged in the urine. Long-term use, especially at high doses, may result in drug-induced memory problems (Gahlinger, 2004; Jansen, 1993). This effect, plus the fact that it is effective at doses lower than those necessary to produce anesthesia, has reportedly made ketamine popular as a date-rape drug.

Aminorex. For a number of years, the drug analog 2-amino-4-methyl-5-phenyl-2-oxazoline has appeared on the streets, usually under the guise of methamphetamine (Karch, 2002). This compound is derived from a diet pill sold in Europe under the brand name of Aminorex in the 1980s; it is easily synthesized (Karch, 2002). Aminorex was classified as a Schedule I compound in April 1989 (Karch, 2002).

The effects of this drug are not well known, but available evidence suggests that it is a CNS stimulant, with effects similar to those of the amphetamines (Karch, 2002). Following a single oral dose of Aminorex, peak blood levels are seen in about 2 hours, and the half-life of Aminorex is approximately 7.7 hours (Karch, 2002). There is no clinical research into the effect on the human body of illicit forms of 2-amino-4-methyl-5-phenyl-2-oxazoline, and the potential for harm from Aminorex-like compounds remains unknown.

Gamma hydroxybutyric acid (GHB). Neurochemists first synthesized gamma hydroxybutyric acid (GHB) in 1960 while conducting research on the neurotransmitter GABA. Initially, there was some interest in the possible use of GHB as a pre-anesthetic, but the vomiting and seizures that occurred when patients recovered from its effects combined with the narrow therapeutic window limited its usefulness for this purpose. Currently, it is only rarely used by physicians in Europe as a presurgical agent (Galloway et al., 1997).

There was little interest in GHB by illicit drug abusers until the 1990s, when bodybuilders began to use it as a legal alternative to the anabolic steroids. Preliminary evidence that GHB might possibly stimulate the production of growth hormones and the fact that it was still legal in the United States focused attention on this compound. But in 2000, GHB was classified as a Schedule I substance[5] (Gahlinger, 2004; Ingels, Rangan, Bellezzo, & Clark, 2000). In response to the government's ban on GHB, users simply switched to any of a number of legal compounds that would be biotransformed into GHB after ingestion, or to illicit sources of this compound. Instructions on how to manufacture GHB are also available on the Internet, allowing amateur chemists to produce their own stockpiles of the drug (Gahlinger, 2004; Li, Stokes, & Woeckener, 1998; Moore & Ginsberg, 1999; Smith, 2001). However, a number of different formulas are available on the Internet, and the purity and potency of the GHB

---

[5]See Appendix 4.

produced will vary with the formula used, so that over-doses are a very real danger for users.

Small amounts of GHB are normally found in the human kidney, heart, muscle tissue, and the brain, where it is thought to function as a neurotransmitter (Drummer & Odell, 2001; Marwick, 1997). In the brain, GHB seems to help mediate sleep cycles and body temperature, control cerebral glucose metabolism, and possibly play a role in memory formation (Gahlinger, 2004). The usual method of administration is oral, although the drug may also be injected into the venous system; effects begin 10–30 minutes after ingestion (Gahlinger, 2004; Klein & Kramer, 2004). Peak plasma levels of GHB are seen within 20–40 minutes of a single oral dose, and it has a half-life of about 20 minutes (Drummer & Odell, 2001; Karch, 2002). The drug's effects might take as long as 60 minutes to develop if it has been mixed with food (Gahlinger, 2004). Depending on the dose ingested, the effects will last 3–6 hours, with larger doses having a longer duration of effect (Klein & Kramer, 2004).

The subjective effects of GHB are similar to those experienced with alcohol (Freese et al., 2002). Users report a sense of euphoria, which at higher doses progresses to dizziness, hypersalivation, hypotonia, and amnesia (Gahlinger, 2004). When mixed with alcohol, GHB's sedating effects are enhanced, and because of this effect it has gained favor as a date-rape drug. Those who use it as a sleep aid report "rebound" insomnia, or a period of reduced alertness, which develops 2–3 hours after the drug was ingested. This effect is thought to be caused by the drug's rapid elimination from the body (Freese et al., 2002). Unfortunately, many law enforcement officials view as unreliable any victim of a date rape that was facilitated by GHB, because of drug-induced changes in perception and anteriograde amnesia (Abramowitz, 2004). Furthermore, GHB has a very narrow detection window, and thus it is rarely collected as evidence when the rape is reported by the victim (Abramowitz, 2004).

Researchers are still not certain how GHB achieves its effects on the user. The GHB molecule is similar to the GABA molecule, but in spite of this similarity it has limited effect on the GABA receptors in the brain. At low dosage levels GHB is thought to inhibit the release of dopamine in the brain, whereas at high levels it has the opposite effect of stimulating the release of dopamine. Clinical evidence suggests that at doses

of 0.1–1.5 mg/kg GHB is able to induce a sleep-like state in the user, initiating both delta sleep and REM sleep (Li et al., 1998). When used at doses of around 10 mg/kg,[6] GHB can induce euphoria and amnesia and can lower inhibitions. Doses of 20–30 mg/kg cause drowsiness and sleep in addition to the effects seen at lower doses. When dosage levels of 40–50 mg/kg are used, the individual will experience sleep. Dosage levels of 60–70 mg/kg cause deep coma and possibly seizures (Chin, Sporer, Cullison, Dyer, & Wu, 1998; Koesters, Rogers, & Rajasingham, 2002).

Side effects of GHB use include nausea, vomiting, cardiopulmonary depression, tunnel vision, ataxia, confusion, agitation, hallucinations, and respiratory failure. The LD_{50} for GHB is only about five times the typical therapeutic dose, giving the compound a very small therapeutic window that becomes even smaller when it is mixed with other CNS depressants (McDowell, 2004). Long-term abusers can become physically dependent on GHB. Following protracted use, withdrawal symptoms such as anxiety, tremor, insomnia, nausea, and hypertension have been reported (Freese et al., 2002; Klein & Kramer, 2004). These symptoms usually start about 12 hours after the last dose and continue for about 12 days in chronic users (Olmedo & Hoffman, 2000). In addition to these withdrawal symptoms, there have been reports of a withdrawal process similar to delirium tremens that begins within 24 hours of the last dose and continues for up to 15 days in heavy abusers who abruptly discontinue the drug (Freese et al., 2002).

Conservative medical care is the best treatment for a GHB overdose or addiction, although intubation and physical restraints may be necessary in extreme cases (Chin et al., 1998; Miro, Nogue, Espinoza, To-Figueras, & Sanchez, 2002). During the process of biotransformation, most of the drug is transformed into carbon dioxide, and only 2% to 5% is excreted from the body in the urine (Drummer & Odell, 2001; Galloway et al., 1997). The elimination half-life of GHB is only 27 minutes (Li et al., 1998). Because of this short elimination half-life, urine toxicology tests can detect GHB in the user's urine for only about 12 hours following ingestion of a single dose (Karch, 2002; Klein & Kramer, 2004; Moore & Ginsberg, 1999). Following

---

[6]Which means 10 mg per kilogram of body weight.

death, natural biochemical processes produce significant amounts of GHB in the blood of the deceased, making the identification of GHB-related death by toxicology testing very difficult (Drummer & Odell, 2001).

It is rare for GHB to be used alone, which is unfortunate because GHB will interact with many other compounds. Its effects are intensified by the concurrent use of other CNS depressants, such as alcohol, hydrocodone, or the benzodiazepines (Klein & Kramer, 2004). When used concurrently with methamphetamines, GHB may cause seizures (Smith, 2001). Patients taking any of the antiviral drugs known as protease inhibitors should not use GHB, for these antiviral compounds alter the liver's ability to biotransform many drugs, including GHB (Drummer & Odell, 2001; Harrington, Woodward, Hooton, & Horn, 1999).

Phenethylamines. There are more than 250 members of this family of compounds, of which *Nexus* is perhaps the best known (Boyer, 2005). Nexus, or 2,5 dimethoxyphenethylamine, is usually ingested orally. A single oral dose of 10–20 mg of 2,5 dimethoxyphenethylamine will cause the user to experience intoxication, euphoria, and visual distortions/hallucinations for 6–8 hours. Side effects include nausea, abdominal cramps, pulmonary problems, and coughing. Nexus is not intended for human use and is illegal in the United States. Virtually nothing is known about its toxicology at this time (Karch, 2002).

Another member of the phenethylamine family of compounds is *2C-T-7*, known by various street names such as 7-Up, Tripstasy, and Blue Mystic (Boal, 2002; Boyer, 2005). The compound, 2,5-dimethoxy-4-(n)-propylthiophenethylamine, is about 12 times as potent as mescaline in terms of psychoactive potential. However, it has a narrow therapeutic window, and the difference between an effective dose and a toxic dose is only a matter of micrograms. It is slowly becoming popular among those who attend "rave" parties. In addition to the visual hallucinations that are desired by the abuser, this compound can cause vomiting, cramps, seizures, and possible death from aspiration (Boyer, 2005).

Tryptamines. The tryptamines are a family of about 200 different compounds, which include the compound 5-MeO-DiPT (which is short for 5-methoxy-N,N-diisopropyltryptamine). This compound is known to abusers by a variety of names, including Foxy (Meatherall & Sharma, 2005) or Foxy Methoxy (Boyer, 2005; Mueller, 2005). The compound began appearing in the late 1990s and was classified as a Schedule I[7] substance by the Drug Enforcement Administration in April 2003 (Mueller, 2005). Chemically, Foxy has a different chemical structure from MDMA, but it has many of the same behavioral effects on the abuser, including the risk of neurological damage (Mueller, 2005).

Because many of these compounds are broken down by first-pass metabolism effect (see Chapter 6), most of the tryptamines must be either snorted or smoked. Little is known about their effects on the user. It is known that Foxy is ingested orally and usually begins to have an effect in 20–30 minutes (Mueller, 2005). It can cause sexual stimulation as well as mild hallucinations. Side effects include restlessness, anxiety, insomnia, and possibly seizures (Meatherall & Sharma, 2005; Mueller, 2005). Some compounds in this group are thought to be able to induce the "serotonin syndrome" (Boyer, 2005). There may be a synergistic effect between Foxy and compounds such as GHB, ketamine, and marijuana, but little is known about its pharmacology or its potential for harm to the user (Mueller, 2005). The best medical treatment is supportive care, and there is little information about how to block the drug's effect or the long-term consequences of tryptamine abuse.

Fentanyl. The fentanyl molecule is easy to manipulate and may be synthesized from a few ordinary industrial chemicals (Langston & Palfreman, 1995). With just a minor change in the molecule of the parent drug, a fentanyl analog can be produced that will extend the drug's effects from the normal 30–90 minutes up to 4–5 hours, or, with the right modifications to the parent drug, even 4–5 *days*, according to the authors. Thus, it is a popular drug for illicit drug manufacturers to produce.

In the early 1980s, a series of fatal narcotic overdoses occurred in California, as street chemists started to produce various designer drugs that were similar to the analgesic fentanyl (discussed in the chapter on narcotic analgesics) (Hibbs, Perper, & Winek, 1991). Kirsch (1986) identified nine different drug analogs to fentanyl that are known or suspected to have been sold on the streets. These drug analogs range widely in potency: The fentanyl analog Benzylfentanyl is one-tenth as potent as

---

[7]See Appendix 4.

morphine; the analog 3-methyl fentanyl is between 1,000 times (Hibbs et al., 1991) and 3,000 times (Kirsch, 1986) more potent than morphine.

The drug 3-methyl fentanyl is also known to chemists as "TMF." A decade ago, this analog of fentanyl was identified as the cause of numerous narcotics overdoses (Hibbs et al., 1991; "A New Market," 1991). The chemical structure of fentanyl makes it possible for the drug molecule to be "snorted," much like cocaine. When it is used intranasally, the drug will be deposited on the blood-rich tissues of the sinuses, where it will be absorbed into the general circulation. Fentanyl can also be smoked. As with cocaine, when fentanyl is smoked, the molecules easily cross into the general circulation through the lungs. Indeed, so rapidly is fentanyl absorbed through the lungs that it is possible for the user to overdose on the medication after just one inhalation ("Take Time to Smell," 1994).

Obviously, given the characteristics of fentanyl, it is safe to assume that analogs of this chemical will present similar abuse profiles. Law-enforcement officials have struggled to deal with the problem of diversion of fentanyl products to illicit users almost from the moment the drug was introduced. But the drug is so powerful that even small amounts have a value to illicit drug users. Some opiate abusers will even scrape the residual medication from transdermal fentanyl patches in order to obtain small amounts of the drug, which will then be smoked or used orally.

Fentanyl is so potent that extremely small doses are effective in humans. To be detected in the blood or urine sample, a special test procedure must be carried out (Evanko, 1991). Routine drug toxicology screens easily miss the small amounts of fentanyl that will be in the blood or urine of a suspected drug user ("Take Time to Smell," 1994). Thus, even a "clean" urine or blood drug toxicology test might not rule out fentanyl use on the part of an addict.

Some opiate abusers have been known to die so rapidly after using fentanyl that they were found with the needle still in their arms (Evanko, 1991). This phenomenon is well documented in cases of narcotic overdoses but is not understood by medicine. Some researchers attribute the rapid death to the narcotic itself; others have suggested that the user's death is caused by the various chemicals added to the drug to cut or dilute it on the street. For example, fentanyl is

so potent that some samples of the drug sold on the street are made up of 0.01% fentanyl, and 99.9% filler (Langston & Palfreman, 1995).

It is difficult to understand the addictive potential of fentanyl. Dr. William Spiegelman (quoted in Gallagher, 1986) observed that "it can take years to become addicted to alcohol, months for cocaine, and one shot for fentanyl" (p. 26). To further complicate matters, street chemists are constantly manipulating the chemical structure of fentanyl, adding a few atoms to the basic fentanyl chain here, snipping a few atoms there, to produce analogs. Unfortunately, fentanyl and its analogs continue to be a significant part of the drug-abuse problem in the United States, and there is no end in sight.

Fry. Fry is found in limited areas of the United States. It is marijuana soaked in formaldehyde and laced with PCP (Klein & Kramer, 2004). These chemicals can induce a toxic psychosis, hallucinations, delusional thinking, panic, paranoia, reduced attention span, and loss of consciousness. Brain and lung damage are also possible as side effects of the formaldehyde (Klein & Kramer, 2004).

Adulterants

Another consequence of the prohibition against the recreational chemicals is that most illicit drugs are rarely sold to the user in their pure form. Adulterants are intermixed with the chemical compounds being sold for a variety of reasons. Some compounds are made in illicit laboratories, and mistakes in "cooking" the batch of a drug can result in adulterants becoming intermixed with the drug being manufactured. Because product reliability is not exactly a major concern, these adulterants are ignored, and the chemicals produced are sold to unsuspecting users. For example, a "high proportion of MDMA pills are adulterated with substances such as caffeine, dextromethorphan, pseudoephedrine, or potent hallucinogens such as LSD, paramethoxyamphetamine (PMA), methylenedioxyamphetamine (MDA) [or other hallucinogenic compounds]" (Gahlinger, 2004, p. 2620).

Most commonly, adulterants are added by middle- and upper-level drug dealers to increase profits. This is known as cutting the drug (Coomber, 1997). By adding an ounce of an inert substance to an ounce of pure cocaine, the dealer obtains 2 ounces of 50% pure cocaine that he or she can then sell. The adulterants added at each stage of the drug manufacturing and distribution process inflate the price of the compound at each stage, increasing profits. The coca paste that is bought from the farmer in South America for $1,000 a kilogram[8] will be adulterated time and time again, until it is about 45% pure when it is sold to illicit users, with the ultimate value of that same kilogram of cocaine being around $70,000 on the streets (Villalon, 2004).

Illegal narcotics are adulterated and the price is inflated in a similar fashion. The farmer in Pakistan who raises opium poppies might be paid $90 for a kilogram of raw opium. The illicit opium is then cut or adulterated at each stage of the production process until it is only about 73% pure (Sabbag, 1994). Heroin is sold in small packets (possibly a small balloon or condom) for between $5 (a "nickel bag") and $10 (a "dime bag") each, and the retail value of a kilogram has become about $290,000 (United Nations, 1997). More than 25% of the contents of each bag is one or more adulterants added along the way, usually by the high-end or mid-level suppliers (Coomber, 1997).

Adulterants are important because of the damage they do to the body. When a person injects an illicit compound, the adulterants are introduced directly into the circulation, bypassing the defensive acids and enzymes of the digestive tract (Leavitt, 2003). Fortunately, in spite of persistent rumors, there is little evidence that illicit drug distributors are adding substances such as ground glass or dust from bricks to compounds being sold to drug abusers (Coomber, 1997). Intuitively, it does not make much sense for a drug dealer to kill his customers—at least not immediately—and such reports appear to be urban legends more than reflections of truth. Identified adulterants fall into one of five categories: (a) various forms of sugar, (b) stimulants, (c) local anesthetics, (d) toxins, and (e) any of a number of inert compounds added to give the product bulk.

In the last decade of the 20th century, various forms of sugar were the most common adulterants (Scaros et al., 1990; Schauben 1990). Adulterants found in illicit narcotics include food coloring, talc powder, starch, powdered milk, baking soda, brown sugar, or on occasion, even dog manure (Scaros et al., 1990), as well

as aspirin, amphetamine compounds, belladonna, caffeine, instant coffee, lactose, LSD, magnesium sulfate, meprobamate, pentobarbital, pepper, secobarbital, and warfarin (Scaros et al., 1990; Schauben 1990).

Marijuana, when purchased on the street, is also frequently adulterated. It is not uncommon for up to half the substance purchased on the street to be seeds and woody stems, which must be removed before the marijuana can be smoked. Further, the marijuana may be laced with other compounds ranging from PCP, cocaine paste, or opium, to toxic compounds such as Raid insect spray (Scaros et al., 1990). Marijuana samples have also been adulterated with dried shredded cow manure (which may expose the user to salmonella bacteria) as well as herbicide sprays such as paraquat (Jenike, 1991). Other substances reportedly found in marijuana samples include alfalfa, apple leaves, catnip, cigarette tobacco, hay, licorice, mescaline, methamphetamine, opium, pipe tobacco, straw, wax, and wood shavings (Schauben, 1990).

When a drug abuser uses a compound that has been adulterated, some or all of the adulterants are introduced into his or her body, increasing the health risks associated with chemical abuse. This is the primary reason that pharmaceuticals are so highly prized among illicit drug users. Pharmaceuticals are of a known quality and potency, and are also unlikely to be contaminated.

Drug Use and Violence: The Unseen Connection

Researchers have recently discovered what police officers have long known: There is a relationship between substance abuse and violence. Approximately 50% of all sexual assaults are committed by men under the influence of alcohol (Abbey, Zawacki, Buck, Clinton, & McAuslan, 2001). As a group, substance abusers are 12 to 16 times as likely to resort to violence as the general population (Marzuk, 1996).

For a number of reasons, the amphetamines and cocaine tend to predispose the user toward violence. One study found that 31% of homicide victims in New York City had cocaine in their bodies at the time of their death (Swan, 1995). Overall, cocaine users are 10 to 50 times as likely to be murdered than are nonusers, according to the

---

[8]Approximately 2.4 pounds.

author. There are a number of reasons for this: Cocaine users tend to associate with people who are more likely to respond with violence and are less likely to avoid situations where violence might occur. Further, individuals under the influence of cocaine might behave in ways that trigger others to respond violently to them, resulting in what is known as a "victim-precipitated homicide."

The disinhibition effects of many recreational drugs may also account for some of the observed tendency toward violence among alcohol/drug abusers. As was discussed in Chapter 7, alcohol is a common factor in violent behaviors. In Kermani and Castaneda's research, "more than half" (1996, p. 2) of those who committed a homicide were actively using chemicals at the time of the crime. But this does not automatically mean that alcohol *caused* the homicide. A significant percentage of homicides were planned in advance, and the murderer then drank in order to bolster his or her courage before committing an act that had been planned in advance. In other cases, the murder was an unplanned act, brought on, at least in part, by the disinhibiting effect of alcohol. Thus, the relationship between alcohol and interpersonal violence is more complex than one of simple cause and effect.

The world of illicit drug use/abuse is a violent one. Drug pushers have been known to attack customers in order to steal their money, armed with the knowledge that the drug user is unlikely to press charges. After all, when someone engages in illegal acts (such as the use of illicit chemicals) or has obtained his or her money through illegal channels (such as burglary), this person is unlikely to report to the police that he or she was victimized by another criminal. Drug pushers have also been known to kill their customers for such reasons as unpaid drug debts and as a warning to others who

might be behind in their payments. One study found that *18%* of all the homicides committed in New York State in 1986 were the result of drug-related debts (Goldstein, 1990). On occasion, drug pushers themselves are shot and possibly just left to die in the street.

At this time, there does not appear to be any end to the drug-related violence. It has been suggested that if drug use were legalized, there would be a significant *decrease* in the level of violence in this country. However, this is only a theory.

Summary

The relationship between criminal activity and substance use or abuse is exceptionally complex, and in this chapter the relationship between alcohol/drug use and crime were briefly explored. Although some criminal activity *does* seem to result from the use or abuse of recreational chemicals, it also has been suggested that many of those who engage in criminal activity and substance use are the types of people who are prone to engage in illegal activities. In such cases, the apparent relationship between substance use and criminal behavior is not a causal one but a complex interaction among the individual's personality, his or her use of chemicals, and his or her tendency to engage in illegal behaviors.

The fact that illicit drug producers are motivated to find new designer drugs in part because of the way drugs are identified and regulated in the United States, and the rewards for finding unregulated drug molecules for sale by consumers of recreational drugs, was discussed. The role that adulterants play in the production and distribution of illicit drugs was examined, and many of the more common adulterants were identified.

Alcohol Abuse Situation Sample Assessment[1]

History and Identifying Information

Mr. John D. is a 35-year-old married white male from —— County, Missouri. He is employed as an electrical engineer for the XXX company, where he has worked for the last 3 years. Prior to this, Mr. D. was in the United States Navy, where he served for 4 years. He received an Honorable Discharge and reported that he had only "a few" minor rules infractions. He was never brought before a court martial, according to Mr D.

Circumstances of Referral

Mr. D. was seen after having been arrested for the charge of driving while under the influence of alcohol. Mr. D. reported that he had been drinking with coworkers to celebrate a promotion at work. His measured blood alcohol level (BAL) was .150, well above the legal limit necessary for a charge of driving while under the influence. Mr. D. reported that he had "seven or eight" mixed drinks in approximately a 2-hour time span. By his report, he was arrested within a quarter hour of the time that he left the bar. After his initial court appearance, Mr. D. was referred to this evaluator by the court, to determine whether he has a chemical-dependency problem.

Drug- and Alcohol-Use History

Mr. D. reports that he first began to drink at the age of 15, when he and a friend would steal beer from his father's supply in the basement. He would drink an occasional beer from time to time after that, and first became intoxicated when he was 17, by his report.

When he was 18, Mr. D. enlisted in the United States Navy, and after basic training he was stationed in the San Diago area. He reported that he was first exposed to chemicals while he was stationed in San Diago and that he tried both marijuana and cocaine while on weekend liberty. Mr. D. reported that he did not like the effects of cocaine and that he used this chemical only once or twice. He did like the effects of marijuana and reported that he would smoke one or two marijuana cigarettes obtained from friends perhaps once a month.

---

[1]This case is entirely fictitious. No similarity between any person, living or dead, is intended, or should be inferred.

During this portion of his life, Mr. D. reports that he would drink about twice a weekend when on liberty. The amount that he would drink ranged from "one or two beers" to 12 or 18 beers. Mr. D. reported that he first had an alcohol-related blackout while he was in the Navy and reported that he "should" have been arrested for driving on base while under the influence of alcohol on several different occasions but was never stopped by the Shore Patrol.

Following his discharge from the Navy at the age of 22, Mr. D. enrolled in college. His chemical use declined to the weekend use of alcohol, usually in moderation, but he reported that he did drink to the point of an alcohol-related blackout "once or twice" in the 4 years he was in college. There was no other chemical use following his discharge from the Navy, and Mr. D. reports that he has not used other chemicals since the age of 20 or 21.

On graduating at the age of 26, Mr. D. began to work for the XXX Company, where he is employed now. He met his wife shortly after that and they were married after a courtship of 1 year. Mr. D.'s wife Pat does not use chemicals other than an "occasional" social drink. Exploration of this revealed that Mrs. D. will drink a glass of wine with a meal about twice a month. She denied other chemical use.

Mrs. D. reported that her husband does not usually drink more than one or two beers, and that he will drink only on weekends. She reported that the night he was arrested was "unusual" for him, in the sense that he is not a heavy drinker. His employer was not contacted, and court records failed to reveal any other arrest records for Mr. D.

Mr. D. admitted to several alcohol-related blackouts, but none since he was in college. He denied seizures, DTs, or alcohol-related tremor. No evidence was noted of ulcers, gastritis, or cardiac problems. His last physical was "normal" according to information provided by his personal physician. There were no abnormal blood chemistry findings, nor did his physician find any evidence suggesting alcoholism. Mr. D. denied having ever been hospitalized for an alcohol-related injury, and there was no evidence suggesting that he has been involved in fights.

On the Michigan Alcoholism Screening Test, Mr. D.'s score of four (4) points would not suggest alcoholism. This information was reviewed in the presence of his wife, who did not suggest that there was any misrepresentation on his test scores. On this administration of the MMPI, there was no evidence of psychopathology noted. Mr. D.'s MacAndrew Alcoholism Scale score fell in the normal range, failing to suggest an addictive disorder at this time.

Psychiatric History

Mr. D. denied psychiatric treatment of any kind. He did admit to having seen a marriage counselor "once" shortly after he married, but reported that overall he and his wife are happy together. Apparently, they had a question about a marital communications issue that was cleared up after one visit, which took place after 3 or 4 years of marriage.

Summary and Conclusions

At this time there is little evidence to suggest an ongoing alcohol problem. Mr. D. would seem to be a well-adjusted young man who drank to the point of excess after having been offered a long-desired promotion at work. This would seem to be an unusual occurrence for Mr. D., who usually limits his drinking to one or two beers on the weekends. No evidence of alcohol-related injuries, accidents, or legal problems was noted.

Recommendations

Recommend light sentence, possibly a fine, limited probation, with no restrictions on license. It is also recommended that Mr. D. attend "DWI School" for 8 weeks, to learn more about the effects of alcohol on driving.

Chemical Dependency Situation Sample Assessment[1]

History and Identifying Information

Mr. Michael S. is a 35-year-old divorced white male who is self-employed. He has been a resident of —— County, Kansas, for the last 3 months. Prior to this, he apparently was living in —— County, New York, according to information provided by Mr. S. On the night of June 6 of this year, Mr. S. was arrested on the charge of possession of a controlled substance. Specifically, Mr. S. was found to be in possession of 2 grams of cocaine, according to police records. This is his first arrest for a drug-related charge in Kansas, although by history he has been arrested on two other occasions for similar charges in New York State. A copy of his police record is attached to this report.

Circumstances of Referral

Mr. Michael S. was referred to the undersigned for a chemical-dependency evaluation, which will be part of his pre-sentence investigation (PSI) for the charge of felony possession of a controlled substance, and the charge of sale of a controlled substance.

Drug- and Alcohol-Use History

Mr. S. reported that he began to use alcohol when he was 13 years of age, and that by the age of 14 he was drinking on a regular basis. Exploration of this revealed that by the time just prior to his 15th birthday, Mr. S. was drinking on weekends with friends. He reported that he first became intoxicated on his 15th birthday but projected responsibility for this onto his friends, who by his report "kept on pouring more and more into the glass until I was drunk."

By the age of 16, Mr. S. was using alcohol "four or five nights a week" and was also using marijuana and hallucinogenics perhaps two or three times a week. He projected responsibility for his expanded chemical use onto his environment, noting that "everybody was selling the stuff, you couldn't walk down the street without people stopping you to ask if you wanted to buy some."

---

[1]This case is entirely fictitious. Any similarity between any person in this report, and any person living or dead, is entirely coincidental.

Also, by the age of 16, Mr. S. was supporting his chemical use through burglaries, which he committed with his friends. He was never caught but volunteered this information informing the undersigned that since the statute of limitations has expired, he does not have to fear being charged for these crimes anymore.

By the age of 21, Mr. S. was using cocaine "once or twice a week." He was arrested for the first time when he was about 22 for possession of cocaine. This was when he was living in the state of ——. After being tried in court, he was convicted of felony possession of cocaine and placed on probation for 5 years. When asked if he used chemicals while he was on probation, Mr. S. responded, "I don't have to answer that."

Mr. S. reported that he first entered treatment for chemical dependency when he was 27 years of age. At that time, he was found to be addicted to a number of drugs, including alcohol, cocaine, and "downers." Although in treatment for 2 months at the chemical dependency unit of —— Hospital, Mr. S. reported that "I left as addicted as when I arrived" and reported with some degree of apparent pride that he had found a way to use chemicals even while in treatment. His chemical use apparently was the reason for his ultimate discharge from this program. While Mr. S. was somewhat vague about the reasons he was discharged, he did report that "they did not like how I was doing" while he was in treatment.

Since that time, Mr. S. has been using cocaine, alcohol, various drugs obtained from a series of physicians, and opiates. Mr. S. was quite vague as to how he would support his chemical use, but noted that "there are ways of getting money, if you really want some."

In the last year, Mr. S. reported, he has been using cocaine "four or five times a week," although on occasion he did admit to having used cocaine "for a whole week straight." He has been sharing needles with other cocaine users from time to time but reported that "I am careful." In spite of this, however, he said he was diagnosed as having Hepatitis B in the last year. He also reported that he had overdosed on cocaine "once or twice," but that he treated this overdose himself with benzodiazepines and alcohol.

In addition to the possible cocaine overdoses noted above, Mr. S. admitted to having experienced chest pain while using cocaine on at least two occasions and has used alcohol or tranquilizers to combat the side effects of cocaine on a regular basis. He has admitted to frequently using tranquilizers or alcohol to help him sleep after using cocaine for extended periods of time. He also admits to having spent money on drugs that was meant for other expenses (loan payments, etc.) and by his report has had at least one automobile repossessed for failure to make payments on the loan.

Mr. S. has been unemployed for at least the last 2 years but is rather vague as to how he supports himself. He apparently was engaged in selling cocaine at the time of his arrest, this being one of the charges brought against him by the police.

Mr. S. had not seen a physician for several years prior to this arrest. During this interview, however, scars strongly suggestive of intravenous needle use were noted on both his arms. When asked about these marks, he referred to them as "tracks," a street term for drug needle scars. This would suggest long-term intravenous drug use by Mr. S. He denied the intravenous use of opiates, but a urine toxicology screen detected narcotics. This would suggest that Mr. S. has not been very open about his narcotic drug use.

On administration of the Michigan Alcoholism Screening Test (MAST), Mr. S. achieved a score of 17 points, a score that is strongly suggestive of alcoholism. He reported that the longest period he has been able to go without using chemicals in the last 5 years was only "hours." His profile on this administration of the Minnesota Multiphasic Personality Inventory (MMPI) was suggestive of a very impulsive, immature individual, who is likely to have a chemical-dependency problem.

Psychiatric History

Mr. S. reported that he has been hospitalized for psychiatric reasons only "once." This hospitalization took place several years ago, while he was living in the state of ——. Apparently, he was hospitalized for observation following a suicide attempt in which he slit his wrists with a razor blade. Mr. S. was unable to recall whether he had been using cocaine prior to this suicide attempt but thought it was "quite possible" that he had experienced a cocaine-induced depression.

Medical History

As noted above, Mr. S. had not seen a physician for several years prior to his arrest. Since the time of his arrest, however, he has been examined by a physician for a cough that he has had for some time. The physician's report (copy enclosed) concluded that Mr. S. is "seropositive" for HIV-1 infection, with a "viral load" count of 4,000 per cc of blood. Appropriate antiviral medications have been prescribed. While it is not possible to determine if he contracted HIV through sharing needles, this is at least a possibility.

Summary and Conclusions

Overall, it is quite apparent that Mr. S. has a long-standing chemical-dependency problem. In spite of his evasiveness and denial, there was strong evidence of significant chemical dependency. Mr. S. seems to support his drug- and alcohol-use through criminal activity, although he is rather vague about this. He has been convicted of drug-related charges in the state of —— and was on probation following this conviction. One might suspect that Mr. S.'s motivation for treatment is quite low at this time, as he has expressed the belief that his attorney will "make a deal for me" so that he will not have to spend time in prison.

Recommendations

1. Given the fact that Mr. S. has contracted HIV and Hepatitis B probably from infected needles, it is strongly recommended that he be referred to the appropriate medical facility for treatment.
2. It is the opinion of this reviewer that Mr. S.'s motivation for treatment is low at this time. If he is referred to treatment, it is recommended that this be made part of his sentencing agreement with the court. If he is incarcerated, chemical-dependency treatment might be made part of his treatment plan in prison.
3. Referral to a therapeutic community should be considered for Mr. S. for long-term residential treatment.

Signed/s/

The "Jellinek" Chart for Alcoholism

Following the publication of earlier editions of *Concepts of Chemical Dependency*, questions were raised concerning my decision as the author not to mention the so-called Jellinek chart in the text. This chart, which is viewed as gospel within the alcohol/drug rehabilitation industry, purports to show the progression from social drinking to alcoholism, then on to recovery. Since the time of its introduction, this chart has been used to illustrate the "unalterable" progression of alcoholism to countless patients who were in the earlier stages of alcohol-use problems as well as to browbeat reluctant individuals into accepting the need for help with their supposed drinking problem. Variations of this chart have been developed for compulsive gambling, steroid abuse, compulsive spending, and both heroin and cocaine addiction, as well as countless other disorders. An example of this chart is provided in Figure A3.1.

The problem is that Jellinek did *not* devise this chart! In spite of the fact that it is often attributed to him, this chart is actually the work of Dr. Maxwell Glatt, a British physician who was so taken by Jellinek's work that he operationalized the *Gamma* subtype of alcoholism in chart form. This chart, which addresses *only* the Gamma subtype of alcoholism as suggested by Jellinek (1960), has mistakenly been accepted by

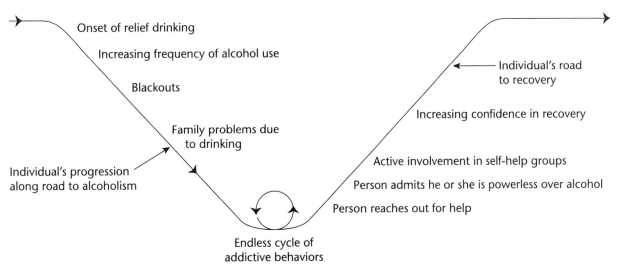

Onset of relief drinking

Increasing frequency of alcohol use

Blackouts

Family problems due to drinking

Individual's progression along road to alcoholism

Endless cycle of addictive behaviors

Individual's road to recovery

Increasing confidence in recovery

Active involvement in self-help groups

Person admits he or she is powerless over alcohol

Person reaches out for help

FIGURE A3.1   Alcohol progression chart often mistakenly called the "Jellinek" chart.

countless alcohol/drug rehabilitation professionals as THE chart that identifies the progression of ALL forms of alcoholism. As a result of this mistake, many patients in rehabilitation programs whose symptoms of alcohol use problems did not "fit" the progression of symptoms suggested in this chart have been subjected to countless hours of confrontation because they were "in denial."

Rather than perpetuate this misunderstanding, the decision was made to not make reference to this chart in the text of *Concepts of Chemical Dependency*.

Drug Classification Schedule

One of the most confusing aspects of drug rehabilitation work for both physicians and mental health professionals is that the legal classification of many of the drugs of abuse is carried out not on the basis of the pharmacological properties of the compound in question but by its perceived abuse potential. Thus, compounds that are perceived to have no accepted medical use in the United States, such as the narcotic analgesic heroin or the hallucinogen MDMA, are lumped together by the Drug Enforcement Administration. Table A4.1 should help you to understand the drug classification schedule now in use in the United States:

TABLE A4.1 Drug Classification Schedule

Schedule	Definition	Examples
Schedule I	Compounds with no accepted medical use	Marijuana, LSD, MDMA, heroin*
Schedule II	Compounds with recognized medical use, but with severe abuse potential	Morphine, methadone, amphetamines
Schedule III	Compounds with recognized medical use, but with moderate abuse potential	Ketamine, acetaminophen with codeine compounds
Schedule IV	Compounds with recognized medical use, but with mild abuse potential	Phenobarbital, benzodiazepines
Schedule V	Compounds with recognized medical use, but with low abuse potential	Buprenorphine

*Heroin has no recognized medical use in the United States. It is used in some other countries for control of acute pain.

Abruptio placentae: A condition in which bleeding starts between the placenta and the wall of the uterus. As the blood accumulates, it gradually separates the placenta from the wall of the uterus, cutting the fetus off from its supply of oxygen. The result may be fatal for both the mother and the infant.

Absorption: The movement of drug molecules from the site of entry, through various cell boundaries, to the site of action.

Acetaldehyde: The first intermediate chemical, or *metabolite*, formed when the alcohol molecule is biotransformed. This occurs through the process known as *oxidation*, and acetaldehyde is quite toxic to the body. In low levels, it is also found in cigarette smoke.

Acetylcholine: One of the major neurotransmitters in the body. Acetylcholine is found mainly in the outer regions of the body, where the central nervous system interacts with body tissues. Acetylcholine is involved in alerting the body to a potential danger or in the communication between the central nervous system and the muscles of the body.

Addiction: A progressive, chronic, primary, relapsing disorder that involves features such as a compulsion to use a chemical, loss of control over the use of a substance, and continued use of a drug in spite of adverse consequences caused by its use.

Adipose tissue: Fat tissue.

Affinity: The strength with which drug molecules bind to the receptor site in the cell wall.

Agonist: A chemical molecule that has the ability, because of its unique structure, to bind with a receptor molecule located in the cell wall. The degree of a "match" between the agonist and the receptor is called the affinity of the agonist molecule. An agonist might be a natural substance or an artifical compound.

Albumin: One of the primary protein molecules found in the general circulation.

Allele: One of the variants of a gene.

Amino acid: Chemical molecules that the body uses to form proteins, which have a variety of functions in the body.

Amphetamine naive: A term that identifies a person as having never used the amphetamines and thus has no acquired tolerance to this class of medications.

Amygdala: A region of the brain shaped like an almond that is found in the temporal lobe, which is part of the brain's limbic system. The amygdala is thought to be concerned with the process of attaching the emotional content to memory as well as modulating emotional responses to external reality.

Analgesic: A compound that will provide relief from pain, without causing a major change in the individual's level of consciousness.

Analog of a drug: A compound that is a variation in the chemical structure of one drug, producing a "new" drug. The original compound is known as the parent drug.

Anandamide: A compound produced in the brain that functions as a neurotransmitter in certain regions of the brain, especially those regions involved in pain perception.

Anhedonia: Inability of a person to take pleasure in activities that he or she once enjoyed. This condition is a feature of some personality disorders, major depression, and schizophrenia.

Anorexia: Loss of desire to eat.

Anorexic: Causing a state of anorexia.

Antagonist: A compound that blocks, or reverses, the effect of an agonist.

Anterograde amnesia: Inability to remember after a specific event, such as a blow to the head or the ingestion of a chemical known to interfere with memory formation. Amnesia-producing drugs include benzodiazepines, barbiturates, and alcohol. *See also* Blackout.

Antidipsotrophic: A compound or behavioral treatment for *dipsomania*.

Antipyretic: Anti-fever.

Antisocial personality disorder (ASPD): A personality pattern marked by a pervasive disregard for the rights of others, repeated violations of the rights of others, impulsiveness, risk taking, disregard for the truth, and self-centeredness. Individuals with ASPD may be very articulate and convincing but tend to be most interested in their own gratification regardless of its effect on others.

Anxiety: An emotional state that can range from mild to severe in intensity; the individual feels that she or he is in some form of imminent danger, although there is no identified threat.

Anxiogenic: A compound or experience that increases the individual's level of anxiety.

Anxioyltic: A compound that decreases the individual's anxiety level.

Apnea: Cessation of normal respiration.

Arrhythmia, cardiac: Disturbance of the normal rhythm of the heart. Depending on the etiology of the arrhythmia, this might prove fatal to the individual.

Aspirative pneumonia: A pneumonia characterized by two components: (a) aspiration of gastric contents into the lungs as a result of a breakdown of the normal body defenses that are supposed to prevent this, and (b) damage to the tissues of the lungs from gastric fluids or bacterial infection (Bartlett, 1999).

Atherosclerosis: A condition in which fatty plaques accumulate in the inner walls of the arteries of the circulatory system. If too much of the artery is obstructed, the blood flow through that artery is obstructed.

Basal ganglia: A region of the brain involved in the exertion of the individual's will on conscious movement. This is where spontaneous movement is initiated. The basal ganglia have indirect connections to the reticular activating system and extensive connections to the cortex of the brain.

Bioavailability: Concentration of the unchanged chemical at the site of action.

Biotransformation: The process, usually carried out in the liver, by which the body alters the chemical structure of a foreign molecule to a form that will allow it to be eliminated from the body, usually by excretion. The process of changing a foreign molecule into a form that can be excreted yields intermediate metabolites, some of which are biologically active.

Blackout: Alcohol-induced memory dysfunction; technically, a state of alcohol-induced anterograde amnesia.

Blind research study: A study in which the data are examined without the researcher knowing whether any given piece of data is from the research sample or the control sample. For example, tissue samples from participants might be examined by a researcher who did not know if the tissue sample came from an alcoholic or a nonalcoholic person.

Botulism: A form of paralysis usually seen when the victim ingests food contaminated by a toxin produced by the microscopic organism *Clostridium botulinum*. The toxin is one of the most potent neurotoxins known to man, and exposure to this agent is potentially fatal.

Carcinogen: A chemical that is known, or strongly suspected of being able, to cause cancer in humans.

Cardiomyopathy: A disease of the heart muscle, in which the muscle tissue becomes flabby and weaker than usual. One or more of the ventricles of the heart might enlarge, and this condition might progress to congestive heart failure.

Cardiotoxin: Any compound that is toxic to the muscle tissue of the heart.

Catecholamines: A family of chemicals, including epinephrine that normally is produced in the adrenal glands, and the neurotransmitters norepinephrine and dopamine. Catecholamines help to regulate varous body functions. For example, epinephrine functions as a vasoconstrictor, whereas norepinephrine and dopamine are neurotransmitters.

Central nervous system (CNS): The brain and spinal cord.

Cerebellum: Located at the base of the brain, this region of the brain is involved in coordination of muscle activity, balance, and some sensorimotor activity.

Cerebrovascular accident (CVA): Once called *stroke*. There are two forms of CVA: the *occlusive* form, in which a blood clot or other material clogs a blood vessel, preventing blood from reaching the brain cells serviced by that vessel; the *hemorrhagic* form, in which a blood vessel ruptures, exposing surrounding neurons to blood (which is toxic to nervous system tissue) and disrupting the blood supply to those neurons serviced by the vessel that has ruptured. Of the two, the occlusive form is by far the most common. *See also* Embolism; Embolus.

Cerebrum: The largest region of the brain, including the cortex.

Cilia: A microscopic, hairlike projection from the cell wall. Cilia are found in many regions of the human body. In the lungs, the motion of the cilia help to push mucus to the top of the lungs, where it is expelled, helping to keep the lungs clean.

Conduct disorder: A condition seen in childhood or adolescence, marked by behaviors that repeatedly violate the rights of others or the age-appropriate norms/rules. Usually, the violation of rules is quite serious, if not extreme, such as running away from home two or more times when there is no physical or sexual abuse situation, violation of parental curfews before the age of 13, vandalism, arson, theft, and the like. Deceitfulness is commonly seen in conduct-disordered children and adolescents, and the child has little empathy for the feelings of others, including those that he or she has hurt. By definition, this condition is not due to any other form of mental illness, such as intellectual impairment or schizophrenia. For a list of the diagnostic criteria for this condition, consult the *Diagnostic and Statistical Manual of Mental Disorders*, 4th edition (Text Revision) (American Psychiatric Association, 2000).

Congestive heart failure: Inadequate heart function, resulting in shortness of breath, fluid accumulation in the extremities, and possible arrhythmias, formation of emboli, and sudden death.

Conjugation: One of the four primary methods of biotransformation used by the liver.

Cortex: The outermost layer of the human brain, where the "higher functions" of thought are generated. This region is intricately folded in upon itself in the adult human brain and contains specialized neurons devoted to such tasks as motor coordination, speech, language interpretation, and processing of sensory information.

COX-1: A subtype of cyclooxygenase found in the human body. Researchers think that COX-1 is normally produced by the body to help regulate the activity of different organs.

COX-2: A subtype of cyclooxygenase found in the human body. Researchers think that COX-2 is produced mainly when body tissues are damaged, helping to trigger the inflammatory response at the site of injury.

CVA: *See* Cerebrovascular accident.

Cross tolerance: A phenomenon in which an individual becomes tolerant to the effects of one substance, such as alcohol, and the tolerance then transfers to other, similar compounds. In the case of alcohol, for example, the alcohol-tolerant individual would also become tolerant to benzodiazepines and barbiturates.

Cyclooxygenase: An enzyme involved in the production of the prostaglandins in the human body. Because one type of prostaglandin is involved in the inflammation response, this enzyme might be said to be indirectly involved in the development of inflammation at the site of injury.

Date rape: Experience in which one partner in a dating relationship will initiate sexual activity with the other partner, even if the other has not expressed an interest in sexual activity. A common part of the date-rape process is the use of drugs by the aggressor to overcome the victim's resistance to the sexual advances.

Dendrite: A thin, branched part of a nerve cell that extends from the body of the neuron toward other nerve cells, collecting information from those neurons through the receptor sites located along the walls of the dendrite.

Dependence: A state in which the body requires the regular use of a compound to continue functioning. *See also* Neuroadaptation.

Depression: An emotional state marked by pervasive and intense sadness and which may include disturbances of the individual's sleep pattern, sex drive, appitite, ability to concentrate, and enthusiasm for daily activities. The depressed individual may experience feelings of worthlessness, may feel guilt about real or imagined past mistakes, and may actively seek to terminate his or her life through the act of suicide.

Diabetes mellitus: A metabolic disorder in which the body loses the ability to regulate the blood sugar level, either through a deficiency in the production of insulin (known as Type 1 diabetes) or through insensitivity to the insulin that is produced (Type 2 diabetes).

Diabetic retinopathy: A complication of diabetes that is the leading cause of blindness in people 20 to 74 years of age.

Dipsomania: Obsolete term for alcohol dependence.

Distribution: How the chemical molecules are moved about in the body. This is usually accomplished by the circulatory system.

Diversion of drugs: A process through which compounds originally prescribed by a physician are used by people for whom those drugs were not prescribed. Sometimes the medications are stolen from drugstores or a person's medicine cabinet. On other occasions an individual with a legitimate need for a desired medication will (for a fee) visit several different doctors in a short period of time to obtain prescriptions from each physician for the same medication. The medications obtained from this process are then sold to other drug abusers.

Dopamine: One of the major neurotransmitters in the body. Dopamine is used as a neurotransmitter by many different regions of the CNS. There are five known subtypes of dopamine found in the CNS.

Dopaminergic: Using dopamine.

Downregulation: A process in which the number of neurotransmitter receptors in a neuron is reduced, increasing the sensitivity of the cell to a certain form of stimulation, because a smaller number of receptor sites will need to be occupied to achieve the critical threshold necessary for the neuron to fire.

Dysentery: A painful infection of the lower intestinal tract, caused by the ingestion of contaminated water. A person with dysentery will develop massive diarrhea that is often mixed with blood and mucus. Unless the fluid loss caused by the diarrhea is rapidly controlled, dysentery can prove rapidly fatal. Dysentery was common in the crowded army camps of the 1700s and 1800s as well as in many cities of that era.

Dysphoria: Acute, transient changes in mood, usually involving such emotions as sadness, sorrow, and depression.

Effective dose (ED): A calculation performed by pharmacologists to estimate the percentage of a population that will respond to a given dose of a chemical. For example, the ED that 95% of the population will respond to is written by pharmacologists as the ED_{95}.

Elimination half-life: The period of time that the body requires to eliminate 50% of a single dose of a drug. Contrast this to the therapeutic half-life of a drug.

Embolism: The process by which a blood vessel is blocked by another substance (a blood clot, fat formation, talc, etc.) known as an embolus. The embolus is transported by the blood from another part of the body and might lodge in any number of different blood vessels. If it lodges in a blood vessel in the lung, the process is called a *pulmonary embolism*; if the embolus lodges in the brain, it is said to cause an *ischemic event, ischemic stroke,* or *cerebrovascular accident.*

Embolus: A formation of fat, or a blood clot, or possibly a foreign substance such as talc introduced into the body when a drug abuser injects a drug contaminated with this substance. The embolus will travel through the bloodstream, propelled by the action of the heart, until it lodges in a blood vessel too small to allow it to move any further. A cork or a plug would be a good analogy.

Enkephalins: Small molecules that belong to the neuropeptide family of chemicals. The enkephalins bind to the opioid receptor sites in the CNS, contributing to the control of mood, movement, behavior, and pain perception.

Excretion: A process by which the body removes waste products or foreign chemicals from the general circulation. This is usually accomplished by the kidneys, although some drugs are excreted from the body in the feces or through the lungs.

False negative: A test result that fails to detect something that is there—for example, the result of a test that failed to detect evidence of drug abuse when it was known that the person had indeed abused a controlled substance.

False positive: A test result that suggests something is true when it is not—for example, a test result that identifies an individual as having used a controlled substance when she or he did not do so.

Fillers: Any of a number of compounds added to a tablet intended for oral ingestion, to give the tablet bulk and form—for example, cornstarch and talc. The chemical properties of these compounds is such that they are usually either destroyed by stomach acid when the medication is taken orally, or they are at least prevented from being absorbed into the body. In the latter case, the filler will harmlessly pass through the body and ultimately be excreted, while the active agent in the tablet is absorbed through the gastrointestinal tract.

First order biotransformation process: A subform of biotransformation in which a set percentage of the medication is biotransformed each hour.

First pass metabolism: A process through which substances absorbed into the body from the small intestine are routed through the liver, allowing that organ to begin to neutralize poisons before they reach the general circulation. As a result of first pass metabolism, the liver is often able to biotransform many medications that are administered orally before they have had a chance to reach the site of action.

Fluoxetine: Generic name of an antidepressant of the selective serotonin reuptake inhibitor (SSRI) class.

Fluvoxamine: Generic name of an antidepressant of the selective serotonin reuptake inhibitor (SSRI) class.

Formication: The sensation of having unseen bugs crawling either on or just under the skin, possibly induced by medications such as amphetamines or cocaine.

Frontal cortex: Region of the brain involved in planning, anticipation of long-term consequences of behavior, focus of attention on a specific task, and so on.

GABA: Shorthand for gamma-amino-butyric acid. GABA is the main inhibitory neurotransmitter in the brain. Neurons that utilize GABA are found in the cortex, the cerebellum, the hippocampus, the superior and inferior colliculi regions of the brain, the amygdala, and the nucleus accumbens.

Gastritis: Inflammation of the lining of the stomach.

Glossitis: A very painful inflammation of the tongue.

Glutamate: A chemical that functions as an excitatory neurotransmitter in certain regions of the brain. Excessive amounts of glutamate can be toxic to the neurons that it comes into contact with.

Half-life: The period of time that it takes for the concentration of a drug in the blood plasma to be reduced by 50% following a single dose. This process depends, in part, on the health of the individual's liver and kidneys.

Harm reduction: An approach to drug abuse that attempts to limit the damage that the drug(s) might cause to the individual's body. This approach is based on the theory that by limiting the amount of damage to the individual, the ultimate cost of that person's chemical abuse to society will be reduced.

HDL: Shorthand for high-density lipoproteins. Sometimes called the "good" cholesterol, HDL help to remove the more dangerous low-density lipoproteins from the body.

Hepatitis: Inflammation of the liver, characterized by jaundice, liver enlargement, possible abdominal and gastric discomfort, abnormal liver function, and in extreme cases scarring of the liver.

Hepatoxicity: Liver failure.

Hippocampus: A portion of the brain that is thought to be involved in the processing of sensory information and in the formation and retrieval of both verbal and emotional memories.

Huff: A slang term meaning to inhale or to use an inhalant.

Hydrolysis: One of the four primary methods of drug biotransformation used by the liver.

Hypertension: Abnormally high blood pressure, usually defined as blood pressure in excess of 140/90 in an adult.

Hypertensive: Related to hypertension.

Hypnotic: A medication designed to help the user become drowsy and fall asleep.

Hyponatremia: Low sodium levels in blood. May be fatal if not corrected.

Hypothalamus: A region of the brain that helps to regulate body temperature.

Iatrogenic disease: A disorder that arises as a complication of the medical treatment of a separate disorder.

IDS-100: *See* Inventory of Drinking Situations.

Intramuscular: Within muscle tissue.

Intranasal method of drug administration: Depositing a compound on the blood-rich tissues of the sinuses where it can be absorbed into the circulation.

Intravenous: Within the veins of the circulatory system.

Inventory of Drinking Situations: A 100-item questionnaire that, when scored, sheds light on situations in which a person is most likely to drink.

Ischemia: Local oxygen deprivation within tissue, usually caused by a reduction in the amount of blood reaching that region of the body, which may result in the destruction of the tissue.

Ischemic stroke: Blockage of a blood vessel in the brain, leading to ischemia in that region of the brain. If this condition is not corrected immediately, those brain cells may be damaged or even die.

Lethal dose level: A calculation performed by scientists to determine the percentage of the general population who will die from exposure to a toxin/chemical. For example, the

lethal dose (LD) at which 95% of the population would die without medical intervention is written as LD_{95}.

LDL: Shorthand for low-density lipoproteins. Sometimes this is called "bad" cholesterol, as plaque tends to be made up of low-density lipoproteins.

Limbic system: Region of the brain thought to be involved in the development and expression of emotions.

Lipids: Fat molecules within the blood, used by the body for various purposes, including formation of cell walls.

Liter: Unit of liquid measure in the metric system of measurement. A liter is 1.056 liquid quarts, or 33.792 liquid ounces.

Locus ceruleus: A region of the brain thought to be involved in the perception of pain and the sensation of anxiety.

"Making" a doctor: Slang term for manipulating a physician into providing a prescription for a desired compound, such as an amphetamine or opioid.

Mean corpuscular volume (MCV): A measure of the average size of a sample of an individual's red blood cells.

Metabolite: One of the compounds that is formed, usually by the liver, during the process of drug biotransformation. Each of the metabolites is a variation of the original parent molecule that has been chemically altered so that the body can eventually remove it from the circulation through the process of elimination.

MI: *See* Myocardial infarction.

Myocardial infarction (MI): Commonly called a heart attack. A process in which the blood supply to a region of the heart is disrupted, possibly by coronary artery disease or by an embolus that blocks a blood vessel leading to the heart. Those heart muscle cells that are deprived of blood may be damaged or in extreme cases may die. This condition can kill the individual if enough cardiac tissue is destroyed; it results in scar tissue formation in those patients who do survive. If the patient survives, his or her cardiac function might be impaired to the point that he or she becomes at risk for later myocardial infarctions, congestive heart failure, the formation of emboli, arrhythmias, and so forth.

N-methyl-D-aspartate: An amino acid that functions as an excitatory neurotransmitter within some regions of the brain.

Narcolepsy: A very rare, lifelong, neurological condition in which the patient experiences sudden attacks of sleep.

Neuroadaptation: A process that takes place within the CNS, in which the neurons make basic changes in how they perform in an attempt to continue normal function in spite of the continued exposure to a chemical that affects the CNS. This process is called neuroadaptation when the individual is using a prescribed medication. This same process was once called *tolerance*, although this term is now used primarily to describe the process of neuroadaptation to drugs of abuse.

Neuron: A nerve cell. Neurons are actually microscopic chemical-electrical generators that produce a small electrical "message" by actively moving sodium and calcium ions back and forth across the cell boundary. Sodium and calcium ions pass through the cell wall through special channels, which are formed by protein molecules in the cell wall. Through a concentration of sodium ions inside the cell, a small electric potential is established. When the neuron fires, calcium ions rush into the cell, replacing the sodium ions, and the cell loses the electric charge that it had built up. The cell then repeats the cycle, pumping calcium ions out and sodium ions back in, to build up another electric charge so that it might fire again. Any chemical that interacts with the protein molecules that form sodium/calcium ion channels in the cell wall of the body's tissues will affect how those cells function.

Neurotoxin: A chemical that destroys nerve cells (neurons).

Neurotransmitter: Any molecule released by a neuron to cause a change in the function of a designated target cell. After being released, the neurotransmitter molecules cross the synapse to bind at a receptor site on the target cell. This then causes the target cell to respond to the chemical message transmitted by the first cell's neurotransmitter molecules.

NMDA: *See* N-methyl-D-aspartate.

Nucleus accumbens: The region of the brain thought to be involved in the pleasure response. Because of this, the nucleus accumbens is also thought to be one region of the brain where drugs are able to cause the sensation of pleasure.

Oliguria: Significant reduction in the amount of urine produced by the kidneys.

Opiophobia: Fear of inducing, or contributing to the development of, an addictive disorder by prescribing too high a dose of narcotic analgesics or by prescribing narcotic analgesics for too long a period of time.

Over-the-counter (OTC) medication: A medication that can be purchased without a prescription. It thus might be sold in various outlets besides a pharmacy, such as a grocery store. Over 600 medications that were once available in the United States only by prescription have now been classified as OTC medications by the Food and Drug Administration (Scheller, 1998).

Oxidation: One of the four primary methods of drug biotransformation used by the liver. In this process, a hydrogen atom is removed from the molecule being biotransformed, or an oxygen atom is added to the molecule, changing its chemical structure in a minor way. Ultimately, the atom in question is changed in such a way that the kidneys can then eliminate the compound from the blood.

Panic attack: The experience of intense feelings of anxiety, often with symptoms such as shortness of breath, rapid heartbeat, a feeling of impending doom, or a feeling that something terrible is about to happen. Panic attacks are usually very short in duration (10–60 minutes) but can cause extreme distress.

Parent compound: The original drug molecule. Usually in reference to its form before it is altered by the process of biotransformation.

Patient year: A statistical concept. For example, 100 patient years means 100 patients, all of whom have a common medical condition, who are followed for 1 year.

Pharmaceuticals: A street term used to describe medications that have been diverted to illicit markets. For example, narcotic analgesics stolen from a pharmacy during a burglary and then sold on the street would be called pharmaceuticals to differentiate them from the drugs produced in illegal laboratories.

Pharmacokinetics: Study of the time course of a drug and its metabolites in the body after it is administered.

Platelets: A part of the body's circulatory system. Disk-shaped platelets circulate in the blood until there is an injury, at which time they help to form a blood clot to stop bleeding.

Polydrug abuse: The abuse of more than one substance at once. Prior to the mid 1970s, individuals with substance-use problems were usually abusing just one chemical, such as alcohol or heroin. This pattern of substance abuse is rarely seen today, except in older individuals whose substance-use pattern was established in the mid 1970s or early 1980s. Currently, it is more common for the individual who has a substance-use problem to be abusing more than one chemical simultaneously.

Polypharmacology: *See* Polydrug abuse.

Potentiate: Often, when similar compounds are ingested, the effects of one drug will intensify that of the other(s), possibly producing lethal results. *See also* Synergistic response.

Prime effect of a drug: The intended effect of a drug. For example, a person with a fever might take some aspirin to lower the fever. The reduction in fever is thus the prime effect of the aspirin. *See also* Side effect of a drug.

Proband: An individual being studied in a genetic investigation.

Prodrug: A compound that is administered to the patient and is then biotransformed by the liver into a compound that is biologically active. Technically, this compound is a metabolite of the parent drug. The parent drug may or may not have a biological action of its own, but the metabolite has a stronger biological action than does the parent drug. This is why the compound is administered to the patient.

Prostaglandins: Any of a family of compounds found in the body that help to mediate the inflammatory response following an injury and also help to control body functions. The prostaglandins function like hormones in the body and are active in very low concentrations.

Rapid eye movement: *See* REM sleep.

Receptor: A protein molecule or group of molecules anchored in the cell wall that allows the cell to receive chemicals from the outside wall. If the chemical molecule transmits a form of information between cells, it is called a *transmitter* molecule. Examples of these include hormones, antigens, and peptides. If the transmitter molecule is from one of the neurons of the CNS, it is referred to as a *neurotransmitter*. Neurotransmitters pass information between neurons.

Receptor site: The region in the cell wall of a neuron where a receptor is located.

Reduction: One of the four primary methods of drug biotransformation used by the liver.

REM sleep: A stage of sleep characterized by rapid eye movement (REM) and usually associated with dream states. Research suggests that the individual usually spends a portion of each sleep cycle in REM sleep and that if this stage of sleep is disrupted for more than a few nights by drugs, a sleep disorder, or inability to sleep, the disruption will have an effect on the individual's ability to function during the waking portion of the day.

REM rebound: A phenomenon in which the individual experiences an increase in the amount of sleep time spent in REM sleep after stopping the use of a CNS depressant, apparently to "catch up" on lost REM sleep. During this period, the individual will experience vivid dreams, which may be quite frightening to the dreamer, and in some cases the nightmares are so disturbing that the patient will begin to use alcohol or drugs again in order to "get a good night's sleep."

Reye's syndrome: A serious medical condition that usually develops in children between the ages of 2 and 12. The condition usually follows a viral infection such as influenza or chickenpox. Symptoms include swelling of the brain, seizures, disturbance of consciousness, a fatty degeneration of the liver, and coma. In about 30% of the cases the syndrome will result in death.

Rhabdomyolysis: Destruction of skeletal muscle tissue on a massive scale. When muscle cells die, they release a chemical known as myoglobin, which helps to store oxygen in the muscle cell. In rhabdomyolysis, massive amounts of myoglobin are released at once. The accumulated myoglobin interferes with kidney function and in extreme cases can result in kidney failure, cardiac arrhythmias, and death.

Rhinitis: Inflammation of the nasal passages.

Rig: Intravenous needle.

Schizophrenia: A psychiatric disorder characterized by delusional thinking, hallucinations, and disorganized behavior.

Secondary hyperparathyroidism: A hormonal disorder that develops when alcohol interferes with the body's ability to regulate calcium levels in the blood for extended periods of time. The calcium in the bones is then reabsorbed into the blood, and the bones become weakened through calcium loss.

Sedative: A drug designed to decrease the individual's activity level, moderate excitement, and calm the patient.

Serotonergic: Activated by or capable of liberating serotonin, especially in transmitting nerve impulses.

Serotonin: One of the major neurotransmitters in the body. Serotonin is used as a neurotransmitter by many different regions of the CNS. There are 15 known subtypes of serotonin found in the CNS, each of which is assumed to control one or more subfunctions within the CNS.

Serotonin syndrome: A rare, drug-induced, neurological disorder that can be life threatening. In spite of the best medical care, approximately 11% of people afflicted with this condition will die. Symptoms of the serotonin syndrome include irritability, confusion, an increase in anxiety, drowsiness, hyperthermia (increased body temperature), sinus tachycardia, dilation of the pupils, nausea, muscle rigidity, and seizures. Although serotonin syndrome may develop as long as 24 hours after the ingestion of a medication or drug that affects the serotonin neurotransmitter system, in 50% of the cases the patient will develop the syndrome within just 2 hours of starting the medication or illicit drug (Mills, 1995). This condition constitutes a medical emergency and should be treated by a physician.

Side effect of a drug: The unintended effect of a chemical in the body. For example, if a person takes some aspirin to control a fever and then experiences gastrointestinal bleeding, the bleeding is an undesired side effect of that compound. *See also* Prime effect of a drug.

"Silent" cardiac ischemia: Episode of cardiac ischemia that is not accompanied by pain or shortness of breath, symptoms that usually occur when the heart muscle is deprived of oxygen. *See* Ischemia.

Single photon emission computed tomography: Imaging through a scanning device that allows scientists to study blood flow patterns in living tissues.

Site of action: The place where a drug has its prime effect.

Sleep apnea: A breathing disorder in which the individual's ability to breathe is disrupted during sleep. Complications of sleep apnea can include high blood pressure, a disruption of the normal heart rate, and even death.

Sleep latency: The period between the time the individual first goes to bed and the time he or she finally falls asleep.

Subdural hematoma: Hemorrhage in the skull, leading to the collection of blood in the space between the membranes surrounding the brain or spinal cord and the skull bones. This condition usually develops as a result of trauma. This process puts pressure on the surrounding tissues of the CNS and can lead to paralysis or even death.

Sublingual method of drug administration: Method of drug administration in which a tablet, capsule, or liquid is placed under the tongue where it can be absorbed quickly into the blood. Some medications and a small number of drugs of abuse can be absorbed through the blood-rich tissues under the tongue.

Suicide: The intentional termination of one's life.

Sumer: The first city-state, located in what is now Iraq. The city-state of Sumer gave rise to the Sumerian empire. It was in Sumer that the art of writing was developed, initially as a system for economic record keeping. Shortly afterward, laws, important events, and the like were also recorded in writing on clay tablets. Many of the tablets are devoted to the process of brewing beer, apparently a favorite beverage in this ancient empire.

Synapse: A microscopic gap between two neurons, across which one neuron will release neurotransmitter molecules to receptor sites in order to transmit a message to the next neuron in that nerve pathway.

Synergistic response: The process by which two or more compounds with the same, or similar, actions multiply the effects of each other.

Synesthesia: A phenomenon wherein information from one sense may "slip over" into another sensory system. A person who is experiencing synesthesia may report being able to "taste" colors or "see" music.

T-helper cell: A form of cell, found in the body's immune system, that helps to activate the body's immune response to a foreign cell.

Temporal lobe: A region of the brain's cortex involved in sensory function, language use, and some aspects of emotions.

Therapeutic half-life: The period of time that the body requires to reduce the effectiveness of a single dose of a drug by 50%.

Therapeutic Index (TI): The ratio between the ED_{50} and the LD_{50}.

Therapeutic threshold: The point at which the concentration of a specific chemical begins to have the desired effect on the user.

Therapeutic window: The dosage range at which the person is taking enough of a pharmaceutical agent to benefit from it, without taking so much that she or he would experience toxic effects from an overdose of that compound.

Thiamine: Also known as vitamin B-1, used by the body to maintain appropriate function of cells in the cardiovascular and nervous systems.

Tolerance: The development of resistance to a drug's effects over time, as the body adapts to the repeated administration of a chemical compound.

Transdermal: Literally, "across the skin."

Type 2 diabetes mellitus: Also known as *adult onset diabetes*. A condition in which the individual's body becomes insensitive to the effects of the insulin being produced. This is the most common form of diabetes, accounting for 85% of all cases of diabetes mellitus.

Ulcer, "bleeding": If a stomach ulcer forms over a blood vessel, the acid will destroy the walls of the blood vessel, allowing blood to escape into the stomach. This is a "bleeding" ulcer. Such bleeding ulcers are a life-threatening emergency. *See also* Ulcer, gastric.

Ulcer, gastric: When stomach acid is brought into contact with the tissues of the stomach, and gradually an area of stomach lining is destroyed by the stomach's acid, the resulting condition is called an ulcer. The condition is usually quite painful.

Upregulation: The process by which a neuron will increase the number of receptors in the cell wall, thus increasing the sensitivity of that neuron to a certain neurotransmitter. This is usually done to compensate for a decrease in the availability of a certain neurotransmitter molecule over time by giving the neurotransmitter molecules more potential receptor sites at which they might bind.

Vasospasm: A phenomenon in which a blood vessel will go into spasms, which interferes with the ability of that vessel to control blood flow. If the vasospasm continues long enough, blood clots may form, which then can cause an occlusion by blocking the blood flow through either an artery or vein.

Ventricular fibrillation: A pattern of rapid and essentially uncoordinated contractions of the lower two chambers of the heart (the ventricles), disrupting the pumping action of the heart.

Viral load test: A procedure that uses DNA technology to provide an estimate of the number of virus particles in a given unit of blood (usually a cubic millimeter). This test is used to estimate the progression of viral infections such as HIV/AIDS and the various hepatitis infections.

Withdrawal: The characteristic process of reverse adaptation, which occurs when a drug that has been repeatedly used over a short period of time is suddenly discontinued. *See also* Tolerance.

Wound botulism: A form of botulism that develops when spores of the microscopic organism *Clostridium botulinum* infect a wound and begin to produce the neurotoxin *botulinum*.

Zero order biotransformation process: A subform of the biotransformation process in which a foreign chemical is metabolized at a set rate, no matter how high the concentration of that chemical in the blood.

REFERENCES

Aanavi, M. P., Taube, D. O., Ja, D. Y., & Duran, E. F. (2000). The status of psychologists' training about and treatment of substance-abusing clients. *Journal of Psychoactive Drugs, 31*, 441–444.

Aase, J. M. (1994). Clinical recognition of FAS. *Alcohol Health & Research World, 18*(1), 5–9.

Abbey, A., Zawacki, T., Buck, P. O., Clinton, A. M., & McAuslan, P. (2001). Alcohol and sexual assault. *Alcohol Research & Health, 25*(1), 43–51.

Abbott, P. H. J., Quinn, D., & Knox, L. (1995). Ambulatory medical detoxification for alcohol. *American Journal of Drug and Alcohol Abuse, 21*, 549–564.

Abel, E. L. (1982). *Drugs and behavior: A primer in neuropsychopharmacology.* Malabar, FL: Robert E. Krieger Publishing Co.

Abramowitz, M. Z. (2004). GHB and date rape. *British Journal of Psychiatry, 185*, 176–177.

Abrams, D. I., Hilton, J. F., Leiser, R. J., Shade, S. B., Elbeik, T. A., Aweeka, F. T., Benowitz, N. L., Bredt, B. M., Kosel, B., Aberg, J. A., Deeks, S. G., Mitchell, T. F., Mulligan, K., Bacchetti, P., McCune, J. M., & Schambelan, M. (2003). Short-term effects of cannabinoids in patients with HIV-1 infection. *Annals of Internal Medicine, 139*, 258–288.

Abrams, M. (2003). The end of craving. *Discover, 24*(5), 24–25.

Abrams, R. C., & Alexopoulos, G. (1987). Substance abuse in the elderly: Alcohol and prescription drugs. *Hospital and Community Psychiatry, 38*, 1285–1288.

Abrams, R. C., & Alexopoulos, G. S. (1998). Geriatric addictions. In *Clinical textbook of addictive disorders* (2nd ed.) (Frances, R. J., & Miller, S. I., eds.). New York: Guilford.

Abt Associates, Inc. (1995a). *Pulse check.* Washington: Office of National Drug Control Policy.

Abt Associates, Inc. (1995b). *What America's users spend on illegal drugs, 1988–1993.* Washington: Office of National Drug Control Policy.

Achord, J. L. (1995). Alcohol and the liver. *Scientific American Science & Medicine, 2*(2), 16–27.

Ackerman, R. J. (1983). *Children of alcoholics: A guidebook for educators, therapists, and parents.* Holmes Beach, FL: Learning Publications, Inc.

Adams, J. K. (1988). Setting free chemical dependency. *Alcoholism & Addiction, 8*(4), 20–21.

Adams, W. L., Yuan, Z., Barboriak, J. J., & Rimm, A. A. (1993). Alcohol-related hospitalizations of elderly people. *Journal of the American Medical Association, 270*, 1222–1225.

Addiction—Part I. (1992a). *Harvard Medical School Mental Health Letter, 9*(4), 1–4.

Addiction—Part II. (1992b). *Harvard Medical School Mental Health Letter, 9*(5), 1–4.

Addiction treatment might be old drugs. (2004). CNN. Retrieved from http://www.cnn.com/2004/HEALTH/conditions/08/30/treating.addiction.ap/index.hmtl.

Adelman, S. A., & Weiss, R. D. (1989). What is therapeutic about inpatient alcoholism treatment? *Hospital and Community Psychiatry, 40*(5), 515–519.

Adger, H., & Werner, M. J. (1994). The pediatrician. *Alcohol Health & Research World, 18*, 121–126.

Adler, J., & Underwood, A. (2002). Aspirin: the oldest new wonder drug. *Newsweek, CXXIX* (21), 60–62.

The agony of "ecstasy." (1994). *Medical Update, 17*(11), 5–6.

Al-Anon's Twelve Steps & Twelve Traditions. (1985). New York: Al-Anon Family Group Headquarters, Inc.

Albertson, T. E., Derlet, R. W., & Van Hoozen, B. E. (1999). Methamphetamine and the expanding complications of amphetamines. *Western Journal of Medicine, 170*, 214–219.

Albertson, T. E., Walby, W. F., & Derlet, R. (1995). Stimulant-induced pulmonary toxicity. *Chest, 108*, 1140–1150.

Alcoholics Anonymous. (1976). New York: Alcoholics Anonymous World Services, Inc.

Alemi, F., Stephens, R. C., Llorens, S., & Orris, B. (1995). A review of factors affecting treatment outcomes: Expected Treatment Outcome Scale. *American Journal of Drug and Alcohol Abuse, 21*, 483–510.

Alexander, D. E., & Gwyther, R. E. (1995). Alcoholism in adolescents and their families. *Pediatric Clinics of North America, 42*, 217–234.

Alexander, M. J. (1996). Women with co-occuring addictive and mental disorders. *American Journal of Orthopsychiatry, 66*, 61–70.

Alibrandi, L. A. (1978). The folk psychotherapy of Alcoholics Anonymous. In *Practical Approaches to Alcoholism Psychotherapy* (Zimberg, S., Wallace, J., & Blume, S., eds.). New York: Plenum Press.

Aligne, C. A., & Stoddard, J. J. (1997). Tobacco and children. *Archives of Pediatric and Adolescent Medicine, 151,* 648–653.

Allen, M. G., & Phillips, K. L. (1993). Utilization review of treatment for chemical dependence. *Hospital and Community Psychiatry, 44,* 752–756.

Alper, J., & Natowicz, M. R. (1992). The allure of genetic explanations. *British Medical Journal, 305,* 666.

Alter, J. (2001). Making marriage work: Communications in recovery. Symposium presented to the Dept. of Psychiatry of The Cambridge Hospital, Boston, MA. March 2.

Alterman, A. I., Erdlen, D. I., LaPorte, D. J., & Erdlen, F. R. (1982). Effects of illicit drug use in an inpatient psychiatric population. *Addictive Behaviors, 7,* 231–242.

Alterman, A. I., McDermott, P. A., Cacciola, J. S., Rutherford, M. I., Boardman, C. R., McKay, J. R., & Cook, T. G. (1998). A typology of antisociality in methadone patients. *Journal of Abnormal Psychology, 107,* 412–422.

Ameling, A., & Povilonis, M. (2001). Spirituality, meaning, mental health, and nursing. *Journal of Psychosocial Nursing, 39*(4), 15–20.

American Academy of Family Physicians. (1990). Effects of fetal exposure to cocaine and heroin. *American Family Physician, 41*(5), 1595–1597.

American Academy of Pediatrics. (1998). Neonatal drug withdrawal. *Pediatrics, 101,* 1079–1089.

American Medical Association. (1993). *Factors contributing to the health care cost problem.* Chicago: American Medical Association.

American Medical Association. (1994). *Drug evaluations annual 1994.* Washington, DC: Author.

American Psychiatric Association. (1990). *Benzodiazepine dependence, toxicity, and abuse.* Washington, DC: American Psychiatric Association.

American Psychiatric Association. (1995). Practice guidelines for the treatment of patients with substance use disorders: alcohol, cocaine, opioids. *American Journal of Psychiatry, 152*(11) (supplement).

American Psychiatric Association. (1996). Practice guidelines for the treatment of patients with nicotine dependence. *American Journal of Psychiatry, 153*(10) (Suppl.).

American Psychiatric Association. (2000). *Diagnostic and statistical manual of mental disorders (4th ed.—Text Revision).* Washington, DC: American Psychiatric Association.

American Society of Health-System Pharmacists. (2002). *AHFS drug information.* Bethesda, MD: Author.

Ames, D., Wirshing, W. C., & Friedman, R. (1993). Ecstasy, the serotonin syndrome, and neuroleptic malignant syndrome—a possible link? *Journal of the American Medical Association, 269,* 869–870.

Amphetamines. (1990). *Harvard Medical School Mental Health Letter, 6*(10), 1–4.

Amtmann, D., Weydt, P., Johnson, K. L., Jensen, M. P., & Carter, G. T. (2004). Survey of cannabis use in patients with amyotrophic lateral sclerosis. *American Journal of Hospice & Palliative Care, 21*(2), 95–104.

Anczak, J. D., & Nogler, R. A. (2003). Tobacco cessation in primary care: Maximizing intervention strategies. *Clinical Medicine & Research, 1*(3), 201–216.

Anda, R. F., Whitfield, C. L., Felitti, V. J., Chapman, D., Edwards, V. J., Dube, S. R., & Williamson, D. F. (2002). Adverse childhood experiences, alcoholic parents, and later risk of alcoholism and depression. *Psychiatric Services, 53,* 1001–1009.

Anderson, C. E., & Loomis, G. A. (2003). Recognition and prevention of inhalant abuse. *American Family Physician, 68,* 869–874, 876.

Anderson, D. J. (1989). An alcoholic is never too old for treatment. *Minneapolis Star Tribune, VIII* (200), p. ex7.

Anderson, D. J. (1993). Chemically dependent women still face barriers. *Minneapolis Star Tribune, XII* (65), p. E8.

Anderson, D. J. (1995). Adult children of alcoholics must deal with anger. *Minneapolis Star Tribune, XIII* (274), p. ex4.

Anderson, R. (1993). AIDS: Trends, predictions, controversy. *Nature, 363,* 393–394.

Angell, M., & Kassirer, J. P. (1994). Alcohol and other drugs—toward a more rational and consistent policy. *The New England Journal of Medicine, 331,* 537–539

Angier, N. (1990). Storming the wall. *Discover, 11*(5), 67–72.

Anker, A. L., & Smilkstein, M. J. (1994). Acetaminophen. *Emergency Medical Clinics of North America, 12,* 335–349.

Annis, H. M., & Davis, C. S. (1991). Relapse prevention. *Alcohol Health & Research World, 15*(3), 204–212.

Anthony, J. C., Arria, A. M., & Johnson, E. O. (1995). Epidemiological and public health issues for tobacco, alcohol, and other drugs. In *Review of psychiatry* (Vol. 14) (Oldham, J. M., & Riba, M. B., eds.). Washington: American Psychiatric Press.

Antman, K., & Chang, Y. (2000). Kaposi's Sarcoma. *New England Journal of Medicine, 342,* 1027–1038.

Anton, R. F. (1994). Medications for treating alcoholism. *Alcohol Health & Research World, 18,* 265–271.

Anton, R. F. (1999). What is craving? Models and implications for treatment. *Alcohol Research & Health, 23,* 165–173.

Antoin, H., & Beasley, R. D. (2004). Opioids for chronic noncancer pain. *Postgraduate Medicine, 116*(3), 37–44.

Antonio, R. (1997). The use & abuse of ephedrine. *Muscle & Fitness, 58*(10), 178–180.

Appleby, L., Dyson, V., Luchins, D. J., & Cohen, L. S. (1997). The impact of substance abuse screening on a public psychiatric inpatient population. *Psychiatric Services, 48,* 1311–1316.

Arehart-Treichel, J. (2004). Homelessness does not lead to increased substance abuse. *Psychiatric News, 39*(12), 9.

Arnett, J. J. (2000). Emerging adulthood. *American Psychologist, 55,* 469–480.

Aronoff, G. M., Wagner, J. M., & Spangler, A. S. (1986). Chemical interventions for pain. *Journal of Consulting and Clinical Psychology, 54,* 769–775.

Ashe, A. R., & Mason, J. D. (2001). Assessing and managing head injury. *Emergency Medicine, 33*(12), 26–39.

Ashton, H. (1992). *Brain function and psychotropic drugs.* New York: Oxford.

Ashton, H. (1994). Guidelines for the rational use of benzodiazepines. *Drugs, 48*(1), 25–40.

Asseo, L. (1993). Drug war clogs system, ABA says. *St. Paul Pioneer Press, 144*(287), p. A2.

Associated Press. (1993). Drug dealers find new prey—the deaf. *San Francisco Examiner, 128*(21), p. B7.

Asthma deaths blamed on cocaine use. (1997). *Forensic Drug Abuse Advisor, 9*(2), 14.

Astrachan, B. M., & Tischler, G. L. (1984). Normality from a health systems perspective. In *Normality and the Life Cycle* (Offer, D., & Sabshin, M., eds.). New York: Basic Books.

Athletes caught using a new steroid—THG. (2003). *Forensic Drug Abuse Advisor, 15*, 76–77.

Autti-Ramo, I. (2000). Twelve-year follow-up of children exposed to alcohol in utero. *Developmental Medicine & Child Neurology, 42*, 406–411.

Avants, S. K., Margolin, P., Chang, T. R., & Birch, S. (1995). Acupuncture for the treatment of cocaine addiction: Investigation of a needle puncture control. *Journal of Substance Abuse Treatment, 12*, 195–205.

Ayd, F. J. (1994). Prescribing anxiolytics and hypnotics for the elderly. *Psychiatric Annals, 24*(2), 91–97.

Ayd, F. J., Janicak, P. G., Davis, J. M., & Preskorn, S. H. (1996). Advances in the pharmacotherapy of anxiety and sleep disorders. *Principles and practice of psychopharmacotherapy, 1*(4), 1–22.

Baber, A. (1998). Addiction's poster child. *Playboy, 45*(5), 29.

Bach, A. K., Wincze, J. P., & Barlow, D. H. (2001). Sexual dysfunction. In *Clinical handbook of psychological disorders* (3rd ed.) (Barlow, D. H., ed.). New York: Guilford.

Back Letter, The. (1994). Steroid-abusing patients: Handle with care. *Archives of General Psychiatry, 51*, 83.

Badon, L. A., Hicks, A., Lord, K., Ogden, B. A., Meleg-Smith, S., & Varner, K. J. (2002). Changes in cardiovascular responsiveness and cardiotoxicity elicited during binge administration of ecstasy. *Journal of Pharmacology and Experimental Therapeutics, 302*, 898–907.

Bagatell, C. J., & Bremner, W. J. (1996). Androgens in men—uses and abuses. *New England Journal of Medicine, 334*, 707–714.

Bagnardi, V., Blangiardo, M., La Vecchia, C., & Corrao, G. (2001). Alcohol consumption and the risk of cancer. *Alcohol Research & Health, 25*, 263–270.

Bahrke, M. S. (1990). Psychological research, methodological problems, and relevant issues. Paper presented at the 1990 meeting of the American Psychological Association, Boston, MA.

Bai-Fang, X., Sobel, S. C., Sigmon, S. L., Walsh, R. E., Johnson, I. A., Liebson, I. A., Nuwayser, E. S., Kerrigan, J. H., & Bigelow, G. E. (2004). Open label trial of an injection depot formulation of buprenorphine in opioid detoxification. *Drug and Alcohol Dependence, 73*(1), 11–22.

Bailey, K. P. (2004). Pharmacological treatments for substance use disorders. *Journal of Psychosocial Nursing, 42*(8), 14–20.

Bald is not beautiful, thallium found in French heroin. (1996). *Forensic Drug Abuse Advisor, 8*(5), 35–36.

Bales, J. (1988). Legalized drugs: Idea flawed, debate healthy. *APA Monitor, 19*(8), 22.

Ballenger, J. C. (1995). Benzodiazepines. In *Textbook of psychopharmacology* (Schatzberg, A. F., & Nemeroff, C. B., eds.). Washington, DC: American Psychiatric Association.

Banerjee, S. (1990). Newest wrinkle for smokers is on their faces. *Minneapolis Star Tribune, VIII* (341), pp. ex1, ex5.

Barbone, F., McMahon, A. D., Davey, P. G., Morris, A. D., Reid, C., McDevitt, D. G., & MacDonald, T. (1998). Association of road-traffic accidents with benzodiazepine use. *The Lancet, 352*, 1331–1336.

Bargh, J. A., & Chartrand, T. L. (1999). The unbearable automaticity of being. *American Psychologist, 54*, 462–479.

Barker, D. (1994). Reasons for tobacco use and symptoms of nicotine withdrawal among adolescent and young adult tobacco users—United States, 1993. *Journal of the American Medical Association, 272*, 1648–1649.

Barki, Z. H. K., Kravitz, H. M., & Berki, T. M. (1998). Psychotropic medications in pregnancy. *Psychiatric Annals, 28*, 486–500.

Barnett, M. (2001). Alternative opioids to morphine in palliative care: A review of current practice and evidence. *Postgraduate Medical Journal, 77*, 371–378.

Barnhill, J. G., Ciraulo, A. M., Ciraulo, D. A., & Greene, J. A. (1995). Interactions of importance in chemical dependence. In *Drug interactions in psychiatry* (2nd ed.) (Ciraulo, D. A., Shader, R. I., Greenblatt, D. J., & Creelman, W., eds.). New York: Williams & Wilkins.

Baron, J. A., Cole, B. F., Sandler, R. S., Haile, R. W., Ahnen, D., Bresalier, R., McKeown-Eyssen, G., Summers, R. W., Rothstein, R., Burke, C. A., Snover, D. C., Church, T. R., Allen, J. I., Beach, M., Beck, G. J., Bond, J. H., Byers, T., Greenberg, E. R., Mandel, J. S., Marcon, N., Mott, L. A., Pearson, L., Saibil, F., & van Stolk, R. (2003). A randomized trial of aspirin to prevent colorectal adenomas. *New England Journal of Medicine, 348*, 891–899.

Barr, A. (1999). *Drink: A social history of America.* New York: Carroll & Graf Publishers, Inc.

Barrera, S. E., Osinski, W. A., & Davidoff, E. (1949/1994). The use of Antabuse (tetraethylthiuramdisulphide) in chronic alcoholics. *American Journal of Psychiatry, 151*, 263–267.

Barre-Sinoussi, F. (1996). HIV as the cause of AIDS. *The Lancet, 348*, 31–35.

Bartecchi, C. E., MacKenzie, T. D., & Schrier, R. W. (1994). The human costs of tobacco use. *The New England Journal of Medicine, 330*, 907–912.

Bartlett, J. G. (1999). *Management of respiratory tract infections* (2nd ed.). New York: Lippincott Williams & Wilkins.

Baselt, R. C. (1996). Disposition of alcohol in man. In *Medicolegal aspects of alcohol* (3rd ed.) (Garriott, J. C., ed.). Tuscon, AZ: Lawyers & Judges Publishing Co.

Bashir, A., & Swartz, C. (2002). Alprazolam-induced panic disorder. *Journal of the American Board of Family Practice, 15,* 69–72.

Batki, S. L. (2001). Methamphetamine and MDMA. Paper presented at symposium, American Society of Addiction Medicine, Washington, DC, November 1.

Batzer, W., Ditzler, T., & Brown, C. (1999). LSD use and flashbacks in alcoholic patients. *Journal of Addictive Diseases, 18*(2), 57–63.

Baughan, D. M. (1995). Barriers to diagnosing anxiety disorder in family practice. *American Family Physician, 52*(2), 447–450.

Baughman, R. D. (1993). Psoriasis and cigarettes. *Archives of Dermatology, 129,* 1329–1330.

Bauman, J. L. (1988). Acute heroin withdrawal. *Hospital Therapy, 13,* 60–66.

Bauman, K. E., & Ennett, S. T. (1994). Peer influence on adolescent drug use. *American Psychologist, 63,* 820–822.

Bayard, M., McIntyre, J., Hill, K. R., & Woodside, J. (2004). Alcohol withdrawal syndrome. *American Family Physician, 1443–1450.*

Bays, J. (1992). The care of alcohol and drug-affected infants. *Pediatric Annals, 21*(8), 485–495.

Bean-Bayog, M. (1988). Alcohol and drug abuse: Alcoholism as a cause of psychopathology. *Hospital and Community Psychiatry, 39,* 352–354.

Bean-Bayog, M. (1993). AA processes and change: How does it work? In *Research on alcoholics anonymous* (McCrady, B. S., & Miller, W. R., eds.). New Brunswick, NJ: Rutgers Center of Alcohol Studies.

Beardsley, T. (1994). The lucky ones. *Scientific American, 270*(5), 20, 24, 28.

Beasley, J. D. (1987). *Wrong diagnosis, wrong treatment: The plight of the alcoholic in America.* New York: Creative Infomatics, Inc.

Beattie, M. (1987). *Codependent no more.* New York: Harper & Row.

Beattie, M. (1989) *Beyond codependency.* New York: Harper & Row.

Beauvais, F. (1998). American Indians and alcohol. *Alcohol Health & Research World, 22,* 253–259.

Beazley, H. (1998). The integration of AA and clinical practice. Symposium presened to the Dept. of Psychiatry at The Cambridge Hospital, Boston, MA.

Becherer, P. R. (1995). Viral hepatitis. *Postgraduate Medicine, 98,* 65–74.

Beck, A. T. (2004). The cognitive-behavioral approach to addiction treatment. Seminar Presented to the Department of Psychiatry at the Cambridge Hospital, Boston, MA, 5 March, 2004.

Beck, A. T., Wright, F. D., Newman, C. F., & Liese, B. S. (1993). *Cognitive therapy of substance abuse.* New York: Guilford.

Beckman, L. J. (1993). Alcoholics Anonymous and gender issues. In *Research on Alcoholics Anonymous* (McCrady, B. S., & Miller, W. R., eds.). New Brunswick, NJ: Rutgers Center of Alcohol Studies.

Beckman, L. J. (1994). Treatment needs of women with alcohol problems. *Alcohol Health & Research World, 18,* 206–211.

Beebe, D. K., & Walley, E. (1991). Substance abuse: The designer drugs. *American Family Physician, 43,* 1689–1698.

Beebe, D. K., & Walley, E. (1995). Smokable methamphetamine ("Ice"): An old drug in a different form. *American Family Physician, 51,* 449–454.

Beeder, A. B., & Millman, R. B. (1995). Treatment strategies for comorbid disorders: Psychopathology and substance abuse. In *Psychotherapy and substance abuse* (Washton, A. M., ed.). New York: Guilford.

Begley, S. (1997). Jagged little pill. *Newsweek, CXXX* (7), 66.

Behnke, M., & Eyler, F. D. (1993). The consequences of prenatal substance use for the developing fetus, newborn and young child. *International Journal of the Addictions, 28,* 1341–1391.

Beitner-Johnson, D., & Nestler, E. J. (1992). Basic neurobiology of cocaine: Actions within the mesolimbic dopamine system. In *Clinician's guide to cocaine addiction.* (Kosten, T. R., & Kleber, H. D., eds.). New York: Guilford.

Belgrade, M. J. (1999). Opioids for chronic nonmalignant pain. *Postgraduate Medicine, 106*(6), 115–124.

Bell, D. C., Montoya, I. D., & Atkinson, J. S. (1997). Therapeutic connection and client progress in drug abuse treatment. *Journal of Clinical Psychology, 53,* 215–224.

Bell, G. L., & Lau, K. (1995). Perinatal and neonatal issues of substance abuse. *Pediatric Clinics of North America, 42,* 261–281.

Bell, N. J., Forthun, L. F., & Sun, S. W. (2000). Attachment, adolescent competencies, and substance use: Developmental considerations in the study of risk behaviors. *Substance Use & Misuse, 35,* 1177–1206.

Bell, R. (1995). Determinants of hospital-based substance abuse treatment programs. *Hospital & Health Services Administration, 39*(1), 93–102.

Bell, R. A., Spangler, J. G., & Quandt, S. A. (2000). Smokeless tobacco use among adults in the southeast. *Southern Medical Journal, 93,* 456–462.

Bell, T. (1996). Abuse or addiction? *Professional Counselor, 11*(5), 12.

Bellack, A. S., & DiClemente, C. C. (1999). Treating substance abuse among patients with schizophrenia. *Psychiaric Services, 50,* 75–80.

Benet, L. Z., Kroetz, D. L., & Sheiner, L. B. (1995). Pharmacokinetics: The dynamics of drug absorption, distribution and elimination. In *The pharmacological basis of therapeutics* (9th ed.) (Hardman, J. G., & Limbird, L. E., eds.). New York: McGraw-Hill.

Benowitz, N. L. (1992). Cigarette smoking and nicotine addiction. *Medical Clinics of North America, 76,* 415–437.

Benowitz, N. L. (1997a). The role of nicotine in smoking-related cardiovascular disease. *Preventive Medicine, 26,* 412–417.

Benowitz, N. L. (1997b). Treating tobacco addiction—Nicotine or no nicotine? The *New England Journal of Medicine*, 337, 1230–1231.

Benowitz, N. L., & Henningfield, J. E. (1994). Establishing a nicotine threshold for addiction. *New England Journal of Medicine*, 331, 123–126.

Benowitz, N. L., & Jacob, P. (1993). Nicotine and cotinine elimination pharmacokinetics in smokers and nonsmokers. *Clincial Pharmacology & Therapeutics*, 53, 316–323.

Benson, R. T., & Sacco, R. L. (2000). Stroke prevention. *Neurologic Clinics of North America*. 19, 309–320.

Benzer, D. G. (1995). Use and abuse of benzodiazepines. Paper presented at the 1995 annual Frank P. Furlano, M.D., memorial lecture, Gunderson-Lutheran Medical Center, La Crosse, WI.

Berenson, D. (1987). Alcoholics Anonymous: From surrender to transformation. *The Family Therapy Networker*, 11(4), 25–31.

Berg, B. J., & Dubin, W. R. (1990). Economic grand rounds: Why 28 days? An alternative approach to alcoholism treatment. *Hospital and Community Psychiatry*, 41, 1175–1178.

Berg, I. K., & Miller, S. D. (1992). *Working with the problem drinker*. New York: Norton.

Berg, J. E. (2003). Mortality and return to work of drug abusers from therapeutic community treatment 3 years after entry. *The Primary Care Companion to the Journal of Clinical Psychiatry*, 5(4), 164–167.

Berg, R., Franzen, M. M., & Wedding, D. (1994). *Screening for brain impairment: A manual for mental health practice* (2nd ed.). New York: Springer Publishing.

Berger, P. A., & Dunn, M. J. (1982). Substance induced and substance use disorders. In *Treatment of mental disorders* (Griest, J. H., Jefferson, J. W., & Spitzer, R. L., eds.). New York: Oxford University Press.

Berger, T. (2000). Nervous system. In *Handbook of alcoholism* (Zernig, G., Saria, A., Kurz, M., & O'Malley, S. S., eds.). New York: CRC Press.

Berkowitz, A., & Perkins, H. W. (1988). Personality characteristics of children of alcoholics. *Journal of Consulting and Clinical Psychology*, 56, 206–209.

Bernstein, E., Tracey, A., Bernstein, J., & Williams, C. (1996). Emergency department detection and referral rates for patients with problem drinking. *Substance Abuse*, 17, 69–76.

Better than well: Society's moral confusion over drugs is neatly illustrated by its differing reactions to Prozac and ecstasy. (1996). *The Economist*, 39(7960), 87–89.

Beullens, J., & Aertgeerts, B. (2004). Screening for alcohol abuse and dependence in older people using DSM criteria: A review. *Aging & Mental Health*, 8(1), 76–82.

Bhandari, M., Sylvester, S. L., & Rigotti, N. A. (1996). Nicotine and cigarette smoking. In *Sourcebook of substance abuse and addiction* (Friedman, L., Fleming, N. F., Roberts, D. H., & Hyman, S. E., eds.). New York: Williams & Wilkins.

Bierut, L. J., Dinwiddie, S. H., Begleiter, H., Crowe, R. R., Hesselbrock, V., Nurnberger, J. I., Porjesz, B., Schuckit, M. A., & Reich, T. (1998). Familial transmission of substance dependence: Alcohol, marijuana, cocaine and habitual smoking. *Archives of General Psychiatry*, 55, 982–988.

Big tobacco's secret kiddie campaign. (1998). *Newsweek*, CXXXI (4), 29.

Bishop, F. M. (2002). Make a difference with SMART recovery. *The Addictions Newsletter*, 9(3), 2, 10.

Bjork, J. M., Grant, S. J., & Hommer, D. W. (2003). Cross-sectional volumetric analysis of brain atrophy in alcohol dependence: Effects of drinking history and comorbid substance use disorder. *American Journal of Psychiatry*, 160, 2038–2045.

Black, C. (1982). *It will never happen to me.* Denver, CO: M.A.C. Printing and Publications.

Black, C. (2003). The legacy of addictions: Looking at family patterns. Symposium presented to the Dept. of Psychiatry at The Cambridge Hospital, Boston, MA, March 7.

Black, R. A., & Hill, D. A. (2003). Over-the-counter medications in pregnancy. *American Family Physician*, 67, 2517–2524.

Blackburn, W. D. (1999). *Approach to the patient with a musculoskeletal disorder.* Caddo, OK: Professional Communications, Inc.

Blair, D. T., & Ramones, V. A. (1996). The undertreatment of anxiety: Overcoming the confusion and stigma. *Journal of Psychosocial Nursing*, 34(6), 9–17.

Blake, R. (1990). Mental health counseling and older problem drinkers. *Journal of Mental Health Counseling*, 12(3), 354–367.

Blansjaar, B. A., & Zwinderman, A. H. (1992). The course of alcohol amnesic disorder: A three-year follow up study of clinical signs. *Acta Psychiatricia Scandinavica*, 86, 240–246.

Blau, M. (1990). Toxic parents, perennial kids: Is it time for adult children to grow up? *Utne Reader*, 42, 60–65.

Bleidt, B. A., & Moss, J. T. (1989). Age-related changes in drug distribution. *U. S. Pharmacist*, 14(8), 24–32.

Bliss, R. E., Garvey, A. J., Heinold, J. W., & Hitchcock, J. L. (1989). The influence of situation and coping on relapse crisis outcomes after smoking cessation. *Journal of Consulting and Clinical Psychology*, 57, 443–449.

Bloch, S., & Pargiter, R. (2002). A history of psychiatric ethics. *Psychiatric Clinics of North America*, 25, 509–524.

Blondell, R. D., Frierson, R. L., & Lippmann, S. B. (1996). Alcoholism. *Postgraduate Medicine*, 100, 69–72, 78–80.

Bloodworth, R. C. (1987). Major problems associated with marijuana abuse. *Psychiatric Medicine*, 3(3), 173–184.

Blue, J. G., & Lombardo, J. A. (1999). Steroids and steroid-like compounds. *Clinics in Sports Medicine*, 18, 667–687.

Blum, D. (1998). Finding strength. *Psychology Today*, 31(3), 32–38, 66–67, 69, 72–73.

Blum, K. (1984). *Handbook of abusable drugs.* New York: Gardner Press, Inc.

Blum, K. (1988). The disease process in alcoholism. *Alcoholism & Addiction, 8*(5), 5–8.

Blum, K., Cull, J. G., Braverman, E. R., & Comings, D. E. (1996). Reward deficiency syndrome. *American Scientist, 84*(2), 132–144.

Blum, K., Noble, E. P., Sheridan, P. J., Montgomery, A., Ritchie, T., Jagadeeswaran, P., Nogami, H., Briggs, A. H., & Cohn, J. B. (1990). Allelic association of human dopamine D2 receptor gene in alcoholism. *Journal of the American Medical Association, 263*(15), 2055–2060.

Blum, K., & Payne, J. E. (1991). *Alcohol and the addictive brain.* New York: The Free Press.

Blum, K., & Trachtenberg, M. C. (1988). Neurochemistry and alcohol craving. *California Society for the Treatment of Alcoholism and Other Drug Dependencies News, 13*(2), 1–7.

Blume, S. B. (1994). Gender differences in alcohol-related disorders. *Harvard Review of Psychiatry, 2*, 7–14.

Blume, S. B. (1998). Addictive disorders in women. In *Clinical textbook of addictive disorders* (2nd ed.) (Frances, R. J., & Miller, S. I., eds.). New York: Guilford.

Blume, S. B., & Zilberman, M. L. (2004). Addiction in women. In *Textbook of substance abuse treatment* (3rd ed.) (Galanter, M., & Kleber, H. D., eds.). Washington, DC: American Psychiatric Press, Inc.

Boal, M. (2002). Designer drug death. *Rolling Stone, 888,* 44–49.

Bode, C., Maute, G., & Bode, J. C. (1996). Prostaglandin E2 and prostaglandin F2a biosynthesis in human gastric mucosa: Effect of chronic alcohol misuse. *Gut, 39,* 348–352.

Bohn, M. (2001). Alcoholism pharmacotherapy. Paper presented at the Contemporary Issues in the Treatment of Alcohol & Drug Abuse Symposium, Milwaukee, WI, June 1.

Bohn, M. J. (1993). Alcoholism. *Psychiatric Clinics of North America, 16,* 679–692.

Bolnick, J. M., & Rayburn, W. F. (2003). Substance use disorders in women: Special considerations during pregnancy. *Obstetric and Gynecological Clinics of North America, 30,* 545–558.

Bonanno, G. A. (2004). Loss, trauma, and human resilience. *American Psychologist, 59,* 20–28.

Bond, W. S. (1989). Smoking's effects on medications. *American Druggist, 200*(1), 24–25.

Bondesson, J. D., & Saperston, A. R. (1996). Hepatitis. *Emergency Medical Clinics of North America, 14,* 695–718.

Bongar, B. (1997). Suicide: What therapists need to know. Seminar presented at the 1997 meeting of the American Psychological Association: Chicago, Illinois.

Bonkovsky, H. L., & Mehta, S. (2001). Hepatitis C: A review and update. *Journal of the American Academy of Dermatology, 44,* 159–179.

Book, S. W., & Randall, C. L. (2002). Social anxiety disorder and alcohol use. *Alcohol Research & Health, 26,* 130–135.

Booth, M. (1996). *Opium: A history.* New York: St. Martin's Griffin.

Bovard, J. (1997). Time out for justice. *Playboy, 44*(12), 54–55.

Bovard, J. (2001). Wanted: Drug czar. *Playboy, 48*(3), 50.

Bovasso, G. B. (2001). Cannabis abuse as a risk factor for depressive symptoms. *American Journal of Psychiatry, 158,* 2033–2037.

Bowden, S. J. (1994). Neuropsychology of alcohol and drug dependence. In *Neuropsychology in clinical practice* (Touyz, S., Byrne, D., & Gilandas, A., eds.). New York: Academic Press.

Bowen, M. (1985). *Family therapy in clinical practice.* Northvale, NJ: Jason Aronson.

Bower, B. (1991). Pumped up and strung out. *Science News, 140*(2), 30–31.

Bowers, D. H. (2000). HIV: Past, present and future. *Postgraduate Medicine, 107,* 109–113.

Boyd, C. (1992). Self-help sickness? *St. Paul Pioneer Press, 143*(346), pp. C1, C4.

Boyd, L. M. (1995). Moved by the spirit. *San Francisco Chronicle, 130*(16), 10.

Boyer, E. W. (2005). Emerging drugs of abuse. Symposium presented to the Dept. of Psychiatry of the Cambridge Hospital, Boston, MA, March 5.

Bracken, P. (2002). *Trauma: Culture, meaning and philosophy.* Philadelphia: Whurr Publishers.

Bradley, K. A., Boyd-Wickizer, J., Powell, S., & Burman, M. L. (1998). Alcohol screening questionnaires in women. *Journal of the American Medical Association, 280,* 166–171.

Bradley, K. A., Bushk, K. R., Epler, A. J., Dobie, D. J., Davis, T. M., Sporleder, J. L., Maynard, C., Burman, M. L., & Kivlahan, D. R. (2003). Two brief alcohol-screening tests from the Alcohol Use Disorders Identification Test (AUDIT). *Archives of Internal Medicine, 163,* 821–829.

Bradshaw, J. (1988a). *Bradshaw on: The family.* Deerfield Beach, FL: Health Communications, Inc.

Bradshaw, J. (1988b). Compulsivity: The black plague of our day. *Lear's Magazine, 42,* 89–90.

Brady, K. T., & Randall, C. L. (1999). Gender differences in substance use disorders. *Psychiatric Clinics of North America, 22,* 241–252.

Brady, T. (1997). Bad hair days: Hair follicle testing offers an alternative to traditional drug tests. *Management Review, 86*(2), 59–62.

Brandt, J., & Butters, N. (1986). The alcoholic Wernicke-Korsakoff syndrome and its relationship to long term alcohol use. In *Neuropsychological assessment of neuropsychiatric disorders.* (Grant, I., & Adams, K. M., eds.). New York: Oxford University Press.

Bravo, G. (2001). What does MDMA feel like? In *Ecstasy: The complete guide* (Holland, J., ed.). Rochester, VT: Park St. Press.

Brecher, E. M. (1972). *Licit and illicit drugs.* Boston: Little, Brown & Co.

Breggin, P. R. (1998). *Talking back to Ritalin.* Monroe, MI: Common Courage Press.

Breggin, P. R. (1999). Letter to the editor. *Journal of the American Medical Association, 281*, 1490–1491.

Breiter, H. C. (1999). The biology of addiction. Symposium presented to the Dept. of Psychiatry of The Cambridge Hospital, Boston, MA, March 6.

Breithaupt, D. (2001). Why health insurers should pay for addiction treatment. *Western Journal of Medicine, 174*, 375–377.

Brekke, J. S., Prindle, C., Woo Bae, S., & Long, J. D. (2001). Risks for individuals with schizophrenia who are living in the community. *Psychiatric Services, 52*, 1358–1366.

Brendel, D., West, H., & Hyman, S. E. (1996). Hallucinogens and phencyclidine. In *Sourcebook of substance abuse and addiction* (Friedman, L., Fleming, N. F., Roberts, D. H., & Hyman, S. E., eds.). New York: Williams & Wilkins.

Brennan, D. F., Betzelos, S., Reed, R., & Falk, J. L. (1995). Ethanol elimination rates in an ED population. *American Journal of Emergency Medicine, 13*, 276–280.

Brennan, P. L., & Moos, R. H. (1996). Late-life drinking behavior: The influence of personal characteristics, life context, and treatment. *Alcohol Health & Research World, 20*, 197–204.

Brenner, D. E., Kukull, W. A., van Belle, G., Bowen, J. D., McCormick, W. C., Teri, L., & Larson, E. B. (1993). Relationship between cigarette smoking and Alzheimer's disease in a population-based case-control study. *Neurology, 43*, 293–300.

Brent, J. A. (1995). Drugs of abuse: An update. *Emergency Medicine, 27*(7), 56–70.

Breo, D. L. (1990). Of MD's and muscles—lessons from two "retired steroid doctors." *Journal of the American Medical Association, 263*, 1697–1705.

Breslau, N., Kilbey, M., & Andreski, P. (1993). Vulnerability to psychopathology in nicotine-dependent smokers: An epidemiologic study of young adults. *American Journal of Psychiatry, 150*, 941–946.

Breslin, J. (1988). Crack. *Playboy, 35*(12), 109–110, 210, 212–213, 215.

Briggs, G. G., Freeman, R. K., & Yaffe, S. J. (1986). *Drugs in pregnancy and lactation* (2nd ed.). Baltimore: Williams and Wilkins.

Brigham, G. S. (2003). 12–step participation as a pathway to recovery: The Maryhaven experience and implications for treatment and research. *Science Practice & Perspectives, 2*(1), 43–51.

Brink, S. (2004). The price of booze. *U.S. News & World Report, 136*(4), 48–50.

Brochu, S., Landry, M., Bergeron, J., & Chiocchio, F. (1997). The impact of a treatment process for substance users as a function of their degree of exposure to treatment. *Substance Use & Misuse, 32*, 1993–2011.

Brodsky, A. (1993). The 12 steps are not for everyone—or even for most. *Addiction & Recovery, 13*(2), 21.

Brody, J. (1991). Hepatitis B still spreading. *Minneapolis Star Tribune, X* (269), p. E4.

Brooks, J. T., Leung, G., & Shannon, M. (1996). Inhalants. In *Source book of substance abuse and addiction* (Friedman, L., Fleming, N. F., Roberts, D. H., & Hyman, S. E., eds.). New York: Williams & Wilkins.

Brophy, J. J. (1993). Psychiatric disorders. In *Current medical diagnosis and treatment* (Tierney, L. M., McPhee, S. J., Papadakis, M. A., & Schroeder, S. A., eds.). Norwalk, CT: Appleton & Lange.

Brower, K. J. (1993). Anabolic steroids. *Psychiatric Clinics of North America, 16*, 97–103.

Brower, K. J. (2001). Alcohol's effects on sleep in alcoholics. *Alcohol Research & Health, 25*(2), 110–124.

Brower, K. J., Aldrich, M. S., Robinson, E. A. R., Zucker, R. A., & Greden, J. F. (2001). Insomnia, self-medication, and relapse to alcoholism. *American Journal of Psychiatry, 158*, 399–404.

Brower, K. J., Blow, F. C., Young, J. P., & Hill, E. M. (1991). Symptoms and correlates of anabolic-androgenic steroid dependence. *British Journal of Addiction, 86*, 759–768.

Brown, R. L. (1997). Stages of change. Paper presented at symposium: Still Getting High—a 30-Year Perspective on Drug Abuse, Gundersen-Lutheran Medical Center, La Crosse, WI, May 2.

Brown, R. L., Leonard, T., Saunders, L. A., Papasoulioutis, O. (1997). A two-item screening test for alcohol and other drug problems. *The Journal of Family Practice, 44*, 151–160.

Brown, R. T., & Braden, N. J. (1987). Hallucinogens. *Pediatric Clinics of North America, 34*(2), 341–347.

Brown, S. (1985). *Treating the alcoholic: A developmental model of recovery*. New York: John Wiley & Sons, Inc.

Brown, S., & Lewis, V. (1995). The alcoholic family: A developmental model of recovery. In *Treating alcoholism* (Brown, S. A., ed.). New York: Jossey-Bass.

Brown, S. A. (1990). Adolescent alcohol expectancies and risk for alcohol abuse. *Addiction & Recovery, 10*(5/6), 16–19.

Brown, S. A. (1995). Introduction. In *Treating alcoholism* (Brown, S. A., ed.). New York: Jossey-Bass.

Brown, S. A., Creamer, V. A., & Stetson, B. A. (1987). Adolescent alcohol expectancies in relation to personal and parental drinking patterns. *Journal of Abnormal Psychology, 96*, 117–121.

Brown, T. M., & Stoudemire, A. (1998). *Psychiatric side effects of prescription and over the counter medications*. Washington, DC: American Psychiatric Association Press, Inc.

Browning, M., Hoffer, B. J., & Dunwiddie, T. V. (1993). Alcohol, memory and molecules. *Alcohol Health & Research World, 16*(4), 280–284.

Brownlee, S., Roberts, S. V., Cooper, M., Goode, E., Hetter, K., & Wright, A. (1994). Should cigarettes be outlawed? *U.S. News & World Report, 116*(15), 32–36, 38.

Brownson, R. C., Novotny, T. E., & Perry, M. C. (1993). Cigarette smoking and adult leukemia. *Archives of Internal Medicine, 153*, 469–475.

Bruner, A. B., & Fishman, M. (1998). Adolescents and illicit drug use. *Journal of the American Medical Association, 280,* 597–598.

Brunette, M. F., Noordsy, D. L., Xie, H., & Drake, R. E. (2003). Benzodiazepine use and abuse among patients with severe mental illness and co-occuring substance use disorders. *Psychiatric Services, 54,* 1395–1401.

Brunswick, M. (1989). More kids turning to inhalant abuse. *Minneapolis Tribune, VII* (356), pp. A1, A6.

Brunton, S. A., Henningfield, J. E., & Solberg, L. I. (1994). Smoking cessation: What works best? *Patient Care, 25*(11), 89–115.

Brust, J. C. M. (1993). Other agents: Phencyclidine, marijuana, hallucinogens, inhalants, and anticholinergics. *Neurologic Clinics of North America, 11,* 555–561.

Brust, J. C. M. (1997). Vasculitis owing to substance abuse. *Neurologic Clinics of North American 15,* 945–957.

Brust, J. C. M. (1998). Acute neurologic complications of drug and alcohol abuse. *Neurologic Clinics of North American 16,* 503–519.

Buber, M. (1970). *I and thou.* New York: Charles Scribner's Sons.

Buchert, R., Thomasius, R., Neleling, B., Petersen, K., Obrocki, J., Jenicke, L., Wilke, F., Wartberg, L., Zapletalova, P., & Clausen, M. (2003). Long-term effects of "ecstasy" use on serotonin transporters of the brain investigated by PET. *Journal of Nuclear Medicine, 44,* 375–384.

Buchert, R., Thomasius, R., Wilke, F., Petersen, K., Nebeling, B., Obrocki, J., Schulze, O., Schmidt, U., & Clausen, M. (2004). A Voxel-based PET investigation on the long-term effects of "ecstasy" consumption on brain serotonin transporters. *American Journal of Psychiatry, 161,* 1181–1189.

Buckley, N. A., Dawson, A. H., Whyte, I. M., & O'Connell, D. L. (1995). Relative toxicity of benzodiazepines in overdose. *British Medical Journal, 310*(6974), 219–222.

Buckley, W. F. (1996). The war on drugs is lost. *National Review, XLVIII* (2), 35–38.

Buckley, W. F. (1997). Save money, cut crime, get real. *Playboy, 44*(1), 129, 192–193.

Budiansky, S., Goode, E. E., & Gest, T. (1994). The cold war experiments. *U.S. News & World Report, 116*(3), 32–38.

Budney, A. J., Moore, B. A., Bandrey, R. G., & Hughes, J. R. (2003). The time course and significance of cannabis withdrawal. *Journal of Abnormal Psychology, 112,* 393–402.

Budney, A. J., Sigmon, S. C., & Higgins, S. T. (2003). Contingency management in the substance abuse treatment clinic. In *Treating substance abuse: Theory and technique* (2nd ed.) (Rotgers, F., Morgenstern, J., & Walters, S. T., eds.). New York: Guilford.

Bufe, C. (1988). A.A.: Guilt and god for the gullible. *Utne Reader, 30,* 54–55.

Bufe, C. (1998). *Alcoholics Anonymous: Cult or cure?* (2nd ed.). Tuscon, AZ: See Sharp Press.

Buffenstein, A., Heaster, J., & Ko, P. (1999). Chronic psychotic illness from methamphetamine. *American Journal of Psychiatry, 156,* 662.

Buhrich, N., Weller, A., & Kevans, P. (2000). Misuse of anticholinergic drugs by people with serious mental illness. *Psychiatric Services, 51,* 928–929.

Buia, C., Fulton, G., Park, A., Shannon, E. M., & Thompson, D. (2000). The lure of ecstasy. *Time, 155*(23), 62–68.

Buka, S. L., Shenassa, E. D., & Niaura, R. (2003). Elevated risk of tobacco dependence among offspring of mothers who smoked during pregnancy: A 30-year perspective study. *American Journal of Psychiatry, 160,* 1978–1984.

Bukstein, O. G. (1994). Treatment of adolescent alcohol abuse and dependence. *Alcohol Health and Research World, 18,* 297–301.

Bukstein, O. G. (1995). *Adolescent substance abuse.* New York: Wiley Interscience.

Bukstein, O. G., Brent, D. A., Perper, J. A., Moritz, G., Baugher, M., Schweers, J., Roth, C., & Balach, L. (1993). Risk factors for completed suicide among adolescents with a lifetime history of substance abuse: a case controlled study. *Acta Psychiatrica Scandinavica, 88,* 403–408.

Burge, S. K., & Schneider, F. D. (1999). Alcohol-related problems: Recognition and intervention. *American Family Physician, 59,* 361–370.

Burke, J. D., Burke, K. C., & Rae, D. S. (1994). Increased rates of drug abuse and dependence after onset of mood or anxiety disorders in adolescence. *Hospital & Community Psychiatry, 45,* 451–455.

Burkett, G., Yasin, S. Y., Palow, D., LaVoie L., & Martinez, M. (1994). Patterns of cocaine binging: Effects on pregnancy. *American Journal of Obstetrics and Gynecology, 171*(2), 372–379.

Burns, D. M. (1991). Cigarettes and cigarette smoking. *Clinics in Chest Medicine, 12,* 631–642.

Bushnell, T. G., & Justins, D. M. (1993). Chosing the right analgesic. *Drugs, 46,* 394–408.

Butterworth, R. F. (1995). The role of liver disease in alcohol-induced cognitive defects. *Alcohol Health & Research World, 19,* 123–129.

Byck, R. (1987). Cocaine use and research: Three histories. In *Cocaine: Clinical and behavioral aspects* (Fisher, S., Rashkin, A., & Unlenhuth, E. H., eds.). New York: Oxford University Press.

Byington, D. B. (1997). Applying relational theory to addictions treatment. In *Gender and addictions* (Straussner, S. L. A., & Zelvin, E., eds.). Northvale, NJ: Jason-Aronson.

Byrd, R. C., & Howard, C. R. (1995). Children's passive and prenatal exposure to cigarette smoke. *Pediatric Annals, 24,* 640–645.

Byrne, C. (1989). Cocaine alley. *Minneapolis Star Tribune, VIII* (215), 29a–32a.

Cabaj, R. P. (1997). Gays, lesbians and bisexuals. In *Substance abuse: A comprehensive textbook* (3rd ed.) (Lowinson, J. H., Ruiz, P., Millman, R. B., & Langrod, J. G., eds.). New York: Williams & Wilkins.

Cadieux, R. J. (1996). Azapirones: An alternative to benzodiazepines for anxiety. *American Family Physician, 53,* 2349–2353.

Caetano, R., Clark, C. L., & Tam, T. (1998). Alcohol consumption among racial/ethnic minorities: Theory and research. *Alcohol Health & Research World, 22,* 229–242.

Cahill, T. (1998). *The gifts of the Jews.* New York: Doubleday.

Calhoun, S. R., Wesson, D. R., Galloway, G. P., & Smith, D. E. (1996). Abuse of flunitrazepam (Rohypnol) and other benzodiazepines in Austin and south Texas. *Journal of Psychoactive Drugs, 28*(2), 183–189.

California judges get tougher on science. (1997). *Forensic Drug Abuse Advisor, 9*(8), 61.

Callahan, E. J. (1980). Alternative strategies in the treatment of narcotic addiction: A review. In *The addictive behaviors* (Miller, W. R., ed.). New York: Pergamon Press.

Callahan, J. (1993). Blueprint for an adolescent suicidal crisis. *Psychiatric Annals, 23*(5), 263–270.

Callaway, J. C., & McKenna, D. J. (1998). Neurochemistry of psychodelic drugs. In *Drug abuse handbook* (Karch, S. B., ed.). New York: CRC Press.

Campbell, G. D. (1994). Overview of community-acquired pneumonia. *Medical Clinics of North America, 78,* 1035–1048.

Campbell, J. W. (1992). Alcoholism. In *Primary care geriatrics* (2nd ed.) (Ham, R. J., & Sloane, P. D., eds.). Boston: Mosby.

Cantor, N. F. (2001). *In the wake of the plague.* New York: The Free Press.

Cape, G. S. (2003). Addiction, stigma and movies. *Acta Psychiatricia Scandinavica, 107,* 163–169.

Cardoni, A. A. (1990). Focus on adinazolam: A benzodiazepine with antidepressant activity. *Hospital Formulary, 25,* 155–158.

Carey, K. B. (1989). Emerging treatment guidelines for mentally ill chemical abusers. *Hospital and Community Psychiatry, 40,* 341–342, 349.

Carey, K. B., Cocco, K. M., & Simons, J. S. (1996). Concurrent validity of clinicians' ratings of substance abuse among psychiatric outpatients. *Psychiatric Services, 47,* 842–847.

Carlin, G. (2001). *Napalm & silly putty.* New York: Hyperion.

Carlson, J. L., Strom, B. L., Morse, L., West, S. L., Soper, K. A., Stolley, P. D., & Jones, J. K. (1987). The relative gastrointestinal toxicity of the nonsteroidal anti-inflammatory drugs. *Archives of Internal Medicine, 147,* 1054–1059.

Carmona, R. H. (2004). *The health consequences of smoking: A report of the Surgeon General.* Washington, DC: Centers for Disease Control.

Carol, G., Smelson, D. A., Losonczy, M. F., & Ziedonis, D. (2001). A preliminary investigation of cocaine craving among persons with and without schizophrenia. *Psychiatric Services, 52,* 1029–1031.

Carpenter, S. (2001). Research on teen smoking cessation gains momentum. *APA Monitor, 32*(6), 54–55.

Carroll, K. M. (1997). New methods of treatment efficacy research. *Alcohol Health & Research World, 21,* 352–359.

Carroll, K. M. (2003). Integrating psychotherapy and pharmacotherapy in substance abuse treatment. In *Treating substance abuse: Theory and technique* (2nd ed.) (Rotgers, F., Morgenstern, J., & Walters, S. T., eds.). New York: Guilford.

Caroll, K. M., & Rounsaville, B. J. (1992). Contrast of treatment-seeking and untreated cocaine abusers. *Archives of General Psychiatry, 49,* 464–471.

Carvey, P. M. (1998). *Drug action in the central nervous system.* New York: Oxford University Press.

Castro, F. G., Barrington, E. H., Walton, M. A., & Rawson, R. A. (2000). Cocaine and methamphetamine: Differential addiction rates. *Psychology of Addictive Behaviors, 14,* 390–396.

Catanzarite, V. A., & Stein, D. A. (1995). "Crystal" and pregnancy methamphetamine-associated maternal deaths. *The Western Journal of Medicine, 162,* 545–547.

Catella-Lawson, F., Reilly, M. P., Kapoor, S. C., Cucchiara, A. J., DeMarco, S., Tournier, B., Vyas, S. N., & Fitzgerald, G. A. (2001). Cyclooxygenase inhibitors and the antiplatlet effects of aspirin. *New England Journal of Medicine, 345,* 1809–1817.

Caton, C. L. M., Gralnick, A., Bender, S., & Simon, R. (1989). Young chronic patients and substance abuse. *Hospitial and Community Psychiatry, 40,* 1037–1040.

"Cat" poses national threat, experts say (methcathione). (1993). *Alcoholism & Drug Abuse Week, 5*(47), 5–6.

Cattarello, A. M., Clayton, R. R., & Leukefeld, C. G. (1995). Adolescent alcohol and drug abuse. In *Review of psychiatry* (Vol. 14) (Oldham, J. M., & Riba, M. B., eds.). Washington, DC: American Psychiatric Press, Inc.

Cavaliere, F. (1995). Substance abuse in the deaf community. *APA Monitor, 26*(10), 49.

Cellucci, T., & Vik, P. (2001). Training for substance abuse treatment among psychologists in a rural state. *Professional Psychology: Research and Practice, 32,* 248–252.

Centers for Disease Control. (1990). Lead poisoning associated with intraveneous methamphetamine use—Oregon, 1988. *Journal of the American Medical Association, 263,* 797.

Centers for Disease Control (2004). *The health consequences of smoking: What it means to you.* Washington, DC: U.S. Government Printing Office.

Cepeda, M. S., Alvarez, H., Morales, O., & Carr, D. B. (2004). Addition of ultralow dose naloxone to postoperative morphine PCA: Unchanged analgesia and opioid requirement but decreased incident of opioid side effects. *Pain, 107,* 41–46.

Ceren, S. L. (2003). Warning: Managed care may be dangerous to your health. *The Independent Practitioner, 23*(2), 77.

Cetaruk, E. W., Dart, E. C., Horowitz, R. S., & Huribut, K. M. (1996). Extended-release acetaminophen overdose. *Journal of the American Medical Association, 275,* 686.

Chan, P., Chen, J. H., Lee, M. H., & Deng, J. F. (1994). Fatal and nonfatal methamphetamine intoxication in the intensive care unit. *Journal of Toxicology: Clinical Toxicology, 32,* 147–156.

Chang, G. (2001). Gender and addictions. Symposium presented to the Dept. of Psychiatry of The Cambridge Hospital, Boston, MA, March 2.

Chapman, C. R., & Okifuji, A. (2004). Pain: Basic mechanisms and conscious experience. In *Psychosocial aspects of pain: A handbook for health care providers* (Dworkin, R. H., & Brietbart, W. S., eds.). Seattle, WA: International Association for the Study of Pain Press.

Chappel, J. N., & DuPont, R. L. (1999). Twelve-step and mutual help programs for addictive disorders. *Psychiatric Clinics of North America, 22,* 425–446.

Charness, M. E., Simon, R. P., & Greenberg, D. A. (1989). Ethanol and the nervous system. *The New England Journal of Medicine, 321*(7), 442–454.

Charney, D. S. (2004). Outpatient treatment of comorbid depression and alcohol use disorders. *Psychiatric Times, XXI* (2), 31–33.

Charney, D. S., Mihis, S. J., & Harris, R. A. (2001). Hypnotics and sedatives. In *The pharmacological basis of therapeutics* (10th ed.) (Hardman, J. G., Limbird, L. E., & Gilman, A. G., eds.). New York: McGraw-Hill.

Chasnoff, I. J. (1988). Drug use in pregnancy: Parameters of risk. *Pediatric Clinics of North America, 3* (6), 1403–1412.

Chasnoff, I. J. (1991a). Cocaine and pregnancy: Clinical and methadologic issues. *Clinics in Perinatology, 18,* 113–123.

Chasnoff, I. J. (1991b). Drugs, alcohol, pregnancy, and the neonate. *Journal of the American Medical Association, 266,* 1567–1568.

Chasnoff, I. J., Anson, A., Hatcher, R., Stenson, H., Iaukea, K., & Randolph, L. A. (1998). Prenatal exposure to cocaine and other drugs. *Annals of the New York Academy of Sciences, 846,* 314–328.

Chassin, L., Curran, P. J., Hussong, A. M., & Colder, C. R. (1996). The relation of parent alcoholism to adolescent substance use: A longitudinal follow-up study. *Journal of Abnormal Psychology, 105,* 70–80.

Chassin, L., & DeLucia, C. (1996). Drinking during adolescence. *Alcohol Health & Research World, 20,* 175–180.

Chatlos, J. C. (1996). Recent developments and a developmental approach to substance abuse in adolescents. *Child and Adolescent Psychiatric Clinics of North America, 5,* 1–27.

Chen, C. K., Lin, S. K., Sham, P. C., Ball, D., Loh, E. W., Hsiao, C. C., Chiang, Y. L., Ree, S.C., & Murray, R. M. (2003). Pre-morbid characteristics and co-morbidity of methamphetamine users with and without psychosis. *Psychological Medicine, 33,* 1407–1414.

Cheng, A. T. A., Gau, S. F., Chen, T. H. H., Chang, J., & Chang, Y. (2004). A 4–year longitudinal study on risk factors for alcoholism. *Archives of General Psychiatry, 61,* 184–191.

Cherny, N. I. (1996). Opioid analgesics: Comparative features and prescribing guidelines. *Drugs, 51,* 713–737.

Cherny, N. I., & Foley, K. M. (1996). Nonopioid and opioid analgesic pharmacology of cancer pain. *Hematology/Oncology Clinics of North America, 10,* 79–102.

Cherubin, C. E., & Sapira, J. D. (1993). The medical complications of drug addiction and the medical assessment of the intravenous drug user: 25 years later. *Annals of Internal Medicine, 119,* 1017–1028.

Chiauzzi, E. (1990). Breaking the patterns that lead to relapse. *Psychology Today, 23*(12), 18–19.

Chiauzzi, E. (1991). *Preventing relapse in the addictions.* New York: Pergamon.

Chick, J. (1993). Brief interventions for alcohol misuse. *British Medical Journal, 307,* 1374.

Chin, R. L., Sporer, K. A., Cullison, B., Dyer, J. E., & Wu, T. D. (1998). Clinical course of gamma hydroxybutyrate overdose. *Annals of Emergency Medicine, 31,* 716–722.

Chopra, D. (1997). *Overcoming addictions.* New York: Three Rivers Press.

Christensen, W. G., Manson, J. E., Seddon, J. M., Glynn, R. J., Buring, J. E., Rosner, B., & Hennekens, C. H. (1992). A prospective study of cigarette smoking and risk of cataract in men. *Journal of the American Medical Association, 268,* 989–993.

Chuck, R. S., Williams, J. M., Goldberg, M. A., & Lubniewski, A. J. (1996). Recurrent corneal ulcerations associated with smokable methamphetamine abuse. *American Journal of Ophthalmology, 121,* 571–573.

Chung, T., Colby, S. M., Barnett, N. P., Rohsenow, D. J., Spirto, A., & Monti, P. M. (2000). Screening adolescents for problem drinking: Performance of brief screens against DSM-IV alcohol diagnoses. *Journal of Studies on Alcohol, 61,* 579–587.

Ciancio, S. G., & Bourgault, P. C. (1989). *Clinical pharmacology for dental professionals* (3rd ed.). Chicago: Year Book Medical Publishers, Inc.

Cigarette smoking-attributable morbidity—United States, 2000. (2004). *Morbidity & Mortality Weekly Report, 52*(35), 842–844.

Ciraulo, D. A. (2004). A pharmacologic approach to treatment. Symposium presented to the Dept. of Psychiatry at The Cambridge Hospital, Boston, MA, March 5.

Ciraulo, D. A., Creelman, W., Shader, R. I., & O'Sullivan, R. O. (1995). Antidepressants. In *Drug interactions in psychiatry* (2nd ed.) (Ciraulo, D. A., Shader, R. I., Greenblatt, D. J., & Creelman, W., eds.). Baltimore: Williams & Wilkins.

Ciraulo, D. A., & Nace, E. P. (2000). Benzodiazepine treatment of anxiety or insomnia in substance abuse patients. *American Journal on Addictions, 9,* 276–284.

Ciraulo, D. A., Piechniczek-Buczek, J., & Iscan, E. N. (2003). Outcome predictors in substance use disorders. *Psychiatric Clinics of North America, 26,* 381–409.

Ciraulo, D. A., Sarid-Segal, O., Knapp, C., Ciraulo, A. M., Greenblatt, D. J., & Shader, R. I. (1996). Liability to alprazolam abuse in daughters of alcoholics. *American Journal of Psychiatry, 153,* 956–958.

Ciraulo, D. A., Shader, R. I., Ciraulo, A., Greenblatt, D. J., & von Moltke, L. L. (1994a). Alcoholism and its treatment. In *Manual of psychiatric therapeutics* (2nd ed.) (Shader, R. I., ed.). Boston: Little, Brown & Co.

Ciraulo, D. A., Shader, R. I., Ciraulo, A., Greenblatt, D. J., & von Moltke, L. L. (1994b). Treatment of alcohol withdrawal. In *Manual of psychiatric therapeutics* (2nd ed.) (Shader, R. I., ed.). Boston: Little, Brown & Co.

Ciraulo, D. A., Shader, R. I., Greenblatt, D. J., & Barnhill, J. G. (1995). Basic concepts. In *Drug interactions in psychiatry* (2nd ed.) (Ciraulo, D. A., Shader, R. I., Greenblatt, D. J., & Creelman, W., eds.). Baltimore: Williams & Wilkins.

Clark, C. M. (1995). Alcoholics Anonymous. *The Addictions Newsletter, 2*(3), 9, 22.

Clark, D. B., Vanyukrov, M., & Cornelius, J. (2002). Childhood antisocial behavior and adolescent alcohol use disorders. *Alcohol Research & Health, 26,* 109–115.

Clark, R. E. (1994). Family costs associated with severe mental illness and substance abuse. *Hospital and Community Psychiatry, 45,* 808–813.

Clark, R. E., Xie, H., & Brunette, M. F. (2004). Benzodiazepine prescription practices and substance abuse in persons with severe mental illness. *Journal of Clinical Psychiatry, 65*(2), 151–155.

Clark, W. G., Bratler, D. C., & Johnson, A. R. (1991). *Goth's medical pharmacology* (13th ed.). Boston, MA: Mosby.

Clark, W. R. (1995). *At war within.* New York: Oxford.

Claunch, L. (1994). Intervention can be used as a tool—or as a weapon against clients. *The Addiction Letter, 10*(4), 1–2.

Clavel, F., & Hance, A. J. (2004). HIV drug resistance. *New England Journal of Medicine, 350,* 1023–1035.

Climko, R. P., Roehrich, H., Sweeney, D. R., & Al-Razi, J. (1987). Ecstasy: A review of MDMA and MDA. *International Journal of Psychiatry in Medicine, 16*(4), 359–372.

Cloninger, C. R., Bohman, M., & Sigvardsson, S. (1981). Inheritance of alcohol abuse: Cross fostering analysis of adopted men. *Archives of General Psychiatry, 38,* 861–868.

Cloninger, C. R., Sigvardsson, S., & Bohman, M. (1996). Type I and Type II alcoholism: An update. *Alcohol Health & Research World, 20*(1), 18–23.

Cloud, J. (2002). Is pot good for you? *Time, 160* (19), 62–66.

Cocaine in the brain. (1994). *Forensic Drug Abuse Advisor, 6*(9), 67.

Cocaine link to heart attack bolstered. (2001). *Science News, 159,* 24.

Cocaine models. (2003). *Forensic Drug Abuse Advisor, 15*(1), 5–6.

Coca leaf production decreases in Colombia. (2003). *Forensic Drug Abuse Advisor, 15*(6), 47.

Cohen, D. A., Richardson, J., & LaBree, L. (1994). Parenting behaviors and the onset of smoking and alcohol use: A longitudinal study. *Pediatrics, 94,* 368–375.

Cohen, G., Fleming, N. S., Glatter, K. A., Haghigi, D. B., Halberstadt, J., McHigh, K. M., & Woolf, A. (1996). Epidemiology of substance use. In *Sourcebook of substance abuse and addiction* (Friedman, L., Fleming, N. F., Roberts, D. H., & Hyman, S. E., eds.). New York: Williams & Wilkins.

Cohen, J., & Levy, S. J. (1992). *The mentally ill chemical abuser: Whose client?* New York: Lexington Books.

Cohen, L. S. (1989). Psychotropic drug use in pregnancy. *Hospital and Community Psychiatry, 40*(6), 566–567.

Cohen, M. (2000). *Counseling addicted women.* Thousand Oaks, CA: Sage.

Cohen, M. S. (1995). HIV and sexually transmitted diseases. *Postgraduate Medicine, 98*(3), 52–64.

Cohen, R. S. (1998). *The love drug.* New York: Haworth Medical Press.

Cohen, S. (1977). Inhalant abuse: An overview of the problem. In *Review of inhalants: Euphoria to dysfunction* (Sharp, C. W., & Brehm, M. L., eds.). Washington, DC: U.S. Government Printing Office.

Cohen, S., Lichtenstein, E., Prochaska, J. O., Rossi, J. S., Gritz, E. R., Carr, C. R., Orleans, C. T., Schoenbach, V. J., Biener, L., Abrams, D., DiClemente, C., Curry, S., Marlatt, G. A., Cummings, K. M., Emont, S. L., Giovino, G., Ossip-Klein, D. (1989). Debunking myths about self-quitting. *American Psychologist, 44,* 1355–1365.

Cohen, S. I. (1995). Overdiagnosis of schizophrenia: Role of alcohol and drug misuse. *The Lancet, 346,* 1541–1542.

Cohn, J. B., Wilcox, C. S., Bowden, C. L., Fisher, J. G., & Rodos, J. J. (1992). Double-blind clorazepate in anxious outpatients with and without depressive symptoms. *Psychopathology, 25* (Suppl. 1), 10–21.

Coker, M. (1997). Overcoming sexism in A.A.: How women cope. In *Gender and addictions* (Straussner, S. L. A., & Zelvin, E., eds.). Northvale, NJ: Jason-Aronson.

Colburn, N., Meyer, R. D., Wrigley, M., & Bradley, E. L. (1993). Should motorcycles be operated within the legal alcohol limits for automobiles? *The Journal of Trauma, 34*(1), 183–186.

Cole, B. S., & Pargament, K. I. (1999). Spiritual surrender: A paradoxical path to control. In *Integrating spirituality into treatment.* Washington, DC: American Psychological Association.

Cole, J. O., & Kando, J. C. (1993). Adverse behavioral events reported in patients taking alprazolam and other benzodiazepines. *Journal of Clinical Psychiatry, 54* (10)(Suppl.), 49–61.

Cole, J. O., & Yonkers, K. A. (1995). Nonbenzodiazepine anxiolytics. In *Textbook of psychopharmacology* (Schatzberg, A. F., & Nemeroff, C. B., eds.). Washington, DC: American Psychiatric Association Press, Inc.

Coleman, D. E., & Baselt, R. C. (1997). Efficacy of two commercial products for altering urine drug test results. *Journal of Toxicology: Clinical Toxicology, 35*(6), 637–642.

Coleman, P. (1989). Letter to the editor. *Journal of the American Medical Association, 261*(13), 1879–1880.

Collette, L. (1988). Step by step: A skeptic's encounter. *Utne Reader, 30*, 69–76.

Collette, L. (1990). After the anger, what then? *The Family Therapy Networker, 14*(1), 22–31.

Collins, E. D., & Kleber, H. D. (2004). Opioids. In *Textbook of substance abuse treatment* (3rd ed.) (Galanter, M., & Kleber, H. D., eds.). Washington, DC: American Psychiatric Press, Inc.

Collins, J. J., & Allison, M. (1983). Legal coercion and retention in drug abuse treatment. *Hospital and Community Psychiatry, 34*, 1145–1150.

Collins, R. L., & McNair, L. D. (2002). Minority women and alcohol use. *Alcohol Research & Health, 26*(4), 251–256.

Comerci, G. D., Fuller, P., & Morrison, S. F. (1997). Cigarettes, drugs, alcohol & teens. *Patient Care, 31*(4), 57–83.

Committee on Addictions of the Group for the Advancement of Psychiatry. (2002). Responsibility and choice in addiction. *Psychiatric Services, 53*, 707–713.

Committee on Child Health Care Financing and Committee on Substance Abuse. (2001). Improving substance abuse prevention, assessment, and treatment financing for children and adolescents. *Pediatrics, 108*, 1025–1029.

Committee on Substance Abuse. (2001a). Alcohol use and abuse: A pediatric concern. *Pediatrics, 108*, 185–189.

Committee on Substance Abuse. (2001b). Tobacco's toll: Implications for the pediatrician. *Pediatrics, 108*, 794–798.

Committee on Substance Abuse and Committee on Children With Disabilities. (1993). Fetal alcohol syndrome and fetal alcohol effects. *Pediatrics, 91*, 1004–1006.

Community Anti-Drug Coalitions of America. (1997). The meth challenge: Threatening communities coast to coast. Interactive live national teleconference. June 19, 1997.

Compton, P., & Athanasos, P. (2003). Chronic pain, substance abuse and addiction. *Nursing Clinics of North America, 38*, 525–537.

Compton, W. M., Cottler, L. B., Jacobs, J. L., Ben-Abdallah, A., & Spitznagel, E. L. (2003). The role of psychiatric disorders in predicting drug dependence treatment outcomes. *American Journal of Psychiatry, 160*, 890–895.

Compton, W. M., Grant, B. F., Colliver, J. D., Glantz, M. D., & Stinson, F. S. (2004). Prevalence of marijuana use disorders in the United States 1991–1992 and 2001–2002. *Journal of the American Medical Association, 291*, 2114–2121.

Concar, D. (1997). Deadly combination. *New Scientist, 155*, 2090–2091.

Cone, E. J. (1993). Saliva testing for drugs of abuse. In *Saliva as a diagnostic fluid* (Malamud, D., & Tabak, L., eds.). New York: Annals of the New York Academy of Sciences.

Cone, E. J., Fant, R. V., Rohay, J. M., Caplan, Y. H., Ballina, M., Reder, R. F., Spyker, D., & Haddox, J. D. (2003). Oxycodone involvement in drug abuse deaths: A DAWN-based classification scheme applied to an Oxycodone postmortem database containing over 1000 cases. *Journal of Analytical Toxicology, 27*, 57–67.

Congeni, J., & Miller, S. (2002). Supplements and drugs used to enhance athletic performance. *The Pediatric Clinics of North America, 49*, 435–461.

Connor, K. R., Li, Y., Meldrum, S., Duberstein, P. R., & Conwell, Y. (2003). The role of drinking in suicidal ideation: Analyses of Project MATCH data. *Journal of Studies on Alcohol, 64*, 402–408.

Connors, G. J., Carroll, K. M., DiClemente, C. C., Longabaugh, R., & Donovan, D. M. (1997). The therapeutic alliance and its relationship to alcoholism treatment participation and outcome. *Journal of Consulting and Clinical Psychology, 65*, 588–598.

Connors, G. J., Donovan, D. M., & DiClemente, C. C. (2001). *Substance abuse treatment and the stages of change.* New York: Guilford.

Consequences of PCP abuse are up. (1994). *The Addiction Letter, 10*(3), 3.

Cook, A. (1995). Ecstasy (MDMA): Alerting users to the dangers. *Nursing Times, 91*, (16), 32–33.

Coomber, R. (1997). The adulteration of illicit drugs with dangerous substitutes—The discovery of a "myth." *Contemporary Drug Problems, 24*(2), 239–271.

Coombs, R. H. (1997). *Drug-impaired professionals.* Cambridge, MA: Harvard University Press.

Cooney, N. L., Zweben, A., & Fleming, M. F. (1995). Screening for alcohol problems and at-risk drinking in health-care settings. In *Handbook of alcoholism treatment approaches* (2nd ed.) (Hester, R. K., & Miller, W. R., eds.). New York: Allyn & Bacon.

Cooper, J. R., Bloom, F. E., & Roth, R. H. (1986). *The biochemical basis of neuropharmacology* (5th ed.). New York: Oxford University Press.

Cooper, J. R., Bloom, F. E., & Roth, R. H. (1996). *The biochemical basis of neuropharmacology* (7th ed.). New York: Oxford University Press.

Cornell, W. F. (1996). Capitalism in the consulting room. *Readings, 11*(1), 12–17.

Cornwell, E. E., Blezberg, H., Velmahos, G., Chan, L. S., Demetriades, D., Stewart, B. M., Oder, D. B., Kahuku, D., Chan, D., Asensio, J. A., & Berne, T. V. (1998). The prevalence and effect of alcohol and drug abuse on cohort-matched critically injured patients. *The American Surgeon, 64*, 461–465.

Corrigan, B. (1996). Anabolic steroids and the mind. *Medical Journal of Australia, 165*, 222–226.

Corwin, J. (1994). Outlook. *U.S. News & World Report, 116*, (23), 15–16.

Cotton, P. (1993). Low-tar cigarettes come under fire. *Journal of the American Medical Association, 270*, 1399.

Cotton, P. (1994). Smoking cigarettes may do developing fetus more harm than ingesting cocaine, some experts say. *Journal of the American Medical Association, 271*, 576–577.

Coughey, K., Feighan, K., Cheney, R., & Klein, G. (1998). Retention in an aftercare program for recovering women. *Substance Use & Misuse 33*, 917–932.

Council on Scientific Affairs. (1990a). Medical and nonmedical uses of anabolicandrogenic steroids. *Journal of the American Medical Association, 264*, 2923–2927.

Council on Scientific Affairs. (1990b). The worldwide smoking epidemic. *Journal of the American Medical Associaion, 263*, 3312–3318.

Cousins, N. (1989). *Head first: The biology of hope.* New York: E. P. Dutton.

Covey, L. W., Sullivan, M. A., Johnston, A., Glassman, A. H., Robinson, M. D., & Adams, D. P. (2000). Advances in non-nicotine pharmacotherapy for smoking cessation. *Drugs, 59*, 17–31.

Cowen, R. (1990). Alcoholism treatment under scrutiny. *Science News, 137*, 254.

Cox, B. J., & Taylor, S. (1999). Anxiety disorders. In *Oxford Textbook of Psychopathology* (Million, T., Blaney, P. H., & Davis, R. D., eds.). New York: Oxford University Press.

CPPD in Puerto Rico, meeting highlights. French heroin. (1996). *Forensic Drug Abuse Advisor, 8*(6), 41–44.

Crack injecting in Chicago—First U.S. reports of dangerous new practice. *Forensic Drug Abuse Advisor, 8* (8), 60.

Craig, R. J. (2004). *Counseling the alcohol and drug dependent client.* New York: Allyn & Bacon.

Craig, T. J. (1996). Drugs to be used with caution in patients with asthma. *American Family Physician, 54*, 947–953.

Creighton, F. J., Black, D. L., & Hyde, C. E. (1991). "Ecstasy" psychosis and flashbacks. *British Journal of Psychiatry, 159*, 713–715.

Critchley, J. A., & Capewell, S. (2003). Mortality risk reduction associated with smoking cessation in patients with coronary heart disease. *Journal of the American Medical Association, 290*, 86–97.

Croft, R. J., Klugman, A., Baldeweg, T., & Gruzelier, J. H. (2001). Electrophysiological evidence of serotonergic impairment in long-term MDMA ("ecstasy") users. *American Journal of Psychiatry, 158*, 1687–1692.

Crowley, T. J. (1988). Substance abuse treatment and policy: Contributions of behavioral pharmacology. Paper presented at the 1988 meeting of the American Psychological Association, Atlanta, Georgia.

Crowley, T. J. (1995). Phencyclidine- (or Phencyclidine-like) related disorders. In *Comprehensive textbook of psychiatry* (6th ed.) (Kaplan, H. I., & Sadock, B. J., eds.). Baltimore: Williams & Wilkins.

Crowley, T. J. (2000). Inhalant-related disorders. In *Comprehensive textbook of psychiatry* (7th ed.) (Kaplan, H. I., & Sadock, B. J., eds.). Baltimore: Lippincott, Williams & Wilkins.

Crowley, T. J., & Sakai, J. T. (2004). Inhalants: Neurobiology of alcohol. In *Textbook of substance abuse treatment* (3rd ed.) (Galanter, M., & Kleber, H. D., eds.). Washington, DC: American Psychiatric Press, Inc.

Cummings, C., Gordon, J. R., & Marlatt, G. A. (1980). Relapse: Prevention and prediction. In *The addictive behaviors.* (Miller, W. R., ed.). New York: Pergamon Press.

Cumsille, P. E., Sayer, A. G., & Graham, J. W. (2000). Perceived exposure to peer and adult drinking as predictors of growth in positive alcohol expectancies during adolescence. *Journal of Consulting & Clinical Psychology, 68*, 531–536.

Cunha, B. A. (1998). TB pneumonia. *Emergency Medicine, 30*(6), 102, 107, 111.

Cunniff, C. (2003). Fetal alcohol syndrome: Diagnosis, treatment and public health. Paper presented at the Continuing Medical Education Symposium, Gundersen-Lutheran Medical Center, La Crosse, WI, May 28.

Cunningham, J. A., Sobell, L. C., Gavin, D. R., Sobell, M. B., & Breslin, F. C. (1997). Assessing motivation for change: Preliminary development and evaluation of a scale measuring the benefits and costs of changing alcohol or drug use. *Psychology of Addictive Behaviors, 11*, 107–114.

Cupp, M. J. (1999). Herbal remedies: Adverse effects and drug interactions. *American Family Physician, 59*, 1239–1244.

Curley, B. (1995). Drugs demand distinction between rights and responsibilities. *Alcoholism & Drug Abuse Week, 7*(19), 5.

Curran, H. V., Collins, R., Fletcher, S., Kee, S. C. Y., Woods, B., & Iliffe, S. (2003). Older adults and withdrawal from benzodiazepine hypnotics in general practice: Effects on cognitive function, sleep, mood and quality of life. *Psychological Medicine, 33*, 1223–1237.

Curran, P. J., Stice, E., & Chassin, L. (1997). The relation between adolescent alcohol use and peer alcohol use: A longitudinal random coefficients model. *Journal of Consulting and Clinical Psychology, 65*, 130–140.

Cyr, M. G., & Moulton, A. W. (1993). The physician's role in prevention, detection, and treatment of alcohol abuse in women. *Psychiatric Annals, 23*, 454–462.

Czeizel, A. E., Kodaj, I., & Lenz, W. (1994). Smoking during pregnancy and congenital limb deficiency. *British Medical Journal, 308*, 1473–1476.

Daeppen, J. B., Gache, P., Landry, U., Sekera, E., Schweizer, V., Gloor, S., & Yersin, B. (2002). Symptom-triggered vs fixed-schedule doses of benzodiazepine for alcohol withdrawal. *Archives of Internal Medicine, 162*, 1117–1121.

Daghestani, A. N., & Schnoll, S. H. (1994). Phencyclidine In *Textbook of substance abuse treatment* (Galanter, M., & Kleber, H. D., eds.). Washington, DC: American Psychiatric Press, Inc.

Daghestani, A. N., Dinwiddie, S. H., & Hardy, D. W. (2001). Antisocial personality disorders in and out of correctional and forensic settings. *Psychiatric Annals, 31*(7), 441–446.

Dance safe. (2001). *Playboy, 48* (1), 157.

D'Andrea, L. M., Fisher, G. L., & Harrison, T. C. (1994). Cluster analysis of adult children of alcoholics. *International Journal of the Addictions, 29*, 565–582.

Danjou, P., Paty, I., Fruncillo, R., Worthington, P., Unruh, M., Cevallos, W., & Martin, P. (1999). A comparison of the residual effects of zaleplon and zolpidem following administration 5 to 2 h before awakening. *British Journal of Clinical Pharmacology, 48*(3), 367–374.

Darton, L. A., & Dilts, S. L. (1998). Opioids. In *Clinical textbook of addictive disorders* (2nd ed.) (Frances, R. J., & Miller, S. I., eds.). New York: Guilford.

D'Aunno, T., & Pollack, H. A. (2002). Changes in methadone treatment practices. *Journal of the American Medical Association, 288,* 850–856.

Davidson, R. (1998). The transtheoretical model. In *Treating addictive behaviors* (2nd ed.) (Miller, W. R., & Heather, N., eds.). New York: Plenum.

Davison, K. P., Pennebaker, J. W., & Dickerson, S. S. (2000). Who talks? *American Psychologist, 55,* 205–217.

Day, E., Bentham, P., Callaghan, R., Kuruvilla, T., & George, S. (2004). Thiamine for Wernicke-Korsakoff Syndrome in people at risk from alcohol abuse. *The Cochrane Database of Systematic Reviews, 2.*

Day, N. L., & Richardson, G. A. (1991). Prenatal marijuana use: Epidemiology, methodologic issues, and infant outcome. *Clinics in Perinatology, 18,* 77–91.

Day, N. L., & Richardson, G. A. (1994). Comparative tetragenicity of alcohol and other drugs. *Alcohol Health & Research World, 18,* 42–48.

DEA. (1995). Press release: 21 June, 1995. Washington, DC: Drug Enforcement Administration.

DeAngelis, T. (1994). Perceptions influence student drinking. *APA Monitor, 25*(12), 35.

DeBellis, M. D., Clark, D. B., Beers, S. R., Soloff, P. H., Boring, A. M., Hall, J., Kersh, A., & Keshavan, M. S. (2000). Hippocampal volume in adolescent-onset alcohol use disorders. *American Journal of Psychiatry, 157,* 737–744.

Decker, S., & Reis, R. K. (1993). Differential diagnosis and psychopharmacology of dual disorders. *Psychiatric Clinics of North America, 16,* 703–718.

Deglamorising cannabis. (1995). *The Lancet, 346,* 1241.

DeJong, W. (1994). Relapse prevention: An emerging technology for promoting long-term abstinence. *International Journal of the Addictions, 29,* 681–785.

Del Boca, F. K., & Hesselbrock, M. N. (1996). Gender and alcoholic subtypes. *Alcohol Health & Research World, 20,* 56–62.

DeLeon, G. (1989). Psychopathology and substance abuse: What is being learned from research in therapeutic communities. *Journal of Psychoactive Drugs, 21*(2), 177–188.

DeLeon, G. (1994). Therapeutic Communities. In *Textbook of substance abuse treatment* (Galanter, M., & Kleber, H. D., eds.). Washington, DC: American Psychiatric Press, Inc.

DeLeon, G. (2004). Therapeutic Communities. In *Textbook of Substance Abuse Treatment* (3rd ed.) (Galanter, M., & Kleber, H. D., eds.). Washington, DC: American Psychiatric Press, Inc.

DeLeon, G., Melnick, G., & Kressel, D. (1997). Motivation and readiness for therapeutic community treatment among cocaine and other drug abusers. *American Journal of Drug and Alcohol Abuse, 23,* 169–190.

DeMaria, P. A., & Weinstein, S. P. (1995). Methadone maintenance treatment. *Postgraduate Medicine, 97*(3), 83–92.

Demers-Gendreau, C. (1998). Diagnosing and treating addictions in college students. Symposium presented to the Dept. of Psychiatry of The Cambridge Hospital, Boston, MA, March 6.

Derlet, R. W. (1989). Cocaine intoxication. *Postgraduate Medicine, 86*(5), 245–248, 253.

Derlet, R. W., & Heischober, B. (1990). Methamphetamine: Stimulant of the 1990's? *The Western Journal of Medicine, 153,* 625–629.

Derlet, R. W., & Horowitz, B. Z. (1995). Cardiotoxic drugs. *Emergency Medicine Clinics of North American, 13,* 771–791.

Dervaux, A., Bayle, F. J., Laqueille, X., Bourdel, M. C., Le Borgne, M. H., Olie, J. P., & Krebs, M. O. (2001). Is substance abuse in schizophrenia related to impulsivity, sensation seeking, or, anhedonia? *American Journal of Psychiatry, 158,* 492–494.

DeVane, C. L., & Nemeroff, C. B. (2002). 2002 guide to psychotropic drug interactions. *Primary Psychiatry, 9*(3), 28–51.

Dewit, D. J. Adlaf, E. M., Offord, D. R., Obborne, A. C. (2000). Age at first alcohol use: A risk factor for the development of alcohol disorders. *American Journal of Psychiatry, 157,* 745–750.

Dewitt, D. E., & Paauw, D. S. (1996). Endocarditis in injection drug users. *American Family Physician, 53,* 2045–2049.

Di Bisceglie, A. M. (1995). Chronic hepatitis B. *Postgraduate Medicine, 98,* 99–103.

Di Bisceglie, A. M., & Bacon, B. R. (1999). The unmet challenges of Hepatitis C. *Scientific American, 281*(4), 80–85.

Dickensheets, S. (2001). Roid rage. *Playboy, 48*(7), 128–129, 156–162.

Dickinson, A. (2000). Smoke screen. *Time, 155*(11), 92.

DiClemente, C. C. (1993). Alcoholics Anonymous and the structure of change. In *Research on Alcoholics Anonymous* (McCrady, B. S., & Miller, W. R., eds.). New Brunswick, NJ: Rutgers Center of Alcohol Studies.

DiClemente, C. C., Bellino, L. E., & Neavins, T. M. (1999). Motivation for change and alcoholism treatment. *Alcohol Health & Research World, 23*(2), 86–92.

DiClemente, C. C., & Prochaska, J. O. (1998). Toward a comprehensive, transtheoretical model of change. In *Treating addictive behaviors* (2nd ed.) (Miller, W. R., & Heather, N., eds.). New York: Plenum.

Dieperink, E., Willenbring, M., & Ho, S. B. (2000). Neuropsychiatric symptoms associated with Hepatitis C and Interferon Alpha: A review. *American Journal of Psychiatry, 157,* 867–876.

Dietch, J. (1983). The nature and extent of benzodiazepine abuse: An overview of recent literature. *Hospital and Community Psychiatry, 34,* 1139–1144.

DiGregorio, G. J. (1990). Cocaine update: Abuse and therapy. *American Family Physician, 41*(1), 247–251.

Dilaudid users may be escaping detection. (1995). *Forensic Drug Abuse Advisor, 7*(3), 26–27.

Diller, L. H. (1998). *Running on Ritalin.* New York: Bantam Books.

Dimeff, L. A., & Marlatt, G. A. (1995). Relapse prevention. In *Handbook of alcoholism treatment approaches* (2nd ed.) (Hester, R. K., & Miller, W. R., eds.). New York: Allyn & Bacon.

Dionne, R. A., & Gordon, S. M. (1994). Nonsteroidal antiinflammatory drugs for acute pain control. *Dental Clinics of North America, 38,* 645–667.

Director, L. (1995). Dual diagnosis: Outpatient treatment of substance abusers with coexisting psychiatric disorders. In *Psychotherapy and SUBSTANCE ABUSE* (Washton, A. M., ed.). New York: Guilford.

Dishion, T. J., McCord, J., & Poulin, F. (1999). When interventions harm. *American Pychologist, 54,* 755–764.

Disney, E. R., Elkins, I. J., McGue, M., & Iacono, W. G. (1999). Effects of ADHD, conduct disorder, and gender on substance use and abuse in adolescence. *American Journal of Psychiatry, 156,* 1515–1521.

Dixit, A. R., & Crum, R. M. (2000). Prospective study of depression and risk of heavy alcohol use in women. *American Journal of Psychiatry, 157,* 751–758.

Djordjevic, M. V., Hoffmann, D., & Hoffmann, I. (1997). Nicotine regulates smoking patterns. *Preventive Medicine, 26,* 435–440.

Dobkin, P. L., Tremblay, R. E., & Sacchitelle, C. (1997). Predicting boys' early-onset substance abuse from father's alcoholism, son's disruptiveness, and mother's parenting behavior. *Journal of Consulting and Clinical Psychology, 65,* 86–92.

Doble, A., Martin, I. L., & Nutt, D. (2004). *Calming the brain.* New York: Martin Dunitz.

Dobs, A. S. (1999). Is there a role for androgenic anabolic steroids in medical practice? *Journal of the American Medical Association, 281,* 1326–1327.

Doghramji, K. (1989). Sleep disorders: A selective update. *Hospital and Community Psychiatry, 40,* 29–40.

Doghramji, K. (2003). When patients can't sleep. *Current Psychiatry, 2*(5), 40–50.

Dolan, K., Rouen, D., & Kimber, J. (2004). An overview of the use of urine, hair, sweat and saliva to detect drug use. *Drug & Alcohol Review, 23*(2), 213–217.

Dole, V. P. (1988). Implications of methadone maintenance for theories of narcotic addiction. *Journal of the American Medical Association, 260,* 3025–3029.

Dole, V. P. (1989). Letter to the editor. *Journal of the American Medical Association, 261*(13), 1880.

Dole, V. P. (1995). On federal regulation of methadone treatment. *Journal of the American Medical Association, 274*(16), 1307.

Dole, V. P., & Nyswander, M. A. (1965). Medical treatment for diacetylmorphine (heroin) addiction. *Journal of the American Medical Association, 193,* 645–656.

Domenico, D., & Windle, M. (1993). Intrapersonal and interpersonal functioning among middle-aged female adult children of alcoholics. *Journal of Consulting and Clinical Psychology, 61,* 659–666.

D'Onofrio, G., Rathlev, N. K., Ulrich, A. S., Fish, S. S., & Freedland, E. S. (1999). Lorazepam for the prevention of recurrent seizures related to alcohol. *The New England Journal of Medicine, 340,* 915–919.

Donovan, D. M. (1992). The assessment process in addictive behaviors. *The Behavior Therapist, 15*(1), 18.

Doran, C. M., Shanahan, M., Mattick, R. P., Ali, R., White, J., & Bell, J. (2003). Buprenorphine versus methadone maintenance: A cost-effectiveness analysis. *Drug and Alcohol Dependence, 71*(3), 295–302.

Dorsman, J. (1996). Improving alcoholism treatment: An overview. *Behavioral Health Management, 16*(1), 26–29.

Doweiko, H. (2002). Dreams as an unappreciated therapeutic avenue for cognitive-behavioral therapists. *Journal of Cognitive Psychotherapy, 16*(1), 29–38.

Downing, C. (1990). The wounded healers. *Addiction & Recovery, 10*(3), 21–24.

Doyle, R. (2001a). Cleaner living. *Scientific American, 285*(5), 25.

Doyle, R. (2001b). Why do prisons grow? *Scientific American, 285*(6), 28.

Draganov, P., Durrence, H., Cox, C., & Reuben, A. (2000). Alcohol-acetaminophen syndrome. *Postgraduate Medicine, 107,* 189–195.

Drake, R. E., Essock, S. M., Shaner, A., Carey, K. B., Minkoff, K., Kola, L., Lynde, D., Osher, F. C., Clark, R. E., & Richards, L. (2001). Implementing dual diagnosis services for clients with severe mental illness. *Psychiatric Services, 52,* 469–476.

Drake, R. E., McHugo, G. J., Clark, R. E., Teague, G. B., Xie, H., Miles, K., & Ackerson, T. H. (1998). Assertive community treatment for patients with co-occurring severe mental illness and substance use disorder: A clinical trial. *American Journal of Orthopsychiatry, 68,* 201–215.

Drake, R. E., & Mueser, K. T. (2002). Co-occuring alcohol use disorder and schizophrenia. *Alcohol Research & Health, 26,* 99–102.

Drake, R. E., Mueser, K. T., Clark, R. E., & Wallach, M. A. (1996). The course, treatment, and outcome of substance disorder in persons with severe mental illness. *American Journal of Orthopsychiatry, 66,* 42–51.

Drake, R. E., & Wallach, M. A. (1993). Moderate drinking among people with severe mental illness. *Hospital and Community Psychiatry, 44,* 780–781.

Dreher, M. C., Nugent, K., & Hudgins, R. (1994). Prenatal marijuana exposure and neonatal outcomes in Jamaica: An ethnographic study. *Pediatrics, 93,* 254–260.

Driessen, M., Meier, S., Hill, A., Wetterling, T., Lang, W., & Junghanns, K. (2001). The course of anxiety, depression and drinking behaviors after completed detoxification in alcoholics with and without comorbid anxiety and depressive disorders. *Alcohol & Alcoholism, 36,* 249–255.

The drug index. (1995). *Playboy, 42*(9), 47.

Drug problems in perspective. (1990). *Health News, 8*(3), 1–10.

Drummer, O. H., & Odell, M. (2001). *The forensic pharmacology of drugs of abuse.* New York: Oxford University Press, Inc.

Dube, S. R., Anda, R. F., Felitti, V. J., Chapman, D. P., Williamson, D. F., & Giles, W. H. (2001). Childhood abuse, household dysfunction, and the risk of attempted suicide throughout the life span. *Journal of the American Medical Association, 286,* 3089–3096.

DuBois, R. N., Sheng, H., Shao, J., Williams, C., & Beauchamp, R. D. (1998). Inhibition of intestinal tumorigenesis via selective inhibition of COX-2. In *Selective COX-2 inhibitors* (Vane, J., & Botting, J., eds.). Hingham, MA: Kluwer Academic Publishers.

Dufour, M. C. (1999). What is moderate drinking? *Alcohol Health & Research World, 23*(1), 5–14.

Duke, S. B. (1996). The war on drugs is lost. *National Review, XLVIII* (2), 47–48.

Dunlop, J., Manghelli, D., & Tolson, R. (1989). Senior alcohol and drug coalition statement of treatment philosophy for the elderly. *Professional Counselor, 4*(2), 39–42.

Dunn, G. E., Paolo, A. M., Ryan, J. J., & Van Fleet, J. (1993). Dissociative symptoms in a substance abuse population. *American Journal of Psychiatry, 150,* 1043–1047.

Dunne, F. J., (1994). Misuse of alcohol or drugs by elderly people. *British Medical Journal, 308,* 608–609.

DuPont, R. L. (2002). Clinical approaches to drug offenders. In *Treatment of drug offenders* (Leukefeld, C. G., Tims, F., & Farabee, D., eds.). New York: Springer.

DuPont, R. L., & Dupont, C. M. (1998). Sedative/hypnotics and benzodiazepines. In *Clinical textbook of addictive disorders* (2nd ed.) (Frances, R. J., & Miller, S. I., eds.). New York: Guilford.

DuRant, R. H., Rickert, V. I., Ashworth, C. S., Newman, C., & Slavens, G. (1993). Use of multiple drugs among adolescents who use anabolic steroids. *The New England Journal of Medicine, 328,* 922–926.

Dwyer, J. (2000). Casualty in the war on drugs. *Playboy, 47*(10), 78–80, 175–176.

Dyehouse, J. M., & Sommers, M. S. (1998). Brief intervention after alcohol-related injuries. *Nursing Clinics of North America, 33,* 93–104.

Dyer, W. W. (1989). *You'll see it when you believe it.* New York: William Morrow and Company, Inc.

Dygert, S. L., & Minelli, M. J. (1993). Heroin abuse progression chart. *Addiction & Recovery, 13*(1), 27–31.

Ecstasy-using HIV patients at risk of death? (1997). *Forensic Drug Abuse Advisor, 9*(7), 49.

Edelson, E. (1993). Fear of blood. *Popular Science, 242*(6), 108–111, 122.

Edmeades, B. (1987). Alcoholics Anonymous celebrates its 50th year. In *Drugs, society and behavior* (Rucker, W. B., & Rucker, M. E., eds.). Guilford, CT: Dashkin Publishing Group, Inc.

Edwards, M. E., & Steinglass, P. (1995). Family therapy treatment outcomes for alcoholism. *Journal of Marital and Family Therapy, 21,* 475–509.

Ehrman, M. (1995). Heroin chic. *Playboy, 42*(5), 66–68, 144–147.

Eidelberg, E., Neer, H. M., & Miller, M. K. (1965). Anticonvulsant properties of some benzodiazepine derivatives. *Neurology, 15,* 223–230.

Eidelman, R. S., Hebert, P. R., Weisman, S. M., & Henneckens, C. H. (2003). An update on aspirin in the primary prevention of cardiovascular disease. *Archives of Internal Medicine, 163,* 2006–2010.

Eisen, S. A., Lyons, M. J., Goldberg, J., & True, W. R. (1993). The impact of cigarette and alcohol consumption on weight and obesity. *Archives of Internal Medicine, 153,* 2457–2463.

Eison, A. S., & Temple, D. L. (1987). Buspirone: Review of its pharmacology and current perspectives on its mechanism of action. *The American Journal of Medicine, 80* (Suppl. 3B), 1–9.

Elders, M. J. (1997). Save money, cut crime, get real. *Playboy, 44*(1), 129, 191–192.

el-Guebaly, N., Cathcart, J., Currie, S., Brown, D., & Gloster, S. (2002). Smoking cessation approaches for persons with mental illness or addictive disorders. *Psychiatric Services, 53,* 1166–1170.

el-Kashen, A. (2001). Medications in development to treat drug addiction. Paper presented at American Society of Addiction Medicine symposium, Washington, DC, November 1.

Elliott, F. A. (1992). Violence. *Archives of Neurology, 49,* 595–603.

Ellis, A., McInerney, J. F., DiGiuseppe, R., & Yeager, R. J. (1988). *Rational emotive therapy with alcoholics and substance abusers.* New York: Pergamon Press.

Ellison, R. C. (2002). Balancing the risks and benefits of moderate drinking. In *Annals of the New York Academy of Sciences* (Vol. 957) (Das, D. K., & Ursini, F., eds.). New York: New York Academy of Sciences, 2002.

Elwood, P. C., Hughes, C., & O'Brien, J. R. (1998). Platelets, aspirin, and cardiovascular disease. *Postgraduate Medical Journal, 74,* 587–591.

Emanuele, M. A., Wezeman, F., & Emanuele, N. V. (2002). Alcohol's effects on female reproductive function. *Alcohol Research & Health, 26*(4), 274–281.

Emonson, D. L., & Vanderbeek, R. D. (1995). The use of amphetamines in the U.S. Air Force tactical operations during Desert Shield and Storm. *Aviation, Space and Environmental Medicine, 66,* (3), 260–263.

Emrick, C. D., Tonigan, S., Montgomery, H., & Little, L. (1993). Alcoholics Anonymous: What is currently known? In *Research on Alcoholics Anonymous* (McCrady, B. S., & Miller, W. R., eds.). New Brunswick, NJ: Rutgers Center of Alcohol Studies.

Enoch, M. A., & Goldman, D. (2002). Problem drinking and alcoholism: Diagnosis and treatment. *American Family Physician, 65,* 441–448.

Epstein, J. F., & Gfroerer, J. C. (1997). *Heroin abuse in the United States*. Rockville, MD: Substance Abuse and Mental Health Services Administration.

Erlich, L. B. (2001). *A textbook of forensic addiction medicine and psychiatry*. Springfield, IL: Charles C Thomas Publisher, Ltd.

Ernst, E. (2002). Complementary therapies for addictions: Not as an alternative. *Addiction, 97*, 1491–1492.

Esmail, A., Meyer, L., Pottier, A., & Wright, S. (1993). Deaths from volatile substance abuse in those under 18 years: Results from a national epidemiological study. *Archives of Disease in Childhood, 69*, 356–360.

Espeland, K. E. (1997). Inhalants: The instant, but deadly high. *Pediatric Nursing, 23*, (1), 82–86.

Estroff, T. W. (1987). Medical and biological consequences of cocaine abuse. In *Cocaine: A clinician's handbook* (Washton, A. M., & Gold, M. S., eds.). New York: The Guilford Press.

Evanko, D. (1991). Designer drugs. *Postgraduate Medicine, 89*(6), 67–71.

Evans, G. D. (1993). Cigarette smoke—radiation hazard. *Pediatrics, 92*, 464.

Evans, K., & Sullivan, J. M. (2001). *Dual diagnosis* (2nd ed.). New York: The Guilford Press.

Ewing, J. A. (1984). Detecting alcoholism: The CAGE questionnaire. *Journal of the American Medical Association, 252*, 1905–1907.

Eyler, F. D., & Behnke, M. (1999). Early development of infants exposed to drugs prenatally. *Clinics in Parinatology, 26*, 107–150.

Facts About Alateen. (1969). New York: Al-Anon Family Group Headquarters.

Fals-Stewart, W., & Lucente, S. (1994). Treating obsessive-compulsive disorder among substance abusers: A guide. *Psychology of Addictive Behaviors, 8*, 14–23.

Fals-Stewart, W., O'Farrell, T. J., & Birchler, G. R. (2003). Family therapy techniques. In *Treating substance abuse: Theory and technique* (2nd ed.) (Rotgers, F., Morgenstern, J., & Walters, S.T., eds.). New York: Guilford.

Farabee, D., Prendergast, M., & Cartier, J. (2002). Alcohol, the "un-drug." *Psychiatric Services, 53*, 1375–1376.

Farber, C. (2000). Science fiction. *Gear, 2*(6), 86–97.

Fariello, D., & Scheidt, S. (1989). Clinical case management of the dually diagnosed patient. *Hospital & Community Psychiatry, 40*, 1065–1067.

Farrell, A. D., & White, K. S. (1998). Peer influences and drug use among urban adolescents: Family structure and parent-adolescent relationship as protective factors *Journal of Consulting and Clinical Psychology, 66*, 248–258.

Farrow, J. A. (1990). Adolescent chemical dependency. *Medical Clinics of North America, 74*, 1265–1274.

Fassinger, R. E. (1991). The hidden minority: Issues and challenges in working with lesbian women and gay men. *The Counseling Psychologist, 19*, 157–176.

Fauci, A. S. (1999). The AIDS epidemic. *New England Journal of Medicine, 341*, 1046–1050.

Fawcett, J., & Busch, K. A. (1995). Stimulants in psychiatry. In *Textbook of psychopharmacology* (Schatzberg, A. F., & Nemeroff, C. B., eds.). Washington, DC: American Psychiatric Association Press, Inc.

FDA revised guidelines, label warnings. (2004). *Forensic Drug Abuse Advisor, 16*(4), 26–27.

Feighner, J. P. (1987). Impact of anxiety therapy on patients' quality of life. *The American Journal of Medicine, 82* (Suppl. A), 14–19.

Fergusson, D. M., Horwood, L. J., Lynskey, M. T., & Madden, P. A. F. (2003). Early reactions to cannabis predict later dependence. *Archives of General Psychiatry, 60*, 1033–1039.

Fernandez-Sola, J., Estruch, R., Grau, J. M., Pare, J. C., Rubin, E., & Urbano-Marquez, A. (1994). The relation of alcoholic myopathy to cardiomyopathy. *Annals of Internal Medicine, 120*, 529–536.

Fetro J. V., Coyle, K. K., & Pham P. (2001). Health-risk behaviors among middle school students in a large majority-minority school district. *Journal of School Health, 71*(1), 30–37.

Fiellin, D. A., Rosenheck, R. A., & Kosten, T. R. (2001). Office-based treatment for opioid dependence: Reaching new patient populations. *American Journal of Psychiatry, 158*, 1200–1204.

Figueredo, V. M. (1997). The effects of alcohol on the heart. *Postgraduate Medicine, 101*, 165–176.

Finch, R. G., & Woodhead, M. A. (1998). Practical considerations and guidelines for the management of community-acquired pneumonia. *Drugs, 56*(1), 31–45.

Fingarette, H. (1988). Alcoholism: The mythical disease. *Utne Reader, 30*, 64–69.

Finger, W. W., Lund, M., & Slagel, M. A. (1997). Medications that may contribute to sexual disorders: A guide to assessment and treatment in family practice. *Journal of Family Practice, 44*, 33–44.

Finkelstein, K. E. (1997). Deadly morals. *Playboy, 44*(8), 80–82, 112–114, 165.

Finnegan, L. P., & Kandall, S. R. (2004). Perinatal substance use. In *Textbook of substance abuse treatment* (3rd ed.) (Galanter, M., & Kleber, H. D., eds.). Washington, DC: American Psychiatric Press, Inc.

Fiore, M. C., Epps, R. P., & Manley, M. W. (1994). A missed opportunity. *Journal of American Medical Association, 271*, 624–626.

Fiore, M. C., Hatsukami, D. K., & Baker, T. B. (2002). Effective tobacco dependence treatment. *Journal of the American Medical Association, 288*, 1768–1771.

Fiore, M. C., Jorenby, D. E., Baker, T. B., & Kenford, S. L. (1992). Tobacco dependence and the nicotine patch. *Journal of the American Medical Association, 268*, 2687–2694.

Fiore, M. C., Novotny, T. E., Pierce, J. P., Giovino, G. A., Hatziandreu, E. J., Newcomb, P. A., Surawicz, T. S., & Davis, R. M. (1990). Methods used to quit smoking in the United States. *Journal of the American Medical Association, 263*, 2760–2765.

Fiore, M. C., Smith, S. S., Jorenby, D. E., & Baker, T. B. (1994). The effectiveness of the nicotine patch for smoking cessation. *Journal of the American Medical Association, 271,* 1940–1947.

Fischer, R. G. (1989). Clinical use of nonsteroidal anti-inflammatory drugs. *Pharmacy Times, 55,* (8), 31–35.

Fischman, M. W., & Haney, M. (1999). Neurobiology of stimulants. In *Textbook of substance abuse treatment* (2nd ed.). Washington, DC: American Psychiatric Association Press, Inc.

Fisher, M. S., & Bentley, K. J. (1996). Two group therapy models for clients with a dual diagnosis of substance abuse and personality disorder. *Psychiatric Services, 47,* 1244–1250.

Fishman, R. H. B. (1996). Normal development after prenatal heroin. *The Lancet, 347,* 1397.

Fishman, S. M., & Carr, D. B. (1992). Clinical issues in pain management. *Contemporary Medicine, 4*(10), 92–103.

Flanagan, P., & Kokotailo, P. (1999). Adolescent pregnancy and substance use. *Clinics in Perinatology, 26,* 185–200.

Flaum, M., & Schultz, S. K. (1996). When does amphetamine-induced psychosis become schizophrenia? *American Journal of Psychiatry, 153,* 812–815.

Fleming, M., Mihic, S. J., & Harris, R. A. (2001). Ethanol. In *The pharmacological basis of therapeutics* (10th ed.) (Hardman, J. G., Limbird, L. E., & Gilman, A. G., eds.). New York: McGraw-Hill.

Fleming, M. F. (1997). Strategies to increase alcohol screening in health care settings. *Alcohol Health & Research World, 21,* 340–347.

Fleming, M. F. (2001). In search of the Holy Grail for the detection of hazardous drinking. *Journal of Family Practice, 50,* 321–322.

Fleming, N. F., Potter, D., & Kettyle, C. (1996). What are substance abuse and addiction? In *Sourcebook of substance abuse and addiction* (Friedman, L., Fleming, N. F., Roberts, D. H., & Hyman, S. E., eds.). New York: Williams & Wilkins.

Fletcher, A. M. (2003). Sober for good: Varied solutions for drinking problems. Symposium presented to the Dept. of Psychiatry at The Cambridge Hospital, Boston, MA, March 8.

Fletcher, J. M., Page, J. B., Francis, D. J., Copeland, K., Naus, M. J., Davis, C. M., Morris, R., Krauskopf, D., & Satz, P. (1996). Cognitive correlates of long-term cannabis use in Costa Rican men. *Archives of General Psychiatry, 53,* 1051–1057.

Fogarty, M. (2003). Depending on cigarettes, counting on science. *The Scientist, 17*(6). Retrieved from http://www.the-scientist.com/yr2003/mar/feature_030324.html

Foley, K. M. (1993). Opioids. *Neurologic Clinics, 11,* 503–522.

Folks, D. G., & Burke, W. J. (1998). Sedative hypnotics and sleep. *Clinics in Geriatric Medicine, 14,* 67–86.

Fonda, D. (2001). Why tobacco won't quit. *Time, 157*(26), 38–39.

Fontham, E. T. H., Correa, P., Reynolds, P., Wu-Williams, A., Buffler, P. A., Greenberg, R. S. Chen, V., Alterman, T., Boyd, P., Austin, D. F., & Liff, J. (1994). Environmental tobacco smoke and lung cancer in nonsmoking women. *Journal of the American Medical Association, 271,* 1752–1759.

Ford, W. E. (2000). Medical necessity and psychiatric managed care. *Psychiatric Clinics of North America, 23,* 309–317.

Fored, C. M., Ejerblad, E., Linblad, P., Fryzek, J. P., Dickman, P. W., Signorello, L. B., Lipworth, L., Elinder, C. G., & Nyren, O. (2001). Acetaminophen, aspirin, and chronic renal failure. *New England Journal of Medicine, 345,* 1801–1808.

Fornazzazri, L. (1988). Clinical recognition and management of solvent abusers. *Internal Medicine for the Specialist, 9*(6), 99–108.

Forstein, M. (2002). Sex, drugs and HIV: A clinician's nightmare. Symposium presented to the Dept. of Psychiatry at The Cambridge Hospital, Boston, MA, February 2.

Fortgang, E. (1999). Is pot bad for you? *Rolling Stone, 87,* 53, 101.

40th anniversary of the first Surgeon General's report on smoking and health. (2004). *Morbidity & Mortality Weekly Report, 53*(3), 49.

Forum. (1991). *Playboy, 38*(1), 52.

Foulks, E. F., & Pena, J. M. (1995). Ethnicity and psychotherapy. *The Psychiatric Clinics of North America, 18,* 607–620.

Frances, R. J. (1991). Should drugs be legalized? Implications of the debate for the mental health field. *Hospital and Community Psychiatry, 42,* 119–120, 125.

Frances, R. J., & Miller, S. I. (1991). Addiction treatment: The widening scope. In *Clinical textbook of addictive disorders* (Frances, R. J., & Miller, S. I., eds.). New York: The Guilford Press.

Frances, R. J., & Miller, S. I. (1998). Addiction treatment. In *Clinical textbook of addictive disorders* (2nd ed.) (Frances, R. J., & Miller, S. I., eds.). New York: Guilford.

Frank, D. A., Augustyn, M., Knight, W. G., Pell, T., & Zuckerman, B. (2001). Growth, development and behavior in early childhood following prenatal cocaine exposure. *Journal of the American Medical Association, 285,* 1613–1625.

Frank, D. A., Bauchner, H., Zuckerman, B. S., & Fried, L. (1992). Cocaine and marijuana use during pregnancy by women intending and not intending to breast feed. *Journal of the American Dietetic Association, 92,* 215–217.

Franken, I. H. A., & Hendriks, V. M. (1999). Predicting outcome of inpatient detoxification of substance abusers. *Psychiatric Services, 50,* 813–817.

Franklin, J. (1987). *Molecules of the mind.* New York: Dell Publishing Co.

Franklin, J. E. (1989). Alcoholism among blacks. *Hospital and Community Psychiatry, 40,* 1120–1122, 1127.

Freeborn, D. (1996). By the numbers. *Minneapolis Star Tribune, XV* (94), p. D2.

Freese, T. E., Miotto, K., & Reback, C. J. (2002). The effects and consequences of selected club drugs. *Journal of Substance Abuse Treatment*, 23(2), 151–156.

Freiberg, P. (1991). Panel hears of families victimized by alcoholism. *APA Monitor*, 22(4), 30.

French, M. T. (1995). Economic evaluation of drug abuse treatment programs: Methodology and findings. *American Journal of Drug and Alcohol Abuse*, 21(1), 111–135.

Frezza, M., DiPadova, C., Pozzato, G., Terpin, M., Baraona, E., & Lieber, C. S. (1990). High blood alcohol levels in women. *The New England Journal of Medicine*, 322, 95–99.

Fricchione, G. (2004). Generalized anxiety disorder. *New England Journal of Medicine*, 251, 675–682.

Fried, P. A. (1995). The Ottawa prenatal prospective study (OPPS): Methadological issues and findings—Its easy to throw the baby out with the bath water. *Live Sciences*, 56, 2159–2168.

Friedman, D. (1987) Toxic effects of marijuana. *Alcoholism & Addiction*, 7(6), 47.

Friedman, R. C., & Downey, J. I. (1994). Homosexuality. *The New England Journal of Medicine*, 331, 923–930.

Friend, T. (1998). Drug errors kill outpatients at a rising rate. *USA Today*, 16(119), p. D1.

Frierson, R. L., Melikian, M., & Wadman, P. C. (2002). Principles of suicide risk assessment. *Postgraduate Medicine*, 112(3), 65–71.

Fromm, E. (1956). *The art of loving*. New York: Harper & Row.

Fromm, E. (1968). *The revolution of hope*. New York: Harper & Row.

Fudala, P. J., & Johnson, R. E. (1995). Clinical efficacy studies of buprenorphine for the treatment of opioid dependence. In *Buprenorphine* (Cowan, A., & Lewis, J. W., eds.). New York: Wiley-Liss.

Fuller, M. A., & Sajatovic, M. (1999). *Drug information handbook for psychiatry*. Cleveland, OH: Lexi-Comp, Inc.

Fuller, P. G., & Cabanaugh, R. M. (1995). Basic assessment and screening for substance abuse in the pediatrician's office. *Pediatric Clinics of North America*, 42, 295–307.

Fuller, R. K. (1995). Antidipsotropic medications. In *Handbook of alcoholism treatment approaches* (2nd ed.) (Hester, R. K., & Miller, W. R., eds.). New York: Allyn & Bacon.

Fuller, R. K., & Hiller-Sturmhofel, S. (1999). Alcoholism treatment in the United States. *Alcohol Health & Research World*, 23(2), 69–77.

Fulton, J. S., & Johnson, G. B. (1993). Using high-dose morphine to relieve cancer pain. *Nursing '93*, 23(2), 35–39.

Fultz, O. (1991). 'Roid rage. *American Health*, X (4), 60–64.

Furst, R. T., Herrmann, C., Leung, R., Galea, J., & Hunt, K. (2004). Heroin diffusion in the mid-Hudson region of New York State. *Addiction*, 99(4), 431–441.

Furstenberg, F. F. (1990). Coming of age in a changing family system. In *At the threshold* (Feldman, S. S., & Elliott, G. R., eds.). Cambridge, MA: Harvard University Press.

Gahlinger, P. M. (2004). Club drugs: MDMA, gamma-hydroxybutyrate (GHB), Rohypnol, and Ketamine. *American Family Physician*, 69, 2919–2927.

Galanter, M. (1993). Network therapy for addiction: A model for office practice. *American Journal of Psychiatry*, 150, 28–36.

Galanter, M., Castaneda, R., & Franco, H. (1991). Group therapy and self-help groups. In *Clinical textbook of addictive disorders* (Frances, R. J., & Miller, S. I., eds.). New York: Guilford.

Gallagher, W. (1986). The looming menace of designer drugs. *Designer*, 7(8), 24–35.

Galloway, G. P. (1997). Anabolic-androgenic steroids. In *Substance abuse: A comprehensive textbook* (3rd ed.) (Lowinson, J. H., Ruiz, P., Millman, R. B., & Langrod, J. G., eds.). New York: Williams & Wilkins.

Galloway, G. P., Frederick, S. L., Staggers, F. E., Gonzales, M., Stalcup, S. A., & Smith, D. E. (1997). Gamma-hydroxybutyrate: An emerging drug of abuse that causes physical dependence. *Addiction*, 92(1), 89–96.

Ganem, D., & Prince, A. M. (2004). Hepatitis B virus infection-natural history and clinical consequences. *New England Journal of Medicine*, 350, 1118–1129.

Gannon, K. (1994). OTC naproxen sodium set to shake OTC analgesics. *Drug Topics*, 138(3), 34.

Garavan, H., Pankiewicz, J., Bloom, A., Cho, J. K., Sperry, L., Ross, T. J., Salmeron, B. J., Risinger, R., Kelley, D., & Stein, E. A. (2000). Cue-induced cocaine craving: Neuroanatomical specificity for drug users and drug stimuli. *American Journal of Psychiatry*, 157, 1789–1798.

Garbarino, J., Dubrow, N., Kostelny, K., & Pardo, C. (1992). *Children in danger*. New York: Josey-Bass.

Garcia-Andrade, C., Wall, T. L., & Ehlers, C. L. (1997). The firewater myth and response to alcohol in mission indians. *American Journal of Psychiatry*, 154, 983–988.

Gardner, E. L. (1997). Brain reward mechanisms. In *Substance abuse: A comprehensive textbook* (3rd ed.) (Lowinson, J. H., Ruiz, P., Millman, R. B., & Langrod, J. G., eds.). New York: Williams & Wilkins.

Garfinkel, D., Zisapel, N., Wainstein, J., & Laudon, M. (1999). Facilitation of benzodiazepine discontinuation by melatonin. *Archives of Internal Medicine*, 159, 2456–2460.

Garrett, L. (1994). *The coming plague*. New York: Farrar, Straus & Giroux.

Garrett, L. (2000). *Betrayal of trust*. New York: Hyperion.

Garriott, J. C. (1996). Pharmacology and toxicology of ethyl alcohol. In *Medicolegal aspects of alcohol* (3rd ed.) (Garriott, J. C., ed.). Tucson, AZ: Lawyers and Judges Publishing Co.

Garro, A. J., Espina, N., & Lieber, C. S. (1992). Alcohol and cancer. *Alcohol Health & Research World*, 16(1), 81–85.

Garry, P. (1995). Oh, judge, can't you make them stop picking on me? *Minneapolis Star Tribune*, XIV (106), p. A10.

Gastfriend, D. R. (2004a). Patient placement criteria. In *Textbook of substance abuse treatment* (3rd ed.) (Galanter, M., &

Kleber, H. D., eds.). Washington, DC: American Psychiatric Press, Inc.

Gastfriend, D. R. (2004b). Patient treatment matching: What works for whom and why. Symposium presented to the Dept. of Psychiatry at The Cambridge Hospital, Boston, MA, March 5.

Gastfriend, D. R., & McLellan, A. T. (1997). Treatment matching. *Medical Clinics of North America, 81,* 945–966.

Gawin, F. H., & Ellinwood, E. H. (1988). Cocaine and other stimulants: Actions, abuse, and treatment. *New England Journal of Medicine, 318,* 1173–1182.

Gawin, F. H., Khalsa, M. E., & Ellinwood, E. (1994). Stimulants. In *Textbook of substance abuse treatment* (Galanter, M., & Kleber, H. D., eds.). Washington, DC: American Psychiatric Press, Inc.

Gawin, F. H., & Kleber, H. D. (1986). Abstinence symptomology and psychiatric diagnosis in cocaine abusers. *Archieves of General Psychiatry, 43,* 107–113.

Gay, G. R. (1990). Another side effect of NSAIDs. *Journal of the American Medical Association, 164,* 2677–2678.

Gazzaniga, M. S. (1988). *Mind matters.* Boston: Houghton-Mifflin.

Gelman, D., Underwood, A., King, P., Hager, M., & Gordon, J. (1990). Some things work! *Newsweek, CXVI* (13), 78–81.

George, A. A., & Tucker, J. A. (1996). Help-seeking for alcohol-related problems: Social contexts surrounding entry into alcoholism treatment or Alcoholics Anonymous. *Journal of Studies on Alcohol, 57,* 449–457.

George, F. R. (1999). Genetic factors in addiction. In *Drugs of abuse and addiction: Neurobehavioral toxicology* (Niesink, R. J. M., Jaspers, R. M. A., Korney, L. M. W., & van Ree, J. M., eds.). New York: CRC Press.

Geppert, C. M. A., & Minkoff, K. (2004). Issues in dual diagnosis: Diagnosis, treatment and new research. *Psychiatric Times, XXI* (4), 103–107.

Gernstein, J. (2003). SMART recovery: A group CBT approach to addictions. Symposium presented to the Dept. of Psychiatry at The Cambridge Hospital, Boston, MA, March 8.

Giacchino, S., & Houdek, D. (1998). Ruptured varicies! *RN, 61*(5), 33–36.

Giacona, N. S., Dahl, S. L., & Hare, B. D. (1987). The role of nonsteroidal antiinflammatory drugs and non-narcotics in analgesia. *Hospital Formulary, 22,* 723–733.

Giannini, A. J. (2000). An approach to drug abuse, intoxication and withdrawal. *American Family Physician, 61,* 2763–2774.

Gilbertson, P. K., & Weinberg, J. (1992). Fetal alcohol syndrome and functioning of the immune system. *Alcohol Health & Research World, 16*(1), 29–38.

Gilliam, M. (1998). *How Alcoholics Anonymous failed me.* New York: William Morrow & Co., Inc.

Gillin, J. C. (1991). The long and the short of sleeping pills. *The New England Journal of Medicine, 324,* 1735–1736.

Gilman, S. (1992). Advances in neurology. *The New England Journal of Medicine, 326,* 1608–1616.

Gitlow, S. (2001). *Substance use disorders.* New York: Lippincott, Williams & Wilkins.

Giunta, C. T., & Compas, B. E. (1994). Adult daughters of alcoholics: Are they unique? *Journal of Studies on Alcohol, 55,* 600–606.

Glantz, J. C., & Woods, J. R. (1993). Cocaine, heroin, and phencyclidine: Obstetric perspectives. *Clinical Obstetrics and Gynecology, 36,* 279–301.

Glantz, S., & Parmley, W. W. (1995). Passive smoking and heart disease. *Journal of the American Medical Association, 273,* 1047–1053.

Glantz, S., & Parmley, W. W. (2001). Even a little second-hand smoke is dangerous. *Journal of the American Medical Association, 286,* 462–463.

Glantz, S. A., Barnes, D. E., Bero, L., Hanauer, P., & Slade, J. (1995). Looking through a keyhole at the tobacco industry. *Journal of the American Medical Association, 274,* 219–224.

Glantz, S. A., Slade, J., Bero, L. A., Hanauer, P., & Barnes, D. E. (1996). *The Cigarette Papers.* Los Angeles: University of California Press.

Glaser, F. B., & Ogborne, A. C. (1982). Does A. A. really work? *British Journal of the Addictions, 77,* 88–92.

Glasser, J. (2002). Cycle of shame. *U.S. News & World Report, 132*(17), 26–33.

Glasser, R. J. (1998). The doctor is not in. *Harper's Magzine, 296*(1774), 35–42.

Glasser, R. J. (2004). We are not immune. *Harper's Magazine, 309*(1850), 35–42.

Glassman, A. H. (1993). Cigarette smoking: Implications for psychiatric illness. *American Journal of Psychiatry, 150,* 546–553.

Glennon, R. A. (2004). Neurobiology of hallucinogens. In *Textbook of substance abuse treatment* (3rd ed.) (Galanter, M., & Kleber, H. D., eds.). Washington, DC: American Psychiatric Press, Inc.

Glick, S. D., & Maisonneuve, I. M. (2000). Development of novel medications for drug addiction. In *New medications for drug abuse* (Glick, S. D., & Maisonneuve, I. B., eds.). New York: New York Academy of Sciences.

Glowa, J. R. (1986). *Inhalants: The toxic fumes.* New York: Chelsea House Publishers.

Godlaski, T. M., Leukefeld, C., & Cloud, R. (1997). Recovery: With and without self-help. *Substance Use & Misuse, 32,* 621–627.

Godwin, C. (2004). What's new in the fight against AIDS. *RN, 67*(4), 46–52.

Gold, M. S. (1989). Opiates. In *Drugs of abuse* (Giannini, A. J., & Slaby, A. E., eds.). Oradell, NJ: Medical Economics Books.

Gold, M. S. (1993). Opiate addiction and the locus coeruleus. *Psychiatric Clinics of North America, 16,* 61–73.

Gold, M. S. (1997). Cocaine (and crack): Clinical aspects. In *Substance abuse: A comprehensive textbook* (3rd ed.) (Lowinson, J. H., Ruiz, P., Millman, R. B., & Langrod, J. G., eds.). New York: Williams & Wilkins.

Gold, M. S., Frost-Pineda, K., & Jacobs, W. S. (2004). Cannabis. In *Textbook of substance abuse treatment* (3rd ed.) (Galanter, M., & Kleber, H. D., eds.). Washington, DC: American Psychiatric Press, Inc.

Gold, M. S., & Miller, N. S. (1997a). Cocaine (and crack): Neurobiology. In *Substance Abuse: A Comprehensive Textbook* (3rd ed.) (Lowinson, J. H., Ruiz, P., Millman, R. B., & Langrod, J. G., eds.). New York: Williams & Wilkins.

Gold, M. S., & Miller, N. S. (1997b). Intoxication and withdrawal from alcohol. In *Manual of therapeutics of addictions* (Miller, N. S., Gold, M. S., & Smith, D. E., eds.). New York: Wiley-Liss.

Gold, M. S., & Miller, N. S. (1997c). Intoxication and withdrawal from marijuana, LSD, and MDMA. In *Manual of therapeutics of addictions* (Miller, N. S., Gold, M. S., & Smith, D. E., eds.). New York: Wiley-Liss.

Gold, M. S., Schuchard, K., & Gleaton, T. (1994). LSD use among US high school students. *Journal of the American Medical Association, 271,* 426–427.

Gold, M. S., & Verebey, K. (1984). The psychopharmacology of cocaine. *Psychiatric Annuals, 14,* 714–723.

Goldberg, I. J. (2003). To drink or not to drink? *New England Journal of Medicine, 348,* 163–164.

Goldberg, R. (2002). Drugs: Divergent views. In *Taking sides: Clashing views on controversial issues in drugs and society* (5th ed.) (Goldberg, R., ed.). New York: McGraw-Hill Dushkin.

Goldkamp, J. S., White, M. D., & Robinson, J. B. (2002). An honest chance: Perspectives on drug courts. Washington, DC: U.S. Department of Justice.

Goldman, B. (1991). How to thwart a drug seeker. *Emergency Medicine, 23*(6), 48–61.

Goldstein, M. Z., Pataki, A., & Webb, M. T. (1996). Alcoholism among elderly persons. *Psychiatric Services, 47,* 941–943.

Goldstein, P. (1990). Drugs and violence. Paper presented at the 1990 meeting of the American Psychological Association, Boston, MA.

Goldstein, R. Z., & Volkow, N. D. (2002). Drug addiction and its underlying neurobiological basis: Neuroimaging evidence for the involvement of the frontal cortex. *American Journal of Psychiatry, 150,* 1642–1652.

Goldstone, M. S. (1993). "Cat": Methcathinone, a new drug of abuse. *Journal of the American Medical Association, 269,* 2508.

Gomberg, E. S. L. (2004). Ethnic minorities and the elderly. In *Textbook of substance abuse treatment* (3rd ed.) (Galanter, M., & Kleber, H. D., eds.). Washington, DC: American Psychiatric Press, Inc.

Goodman, E., & Capitman, J. (2000). Depressive symptoms and cigarette smoking among teens. *Pediatrics, 106,* 748–755.

Goodnough, L. T., Brecher, M. E., Kanter, M. H., & AuBuchon, J. P. (1999). Transfusion medicine. *The New England Journal of Medicine, 340,* 438–447.

Goodwin, D. W., & Warnock, J. K. (1991). Alcoholism: A family disease. In *Clinical textbook of addictive disorders.* (Frances, R. J., & Miller, S. I., eds.). New York: The Guilford Press.

Gorbach, S. L., Mensa, J., & Gatell, J. M. (1997). *Pocket book of antimicrobial therapy & prevention.* Baltimore, MD: Williams & Wilkins.

Gordis, E. (1995). The National Institute on Alcohol Abuse and Alcoholism. *Alcohol Health & Research World, 19,* 5–11.

Gordis, E. (1996). Alcohol research. *Archives of General Psychiatry, 53,* 199–201.

Gordon, S. C. (2000). Antiviral therapy for chronic hepatitis B and C. *Postgraduate Medicine, 107,* 135–144.

Gorman, D. M. (2003). The best of practices, the worst of practices: The making of science-based primary intervention programs. *Psychiatric Services, 54,* 1087–1089.

Gorski, T. T. (1992). Diagnosing codependence. *Addiction & Recovery, 12*(7), 14–16.

Gorski, T. T. (1993). Relapse prevention. *Addiction & Recovery, 13*(2), 25–27.

Gossop, M., Battersby, M., & Strang, J. (1991). Self-detoxification by opiate addicts. *British Journal of Psychiatry, 159,* 208–212.

Gottesman, J. (1992). Little is known about effects of steroids on women. *Minneapolis Star Tribune, XI* (211), p. C7.

Gottlieb, A. M. (1997). Crisis of consciousness. *Utne Reader, 79,* 45–48.

Gottlieb, A. M., Killen, J. D., Marlatt, G. A., & Taylor, C. B. (1987). Psychological and pharmacological influences in cigarette smoking withdrawal: Effects of nicotine gum and expectancy on smoking withdrawal symptoms and relapse. *Journal of Clinical and Consulting Psychology, 55,* 606–608.

Gottlieb, M. I. (1994). Alcohol and pregnancy: A potential for disaster. *Emergency Medicine, 26*(1), 73–79.

Gourlay, S. G., & Benowitz, N. L. (1995). Is clonidine an effective smoking cessation therapy? *Drugs, 50,* 197–207.

Gouzoulis-Mayfrank, E., Daumann, J., Tuchtenhagen, F., Pelz, S., Becker, S., Kunert, H. J., Fimm, B., & Sass, H. (2000). Impaired cognitive performance in drug free users of recreational ecstasy (MDMA). *Journal of Neurology, Neurosurgery and Psychiatry, 68,* 719–725.

Graedon, J., & Ferguson, T. (1993). *The aspirin handbook.* New York: Bantam.

Graedon, J., & Graedon, T. (1991). *Graedons' best medicine.* New York: Bantam Books.

Graedon, J., & Graedon, T. (1995). *The people's guide to deadly drug interactions.* New York: St. Martin's Press.

Graedon, J., & Graedon, T. (1996). *The people's pharmacy— Revised.* New York: St. Martin's Griffin.

Graham, B. (1988). The abuse of alcohol: Disease or disgrace? *Alcoholism & Addiction, 8*(4), 14–15.

Graham, J. R. (1990). *MMPI-2 assessing personality and psychopathology.* New York: Oxford University Press.

Graham, M. (1989). One toke over the line. *The New Republic, 200*(16), 20–22.

Grant, I. (1987). Alcohol and the brain: Neuropsychological correlates. *Journal of Clinical and Consulting Psychology,* 55, 310–324.

Grant, I., Gonzalez, R., Carey, C. L., Natarajan, L., & Wolfson, T. (2003). Non-acute (residual) neurocognitive effects of cannabis use: A meta analytic study. *Journal of the International Neuropsychological Society,* 9(5), 929–934.

Grant, J. E., Kushner, M. G., & Kim, S. W. (2002). Pathological gambling and alcohol use disorder. *Alcohol Research & Health,* 26, 143–150.

Graumlich, J. F. (2001). Preventing gastrointestinal complications of NSAIDS. *Postgraduate Medicine,* 109(5), 117–128.

Gray, M. (1998). *Drug crazy.* New York: Routledge.

Green, J. (2002). *Cannabis.* New York: Thunder's Mouth Press.

Green, K. (1998). Marijuana smoking vs cannabinoids for glaucoma therapy. *Archives of Ophthalmology,* 116, 1433–1437.

Greenberg, D. A. (1993). Ethanol and sedatives. *Neurologic Clinics,* 11, 523–534.

Greene, M. A., & Gordon, D. E. (1998). Lessons of the new genetics. *Family Therapy Networker,* 22(2), 26–41.

Greener, M. (2003). The COX continuum. *The Scientist,* 17(14), 31.

Greenfield, S. F. (2003). Gender differences in addiction: Findings and treatment implications. Symposium presented to the Dept. of Psychiatry at The Cambridge Hospital, Boston, MA, March 7.

Greenfield, S. F., & Hennessy, G. (2004). Assessment of the patient. In *Textbook of substance abuse treatment* (3rd ed.) (Galanter, M., & Kleber, H. D., eds.). Washington, DC: American Psychiatric Press, Inc.

Greydanus, D. E., & Patel, D. R. (2003). Substance abuse in adolescents: A complex conundrum for the clinician. *Pediatric Clinics of North America,* 50, 1179–1223.

Griffin, K. W., Botvin, G. J., Scheier, L. M., Diaz, T., & Miller, N. L. (2000). Parenting practices as predictors of substance use, delinquency, and aggression among urban minority youth: Moderating effects of family structure and gender. *Psychology of Addictive Behaviors,* 14, 174–184.

Griffin, M. L., Weiss, R. D., Mirin, S. M., & Lang, U. (1989). A comparison of male and female cocaine abusers. *Archives of General Psychiatry,* 46, 122–126.

Griffiths, H. J., Parantainen, H., & Olson, P. (1994). Alcohol and bone disorders. *Alcohol Health & Research World,* 17, 299–304.

Grinfeld, M. J. (2001). Decriminalizing addiction. *Psychiatric Times,* XVIII (3), 1, 5, 6.

Grinspoon, L., & Bakalar, J. B. (1990). What is phencyclidine? *The Harvard Medical School Mental Health Letter,* 6(7), 8.

Grinspoon, L., & Bakalar, J. B. (1993). *Marijuana: The forgotten medicine.* New Haven, CT: Yale University Press.

Grinspoon, L., & Bakalar, J. B. (1995). Marijuana as medicine. *Journal of the American Medical Association,* 273, 1875–1876.

Grinspoon, L., & Bakalar, J. B. (1997a). Marijuana. In *Substance abuse: A comprehensive textbook* (3rd ed.) (Lowinson, J. H., Ruiz, P., Millman, R. B., & Langrod, J. G., eds.). New York: Williams & Wilkins.

Grinspoon, L., & Bakalar, J. B.(1997b). Smoke screen. *Playboy,* 44(6), 49–53.

Group for the Advancement of Psychiatry. (1991). Substance abuse disorders: A psychiatric priority. *American Journal of Psychiatry,* 148, 1291–1300.

Grover, S. A., Gray-Donald, K., Joseph, L., Abrahamowicz, M., & Coupal, L. (1994). Life expectancy following dietary modification or smoking cessation. *Archives of Internal Medicine,* 154, 1697–1704.

Gruber, A. J., & Pope, H. G. (2002). Marijuana use among adolescents. *The Pediatric Clinics of North America,* 49, 389–413.

Gruber, A. J., Pope, H. G., Hudson, J. I., & Yurgelun-Todd, D. (2003). Attributes of long-term heavy cannabis users: A case-controlled study. *Psychological Medicine,* 33, 1415–1422.

Guilbert, T., & Krawiec, M. (2003). Natural history of asthma. *The Pediatric Clinics of North America,* 50, 523–538.

Guslandi, M. (1997). Gastric toxicity of antiplatelet therapy with low-dose aspirin. *Drugs,* 53, 1–5.

Gutstein, H. B., & Akil, H. (2001). Opioid analgesics. In *The pharmacological basis of therapeutics* (10th ed.) (Hardman, J. G., Limbird, L. E., & Gilman, A. G., eds.). New York: McGraw-Hill.

Guydish, J., Werdeger, D., Sorensen, J. L., Clark, W., & Acampora, A. (1998). Drug abuse day treatment: A randomized clinical trial comparing day and residential treatment programs. *Journal of Consulting and Clinical Psychology,* 66, 280–289.

Haack, M. R. (1998). Treating acute withdrawal from alcohol and other drugs. *Nursing Clinics of North America,* 33, 75–92.

Hager, M., & Reibstein, L. (1998). Do you have hepatitis C? *Newsweek,* CXXXI (18), 83.

Hahn, I. H. & Hoffman, R. S. (2001). Cocaine use and acute myocardial infarction. *Emergency Medicine Clinics of North America,* 19, 493–510.

Hale, T. W. (2003). Medications in breastfeeding mothers of preterm infants. *Pediatric Annals,* 32, 337–347.

Hall, S. M., Havassy, B. E., & Wasserman, D. A. (1991). Effects of commitment to abstinence, positive moods, stress and coping on relapse to cocaine use. *Journal of Consulting and Clinical Psychology,* 59, 526–532.

Hall, W., & Degenhardt, L. (2005). Cannabis-related disorders. In *Kaplan & Sadock's comprehensive textbook of psychiatry* (8th ed.) (Sadock, B. J. & Sadock, V. A., eds.). New York: Lippincott, Williams & Wilkins.

Hall, W., & Sannibale, C. (1996). Are there two types of alcoholism? *The Lancet,* 348, 1258.

Hall, W., & Solowij, N. (1998). Adverse effects of cannabis. *The Lancet, 352,* 1611–1616.

Hall, W. C., Talbert, R. L., & Ereshefsky, L. (1990). Cocaine abuse and its treatment. *Pharmacotherapy, 10*(1), 47–65.

Halushka, M. K., & Halushka, P. V. (2002). Why are some individuals resistant to the cardioprotective effects of aspirin? *Circulation, 105,* 1620–1622.

Hamner, M. B. (1993). PTSD and cocaine abuse. *Hospital and Community Psychiatry, 44,* 591–592.

Hampson, A. J., Grimaldi, M., Lolic, M., Wink, D., Rosenthal, R., & Axelrod, J. (2002). Neuroprotective antioxidants from marijuana. *Annals of the New York Academy of Sciences, 939,* 274–282.

Haney, M. (2004). Neurobiology of stimulants. In *Textbook of substance abuse treatment* (3rd ed.) (Galanter, M., & Kleber, H. D., eds.). Washington, DC: American Psychiatric Press, Inc.

Hankinson, S. E., Willett, W. C., Colditz, G. A., Seddon, J. M., Rosner, B., Speizer, F. E., & Stampfer, M. J. (1992). A prospective study of cigarette smoking and risk of cataract surgery in women. *Journal of the American Medical Association, 268,* 994–998.

Hanners, D. (1998). Scientists paid to write on tobacco. *St. Paul Pioneer Press, 150*(100), pp. A1, A5.

Harkness, R., & Bratman, S. (2003). *Mosby's handbook of drug-herb and drug-supplement interactions.* Philadelphia: Mosby.

Harrell, A., & Kleiman, M. (2002). Drug testing in criminal justice settings. In *Treatment of drug offenders* (Leukefeld, C. G., Tims, F., & Farabee, D., eds.). New York: Springer Publishing Co.

Harrington, R. D., Woodward, J. A., Hooton, T. M., & Horn, J. R. (1999). Life-threatening interactions between HIV-1 Protease inhibitors and the illicit drugs MDMA and gamma-hydroxybutyrate. *Archives of Internal Medicine, 159,* 2221–2224.

Harrison, P. A., Fulkerson, J. A., & Beebe, T. J. (1998). DSM-IV substance use disorder criteria for adolescents: A critical examination based on a statewide school survey. *American Journal of Psychiatry, 155,* 486–492.

Hart, K. E., & Fiissel, D. L. (2003). Do adult offspring of alcoholics suffer from poor mental health? A three-group comparison controlling for self-report bias. *Canadian Journal of Nursing, 35,* 52–72.

Hart, R. H. (1997). On the cannabinoid receptor: A study in molecular psychiatry. *Psychiatric Times, XIV* (7), 59–60.

Hartman, D. E. (1995). *Neuropsychological toxicology* (2nd ed.). New York: Plenum.

Hartmann, P. M. (1995). Drug treatment of insomnia: Indications and newer agents. *American Family Physician, 51*(1), 191–194.

Hartwell, S. W. (2004). Comparison of offenders with mental illness only and with offenders with dual diagnosis. *Psychiatric Services, 55,* 145–150.

Harwitz, D., & Ravizza, L. (2000). Suicide and depression. *Emergency Medicine Clinics of North America, 18,* 263–271.

Hasin, D. S., & Grant, B. F. (2002). Major depression in 6050 former drinkers. *Archives of General Psychiatry, 59,* 794–800.

Hatsukami, D. K., & Fischman, M. W. (1996). Crack cocaine and cocaine hydrochloride. *Journal of the American Medical Association, 276,* 1580–1588.

Hawkes, C. H. (1992). Endorphins: The basis of pleasure? *Journal of Neurology, Neurosurgery and Psychiatry, 55,* 247–250.

Hawley, T. L., Halle, T. G., Drasin, R. E., & Thomas, N. G. (1995). Children of addicted mothers: Effects of the "crack epidemic" on the caregiving environment and the development of preschoolers. *American Journal of Orthopsychiatry, 65*(3), 364–379.

Hayner, G. N., & McKinney, H. (1986). MDMA: The dark side of ecstasy. *Journal of Psychoactive Drugs, 18*(4), 341–347.

Hays, J. T., Hurt, R. D., Rigotti, N. A., Niaura, R., Gonzales, D., Durcan, M. J., Sachs, D. P. L., Wolter, T. D., Buist, S., Johnston, J. A., & White, J. D. (2001). Sustained-release bupropion for pharmacologic relapse prevention after smoking cessation. *Annals of Internal Medicine, 135,* 423–433.

He, J., Whelton, P. K., Vu, B., & Klag, M. J. (1998). Aspirin and risk of hemorrhagic stroke. *Journal of the American Medical Association, 280,* 1930–1935.

Health spending criticized. (1996). *Wisconsin State Journal, 157*(260), pp. A1, A3.

Heath, A. W., & Stanton, M. D. (1998). Family-based treatment. In *Clinical textbook of addictive disorders* (2nd ed.) (Frances, R. J., & Miller, S. I., eds.). New York: Guilford.

Heath, D. B. (1994). Inhalant abuse. *Behavioral Health Management, 14*(3), 47–48.

Heesch, C. M., Negus, B. H., Steiner, M., Snyder, R. W., McIntire, D. D., Grayburn, P. A., Ashcraft, J., Hernandez, J. A., & Eichorn, E. J. (1996). Effects of in vivo cocaine administration on human platelet aggregation. *The American Journal of Cardiology 78,* 237–239.

Hegab, A. M., & Luketic, V. A. (2001). Bleeding exophateal varices. *Postgraduate Medicine, 109*(2), 75–76, 81–86, 89.

Heil, S. H., & Subramanian, M. G. (1998). Alcohol and the hormonal control of lactation. *Alcohol Health & Research World, 22*(3), 178–184.

Heimel, C. (1990). It's now, it's trendy, it's codependency. *Playboy, 37*(5), 43.

Heinz, A., Dufeu, P., Kuhn, S., Dettling, M., Graf, K., Kurten, I., Rommelspacher, H., & Schmidt, L. G. (1996). Psychopathological and behavioral correlates of dopaminergic sensitivity in alcohol-dependent patients. *Archives of General Psychiatry, 53,* 1123–1128.

Heinz, A., Ragan, P., Jones, D. W., Hommer, D., Williams, W., Knable, M. B., Gorey, J. G., Doty, L., Geyer, C., Lee, K. S., Coppola, R., Weinberger, D. R., & Linnoila, M. (1998). Reduced central serotonin transporters in alcoholism. *American Journal of Psychiatry, 155,* 1544–1549.

Heller, A., Bubula, N., Lew, R., Heller, B., & Won, L. (2001). Gender-dependent enhanced adult neurotoxic response to methamphetamine following fetal exposure to the drug. *Journal of Pharmacology and Experimental Therapeutics, 298,* 1–11.

Hellman, R. E., Stanton, M., Lee, J., Tytun, A., & Vachon, R. (1989). Treatment of homosexual alcoholics in government-funded agencies: Provider training and attitudes. *Hospital and Community Psychiatry, 40,* 1163–1168.

Helzer, J. E., Robins, L. N., Taylor, J. R., Carey, K., Miller, R. H., Combs-Orme, T., & Farmer, A. (1985). The extent of long-term moderate drinking among alcoholics discharged from medical and psychiatric treatment facilities. *The New England Journal of Medicine, 312,* 1678–1682.

Henderson, L. A. (1994a). About LSD. In *LSD: Still with us after all these years.* (Henderson, L. A., & Glass, W. J., eds.). New York: Lexington Books.

Henderson, L. A. (1994b). Adverse reactions. In *LSD: Still with us after all these years* (Henderson, L. A., & Glass, W. J., eds.). New York: Lexington Books.

Henderson, T. A., & Fischer, V. W. (1994). Effects of methylphenidate (Ritalin) on mammalian myocardial ultrastructure. *American Journal of Cardiovascular Pathology, 5*(1), 68–78.

Hennessey, M. B. (1992). Identifying the woman with alcohol problems. *Nursing Clinics of North America, 27,* 917–924.

Henningfield, J. E. (1995). Nicotine medications for smoking cessation. *New England Journal of Medicine, 333,* 1196–1203.

Henningfield, J. E., & Nemeth-Coslett, R. (1988). Nicotine dependence. *Chest, 93*(2), 37s-55s.

Henretig, F. (1996). Inhalant abuse in children and adolescents. *Pediatric Annals, 25*(1), 47–52.

Henry, J., & Rella, J. (2001). Medical risks associated with MDMA use. In *Ecstasy: The complete guide* (Holland, J., ed.). Rochester, VT: Park St. Press.

Henry, J. A. (1996). Management of drug abuse emergencies. *Journal of Accident & Emergency Medicine, 13,* 370–372.

Henry, J. A., Jeffreys, J. A., & Dawling, S. (1992). Toxicity and deaths from 3,4–methylenedioxymethamphetamine ("ecstasy"). *The Lancet, 340,* 384–387.

Henry, K., Stiffman, M., & Feldman, J. (1997). Antiretroviral therapy for HIV infection. *Postgraduate Medicine, 102,* (4), 100–120.

Herman, R. (1988). The twelve-step program: Cure or cover? *Utne Reader, 30,* 52–53.

Herman, R. (1993). Alcohol debate may drive you to drink. *St. Paul Pioneer Press, 144*(356), p. G11.

Herning, R. I., Better, W. E., Tate, K., & Cadet, J. L. (2001). Marijuana abusers are at increased risk for stroke: Preliminary evidence from cerebrovascular perfusion data. *Annals of the New York Academy of Sciences, 939,* 413–415.

Heroin encephalophy. (2002). *Forensic Drug Abuse Advisor, 14*(2), 12.

Herrera, S. (1997). The morphine myth. *Forbes, 159,* 258–260.

Hester, R. K. (1994). Outcome research: Alcoholism. In *Textbook of substance abuse treatment* (Galanter, M., & Kleber, H. D., eds.). Washington, DC: American Psychiatric Press, Inc.

Hester, R. K., (1995). Self-control training. In *Handbook of alcoholism treatment approaches.* (Hester, R. K., & Miller, W. R., eds.). New York: Allyn & Bacon.

Hester, R. K., & Squires, D. D. (2004). Outcome research. In *Textbook of substance abuse treatment* (3rd ed.) (Galanter, M., & Kleber, H. D., eds.). Washington, DC: American Psychiatric Press, Inc.

Hibbs, J., Perper, J., & Winek, C. L. (1991). An outbreak of designer drug-related deaths in Pennsylvania. *Journal of the American Medical Association, 265,* 1011–1013.

Higgins, J. P., Wright, S. W., & Wrenn, K. D. (1996). Alcohol, the elderly, and motor vehicle crashes. *American Journal of Emergency Medicine, 14,* 265–267.

Hilditch, T. (2000). Ya ba. *Gear, 2*(11), 86–88.

Hill, D. B., & Kugelmas, M. (1998). Alcoholic liver disease. *Postgraduate Medicine, 103,* 261–275.

Hill, P., Dwyer, K., Kay, T., & Murphy, B. (2002). Severe chronic renal failure in association with oxycodone addiction: A new form of fibillary glomerulopathy. *Human Pathology, 33,* 783–787.

Hill, S. Y. (1995). Vulnerability to alcoholism in women. In *Recent developments in alcoholism* (Vol. 12) (Galanter, M., ed.). New York: Plenum Press.

Hiller, M. L., Knight, K., Rao, S. R., & Simpson, D. D. (2002). Assessing and evaluating mandated correctional substance abuse treatment. In *Treatment of drug offenders* (Leukefeld, C. G., Tims, F., & Farabee, D., eds.). New York: Springer.

Hilts, P. J. (1994). Labeling on cigarettes called a smoke screen. *St. Paul Pioneer Press, 146*(5), pp. A1, A6.

Hilts, P. J. (1996). *Smoke screen.* New York: Addison-Wesley Publishing Co.

Hines, L. M., Stampfer, K. M. J., Ma, J., Gaziano, J. M., Ridker, P. M., Hankinson, S. E., Sacks, F., Rimm, E. B., & Hunter, D. J. (2001). Genetic variation in alcohol dehydrogenase and the beneficial effect of moderate alcohol consumption on myocardial infarction. *New England Journal of Medicine, 344,* 549–555.

Hines, S. E. (2002). Progress against hepatitis C infection. *Patient Care, 36*(3), 11–20.

Hingson, R. (1996). Prevention of drinking and driving. *Alcohol Health & Research World, 20,* 219–226.

Hingson, R. (2003). College age drinking. Symposium presented to the Dept. of Psychiatry at The Cambridge Hospital, Boston, MA, March 7.

Hirsch, D., Paley, J. E., & Renner, J. A. (1996). Opiates. In *Sourcebook of substance abuse and addiction* (Friedman, L., Fleming, N. F., Roberts, D. H., & Hyman, S. E., eds.). New York: Williams & Wilkins.

Hirschfeld, R. M. A., & Davidson, L. (1988). Risk factors for suicide. In *Review of psychiatry* (Vol. 7) (Frances, A. J., & Hales, R. E., eds.). Washington, DC: American Psychiatric Association Press, Inc.

Hitchcock, H. C., Stainback, R. D., & Roque, G. M. (1995). Effects of halfway house placement on retention of patients in substance abuse aftercare. *American Journal of Drug and Alcohol Abuse, 21*, 379–391.

Hobbs, W. R., Rall, T. W., & Verdoorn, T. A. (1995). Hypnotics and sedatives; ethanol. In *The pharmacological basis of therapeutics* (9th ed.) (Hardman, J. G., & Limbird, L. E., ed.). New York: McGraw-Hill.

Hoberman, J. M., & Yesalis, C. E. (1995). The history of synthetic testosterone. *Scientific American, 272*(2), 76–81.

Hobson, J. A. (2001). *The dream drugstore.* Cambridge, MA: The MIT Press.

Hoegerman, G., & Schnoll, S. (1991). Narcotic use in pregnancy. *Clinics in Perinatology, 18*, 52–76.

Hoeksema, H. L., & de Bock, G. H. (1993). The value of laboratory tests for the screening and recognition of alcohol abuse in primary care patients. *The Journal of Family Practice, 37*, 268–276.

Hoffman, B. B., & Lefkowitz, R. J. (1990). Catecholamines and sympathomimetic drugs. In *The pharmacological basis of therapeutics* (8th ed.) (Gilman, A. G., Rall, T. W., Nies, A. S., & Taylor, P., eds.). New York: Pergamon Press.

Hoffman, R. S., & Hollander, J. E. (1997). Evaluation of patients with chest pain after cocaine use. *Critical Care Clinics of North America, 13*, 809–828.

Hoffmann, N. G., Belille, C. A., & Harrison, P. A. (1987). Adequate resources for a complex population? *Alcoholism & Addiction, 7*(5), 17.

Hoffnagle, J. H., & Di Bisceglie, A. M. (1997). The treatment of chronic viral hepatitis. *The New England Journal of Medicine, 336*, 347–356.

Hogan, C. M., & Hammer, S. M. (2001). Host determinants in HIV infection and disease. *Archives of Internal Medicine, 134*, 761–776.

Hogan, M. J. (2000). Diagnosis and treatment of teen drug use. *Medical Clinics of North America, 84*, 927–966.

Holden, C. (1998). New clues to alcoholism risk. *Science, 280*, 1348–1349.

Holder, H., Longabaugh, R., Miller, W. R., & Rubonis, A. V. (1991). The cost effectiveness of treatment for alcoholism: A first approximation. *Journal of Studies on Alcohol, 52*, 517–540.

Holland, W. W., & Fitzsimons, B. (1991). Smoking in children. *Archives of Disease in Childhood, 66*, 1269–1270.

Hollander, J. E. (1995). The management of cocaine-associated myocardial ischemia. *New England Journal of Medicine, 333*, 1267–1271.

Hollander, J. E., Hoffman, R. S., Burnstein, J. L., Shih, R. D., & Thode, H. C. (1995). Cocaine-associated myocardial infarction. *Archives of Internal Medicine, 155*, 1081–1086.

Hollander, J. E., Shih, R. D., Hoffman, R. S., Harchelroad, F. P., Phillips, S., Brent, J., Kulig, K., & Thode, H. C. (1997). Predictors of coronary artery disease in patients with cocaine-associated myocardial infarction. *American Journal of Medicine, 102*, 159–163.

Hollander, J. E., Todd, K. H., Green, G., Heilpern, K. L., Karras, D. J., Singer, A. J., Brogan, G. X., Funk, J. P., & Strahan, J. B. (1995). Chest pain associated with cocaine: An assessment of prevalence in suburban and urban emergency departments. *Annals of Emergency Medicine, 26*, 671–676.

Holleran, R. S. (2002). The problem of pain in emergency care. *Nursing Clinics of North America, 37*, 67–78.

Holloway, M. (1991). Rx for addiction. *Scientific American, 264*(3), 94–103.

Holloway, R. (1998). Doubtful demons. *Nursing Times, 94*(21), 34–36.

Holm, K. J., & Goa, K. L. (2000). Zolpidem. *Drugs, 59*, 865–889.

Hommer, D. W., Momenan, R., Kaiser, E., & Rawlings, R. R. (2001). Evidence of a gender-related effect of alcoholism on brain volumes. *American Journal of Psychiatry, 158*, 198–204.

Hong, R., Matsuyama, E., & Nur, K. (1991) Cardiomyopathy associated with smoking of crystal methamphetamine. *Journal of the American Medical Association, 265*, 1152–1154.

Hopewell, P. C. (1996). Mycobacterium tuberculosis an emerging pathogen? *Western Journal of Medicine, 164*, 33–35.

Hopfer, C. J., Mikulich, S. K., & Crowley, T. J. (2000). Heroin use among adolescents in treatment for substance use disorders. *Journal of the American Academy of Child and Adolescent Psychiatry, 39*, 1316–1323.

Hopkins, G. L. (1998). Why people abuse drugs. *Vibrant Life, 14*(1), 4–6.

Hopko, D. R., Lachar, D., Bailley, S. E., & Varner, R. V. (2001). Assessing predictive factors for extended hospitalization at acute psychiatric admission. *Psychiatric Services, 52*, 1367–1373.

Horgan, J. (1989). Lukewarm turkey: Drug firms balk at pursuing a heroin-addiction treatment. *Scientific American, 260*(3), 32.

Horney, K. (1964). *The neurotic personality of our time.* New York: W. W. Norton & Co.

Horvath, A. T. (2000). SMART recovery. *The Addictions Newsletter, 7*(2), 11.

Hough, D. O., & Kovan, J. R. (1990). Is your patient a steroid abuser? *Medical Aspects of Human Sexuality, 24*(11), 24–32.

House, M. A. (1990). Cocaine. *American Journal of Nursing, 90*(4), 40–45.

Howard, D. L., & McCaughrin, W. C. (1996). The treatment effectiveness of outpatient substance misuse treatment organizations between court-mandated and voluntary clients. *Substance Use & Misuse, 31*, 895–925.

Howard, G., Wagenknecht, L. E., Burke, G. L., Diez-Roux, A., Evans, G. W., McGovern, P., Nieto, J., & Tell, G. S. (1998). Cigarette smoking and the progression of atherosclerosis. *Journal of the American Medical Association, 279*, 119–124.

Howard, M. O., Kivlahan, D., & Walker, R. D. (1997). Cloninger's tridimensional theory of personality and psychopathology: Applications to substance use disorders. *Journal of Studies on Alcohol, 58*, 48–67.

How he won the war. (1996). *60 Minutes.* XXVIX (13). Livingston, NJ: Burrelle's Information Services.

Howland, R. H. (1990). Barriers to community treatment of patients with dual diagnoses. *Hospital & Community Psychiatry, 41*, 1136–1138.

Hser, Y., Anglin, M. D., & Powers, K. (1993). A 24-year follow-up of California narcotics addicts. *Archives of General Psychiatry, 50*, 577–584.

Hser, Y., Evans, E., Huang, D., & Anglin, M. D. (2004). Relationship between drug treatment services, retention, and outcomes. *Psychiatric Services, 55*, 767–774.

Hser, Y., Hoffman, V., Grella, C. E., & Anglin, M. D. (2001). A 33-year follow-up of narcotics addicts. *Archives of General Psychiatry, 58*, 503–508.

Hubbard, J. B., Franco, S. E., & Onaivi, E. S. (1999). Marijuana: Medical implications. *American Family Physician, 60*, 2583–2593.

Huddleston, C. W., Freeman-Wilson, K., & Boone, D. L. (2004). *Painting the current picture: A national report card on drug courts and other problem solving court programs in the United States.* Alexandria, VA: National Drug Court Institute.

Huffing can kill your child. (2004). CBS Evening News. Retrieved June 4, 2004, from http://www.cbsnews.com/stories/2004/06/01eveningnews/main620528.shtml

Hughes, J. R (1992). Tobacco withdrawal in self-quitters. *Journal of Consulting and Clinical Psychology, 60*, 689–697.

Hughes, J. R. (2000). Nicotine-related disorders. In *Comprehensive textbook of psychiatry* (7th ed.) (Kaplan, H. I., & Sadock, B. J., eds.). Baltimore: Lippincott, Williams & Wilkins.

Hughes, J. R., Gust, S. W., Skoog, K., Keenan, R. M., & Fenwick, J. W. (1991). Symptoms of tobacco withdrawal. *Archives of General Psychiatry, 48*, 52–59.

Hughes, J. R., Rose, G. L., & Callas, P. W. (2000). Nicotine is more reinforcing in smokers with a past history of alcoholism than in smokers without this history. *Alcoholism: Clinical and experimental research, 24*, 1633–1638.

Hughes, R. (1993). Bitch, bitch, bitch. . . . *Psychology Today, 26*(5), 28–30.

Hughes, T. L., & Wilsnack, S. C. (1997). Use of alcohol among lesbians: Research and clinical implications. *American Journal of Orthopsychiatry, 67*, 20–36.

Humphreys, K. (1997). Clinicians' referral and matching of substance abuse patients to self-help groups after treatment. *Psychiatric Services, 48*, 1445–1449.

Humphreys, K. (2003). A research-based analysis of the Moderation Management controversy. *Psychiatric Services, 54*, 621–622.

Humphreys, K., & Moos, R. H. (1996). Reduced substance-abuse-related health care costs among voluntary participants in Alcoholics Anonymous. *Psychiatric Services, 47*, 709–713.

Humphreys, K., Moos, R. H., & Finney, J. W. (1995). Two pathways out of drinking problems without professional treatment. *Addictive Behaviors, 20*, 427–441.

Humphreys, K., Moos, R. H., & Finney, J. W. (1996). Life domains, Alcoholics Anonymous, and role incumbency in the 3 year course of problem drinking. *The Journal of Nervous and Mental Disease, 184*, 475–481.

Humphreys, K., & Rappaport, J. (1993). From the community mental health movement to the war on drugs. *American Psychologist, 48*, 892–901.

Hung, J. (2003). Aspirin for cardiovascular disease prevention. *Medical Journal of Australia, 179*, 147–152.

Hunter, M., & Kellogg, T. (1989). Redefining ACA characteristics. *Alcoholism & Addiction, 9*(3), 28–29.

Hurcom, C., Copello, A., & Orford, J. (2000). The family and alcohol: Effects of excessive drinking and conceptualizations of spouses over recent decades. *Substance Use & Misuse, 35*, 473–502.

Hurt, R. D., Offord, K. P., Croghan, I. T., Gomez-Dahl, L., Kottke, T. E., Morse, R. M., & Melton, J. (1996). Mortality following inpatient addictions treatment. *Journal of the American Medical Association, 275*, 1097–1103.

Hurt, R. D., & Robertson, C. R. (1998). Prying open the door to the tobacco industry's secrets about nicotine. *Journal of the American Medical Association, 280*, 1173–1181.

Husak, D. N. (2004). The moral relevance of addiction. *Substance Use & Misuse, 39*, 399–436.

Hussar, D. A. (1990). Update 90: New drugs. *Nursing 90, 20*(12), 41–51.

Hutchison, R. (2004). COX-2—Selective NSAIDS. *American Journal of Nursing, 104*(3), 52–55.

Hyman, S. E. (1988). *Manual of psychiatric emergencies* (2nd ed.). Boston: Little, Brown & Co.

Hyman, S. E. (1996). Drug abuse and addiction. In *Scientific American medicine.* (Rubenstein, E., & Federman, D. D., eds.). New York: Scientific American Press.

Hyman, S. E., & Cassem, N. H. (1995). Alcoholism. In *Scientific American medicine.* (Rubenstein, E., & Federman, D. D., eds.). New York: Scientific American Press.

Hyman, S. E., & Nestler, E. J. (2000). Basic molecular neurobiology. In *Comprehensive textbook of psychiatry* (7th ed.) (Sadock, B. J., & Sadock, V. A., eds.). Philadelphia: Lippincott, Williams & Wilkins.

Hymowitz, N., Feuerman, M., Hollander, M., & Frances, R. J. (1993). Smoking deterrence using silver acetate. *Hospital and Community Psychiatry, 44*, 113–114, 116.

Ibogaine and minimium sentencing hot topics at DPF meeting. (1994). *Forensic Drug Abuse Advisor, 6*(10), 78–79.

Ice overdose. (1989). *The Economist, 313*(7631), 29–31.

Iggers, J. (1990). The addiction industry. *Minneapolis Star Tribune, IX* (102), pp. E1, E4, ex10.

Imhof, J. E. (1995). Overcoming countertransference. In *psychotherapy and substance abuse* (Washton, A. M., ed.). New York: Guilford.

Ingels, M., Rangan, C., Bellezzo, J., & Clark, R. F. (2000). Coma and respiratory depression following the ingestion of GHN and its precursors: Three cases. *Journal of Emergency Medicine, 19,* 47–50.

Iqbal, M. M., Sobhan, T., & Ryals, T. (2002). Effects of commonly used benzodiazepines on the fetus, the neonate and the nursing infant. *Psychiatric Services, 53,* 39–49

Ireland, T. (2001). The abuse connection. *Counselor, 2*(3), 14–20.

Irvin, J. E., Bowers, C. A., Dunn, M. E., & Wang, M. C. (1999). Efficacy of relapse prevention: A meta-analytic review. *Journal of Consulting and Clinical Psychology, 67,* 563–570.

Isaacson, J. H., & Schorling, J. B. (1999). Screening for alcohol problems in primary care. *Medical Clinics of North America, 83,* 1547–1563.

Is cocaethylene cardiotoxic? (2002). *Forensic Drug Abuse Advisor, 14*(9), 67–68.

Isenhart, C. E., & Silversmith, D. J. (1996). MMPI-2 response styles: Generalization to alcoholism assessment. *Psychology of Addictive Behaviors, 10,* 115–123.

Isensee, B., Hans-Ulrich, W., Stein, M. B., Hofler, M., & Lieb, R. (2003). Smoking increases the risk of panic. *Archives of General Psychiatry, 60,* 692–700.

Iverson, L. (2005). Long-term effects of exposure to cannabis. *Current Opinion in Pharmacology, 5,* 69–72.

Jackson, L. M., & Hawkey, C. J. (2000). COX-2 selective nonsteroidal anti-inflammatory drugs. *Drugs, 59*(6), 1207–1216.

Jackson, T. R. (2002). Treatment practice and research issues in improving opioid treatment outcomes. *Science & Practice Perspectives, 1*(1), 22–27.

Jackson, V. A., Sesso, H. D., Buring, J. E., Gaziano, M. (2003). Alcohol consumption and mortality in men with preexisting cerebrovascular disease. *Archives of Internal Medicine, 163,* 1189–1193.

Jacob, T., Waterman, B., Heath, A., True, W., Bucholz, K. K., Haber, R., Scherrer, J., & Fu, Q. (2003). Genetic and environmental effects on offspring alcoholism. *Archives of General Psychiatry, 60,* 1265–1272.

Jacobs, E. J., Thun, M. J., & Apicella, L. F. (1999). Cigar smoking and death from coronary heart disease in a prospective study of U.S. men. *Archives of Internal Medicine, 159,* 2413–2418.

Jaffe, J. H. (1989). Drug dependence: Opioids, nonnarcotics, nicotine (tobacco) and caffeine. In *Comprehensive textbook of psychiatry/V.* (Kaplan, H. I., & Sadock, B. J., eds.). Baltimore: Williams & Wilkins.

Jaffe, J. H. (1990). Drug addiction and drug abuse. In *The pharmacological basis of therapeutics* (8th ed.) (Gilman, A. G., Rall, T. W., Nies, A. S., & Taylor, P., eds.). New York: Macmillan Publishing Co.

Jaffe, J. H. (1992). Opiates: Clinical aspects. In *Substance abuse: A comprehensive textbook* (2nd ed.) (Lowinson, J. H., Ruiz, P., Millman, R. B., & Langrod, J. G., eds.). New York: Williams & Wilkins.

Jaffe, J. H., (2000a). Amphetamine (or amphetaminelike) disorders. In *Comprehensive textbook of psychiatry* (7th ed.) (Kaplan, H. I., & Sadock, B. J., eds.). Baltimore: Lippincott, Williams & Wilkins.

Jaffe, J. H., (2000b). Cocaine-related disorders. In *Comprehensive textbook of psychiatry* (7th ed.) (Kaplan, H. I., & Sadock, B. J., eds.). Baltimore: Lippincott, Williams & Wilkins.

Jaffe, J. H., (2000c). Opioid-related disorders. In *Comprehensive textbook of psychiatry* (7th ed.) (Kaplan, H. I., & Sadock, B. J., eds.). Baltimore: Lippincott, Williams & Wilkins.

Jaffe, J. H., & Jaffe, A. B. (2004). Neurobiology of opioids. In *Textbook of substance abuse treatment* (3rd ed.) (Galanter, M., & Kleber, H. D., eds.). Washington, DC: American Psychiatric Press, Inc.

Jaffe, J. H., Knapp, C. M., & Ciraulo, D. A. (1997). Opiates: Clinical aspects. In *Substance abuse: A comprehensive textbook* (3rd ed.) (Lowinson, J. H., Ruiz, P., Millman, R. B., & Langrod, J. G., eds.). New York: Williams & Wilkins.

Jaffe, J. H., & Martin, W. R. (1990). Opioid analgesics and antagonists. In *The pharmacological basis of therapeutics* (8th ed.) (Gilman, A. G., Rall, T. W., Nies, A. S., & Taylor, P., eds.). New York: Macmillan Publishing Co.

Jaffe, J. H., Rawson, R. A., & Ling, W. H. (2005). Cocaine-related disorders. In *Kaplan & Sadock's comprehensive textbook of psychiatry* (8th ed.) (Kaplan, V. A., & Sadock, B. J., eds.). New York: Lippincott, Williams & Wilkins.

James, L. P., Farrar, H. C., Komoroski, E. M., Wood, W. R., Graham, C. J., & Bornemeier, R. A. (1998). Sympathomimetic drug use in adolescents presenting to a pediatric emergency department with chest pain. *Journal of Toxicology: Clinical Toxicology, 36,* 321–329.

Jamison, K. R. (1999). *Night falls fast.* New York: Knopf.

Jansen, K. L. R. (1993). Non-medical use of ketamine. *The Lancet, 306,* 601–602.

Japenga, A. (1991). You're tougher than you think! *Self, 13*(4), 174–175, 187.

Jarvik, M. E., & Schneider, N. G. (1992). Nicotine. In *Substance abuse: A comprehensive textbook* (2nd ed.) (Lowinson, J. H., Ruiz, P., Millman, R. B., & Langrod, J. G., eds.). New York: Williams & Wilkins.

Jellinek, E. M. (1952). Phases of alcohol addiction. *Quarterly Journal of Studies on Alcohol, 13,* 673–674.

Jellinek, E. M. (1960). *The disease concept of alcoholism.* New Haven, CT: College and University Press.

Jenike, M. A. (1991). Drug abuse. In *Scientific American medicine* (Rubenstein, E., & Federman, D. D., eds.). New York: Scientific American Press, Inc.

Jenkins, A. J., & Cone, E. J. (1998). Pharmacokinetics: Drug absorption, distribution, and elimination. In *Drug abuse handbook* (Karch, S. B., ed.). New York: CRC Press.

Jenkins, S. C., Tinsley, J. A., & Van Loon, J. A. (2001). *A pocket reference for psychiatrists* (3rd ed.). Washington, DC: American Psychiatric Press, Inc.

Jensen, G. B., & Pakkenberg, B. (1993). Do alcoholics drink their neurons away? *The Lancet, 342,* 1201–1204.

Jensen, J. G. (1987a). Step Three: Turning it over. In *The Twelve Steps of Alcoholics Anonymous*. New York: Harper & Row.

Jensen, J. G. (1987b). Step Two: A promise of hope. In *The Twelve Steps of Alcoholics Anonymous*. New York: Harper & Row.

Jentsch, J. D., Redmond, D. E., Elsworth, J. D., Taylor, J. R., Youngren, K. D., & Roth, R. H. (1997). Enduring cognitive deficits and cortical dopamine dysfunction in monkeys after long-term administration of phencyclidine. *Science*, 277, 953–955.

Jersild, D. (2001). *Happy hours*. New York: Harper Collins.

Joe, G. W., Simpson, D. D., Dansereau, D. F., & Rowan-Szal, G. A. (2001). Relationships between counseling rapport and drug abuse treatment outcomes. *Psychiatric Services*, 52, 1223–1229.

Johns, A. (2001). Psychiatric effects of cannabis. *British Journal of Psychiatry*, 178, 116–122.

Johnson, B. A., Ait-Daoud, N., Akhtar, F. Z., & Ma, J. Z. (2004). Oral topiramate reduces the consequences of drinking and improves the quality of life of alcohol-dependent individuals. *Archives of General Psychiatry*, 61, 905–912.

Johnson, B. A., Ait-Daoud, N., Bowden, C. L., DiClemente, C. C., Roache, J. D., Lawson, K., Javors, M. A., & Ma, J. Z. (2003). Oral topiramate for treatment of alcohol dependence: A randomised control trial. *The Lancet*, 361, 1677.

Johnson, B. A., Devous, M. D., Ruiz, P., & Ait-Daoud, N. (2001). Treatment advances for cocaine-induced ischemic stroke: Focus on dihydropyridine-class calcium channel antagonists. *American Journal of Psychiatry*, 158, 1191–1198.

Johnson, B. A., Roache, J. D., Javors, M. A., DiClemente, C. C., Cloninger, C. R., Prihoda, T. J., Bordnick, P. S., Ait-Daoud, N., & Hensler, J. (2000). Ondansetron for reduction of drinking among biologically predisposed alcoholic patients. *Journal of the American Medical Association*, 284, 963–970.

Johnson, H. L., Nusbaum, B. J., Bejarano, A., & Rosen, T. S. (1999). An ecological approach to development in children with prenatal drug exposure. *American Journal of Orthopsychiatry*, 69, 448–456.

Johnson Institute. (1987). *The family enablers*. Minneapolis: The Johnson Institute.

Johnson, J. L., & Hirsch, C. S. (2003). Aspiration pneumonia. *Postgraduate Medicine*, 113(3), 99–112.

Johnson, M. D. (1990). Anabolic steroid use in adolescent athletes. *The Pediatric Clinics of North America*, 37, 1111–1123.

Johnson, M. R., & Lydiard, R. B. (1995). The neurobiology of anxiety disorders. *The Psychiatric Clinics of North America*, 18, 681–725.

Johnson, R. A., Hoffmann, J. P., & Gerstein, D. R. (1996). *The relationship between family structure and adolescent substance use*. Rockville, MD: U.S. Department of Health and Human Services.

Johnson, V. E. (1980). *I'll quit tomorrow*. San Francisco: Harper & Row.

Johnston, L. D., O'Malley, P. M., & Bachman, J. G. (2000a). *National survey results on drug use from the monitoring the future study, 1975–1999* (Vol. I). Rockville, MD: U.S. Department of Health and Human Services.

Johnston, L. D., O'Malley, P. M., & Bachman, J. G. (2000b). *National survey results on drug use from the monitoring the future study, 1975–1999* (Vol. II). Rockville, MD: U.S. Department of Health and Human Services.

Johnston, L. D., O'Malley, P. M., & Bachman, J. G. (2003a). *National survey results on drug use from the monitoring the future study, 1975–2003* (Vol. I). Rockville, MD: U.S. Department of Health and Human Services.

Johnston, L. D., O'Malley, P. M., & Bachman, J. G. (2003b). *National survey results on drug use from the monitoring the future study, 1975–2003* (Vol. II). Rockville, MD: U.S. Department of Health and Human Services.

Johnston, L. D., O'Malley, P. M., Bachman, J. G., & Schulenberg, J. E. (2004a). *National survey results on drug use from the monitoring the future study, 1975–2003* (Vol. I). Rockville, MD: U.S. Department of Health and Human Services.

Johnston, L. D., O'Malley, P. M., Bachman, J. G., & Schulenberg, J. E. (2004b). *National survey results on drug use from the monitoring the future study, 1975–2003* (Vol. II). Rockville, MD: U.S. Department of Health and Human Services.

Johnston, S. C., & Pelletier, L. L. (1997). Enhanced hepatoxicity of acetaminophen in the alcoholic patient. *Medicine*, 76(3), 185–191.

Jones, A. L., Jarvie, D. R., McDermid, G., & Proudfoot, A. T. (1994). Hepatocellular damage following amphetamine intoxication. *Journal of Toxicology*, 32(4), 435–445.

Jones, A. W. (1996). Biochemistry and physiology of alcohol: Applications to forensic sciences and toxicology. In *Medicolegal aspects of alcohol* (3rd ed.) (Garriott, J. C., ed.). Tuscon, AZ: Lawyers & Judges Publishing Co.

Jones, E. M., Knutson, D., & Haines, D. (2003). Common problems in patients recovering from chemical dependency. *American Family Physician*, 68, 1971–1978.

Jones, R. L. (1990). Evaluation of drug use in the adolescent. In *Clinical management of poisoning and drug overdoses* (2nd ed.) (Haddad, L. M., & Winchester, J. F., eds.). New York: W. B. Saunders.

Jones, R. T. (1987). Psychopharmacology of cocaine. In *Cocaine: A clinician's handbook* (Washton, A. G., & Gold, M. S., eds.). New York: The Guilford Press.

Jones, R. T., & McMahon, J. (1998). Alcohol motivations as outcome expectancies. In *Treating addictive behaviors* (2nd ed.) (Miller, W. R., & Heather, N., eds.). New York: Plenum.

Jones-Webb, R. (1998). Drinking patterns and problems among African-Americans: Recent findings. *Alcohol Health & Research World*, 22, 260–264.

Jonnes, J. (1995). The rise of the modern addict. *The American Journal of Public Health*, 85(8), 1157–1162.

Jonnes, J. (2002). Hip to be high: Heroin and popular culture in the twentieth century. In *One hundred years of heroin* (Musto, D. F., Korsmeyer, P., & Maulucci, T. W., eds.). Westport, CT: Auburn House.

Jorenby, D. E. (1997). Effects of nicotine on the central nervous system. *Hospital Practice: A Special Report*, 38(4), 17–20.

Jorgensen, E. D. (2001). Dual diagnosis in treatment resistent adolescents. Symposium presented to the Dept. of Psychiatry at The Cambridge Hospital, Boston, MA, March 3.

Joseph, H. (2004). Feedback/feedforward. *Addiction Treatment Forum*, 13(2), 3–4.

Joshi, N. P., & Scott, M. (1988). Drug use, depression, and adolescents. *The Pediatric Clinics of North America*, 35(6), 1349–1364.

Judd, L. L., & Huey, L. Y. (1984). Lithium antagonizes ethanol intoxication in alcoholics. *The American Journal of Psychiatry*, 141, 1517–1521.

Juergens, S. M. (1993). Benzodiazepines and addiction. *Psychiatric Clinics of North America*, 16, 75–86.

Juhnke, G. A. (2002). *Substance abuse assessment and diagnosis.* New York: Brunner-Routledge.

Julien, R. M. (1992). *A primer of drug action* (6th ed.). New York: W. H. Freeman & Co.

Kacso, G., & Terezhalmy, G. T. (1994). Acetylsalicylic acid and acetaminophen. *Dental Clinics of North America*, 38, 633–644.

Kadushin, C., Reber, E., Saxe, L., & Livert, D. (1998). The substance use system: Social and neighborhood environments associated with substance use and misuse. *Substance Use & Misuse*, 33, 1681–1710.

Kaiser, D. (1996). Not by chemicals alone: A hard look at "psychiatric medicine." *Psychiatric Times*, XIII (12), 41–44.

Kalb, C., Raymond, J., Pierce, E., Smith, S., Wagner, J. P., Gordon-Thomas, J., & Wirzbicki, A. (2001). Playing with pain killers. *Newsweek*, CXXXVII (15), 44–48.

Kalichman, S. C., Heckman, T., Kochman, A., Sikkema, K., & Bergholte, J. (2000). Depression and thoughts of suicide among middle-aged and older persons living with HIV-AIDS. *Psychiatric Services*, 51, 903–907.

Kalivas, P. W. (2003). Predisposition to addiction: Pharmacokinetics, pharmacodynamics, and brain circuitry. *American Journal of Psychiatry*, 160, 1–3.

Kaltenbach, K. (1997). Maternal and fetal effects. Paper presented at NIDA conference: Heroin Use and Addiction, Washington, DC, September 29–30.

Kaminer, W. (1992). *I'm dysfunctional, you're dysfunctional.* New York: Addison-Wesley Publishing.

Kaminer, Y. (1994). Adolescent substance abuse. In *Textbook of substance abuse treatment* (Galanter, M., & Kleber, H. D., eds.). Washington, DC: American Psychiatric Press, Inc.

Kaminer, Y. (1999). Addictive disorders in adolescents. *Psychiatric Clinics of North America*, 22, 275–288.

Kaminer, Y. (2001). Adolescent substance abuse treatment: Where do we go from here? *Psychiatric Services*, 52, 147–149.

Kaminer, Y., & Bukstein, O. G. (1998). Adolescent substance abuse. In *Clinical textbook of addictive disorders* (2nd ed.) (Frances, R. J., & Miller, S. I., eds.). New York: Guilford.

Kaminer, Y., & Frances, R. J. (1991). Inpatient treatment of adolescents with psychiatric and substance abuse disorders. *Hospital and Community Psychiatry*, 42, 894–896.

Kaminer, Y., & Tarter, R. E. (2004). Adolescent substance abuse. In *Textbook of substance abuse treatment* (3rd ed.) (Galanter, M., & Kleber, H. D., eds.). Washington, DC: American Psychiatric Press, Inc.

Kaminski, A. (1992). *Mind-altering drugs.* Madison, WI: Wisconsin Clearinghouse, Board of Regents, University of Wisconsin System.

Kanayama, G., Cohane, G. H., Weiss, R. D., & Pope, H. G. (2003). Past anabolic-androgenic steroid use among men admitted for substance abuse treatment: An underrecognized problem? *Journal of Clinical Psychiatry*, 64, 156–160.

Kandall, S. R. (1999). Treatment strategies for drug-exposed neonates. *Clinics in Perinatology*, 26, 231–243.

Kandall, S. R., Doberczak, T. M., Jantunen, M., & Stein, J. (1999). The methadone maintained pregnancy. *Clinics in Perinatology*, 26, 173–181.

Kandall, S. R., Gaines, J., Habel, L., Davidson, G., & Jessop, D. (1993). The relationship of maternal substance abuse to subsequent sudden infant death syndrome in offspring. *The Journal of Pediatrics*, 123, 120–126.

Kandel, D. (1997). Sequencing of drug involvement: Marijuana and heroin. Paper presented at NIDA conference: Heroin Use and Addiction, Washington, DC, September 29–30.

Kandel, D. B., & Chen, K. (2000). Types of marijuana users by longitudinal course. *Journal of Studies on Alcohol*, 61, 367–378.

Kandel, D. B., & Davies, M. (1996). High school students who use crack and other drugs. *Archives of General Psychiatry*, 53, 71–80.

Kandel, D. B., & Raveis, V. H. (1989). Cessation of illicit drug use in young adulthood. *Archives of General Psychiatry*, 46, 109–116.

Kandel, D. B., Yamaguchi, K., & Chen, K. (1992). Stages of progression in drug involvement from adolescence to adulthood: Further evidence for the gateway theory. *Journal of Studies on Alcohol*, 53(5), 447–458.

Kanwischer, R. W., & Hundley, J. (1990). Screening for substance abuse in hospitalized psychiatric patients. *Hospital and Community Psychiatry*, 41, 795–797.

Kaplan, H. I., & Sadock, B. J. (1996). *Concise textbook of clinical psychiatry.* Baltimore: Williams & Wilkins.

Kaplan, H. I., Sadock, B. J., & Grebb, J. A. (1994). *Synopsis of psychiatry* (7th ed.). Baltimore: Williams & Wilkins.

Karam-Hage, M. (2004). Treating insomnia in patients with substance use/abuse disorders. *Psychiatric Times*, XXI (2), 55–56.

Karan, L. D., Haller, D. L., & Schnoll, S. H. (1998). Cocaine and stimulants. In *Clinical textbook of addictive disorders*

(2nd ed.) (Frances, R. J., & Miller, S. I., eds.). New York: Guilford.

Karch, S. B. (1996). *The pathology of drug abuse* (2nd ed.). New York: CRC Press.

Karch, S. B. (2002). *The pathology of drug abuse* (3rd ed.). New York: CRC Press.

Karhunen, P. J., Erkinjuntti, T., & Laippala, P. (1994). Moderate alcohol consumption and loss of cerebellar Purkinje cells. *British Medical Journal, 308,* 1663–1667.

Karlen, A. (1995). *Man and microbes.* New York: G. P. Putnam's Sons.

Karsan, H. A., Rojter, S. E., & Saab, S. (2004). Primary prevention of cirrhosis. *Postgraduate Medicine, 115,* 25–30.

Karst, M., Salim, K., Burstein, S., Conrad, I., Hoy, L., Schneider, U. (2003). Analgesic effect of the synthetic cannaboinoid CT-3 on chronic neuropathic pain. *Journal of the American Medical Association, 290,* 1757–1762.

Kashkin, K. B. (1992). Anabolic steroids. In *Substance abuse: A comprehensive textbook* (2nd ed.) (Lowinson, J. H., Ruiz, P., Millman, R. B., & Langrod, J. G., eds.). New York: Williams & Wilkins.

Kashkin, K. B., & Kleber, H. D. (1989). Hooked on hormones? An anabolic steroid addiction hypothesis. *Journal of the American Medical Association, 262,* 3166–3173.

Kassirer, J. P. (1997). Federal foolishness and marijuana. *New England Journal of Medicine, 336,* 366–367.

Katz, S. J., & Liu, A. E. (1991). *The codependency conspiracy.* New York: Warner Books.

Katz, W. A. (2000). *Pain management in rheumatologic disorders.* Philadelphia: Drugsmartz Publications.

Kauffman, E., Dore, M. M., & Nelson-Zlupko, L. (1995). The role of women's therapy groups in the treatment of chemical dependence. *American Journal of Orthopsychiatry, 65,* 355–363.

Kauffman, J. (2003). Recovery and methadone treatment. Symposium presented to the Dept. of Psychiatry at The Cambridge Hospital, Boston, MA, March 8.

Kauffman, J. F. (2003). Methadone treatment and recovery for opioid dependence. *Primary Psychiatry, 10*(9), 61–64.

Kaufman, E., & McNaul, J. P. (1992). Recent developments in understanding and treating drug abuse and dependence. *Hospital and Community Psychiatry, 43,* 223–236.

Kaufman, M. J., Levin, J. M., Ross, M. H., Lange, N., Rose, S. L., Kukes, T. J., Mendelson, J. H., Lukas, S. E., Cohen, B. M., & Renshaw, P. F. (1998). Cocaine-induced vasoconstriction detected in humans with magnetic resonance angiography. *Journal of the American Medical Association, 279,* 376–380.

Kavanagh, D. J., McGrath, J., Saunders, J. B., Dore, G., & Clark, D. (2002). Substance misuse in patients with schizophrenia. *Drugs, 62*(5), 743–756.

Kaye, A. D., Gevirtz, C., Bosscher, H. A., Duke, J. B., Frost, E. A., Richards, T. A., & Fields, A. M. (2003). Ultra-rapid opiate detoxification: a review. *Canadian Journal of Anesthesia, 50*(7), 633–671.

Keller, D. S. (2003). Exploration in the service of relapse prevention: A psychoanalytic contribution to substance abuse treatment. In *Treating substance abuse: Theory and technique* (2nd ed.) (Rotgers, F., Morgenstern, J., & Walters, S.T., eds.). New York: Guilford.

Keller, R. W., & Snyder-Keller, A. (2000). Prenatal cocaine exposure. In *New Medications for Drug Abuse* (Glick, S. D., & Maisonneuve, I. B., eds.). New York: New York Adacemy of Sciences.

Kelly, A. E., & Saucier, J. (2004). Is your patient suffering from alcohol withdrawal? *RN, 67*(2), 27–31.

Kelly, V. A., & Myers, J. E. (1996). Parental alcoholism and coping: A comparison of female children of alcoholics with female children of nonalcoholics. *Journal of Counseling & Development, 74,* 501–504.

Kendler, K. S., & Prescott, C. A. (1998). Cocaine use, abuse and dependence in a population-based sample of female twins. *British Journal of Psychiatry, 173,* 345–350.

Kendler, K. S., Thornton, L. M., & Pedersen, N. L. (2000). Tobacco consumption in Swedish twins reared apart and reared together. *Archives of General Psychiatry, 57,* 886–892.

Kenford, S. L., Fiore, M. C., Jorenby, D. E., Smith, S. S., Wetter, D., & Baker, T. B. (1994). Predicting smoking cessation. *Journal of the American Medical Association, 271,* 589–594.

Kerfoot, B. P., Sakoulas, G., & Hyman, S. E. (1996). Cocaine. In *Sourcebook of substance abuse and addiction* (Friedman, L., Fleming, N. F., Roberts, D. H., & Hyman, S. E., eds.). New York: Williams & Wilkins.

Kermani, E. J., & Castaneda, R. (1996). Psychoactive substance use in forensic psychiatry. *American Journal of Drug and Alcohol Abuse, 22,* 1–28.

Kessler, D. A. (1995). Nicotine addiction in young people. *The New England Journal of Medicine, 333,* 186–189.

Kessler, R. C., Aguilar-Gaxiola, S., Berglund, P. A., Caraveo-Anduaga, J. J., DeWit, D. J., Greenfield, S. F., Kolody, B., Olfson, M., & Vega, W. A. (2001). Patterns and predictors of treatment seeking after onset of a substance use disorder. *Archives of General Psychiatry, 58,* 1065–1971.

Kessler, R. C., Crum, R. M., Warner, L. A., Nelson, C. B., Schulenberg, J., & Anthony, J. C. (1997). Lifetime co-occurence of DSM-III-R alcohol abuse and dependence with other psychiatric disorders in the National Comorbidity Survey. *Archives of General Psychiatry, 54,* 313–321.

Kessler, R. C., McGonagle, K. A., Zhao, S., Nelson, C. B., Hughes, M., Eshleman, S., Hans-Ulrich, W., & Kendler, K. S. (1994). Lifetime and 12 month prevalence of DSM-III-R psychiatric disorders in the United States. *Archives of General Psychiatry, 51,* 8–19.

Khan, J. O., & Walker, B. D. (1998). Acute human immunodeficiency virus type 1 infection. *The New England Journal of Medicine, 339,* 33–39.

Khantzian, E. J. (2003a). Introductory comments by moderator. Symposium presented to the Dept. of Psychiatry at The Cambridge Hospital, Boston, MA, March 8.

Khantzian, E. J. (2003b). The self-medication hypothesis revisited: The dually diagnosed patient. *Primary Psychiatry, 10*(9), 47–48, 53–54.

Khantzian, E. J. (2004). The self-medication hypothesis revisited: Treatment implications. Symposium presented to the Dept. of Psychiatry at The Cambridge Hospital, Boston, MA, March 6.

Khantzian, E. J., Mack, J. E., & Schatzberg, A. F. (1999). Heroin use as an attempt to cope. In *Treating addiction as a human process* (Khantzian, E. J., ed.). New York: Aronson.

Khat calls. (2004). *Forensic Drug Abuse Advisor, 16*(3), 19–21.

Kick, S. D. (1999). Evaluation and management of chronic alcohol abuse. *Hospital Practice, 34*(4), 95–106.

Kiefer, F., Jahn, H., Tarnaske, T., Helwig, H., Briken, P., Holzbach, R., Kampf, P., Stracke, R., Baehr, M., Naber, D., & Wiedermann, K. (2003). Comparing and combining naltrexone and acamprosate in relapse prevention of alcoholism. *Archives of General Psychiatry, 60,* 92–99.

Kilbourne, J. (2002). Deadly persuasion: Advertising and addiction. Symposium presented to the Dept. of Psychiatry at The Cambridge Hospital, Boston, MA, February 2.

Kilpatrick, D. G., Acierno, R., Saunders, B., Resnick, H. S., Best, C. L., & Schnurr, P. P. (2000). Risk factors for adolescent substance abuse and dependence: Data from a national sample. *Journal of Consulting and Clinical Psychology, 2000,* 19–30.

King, G. R., & Ellinwood, E. H. (1997). Amphetamines and other stimulants. In *Substance abuse: A comprehensive textbook* (3rd ed.) (Lowinson, J. H., Ruiz, P., Millman, R. B., & Langrod, J. G., eds.). New York: Williams & Wilkins.

King, M., McKeown, E., Warner, J., Ramsay, A., Johnson, K., Clive, C., Wright, L., Blizard, R., & Davidson, O. (2003). Mental health and quality of life of gay men and lesbians in England and Wales: Controlled, cross-sectional study. *The British Journal of Psychiatry, 183,* 552–558.

Kintz, P. (2002). A new series of 13 buprenorphine-related deaths. *Clinical Biochemistry, 35*(7), 513–516.

Kirchner, J. T. (1999). Hepatitis C: Who should we be treating? *American Family Physician, 59*(2), 273–275.

Kirsch, M. M. (1986). *Designer drugs.* Minneapolis: Comp-Care Publications.

Kishline, A. (1996). A toast to moderation. *Psychology Today, 29*(1), 53–56.

Kitchens, J. M. (1994). Does this patient have an alcohol problem? *Journal of the American Medical Association, 272,* 1782–1787.

Kitridou, R. C. (1993). The efficacy and safety of oxaproxzin versus aspirin: Pooled results of double-blind trials in rheumatoid arthritis. *Drug Therapy, 23*(Suppl.), 21–25.

Kivlahan, D. R., Heiman, J. R., Wright, R. C., Mundt, J. W., & Shupe, J. A. (1991). Treatment cost and rehospitalization rate in schizophrenic outpatients with a history of substance abuse. *Hospital and Community Psychiatry, 42,* 609–614.

Klar, H. (1987). The setting for psychiatric treatment. In *American Psychiatric Association annual review* (Vol. 6). Washington, DC: American Psychiatric Association Press, Inc.

Klass, P. (1989). Vital signs. *Discover, 10*(1), 12–14.

Klatsky, A. L. (2002). Alcohol and wine in health and disease forward. In *Annals of the New York Academy of Sciences* (Vol. 957) (Das, D. K., & Ursini, F., eds.). New York: New York Academy of Sciences, 2002.

Klatsky, A. L. (2003). Drink to your health? *Scientific American, 288*(2), 74–81.

Kleber, H. D. (1991). Tracking the cocaine epidemic. *Journal of the American Medical Association, 266,* 2272–2273.

Kleber, H. D. (1997). Overview of treatment and psychiatric comorbidity. Paper presented at NIDA conference: Heroin Use and Addiction, Washington, DC, September 29–30.

Kleber, H. D. (2002). Methadone: The drug, the treatment, the controversy. In *One hundred years of heroin* (Musto, D. F., Korsmeyer, P. I., & Maulucci, T. W., eds.). Westport, CT: Auburn House.

Klein, J. M., & Miller, S. I. (1986). Three approaches to the treatment of drug addiction. *Hospital and Community Psychiatry, 37,* 1083–1085.

Klein, M., & Kramer, F. (2004). Rave drugs: Pharmacological considerations. *AANA Journal, 72*(1), 61–67.

Kleinig, J. (2004). Ethical issues in substance use intervention. *Substance Use & Misuse, 39*(3), 369–398.

Kleinman, S., Busch, M. P., Hall, L., Thomson, R., Glynn, S., Gallahan, D., Ownby, H. E., & Williams, A. E. (1998). False-positive HIV-1 test results in a low-risk screening setting of voluntary blood donation. *Journal of the American Medical Association, 280,* 1080–1085.

Klesges, R. C., Winders, S. E., Meyers, A. W., Eck, L. H., Ward, K. D., Hultquist, C. M., Ray, J. W., & Shadish, W. R. (1997). How much weight gain occurs following smoking cessation? A comparison of weight gain using both continuous and point prevalence abstinence. *Journal of Consulting and Clinical Psychology, 65,* 286–291.

Kline, A. (1996). Pathways into drug user treatment: The influence of gender and racial/ethnic identity. *Substance Use & Misuse, 31,* 323–342.

Klinger, R. L., & Cabaj, R. P. (1993). Characteristics of gay and lesbian relationships. In *Review of psychiatry* (Vol. 12) (Oldham, J. M., Riba, M. B., & Tasman, A., eds.). Washington, DC: American Psychiatric Association.

Klirsfeld, D. (1998). HIV disease and women. *Medical Clinics of North America, 82,* 335–357.

Klonoff-Cohen, H. S., Edelstein, S. L., Lefkowitz, E. S., Srinivasen, I. P., Kaegi, D., Chang J. C., & Wiley, K. J. (1995). The effect of passive smoking and tobacco exposure through breast milk on Sudden Infant Death Syndrome. *Journal of the American Medical Association, 173,* 795–798.

Kluge, E. H. W. (2000). Social values, socioeconomic resources, and effectiveness coefficients. *Annals of the New York Academy of Sciences, 913,* 23–31.

Knapp, C. (1996). *Drinking: A love story.* New York: The Dial Press.

Knauer, S. (2002). *Recovering from sexual abuse, addictions, and compulsive behaviors.* New York: Haworth Social Work Practice Press.

Knight, J. R. (2000). Screening for adolescent substance abuse. Symposium presented to the Dept. of Psychiatry at The Cambridge Hospital, Boston, MA, March 3.

Knight, J. R. (2002). Adolescent substance abuse: New strateties for early identification and intervention. Symposium presented to the Dept. of Psychiatry at The Cambridge Hospital, Boston, MA, February 1.

Knight, J. R. (2003). No dope. *Nature, 426*(2963), 114–115.

Knight, J. R. (2005). Adolescent substance abuse: New strategies for early identification and intervention. Symposium presented to the Dept. of Psychiatry of the Cambridge Hospital, Boston, MA, March 4.

Koenig, H. G. (2001). Religion, spirituality and medicine: How are they related and what does it mean? *Mayo Clinic Proceedings, 76,* 1189–1191.

Koesters, S. C., Rogers, P. D., & Rajasingham, C. R. (2002). MDMA ("ecstasy") and other "club drugs": The new epidemic. *Pediatric Clinics of North America, 49,* 415–433.

Kofoed, L., Kania, J., Walsh, T., & Atkinson, R. M. (1986). Outpatient treatment of patients with substance abuse and coexisting psychiatric disorders. *The American Journal of Psychiatry, 143,* 867–872.

Kofoed, L., & Keys, A. (1988). Using group therapy to persuade dual-diagnosis patients to seek substance abuse treatment. *Hospital & Community Psychiatry, 39,* 1209–1211.

Kolodner, G., & Frances, R. (1993). Recognizing dissociative disorders in patients with chemical dependency. *Hospital and Community Psychiatry, 44,* 1041–1044.

Komro, K. A., & Toomey, T. L. (2002). Strategies to prevent underage drinking. *Alcohol Research & Health, 26*(1), 5–13.

Kondro, W. (2003). Athlete's "designer steroid" leads to widening scandal. *The Lancet, 362,* 1466.

Konstan, M. W., Byard, P. J., Hoppel, C. L., & Davis, P. B. (1995). Effect of high-dose ibuprofen in patients with cystic fibrosis. *The New England Journal of Medicine, 332,* 848–854.

Konstan, M. W., Hoppel, C. L., Chai, B., Davis, P. B. (1991). Ibuprofen in children with cystic fibrosis: Pharmacokinetics and adverse effects. *Journal of Pediatrics, 118,* 956–965.

Kosten, T. R., & George, T. P. (2002). The neurobiology of opioid dependence: Implications for treatment. *Science & Practice Perspectives, 1*(1), 13–20.

Kosten, T. R., & O'Connor, P. G. (2003). Management of drug and alcohol withdrawal. *New England Journal of Medicine, 348,* 1786–1795.

Kosten, T. R., & Sofuoglu, M. (2004). Stimulants. In *Substance abuse: A comprehensive textbook* (3rd ed.) (Lowinson, J. H., Ruiz, P., Millman, R. B., & Langrod, J. G., eds.). New York: Williams & Wilkins.

Kotulak, R. (1992). Recent discoveries about cocaine may help unlock secrets of brain. *Saint Paul Pioneer Press, 143*(345), p. C4.

Kotz, M., & Covington, E. C. (1995). Alcoholism. In *Conn's current therapy* (Rakel, R. E., ed.). Philadelphia, PA: W. B. Saunders Co.

Kouri, E. M., Pope, H. G., & Lukas, S. E. (1999). Changes in aggressive behavior during withdrawal from long-term marijuana use. *Psychopharmacology, 143,* 302–308.

Kovalesky, A. (2004). Women with substance abuse concerns. *Nursing Clinics of North America, 39,* 205–217.

Kozlowski, L. T., Wilkinson, A., Skinner, W., Kent, W., Franklin, T., & Pope, M. (1989). Comparing tobacco cigarette dependence with other drug dependencies. *Journal of the American Medical Association, 261,* 898–901.

Kraft, M. K., Rothbard, A. B., Hadley, T. R., McLellan, A. T., & Asch, D. A. (1997). Are supplementary services provided during methadone maintenance really cost effective? *American Journal of Psychiatry, 154,* 1214–1219.

Krain, A., Wisnivesky, J. P., Garland, E., & McGinn, T. (2004). Prevalence of human immunodeficiency virus testing in patients with Hepatitis B and C infection. *Mayo Clinic Proceedings, 79,* 51–56.

Krambeer, L. L., von McKnelly, W., Gabrielli, W. F., & Penick, E. C. (2001). Methadone therapy for opioid dependence. *American Family Physician, 63,* 2404–2410.

Kranzler, H. R., Amin, H., Modesto-Lowe, V., & Oncken, C. (1999). Pharmacologic treatments for drug and alcohol dependence. *Psychiatric Clinics of North America, 22,* 401–423.

Kranzler, H. R., Burleson, J. A., Del Boca, F. K., Babor, T. F., Korner, P., Brown, J., & Bohn, T. F. (1994). Buspirone treatment of anxious alcoholics. *Archives of General Psychiatry, 51,* 720–731.

Kreeger, K. (2003). Inflammation's infamy. *The Scientist, 17*(4), 28.

Kreek, M. J. (1997). History and effectiveness of methadone treatment. Paper presented at NIDA conference: Heroin Use and Addiction, Washington, DC, September 29–30.

Kreek, M. J. (2000). Methadone-related opioid agonist pharmacotherapy for heroin addiction. In *New medications for drug abuse* (Glick, S. D., & Maisonneuve, I. B., eds.). New York: New York Adacemy of Sciences.

Kriechbaum, N., & Zernig, G. (2000). Adolescent patients. In *Handbook of alcoholism* (Zernig, G., Saria, A., Kurz, M., & O'Malley, S. S., eds.). New York: CRC Press.

Kriegstein, A. R., Shungu, D.C., Millar, W. S., Armitage, B. A., Brust, J. C., Chillrud, S., Goldman, J., & Lynch, T. (1999). Leukoencephalopathy and raised brain lactate from heroin vapor inhalation ("chasing the dragon"). *Neurology, 53,* 1765–1773.

Krishnan-Sarin, S. (2000). Heritability. In *Handbook of alcoholism* (Zernig, G., Saria, A., Kurz, M., & O'Malley, S. S., eds.). New York: CRC Press.

Kritz, H., Schmid, P., & Sinzinger, H. (1995). Passive smoking and cardiovascular risk. *Archives of Internal Medicine, 155,* 1942–1948.

Kryger, M. H., Steljes, D., Pouliot, Z., Neufeld, H., & Odynski, T. (1991). Subjective versus objective evaluation of hypnotic efficacy: Experience with Zolpidem. *Sleep, 14*(5), 399–407.

Krystal, J. H., Cramer, J. A., Krol, W. F., Kirk, G. F., & Rosenheck, R. A. (2001). Naltrexone in the treatment of alcohol dependence. *New England Journal of Medicine, 345,* 1734–1739.

Kuiken, C., Thakallapalli, R., Eskild, A., & de Ronde, A. (2000). Genetic analysis reveals epidemiologic patterns in the spread of human immunodeficiency virus. *American Journal of Epidemiology, 152,* 814–822.

Kuhl, D. (2002). *What dying people want.* New York: Public Affairs.

Kumpfer, K. L. (1997). Focus on families: Prevention in action. Paper presented at NIDA conference: Heroin Use and Addiction, Washington, DC, September 29–30.

Kunitz, S. J., & Levy J. E. (1974). Changing ideas of alcohol use among Navaho Indians. *Quarterly Journal of Studies on Alcohol, 46,* 953–960.

Kuper, H., Boffetta, P., & Adami, H. O. (2002). Tobacco use and cancer causation: Association by tumour type. *Journal of Internal Medicine, 252,* 206–224.

Kurtz, E. (1979). *Not God: A history of Alcoholics Anonymous.* Center City, MN: Hazelden.

Kurutz, S. (2003). Kill 'em all. *Playboy, 50*(9), 49.

Kushner, M. G., Sher, K. J., & Beitman, B. D. (1990). The relation between alcohol problems and the anxiety disorders. *American Journal of Psychiatry, 147,* 685–695.

Kviz, F. J., Clark, M. A., Crittenden, K. S., Warnecke, R. B., & Freels, S. (1995). Age and smoking cessation behaviors. *Preventative Medicine, 24,* 297–307.

Lacks, P., & Morin, C. M. (1992). Recent advances in the assessment and treatment of insomnia. *Journal of Consulting and Clinical Psychology, 60,* 586–594.

Lacombe, P. S., Bicente, J. A. G., Pages, J. C., & Morselli, P. L. (1996). Causes and problems of nonresponse or poor response to drugs. *Drugs, 51,* 552–570.

Laine, C., Hauck, W. W., Gourevitch, M. N., Rothman, J., Cohen, A., & Turner, B. J. (2001). Regular outpatient medical and drug abuse care and subsequent hospitalization of persons who use illicit drugs. *Journal of the American Medical Association, 285,* 2355–2362.

Lala, S., & Straussner, A. (1997). Gender and substance abuse. In *Gender and addictions* (Straussner, S. L. A., & Zelvin, E., eds.). Northvale, NJ: Jason-Aronson.

Lamar, J. V., Riley, M., Smghabadi, R. (1986). Crack: A cheap and deadly cocaine is spreading menace. *Time, 128,* 16–18.

Land, W., Pinsky, D., & Salzman, C. (1991). Abuse and misuse of anticholinergic medications. *Hospital and Community Psychiatry, 42,* 580–581.

Landry, G. L., & Primos, W. A. (1990). Anabolic steroid abuse. *Advances in Pediatrics, 7,* 185–205.

Landry, M. J. (1997). *Overview of addiction treatment effectiveness.* Rockville, MD: U.S. Department of Health and Human Services.

Lange, W. R., White, N., & Robinson, N. (1992). Medical complications of substance abuse. *Postgraduate Medicine, 92,* 205–214.

Langone, J. (1989). Hot to block a killer's path. *Time, 133*(5), 60–62.

Langston, J. W., & Palfreman, J. (1995). *The case of the frozen addicts.* New York: Pantheon Books.

Larimer, M. E., & Kilmer, J. R. (2000). Natural history. In *Handbook of alcoholism* (Zernig, G., Saria, A., Kurz, M., & O'Malley, S. O., eds.). New York: CRC Press.

Larson, K. K. (1982). Birthplace of "The Minnesota Model." *Alcoholism, 3*(2), 34–35.

Latimer, W. W., Newcomb, M., Winters, K. C., & Stinchfield, R. D. (2000). Adolescent substance abuse treatment outcome: the role of substance abuse problem severity, psychosocial, and treatment factors. *Journal of Consulting and Clinical Psychology, 68,* 684–696.

Launer, L. J. (2003). Nonsteroidal anti-inflammatory drugs and Alzheimer's disease. What's next? *Journal of the American Medical Association, 289,* 2865–2867.

Laurence, D. R., & Bennett, P. N. (1992). *Clinical pharmacology* (7th ed.). New York: Churchill Livingstone.

Lawental, E., McLellan, A. T., Grissom, G. R., Brill, P., & O'Brien, C. (1996). Coerced treatment for substance abuse problems detected through workplace urine surveillance: Is it effective? *Journal of Substance Abuse, 8,* 115–128.

Lawson, C. (1994). Flirting with tragedy: Women who say yes to drugs. *Cosmopolitan, 217*(1), 138–141.

Layne, G. S. (1990). Schizophrenia and substance abuse. In *Managing the dually diagnosed patient* (O'Connell, D. F., ed.). New York: The Haworth Press.

Lazarou, J., Pomeranz, B. H., & Corey, P. N. (1998). Incidence of adverse drug reactions in hospitalized patients. *Journal of the American Medical Association, 279,* 1200–1205.

Leavitt, F. (2003). *The real drug abusers.* New York: Rowman & Littlefield, Publishers.

LeBon, O., Basiaux, P., Streel, E., Tecco, J., Hanak, C., Hansenne, M., Ansseau, M., Pele, I., Berbanck, P., & Dupont, S. (2004). Personality profile and drug of choice: A multivariate analysis using Cloninger's TCI and heroin addicts, alcoholics, and a random population group. *Drug & Alcohol Dependence, 73*(2), 175–182.

LeBon, O., Verbanck, P. Hoffman, G., Murphy, J. R., Staner, L., DeGroote, D., Mampuza, S., Den Dulk, A, Vacher, C., Kornreich, C., & Pelc, I. (1997). Sleep in detoxified alcoholics: Impairment of most standard sleep parameters and increased risk for sleep apnea. *Journal of Studies on Alcohol, 58,* 30–36.

Lee, E. W., & D'Alonzo, G. E. (1993). Cigarette smoking, nicotine addiction, and its pharmacologic treatment. *Archives of Internal Medicine, 153,* 34–48.

Lee, M. T., Garnick, D. W., Miller, K., & Horgan, C. M. (2004). Adolescents with substance abuse: Are health plans missing them? *Psychiatric Services* 55, 116.

Lee, W. M. (1997). Hepatitis B virus infection. *The New England Journal of Medicine*, 337, 1733–1745.

Leeds, J., & Morgenstern, J. (2003). Psychoanalytic theories of substance abuse. In *Treating substance abuse: Theory and technique* (2nd ed.) (Rotgers, F., Morgenstern, J., & Walters, S. T., eds.). New York: Guilford.

Leeper, K. V., & Torres, A. (1995). Community-acquired pneumonia in the intensive care unit. *Clinics in Chest Medicine*, 16, 155–171.

Lehman, A. F., Myers, C. P., & Corty, E. (1989) Assessment and classification of patients with psychiatric and substance abuse syndromes. *Hospital & Community Psychiatry*, 40, 1019–1025.

Lehman, L. B., Pilich, A., & Andrews, N. (1994). Neurological disorders resulting from alcoholism. *Alcohol Health & Research World*, 17, 305–309.

Lehrman, S. (2004). Sobering shift. *Scientific American*, 290(4), 22, 24.

Leinwand, D. (2000). New drugs, younger addicts fuel push to shift treatment from methadone clinics. *USA Today* 18(179), 1, 2.

Lemanski, M. J. (1997). The tenacity of error in the treatment of addiction. *The Humanist*, 57(3), 18–24.

Lemonick, M. D., Lafferty, E., Nash, J. M., Park, A., & Thompson, D. (1997). The mood molecule. *Time*, 150(13), 74–82.

Lender, M. E. (1981). The disease concept of alcoholism in the United States: Was Jellinek first? *Digest of Alcoholism Theory and Application*, 1(1), 25–31.

Leo, J. (1990). The it's-not-my-fault syndrome. *U.S. News & World Report*. 109(12), 16.

Leonard, K. E., & Mudar, P. (2003). Peer and partner drinking and the transition to marriage: A longitudinal examination of selection and influence processes. *Psychology of Addictive Behaviors*, 17, 115–125.

Leonard, K. E., & Roberts, R. J. (1996). Alcohol in the early years of marriage. *Alcohol Health & Research World*, 20, 192–196.

Leshner, A. I. (1997a). Drug abuse and addiction treatment research—the next generation. *Archives of General Psychiatry*, 54, 691–694.

Leshner, A. I. (1997b). Drug abuse and addiction are biomedical problems. *Hospital Practice—A Special Report*, 38(4), 2–4.

Leshner, A. I. (1998). Addiction is a brain disease, and it matters. *Science*, 278, 45–47.

Leshner, A. I. (1999). Research shows effects of prenatal cocaine exposure are subtle but significant. *NIDA Notes*, 14(3), 3–4.

Leshner, A. I. (2001a). Addiction and the brain. Symposium presented to the Dept. of Psychiatry of The Cambridge Hospital, Boston, MA, March 2.

Leshner, A. I. (2001b). Recent developments in drug addiction research. Paper presented at American Society of Addiction Medicine symposium, Washington, DC, November 2.

Lessard, S. (1989). Busting our mental blocks on drugs and crime. *Washington Monthly*, 21(1), 70.

Lester, B. M., El Sohly, M., Wright, L., Smeriglio, V. L., Verter, J., Bauer, C. R., Shankaran, S., Bada, H. S., Walls, H. C., Huestis, M. A., Finnegan, L. P., & Maza, P. L. (2001). The maternal lifestyle study: Drug use by meconium toxicology and maternal self report. *Pediatrics*, 107, 309–317.

Lester, D. (2000). Alcoholism, substance abuse, and suicide. In *Comprehensive textbook of suicidology* (Maris, R. W., Berman, A. L., & Silverman, M. M., eds.). New York: Guilford.

Levant, R. F. (2000). Rethinking healthcare costs. *The Independent Practitioner*, 20, 246–248.

Levin, J. D. (2002). *Treatment of alcoholism and other addictions*. Northvale, NJ: Jacob Aronson, Inc.

Levisky, J. A., Karch, S. B., Bowerman, D. L., Jenkins, W. W., Johnson, D. G., & Davies, D. (2003). False positive RIA for methamphetamine following ingestion of an ephedra-derived herbal product. *Journal of Analytical Toxicology*, 27(3), 123–124.

Levy, S. J., & Rutter, E. (1992). *Children of drug abusers*. New York: Lexington Books.

Levy, T. M., & Orlans, M. (1998). *Attachment, trauma and healing*. Washington, DC: CWLA Press.

Lewis, D. C. (1997). The role of the generalist in the care of the substance-abusing client. *Medical Clinics of North America*, 81, 831–843.

Lewis, J. A., Dana, R. Q., & Blevins, G. A. (1988). *Substance abuse counseling*. Pacific Grove, CA: Brooks/Cole.

Lewis, J. W. (1995). Buprenorphine—medicinal chemistry. In *Buprenorphine* (Cowan, A., & Lewis, J. W., eds.). New York: Wiley Interscience.

Lewis, M. L. (1937). Alcohol and family casework. *Social Casework*, 35, 8–14.

Li, G., Baker, S. P., Smialek, J. E., & Soderstrom, C. A. (2001). Use of alcohol as a risk factor for bicycling injury. *Journal of the American Medical Association*, 285, 893–896.

Li, J., Stokes, S. A., & Woeckener, A. (1998). A tale of novel intoxication: A review of the effects of gamma hudroxy-butyric acid with recommendations for management. *Annals of Emergency Medicine*, (28) 729–736.

Liberto, J. G., Oslin, D. W., & Ruskin, P. E. (1992). Alcoholism in older persons: A review of the literature. *Hospital and Community Psychiatry*, 43, 975–984.

Lieber, C. S. (1995). Medical disorders of alcoholism. *The New England Journal of Medicine*, 333, 1058–1065.

Lieber, C. S. (1996). Metabolic basis of alcoholic liver disease. Paper presented at the 1996 annual Frank P. Furlano, M.D., memorial lecture, Gunderson-Lutheran Medical Center, La Crosse, WI.

Lieber, C. S. (1998). Hepatic and other medical disorders of alcoholism: From pathogenesis to treatment. *Journal of Studies on Alcohol*, 59(1), 9–25.

Lieber, C. S. (2001). Alcohol and hepatitis C. *Alcohol Research & Health, 25,* 245–254.

Liebschutz, J. M., Mulvey, K. P., & Samet, J. H. (1997). Victimization among substance-abusing women. *Archives of Internal Medicine, 157,* 1093–1097.

Lieveld, P. E., & Aruna, A. (1991). Diagnosis and management of the alcohol withdrawal syndrome. *U.S. Pharmacist, 16*(1), H1–H11.

Lindman, R. E., Sjoholm, B. A., & Lang, A. R. (2000). Expectations of alcohol-induced positive affect: A cross-cultural comparison. *Journal of Studies on Alcohol, 61,* 681–687.

Linehan, M. M. (1993). *Skills training manual for treating borderline personality disorder.* New York: Guilford.

Lingeman, R. R. (1974). *Drugs from A to Z: A dictionary.* New York: McGraw Hill.

Linszen, D. H., Dingemans, P. M., & Lenior, M. E. (1994). Cannabis abuse and the course of recent-onset schizophrenic disorders. *Archives of General Psychiatry, 51,* 273–279.

Lipkin, M. (1989). Psychiatry and medicine. In *Comprehensive textbook of psychiatry/V.* (Kaplan, H. I., & Sadock, B. J., eds.). Baltimore: Williams & Wilkins.

Lipscomb, J. W. (1989). What pharmacists should know about home poisonings. *Drug Topics, 133*(15), 72–80.

Lisanti, P., & Zwolski, K. (1997). Understanding the devastation of AIDS. *American Journal of Nursing, 97*(7), 26–34.

Lit, E., Wiviott-Tishler, W., Wong, S., & Hyman, S. (1996). Stimulants: Amphetamines and caffeine. In *Sourcebook of substance abuse and addiction* (Friedman, L., Fleming, N. F., Roberts, D. H., & Hyman, S. H., eds.). New York: Williams & Wilkins.

Litten, R. Z. (2001). Medications in development to treat alcoholism. Paper presented at American Society of Addiction Medicine symposium, Washington, DC, November 1.

Little, H. J. (2000). Behavioral mechanisms underlying the link between smoking and drinking. *Alcohol Research & Health, 24,* 215–224.

Little, R. E., Anderson, K. W., Ervin, C. H., Worthington-Roberts, B., & Clarren, S. K. (1989). Maternal alcohol use during breast-feeding and infant mental and motor development at one year. *The New England Journal of Medicine, 321,* 425–430.

Littleton, J. (2001). Alcohol and nicotine: A pharmacological balancing act? Paper presented at American Society of Addiction Medicine symposium, Washington, DC, November 3.

Liu, S., Siegel, P. Z., Brewer, R. D., Mokdad, A. H., Sleet, D. A., & Serdula, M. (1997). Prevalence of alcohol-impaired driving. *Journal of the American Medical Association, 277,* 122–125.

Lively, K. (1996). The "date rape drug": Colleges worry about reports of use of Rohypnol, a sedative. *The Chronicle of Higher Education, 42*(42), A29.

Løberg, T. (1986). Neuropsychological findings in the early and middle phases of alcoholism. In *Neuropsychological assessment of neuropsychiatric disorders.* (Grant, I., & Adams, K. M., eds.). New York: Oxford University Press.

Loebl, S., Spratto, G. R., & Woods, A. L. (1994). *The nurse's drug handbook* (7th ed.). New York: Delmar Publishers, Inc.

Loiselle, J. M., Baker, M. D., Templeton, J. M., Schwartz, G., & Drott, H. (1993). Substance abuse in adolescent trauma. *Annals of Emergency Medicine, 22,* 1530–1534.

London, E. D., Simon, S. L., Berman, S. M., Mandelkern, M. A., Lichtman, A. M., Bramen, J., Shinn, A. K., Miotto, K., Learn, J., Dong, Y., Matochik, J. A., Kurian, V., Newton, T., Woods, R., Rawson, R., & Ling, W. (2004). Mood disturbances and regional cerebral metabolic abnormalities in recently abstinent methamphetamine abusers. *Archives of General Psychiatry, 61,* 73–84.

Longo, L. P., & Johnson, B. (2000). Addiction: Part I. *American Family Physician, 61,* 2121–2128.

Longo, L. P., Parran, T., Johnson, B., & Kinsey, W. (2000). Addiction: Part II. *American Family Physician, 61,* 2401–2408.

Lopez, W., & Jeste, D. V. (1997). Movement disorders and substance abuse. *Psychiatric Services, 48,* 634–636.

Louie, A. K. (1990). Panic attacks—When cocaine is the cause. *Medical Aspects of Human Sexuality, 24*(12), 44–46.

Lourwood, D. L., & Riedlinger, J. E. (1989). The use of drugs in the breast feeding mother. *Drug Topics, 133*(21), 77–85.

Lovett, A. R. (1994, May 5). Wired in California. *Rolling Stone,* 39–40.

Lowe, C. (2004). Addiction in the workplace. *Behavioral Health Management, 24*(5), 27–29.

Lund, N., & Papadakos, P. J. (1995). Barbiturates, neuroleptics, and propofol for sedation. *Critical Care Clinics, 11,* 875–885.

Lundeen, E. (2002). On the implications of drug legalization. *The Independent Practitioner, 22*(2), 175–176.

Lynam, D. R., Milich, R., Zimmerman, R., Novak, S. P., Logan, T. K., Martin, C., Leukefeld, C., & Clayton, R. (1999). Project DARE: No effects at 10–year follow-up. *Journal of Consulting and Clinical Psychology, 67,* 590–593.

Lynskey, M. T., & Hall, W. (2001). Attention deficit hyperactivity disorder and substance use disorders: Is there a causal link? *Addiction, 96,* 815–822.

Maas, E. F., Ashe, J., Spiegel, P., Zee, D. S., & Leigh, R. J. (1991). Acquired pendular nystagmus in toluene addiction. *Neurology, 41,* 282–286.

MacCoun, R., & Reuter, P. (1998). Interpreting Dutch cannabis policy: Reasoning by analogy in the legalization debate. *Science, 278,* 47–52.

MacCoun, R., & Reuter, P. (2001). Evaluating alternative cannabis regimes. *British Journal of Psychiatry, 178,* 123–128.

MacCoun, R. J. (1998). Towards a psychology of harm reduction. *American Psychologist, 53*(11), 1199–1208.

Macfadden, W., & Woody, G. E. (2000). Cannabis-related disorders. In *Comprehensive textbook of psychiatry* (7th ed.) (Sadock, B. J., & Sadock, V. A., eds.). New York: Lippincott Williams & Wilkins.

MacKenzie, T. D., Bartecchi, C. E., & Schrier, R. W. (1994). The human costs of tobacco use. *The New England Journal of Medicine, 330,* 907–912.

Madras, B. K. (2002). Addictions: A biological disease? Symposium presented to the Dept. of Psychiatry at The Cambridge Hospital, Boston, MA, February 1.

Magellan slashes fees: An outrage or opportunity? (1999). *American Association of Practicing Psychologist, 2*(1), 5, 7.

Maguire, J. (1990). *Care and feeding of the brain.* New York: Doubleday.

Maher, B. (2002). *When you ride ALONE you ride with bin Laden.* Beverly Hills, CA: New Millennium Press.

Mailer, N. (2004). Immodest proposals. *Playboy, 51*(1), 90–94, 198, 266, 268, 270, 272.

Maisto, S. A., & Connors, G. J. (1988). Assessment of treatment outcome. In *Assessment of addictive disorders* (Donovan, D. M., & Marlatt, G. A., eds.). New York: Guilford.

Makkai, T. (2003). Substance use, psychological distress and crime. *Medical Journal of Australia, 179,* 399–400.

Males, M. (1992). Tobacco: Promotion and smoking. *Journal of the American Medical Association, 267,* 3282.

Malinin, A. I., Callahan, K. P., & Serebruany, V. L. (2001). Paradoxical activation of major platelet receptors in the methadone-maintained patients after a single pill of aspirin. *Thrombosis Research, 104,* 297–299.

Malow, R. M., Devius, J. G., & Rosenberg, R. (2001). Enhanced cognitive-behavioral HIV prevention for adolescents abusing alcohol and other drugs. *The Addictions Newsletter, 8*(3), 2, 7.

Mamer, M., Penn, A., Wildmer, K., Levin, R. I., & Maslansky, R. (2003). Coronary artery disease and opioid use. *American Journal of Cardiology, 93,* 1295–1297.

Mandell, L. A., & Niederman, M. S. (1999). *Guide to prognosis and management of community-acquired pneumonia (CAP) & hospital-acquired pneumonia (HAP).* Greenwood Lake, NY: Sheffield Dawson Publishers, LTD.

Manderson, D. R. A. (1998). Drug abuse and illicit drug trafficking. *Medical Journal of Australia, 12,* 588–589.

Manfredi, R. L., Kales, A., Vgontzas, A. N., Bixler, E. O., Isaac, M. A., & Falcone, C. M. (1991). Buspirone: Sedative or stimulant effect? *American Journal of Psychiatry, 148,* 1213–1217.

Mann, C. C., & Plummer, M. L. (1991). *The aspirin wars.* New York: Knopf.

Mann, J. (1994). *Murder, magic and medicine.* New York: Oxford.

Mannino, D. M., Moorman, J. E., Kingsley, B., Rose, D., & Repace, J. (2001). Health effects related to environmental tobacco smoke exposure in children in the United States. *Archives of Pediatric and Adolescent Medicine, 155,* 36–41.

Mansvelder, H. D., Keath, J. R., & McGehee, D. S. (2002). Synaptic mechanisms underlie nicotine-induced excitability of brain/ reward areas. *Neuron, 33,* 905–919.

Maranto, G. (1985). Coke: The random killer. *Discover, 12*(3), 16–21.

Marcus, D. A. (2003). Tips for managing chronic pain. *Postgraduate Medicine, 113*(4), 49–50, 55–56, 59–60, 63–66, 98.

Margolin, A., Kleber, H. D., Avants, S. K., Konefal, J., Gawin, F., Stark, E., Sorensen, J., Midkiff, E., Wells, E., Jackson, T. R., Bullock, M., Culliton, P. D., Boles, S., & Vaughan, R. (2002). Acupuncture for the treatment of cocaine addiction. *Journal of the American Medical Association, 287,* 55–63.

Marijuana and breast feeding. (1990). *Pediatrics for Parents, 11*(10), 1.

Marijuana arrests. (2003). *Forensic Drug Abuse Advisor, 15,* 7.

Marijuana-related deaths? (2002). *Forensic Drug Abuse Advisor, 14*(1), 1–2.

Marik, P. E. (2001). Aspiration pneumonitis and aspiration pneumonia. *New England Journal of Medicine, 344,* 665–671.

Marinelli-Casey, P., Domier, C. P., & Rawson, R. A. (2002). The gap between research and practice in substance abuse treatment. *Psychiatric Services, 53,* 984–987.

Markarian, M., & Franklin, J. (1998). Substance abuse in minority populations. In *Clinical textbook of addictive disorders* (2nd ed.) (Frances, R. J., & Miller, S. I., eds.). New York: Guilford.

Markel, H. (2000). Easy answer might not be the right one. *The New York Times, CL* (51551), p. D8.

Markel, H. (2004). *When germs travel.* New York: Pantheon Books.

Market update. (1993). *The Economist, 329*(7830), 68.

Marlatt, G. A. (1994). Harm reduction: A public health approach to addictive behavior. *Division on Addictions Newsletter, 2*(1), 1, 3.

Marlatt, G. A., Baer, J. S., Kivlahan, D. R., Dimeff, L. A., Larimer, M. E., Quigley, L. A., Somers, J. M., & Williams, E. (1998). Screening and brief intervention for high-risk college student drinkers: Results from a 2 year follow-up assessment. *Journal of Consulting and Clinical Psychology, 66,* 604–615.

Marlowe, D. B., & DeMatteo, D. S. (2003). Drug policy by analogy: Well, it's like this . . . *Psychiatric Services, 54,* 1455–1456.

Marlowe, D. B., & DeMatteo, D. S. (2004). In reply. *Psychiatric Services, 56,* 720.

Marmor, J. B. (1998). Medical marijuana. *Western Journal of Medicine, 168,* 540–543.

Marsano, L. (1994). Alcohol and malnutrition. *Alcohol Health & Research World, 17,* 284–291.

Marshall, J. R. (1994). The diagnosis and treatment of social phobia and alcohol abuse. *Bulletin of the Menninger Clinic, 58,* A58–A66.

Marsicano, G., Wotjak, C. T., Azad, S. C., Bisogno, T., Rammes, G., Cascio, M. G., Herman, H. Tang, J.,

Hofmann, C., Ziegigansberger, W., De Marzo V., & Lutz B. (2002). The endogenous cannabinoid system controls extinction of aversive memories. *Nature, 418*, 530–534.

Marston, H. M., Reid, M. E., Lawrence, J. A., Olverman, H. J., & Butcher, S. P. (1999). Behavioral analysis of the acute and chronic effects of MDMA treatment in the rat. *Psychopharmacology, 144*, 67–76.

Martensen, R. L. (1996). From Papal endorsement to southern vice. *Journal of the American Medical Association, 276*, 1615.

Martin, B. R. (2004). Neurobiology of marijuana. In *Textbook of substance abuse treatment* (3rd ed.) (Galanter, M., & Kleber, H. D., eds.). Washington, DC: American Psychiatric Press, Inc.

Martin, C. S., & Winters, K. C. (1998). Diagnosis and assessment of alcohol use disorders among adolescents. *Alcohol Health & Research World, 22*, 95–101, 104.

Martin, J. E., & Booth, J. (1999). Behavioral approaches to enhance spirituality. In *Integrating spirituality into treatment*. Washington, DC: American Psychological Association.

Martin, P. J., Enevoldson, T. P., & Humphrey, P. R. D. (1997). Causes of ischaemic stroke in the young. *Postgraduate Medical Journal, 73*, 8–16.

Marvel, B. (1995). AA's "higher power" challenged. *St Paul Pioneer Press, 147*(44), p. A4.

Marwick, C. (1997). Coma-inducing drug GHB may be reclassified. *Journal of the American Medical Association, 277*, 1505–1506.

Marzuk, P. M. (1996). Violence, crime, and mental illness. *Archives of General Psychiatry, 53*, 481–486.

Marzuk, P. M., Tardiff, K., Leon, A. C., Hirsch, C. S., Stajic, M., Portera, L., Hartwell, N., & Iqbal, M. I. (1995). Fatal injuries after cocaine use as a leading cause of death among young adults in New York City. *The New England Journal of Medicine, 332*, 1753–1757.

Mash, D. C., Ouyang, Q., Pablo, J., Basile, M., Izenwasser, S., Lieberman, A., & Perrin, R. J. (2003). Cocaine abusers have an overexpression of synuclein in dopamine neurons. *Journal of Neuroscience, 23*, 2564–2571.

Mason, B. J., Salvato, F. R., Williams, L. D., Ritvo, E. C., & Cutler, R. B. (1999). A double-blind, placebo-controlled study of oral nalmefene for alcohol dependence. *Archives of General Psychiatry, 56*, 719–724.

Masse, L. C., & Tremblay, R. E. (1997). Behavior of boys in kindergarten and onset of substance use during adolescence. *Archives of General Psychiatry, 52*, 62–68.

Masten, A. S. (2001). Ordinary magic: Resilience processes in development. *American Psychologist, 56*, 227–238.

Mathers, D. C., & Ghodse, A. D. (1992). Cannabis and psychiatric illness. *British Journal of Psychiatry, 161*, 648–653.

Mathew, J., Addai, T., Ashwin, A., Morrobel, A., Maheshwari, P., & Freels, S. (1995). Clinical features, site of involvement, bacteriologic findings and outcome of infection endocarditis in intraveneous drug users. *Archives of Internal Medicine, 155*, 1641–1649.

Mathew, R. D., Wilson, W. H., Blazer, D. G., & George, L. K. (1993). Psychiatric disorders in adult children of alcoholics: Data from the epidemiologic catchment area project. *American Journal of Psychiatry, 150*, 793–800.

Mathias, R. (1995). NIDA survey provides first national data on drug use during pregnancy. NIDA *Notes, 10*(1), 6–7.

Mathias, R. (2002). Chronic solvent abusers have more brain abnormalities and cognitive impairments than cocaine abusers. NIDA *Notes, 17*(4), 5–6, 12.

Mattick, R. P., & Hall, W. (1996). Are detoxification programs effective? *The Lancet, 347*, 97–100.

Mattila, M. A. K., & Larni, H. M. (1980). Flunitrazepam: A review of its pharmacological properties and therapeutic use. *Drugs, 20*, 353–374.

Mattson, S. N., & Riley, E. P. (1995). Prenatal exposure to alcohol. *Alcohol Health & Research World, 19*, 273–278.

Matuschka, P. R. (1985). The psychopharmacology of addiction. In *Alcoholism and substance abuse: Strategies for clinical intervention* (Bratter, T. E., & Forrest, G. G., eds.). New York: The Free Press.

Maxmen, J. S., & Ward, N. G. (1995). *Psychotropic drugs fast facts* (2nd ed.). New York: W. W. Norton & Co.

May, D. (1999). Testing by necessity. *Occupational Health & Safety, 68*(4), 48, 50–51.

May, G. G. (1988). *Addiction & grace.* New York: Harper & Row.

May, G. G. (1991). *The awakened heart.* New York: Harper & Row.

Mayo Foundation for Medical Education and Research. (1989). America's drug crisis. In *Mayo Clinic Health Letter.* Rochester, MN: Author.

McAllister, J. F. O., Brfant-Zawadzki, A., de la Cal, M., Frank, S., Gerard, N., Le Quesne, N., Ruairi, T. M., & Walker, J. (2001). Europe goes to pot. *Time, 158*(7), 60–61.

McAnalley, B. H. (1996). Chemistry of alcoholic beverages. In *Medicolegal aspects of alcohol* (3rd ed.) (Garriott, J. C., ed.). Tucson, AZ: Lawyers and Judges Publishing Co.

McCaffery, M., & Ferrell, B. R. (1994). Understanding opioids and addiction. *Nursing 94, 24*(8), 56–59.

McCann, U. D., Szabo, Z., Scheffel, U., Dannals, R. F., & Ricaurte, G. A. (1998). Positron emission tomographic evidence of toxic effect of MDMA ("ecstasy") on brain serotonin neurons in human beings. *The Lancet, 352*, 1433–1437.

McCarthy, J. J., & Borders, O. T. (1985). Limit setting on drug abuse in methadone maintenance patients. *American Journal of Psychiatry, 142*, 1419–1423.

McCaul, M. D., & Furst, J. (1994). Alcoholism treatment in the United States. *Alcohol Health & Research World, 18*, 253–260.

McClosky, M. S., & Berman, M. E. (2003). Alcohol intoxication and self-aggressive behavior. *Journal of Abnormal Psychology, 112*, 306–311.

McCollister, K. E., & French, M. T. (2002). The economic cost of substance-abuse treatment in criminal justice settings. In *Treatment of drug offenders* (Leukefeld, G. G., Tims, F., & Farabee, D., eds.). New York: Springer Publishing Co.

McCrady, B. S. (1994). Alcoholics Anonymous and behavior therapy: Can habits be treated as diseases? Can diseases be treated as habits? *Journal of Consulting and Clinical Psychology, 62,* 1159–1166.

McCrady, B. S. (2001). Alcohol use disorders. In *Clinical handbook of psychological disorders* (3rd ed.) (Barlow, D. H., ed.). New York: Guilford.

McCrady, B. S., & Delaney, S. I. (1995). Self-help groups. In *Handbook of alcoholism treatment approaches* (2nd ed.) (Hester, R. K., & Miller, W. R., eds.). New York: Allyn & Bacon.

McCrady, B. S., & Epstein, E. E. (1995). Marital therapy in the treatment of alcoholism. In *Clinical handbook of couple therapy* (Jacobson, N. S., & Gurman, A. S., eds.). New York: Guilford.

McCrady, B. S., & Irvine, S. (1989). Self-help groups. In *Handbook of alcoholism treatment approaches* (Hester, R. K., & Miller, W. R., eds.). New York: Pergamon Press.

McCrady, B. S., & Langenbucher, J. W. (1996). Alcohol treatment and health care system reform. *Archives of General Psychiatry, 53,* 737–746.

McCusker, J., Stoddard, A., Frost, R., & Zorn, M. (1996). Planned versus actual duration of drug abuse treatment. *Journal of Nervous and Mental Disease, 184,* 482–489.

McCutchan, J. A. (1990). Virology, immunology, and clinical course of HIV infection. *Journal of Clinical and Consulting Psychology, 58,* 5–12.

McDargh, J. (2000). The role of spirituality in the recovery process. Symposium presented to the Dept. of Psychiatry of The Cambridge Hospital, Boston, MA, March 4.

McDonough, J. (1998). Acetaminophen overdose. *American Journal of Nursing, 98,* (3), 52.

McDowell, D. M. (2004). MDMA, Ketamine, GHB, and the "club drug" scene. In *Textbook of substance abuse treatment* (3rd ed.) (Galanter, M., & Kleber, H. D., eds.). Washington, DC: American Psychiatric Press, Inc.

McElhatton, P. R., Bateman, D. N., Evans, C., Pughe, K. R., & Thomas, S. H. L. (1999). Congenital abnomalies after prenatal ecstasy exposure. *The Lancet, 354,* 1441.

McEnroe, P. (1990). Hawaii is fighting losing battle against the popularity of drug "ice." *Minneapolis Star Tribune, IX* (44), pp. A1, A20.

McFadden, E. R. & Hejal, R. B. (2000). The pathobiology of acute asthma. *Clinics in Chest Medicine, 21,* 213–224.

McGowan, R. (1998). Finding God in all things: Ministering to those suffering from addictions. Symposium presented to the Dept. of Psychiatry of The Cambridge Hospital, Boston, MA, March 7.

McGuire, L. (1990). The power of non-narcotic pain relievers. *RN, 53*(4), 28–35.

McGuire, P., & Fahy, T. (1991). Chronic paranoid psychosis after misuse of MDMA ("ecstasy"). *British Medical Journal, 302,* 697.

McHugh, M. J. (1987). The abuse of volatile substances. *The Pediatric Clinics of North America, 34*(2), 333–340.

McKay, A., Koranda, A., & Axen, D. (2004). Using a symptom-triggered approach to manage patients in acute alcohol withdrawal. *MEDSURG Nursing, 13*(1), 15–20, 31.

McKay, J. R., McLellan, T., Alterman, A. I., Cacciola, J. S., Rutherford, M. J., & O'Brian, C. P. (1998). Predictors of participation in aftercare sessions and self-help groups following completion of intensive outpatient treatment for substance abuse. *Journal of Studies on Alcohol, 59,* 152–162.

McLellan, A. T. (2001). Is addiction treatment effective: Compared to what? Symposium presented to the Dept. of Psychiatry of The Cambridge Hospital, Boston, MA, March 2.

McLellan, A. T., Arndt, I. O., Metzger, D. S., Woody, G. E., & O'Brien, C. P. (1993). The effects of psychosocial services in substance abuse treatment. *Journal of the American Medical Association, 269,* 1953–1959.

McLellan, A. T., Lewis, D. C., O'Brien, C. P., & Kleber, H. D. (2000). Drug dependence, a chronic medical illness. *Journal of the American Medical Association, 284,* 1689–1695.

McMahon, F. J. (2003). Molecular genetics. In *Molecular neurobiology for the clinician* (Charney, D. S., ed.). Washington, DC: American Psychiatric Publishing, Inc.

McPhillips, M. A., Strang, J., & Barnes, T. R. E. (1998). Hair analysis. *British Journal of Psychiatry, 173,* 287–290.

McRae, A. L., Brady, K. T., & Sonne, S. C. (2001). Alcohol and substance abuse. *Medical Clinics of North America, 85,* 779–801.

McWilliams, P. (1993). Ain't nobody's business. *Playboy, 40*(9), 49–52.

McWilliams, P. (1999). The general's loophole. *Playboy, 46*(12), 61.

Meatherall, R., & Sharma, P. (2005). Foxy, a designer tryptamine hallucinogen. *Journal of Analytical Toxicology, 27*(5), 313–317.

Medical Economics Company. (1989). Anabolic steroid abuse and primary care. *Patient Care, 23*(8), 12.

Medical Economics Company. (2000). *Physicians' desk reference* (54th ed.). Oradell, NJ: Author.

Medical reprieve. (2003). *Playboy, 50*(3), 60.

Mee-Lee, D. (2002). Clinical implications of four generations of addiction treatment: We've come a long way baby—Or have we? Symposium presented to the Dept. of Psychiatry at The Cambridge Hospital, Boston, MA, February 1.

Meer, J. (1986). Marijuana in the air: Delayed buzz bomb. *Psychology Today, 20,* 68.

Meier, B. (2003). *Pain killer: A "wonder" drug's trail of addiction and death.* New York: Rodale.

Meldrum, M. L. (2003). A capsule history of pain management. *Journal of the American Medical Association, 290,* 2470–2475.

Melnick, G., De Leon, G., Hawke, J., Jainchill, N., & Kressel, D. (1997). Motivation and readiness for therapeutic community treatment among adolescents and adult substance abusers. *American Journal of Alcohol Abuse, 24*, 485–506.

Melzack, R. (1990). The tragedy of needless pain. *Scientific American, 262*(2), 27–33.

Mendelson, J. H., & Mello, N. K. (1996). Management of cocaine abuse and dependence. *The New England Journal of Medicine, 334*, 965–972.

Mendelson, J. H., & Mello, N. K. (1998). Cocaine and other commonly abused drugs. In *Harrison's principles of internal medicine* (14th ed.) (Fauci, A. S., Martin, J. B., Braunwald, E., Kasper, D. L., Isselbacher, K. J., Hauser, S. L., Wilson, J. D., & Longo, D. L., eds.). New York: McGraw-Hill.

Mendelson, W. B., & Rich, C. L. (1993). Sedatives and suicide: The San Diego study. *Acta Psychiatrica Scandinavica, 88*, 337–341.

Mendoza, R., & Miller, B. L. (1992). Neuropsychiatric disorders associated with cocaine use. *Hospital and Community Psychiatry, 43*, 677–678.

Mendyk, S. L., & Fields, D. W. (2002). Acute psychotic reactions: Consider "Dip Dope" intoxication. *Journal of Emergency Nursing, 28*, 432–435.

The men who created crack. (1991). *U.S. News & World Report, 111*(8), 44–53.

Merikangas, K. R., Dierker, L. C., & Szatmari, P. (1998). Psychopathology among offspring of parents with substance abuse and/or anxiety disorders: A high risk study. *Journal of Child Psychology & Psychiatry, 39*, 711–720.

Merikangas, K. R., Stolar, M., Stevens, D. E., Goulet, J., Preisig, M. A., Fenton, B., Zhang, H., O'Malley, S. S., & Rounsaville, B. J. (1998). Familial transmission of substance use disorders. *Archives of General Psychiatry, 55*, 973–979.

Merikle, E. P. (1999). The subjective experience of craving: An exploratory analysis. *Substance Use & Misuse, 34*, 1011–1015.

Merlotti, L., Roehrs, T., Koshorek, G., Zorick, F., Lamphere, J., & Roth, T. (1989). The dose effects of zolpidem on the sleep of healthy normals. *Journal of Clinical Psychopharmacology, 9*(1), 9–14.

Mersey, D. J. (2003). Recognition of alcohol and substance abuse. *American Family Physician, 67*, 1529–1532, 1535–1536.

Merton, T. (1961). *New seeds of contemplation*. New York: New Directions Publishing.

Merton, T. (1978). *No man is an island*. New York: New Directions Publishing.

Methadone-Cipro interactions. (2002). *Forensic Drug Abuse Advisor, 14*(1), 5–6.

Methadone dose debate continues. (2003). *Addiction Treatment Forum, 12*(1), 1, 3, 7.

Metzner, R. (2002). The role of psychoactive plant medicines. In *Hallucinogens* (Grob, C. S., ed.). New York: Penguin Putnam, Inc.

Meyer, R. (1988). Intervention: Opportunity for healing. *Alcoholism & Addiction, 9*(1), 7.

Meyer, R. E. (1989). Who can say no to illicit drug use. *Archives of General Psychiatry, 46*, 189–190.

Meyer, R. E. (1992). New pharmacotherapies for cocaine dependence . . . revisited. *Archives of General Psychiatry, 49*, 900–904.

Meyer, R. E. (1994). What for, alcohol research? *American Journal of Psychiatry, 151*, 165–168.

Meyer, R. E. (1996). The disease called addiction: Emerging evidence is a 200-year debate. *The Lancet, 347*, 162–166.

Meyers, B. R. (1992). *Antimicrobial therapy guide*. Newtown, PA: Antimicrobial Prescribing, Inc.

Meza, E., & Kranzler, H. R. (1996). Closing the gap between alcoholism research and practice: The case for pharmacotherapy. *Psychiatric Services, 47*, 917–920.

Michelson, J. B., Carroll, D., McLane, N. J., & Robin, H. S. (1988). Drug abuse and ocular disease. In *Surgical treatment of ocular inflammatory disease* (Michelson, J. B., & Nozik, R. A., eds.). New York: J. B. Lippincott Co.

Middleman, A. B., & DuRant, R. H. (1996). Anabolic steroid use and associated health risk behaviors. *Sports Medicine, 21*, 251–255.

Milberger, S., Biederman, J., Faraone, S. V., Chen, L., & Jones, J. (1996). Is maternal smoking during pregnancy a risk factor for attention deficit hyperactivity disorder in children? *American Journal of Psychiatry, 153*, 1138–1142.

Miles, H., Johnson, S., Amponsah-Afuwape, S., Finch, E., Leese, M., & Thornicroft, G. (2003). Characteristics of subgroups of individuals with psychotic illness and a comorbid substance use disorder. *Psychiatric Services, 54*, 554–561.

Miles, S. A. (1996). Pathogenesis of AIDS-related Kaposi's Sarcoma. *Hematology/Oncology Clinics of North America, 10*, 1011–1021.

Milhorn, H. T. (1991). Diagnosis and management of phenocyclidine intoxication. *American Family Physician, 43*, 1293–1302.

Milhorn, H. T. (1992). Pharmacologic management of acute abstinence syndromes. *American Family Physician, 45*, 231–239.

Milin, R., Loh, E., Chow, J., & Wilson, A. (1997). Assessment of symptoms of attention-deficit hyperactivity disorder in adults with substance use disorders. *Psychiatric Services, 48*, 1378–1380.

Miller, A. (1988). *The enabler*. Claremont, CA: Hunter House.

Miller, B. A., & Downs, W. R. (1995). Violent victimization among women with alcohol problems. In *Recent developments in alcoholism* (Vol. 12) (Galanter, M., ed.). New York: Plenum Press.

Miller, L., Davies, M., & Greenwald, S. (2000). Religiosity and substance use and abuse among adolescents in the National Comorbidity Survey. *Journal of the American Academy of Child and Adolescent Psychiatry, 39*, 1190–1197.

Miller, N. S. (1994). Psychiatric comorbidity: Occurrence and treatment. *Alcohol Health & Research World, 18*, 261–264.

Miller, N. S. (1999). Mortality risks in alcoholism and effects of abstinence and addiction treatment. *Psychiatric Clinics of North America, 22*, 371–383.

Miller, N. S., & Gold, M. S. (1991a). Abuse, addiction, tolerance, and dependence to benzodiazepines in medical and nonmedical populations. *American Journal of Drug and Alcohol Abuse, 17*(1), 27–37.

Miller, N. S., & Gold, M. S. (1991b). Organic solvent and aerosol abuse. *American Family Physician, 44*, 183–190.

Miller, N. S., & Gold, M. S. (1998). Management of withdrawal syndromes and relapse prevention in drug and alcohol dependence. *American Family Physician, 58*(1), 139–146.

Miller, S. I., Frances, R. J., & Holmes, D. J. (1988). Use of psychotropic drugs in alcoholism treatment: A summary. *Hospital & Community Psychiatry, 39*, 1251–1252.

Miller, S. I., Frances, R. J., & Holmes, D. J. (1989). Psychotropic medications. In *Handbook of alcoholism treatment approaches* (Hester, R. K., & Miller, W. R., eds.). New York: Pergamon Press.

Miller, W. R. (1976). Alcoholism scales and objective measures. *Psychological Bulletin, 83*, 649–674.

Miller, W. R. (1995). Increasing motivation for change. In *Handbook of alcoholism treatment approaches* (2nd ed.) (Hester, R. K., & Miller, W. R., eds.). New York: Allyn & Bacon.

Miller, W. R. (1998). Enhancing motivation for change. In *Treating addictive behaviors* (2nd ed.) (Miller, W. R., & Heather, N., eds.). New York: Plenum.

Miller, W. R. (2003). What really motivates change? Reflections on 20 years of motivational interviewing. Symposium presented to the Dept. of Psychiatry at The Cambridge Hospital, Boston, MA, March 7.

Miller, W. R., Andrews, N. R., Wilbourne, P., & Bennett, M. E. (1998). A wealth of alternatives. In *Handbook of alcoholism treatment approaches* (2nd ed.) (Hester, R. K., & Miller, W. R., eds.). New York: Allyn & Bacon.

Miller, W. R., & Brown, S. A. (1997). Why psychologists should treat alcohol and drug problems. *American Psychologist, 52*, 1269–1279.

Miller, W. R., & Cervantes, E. A. (1997). Gender and patterns of alcohol problems: Pretreatment responses of women and men to the comprehensive drinker profile. *Journal of Clinical Psychology, 53*, 263–277.

Miller, W. R., Genefield, G., & Tonigan, J. S. (1993). Enhancing motivation for change in problem drinking: A controlled comparison of two therapist styles. *Journal of Consulting and Clinical Psychology, 61*, 455–462.

Miller, W. R., & Harris, R. J. (2000). A simple scale of Gorski's warning signs for relapse. *Journal of Studies on Alcohol, 61*, 759–765.

Miller, W. R., & Hester, R. K. (1980). Treating the problem drinker: Modern approaches. In *The addictive behaviors* (Miller, W. R., ed.). New York: Pergamon Press.

Miller, W. R., & Hester, R. K. (1986). Inpatient alcoholism treatment. *American Psychologist, 41*(7), 794–806.

Miller, W. R., & Hester, R. K. (1995). Treating alcohol problems: Toward an informed eclecticism. In *Handbook of alcoholism treatment approaches* (2nd ed.) (Hester, R. K., & Miller, W. R., eds.). New York: Allyn & Bacon.

Miller, W. R., & Kurtz, E. (1994). Models of alcoholism used in treatment: Contrasting AA and other perspectives with which it is often confused. *Journal of Studies on Alcohol, 55*, 159–166.

Miller, W. R., & McCrady, B. S. (1993). The importance of research on Alcoholics Anonymous. In *Research on Alcoholics Anonymous* (McCrady, B. S., & Miller, W. R., eds.). New Brunswick, NJ: Rutgers Center of Alcohol Studies.

Miller, W. R., & Rollnick, S. (2002). *Motivational Interviewing* (2nd ed.). New York: Guilford Press.

Miller, W. R., Walters, S., & Bennett, M. E. (2001). How effective is alcoholism treatment in the United States? *Journal of Studies on Alcohol, 62*, 211–220.

Miller, W. R., Westerberg, V. S., & Waldron, H. B. (1995). Evaluating alcohol problems in adults and adolescents. In *Handbook of alcoholism treatment approaches* (2nd ed.) (Hester, R. K., & Miller, W. R., eds.). New York: Allyn & Bacon.

Millman, R. B., & Beeder, A. B. (1994). Cannabis. In *Textbook of substance abuse treatment* (Galanter, M., & Kleber, H. D., eds.). Washington, DC: American Psychiatric Press, Inc.

Millon, T. (1981). *Disorders of personality*. New York: John Wiley.

Mills, K. C. (1995). Serotonin syndrome. *American Family Physician, 52*, 1475–1482.

Milne, D. (2003). Experts desperately seeking meth abuse prevention, treatment. *Psychiatric News, XXXVIII* (1), 12.

Minkoff, K. (1989). An integrated treatment model for dual diagnosis of psychosis and addiction. *Hospital and Community Psychiatry, 40*, 1031–1036.

Minkoff, K. (1997). Substance abuse versus substance dependence. *Psychiatric Services, 48*, 867.

Minkoff, K. (2001). Developing standards of care for individuals with co-occuring psychiaric and substance use disorders. *Psychiatric Services, 52*, 597–599.

Mirin, S. M., Weiss, R. D., & Greenfield, S. F. (1991). Psychoactive substance use disorders. In *The practitioner's guide to psychoactive drugs* (3rd ed.) (Galenberg, A. J., Bassuk, E. L., & Schoonover, S. C., eds.). New York: Plenum Medical Book Co.

Miro, O., Nogue, S., Espinoza, G., To-Figueras, J., & Sanchez, S. (2002). Trends in illicit drug emergencies: The emerging role of gamma hydroxybutyrate. *Clinical Toxicology, 40*, 129–135.

Mitra, S. C., Ganesh, V., & Apuzzio, J. J. (1994). Effect of maternal cocaine abuse on renal arterial flow and urine output in the fetus. *American Journal of Obstetrics and Gynecology, 171*, 1556–1560.

Mittleman, M. A., Lewis, R. A., Maclure, M., Sherwood, J. B., & Muller, J. E. (2001). Triggering myocardial infarction by marijuana. *Circulation, 103*, 2805–2809.

Modesto-Lowe, V., & Kranzler, H. R. (1999). Diagnosis and treatment of alcohol-dependent patients with comorbid psychiatric disorders. *Alcohol Research & Health, 23*(2), 144–149.

Moe, V., & Slinning, K. (2001). Children prenatally exposed to substances: Gender-related differences in outcome from infancy to 3 years of age. *Infant Mental Health Journal, 22*(3), 334–350.

Moeller, F. G., & Dougherty, D. M. (2001). Antisocial personality disorder, alcohol, and aggression. *Alcohol Research & Health, 25*(1), 5–11.

Mokdad, A. H., Marks, J. S., Stroup, D. F., & Gerberding, J. L. (2004). Actual causes of death in the United States, 2000. *Journal of the American Medical Association, 291*, 1238–1245.

Moliterno, D. J., Willard, J. E., Lange, R. A., Negus, B. H., Boehrer, J. D., Glamann, B., Landau, C., Rossen, J. D., Winniford, M. D., & Hillis, L. D. (1994). Coronary-artery vasoconstriction induced by cocaine, cigarette smoking, or both. *The New England Journal of Medicine, 330*, 454–459.

Monforte, R., Estruch, R., Valls-Sole, J., Nicolas, J., Villalta, J., & Urbano-Marquez, A. (1995). Autonomic and peripheral neuropathies in patients with chronic alcoholism. *Archives of Neurology, 51*, 45–51.

Monroe, J. (1994). Designer drugs: CAT & LSD. *Current Health, 20*(1), 13–16.

Monroe, J. (1995). Inhalants: Dangerous highs. *Current Health, 22*(1), 16–20.

Monti, P. M. (2003). Identifying risk and brief intervention with adolescent alcohol problems. Symposium presented to the Dept. of Psychiatry at The Cambridge Hospital, Boston, MA, March 7.

Monti, P. M., Kadden, R. M., Rohsenow, D. J., Cooney, N. L., & Abrams, D. B. (2002). *Treating alcohol dependence* (2nd ed.). New York: Guilford.

Moon, D. B., Hecht, M. L., Jackson, K. M., & Spellers, R. E. (1999) Ethnic and gender differences and similarities in adolescent drug use and refusals of drug offers. *Substance Use & Misuse, 34*, 1059–1083.

Moore, M. H. (1991). Drugs, the criminal law, and the administration of justice. *The Milbank Quarterly, 69*(4), 529–560.

Moore, M. K., & Ginsberg, L. (1999). The date rapist's scary new weapon. *Cosmopolitan, 226*(2), 202.

Moore, R. A. (1995). Analysis. In *Buprenorphine* (Cowan, A., & Lewis, J. W., eds.). New York: Wiley Interscience.

Moos, R. H. (2003). Addictive disorders in context: Principles and puzzles of effective treatment and recovery. *Psychology of Addictive Behaviors, 17*, 3–12.

Moos, R. H., King, M. J., & Patterson, M. A. (1996). Outcomes of residential treatment of substance abuse in hospital and community-based programs. *Psychiatric Services, 47*, R68–74.

Moos, R. H., & Moos, B. S. (1995). Stay in residential facilities and mental health care as predictors of readmission for patients with substance use disorders. *Psychiatric Services, 46*, 66–72.

Moos, R. H., Moos, B. S., & Andrassy, J. M. (1999). Outcomes of four treatment approaches in community residential programs for patients with substance use disorders. *Psychiatric Services, 50*, 1577–1583.

Morabia, A., Bernstein, M., Heritier, S., & Khatchatrian, N. (1996). Relation of breast cancer with passive and active exposure to tobacco. *American Journal of Epidemiology, 143*, 918–928.

Morey, L. C. (1996). Patient placement criteria. *Alcohol Health & Research World, 20*, 36–44.

Morgan, B. W., Barnes, L., Parramore, C. S., & Kaufmann, R. B. (2003). Elevated blood lead levels associated with the consumption of moonshine among emergency department patients in Atlanta, Georgia. *Annals of Emergency Medicine, 42*, 351–358.

Morgan, M. J. (1999). Memory deficits associated with recreational "ecstasy" (MDMA). *Psychopharmacology, 141*, 30–36.

Morgan, T. J. (2003). Behavioral treatment techniques for psychoactive substance use disorders. In *Treating substance abuse: Theory and technique* (2nd ed.) (Rotgers, F., Morgenstern, J., & Walters, S.T., eds.). New York: Guilford.

Morgenstern, J., Labouvie, E., McCrady, B. S., Kahler, C. W., & Frey, R. M. (1997). Affiliation with Alcoholics Anonymous after treatment: A study of its therapeutic effects and mechanisms of actions. *Journal of Consulting and Clinical Psychology, 65*, 768–777.

Morrison, M. A. (1990). Addiction in adolescents. *The Western Journal of Medicine, 152*, 543–547.

Morrison, S. F., Rogers, P. D., & Thomas, M. H. (1995). Alcohol and adolescents. *Pediatric Clinics of North America, 42*, 371–387.

Morse, R. M., & Flavin, D. K. (1992). The definition of alcoholism. *Journal of the American Medical Association, 268*, 1012–1014.

Mortensen, M. E., & Rennebohm, R. M. (1989). Clinical pharmacology and use of nonsteroidal anti-inflammatory drugs. *Pediatric Clinics of North America, 36*, 1113–1139.

Morton, H. G. (1987). Occurrence and treatment of solvent abuse in children and adolescents. *Pharmacological Therapy, 33*, 449–469.

Morton, W. A., & Santos, A. (1989). New indications for benzodiazepines in the treatment of major psychiatric disorders. *Hospital Formulary, 24*, 274–278.

Mosier, W. A. (1999). Alcohol addiction: Identifying the patient who drinks. *Journal of the American Academy of Physician's Assistants, 12*(5), 25–26, 28–29, 35–36, 38, 40.

Motluk, A. (2004). Intemperate society. *New Scientist, 183*(2461), 28–33.

Mott, S. H., Packer, R. J., & Soldin, S. J. (1994). Neurologic manifestations of cocaine exposure in childhood. *Pediatrics, 93*, 557–560.

Movig, K. L. L., Mathijssen, M. P. M., Nagel, P. H. A., van Egmond, J., de Gier, J., Leufkens, H. G. M., & Egberts, A. C. G. (2004). Psychoactive substance use and the risk of motor vehicle accidents. *Accident Analysis and Prevention, 36,* 631–636.

Moylan, D. W. (1990). Court intervention. *Adolescent Counselor, 2*(5), 23–27.

Mueller, A. A. (2005). New drugs of abuse update: Foxy Methoxy. *Journal of Emergency Nursing, 30*(5), 507–508.

Mueller, P. S., Plevak, D. J., & Rummans, T. A. (2001). Religious involvement, spirituality, and medicine: Implications for clinical practice. *Mayo Clinic Proceedings, 76,* 1225–1235.

Mueller, T. I., Lavori, P. W., Keller, M. B., Swartz, A., Warshaw, M., Hasin, D., Coryell, W., Endicott, J., Rice, J., & Akiskall, H. (1994). Prognostic effect of the variable course of alcoholism on the 10 year course of depression. *American Journal of Psychiatry, 151,* 701–706.

Mueser, K. T., Bellack, A. S., & Blanchard, J. J. (1992). Comorbidity of schizophrenia and substance abuse: Implications for treatment. *Journal of Counseling and Clinical Psychology, 60,* 845–856.

Mukamal, K. J., Conigrave, K. M., Mittleman, M. A., Camargo, C. A., Stampfer, M. J., Willett, W. C., & Rimm, E. B. (2003). Roles of drinking in pattern and type of alcohol consumed in coronary heart disease in men. *New England Journal of Medicine, 348,* 109–118.

Mundle, G. (2000). Geriatric patients. In *Handbook of Alcoholism* (Zernig, G., Saria, A., Kurz, M., & O'Malley, S. S., eds.). New York: CRC Press.

Murphy, G. E., Wetzel, R. D., Robins, E., & McEvoy, L. (1992). Multiple risk factors predict suicide in alcoholism. *Archives of General Psychiatry, 49,* 459–463.

Murphy, S. L., & Khantzian, E. J. (1995). Addiction as a self-medication disorder: Application of ego psychology to the treatment of substance abuse. In *Psychotherapy and substance abuse* (Washton, A. M., ed.). New York: Guilford.

Musto, D. F. (1991). Opium, cocaine and marijuana in American history. *Scientific American, 265*(1), 40–47.

Musto, D. F. (1996). Alcohol in American history. *Scientific American, 274*(4), 78–83.

Myers, B. J., Dawson, K. S., Britt, G. C., Lodder, D. E., Meloy, L. D., Saunders, M. K., Meadows, S. L., & Elswick, R. K. (2003). Prenatal cocaine exposure and infant performance on the Brazelton Neonatal Behavioral Assessment Scale. *Substance Use & Misuse, 38*(14), 2065–2096.

Mylonakis, E., Paliou, M., & Rich, J. D. (2001). Plasma viral load testing in the management of HIV infection. *American Family Physician, 63,* 483–490.

Nace, E. P. (1987). *The treatment of alcoholism.* New York: Brunner/Mazel.

Nace, E. P. (1997). Alcoholics Anonymous. In *Substance abuse: A comprehensive textbook* (3rd ed.) (Lowinson, J. H., Ruiz, P., Millman, R. B., & Langrod, J. G., eds.). New York: Williams & Wilkins.

Nace, E. P. (2003). The importance of Alcoholics Anonymous in changing destructive behavior. *Primary Psychiatry, 10*(9), 65–68, 71–72.

Nace, E. P., & Isbell, P. G. (1991). Alcohol. In *Clinical textbook of addictive disorders* (Frances, R. J., & Miller, S. I., eds.). New York: Guilford.

Nadelmann, E., & Wenner, J. S. (1994, May 5). Towards a sane national drug policy. *Rolling Stone,* 24–26.

Nadlemann, E. A. (1989). Drug prohibition in the United States: Costs, consequences, and alternatives. *Science, 245,* 939–946.

Nadlemann, E. A. (2002). Commonsense drug policy. In *Taking sides: Clashing views on controversial issues in drugs and society* (5th ed.) (Goldberg, R., ed.). New York: McGraw-Hill Dushkin.

Nadelmann, E. A., Kleiman, M. A. R., & Earls, F. J. (1990). Should some illegal drugs be legalized? *Issues in Science and Technology, VI* (4), 43–49.

Nahas, G. G. (1986). Cannabis: Toxicological properties and epidemiological aspects. *The Medical Journal of Australia, 145,* 82–87.

Naimi, T. S., Brewer, R. D., Mokdad, A., Denny, C., Serdula, M. K., & Marks, J. S. (2003). Binge drinking among U.S. adults. *Journal of the American Medical Association, 289,* 70–75.

Najm, W. (1997). Viral hepatitis: How to manage type C and D infections. *Geriatrics, 52*(5), 28–37.

Narcotics Anonymous World Service Office, Inc. (1976). *The Group.* Van Nuys, CA: Author.

Narcotics Anonymous World Service Office, Inc. (1982). *Narcotics Anonymous.* Van Nuys, CA: Author.

Narcotics Anonymous World Service Office, Inc. (1983). *The triangle of self-obsession.* New York: Author.

Nathan, P. E. (1988). The addictive personality is the behavior of the addict. *Journal of Consulting and Clinical Psychology, 56,* 183–188.

Nathan, P. E. (1991). Substance use disorders in the DSM-IV. *Journal of Abnormal Psychology, 100,* 356–361.

National Academy of Sciences. (1990). *Treating drug problems* (Vol. 1). Washington, DC: National Academy Press.

National Center on Addiction and Substance Abuse at Columbia University. (2000). CASA releases physician survey. Press release, May 10, 2000.

National Commission on Marihuana and Drug Abuse. (1972). *Marihuana: A signal of misunderstanding.* Washington, DC: U.S. Government Printing Office.

National Commission on Marihuana and Drug Abuse. (1973). *Drug use in America: Problem in perspective.* Washington, DC: U.S. Government Printing Office.

National Foundation for Brain Research. (1992). *The cost of disorders of the brain.* Washington, DC: Author.

National Institute on Alcohol Abuse and Alcoholism. (1993a). Alcohol and cancer. *Alcohol Alert.* Washington, DC: Author.

National Institute on Alcohol Abuse and Alcoholism. (1993b). Alcohol and the liver. *Alcohol Alert.* Washington, DC: Author.

National Institute on Alcohol Abuse and Alcoholism. (1993c). Alcohol and nutrition. *Alcohol Alert.* Washington, DC: Author.

National Institute on Alcohol Abuse and Alcoholism. (1994). Alcohol and hormones. *Alcohol Alert.* Washington, DC: Author.

National Institute on Alcohol Abuse and Alcoholism. (1995). Alcohol-medication interactions. *Alcohol Alert.* Washington, DC: Author.

National Institute on Alcohol Abuse and Alcoholism. (1996). Drinking and driving. *Alcohol Alert.* Washington, DC: Author.

National Institute on Alcohol Abuse and Alcoholism. (1998). Alcohol and tobacco. *Alcohol Alert,* 39. Washington, DC: Author.

National Institute on Alcohol Abuse and Alcoholism. (2002). Alcohol and minorities: An update. *Alcohol Alert.* Washington, DC: Author.

National Institute on Drug Abuse. (1991). *National household survey on drug abuse: Population estimates 1990.* Rockville, MD: U.S. Government Printing Office.

National traffic death toll total highest since 1990. (2003). *La Crosse Tribune, 100*(4), p. A8.

Nazi meth on the rise. (2003). *Forensic Drug Abuse Advisor, 15,* 77–78.

Neeleman, J., & Farrell, M. (1997). Suicide and substance misuse. *British Journal of Psychiatry, 171,* 303–304.

Neergaard, L. (2004). Dieters, bodybuilders will lose ephedra; FDA ban takes effect April 12. *Milwaukee Journal Sentinel, 122*(84), 3A.

Negus, S. S., & Woods, J. H. (1995). Reinforcing effects, discriminative stimulus effects, and physical dependence liability of buprenorphine. In *Buprenorphine* (Cowan, A., & Lewis, J. W., eds.). New York: Wiley Interscience.

Nelipovich, M., & Buss, E. (1991). Investigating alcohol abuse among persons who are blind. *Journal of Visual Impairment & Blindness, 85,* 343–345.

Nelson, E. C., Heath, A. C., Bucholz, K. K., Madden, P. A. F., Fu, Q., Knopik, V., Lynskey, M. T., Whitfield, J. B., Statham, D. J., & Martin, N. G. (2004). Genetic epidemiology of alcohol-induced blackouts. *Archives of General Psychiatry, 61,* 257–263.

Nelson, H. D., Nevitt, M. C., Scott, J. C., Stone, K. L., & Cummings, S. R. (1994). Smoking, alcohol, and neuromuscular and physical function in older women. *Journal of the American Medical Association, 272,* 1825–1831.

Nelson, S., Mason, C., Kolls, J., & Summer, W. (1995). Pathophysiology of pneumonia. *Clinics in Chest Medicine, 16,* 1–12.

Nelson, T. (2000). Pharmacology of drugs of abuse. Seminar presented by the Division of Continuing Studies, University of Wisconsin—Madison, 29–31 March, 2000.

Nemeroff, C. B., Compton, M. T., & Berger, J. (2001). The depressed suicidal patient. In *Annals of the New York Academy of Sciences, 932,* 1–23.

Nesse, R. M., & Berridge, K. C. (1997). Psychoactive drug use in evolutionary perspective. *Science, 278,* 63–66.

Nestler, E. J. (1997). Basic neurobiology of heroin addiction. Paper presented at NIDA conference: Heroin Use and Addiction, Washington, DC, September 29.

Nestler, E. J., Hyman, S. E., & Malenka, R. C. (2001). Molecular neuropharmacology. In *From molecules to managed care* (Schultz, T. K., ed.). Chevy Chase, MD: American Society of Addiction Medicine.

Newcomb, M. D. (1996). Adolescence: Pathologizing a normal process. *The Counseling Psychologist, 24,* 482–490.

Newcomb, M. D., & Bentler, P. M. (1989). Substance use and abuse among children and teenagers. *American Psychologist, 44,* 242–248.

Newcomb, M. D., Galaif, E. R., & Carmona, J. V. (2001). The drug-crime nexus in a community sample of adults. *Psychology of Addictive Behaviors, 15,* 185–193.

New drug "ice" grips Hawaii, threatens mainland. (1989). *Minneapolis Star Tribune, VIII* (150), p. A12.

Newell, T., & Cosgrove, J. (1988). Recovery of neuropsychological functions during reduction of PCP use. Paper presented at the 1988 annual meeting of the American Psychological Association, Atlanta, GA.

A new market for a lethal drug. (1991). *Newsweek, CXVII* (7), 58.

Newton, R. E., Marunycz, J. D., Alderdice, M. C., & Napoliello, M. J. (1986). Review of the side effects of buspirone. *The American Journal of Medicine, 80* (Suppl. 3B), 17–21.

Nicastro, N. (1989). Visual disturbances associated with over-the-counter ibuprofen in three patients. *Annuals of Ophthalmology, 21,* 447–450.

Nielson, D. A., Virkkunen, M., Lappalainen, J., Eggert, M., Brown, G. L., Long, J. C., Goldman, D., & Linnoila, M. (1998). A tryptophan hydroxylase gene marker for suicidality and alcoholism. *Archives of General Psychiatry, 55,* 593–602.

Nisbet, P. A. (2000). Age and the lifespan. In *Comprehensive textbook of suicidology* (Maris, R. W., Berman, A. L., & Silverman, M. M., eds.). New York: Guilford.

Nishino, S., Mignot, E., & Dement, W. C. (1995). Sedative-hypnotics. In *Textbook of psychopharmacology* (Schatzberg, A. F., & Nemeroff, C. B., eds.). Washington, DC: American Psychiatric Association Press, Inc.

Noble, E. P., Blum, K., Ritchie, T., Montgomery, A., & Sheridan, P. F. (1991). Allelic association of the D2 dopamine receptor gene with receptor-binding characteristics in alcoholism. *Archives of General Psychiatry, 48,* 648–654.

Noble, S. L., King, D. S., & Olutade, J. I. (2000). Cyclooxygenase-2 enzyme inhibitors: Place in therapy. *American Family Physician, 61,* 3669–3676.

Norris, D. (1994). War's "wonder" drugs. *America's Civil War, 7*(2), 50–57.

Norris, K. (1998). *Amazing grace.* New York: Riverhead Books.

North, C. S. (1996). Alcoholism in women. *Postgraduate Medicine, 100*, 221–224, 230–232.

Norton, R. L., Burton, B. T., & McGirr, J. (1996). Blood lead of intravenous drug users. *Journal of Toxicology: Clinical Toxicology, 34*(4), 425–431.

Not enough data on how long marijuana users test positive. (1995). *Forensic Drug Abuse Advisor, 7*(9), 66–68.

Novello, A. C., & Shosky, J. (1992). From the Surgeon General, U.S. Public Health Service. *Journal of the American Medical Association, 268*, 961.

Nowak, M. A., & McMichael, A. J. (1995). How HIV defeats the immune system. *Scientific American, 273*(2), 58–65.

Nowak, R. (2004). How our brains fend off madness. *New Scientist, 183* (2462), 13.

Nowinski, J. (2003). Facilitating 12–Step recovery from substance abuse and addiction. In *Treating substance abuse: Theory and technique* (2nd ed.) (Rotgers, F., Morgenstern, J., & Walters, S.T., eds.). New York: Guilford.

Noxon, C. (2002). The trouble with rehab. *Playboy, 49*(3), 86–88, 152, 154, 156–157.

Nunes, J. V., & Parson, E. B. (1995). Patterns of psychoactive substance use among adolescents. *American Family Physician, 52*, 1693–1697.

Nutt, D. J. (1996). Addiction: Brain mechanisms and their treatment implications. *The Lancet, 347*, 31–36.

Nyffeler, T., Stabba, A., & Sturzenegger, M. (2003). Progressive myelopathy with selective involvement of the lateral and posterior columns after inhalation of heroin vapour. *Journal of Neurology, 250*, 496–498.

O'Brien, C. P. (1997). Progress in the science of addiction. *American Journal of Psychiatry, 154*, 1195–1197.

O'Brien, C. P. (1998). A range of research-based pharmacotherapies for addiction. *Science, 278*, 66–70.

O'Brien, C. P. (2001). Drug addiction and drug abuse. In *Pharmacological basis of therapeutics* (10th ed.) (Hardman, J. G., Limbird, L. E., & Gilman, A. G., eds.). New York: McGraw-Hill.

O'Brien, C. P. (2004). The mosaic of addiction. *American Journal of Psychiatry, 161*, 1741–1742.

O'Brien, C. P., & McLellan, A. T. (1996). Myths about the treatment of addiction. *The Lancet, 347*, 237–240.

O'Brien, P. E., & Gaborit, M. (1992). Codependency: A disorder separate from chemical dependency. *Journal of Clinical Psychology, 48* (1), 129–136.

Ochs, L. (1992). EEG treatment of addictions. *Biofeedback, 20*(1), 8–16.

O'Connor, P. G. (2000). Treating opioid dependence—New data and new opportunities. *New England Journal of Medicine, 343*, 1332–1333.

O'Connor, P. G., Chang, G., & Shi, J. (1992). Medical complications of cocaine use. In *Clinician's guide to cocaine addiction* (Kosten, T. R., & Kleber, H. D., eds.). New York: Guilford.

O'Dell, K. J., Turner, N. H., & Weaver, G. D. (1998). Women in recovery from drug misuse: An exploratory study of their social networks and social support. *Substance Use & Misuse, 33*, 1721–1734.

O'Donnell, M. (1986). The executive ailment: "Curable only by death." *International Management, 41*(7), 64.

O'Donovan, M. C., & McGuffin, P. (1993). Short acting benzodiazepines. *British Medical Journal, 306*, 182–183.

Oetting, E. R., Deffenbacher, J. L., & Donnermeyer, J. F. (1998). Primary socialization theory: The role played by personal traits in the etiology of drug use and deviance. II. *Substance Use & Misuse, 33*, 1337–1366.

O'Farrell, T. J. (1995). Marital and family therapy. In *Handbook of alcoholism treatment approaches* (2nd ed.) (Hester, R. K., & Miller, W. R., eds.). New York: Allyn & Bacon.

Office of National Drug Control Policy. (2001). *National drug control strategy*. Washington, DC: U.S. Government Printing Office.

Office of National Drug Control Policy. (2002). *The price of illicit drugs*. Washington, DC: U.S. Government Printing Office.

Office of National Drug Control Policy. (2004). *National drug control strategy*. Washington, DC: U.S. Government Printing Office.

Ogborne, A. C. (1993). Assessing the effectiveness of Alcoholics Anonymous in the community: Meeting the challenges. In *Research on Alcoholics Anonymous* (McCrady, B. S., & Miller, W. R., eds.). New Brunswick, NJ: Rutgers Center of Alcohol Studies.

Ogborne, A. C., & Glaser, F. B. (1985). Evaluating Alcoholics Anonymous. In *Alcoholism and substance abuse: Strategies for clinical intervention* (Bratter, T. E., & Forrest, G. G., eds.). New York: The Free Press.

Olds, D. L., Henderson, C. R., & Tatelbaum, R. (1994). Intellectual impairment in children of women who smoke cigarettes during pregnancy. *Pediatrics, 93*, 221–227.

Oliwenstein, L. (1988). The perils of pot. *Discover, 9*(6), 18.

Olmedo, R., & Hoffman, R. S. (2000). Withdrawal syndromes. *Emergency Medical Clinics of North America, 18*, 273–288.

Olmstead, T., White, W. D., & Sindelar, J. (2004). The impact of managed care on substance abuse treatment services. *Health Services Research, 39*(2) 319–343.

Olson, D. H., Mylan, M. M., Fletcher, L. A., Nugent, S. M., Lynch, J. W., & Willenbring, M. L. (1997). A clinical tool for rating response to civil commitment for substance abuse treatment. *Psychiatric Services, 48*, 1317–1322.

Olson, J. (1992). *Clinical pharmacology made ridiculously simple*. Miami, FL: MedMaster, Inc.

O'Malley, S., Adamse, M., Heaton, R. K., Gawin, F. G. (1992). Neuropsychological impairment in chronic cocaine abusers. *American Journal of Drug and Alcohol Abuse, 18*(2), 131–144.

ONDCP gives rundown on treatment P approaches. (1990). *Alcoholism & Drug Abuse Week, 2*(26), 3–5.

Ordorica, P. I., & Nace, P. E. (1998). Alcohol. In *Clinical textbook of addictive disorders* (2nd ed.) (Frances, R. J., & Miller, S. I., eds.). New York: Guilford.

Osher, F. C., & Drake, R. E. (1996). Reversing a history of unmet needs: Approaches to care for persons with co-occuring addictive and mental disorders. *American Journal of Orthopsychiatry*, 66, 4–11.

Osher, F. C., Drake, R. E., Noordsy, D. L., Teague, G. B., Hurlbut, S. C., Biesanz, J. C., & Beaudett, M. S. (1994). Correlates and outcomes of alcohol use disorder among rural outpatients with schizophrenia. *Journal of Clinical Psychiatry*, 55, 109–113.

Osher, F. C., & Kofoed, L. L. (1989). Treating patients with psychiatric and psychoactive substance abuse disorders. *Hospital and Community Psychiatry*, 40, 1025–1030.

Ostrea, E. M., Ostrea, A. R., & Simpson, P. M. (1997). Mortality within the first 2 years in infants exposed to cocaine, opiate or cannabinoid during gestation. *Pediatrics*, 100, 79–84.

Other AAFS highlights. (1995). *Forensic Drug Abuse Advisor*, 7(3), 18.

Otsuka, R., Watanabe, H., Hirata, K., Tokai, K., Muro, T., Yoshiyama, M., Takeuchi, K., & Yoshikawa, J. (2001). Acute effects of passive smoking on the coronary circulation in healthy young adults. *Journal of the American Medical Association*, 286, 436–441.

Ott, A., Slooter, A. J. C., Hofman, A., van Harskamp, F., Witteman, J. C. M., Broeckhoven, C. V., & van Duijn, C. M. (1998). Smoking and risk of dementia and Alzheimer's disease in a population-based cohort study: The Rotterdam study. *The Lancet*, 351, 1840–1843.

Otto, R. K., Lang, A. R., Megargee, E. I., & Rosenblatt, A. I. (1989). Ability of alcoholics to escape detection by the MMPI. *Critical Items*, 4(2), 2, 7–8.

Ouimette, P. C., Finney, J. W., & Moos, R. H. (1997). Twelve-Step and cognitive-behavioral treatment for substance abuse: A comparison of treatment effectiveness. *Journal of Consulting and Clinical Psychology*, 65, 230–240.

Overman, G. P., Teter, C. J., & Guthrie, S. K. (2003). Acamprosate for the adjunctive treatment of alcohol dependence. *The Annals of Pharmacotherapy*, 37, 1090–1099.

Owen, R. R., Fischer, E. P., Booth, B. M., & Cuffel, B. J. (1996). Medication noncompliance and substance abuse among patients with schizophrenia. *Psychiatric Services*, 47, 853–858.

Page, J. (2001). Take two aspirin and call me in the morning. *Smithsonian*, 32(5), 96–105.

Pagliaro, L. A., & Pagliaro, A. M. (1998). *The pharmacologic basis of therapeutics*. New York: Brunner-Mazel.

Pairet, M., van Ryn, J., Mauz, A., Schierok, H., Diederen, W., Turck, D., & Engelhardt, G. (1998). Differential inhibition of COX-1 and COX-2 by NSAIDS: A summary of results obtained using various test systems. In *Selective COX-2 inhibitors* (Vane, J., & Botting, J., eds.). Hingham, MA: Kluwer Academic Publishers.

Palella, F. J., Delaney, K. M., Moorman, A. C., Loveless, M. O., Fuhrer, J., Satten, G. A., Aschman, D. J., & Holmberg, S. D. (1998). Declining morbidity and mortality among paients with advanced human immunodeficiency virus infection. *The New England Journal of Medicine*, 338, 853–860.

Palmer, N. D., & Edmunds, C. N. (2003). Victims of sexual abuse and assault: Adults and children. In *Victim assistance*. New York: Springer.

Palmstierna, T. (2001). A model for predicting alcohol withdrawal delirium. *Psychiatric Services*, 52, 820–823.

Pape, P. A. (1988). EAP's and chemically dependent women. *Alcoholism & Addiction*, 8(6), 43–44.

Pappagallo, M. (1998). The concept of pseudotolerance to opioids. *Journal of Pharmacological Care and Symptom Control*, 6, 95–98.

Pappas, N. (1990). Dangerous liaisons: When food and drugs don't mix. *In Health*, 4(4), 22–24.

Pappas, N. (1995). Secondhand smoke: Is it a hazard? *Consumer Reports*, 60(1), 27–33.

Parini, S. (2003). Hepatitis C. *Nursing 2003*, 33(4), 57–63.

Paris, P. M. (1996). Treating the patient in pain. *Emergency Medicine*, 28(9), 66–76, 78–79, 83–86, 90.

Park, A. (2000). When did AIDS begin? *Time*, 155(6), 66.

Parker, G. B., Barrett, E. A., & Hickie, I. B. (1992). From nurture to network: Examining links between perceptions of parenting received in childhood and social bonds in adulthood. *American Journal of Psychiatry*, 149, 877–885.

Parker, R. N. (1993). The effects of context on alcohol and violence. *Alcohol Health & Research World*, 17(2), 117–122.

Parras, F., Patier, J. L., & Ezpeleta, C. (1988). Lead contaminated heroin as a source of inorganic lead intoxication. *The Staff*, 316, 755.

Parrott, A., Morinan, A., Moss, M., & Scholey, A. (2004). *Understanding drugs and behavior*. New York: John Wiley & Sons, Ltd.

Parrott, A. C. (1999). Does cigarette smoking cause stress? *American Psychologist*, 54, 817–820.

Parry, A. (1992). Taking heroin maintenance seriously: The politics of tolerance. *The Lancet*, 339, 350–351.

Parsons, O. A., & Nixon, S. J. (1993). Neurobehavioral sequelae of alcoholism. *Behavioral Neurology*, 11, 205–218.

Parthasarathy, S., Weisner, C., Hu, T. W., & Moore, C. (2000). Association of outpatient alcohol and drug treatment with health care utilization and cost: Revisiting the offset hypothesis. *Journal of Studies on Alcohol*, 62, 89–97.

Passaro, D. J., Werner, S. B., McGee, J., Mac Kenzie, W. R., & Vugia, D. J. (1998). Wound botulism associated with black tar heroin among injecting drug users. *Journal of the American Medical Association*, 279, 859–863.

Patel, K., & McHutchison, J. G. (2003). Current therapies for chronic hepatitis B. *Postgraduate Medicine*, 114, 48–52, 57–59, 62.

Patkar, A. A., Vergare, M. J., Batka, V., Weinstein, S. P., & Leone, F. T. (2003). Tobacco smoking: Current concepts in etiology and treatment. *Psychiatry*, 66(3), 183–199.

Paton, A. (1996). The detection of alcohol misuse in accident and emergency departments grasping the opportunity. *Journal of Accident & Emergency Medicine, 13,* 306–308.

Patrick, D. D. (2003). Dual diagnosis' substance-related and psychiatric disorders. *Nursing Clinics of North America, 38,* 67–73.

Paul, J. P., Stall, R., & Bloomfield, K. A. (1991). Gay and alcoholic. *Alcoholic Health & Research World, 15,* 151–160.

Payan, D. G., & Katzung, B. G. (1995). Nonsteroidal antiinflammatory drugs: Nonopioid analgesics; drugs used in gout. In *Basic & clinical pharmacology* (Katzung, B. G., ed.). Norwalk, CT: Appleton & Lange.

Pearlman, B. L. (2004). Hepatitis C infection: A clinical review. *Southern Medical Journal, (97),* 365–373.

Pearlson, G. D., Jeffery, P. J., Harris, G. J., Ross, C. A., Fischman, M. W., & Camargo, E. E. (1993). Correlation of acute cocaine-induced changes in local cerebral blood flow with subjective effects. *American Journal of Psychiatry, 150,* 495–497.

Pearson, M. A., Hoyme, E., Seaver, L. H., & Rimsza, M. E. (1994). Toluene embryopathy: Delineation of the phenotype and comparison with fetal alcohol syndrome. *Pediatrics, 93,* 211–215.

Peart, J., & Gross, G. (2004). Morphine-tolerant mice exhibit a profound and persistent cardioprotective phenotype. *Circulation, 109,* 1219–1222.

Pechnick, R. N., & Ungerleider, J. T. (2004). Hallucinogens. In *Textbook of substance abuse treatment* (3rd ed.) (Galanter, M., & Kleber, H. D., eds.). Washington, DC: American Psychiatric Press, Inc.

Peck, M. S. (1978). *The road less traveled.* New York: Simon & Schuster.

Peck, M. S. (1993). *Further along the road less traveled.* New York: Simon & Schuster.

Peck, M. S. (1997a). *Denial of the soul.* New York: Harmony Books.

Peck, M. S. (1997b). *The road less traveled & beyond.* New York: Simon & Schuster.

Peele, S. (1985). *The meaning of addiction.* Lexington, MA: D. C. Heath & Co.

Peele, S. (1989). *Diseasing of America.* Lexington, MA: D. C. Heath & Co.

Peele, S. (1994). Hype overdose: Why does the press automatically accept reports of heroin overdoses, no matter how thin the evidence? *National Review, 46(21),* 59–61.

Peele, S. (1998). All wet. *The Sciences, 38(2),* 17–21.

Peele, S. (2004a). Is AA's loss psychology's gain? *Monitor on Psychology, 35(7),* 86.

Peele, S. (2004b). The surprising truth about addiction. *Psychology Today, 37(3),* 43–46.

Peele, S., Brodsky, A., & Arnold, M. (1991). *The truth about addiction and recovery.* New York: Simon & Schuster.

Peluso, E., & Peluso, L. S. (1988). *Women & drugs.* Minneapolis: CompCare Publishers.

Peluso, E., & Peluso, L. S. (1989). Alcohol and the elderly. *Professional Counselor, 4(2),* 44–46.

Penick, E. C., Nickel, E. J., Cantrell, P. F., Powell, B. J., Read, M. R., & Thomas, M. M. (1990). The emerging concept of dual diagnosis: An overview and implications. In *Managing the dually diagnosed patient* (O'Connell, D. F., ed.). New York: The Halworth Press.

Peniston, E. G., & Kulkosky, P. J. (1990). Alcoholic personality and Alpha-Theta brainwave training. *Medical Psychotherapy, 3,* 37–55.

Pepper, B. (2004). Responding to co-occuring disorders: Status report. *Psychiatric Services, 55,* 343.

Perneger, T. V., Whelton, P. K., & Klag, M. J. (1994). Risk of kidney failure associated with the use of acetaminophen, aspirin, and nonsteroidal antiinflammatory drugs. *The New England Journal of Medicine, 331,* 1675–1679.

Peroutka, S. J. (1989). "Ecstasy": A human neurotoxin? *Archives of General Psychiatry, 46,* 191.

Perry, J. C., & Cooper, S. H. (1989). An empirical study of defense mechanisms. *Archives of General Psychiatry, 46,* 444–452.

Peters, H., & Theorell, C. J. (1991). Fetal and neonatal effects of maternal cocaine use. *Journal of Obstetric, Gynecologic, and Neonatal Nursing, 20(2),* 121–126.

Peters, R., Copeland, J., & Dillon, P. (1999). Anabolic-androgenic steroids: User characteristics, motivations and deterrents. *Psychology of Addictive Behaviors, 13(3),* 232–242.

Petersen, J. R. (1999). Snitch culture. *Playboy, 46(6),* 51.

Petersen, J. R. (2000). My millennium fix. *Playboy, 47(1),* 53–54.

Peterson, A. M. (1997). Analgesics. *RN, 60(4),* 45–50.

Peto, R., Chen, Z., & Boreham, J. (1996). Tobacco—The growing epidemic in China. *Journal of the American Medical Association, 275,* 1683–1684.

Peto, R., Lopez, A. D., Boreham, J., Thun, M., & Heath, C. (1992). Mortality from tobacco in developed countries: Indirect estimation from national vital statistics. *The Lancet, 339,* 1268–1278.

Petrakis, I. L., Gonzalez, G., Rosenheck, R., & Krystal, J. H. (2002). Comorbidity of alcoholism and psychiatric disorders. *Alcohol Research & Health, 26(2),* 81–89.

Pettine, K. A. (1991). Association of anabolic steroids and avascular necrosis of femoral heads. *The American Journal of Sports Medicine, 19(1),* 96–98.

Pettit, J. L. (2000). Melatonin. *Clinician Reviews, 10(6),* 87–88, 91.

Peyser, H. S. (1989). Alcohol and drug abuse: Underrecognized and untreated. *Hospital and Community Psychiatry, 40(3),* 221.

Pfefferbaum, A., Rosenbloom, M., Deshmukh, A., & Sullivan, E. V. (2001). Sex differences in the effects of alcohol on brain structure. *American Journal of Psychiatry, 158,* 188–197.

Pfefferbaum, A., Rosenbloom, M. J., Serventi, K., & Sullivan, E. V. (2004). Brain volumes, RBC status, and hepatic function in alcoholics after 1 and 4 weeks of sobriety: Predictors of outcome. *American Journal of Psychiatry, 161,* 1190–1196.

Pfefferbaum, A., Sullivan, E. V., Rosenbloom, M. J., Mathalon, D. H., & Lim, K. O. (1998). A controlled study of cortical gray matter and ventricular changes in alcoholic men over a 5 year interval. *Archives of General Psychiatry, 55*, 905–912.

Phelps, D. (1996). Records suggest nicotine enhanced. *Minneapolis Star Tribune, XV* (5), pp. A1, A22.

Phillips, A., Savigny, D., & Law, M. M. (1995). As Canadians butt out, the developing world lights up. *Canadian Medical Journal, 153*, 1111–1114.

Phillips, A. N., Wannamethee, M. W., Thomson, A., & Smith, G. D. (1996). Life expectancy in men who have never smoked and those who have smoked continuously: 15 year follow up of large cohort of middle aged British men. *British Medical Journal, 313*, 907–908.

Physicians' Desk Reference (58th ed.). (2004). Montvale, NJ: Thomson PDR.

Pies, R. W. (2003). Antidepressants and alcohol: How do they "mix"? Symposium presented to the Dept. of Psychiatry at The Cambridge Hospital, Boston, MA, March 7.

Piette, J. D., Heisler, M., & Wagner, T. H. (2004). Cost-related medication underuse. *Archives of Internal Medicine, 164*, 1749–1755.

Pihl, R. O. (1999). Substance abuse: Etiological considerations. In *Oxford textbook of psychopathology* (Millon, T., Blaney, P. H., & Davis, R. D., eds.). New York: Oxford University Press.

Pirisi, A., & Sims, S. (1997). Why we're so paranoid about pills. *Remedy, IV* (5), 20–25.

Pirkle, J., Flegal, K. M., Bernert, J. T., Brody, D. J., Etzel, R. A., & Maurer, K. R. (1996). Exposure of the U.S. population to environmental tobacco smoke. *Journal of the American Medical Association, 275*, 1233–1240.

Pirozzolo, F. J., & Bonnefil, V. (1995). Disorders appearing in the perinatal and neonatal period. In *Pediatric neuropsychology* (Batckhelor, E. S., & Dean, R. S., eds.). New York: Allyn & Bacon.

Plessinger, M. A., & Woods, J. R. (1993). Maternal, placental, and fetal pathophysiology of cocaine exposure during pregnancy. *Clinical Obstetrics and Gynecology, 36*, 267–278.

Pliszka, S. R. (1998). The use of psychostimulants in the pediatric patient. *Pediatric Clinics of North America, 45*, 1085–1098.

Polen, M. R., Sidney, S., Tekawa, I. S., Sadler, M., & Friedman, G. D. (1993). Health care use by frequent marijuana smokers who do not smoke tobacco. *Western Journal of Medicine, 158*, 596–601.

Politicians discover the drug war. (1996). *Forensic Drug Abuse Advisor, 8*(9), 70–72.

Polivy, J., & Herman, C. P. (2002). If at first you don't succeed. *American Psychologist, 57*, 677–689.

Pollock, N. K., & Martin, C. S. (1999). Diagnostic orphans: Adolescents with alcohol symptoms who do not qualify for a DSM-IV abuse or dependence diagnosis. *American Journal of Psychiatry, 156*, 897–901.

Pomerantz, R. J. (1998). How HIV resists eradication. *Hospital Practice, 33*(9), 87–90, 93–95, 99–101.

Pomerantz, R. J. (2003). Cross-talk and viral reservoirs. *Nature, 424*, 136–137.

Pomerleau, O. D., Collins, A. C., Shiffman, S., & Pomerleau, C. S. (1993). Why some people smoke and others do not: New perspectives. *Journal of Clinical and Consulting Psychology, 61*, 723–731.

Ponnappa, B. C., & Rubin, E. (2000). Modeling alcohol's effects on organs in animal models. *Alcohol Research & Health, 24*(2), 93–104.

Pope, H. G., & Brower, K. J. (2004). Anabolic-androgenic steroids. In *Textbook of substance abuse treatment* (3rd ed.) (Galanter, M., & Kleber, H. D., eds.). Washington, DC: American Psychiatric Press, Inc.

Pope, H. G., & Brower, K. J. (2005). Anabolic-androgenic steroid abuse. In *Kaplan & Sadock's comprehensive textbook of psychiatry* (8th ed.) (Sadock, B. J., & Sadock, V. A., eds.). New York: Lippincott, Williams & Wilkins.

Pope, H. G., Gruber, A. J., Hudson, J. I., Huestis, M. A., & Yurgelun-Todd, D. (2001). Neuropsychological performance in long-term cannabis users. *Archives of General Psychiatry, 58*, 909–915.

Pope, H. G., & Katz, D. L. (1987). Bodybuilder's psychosis. *The Lancet. 334*, 863.

Pope, H. G., & Katz, D. L. (1988). Affective and psychotic symptoms associated with anabolic steroid use. *American Journal of Psychiatry, 145*, 487–490.

Pope, H. G., & Katz, D. L. (1990). Homicide and near-homicide by anabolic steroid users. *Journal of Clinical Psychiatry, 51*(1), 28–31.

Pope, H. G., & Katz, D. L. (1991). What are the psychiatric risks of anabolic steroids? *The Harvard Mental Health Letter, 7*(10), 8.

Pope, H. G., & Katz, D. L. (1994). Psychiatric and medical effects of anabolic-androgenic steroid use. *Archives of General Psychiatry, 51*, 375–382.

Pope, H. G., Katz, D. L., & Champoux, R. (1986). Anabolic-androgenic steroid use among 1,010 college men. *The Physician and Sports Medicine, 17*(7), 75–81.

Pope, H. G., Kouri, E. M., & Hudson, J. I. (2000). Effects of supraphysiologic doses of testosterone on mood and aggression. *Archives of General Psychiatry, 57*, 133–140.

Pope, H. G., Phillips, K. A., & Olivardia, R. (2000). *The Adonis complex: The secret crisis of male body obsession.* New York: The Free Press.

Pope, H. G., & Yurgelun-Todd, D. (1996). The residual cognitive effects of heavy marijuana use in college students. *Journal of the American Medical Association, 275*, 521–527.

Porcerelli, J. H., & Sandler, B. A. (1998). Anabolic-pandrogenic steroid abuse and psychopathology. *The Psychiatric Clinics of North America, 21*, 829–833.

Post, R. M., Weiss, S. R. B., Pert, A., & Uhde, T. W. (1987). Chronic cocaine administration: Sensitization and kindling effects. In *Cocaine: Clinical and behavioral aspects*

(Fisher, S., Rashkin, A., & Unlenhuth, E. H., eds.). New York: Oxford University Press.

Potenza, M. N., Fiellin, D. A., Heninger, G. R., Rounsaville, B. J., & Mazure, C. M. (2002). Gambling: An addictive behavior with health and primary care implications. *Journal of General Internal Medicine*, 17(9), 721–732.

Potenza, M. N., Kosten, T. R., & Rounsaville, B. J. (2001). Pathological gambling. *Journal of the American Medical Association*, 286, 141–144.

Potter, J. D. (1997). Hazards and benefits of alcohol. *The New England Journal of Medicine*, 337, 1763–1764.

Potter, W. Z., Rudorfer, M. V., & Goodwin, F. K. (1987). Biological findings in bipolar disorders. In *American Psychiatric Association Annual Review* (Vol. 6). Washington, DC: American Psychiatric Association Press, Inc.

Potterton, R. (1992). A criminal system of justice. *Playboy*, 39(9), 46–47.

Prater, C. D., Miller, K. E., & Zylstra, R. G. (1999). Outpatient detoxification of the addicted or alcoholic patient. *American Family Physician*, 60, 1175–1183.

Predicting drug-related impairment. (2004). *Forensic Drug Abuse Advisor*, 16(3), 21–22.

Prescott, C. A., & Kendler, K. S. (1999). Genetic and environmental contributions to alcohol abuse and dependence in a population-based sample of male twins. *American Journal of Psychiatry*, 156, 34–40.

Preston, K. L., Epstein, D. H., Cone, E. J., Wtsadik, A. T., Huestis, M. A., & Moolchan, E. D. (2002). Urinary elimination of cocaine metabolites in chronic users during cessation. *Journal of Analytical Toxicology*, 27, 393–400.

Preston, R. (1999). The demon in the freezer. *The New Yorker*, LXXV (18), 44–61.

Preuss, U. W., Schuckit, M. A., Smith, T. L., Danko, G. P., Bucholz, K. K., Hesslebrock, V., & Kramer, J. R. (2003). Predictors and correlates of suicide attempts over 5 years in 1,237 alcohol-dependent men and women. *American Journal of Psychiatry*, 160, 56–63.

Preuss, U. W., & Wong, W. M. (2000). Comorbidity. In *Handbook of Alcoholism* (Zernig, G., Saria, A., Kurz, M., & O'Malley, S. S., eds.). New York: CRC Press.

Pristach, C. A., & Smith, C. M. (1990). Medication compliance and substance abuse among schizophrenic patients. *Hospital and Community Psychiatry*, 41, 1345–1348.

Prochaska, J. O. (1998). Stage model of change. Paper presented at symposium, Gundersen-Lutheran Medical Center, La Crosse, WI, September 17.

Prochaska, J. O. (2002). Stages of change: 25 years of addiction treatment. Symposium presented to the Dept. of Psychiatry at The Cambridge Hospital, Boston, MA, February 1.

Prochaska, J. O., DiClemente, C. C., & Norcross, J. C. (1992). In search of how people change. *American Psychologist*, 47, 1102–1114.

Pursch, J. A. (1987). Mental illness and addiction. *Alcoholism & Addiction*, 7(6), 42.

Purow, D. B., & Jacobson, I. M. (2003). Slowing the progression of chronic hepatitis B. *Postgraduate Medicine*, 114, 65–76.

Putnam, F. W. (1989). *Diagnosis and treatment of multiple personality disorder*. New York: The Guilford Press.

Quinolones may cause false positive opiate tests. (2002). *Forensic Drug Abuse Advisor*, 14(1), 2–3.

Qureshi, A., & Lee-Chiong, T. (2004). Medications and their effects on sleep. *Medical Clinics of North America*, 88, 751–766.

Rabinowitz, J., Cohen, H., & Kotler, M. (1998). Outcomes of ultrarapid opiate detoxification combined with naltrexone maintenance and counseling. *Psychiatric Services*, 49, 831–834.

Rabinowitz, J., & Marjefsky, S. (1998). Predictors of being expelled from and dropping out of alcohol treatment. *Psychiatric Services*, 49, 187–189.

RachBeisel, J., Scott, J., & Dixon, L. (1999). Co-occurring severe mental illness and substance use disorders: A review of recent research. *Psychiatric Services*, 50, 1427–1434.

Racine, A., Joyce, T., & Anderson, R. (1993). The association between prenatal care and birth weight among women exposed to cocaine in New York City. *Journal of the American Medical Association*, 270, 1581–1586.

Rado, T. (1988). The client with a dual diagnosis—A personal perspective. *The Alcohol Quarterly*, 1(1), 5–7.

Rains, V. S. (1990). Alcoholism in the elderly—The hidden addiction. *Medical Aspects of Human Sexuality*, 24(10), 40–42, 43.

Rall, T. W. (1990). Hypnotics and sedatives. In *The pharmacological basis of therapeutics* (8th ed.) (Gilman, A. G., Rall, T. W., Nies, A. S., & Taylor, P, eds.). New York: Pergamon Press.

Ramaekers, J. G., Berghaus, G., van Laar, M., & Drummer, O. H. (2004). Dose-related risk of motor vehicle crashes after cannabis use. *Drug & Alcohol Dependence*, 73(2), 109–119.

Ramcharan, S., Meenhorst, P. L., Otten, J. M. M. B., Koks, C. H. W., de Boer, D., Maes, R. A. A., & Beijnen, J. H. (1998). Survival after massive ecstasy overdose. *Journal of Toxicology: Clinical Toxicology*, 36, 727.

Ramlow, B. E., White, A. L., Watson, D. D., & Leukefeld, C. G. (1997). The needs of women with substance use problems: An expanded vision for treatment. *Substance Use & Misuse*, 32, 1395–1404.

Ramsay, J. R. & Newman, C. F. (2000). Substance abuse. *In Cognitive-behavioral strategies in crisis intervention* (2nd ed.) (Dattilo, F. M., & Freeman, A., eds.). New York: Guilford.

Rand, L. (1995). A different road. *Chicago Tribune*, 148(53), Tempo section: 1, 7.

Randall, T. (1992). Medical news & perspectives. *Journal of the American Medical Association*, 268, 1505–1506.

Randle, K. D., Estes, R., & Cone, W. P. (1999). *The abduction enigma*. New York: Forge.

Randolph, W. M., Stroup-Benham, C., Black, S. A., & Markides, K. S. (1998). Alcohol use among Cuban-Americans, Mexican-Americans, and Puerto-Ricans. *Alcohol Health & Research World*, 22, 265–269.

Rapoport, R. J. (1993). The efficacy and safety of oxaproxzin versus aspirin: Pooled results of double-blind trials in osteoarthritis. *Drug Therapy, 23*(Suppl.), 3–8.

Raskin, V. D. (1994). Psychiatric aspects of substance use disorders in childbearing populations. *Psychiatric Clinics of North America, 16,* 157–165.

Rasymas, A. (1992). Basic pharmacology and pharmacokinetics. *Clinics in Podiatric Medicine and Surgery, 9,* 211–221.

Rathbone-McCuan, E., & Stokke, D. (1997). Lesbian women and substance abuse. In *Gender and addictions* (Straussner, S. L. A., & Zelvin, E., eds.). Northvale, NJ: Jason-Aronson.

Raut, C. P., Stephen, A., & Kosopsky, B. (1996). Intrauterine effects of substance abuse. In *Sourcebook of substance abuse and addiction* (Friedman, L., Fleming, N. F., Roberts, D. H., & Hyman, S. E., eds.). New York: Williams & Wilkins.

Ravel, R. (1989). *Clinical laboratory medicine: Clinical application of laboratory data* (5th ed.). Chicago: Year Book Medical Publishers, Inc.

Raw data. (1990). *Playboy, 37*(1), 16.

Rawson, R. A., Gonzales, R., & Brethen, P. (2002). Treatment of methamphetamine use disorders: An update. *Journal of Substance Abuse Treatment, 23,* 145–150.

Ray, O. S., & Ksir, C. (1993). *Drugs, society and human behavior* (6th ed.). St. Louis: C. V. Mosby.

Redfearn, P. J., Agrawal, N., & Mair, L. H. (1998). An association between the regular use of 3,4 methylendioxymethamphetamine (ecstasy) and excessive wear of the teeth. *Addiction, 93*(5), 745–748.

Redman, G. L. (1990). Adolescents and anabolics. *American Fitness, 8*(3), 30–33.

Reeves, D., & Wedding, D. (1994). *The clinical assessment of memory.* New York: Springer Publishing Co.

Rehman, Q., & Sack, K. E. (1999). When to try COX-2 specific inhibitors. *Postgraduate Medicine, 106,* 95–105.

Reid, M. C., & Anderson, P. A. (1997). Geriatric substance use disorders. *Medical Clinics of North America, 81,* 999–1016.

Reiman, E. M. (1997). Anxiety. In *The practitioner's guide to psychoactive drugs* (4th ed.) (Gelenberg, A. J., & Bassuk, E. L., eds.). New York: Plenum.

Reinisch, J. M., Sanders, S. A., Mortensen, E. L., & Rubin, D. B. (1995). In utero exposure to phenobarbital and intelligence deficits in adult men. *Journal of the American Medical Association, 174,* 1518–1525.

Reiser, M. F. (1984). *Mind, brain, body.* New York: Basic Books, Inc.

Reisine, T., & Pasternak, G. (1995). Opioid analgesics and antagonists. In *The pharmacological basis of therapeutics* (9th ed.) (Hardman, J. G., & Limbird, L. E., eds.). New York: McGraw-Hill.

Renaud, S., & DeLorgeril, M. (1992). Wine, alcohol, and the French paradox for coronary heart disease. *The Lancet, 339,* 1523–1526.

Reneman, L., Booij, J., Schmand, B., van den Brink, W., & Gunning, B. (2000). Memory disturbances in "ecstasy" users are correlated with an altered brain serotonin neurotransmission. *Psychopharmacology, 148,* 322–324.

Renerman, L., Lavalaye, J., Schmand, B., de Wolff, F. A., van den Brink, W., den Heeten, G. J., & Booij, J. (2001). Cortical serotonin transporter density and verbal memory in individuals who stopped using 3,4–methylenedioxymethamphetamine (MDMA or "ecstasy"). *Archives of General Psychiatry, 58,* 901–906.

Renner, J. A. (2001). Dual diagnosis in treatment resistant adults. Symposium presented to the Dept. of Psychiatry at The Cambridge Hospital, Boston, MA, March 3.

Renner, J. A. (2004). Alcoholism and alcohol abuse. In *Massachusetts General Hospital psychiatry update and board preparation* (2nd ed.) (Stern, T. A., & Herman, J. B., eds.). New York: McGraw-Hill.

Report of the Institute of Medicine committee on the efficacy and safety of Halcion. (1999). *Archives of General Psychiatry, 56,* 349–352.

Research on nitrites suggests drug plays role in AIDS epidemic. (1989). *AIDS Alert, 4*(9), 153–156.

Restak, R. (1984). *The brain.* New York: Bantam Books.

Restak, R. (1991). *The brain has a mind of its own.* New York: Harmony Books.

Restak, R. (1994). *Receptors.* New York: Bantam Books.

Revkin, A. C. (1989). Crack in the cradle. *Discover, 10*(9), 63–69.

Rexrode, K. M., Buring, J. E., Glynn, R. J., Stampfer, M. J., Youngman, L. D., & Gaziano, J. M. (2001). Analgesic use and renal function in men. *Journal of the American Medical Association, 286,* 315–321.

Reynaud, M., Schwan, R., Loiseaux-Meunier, M. N., Albuisson, E., & Deteix, P. (2001). Patients admitted to emergency services for drunkenness: Moderate alcohol users or harmful drinkers. *American Journal of Psychiatry, 158,* 96–99.

Reynolds, E. W., & Bada, H. S. (2003). Pharmacology of drugs of abuse. *Obstetrics and Gynecology Clinics of North America, 30,* 501–522.

Rhee, S. H., Hewitt, J. K., Young, S. E., Corley, R. P., Crowley, T. J., & Stallings, M. C. (2003). Genetic and environmental influences on substance initiation, use, and problem use in adolescents. *Archives of General Psychiatry, 60,* 1256–1264.

Rice, C., & Duncan, D. F. (1995). Alcohol use and reported physician visits in older adults. *Preventive Medicine, 24,* 229–234.

Rice, D. P. (1993). The economic cost of alcohol abuse and alcohol dependence: 1990. *Alcohol Health & Research World, 17*(1), 10–11.

Richards, J. R. (2000). Rhabdomyolsis and drugs of abuse. *Journal of Emergency Medicine, 19,* 51–56.

Richardson, S. (1995). The race against AIDS. *Discover, 16*(5), 28–32.

Rickels, K., Schweizer, E., Csanalosi, I., Case, W. G., & Chung, H. (1988). Long-term treatment of anxiety and risk of withdrawal. *Archives of General Psychiatry, 45,* 444–450.

Rickels, K., Schweizer, E., Case, W. G., Greenblatt, D. J. (1990). Long-term therapeutic use of benzodiazepines: I. Effects of abrupt discontinuation. *Archives of General Psychiatry, 47,* 899–907.

Rickels, L. K., Giesecke, M. A., & Geller, A. (1987). Differential effects of the anxiolytic drugs, diazepam and buspirone on memory function. *British Journal of Clinical Pharmacology, 23,* 207–211.

Ridker, P. M., Cushman, M., Stampfer, M. J., Tracy, R. P., & Hennekens, C. H. (1997). Inflammation, aspirin, and the risk of cardiovascular disease in apparently healthy men. *The New England Journal of Medicine, 336,* 973–979.

Ries, R. K., & Ellingson, T. (1990). A pilot assessment at one month of 17 dual diagnosis patients. *Hospital and Community Psychiatry, 41,* 1230–1233.

Ries, R. K., Russo, J., Wingerson, D., Snowden, M., Comtois, K. A., Srebnik, D., & Roy-Byrne, P. (2000). Shorter hospital stays and more rapid improvement among patients with schizophrenia and substance disorders. *Psychiatric Services, 51,* 210–215.

Riggs, P. D. (2003). Treating adolescents for substance abuse and comorbid psychiatric disorders. *Science & Practice Perspectives, 2*(1), 18–28.

Rigler, S. K. (2000). Alcoholism in the elderly. *American Family Physician, 61,* 1710–1716.

Riley, J. A. (1994). Dual diagnosis. *Nursing Clinics of North America, 29,* 29–34.

Rimm, E. B., Chan, J., Stampfer, M. J., Colditz, G. A., & Willett, W. C. (1995). Prospective study of cigarette smoking, alcohol use, and the risk of diabetes in men. *British Medical Journal, 310,* 555–559.

Ringwald, C. D. (2002). *The soul of recovery.* New York: Oxford University Press.

Ritalin may increase risk of cocaine use later. (1998). *Alcoholism & Drug Abuse Week, 10*(17), 8.

Ritsher, J. B., Moos, R. H., & Finney, J. W. (2002). Relationship of treatment orientation and continuing care to remission among substance abuse patients. *Psychiatric Services, 53,* 595–601.

Ritz, M. C. (1999). Molecular mechanisms of addictive substances. In *Drugs of abuse and addiction: Neurobehavioral toxicology* (Niesink, R. J. M., Jaspers, R. M. A., Korney, L. M. W., & van Ree, J. M., eds.). New York: CRC Press.

Rivara, F. P., Mueller, B. A., Somes, G., Mendoza, C. T., Rushforth, N. B., & Kellerman, A. L. (1997). Alcohol and illicit drug use and the risk of violent death in the home. *Journal of the American Medical Association, 278,* 569–575.

Roane, K. R. (2000). A scourge of drugs strikes a pious place. *U.S. News & World Report, 128*(9), 26–28.

Robbins, A. S., Manson, J. E., Lee, I., Satterfield, S., & Hennekens, C. H. (1994). Cigarette smoking and stroke in a cohort of U.S. male physicians. *Annals of Internal Medicine, 120,* 458–462.

Roberts, D. H., & Bush, B. (1996). Inpatient management issues and pain management. In *Sourcebook of substance abuse and addiction* (Friedman, L., Fleming, N. F., Roberts, D. H., & Hyman, S. E., eds.). New York: Williams & Wilkins.

Roberts, D. J. (1995). Drug abuse. In *Conn's current therapy* (Rakel, R. E., ed.). Philadelphia: W. B. Saunders Co.

Roberts, J. R., & Tafure, J. A. (1990). Benzodiazepines. In *Clinical management of poisoning and drug overdose* (2nd ed.) (Haddad, L., & Winchester, J. F., eds.). Philadelphia: W. B. Saunders Co.

Roberts, L. J., & Leonard, K. E. (1998). An empirical typology of drinking partnerships and their relationship to marital functioning and drinking consequences. *Journal of Marriage and Family, 60,* 515–526.

Roberts, R. O., Jacobson, D. J., Girman, C. J., Rhodes, T., Lieber, M. M., & Jacobsen, S. J. (2002). A population-based study of daily nonsteroidal anti-inflammatory drug use and prostate cancer. *Mayo Clinic Proceedings, 77,* 219–225.

Robinson, D. J., Lazo, M. C., Davis, T., & Kufera, J. A. (2000). Infective endocarditis in intravenous drug users: Does HIV status alter the presenting temperature and white cell count? *Journal of Emergency Medicine, 19,* 5–11.

Robson, P. (2001). Therapeutic aspects of cannabis and cannabinoids. *British Journal of Psychiatry, 178,* 107–115.

Rochester, J. A., & Kirchner, J. T. (1999). Ecstasy (3,4–Methylenedioxymethamphetamine): History, neurochemistry and toxicity. *Journal of the American Board of Family Practice, 12,* 137–142.

Roden, D. M. (2004). Drug-induced prolongation of the QT interval. *New England Journal of Medicine, 350,* 1013–1022.

Rodgers, J. E. (1994). Addiction—A whole new view. *Psychology Today, 27*(5), 32–38, 72, 74, 76, 79.

Rodman, M. J. (1993). OCT interactions. *RN, 56*(1), 54–60.

Roehling, P., Koelbel, N., & Rutgers, C. (1994). Codependence—Pathologizing feminity? Paper presented at the 1994 annual meeting of the American Psychological Association, Los Angeles, CA.

Roehrs, T., & Roth, T. (1995). Alcohol-induced sleepiness and memory function. *Alcohol Health & Research World, 19*(2), 130–135.

Rogers, C. R. (1961). *On becoming a person.* Boston: Houghton-Mifflin Co.

Rogers, J., Buchanan, T., Scholey, A. B., Heffernan, T. M., Ling, J., & Parrott, A. C. (2003). Patterns of drug use and the influence of gender on self-reports of memory ability in ecstasy users: A web-based study. *Journal of Psychopharmacology, 17*(4), 389–396.

Rogers, P. D., Harris, J., & Jarmuskewicz, J. (1987). Alcohol and adolescence. *The Pediatric Clinics of North America, 34*(2), 289–303.

Rohde, P., Lewinsohn, P. M., Kahler, C. W., Seeley, J. R., & Brown, R. A. (2001). Natural course of alcohol use disorders from adolescence to young adulthood. *Journal of the American Academy of Child and Adolescent Psychiatry, 40,* 83–90.

Rohypnol and date rape. (1997). *Forensic Drug Abuse Advisor,* 9(1), 1–2.

Rohypnol use spreading throughout southern U.S. (1995). *Substance Abuse Letter,* 2(1), 1, 6.

Roine, R., Gentry, T., Hernandez-Munoz, R., Baraona, E., & Lieber, C. S. (1990). Aspirin increases blood alcohol concentrations in humans after ingestion of alcohol. *Journal of the American Medical Association, 264,* 2406–2408.

Rold, J. F. (1993). Mushroom madness. *Postgraduate Medicine, 78*(5), 217–218.

Romach, M. K., Glue, P., Kampman, K., Kaplan, H. L., Somer, G. R., Poole, S., Clarke, L., Coffin, V., Cornish, J., O'Brien, C. P., & Sellers, E. M. (1999). Attenuation of the euphoric effects of cocaine by the Dopamine D1/D5 antagonist Ecopipam (SCH 39166). *Archives of General Psychiatry, 56,* 1101–1106.

Roman, P. M., & Blum, T. C. (1996). *American Journal of Health Promotion, 11*(2), 136–149.

Rome, H. P. (1984). Psychobotanica revisited. *Psychiatric Annuals, 14,* 711–712.

Rootes, L. E., & Aanes, D. L. (1992). A conceptual framework for understanding self-help groups. *Hospital and Community Psychiatry, 43,* 379–381.

Rose, G. S. (2001). Motivational interviewing. Symposium presented to the Dept. of Psychiatry of The Cambridge Hospital, Boston, MA, March 2.

Rose, J. E., Behm, F. M., Westman, E. C., Mathew, R. J., London, E. D., Hawk, T. C. Turkington, T. G., & Coleman, R. E. (2003). PET studies of the influences of nicotine on neural systems in cigarette smokers. *American Journal of Psychiatry, 160,* 323–333.

Rose, K. J., (1988). *The body in time.* New York: John Wiley & Sons, Inc.

Rosenbaum, J. F. (1990). Switching patients from alprazolam to clonazepam. *Hospital and Community Psychiatry, 41,* 1302.

Rosenbaum, J. F., & Gelenberg, A. J. (1991). Anxiety. In *The practitioner's guide to psychoactive drugs* (3rd ed.) (Gelenberg, A. J., Bassuk, E. L., & Schoonover, S. C., eds.). New York: Plenum.

Rosenbaum, R. (1999). *Zen and the heart of psychotherapy.* New York: Brunner/Mazel.

Rosenberg, A. (1996). Brain damage caused by prenatal alcohol exposure. *Scientific American Medicine, 3*(4), 42–51.

Rosenberg, C. E. (2002). The tyranny of diagnosis: Specific entities and individual experience. *The Milbank Quarterly, 80* (2), 237–260.

Rosenberg, H. (1997). Use and abuse of illicit drugs among older people. In *Older adults' misuse of alcohol, medicines and other drugs* (Gurnack, A. M., ed.). New York: Springer Publishing Co.

Rosenberg, N. (1989). Nervous systems effects of toluene and other organic solvents. *The Western Journal of Medicine, 150,* 571–573.

Rosenbloom, D. L. (2000). The community perspective on addictions: joining together. Symposium presented to the Dept. of Psychiatry at The Cambridge Hospital, Boston, MA, March 3.

Rosenblum, M. (1992). Ibuprofen provides longer lasting analgesia than fentanyl after laparoscopic surgery. *Journal of the American Medical Association, 267,* 219.

Rosenthal, E. (1992). Bad fix. *Discover, 13*(2), 82–84.

Ross, A. (1991). Poland's dark harvest. *In Health, 5*(4), 66–70.

Ross, G. R. (2002). Child and adolescent alcohol and drug use. Seminar presented by the Cross Country University, Milwaukee, WI, June 6, 2002.

Ross, S. M., & Chappel, J. N. (1998). Substance use disorders. *The Psychiatric Clinics of North America, 21,* 803–828.

Rosse, R. B., Collins, J. P., Fay-McCarthy, M., Alim, T. N., Wyatt, R. J., & Deutsch, S. I. (1994). Phenomenologic comparison of the idiopathic psychosis of schizophrenia and drug-induced cocaine and phencyclidine psychosis: A retrospective study. *Clinical Neuropharmacology, 17,* 359–369.

Rothenberg, L. (1988). The ethics of intervention. *Alcoholism & Addiction, 9*(1), 22–24.

Rothman, R. B., Vu, N., Partilla, J. S., Roth, B. L., Hufeisen, S. J., Compton-Toth, B. A., Birkes, J., Young, R., & Glennon, R. A. (2003). In vitro characterization of ephedrine-related stereoisomers at biogenic amine transporters and the receptorome reveals selective actions as norepinephrine transporter substrates. *Journal of Pharmacology and Experimental Therapeutics, 307,* 138–145.

Rothwell, P. M., & Grant, R. (1993). Cerebral venous sinus thrombosis induced by "ecstasy." *Journal of Neurology, Neurosurgery and Psychiatry, 56,* 1035.

Rouse, S. V., Butcher, J. N., & Miller, K. B. (1999). Assessment of substance abuse in psychotherapy clients: The effective of the MMPI-2 substance abuse scales. *Psychological Assessment 11*(1), 101–1–7.

Rowe, C. (1998). Just say no. *Playboy, 45*(10), 44–45.

Roy, A. (1993). Risk factors for suicide among adult alcoholics. *Alcohol Health & Research World, 17,* 133–136.

Roy, A. (2001). Characteristics of cocaine-dependent patients who attempt suicide. *American Journal of Psychiatry, 158,* 1215–1219.

Roy, A. (2003). Characteristics of HIV patients who attempt suicide. *Acta Psychiatrica Scandinavica, 107,* 41–44.

Royko, M. (1990). Drug war's over: Guess who won. *Playboy. 37*(1), 46.

Ruben, D. H. (2001). *Treating adult children of alcoholics.* New York: Academic Press.

Rubin, E., & Doria, J. (1990). Alcoholic cardiomyopathy. *Alcohol Health & Research World, 14*(4), 277–284.

Rubin, R. H. (1993). Acquired immunodeficiency syndrome. In *Scientific American medicine* (Rubenstein, E., & Federman, D. D., eds.). New York: Scientific American Press, Inc.

Rubino, F. A. (1992). Neurologic complications of alcoholism. *Psychiatric Clinics of North America, 15,* 359–372.

Rubins, J. B., & Janoff, E. N. (1997). Community-acquired pneumonia. *Postgraduate Medicine, 102*(6), 45–60.

Rubinstein, L., Campbell, F., & Daley, D. (1990). Four perspectives on dual diagnosis: Overview of treatment issues. In *Managing the dually diagnosed patient* (O'Connell, D. F., ed.). New York: The Halworth Press.

Russell, J. M., Newman, S. C., & Bland, R. C. (1994). Drug abuse and dependence. *Acta Psychiatrica Scandinavica, Supplement 376*, 54–62.

Russo, M. W. (2004). Hepatitis B. *Emergency Medicine, 36*(3), 37–44.

Rustin, T. (1988). Treating nicotine addiction. *Alcoholism & Addiction, 9*(2), 18–19.

Rustin, T. (1992). Review of nicotine dependence and its treatment. Consultation to La Crosse addiction treatment programs, Lutheran Hospital and St. Francis Hospitals. Symposium conducted for staff, Lutheran Hospital, La Crosse, WI, August.

Rustin, T. (2000). Assessing nicotine dependence. *American Family Physician, 62*, 579–584.

Rx drugs. (1992). *60 Minutes*. XXV (15). Livingston, NJ: Burrelle's Information Services.

Rychtarik, R. G., Connors, G. J., Whitney, R. B., McGillicuddy, N. B., Fitterling, J. M., & Wirtz, P. W. (2000). Treatment settings for persons with alcoholism: Evidence for matching clients to inpatient versus outpatient care. *Journal of Consulting and Clinical Psychology, 68*, 277–289.

Ryglewicz, H., & Pepper, B. (1996). *Lives at risk*. New York: The Free Press.

Saag, M. S. (1997). Use of HIV viral load in clinical practice: Back to the future. *Annals of Internal Medicine, 126*, 983–986.

Saal, D., Dong, Y., Bonci, A., & Malenka, R. C. (2003). Drugs of abuse and stress trigger a common synaptic adaptation in dopamine neurons. *Neuron, 37*(4), 577–582.

Sabbag, R. (1994, May 5). The cartels would like a second chance. *Rolling Stone*, 35–37, 43.

Sacco, R. L. (1995). Risk factors and outcomes for ischemic stroke. *Neurology, 45* (Suppl. 1), S10–S14.

Sacks, O. (1970). *The man who mistook his wife for a hat*. New York: Harper & Row.

Sadock, B. J., & Sadock, V. A. (2003). *Kaplan and Sadock's synopsis of psychiatry* (9th ed.). New York: Lippincott, Williams & Wilkins.

Saffer, H. (2002). Alcohol advertising and youth. *Journal of Studies on Alcohol* (Suppl. 14), 173–181.

Sagar, S. M. (1991). Toxic and metabolic disorders. In *Manual of neurology* (Samuels, M. A., ed.). Boston: Little, Brown & Co.

Saitz, R. (1998). Introduction to alcohol withdrawal. *Alcohol Health & Research World, 22*(1), 5–12.

Saitz, R., Ghali, W. A., & Moskowitz, M. A. (1997). The impact of alcohol-related diagnoses on pneumonia outcomes. *Archives of Internal Medicine, 157*, 1446–1452.

Saitz, R., & O'Malley, S. S. (1997). Pharmacotherapies for alcohol abuse. *Medical Clinics of North America, 81*, 881–907.

Salloway, S. (1998) The nucleus accumbens: A key structure mediating substance abuse and reward. *Psychiatric Times, XV* (4), 62–64.

Samenuk, D., Link, M. S., Homoud, M. K., Contreras, R., Theohardes, T. C., Wang, P. J., & Estes, N. A. M. (2002). Adverse cardiovascular events temporally associated with Ma Huang, an herbal source of ephedrine. *Mayo Clinic Proceedings, 77*, 12–16.

Sampson, H. W. (2002). Alcohol and other risk factors affecting osteoporosis risk in women. *Alcohol Research & Health, 26*(4), 292–298.

Sanchez, L. M., & Turner, S. M. (2003). Practicing psychology in the era of managed care. *American Psychologist, 58*, 116–129.

Sanders, S. R. (1990). Under the influence. *The Family Therapy Networker, 14*(1), 32–37.

Sandler, R. S., Halabi, S., Baron, J. A., Budinger, S., Paskett, E., Keresztes, R., Petrelli, N., Pipas, M., Karp, D. D., Loprinzi, C. L., Steinback, G., & Schilsky, R. (2003). A randomized trial of aspirin to prevent colorectal adenomasa in patients with previous colorectal cancer. *New England Journal of Medicine, 348*, 883–890.

Sands, B. F., Creelman, W. L., Ciraulo, D. A., Greenblatt, D. J., & Shader, R. I. (1995). Benzodiazepines. In *Drug interactions in psychiatry* (2nd ed.) (Ciraulo, D. A., Shader, R. I., Greenblatt, D. J., & Creelman, W., eds.). Baltimore: Williams & Wilkins.

Sands, B. F., Knapp, C. M., & Ciraulo, D. A. (1993). Medical consequences of alcohol-drug interactions. *Alcohol Health & Research World, 17*, 316–320.

Sanford, L. T. (2004). The power of shame in addiction treatment. Symposium presented to the Dept. of Psychiatry at The Cambridge Hospital, Boston, MA, March 5.

Sanna, P. P., & Koob, G. F. (2004). Cocaine's long run. *Nature Medicine, 10*(4), 340–341.

Sapolsky, R. (1997). A gene for nothing. *Discover, 18*(10), 40–46.

Sapolsky, R. (1998). Is biology destiny? *Family Therapy Networker, 22*(2), 33–35.

Sarid-Segal, O., Creelman, W. L., Ciraulo, D. A., & Shader, R. I. (1995). Lithium. In *Drug interactions in psychiatry* (2nd ed.) (Ciraulo, D. A., Shader, R. I., Greenblatt, D. J., & Creelman, W., eds.). Baltimore: Williams & Wilkins.

Satel, S. L. (2000). The limits of drug treatment and the case for coercion. Symposium presented to the Dept. of Psychiatry at The Cambridge Hospital, Boston, MA, March 3.

Satel, S. L., & Edell, W. S. (1991). Cocaine-induced paranoia and psychosis proneness. *American Journal of Psychiatry, 148*, 1708–1711.

Satel, S. L., Kosten, T. R., Schuckit, M. A., & Fischman, M. W. (1993). Should protracted withdrawal from drugs be included in DSM-IV? *American Journal of Psychiatry, 150*, 695–704.

Satel, S. L., Price, L. H., Palumbo, J. M., McDougle, C. J., Krystal, J. H., Gawin, F., Charney, D. S., Heninger, G. R., & Kleber, H. D. (1991). Clinical phenomenology and neurobiology of cocaine abstinence: A prospective inpatient study. *American Journal of Psychiatry, 148,* 1712–1716.

Sattar, S. P., & Bhatia, S. (2003). Bendodiazepine for substance abusers: Yes or no? *Current Psychiatry, 2*(5), 25–34.

Saum, C. A., & Inciardi, J. A. (1997). Rohypnol misuse in the United States. *Substance Use & Misuse, 32,* 723–731.

Saunders, J. B., Aasland, O. G., Babor, T. F., de la Fuente, J. R., & Grant, M. (1993). Development of the alcohol use disorders identification test (AUDIT): WHO collaboratives project on early detection of persons with harmful alcohol consumption—II. *Addiction, 88,* 791–804.

Sauret, J. M., Marinides, G., & Wang, G. K. (2002). Rhabdomyolysis. *American Family Physician, 65,* 907–912.

Savage, S. R. (1993). Opium: The gift and its shadow. *Addiction & Recovery, 13*(1), 38–39.

Savage, S. R. (1999). Opioid use in the management of chronic pain. *Medical Clinics of North America, 83,* 761–786.

Savitch, C. (1998). Planes, trains and tuberculaids. *The Saturday Evening Post, 270*(4), 50–51.

Sax, P. E. (2003). HIV infection. In *Antibiotic essentials* (Cunha, B. A., ed.). Royal Oak, MI: Physician's Press.

Sbriglio, R., & Millman, R. B. (1987). Emergency treatment of acute cocaine reactions. In *Cocaine: A clinician's handbook* (Washton, A. M., & Gold, M. S., eds.). New York: The Guilford Press.

Scarf, M. (1980). *Unfinished business.* New York: Ballantine Books.

Scaros, L. P., Westra, S., & Barone, J. A. (1990). Illegal use of drugs: A current review. *U.S. Pharmacist, 15*(5), 17–39.

Schachter, H. M., Pham, B., King, J., Langford, S., & Moher, D. (2002). How efficacious and safe is short-acting methylphenidate for the treatment of attention-deficit disorder in children and adolescents? A meta-analysis. *Canadian Medical Association Journal, 165*(11), 1475–1488.

Schafer, J., & Brown, S. A. (1991). Marijuana and cocaine effect expectancies and drug use patterns. *Journal of Consulting and Clinical Psychology, 59,* 558–565.

Schaler, J. A. (2000). *Addiction is a choice.* Chicago: Open Court.

Schauben, J. L. (1990). Adulterants and substitutes. *Emergency Medicine Clinics of North America, 8,* 595–611.

Scheer, R. (1994a). The drug war's a bust. *Playboy, 41*(2), 49.

Scheer, R. (1994b). Fighting the wrong war. *Playboy, 41*(10), 49.

Schenker, S., & Speeg, K. V. (1990). The risk of alcohol intake in men and women. *The New England Journal of Medicine, 322,* 127–129.

Schiavi, R. C., Stimmel, B. B., Mandeli, J., & White, D. (1995). Chronic alcoholism and male sexual function. *American Journal of Psychiatry, 152,* 1045–1051.

Schiff, E. R., & Ozden, N. (2003). Hepatitis C and alcohol. *Alcohol Research & Health, 27*(3), 232–239.

Schiødt, F. V., Rochling, F. A., Casey, D. L., & Lee, W. M. (1997). Acetaminophen toxicity in an urban county hospital. *The New England Journal of Medicine, 337,* 1112–1117.

Schirmer, M., Wiedermann, C., & Konwalinka, G. (2000). Immune system. In *Handbook of alcoholism* (Zernig, G., Saria, A., Kurz, M., & O'Malley, S. S., eds.). New York: CRC Press.

Schlaepfer, T. E., Strain, E. C., Greenberg, B. D., Preston, K. L., Lancaster, E., Bigelow, G. E., Barta, P. E., & Pearlson, G. D. (1998). Site of opioid action in the human brain: Mu and kappa agonists subjective and cerebral blood flow effects. *American Journal of Psychiatry, 155,* 470–473.

Schlosser, E. (1994). Marijuana and the law. *The Atlantic Monthly, 274*(3), 84–86, 89–90, 92–94.

Schlosser, E. (2003). *Reefer madness.* New York: Houghton Mifflin Co.

Schmid, H., Bogt, T. T., Godeau, E., Hublet, A., Dias, S. F., & Fotiou, A. (2003). Drunkenness among young people: A cross-national comparison. *Journal of Studies on Alcohol, 64,* 650–661.

Schmitt, J. K., & Stuckey, C. P. (2004). AIDS—No longer a death sentence, still a challenge. *Southern Medical Journal, 97*(4), 329–330.

Schmoke, K. (1996). The war on drugs is lost. *National Review, XLVIII* (2), 40–42.

Schmoke, K. (1997). Save money, cut crime, get real. *Playboy, 44*(1), 129, 190–191.

Schneiderman, H. (1990). What's your diagnosis? *Consultant, 30*(7), 61–65.

Schnoll, S. H., & Weaver, M. F. (2004). Phencyclidine and ketamine. In *Textbook of substance abuse treatment* (3rd ed.) (Galanter, M., & Kleber, H. D., eds.). Washington, DC: American Psychiatric Press, Inc.

Schoenbaum, M., Zhang, W., & Strum, R. (1998). Costs and utilization of substance abuse care in a privately insured population under managed care. *Psychiatric Services, 49,* 1573–1578.

Schorling, J. B., & Buchsbaum, D. G. (1997). Screening for alcohol and drug abuse. *Medical Clinics of North America, 81,* 845–865.

Schottenfeld, R. S. (2004). Opioids maintenance treatment. In *Textbook of substance abuse treatment* (3rd ed.) (Galanter, M., & Kleber, H. D., eds.). Washington, DC: American Psychiatric Publishing.

Schottenfeld, R. S., Pakes, J. R., Oliveto, A., Ziedonis, D., & Kosten, T. R. (1997). Buprenorphine vs. methadone maintenance treatment for concurrent opioid dependence and cocaine abuse. *Archives of General Psychiatry, 54,* 713–720.

Schroeder, B. E., Holahan, M. R., Landry, C. F., & Kelley, A. E. (2000). Morphine-associated environmental cues elicit condition gene expression. *Synapse, 37* (2), 1–13.

Schrof, J. M. (1992). Pumped up. *U.S. News & World Report, 112*(21), 54–63.

Schuckit, M. A. (1994). Low level of response to alcohol as a predictor of future alcoholism. American Journal of Psychiatry, 151, 184–189.

Schuckit, M. A. (1995a). Alcohol related, disorders. In *Comprehensive textbook of psychiatry* (6th ed.) (Kaplan, H. I., & Sadock, B. J., eds.). Baltimore: Williams & Wilkins.

Schuckit, M. A. (1995b). *Drug and alcohol abuse: A Clinical guide to diagnosis and treatment* (4th ed.). New York: Plenum Press.

Schuckit, M. A. (1996a). Alcohol, anxiety and depressive disorders. *Alcohol Health & Research World, 20,* 81–86.

Schuckit, M. A. (1996b). Recent developments in the pharmacology of alcohol dependence. *Journal of Consulting and Clinical Psychology, 64,* 669–676.

Schuckit, M. A. (1998). Alcohol and alcoholism. In *Harrison's principles of internal medicine* (14th ed.) (Fauci, A. S., Martin, J. B., Braunwald, E., Kasper, D. L., Issebacher, K. J., Hauser, S. L., Wilson, J. D., & Longo, D. L., eds.). New York: McGraw-Hill.

Schuckit, M. A. (2000). *Drug and alcohol abuse: A clinical guide to diagnosis and treatment* (5th ed.). New York: Plenum Press.

Schuckit, M. A. (2001). Nature, nurture and the genetics of alcoholism. Paper presented at the Contemporary Issues in the Treatment of Alcohol & Drug Abuse Symposium, Milwaukee, WI, June 1.

Schuckit, M. A., Daeppen, J. B., Tipp, J. E., Hellelbrock, M., & Bucholz, K. K. (1998). The clinical course of alcohol-related problems in alcohol dependent and nonalcohol dependent drinking women and men. *Journal of Studies on Alcohol, 59,* 581–590.

Schuckit, M. A., Klein, J., Twitchell, G., & Smith, T. (1994). Personality test scores as predictors of alcoholism almost a decade later. *American Journal of Psychiatry, 151,* 1038–1042.

Schuckit, M. A., & Smith, T. L. (1996). An 8-year follow-up of 450 sons of alcoholic and control subjects. *Archives of General Psychiatry, 53,* 202–210.

Schuckit, M. A., Smith, T. L., Anthenelli, R., & Irwin, M. (1993). Clinical course of alcoholism in 636 male inpatients. *American Journal of Psychiatry, 150,* 786–792.

Schuckit, M. A., & Tapert, S. (2004). Alcohol. In *Textbook of substance abuse treatment* (3rd ed.) (Galanter, M., & Kleber, H. D., eds.). Washington, DC: American Psychiatric Press, Inc.

Schuckit, M. A., Zisook, S., & Mortola, J. (1985). Clinical implications of DSM-III diagnoses of alcohol abuse and alcohol dependence. *American Journal of Psychiatry, 142,* 1403–1408.

Schultz, C. H. (2002). Earthquakes. In *Disaster medicine* (Hogan, D. E., & Burstein, J. L., eds.). New York: Lippincott, Williams & Wilkins.

Schutte, K. K., Moos, R. H., & Brennan, P. L. (1995). Depression and drinking behavior among women and men: A three-wave longitudinal study of older adults. *Journal of Consulting and Clinical Psychology, 63,* 810–822.

Schwartz, R. H. (1987). Marijuana: An overview. *The Pediatric Clinics of North America, 34*(2), 305–317.

Schwartz, R. H. (1989). When to suspect inhalant abuse. *Patient Care, 23*(10), 39–50.

Schwartz, R. H. (1995). LSD. *Pediatric Clinics of North America, 42,* 403–413.

Schwartz, R. H. (1996). Let's help young smokers quit. *Patient Care, 30*(8), 45–51.

Schwartz, R. H., & Miller, N. S. (1997). MDMA (ecstasy) and the rave: A review. *Pediatrics, 100,* 705–708.

Schweizer, E., & Rickels, K. (1994). New and emerging clinical uses of buspirone. *Journal of Clinical Psychiatry, 55*(5)(Suppl.), 46–54.

Schwertz, D. W. (1991). Basic principles of pharmacologic action. *Nursing Clinics of North America, 26,* 245–262.

Science and Technology Committee Publications. (1998). *Cannabis: The scientific and medical evidence.* London, England: House of Lords.

Scientists call for stronger warnings for acetaminophen. (2002). *La Crosse Tribune, 99*(153), pp. A1, A8. (From the *Los Angeles Times.*)

Scott, I. (1998). A hundred-year habit. *History Today, 48*(6), 6–8.

Screening for alcohol problems—An update. (2002). *Alcohol Alert, 56,* 1–3.

Secondhand crack smoke is not an acceptable excuse. (1995). *Forensic Drug Abuse Advisor, 7*(10), 75–76.

Segal, B., & Duffy, L. K. (1999). Biobehavioral effects of psychoactive drugs. In *Drugs of abuse and addiction: Neurobehavioral toxicology* (Niesink, R. J. M., Jaspers, R. M. A., Korney, L. M. W., & van Ree, J. M., eds.). New York: CRC Press.

Segal, R., & Sisson, B. V. (1985). Medical complications associated with alcohol use and the assessment of risk of physical damage. In *Alcoholism and substance abuse: Strategies for clinical intervention* (Bratter, T. E., & Forrest, G. G., eds.). New York: The Free Press.

Seidman, S. N., & Rieder, R. O. (1994). A review of sexual behavior in the United States. *American Journal of Psychiatry, 151,* 330–341.

Seilhamer, R. A., Jacob, T., & Dunn, N. J. (1993). The impact of alcohol consumption on parent-child relationships in families of alcoholics. *Journal of Studies on Alcohol, 54*(2), 189–198.

Sekine, Y., Iyo, M., Ouchi, Y., Matsunaga, T., Tsukada, H., Okada, H., Yoshikawa, E., Fatatsubashi, M., Takei, N., & Mori, N. (2001). Methamphetamine-related psychiatric symptoms and reduced brain dopamine transporters studied with PET. *American Journal of Psychiatry, 158,* 1206–1214.

Selim J. (2001). It's a hard habit to break. *Discover, 22*(10), 23.

Sellers, E. M., Ciraulo, D. A., DuPont, R. L., Griffiths, R. R., Kosten, T. R., Romach, M. K., & Woody, G. E. (1993). Alprazolam and benzodiazepine dependence. *Journal of Clinical Psychiatry, 54*(10)(Suppl.), 64–74.

Selzer, M. (1971). The Michigan Alcoholism Screening Test: The quest for a new diagnostic instrument. *American Journal of Psychiatry, 127,* 1653–1658.

Senchak, M., Leonard, K. E., Greene, B. W., & Carroll, A. (1995). Comparisons of adult children of alcoholic, divorced and control parents in four outcome domains. *Psychology of Addictive Behaviors, 9*(3), 147–156.

Setola, V., Hufeisen, S. J., Grande-Allen, J., Vesely, I., Glennon, R. A., Blough, B., Rothman, R. B., & Roth, B. L. (2003). 3,4–methylenedioxymethamphetamine (MDMA, "ecstasy") induces fenfluramine-like proliferative actions on human cardiac valvular interstitial cells in vitro. *Molecular Pharmacology, 63*, 1223–1229.

Sexson, W. R. (1994). Cocaine: A neonatal perspective. *International Journal of the Addictions, 28*, 585–598.

Seymour, J. (1997). Old diseases, new danger. *Nursing Times, 93*(14), 22–24.

Shader, R. I. (1994). A perspective on contemporary psychiatry. In *Manual of psychiatric therapeutics* (2nd ed.). Boston: Little, Brown & Co.

Shader, R. I., & Greenblatt, D. J. (1993). Use of benzodiazepines in anxiety disorders. *The New England Journal of Medicine, 328*, 1398–1405.

Shader, R. I., Greenblatt, D. J., & Ciraulo, D. A. (1994). Treatment of physical dependence on barbiturates, benzodiazepines, and other sedative-hypnotics. In *Manual of psychiatric therapeutics* (2nd ed.). Boston: Little, Brown & Co.

Shaffer, H. J. (2001). What is addiction and does it matter? Symposium presented to the Dept. of Psychiatry of The Cambridge Hospital, Boston, MA, March 2.

Shaffer, H. J., & Robbins, M. (1995). Psychotherapy for addictive behavior: A stage-change approach to meaning making. In *Psychotherapy and substance abuse* (Washton, A. M., ed.). New York: Guilford.

Shalala, D. E. (1997). Introductory remarks. Paper presented at NIDA conference: Heroin Use and Addiction, Washington, DC, September 29–30.

Shannon, E. (2000). The world's best pot now comes from Vancouver. *Time, 155*(10), 66.

Shannon, M. T., Wilson, B. A., & Stang, C. L. (1995). *Drugs and nursing implications* (8th ed.). Norwalk, CT: Appleton & Lange.

Shapiro, D. (1981). *Anatomy and rigid character.* New York: Basic Books.

Sharara, A. I., Hunt, C. M., & Hamilton, J. D. (1996). Hepatitis C. *Annual of Internal Medicine, 125*, 658–668.

Sharma, P. (2003). Tylenol, the wonder drug. Paper presented at the Continuing Medical Education Symposium, Gundersen-Lutheran Medical Center, La Crosse, WI, March 5.

Sharp, M. J., & Getz, J. G. (1998). Self-process in comorbid mental illness and drug abuse. *American Journal of Orthopsychiatry, 68*, 639–644.

Shea, S. C. (2002). *The practical art of suicide assessment,* New York: John Wiley & Sons.

Shear, M. K. (2003). Optimal treatment of anxiety disorders. *Patient Care, 37*(5), 18–32.

Shedler, J., & Block, J. (1990). Adolescent drug use and psychological health. *American Psychologist, 45*, 612–630.

Shekelle, P. G., Hardy, M. L., Morton, S. C., Maglione, M., Mojica, W. A., Suttorp, M., Rhodes, S. L., Jungvig, L., & Gagne, J. (2003). Efficacy and safety of ephedra and ephedrine for weight loss and athletic performance. *Journal of the American Medical Association, 289*, 1537–1545.

Shenk, J. W. (1999). America's altered states. *Harper's Magazine, 298*(1788), 38–52.

Shepard, D. S., Larson, M. J., & Hoffmann, N. G. (1999). Cost-effectiveness of substance abuse services. *Psychiatric Clinics of North America, 22*, 385–400.

Shepherd, S. M., & Jagoda, A. S. (1990). PCP. In *Clinical management of poisoning and drug overdose* (2nd ed.) (Haddad, L.D., & Winchester, J. F., eds.). Philadelphia: W. B. Saunders Co.

Sher, K. J. (1991). *Children of alcoholics.* Chicago: University of Chicago Press.

Sher, K. J. (1997). Psychological characteristics of children of alcoholics. *Alcohol Health & Research World, 21*(3), 247–254.

Sher, K. J., Walitzer, K. S., Wood, P. K., & Brent, E. E. (1991). Characteristics of children of alcoholics: Putative risk factors, substance use and abuse, and psychopathology. *Journal of Abnormal Psychology, 100*, 427–448.

Sheridan, E., Patterson, H. R., & Gustafson, E. A. (1982). *Falconer's the drug, the nurse, the patient* (7th ed.). Philadelphia: W. B. Saunders.

Sherman, C. (1994). Kicking butts. *Psychology Today, 27*(5), 40–45.

Sherman, C. (2000a). Acamprosate proven effective for alcohol tx. *Clinical Psychiatry News, 28*(7), 14.

Sherman, C. (2000b). Anticonvulsants may help treat benzodiazepine, cocaine withdrawal. *Clinical Psychiatry News, 28*(7), 14.

Sherman, C. B. (1991). Health effects of cigarette smoking. *Clinics in Chest Medicine, 12* 643–658.

Shiffman, L. B., Fischer, L. B., Zettler-Segal, M., & Benowitz, N. L. (1990). Nicotine exposure among nondependent smokers. *Archives of General Psychiatry, 47*, 333–340.

Shiffman, S. (1992). Relapse process and relapse prevention in addictive behaviors. *The Behavior Therapist, 15*(1), 99–11.

Shih, R. D., & Hollander, J. E. (1996). Management of cocaine-associated chest pain. *Hospital Physician, 32*(11), 11–20, 45.

Shipley, R., & Rose, J. (2003). *Quit smart.* Durham, NC: QuitSmart Smoking Resources, Inc.

Shivani, R., Goldsmith, R. J., & Anthenelli, R. M. (2002). Alcoholism and psychiatric disorders. *Alcohol Research & Health, 26*, 90–98.

Shute, N., Licking, E. F., & Schultz, S. (1998). Hepatitis C: A silent killer. *U.S. News & World Report, 124*(24), 60–66.

Shute, N., & Tangley, L. (1997). The drinking dilemma. *U.S. News & World Report, 123*(9), 54–65.

Siebert, C. (1996). Are we more than ever at the mercy of our genes? *Minneapolis Star Tribune, XIV* (286), p. A13.

Siegel, B. S. (1986). *Love, medicine & miracles.* New York: Harper & Row.

Siegel, B. S. (1989). *Peace, love & healing.* New York: Harper & Row.

Siegel, R. K. (1982). Cocaine smoking disorders: Diagnosis and treatment. *Psychiatric Annals, 14,* 728–732.

Siegel, R. K. (1991). Crystal meth or speed or crank. *Lear's, 3*(1), 72–73.

Siegel, R. L. (1986). Jungle revelers: When beasts take drugs to race or relax, things get zooey. *Omni, 8*(6), 70–74, 100.

Sigvardsson, S., Bohman, M., & Cloninger, R. (1996). Replication of the Stockholm adoption study. *Archives of General Psychiatry, 53,* 681–687.

Simkin, D. R. (2002). Adolescent substance use disorders and comorbidity. *Pediatric Clinics of North America, 49,* 463–477.

Simmons, A. L. (1991). A peculiar dialect in the land of 10,000 treatment centers. *Minneapolis Star Tribune, X*(24), p. A23.

Simon, D., & Burns, E. (1997). *The corner.* New York: Broadway Books.

Simon, E. J. (1997). Opiates: Neurobiology. In *Substance abuse: A comprehensive textbook* (3rd ed.) (Lowinson, J. H., Ruiz, P., Millman, R. B., & Langrod, J. G., eds.). Baltimore: Williams & Wilkins.

Simons, A. M., Phillips, D. H., & Coleman, D. V. (1993). Damage to DNA in cervical epithelium related to smoking tobacco. *British Medical Journal, 306,* 1444–1448.

Singer, L. T., Arendt, R., Minnes, S., Farkas, K., Salvator, A., Kirchner, H. L., & Kliegman, R. (2002). Cognitive and motor outcomes of cocaine-exposed infants. *Journal of the American Medical Association, 287,* 1952–1960.

Singer, L. T., Minnes, S., Short, E., Arendt, R., Farkas, K., Lewis, B., Klein, N., Russ, S., Min, M. O., & Kirchner, H. L. (2004). Cognitive outcomes of preschool children with prenatal cocaine exposure. *Journal of the American Medical Association, 291*(20), 2448–2456.

Singh, R. A., Mattoo, S. K., Malhotra, A., & Varma, V. K. (1992). Cases of buprenorphine abuse in India. *Acta Psychiatrica Scandinavica, 86,* 46–48.

Sinha, G. (2001). Out of control? *Popular Science, 258*(6), 48–52.

Sinha, R. (2000). Women. In *Handbook of alcoholism* (Zernig, G., Saria, A., Kurz, M., & O'Malley, S. S., eds.). New York: CRC Press.

Sjogren, M. H. (1996). Serologic diagnosis of viral hepatitis. *Medical Clinics of North America, 80,* 929–956.

Sklair-Tavron, L., Ski, W. X., Lane, S. B., Harris, H. W., Bunny, B. S., & Nestler, E. J. (1996). Chronic morphine induces visible changes in the morphology of mesolimbic dopamine neurons. *Proceedings of the National Academy of Sciences, 93,* 11202–11207.

Skog, O. J., & Duckert, F. (1993). The development of alcoholics' and heavy drinkers' consumption: A longitudinal study. *Journal of Studies on Alcohol, 54,* 178–188.

Slaby, A. E., Lieb, J., & Tancredi, L. R. (1981). *Handbook of psychiatric emergencies* (2nd ed.). Garden City, NY: Medical Examination Publishing Co., Inc.

Slade, J., Bero, L. A., Hanauer, P., Barnes, D. E., & Glantz, S. A. (1995). Nicotine and addiction. *Journal of the American Medical Association, 274,* 225–233.

Sleeping pills and antianxiety drugs. (1988). *Harvard Medical School Mental Health Letter, 5*(6), 1–4.

Slovut, G. (1992). Sports medicine. *Minneapolis Star Tribune, X*(353), p. C20.

Slutske, W. S., Heath, A. C., Madden, P. A. F., Bucholz, K. K., Statham, D. J., & Martin, N. G. (2002). Personality and the genetic risk for alcohol dependence. *Journal of Abnormal Psychology, 111,* 124–133.

Small, M. F. (2002). What you can learn from drunk monkeys. *Discover, 23*(7), 40–47.

Smith, B. H., Molina, B. S. G., & Pelham, W. E. (2002). The clinically meaningful link between alcohol use and attention deficit hyperactivity disorder. *Alcohol Research & Health, 26,* 122–129.

Smith, D. (1997). Prescription drug abuse. Paper presented at the WisSAM Symposium: Still Getting High—a 30-Year Perspective on Drug Abuse, Gundersen-Lutheran Medical Center, La Crosse, WI, May.

Smith, D. (2001). All the rave—What's pop in substance abuse. Paper presented at the Contemporary Issues in the Treatment of Alcohol & Drug Abuse Symposium, Milwaukee, WI, June 1.

Smith, D. E., & Wesson, D. R. (2004). Benzodiazepines and other sedative-hypnotics. In *Textbook of substance abuse treatment* (3rd ed.) (Galanter, M., & Kleber, H. D., eds.). Washington, DC: American Psychiatric Press, Inc.

Smith, G. S., Keyl, P. M., Hadley, J. A., Bartley, C. L., Foss, R. D., Tolbert, W. G., & McKnight, J. (2001). Drinking and recreational boating fatalities. *Journal of the American Medical Association, 286,* 2974–2980.

Smith, G. T. (1994). Psychological expectancy as mediator of vulnerability to alcoholism. In *Types of alcoholics* (Babor, T. F., Hesselbrock, V., Meyer, R. E., & Shoemaker, W., eds.). New York: New York Academy of Sciences.

Smith, G. T., Goldman, M. S., Greenbaum, P. E., & Christiansen, B. A. (1995). Expectancy for social facilitation from drinking: The divergent paths of high-expectancy and low-expectancy adolescents. *Journal of Abnormal Psychology, 104,* 32–40.

Smith, J. E., Meyers, R. J., & Delaney, H. D. (1998). The community reinforcement approach with homeless alcohol-dependent individuals. *Journal of Consulting and Clinical Psychology, 66,* 541–548.

Smith, J. W. (1997). Medical manifestations of alcoholism in the elderly. In *Older adults' misuses of alcohol, medicines and other drugs* (Gurnack, A. M., ed.). New York: Springer.

Smith, L. M., Chang, L., Yonekura, M. L., Gilbride, K., Kuo, J., Poland, R. E., Walot, I., & Ernst, T. (2001). Brain proton magnetic resonance spectroscopy and imaging in children exposed to cocaine in utero. *Pediatrics, 107,* 227–231.

Smith, L. M., Chang, L., Yonekura, M. L., Grob, C., Osborn, D., & Ernst, T. (2001). Brain proton magnetic resonance spectroscopy in children exposed to methamphetamine in utero. *Neurology, 57*(2), 255–260.

Smith, S. G. T., Touquet, R., Wright, S., & Das Gupta, N. (1996). Detection of alcohol misusing patients in accident and emergency departments: The Paddington alcohol test (PAT). *Journal of Accident & Emergency Medicine, 13,* 308–312.

Smith, T. (1994). How dangerous is heroin? *British Medical Journal, 307,* 807.

Smithson, M., McFadden, M., Mwesigye, S. E., & Casey, T. (2004). The impact of illicit drug supply reduction on health and social outcomes: The heroin shortage in the Australian capital territory. *Addiction, 99,* 340–348.

Smolowe, J. (1997). Sorry, pardner. *Time, 146*(26), 4–12.

Smothers, B. A., Yahr, H. T., & Ruhl, C. (2004). Detection of alcohol use disorders in general hospital admissions in the United States. *Archives of Internal Medicine, 164,* 749–756.

Smucker, W. D., & Hedayat, M. (2001). Evaluation and treatment of ADHD. *American Family Physician, 64,* 817–829.

Snyder, S. H. (1986). *Drugs and the brain.* New York: Scientific American Books, Inc.

Sobell, M. B., & Sobell, L. C. (1993). *Problem drinkers.* New York: Guilford Press.

Sokol, R. J., Delaney-Black, V., & Nordstrom, B. (2003). Fetal alcohol spectrum disorder. *Journal of the American Medical Association, 290,* 2996–2999.

Solomon, D. H., Glynn, R. J. Levin, R., & Avorn, J. (2002). Nonsteroidal anti-inflammatory drug use and acute myocardial infarction. *Archives of Internal Medicine, 162,* 1099–1104.

Solomon, J., Rogers, A., Katel, P., & Lach, J. (1997). Turning a new leaf. *Newsweek, CXXIX* (13), 50.

Solotaroff, P. (2002). Killer bods. *Rolling Stone, 889,* 54–56, 58–59, 72, 74.

Solowij, N., Stephens, R. S., Roffman, R. A., Babor, T., Kadden, R., Miller, M., Christiansen, K., McRee, B., & Vendetti, J. (2002). Cognitive functioning of long-term heavy cannabis users seeking treatment. *Journal of the American Medical Association, 287,* 1123–1131.

Solvent abuse puts teens at risk. (2003). *BBC News,* 22 October, 2003.

Sonne, S. C., & Brady, K. T. (1999). Substance abuse and bipolar comorbidity. *Psychiatric Clinics of North America, 22,* 609–627.

Sonne, S. C., & Brady, K. T. (2002). Bipolar disorder and alcoholism. *Alcohol Research & Health, 26,* 103–108.

Sorensen, J. L., Masson, C. L., & Perlman, D. C. (2002). HIV/hepatitis prevention in drug abuse treatment programs: Guidance from research. *Science & Practice Perspectives, 1*(1), 4–11.

South American drug production increases. (1997). *Forensic Drug Abuse Advisor, 9*(3), 18.

Soyka, M. (2000). Alcohol-induced psychotic disorders. In *Handbook of alcoholism* (Zernig, G., Saria, A., Kurz, M., & O'Malley, S. S., eds.). New York: CRC Press.

Spanagel, R., & Hoelter, S. M. (2000). Controversial research areas. In *Handbook of alcoholism* (Zernig, G., Saria, A., Kurz, M., & O'Malley, S. S., eds.). New York: CRC Press.

Spangler, J. G., & Salisbury, P. L. (1995). Smokeless tobacco: Epidemiology, health effects and cessation strategies. *American Family Physician, 52,* 1421–1430.

Spear, L. P. (2002). The adolescent brain and the college drinker: Biological basis of propensity to use and misuse alcohol. *Journal of Studies on Alcohol* (Suppl. 14), 71–81.

Spencer, T., Biederman, J., Wilens, T., Faraone, S., Prince, J., Gerard, K., Doyle, R., Parekh, A., Kagan, J., & Bearman, S. K. (2001). Efficacy of a mixed amphetamine salts compound in adults with Attention Deficit/Hyperactivity Disorder. (2001). *Archives of General Psychiatry, 58,* 775–782.

Spiegel, R. (1996). *Psychopharmacology: An introduction* (3rd ed.). New York: John Wiley & Sons.

Spiller, H. A., & Krenzelok, E. P. (1997). Epidemiology of inhalant abuse reported to two regional poison centers. *Journal of Toxicology: Clinical Toxicology, 35,* 167–174.

Spindler, K. (1994). *The man in the ice.* New York: Harmony Books.

Spohr, H. L., Williams, J., & Steinhausen, H. C. (1993). Prenatal alcohol exposure and long-term consequences. *The Lancet, 341,* 907–910.

Sporer, K. A., & Khayam-Bashi, H. (1996). Acetaminophen and salicylate serum levels in patients with suicidal ingestion or altered mental states. *American Journal of Emergency Medicine, 14,* 443–446.

Springborn, W. (1987). Step one: The foundation of recovery. In *The twelve steps of Alcoholics Anonymous.* New York: Harper & Row.

Squires, S. (1990). Popular painkiller ibuprofen is linked to kidney damage. *Minneapolis Star Tribune, VIII* (315), 1E, 4E.

Srisurapanont, M., Marsden, J., Sunga, A., Wada, K., & Monterio, M. (2003). Psychotic symptoms in methamphetamine psychotic in-patients. *International Journal of Neuropsychopharmacology, 6*(4), 347–352.

Stahl, S. M. (2000). *Essential psychopharmacology* (2nd ed.). New York: Cambridge University Press, Inc.

Stamp out drugs. (2003). *Playboy, 50*(7), 52.

Steele, T. E., & Morton, W. A. (1986). Salicylate-induced delirium. *Psychosomatics, 27*(6), 455–456.

Stein, B., Orlando, M., & Sturm, R. (2000). The effect of copayments on drug and alcohol treatment following inpatient detoxification under managed care. *Psychiatric Services, 51,* 195–198.

Stein, J. A., Newcomb, M. D., & Bentler, P. M. (1993). Differential effects of parent and grandparent drug use on behavior problems of male and female children. *Developmental Psychology, 29,* 31–43.

Stein, M. D., Freedberg, K. A., Sullivan, L. S., Savetsky, J., Levenson, S. M., Hingson, R., & Samet, J. H. (1998). Sexual ethics. *Archives of Internal Medicine, 158,* 253–257.

Stein, M. D., & Friedmann, P. D. (2001). Generalist physicians and addiction care. *Journal of the American Medical Association, 286,* 1764–1765.

Stein, S. M., & Kosten, T. R. (1992). Use of drug combinations in treatment of opioid withdrawal. *Journal of Clinical Psychopharmacology, 12*(3), 203–209.

Stein, S. M., & Kosten, T. R. (1994). Reduction of opiate withdrawal-like symptoms by cocaine abuse during methadone and buprenorphine maintenance. *American Journal of Drug and Alcohol Abuse, 20*(4), 445–459.

Steinberg, N. (1994, May 5). The cartels would like a second chance. *Rolling Stone,* 33–34.

Steinberg, W., & Tenner, S. (1994). Acute pancreatitis. *New England Journal of Medicine, 330,* 1198–1210.

Steinberger, H. (2001). Faith-based or science-based and secular options in self-help? *The Additions Newsletter, 8*(3), 13.

Steinbrook, R. (2004). The AIDS epidemic in 2004. *New England Journal of Medicine, 351,* 115–117.

Steinglass, P., Bennett, L. A., Wolin, S. J., & Reiss, D. (1987). *The alcoholic family.* New York: Basic Books.

Sternbach, H. (2003). Serotonin syndrome. *Current Psychiatry, 2*(5), 14–24.

Sternbanch, G. L., & Varon, J. (1992). Designer drugs. *Postgraduate Medicine, 91,* 169–176.

Steroids and growth hormones make users "really ripped." (2003). *Forensic Drug Abuse Advisor, 15,* 74–76.

Stetter, F. (2000). Psychotherapy. In *Handbook of alcoholism* (Zernig, G., Saria, A., Kurz, M., & O'Malley, S. S., eds.). New York: CRC Press.

Stevens, R. S., Roffman, R. A., & Simpson, E. E. (1994). Treating adult marijuana dependence: A test of the relapse prevention model. *Journal of Consulting and Clinical Psychology, 62,* 92–99.

Stimac, D., Milic, S., Dintinjana, R. D., Kovac, D., & Ristic, S. (2002). Androgenic/anabolic steroid-induced toxic hepatitis. *Journal of Clinical Gastroenterology, 35,* 350–352.

Stimmel, B. (1997a). Drug abuse and social policy in America: The war that must be won. Paper presented at the 1997 annual Frank P. Furlano, M.D. memorial lecture, Gunderson-Lutheran Medical Center, La Crosse, WI.

Stimmel, B. (1997b). *Pain and its relief without addiction.* New York: The Harworth Medical Press.

Stitzer, M. (2003). Nicotine addiction and tobacco dependence. Seminar presented at the 2003 meeting of the American Psychological Association: Toronto, Canada.

Stocker, S. (1997). Compounds show strong promise for treating cocaine addiction. *NIDA Notes, 12*(3), 12–13.

Stocker, S. (1999a). Cocaine's pleasurable effects may involve multiple chemical sites in the brain. *NIDA Notes, 14*(2), 5–7.

Stocker, S. (1999b). Medications reduce incidence of substance abuse among ADHD patients. *NIDA Notes, 14*(4), 6–8.

Stockwell, T., & Town, C. (1989). Anxiety and stress management. In *Handbook of alcoholism treatment approaches* (Hester, H. K., & Miller, W. R., eds.). New York: Pergamon Press.

Stolberg, S. (1994). Aspirin isn't just for headaches. *Minneapolkis Star Tribune, XIII* (179), p. A4.

Stone, J. (1991). Light elements. *Discover, 12*(1), 12–16.

Stoschitzky, K. (2000). Cardiovascular system. In *Handbook of alcoholism* (Zernig, G., Saria, A., Kurz, M., & O'Malley, S. S., eds.). New York: CRC Press.

Strain, E. C., Stitzer, M. L., Liebson, I. A., & Bigelow, G. E. (1994). Comparison of buprenorphine and methadone in the treatment of opioid dependence. *American Journal of Psychiatry, 151,* 1025–1030.

Strang, J., Johns, A., & Caan, W. (1993). Cocaine in the UK—1991. *British Journal of Psychiatry, 162,* 1–13.

Strauch, B. (2003). *The primal teen.* New York: Doubleday.

Streissguth, A. P., Aase, J. M., Clarren, S. K., Randels, S. P., LaDue, R. A., & Smith, D. F. (1991). Fetal alcohol syndrome in adolescents and adults. *Journal of the American Medical Association, 265,* 1961–1967.

Strong medicine. (1995). *Harvard Medical School Mental Health Letter, 20*(6), 4–6.

Sturmi, J. E., & Diorio, D. J. (1998). Anabolic agents. *Clinics in Sports Medicine, 17,* 261–282.

Supernaw, R. B. (1991). Pharmacotherapeutic management of acute pain. *U.S. Pharmacist, 16*(2), H1–H14.

Sussman, N. (1988). Diagnosis and drug treatment of anxiety in the elderly. *Geriatric Medicine Today, 7* (10), 1–8.

Sussman, N. (1994). The uses of buspirone in psychiatry. *Journal of Clinical Psychiatry, 55*(5) (Suppl.), 3–19.

Sussman, N., & Westreich, L. (2003). Chronic marijuana use and the treatment of mentally ill patients. *Primary Psychiatry, 19*(9), 73–76.

Suter, P. M., Schultz, Y., & Jequier, E. (1992). The effect of ethanol on fat storage in healthy subjects. *The New England Journal of Medicine, 326,* 983–987.

Sutherland, G., Stapleton, J. A., Russell, M. A. H., Jarvis, M. J., Hajek, P., Belcher, M., & Feyerabend, C. (1992). Randomised controlled trial of nasal nicotine spray in smoking cessation. *The Lancet, 340,* 324–329.

Svikis, D. S., Zarin, D. A., Tanielian, T., & Pincus, H. A. (2000). Alcohol abuse and dependence in a national sample of psychiatric patients. *Journal of Studies on Alcohol, 61,* 427–430.

Svitil, K. A. (2003). What, me worry about SARS? *Discover, 24*(8), 19–20.

Swan, N. (1994). Research demonstrates long-term benefits of methadone treatment. *NIDA Notes, 9*(4), 1, 4–5.

Swan, N. (1995). 31% of New York murder victims had cocaine in their bodies. *NIDA Notes, 10*(2), 1, 4.

Swan, N. (1998). Drug abuse cost to society set at $97.7 billion, continuing steady increase since 1975. *NIDA Notes, 13*(4), 1, 12.

Swendsen, J. D., Conway, K. P., Rounsaville, B. J., & Merikangas, K. R. (2002). Are personality traits familial risk factors for substance use disorders? Results of a controlled family study. *American Journal of Psychiatry, 159,* 1760–1766.

Swift, R., & Davidson, D. (1998). Alcohol hangover. *Alcohol Health & Research World, 22,* 54–60.

Swift, R. M., Whelihan, W., Kuznetsov, O., Buongiorno, G., & Hsuing, H. (1994). Naltrexone-induced alterations in human ethanol intoxication. *American Journal of Psychiatry, 151,* 1463–1467.

Szabo, G. (1997). Alcohol's contribution to compromised immunity. *Alcohol Health & Research World, 21* 30–41.

Szarewski, A., Jarvis, M. J., Sasieni, P., Anderson, M., Edwards, R., Steele, S. J., & Buillebaud, J. C. (1996). Effect of smoking cessation on cervical lesion size. *The Lancet, 347,* 941–943.

Szasz, T. S. (1972). Bad habits are not diseases: A refutation of the claim that alcoholism is a disease. *The Lancet, 319,* 83–84.

Szasz, T. S. (1988). A plea for the cessation of the longest war of the twentieth century—The war on drugs. *The Humanistic Psychologist, 16*(2), 314–322.

Szasz, T. S. (1996). The war on drugs is lost. *National Review, XLVIII* (2), 45–47.

Szasz, T. S. (1997). Save money, cut crime, get real. *Playboy, 44*(1), 129, 190.

Szwabo, P. A. (1993). Substance abuse in older women. *Clinics in Geriatric Medicine, 9,* 197–208.

Tabakoff, B., & Hoffman, P. L. (1992). Alcohol: Neurobiology. In *Substance abuse: A comprehensive textbook* (2nd ed.) (Lowinson, J. H., Ruiz, P., Millman, R. B., & Langrod, J. G., eds.). New York: Williams & Wilkins.

Tabakoff, B., & Hoffman, P. L. (2004). Neurobiology of alcohol. In *Textbook of substance abuse treatment* (3rd ed.) (Galanter, M., & Kleber, H. D., eds.). Washington, DC: American Psychiatric Press, Inc.

Tabor, B. L., Smith-Wallace, T., & Yonekura, M. L. (1990). Parinatal outcome associated with PCP versus cocaine use. *American Journal of Drug and Alcohol Abuse, 16,* 337–349.

Taha, A. S., Dahill, S., Sturrock, R. D., Lee, F. D., & Russell, R. I. (1994). Predicting NSAID related ulcers—Assessment of clinical and pathological risk factors and importance of differences in NSAID. *Gut, 35,* 891–895.

Takanishi, R. (1993). The opportunities of adolescence—Research, interventions, and policy. *American Psychologist, 48,* 85–87.

Take time to smell the fentanyl. (1994). *Forensic Drug Abuse Advisor, 6*(5), 34–35.

Take 2 aspirins and come back in 76 years. (1994). *U.S. News & World Report, 117*(12), 24.

Talley, N. J. (1993). The effects of NSAIDs on the gut. *Contemporary Internal Medicine, 5*(2), 14–28.

Talty, S. (2003). The straight dope. *Playboy, 50*(11), 89–92.

Taming drug interactions. (2003). *Addiction Treatment Forum, 12*(4), 1, 6.

Tanhehco, E. J., Yasojima, K., McGeer, P. L., & Lucchesi, B. R. (2000). Acute cocaine exposure up-regulates complement expression in rabbit heart. *Journal of Pharmacology and Experimental Therapeutics, 292,* 201–208.

Tanner, S. (1995). Steroids: A breakfast of champions. *Orthopaedic Nursing, 14*(6), 26–30.

Tantisiriwat, W., & Tebas, P. (2001). HIV infection and AIDS. In *The Washington manual of medical therapeutics* (30th ed.) (Ahya, S. N., Flood, K., & Paranjothi, S., eds.). New York: Lippincott, Williams & Wilkins.

Tapert, S. F., Cheung, E. H., Brown, G. S., Frank, L. R., Paulus, M. P., Schweinsburg, A. D., Meloy, M. J., & Brown, S. A. (2003). Neural response to alcohol stimuli in adolescents with alcohol use disorder. *Archives of General Psychiatry, 60,* 727–735.

Tarter, R. E., Ott, P. J., & Mezzich, A. C. (1991). Psychometric assessment. In *Clinical textbook of addictive disorders* (Frances, R. J., & Miller, S. I., eds.). New York: The Guilford Press.

Tashkin, D. P. (1990). Pulmonary complications of smoked substance abuse. *The Western Journal of Medicine, 152,* 525–531.

Tashkin, D. P. (1993). Is frequent marijuana smoking harmful to health? *The Western Journal of Medicine, 158,* 635–637.

Tashkin, D. P., Kleerup, E. P., Koyal, S. N., Marques, J. A., & Goldman, M. D. (1996). Acute effects of inhaled and IV cocaine on airway dynamics. *Chest, 110,* 907–914.

Tate, C. (1989). In the 1800's, antismoking was a burning issue. *Smithsonian, 20*(4), 107–117.

Tate, J. C., Stanton, A. L., Green, S. B., Schmitz, J. M., Le, T., & Marshall, B. (1994). Experimental analysis of the role of expectancy in nicotine withdrawal. *Psychology of Addictive Behaviors, 8,* 169–178.

Tavris, C. (1990). One more guilt trip for women. *Minneapolis Star Tribune, VIII,* (341), p. A21.

Tavris, C. (1992). *The mismeasure of woman.* New York: Simon & Schuster.

Tavris, C. (1998). A grain of salt. *Family Therapy Networker, 22*(2), 42–43, 109.

Taylor, D. (1993). Addicts' abuse of sleeping pills brings call for tough curbs. *The Observer, 10531,* 6.

Taylor, M. L. (2004). Drug courts for teenagers can be effective. *La Crosse Tribune, 101*(61), 16.

Taylor, S., McCracken, C. F. M., Wilson, K. C. M., & Copeland, J. R. M. (1998). Extended and appropriateness of benzodiazepine use. *British Journal of Psychiatry, 173,* 433–438.

Taylor, W. A., & Gold, M. S. (1990). Pharmacologic approaches to the treatment of cocaine dependence. *Western Journal of Medicine, 152,* 573–578.

Teich, J. L. (2000). Monitoring change in behavioral health care. *Psychiatric Clinics of North America, 23,* 297–308.

Teicher, M. H. (2002). The neurobiology of child abuse. *Scientific American, 286*(3), 68–75.

Telenti, A., & Iseman, M. (2000). Drug-resistant tuberculosis. *Drugs, 59*(2), 171–179.

Terry, M. B., Gammon, M. D., Zhang, F. F., Tawfik, H., Teitelbaumn, S. L., Britton, J. A., Subbaramaiah, K., Dannenberg, A. J., & Neugut, A. I. (2004). Association of frequency and duration of aspirin use and hormone receptor status with breast cancer risk. *Journal of the American Medical Association, 291*, 2433–2440.

Terwilliger, E. G. (1995). Biology of HIV-1 and treatment strategies. *Emergency Medicine Clinics of North America, 13*, 27–42.

Thompson, P. M., Hayashi, K. M., Simon, S. L., Genga, J. A., Hong, M. S., Sui, Y., Lee, J. Y., Toga, A. W., Ling, W., & London, E. D. (2004). Structural abnormalities in the brains of human subjects who use methamphetamine. *Journal of Neuroscience, 24*, 6028–6036.

Timko, C., Moos, R. H., Finney, J. W., & Lesar, M. D. (2000). Long-term outcomes of alcohol use disorders: Comparing untreated individuals with those in Alcoholics Anonymous and formal treatment. *Journal of Studies on Alcohol, 61*, 529–540.

Tinsley, J. A., Finlayson, R. E., & Morse, R. M. (1998). Developments in the treatment of alcoholism. *Mayo Clinic Proceedings, 73*, 857–863.

Tip sheet. (2004). *Playboy, 51*(5), 26.

Tobin, J. W. (1992). Is A.A. "treatment"? You bet. *Addiction & Recovery, 12*(3), 40.

Tolmetin foils EMIT assay. (1995). *Forensic Drug Abuse Advisor, 7*(3), 23.

Toneatto, T., Sobell, L. C., Sobell, M. B., & Leo, G. I. (1991). Psychoactive substance use disorder (Alcohol). In *Adult psychopathology & diagnosis* (2nd ed.) (Hersen, M., & Turner, S. M., eds.). New York: Wiley.

Toneatto, T., Sobell, L. C., Sobell, M. B., & Rubel, E. (1999). Natural recovery from cocaine dependence. *Psychology of Addictive Behaviors, 13*, 259–268.

Tonigan, J. S., & Hiller-Sturmhofel, S. (1994). Alcoholics Anonymous: Who benefits? *Alcohol Health & Research World, 18*, 308–310.

Tonigan, J. S., & Toscova, R. T. (1998). Mutual-help groups. In *Treating addictive behaviors* (2nd ed.) (Miller, W. R., & Heather, N., eds.). New York: Plenum.

Torrens, M., San, L., & Cami, J. (1993). Buprenorphine versus heroin dependence: Comparison of toxicologic and psychopathologic characteristics. *American Journal of Psychiatry, 150*, 822–824.

Trabert, W., Caspari, D., Bernhard, P., & Biro, G. (1992). Inappropriate vasopressin secretion in severe alcohol withdrawal. *Acta Psychiatrica Scandinavica, 85*, 376–379.

Trachtenberg, M. C., & Blum, K. (1987). Alcohol and opioid peptides: Neuropharmacolical rationale for physical craving of alcohol. *American Journal of Drug and Alcohol Abuse, 13*(3), 365–372.

Treadway, D. (1990). Codependency: Disease, metaphor, or fad? *Family Therapy Networker, 14*(1), 39–43.

Treatment protocols for marijuana dependence are starting to emerge. (1995). *The Addiction Letter, 11*(8), 1–2.

Treisman, G. J., Angelino, A. F., & Hutton, H. E. (2001). Psychiatric issues in the management of patients with HIV infection. *Journal of the American Medical Association, 286*, 2857–2864.

Tresch, D. D., & Aronow, W. S. (1996). Smoking and coronary artery disease. *Clinics in Geriatric Medicine, 12*, 23–32.

Trevisan, L. A., Boutros, N., Petrakis, I. L., & Krystal, J. H. (1998). Complications of alcohol withdrawal. *Alcohol Health & Research World, 22*(1), 61–66.

Trichopoulos, D., Mollo, F., Tomatis, L., Agapitos, E., Delsedime, L., Zavitsanos, X., Kalandidi, A., Katsouyanni, K., Riboli, E., & Saracci, R. (1992). Active and passive smoking and pathological indicators of lung canger risk in an autopsy study. *Journal of the American Medical Association, 268*, 1697–1701.

Tronick, E. Z. & Beeghly, M. (1999). Prenatal cocaine exposure, child development, and the compromising effects of cumulative risk. *Clinics in Perinatology, 26*, 151–171.

Truog, R. D., Berde, C. B., Mitchell, C., & Grier, H. E. (1992). Barbiturates in the care of the terminally ill. *The New England Journal of Medicine, 327*, 1678–1682.

Tsai, G., Gastfriend, D. R., & Coyle, J. T. (1995). The glutamatergic basis of human alcoholism. *American Journal of Psychiatry, 152*, 332–340.

Tsuang, M. T., Lyons, M. J., Meyer, J., Doyle, T., Eisen, S. A., Goldberg, J., True, W., Lin, N. Toomey, R., & Eaves, L. (1998). Co-occurance of abuse of different drugs in men. *Archives of General Psychiatry, 55*, 967–972.

Tucker, J. A., & Sobell, L. C. (1992). Influences on help-seeking for drinking problems and on natural recovery without treatment. *The Behavior Therapist, 15*(1), 12–14.

Tuncel, M., Wang, Z., Arbique, D., Fadel, P. J., Victor, R. G., & Vongpatanasin, W. (2002). Mechanism of the blood pressure-raising effect of cocaine in humans. *Circulation, 105*, 1054–1059.

Turbo, R. (1989). Drying out is just a start: Alcoholism. *Medical World News, 30*(3), 56–63.

Tweed, S. H. (1998). Intervening in adolescent substance abuse. *Nursing Clinics of North America, 33*, 29–45.

Tweed, S. H., & Ryff, C. D. (1991). Profiles of wellness amidst distress. *Journal of Studies on Alcohol, 52*, 133–141.

Twelve Steps and Twelve Traditions. (1981). New York: Alcoholics Anonymous World Services, Inc.

Twerski, A. J. (1983). Early intervention in alcoholism: Confrontational techniques. *Hospital & Community Psychiatry, 34*, 1027–1030.

Tyas, S., & Rush, B. (1993). The treatment of disabled persons with alcohol and drug problems: Results of a survey of addiction services. *Journal of Studies on Alcohol, 54*, 275–282.

Tyler, D. C. (1994). Pharmacology of pain management. *Pediatric Clinics of North America, 41*, 59–71.

Tyrer, P. (1993). Withdrawal from hypnotic drugs. *British Medical Journal, 306*, 706–708.

Uhde, T. W., & Trancer, M. E. (1995). Barbiturates. In *Comprehensive textbook of psychiatry* (6th ed.) (Kaplan, H. I., & Sadock, B. J., eds.). Baltimore: Williams & Wilkins.

Uhl, M., & Sachs, H. (2004). Cannabinoids in hair: Strategy to prove marijuana/hashish consumption. *Forensic Science International, 145*, 143–147.

Understanding anonymity. (1981). New York: Alcoholics Anonymous World Services, Inc.

Ungvarski, P. J., & Grossman, A. H. (1999). Health problems of gay and bisexual men. *Nursing Clinics of North America, 34*, 313–326.

United Nations. (1997). *World drug report.* New York: Oxford University Press.

United Nations. (2000). *World drug report 2000.* New York: Oxford University Press.

United Nations. (2003). *Ecstasy and amphetamines: Global survey, 2003.* New York: United Nations Office of Drug Control Policy.

United Nations. (2004). *World drug report. Volume 1: Analysis.* Retrieved June 26, 2004, from http://www.unodc.org/unodc/en/world_drug_report.html

United States Department of Health & Human Services. (1999). Tobacco use—United States, 1900–1999. *Morbidity and Mortality Weekly Report, 48*(43), 986–993.

United States Pharmacopeial Convention, Inc. (1990). *Advice for the patient* (10th ed.). Rockville, MD: USPC Board of Trustees.

University of California, Berkeley. (1990a). Codependency. *The Wellness Letter, 7*(1), 7.

University of California, Berkeley. (1990b). Marijuana: What we know. *The Wellness Letter, 6*(6), 2–4.

University of California, Berkeley. (1990c). Women's magazines: Whose side are they on? *The Wellness Letter, 7*(3), 7.

Unterwald, E. M. (2001). Regulation of opioid receptors by cocaine. *Annals of the New York Academy of Sciences, 937*, 75–92.

Unwin, B. K., Davis, M. K., & De Leeuw, J. B. (2000). Pathologic gambling. *American Family Physician, 61*, 741–749.

Urbano-Marquez, A., Estruch, R., Fernandez-Sala, J., Nicholas, J. M., Pare, C., & Rubin, E. (1995). The greater risk of alcoholic cardiomyopathy and myopathy in women compared with men. *Journal of the American Medical Association, 274*, 149–154.

Uva, J. L. (1991). Alcoholics Anonymous: Medical recovery through a higher power. *Journal of the American Medical Association, 266*, 3065–3068.

Vail, B. A. (1997). Management of chronic viral hepatitis. *American Family Physician, 55*, 2749–2756.

Vaillant, G. E. (1983). *The natural history of alcoholism.* Cambridge, MA: Harvard University Press.

Vaillant, G. E. (1990). We should retain the disease concept of alcoholism. *The Harvard Medical School Mental Health Letter, 9*(6), 4–6.

Vaillant, G. E. (1995). *The natural history of alcoholism revisited.* Cambridge, MA: Harvard University Press.

Vaillant, G. E. (1996). A long-term follow-up of male alcohol abuse. *Archives of General Psychiatry, 53*, 243–249.

Vaillant, G. E. (2000). Alcoholics Anonymous: Cult or magic bullet? Symposium presented to the Dept. of Psychiatry at The Cambridge Hospital, Boston, MA, March 4.

Vaillant, G. E., & Hiller-Sturmhofel, S. (1996). The natural history of alcoholism. *Alcohol Health & Research World, 20*, 152–161.

Valenzuela, C. F., & Harris, R. A. (1997). Alcohol: Neurobiology. In *Substance abuse: A comprehensive textbook* (3rd ed.) (Lowinson, J. H., Ruiz, P., Millman, R. B., & Langrod, J. G., eds.). New York: Williams & Wilkins.

Vanable, P. A., King, A. C., & de Wit, H. (2000). Psychometric screening instruments. In *Handbook of alcoholism* (Zernig, G., Saria, A., Kurz, M., & O'Malley, S. S., eds.). New York: CRC Press.

Vandeputte, C. (1989). Why bother to treat older adults? The answer is compelling. *Professional Counselor, 4*(2), 34–38.

Van Etten, M. L., Neumark, Y. D., & Anthony, J. C. (1999). Male-female differences in the earliest stages of drug involvement. *Addiction, 94*, 1413–1419.

Vastag, R. (2003). In-office opiate treatment "not a panacea." *Journal of the American Medical Association, 290*, 731–732.

Vega, C., Kwoon, J. V., & Lavine, S. D. (2002). Intracranial aneurysms: Current evidence and clinical practice. *American Family Physician, 66*(4), 601–608.

Veld, B. A., Ruitenberg, A., Hofman, A., Launer, L. J., van Duijn, C. M., Stijnen, T., Breteler, M. M. B., & Stricker, B. H. C. (2001). Nonsteroidal antiinflammatory drugs and the risk of Alzheimer's disease. *New England Journal of Medicine, 345*, 1515–1521.

Verebey, K. G., & Buchan, B. J. (1997). Diagnostic laboratory: Screening for drug abuse. In *Substance abuse: A comprehensive textbook* (3rd ed.) (Lowinson, J. H., Ruiz, P., Millman, R. B., & Langrod, J. G., eds.). New York: Williams & Wilkins.

Verebey, K., Buchan, B. J., & Turner, C. E. (1998). Laboratory testing. In *Clinical textbook of addictive disorders* (2nd ed.) (Frances, R. J., & Miller, S. I., eds.). New York: Guilford.

A very venerable vintage. (1996). *Minneapolis Star Tribune,* XV (63), p. A16. (From the *Los Angeles Times*)

Victor, M. (1993). Persistent altered mentation due to ethanol. *Neurologic Clinics, 11*, 639–661.

Vik, P. W., Cellucci, T., Jarchow, A., & Hedt, J. (2004). Cognitive impairment in substance abuse. *Psychiatric Clinics of North America, 27*, 97–109.

Villalon, C. (2004). Cocaine country. *National Geographic, 206*(1), 34–55.

Vincenzo, B., Pearl, L., Hill, M. K., Cherpes, J., Chennat, J., & Kaltenback, K. (2003). Maternal methadone dose and neonatal withdrawal. *American Journal of Obstetrics and gynecology, 189*(2), 312–317.

Voelker, R. (1994). Medicinal marijuana: A trial of science and politics. *Journal of the American Medical Association, 271,* 1645–1648.

Volkow, N. D. (2004). Addictions and the brain. Symposium presented to the Dept. of Psychiatry at The Cambridge Hospital, Boston, MA, March 6.

Volkow, N. D., Hitzemann, R., Wang, G. J., Fowler, J. S., Burr, G., Pascani, K., Dewey, S. L., & Wolf, A. P. (1992). Decreased brain metabolism in neurologically intact healthy alcoholics. *American Journal of Psychiatry, 149,* 1016–1022.

Volkow, N. D., & Swanson, J. M. (2003). Variables that affect the clinical use and abuse of methylphenidate in the treatment of ADHD. *American Journal of Psychiatry, 160,* (11), 1909–1918.

Volkow, N. D., Wang, G. J., Fowler, J. S., Gatley, S. J., Logan, J., Ding, Y. S., Hitzemann, R., & Pappas, N. (1998). Dopamine transporter occupancies in the human brain induced by therapeutic doses of oral methylphenidate. *American Journal of Psychiatry, 155,* 1325–1331.

Volkow, N. D., Wang, G. J., Fowler, J. S., Logan, J., Gatley, S. J., Gifford, A., Hitzemann, R., Ding, Y. S., & Pappas, N. (1999). Prediction of reinforcing responses to psychostimulants in humans by brain dopamine D2 receptor levels. *American Journal of Psychiatry, 156,* 1440–1443.

Volpe, J. J. (1995). *Neurology of the newborn* (3rd ed.). Philadelphia: W. B. Saunders.

Volpicelli, J., Balaraman, G., Hahn, J., Wallace, H., & Bux, D. (1999). The role of uncontrolled trauma in the development of PTSD and alcohol addiction. *Alcohol Research & Health, 23,* 256–262.

Vourakis, C. (1998). Substance abuse concerns in the treatment of pain. *Nursing Clinics of North America, 33,* 47–60.

Vuchinich, R. E. (2002). President's column. *The Addictions Newsletter, 10*(1), 1, 5.

Wadler, G. I. (1994). Drug use update. *Medical Clinics of North America, 78,* 439–455.

Wakefield, J. C. (1992). The concept of mental disorder. *American Psychologist, 47,* 373–388.

Wallace, J. (2003). Theory of 12–step oriented treatment. In *Treating substance abuse: Theory and technique* (2nd ed.) (Rotgers, F., Morgenstern, J., & Walters, S. T., eds.). New York: Guilford.

Wallen, M. C., & Weiner, H. D. (1989). Impediments to effective treatment of the dually diagnosed patient. *Journal of Psychoactive Drugs, 21,* 161–168.

Walker, J. D. (1993). The tobacco epidemic: How far have we come? *Canadian Medical Association Journal, 148,* 145–147.

Walker, S. (1996). *A dose of sanity.* New York: Wiley.

Walsh, D. C., Hingson, R. W., Merrigan, D. M., Levenson, S. M., Cupples, L. A., Herren, T., Coffman, G. A., Becker, C. A., Barker, T. A., Hamilton, S. A., McGuire, T. G., & Kelly, C. A. (1991). A randomized trial of treatment options for alcohol-abusing workers. *The New England Journal of Medicine, 325,* 775–782.

Walsh, J. K., Pollak, C. P., Scharf, M. B., Schweitzer, P. K., & Vogel, G. W. (2000). Lack of residual sedation following middle of the night Zaleplon administration in sleep maintenance insomnia. *Clinical Neuropharmacology, 23*(1), 17–21.

Walsh, K., & Alexander, G. (2000). Alcoholic liver disease. *Postgraduate Medicine, 76,* 280–286.

Walter, D. S., & Inturrisi, C. E. (1995). Absorption, distribution, metabolism, and excretion of buprenorphine in animals and humans. In *Buprenorphine* (Cowan, A., & Lewis, J. W., eds.). New York: Wiley Interscience.

Walters, G. D. (1994). The drug lifestyle: One pattern or several? *Psychology of Addictive Behaviors, 8,* 8–13.

Walters, S. T., Rotgers, F., Saunders, B., Wilkinson, C., & Towers, T. (2003). Theoretical perspectives on motivation and addictive behaviors. In *Treating substance abuse: Theory and technique* (2nd ed.) (Rotgers, F., Morgenstern, J., & Walters, S. T., eds.). New York: Guilford.

Walton, S. (2002). *Out of it: A cultural history of intoxication.* New York: Harmony Books.

Wannamethee, S. G., Camargo, C. A., Manson, J. A. E., Willett, W. C., & Rimm, E. B. (2003). Alcohol drinking patterns and risk of Type 2 Diabetes Mellitus among younger women. *Archives of Internal Medicine, 163,* 1329–1336.

Wareing, M., Risk, J. E., & Murphy, P. N. (2000). Working memory deficits in current and previous users of MDMA ("ecstasy"). *British Journal of Psychiatry, 91.* 181–188.

Warn, D. J. (1997). Recovery issues of substance-abusing gay men. In *Gender and addictions* (Straussner, S. L. A., & Zelvin, E., eds.). Northvale, NJ: Jason-Aronson.

Warner, E. A. (1995). Is your patient using cocaine? *Postgraduate Medicine, 98,* 173–180.

Warren, K. R., & Foudin, L. L. (2001). Alcohol related birth defects—The past, present, and future. *Alcohol Research & Health, 25*(3), 153–158.

Washton, A. M. (1990). Crack and other substance abuse in the suburbs. *Medical Aspects of Human Sexuality, 24,* (5) 54–58.

Washton, A. M. (1995). Clinical assessment of psychoactive substance use. In *Psychotherapy and substance abuse* (Washton, A. M., ed.). New York: Guilford.

Washton, A. M., & Rawson, R. A. (1999). Substance abuse treatment under managed care: A provider perspective. In *Textbook of substance abuse treatment* (2nd ed.). Washington, DC: American Psychiatric Association Press, Inc.

Washton, A. M., Stone, N. S., & Hendrickson, E. C. (1988). Cocaine abuse. In *Assessment of addictive behaviors* (Donovan, D. M., & Marlatt, G. A., eds.). New York: The Guilford Press.

Watkins, K. E., Burnam, A., Kung, F. Y., & Paddock, S. (2001). A national survey of care for persons with co-occuring mental and substance use disorders. *Psychiatric Services, 52,* 1062–1068.

Watson, C. G., Hancock, M., Gearhart, L. P., Mendez, C. M., Malovrh, P., & Raden, M. (1997). A comparative outcome study of frequent, moderate, occasional, and nonattenders of Alcoholics Anonymous. *Journal of Clinical Psychology, 53,* 209–214.

Watson, C. G., Hancock, M., Malovrh, P., Gearhart, L. P., & Raden, M. (1996). A 48 week natural history follow-up of alcoholics who do and do not engage in limited drinking after treatment. *Journal of Nervous and Mental Disease, 184,* (10), 623–627.

Watson, J. M. (1984). Solvent abuse and adolescents. *The Practitioner, 228,* 487–490.

Watson, S. J., Benson, J. A., & Joy, J. E. (2000). Marijuana and medicine: Assessing the science base. *Archives of General Psychiatry, 57,* 547–552.

Weathermon, R., & Crabb, D. W. (1999). Alcohol and medication interactions. *Alcohol Research & Health, 23*(1), 40–54.

Weathers, W. T., Crane, M. M., Sauvain, K. J., & Blackhurst, D. W. (1993). Cocaine use in women from a defined population: Prevalence at delivery and effects on growth in infants. *Pediatrics, 91,* 350–354.

Weaver, M. F., Jarvis, M. A. E., & Schnoll, S. H. (1999). Role of primary care physician in problems of substance abuse. *Archives of Internal Medicine, 159,* 913–924.

Webb, S. T. (1989). Some developmental issues of adolescent children of alcoholics. *Adolescent Counselor, 1*(6), 47–48, 67.

Wechsler, H. (2002). Heavy alcohol use on American college campuses: Causes and solutions. Symposium presented to the Dept. of Psychiatry at The Cambridge Hospital, Boston, MA, February 1.

Weddington, W. W. (1993). Cocaine. *Psychiatric Clinics of North America, 16,* 87–95.

Wegscheider-Cruse, S. (1985). *Choice-making.* Pompano Beach, FL: Health Communications.

Wegscheider-Cruse, S., & Cruse, J. R. (1990). *Understanding co-dependency.* Pompano Beach, FL: Health Communications.

Weil, A. (1986). *The natural mind.* Boston: Houghton-Mifflin Co.

Weiner, H. R. (1997). HIV: An update for primary care physicians. *Emergency Medicine, 29*(9), 52–62.

Weiner, D. A., Abraham, M. E., & Lyons, J. (2001). Clinical characteristics of youths with substance use problems and implications for residential treatment. *Psychiatric Services, 52,* 793–799.

Weingardt, K. R., Baer, J. S., Kivlahan, D. R., Roberts, L. J., Miller, E. T., & Marlatt, G. A. (1998). Episodic heavy drinking among college students: Methodological issues and longitudinal perspectives. *Psychology of Addictive Behaviors, 12,* 155–167.

Weisner, C., & Schmidt, L. (1992). Gender disparities in treatment for alcohol problems. *Journal of the American Medical Association, 268,* 1872–1876.

Weiss, C. J., & Millman, R. B. (1998). Hallucinogens, phencyclidine, marijuana, inhalants. In *Clinical textbook of addictive disorders* (2nd ed.) (Frances, R. J., & Miller, S. I., eds.). New York: Guilford.

Weiss, R. D., Greenfield, S. H., & Mirin, S. M. (1994). Intoxication and withdrawal syndromes. In *Handbook of psychiatric emergencies* (3rd ed.) (Hyman, S. E., & Tesar, G. E., eds.). Boston: Little, Brown & Co.

Weiss, R. D., Griffin, M. L., Gallop, R., Luborsky, L., Siqueland, L., Frank, A., Onken, L. S., Daley, D. C., & Gastfriend, D. R. (2000). Predictors of self-help group attendance in cocaine dependent patients. *Journal of Studies on Alcohol, 61,* 714–719.

Weiss, R. D., Griffin, M. L., Mazurick, C., Berkman, B., Gastfriend, D. R., Frank, A., Barber, J. P., Blaine, J., Salloum, I., & Moras, K. (2003). The relationship between cocaine craving, psychosocial treatment, and subsequent cocaine use. *American Journal of Psychiatry, 160,* 1320–1325.

Weiss, R. D., & Mirin, S. M. (1988). Intoxication and withdrawal syndromes. In *Handbook of psychiatric emergencies* (2nd ed.) (Hyman, S. E., ed.). Boston: Little, Brown & Co.

Wells-Parker, E. (1994). Mandated treatment. *Alcohol Health & Research World, 18,* 302–306.

Welsby, P. D. (1997). An HIV view of the human condition. *Postgraduate Medicine, 73,* 609–610.

Wender, P. H. (1995). *Attention-deficit hyperactivity disorder in adults.* New York: Oxford University Press.

Werner, E. E. (1989). High-risk children in young adulthood. A longitudinal study from birth to 32 years. *American Journal of Orthopsychiatry, 59,* 72–81.

Werner, M. J., Walker, L. S., & Greene, J. W. (1995). Relation of alcohol expectancies to changes in problem drinking among college students. *Archives of Pediatric and Adolescent Medicine, 149,* 733–739.

Werner, R. M., & Pearson, T. A. (1998). What's so passive about passive smoking? *Journal of the American Medical Association, 279,* 157–158.

Wertz, J. M., & Sayette, M. A. (2001). A review of the effects of perceived drug use opportunity on self-reported urge. *Experimental and Clinical Psychopharmacology, 9,* 3–13.

Wesson, D. R., & Ling, W. (1996). Addiction medicine. *Journal of the American Medical Association, 275,* 1792–1793.

West, R., & Hajek, P. (1997). What happens to anxiety levels on giving up smoking? *American Journal of Psychiatry, 154,* 1589–1592.

Westermeyer, J. (1987). The psychiatrist and solvent-inhalent abuse: Recognition, assessment and treatment. *American Journal of Psychiatry, 144,* 903–907.

Westermeyer, J. (1995). Cultural aspects of substance abuse and alcoholism. *The Psychiatric Clinics of North America, 18,* 589–620.

Westermeyer, J. (2001). Detection and diagnosis of alcoholism in hospitalized patients. *Mayo Clinic Proceedings, 76,* 457–458.

Westermeyer, J., Eames, S. L., & Nugent, S. (1998). Comorbid dysthymia and substance disorder: Treatment history and cost. *American Journal of Psychiatry, 155,* 1556–1560.

Westman, E. C. (1995). Does smokeless tobacco cause hypertension? *Southern Medical Journal, 88,* 716–720.

Wetli, C. V. (1987). Fatal reactions to cocaine. In *Cocaine: A clinician's handbook* (Washton, A. M., & Gold, M. S., eds.). New York: The Guilford Press.

Wetter, D. W., Young, T. B., Bidwell, T. R., Badr, M. S., & Palta, M. (1994). Smoking as a risk factor for sleep-disordered breathing. *Archives of Internal Medicine, 154,* 2219–2224.

Wexler, B. E., Gottschalk, C. H., Fulbright, R. K., Prohovnik, I., Lacadie, C. M., Rounsaville, B. J., & Gore, J. C. (2001). Functional magnetic resonance imaging of cocaine craving. *American Journal of Psychiatry, 158,* 86–95.

Wheeler, K., & Malmquist, J. (1987). Treatment approaches in adolescent chemical dependency. *The Pediatric Clinics of North America, 34,* (2), 437–447.

Whitcomb, D. C., & Block, G. D. (1994). Association of acetaminophen hepatotoxicity with fasting and ethanol use. *Journal of the American Medical Association, 272,* 1845–1850.

White, A. M. (2003). What happened? Alcohol, memory blackouts, and the brain. *Alcohol Research & Health,* 27(2), 186–196.

White, P. T. (1989). Coca. *National Geographic,* 175(1), 3–47.

Whitman, D., Friedman, D., & Thomas, L. (1990). The return of skid row. *U.S. News & World Report,* 108(2), 27–30.

Whitworth, A. B., Fischer, F., Lesch, O. M., Nimmerrichter, A., Oberbauer, H., Platz, T., Potgieter, A., Walter, H., & Fleischhacker, W. W. (1996). Comparison of acamprosate and placebo in long-term treatment of alcohol dependence. *The Lancet, 347,* 1438–1442.

Why confirmatory testing is always a necessity. (1997). *Forensic Drug Abuse Advisor,* 9(4), 25.

Wijetunga, M., Bhan, R., Lindsay, J., & Karch, S. (2004). Acute coronary syndrome and crystal methamphetamine use: A case series. *Hawaii Medical Journal,* 63(1), 8–13.

Wilcox, C. M., Shalek, K. A., & Cotsonis, G. (1994). Striking prevalence of over-the-counter nonsteroidal anti-inflammatory drug use in patients with upper gastrointestinal hemorrhage. *Archives of Internal Medicine, 154,* 42–46.

Wild, T. C., Cunningham, J., & Hobdon, K. (1998). When do people believe that alcohol treatment is effective? The importance of perceived client and therapist motivation. *Psychology of Addictive Behaviors, 12,* 93–100.

Wilens, T. E. (2004a). Attention deficit/hyperactivity disorder and the substance use disorders: The nature of the relationship, subtypes at risk, and treatment issues. *Psychiatric Clinics of North America, 27,* 283–301.

Wilens, T. E. (2004b). Attention deficit/hyperactivity disorder and the substance use disorders: The nature of the

relationship, who is at risk, and treatment issues. *Primary Psychiatry,* 11(7), 63–70.

Wilkinson, R. J., Liewelyn, M., Toossi, A., Patel, P., Pasvol, G., Lalvani, A., Wright, D., Latif, M., & Davidson, R. N. (2000). Influence of vitamin D deficiency and vitamin D receptor polymorphisms on tuberculosis among Gujarati Asians in West London: A case-control study. *The Lancet, 355,* 618–621.

Will, G. F. (2002). Eurasia and the epidemic. *Newsweek,* CXL (20), 80.

Willenbring, M. L. (2004). Treating co-occuring substance use disorders and hepatitis C. *Psychiatric Times,* XXI (2), 53–54.

Williams, B. R., & Baer, C. L. (1994). *Essentials of clinical pharmacology in nursing* (2nd ed.). Springhouse, PA: Springhouse Corp.

Williams, D. A. (2004). Evaluating acute pain. In *Psychosocial aspects of pain: A handbook for health care providers* (Dworkin, R. H., & Breitbart, W. S., eds.) Seattle, WA: IASP Press.

Williams, E. (1989). Strategies for intervention. *The Nursing Clinics of North America,* 24(1), 95–107.

Williams, H., Dratcu, L., Taylor, R., Roberts, M., & Oyefeso, A. (1998). "Saturday night fever": Ecstasy related problems in a London accident and emergency department. *Journal of Accident and Emergency Medicine, 15,* 322–326.

Williams, T. (2000). High on hemp: Ditchweed digs in. *Utne Reader, 98,* 72–77.

Willoughby, A. (1984). *The alcohol troubled person: Known and unknown.* Chicago: Nelson-Hall.

Wills, T. A., McNamara, G., Vaccaro, D., & Hirky, A. E. (1996). Escalated substance use: A longitudinal grouping analysis from early to middle adolescence. *Journal of Abnormal Psychology, 105,* 166–180.

Wills, T. A., Sandy, J. M., Yaeger, A. M., Cleary, S. D., & Shinar, O. (2001). Coping dimensions, life stress and adolescent substance use: A latent growth analysis. *Journal of Abnormal Psychology, 110,* 309–323.

Wilsnack, S. C., & Wilsnack, R. W. (1995). *Drinking and problem drinking in U.S. women: Recent developments in alcoholism* (Vol. 12) (Galanter, M., ed.). New York: Plenum Press.

Wilsnack, S. C., Wilsnack, R. W., & Hiller-Sturmhoffel, S. (1994). How women drink. *Alcohol Health & Research World, 18,* 173–181.

Wilson, F., & Kunsman, K. (1997). The saliva solution: New choices for alcohol testing. *Occupational Health & Safety,* 66(4), 40–43.

Wilson, L., & French, S. (2002). Cocathylene's effect on coronary artery blood flow and cardiac function in a canine model. *Clinical Toxicology, 40,* 434–456.

Wilson, W. H., & Trott, K. A. (2004). Psychiatric illness associated with criminality. Retrieved on March 5, 2004, from http://www.emedicine.com/med/topic3485.htm

Wilson-Tucker, S., & Dash, J. (1995). Legal—But lethal: Fighting the newest health threat to our kids. *Family Circle,* 108(14), 21–24.

Winchester, J. F. (1990). Barbiturates, methaqualone and primidone. In *Clinical management of poisoning and drug overdose* (2nd ed.) (Haddad, L. M., & Winchester, J. F., eds.). Philadelphia: W. B. Saunders.

Windle, M., Windle, R. C., Scheidt, D. M., & Miller, G. B. (1995). Physical and sexual abuse and associated mental disorders among alcoholic inpatients. *American Journal of Psychiatry, 152,* 1322–1328.

Winecker, R. E., & Goldberger, B. A. (1998). Urine specimen suitability for drug testing. In *Drug abuse handbook* (Karch, S. B., ed.). New York: CRC Press.

Winegarden, T. (2001). Antipsychotic use in special populations. Teleconference sponsored by Astra-Zeneca Pharmaceuticals. La Crosse, WI, September 9, 2001.

Wing, D. M. (1995) Transcending alcoholic denial. *Image, 27,* 121–126.

Wingerchuk, D. (2004). Cannabis for medical purposes: Cultivating science, weeding out the fiction. *The Lancet, 364*(9431), 315–316.

Wiseman, B. (1997). Confronting the breakdown of law and order. *USA Today, 125,* (2620), 32–34.

Wisneiwski, L. (1994). Use of household products as inhalants rising among young teens. *Minneapolis Star Tribune, XIII* (9), p. ex8.

Witkiewitz, K., & Marlatt, G. A. (2004). Relapse prevention for alcohol and drug problems: That was Zen, this is Tao. *American Psychologist, 59*(4), 224–235.

Witkin, G. (1995). A new drug gallops through the west. *U.S. News & World Report, 119*(19), 50–51.

Witkin, G., & Griffin, J. (1994). The new opium wars. *U.S. News & World Report, 117* (114), 39–44.

Woititz, J. G. (1983). *Adult children of alcoholics.* Pompana Beach, FL: Health Communications, Inc.

Wolin, S. J., & Wolin, S. (1993). *The resilient self.* New York: Villard Books.

Wolin, S. J., & Wolin, S. (1995). Resilience among youth growing up in substance-abusing families. *Pediatric Clinics of North America, 42,* 415–429.

Woods, A. R., & Herrera, J. L. (2002). Hepatitis C: Latest treatment guidelines. *Consultant, 42,* 1233–1243.

Woods, J. H., Katz, J. L., & Winger, G. (1988). Use and abuse of benzodiazepines. *Journal of the American Medical Association, 260*(23), 3476–3480.

Woods, J. H., & Winger, G. (1997). Abuse liability of flunitrazepam. *Journal of Psychopharmacology, 17* (Suppl. 3), 1S-57S.

Woods, J. R. (1998). Maternal and transplacental effects of cocaine. *Annals of the New York Academy of Sciences, 846,* 1–11.

Woody, G. E., McLellan, A. T., & Bedrick, J. (1995). Dual diagnosis. In *Review of psychiatry* (Vol. 14) (Oldham, J. M., & Riba, M. B., eds.). Washington, DC: American Psychiatric Association Press, Inc.

Woolf, A. D., & Shannon, M. W. (1995). Clinical toxicology for the pediatrician. *Pediatric Clinics of North America, 42,* 317–333.

Work Group on HIV/AIDS (2000). Practice guideline for the treatment of patients with HIV/AIDS. *American Journal of Psychiatry, 157*(11)(Suppl.).

Wright, K. (1999). A shot of sanity. *Discover, 20*(6), 47–48.

Wright, K. (2001). Does aspirin help prevent cancer? *Discover, 22*(6), 29–30.

Wu, L., & Schlenger, W. E. (2004). Private health insurance coverage for substance abuse and mental health services, 1995 to 1998. *Psychiatric Services, 55,* 180–182.

Wuethrich, B. (2001). Getting stupid. *Discover, 22*(3), 56–63.

Yablonsky, L. (1967). *Synanon: The tunnel back.* Baltimore: Penguin Books.

Yalom, I. D. (1985). *The theory and practice of group psychotherapy* (3rd ed.). New York: Basic Books.

Yancey, P. (2000). *Reaching for the invisible God.* Grand Rapids, MI: Zondervan Publishing Co.

Yancey, P. (2003). *Rumors of another world.* Grand Rapids, MI: Zondervan Publishing Co.

Yeager, K. R., & Gregoire, T. K. (2000). Crisis intervention application in brief solution-focused therapy in addictions. In *Crisis intervention handbook* (2nd ed.) (Roberts, A. R., ed.). New York: Oxford University Press.

Yesalis, C. E., Kennedy, N. J., Kopstein, A. N., & Bahrke, M. S. (1993). Anabolic-androgenic steroid use in the United States. *Journal of the American Medical Association, 270,* 1217–1221.

Yip, L., Dart, R. C., & Gabow, P. A. (1994). Concepts and controversies in salicylate toxicity. *Emergency Medical Clinics of North America, 12,* 351–364.

Yost, D. A. (1996). Alcohol withdrawal syndrome. *American Family Physician, 54,* 657–664.

Yost, J. H., & Morgan, G. J. (1994). Cardiovascular effects of NSAIDS. *Journal of Musculoskeletal Medicine, 11*(10), 22–34.

Youngstrom, N. (1990a). Debate rages on: In- or outpatient? *APA Monitor, 21*(10), 19.

Youngstrom, N. (1990b). The drugs used to treat drug abuse. *APA Monitor, 21*(10), 19.

Yu, K., & Daar, E. S. (2000). Primary HIV infection. *Postgraduate Medicine, 107,* 114–122.

Zajicek, J., Fox, P., Sanders, H., Wright, D., Vickery, J., Nunn, A., & Thompson, A. (2003). Cannabinoids for treatment of spasticity and other symptoms related to multiple sclerosis (CAMS study): Multicentre randomised placebo-controlled trial. *The Lancet, 362*(8), 1517–1526.

Zakhari, S. (1997). Alcohol and the cardiovascular system. *Alcohol Health & Research World, 21,* 21–29.

Zarek, D., Hawkins, D., & Rogers, P. D. (1987). Risk factors for adolescent substance abuse. *The Pediatric Clinics of North America, 34*(2), 481–493.

Zealberg, J. J., & Brady, K. T. (1999). Substance abuse and emergency psychiatry. *Psychiatric Clinics of North America, 22,* 803–817.

Zeese, K. B. (2002). From Nixon to now. *Playboy, 49*(9), 49.

Zelvin, E. (1997). Codependency issues of substance-abusing women. In *Gender and addictions* (Straussner, S. L. A., & Zelvin, E., eds.). Northvale, NJ: Jason-Aronson.

Zernig, G., & Battista, H. J. (2000). Drug interactions. In *Handbook of alcoholism* (Zernig, G., Saria, A., Kurz, M., & O'Malley, S. S., eds.). New York: CRC Press.

Zerwekh, J., & Michaels, B. (1989). Co-dependency. *The Nursing Clinics of North America, 24*(1), 109–120.

Zevin, S., & Benowitz, N. L. (1998). Drug-related syndromes. In *Drug abuse handbook* (Karch, S. B., ed.). New York: CRC Press.

Zickler, P. (1999). NIDA studies clarify developmental effects of prental cocaine exposure. *NIDA Notes, 14*(3), 5–7.

Zickler, P. (2001). NIDA scientific panel reports on prescription drug misuse and abuse. *NIDA Notes, 16*(3), 1, 5.

Ziedonis, D., & Brady, K. (1997). Dual diagnosis in primary care. *Medical Clinics of North America, 81*, 1017–1036.

Zimberg, S. (1978). Psychosocial treatment of elderly alcoholics. In *Practical approaches to alcoholism psychotherapy* (Zimberg, S., Wallace, J., & Blume, S. B., eds.). New York: Plenum Press.

Zimberg, S. (1995). The elderly. In *Psychotherapy and substance abuse* (Washton, A. M., ed.). New York: Guilford.

Zimberg, S. (1996). Treating alcoholism: An age-specific intervention that works for older patients. *Geriatrics, 51*(10), 45–49.

Zisserson, R. N., & Oslin, D. W. (2004). Alcoholism and at-risk drinking in the older population. *Psychiatric Times, XXI* (2), 50–53.

Zito, J. M. (1994). *Psychotherapeutic drug manual* (3rd ed.). New York: John Wiley & Sons, Inc.

Zoldan, J. (2000). The treatment of denial in recovery: Moving from denial of acceptance towards acceptance of denial. Symposium presented to the Dept. of Psychiatry at The Cambridge Hospital, Boston, MA, March 4.

Zubaran, C., Fernandes, J. G., & Rodnight, R. (1997). Wernicke-Korsakoff syndrome. *Postgraduate Medical Journal, 73*, 27–31.

Zucker, R. A., & Gomberg, E. S. L. (1986). Etiology of alcoholism reconsidered: The case for a biopsychosocial process. *American Psychologist, 41*, 783–794.

Zuckerman, B., & Bresnahan, K. (1991). Developmental and behavioral consequences of prenatal drug and alcohol exposure. *Pediatric Clinics of North America, 38*, 1387–1406.

Zuckerman, B., Frank, D. A., & Mayes, L. (2002). Cocaine-exposed infants and developmental outcomes. *Journal of the American Medical Association, 287*, 1990–1991.

Zuger, A. (1994). Meningitis mystery. *Discover, 15*(3), 40–43.

Zukin, S. R., Sloboda, Z., & Javitt, D. C.. (1997). Phencyclidine. In *Substance abuse: A comprehensive textbook* (3rd ed.) (Lowinson, J. H., Ruiz, P., Millman, R. B., & Langrod, J. G., eds.). New York: Williams & Wilkins.

Zukin, S. R., & Zukin, R. S. (1992). Phencyclidine. In *Substance abuse: A comprehensive textbook* (2nd ed.) (Lowinson, J. H., Ruiz, P., Millman, R. B., & Langrod, J. G., eds.). New York: Williams & Wilkins.

Zweben, J. E. (1995). Integrating psychotherapy and 12–Step approaches. In *Psychotherapy and substance abuse* (Washton, A. M., ed.). New York: Guilford.

Zweig, C., & Wolf, S. (1997). *Romancing the shadow.* New York: Ballantine Books.

INDEX